Born in Shropshire in 1974, Domi[nic]... [studied at]
Oxford, the University of St And[rews]...
history at the University of Shef[field]...
Rothermere Institute, University [of Oxford]...
first volume of Dominic Sandbrook['s history,]
Had It So Good: A History of Britain from...

Praise for *White Heat*:

'*White Heat* is a triumph. Its 800-odd pages successfully integrate a blow-by-blow political history of the era dominated by Harold Wilson with an amazingly full social and cultural history of the same period . . . Extraordinarily enlightening . . . as this splendid book reminds us, it was fun while it lasted'
Jane Stevenson, *Daily Telegraph*

'They say that if you can remember the sixties you weren't there. For all those in need of reminding, Dominic Sandbrook's brilliant analysis of the era looks at political and everyday life as well as the free love, dope-fuelled existence of the pop stars, models and hippies'
Books of the Year, *Daily Mail*

'An active pleasure to read. This is a deftly written and evocative account of the day before yesterday, a period about which we – including our governing class – know far too little'
Books of the Year, *Mail on Sunday*

'Humorously written exposition of the creative and optimistic society that emerged after the Second World War, but which could not find the economic answer to post-imperial decline'
Books of the Year, *Financial Times*

'An epic account of mid-twentieth century Britain which is hugely enjoyable, funny, contentious, and shows a sharp eye for telling detail'
Books of the Year, *Sunday Herald*

'Entertaining'
D. J. Taylor, Books of the Year, *Times Literary Supplement*

'Dominic Sandbrook demolishes the myth that traditional society was swept aside by flower power, free love and student unrest'
Leo McKinstry, *The Times*

'A socio-politico-cultural extravaganza on the sixties. While the key images are given full weight, Sandbrook reveals that most of the nation remained warily conservative. Riveting even if you didn't live through it'
John Walsh, *Independent*

'Sandbrook was not around at the time, which may account for his wonderful gift for breathing new life into these all-too-familiar stories, and also for the fresh eye which allows him to take a new angle on all the hoary old myths . . . He covers every aspect of the "Swinging Sixties", scrupulously careful throughout to avoid either demonising or romanticising what was almost certainly the least distinguished and most worthless cast of characters ever to take centre stage in British history . . . An extraordinary story . . . not to be missed'
Peregrine Worsthorne, *Evening Standard*

'We were knocked out by the young Oxford historian's first book, a blockbuster on the years 1956–63, *Never Had It So Good*. This proved a winning format and he has followed through on his success in the same easy-to-read style . . . Sandbrook tells this story with unflagging relish . . . [and] undaunted zeal . . . This is history of a commendably inclusive range. There is something for everybody'
Peter Clarke, *Sunday Times*

'An outstanding feat on the part of a young man who has not only read, marked and learnt but has also inwardly digested a decade and more of recent British history to the great benefit of the rest of us . . . If you want an updated version of the Bayeux Tapestry then this is the book for you'
Anthony Howard, *Sunday Telegraph*

'The financial crisis that the Labour administrations of the 1960s stumbled and reeled their way through are the backbone of Dominic Sandbrook's wondrously all-encompassing account of the decade in Britain . . . The grip derives from Sandbrook's sense of drama, the sense of drama from his ability to see both sides of an argument . . . What we need now is an explanation for why the seventies were such a washout. Come on Sandbrook: the age of flares awaits your flair for ages'
Christopher Bray, *New Statesman*

'Skilfully marshals a vast array of facts into a clear and competent narrative . . . covering not just politics, but the arts, social trends, fashion and popular culture . . . Written with sense and judgement'
Vernon Bogdanor, *Financial Times*

'His chosen period coincided with a wave of self-conscious novelty and experiment, and the book, well organised and balanced, sets up a counterpoint between public events and developments in fashion, social attitudes and culture (both high and popular)'
Adam Mars-Jones, *Observer*

WHITE HEAT

A History of Britain in the
Swinging Sixties

DOMINIC SANDBROOK

ABACUS

ABACUS

First published in Great Britain in 2006 by Little, Brown
This paperback edition published in 2007 by Abacus
Reprinted 2008

Copyright © Dominic Sandbrook 2006

The moral right of the author has been asserted.

All rights reserved.
No part of this publication may be reproduced, stored in a retrieval system, or transmitted, in any form or by any means, without the prior permission in writing of the publisher, nor be otherwise circulated in any form of binding or cover other than that in which it is published and without a similar condition including this condition being imposed on the subequent purchaser.

A CIP catalogue record for this book
is available from the British Library.

ISBN 978-0-349-11820-8

Typeset in Spectrum by M Rules
Printed and bound in Great Britain by Clays Ltd, St Ives plc

Abacus
An imprint of
Little, Brown Book Group
100 Victoria Embankment
London EC4Y 0DY

An Hachette Livre UK Company

www.littlebrown.co.uk

*In memory of my grandfather
Norman Daker, 1915–1996*

CONTENTS

Acknowledgements ix
Preface xiii

PART ONE: THE NEW BRITAIN

1. Let's Go with Labour — 3
2. The Ten Faces of Harold — 20
3. The Space Age — 44
4. This is Tomorrow — 65
5. The Hundred Days — 86
6. Introducing the Turds — 101
7. Special Relations — 120
8. Enter the Stones — 133
9. Women! Win Mr Heath! — 156

PART TWO: ENGLAND SWINGS

10. Britain in 1965 — 183
11. The Wild Ones — 203
12. Dedicated Followers of Fashion — 228
13. The Swinging City — 251
14. The Day It All Stopped — 277
15. The Face of '66 — 300
16. Is Britain Civilised? — 326
17. Sowing Dragons' Teeth — 343
18. The Yorkshire Walter Mitty — 367

PART THREE: THE END OF ILLUSIONS

19	Carry On England	395
20	The Pound in Your Pocket	415
21	I Was Lord Kitchener's Valet	434
22	Heavens Above!	457
23	Love Without Fear	477
24	The Arctic Winter of the Treasury	501
25	Play Power	520
26	Sympathy for the Devil	545
27	Why Lucky Jim Turned Right	570

PART FOUR: I'M BACKING BRITAIN

28	The Other England	597
29	Streets in the Sky	620
30	Wilson Must Go	641
31	Back Britain, Not Black Britain	661
32	Desperate Housewives	687
33	In Place of Strife	705
34	Children of Wrath	732
35	The Carnival Is Over	759

Epilogue	789
Notes	795
Select Bibliography	907
Index	927

ACKNOWLEDGEMENTS

Like its predecessor, *Never Had It So Good*, this book was conceived and partially written while I was a lecturer in history at the University of Sheffield. As before, I am delighted to thank my erstwhile colleagues for their advice and support, notably Pertti Ahonen, Mike Braddick, Flurin Condrau, Simon Hall, Ian Kershaw, Zoë Laidlaw, Simon Loseby, Patrick Renshaw, Barbara Schmucki, Ted Vallance and Nik Wachsmann. Robert Cook, Hugh Wilford and Joe Street were particularly generous with their encouragement and I have benefited from their close knowledge of Birmingham, beards and the Black Country. Karen Harvey was a great source of help on mini-skirts.

My former associates in the Age of Nixon, whose commitment to the late president reached mind-boggling proportions, ensured that I departed South Yorkshire in suitably melodramatic style. Afterwards, I was lucky to benefit from the superb facilities and support of the Rothermere American Institute at Oxford. In particular, I am grateful to Paul Giles, Cheryl Hudson, Andrea Beighton and Laura Lauer, while Richard Carwardine, Gareth Davies and Stephen Tuck could hardly have been more welcoming. My thanks also go to the various librarians in London, Oxford, Cambridge and Sheffield without whom researching this book would have been so much more difficult, and of course to the hundreds of historians whose works I have used. Anyone writing a book of this kind runs up enormous debts to those who have gone before, and I have tried to acknowledge them in the endnotes and bibliography.

For their comments on drafts of the manuscript, I am grateful to Andrew Clark, Joe Guinan, Simon Hall, Simon Hooper, Martin O'Neill, Andrew Preston and Hugh Wilford. For hospitality during my various research trips, I am indebted to Simon Hooper and Lauren Stewart; James Davis, Kaele Stokes and Ed Meek; and Nathan Bavidge and Vicky Scahill. Pat Thane and her colleagues at the Institute of Historical Research made me very welcome and asked difficult questions when I came to talk about my work. Max Hastings, Tom Holland and Richard Thorpe were terrific sources of encouragement and advice. Thomas Matthews-Boehmer gave me the benefit of his rigorous historical judgement. And Sam Leith, Caroline Gascoigne, Andrew Holgate, Katie Law and Andy Neather kept me well supplied with books and other distractions.

As always, I am grateful to Andrew Wylie and his staff for their immense professionalism and for enabling me to write for a living. I am particularly indebted to Michal Shavit for all her support and hard work over the last few years. The team at Little, Brown were as friendly, helpful and accomplished as ever, and I want to thank Sarah Allman, Richard Beswick, Caroline Brown, Roger Cazalet, Kerry Chapple, Jenny Fry, Steve Guise, Duncan Spilling and Stephanie Young, as well as anyone else I may have overlooked. Susan de Soissons is a publicist without peer, and Iain Hunt guided the manuscript to publication with his usual supreme patience and skill.

Finally, I want to thank my parents for their unwavering encouragement, Alex and Susie for the entertainment, and Catherine Morley for her wonderful, selfless love and support. And to my editor, Tim Whiting, I owe a very special debt. Since we first met as schoolboys studying history with the incomparable Roy Allen, he has been an irascible tennis opponent, an unconvincing Welshman, a marvellous editor and, above all, a steadfast friend. I could not have wished for a better partner in crime over the last sixteen years. It is just a shame that he never did persuade Martin Amis to come to the Gobi Desert all those years ago.

[The scientific] revolution cannot become a reality unless we are prepared to make far-reaching changes in economic and social attitudes which permeate our whole system of society.

The Britain that is going to be forged in the white heat of this revolution will be no place for restrictive practices or for outdated methods on either side of industry . . . In the Cabinet room and the boardroom alike, those charged with the control of our affairs must be ready to think and to speak in the language of our scientific age.

Harold Wilson, 1 October 1963

PREFACE

Shortly after eight o'clock on the morning of Sunday, 24 January 1965, Sir Winston Churchill died. He had fought on for twelve days following the last of many strokes; this time, his indomitable spirit was not enough to save him. Almost immediately, Britain became a nation in mourning. Flags were lowered to half-mast, prayers were offered in parish services, and the lights of Piccadilly Circus were dimmed that evening in tribute. The Prime Minister, Harold Wilson, immediately announced that Churchill's body would lie in state for three days at Westminster Hall, before a full state funeral at St Paul's the following Saturday. 'Tonight,' he told the British people in a televised address, 'our nation mourns the loss of the greatest man any of us have ever known.'[1]

In the days that followed, some 320,000 people waited for four hours or more to pay their respects to their fallen leader. Even at one in the morning, the government minister Richard Crossman saw a 'stream of people pouring down the steps of Westminster Hall towards the catafalque'.[2] The BBC's commentator Richard Dimbleby, himself struggling against the cancer that was to kill him, told his audience: 'I have stood for half an hour . . . watching this silent flow of people, imagining who they were and where they came from, and realising that this is simply the nation, with its bare heads, and its scarves, and its plastic hoods, and its shopping bags, and its puzzled little children'.[3]

Churchill's funeral, held at St Paul's Cathedral on Saturday, 30 January 1965, was one of the great national events of the decade. Although the leaders of more than a hundred different countries were in attendance, it was above all a fiercely patriotic celebration of national history. Hundreds of thousands of people, young and old, rich and poor, lined the streets as the former Prime Minister's coffin was brought from Westminster to the City of London on a gun carriage escorted by air crews who had fought in the Battle of Britain. Eight guardsmen bore the coffin into the cathedral; ahead of them walked twelve pall-bearers, old comrades from the war years, among them three former Prime Ministers. 'What a setting for this last farewell,' commented *The Times*:

> On every side the nation's past heroes and glories – Nelson and Wellington, Abercromby and Cornwallis, Gordon and Howe, Roberts and Melbourne, Jellicoe and Beatty. Inkerman, Waterloo, Quatre-Bras and Salamanca, Crimea and Khartum, Corunna and Trafalgar . . . Once again the great cathedral was fulfilling the words of Tennyson:
>
>> *Warriors carry the warrior's pall*
>> *And sorrow darkens hamlet and hall . . .*
>> *And the sound of the sorrowing anthem roll'd*
>> *Thro' the dome of the golden cross.*

After the thirty-minute service, Churchill's coffin was carried back to the gun carriage, and escorted down towards Tower Pier. On Tower Hill, the crowds pressed as thick and silent as ever, thirty deep in places. At the pier, with bagpipes wailing out a lingering lament, the coffin was transferred to a waiting launch for the short journey across the Thames, in itself a signal honour and the first river procession of this kind since the funeral of Nelson. As the launch pushed off, the bagpipes fell silent and the Royal Marine band burst into 'Rule, Britannia'. And as the boat headed south across the river, the dockers' cranes on the wharves opposite dipped their long necks, 'like dinosaurs', wrote one observer, 'in an eery, impressive civilian salute'.[4]

On the south bank of the Thames, the coffin was loaded into a hearse and driven the short distance to Waterloo Station. There it was carried onto a special locomotive, the 'Winston Churchill', for the journey to its final resting-place in Bladon, Oxfordshire. As before, the route was lined with thousands of mourners and well-wishers. Churchill's wartime private secretary, Sir Leslie Rowan, was on the train, and remembered seeing two figures who 'epitomised for me what Churchill really meant to ordinary people: first on the flat roof of a small house a man standing at attention in his RAF uniform; and then in a field, some hundred yards away from the track, a simple farmer stopping work and standing, head bowed and cap in hand'.[5]

Looking back on Churchill's funeral a few years later, the journalist Bernard Levin wrote that it had been 'one of the great public ceremonies of history'.[6] But its real impact fell not on the great and the good, but on the millions of ordinary Britons for whom Winston Churchill was a genuinely heroic figure. Not only did hundreds of thousands of people pay their respects to the dead man in person, but an estimated national audience of more than twenty-five million watched the funeral live on television.[7] One reporter noted the 'surprising number of young people who seemed to have come, not out of curiosity but out of reverence for the man'.[8] Many were not afraid to show their emotions, and the *Daily Express* commented that 'for a British crowd, the tears were surprisingly copious. People dashed at their eyes with handkerchiefs, gripped by what was clearly a sharp and personal sense of grief.'[9] On television, Richard Dimbleby suggested that there had not been 'in the whole history of our land a state funeral or an occasion which has touched the hearts of people quite as much as this one is doing today'.[10]

Bernard Levin was not alone in seeing Churchill's funeral as 'one of the great watersheds of history'.[11] On both left and right, commentators agreed that with the great man gone, all that remained was the gloomy reality of national decline. Looking around him in St Paul's Cathedral, Richard Crossman reflected on 'what a faded, declining establishment surrounded me. Aged marshals, grey, dreary ladies, decadent Marlboroughs and Churchills. It was a dying congregation gathered there and I am afraid the Labour Cabinet didn't look too distinguished either. It felt like the end of an epoch, possibly even the end of a nation.'[12] And in the *Observer* the following day, Patrick O'Donovan commented that 'this was the last time such a thing could happen . . . This was the last time that London would be the capital of the world. This was an act of mourning for the Imperial past. This marked the final act in Britain's greatness. This was a great gesture of self-pity, and after this the coldness of reality and the status of Scandinavia.'[13]

The significance of Churchill's funeral seemed all the greater because his life appeared to encapsulate all that Britain had undergone since the Victorian period, from music halls and cavalry charges to tanks and telephones, from the age of empires to the Common Market. Churchill had finally left Downing Street in April 1955, and since then the country seemed to have been in the grip of unrelenting change. The Suez Crisis had exposed the decline of Britain's diplomatic power and prestige, the colonies in Africa and Asia had fallen away with giddying speed and thousands of non-white immigrants had flocked to build new lives in Britain itself. The days of imperial glory and gunboat diplomacy were long gone, and George Orwell's vision of Britain as 'a cold and unimportant little island where we should all have to work very hard and live mainly on herrings and potatoes' seemed too close for comfort.[14]

Yet contrary to Orwell's gloomy prediction, the end of the empire heralded an age not of austerity but of affluence. Under the ebullient Harold Macmillan, Churchill's old party reaped the rewards of an unprecedented economic boom based on full employment, rising incomes and rampant consumerism. People took home more money than ever before and spent it on a bewildering array of new appliances, luxuries and entertainments, from cars and motorbikes to cookers and washing machines. In coffee bars, jazz clubs, Italian restaurants and high-street showrooms, the affluent society was in full swing. The BBC and ITV battled for the allegiance of tens of millions of television viewers, while record companies and fashion designers raced to tap the new teenage market. Cliff Richard and James Bond, *Coronation Street* and *Doctor Who*, the Shadows and the Beatles: all were emblematic of an age in which, as Macmillan famously put it, 'most of our people have never had it so good'.

Despite the dazzling consumerism of the affluent society, however, a vein of dissatisfaction ran through British political culture. Thanks partly to the burden of maintaining a military presence abroad, Macmillan's government struggled to maintain a healthy balance of payments, and was occasionally forced to administer doses of economic deflation to stop people buying too many imports. Critics and satirists argued that the country was hidebound by anachronism and amateurism, and in the summer of 1963 Macmillan was almost engulfed by the Profumo sex scandal, which seemed to knit together a host of contemporary anxieties about materialism, promiscuity, subversion and corruption. Although Macmillan survived the furore, he was shortly struck down by ill health and decided to resign, prompting a bewildering and murky battle to succeed him. The victor was the aristocratic Foreign Secretary, the Earl of Home, a likeable and decent man, but an unlikely figurehead for the age of consumerism. At the beginning of 1964, few observers expected Home to last long. Instead it was his opponent, the quick-witted Labour leader Harold Wilson, full of talk about science, modernisation and the possibilities of the future, who seemed more likely to embody the spirit of the sixties.

In my last book, *Never Had It So Good*, I described the British experience during the late fifties and early sixties, tracing the story of affluence and decline from the Suez Crisis in 1956 to the rise of the Beatles in 1963.[15] One of the arguments of the book was that the national mood was very different from the optimistic hedonism often associated with the 1960s. It was certainly true that millions of people were wealthier and more comfortable than ever, and the fruits of the affluent society were obvious to anyone who cared to look. But at the same time, the newspapers were full of laments for Britain's lost greatness, and many people complained that the social and cultural changes of the sixties were creating a society of materialism, alienation and immorality.

In writing both *Never Had It So Good* and the present book, which takes the story from 1964 to 1970, I have tried to avoid the predictable and tiresome ritual of either romanticising or demonising the sixties. Indeed, I have lost count of the number of magazine features and newspaper editorials devoted to the supposed decadence or utopianism of the period. Almost all of these accounts concentrate overwhelmingly on the activities of a relatively small, well-educated minority, usually people who were in their teens or twenties at the time and went on to become well-paid writers, journalists, publishers and so on.

But as we will see, for millions of other people, the reality of daily life was rather different. Change often came slowly to provincial towns and rural villages, and the joke that everything 'reached Hull about five years after it reached everywhere else' carried more than a ring of truth.[16] Many of the best-known changes of the period, like the growth of television, the introduction of the mini-skirt or the development of the Pill, provoked considerable unease or anger in some sections of the population, and although it is always tempting to reduce the period to a parade of gaudy stereotypes, the reality was both more complicated and, ultimately, more interesting.

Although *White Heat* follows on directly from the end of *Never Had It So Good*, it can easily be read as a single volume in its own right. It begins with Harold Wilson's coronation as the leader of the Labour Party and his promise to harness the power of science to build a modern, classless 'New Britain'. At one level, the story of the book is that of Wilson's dream between 1964 and 1970, showing how the high hopes of the mid-sixties curdled into the disillusionment with which Britain entered the seventies. But although this political narrative provides the backbone to the book, there is more to the story than the activities of Westminster politicians, and I have turned to other issues whenever appropriate: science and technology, art and design, pop music and fashion, religion and sexual morality, and so on. This means that *White Heat* is quite a long book, not least because some areas, such as the origins of the conflict in Northern Ireland, really deserve books of their own. Even so, Scottish and Welsh readers may complain that there is too much about England and not enough about the other parts of the United Kingdom. Although I have found room for some Scottish Mods and Welsh dolly birds, I decided to leave the rebirth of Welsh and Scottish nationalism until my next book, which will cover the 1970s.

One reviewer complained of *Never Had It So Good* that there was not enough about Mao Tse-tung, the Cuban revolution or the French war in Algeria. I am not convinced that these things belong in a book about the British national experience, and in *White Heat*, too, I have concentrated on Britain itself, with occasional excursions into the United States, Rhodesia, Aden and so on. Another reviewer thought that the last book contained rather too much about Harold Macmillan's prostate gland, but when it comes to the questions of anecdotes and personal colour, I am equally unrepentant. If my first volume had quite a lot to say about Macmillan's prostate, this book has just as much to say about Harold Wilson's dining arrangements, George Brown's drinking habits or Mary Quant's hairstyle. History should be entertaining as well as informative, and I make no apology for trying to tell as good a story as I can.

Finally, a word on the title. Contemporary writers regularly described Britain, and specifically London, as 'swinging'; as one journalist put it, the term suggested 'wealth, sex appeal, fame, youth, talent, novelty, and quick success'.[17] One of Harold Wilson's possible campaign slogans in 1964 was 'Tories Dodgy – Labour Swinging', and although this was never used, it reflected his emphasis on youth, optimism and innovation. As the youngest Prime Minister of the century, Wilson was keen to pose as the figurehead of the new swinging Britain, and his rhetoric about 'the white heat of this revolution' captured the scientific optimism of the mid-sixties. But as the coverage of Churchill's funeral suggests, many observers did not share his optimism. The affluent society was not universally popular, and confident visions of the New Britain were intermingled with gloomy predictions of national decline. And as we will see, it is the tension between them that provides the story of this book.

PART ONE

THE NEW BRITAIN

1

LET'S GO WITH LABOUR

Why I'm Voting Labour
VOTER 1: Because I believe a vast amount of talent and energy, especially among the young, will be released if we give Labour a chance to make a new Britain.
VOTER 2: The Britain of the future shall be a classless one where all petty snobbisms of accent, dress, education will be defunct . . . a society which seeks to harness the talents of all in the best possible manner.
VOTER 3: I shall vote for the party of teachers and trained economists, the Labour Party; not the party of company directors and blimps.
VOTER 4: They appear to be bursting with ideas for 'putting Britain back on the map' again, and this infectious zeal has spread throughout their party.

Sun, 30 September, 2 October and 6 October 1964

On the first day of October 1963, as the earliest whispers of dawn were edging across the clifftops of the Yorkshire resort of Scarborough, the new leader of the Labour Party nervously paced up and down the carpet of his hotel suite. Harold Wilson was due to address his party conference later that morning, but his speech was still not finished. At nine the previous evening, dragging himself away from the bonhomie of the conference bars, Wilson had casually remarked to his political secretary: 'I still don't know what to say. I think I'll go to bed and do it early in the morning.' 'No,' Marcia Williams replied, 'you will do it now.' But when they got up to Wilson's suite, the Leader of the Opposition was still searching for a theme. Williams thought for a minute, and then offered a suggestion: 'What about the Science Committee stuff?'[1]

Twelve hours later, tired but confident, Wilson rose to address the conference for the first time as Labour leader. His subject was 'Labour and the Scientific Revolution', and as his flat Yorkshire vowels echoed around the hall, legions of pressmen frantically scribbled down his words for the next morning's papers. He was speaking not only to the faithful members of his party, but to a nationwide electorate that was expecting a general election within the next twelve months. Four years earlier, basking in the summer of the affluent society, the Conservatives had coasted to re-election. But now, at the end of 1963, the government looked weary and vulnerable, its energies sapped by economic jitters and spy scandals. By contrast, Wilson promised dynamic leadership, industrial modernisation and a new commitment to scientific change. And as his speech neared its end, he hit upon the phrase that would define his appeal in 1964. Socialism, he said, would be recast 'in terms of the scientific revolution':

> But that revolution cannot become a reality unless we are prepared to make far-reaching changes in economic and social attitudes which permeate our whole system of society.
>
> The Britain that is going to be forged in the white heat of this revolution will be no place for restrictive practices or for outdated methods on either side of industry . . . In the Cabinet room and the boardroom alike, those charged with the control of our affairs must be ready to think and to speak in the language of our scientific age.[2]

With its promise of democratic, scientific professionalism, the 'White Heat' speech set the tone for Wilson's leadership of the Labour Party and caught the mood of the moment. *The Times*, for instance, thought that it was the most successful speech he had ever delivered, and noted that 'the audience showed a fervour that hardly knew any bounds when he sat down'.[3] The Labour papers were even more enthusiastic, and *Tribune* called the speech 'an historic utterance which established Labour unchallenged as the party of Britain's destiny'.[4] In the *Guardian*, John Cole wrote that it 'probably did as much as long months of work at Westminster to establish him in the public mind as the kind of man who would make a Prime Minister'.[5] 'Harold Wilson will not just be a good Prime Minister,' wrote James Cameron in the staunchly Labour *Daily Herald*. 'He may well be a great one . . . Wilson's startling essay into political science-fiction may well be held by experts to be the most vital speech he has ever made. Here at last [is] the twentieth century.'[6]

As Harold Wilson looked forward to the forthcoming general election, he had every reason to feel confident. On the one hand, he cultivated an appearance of classless professionalism, aiming to tap the contemporary faith in technical expertise and appeal to working-class and lower-middle-class voters who had bettered themselves during the economic boom of the late fifties. Asked which class he belonged to, he replied: 'Well someone who started at elementary school in Yorkshire and became an Oxford don — where do you put him in this class spectrum? I think these phrases are becoming more and more meaningless.'[7]

At the same time, Wilson played up his humble roots and Yorkshire background, emphasising to interviewers that he owed his success to plain living, hard work and ordinary values. He took care to be photographed in a sweater, talked a lot about his wife and family, and regularly sucked on a pipe in interviews and public appearances despite the fact that he actually preferred cigars. Unlike Harold Macmillan, who relaxed by reading classical poetry or nineteenth-century novels, Wilson declared that he enjoyed *Coronation Street* because 'the people in it seem to be real'.[8] Like the actors and writers of the New Wave, or even the members of the Beatles, he projected himself as a cheeky outsider with self-consciously 'ordinary' tastes. He told the *Daily Express*:

> The Right-Wing Establishment has never tried to embrace me or buy me off. That's probably a compliment. Lady Whatsit or Lord So-and-So haven't plied me with invitations. I don't do much socializing and my tastes are simple. If I had the choice between smoked salmon and tinned salmon I'd have it tinned. With vinegar. I prefer beer to champagne and if I get the chance to go home I have a North Country high tea — without wine.[9]

Wilson's strategy worked brilliantly. Even his gentle Yorkshire accent struck the right note, and contemporary observers agreed that here was a modern, professional politician with his roots in the North and his mind on the future. At the beginning of 1963, Labour had enjoyed a 9 per cent lead over the Conservatives. By March the gulf had widened to 17 per cent; by June, with Macmillan engulfed by the Profumo scandal, it was 20 per cent.[10]

Wilson himself, meanwhile, was staggeringly popular. The *Telegraph* reminded its readers that he was 'the first product of the sixth form of a grammar school to come out on top'.[11] 'His speeches glitter, cascade with wit,' said the *Observer*. 'Vain but not conceited, with a hard inner assurance, dependable and industrious . . . Harold Wilson is a contemporary, classless figure.'[12] Throughout the year his approval ratings hovered at around 65 per cent, the highest for a Labour leader in living memory; by contrast, Macmillan's replacement, the former Lord Home, was struggling even to win over his own party.[13] By the end of 1963, barely three in ten voters expected that the Conservatives would be able to hold off Wilson in the forthcoming general election, and his triumphant arrival in Downing Street seemed only a matter of time.[14]

Labour had begun planning the details of their election campaign even before Wilson took over as leader. As early as 1962 the market researcher Mark Abrams had begun working out how the party might best appeal to the so-called 'middle majority' of white-collar, professional workers, younger voters and women.[15] In May 1963 the party launched an expensive advertising campaign to persuade middle-class voters that Labour stood for prosperity and progress. The campaign was also designed to 'sell' Wilson to the electorate, so the first advertisements carried a large photograph of the leader with the caption: 'Harold Wilson explains Labour's New Plans for making Britain Dynamic and Prosperous Again'. The party's advertising men adopted the slogan 'Let's Go with Labour and we'll get things done', while the campaign symbol, borrowed from the television show *Sunday Night at the London Palladium*, was a thumbs-up sign. There were 'Let's Go' stickers, badges, balloons and posters, all bearing the thumbs-up motif or a picture of Wilson, and the general impression was one of slickness and vigour, which perfectly matched the Labour leader's rhetoric.[16]

Campaign advertising on this scale was often seen as an example of the so-called Americanisation of British politics, and Labour's strategists had indeed been inspired by John F. Kennedy's presidential campaign of 1960.[17] Although Kennedy was actually a pretty cautious politician, he had plenty of admirers on the eastern side of the Atlantic.[18] The extent of Wilson's infatuation with Kennedy was captured by an interview he gave in March 1964. He thought that Kennedy was 'the most full-time and active President there's ever been in this century', that he had 'shifted the whole idea to a younger generation' and that he had pioneered the 'basing of decisions on an intellectual process'.[19] Unfortunately, the President's untimely demise at the end of 1963 meant that he was a rather unpropitious role model, but Wilson had an ideal replacement in mind. By a remarkable stroke of luck, this just happened to be the new President. 'I'm not a Kennedy,' he told a press conference later that year. 'I'm a [Lyndon] Johnson. I fly by the seat of my pants.'[20]

Kennedy's 'New Frontier' programme was also the direct inspiration for the second stage of Wilson's campaign, which was based on the theme of the 'New Britain'. Its chief tactician was Anthony Wedgwood Benn, a newcomer to the leader's inner circle who had fought a long battle to disclaim his peerage and had the reputation of a technological whizz-kid.* As a former television producer, Benn was an enthusiastic champion of the new public relations and advertising techniques.[21] By the end of 1963 he was effectively Wilson's principal speechwriter and adviser, although Wilson was not keen to share the limelight. 'Harold doesn't want any people to know that anyone helps him at all,' Benn wrote in his diary. 'He wants it all to be his show . . . Kennedy never minded it being known that he had speech writers and advisers but Harold does.'[22]

On 3 December Wilson called Benn over for a meeting to discuss the election. As luck would have it, Benn's wife Caroline had recently helped him to prepare a few suggestions for the Labour leader. Benn's main idea was that Wilson should mount a new public relations offensive in the New Year, setting out 'the programme of a Labour government. This programme must have a specific name like the "New Britain" programme – an idea Caroline had suggested – comparable to Kennedy's "New Frontier".'[23] The theme would be 'regeneration', which Benn thought had 'a spiritual flavour and a suggestion of youth (new generation) about it which differentiates it more forcibly from Tory philosophy'.[24] Wilson liked the idea: two weeks later, he told Benn to get cracking on the address to launch the 'New Britain' campaign. 'He is delighted with it,' Benn wrote proudly, 'and I can see I am firmly entrenched as his speech writer.'[25]

On 19 January, Wilson kicked off his New Year offensive with a much-reported speech at Birmingham Town Hall. It was pure Benn:

> I want to speak to you today about a new Britain and how we intend to bring home to our people the excitement there will be in building it.
>
> For 1964 is the year in which we can take our destiny into our own hands again.
>
> Since the war, the world has been rushing forward at an unprecedented, an exhilarating speed. In two decades, the scientists have made more progress than in the past two thousand years. They have made it possible for man to reach out to the stars, and to bring abundance from the earth. They have made it possible to end the dark ages of poverty and want, to take mankind forward to a future which our fathers could not have dreamed possible.

---

*Benn was not widely known as 'Tony' until the 1970s. Before then his colleagues usually called him 'Wedgie'.

'This is what 1964 can mean,' Wilson told his audience, his voice echoing around the grand old Victorian building:

> A chance for change. More, a time for resurgence.
> A chance to sweep away the grouse-moor conception of Tory leadership and refit Britain with a new image, a new confidence.
> A chance to change the face and future of Britain.[26]

Throughout much of his first year at the helm, Wilson had assumed that in the election he would be facing the veteran Prime Minister, Harold Macmillan. In October 1963, however, Macmillan unexpectedly resigned after being taken ill with prostate trouble. Wilson and his aide were greatly disappointed. 'As long as he [has] Macmillan opposite him,' one adviser noted, 'old, effete, worn out, a cynical dilettante, the contrast between Harold's character and Macmillan is an overwhelming advantage to Harold and the Labour Party.'[27]

The potential successor who most worried Wilson was the Chancellor, Reginald Maudling, an extremely bright character with a well-deserved reputation for louche self-indulgence.[28] However, Maudling shot himself in the foot with a lacklustre speech at the Conservative Party conference, and to general surprise the successor turned out to be Lord Home, the aristocratic and old-fashioned Foreign Secretary. When Wilson heard the news he was, according to one adviser, 'ecstatic with pleasure'.[29] Benn, too, was delighted. He thought that Home would be 'a dud when it comes to exciting the electorate and Wilson will run rings round him'.[30]

Although Home disclaimed his peerage and took office as Sir Alec Douglas-Home, it was hard for him to shake off the label of 'the fourteenth Earl of Home'. He had the image of a good-natured amateur who had somehow bumbled his way to the political summit, rather as if one of P. G. Wodehouse's heroes had woken up one day and found himself in 10 Downing Street. When interviewed by the *Observer* in September 1962, Home had remarked: 'When I have to read economic documents I have to have a box of matches and start moving them into position to simplify and illustrate the points to myself.'[31] In short, he was the ideal target for Wilson's attacks on the inadequacies of the old Establishment. As Noël Annan put it, 'the aristocrat in tweeds' was up against 'the technocrat in a white coat'; as David Frost told the viewers of *That Was The Week That Was*, it was 'Dull Alec versus Smart Alec'.[32]

To make matters worse, Home was notoriously ill suited to television, and when he arrived in the studio for one early appearance as Prime Minister he had a depressing exchange with the make-up assistant:

HOME: Can you not make me look better than I do on television? I look rather scraggy, like a ghost.
MAKE-UP LADY: No.
HOME: Why not?
MAKE-UP LADY: Because you have a head like a skull.
HOME: Does not everybody have a head like a skull?
MAKE-UP LADY: No.[33]

Direct comparisons between Home and Wilson showed that the latter was much more popular. Only 54 per cent told NOP that Home was 'tough'; the corresponding figure for Wilson was 80 per cent.[34] 'We are sick of seeing old men dressed in flat caps and bedraggled tweeds strolling with a 12 bore,' wrote one Tory supporter to Central Office. 'For God's sake, what is your campaign manager doing? These photographs of Macmillan's ghost with Home's face date [to] about 1912.'[35]

Unlike Wilson, Home was distinctly uncomfortable with the rhetoric of modernisation. In December 1963, he told an adviser that he wanted to speak for 'people who live close to nature', who were 'natural conservatives – slow thinkers but sound', and that he hoped to keep Britain 'in the First XI and not only that but one of the four opening batsmen'.[36] As one of Home's more acerbic Conservative critics later put it, the contest between the two philosophies was reminiscent of 'a horse-drawn plough competing with one pulled by a tractor'.[37] But Home's advisers prevailed upon him to adopt the message of modernisation.[38] The day after Wilson's Birmingham speech, he gave a riposte in Swansea, promising 'modernisation ... efficiency ... expansion' and calling Labour 'as stuffy and dated as a Victorian front parlour'. 'Their Luddism', he insisted, 'belongs to the nineteenth century, their vocabulary to the twenties and their economic planning ideas are a hangover from the days of post-war shortage and rationing.'[39] The effect was rather ruined, however, by Home's nervous delivery: as one account put it, 'there were constant dropped negatives, garbled statistics and pure howlers'.[40]

This pattern was repeated in Newcastle two months later, when Home tried to emulate Wilson's appeal to the young. 'To any young person looking for a full life, I say "Jump on the Conservative bandwagon,"' he declared enthusiastically. 'It is delivering the goods and it goes places and it will never, I promise you, get stuck in the mud.'[41] Young voters were widely seen as the key to victory, and Home's book of campaign speeches, *Peaceful Change*, boasted a section entitled 'I Call on British Youth' which opened with the obviously disingenuous words: 'Few subjects fascinate the Prime Minister more than youth.'[42] For his Newcastle speech, Home's speechwriters had included a joke about the Beatles designed to show the Prime Minister's grasp of contemporary culture. He was supposed to say: 'I am too modest to claim that the country loves us, but *you know that can't be bad*.' Unfortunately, Home clearly did not understand the reference, and to the audience's bewilderment, he ended up saying: 'You know, er, that can't be too bad.'[43]

To be fair to Home, it was hardly easy to lead a government that had largely run out of steam. During the spring of 1964, for example, he became bogged down in an internal Conservative battle over the complicated issue of Resale Price Maintenance (RPM), the mechanism by which manufacturers could dictate the price at which their goods were sold. Although both major parties had long thought about abolishing it, they were inhibited from doing so for fear of alienating shopkeepers, who thought that it protected them from the supermarkets and chain stores. The new President of the Board of Trade, Edward Heath, argued that the abolition of RPM would be an ideal way to demonstrate the Conservatives' modernising credentials.[44] Many Conservative backbenchers, however, were worried that this would lose them the shopkeeper's vote, and Heath only steamrollered the proposal through Cabinet by threatening to resign unless he got his way.[45] On 11 March, 22 Conservatives voted against the bill and 25 abstained, the biggest revolt since the fall of Chamberlain in 1940.[46] Not only did the whole business make Home and Heath very unpopular with their backbenchers, it also ensured that the right-wing press was in rebellious mood in the months running up to the election.[47] Indeed, many Tories thought that the leadership should have gone not to Home but to R. A. Butler, his experienced Foreign Secretary. Butler himself made little secret of his belief that Home did not have the brains for the job. 'Mind you,' he would say at the end of some typically indiscreet anecdote, 'Alec's a good man really.'[48]

Harold Wilson, by contrast, did not underestimate his rival. He often remarked that Home was 'going down well with the Tory women', and he worried that the Prime Minister's unpretentious decency might win over the electorate. 'I was given a book on my eighth birthday called *Test*

Match Surprise by Jack Hobbs,' Wilson told a journalist. 'It was about a cricketing peer, Lord Ravensdale, if I remember rightly, who gets attacked by the press but goes on to make 51 in the second innings, and to take 5 for 50.'[49]

And, just as Wilson feared, by the spring of 1964 Home was beginning to contemplate a Test Match Surprise of his own. Most historians agree that Home's leadership was surprisingly effective; indeed, his poll ratings were consistently higher than Macmillan's in his final year.[50] His palpable decency and modesty were slowly winning round the critics on his own backbenches. His performances in the Commons and on the stump had begun to pick up; indeed, *The Times* commended his 'cheerful confidence and unforced humour'.[51] Thanks to Reginald Maudling's generous 1963 Budget, the economy was booming: unemployment was low, demand and production were up, and what commentators called a 'dash for growth' was under way. In April, Home confirmed that the date of the election would be 15 October, which his advisers thought would give him time to claw back Wilson's lead in the polls.[52] An expensive Conservative advertising campaign reminded voters that their living standards had dramatically improved over the previous thirteen years. 'Conservatives Give Prosperity', ran the slogan on one poster: 'Don't chuck it away'. 'It's Your Standard of Living', proclaimed another: 'Keep It'.[53]

'We are all extremely anxious now about the way the political situation is developing,' Benn recorded on 6 July. 'Harold is principally concerned with his own position and we have lost the initiative.'[54] He was quite right: slowly but surely, the Tories were chipping away at Wilson's lead. The summer of 1964 was unusually warm, and from the beginning of June onwards the country enjoyed almost unbroken sunshine and blue skies. The seaside resorts recorded their best season in living memory; teenagers lazed contentedly to the sound of the Beatles and the Rolling Stones; couples strolled down the high streets contemplating future purchases; and all appeared to be right with the world.[55] In August, Gallup found that 46 per cent of the electorate approved of the government's record, up from 32 per cent in July 1963.[56] Labour's lead had been almost 20 per cent at the end of May; by July it was down to 7 per cent; by August it was 5 per cent; and as September began, it was a mere 2 per cent.[57]

With the outcome of the election now in serious doubt, Labour's campaign kicked off on 12 September with a rally at the Empire Pool, Wembley. The line-up was designed to convey the right mixture of working-class traditionalism and slick, fashionable modernity, so the audience were treated not only to the Grimethorpe Colliery Brass Band and the Welsh Male Voice Choir but to performances by Humphrey Lyttleton's jazz band, Harry Corbett and Vanessa Redgrave.[58] 'On the one hand,' Wilson told his cheering audience, 'you have a tired Administration which no longer has anything to offer the country, no objectives, no horizons, no heights to conquer . . . On the other hand, we in the Labour Party think Britain can do better. We do not feel that what we have so far achieved is good enough.'[59] Despite the erosion of his lead in the polls, he had no intention of abandoning the emphasis on modernisation that had initially served him so well. 'Interviewed' by Benn for a party political broadcast, Wilson promised 'something like President Kennedy had . . . a programme of a hundred days of dynamic action'.[60]

The Labour manifesto, *Let's Go with Labour for the New Britain*, published that same week, began in familiar fashion, promising a 'New Britain – mobilizing the resources of technology under a national plan; harnessing our national wealth in brains, our genius for scientific invention and medical discovery; reversing the decline of the thirteen wasted years', and so on.[61] There were promises to set up special Ministries of Technology and of Economic Affairs, which would work on a long-term national plan for the economy; there were pledges to increase National Insurance payments and benefits for the old, the sick and the unemployed; there were commitments to abolish prescription charges, build more hospitals, scrap the eleven-plus and undertake 'a programme of massive expansion in higher, further and university education'. Modernisation was the overarching theme, and it was noticeable that while Labour manifestos of the fifties had talked a great deal about the poor and the dispossessed, this edition preferred to discuss 'the go-ahead people with a sense of national purpose'. Indeed, many contemporary observers thought that it had been carefully designed to 'increase the middle-class appeal of the party'.[62]

By contrast, the Conservatives preferred to wallow in the joys of prosperity.[63] Their most notable television broadcast told the story of a housewife whose husband seems to have forgotten their wedding anniversary:

> She leant on her vacuum cleaner and sulked. A Conservative canvasser called. No thanks, she said, we're Labour here. Just then the husband rang to say that her present was down in a show-room – a car. A Labour canvasser called – a pompous, duffle-coated intellectual who prated

about Harold Wilson's views on international liquidity. She thought back to the days of the Labour Government — coupons, queues, shortages — and compared this with the affluence of her home — washing machine, refrigerator and now a car. By the end of the film she has come to realize that whatever her husband's prejudice, Labour had nothing to offer her.

Many commentators hated the broadcast, seeing it as the worst kind of slick, Americanised television advertising. But the party's vice-chairman, Lord Poole, was unrepentant. 'In any election,' he said, 'you've got to have a bloody good bit of rough stuff . . . After all, if you don't parade the circus down the street no one will buy a ticket for the night.'[64]

Unfortunately for the Conservatives, their own spokesmen were rarely as successful as their campaign broadcasts. Home had been given extensive coaching to prepare for his speaking tours and television appearances, but he began the campaign with a hideous gaffe on the BBC's *Election Forum*, referring to old-age pensions as 'donations' as though he were some relic of Victorian paternalism. A Vicky cartoon in the *Evening Standard* was typical of the general reaction: two old men are sitting reading about the government pension scheme, with one telling the other: 'Sir Alec says he'll give us a donation when we're a bit older.'[65] And in contrast to Wilson, Home evidently found it hard to adjust to the requirements of television. The producer of *Election Forum* later recalled:

> Wilson arrived early: polite, wary and prepared, with a posse of advisers. He ate cold ham and salad with the production staff and went to the studio with the air of a serious politician dealing with an important situation. Home arrived shortly before the programme started, accompanied only by the Director of the Conservative Research Department. He looked so exhausted that his skin appeared to be drawn tightly over his skull. His answers to the questions fired at him seemed totally unprepared.[66]

But contrary to political myth, many of Home's contemporaries thought that he was surprisingly effective. Robin Day, the BBC's most forceful and controversial interviewer, wrote that although Home lacked Wilson's sharp eloquence, he 'spoke crisply, lucidly and incisively', and 'sounded more straight-forward than either Macmillan or Wilson'.[67] 'He was quite an impressive man,' recalled the Labour MP Dick Taverne. 'He was very direct on television . . . His directness and candour contrasted quite well with Harold, although the public didn't see it that way.'[68] Even Tony Benn later admitted that he had been too quick to dismiss Home's old-fashioned appeal. 'It was easy for Wilson to make fun of him,' he mused, 'but he had a certain straightness about him – "good old Alec Home" . . . And he campaigned very powerfully. I think he's a much underestimated figure.'[69]

While Home's modesty drew admiration from even his greatest critics, Wilson ran a highly personalised, almost presidential campaign. Some journalists loved it; indeed, they were so keen to cast him as the British answer to President Kennedy that their reports might have been written by the Labour leader himself. For instance, on a visit to Liverpool:

> Hundreds of children followed him round during the day. They asked for autographs, they chanted his name and yelled 'Yeah, yeah, yeah', which, in Merseyside, is an honour otherwise given only to Beatles. At one time in the afternoon a crowd of children actually mobbed Wilson and injured his arm. His extraordinary Pied Piper effect on the young is something quite unprecedented in British politics, and a little uncanny. For instance children, and sometimes grown-ups, made a point of touching his car, and then gazing at the hand which had received such magical blessing.[70]

Most of Wilson's own colleagues, however, were rather put out by his personalised campaigning style. 'Of course we've all been downgraded because Harold is absolutely determined to be the sole man,' grumbled Richard Crossman at the beginning of September.[71] *The Times* remarked that no party leader in recent history had taken so much upon himself, and the journalist Anthony Howard later recalled that the campaign 'was really run by two people, Harold Wilson and Marcia Williams'.[72]

Wilson's closeness to his political secretary did not go unnoticed. Back in March, the romantic novelist and staunch anti-socialist Barbara Cartland had publicly accused them of having an affair, and nine days before the polls opened, Quintin Hogg responded to heckling about the Profumo scandal with a characteristically impulsive rebuke: 'If you can tell me there are no adulterers on the front bench of the Labour Party you can talk to me about Profumo.' As it turned out, the row quickly blew over; but the gossip about Wilson's relationship with Marcia Williams did not go away, and would return to trouble him later in the decade.[73]

Despite Wilson's supposed appeal to children, as the campaign entered its final weeks the two parties could hardly have been closer. The weather was beautiful: 'the most perfect autumn I can remember,' wrote Crossman, 'on and on, lovely warm sunshine, mists in the early morning, the farm amazingly dry'.[74] Labour's lead had finally evaporated at the end of September, and some polls in the next few days even showed the Conservatives taking the lead.[75] At this point, however, luck deserted them. Home was having severe problems with hecklers; one meeting at Putney Bridge was particularly notable:

> The longer Home soldiered on with his set speech, the angrier they became, and so in turn did the Tories in the audience. Some middle-aged ladies clouted the children with rolled umbrellas. Another took out a bag of pepper and scattered it in their eyes. A purple-faced steward walked up to a scrawny, pale heckler and yelled, 'Shut up, you ignorant turd!' straight in his face. More fighting broke out, the police came in, and uproar silenced Sir Alec.[76]

The greatest debacle, however, was Home's final set-piece speech of the campaign at the Bull Ring in Birmingham, where the Prime Minister was systematically shouted down by hundreds of hecklers yelling: 'Tories out! We want Wilson!' Home struggled to carry on, but his speech was almost completely inaudible, with only the occasional scrap floating over 'like the sound of a single flute in a Wagner storm scene'.[77] To make matters worse, he was also confronted by an alarming apparition in the front row of the crowd: a Homosaurus, a cardboard monster with 'the body of a prehistoric reptile and the face of Sir Alec'.[78] It was hardly surprising that, with the Homosaurus staring back at him, he should have found it so difficult to quell the hecklers. Finally, after an hour of torment, Home attempted to leave the stage, but even this proved difficult as his retinue literally had to fight their way up the aisle to shepherd him out, while the Prime Minister dodged the kicks and blows of his assailants.[79]

On television the whole business looked terrible. Home later admitted that he appeared 'hunted', and the general atmosphere of chaos and fury was the worst kind of publicity. Like his party chairman, Lord Blakenham, Home thought that the Bull Ring speech was the point on which the campaign turned.[80] The sense of Tory anxiety was heightened a few days later by a disastrously indiscreet interview given by Rab Butler to George Gale of the

Daily Express. 'We're running neck and neck,' Butler remarked. 'I'll be very much surprised if there's much in it – say 20 seats either way. But things might start slipping in the last few days . . . They won't slip towards us.'[81]

On polling day, Thursday 15 October, the weather changed at last. After three months of sunshine, it was wet and misty across the country. In the morning's newspapers both Gallup and NOP had Labour ahead, but only by the tiniest of margins, while the *Daily Express* gave the Conservatives a lead of 1 per cent.[82] One of Wilson's great concerns had already been allayed. The BBC were due to show an episode of *Steptoe and Son* that evening at eight and he was worried that the audience, whom he thought would be Labour voters, would stay in and watch television rather than go out and vote. Under pressure, the BBC director-general Hugh Carleton Greene agreed to postpone the programme by an hour. 'Thank you very much, Hugh,' Wilson replied. 'That will be worth a dozen or more seats to me.' Asked to suggest an alternative programme to fill the slot, the Labour leader thought and then said: '*Oedipus Rex*, Greek tragedy.'[83]

Sir Alec Douglas-Home spent election night nervously watching the returns on television in Downing Street, surrounded by his staff, his family and tables groaning with food and drink.[84] Wilson, meanwhile, watched the early returns with his wife and closest advisers in his suite in the Adelphi Hotel in Liverpool, armed with a slide-rule and a telephone. At midnight he was driven to his own constituency in Huyton for the count. By this stage it was clear that the overall result was going to be extremely close, but it was still impossible to tell who had won. Home, who knew that the decision would not come until the following day, had already retired to bed. Wilson, typically hyperactive, stayed up until four, slept for a couple of hours, and then caught an eight o'clock train down to London. A small crowd cheered as he climbed into his compartment, but the tired Labour leader could only manage a feeble wave. As the train rattled south his staff huddled around a little radio, desperate to hear the latest results, but there was still no definitive verdict. Marcia Williams was terrified that 'Harold would step into the train ahead and step out at Euston behind'.[85] At about eleven-thirty, as the train approached London, Wilson announced that he was sure he had lost: 'It's no good. We shan't make it. I've checked with the slide-rule. We've lost by one seat.'[86]

At midday the train pulled into Euston and the Wilson party disembarked to desultory cheers from a waiting crowd. Within the hour it was indeed pretty much all over, but not as the Labour leader had forecast. The last marginal constituencies were falling not to the Tories but to Labour, and at ten to three in the afternoon the returning officer at Brecon and Radnor announced that Labour had held the seat, giving them 315 MPs and an overall majority in the new Parliament. Half an hour later, dressed in top hat and tails, Home emerged from Downing Street and told the press that he was on his way to Buckingham Palace. Wilson had done it, and a further half-hour after that came the telephone call that he had been dreaming about all his life. 'Would it', asked Sir Michael Adeane, the Queen's private secretary, 'be convenient for you to come round and see Her Majesty?'[87]

The election could hardly have been closer. Labour had a majority of just five seats, which was far smaller than Wilson had hoped for. If a mere nine hundred voters in eight crucial constituencies had voted for the Conservatives instead of Labour, or even abstained, then Home would have stayed in office.[88] Wilson's supporters often claimed that his modernising style and message had won it, but in reality there was little evidence that this was the case. In 1964, Labour actually polled ten thousand *fewer* votes than in 1959, when they had lost.[89] At the same time the Tory vote fell by almost two million so there is a strong argument that the election had really been decided not by Wilson but by the alienation of the Conservative faithful.[90] The big winners, unexpectedly, were the Liberals, who had benefited from the genial leadership of Jo Grimond and the campaign services of Honor Blackman, the fashionable star of *The Avengers*. They had won three million votes, doubling their tally in the previous election, and many of their new supporters were probably former Conservatives who did not want to vote for Wilson. However, thanks to the electoral system, the Liberal revival did not translate into parliamentary strength, and they won just nine seats in the new House of Commons.[91]

In the end, Wilson's margin of victory was so narrow that few observers could resist wondering what might have happened had history taken a different course. If the news of Nikita Khrushchev's fall from power in the Soviet Union, announced late on polling day, had come a little earlier, it is plausible that anxious voters might have rallied to the incumbent government.[92] Many historians have cast Home as a likeable but inevitable loser, but actually his performance in dragging the Tories back to the brink of victory was an impressive achievement in itself. Indeed, if those nine hundred voters had acted differently, he would have entered the textbooks as a plucky underdog who unexpectedly saved his party from certain defeat. The majority of his Conservative colleagues, however, felt that if Home had been able to come so close, then a different leader might well have won. Wilson himself believed that he would have lost had Rab Butler been the Conservative leader.[93] Even Harold Macmillan, who had engineered Home's succession, admitted that 'he could not impress himself on Parlt or people enough for a PM'. Home, he thought, 'didn't have enough fire in his belly'; maybe it would have been better if Butler had succeeded him after all.[94]

The premiership of Sir Alec Douglas-Home had lasted a mere 362 days.*
He left Downing Street later that afternoon by the garden gate, although Wilson generously offered him the hospitality of Chequers until he had sorted out somewhere else to live.[95] Home and his wife had been extremely popular with the Downing Street staff; one official recalled that 'as the election results came in, lots of the garden room girls were in tears at the thought of losing two very nice people'.[96] The Prime Minister's former neighbour at number 11, meanwhile, spent the afternoon loading boxes full of his possessions into a van by the back gate. The ritual transfer of power could be cruel: at one point, struggling with a packing case of 'ageing toys and half-empty bottles of ketchup', Reginald Maudling looked up and saw Wilson's adviser Thomas Balogh 'framed in the window next door to the Cabinet Room, with a wide grin'.[97] However, it was never easy to keep Maudling's spirits down for long. 'I shall have to look for a job and make some money,' he mused, gazing out of the windows on to Horse Guards Parade for one last time. 'It's exciting. It won't be such hard work and I'll probably be better paid.'[98]

Home's defeat meant the end of an era in British politics. In material terms, most voters had never been better off; earnings were rising, prices were relatively stable, unemployment was negligible and the high streets were awash with consumer goods.[99] Yet at the same time, Wilson had been able to profit from an underlying sense of insecurity: resentment at the collapse of British power abroad; unease at the Conservatives' failure to embrace the spirit of modernisation; anxieties about materialism and cultural decadence; fears of falling behind Britain's international competitors. The paradoxical result was that although the Conservatives had presided over an increasingly affluent society, they left office unlamented by all but their staunchest partisans.[100]

Meanwhile, on the afternoon of Friday, 16 October, as Harold Wilson's car headed through the drizzle towards Buckingham Palace, he could be

---

*This made it the briefest premiership since that of Andrew Bonar Law in 1922–3 (209 days).

forgiven for basking in his victory. 'We've waited thirteen years for this,' Wedgwood Benn triumphantly wrote in his diary.[101]

Now, at last, the new age could begin. The Labour leader had promised 'the ending of economic privilege, the abolition of poverty in the midst of plenty, and the creation of real equality of opportunity'. He had promised that 'the British [will] again become the go-ahead people with a sense of national purpose'.[102] Above all, he had promised a 'New Britain', and at last he would have the chance to build it. It was hardly surprising that the new Prime Minister was, in the words of one watching journalist, 'dazed and almost green with excitement'.[103] It was, he wrote to a friend, the beginning of 'a tremendous adventure'.[104]

2

THE TEN FACES OF HAROLD

NIGEL: Now listen. The days of the kow-towing little runt of a scholarship boy, you know, they're over, they're finished!

Dennis Potter, *Stand up for Nigel Barton* (1965)

Anyway, come the evening of the Browns' visit, the Callaghans duly arrived . . . and Jim and Audrey were getting on very agreeably with Sophie talking about their new squeezeematic window-cleaning mop, when there came a tremendous crash at the front door and George burst in, tripping over the door-mat and looking very tired. 'Quick,' cried Sophie, leaping up, 'put on a soothing record,' so I hastily selected Mantovani's 'Moonlight Serenade' and slipped it over the spindle.

'Mrs Wilson's Diary', *Private Eye*, 5 March 1965

Shortly after four o'clock on the afternoon of Friday, 16 October 1964, a sleek black Daimler eased through the rain into the forecourt of Buckingham Palace. Harold Wilson had dreamed of this moment since, as a cheeky eight-year-old boy, he had posed for a photograph on the steps of 10 Downing Street. Now, at forty-eight, he was to be the youngest Prime Minister since the Earl of Rosebery in 1894, and he was determined to show the public that he was a modern man, a husband and a father as well as a national leader. With him in the car were his wife Mary and his elder son Robin, and their presence at his side as he walked into the Palace came as a mild surprise to the royal officials, who were used to seeing their new Prime Ministers on their own. 'The arrival of Wilson was taken calmly,' recalled the Queen's assistant private secretary, Sir Martin Charteris. 'There was no feeling of a problem, though when he came to the Palace with his family it was a bit of a culture shock.'[1]

Wilson himself was in a daze of relief, excitement and shock. His meeting with the Queen was brief and straightforward. 'She simply asked me if I could form an administration,' he later recalled, and he 'was made Prime

Minister on the spot'.[2] Apart from a shared interest in the values of the Scout movement, he had little in common with his monarch, and nostalgic conversations about 'rubbing two sticks together' could only last them so long. However, these two superficially incompatible individuals eventually got on very well. The Queen saw Wilson as an intriguing, even amusing character whose background and values were completely different from those she usually encountered. Wilson, meanwhile, treasured their relationship as evidence of his own success. Like many of his working-class supporters, he liked the pomp and circumstance associated with the monarchy and found it hard to hide his excitement at being part of it himself.[3] He enjoyed his regular Tuesday audiences with the monarch, and, according to Palace gossip, used to 'talk to her as if she were a member of his Cabinet', which both of them evidently enjoyed. 'His Audiences got longer and longer,' recalled one political aide. 'Once he stayed for two hours, and was asked to stay for drinks. Usually prime ministers only see her for twenty or thirty minutes, and it is not normal for them to be offered drinks by the monarch.'[4]

Harold Wilson's obvious admiration for the Royal Family was only one of many aspects of his personality that often baffled his ministers. Indeed, although Wilson was the dominant British political figure of the 1960s and 1970s, holding power for almost eight years and winning four out of five general elections, he always remained something of an enigma: ambiguous, contradictory, even unfathomable.

Like many of his Cabinet colleagues, Wilson had studied at Oxford in the highly charged atmosphere on the eve of the Second World War. But in contrast to the likes of Crossman, Healey, Jenkins, Crosland and Benn, he displayed very little interest in radical ideas or student politics. He did not join the Labour Club: indeed, he wrote to his parents that it was 'very petty'. He never took part in the controversial Oxford Union debates of the day.[5] He did join the university's Liberal Club, but few of his contemporaries thought that he was particularly interested in politics. Indeed, he was noted more for his 'political blandness' than for any strong convictions, and his name was almost never mentioned in the Liberal Club's magazine. One fellow member could not recall 'his taking any strong political line at any time and certainly I had no indication that he was likely to join Labour'.[6] 'I could have told that he was not a Tory,' wrote a tutor who taught him politics for two years. 'That is all.'[7]

While the student politicians who were to become ministers in his governments were busily running for office, dashing off angry articles or dining with intellectual celebrities, Wilson remained a comparative nonentity. At the same time that the likes of Crosland and Jenkins were indulging themselves at lively parties, he struggled to save money and secluded himself in his room working on his tutorial essays. This was a more mundane experience, but it was also a more common one. And while Wilson was superficially a more mundane character than his future colleagues, he was also a more successful one. It was his lack of interest in political ideology, his simple, homely tastes, his very ordinariness, that explained why he rose to the top of the greasy pole, while his extravagantly gifted contemporaries fell by the wayside.

Wilson once claimed that he had grown up in a town where 'more than half the children in my class never had boots and shoes on their feet'.[8] This was a gross exaggeration. Although he often liked to portray himself as working class, he had been born in 1916 into a respectable lower-middle-class family just outside Huddersfield. The Wilson family could have been an advertisement for the values of the Nonconformist middle class: they were solid, sober citizens, well turned-out, hard-working, and a little dull. One biographer sums up the ethos of the Wilson household as 'eager striving', and Harold himself was no different.[9] Friends and teachers remembered the chubby boy as something of a school swot, or even a prig. His teachers remarked on his prodigious memory, which meant at only six or seven he could reproduce tables of figures with barely a single mistake.[10] He was always aware of current affairs: when he went into hospital for appendicitis, the seven-year-old Harold reminded his visiting parents that they should go and vote for Philip Snowden, a prominent Labour politician whose puritanical respectability went down well with the Wilson family.[11]

But Harold's greatest enthusiasm, and the hobby that shed most light on his personality, was Scouting. At twelve he won a competition in the *Yorkshire Post* by writing a hundred words about his hero, Robert Baden-Powell; he was a regular and enthusiastic participant in Scout camps; and as Labour leader, he told an interviewer that the Fourth Scout Law, 'A Scout is a friend to all and a brother to every other Scout', was one of the guiding principles of his life.[12] As one writer puts it, Scouting never lost its 'semi-mystical significance' for Wilson, being the practical application of his parents' Congregationalist principles.[13] Yet to many of his colleagues, especially the intellectuals who had won such honours at Oxford in the thirties,

Scouting was the typically middle-class enthusiasm of an embarrassingly middlebrow man. 'No man can be the kind of boy scout Harold is and read aloud Kipling's *If* as often as he reads it to me without a great deal of self-deception in his make-up,' remarked Richard Crossman. 'It's because he is unreflective and unphilosophical.'[14]

Despite the contempt in which Wilson's old Oxford contemporaries often held him, in many ways his university career was no less impressive than theirs. He had modest tastes and took no great pleasure in lavish meals and drinking sessions, but he was also extremely short of money; not only did he send his washing home to Yorkshire to save on laundry bills, but his mother used to send him meat and biscuits in the post.[15] He regularly sent proud letters to his parents telling them how many hours he had put in at his desk: in March 1935, for example, he boasted that he had 'touched 10 hours one day' and reached '46 hours for the week', not including lectures and tutorials. Seven or eight hours a day, at a time when many students spent as much time in the pub as over their books, struck him as a decent record.[16]

Wilson was, in short, the classic swot: as he told an interviewer in October 1964, he had 'always been driven by a feeling that there is something to be done and I really ought to be doing it . . . Even now I feel myself saying that if I spend an evening enjoying myself, I shall work better next day, which is only a kind of inversion of the old feeling of guilt.'[17] Yet he was also exceptionally clever. Ben Pimlott even calls him 'the outstanding student of his generation'.[18] He was awarded the best PPE First of the decade, and his examination results were simply incredible. Of his eighteen papers, only one fell below the alpha grade, and his economic theory paper was awarded the first alpha-plus in the history of the subject.[19] The historian Kenneth Morgan, who was later taught by Wilson's old tutor, found that he 'considered Wilson the best student he ever had'.[20]

Perhaps not surprisingly, there was a solitary side to Wilson's character, and he had no intimate friends. 'I am not wasting time going to see people and messing about in their rooms,' he wrote to his parents, 'for this [academic work] is more interesting.'[21] Yet when he did venture out, he was a relatively popular figure, with something of the overgrown Boy Scout about him. He was known to be boastful, an unreliable storyteller and an inveterate show-off, but he was also cheerful and kind-hearted.[22]

These were qualities that appealed to his future wife, Gladys Mary Baldwin, whom Wilson had met at the local tennis club shortly before going up to Oxford.* Like Wilson, Mary took her religion very seriously. She was a quiet, thoughtful girl, impressed despite herself by young Harold's self-promoting enthusiasm. Only three weeks after their first meeting, he predicted that he would marry her. As a family joke later had it, if she had believed him, it would have been a short romance.[23] It would perhaps also have been short-lived if she had known how Wilson's career would develop: she had no interest whatsoever in politics. 'She really doesn't want to be the Prime Minister's wife and would love to be the wife of an Oxford don,' recorded Tony Benn in 1965.[24]

Wilson's political journey began in 1937 with his appointment as a research assistant to Sir William Beveridge, the future author of the famous report on social insurance that became the blueprint for the post-war welfare state. His life in Oxford was interrupted by the outbreak of war, and Wilson joined the Economic Section of the Cabinet Secretariat, which was something of a hothouse for promising young minds. He eventually became a statistician in the Mines Department of the Board of Trade, where he made a great impression on another brilliant young economic adviser, Hugh Gaitskell.[25] By now Wilson was set on a political career. He had already begun to take a keen interest in the Labour Party, and in the post-war election of July 1945, not yet thirty, he was duly elected as MP for Ormskirk in Lancashire. Many contemporaries thought that he was something of a dull dog, fascinated by committees and statistics, but they also recognised his youthful talent. In 1947, promoted to the position of President of the Board of Trade, he became the youngest Cabinet minister since 1806.[26]

Wilson's elevation to the Cabinet marked him out as a direct rival to Gaitskell, who was Labour's other rising star of the late 1940s. The two men first fell out in 1949, but their mutual suspicion was based as much on personality as on policy.[27] A year later, Gaitskell wrote in his diary that Wilson might be 'extremely able', but offended too many people 'by being so swollen headed', and was so 'impersonal' that 'you don't feel really that he would ever have any close friends'.[28]

The truth was that Gaitskell and his Hampstead friends, Anthony Crosland and Roy Jenkins, looked down on Wilson as socially gauche, intellectually narrow and irredeemably middlebrow. Despite living barely half a mile from

---

*During their courtship and the early years of their marriage, she used the name Gladys. By the middle of the fifties, however, she was generally called by her second name, and it is as Mary Wilson that she is best known.

Gaitskell and his friends, Wilson almost never socialised with them. He was not interested in dancing and dinner parties; instead, he spent his free time at home with his family, helping the local Scouts, listening to Gilbert and Sullivan, playing with a Meccano set with his children, whacking a golf ball, and, on Sunday evenings, enjoying his favourite meat pie with HP sauce.[29] He did not really have any hobbies outside politics and had little interest in the arts. On holiday he would reread the detective novels of Agatha Christie and Dorothy L. Sayers, or the popular histories of Arthur Bryant, before inventing an excuse to get back to work.[30] His were the values, in short, of the typical lower-middle-class, suburban Englishman. 'Even his taste in paintings reflects his "Englishness",' wrote his loyal political secretary, Marcia Williams. 'His favourite painter is Lowry – because Lowry's world is a world Harold Wilson understands.'[31]

Wilson drew criticism throughout his career for his supposed lack of ideological commitment. When Philip Ziegler, his authorised biographer, admitted that he was 'far from being a committed socialist', Wilson replied cheerfully: 'That's lucky. Nor am I!'[32] On another occasion, he told the *Guardian* correspondent John Cole: 'I don't like theory. I got an alpha-plus in economic theory, but I never understood it. I think my examiner must have been very kind. Or perhaps he didn't understand it either.'[33] There was a strong element of self-mockery about this, but also more than a grain of truth. Wilson was always suspicious of abstractions, and he was most at home devising tactics to solve practical, short-term problems. He consistently sought compromise rather than conflict, he disliked dogmatic extremes, and he invariably spent a long time looking before he leapt.[34] For all his political precocity, he was still the hard-working character who had preferred the quiet backwater of the Oxford Liberal Club to the fevered arguments of the Labour Club. Socialism, to Wilson, was little different from Scouting. He was not somebody who would keenly debate the finer points of socialist theory into the small hours, but a brilliant tactician adept at tying and untying the most intricate of knots.[35]

The defining moment of Wilson's early political career came in April 1951. Gaitskell, who had been Chancellor for just a few months, had come up with a scheme to cut spending on the NHS in order to pay for Britain's Cold War rearmament programme, and when Aneurin Bevan, the champion of the Labour left, resigned from the Cabinet in protest, Wilson unexpectedly joined him in exile. This surprised many observers because Wilson had until then been seen as a cautious, moderate figure.[36] In fact, although he was henceforth associated with the Bevanite camp, he was never really a great firebrand of the left. Circumstances forced him to hobnob with the Bevanites, but in reality he was always a man of the centre.[37] Bevan himself was always suspicious of Wilson's motives. 'He's much more dangerous than Gaitskell,' he remarked in 1958, 'because he isn't honest and he isn't a man of principle but a sheer, absolute careerist, out for himself alone.'[38]

Such accusations of opportunism, inconsistency and untrustworthiness dogged Wilson throughout his career. In 1963 a cartoon in *Private Eye* lampooned him as 'Harold Willsoon, a very clever little politician. The reason why he is called Willsoon is that whenever anyone has said "Oh, not even Harold would do a thing like that", you can be absolutely certain that he will soon.'[39] A year later, Walter Terry remarked in the *Daily Mail* on the 'ten faces of Harold': Huddersfield Harold, American Harold, Basic Harold, 'Nationalize 'em Harold', Orthodox Harold, Intelligentsia Harold, Dynamic Harold, Little Englander Harold, Capitalist Harold and Russian Harold. Some of his Labour colleagues mused privately that ten faces might have been an underestimate.[40]

This was harsh, but even Wilson's staunchest defenders would have to admit that it had the ring of truth. Wilson *was* a brilliant opportunist, he did often give two answers to the same question, and his colleagues universally remarked on his artfulness. Tony Benn and James Callaghan both called him 'devious', and Richard Crossman wrote that he had 'a really elegant ability to be imprecise, to steer a non-committal hedging course and to say things which aren't quite right in order to avoid any commitment'. One opponent later commented: 'There are two things I dislike about Wilson. His face!'[41] In fact, much of this two-facedness was rooted in his dislike of personal arguments. The American Secretary of State Henry Kissinger wrote that he was 'touchingly eager for approval, especially from those he respected'.[42] But the same eagerness to please that had stood Wilson in such good stead as a schoolboy and Boy Scout would serve him less well as the leader of his party.

In later years, some of Wilson's old colleagues were so keen to point out his insecurities that they overlooked his undoubted political strengths. By the late fifties, he was back at Labour's top table as Shadow Chancellor, and had managed to carve out a new reputation as something of a wit. The intricate, interminable lectures about economic statistics had largely gone; instead, Wilson had a new rhetorical approach, full of homely aphorisms and witty flourishes. 'Epigram followed epigram,' wrote Harold Macmillan of his opponent, 'and the continual flashes of wit were from time to time relieved by more serious arguments.'[43] He was also an unusually considerate politician, loyal to his friends, charitable to his colleagues, and generous to his secretaries and officials. Benn called him 'an extremely kind man'; Lord Longford thought that he was 'a very nice, in particular a very kind man'; and even Sir Gerald Nabarro, one of his fiercest Conservative critics, wrote of his 'outstanding kindness, charm and generosity'.[44]

And despite his famous eagerness to be liked, Wilson was also a supremely resilient politician, patient and cool under fire. Much of this was rooted in his unflagging self-confidence; indeed, his perpetual good cheer often irritated those around him.[45] But Wilson's optimism could also be a tremendous asset: it kept him upright, still fighting, on occasions when other men might have crumbled. 'His image of himself', observed Richard Crossman in 1965, 'is as a gritty, practical Yorkshireman, a fighter, the Britisher who doesn't give in, who doesn't switch, who hangs on.'[46]

When Gaitskell died unexpectedly in January 1963, Wilson was one of the obvious favourites to succeed him. His leading rival, and the standard-bearer of the party right, was George Brown. The son of a lorry driver, Brown had been born in Lambeth in 1914 and was one of the few prominent Labour politicians of the sixties with genuine working-class roots. As a salesman and then a trade unionist, he had slowly worked his way up the political ladder, and by the time he was elected as Gaitskell's deputy in 1960, he was widely seen as the most popular and charismatic figure on the right wing of the party.[47]

Two more different characters than Wilson and Brown could barely have been imagined. Comparing the two men in March 1968, Crossman noted: 'Harold can be tender-hearted but he's also cool, careful, prim, nonconformist, intellectual, bookish: George is none of these things. He's tough and crude and yet brilliant and imaginative.'[48] To borrow the words of his biographer, Brown was also 'accident-prone, outspoken to an extent rare among modern politicians, intensely patriotic, hard-working, even harder drinking, quick as a Gascon to take offence in any company – and as swift to apologise for any offence given: he probably wrote more letters of apology than any politician in history'.[49]

Despite his indisputable political ability, Brown was a deeply flawed individual. Even one of his political patrons, the former Chancellor Hugh Dalton, thought that he was 'very awkward, vain, sensitive and fundamentally self-seeking and unfaithful'. Much of this was rooted in Brown's resentment of his colleagues; as Dalton noted, he was 'terribly class-conscious and prickly' and found 'it difficult to be a really good comrade with an "intellectual", defined as a person who has been at Public School and University'.[50] Similarly, Crossman recorded that although Brown was 'the most gifted, certainly the most imaginative' of his colleagues, 'he had a huge chip on his shoulder. For years George detested me because I was an intellectual from the universities. He openly detested such people. He sloshed them, he smashed them, he sneered at them and he grew famous as the Party's hatchet man to deal with left-wing intellectuals.'[51] Indeed, on one occasion in 1957, having taken offence to an article Crossman had written in the *Daily Mirror*, the diminutive Brown physically attacked him in a Commons corridor, only to find himself a moment later in a heap on the ground with Crossman sitting on top of him.[52]

If that were not enough, Brown's personal life was also messy, to say the least. His marriage was often less of a partnership than a running battle; indeed, at dinner parties his wife Sophie would frequently spend much of the evening insulting her husband, and it was quite normal for them to leave separately.[53] Part of the problem was that by the early sixties Brown was effectively an alcoholic: he would begin drinking whisky at lunchtime, and would then liberally top it up throughout the day, so he was usually drunk by the time he appeared in the Commons in the evening. 'He started two gins ahead of everybody else,' one of his friends later recalled. 'He'd go mad, suddenly berserk, on a couple of glasses of wine . . . Alcohol, no matter how small the amount, used to change him, change his personality so that he became very aggressive.'[54]

It was obvious to anyone who knew anything about Labour Party politics that the struggle for the leadership between Wilson and Brown would be particularly bitter. As one observer recorded, Brown nursed 'a pestilential hatred and contempt' for his Oxford-educated rival, partly on genuine political grounds but also because of their temperamental differences.[55] The strength of his hatred was not necessarily unusual, for many of Gaitskell's friends also detested Wilson. Tony Benn recalled that 'they just loathed him. They thought his economics were phoney, that his principles didn't exist.'[56] This was made even worse by their mutual social distaste: while Wilson resented the exclusive cultural snobbery of Gaitskell's Hampstead friends, they joked that he was a suburban dullard with 'flying ducks on the wall'.[57] And even many members of the party rank and file hated Wilson: one group of workers from the Hammersmith bus garage wrote to tell him 'what a dirty, treacherous, back-stabbing Bastard we think you are. You sit on the fence to see which way the cat jumps, and then you try to stab Hugh in the back.'[58]

As the campaign for the party leadership began, the one thing that united Gaitskell's old friends was a determination to prevent Wilson from succeeding him. As the obvious right-wing candidate, Brown was widely expected to win and was understandably confident. The problem, however, was that many of his natural allies were worried about being led by a man with such a record of instability and bad behaviour. The moderate Benn, for instance, thought that Gaitskell's death was 'a disaster because it looks as if George Brown will succeed him and for a number of reasons he is totally unsuited to be Leader of the Party'.[59] Even more revealing was the attitude of Anthony Crosland, the leading intellectual of the right, who had been extremely close to Gaitskell. Crosland complained that he was being given a choice between 'a crook and a drunk', and refused to contemplate voting for Brown. Indeed, he went to Brown's office and told him so, with the predictable result that Brown exploded with rage and then sent him an emotional letter of apology the following day.[60]

Instead, Crosland backed another candidate from the right of the party, James Callaghan, who was seen as a dark horse putting down a marker for the future. Like Brown, Callaghan was a trade unionist from a humble background; he was less charismatic, but a much steadier politician.[61] Brown, of course, was furious: he had 'absolute contempt' for Callaghan and did not bother to hide his scorn for his backers. In the middle of the campaign, sitting next to Callaghan on the opposition front bench, he turned to him and said: 'You must have a pretty good conceit of yourself to think that you can be leader of the Labour Party – why are you doing it?' Callaghan stared at him and then replied: 'Because a lot of people think I'd make a better job of it than you.'[62]

With the right divided, Wilson's path to the top was clear. On the first ballot, on 7 February 1963, he won 115 votes to Brown's 88 and Callaghan's 41. Brown was appalled. 'What a shit, what a bastard', he spat at one Callaghan voter as he walked through the Commons lobby.[63] A week later, it was all over: Wilson won the second ballot by 144 votes to 103. It had been a leadership contest of rare bitterness, with smears and insults being flung from all sides.[64] As acting leader, Brown had the unenviable duty of reading out the results himself. Although Wilson then gave a magnanimous speech asking him to stay on as his deputy, Brown immediately disappeared to Scotland without telling anyone where he was going.[65] This was a public sulk of impressive, although infantile, proportions, and for Wilson it was extremely embarrassing because it meant that he was unable to name his Shadow Cabinet team. Eventually, five days later, Brown did return and accepted the post of deputy leader, but the damage had been done. Wilson never forgot how he had been publicly humiliated. 'He will have to go in the end,' he told a friend, 'but it will have to be at a time of our making, when it suits us. And when we do drop him, you won't even hear a splash.'[66]

Many of the old Gaitskellites found it hard to conceal their misery at Wilson's victory. Dining with a triumphant Richard Crossman shortly after the second ballot, Roy Jenkins snapped: 'The fact is that Harold is a person no one can like, a person without friends.'[67] Anthony Crosland, after listening impatiently to a defence of Wilson's virtues, exploded: 'But the bloody man plays golf!'[68] Another revisionist, Bill Rodgers, later said that he 'felt rather as though Wilson had killed my father and married my mother — that was the sort of feeling I had. I never really could adjust to Harold Wilson.'[69]

The press, by contrast, was almost unanimous in its praise for the new Labour leader. The right-wing *Financial Times*, for example, concluded that 'on grounds of intellectual ability, experience, political acumen and the cool toughness in action needed by a Party leader, Harold Wilson was Labour's obvious choice'.[70] And Wilson's Conservative opponents also acknowledged that they were facing a formidable adversary. 'I thought you would win, and you did,' wrote Lord Hailsham in a letter of congratulation. 'I am sure your followers chose their ablest man.'[71] The Prime Minister agreed. 'Wilson is an able man, far more able than Brown,' wrote Harold Macmillan in his diary. 'He is good in the House and in the country — and, I am told, on T.V.'[72]

On the eve of his election Wilson told a friend that he was not going to waste his time on endless press interviews: 'And no social life either. That was another of Hugh's mistakes. A leader cannot afford it. Mary and I will have none of it whatsoever. We have a serious job to do.'[73] He was as good as his word, although this was not the image that was presented to the world. In fact, Wilson's public relations during the first months of his leadership were stunningly successful. By immediately staking out moderate positions on every issue from nationalisation to Europe, he put an end to the quarrelling that had inflicted so much damage on the party since the early 1950s. The old Bevanites kept quiet because they felt that, deep down, the new leader was one of them; the Gaitskellites, meanwhile, were impressed by his willingness to listen to their opinions and copy their rhetoric. After all the arguments of the Gaitskell years, Wilson's emollient approach was a blessed relief. Party unity, not ideological purity, was the priority now, and it paid off handsomely. On the afternoon of 16 October, as Wilson's Daimler glided away from Buckingham Palace, with the new Prime Minister, his wife and son grinning delightedly in the back, many Labour supporters had never been happier.[74]

As soon as Wilson had been shown around his new home, he began to think about putting together his first Cabinet. In opposition he had been careful to keep the revisionist right happy; to his old Bevanite cronies, he joked that he was 'running a Bolshevik Revolution with a Tsarist Shadow Cabinet'.[75] In government he kept up the same careful balancing act, and when the Cabinet assembled for the first time on 19 October, it was dominated by Gaitskell's old friends rather than Wilson's left-wing associates. Only six out of twenty-three had voted for Wilson as Labour leader, and what was more, the right controlled all the key economic offices as well as foreign affairs and defence.[76]

The two most powerful figures, apart from the Prime Minister himself, were James Callaghan and George Brown, both men of the right. Callaghan, the Chancellor of the Exchequer, was regarded by some of his Oxbridge-educated colleagues as rather a lightweight, and Wilson was thought to have given him the Treasury so that he could run it himself.[77] Ironically, events were to show that Callaghan was one of the period's few genuine political heavyweights, and his record of holding all three major offices of state (Treasury, Home Office and Foreign Office) as well as the premiership remains unmatched by any other British politician before or since.

Born in 1912, Jim Callaghan had been brought up in Portsmouth in an atmosphere of fierce religiosity, dominated by the activities of the local Baptist chapels and the precepts of his extremely pious mother. His character was strongly marked by the religious experience of his youth. Adultery, homosexuality, pornography, drug-taking and other apparent moral depredations all left him with a deep sense of distaste, and during the late sixties his moral rectitude was often mocked by his more well-heeled Cabinet colleagues.[78] Portsmouth itself also left a deep mark on the young Callaghan; as he put it himself, 'the sea was the whole of our daily lives'.[79] The Royal Navy, in which he served during the Second World War, meant everything to him: he treasured the memory of his father, a chief petty officer, collected naval prints and photographs, used seafaring imagery in his speeches and generally exhibited the robust, patriotic populism of someone who had grown up in one of the British Empire's historic ports.[80]

As a boy, Callaghan had known poverty and hardship, especially after the early death of his father, but he was not quite working class, more naval lower middle class. Although touchy and defensive if patronised, he was a tough, self-reliant character and an enthusiastic team player. Like George Brown, he worked his way up through the trade union ranks into Parliament, and he always took his roots as a union man very seriously.[81] In 1947 he was given junior office in Attlee's Labour government and was widely seen as a coming man. Admittedly, he was not a brilliant young meteor like Wilson, but he was physically imposing, articulate and sensible, a solid man of the centre who knew his own mind and reflected the values of the party at large.[82] In the fifties he became close to Gaitskell, but the Hampstead scene was altogether too stuck-up and self-regarding for the self-consciously ordinary Callaghan. And he was also remarkably good on television, communicating confidence and straightforwardness. In an age when the television was becoming a vital tool of political communication, this was a valuable asset.[83]

Callaghan's elevation to the Treasury was his first Cabinet appointment, and since most of his immediate predecessors were regarded as failures, some contemporaries doubted that he would be able to cope. He had never been to university, had no real experience of business or industry, and made no pretence of knowing much about economic theory.[84] However, these were not necessarily terminal disadvantages, and while Shadow Chancellor he attended a series of seminars at Nuffield College, Oxford, in an attempt to educate himself before taking office.[85] As his colleague Edmund Dell later put it, his 'self-deprecating modesty, added to an easy manner and an assured understanding of his audience, made him a master of the House of Commons'. Dell noted that Callaghan was 'aware that he himself was no expert, and with his customary, and attractive, candour, he was prepared to admit it openly'.[86]

Callaghan was also almost effortlessly good at winning public sympathy; one commentator wrote that to watch him campaigning in his Cardiff constituency was 'to see a master craftsman at work, his technique tempered by a genuine humanity and directness'.[87] Although his bright young colleagues doubted his intellect, Callaghan was steady, pragmatic and popular, qualities that arguably counted for much more in the game of politics. Perhaps his most revealing association was his role as a parliamentary consultant for the Police Federation. Even though he gave up the position when he took office in October 1964, Callaghan was still portrayed by cartoonists as 'PC Jim', the 'political reincarnation' of the titular character from the television series *Dixon of Dock Green*: reassuring, decent and dependable.[88]

Decency and dependability were not qualities that many observers associated with the other heavyweight of the right, George Brown, who was Labour's deputy leader and the new First Secretary at the Department of Economic Affairs. Brown, who had finally managed to hide his disappointment at losing the leadership election to Wilson, did have some very impressive qualities: he was energetic, charismatic and quick-witted, and in a government of academics he could point to genuine working-class roots and a history of hard work.[89] But he had already given an extraordinary demonstration of his unreliability during the last year of the Conservative government. On 22 November 1963, after the assassination of President Kennedy, he was invited to appear on the ITV programme *This Week* and offer a tribute. He had met Kennedy three times in his life, for a grand total of about two hours, and on the last occasion Kennedy had invited Brown's daughter, who lived in New York, to join them. Brown therefore had good reason to be mournful, although perhaps not to behave as he did.

The other guests, to whom Brown was introduced in the hospitality suite, included the American actor Eli Wallach. Brown, who had already had a few drinks, tried to make small talk with Wallach, but the actor was clearly still upset by the news about Kennedy. Brown then loudly asked 'why actors were so conceited', accused Wallach of always carrying 'a newspaper in his pocket with his name in prominent headlines', and mocked him for having never heard of Ted Willis, the author of *Dixon of Dock Green* and a speechwriter for Harold Wilson. Wallach leapt to his feet, called Brown a 'bastard' and threatened to leave unless he was silenced. Brown then made another remark about conceited American actors, at which Wallach took off his jacket and shouted: 'Come outside and I'll knock you off your can!' At this point general anarchy ensued, with the production team wrestling the infuriated Wallach to the ground, but after a short interval the two men were persuaded to shake hands. As Wallach left the room to go down to the studio, Brown could not resist having the last word. 'And now you'll know who Ted Willis is!' he shouted after the disappearing actor.[90]

With any other politician, this would have been enough excitement for one evening. However, it was merely the prelude to the real action of the night, Brown's televised tribute to Kennedy. Bearing in mind that

Brown had spent less time with Kennedy than most people spend with their dentist, his answers to Kenneth Harris's questions were bizarre to say the least:

> HARRIS: I know you met President Kennedy once or twice. Did you get to know him as a man?
> BROWN: *(glaring ferociously)*. Now, you're talking about a man who was a very great friend of mine. We understood what the world was about, and what the division between East and West was about. I think it is a terrible tragedy . . . Jack Kennedy, who I liked, who I was very near to . . . *(close to tears)* I remember it's not many weeks ago I was over there with my daughter who lives in New York. We were walking across the garden, and she was talking to Jackie across the garden. One is terribly hurt by this loss . . .

Throughout the interview Brown referred to his close friends 'Jack' and 'Jackie', waved his arms around wildly, slurred his words, and generally struggled to maintain both his composure and some semblance of sobriety. Nobody watching the programme could be sure that he would not, say, burst into tears or physically assault the interviewer, and his performance was, as his biographer admits, 'deeply, excruciatingly, embarrassing, a compound of maudlin sentimentality, name-dropping and aggression'.[91]

Of all the anecdotes about Brown's misbehaviour, the Kennedy incident was probably the most important in terms of his public image. His Labour colleagues were horrified. Richard Crossman, watching on television, thought it was 'awful', while Benn, who saw the performance and heard about the Wallach fracas from a television producer a couple of days later, described Brown as 'an absolute disgrace'.[92] Brown was compelled to make a personal apology to a meeting of the parliamentary party, and Wilson very cleverly used the incident to undermine the credibility of his erstwhile rival.[93] The *People*, a stalwart Labour newspaper, spoke for Fleet Street in general when it called Brown 'turbulent', 'intoxicated with the exuberance of his own emotions' and 'far too erratic'.[94] Meanwhile, letters flooded into Brown's office from ordinary people who had seen the programme. 'You are not fit for any public role, and not worthy to sit in our Parliament,' said one. A woman from Renfrewshire summed up the general feeling: 'On a solemn occasion you were as pissed as a coot . . . You are a disgrace to the nation. Brother, you are on your way – OUT.'[95]

After obtaining various promises of good behaviour, Wilson kept Brown on the team, and in the new government he was given the flagship Department of Economic Affairs. However, since he was effectively an alcoholic, there was no guarantee that he would not offend again. Even in September 1964, at the meeting to approve Labour's manifesto, Benn observed that Brown was drunk and incapable of answering a simple question.[96] He would be back in the headlines again before too long.

At the beginning of his administration, Wilson was not particularly close to either Callaghan or Brown. He preferred to confide in protégés like Benn, who became the new Postmaster General, or old associates like Richard Crossman and Barbara Castle, who went to Housing and Overseas Development respectively.[97] Both Castle and Crossman later published detailed diaries of their time in government, which means that most accounts of the Wilson governments give them prominent roles. Castle was the only female Cabinet minister and also probably the only one who 'felt a real human sympathy' with Wilson. Passionate, impulsive and entirely devoted to politics, she was one of the government's most colourful and popular figures, although her colleagues often became impatient with her ardent outbursts.[98]

Crossman was a very different character, a former Oxford don whose socialism was rooted in temperamental rebelliousness and who was one of the most magnetic personalities of Wilson's administration.[99] The political historian and Labour MP David Marquand, who had been one of his students, called him 'a big, powerful, untidy, bear-like man . . . radiating physical and intellectual vitality and coruscating with mischief'.[100] He was a brilliant, unpredictable lecturer, an accomplished journalist and an engaging diarist whose recollections were often completely unreliable but never less than entertaining. He liked to think of himself as Wilson's mentor, and once praised him as the only Labour MP 'who is not afraid of my brutal brain power'.[101] The reality was that Wilson took his advice less often than Crossman liked to think, although this was not necessarily reflected in the latter's famous diaries. 'I sometimes wondered if he knew how to distinguish what he said to the Prime Minister from what the Prime Minister said to him,' remarked John Cole.[102]

Indeed, Crossman was a reckless and scurrilous gossip and was often seen as a congenital traitor; even before he entered Parliament, people called him 'double-Crossman', and the standing joke was that you either disliked and distrusted him, or liked and distrusted him.[103] His unreliability also extended to his performance as a minister: on one occasion, he treated himself to an expensive solo dinner at Prunier, an exclusive seafood restaurant in St James's, only to leave a pile of confidential Cabinet papers under his seat, where they were found by a fellow-diner who leaked them to the *Express*.[104] And he was notorious for falling asleep in Cabinet, although whenever he was awake and on form he always kept his colleagues on their toes.[105]

In his intellectual brilliance and temperamental unreliability, Crossman was a good representative of Wilson's most celebrated and talented ministers. No government had a more impressive academic pedigree. Eleven of the twenty-three original Cabinet ministers, including Wilson himself, had been to Oxford, and by 1966 the Cabinet boasted no fewer than eight Oxford Firsts, a British political record.[106] The fact that the government was so talented perhaps explains why it was also so prone to factionalism. The likes of Crossman, Healey, Jenkins and Crosland were deeply convinced of their own intellectual pre-eminence, and this did not always make for happy coexistence. Richard Ingrams, the editor of *Private Eye*, commented in 1971 that not only did they like to wash their dirty linen in public, but they gossiped 'much more than the Conservatives . . . the average Labour MP will tell you two or three malicious stories about his colleagues within five minutes of acquaintance'.[107]

Ironically for a team that had trumpeted its attachment to science and technology, none of Wilson's ministers had experience of industry, business or commercial technology; in very broad terms, they were a government of Oxford academics and trade unionists purporting to be scientific innovators.[108] What was more, the fact that Labour had been in opposition for thirteen years meant that very few of them had any experience of administration or government. Only three had been in Cabinet before, and only half the Cabinet had even held junior office.[109] 'I still had everything to learn,' recalled Denis Healey. 'I knew nothing about running a department, or about fighting my corner in the never-ending battles of Whitehall.'[110] Many other ministers struggled to get to grips with their new responsibilities. Tony Benn's private secretary came to pick him up in an enormous Austin Princess and, when the new Postmaster General got in the car, asked him: 'How do you intend to play, minister?', to which the baffled Benn had no ready answer.[111]

The life of a successful minister was one of endless, often unrewarded hard graft: as Secretary of State for Defence, Denis Healey worked 'harder than I had ever imagined' for ten to twelve hours a day and another three or four hours every night, for five or six days a week, not including tours abroad, conferences and summit meetings.[112] Wilson's political secretary Marcia Williams summed it up well when she remarked that government was 'not as happy and pleasant as you thought it would be . . . Suddenly you enter a door and it shuts behind you and you can't just say, "Help, let me out!", you're there and you make the best of a bad job and you try and work out day to day what you are going to do.'[113]

Williams was the most influential member of what contemporaries called the 'Kitchen Cabinet'. While previous Prime Ministers had employed personal advisers and speechwriters, Wilson was the first to bring into Downing Street a large personal retinue, rather like the entourage that accompanies an American President into office.[114] The Kitchen Cabinet was a fluid, informal group, with Williams at its centre; other key figures included the economic adviser Thomas Balogh, the political press secretary Gerald Kaufman, Wilson's parliamentary private secretary Peter Shore, the Paymaster General George Wigg and, from time to time, Benn and Crossman.[115] The only thing they had in common was their personal loyalty to Wilson himself. Wigg, for example, was a lugubrious bloodhound with responsibility for liaising with the security services. Obsessed with plots and scandals, he encouraged the Prime Minister to see conspiracies around every corner.[116] Balogh, a Hungarian-born Oxford economist, was another suspicious and conspiratorial character as well as a great enthusiast for government planning of the economy. Along with another Hungarian-born economic adviser, Nicholas Kaldor, he was distrusted by the civil service and regularly lampooned in the press.[117]

But by far the most controversial member of the group was Marcia Williams herself. The daughter of a Northamptonshire builder, she was a scholarship girl who had met Wilson while working as a Labour Party secretary. She was fiercely loyal not only to the party but to Wilson himself, and her uncompromising, tempestuous personality often made her unpopular with his colleagues. It also filled a gap in his life. As we have seen, while he was obsessed with politics, his wife Mary was completely uninterested in it. Marcia Williams was therefore the ideal professional companion, and her ferocious temperament was the ideal counterpoint to Wilson's cool detachment.[118] Their intellectual and personal intimacy was, as one biographer puts it, 'plain for all to see'.[119] Joe Haines, who became Wilson's press secretary in 1969, summed up their relationship best:

She met for a great many years a deep craving within him: for someone else to whom politics was meat and drink and the very air that was breathed; someone who, at her best, had a political mind capable of testing and matching his; someone who, again at her best, possessed a deadly ability to slash her way through the woolliness and verbiage of political argument to get to the heart of an issue. Someone who was prepared to devote all her time to Harold Wilson's service; and someone who, at the very worst moments, was always there.[120]

Williams' contribution to Wilson's success was often underestimated; she was an excellent organiser and a loyal confidante, as well as being effectively his 'political wife'.[121] Her brother drove Wilson's car in the 1964 election campaign and played golf with him; her sister became Mary Wilson's personal secretary; her father even cooked the first meal that Harold and Mary Wilson ate in 10 Downing Street after the election.[122] She even arranged their holidays, organised their finances and paid their domestic bills.[123] Predictably, there were plenty of rumours that Wilson and his secretary were having an affair. *Private Eye* regularly alluded to their supposed liaison throughout the sixties, and in Westminster and Fleet Street circles, it was taken as an established fact, even though conclusive evidence never surfaced.[124] Wilson's biographer Philip Ziegler concludes that their relationship really resembled that between father and daughter: it was 'sexual, in the sense that it could only have existed between man and woman, but there is not the slightest reason to believe that it ever contained any element of physical sexuality in it'.[125]

The gossip about Marcia Williams' relationship with her employer was rooted in her widespread unpopularity. While Wilson was reluctant to make enemies, she specialised in it.[126] Soon after arriving in Downing Street she announced that the official typists, or 'garden room girls', were upper-class Conservatives and must be purged immediately, along with various other civil servants who worked in No. 10. No such purge took place, but it was a good example of Williams' attitude to those whom she suspected of disloyalty.[127] Apart from Wilson himself, she was probably the single most influential figure in Downing Street, and officials frequently heard her shouting and screaming at the Prime Minister in order to get her way.[128] She did have her admirers – in November 1965 Benn called her 'infinitely the most able, loyal, radical and balanced member of Harold's personal team'. But many Labour MPs, especially on the right, abhorred her.[129] 'You stand for sod all, you're nothing, you're out as far as I'm concerned,' shouted Bob Mellish, a Docklands bruiser who later became the Chief Whip, after one altercation.[130]

In complete contrast, Mary Wilson hated Downing Street. Life as the Prime Minister's wife could not have been more different from her original dream of wedded bliss with an Oxford don. 'She started with a deep suspicion that everyone disliked and despised her,' commented one official. 'She walked about looking terribly unhappy.' State dinners and functions filled her with particular dread; at one, a civil servant's wife found her in tears in the ladies', saying: 'I can't take it any more.'[131] The fact that Wilson palpably loved being Prime Minister, and expected her to revel in his success, only made matters worse. In March 1966 Crossman recorded a conversation with him about Mary's appearance at a campaign rally:

> I said that Mary must hate it. 'Oh no,' he said. 'She liked the meeting a great deal.' As I was going downstairs I ran into Mary and said, 'I hear you really enjoyed last night after all.' 'Enjoyed it?' she said, with agony on her face. 'Who told you that? That man?' Her relationship with Harold is fascinating. I am sure they are deeply together but they are now pretty separate in their togetherness.[132]

Given Mary's complete lack of interest in politics, it was quite understandable that she found most of Wilson's colleagues hard to get on with. *Private Eye*'s regular feature 'Mrs Wilson's Diary', which was both unfair and hilariously effective, portrayed her as a suburban ingénue lost in the cynical world of politics. The diary entries were full of references to baked beans, cups of tea, HP Sauce, 'Quaker Puffs', and 'my plaster ducks all nicely arranged in the lounge'.[133] Thanks to *Private Eye*, she even became a personification of the supposedly banal, commercialised tastes of the affluent society: the entry for 3 September 1965, for instance, had her cooking 'some Birds Eye Frozen Cod-fingers and Broccoli' with 'Yellow Cling Peaches with banana-flavoured topping' for lunch, while Harold contents himself with 'a piece of Krispiwheet and a portion of Dairylea Processed Cheese'.[134]

The ordinariness of Wilson's tastes was not just a satirical invention. Crossman commented in 1965 that the Prime Minister had 'no social life', which was not quite true, because he did accumulate some dubious cronies and golfing partners from the world of business. In general, however, he led a very quiet life.[135] He bought few books; he had no interest in concerts or the theatre; he disliked dinner parties; he even wore cheap, off-the-peg suits.[136] In May 1965 Crossman went up to the Downing Street flat with him for lunch and was aghast to be confronted by 'a plate with a piece of steak, two veg and a bit of cold salad' as well as 'two tins of Skol beer'. 'Nothing could be more deeply *petit bourgeois* than the way he lives in those crowded little servants' quarters up there,' he wrote despairingly.[137] In March 1968 he bravely accepted an invitation to go up for dinner with Harold and Mary and discovered that nothing had changed:

> I hadn't talked to her for some time and she said to me rather awkwardly, 'I remember the only time you came to see us at our house in Hampstead. I offered you Nescafé and you said you'd rather not and we went out to a restaurant and there you got some ordinary coffee. So I suppose you don't like tinned salmon but that's all we've got tonight apart from a bit of cold ham.' We were sitting in that miserable little dining-room and there on the table-cloth was a bit of mutton wrapped up in Cellophane, a bit of butter on a plate, a couple of tomatoes and some lettuce, and beside them a very large tin of salmon which had by now been emptied out into a potato dish.[138]

Wilson prided himself on the fact that as Prime Minister he retained his common touch. 'One's overwhelming impression of him', wrote Barbara Castle in 1966, 'is always of informality to the point of rakishness.'[139] On one occasion she arrived early for a meeting and 'found a geranium flag-seller for the blind waiting in the hall with a blind soldier': the first appointment in Wilson's diary. 'They were delighted with their few words with him,' she recorded, 'and since there were no press or photographers there it *must* mean that he has a naturally kind heart.'[140]

Indeed, some of Wilson's closest colleagues thought that he was nice to a fault. A year after the election, Crossman reflected on his leader's 'reluctance to have a scene or sack anybody'.[141] Callaghan also considered that Wilson should have been 'more ruthless in laying down the law'. He was, said Callaghan, 'a kindly man who does not enjoy knocking heads together, nor does he easily ride roughshod over his colleagues' feelings'.[142] Even the loyal Marcia Williams later admitted that he was 'curiously soft' and 'incapable of showing that streak of hardness and toughness with colleagues that is really necessary':

Very often people who were totally opposed to him personally would mortally offend him, but instead of telling them exactly what he thought of them, he would be extraordinarily nice and polite to them . . .

We had a joke about Harold and his decisions to tell his colleagues exactly what he thought about them and to put things right when they were going badly wrong. We always used to say: 'Ah! He has his feather duster out again.'[143]

Shortly after taking office, Wilson told Crossman that he planned to 'sit back and study strategy and leave you chaps to do the tactics and detailed work in your Departments'.[144] In fact this was a very inaccurate description of his style of leadership. Work took up almost all of Wilson's waking life; one biographer calls his daily routine 'puritanically simple' and 'monastic'.[145] Williams recorded that he was always at his desk at eight, having already read the morning papers in bed, and then worked a sixteen-hour day before glancing at the first editions and retiring upstairs.[146] He had no interest in food and made little time for meals, although he did like to have a few glasses of whisky or brandy in the evening.[147] The pretence of 'sitting back' was rapidly abandoned; in 1970 he told Crossman that his was 'a full-time job':

I can tell you this, I have never read a book in No. 10. At Chequers I've read a book but, unlike Sir Alec Douglas-Home, who used to go downstairs to the big room and read novels, I don't. I've got to cover everything . . .

After all, let's be clear about it. Macmillan was an idle man, who just didn't work as Prime Minister, and Douglas-Home was idle. I am not an idle man. I have never worked harder than I do here.[148]

The notion that Macmillan and Home were idle was quite ridiculous, but it was revealing that Wilson believed it. As Ben Pimlott points out, the obvious comparison was not with his Conservative predecessors but with one of his Conservative successors, Margaret Thatcher. Both came from provincial lower-middle-class, Nonconformist backgrounds; both went to grammar school and Oxford; and both rose to the premiership despite the condescension of their colleagues.[149] Both prided themselves on their discipline and hard work, and, like Thatcher, Wilson was convinced that he knew his ministers' briefs better than they did, endlessly badgering them with suggestions and advice. He thought nothing of dashing off a memo on machine-tool production or on traffic jams caused by heavy lorries in Parliament Square.[150] Barbara Castle compared him with 'a juggler with a dozen balls in the air at the same time'.[151] Wilson himself preferred a different analogy. Shortly after accompanying Callaghan to a rugby match at Cardiff Arms Park, he wrote to his Chancellor: 'I see my job as a scrum half who can sometimes get the ball, hare off round the blind side of the scrum & go off diagonally to the far corner flag & generally open up the game.' He evidently did not know much about rugby, but the point was made.[152]

As Wilson contemplated his first months in power, he knew exactly what he wanted. A few months earlier he had promised 'a hundred days of dynamic action', just like President Kennedy.[153] The close result of the election, however, gave him a majority of just five seats and no room for manoeuvre at all. He had to manage his party with care, because despite the apparent calm of the last two years his backbenchers were still deeply divided between left and right. They were, as a group, increasingly middle class; there were more academics, teachers, journalists and managers than ever before, more concerned about their own ideological commitments than about tribal loyalty to the Labour movement.[154] The tiny majority meant that Wilson could not afford to antagonise any particular group. It also meant that for critical votes, seriously ill or elderly Labour MPs had to be rushed to Westminster to preserve the government's majority, with doctors on hand in case the pressure became too much.[155]

Wilson's new ministers were under no illusions: the goal, said Denis Healey, was to 'keep the ship afloat and take advantage of any favourable tide to increase our majority'.[156] At the same time, the Prime Minister was keen to create an impression of 'activity and reforming zeal', as promised in his rhetoric about the hundred days. When Parliament met on a gloomy, foggy 3 November for the Queen's Speech, it was treated to a long list of Labour's manifesto promises, from higher pensions and the abolition of prescription charges to a free vote on the death penalty and the renationalisation of the steel industry.[157] Wilson wanted to cultivate the appearance of continuous, imaginative action, with himself at the centre; as one historian puts it, he was 'like a juggler, spinning plates on sticks, moving rapidly from one to the next to keep all in motion, while maintaining a witty patter to the audience at the same time'.[158] The crucial task was to keep the party together and prepare the ground for the next general election. 'You can't keep a Government together by the skin of your nose,' said the journalist James Margach, interviewing him as the results came in. 'I'll pilot it by the seat of my pants then,' replied Wilson. 'The main thing is to get in there, form a Government and then control events and time the next election.'[159]

3

THE SPACE AGE

> This is the age of the push-button, Mr Steed . . . As a journalist you'll appreciate that we human beings are fallible, temperamental, and so often unreliable. The machine, however, is obedient, and invariably more competent.
>
> 'The Cybernauts', *The Avengers* (1965)

> STEED: Do you know, we should be very grateful.
> EMMA: For what, pray?
> STEED: For living in the twentieth century, the world of thermostats, computers, transistors –
> EMMA: Not forgetting automatic toasters.
>
> 'Return of the Cybernauts', *The Avengers* (1967)

Just before eleven o'clock on the morning of Friday, 8 October 1965, Harold Wilson's car drew into the narrow streets of Fitzrovia for the official opening of the new Post Office Tower. At more than six hundred feet tall, the narrow, piercing cylinder of glass and steel was at once the capital's tallest building, the centrepiece of Britain's brand-new telecommunications network, and an uncompromising statement of technological optimism. Building work had begun four years earlier, under the direction of Eric Bedford, the chief architect at the Ministry of Works, and had cost two million pounds, making the new edifice one of the most expensive buildings in the country. Sixteen utility platforms of radio, ventilation and power units soared above the Georgian streets of bohemian London, supporting a vast array of microwave antennae, aerials and dishes beaming calls and signals to smaller towers across the nation.[1]

The tower's inaugural ceremonies passed off smoothly enough. Wilson made a cheerful ceremonial telephone call to test the new equipment, unveiled a plaque near the entrance, and then took a lift thirty-four floors above the capital to look across the skyline. He was accompanied not only by his wife Mary and his private secretary Marcia Williams, but also by a nervous gaggle of senior officials from the Post Office and the current Postmaster General, Anthony Wedgwood Benn.

Lampooned by *Private Eye* as 'Wedgie the Whizz', Benn was the government's most enthusiastic champion of technology and modernisation, although he recorded in his diary that the tower had endured more than its fair share of teething troubles. Even when Wilson went up to the observation gallery, Benn noted, 'it was so misty we could hardly see anything at all'.[2] Despite this bad luck, however, the opening was generally considered a success, and eight months later Benn returned to the tower to give the Queen a guided tour. 'Afterwards,' he recorded, 'we went up and had tea with Billy Butlin, revolving in his restaurant. She was obviously not interested in the technical aspects but I think enjoyed seeing London from such a height. I suggested that there ought to be a state banquet in which all the guests went by the top table every twenty minutes.'[3]

Sir Billy Butlin's revolving restaurant was by far the most intriguing and newsworthy aspect of the new building. Built on a circular platform that slowly revolved on nylon wheels, it completed a full turn every twenty-two minutes and gave diners an unbeatable view of the London skyline. It was opened to the public in yet another official ceremony on 19 May 1966, with Benn and Butlin gamely tucking into prawn cocktails and T-bone steaks for the benefit of the cameras, and proved a tremendous hit. In the first twelve months alone, one and a half million visitors paid four shillings for entrance to the tower, where they could stare out at the capital from two different observation galleries, browse in the souvenir shop and throw coins into the charity wishing well. Whether the tower was quite ready for such attention was another matter. As Benn privately noted, its organisation was 'appalling', with only two lifts, each holding fourteen people, having 'to be used continually to take 400 people to the top and bring them down again'.[4] But such was the demand for places in the revolving restaurant that visitors were advised to book well in advance, although the staff found the whole thing rather dizzying and nicknamed it the 'revolting restaurant'.[5]

The Post Office Tower was more than a building; it was a symbol of what *Private Eye* mockingly called 'Benn's HoverBritain'.[6] Indeed, barely a month after the tower had been opened to the public, it was playing a central role in the BBC's science-fiction series *Doctor Who*. In 'The War Machines', which began in June 1966, the Doctor and his friends find themselves in contemporary London, a place of dolly birds, swinging nightclubs and a megalomaniac computer, WOTAN, which controls an army of War Machines from its headquarters at the summit of the Post Office Tower. Unfortunately, BBC research suggested that the show's six million viewers were less than impressed, largely because audiences found that 'the whole idea of a computer able to think for itself, and with power over human beings as well as machines, was "preposterous"'. 'I like science fiction,' said one disgruntled viewer, 'but this is ridiculous.'[7]

The success of the Post Office Tower as an iconic tourist attraction owed a great deal to the contemporary enthusiasm for science and technology. Instead of being seen as technical, desiccated and boring, science was regarded as inherently exciting and dynamic, and its place in the national imagination was confirmed not merely by the success of *Doctor Who* but also by the popularity of Dan Dare, toy space rockets and chemistry sets.[8] Indeed, by the time that the Post Office Tower was opened to the public, British science had been enjoying something of a thirty-year golden age. If the 1930s had been the heroic years of Lord Rutherford's Cavendish laboratory at Cambridge and the great breakthrough in nuclear physics, then the decades that followed had been no less exhilarating. The mobilisation of science to fight the Nazis had produced plenty of impressive benefits in peacetime, from nuclear power and radar to infra-red and improved antibiotics. Perhaps the most common if apparently mundane example was polythene, which had been developed by ICI in 1939 to insulate electrical equipment. After the war, it became one of the most ubiquitous of all plastics, used to wrap and contain food in almost every household in the nation, and by the early sixties its production ran into millions of tonnes.[9]

In the decades that followed, British scientists consistently earned international renown for their work on everything from geophysics and fluid mechanics to radio astronomy and molecular biology, and British science continued to win more than its fair share of Nobel prizes. Sir Bernard Lovell developed the world's most advanced radio telescope at Jodrell Bank; Ernst Chain and Howard Florey made the breakthrough in penicillin culture that allowed it to become a ubiquitous, marketable drug; Dorothy Hodgkin worked out the molecular structure of vitamin B12. Indeed, only the United States, which enjoyed far greater funding and resources, could point to a comparable record of achievement. The most renowned discovery of all came in 1953, when Francis Crick and James Watson worked out the double helix structure of DNA, the genetic carrier from generation to generation, and their satisfaction was all the greater for the knowledge that they had narrowly beaten the American chemist Linus Pauling to the same breakthrough.[10]

For anyone interested in science, these were exciting times, and although the double-helix discovery failed to attract much – or indeed any – attention from the popular press, there is no doubt that scientific discoveries did have a tremendous impact on daily life in the fifties and sixties. Medical science in particular was booming; and thanks to the NHS, patients across the country reaped the rewards of the latest researches. Many of the advances of modern medicine were actually based on breakthroughs in other fields of science and technology. The development of X-ray equipment, for instance, drew on the research of the photographic industry; analgesics and sulphonamides came from chemical engineering; and even hearing aids were inspired by the development of the transistor radio. The march of medical science was so rapid that, by the sixties, NHS doctors were regularly carrying out intricate kidney and liver operations, blood transfusions and complicated heart surgery, and by 1969 there was serious talk of transplant surgery and genetic engineering.[11]

The everyday impact of the new technology went well beyond the hospitals. In 1962 Anthony Sampson wrote that 'an alarming new master-manager' was making its presence felt in the boardroom:

> a brain which can remember everything about everyone, which can check figures, write cheques, calculate turnovers and notice exceptions in every factory and shop. No manager can ignore the influence of the neat grey machines, with their menacing names – Leo, Pegasus, Orion – silently working in their air conditioned rooms, disgorging their tickertapes of figures. The computer is still in its infancy in Britain, which has only about two hundred of them (compared with four thousand in America), of which sixty are in industry; but clearly computers will eventually have drastic effect on managers.[12]

One of Britain's first major computer developments, as Sampson acknowledged, was LEO, a monstrous machine that consisted of three thousand valves wired together from floor to ceiling of an entire room. LEO stood for Lyons Electronic Office; it had been specially built at Cambridge for the Lyons tea-shop company. It began running their bakery operations in 1951 and managing the payroll three years later.[13]

Although it might seem surprising that the world's first office computer was made for a company more famous for Swiss rolls and Earl Grey tea, the link between technology and consumerism was arguably never stronger than in the fifties and sixties. During the war years, scientific progress had been driven by the desperate need to defeat Nazi Germany; now the equivalent pressures came not only from the Cold War but from the demands of commerce and consumerism. Electrical appliances like televisions, washing machines and refrigerators were becoming commonplace in British homes, and scientific research was also being channelled into the development of detergents, disinfectants, frozen foods, synthetic fabrics, plastics and polishes. Since only the very poorest or most isolated members of society remained untouched by the pace of scientific change, technology and affluence appeared to be advancing hand in hand. In the words of one observer, there emerged in the mid-1950s

> a dawning realization that, thanks to the miraculous advance of technology, an entirely new kind of material prosperity was coming into being . . . There was suddenly much more money around than would have seemed imaginable to any previous generation, and every year that passed seemed to bring yet more technical marvels, more change – transistor radios, jet airliners, computers, motorways, new kinds of architecture in steel, concrete and glass.[14]

Unlike *Doctor Who*'s deranged computer WOTAN, LEO was more interested in the price of cream buns than in seizing control of Greater London, but the development of the office computer – or 'robot', as many people insisted on calling it – did not go unnoticed. As early as 1955, the *Mirror* published a week-long investigation into the 'Robot Revolution':

> They can bake pies. They can make motors. They can answer the telephone. They can fashion jib-bores. They can add up, subtract, divide. They can write. They can speak. They can pen love-letters. They can do all these things without any help from you. Whatever your job is, the chances are that one of these machines can do it faster and better than you can.

Automation, according to the *Mirror*, would bring a four-day week and higher salaries, although office boys and factory girls would have to retrain to take care of the machines that would be doing their jobs. The Robot Revolution, the paper concluded, might well 'bring about something which Socialists fundamentally believe in — a shorter working week for all, less drudgery for all, and therefore more leisure for all'.[15] Other observers, however, were rather less optimistic. 'A big computer', one consultant remarked, 'can put a giant corporation back into being a one-man firm.' Anthony Sampson, too, predicted that computers would put thousands of people out of work. 'Rather as television can by-pass the small salesman,' he wrote, 'so computers may by-pass the small manager.'[16]

It was not surprising, then, that popular culture in the sixties often reflected fears of mechanisation, technology and uncontrollable computers. Television adventure series like *The Avengers*, for instance, regularly fell back on mad computers, modernisation-crazed scientists and armies of killing machines for their villains. In one of the most popular episodes, 'The Cybernauts' (1965), the heroes uncover a plot by Dr Armstrong, the chairman of United Automation, to bring about 'government by automation' under the aegis of his humanoid Cybernaut robots. Human beings, Armstrong explains, are 'fallible', while machines are 'invariably more competent' and represent 'the ultimate in human achievement'. John Steed, the dashing hero, is less impressed; he denounces the dream of a 'cybernetic police state' run by 'push-button bobbies', and inevitably wins the day.

In 1966, meanwhile, in 'The House That Jack Built', the heroine Emma Peel is trapped inside a futuristic house lined with corridors painted in swirling Pop and Op Art patterns and humming with electronic noise. The architect, it turns out, is Professor Keller, an automation expert whom she had dismissed years before from her late father's company when his robotic obsession had spilled over into misanthropic mania. Keller is long dead, but a machine plays back his chilling recorded message:

> This house is a machine — an indestructible machine, powered by solar energy . . . This machine will last for a thousand years, perhaps forever. An indestructible monument to my ingenuity. And yet the means of your destruction. You see, Mrs Peel, the mind of a machine cannot reason, therefore it cannot lose its reason. That is the machine's ultimate superiority. Its mind has no breaking point. But your mind has. When the experiment is concluded, the machine will continue to function perfectly, but you, Mrs Peel, will be quite, quite mad.[17]

Emma Peel survives, of course; her imagination outwits the machine, which promptly self-destructs.

These were not isolated themes: they were also increasingly common in *Doctor Who*. In 1968 the time-travelling Doctor and his friends once again find themselves in Swinging London, and this time they are up against an army of gleaming Cybermen.[18] A race of men who have gradually replaced flesh and blood with metal and plastic, and have lost all human feeling and compassion, the Cybermen were a perfect example of contemporary fears about scientific progress. They were the creation of the programme's scientific adviser, Dr Kit Pedler, an ophthalmologist from the University of London. As he explained to the *Radio Times*, he 'foresaw a time when spare part surgery — the replacement of limbs and organs — would become as commonplace as changing a shirt, and that eventually people might have so many prosthetic parts that they would become uncertain whether they were human or machine'.[19]

Most politicians and civil servants in the fifties and sixties, impressed by the wartime impact of penicillin, radar and atomic power, were more interested in encouraging the development of new technology than in taking precautions against cybernetic invasion. In 1945 the Percy Report had recommended a rapid increase in the numbers of engineering students, and a year later the Barlow Committee recommended that steps should be taken to double the number of annual science graduates. 'Never before', said the Barlow Report, 'has the importance of science been so widely recognised, or so many hopes of future progress and welfare founded upon the scientist.'[20]

Although successive governments were lambasted for not doing enough to promote scientific expertise, it was extremely unfair to imagine that the British political classes were befuddled by a kind of amateurish anachronism. Between 1945 and 1964, government spending on non-military scientific research and development rose from almost £7 million to over £150 million, which, allowing for inflation, represented a tenfold increase.[21] In the sixties Britain spent some 2.3 per cent of GNP on scientific research, which was admittedly less than the 3 per cent spent by the United States and the Soviet Union, but still outstripped West Germany (1.8 per cent) and France (1.5 per cent).[22] Scientific advisers like Henry Tizard and Solly Zuckerman cut influential figures in Whitehall, and in 1959 Harold Macmillan appointed the charismatic if slightly implausible figure of Viscount Hailsham as the country's first Minister for Science and Technology.[23]

Even the Royal Family was associated with the popular vogue for science and technology, thanks to the Duke of Edinburgh, who served from 1951 as president of the British Association for the Advancement of Science and made a notable impact in his inaugural lecture, entitled 'The British Contribution to Science and Technology in the Past Hundred Years'. The effect was slightly tarnished for insiders by the fact that the speech had actually been written by a panel of eminent scientists; indeed, the Duke confessed to the secretary of the association: 'The more I read the material you have been sending me the more confused I get.'[24] However, given the dizzying advance of British science in the preceding years, this was not necessarily cause for great shame, and the Duke's modernising image survived unscathed.

Despite the impressive advances of British science during the 1950s and their manifest repercussions everywhere from the kitchen to the shop floor, the country's politicians were never able to dispel the nagging suspicion that instead of surging ahead in the great technological race, Britain was really falling behind. The image of the nation as a doddering relic, hidebound by privilege and struggling to keep up with its younger competitors, owed much to a particular kind of political dissatisfaction with the Conservative government, and it reached its peak in the early sixties at exactly the same point when Harold Macmillan's administration was running out of steam. Between 1961 and 1964, the *Financial Times*' industrial editor Michael Shanks published his manifesto *The Stagnant Society*, Anthony Sampson examined the *Anatomy of Britain* and Anthony Hartley produced *A State of England*. In October 1962 the journal *New Society*, which promised to take a long look at Britain's social and economic problems, made its first appearance, and in July 1963 the highbrow periodical *Encounter* devoted a special issue to the supposed 'Suicide of a Nation'.[25]

Given the tremendous technological advances and consumer affluence of the period, this torrent of rather depressing self-analysis looks more like a disguised attack on the Macmillan government than a serious response to a genuine problem. After all, the average wage and the standard of living had both grown rapidly since the end of the Second World War, and most ordinary people led far more prosperous and comfortable lives than they had done just ten years before. On the other hand, the criticism did reflect popular unease at some of the changes that British society had undergone during the period of affluence. It allowed people to voice their frustration at the undoubted decline of Britain's international prestige, and it also represented an excellent way of attacking the government. As the historian Jim Tomlinson remarks, it was based more on 'Mickey Mouse sociology' and a desire to bash the Tories than on serious analysis of the country's position.[26]

But it nevertheless encouraged the feeling among some scientists that they were being treated poorly by an amateurish and antiquated society. The most famous spokesman for this position was the novelist C. P. Snow, a grammar-school boy from Leicester who moved in stately progression from a Cambridge fellowship to civil service work in the war, a stint as a civil service commissioner with responsibility for scientific recruitment, and a post at the Ministry of Technology in the first Wilson government. Snow's novels, which attracted considerable attention in the fifties and sixties but largely disappeared into obscurity thereafter, followed the life of Lewis Elliot, a provincial outsider who moves smoothly through the worlds of the law, big business, the civil service, secret atomic research and so on. Like his creator, Elliot owes his advancement in part to his reputation as a scientist; towards the end of the cycle, he is knighted, becomes a senior government adviser, and ends up as a junior minister. He is the quintessential example of what Snow saw as the 'new men', a national elite based on merit rather than breeding and on scientific expertise rather than literary erudition.[27]

The most famous articulation of Snow's faith in the 'new men' came in 1959, when he was invited to deliver the Rede Lecture at Cambridge. In his address, entitled 'The Two Cultures and the Scientific Revolution', he examined the 'gulf of mutual incomprehension' between science and the arts in modern Britain. For Snow, it was deplorable that British intellectuals were ignorant of, say, the Second Law of Thermodynamics, and he complained that 'traditional culture' had 'an "unscientific", even an "anti-scientific" flavour'. Literary intellectuals, he concluded, were 'natural Luddites'; by contrast, scientific culture contained 'a great deal of argument, usually much more rigorous, and almost always at a higher conceptual level, than the literary persons' arguments'. Scientists had 'the future in their bones', but 'traditional' intellectuals responded only 'by wishing the future did not exist'.[28]

Snow's rather fatuous argument would probably have been forgotten had it not been for the furious response of F. R. Leavis, the intemperate Cambridge don and literary critic. Leavis waited until 1962 and his Richmond Lecture, again in Cambridge, before delivering his broadside, and he secured the attention of the press by first barring all reporters from attending the lecture, entitled 'The Significance of C. P. Snow', and then publishing the whole thing in the *Spectator*. He was out not to wound but to kill; as one commentator remarks, it is 'not just that no two stones of Snow's argument are left standing: each and every pebble is pulverized; the fields are salted; and the entire population is sold into slavery'.[29] Leavis attacked 'the preposterous and menacing absurdity of C. P. Snow's consecrated public standing', dismissed his 'embarrassing vulgarity of style' and 'complete ignorance' of history and literature, and announced that it was 'ridiculous to credit him with any capacity for serious thinking about the problems on which he offers to advise the world'. And in case any of his listeners had missed the point, Leavis added that Snow was 'of course, a – no, I can't say that; he isn't: Snow thinks of himself as a novelist . . . [but] his incapacity as a novelist is . . . total'. 'As a novelist,' he continued witheringly, 'he doesn't exist; he doesn't begin to exist. He can't be said to know what a novel is . . . Not only is he not a genius, he is intellectually as undistinguished as it is possible to be.'[30]

Since Snow was an established member of London's intellectual elite, it was no surprise that his highbrow friends rallied to his side. The *Spectator* printed more than thirty letters responding to Leavis's lecture, all but five of which took up the cudgels on Snow's behalf. Lord Boothby, for example, attacked Leavis's 'reptilian venom' and declared that there was 'not a single constructive thought in his lecture'; other correspondents criticised his 'bemused drivelling', his 'insincerity, incapacity and envy' and his 'ill-mannered, self-centred and destructive behaviour'.[31] All in all, it was easily the most vehement and engaging intellectual feud of the decade. On the other hand, neither man had emerged with any great distinction from the affair, and what was more, it really only amounted to a rehash of a much more genteel debate conducted between Matthew Arnold and T. H. Huxley in the 1880s. Although Leavis had triumphantly succeeded in besmirching Snow's reputation as a novelist, he did not manage to destroy his case about the place of science in British culture. Indeed, during the 1980s, several influential historians, notably Martin Wiener and Correlli Barnett, argued that in effect Snow had been right, and that national economic failure could be attributed to the persistent anti-scientific and anti-technical bias of British culture and education.[32]

At the time, this sort of analysis went down very well on the political left as well as in influential journals like *The Economist*, *Encounter* and the *New Statesman*. Indeed, barely a week seemed to go by without one of them attacking the dusty old Establishment and calling for educational reform or technological modernisation. Since their principal target was usually Macmillan's exhausted government, Labour were the obvious beneficiaries.[33] Indeed, Wilson himself had always been keen on the rhetoric of scientific progress. At his very first public meeting as a Labour parliamentary candidate, in 1944, he had hailed the 'great industrial and technical revolution' that meant Britain was now 'a totally different world'.[34]

By the end of the fifties Wilson was already specialising in the kind of language for which he became famous six years later. 'This is an age of *sputniks* and space travel and of scientific achievement proceeding at a staggering rate,' he remarked in 1957. 'All this produces a new challenge to any Government, and that is why it is a tragedy that this country, which seemed to be leading the world, is still governed by a group of obsolete Edwardians.'[35] Like other Labour politicians of the day, he identified technological progress and economic growth as the solutions to almost every conceivable problem.[36] 'This is our message for the sixties,' he told the party conference in 1960, 'a Socialist-inspired scientific and technological revolution releasing energy on an enormous scale and deployed not for the destruction of mankind but for enriching mankind beyond our wildest dreams.'[37]

Wilson was not alone in his attachment to science and modernisation. In October 1959, when the Conservatives won their third consecutive general election, it was widely assumed that Labour's traditional working-class base had been eroded by consumer affluence and social change. The pollster Mark Abrams even argued that unless the party rapidly modernised itself, it was likely to fall victim to 'a permanent and continuing swing' towards Conservatism.[38] The old cloth-cap image, according to Abrams, had to go; instead, the party should appeal to 'ambitious people, middle-class people, young people, office workers and scientists'.[39]

Although this argument cut little ice with the Labour left, which instinctively recoiled from the values of Macmillan's affluent society, it made a great impression on Hugh Gaitskell, who was keen to find a rationale for modernising his party and pushing it further towards the centre. Gaitskell warned the 1959 Labour Party conference that the advent of 'TV, new gadgets like refrigerators and washing machines, the glossy magazines with their special appeal to women and even the flood of new cars on the home markets' meant that 'more and more people are beginning to turn to their own personal affairs and to concentrate on their own material advance'. And he argued that Labour had to change the very nature of their appeal; after all, 'the typical worker of the future is more likely to be a skilled man in a white overall, watching dials in a bright new modern factory, than a badly paid cotton operative working in a dark and obsolete nineteenth-century mill'.[40]

In welcoming the opportunities of this new world of affluence and technology, Gaitskell and Wilson were following the example of one of their most talented contemporaries, the suave young intellectual Anthony Crosland. In 1956 Crosland had published *The Future of Socialism*, which had attracted glowing reviews and was considered by commentators of all parties to be the most important book on socialism since the war.[41] Crosland was a keen admirer of the new sociology of the fifties, as well as the ideas of the Canadian economist John Kenneth Galbraith.[42] He assumed that Britain was on the verge of a revolutionary new age of rapid economic growth, and that the old appeals to working-class solidarity were as outdated as the old reliance on nationalisation and public ownership.[43] Given the popularity of televisions, annual holidays and kitchen appliances, Crosland thought that Labour would be 'ill-advised to continue making a largely proletarian class appeal when a majority of the population is gradually attaining a middle-class standard of life, and distinct symptoms of a middle-class psychology'.[44] In a particularly famous passage, he argued that socialists should turn their attention to

> more important spheres – of personal freedom, happiness and cultural endeavour: the cultivation of leisure, beauty, grace, gaiety, excitement, and of all the proper pursuits, whether elevated, vulgar, or eccentric, which contribute to the varied fabric of a full private and family life . . . We need not only higher exports and old-age pensions, but more open-air cafés, brighter and gayer streets at night, later closing-hours for public houses, more repertory theatres, better and more hospitable hoteliers and restaurateurs, brighter and cleaner eating-houses, more riverside cafés, more pleasure-gardens on the Battersea model, more murals and pictures in public places, better designs for furniture and pottery and women's clothes, statues in the centre of new housing estates, better-designed street lamps and telephone kiosks, and so on ad infinitum . . .
>
> Now the time has come for . . . a greater emphasis on private life, on freedom and dissent, on culture, beauty, leisure and even frivolity. Total abstinence and a good filing system are not now the right signposts to the socialist Utopia: or at least, if they are, some of us will fall by the wayside.[45]

Crosland's book was immensely influential, underpinning the kind of liberal progressivism that Labour represented in the sixties. For despite all the attention given to Harold Wilson in 1963 and 1964, the modernisation of Labour's appeal and message had long been under way. Even in 1959 the party's campaign literature had been full of references to 'scientific progress', 'the age of automation and atomic power' and 'the age of the Sputnik'.[46] And in 1960 and 1961, the party's general secretary, Morgan Phillips, prepared two controversial documents arguing for the 'scientific revolution', 'a national plan with targets for individual industries' and a National Industrial Planning Board to encourage 'speedy and purposive industrial investment'.[47]

Wilson's real accomplishment, therefore, was to take these themes and weave them into a slick, resonant argument. Instead of attacking the Conservatives on the traditional Labour grounds of inequality, poverty and inhumanity, he blamed them for not doing enough to encourage economic growth, reform the education system or modernise industry. 'Twelve Wasted Years' was the title of one Labour pamphlet issued in September 1963, decrying 'years of stagnation at home and lost influence abroad'.[48] Science was to be at the forefront of Labour's bid to reverse the country's decline, and Wilson surrounded himself with a team of eminent advisers such as the physicist Patrick Blackett, the chemist Howard Florey and the mathematician Jacob Bronowski.[49] When he was asked what he associated socialism with in the modern age, he replied that 'if there was one word it was science'.[50] Obligingly, the press played along. 'Labour Mobilises the Scientists' read one headline. 'The Tories in Danger of Losing the Battle of Brains' proclaimed another.[51]

The beauty of this approach was that it also allowed Wilson to draw together the different factions of the Labour Party behind the banner of modernisation, while also reaching out to white-collar voters.[52] The old image of cloth-capped trade unionists bickering with slightly deranged Hampstead intellectuals was no more; instead, commented *The Economist* in June 1964, it had been superseded by 'Mr Wilson's capture of the more positive image of the white laboratory coat'.[53] Indeed, Wilson himself was widely seen as the living embodiment of science and efficiency. Again and again in interviews he talked about 'cutting edges', 'hard facts' and 'tough decisions', while promising a 'dynamic', 'purposive' and 'thrusting' administration, fit for the 'jet-age'.[54] 'We need a shake-up in industry,' he commented in July 1963, with one eye obviously on Westminster. 'There's still too much dead wood – too many directors sitting in boardrooms not because they can produce or sell, but because of their family background. To make industry dynamic, we need vigorous young executives, scientists and sales experts chosen for their abilities – not their connections.'[55]

All this talk of modernisation reflected the wide intellectual enthusiasm in the early sixties for science and planning, and it was an integral part of the general optimism with which many commentators looked ahead. Indeed, what was incongruous about the Snow–Leavis debate was that it took place at a time when British science was more self-confident than ever before. In 1962 Anthony Sampson pointed out that although scientists, engineers and doctors were still regarded as a 'separate breed', they enjoyed more prestige than at any time in living memory:

> Men accustomed before the war to scrounge for equipment as government 'boffins' or university pariahs, have found themselves wooed by government and industry with new labs, vast equipment, nervous respect and multiplied staff. 'The feeling of being a depressed class has quite gone', said one science knight: '. . . Now the scientists are the privileged class.'[56]

This enthusiasm for science and technology was not, of course, confined to Britain. Across the Atlantic, it was even more marked, and in January 1961 the news magazine *Time* awarded its 'Man of the Year' prize to a group of fifteen American scientists, with the explanation that 'Science is at the apogee of its power'.[57]

Many historians argue that Western society in these years underwent a 'technological revolution', with repercussions in 'the urban landscape and rural environment, the working day, domestic chores and the pursuit of leisure, the role of women, and the nature of education'.[58] Persuasive as it is, this idea still has its flaws. Not only were many of the changes attributed to the sixties actually under way as early as the inter-war years, but in many ways the new technological possibilities of the affluent society strengthened rather than undermined existing attitudes and habits. At the time, however, most commentators were keener to celebrate change than to acknowledge continuity, not least because change made for a better story and attracted younger readers. Indeed, although British politics and popular culture in the late 1950s had been marked by a deep sense of conservatism, press headlines regularly announced not only the 'Age of Boom' but the 'Jet Age', the

'Atom Age', the 'Electronic Age' and the 'Space Age'. Even the passing of the last steam locomotive in 1957 was taken to mark the end of the Victorian Steam Age and the onset of a new 'state of mind . . . when the limits of the Possible were suddenly removed'.[59]

For many observers, the most exciting technological development of the post-war years was the race between Soviet and American scientists to explore the vast expanses of space. When the first *Sputnik* satellite was launched into orbit in 1957, the *Daily Express* ran the enormous banner headline 'SPACE AGE IS HERE' above the news that a Soviet 'man-made moon' was circling the earth.[60] But although public interest in the conquest of space was greatly strengthened by the *Sputnik* launch, it had already been evident for several years. Since April 1950, for example, the smart, colourful *Eagle*, a weekly comic paper for children, had attracted millions of readers largely thanks to the escapades of 'Dan Dare, Pilot of the Future', a flying ace in the International Space Fleet and a dashing British hero for the Space Age.[61] In the mid-fifties popular enthusiasm for rocketry, air power and space travel reached a peak never matched before or since. It takes little imagination to spot the link with Britain's experience in the Second World War; the Battle of Britain was already well on the way to becoming a legend of national courage, and it was no coincidence that the comic *Rocket*, billed as 'The First Space-Age Weekly', purported to be edited by Douglas Bader. Words like *astronaut, cosmonaut, countdown* and *blast-off* found their way into everyday conversation, while a revealing cliché of the era held that every boy wanted to be an astronaut and every girl wanted to marry one.[62]

Toy companies were quick to pounce. While waiting for the anticipated call from NASA, aspiring astronauts could content themselves with the Dan Dare Cosmic Ray Gun, the De Luxe Sputnik or the Friction-Powered Gemini Space Capsule. To stave off pangs of hunger during the long journey towards the outer planets, the would-be Yuri Gagarin would be wise to stock up on Space Patrol sweet cigarettes and Sky Ray or Zoom lollipops, while even boxes of Quaker Puffed Wheat, marketed as 'the shot from guns cereal' that would 'launch big and little space men', came with a free 'Spinning Sputnik', which looked suspiciously like a standard flying saucer.[63] And the Space Age craze was not limited to the playground. In 1962, for example, the Tornados topped the singles charts on both sides of the Atlantic with their instrumental recording 'Telstar', a rare example of a chart hit inspired by a communications satellite. And there were even Space

Age restaurants in Hyde Park and at the Theatre Royal in York, in which diners could tuck in to their prawn cocktails confident in the knowledge that they were embracing the spirit of the brave new Britain.[64]

Public enthusiasm for modernity in the so-called Space Age probably owed as much to a belated reaction to the austerity of the early fifties as it did to scientific innovation and suburban affluence. Christopher Booker, the former editor of *Private Eye*, noted that newspapers like the *Observer* and the *Sunday Times* were always looking for 'any new excitement that happened to be in the air, whether joining the Common Market or candy-striped shirts, economic "growth" or features on leather jacketed "ton-up kids"'. The upper-middle-class press had fallen victim to a nasty case of 'neophilia': literally, love of the new.[65] In 1961, above a large and admiring photograph of a West German monorail, the *Observer* asked: 'Must Britain Be In a Mess?' 'Much more research and enterprise', the article explained, 'are needed in Britain to develop the fast, compact forms of public transport which are now technically possible.' Since the monorail was new, it apparently followed that it represented the future; not for nothing were the villains' headquarters in James Bond films typically equipped with a functioning monorail. A year later the same newspaper made another bid 'to assert the dynamic importance of the Hovercraft'.[66]

Even sport was not immune from the cult of novelty. In April 1961, for example, Anthony Crosland suggested that the Double-winning Tottenham side might be 'the first really professional football team' and a sign of 'a more general breakthrough, of a shift in the national mood from complacency to dynamism'.[67] The love of the new was not confined to politicians and journalists, either, but was implicit in the consumer trends of the period. The model Lesley Hornby, or Twiggy, later recalled her childhood in the early sixties:

> Anything modern was wonderful, and anything old was terrible. It has a lot to do with the middle-class, suburban way of thinking, to revere new things, everything up to date, up to the minute, brand new and streamlined and contemporary – that's what everything has to be – houses, home décor, ornaments, clothes! . . . In the sixties, anyway, everything had to be in fashion immediately and then out again, constantly changing.[68]

It is too simplistic to say, as some historians do, that the sixties were 'utopian years'; this faith in a bright technological future was far from universal, and as the examples of the Cybernauts and the Cybermen might suggest, many people were deeply afraid of economic and political decline, social change or cultural collapse.[69] But until the middle of the sixties, politicians and journalists alike emphasised the rewards of science and innovation, not its dangers. Indeed, between about 1956 and 1964, British popular culture *did* exhibit an intangible and distinctive sense of confidence, closely associated with rising wages, full employment, rampant materialism and technological change. This was, after all, the heyday of James Bond, that most conspicuous of consumers. 'When did you last hear the word austerity?' asked *Queen* magazine at the turn of the decade:

> This is the last time you will see it in this issue. At this minute there is more money in Britain than ever before. Nearly two thousand million pounds is pouring out of pockets and wallets and handbags and changing into air tickets and oysters, television sets and caviar, art treasures and vacuum cleaners, cigars and refrigerators. Britain has launched into an age of unparalleled lavish living. It came unobtrusively. But now, you are living in a new world. Turn the page if you want proof that you are living in an age of BOOM.[70]

'At the gates of the new decade', said *The Economist* a few months later, 'the main peril, blinding our eyes to what we could achieve, seems almost to be smugness.'[71]

In August 1964, despite the occasional stuttering of the economy under Harold Macmillan's various Chancellors, *Queen*'s 'age of BOOM' was still in full swing. Indeed, thanks to the munificence of the last Tory Chancellor, Reginald Maudling, Britain was enjoying a reckless surge of growth and prosperity, and as shoppers strolled down their local high streets in the glorious late summer sunshine, they were surrounded by all the trappings of the affluent society: car and television showrooms, crowded supermarkets, teenagers chatting over their mopeds, radios blaring out the latest hits by the Beatles and the Rolling Stones. Both the *Sunday Times* and the *Sunday Telegraph* were already producing glossy guides to this new world of consumerism and luxury, with fashion tips by Mary Quant for the housewife and short stories by Ian Fleming for her husband, but this new Britain still seemed to lack its own definitive chronicle.

Then, on 15 September, a new publication appeared on the shelves of newsagents across the country. The launch of the *Sun*, three days after the beginning of Labour's election campaign and two days before the premiere of *Goldfinger*, was in itself a striking indication of how much times and tastes had changed. 'Good Morning!' exclaimed its exuberant front page. 'Yes, it's time for a new newspaper . . . The *Sun* is here! The only newspaper born of the age that we live in.'[72]

The *Sun* had been born from the ashes of the *Daily Herald*, the old trade union paper, which had been haemorrhaging money and readers.[73] Its founders, the newspaper baron Cecil Harmsworth King and his editorial director Hugh Cudlipp, commissioned a series of expensive market surveys by Mark Abrams, who had already produced several influential analyses of teenage consumerism as well as Harold Wilson's advertising campaign in 1964. Abrams reported that the *Herald*'s old working-class readers were 'rising in status', becoming drawn to a new era of 'consumer politics' as they acquired cars and televisions.[74] Intrigued by this vision of a Britain that would be forged anew in the white heat of mass consumerism, King and Cudlipp decided to relaunch the *Herald* as a paper for women and the young, the fashionable audiences of the early sixties and also those most likely to impress advertisers.[75] As King told anyone who would listen, the new paper would be 'deliberately geared to the mental attitudes and new interests of the mid-1960s'.[76]

The editorial column of the *Sun*'s first issue spelled out its commitment to the new age of affluence and science:

> It is an independent newspaper designed to serve and inform all those whose lives are changing, improving, expanding in these hurrying years.
>
> We welcome the age of automation, electronics, computers. We will campaign for the rapid modernisation of Britain – regardless of the vested interests of managements or workers . . .
>
> The *Sun* is a newspaper with a social conscience. A radical newspaper ready to praise or criticise without preconceived bias. Championing progressive ideas. Fighting injustice. Exposing cruelty and exploitation.

It was, quite simply, the paper of the future: progressive, classless and free-thinking. 'Look at how life has changed,' the editorial pointed out:

> Five million Britons now holiday abroad every year. Half our population is under 35 years of age. Steaks, cars, houses, refrigerators, washing-machines are no longer the prerogative of the 'upper crust', but the right

of all. People believe, and the *Sun* believes with them, that the division of Britain into social classes is happily out of date . . .

For all these millions of people with lively minds and fresh ambitions the *Sun* will stimulate the new thinking, hoping to produce among its readers the leaders of tomorrow, knowing that they are more likely to emerge from a college of advanced technology than from Eton or Harrow.[77]

The IPC Group spent almost £400,000 on advertising alone, from posters to television commercials, all branded with the device of a blazing sun and the slogan 'Time for a new newspaper, born of the age we live in'. More than three million copies of the first issue were produced to meet the expected demand, more than twice the print run of the old *Herald*. King and Cudlipp threw a lavish champagne party at the Café Royal to celebrate the launch of the newspaper that would surely capture the spirit of the Space Age.[78]

And then, nemesis. The *Sun* sold well over three million copies on its first day, but readers were obviously not impressed. 'It is appalling,' wrote a disappointed Tony Benn, who might have been expected to admire its emphasis on technology and novelty:

It is a pale wishy-washy imitation of the *Daily Mail* and I don't honestly see how it can survive as a daily. It is the product of market research, without any inner strength and message. There is little hard news — pages of fluffy features and nothing hard to bite on. I am afraid that it may not be as much of a help to us between now and polling day as we had hoped.[79]

Within four days the *Sun*'s circulation was down to 1.75 million; within a couple of weeks it was sinking back down towards the level of the *Herald*. By the last years of the decade its readership had fallen to some 800,000. In the middle of 1969 the IPC board decided to stop losing money on an obviously unsuccessful venture, and at the end of the year they sold it for a nominal fee to an Australian businessman called Rupert Murdoch.[80]

The failure of the *Sun* should have been a warning that for all the excitement about the Space Age, the path of change did not always run smooth. Mark Abrams had correctly identified how British society would evolve in the future, but he was wrong to imagine that the transformation would happen overnight, that people would welcome it with open arms, or that they would want to read a newspaper associated so closely with how things might be, not how they were. Technology had changed people's daily lives, of course. Thanks to the new household appliances, women were liberated from the backbreaking chores of housework; thanks to the car, they travelled wherever and whenever they wanted; thanks to the television, they were drawn into a truly national popular culture. But most parts of the United Kingdom were as yet unreachable by monorail, and old habits died hard. Although Labour had downplayed the issue of poverty in their election campaign, in most communities class boundaries still seemed as strong as ever, more than ten thousand people were homeless, and as we will see, more than five million were living in poverty.

Even at the peak of Wilson's enthusiasm for Space Age socialism, a few dissenting voices pointed out the weaknesses of his programme. *The Times* commented after the 'white heat' speech that he had done 'far more to describe the problems of the future than to show exactly how his broad proposals could be worked', and that he 'scarcely did more than sketch the outline of what a Labour government will do for science and technology'.[81] Edmund Dell, then a Labour parliamentary candidate, thought that Wilson's address was 'a clever patchwork designed to appeal to a wide variety of audiences' but that there was 'nothing in the speech by way of detailed substance'.[82] The *Spectator* even questioned whether Wilson's vision of the future had 'anything particular to do with the humanitarian socialism' of Labour Party tradition. After all, the image of 'a Britain pulsing with dynamic energies where technologists and scientists will be valued at their proper financial worth [was] hardly that of a more just or a more humane society . . . [but rather] a society of technocratic privilege, high salaries and early coronary thrombosis'.[83]

Above all, Wilson's vision was based on an unshakeable optimism about continuing economic growth. Again and again he talked about increasing production and investment without ever explaining how this was to be achieved. Again and again he told audiences that Labour's spending commitments would be met by greater growth and efficiency, apparently without ever considering that the economy might not immediately expand to order. He talked a great deal about the case for economic planning, but said next to nothing about how this would work in practice. Similarly, he repeatedly told his listeners that better education was the key to greater productivity; but there was no very convincing evidence that this was the case.[84] It is not surprising that many historians are so hard on Wilson's scientific rhetoric: 'an obscure and clouded vision', according to Vernon Bogdanor, for whom the label of 'thirteen wasted years' might be better applied to a Labour Party that had no new radical ideas, no coherent economic policy and no realistic appreciation of the country's problems.[85]

This was hardly Wilson's fault alone. Almost every other senior Labour figure of the day shared his complacency about the inevitable march of affluence and his faith that Britain would be reborn in the white heat of science and technology.[86] 'There exists at this moment a fantastic wealth of new scientific and technological knowledge, of new techniques and new processes, which if applied to industry would revolutionize Britain overnight,' wrote the journalist and academic Goronwy Rees. 'In this sense it is not true to say that Britain's problems are primarily economic ones; the means already exist by which those problems can be overcome.'[87]

That these wonderful new techniques might have unanticipated, even counter-productive consequences did not occur to him. Indeed, few people in the autumn of 1964 wondered what would happen if modernisation failed to reverse Britain's competitive fortunes, if economic growth came to an end, if the dreams of the Space Age, like the launch of the newspaper of tomorrow, turned sour. Either way, they were about to find out.

4

THIS IS TOMORROW

Pop Art: Way In or Way Out?

Sunday Times Colour Section, 26 January 1964

Taste is constantly on the move . . . People have become enormously aware of colour and design, and they are prepared to have more exciting things provided that they are less expensive and more expendable . . . 'Expendability' is no longer a dirty word.

Terence Conran, *The Ambassador*, August 1965

On 11 May 1964, at Brompton Cross on the Fulham Road, Chelsea, a new shop selling furniture, fabrics and household goods opened its doors for the first time. It was the brainchild of Terence Conran, an upper-middle-class designer in his early thirties, whose optimistic faith in all things modern and keen eye for a commercial opportunity made him one of the emblematic figures of the fifties and sixties.

Born in Surrey, Conran had studied textile design and worked in a minor capacity on the Festival of Britain, the nationwide celebration of science and art to mark the hundredth anniversary of the Great Exhibition. A year later he set up a furniture-making business in a studio he shared with the Pop artist Eduardo Paolozzi, and then, in 1953, he opened his first Soup Kitchen, selling mugs of soup, French cheeses and fresh bread in a tiled café clattering with the sound of a Gaggia coffee machine. Throughout the fifties and sixties Conran hovered on the fringes of Chelsea's well-heeled bohemian circuit and shared many of its values: a love of the modernist look, for example, and the adoration of all things French and Italian. Asked later to find ten words to describe himself, he said: 'Ambitious, mean, kind, greedy, frustrated, emotional, tiresome, intolerant, shy, fat.'[1]

In the fifties Terence Conran might not have been fat, but he was certainly ambitious. By the end of the decade he had established both of his major manufacturing enterprises, Conran Fabrics and Conran Furniture, as well as the Conran Design Group. He was greatly influenced by American and Scandinavian modernism and was particularly impressed by American methods of production and marketing. By the early sixties he had opened an enormous new factory at Thetford in Norfolk, full of the latest machinery for mass-producing furniture at the cheapest possible cost. In 1962 he proudly launched the new Summa range of domestic furniture, based on the clean, stark lines of Scandinavian design. It was 'designed to match the mood of present day living', explained the advertisements. 'What people want now for their homes is lively practical furniture in good basic shapes and warm unspoilt materials – natural timbers, leather, canvas – set off by bright fabrics.'[2]

Conran was convinced that the Summa range would be a success, but to his enormous frustration, only two furniture outlets in the capital, Heal's and Woodland's, were interested in stocking it. By the end of 1963, therefore, he had decided that it was time to appeal directly to the customers. The fashion designer Mary Quant, one of Conran's good friends from the so-called Chelsea Set, had already pointed the way with her own boutique on the King's Road, and Conran decided to follow suit. He picked the location carefully. The people who lived in the Fulham Road were exactly the kind of customers he had in mind: young, affluent and, above all, interested in looking 'with-it'. All he needed now was a name, and he eventually found it in *Roget's Thesaurus*. And so, in May 1964, Habitat was born.[3]

Habitat would never have caught the public's imagination had it not built on the deeper economic and cultural trends of the late fifties and early sixties, from the changing values of art and design to the unprecedented boom in consumer spending and home ownership. The contemporary enthusiasm for science and technology was closely associated with the new cult of domesticity. At the 1959 *Daily Mail* Ideal Home Exhibition, for example, there was a diorama of the new nuclear reactor at Dounreay in Scotland, as well as a Hall of Science and Technology, with examples of British work in everything from radio astronomy to underwater television. One display featured the thirty-five British scientists who had won a Nobel prize, while the final courtyard celebrated British inventions that had spread around the world, from postage stamps to penicillin. Just a few yards away, there were demonstrations of electric cookers, Electrolux vacuum cleaners and the first fully automatic dishwasher in Europe, made by Kenwood and tested for the cameras by the Duke of Bedford.[4]

Science was not merely changing the wider world; it was also, perhaps more importantly, changing the suburban home. Three years earlier, the Ideal Home Exhibition had mounted a special display on the House of the Future. Designed by Alison and Peter Smithson, two experimental young architects associated with the Brutalist movement, this one-bedroom town house was built around a small central garden. Moulded out of plaster impregnated with plastic, the house had soundproof exterior walls, an entirely transparent wall to the garden, and a double-curved roof, covered with aluminium foil. The living room was largely empty apart from a few perspex chairs, but at the touch of a button a coffee table would rise out of the floor. The bathroom included a shower that both washed and dried the occupant and a sunken bath that filled from the bottom at a pre-determined temperature. The bedroom contained only a bed with a thin nylon sheet, since the central heating meant there would be no need for more bedclothes. Other features included a 'loud-speaker' telephone that recorded messages, an oven that cooked by 'micro-waves', a trolley for keeping food warm, and a 'waste-disposal unit' beneath the pedal-operated kitchen sink.

The Smithsons, who were photographed living in their House of the Future, wore nylon clothes made by the sportswear designer Teddy Tinling. 'The clothes worn by the man are plain and unembellished,' he explained:

> This is in keeping with the times, a kind of Superman trend to fit in with the Space Age. I am sure that the trend, already beginning, for more colour in men's clothing, will develop. Especially in the house, men will revert to the bright colours which they wore before the Industrial Revolution. Out-of-doors [women's] clothes will have to be almost as severe as men's. A woman's space suit, for example, will be much the same as a man's. As a reaction to this, I feel sure she will want light, pretty clothes to wear in her well-heated home. Through history women have emphasised their femininity by décolleté necklines, and our woman of the future will be no exception.[5]

For those housewives who could afford to install refrigerators, washing machines and televisions in their new suburban homes, the House of the Future was already a reality. From the early fifties onwards, the design of the British home had increasingly reflected the optimism, leisure and domesticity associated with the affluent society, all rendered in a self-consciously modern style that was known as 'Contemporary'. This new look held sway from roughly the end of the forties until the early sixties, giving a sense of coherence not only to architecture and industrial design but to paintings, sculpture, furniture and furnishings.[6]

Contemporary design's obvious hallmark was its sheer colourfulness: technological advances meant that designers could use cheap dyeing techniques to draw stark contrasts between primary colours in a way that seemed invigorating at the time but would strike later generations as rather garish. Furniture design tended to be organic and curvilinear, while decorative patterns for wallpaper, curtains and carpets similarly combined 'natural', organic shapes with spiky abstract doodles reminiscent of the artworks of Joan Miró and Paul Klee. The aim was to create an overall impression of innovation, brightness and adventure, often exploiting the novelty of plastic, aluminium and synthetic fabrics. The Bakelite company, for example, tried to interest consumers in its 'Warerite' range of laminated plastics, 'for here and now, the materials of today . . . Gay and exuberant. Cool, calm or restless . . . Always clean, clinical, smooth and functional.'[15]

The success of Contemporary design in Britain was closely linked to the advent of affluence and the fact that growing numbers of people, both middle class and working class, had money to spend on home improvements. Spending on household items had increased by a staggering 115 per cent over the course of the 1950s, and in a self-consciously modern era young middle-class couples were keen to have the latest style for their new homes.[16] This meant a break with the deliberately traditional, respectable look of the thirties and forties – the faux-mahogany sideboards, the heavy, rounded armchairs and the enormous three-piece suites in floral fabrics – in favour of the cleaner lines, natural woods and lively colours of Contemporary. Front doors were brightly painted in primary colours, interior walls were decorated with bright, busy wallpaper and often one particular wall, usually with the fireplace, was papered with an even more gaudy design to make it 'stand out' from the rest.[17] Meanwhile, old symbols of gentility like pianos and handed-down china were carted off to junk shops and jumble sales. 'If you had a nice old panelled door, you had to put hardboard over it, with beading all around,' one critic later explained. 'Same with fireplaces. Then you'd invite people in to come and look at the desecration.'[18]

Popular interest in home furnishings reflected the aspirations and insecurities of an increasingly mobile, suburban society, in which the physical appearance of the home became emblematic of the taste and status of the entire family. The most famous replacement for all the old furniture that had been thrown away was the G-Plan range, launched in 1953 by E. H. Gomme and Sons and based on the principle of supplying solid, fashionable furniture at a price that most ordinary people could afford. Rather like the Ikea furniture popular half a century later, the G-Plan range was simple, cheap and dependable. This helped to ensure its popularity with younger couples furnishing their first home: as one Rotherham woman later explained, the G-Plan was a 'status symbol', supposedly reflecting the affluence, ambition and modernity of the home's occupants.[19]

By the beginning of the sixties imitations of the G-Plan could be found in shops from Harrod's to Woolworth's. Yet although the popularity of Contemporary with the middle-class young was beyond question, its ubiquity is often overstated. Older people often saw little reason to buy the latest style when they had perfectly serviceable furniture already, while thousands of couples, lacking the funds to splash out on an entire range of G-Plan furniture, were content to make do with what they had inherited or picked up cheaply. Surveys suggested that although many people would have quite liked a house kitted out in the latest style, when it came to parting with their own money they were rather more cautious, opting for the familiar rather than the new.[20]

Despite the innovations of Contemporary design, Britain entered the 1960s as something of a minnow in design terms, and British products did not have a very good international reputation. But change was in the air. Younger designers like Robert Welch and Robin Day were already making names for themselves at home and abroad, while the Council of Industrial Design, which had been established at the end of 1944, had been working hard to encourage 'good', modern design through its official journal, *Design*. Its director, George Russell, was a great admirer of mass production and mechanisation, and he encouraged the development of affordable designs that were both practical and pleasing to the eye. In 1956 he had established a new Design Centre in London, which soon had its own award scheme and index of approved designs, and in its first twelve months the Centre's enormous exhibitions of British products had attracted some 700,000 visitors. Suddenly design was popular, and although few people realised it at the time, British designers were on the brink of a new era of international acclaim.[21]

Design was not the only field in which the white heat of the technological revolution brought new opportunities and a new style. For those who worked in the visual arts, the late 1950s and 1960s were golden years. Britain had more art schools, per head, than any other country in the world. Many attracted working-class or lower-middle-class students with poor academic results but some vague glimmers of creativity. Entrance standards were less than exacting, and often the courses were relatively flexible and undemanding, so art colleges became, as George Melly put it, 'the refuge of the bright but the unacademic, the talented, the non-conformist, the lazy, the inventive and the indecisive'.[22] Indeed, the general ease and bohemianism of the art schools made them excellent breeding grounds for new musical trends; there was plenty of time for aspiring musicians to rehearse, and so it was in the art schools that initially uncommercial kinds of music, from rhythm and blues to psychedelic rock, first took hold.[23] But the art schools were not merely creative hothouses for bohemian musicians; they also ensured that at the beginning of the 1960s Britain had probably the best system of art education in the world.[24]

British art in the fifties did not command much attention among the public at large. The reputation of the painter Francis Bacon was growing rapidly, but he was hardly a household name. The dominant schools of the period were, first, the sombre Neo-Romanticism of painters like Graham Sutherland and John Craxton, and, second, the so-called 'Kitchen Sink' school of painters like John Bratby, whose thick, grim paintings of shabby breakfast tables did not endear him to the lay public.[25] Modern innovations, like American Abstract Expressionism, did not initially make much of an impact on the British artistic scene; to younger artists and curators who were keen to keep up with the latest international developments, this was a source of great frustration.[26]

Perhaps the most influential member of this new generation was Bryan Robertson, a bright, free-thinking curator in his early thirties, whose Whitechapel Art Galley was one of the few places in London, and indeed in Britain, which exhibited contemporary art. Its most celebrated exhibition opened in August 1956. Entitled 'This is Tomorrow', it consisted of twelve installations, each assembled by a different group of artists to represent their vision of the future. Most observers were drawn to the second installation, a 'fun house' by Richard Hamilton, John McHale and John Voelcker, in which the visitor moved through a corridor of disorientating black-and-white optical patterns before coming face-to-face with a collage of film posters, screens showing colour war films and television commercials for Pepsi and orange juice, another collage of magazine food advertisements, a giant bottle of Guinness, a reproduction of van Gogh's *Sunflowers* and enormous images of Marilyn Monroe and the character Robbie the Robot from the film *Forbidden Planet*.

Hamilton's poster advertising the installation was also steeped in images drawn from advertising and popular culture, and became emblematic not only of the exhibition but of the direction of British art in the late fifties and sixties. Entitled, *Just what is it that Makes Today's Homes so Different, so Appealing?*, it presented another collage, this time featuring the body-builder Charles Atlas, who is holding a giant phallic lollipop on which is engraved the word 'POP', and a semi-naked beauty posing in a living room crammed with images of the affluent society: a vacuum cleaner, a tin of ham, a television, a cassette recorder. The insignia of the Ford motor company is emblazoned on the lampshade; the blown-up cover of a teenage comic is framed on the wall; the window opens on to the illuminated forecourt of a cinema; overhead glowers an image of the Moon, the ultimate objective of the space race.[27]

Hamilton's fascination with modern consumer culture typified what came to be known as Pop Art. Pop presented a world drenched in affluence, in which, as one account has it, lives and identities 'were visualised through television and advertising, a world of mass production and mass mediation'.[28] Hamilton himself offered the best definition of the new movement in 1957:

> Popular (designed for a mass audience)
> Transient (short term solution)
> Expendable (easily forgotten)
> Low cost
> Mass produced
> Young (aimed at youth)
> Witty
> Sexy
> Gimmicky
> Glamorous
> Big Business.[29]

But although it was Hamilton who first popularised and defined Pop Art, it was not his creation alone. Eduardo Paolozzi, for example, had been producing collages of images from American magazines since the late 1940s, such as *It's a Psychological Fact Pleasure Helps Your Disposition* (1948), which showed two housewives cheerfully cleaning a gleaming modern kitchen and a colourful child's bedroom. Four years later, Paolozzi had joined Hamilton and a group of like-minded artists, including Alison and Peter Smithson and the critics Lawrence Alloway and Reyner Banham, to form the Independent Group, a faction within the Institute of Contemporary Arts which initially wanted to emphasise the relationship between art, technology and the mass media. It was this group that became the nucleus of the Pop movement.[30]

Fascinated by technology, advertising and American popular culture, Pop Art eagerly embraced the modern world with an enthusiasm that put even Harold Wilson to shame. Its optimistic visual appearance dazzled the viewer with bright, bold primary colours that owed more to the supposedly 'low' art of comic-books and magazines than to the traditions of fine art. Indeed, unlike Modernism, which had been very much a movement of elites, Pop Art was determinedly democratic. For the design historian Philippe Garner, it embraced 'a never-mind-about-tomorrow, brash, superficial modern; the modern of billboards and supermarkets; modern in the sense of being part of a collective wish-fulfilment fantasy of up-to-the-minute consumer gadgetry, packaging, advertising and fashion'.[31] This 'never-mind-about-tomorrow' ethos, reflecting the values of a newly affluent society, was central to the Pop artists and prevailed throughout much of the sixties. As late as 1967, the editor of *Art and Artists*, Mario Amaya, was still proclaiming the brash and disposable values of the Pop movement:

> Such art is by its very nature transitory. Its freshness, its excitement, its uniqueness, depend upon quick change, newness for its own sake, the expendable, the gimmicky, the cheap, the mass-produced, the deliberately offensive and ugly; in fact, all the things which we have been taught to abhor in a work of art.[32]

As these words suggest, there was a strong element of generational revolt in the rise of Pop Art, a revolt by younger artists against the paternalistic 'mandarin values' of the artistic establishment. At the Whitechapel This is Tomorrow Exhibition the organisers listed among their pet hates 'the English Way of Life, personal freshness, those who insist on individuality, beauty or refinement, phone bills and church'.[33] As the critic John Russell later explained, Pop Art was a resistance movement . . . directed against the Establishment in general and the art-Establishment in particular . . . Pop was meant as a cultural break, signifying the firing-squad, without mercy or reprieve, for the kind of people who believed in the Loeb classics, holidays in Tuscany, drawings by Augustus John, signed pieces of French furniture, leading articles in the *Daily Telegraph* and very good clothes that lasted for ever.[34]

Like the lower-middle-class Movement writers who came to prominence at about the same time, the Pop artists disliked what they saw as the snobbery of the metropolitan elite and preferred to emphasise their fondness for American popular culture.[35] According to the critic Robert Hughes, the Pop artists saw the United States as 'a mythical world of innocent plenty, far from the austerities of a victorious but pinched England'.[36] The young art dealer Robert Fraser, who would later come to the public's attention as a friend of the Beatles and the Rolling Stones, explained that there were 'very few English people who are interested in what one might call modern or contemporary art', whereas Americans 'have aesthetic leanings anyway, and have been able to fulfil their lifestyle and social desires by buying art, or supporting music . . . Also, they believe in what is going on now, whereas there is not this feeling here in this country'.[37]

At the beginning of the fifties, Pop Art had been the province of a few young, relatively obscure members of the Independent Group. Ten years later, however, it was hard to overstate its influence. Hamilton and Paolozzi both taught at the Royal College of Art, and it was from there that a 'second wave' of Pop artists emerged at the turn of the decade. In February 1961 the Young Contemporaries Exhibition, designed to show off the talents of the latest bright young things, was dominated by artists working in the shadow of Pop, from David Hockney to Peter Blake. The Pop critic Lawrence Alloway, who was on the selection committee, explained that their aim was to 'connect their art with the city', drawing on 'popular art' and 'the play of signs', including 'real objects, same size representation, sketchy notation, printing and writing'.[38]

A year later four of this new generation were profiled in Ken Russell's BBC film *Pop Goes the Easel*, which was broadcast as part of the *Monitor* series and brought Pop Art to the attention of millions of hitherto oblivious viewers. In the same month, February 1962, the first edition of the *Sunday Times Colour Section* ran a feature on Peter Blake, 'Pioneer of Pop Art'. The following year, meanwhile, five of the new Pop artists were selected for the Paris

Biennale, and, for the first time, Pop Art was admitted into the Royal Academy's summer show. Not only had Pop conquered London, it was conquering the world: Alloway was appointed as the curator of the Solomon Guggenheim Museum in New York, and during the rest of the sixties British painters and sculptors were widely exhibited and discussed not only in Europe but in artistic circles across the United States, which had not previously been very interested in British art.[39]

Of course it does little justice to the individual talents of the artists of the 1960s to lump them all together in one movement. But there was nevertheless an undeniable sense in the early sixties that Pop Art was carrying all before it, and the RCA 'second wave' generation revelled in their exploitation of consumerism. Derek Boshier, for example, painted a packet of cornflakes in *Special K* (1961) and a man made of toothpaste in *The Identi-Kit Man* (1962), while the abstract painter Richard Smith, fascinated by communications and marketing, incorporated images from commercial advertising into works like *Gift Wrap* (1963), which plays with the three-dimensional form of cigarette packets.[40]

By contrast, Peter Blake, who had shared a studio with Smith at the RCA and emerged as one of the best-known artists of the period, had a slightly different approach, more nostalgic and self-consciously English, drawing on folk and Victorian art as well as images of his favourite film stars and musical heroes. In his wall-mounted relief *Toy Shop* (1962), for instance, Blake lovingly recreated the window of an English village shop from the 1950s, complete with little toys evoking his childhood memories. This meant that he was ideally suited to produce what became his most famous creation, the cover design of the Beatles' album *Sgt. Pepper's Lonely Hearts Club Band* (1967), since his brand of domestic nostalgia not only matched the Beatles' own but nicely suited the contemporary fashion for Victorian revivalism.[41]

Probably the only British artist of the sixties whose fame outstripped Blake's was David Hockney. A grammar-school boy from Bradford, Hockney denied being a Pop artist, and was even alleged to have stormed out of a private viewing of his own work in 1963 shouting 'I am not a Pop painter', which, for some observers, was the final proof that he was. Hockney was more versatile than any of his contemporaries: in addition to being a successful painter in a deliberately rough style, he produced photographs, posters, book illustrations and even set designs. His colourful persona was an important part of his appeal. By the early sixties he had bleached his hair and taken to wearing horn-rimmed glasses and a gold lamé jacket, which he wore to receive the RCA Gold Medal in 1962. This all contributed to his growing notoriety, but he was so successful that soon after graduating from the RCA he was financially independent and, unlike many of his peers, did not have to teach for a living.

Hockney promptly moved to Los Angeles, a city devoted to consumerism, communications and mass entertainment, abandoned oils in favour of acrylics and produced a series of ironic, brightly coloured paintings of contemporary Californian interiors, shimmering Beverly Hills swimming pools and celebrated friends, perhaps most famously *Mr and Mrs Clark and Percy* (1970), a double portrait of the fashion designers Ossie Clark and Celia Birtwell and their cat, Percy. By the late sixties Hockney's paintings hung everywhere from Amsterdam to Chicago.[42] He was, wrote one commentator in 1967, 'the king of Pop art in Britain . . . one of the rare artists who has made such an instant success that he has never had to work at anything but his art'.[43] Yet Hockney himself always shunned the label. 'Pop Art was a figment of the critics' imaginations,' he later said. 'I've always despised the idea of pop. I have no interest in popular music or culture and never have had.'[44]

The fact that, despite his denials, Hockney was widely seen as a Pop artist was testament to the enormous success of Pop Art, not least in its impact on design, architecture, the cinema and other related fields, from women's mini-dresses to James Bond posters. 'Pop Art: Way In or Way Out?' asked the cover of the *Sunday Times Colour Section* in January 1964. The answer, it appeared, was 'Way In'.[45] Older artists, like Graham Sutherland, were dismissed as fusty and outdated, while the evolving genius of the sculptor Henry Moore was often overlooked in favour of the radical abstractions of his former pupil, Anthony Caro, whose obsession with surface and newness suited the tenor of the times.[46]

Still, the London art scene appeared to be booming during the 1960s. In 1955 the Tate Gallery had attracted 480,000 visitors; in 1965, it attracted almost 760,000. A year later, some 140,000 people paid ten shillings each to attend the Royal Academy's Bonnard Exhibition, which had to be extended to meet the demand, while that summer a sculpture exhibition in Battersea Park attracted a record attendance of 61,000. There were reports that more art students were choosing to stay in London instead of disappearing to Paris or Rome, and Thames & Hudson enjoyed sensational sales for their new range of paperback art books.[47] As a commercial proposition, too, art was suddenly extremely attractive: sales were booming, Arts Council subsidies for artists were higher than ever, and corporate sponsorship was pouring into contemporary art. Between 1950 and 1960, the number of commercial galleries in London had more than doubled, and more appeared in the sixties. The Waddington Galleries opened in 1958 and 1966; the Grabowski Gallery in 1959; the Robert Fraser Gallery in 1962; the Kasmin Gallery in 1963; the Signals Gallery in 1964; and the notorious Indica Gallery in 1966. These were merely the most prominent of a bumper crop: fifteen new galleries were reported to have opened in London in 1961 alone, and by the middle of the decade almost a hundred different commercial art galleries were competing for exhibitors and for customers.[48]

Of all these establishments, the most infamous was the Robert Fraser Gallery. An Old Etonian, a former officer in the King's African Rifles and the son of an exceedingly respectable City banker, Fraser was nevertheless a rather dissolute, bohemian figure, who had spent his early twenties in New York learning about the art world. At twenty-five he returned to London to open his own gallery at 69 Duke Street, in which he planned to bring the latest American art to his clients' attention; and thanks to his connections, he was able to attract an impressive crowd to the opening in April 1962.[49] Fraser subsequently acquired a reputation for unreliability and generally erratic behaviour, not least because of his association with the likes of Paul McCartney and Mick Jagger, and his increasing use of hard drugs. Thanks to his friendship with the leading pop stars of the day, he became a well-known figure around town, always suavely turned out, chatting easily to titled peers and bass guitarists in his Etonian drawl and enthusiastically introducing the likes of Jagger and Keith Richards to the pleasures of the hookah pipe. This greatly contributed to the notoriety of his gallery, which regularly appeared in newspaper and magazine reports about the lives of the swinging set.[50] There is little doubt, however, that Fraser's gallery was a genuine success. Bryan Robertson later remembered that it 'made an extraordinary impression from the beginning, because of its obvious sophistication and style'.[51] 'I like to see an extreme approach,' Fraser told an interviewer. 'I like to see artists who are provoking and breaking new ground.'[52]

Fraser invited most of the rising stars of British art to exhibit at his gallery, but of them all, the one who was most closely associated with the spirit of the mid-sixties was not any of the painters affiliated with Pop, but the black-and-white 'Optical' painter Bridget Riley. Born in 1931, Riley had been educated at Cheltenham Ladies' College, Goldsmiths and the RCA, but at the age of thirty she was still an unknown, working as a draughtsman for the advertising company J. Walter Thompson. Happily, a chance encounter with the director of Gallery One, a small avant-garde gallery in London, led to her first solo show in May 1962. A year later she exhibited again in the same gallery, attracting more interest and reviews; in 1964 she was part of the first Whitechapel New Generation programme; and in 1965 her paintings were heavily featured in New York, in the Museum of Modern Art's show The Responsive Eye. Riley's success can be gauged by the fact that three years later, selected to represent Britain in the Venice Biennale, she became the first British entrant and the first woman from any country to win the International Prize for Painting. 'No painter, dead or alive, has ever made us more aware of our eyes than Bridget Riley,' commented the *New Statesman* in 1971.[53]

Riley was the most famous exponent of what came to be called Op Art, the term Op being a catchy abbreviation of 'optical'. Until 1967 she painted in black and white only, trying, as she put it, 'to create [a] paradox, something that moves and does not move'. Working from precise geometric patterns, she created shimmering optical illusions that both fascinated and bewildered the eye, hovering between two and three dimensions, 'constancy' and 'movement'.[54] Her technique was nothing revolutionary; what appealed to observers in the sixties, however, was what one writer calls the art of 'psychological transformation'. In paintings like *Fall* (1963), with its shifting optical frequencies created by the repetition of a single curving black line, the eye struggles to make sense of the intense and bewildering pattern, and the painting therefore seems to defy contemplation. This greatly appealed to audiences in the mid-sixties, not least because the clean black-and-white geometry of Riley's paintings had the right overtones of science and modernity, and the 'Op Art look' was one of the most obvious examples of the increasing commercialisation of avant-garde art. Indeed, it is hard to think of another innovation in the fine arts that became so quickly assimilated into the commercial mainstream.[55]

Riley recognised, however, that this would do her no good at all. If her art became nothing more than another consumer trend, it would inevitably fall out of fashion as quickly as it had arrived, and she was horrified when fashion designers began copying her patterns for their coats and dresses.[56] But she was fighting a losing battle. As far as the media were concerned, Op was modern, young and sophisticated, and its beguiling black-and-white patterns were ideally suited for reproduction in popular culture. Few phenomena better illustrated the close association in the sixties between art and commerce, or indeed between the different arts themselves. Indeed, one of the most obvious characteristics of British culture in the sixties was the sense that people in very different fields were drawing on one another's work, so that there seemed to be some vague connection between, say, the paintings of Bridget Riley, the designs of Mary Quant, the furniture of Terence Conran, the photography of David Bailey and the music of the Rolling Stones.

In the case of Op Art there were Op dresses, Op posters, Op carpets, Op earrings, Op magazine advertisements and even Op haircuts, courtesy of Vidal Sassoon. On the big screen James Bond and his imitators moved through an Op Art world; on the small screen the heroines of *The Avengers* dressed in Op-themed fashions and confronted their adversaries in gleaming black-and-white corridors. Op even conquered the world of interior decorating: in 1966, Heal's produced a series of Op-patterned fabrics with names like Impact and Illusion, while in their Palladio 7 wallpaper collection the Wall Paper Manufacturers Ltd brought out a series of black-and-white wallpapers in circular patterns that could be hung vertically, horizontally or upside-down to get the desired optical effect.[57]

One reason why Op Art proved so popular in the design world was that it captured a sense of geometric precision, emblematic not only of the Space Age but of Harold Wilson's technological revolution. As a survey of British furniture published in 1964 put it, 'logical thinking' was all the rage.[58] Soft swirls of colour were replaced by perfect geometrical shapes; abstraction, informality and improvisation were replaced by symmetry, rigidity and repetition. Just as Wilson's Ministry of Technology hoped to revive the economy through 'purposive planning' and encouraged corporate mergers in the belief that bigger was better, so large organisations like the Council of Industrial Design or the London Fashion House Group urged designers to coordinate their marketing strategies and incorporate the latest technology into their operations. And, like Wilson's faith in planning, this had its roots in a broader 'confidence in the value of science and technology, and of the perceived benefits that a controlled "scientific" approach could bring to the designer, the manufacturer and the consumer'. The geometric, Op Art look was not merely new and fashionable; it was 'the embodiment of moral and aesthetic certainty'.[59]

By the middle of the sixties affluent young shoppers could hardly move for 'scientific' designs teeming with circles, cylinders, tubes, domes, squares, diamonds, cubes, triangles, cones and pyramids. Between 1962 and 1964, for example, Heal's, one of the most innovative and fashionable London stores, offered a series of geometrical fabric patterns with titles like Symmetry, Recurrence, Reciprocation, Alternation and Repetition.[60] Carpets often had circular or oval motifs, and they went nicely with the rigidly geometric and exceedingly fashionable patterns of the latest wallpaper. Pots, mugs, jewellery, lampshades, even public buildings like the Post Office Tower in London and the Rotunda in Birmingham: all were heavily based on the clean, confident geometric shapes that typified the 'look' of the mid-sixties.[61] Even the humble cigarette lighter was not immune: in 1968 the prominent designer Kenneth Grange produced a lighter for Ronson in the form of a gleaming white, oval egg, the top of which opened to reveal the lighter mechanism. White was the colour of space travel and, by extension, the Space Age, while the lighter itself was smooth, streamlined and perfectly formed. Few products better captured the modernising spirit of the sixties.[62]

All of these designs reflected not only a close interest in science and technology, but an overriding preoccupation with the future. Designers were working in an era which had seen the end of rationing and austerity, the birth of the supermarket, the rapid development of television and the spread of labour-saving appliances, and in which full employment and high incomes were taken for granted. In a world in which the launch of the first artificial satellite had been followed by the first manned space flight, it was hardly surprising that their imaginations ran riot. The gleaming white, silver and black 'Space Age look', therefore, was not only modern: it was progressive, confident and democratic, emphasising freedom, leisure and fulfilment.[63]

The heyday of the Space Age look lasted from the late 1950s until about 1965 or 1966. A useful barometer of the general mood was the *Daily Mail* Ideal Home Exhibition, which, having scored an undisputed hit with the Smithsons' House of the Future in 1956, tried to repeat the trick in the years that followed. The 1962 exhibition boasted a stand of the latest gadgets, among which were a television consisting of a swivelling screen with the workings concealed in a drawer beneath, an electroplating kit powered by a torch battery, and, rather oddly, a combined bed warmer, table lamp, inspection lamp, vaporiser and feeding-bottle heater, a gadget that would not have disgraced James Bond himself.[64] Indeed, some designers openly acknowledged the influence of the cinema and television. In 1965 Michael Wolff even wrote in the *Journal of the Society of Industrial Arts* that 'the sort of designers in Britain who have really given people a bang in the last two years are Ken Adams, Art

Director of the James Bond films; Frederick Starke with his clothes for Cathy Gale [from *The Avengers*]; and Ray Cusick, with his Daleks [from *Doctor Who*]'.[65]

In many respects, however, the designers of the late fifties and sixties were eminently practical, drawing on the innovations of science and technology, and exploiting the potential of materials like nylon, Terylene, Formica and so on. Formica, for example, was not only durable and heat-resistant, but exciting, fashionable and labour-saving, as magazine advertisements explained:

> Isn't life COLOURFUL with clean-at-a-wipe Formica!
> The cheering colours of 'FORMICA' Laminated Plastic beckon you to a workaday life that is free from needless drudgery! This tough jewel-bright surface cuts out scrubbing and scouring for good and all. A quick wipe with a damp cloth leaves 'FORMICA' shining-clean . . .
> Isn't it time you claimed your share of the extra leisure 'FORMICA' offers to every woman?

The accompanying picture, showing a smiling housewife brandishing a sparkling white cloth while her husband moves to embrace her, offered a hint of what purchasers might get up to in all that extra leisure time, and the advertisement helpfully added that 'beautiful' Formica could be bought on 'nursery furniture', as well as 'coffee tables, tea trolleys, bookcases [and] dressing tables'.[66] This evidently went down very well with consumers. 'We had Formica on the draining board, on the bath top, we had it on the coffee table,' recalled one Derbyshire man. 'It came in a wide variety of colours so you could match everything into your colour scheme . . . It was great. It offered up a world of possibilities for the home decorator.'[67]

Formica was only one of a number of synthetic materials that were extremely popular in the sixties, especially for young couples who wanted to establish their own modern, sophisticated identity in contrast to the ageing furnishings of their parents. Plastic in all its forms was colourful, hard-wearing and cheap, and the general assumption, as exemplified by dozens of science-fiction films, was that the future would be kitted out almost entirely in plastic. By far the most successful example was Robin Day's famous chair, created in 1963. It was the first chair to be made from Shell's new plastic, polypropylene, with a plain seat resting on aluminium legs, and its success rested on two things. First, it was cheap and easy to make, since one injection mould could produce four thousand seat shells a week; and second, the chairs could be stacked on top of one another, making them easy to store and transport. For decades afterwards Day's chairs were ubiquitous in schools, hospitals and similar institutions across the world. To later generations, few British innovations of the sixties would seem so mundane; yet few were so successful.[68]

Day's chairs also proved much more enduring than some of their more immediately eye-catching rivals. In 1967 the *Daily Telegraph* announced that inflatable chairs had come to the rescue of the 'no-space generation' and promised that 'these unusual blow-up pieces are going to affect the design of furniture in a decisive kind of way'.[69] There was also a brief vogue for paper furniture, like the cardboard chair designed by Peter Murdoch, another RCA graduate, in 1963. Murdoch had originally intended his chairs to be for children, but they were soon being sold to fashion-conscious consumers with the slogan: 'Fibreboard furniture for the young – Designed to last!' Laminated, washable and covered in bright designs inspired by Pop and Op Art, Murdoch's cardboard chairs were extremely cheap to make, since they could be stamped from a printed sheet at the rate of one a second, and they cost a mere thirty shillings apiece.[70] Paper furniture even made it into the Ideal Home Exhibition in 1966, although in the long run it was not much more successful than its inflatable equivalent.[71]

The whole point about inflatable and paper furniture was that it exploited the broader fascination with expendability. In an age of relative if sometimes overstated abundance, there was no shame in buying something that would last for only a couple of years: quite the reverse. The manufacturers of paper chairs were counting on consumers to buy something that was temporarily fashionable, throw it away after a brief period of use, and then look for the next 'in' thing. 'Where are all the three-piece suites?' asked the title of an article in the May 1967 issue of the painfully fashionable magazine *Nova*:

> Let the kids beat up the furniture, scratch the table or even paint all over the chairs – for you can buy very cheap, well-designed expendable furniture. When it gets broken, marked or stained, you can throw it away. Cheap materials and mass-produced methods are providing the consumer market with a whole range of goods which are efficient – and so cheap that you can discard them when you like without feeling guilty. Everything is changing at such a rate today that it is a drawback not to be able to change your belongings too, at frequent intervals.

As Terence Conran told an interviewer: 'Taste is constantly on the move . . . People have become enormously aware of colour and design, and they are prepared to have more exciting things provided that they are less expensive and more expendable . . . "Expendability" is no longer a dirty word.'[72]

To older observers, especially those who had lived through the austerity of the thirties and forties, there was something bewildering about a 'here today, gone tomorrow' consumer culture. But for many people, especially in the media, the assumption was that the current economic golden age would last indefinitely. Throughout the sixties incomes continued to rise, unemployment remained little more than nominal and spending on household appliances increased by more than 100 per cent.[73] With more money swilling around, habits, goods and activities that had once been reserved for the wealthy were now open to a much broader swath of the population, and the very act of shopping itself became emblematic of post-war modernity. For young people making their own homes for the first time, for instance, shopping allowed them to carve out their own identities, distinct from those of their parents. Women's magazines offered plenty of advice about furnishings and design to the young housewife, while the *Sunday Times Colour Section* countered with its famous 'Design for Living' pages, aimed at the affluent middle-class couples who made up the newspaper's target readership.[74]

As far as 'Design for Living' and its imitators were concerned, the crucial thing was to look modern. Modular furniture, glass tables, inflatable chairs, brilliant white walls and geometrical tableware all created the right impression of space, youth and modernity. One problem was that millions of people lived not in specially built open-plan villas but in flats, narrow terraces or semi-detached houses, so the sixties were boom years for renovations, knocking down walls and generally bashing houses about. One woman later recalled that her mother spent a fortune 'stripping things out of [her Edwardian] house, and gradually painting nearly everywhere white with bits of pine and metal strips and bright-coloured plastic and knocking down the odd wall for the new open-plan effect'.[75] Another, whose mother and stepfather owned a semi-detached house in Weymouth, remembered that 'they ripped out all the inside walls downstairs and had black and white tiles put in through the hallway into the back'. As for the living room:

> All the walls were white. The old-fashioned tile fireplace came out to give a hole in the wall with a stainless steel strip around it. I think there was

a rocking chair in there. Then there were shelves in the alcoves with the stereo – or record player as you would have called it then – oh, and there was a studio couch which could be turned into a bed and a table and chairs in one corner. It was very, very sixties, that room.[76]

But the two rooms that were most affected by the technological and economic changes of the post-war decades were the bathroom and the kitchen. In 1950 a survey found that nearly half of all homes had no bathroom, but this picture was changing rapidly. Over the course of the 1960s, the number of homes without a bathroom fell from 3.2 million to 1.5 million. To people who had previously made do with a tin bath and an outside toilet, this was no mean improvement. As one man put it: 'Just the thought of it was wonderful. To be able to walk in, open a tap and have hot running water and a nice warm bath.'[77] The kitchen, meanwhile, was the most important room in the home, as the centre of the housewife's operations and the focus for her identity as a so-called 'kitchen goddess'. The nature of the kitchen had already been changing before the Second World War as more and more middle-class families, especially those without servants, chose to eat in a larger and more comfortable kitchen rather than decamp to a dining room.[78] The new kitchens of the fifties and sixties were therefore based on a model first popularised in the 1930s: a large table in the middle, surrounded by stainless-steel sink units and kitchen cabinets in the latest style. The overall look tended to emphasise light, 'hygienic' colours like cream and white, which of course went nicely with the cult of the Space Age in the early sixties.[79]

Although the late 1960s are usually associated with economic decline, the broad picture as far as most consumers were concerned remained, by the standards of other periods, outstandingly bright. The number of cars on the roads, for example, increased during the Wilson years by some three million; similarly, the proportion of householders owning their own property rose from 46 to 50 per cent, and the figures for ownership of electrical appliances continued their inexorable rise.[80] Even in the houses of the poorest, as in the St Ann's district of Nottingham, appliances could be found: televisions, vacuum cleaners, washing machines and so on, although they were bought on credit and were often inferior to similar goods in middle-class homes.[81] The popularity of appliances like these opened up yet more opportunities for designers, the most famous example being Kenneth Grange, who came up with the redesign for the enormously popular

Kenwood Chef food mixer in 1961. Simple, clean and perfectly white, the Kenwood Chef typified the Space Age modernism of the early sixties. And it also made Grange's name, helping to win him further contracts with companies like Kodak, Wilkinson and Morphy Richards, and even elevating him into the category of the 'young meteors' that Jonathan Aitken interviewed for his book about Swinging London in 1967.[82]

The Kenwood Chef was a good example of the way in which the evolution of design in the sixties was closely associated with, and ultimately depended upon, the booming consumer economy. Designers needed manufacturers, marketers and retailers to make, promote and sell their products; without them, nobody would have heard of Robin Day or Kenneth Grange. In many cases, British designers owed their success as much to their skill in tapping the market and finding the right manufacturers and retailers as they did to the intrinsic qualities of their products.[83] 'The 1960s', explains one account, 'was the age of the entrepreneur, and for those with design skills, commercial intuition and personal drive, there were large and lucrative markets to be exploited and considerable fortunes to be made.'[84]

More than any other entrepreneur of the sixties, Terence Conran personified the cultural and economic trends of the day. When Habitat opened its doors in May 1964, it was a superb symbol of the association between design and commerce and rapidly became one of the iconic institutions of the decade. There were painted wood chairs from Italy, pine furnishings from Scandinavia and great piles of Mediterranean chicken bricks, butcher's blocks, knives, pots and pans. However, it was not only the sheer range and style of what Conran was selling that was new, but the way in which he was selling it. Products were piled on deep pine shelves, and customers were encouraged simply to pick up a basket and wander around. Habitat's very appearance was deliberately democratic; its target customers were fashion-conscious, affluent middle-class couples in their twenties and thirties, and no expense was spared to create the right impression of welcoming informality. The walls were whitewashed brick, the floor was lined with quarry tiles, the interior was lit from spotlights in the wooden ceiling, jazz music played on a central record player, and the overall effect was of 'simplicity, clarity and openness'. Even the shop assistants were encouraged to have fashionable bobbed haircuts and wear the latest Mary Quant dresses.[85]

In later years, as Conran's ambitions and self-worth expanded to match his ballooning waistline, it was easy to mock his achievement. His friend

John Kasmin, owner of the Kasmin Art Gallery, remarked that 'the problem with Terence is that he wants everybody to have a better salad bowl', while the critic Stephen Bayley commented that Conran 'could never quite appreciate that there were, somewhere, in places he had probably never visited, harassed individuals who would actually choose easy-care nylon sheets rather than his preferred river-washed, air-dried linen'.[86] But the importance and popularity of Habitat in the sixties and seventies are beyond question. In October 1966 Conran opened a second branch on Tottenham Court Road, as well as launching the first breezy Habitat catalogue; in 1967 he opened branches in Manchester and Kingston-upon-Thames; and by the end of the decade he had nine shops around the country, all catering to thousands of enthusiastic customers.[87]

Although it was true that Conran tended to sell to urban, affluent, middle-class consumers, Habitat's products were copied by almost every furniture, linen, tableware and department store in the land, so within ten years or so there were few households that did not have at least one or two products that traced their lineage back to Conran and his imitators. Unlike so many of the fashionable boutiques of the sixties, Habitat was built to last. Its products were invariably practical, good looking and well made, and even four decades later some branches were still trading in their original locations, with strikingly similar products. It was, quite simply, the most important retailing institution since the war, tying together the latest developments in design, production and marketing in an irresistible combination that its competitors then scrambled to copy.[88] And more than the Post Office Tower, the House of the Future or any utopian technological vision of the period, it was Habitat, with its idealised ethos of economic wealth, artistic effervescence and technological sophistication, that pointed the way to a better tomorrow in Harold Wilson's New Britain.

5

THE HUNDRED DAYS

> I said to Harold, '. . . We haven't even got across the image of a new era. Don't pretend. Let's say instead that we have only built the skirting, and ask people to give us a chance to build the whole house.' He said, 'That's a fine idea.' And I replied, 'You know, any idea of our being a Kennedy regime is absurd.' He looked at me and he said, 'I suppose you're right, Dick. You can't really sell a Yorkshire terrier as a borzoi hound.'
>
> Richard Crossman's diary, 25 September 1965

In the early evening of 16 October 1964, Harold Wilson made his first ministerial appointment, confirming Jim Callaghan as Chancellor of the Exchequer. Callaghan was understandably emotional, and after embracing a surprised Wilson, he made his way for the first time down the narrow corridor that led from No. 10 to the Chancellor's residence next door. There, in the study of No. 11, his new permanent secretary, Sir William Armstrong, was waiting. 'He handed me a foolscap typed volume at least two inches thick of background economic information,' Callaghan recalled, 'with a polite intimation that I might wish to read it before the morrow. It began with the words "We greet the Chancellor", but the rest of the contents were not so happy.'[1]

The news was appalling. According to the documents, the new government had inherited a deficit that had been growing for weeks and was now thought to be as much as £800 million. The pound itself was under immediate threat, and severe cuts in public spending and increases in taxation were almost inevitable.[2] The Treasury's senior economic adviser, Sir Alec Cairncross, later admitted that the civil servants had deliberately painted the blackest possible picture; they wanted the new Chancellor to make a decision immediately, and they wanted to show their new masters that there were no easy choices in government.[3] The news had the effect they wanted. 'The size of the deficit was a complete surprise,' recalled Jack Diamond, the new Chief Secretary to the Treasury. 'It was a terrible mess. Just unheard of, figures at that level. We'd been expecting some difficulties but not such a mess as that.'[4]

Successive Chancellors had been struggling with the balance of payments and the value of sterling for years. Put very simply, there were two interlinked problems. First, the pound was overvalued on the international exchange markets at $2.80 and was increasingly unpopular with foreign speculators. Second, the balance of payments was constantly under pressure not only because of consumer demand for imports, but because of the bill for maintaining Britain's world role overseas, which had to be paid for in sterling. Governments continually urged British manufacturers to produce more goods for export, in order to try to reduce the deficit. But the danger was that rising production and economic growth would only encourage people to spend more money on imports, making the haemorrhage of sterling out of the country even worse. So the Conservative and Labour governments of the sixties faced the same delicate balancing act. They needed to promote economic growth to meet their goals of prosperity and popularity; at the same time, they had to encourage businesses to produce goods for foreign as well as domestic markets; and, simultaneously, they had somehow to restrain consumers from spending too much on imports. To compound their difficulties, international trade was becoming more competitive in the sixties, so the British share of export markets was bound to come under threat.

In later years the historians pointed the finger of blame for the deficit at Callaghan's predecessor, the debonair Conservative Chancellor Reginald Maudling. In April 1963, with one eye on the election and hoping to break out of a stuttering 'stop–go' growth cycle, Maudling had thrown caution to the wind and cut taxes by £260 million, unleashing the so-called 'Dash for Growth'.[5] But by the beginning of 1964 it was clear that a reckless boom was under way. British consumers were lavishing millions on imports, and the current-account deficit was sliding further and further into the red.[6] Maudling had not broken out of the stop–go cycle; he had exacerbated it, and in February 1964 he was compelled to raise bank rate to 5 per cent. Two months later, in his second Budget, he admitted that the balance of payments was bound to worsen, but he refused to impose heavy tax increases, not least because they would severely damage the Tories' re-election prospects.[7]

Maudling's complacency proved expensive. At the end of April, Sir Alec

Cairncross warned him that the current rate of growth was unsustainable, and by June Treasury officials were talking about a possible deficit of several hundred million pounds.[8] While still breezily denying that there was anything wrong, Maudling asked them to prepare emergency plans for whoever won the election.[9] Since unemployment was negligible and the high streets were booming, the public was still largely oblivious to the looming disaster. But in Whitehall there was a growing sense of alarm. On 28 August Lord Cromer, the Governor of the Bank of England, wrote to the Treasury expressing his 'considerable misgivings about the direction in which our financial affairs are going', and added that he had asked Maudling to convey his fears to the Prime Minister.[10] By 14 September there were rumours in the City that Britain was planning to negotiate a loan from the International Monetary Fund or a $500 million swap arrangement with the United States. And by the eve of the election, Treasury officials had revised their deficit prediction to £600 million or even higher.[11]

Despite their political differences, Maudling and Callaghan were good friends, and the latter recalled that they used to meet regularly to have a couple of drinks and 'talk privately and frankly' about their concerns. On 18 June Callaghan visited his opposite number in the Chancellor's room at the Commons for the last time before the election. 'Maudling was his usual unruffled, amiable self,' he wrote, 'reflectively sipping a large whisky and soda.' While the Chancellor admitted that the balance of payments was looking less than healthy, he nonetheless maintained that there was no cause for panic. Maudling certainly did not communicate any great sense of disquiet, although he confided that he expected to lose the election, and suggested that Callaghan should think about organising a loan from the European central banks after he took office.[12]

Four months later, early on the morning of Saturday, 17 October, Callaghan sat at Maudling's old desk in the study of 11 Downing Street, reading his Treasury brief in stunned horror. He had guessed that the situation was serious, but had never envisaged a deficit of £800 million. Upstairs, in the flat, Maudling was finishing packing for the journey into opposition. On his way out, carrying a great pile of suits over his arm, he stuck his head around the door of his old study. 'Good luck, old cock,' he said cheerfully to his successor. 'Sorry to leave it in such a mess.' Then he smiled, stuck his trilby on his head, and sauntered off.[13]

At eleven Callaghan walked through the connecting corridor into No. 10 to take his first, vital decision as Chancellor. In the Cabinet Room, Wilson and George Brown, the latter in his capacity as deputy leader and head of the new Department of Economic Affairs, were waiting for him. Callaghan takes up the story:

> From where I sat I could see the autumn colours in St James's Park, heightened by the bright sunshine, and I felt we were beginning a great adventure. We had discussed our early action often enough, and the first item on our informal agenda did not take long to dispose of. It was to decide formally whether to devalue the pound. We did not need to call in the officials for each of us knew before the Prime Minister began what our answer would be, and we quickly reached a unanimous conclusion to maintain sterling's exchange rate.[14]

Devaluation, as far as they were concerned, was not an option. The very word was left out of minutes of their meetings that day, and there was to be no discussion of it for another eighteen months. Instead, Callaghan set to work on an emergency Budget to be presented in November, in which he intended to propose cuts and tax increases that would reduce purchasing power, ease demand for imports and take the pressure off the beleaguered pound.[15]

This decision has often been identified as the turning point in the history of Wilson's government, dooming them to a long, draining battle to defend an overvalued pound. In 1975 Anthony Crosland reflected that it was the 'central failure' of the administration, in that it 'constrained public expenditure . . . antagonised the trade unions and alienated large groups of workers . . . killed the National Plan and . . . frustrated policies for improving the industrial structure'.[16] Edmund Dell, himself a new Labour MP in 1964, wrote that right at the very beginning of the government, its three leading ministers had rushed into a decision that 'made Callaghan's task as Chancellor impossible' and committed themselves 'to endless difficulties and possibly destruction'.[17]

Many historians have suggested that Wilson and his ministers decided against devaluation for self-interested political reasons rather than economic ones.[18] 'The Conservatives would have crucified us,' Callaghan explained later, pointing out that it had taken years for Labour to live down the humiliating devaluation of 1949, and that if he had devalued in October 1964, 'the Tory Opposition as well as the press would have hammered home day after day that devaluation was always Labour's soft option, and took place whenever a Labour Government was elected'.[19] These thoughts were uppermost in Wilson's mind, too. A month after the fateful decision, Crossman privately suggested to him that 'devaluation was the only thing left and should be got over as quickly as possible'. Wilson was having none of it. 'You're talking nonsense,' he replied. 'Devaluation would sweep us away. We would have to go to the country defeated.' For years he had been telling audiences that 'a second devaluation would be regarded all over the world as a defeat', and he hated the idea of making Labour the party of devaluation once again.[20]

Wilson also knew that devaluation would inevitably be accompanied by severe cuts in public spending and a rapid slowdown in consumer growth in order to release economic resources for exports. This would mean abandoning the manifesto pledges on which Labour had come to office and breaking his promises to spend more on national insurance benefits, the NHS, pensions and education. Since a second election was likely in a year or two, it would be a disaster.[21] As George Brown pointed out, the heavy deflation necessary to make devaluation work would predominantly hurt the working-class voters that Labour was supposed to be protecting.[22] And as far as Wilson was concerned, the value of the pound was a question of patriotism and international prestige. 'Look at this government,' he imagined his foreign contemporaries saying, 'every time they get into trouble, even a small trouble, they devalue.'[23]

Wilson's critics often blame him for allowing 'questionable political calculations' to cloud his economic judgement, but this is very unfair.[24] Callaghan's Treasury advisers were strongly opposed to devaluation, arguing that it would represent a severe blow to the prestige of sterling and would effectively be betraying those countries, like Malaysia, for example, that had invested in the British currency. The briefing notes prepared for the new Chancellor called it 'an act of desperation that would have far-reaching consequences', and pointed out that quite apart from the inflationary pressures at home, it was likely to be a severe shock to world trade and would probably heap further pressure on the dollar, thereby alienating Britain's American allies.[25] Most economists were also opposed, as were Sir William Armstrong, the senior Treasury civil servant, and Lord Cromer, the Governor of the Bank of England.[26] Thomas Balogh, Wilson's economic adviser, thought that it would be merely a short-term fix to a long-term problem, which was the underperformance of British industry, and he argued that it would be better to concentrate on increasing productivity and development.[27]

In short, there seemed to be excellent economic motives, as well as the obvious political ones, for resisting the temptation, and even if Wilson and Callaghan had devalued in 1964, there is no reason to believe that it would have been a marvellous cure for Britain's economic ills.[28]

For Wilson, there was no going back. 'It was the first day or never,' he told President Johnson's chief economic adviser; 'now it's never.' In a letter to the American President, he wrote that he had ruled out devaluation 'for all time'.[29] The problem was that he had now staked his reputation, his personal prestige and his trustworthiness on defending the pound, and every time that he tried to reassure the markets by reiterating his opposition to devaluation, he dug himself deeper into the trench. Changing course, once that course had been set, would mean sacrificing his own credibility, and so for Wilson the defence of sterling became what one historian calls 'a kind of fetish'.[30] This explains why the very word 'devaluation' became such a taboo in government circles. 'It was a forbidden word,' recalled Barbara Castle. 'It was almost the F word in cabinet. You weren't allowed even to mention it.'[31] George Brown, melodramatic as ever, told his junior minister Anthony Crosland that 'the subject was never, *never* to be mentioned again', and whenever he wanted to refer to it himself, he would 'purse his lips and put a finger in front – and that meant devaluation'.[32]

The obvious temptation, both then and later, was to blame Maudling and the Conservatives for the hideous situation they had bequeathed to their successors. There was no doubt that Maudling's reckless over-optimism had driven up the deficit, but it is too easy to hold him responsible for everything that followed. The irony was that during Maudling's spell at the Treasury, his Labour critics had accused him of being too hard-hearted, not too generous. When Maudling presented his notorious Budget in April 1963, two of the most celebrated brains on the Labour benches, Anthony Crosland and Roy Jenkins, agreed that he was far too parsimonious. Crosland said that he had 'acted on the cautious side', while Jenkins condemned his 'half-hearted approach to expansion'. This was hardly a record of which to be proud.[33]

Indeed, there is little evidence that anybody on the Labour benches had thought very hard about the problems of sterling before they took office in 1964. For the fundamental problem, putting aside Maudling's self-indulgence, was the fact that successive British governments had been trying to pay two bills at once with limited assets: first, the bill for their continued status as a supposed Great Power; and second, the bill for a modern, affluent consumer society. Britain insisted on maintaining expensive military bases abroad, not to mention the troops serving on the Rhine and in trouble-spots like Malaysia and Aden, while still preserving the pound as an international reserve currency. This heavy spending on foreign aid and military establishments overseas, not the exaggerated imbalance between imports and exports, was the real drain on the nation's finances. In fact the deficit in 1964 was never as much as £800 million; the Treasury had overestimated the severity of the crisis. It was the determination to maintain Britain's world role that was the real problem, but this was something to which Wilson and Callaghan had given very little thought.[34]

Wilson held his first Cabinet meeting on Monday, 19 October, although it was no more than a formality. Crossman, among others, was disgruntled to hear that they were not going to be given the full details of their economic inheritance, and described the scene as 'an absolute farce'. 'Naturally you won't want to be told, for fear of the information leaking, how serious the situation is,' said George Brown. 'You won't want to be told what methods we shall take but we shall take them.'[35] What these methods were did not become clear until later in the week, when Callaghan and Brown announced that they had devised a scheme to deal with the balance of payments crisis, namely a 15 per cent surcharge on all imports. In itself, the surcharge was clearly not a viable alternative to devaluing the pound, and neither did it inspire much confidence abroad. Although it did save about £150 million a year in imports, the surcharge ultimately provoked such ferocious opposition and dire threats of retaliation abroad that in February 1965 it was cut to 10 per cent and was finally abolished a year later.[36]

The surcharge experiment was a bad beginning for the new government, and matters were about to get worse. On 11 November Callaghan presented an emergency Budget to the Commons. The constant shadow of the deficit and the expected inflationary pressures of the import surcharge meant that the Budget needed to be deflationary, but the new government was committed to spending more public money in the form of increased pensions and social security benefits and the abolition of prescription charges. The Budget did increase income and petrol taxes, but the impact of this new spending meant that its effect was only mildly deflationary. Callaghan also announced that he would introduce capital gains tax and corporation tax the following year, but he was unable to provide any details about rates, regulations or expected revenue.[37]

The package had clearly been put together in a rush and it failed to appease any of its possible constituencies. Cairncross thought it was symptomatic of a 'remarkably amateurish and ramshackle' approach to handling the economy; the *Guardian* called it 'a costly blunder'; and most importantly, the markets were distinctly unimpressed.[38] On 20 November, with share prices tumbling and the Bank of England haemorrhaging gold and exchange reserves, rumours circulated that the pound was going to be devalued after all.[39] 'Government Faced by Financial Crisis' read the headline in the following day's *Times*: 'Pressure on the Pound in All European Capitals'.[40]

Economic management is far from an exact science. Nevertheless, most historians agree that Wilson and Callaghan blundered badly in not adopting a policy of severe tax rises and spending cuts as soon as they took office. Their motives were understandable: they wanted to carry out their manifesto commitments, they were ideologically committed to economic growth, and they were worried about the impact on the electorate. Had they immediately deflated the economy, however, they would have won some breathing space to defend the pound and prepare the ground for expansion later in the decade. Instead, they found themselves trapped in a cycle of apparently endless sterling crises. Since they never won the confidence of the markets, the story of the Wilson administration would be that of a gruelling rearguard action against interminable pressure on the pound.[41] In the words of the Labour MP Edmund Dell, the years that followed were 'among the unhappiest in the history of British economic management'.[42]

The first serious attack on sterling peaked in the last ten days of November 1964. Callaghan later wrote that he had never 'experienced anything more frustrating than sitting at the Chancellor's desk watching our currency reserves gurgle down the plughole day by day and knowing that the drain could not be stopped'. He could not even share his troubles with others, because the officials at the Bank of England insisted that the losses be kept a secret so as not to encourage the speculators. Each day, Callaghan remembered, was the same, an exhausting 'game of bluff' in which he tried to outguess the markets. 'It was like swimming in a heavy sea,' he wrote. 'As soon as we emerged from the buffeting of one wave, another would hit us before we could catch our breath.'[43]

The pressure inevitably took its toll. On 24 November Crossman was sitting at a packed meeting of the parliamentary party when Brown came in, sat next to him and muttered: 'The situation is desperate. It's the worst we've ever had.' Minutes later Callaghan appeared on the other side of him and said exactly the same thing.[44] The Chancellor was taking it hard, and Crossman noted that he was 'heavy and gloomy . . . obviously overawed by the situation and full of self-pity'.[45] Callaghan later admitted that he relied on Wilson's experience in those first weeks, often trooping disconsolately through to No. 10 for advice and support.[46] Wilson, meanwhile, was keen for their colleagues to know who had lost his nerve, and who had kept it. 'I had to put another backbone into the Chancellor today,' he used to remark to his officials.[47] 'I'm having to hold his hand,' he boasted to Crossman. 'His nerve isn't very good these days.'[48]

On 23 November the inner triumvirate of Wilson, Callaghan and Brown agreed to raise bank rate by 2 per cent to try to appease the markets. Unfortunately, instead of being impressed, foreign investors read it as another indication of panic, and by the end of the following day the Bank of England had spent almost a third of its foreign exchange reserves to support sterling. Taking into account the Bank of England's arrangements with other central banks in Europe and the United States, this meant it had about £800 million left to support the pound, which, if the current trend continued, meant that sterling had only days left.[49]

That night, Lord Cromer and his deputy requested a meeting with Wilson and Callaghan. The Governor of the Bank of England brought a stark message: either Wilson must announce an emergency package of deflationary cuts and withdraw his plans for the nationalisation of steel, or the markets would have their head. Wilson, furious to be lectured by an unelected official who was no friend to the Labour Party, promptly exploded. He reminded Cromer that he intended to carry out his manifesto promises, and added that if necessary he would float the pound and call an immediate general election on the theme of 'the bankers against the people'. Cromer angrily retorted that 'to go to the country on that issue would mean putting Party before Country', but he was clearly stunned by Wilson's vehemence.[50]

Temporarily at least, the Prime Minister had won the day, and Cromer agreed to renew his efforts to raise international support for the pound. After spending almost all night on the telephone, he pulled it off. By the following day Cromer had persuaded his foreign colleagues to put together an aid package of some $3000 million, much of it from the American Federal Reserve. Almost immediately the pressure lessened and the crisis receded. The Bank had spent some £600 million to keep the pound at its current level, and Britain not only had to defer its existing loans from the United States, but also had to negotiate IMF assistance to repay the short-term loans that had saved the pound on this occasion.[51]

The confrontation between Wilson and Cromer illustrated the central dilemma facing the Labour government during the sixties. On the one hand, they had been elected on a programme of modernisation, growth and promises to overhaul the welfare state; not to carry out their commitments would mean abandoning their principles and betraying their supporters. On the other, they had inherited a parlous financial situation and were struggling to win the trust of the exchange markets; to stick with their commitments would mean risking the future of the pound and the health of the economy.

Instead of spelling out this dilemma in public, Wilson kept it quiet, so as not to alienate the voters or alarm foreign investors. At the party conference on 12 December, he struck an upbeat note. Already the Kennedy analogy had been forgotten; now, switching guises with remarkable facility, he portrayed himself as the new Churchill:

> I believe that our people will respond to this challenge because our history shows that they misjudge us who underrate our ability to move, and to move decisively, when the need arises. They misjudged our temper after Dunkirk, but we so mobilised our talent and untapped strength that apparent defeat was turned into a great victory. I believe that the spirit of Dunkirk will once again carry us through to success.[52]

Crossman recorded that Wilson 'did extremely well' and the delegates clearly loved it, but he could not hide his own misgivings:

> It didn't seem to me that he struck the right Prime Ministerial note and he certainly didn't steel our people for the difficulties ahead. As Minister for Housing I know quite well that I've got to explain the fact that the local authorities aren't going to get the money to build the houses. They will have to cut back their housing programme . . . The fact is, deflation is really starting. That's what I feel in my bones. But it hasn't been said and Harold Wilson blithely denies it.[53]

At the beginning of 1965 there were signs that the picture might be improving. Exports were comfortably outweighing imports, and the current-account deficit was finally coming back under control. Wilson, whose capacity for looking on the bright side often amazed his colleagues, was full of confidence for the year ahead. On 4 February he told his backbenchers that the crisis was 'now virtually over. The future is bright with promise.'[54] Other ministers were much less sanguine. Three days into the New Year, Crossman privately predicted 'a pretty rough time' in the months ahead, partly due to the fact that they had come 'into office with very halfbaked plans'.[55] Ten days later, Benn was even more pessimistic:

> Defence, colour television, Concorde, rocket development – these are all issues raising economic considerations that reveal this country's basic inability to stay in the big league. We just can't afford it. The real choice is, do we stay in with Europe or do we become an American satellite? . . . I was always against the Common Market but the reality of our isolation is being borne in on me all the time. This country is so decrepit and hidebound that only activities in a wider sphere can help us to escape from the myths that surround our politics.[56]

Although the government's attention in the early months of 1965 was largely devoted to the country's parlous finances, other problems were not slow to intrude. One of the sub-plots of the October election had been the fate of Patrick Gordon Walker, a leading Gaitskellite and Wilson's choice as the new Foreign Secretary. Gordon Walker represented Smethwick, in the West Midlands, and many observers were horrified when he unexpectedly lost his seat after a notorious anti-immigration campaign by his Conservative opponent, Peter Griffiths. One of the slogans associated with Griffiths's campaign had been 'If you want a nigger neighbour, vote Labour', and it was no surprise that many leading Conservatives immediately distanced themselves from Smethwick's new MP.* Wilson invited Gordon Walker to serve as Foreign Secretary anyway, despite his defeat, and a new, relatively safe seat was found for him in the East London constituency of Leyton.

The by-election was scheduled for 21 January and proved a disaster. Gordon Walker was greeted at his nomination by a man who had blackened his face with boot polish and carried a placard reading: 'Gordon Walker – The Race Mixing Candidate – Make Britain Black', and anti-immigration

---

*See Chapter 31.

campaigners paraded outside his headquarters dressed in monkey suits and armed with placards reading: 'We immigrants are voting for Gordon Walker'.[57] He had become a target of the anti-immigrant far right, and his election meetings were frequently marred by shouting and scuffles, including one notable set-to when the Defence Secretary, Denis Healey, landed a punch on the neo-fascist campaigner Colin Jordan.[58] In the end, Gordon Walker lost by 205 votes. Although Wilson had never much liked him anyway, the government had been publicly humiliated. After months of success, the polls were finally beginning to turn against Labour, and in February 1965 Gallup put the two parties neck and neck for the first time in three years.[59]

Wilson met his Kitchen Cabinet the following morning and told them that 'he could not allow the drift to go on'.[60] At Cabinet, four days later, there was a heated discussion about strategy. Callaghan argued that they should be more honest with the public, explaining the economic dilemma and offering them nothing but 'blood, sweat and tears'. Brown completely disagreed: they had been 'guilty of too much morality and not enough politics'. The government's majority was already down to just three, so they could be brought down by 'a couple of appendicitis operations' or 'a single car accident'. 'We must now', said the Deputy Prime Minister, 'have nothing but short-term tactics and prepare an offensive designed to put the blame back on the Tories.'[61] Either way, what passed for Wilson's honeymoon was clearly over. 'I felt an epoch had ended,' wrote Crossman on the night of the Leyton result; 'Ironically enough this was the ninety-ninth of Harold's famous Hundred Days.'[62]

The new emphasis on 'short-term tactics' did not sit easily beside Callaghan's determination to insist on an austere Budget in the spring of 1965. Even as his colleagues tried to think of new ways to restore the government's popularity, the Chancellor was warning them that Britain was eventually going to have to repay its overseas loans. If they wanted to borrow more money, he said, 'the bankers would expect us to introduce deflationary measures as the price of their support'.[63] This did not go down very well with Callaghan's colleagues on the left, who were greatly disgruntled at the thought of abandoning their spending plans at the behest of the markets. At one Cabinet meeting, Barbara Castle declared: 'The Tories have got on all right without financial rectitude for fifteen years', at which, she noticed, 'Harold buried his head in his hands in silent laughter while Wedgie Benn recoiled in horror'.[64]

Callaghan, however, was undeterred, and when he presented his Budget on 6 April, it was an exercise in deflation. Not only did he introduce corporation and capital gains taxes, but he increased the duty on beer, spirits, tobacco and car licences, all of which produced an extra £475 million in government revenue.[65] There were squeals of anguish from some quarters: one City gentleman interviewed on television denounced the Budget as a step towards 'a Communist state' and threatened to 'fight like hell on the beaches, and on the streets and in the farms'. Most City observers, however, were pleased to see some financial rigour, and even Callaghan's more radical colleagues were appeased by the new taxes on business.[66] The loudest protests came, rather ominously, from George Brown, who privately told Wilson that deflation on this scale seemed 'a very old-fashioned way of running our affairs'. Since Brown had no better ideas, his advice was roundly ignored.[67]

Late spring and summer did not bring much improvement. In May the government effectively abandoned its plans for the nationalisation of the steel industry, which had been promised in the Labour manifesto. Nationalisation was dear to the hearts of many activists in the Labour movement, and Wilson had hoped that he could unite his party around an issue that differentiated it from the Conservatives. The problem was that two discontented backbenchers from the Labour right, Woodrow Wyatt and Desmond Donnelly, had other ideas. Both were fervently opposed to steel nationalisation and threatened to vote against the bill, which might, given Labour's thin majority, bring down the government. In the end Wilson gave way, and nobody was very surprised when the bill was dropped from the next Queen's Speech.[68] In truth there was little else that the government could do, but it was an important symbolic moment. From now on, first backbenchers, then journalists and eventually ordinary voters began to wonder whether the government was quite as brave and honest as they had thought, or whether they were just another group of shop-worn, cynical politicians.[69]

By the beginning of June, Wilson was keen to find some way to break Labour's slow decline in the polls. His solution was to cut bank rate; after all, he argued, the economic situation was on the mend, so why not give the electorate a bit of a boost? On 3 June, he explained his reasoning to the Cabinet:

> We were in a 'rut, groove, corner': no room for manoeuvre: and the time had now come to break out. If we did not lower bank rate now, we should probably never have another chance . . . If the whole thing went

wrong, we should be in a mess. He did not underestimate the risk. But there was a sporting chance that it would enable us to break out, politically as well as economically. He personally strongly recommended it to Cabinet.[70]

The Cabinet agreed, and the rate was cut by 1 per cent. Unfortunately, the international financiers did not take to the measure as well as Wilson had hoped, and after complaints from Washington, the Chancellor was forced to contemplate yet another deflationary package.[71]

Wilson, meanwhile, blamed 'political malice' on the part of the bankers and speculators rather than any shortcomings of his own.[72] On 24 July, in a speech at Newport, he publicly questioned 'the motives of those who at home and abroad want to sell Britain short'.[73] As Edmund Dell later pointed out, Wilson seemed to believe that since he had a mandate from the British electorate, the bankers and the speculators had no business doubting the viability of the national economy or the value of the pound. But this was nonsense. The bankers were not motivated by anti-socialist spite, but by cold financial calculations. Try as he might, the Prime Minister could not simply wish away the bad news.[74] And by now, even the government's senior officials were tiring of his refusal to face the gravity of the situation. 'The PM did most of the talking,' recorded Cairncross after one meeting in May, 'and it trod the familiar path from gimmicks to autobiography and then hot foot to the failings of statistics, this government's favourite alibi.'[75]

While Wilson was blaming the speculators, the statisticians and various other malefactors, yet another package of cuts was put together. As was becoming usual on these occasions, there were howls of protest from ministers who saw their own projects disappear before their eyes. Crossman, who was fighting hard to save his housing schemes, had already complained that 'Tory priorities were prevailing over our own socialist loyalties', and he was disgruntled to find that when the package was presented to the Cabinet on 27 July, they were asked to 'take it or leave it as it stands'.[76] Anthony Crosland argued that Callaghan's path led 'straight into stagnation and Tory policies' and pointed out that there was 'no guarantee these steps would do the trick'. The alternative was 'to devalue now by refusing to adopt Tory remedies'. However, this was never likely, and in the end the Cabinet agreed to support the new round of cuts. 'Our people took the statement in numbed silence,' recorded Barbara Castle, 'but morale that night in the tea-room was pretty low.'[77]

Crosland's intervention had exposed the central flaw in the government's economic strategy. By committing themselves to defend the value of the pound, they had found themselves at the mercy of foreign speculators, forced to deflate the economy and to abandon their cherished manifesto commitments. Worse, there was no clear end in sight: the cycle of deflation might drag on for years. But Crosland and Castle were not the only ones to have doubts: many of Callaghan's own officials were beginning to wonder whether it might not be best to devalue and be done with it.[78] At the same time, Wilson's closest economic advisers, Balogh, Kaldor and Robert Neild, had also come to the conclusion that devaluation might be better than endless 'repressive measures'. The great obstacle, of course, was that Wilson had categorically ruled it out, which meant that he would be destroying his own credibility if he went along with their advice.[79] As Richard Crossman recognised, however, Wilson was taking an enormous risk: 'If you commit yourself to the view that devaluation is the end of everything and then fail to defend the pound, then it really is the end and you go down in catastrophe . . . Defending the pound by frantic cuts and then in the end finding we would have to devalue makes no sense at all.'[80]

The one consolation was that, so far, the electorate had yet to feel the pinch; in fact the government's failure to deflate the economy adequately meant that the crisis had had little impact on the ordinary voter. But although polls showed that the public still held the Conservatives responsible for the current mess, they also suggested that Labour would lose a general election if it were held immediately. Wilson's own reputation had taken a buffeting, too: in June his personal approval rating had fallen below 50 per cent for the first time, a decline of 15 per cent in two months.[81] 'We have taken a terrible beating,' wrote Crossman as the Commons broke for its summer recess, 'and our own people are disheartened and the press is utterly vicious. Terrible times. We can still pick up but I'm pretty sure we wouldn't be able to pick up after the next package Callaghan wants to put through in defence of sterling.'[82]

6

INTRODUCING THE TURDS

> Those who flock around the Beatles, who scream themselves into hysteria, whose vacant faces flicker over the TV screen, are the least fortunate of their generation, the dull, the idle, the failures.
>
> Paul Johnson, 'The Menace of Beatlism', *New Statesman*, 29 February 1964

Just after six on the evening of Friday, 9 August 1963, to the sound of Manfred Mann's '5–4–3–2–1' and with the promise that 'The weekend starts here!', a new pop music show made its first appearance on British television. Filmed in a tiny studio packed with fashionably dressed teenagers, *Ready, Steady, Go!* had been carefully designed by London's independent television company, Associated Rediffusion, to attract younger audiences on Friday nights. It was not by any means the first time that television had tried to come to terms with pop music and youth culture, but *Ready, Steady, Go!* was different. Its sets were designed to resemble Pop or Op Art paintings; its camera angles were deliberately jerky and unrehearsed; its studio audiences were auditioned for their look and dancing ability; and its live acts were carefully chosen to get the right air of novelty and excitement. The show's most celebrated presenter, a former secretary called Cathy McGowan, was the same age as the national audience; she wore all the latest trendy shifts and mini-dresses; and she spoke with an earnest, ceaseless barrage of teenage slang, praising whatever was 'fab' or 'smashing', and damning all that was 'square' or 'out'.[1] 'The atmosphere', one observer wrote later, 'was that of a King's Road party where the performers themselves had only just chanced to drop by.'[2]

Although earlier shows like *Six-Five Special* had been popular with teenage audiences, none of them had quite the appeal of *Ready, Steady, Go!*. It was, one fashion-obsessed teenager later wrote, 'our bible . . . the TV programme that you would *not* miss.'[3] Indeed, the programme was soon so popular with teenagers that if a single was performed for the first time on the programme, it was very likely to be catapulted straight into the Top Ten. McGowan became a self-proclaimed voice of youth, her attitudes and opinions regularly sought by journalists hoping to gauge the mood of the nation's adolescents. '[She] was our heroine', one teenage admirer later recalled, 'I'd sit and drool over her clothes. She was a heroine to us because she was one of us.'[4]

And thanks to the enthusiastic salesmanship of McGowan and her fellow presenters, the emerging youth culture that had once been confined to the capital or to the great cities could now be seen and copied almost immediately from Cornwall to the Highlands. 'It plugged in direct to the centre of the scene,' wrote the jazz critic George Melly, 'and only a week later transmitted information as to clothes, dances, gestures, even slang to the whole British teenage Isles.' *Ready, Steady, Go!*, he thought, had 'made pop work on a truly national scale', diffusing the latest trends and fashions from the capital to the furthest corners of the country, so that 'it was almost possible to feel a tremor of pubescent excitement from Land's End to John O'Groats'.[5]

Newspaper columnists had first drawn attention to the new teenage culture in the late fifties. In an era of free education and healthcare, teenagers were bigger, healthier, more sexually mature, more economically independent and more culturally assertive, and although many people chose to see this as a social threat, others recognised it as a commercial opportunity. As the sixties began there were more than five million teenagers in Britain, accounting for a tenth of the nation's total personal income and spending more than £800 million a year, mostly on clothing and entertainment.[6] Many institutions, such as cinemas, dance halls, magazine publishers and record shops, had become highly dependent on teenage patronage. Teenagers bought more than a third of all bicycles and motorbikes, for example, as well as a third of all cosmetic products, film tickets and tickets for public entertainments in general. They also made up almost half of the market for records and record players.[7]

Teenage affluence was undoubtedly the single biggest factor in explaining the spectacular development of popular music between the mid-fifties and the early sixties. Popular music itself was not of course anything new, but as the fifties progressed and retailers began selling more and more records, so the tastes of the young, the keenest and most reliable shoppers, began to dominate the market. In 1955 British listeners bought just over 4 million 45-rpm singles a year; by 1960, they were buying 52 million; and by 1963, 61 million.[8] Record companies and retailers recognised that they would make more money if they emphasised styles that appealed to the young, rather than the romantic ballads and big-band music that appealed to their parents. This explains why the late fifties saw such a rapid turnover of musical styles, as record companies tore through different genres in the hunt for the latest teenage craze. Rock and roll music, imported from the United States in the forms of Bill Haley and Elvis Presley, was merely one craze among many. Home-grown equivalents, like Tommy Steele, Billy Fury, Adam Faith and Cliff Richard, had enjoyed considerable chart success, but by 1961 the rock and roll craze had obviously peaked. By far the most popular musical artist in the country, Cliff Richard, was already moving away from rock and roll into family-oriented ballads, and record executives were generally of the opinion that rock and roll music was 'finished' and ripe for replacement by a new fad, perhaps calypso music, cha-cha or 'trad' jazz.[9]

This was the context for the sensational rise of the Beatles between October 1962, when their first single reached number seventeen in the chart, and December 1963, by which time their conquest of the British music scene had reached almost unimaginable proportions. On Christmas Day they held the top two spots in the singles chart with 'I Want to Hold Your Hand' and 'She Loves You', as well as the top two places in the album chart. Their most recent album, *With the Beatles*, was selling so quickly that it also held fifteenth place in the *singles* chart, while three more records, the EPs 'Twist and Shout', 'Beatles' Hits' and 'Beatles' No. 1', were also selling strongly enough to occupy places in the Top Thirty.[10]

Much of this success, of course, was down to the members of the group themselves: their ability to turn out a catchy 'beat' tune that appealed to both adults and teenagers; their cheeky, irrepressible personalities, which made them popular with journalists and fans alike; their electrically amplified guitar-based sound, which stood out in a market swollen with solo singers; and, above all, their ambition, hard work and sheer talent, which meant that they never rested on their laurels, but reacted to each success as though it were a fresh challenge.[11] But the Beatles' success can also be seen in a different light, almost as an accident waiting to happen. If they had not broken through, it is quite likely that some other, doubtless inferior group would have done so. Thanks to the spread of cheap radios and record players, music was more accessible than ever before, not only played in concert halls, pubs and restaurants, but enjoyed in the privacy of the office, the living room and the teenage bedroom.[12] The national press paid far more attention to popular music and teenage tastes than before; even the *Daily Telegraph* was about to start printing a weekly Top Ten.[13] As a breathless report in the *Daily Mirror* in October 1963 put it, there were now five and a half million 'spendagers' in Britain, buying more than fifty million records a year and spending an annual total of some one billion pounds.[14] Magazines devoted to pop music were thriving: *Fabulous* was selling 900,000 copies a week at a shilling apiece, while *Rave* cost 2s 6d but still accounted for some 250,000 sales a month.[15] With eight out of ten records sold being 45rpm singles, the potential for a home-grown act to win over the newspapers, inspire teenage adulation and sell millions of records was simply much greater than ever.[16]

A classic example of the new importance of pop music was the establishment of pirate radio stations, broadcasting from ships and rigs anchored just outside British territorial waters. The most popular was Radio Caroline, set up under the Panamanian flag on an old passenger ferry moored three miles off the Harwich coast. It first began broadcasting on 29 March 1964, making a star of the irreverent young disc jockey Simon Dee, and within a year Radio Caroline and its buccaneering competitors commanded an audience of several million listeners. Some were based on ships or minesweepers, others in maritime forts and towers. All benefited from new multi-track tape technology that made it possible to combine hit records, commercials, station jingles and the disc jockey's patter in a seamless blend of sound, while the disc jockeys themselves cultivated a youthful, cheeky, classless style that was only occasionally interrupted by bouts of seasickness.[17] The rivalry between the stations, from Radio London and Radio Scotland to Radio City and Radio Invicta, was intense. Sabotage was common, and one man was even killed during a midnight raid on Radio City's base in a Thames estuary fort. After constant pressure from the BBC, the Marine Broadcasting (Offences) Act finally closed down the pirate stations in 1967; but having learned its lesson, the Corporation then stepped in to capture their best disc jockeys for its own new station, Radio One.[18]

Interviewed for a BBC documentary in the mid-sixties, one teenage pop aficionado tried to explain his devotion to the genre. 'It's our culture, our entertainment, our form of art,' he said. 'Most people won't listen to anything else but pop music. You get the beat, get the urge to dance, you know, chat a bird up and start dancing. Your feet are tapping and then your hands start. It just builds up inside of you.'[19] But pinning down exactly what pop music meant to listeners in the mid-sixties is not an easy business. In all probability, only a minority were particularly drawn to the lyrics: relatively few pop songs of the early sixties were notable for great wit, originality or verbal sophistication. Others listened for the melody, or the general 'sound' of the group. But probably the biggest number were, as the critic Ian MacDonald argues, attracted to the cultural associations of the performers, 'the attitudes, the clothes, the moves, the atmosphere'. All the evidence of record-buying in the sixties, as well as in the decades that followed, suggests that most young consumers ultimately judged musical acts more by the cultural and social values they projected than by the lyrical originality or musical expertise of their performances.[20]

One of the most important of these values was amateurishness, which became increasingly prominent after the Beatles' breakthrough in 1963. In the fifties, singers and groups had been carefully assembled and groomed by professional managers, with music written and arranged for them by professional writers. By the beginning of 1964, however, the future clearly lay with young groups who wrote their own music and made their own decisions about their look, sound and direction. This meant that popular music was, in a sense, democratised and brought closer to the audience. As MacDonald explains, the balance of power had shifted from 'a corps of professionals – managers, songwriters, producers, publishers, record executives, radio station proprietors and record shop owners – to a body of young amateurs whose connection with the industry's audience was as close as could be'.[21]

During the late fifties rock and roll music had received an extremely frosty welcome from the British press. *Melody Maker*, then the bible of the jazz fraternity, called it 'the antithesis of . . . good taste and musical integrity', while the *Daily Mail* labelled it 'deplorable', 'tribal' and 'the Negro's revenge'.[22] However, what was striking about the press coverage of the beat boom in 1963 was that it was so overwhelmingly positive. At the time, the newspapers already had their knives out for Harold Macmillan's Conservative government, and the likes of the Beatles offered a refreshing contrast with the alleged decadence of the old order. The *Mirror* welcomed the Beatles' supposed preference for 'tea and cakes rather than Dry Martini with a twist of lemon'; the *Evening Standard* announced that they had won over 'the grown ups and the husbands'; and after the group's successful turn at the Royal Variety Performance that autumn, the *Mirror* exclaimed:

> Fact is that Beatle People are everywhere. From Wapping to Windsor. Aged seven to seventy. And it's plain to see why these four cheeky, energetic lads from Liverpool go down so big.

They're young, new. They're high-spirited, cheerful. What a change from the self-pitying moaners, crooning their lovelorn tunes from the tortured shallows of lukewarm hearts.

The Beatles are whacky. They wear their hair like a mop — but it's WASHED, it's super clean. So is their fresh young act. They don't have to rely on off-colour jokes about homos for their fun . . .

Youngsters like the Beatles are doing a good turn for show business — and the rest of us — with their new sounds, new looks.

Good luck Beatles![23]

Some commentators, however, found the Beatles' success almost too much to bear. The most notorious example was the wrathful *New Statesman* columnist Paul Johnson, who devoted an article in February 1964 to 'The Menace of Beatlism'. Watching the studio audience for *Juke Box Jury*, he saw

> a bottomless pit of vacuity . . . the huge faces bloated with cheap confectionery and smeared with chain store make-up, the open, sagging mouths and glazed eyes, the hands mindlessly drumming in time to the music, the broken stiletto heels, the shoddy, stereotyped, 'with-it' clothes: here, apparently is a collective portrait of a generation enslaved by a commercial machine.

What was even worse, however, was what all of this represented: a contemporary obsession with modernity, youth and gimmickry. 'You can see writers of distinction,' Johnson wrote angrily,

> squatting on the bare boards of malodorous caverns, while through the haze of smoke, sweat and cheap cosmetics comes the monotonous braying of savage instruments . . . Bewildered by a rapidly changing society, excessively fearful of becoming out of date, our leaders are increasingly turning to young people as guides and mentors — or, to vary the metaphor, as Geiger-counters to guard them against the perils of mental obsolescence . . . Indeed, whatever youth likes must be good: the supreme crime, in politics and culture alike, is not to be 'with it'.[24]

Although it is tempting to dismiss Johnson's furious indictment of 'Beatlism' as the splenetic outpourings of a famously angry columnist, it is not difficult to see what had provoked him. There was, after all, something rather ludicrous in the rush of politicians to embrace the Beatles, what with Edward Heath praising them as 'the salvation of the corduroy industry' and Sir Alec Douglas-Home feebly attempting to invoke their lyrics in his speeches.[25] Similarly, the spectacle of the music critic of *The Times* praising the Beatles' 'chains of pandiatonic clusters', 'Aeolian cadences', and 'autocratic but not by any means ungrammatical attitude to tonality' did rather smack of the ridiculous.[26]

Throughout the Beatles' career, meanwhile, a large proportion of the population, especially among those over thirty, remained completely indifferent to their music. Many people probably shared the attitude of *Private Eye*, which never treated the Beatles with anything less than amused contempt. Indeed, the group's very first appearance in the magazine, a brilliant parody of Maureen Cleave's pop articles in the *Evening Standard*, set the tone for the *Eye*'s coverage of popular music for the next forty years:

Pop Scene

By Maureen Cleavage

INTRODUCING THE TURDS

I want you to meet four very young and very exciting Turds.

They're from the new Beat Centre of Rochdale and they're swinging into the charts with their first waxing 'Chain Stagger'.

YOUNG

Yesterday, I popped into the studio and talked to them.

The Turds are something new. Irreverent, greedy, short and acned, there is a trendy look about them that sets a 60s pace, as up to date as next year's Courrèges underwear.

The leader of the group Spiggy Topes explained: 'Actually we don't have a leader. In our eyes all Turds are equal.'

EXCITING

... The Turds like everyone else in the world are classless and horrible. The Turds started at the bottom and are already dominating the thinking of pacey people.

I think the Turds are going to be with us for a long time.

(God help us all. Ed.)[27]

For all their commercial success, it was quite possible to imagine that, at the end of 1963, the Beatles had peaked. At home there were simply no more worlds for them to conquer: they had occupied the singles and album charts as their own personal fiefdoms, written best-selling songs for other performers, taken all the applause at the Royal Variety Performance and made a string of highly successful television appearances. Only international success on a scale hitherto denied to any British musical act could conceivably keep them writing and performing at the highest level. 'We would be daft to sit back on our laurels,' explained Paul McCartney. 'We'll be facing a lot of big challenges this year and we are determined to really go ahead and face them. I suppose America is our biggest challenge. It would knock us out to go over there and make good.'[28]

However, this was by no means certain. Contrary to popular myth, British acts like Lonnie Donegan, Acker Bilk and the Shadows had already done well on the other side of the Atlantic, but the most obvious precedent was that of Cliff Richard, the leading British rock and roll singer of the early sixties, whose single American tour had not been a resounding success. As 1964 began, only an infinitesimal minority of Americans had ever heard of the Beatles. 'We don't think the Beatles will do anything in this market,' the senior executive of Capitol, the group's American record company, told their producer George Martin.[29] However, the Beatles' manager, the dapper and driven Brian Epstein, was adamant that his boys must be given their chance to impress American audiences, and he persuaded Capitol to release 'I Want to Hold Your Hand', and to prepare for a two-week American tour in February.

'I Want to Hold Your Hand' was the climax of what MacDonald calls John Lennon and Paul McCartney's 'fifty–fifty' period, in which they wrote as a collaborative duo, instead of simply refining each other's efforts.[30] By the time of its British release in November 1963 it had already chalked up more than a million advance orders, enough to propel it immediately to number one. In the United States, by contrast, it did not come out until after Christmas, and apparently faced an uphill struggle because the Beatles were so little known. This made its success all the more striking. The single was released on 26 December and, thanks to its popularisation by a number of disc jockeys who liked the group, sold 250,000 copies within three days. By 10 January, sales had topped one million.[31]

In Britain, meanwhile, the Beatles were preparing to depart for France on a kind of warm-up tour for their American adventure the following month. They were not particularly popular in France, where music from across the Channel was generally held in low regard, and the tour did not go well, with the media indifferent and audiences listless. On 17 January the group played an evening concert in the Olympia Theatre, Paris, which was followed by a mass brawl between cameramen and the police. Later that night, as the group sat in their hotel suite and licked their wounds, Brian Epstein took a telephone call from the United States. When the photographer Dezo Hoffman came in moments later, he found the group and their entourage 'in a state of eerie quiet':

> Brian was there as well . . . He was sitting in a chair and the Beatles were sitting on the floor around him. He said the news had come through that 'I Want to Hold Your Hand' was Number One in the American Top Hundred. The Beatles couldn't even speak – not even John Lennon. They just sat on the floor like kittens at Brian's feet.[32]

The Beatles' initial success in the United States is impossible to explain away. At the end of 1963 they had been almost completely unknown, a British act trying to conquer the charts in a country that credited itself with the invention of rock and roll music and that had proved largely resistant to foreign musical invaders. Just two weeks later they were the most famous group in the world. American record executives had initially believed that the Beatles sounded 'too raw and raucous' for white audiences; now they had the proof that white teenagers actually preferred their uninhibited sound to the formulaic ballads that had dominated the American charts for much of 1963.[33] This was, of course, the perfect prelude to the Beatles' impending American tour. 'It's going to be fab!' Lennon told an interviewer. 'None of us is nervous about our personal appearances or anything like that. The Americans are just going to get exactly the same as the British, French and the rest of them.'[34]

Capitol, however, were leaving nothing to chance. Before the Beatles had even arrived in New York, their record company had spent an unprecedented fifty thousand dollars, ten times as much as they had ever spent promoting any other artist, on posters, badges, car stickers and the like, carrying the message 'The Beatles Are Coming'. Four-page brochures were sent to disc jockeys across the United States; Capitol executives were photographed looking ridiculous in Beatle wigs; and teenagers were effectively bribed by two local radio stations to welcome the Beatles at Kennedy

Airport, their reward being a dollar and a free Beatles T-shirt each.[35] Not surprisingly, when the group did touch down on the afternoon of 7 February, they were met by some five thousand screaming, overexcited fans, packed in behind the thick glass of the terminal building.[36]

It was the Beatles' reaction to this reception that cemented their place in the hearts of their American admirers. Where other groups might have been overawed, the Beatles reacted with the same cheeky good humour that had served them so well at similar occasions in Britain. At their first press conference, held in the airport itself, the group made it very clear that they did not take themselves too seriously, and although the exchange hardly touched the pinnacle of comic genius claimed by their admirers, it was nevertheless a refreshing contrast to the painfully earnest formality of most American acts:

Q: What do you think of Beethoven?
RINGO: Great, especially his poems. [*Aside, to others*] I'm sick of that one.
Q: Can you explain your strange English accents?
GEORGE: It's not English, it's Liverpudlian.
Q: In Detroit, there's people handing out car stickers saying, 'Stamp Out the Beatles'.
PAUL: Yeah, well, we've got two answers to that. First of all, we're bringing out a 'Stamp Out Detroit' campaign — [*Laughter from reporters makes second answer inaudible*] . . .
Q: How many of you are bald, so that you have to wear those wigs?
RINGO: All of us.
PAUL: I'm bald.
JOHN: Oh, we're all bald.
PAUL: Please don't tell anyone, please.
JOHN: And deaf and dumb, too.[37]

Despite their relaxed appearance, however, the Beatles were terribly excited by their ecstatic welcome. 'We thought, "Wow! God, we have really made it,"' Paul McCartney later recalled. 'I remember, for instance, the great moment of getting in the limo and putting on the radio and hearing a radio commentary on *us* . . . It was like a dream. The greatest fantasy ever.'[38]

All in all, the tour was a triumph. The group were so popular with their fans, especially teenage girls, that by the time they performed at the

Washington Coliseum on 11 February, their devotees were all armed with jelly beans. These they hurled at the stage in the belief that this would endear them to George Harrison, who was said to be a great lover of jelly babies. Although this left Harrison himself bruised and disgruntled, the Beatles' watching families were delighted at the warmth of their reception. 'I was sitting next to Cynthia [Lennon],' recalled Harrison's sister Louise, 'and we were both kind of sitting there with goose bumps, listening to the tremendous amount of vibrations that were in the theatre. For she and I, sitting together, to think that it's our guys that this is all for was wonderful. I had tears running down my face because it was so overwhelming.'[39]

A further indication of the group's popularity, if any were needed, came a few hours later, when they arrived for a private reception at the British Embassy in Washington. The ambassador had invited all his friends to come and meet the Beatles, so the four tired musicians found themselves mobbed by socialites as though, as Ringo put it, they were 'something in a zoo'. Some of the eminent guests became so overexcited that at one point a minor scuffle broke out among a group of women all trying to have their albums signed; in the confusion another British debutante managed to force her way through to Ringo and cut off a lock of his hair. The Beatles were not pleased by the incident; indeed, it was considered such a diplomatic faux pas that the Foreign Secretary was forced to deny in the House of Commons that Embassy staff had manhandled the country's favourite musicians.[40]

The undoubted highlight of the tour, however, was the Beatles' appearance on *The Ed Sullivan Show*, which was filmed in New York City and broadcast on 9 February by CBS, one of the three major American networks. The group only appeared for just over thirteen minutes, playing five songs, but the programme nevertheless represented a milestone in their international career. More than 73 million viewers tuned in, which was not only the biggest audience in the history of the programme, but the biggest audience in the history of American television. Observers claimed that the streets of New York were eerily deserted as people huddled in front of their television sets; the police reported that the crime rate had dropped for the evening; and even the evangelist Billy Graham broke his rule about not watching television on the Sabbath so that he could see what was getting his daughters so excited.[41] 'The Beatles are not such bad chaps after all,' the *Washington Post* reassured its readers the next day. 'They behaved in a more civilized manner than most of our own rock 'n' roll heroes. Except for the outrageous bath-mat coiffure, the four young men seemed downright conservative . . . asexual and homely.'[42]

Given that just two months before the Beatles had been almost completely unknown in the United States, their success in the spring of 1964 simply beggared belief. No American artist came close to competing with them. 'They showed us a trick or two,' remarked the rock and roll singer Jerry Lee Lewis. 'Cut them down like wheat before the sickle.'[43] Beatles merchandise was everywhere: in the aftermath of the group's triumphant appearance on *The Ed Sullivan Show*, 100,000 Beatles dolls poured into the shops of New York, while various companies were producing an estimated total of 35,000 Beatles wigs a day. There were masks, pens, bow ties, edible records and even 'Beatle nut' ice creams, and the *Wall Street Journal* predicted that the American public would snap up some 5 million dollars' worth of Beatles products before 1964 was over.[44] And their chart success was simply phenomenal. For three weeks that spring, the Beatles accounted for almost two-thirds of all records sold in the United States, and at one point in April they had twelve different records in the *Billboard* Hot 100, occupying numbers 1, 2, 3, 4, 5, 31, 41, 46, 58, 65, 68 and 79. If that were not enough, on the other side of the border they managed to hold no fewer than nine of the places in the Canadian Top Ten.[45]

Back home, meanwhile, the newspapers were ecstatic. 'YEAH! YEAH! USA!' roared a triumphant headline in the *Mirror*, while an editorial proudly declared: 'Everyone, everywhere is catching it. It is called Beatlemania.'[46] When the group returned home on 22 February, their arrival in London was covered by the BBC's flagship sports programme *Grandstand*, with the four stars being interviewed at the airport by an earnest David Coleman.[47] 'They herald a cultural movement among the young which may become part of the history of our time,' the Cabinet minister William Deedes told a meeting of the Young Conservatives, adding that their achievements were 'important and heartening'.[48] And even the supposedly stuffy Sir Alec Douglas-Home was roused to warn: 'If any country is in deficit with us, I have only to say the Beatles are coming . . . Let me tell you why they have had a success in the United States – it is because they are a band of very natural, very funny young men.'[49]

The Beatles' success undoubtedly owed a good deal to the fact that at the beginning of 1964 the American pop scene was in a fairly moribund condition. As one account puts it, the *Billboard* charts were 'sodden with Bobby-ballads, forgettable instrumentals and edifying anthems', and the Beatles were much more exuberant, irreverent and hard-hitting than most of their American competitors.[50] Their appeal to the American heartland can be gauged by the ubiquity of their imitators: as well as the Monkees, an accomplished although irritatingly zany group created for a television show, they had to contend with the likes of the Liverpools, whose album notes advised their fans that they were 'four *liver*-uppers who have *pooled* their talents', and the Liverpool Kids, the cover of whose album *Beattle Mash* betrayed their identity, not as kids, but as three outstandingly unattractive middle-aged men with thinning hair. Perhaps the most striking of these groups, though, were the Beatle Buddies, who were photographed in exactly the same poses as the real Fab Four on *Meet the Beatles* but who resembled, in the words of one American account, 'four tough broads who look only recently paroled from a maximum-security penitentiary'. The Beatle Buddies' sleeve notes described them as 'cute and talented' with 'looks and sound destined to last long after the [real] Beatles are gone'; sadly, this prediction turned out to be somewhat wide of the mark.[51]

Before the Beatles' first tour of the United States, the assumption had been that musical traffic across the Atlantic was fundamentally one-way. While British teenagers had been extremely keen to buy the latest records by the likes of Elvis Presley and Buddy Holly, their American counterparts had been less eager to snap up singles by, say, Cliff Richard or Billy Fury. In the years before 1964, British artists had held the top spot in the American charts for a grand total of four weeks, a pretty feeble tally that testified to their general lack of influence on the western shores of the Atlantic.[52]

With the success of the Beatles, however, this picture of American musical dominance began to change. In the last week of July 1964, for example, not only did the Beatles have four albums in the American *Billboard* LP chart, but they were joined by four other British acts: the Dave Clark Five, the Searchers, the Rolling Stones and Peter and Gordon.[53] The singles charts offered even more striking evidence of the success of the so-called 'British Invasion'. In 1962 and 1963 a total of 212 singles had made the *Billboard* Top Ten, of which a paltry 3 had been British in origin. In 1964, however, British acts accounted for no fewer than 32 of the 100 singles to make the Top Ten; in 1965 they accounted for 36 out of 110; and in 1966, 30 out of 124.[54] And British acts not only had a significant foothold in the American chart but tended to do disproportionately well within it. Nine different British singles reached number one in the *Billboard* chart in 1964, and twelve the following year; indeed, in those years British acts held the top spot for no fewer than 52 weeks. 'All any English band with a working-class accent had to do was show up at the airport,' wrote one American observer afterwards, with pardonable exaggeration.[55]

Although the British Invasion is often equated with the 'beat boom' of 1963 to 1965, this is not quite accurate. Some acts that did very well in the United States, like Petula Clark and the Bachelors, were not playing beat music at all.[56] In general, however, it is true that many British groups played up to a common image. Beat music, based on the now conventional formula of two rhythm guitarists, a bass guitarist and a drummer, had swept the country in 1963 and 1964 and hundreds of different groups, each with their own mildly distinctive style, were competing to become the new Beatles. In Merseyside alone there were the Pacemakers, the Searchers, the Mojos and the Undertakers; in Birmingham there were the Applejacks, the Fortunes and the Ivy League; in Manchester the Hollies, the Dakotas, the Hermits and the Dreamers.[57] Since the British market was so crowded, it was not surprising that many chose to seek their future in the United States, rather as the Beatles themselves had moved to Hamburg a few years before because there was so much competition in Liverpool.

Success in the United States was based not only on musical talent but on a group's ability to project the right kind of sanitised, exaggerated Britishness. 'In corporate character,' explains Alan Clayson, 'they adhered closely to a Hollywood movie idea of Britain, the mythical land of Good Queen Bess, Robin Hood, fish 'n' chips, Oxford-and-Cambridge, Beefeaters, monocled cads, kilted Scotsmen and hello-hello-hello policemen.'[58] The quintessential example was Herman's Hermits, a Manchester beat quintet who recorded a British number one with 'I'm Into Something Good' in August 1964. A few months later the group recast themselves as a kind of walking self-parody of nostalgic Britishness and proceeded to launch an astonishingly successful assault on the American charts. Their new singles were either cover versions of long-forgotten vaudeville classics, like 'Two Lovely Black Eyes' and 'Mrs Brown You've Got a Lovely Daughter', or catchy advertisements for their own nationality, like 'I'm Henry the Eighth I Am' and 'Je Suis Anglais'. Some of these singles were not even released in Britain itself; indeed, as far as the domestic music press were concerned, the group's latest records were nothing more than ludicrous concessions to the wilder extremes of American taste. However, with more than ten million American sales in 1965 and 1966, the group could afford to ignore the domestic market and concentrate on their overseas admirers, and as late as 1970 their records were still going down very nicely with American audiences.[59]

For all their popularity, Herman's Hermits never really threatened the Beatles' domination of the singles charts at home or abroad. Instead, the Fab

Four's most plausible competitors, at least as far as the newspapers were concerned, came in the form of a five-man group from North London. In the second week of January 1964, just before the Beatles conquered the American charts, 'I Want to Hold Your Hand' was finally deposed from the top spot in the British singles chart by the Dave Clark Five's new single 'Glad All Over'. 'TOTTENHAM SOUND HAS CRUSHED THE BEATLES' screamed the front page of the *Daily Express* after the announcement of the Five's number one.[60] The *Mirror* fêted the eponymous Clark, the group's drummer and vocalist, as 'the boy who beat the Beatles', and the *Daily Mail* ran a cartoon in which a group of teenage girls, waiting outside the stage door at a Dave Clark Five concert, stare contemptuously across the road at an apparently indifferent contemporary. 'She *must* be old,' read the caption, 'she can remember when the Beatles were top-of-the-pops!'[61]

As it turned out, however, the Tottenham Sound never posed a serious threat to the Beatles' musical hegemony. Although the Dave Clark Five were a perfectly accomplished beat group with an infectious devil-may-care style, they could not match the ambition, eclecticism or sheer talent of their Liverpudlian rivals. The Beatles' success depended not only on luck and timing, but on their knack of spotting trends before their competitors did, their skill at reinventing themselves to anticipate the interests of their audiences, and, above all, their songwriting ability. While the Beatles went from strength to strength, the Dave Clark Five enjoyed a patchy chart career over the next two years, especially as beat singles began to slip from fashion.

What made the Dave Clark Five different from other beat groups, though, was their enormous popularity in the United States. Like Herman's Hermits, the Five became much more successful across the Atlantic than they had ever been at home, and they pulled off a remarkable series of seventeen consecutive *Billboard* Top Forty hits with catchy, thumping songs such as 'I Like It Like That' and 'Over and Over'. Unlike rival groups such as the Rolling Stones, the Kinks and the Who, the Dave Clark Five were not really interested in graduating from chart-topping singles to anything more ambitious, and in appearance they were much more respectable than their British contemporaries, which explains why they were so successful in the relatively conservative American singles market. What was remarkable about this was that at home they were only moderately popular; as Adam Clayson remarks, their releases in Britain were little more than 'market research for the States'. Indeed, by 1965 they were making biannual trips across the Atlantic and concentrating almost entirely on the American market, even overtaking the Beatles at one point as Britain's prominent and successful musical export.[62]

Many beat groups subsided into obscurity after 1964, the turbulent tides of musical fashion having left them high and dry. The obvious exception, and by far the most talented of all the Beatles' rivals, was another group from North London, the Kinks. The prime movers in the Kinks were two brothers, Ray and Dave Davies, who had been brought up in the leafy Edwardian suburb of Muswell Hill.[63] The Davies brothers' roots remained extremely important to them: in 1971 they even released an album called *Muswell Hillbillies*, and more than any other group of the sixties they exemplified the way in which British pop music drew on domestic cultural traditions as well as on the often rather exaggerated influence of the United States. This was not immediately apparent, however, when they released their most celebrated single, 'You Really Got Me', in August 1964. It was easily the most aggressive single of the year. As one account puts it:

> Without warning, the rasping, distorted guitar chops out five notes, again and again, heavier and nastier than anything on a British radio before. Then there's a voice, steadily growing ecstatic, driven so wild by a girl that, according to the singer, '*I don't know what I'm doing*'. A full band is rising behind him, but every time the record approaches climax it pulls back. Finally the singer gasps '*Oh . . . no!*' and falls from the [microphone] as the guitar screams. The single fades, self-contained and complete. Two minutes, 11 seconds, and The Kinks are born.[64]

For some historians of British popular music, 'You Really Got Me', with its deliberately distorted guitar sound, prefigured the belligerent excesses of the 'heavy' rock music that became popular at the end of the sixties.[65] Other critics point to a slightly different legacy, arguing that with their 'white neuroticism' and 'superhuman drive', the Kinks anticipated the urban nihilism of the late seventies.[66] But in the late summer of 1964, all that mattered was that the single charged to the top of the charts, selling more than a million copies and instantly transforming the Kinks' reputation. A few weeks later it made it into the American Top Ten, and in October the Kinks' new single, 'All Day and All of the Night', peaked at number two. By January 1965, when 'Tired of Waiting for You' became the group's second number one, most observers assumed that the Kinks would join the Beatles at the summit of international pop music.[67]

INTRODUCING THE TURDS

At this point, however, their career began to falter, not because of any deficiency of talent or application, but because the group's spectacular and violent feuding was beginning to alienate their promoters. The Davies brothers regularly fell out with each other in the most ferocious and public way, and the group began to acquire a reputation for being 'difficult'. When they played at the *New Musical Express* Poll Winners Show at Wembley in April 1965, for example, Dave Davies was already on bail after a brawl with the Danish police, while his brother stormed off the stage after hearing that the group had been beaten to the Best Newcomer award by the Rolling Stones. Not long afterwards a particularly savage fight broke out between the members of the group themselves while they were playing in Cardiff. Half-way through the concert, Dave Davies, who was wearing dark glasses to disguise the black eyes he had suffered in previous brawls, attempted to kick over the group's drum kit; in response, the drummer, Mick Avory, slashed Davies's head open with one blow from a cymbal and then fled the stage in the belief that he had literally decapitated his own guitarist. Amazingly enough, Ray Davies carried on singing nonchalantly throughout, and the audience remained dancing where they were in the belief that this was all part of the act.[68]

In the more conservative climate of the United States, however, this sort of stuff went down very badly. Some American critics had been genuinely shocked by the Beatles' 'long' hair, considering it dangerously subversive, so it was hardly surprising that the much more volatile Kinks soon found themselves in trouble. In June 1965, in the searing heat of a Los Angeles television studio, Ray Davies came to blows with an American union official who had called the group 'Commie wimps' and branded Davies a 'talentless fuck'. The net result was that the Kinks were effectively blacklisted by the American Federation of Musicians and were unable to tour in the United States until the very end of the decade.[69] This was an enormous blow to the group's hopes of international stardom, and despite the fact that only the Beatles matched their musical ingenuity, originality and flair, the Kinks never quite won the acclaim they deserved. However, since the American avenue had been closed to them, they were able to indulge some of their more esoteric and less obviously commercial interests, devoting themselves to self-expression rather than the pursuit of profit. 'Being a Kink is an art, only I'm dabbling in sounds, not pictures,' Ray Davies had told an interviewer in December 1964.[70] With their third hit single, 'Tired of Waiting For You', the group had already exhibited a quieter, more reflective side, and over the next few years eight more Top Ten hits cemented their reputation as the thinking man's pop group, as we will see.[71]

From a purely commercial point of view, this was a high point for the record industry. In 1964 the British public bought more than a hundred million records, an all-time peak that was never exceeded. The enthusiasm of audiences, the interest of the press and the general cultural cachet of pop music had never been more intense and would not, perhaps, ever be so again.[72] But it is important to bear in mind that, for all the attention given to beat music in 1964, it was not the only popular musical genre of the day. At the beginning of May, for example, the Top Twenty albums included nine beat or rhythm and blues LPs, two Broadway cast recordings, two collections of ballads, a West End revue album, a gospel album, a film soundtrack, an album of comedy songs and a collection of light instrumental music. Older listeners in particular kept up their interests in ballads, instrumental and light classical music, and it would be wrong to think that the dominance of pop music went entirely unchallenged.[73]

All the same, pop was comfortably the most controversial and influential genre of the day. Indeed, the success of groups like the Beatles and the Kinks, not to mention other competitors from the Rolling Stones and the Animals to the Yardbirds and the Who, has often led commentators to see the mid-sixties as something of a musical golden age. The *NME* Top Thirty published on 15 July 1964, for instance, began with the following five songs:

1 A Hard Day's Night (The Beatles)
2 It's All Over Now (The Rolling Stones)
3 House of the Rising Sun (The Animals)
4 Hold Me (P. J. Proby)
5 I Just Don't Know What to Do with Myself (Dusty Springfield)[74]

The singles chart published at the beginning of December was no less impressive:

1 I Feel Fine (The Beatles)
2 Little Red Rooster (The Rolling Stones)
3 I'm Gonna Be Strong (Gene Pitney)

4 Downtown (Petula Clark)
5 All Day and All of the Night (The Kinks)
6 Baby Love (The Supremes)[75]

Of course, there is often something rather irritating about the frequent suggestion that the 1960s represented a cultural high-water mark, after which all was parody and decline. Nonetheless, there is no doubt that, for record buyers, these were extraordinarily exciting times. As the critic Ian MacDonald points out, when pop devotees in the sixties bought a new single by the Beatles, the Rolling Stones or the Kinks, 'they never knew from bar to bar what was coming next', such was the premium placed on originality and 'creative unexpectedness', and so fluid were the parameters of the new popular music.[76]

And it is hard to disagree with MacDonald's conclusion that the most original, provocative and simply entertaining popular music of modern times was made during the mid-sixties. Pop music was then 'a new, half-invented art form', which allowed artists to experiment with eclectic musical styles, instruments and lyrical approaches; at the same time, competition for sales was intense, so musicians felt obliged to push the boundaries of the form in order to attract audiences who valued novelty and experiment.[77]

In the fifties and early sixties, pop music had been widely criticised as hollow, trivial, even corrupt; but now, in the eyes of the press, it had suddenly become an example of cultural creativity and a source of national pride. Thanks to the success of the British Invasion, groups like the Beatles had turned into national ambassadors, carrying the gospel of the New Britain across the globe.

Pop was in danger of becoming respectable, but it would not last. Soon the Fab Four would have serious competition, from a group that would become synonymous with the excesses of the swinging sixties – the Rolling Stones.

7

SPECIAL RELATIONS

ANNE: For what, tell me that? . . . Labour colonial secretaries hobnobbing with corrupt old sheiks. Labour defence secretaries paying for Polaris on the never-never. Harold being buddy-buddy with Lyndon. That's what for, Nigel. That's your Signpost for the Sixties!

Dennis Potter, *Vote, Vote, Vote for Nigel Barton* (1965)

> O fateful land that bears the name
> Of Mr Cecil Rhodes
> Who knows the nameless deeds of shame
> That UDI forebodes?

'Mrs Wilson's Diary', *Private Eye*, 29 October 1965

On 11 December 1964 Harold Wilson assembled his Cabinet to fill them in on the details of his first trip to Washington as Prime Minister. He was clearly glowing with enthusiasm and pleasure after his reception in the White House, and was eager to share his news with his colleagues. On the economy, for instance, he reported that 'President Lyndon Johnson had shown himself deeply concerned about our situation and virtually promised us all aid short of war. He also expressed an appreciation of the help which we had given him during the election and all that Harold Wilson's speeches had meant for him.' At this last comment, Richard Crossman noted, some ministers had to struggle not to burst out laughing, 'but I fear the humour was entirely unconscious'. Wilson, however, was cock-a-hoop with pride and looking forward to a new era in Anglo-American relations. 'They want us with them,' he said confidently. 'They want our new constructive ideas after the epoch of sterility. We are now in a position to influence events more than ever before for the last ten years.'[1]

From the very first day that he came into office, Harold Wilson was a keen proponent of Britain's supposedly special relationship with the United

States. In their thirteen long years of opposition, Labour's leaders had been unstinting in their support for the Cold War and many of the party's young revisionist intellectuals made no secret of their admiration for all things American.[2] The party had a strong tradition of pro-American 'Atlanticism' going back to the 1940s, and by the time Labour regained power in 1964, the links between the two countries had become even stronger. To take one example, Britain had become dependent on the Americans for its nuclear technology, notably the Polaris nuclear submarine system for which Harold Macmillan had negotiated in 1962. Instead of having its own independent deterrent, as had been promised in the fifties, Britain had ended up as a kind of nuclear client state, with American bombers stationed on its soil and Polaris submarines, controlled from Washington, drifting beneath the waters of the Firth of Clyde.[3]

The new government was well aware that, given Britain's dependence on the United States, they had to tread carefully. Two months before the election, Patrick Gordon Walker, the foreign affairs spokesman, noted that 'we must base our policy on the alliance with the US'.[4] Accordingly, as soon as he had taken office, Wilson sent his new Foreign Secretary off to Washington to assure the Americans of his continued support.[5] This first meeting passed off successfully, and in the months that followed Wilson and Callaghan made sure to keep the Americans informed about their various financial manoeuvres. During the sterling crisis of November 1964, Wilson sent two officials across the Atlantic to consult the Americans about increasing bank rate, and in March 1965 President Johnson's chief economic adviser told him that 'in spite of the British secrecy, Jim Callaghan told me last November 7 – for your eyes only – what was going to be in their Budget a few days later'.[6] Had word of this leaked out in Britain it would have been extremely damaging for Callaghan and Wilson, but it reflected their enormous belief and confidence in the American alliance.

When Gordon Walker lost the Leyton by-election in January 1965 Wilson replaced him with Michael Stewart, a former schoolmaster and a quiet, dry man who was often underestimated by his colleagues.[7] However, being a tortoise in a Cabinet overloaded with preening hares was not necessarily such a bad thing. Wedgwood Benn recognised that Stewart was 'a nice, sincere guy who is basically right-wing but is humane and civilised'.[8] Wilson certainly saw him as pragmatic and dependable, and, as time went on, increasingly came to rely on him.[9] Like his predecessor, Stewart had close links with American officials: both he and his opposite number, the

Secretary of State Dean Rusk, were alumni of St John's College, Oxford. It was no surprise, then, that he deeply believed in Britain's world role, in the Cold War and in the Atlantic alliance, and as the decade progressed he remained faithful to these commitments despite their growing unpopularity in his party.[10]

Quite apart from the exigencies of the Cold War, there were obvious reasons for Wilson to court the Americans. Their financial muscle would be vital in another sterling crisis, and he also wanted their support in dealing with the recalcitrant colony of Southern Rhodesia. President Johnson, meanwhile, wanted to make sure that Britain would maintain its military bases east of Suez and he also wanted British support for the Americans' increasingly costly commitment in South Vietnam. The issue of Vietnam dominated relations between the two countries for the remainder of the sixties, and it also had a profound effect on Wilson's standing within his own party.[11] However, as the American presence in Vietnam increased during the early months of 1965, culminating in the arrival of the Marines in March, Wilson's position became rather more complicated. Even at this early stage, some British diplomats were already reporting that the cause was lost, and few officials approved of the Americans' heavy-handed military strategy.[12]

British officials already had experience of fighting guerrillas in South-East Asia. Between 1948 and 1960 they had successfully staved off a Communist rebellion in Malaya, and in 1965 British forces were still engaged in the 'Confrontation' with Indonesia over the disputed Malaysian border in Borneo.[13] Some historians even argue that Britain's involvement in Malaysia was a blessing in disguise, since it tied up troops and resources that might otherwise have been sent to Vietnam.[14] Either way, by February 1965 Wilson was sufficiently alarmed by the escalation of American operations in Vietnam to stay up until three-thirty in the morning so that he could ring the President and suggest that he fly over to Washington and give him some advice. Johnson's reaction suggested how much he valued Wilson's counsel. 'I won't tell you how to run Malaysia and you don't tell us how to run Vietnam,' he shouted. 'If you want to help us some in Vietnam send us some men and send us some folks to deal with these guerrillas. Now if you don't feel like doing that, go on with your Malaysian problem.'[15]

Despite his doubts, though, Wilson had no intention of breaking publicly with the President. The problem was that many of his own backbenchers deeply objected to the Americans' brutal bombing raids on North Vietnam. On 4 March forty-nine MPs put down a motion calling for the government to disavow American policy; in June fifty MPs signed a private letter to Wilson expressing their anxiety at the escalation of the conflict; and in September, at the party conference, a succession of speakers attacked his reluctance to criticise the American bombing.[16] But Wilson stuck to his guns. On 19 July he warned the House that if the Americans pulled out of Vietnam the results would be 'incalculable', since 'friend and potential foe throughout the world would begin to wonder whether the United States might be induced also to abandon other allies when the going got rough'.[17]

Given his dependence on American support for the pound, as well as for British policy in Malaysia and Rhodesia, it is hard to see what else Wilson could have done at this stage, and most historians acknowledge that he was in an impossible position.[18] However, he had not impressed those backbenchers who thought that the Americans were conducting themselves like war criminals, among them the saturnine Conservative Enoch Powell, who despised the American alliance. Powell complained that under Labour Britain was behaving like 'an American satellite'. In Vietnam, he said, Wilson had acted as 'an obedient commentator', issuing statements of approval when the Americans bombed North Vietnam, when they stopped bombing, and even when they started again. He wanted to know if Wilson was planning to go even further, to commit British forces to fight in the Indochinese jungle, a step that Powell thought would be 'intolerable'.[19] Powell suspected that the commitment of British forces might 'come about as part of a package deal arising from pressure on sterling, or a bout of short term insolvency': in other words, as part of a deal whereby the Americans would bail out the pound and a grateful Wilson would send troops to Vietnam.[20] He had an unexpected ally in the left-wing Labour backbencher, William Warbey, who in September 1965 had published a book entitled *Vietnam: The Truth*, accusing Wilson of having agreed a deal in which 'America supports the pound, and Britain supports America in Vietnam'.[21]

These suspicions were not necessarily misplaced. The Americans did support the pound, largely because they were worried that if it were devalued, pressure might fall on the dollar in its turn. But by the middle of 1965, when Britain found itself in yet another sterling crisis, they were beginning to think of precisely the deal that Powell had outlined. In July Johnson's National Security Adviser, the peculiarly named McGeorge Bundy, told him:

> we want to make very sure that the British get it into their heads that it makes no sense for us to rescue the Pound in a situation in which there

is no British flag in Vietnam, and a threatened British thin-out in both east of Suez and in Germany. What I would like to say to [them] myself, is that a British Brigade in Vietnam would be worth a billion dollars at the moment of truth for Sterling.[22]

Johnson and Bundy had their opportunity just a month later, when, despite Callaghan's efforts, the pound came under renewed pressure. 'A gloomy session at the Bank,' recorded Cecil King, the newspaper baron and Bank of England director, on 5 August. 'There has been a run on gold and a run on sterling, and the reserves are in sight of exhaustion.'[23] Devaluation was out and more deflation was politically unpalatable, so Callaghan was sent back to Washington to negotiate a new American rescue package for the pound.[24] Johnson's advisers had already put together a set of stringent conditions. First, the British would be 'told that under any and all circumstances devaluation of the pound is unthinkable and cannot be permitted'. Next, they must agree to implement a statutory incomes policy in order to prevent rampant wage inflation. Finally, they must agree 'to maintain fully their worldwide defense commitments', which meant no withdrawal from their bases east of Suez.[25]

Callaghan agreed the economic aspects of the package in Washington at the end of August, and they were reluctantly approved by an emergency meeting of the Cabinet on 1 September.[26] Prudently, if dishonestly, Wilson and Callaghan took care to conceal from their colleagues the fact that they were dancing to the Americans' tune; instead, they pretended that the statutory incomes policy was entirely their own idea. The trade unions, after strenuous persuasion by George Brown, very gloomily agreed to the package, and on 9 September the Bank of England, the Federal Reserve and the European central banks finalised a £350 million deal to support the pound.[27]

As for the Americans' third condition, governing Britain's defence policy, this had not been mentioned at all to the Cabinet. Instead, it was secretly agreed in London on 10 September by George Ball, an emissary from the White House, and Bundy then reported to Johnson: 'George Ball really put it to the British on Singapore and our support of the pound . . . You will notice that it took two talks for Wilson to agree to the association between our defense of the pound and their overseas commitments. The one thing which he was apparently trying to avoid was a liability in Vietnam.'[28] On the same day the Federal Reserve and the European central banks simultaneously placed enormous orders for sterling on the exchange markets, stunning the speculators and restoring faith in the pound. The deal had done the trick; at last the government had a respite from the endless succession of sterling crises, and for the rest of 1965 the pound was safe.[29]

In their memoirs both Wilson and Callaghan played down talk of their secret arrangement with the Americans.[30] Only four ministers – Wilson, Callaghan, Brown and the President of the Board of Trade, Douglas Jay – knew that there had been any kind of deal, and probably only Wilson himself knew the full extent of the unwritten contract. Unfortunately, they all found it very difficult to keep their mouths shut. As early as 12 September Jay publicly reminded George Brown that 'we can't reflate this autumn without breaking the pledges which James Callaghan made to [the Americans] in Washington'. The Chancellor immediately intervened to say 'there was some misunderstanding since he had made no pledges at all', but as Crossman remarked, 'if a denial ever completely confirmed a statement it was Callaghan's on that occasion'.[31] Similarly, in February 1966 George Brown admitted to Barbara Castle that they were being tough on union pay claims because 'Harold said something to Johnson about it'.[32] And just a few days later Crossman recorded that Wilson had come out with 'a very characteristic chain of utterances':

> First he repeated time after time that the Americans had never made any connection between the financial support they gave us and our support for them in Vietnam. Then about ten minutes later he was saying, 'Nevertheless, don't let's fail to realize that their financial support is not unrelated to the way we behave in the Far East: any direct announcement of our withdrawal, for example, could not fail to have a profound effect on my personal relations with LBJ and the way the Americans treat us.'[33]

On the face of it, without consulting his colleagues or telling the public, Wilson had handed over to President Johnson the right to dictate not only Britain's foreign and defence policies, but also its internal economic affairs. However, this was not simply a tale of slavish self-abasement.[34] It is hard to think of a single policy that was adopted primarily as a result of American pressure; in fact, Wilson probably found it easy to make a deal with the United States because their demands tallied with what he wanted to do. This is not to underestimate American influence. Thanks to the demands of the nuclear alliance, the problems in Malaysia and Rhodesia and above all the weakness of the pound, Britain was probably more dependent on the United States in the sixties than at any time since the late forties.[35] But it is not true that in September 1965 Wilson sold his soul to Washington in a Faustian pact that saved sterling while surrendering control of British policy.[36] Paradoxically, it was Wilson, fighting from the weakest of positions, who had got the better of the deal, because it allowed him to carry out policies that he had always supported anyway. Whether they were the right policies, however, was another matter.

The prospect of British involvement in Vietnam was still very far from voters' minds as they enjoyed the last summer days of 1965. It had been the summer of *Help!* and the Who, plastic raincoats and the Post Office Tower, Swinging London and the Op Art look. But there were already signs that Wilson's relationship with Johnson was damaging his popularity, above all with his own Labour activists. On 30 April the cover of *Private Eye* had featured probably the most famous cartoon of Wilson ever published, the scathing handiwork of Gerald Scarfe. 'VIETNAM', read the caption: 'WILSON RIGHT BEHIND JOHNSON'. The picture showed two grotesque figures: first, the exaggerated, big-eared American President, a pistol hanging from his belt and his trousers pulled down to reveal his behind; beside him, a midget-like Wilson, his hands on Johnson's belt and his tongue flickering obscenely towards the presidential posterior. 'I've heard of a special relationship,' Johnson is saying, 'but this is ridiculous.'[37]

As the summer gave way to autumn, with the pound apparently safe from the speculators, George Brown hard at work on his National Plan and the Rolling Stones riding high in the singles charts, Harold Wilson began to spend more and more time puzzling over the most intractable legacy of Britain's colonial empire: the problem of Rhodesia.

At the beginning of the sixties, the self-governing territory of Southern Rhodesia had one of the largest white settler communities in Africa. More than 200,000 Europeans controlled a system of racial segregation that gave little voice to Southern Rhodesia's population of more than two million blacks, and many observers were struck by the similarities with the apartheid system in neighbouring South Africa. The settler issue made it difficult for the British governments of the fifties to disengage from Rhodesia as swiftly as they had done elsewhere in Africa, but no easy solution presented itself. In 1953 the Conservative government had invented a Central African Federation for Nyasaland, Northern and Southern Rhodesia, but this fell apart ten years later. Nyasaland and Northern Rhodesia, which both had much smaller white minorities, duly became independent in 1964 as Malawi and Zambia respectively – leaving Southern Rhodesia isolated and uncertain.

Profiting from cheap black labour and a steady flow of raw materials from the north, Southern Rhodesia entered the sixties with a booming economy. Its white settlers enjoyed an extremely comfortable standard of living: fine weather, high wages, low taxes and an average of two servants per household.[38] People joked that Rhodesia was 'Basingstoke-in-the-Bush': as one account has it, 'a parody of a pre-war middle-class suburb transported across the Equator, complete with its tennis and golf clubs, and populated by aggressively hearty men in shorts, blazers and cravats, who talked of nothing but sport, and women who knew their place'.[39] This existence depended, however, on the complete subordination of the black majority. Floggings and harsh prison terms for blacks were common, and political, commercial and cultural power was reserved for whites only. According to one Rhodesian policeman interviewed by the *Sun*, the black man was 'muck to be kicked and kept down there'.[40] 'Britain's not bloody well going to make us live under a bunch of fucking monkeys,' one recent arrival from Scotland remarked. 'Look at South Africa, that's how to fix them.'[41]

These sentiments were perfectly represented in the person of the Rhodesian Prime Minister, Ian Smith. A middle-aged farmer of limited horizons, he had flown for the RAF during the war, idolised Sir Winston Churchill, and was interested mainly in rugby and cattle. Nevertheless, he was extremely popular among his fellow-settlers and proved an unyielding, even cunning negotiator. He regarded the British as traitors to the settlers' cause, and refused to deny rumours that he might make a unilateral declaration of independence, or UDI, based on white minority rule. This proved extremely popular with his domestic audience: on 7 May 1965 all fifty white seats in the Salisbury parliament fell to the Rhodesian Front. With his political base secured, Smith then moved to prepare the ground for independence. He already controlled Rhodesian radio and television; now he replaced the High Commissioner in London with a regime loyalist and installed another hardliner as his army chief of staff. UDI was not yet inevitable, but, day by day, it was becoming more likely.[42]

Wilson had strong feelings on racial issues, and he accepted Britain's responsibility for the affairs of the troubled territory. On the other hand, he knew that any military conflict would be extremely controversial at home, where many people had voiced their sympathy for their white 'kith and kin' in Africa. As even his fiercest critics admit, his administration had 'virtually no cards in its hands against an intransigent, embittered and introverted government in Rhodesia' that appeared bent on illegally seizing independence.[43] Wilson therefore found himself trapped between appeasing Smith's demands on the one hand, and pushing him into a unilateral declaration of independence on the other. In the autumn of 1965 he publicly warned the Rhodesians that if they declared independence, Britain would sever all diplomatic and economic ties, thereby inflicting 'disastrous economic damage' on the rebel regime.[44] Over the next few months, desultory negotiations continued with the Smith regime, with the British insisting that black majority rule must be the basis of any independence, and the Rhodesian settlers defiantly holding out.[45]

In October 1965 the drama began to move towards its inevitable conclusion. Early in the month, Smith flew to London for talks, but he had no intention of reaching a settlement, and after five days the summit broke up.[46] On the night of Smith's return flight to Rhodesia, Wilson made a televised appeal: 'I know I speak for everyone in these islands, all parties, all our people, when I say to Mr Smith, "Prime Minister, think again."' Instead, Smith was surer than ever of his ground, and on 19 October the Rhodesian Security Council secretly agreed to declare independence at the first opportunity. Meanwhile, Wilson, ever the optimist, had decided on a spectacular move to break the deadlock. On 21 October, to the horror of his colleagues, he decided to fly to Salisbury for a last attempt to sway the Rhodesians.[47]

The Prime Minister arrived in the Rhodesian capital on 25 October to a frosty reception from the settler government. The Rhodesians treated him with open contempt: at an official dinner, one aristocratic settler performed a bizarre belly dance in front of Wilson's irritated face, deliberately brushing against him with every motion of the dance. All in all, the visit was a disaster. By his own account, Wilson felt sick at the heat, the weight of racial oppression and the unconcealed hostility and indifference of his hosts, and he flew back to London five days later having made no real progress.[48] Tired and disillusioned, he then made his greatest tactical mistake. The only thing that inhibited Smith and his supporters from declaring UDI was their fear that Britain might respond with military force, because the Rhodesians knew that their own army and air force could not resist for long. Wilson had already told Smith in London that he had no intention of sending in British troops, but the Rhodesian leader could not be entirely sure. In Salisbury

Wilson had repeated his promise and then, on 30 October, he gave the same assurance to the British public in a national radio broadcast: 'If there are those in this country who are thinking in terms of a thunderbolt, hurtling through the sky and destroying their enemy, a thunderbolt in the shape of the Royal Air Force, let me say that this thunderbolt will not be coming.'[49] Smith was ecstatic. Wilson had given a public promise that he could not break, and the Rhodesian Front could therefore proceed immediately to a declaration of independence.[50]

On 5 November Smith declared a state of emergency. Five days later word reached Downing Street that UDI was imminent, and at six the following morning Wilson made one final telephone call to Smith, recording the conversation for posterity. Ben Pimlott likens the apologetic tone to 'the break-up of a stormy love affair, in which there was still some lingering affection, rather than a declaration of legal war'.[51] When his Cabinet arrived later that morning, Wilson remarked that Smith had been 'astonishingly calm — almost friendly — the calm of the madman'. Then, Barbara Castle recalled, at just after quarter past eleven, 'a message was brought in to the PM, who said, "As of five minutes ago a UDI was declared." A solemn moment.'[52] 'We have been waiting for it for a long time,' remarked Tony Benn, 'but now it has come there is a sense of relief.'[53]

That afternoon Wilson publicly denounced the settlers' illegal declaration of independence as a 'tragedy affecting a great people, including many thousands who have made their homes there and who are plunged into a maelstrom not of their own making, and of millions more who are denied the inalienable human right of self-expression and self-determination'. He promised an end to all British links with the 'rebel regime', but did not make any mention of using force to retrieve the situation.[54] This was not so much a matter of timidity as of sheer practicality. The Rhodesian settlers were in complete control of the country and only a major military operation could dislodge them. 'It will split the country from top to bottom,' thought Crossman; 'we haven't got the troops and if we had it would be geographically impossible to put them in.'[55]

In fact Britain did have the troops, but the Defence Secretary, Denis Healey, told his colleagues that it would take months to assemble the five battalions necessary and fly them into Rhodesia, so 'there would be no chance of surprise'. He added that 'South Africa might intervene — and we couldn't take her on — and we should need a pre-emptive strike in which we couldn't be sure of the loyalty of our forces'.[56] Indeed, in his memoirs

Healey recalled that there had been 'mutinous muttering' among senior army officers who disliked the idea of taking on the 'kith and kin' alongside whom they had fought in the Second World War.[57] He also thought that an invasion would 'embitter the white population beyond any hope of collaboration', while Wilson predicted that an invasion would mean 'a bloody war turning into a bloody civil war'.[58] He had only to look to the worsening American experience in Vietnam for a daily reminder of the dangers of rash military adventures.

There were also persuasive political reasons for avoiding force. Crossman noted that 'the last thing the British public wants to see is the use of force or sanctions in Rhodesia. They are prepared to see us standing up for what is right but they wouldn't tolerate a war against fellow white men who are also British subjects.'[59] Opinion polls consistently found strong public opposition to military intervention. What was more, Wilson's tiny majority meant that any military strategy would be vulnerable to the whims of two or three Labour backbenchers. Most of his Cabinet ministers felt that an invasion would be reckless and dangerous. And he could hardly count on the Conservatives for support, because several dozen of their backbenchers openly sided with the rebels.[60]

Wilson does not seem to have suffered great anguish over the rebellion of the Rhodesian settlers, and he evidently enjoyed the opportunity to play the international statesman. In an interview in October for the *Sunday Telegraph* he had once again taken up the Kennedy mantle, and described Rhodesia as 'my Cuba'.[61] Similarly, at lunch with Cecil King in December he declared that he had 'constantly in mind Suez, Cuba and the Bay of Pigs'.[62] In 'Mrs Wilson's Diary', *Private Eye* had great fun with his statesmanlike pretensions:

> All this week Harold has been very silent at his food, reading a large book called 'Kennedy'. I happened to pick it up the other day and found that the chapter on Cuba was heavily underlined and fell open first as it was so well thumbed . . .
>
> The other evening I slipped in quietly to take him his hot drink late at night. Imagine my surprise to see Harold sitting at his desk, looking at himself in a mirror and saying, 'Good evening. This is a midnight broadcast from London. I am speaking to you at a time of crisis for the whole free world. I appeal to Prime Minister Smith to step down this instant, or the Royal Navy will not hesitate to deliver our ultimate deterrent. God

bless you all.' He then put on a record of 'Land of Hope and Glory', and was just straightening his quiff in the mirror when the telephone rang and I had to betray my presence with a light cough.[63]

Most of Wilson's colleagues agreed that he had got carried away. Crossman complained that 'since the summer Harold Wilson has been more and more obsessed with Rhodesia and Vietnam and less and less actively concerned with the home front'.[64] Even Marcia Williams remarked that he had 'completely taken off and got out of touch with the real problems at home'.[65] Yet the public evidently respected him for it: his lead in the polls actually increased after the Rhodesian UDI.[66]

Wilson had given surprisingly little thought to the means of defeating the Smith regime if the worst happened. A programme of economic warfare was quickly put into operation, and the government expelled the rebel regime from the sterling area, froze Rhodesian reserves in London, blocked access to the City's financial markets and eventually seized Rhodesian bank assets.[67] But since none of this had any immediate effect, there were murmurs of disquiet within the Cabinet. On 18 November Callaghan put the case for tougher measures and a 'quick kill'; his fear, shared by Crossman, was that 'if we fail to bring Smith to heel in the next two months, Wilson will soon fall from the height of popularity'.[68] Ten days later Crossman reflected that UDI had been followed by 'an awkward hiatus':

> We are sitting here in London and the so-called rebels are sitting quite happily there in Salisbury. We have no means of enforcing law and order on the rebels, whereas the rebels obviously have every means of maintaining law and order in defiance of us. This week people began to ask whether this is all the Government had up its sleeve; and the answer seems to be an uncomfortable 'Yes, that's all.'[69]

The Rhodesian regime's one obvious weakness was its dependence on imported oil, and in December Wilson finally acceded to the demands of the United Nations and imposed oil sanctions. By the middle of January 1966 Britain had effectively cut off the flow of oil to Rhodesia from its one principal source, the port of Beira in neighbouring Mozambique.[70] Wilson's famous optimism, which so often irritated his ministers, was now in evidence once again. He was genuinely convinced that the sanctions would bring down Smith's regime. At lunch with Cecil King just before Christmas he was 'friendly, relaxed and confident . . . that he can bring down Smith and get him to talk terms'. He was even thinking ahead to Rhodesia's future: 'direct British rule for an indefinite period, but of the order of ten years', with a multi-racial Cabinet from the start and 'a strenuous effort to educate the Africans up to the standards of literacy etc. required for self-government'.[71] Three days into the New Year he cheerfully told Castle that 'sanctions were really beginning to bite . . . and Smith was getting desperate'.[72] On 11 January in Nigeria he told the sceptical Commonwealth Prime Ministers that the rebellion would end 'within a matter of weeks rather than months'.[73] It was a brave forecast, but the press believed it. Under the headline 'Wilson's Timetable for Defeat of Rebel Regime', the *Sun* had already printed an apparently leaked story predicting Smith's surrender by March; other newspapers now followed suit.[74]

The predictions were wrong. Sanctions never came close to provoking serious economic collapse or widespread white dissent. It was never entirely clear whether they were supposed to be buying time for some other measure, appeasing the United Nations or toppling the Smith regime on their own.[75] If the sanctions were supposed to be bringing down Smith, they proved singularly ineffective. Rhodesia's borders were impossible to patrol and her immediate neighbours, the apartheid regime in South Africa and the Portuguese colony of Mozambique, made only token efforts to enforce the sanctions. Oil shipments were reaching Rhodesia within days of Wilson's rash prediction in Lagos, while foreign subsidiaries of international oil companies, which were not covered by British sanctions laws, continued to sell oil to the rebels through South Africa.[76]

By the spring of 1966 it looked increasingly unlikely that sanctions would bring the 'quick kill' Wilson had wanted. Zambia, the former colony to Rhodesia's north, refused to enforce a full embargo, and on 3 March Smith audaciously announced the suspension of petrol rationing. Britain's international reputation was badly tarnished, and at home Wilson looked less like a cunning statesman and more like a self-deluding fantasist. Weeks had turned into months after all; and months looked as though they might turn into years.[77]

8

ENTER THE STONES

Jagger is a lad of good general character though he has been rather slow to mature. The pleasing quality which is now emerging is that of persistence when he makes up his mind to tackle something . . .

Jagger's development now fully justifies me in recommending him for a Degree Course and I hope you will be able to accept him.

> Michael Jagger's reference from the headmaster of
> Dartford Grammar School, 1960

Mick Jagger lips. Order now. Be with the in-crowd. Full details from your local lip dealers.

> Classified newspaper advertisement, 1965

In April 1963 a young man called Andrew Loog Oldham was on the hunt for a rock and roll band. The son of a Dutch-American air force officer who had been killed in the Second World War, Oldham was just nineteen, with expensive tastes and lofty ambitions. He was, said one observer, 'calculatedly vicious and nasty, but pretty as a stoat'.[1] A driven, even ruthless character, he had spent his teens working as an odd-job boy for the designer Mary Quant before moving into public relations and pop music promotion. His dream was to manage his own pop group to rival the Beatles, for whom he had done a little work earlier that year.[2]

One evening towards the end of April, Oldham went out for a drink with Peter Jones, the editor of *Record Mirror*. Jones remarked that he had been hearing a lot about a rhythm and blues group who had been playing regularly at the Crawdaddy Club in the Station Hotel, Richmond. 'There might be something there for you,' he said casually. 'It looks like rhythm 'n' blues will make it big soon, so why not have a look at them?'[3]

That Sunday, 28 April 1963, Oldham caught the train from North London to Richmond to see what Jones had been talking about. When he arrived, he almost immediately bumped into a young couple quarrelling in a darkened alley between the railway station and the Station Hotel, one of whom, he discovered, was the group's lead singer. Oldham remembered the young man's reaction:

> He gave me a look that asked me everything about myself in one moment – as in 'What are you doing with the rest of my life?' His lips looked at you, seconding that first emotion. He was thin, waistless, giving him the human form of a puma with a gender of its own; the girl was a bridge to reality. They were both very earnest, hurt and similar: pale skins, brown hair and flashing eyes. And both very attractive in their similarity, in heat.[4]

Half an hour later Oldham watched as the singer took the stage in the dark and sweat-sodden club with the five other members of his group. And although he knew almost nothing about rhythm and blues, and was interested in the group primarily as a way of making money, Oldham was simply blown away:

> I'd never seen anything like it. They came on to me. All my preparations, ambitions and desires had just met their purpose. It was a feeling of all the elements falling into the right place and time, catching all the dualities. The music was authentic and sexually driven by the three on stools and the bottom end behind them. It reached out and went inside me – totally. It satisfied me. I was in love . . . I heard what I'd always wanted to hear. I wanted it; it already belonged to me. Everything I'd done up until now was a preparation for this moment. I saw and heard what my life, thus far, had been for.

Andrew Oldham had found his rock and roll band, the Rolling Stones had found their manager, and they were on their way to fame and fortune.[5]

For many historians, the most important single influence on the British pop music of the 1960s was the heritage of the black American music produced earlier in the century.[6] 'Rhythm and blues', as it was called during the forties and fifties, drew on the heritage of classic blues music, but the term was basically just a euphemism for contemporary black music, coined because the American charts were subject to strict racial segregation.[7] Unlike the old blues, 'rhythm and blues' was aggressive, hedonistic and upbeat, and it catered for an increasingly urban, affluent and self-confident black audience.[8] It did not, however, appeal to white audiences, and when white artists like Elvis Presley performed black or black-inspired music, it was marketed as 'rock and roll'.[9] Although rock and roll had been very successful in Britain in the late fifties, too, it seemed unlikely that rhythm and blues would have the same appeal. As the bandleader Ted Heath told a journalist, it would never take off, because it was 'primarily for the coloured population'.[10]

As it turned out, however, blues music proved much more popular than Heath had anticipated. Since the dividing line between blues and jazz was always pretty vague, British jazz musicians like Chris Barber were not averse to flirting with the blues.[11] Indeed, Barber was one of the key figures in the popularisation of blues music: as one writer puts it, 'by providing a base first for skiffle and then for the blues, he was virtually a founding father of what came next: a British rock scene'.[12] The other key figures were Alexis Korner, a raffish young musician whose passion for the blues was second to none, and his great friend Cyril Davies, a dishevelled scrap-yard panel-beater and the most accomplished British blues musician of his generation. Both Korner and Davies had played jazz and skiffle during the mid-1950s, and they ran a blues club at the Round House pub on Wardour Street. In 1960, however, they were effectively forced out for using light amplification, which was considered heretical by many jazz aficionados. As a result they ended up joining Barber, whose band was moving further away from jazz into blues, with Korner on electric guitar and Davies on harmonica.[13]

Although the collaboration between Barber, Korner and Davies did not last very long, it proved immensely influential in the history of British rock music. The sound was 'a synthesis of guitar-led vocals and free-flowing jazz rhythms', an extremely attractive blend for young listeners who were bored of rock and roll, ballads and trad jazz. When the Barber band played in Cheltenham in 1961, they made a great impression on one earnest young devotee called Brian Jones, who stayed behind after the concert for a drink in a nearby wine bar with Alexis Korner. Korner promised his young admirer that if he ever came to London, he would be delighted to put him up, and this meeting would prove a pivotal moment in the genesis of the Rolling Stones.[14]

In the meantime, Korner and Davies formed their own group playing nothing but rhythm and blues, which they called Blues Incorporated. Tired of the constant struggle to secure dates at jazz clubs where blues was frowned upon, they decided to open their own club in a damp basement in Ealing, West London. A hundred people came to the first night on 17 March 1962, but within a month the attendance had doubled and the tiny club was bursting at the seams. The admission charge of five shillings included membership for a year, and thanks to a limited advertising campaign in magazines like the *NME* and *Jazz News*, the Ealing club soon had a membership list of more than eight hundred people, some living as far away as Scotland.[15] Regular, often overawed young visitors in the early days included such characters as Brian Jones, Mick Jagger and Keith Richards (all later of the Rolling Stones), Paul Jones (of Manfred Mann), Jack Bruce (Manfred Mann and Cream) and Ginger Baker (Cream). Not only did Korner have extremely eclectic tastes, but he encouraged young fans to participate on stage, if they were any good. Jagger later remembered that it was 'a Mecca for anyone interested in the blues':

> We went every Saturday . . . and soon got up the courage to get up and have a go ourselves. I saw people my own age getting up – like Paul Jones and Brian Jones – and I thought to myself, 'They're not that brilliant. I can do as well as that.' So I got up and sang 'Got My Mojo Working' . . . and before I knew what was happening, I was one of the band's featured vocalists . . . That's how it all started.[16]

Rhythm and blues was almost completely ignored by the press in the first years of the sixties, which was hardly surprising since it had made no impact on the charts. Yet there already existed a rudimentary blues infrastructure allowing suburban teenagers to seek out obscure records and even to take up guitars themselves. Most blues clubs were situated in London and the South-East, especially on the western fringes of the capital, where devotees flocked to the likes of the Crawdaddy, the Eel Pie Island Hotel and the Crown. But soon there were plenty of clubs in the provinces, too: the Olympia in Reading; the R&B Club in Andover; the Wooden Bridge Hotel in Guildford; the St Andrews Hall in Norwich; the Rhythm and Blues Club in Belfast; and the Downbeat in the docks of Newcastle. Shops like Violet May's in Sheffield stocked obscure imported LPs by classic blues artists as well as more recent records by the likes of Chuck Berry. Indeed, in many ways it was easier for white British teenagers to follow an interest in black American music than it was for their American counterparts, who were inhibited by the racial politics of the day.[17]

By the end of 1963 older jazz clubs like the Marquee and the Flamingo, having sensed which way the wind was blowing, had scaled down their live jazz performances in order to make room for rhythm and blues groups and capitalise on what seemed likely to become the next musical craze.[18] By the following March the capital alone boasted twenty-eight different blues clubs catering for some ten thousand people each week. Even on Mondays, London's blues clubs attracted a minimum of three thousand fans, all of which meant that blues was rapidly overtaking jazz in the nation's affections.[19] In August the National Jazz and Blues Festival brought together jazz musicians like Humphrey Lyttleton with blues performers like the Rolling Stones and the Yardbirds. But this was virtually the last instance of collaboration between jazz and blues, because the blues groups were already becoming far too popular to spend their time playing at jazz festivals. Having flirted with nationwide appeal between about 1960 and 1962, jazz was destined to remain a rather intellectual minority interest. Rhythm and blues, by contrast, was heading for the top.[20]

The striking thing about the rhythm and blues boom of the early sixties was that it was very closely associated with the nation's art schools. The other great pioneer of the British blues movement, John Mayall, had formed his first band while at art college in Manchester. As the leader of the Bluesbreakers, Mayall nurtured the careers of an extraordinary series of British rock musicians, from Mick Fleetwood and Jack Bruce to Eric Clapton and Mick Taylor.[21] Among other bands with roots in the art college jazz and blues scene were the Kinks, the Rolling Stones, the Animals, the Yardbirds, the Pretty Things, the Move and Pink Floyd. The art schools in the suburbs of London, where blues had a stronger foothold than anywhere else, were particularly notable for churning out the stars of the future: Keith Richards, Dick Taylor and Phil May from Sidcup, for example; Pete Townshend, Ronnie Wood and Freddie Mercury from Ealing; Eric Clapton and Keith Relf from Kingston; Jeff Beck from Wimbledon; Ray Davies from Hornsey; Syd Barrett from Camberwell; Jimmy Page from Sutton; Charlie Watts from Harrow, and so on.[22]

Rhythm and blues fitted nicely with the dissenting spirit of the art schools. As the music of the black American city, it allowed suburban British bohemians to portray themselves as cosmopolitan rebels, and as one student put it, 'there was a cachet about liking and having really obscure blues records'.[23] And the art school was also the ideal environment for young men who wanted to set up bands of their own, providing them with a ready-made stage and a captive audience who put a higher premium on artifice and 'authenticity' than on smooth musical professionalism. The art school experience was crucial in forging the British pop of the sixties, encouraging a general spirit of surprise, experiment and whimsy that was very different from the ponderous earnestness of contemporary American music.[24]

A good example of the close relationship between the old jazz scene, the art schools and the new popularity of rhythm and blues was a Tyneside group that first came to public attention in July 1964. In many ways the Animals were the quintessential provincial rhythm and blues group. Their hoarse, charismatic vocalist, Eric Burdon, carried off a very good impersonation of his black American heroes, and since his own background included a stint as a trombonist in a college jazz band, he was an excellent example of the jazz-blues crossover of the early sixties.[25] In the summer of 1964 his group struck gold with 'The House of the Rising Sun', a traditional American ballad telling the story of a life ruined by prostitution at a New Orleans bawdy house. Executives at the Animals' record company thought that it was too sombre, too slow and, above all, too long, but the result was a stunning success. As a hard-driving blues band, the Animals gave the song an aggressive, compelling sound, while Burdon's growling delivery fascinated listeners who would never normally have contemplated buying a ballad about a brothel. The single shot to the top of the British chart in July 1964, then became an American number one and eventually sold more than eight million copies across the world.[26]

Just as 'You Really Got Me' had transformed the fortunes of the Kinks, so the success of 'The House of the Rising Sun' turned the Animals into a highly successful chart outfit, and in the next eighteen months they recorded five more Top Ten hits. As one writer puts it, it took the intervention of British groups like the Animals to open 'the eyes of young Americans at last to their own musical heritage'.[27] (In fact, although the song is sometimes cited as an example of the so-called Americanisation of popular culture, it was partly based on a seventeenth-century English folk melody.) Young white British musicians had few qualms about performing 'black' music, but had they been American, they would probably have been inhibited from doing so for fear of transgressing that country's tortured racial codes.[28]

Indeed, British musicians were often shocked by the grim reality of American racial attitudes. Mick Jagger complained that when the Rolling Stones played in Alabama, the authorities prevented black fans from attending their concerts. 'Materially America is fantastic,' he mused. 'It's just the people who are so bloody awful.'[29] Similarly, Eric Burdon recalled that on one of the Animals' tours in the mid-sixties, they played a concert in the city of Mobile, Alabama, after which a pretty white girl came and asked for his autograph.

> During the conversation I mentioned that Otis Redding had played there the night before. She said, 'Yeh man, he's too much, isn't he? I think his recording of *My Girl* is fantastic.' I told her, 'Yeh, it's my favourite record too.' Then I asked her if she had seen him perform. She said, 'Did I see him? You got to be joking, man, the place was full of niggers.'[30]

Of all the British blues groups, by far the most famous was the band that Andrew Loog Oldham had discovered in Richmond on 28 April 1963. Easily the most controversial British musical act of the sixties, the Rolling Stones were the only group genuinely to match the popularity of the Beatles. And more than any other group, it was the Stones who did most to define the sound, the look and the style of rock music (as opposed to pop) worldwide for the next few decades.

The Rolling Stones can trace their origins to a chance meeting in the autumn of 1961. Early on the drizzly morning of Tuesday, 25 October, a seventeen-year-old graphic-design student called Keith Richards arrived at Dartford station to catch the train to Sidcup Art College, where he spent most of his time setting fire to dustbins and playing the guitar. Standing on the platform, he noticed the vaguely familiar face of Mike Jagger, an old primary-school classmate who was now studying economics at the London School of Economics. Mike was carrying four or five blues records that he had imported from the United States by mail order, and Keith was excited to see that they included some of his favourites, like Chuck Berry and Muddy Waters. Although they had not seen each other for several years, the two boys struck up a conversation and discovered that they shared a mutual friend, another teenage blues fan called Dick Taylor. Mike mentioned that he and Taylor had formed their own amateur 'group', Little Boy Blue and the Blue Boys, who performed in the privacy of their own bedrooms. Would Keith like to come and play the guitar with them? Indeed he would: as his mother recalled, when he arrived home that evening, he could hardly wait to tell her about the encounter with Mike Jagger and the invitation to join the Blue Boys. 'He was really excited about that meeting,' she remembered. 'He'd been playing guitar for ages, but always on his own. He was too shy to join in with anyone else, although Dick Taylor had often asked him.'[31]

For two men who were to become icons of youthful rebellion and decadent excess, both Keith Richards and Mick Jagger had strikingly ordinary early lives. Richards's mother and father worked as a light-bulb factory supervisor and a part-time baker's shop assistant, respectively, and he grew up as a good-natured if rather undisciplined boy on a brand-new council estate in Dartford. Expelled from Dartford Technical College in 1958, he had pitched up at Sidcup Art College more from a desire to avoid working than any real interest in art.[32] By contrast, Michael Jagger was a rather more ambitious figure, although he too lost interest in his studies in his teens and became something of an irritant to his teachers. Like Richards, Jagger was a child of the Second World War, but his background was slightly more prosperous, and his father was a lecturer in physical education. Young Mike was clearly bright: he passed his eleven-plus, attended the local grammar school, and won a place at the prestigious LSE.[33] His real passion, however, was the blues, and as a teenager he spent every Saturday afternoon hanging around the jazz shops on the Charing Cross Road and practising his vocals with Dick Taylor and the other Blue Boys. The only adult who heard them play was Taylor's mother; with remarkable prescience, she told Jagger that 'he'd got something special'.[34]

Both Richards and Jagger exemplified the links between the new popular music and the bohemianism of higher education in the early sixties. Richards spent most of his time at Sidcup talking to the other art students about music and practising his guitar chords, all of which kept up his image as an outlaw. At the LSE, meanwhile, Mike Jagger cultivated a generally shabby, rebellious appearance, affected a strangled Cockney accent of which there had previously been no evidence, and took to calling himself 'Mick' rather than 'Mike', because the former supposedly sounded more down-to-earth.[35]

The bohemian scene through which the young Jagger moved at the LSE was not very different from that inhabited by Brian Jones, the third member of the triumvirate who founded the Rolling Stones. Jones was a year older than his two collaborators in the Rolling Stones, and came from a distinctly middle-class background. He had been born in the genteel spa town of Cheltenham, and grew up in an atmosphere of suburban respectability. A very bright boy, he too passed his eleven-plus and went to Cheltenham Grammar School. Indeed, he was easily the most academically gifted of the Stones, with nine O-level passes and two A-levels, in physics and chemistry.[36]

However, by the time Jones was sixteen or so, he had already embarked on a career of dissolution that made Keith Richards look positively conformist by comparison. In 1958 a fourteen-year-old pupil at the girls' grammar school became pregnant and named Jones as the father, and it became well known that he was unusually sexually active for his age, scorning contraceptives and working his way through a series of girlfriends with the zeal of a collector. In 1960 another of his conquests, a married woman from Guildford who had spent just one night with him, gave birth to a daughter, and a year later he fathered yet another child, who was brought up by his very occasional girlfriend, Pat Andrews. Meanwhile, Jones was idling his way through an incongruous string of jobs, including stints as a coalman and a trainee in the office of the borough architect.[37]

Although Jones was very good looking, which explains his great success at acquiring female company, he was neither reliable nor secure. Bill Wyman, who generally liked his old collaborator, comments that he was 'a preening peacock, gregarious, artistic, desperately needing assurance from his peers'.[38] And while most of the pop stars of the sixties occasionally behaved in ways that were selfish, self-indulgent or merely ridiculous, probably only John Lennon rivalled Jones for sheer nastiness. 'Because of Brian's particular insecurities, he was very heavy on anyone else's insecurity,' remarked his musical patron Alexis Korner. 'Obviously I dug Brian, but he could be very mean. Just plain evil, like twisting words and finding a way of saying something that would hurt, without it sounding like that at the time.'[39] Similarly, while many of Jones's musical contemporaries treated women with casual disregard, his own behaviour was simply appalling. It was not unknown, for example, for him to beat up girlfriends if they stood up to him; even girls who spent just one night with him would reappear the following morning 'battered and bruised'.[40]

Cheltenham in the early sixties boasted a very small bohemian set, largely made up of art students, aspiring musicians and CND supporters who gathered in coffee bars like the Aztec and the Waikiki and listened to jazz.[41] Through this circle, Jones steadily graduated from jazz to blues, but what made him unusual was the sheer intensity of his interest. He was unquestionably more knowledgeable than either of his Dartford counterparts; as Bill Wyman puts it, he 'nursed an absolute fervour for true American blues', and it was this 'obsession' that made the Rolling Stones 'different from every other pop group'.[42] It was this intensity that made him seek out Alexis Korner after the Barber band played in Cheltenham in 1961, and it also impelled him to follow Korner to London not long afterwards.

There he took a job as an appliance salesman and spent his evenings drifting through various clubs, keen to start his own group playing traditional American blues.[43]

In May 1962 Jones placed a classified advertisement in *Jazz News*, appealing for four like-minded musicians to join his new band. The first successful applicant was Ian Stewart, a down-to-earth Scottish jazz pianist who was impressed by Jones's seriousness and knowledge of American music.[44] A few weeks later they began playing with three blues enthusiasts whom they had met through Alexis Korner. Mick Jagger, Keith Richards and Dick Taylor were regular visitors to Korner's Ealing club, and Jagger occasionally appeared onstage as a singer with Blues Incorporated. After various rehearsals, Jones and his friends settled on their line-up and arranged their first performance at the Marquee in place of Blues Incorporated, who were appearing on the BBC show *Jazz Club*. On 11 July *Jazz News* reported:

> Mick Jagger, R&B vocalist, is taking a rhythm and blues group into the Marquee tomorrow night (Thursday) while Blues Inc. is doing its *Jazz Club* gig.
>
> Called 'The Rolling Stones' ('I hope they don't think they're a rock 'n' roll outfit,' says Mick), the line-up is: Jagger (vocals), Keith Richards, Elmo Lewis (guitars), Dick Taylor (bass), 'Stu' (piano), Mick Avery (drums).

'Elmo Lewis' was Jones, who had adopted what he thought was a suitable blues pseudonym; 'Stu' was Ian Stewart; 'Mick Avery' was actually Mick Avory, the future Kinks drummer; and the group's name was inspired by the Muddy Waters song 'Rollin' Stone Blues'.[45] As Jagger had told *Jazz News*, they were very definitely a blues band, not a 'rock 'n' roll outfit'. That Jagger had been quoted at all, rather than 'Elmo Lewis', was also slightly misleading, for Brian Jones was the acknowledged 'leader' of the group, the 'inventor and inspiration', without whom the Rollin' Stones would never have existed.[46]

Although rhythm and blues was on the rise in 1962, the Rollin' Stones initially found it very hard going. They had great difficulty securing bookings, were rejected by many fans for being too raucous, and generally struggled to make ends meet. The few concerts they did play tended to be at the Marquee, where they met with indifference and abuse from regular patrons, and weekend dances in suburban church halls and sports clubs.

Mick Avory had little feel for rhythm and blues and never became a permanent fixture, while Dick Taylor left just before Christmas to begin a course at the Royal College of Art. Jagger, meanwhile, was still spending his days at the LSE, leaving Richards and Jones alone in the shabby flat they shared at 102 Edith Grove, Chelsea, idling around the house for hours making faces at each other.[47]

For all the glitter of Macmillan's affluent society in the early years of the sixties, it was no fun being poor. The flat was almost stereotypically awful: two rooms in an extremely dingy house, with 'peeling wallpaper, grubby furniture, filthy curtains and naked light bulbs that functioned at the behest of a single, ironclad electric meter'.[48] The winter of 1962–3 was one of the worst in living memory: the water pipes froze solid, and they could not even pull the chain on their grubby toilet. The three musicians lived on potatoes and eggs liberated from local grocery shops and stale bread scavenged from their neighbours' parties; their laundry was sent to Keith Richards' mother Doris, who also used to send them cash and even food parcels. When their new bass player visited his colleagues' flat in December, he thought it 'looked like it was bomb-damaged . . . piled high with dirty dishes, and filth everywhere'. If that were not enough, 'their habits were disgusting': the three young men used to spit on the walls and then write an appropriate caption next to their dried spittle: 'Yellow Humphrey', say, or 'Polka-dot Perkins'. And their taste in entertainment was peculiar, to say the least. They had wired up a microphone in their bathroom, so that any guest would be entertained with tape recordings of his own ablutions as well as notable performances by previous visitors.[49]

Despite their spectacular lack of success, by January 1963 the Rollin' Stones had acquired two new members. The first to join was a young working-class man from Penge, who was six years older than Jagger and Richards, already had a wife and child, and had little sympathy with their bohemian lifestyle. Bill Perks had grown up in considerable poverty in the forties, managed to win a scholarship to the local grammar school and, after a period of National Service, became a storekeeper with an engineering firm. By this point he had changed his name to Bill Wyman, imitating a friend from his conscript days with the RAF in West Germany.[50] Wyman was initially suspicious of the Stones' 'bohemian and arty' appearance, which offended the smart standards of the pop circles in which he moved. He also had little interest in their obscure blues favourites, but since his equipment was far better than anything they had ever used, they were happy to welcome him aboard.[51] All the same, Wyman knew that the three flat-sharers resented his marriage, his fatherhood and his regular income, and throughout his time with the Rolling Stones, he never quite shook off the feeling of being an outsider.[52]

The other newcomer was Charlie Watts, an extremely accomplished drummer who had recently given up playing with Blues Incorporated because he wanted to concentrate on his career as a graphic designer. Another working-class Londoner, Watts was a lugubrious, rather mournful-looking character. His real interest was modern jazz, and as a teenager in the fifties he had learned his drumming skills by playing along to jazz records. However, he felt that rhythm and blues was likely to be the more successful genre in the short term, and in January 1963 he finally yielded to the entreaties of the Rollin' Stones to come and play with them.[53] Unlike the other members of the group, Watts remained indifferent throughout to the pleasures and perils of stardom, reserving his enthusiasm for jazz music, his wife Shirley, and his various collections of silver, model soldiers and American military memorabilia. Although he was a quite different character from the Beatles' drummer Ringo Starr, he fulfilled a strikingly similar role, keeping his feet on the ground and representing the calm, unflappable centre around which his fellow musicians giddily revolved.[54]

The Rollin' Stones' first big break came in February 1963. As luck would have it, Giorgio Gomelsky, a black-bearded Georgian émigré and jazz connoisseur, had opened a new club, the Crawdaddy, on Sunday nights at the Station Hotel in Richmond, and was on the lookout for new groups. After weeks of pestering, Jones finally persuaded him to engage the Stones. Their first performance, on 24 February 1963, went very well: they were far more aggressive than most rhythm and blues groups, and the audience clearly enjoyed themselves.[55] One watching promoter observed:

> I honestly didn't know whether to laugh at the Stones or call for an animal trainer. I'd never seen anything like them. It was a matter of atmosphere. They seemed in a world of their own as they played music that electrified the whole place. Kids watching had never sampled this sort of thing and didn't know what to make of it at first. But they'd heard a sound that knocked most of the other groups right off the scene.[56]

By the late spring of 1963 the Rollin' Stones had established a reputation for the raw vigour of their performances and the unbridled enthusiasm of their fans. On 13 April the group had their first press coverage in the *Richmond and Twickenham Times*, a clipping that Brian Jones proudly carried around for months. Interestingly, the writer saw the band not as a pop act like the Beatles but as a jazz group, noting their appeal to 'jazz beatniks' rather than the teenage girls who tended to buy pop singles. On the club's first night, he observed, there had been about fifty people; now there were more than three hundred every Sunday, wearing 'long hair, suede jackets, gaucho trousers and Chelsea boots' which marked them out as 'funny' in the eyes of the Station Hotel's regulars. And in an increasingly common aside, the writer remarked that 'physically the Rollin' Stones also provide visual entertainment', with their 'hair worn Piltdown-style, brushed forward from the crown like the Beatles pop group'. His conclusion, however, was reassuring enough. 'The Stones', he said, 'will go on Rolling.'[57]

The most promising sign of the Rollin' Stones' growing prestige came the very next evening. Soon after the band had begun their weekly set, they noticed four shadowy figures slipping into the back of the audience. 'I became very nervous,' Bill Wyman recalled, 'and said to myself: "Shit, that's the *Beatles*!"' The Liverpudlian chart-toppers had dropped in after filming for television in Twickenham, and they were happy to share a few drinks with their young rivals. At this stage the Beatles were already national stars, while, for all their success in Richmond, the Stones were, to put it bluntly, nobodies. Still, the two groups got on pretty well, and the Beatles invited their new friends to their concert at the Royal Albert Hall the following Thursday. The Rollin' Stones were clearly delighted, and on the day Jagger, Richards and Jones even carried the Beatles' guitars in for them so that they did not have to buy tickets, a moment that clearly illustrated the balance of power between the two groups.

These encounters meant a great deal to the Rollin' Stones. Wyman noticed that Brian Jones was excited for days afterwards, and 'seemed desperate for success'.[58] Wyman even thought that Jones, Jagger and Richards 'idolized' and were 'totally starstruck by the Beatles'. This was not a temporary infatuation: even after they had become international stars in their own right, the more prominent members of the Rolling Stones still regarded the Beatles with great admiration, copying their innovations and even turning up to nightclubs where the Beatles might be present.[59] Indeed, although the press continually presented the two groups as keen rivals, it makes more sense to see them as contemporaries and friends, albeit with the Stones as very much the junior partners.

It was two weeks after their encounter with the Beatles that the Rollin' Stones met Andrew Loog Oldham for the first time. Oldham was enormously impressed by the band's performance at the Crawdaddy and by the beginning of May had signed a three-year management deal with them. Despite all his patter, however, he was a mere nineteen years old and had no real experience of managing a successful group. He therefore took on a partner, Eric Easton, a balding, blunt Lancastrian, steeped in showbiz. Easton is often overlooked by chroniclers of the Rolling Stones, but his role illustrates the extent to which the pop groups of the sixties embraced the showbusiness traditions of the past.[60] Oldham and Easton rapidly lined up a record deal with Decca's A&R chief Dick Rowe, who had the unenviable reputation as 'the man who had turned down the Beatles' and was desperate to make up for his mistake. Rowe had already heard about the Rollin' Stones from George Harrison, so the deal with Decca was relatively straightforward.[61]

Oldham now took the opportunity to present two important changes to his new charges. First, he told Jones and Jagger that Decca had signed them as the 'Rolling', not 'Rollin'', Stones, adding caustically: 'How can you expect people to take you seriously when you can't even spell your name properly?' And second, he persuaded them that a group with six people was too unwieldy and added that Ian Stewart, the pianist, 'was ugly and spoiled the "look" of the group'.[62] Just as the Beatles had dumped their drummer Pete Best on the orders of George Martin, the Stones now proved equally ruthless. Unlike Best, though, Stewart elected to stay with the band that had dismissed him, becoming their driver, road manager and 'guardian' of their blues roots for the next twenty years. Brian Jones rather rashly promised Stewart that he would have 'a sixth of everything', a pledge that was never kept and which weighed heavily on the consciences of some of his colleagues.[63]

At precisely the point when Oldham was taking charge of the Rolling Stones, the Beatles were decisively strengthening their grip on the domestic charts. It was not surprising, therefore, that Oldham initially modelled his new charges on the Liverpudlians, even down to their neat stage suits. On 4 May Oldham and Easton took the boys to Carnaby Street and chose a set of matching jackets with velvet half-collars, round-collared shirts, thin ties and Cuban-heeled boots. Only Wyman agreed to wear the full ensemble, although he grumbled that Oldham was 'attempting to make us look like the Beatles'.[64] Indeed, at this stage, the Rolling Stones were seen not as rebels but as inheritors of existing pop traditions, and Keith Richards was even persuaded to drop the *s* from his surname so that he would have 'a more pop sound', like Cliff Richard.[65]

From the middle of 1963 onwards, the Rolling Stones' star began inexorably to rise. On 11 May the *Record Mirror* reported:

> At the Station Hotel, Richmond, the hip kids throw themselves about to the new 'jungle music' like they never did in the more restrained days of Trad. And the combo they writhe and twist to is called The Rolling Stones. Maybe you haven't heard of them — if you live far from London, the odds are you haven't. But by gad you will! The Stones are destined to be the biggest group in the R&B scene, if that scene continues to flourish.[66]

To the public at large, however, the Rolling Stones were still almost entirely unknown, and their first single, a Chuck Berry cover, 'Come On', met a fairly lukewarm reception, peaking at number twenty-six in the *NME* chart. The singer Craig Douglas told *Melody Maker* that the song was 'very, very ordinary . . . If there was a Liverpool accent it might get somewhere but this is definitely no hit.'[67]

But despite the relative disappointment of 'Come On', the Stones continued to gather momentum. Both Wyman and Watts left their jobs in order to devote themselves to the band, and Eric Easton arranged for the Rolling Stones to spend the next few months touring the country supporting visiting American acts. It was hard work, but since it was what the band had dreamed of for more than a year, it was worth it. And it also had its comic moments, like the matinée at the Co-op Ballroom, Nuneaton, where the Stones 'faced a room full of kids aged from about six to ten, who were in the middle of their afternoon tea'. Few audiences were as unforgiving as these diminutive connoisseurs from Warwickshire. 'They didn't appreciate R&B,' Bill Wyman sadly recalled, 'and the little perishers proceeded to throw cream cakes at us throughout our set.'[68]

On 30 September the last member of the Rolling Stones with a foot in the 'real', non-musical world made his mind up to concentrate on the group. 'I have been offered a really excellent opportunity in the entertainment world,' Mick Jagger wrote to the Kent Education Committee, explaining his decision to leave the London School of Economics.[69] Indeed, the popularity of his group was growing steadily. When the *New Musical Express* conducted its annual poll at the end of 1963, the Rolling Stones finished sixth in the 'British Vocal Group' category and fifth in the 'British

Small Group' section. Clearly there was still some way to go: in the Vocal Group poll they had picked up 745 votes, which looked pretty feeble when compared with the Beatles' 18,623.[70]

Meanwhile, the Beatles had already offered their friends a new single, 'I Wanna Be Your Man,' written by McCartney and Lennon. Thanks to its association with the Fab Four, this latest release peaked in December at number thirteen. The Stones were inexorably inching their way up the charts, and at last the national media were beginning to take note. As 1964 began, the *Daily Sketch* asked:

> Who would have thought a few months ago that half Britain's teenagers would end the year with heads like hairy pudding-basins? The Stones look straight out of the Stone Age. Already, with just one disc in the hit parade, they've reached fifth place in *Melody Maker*'s ratings. Their success seems to lie in their off-handedness. 'We just please ourselves,' they say. But remember, millions of teenagers in 1964 may end up looking like them.[71]

Pop chroniclers often characterise 1964 as the year of the Rolling Stones, just as 1963 had belonged to the Beatles. In fact, the Stones were nowhere near as successful in 1964 as the Beatles had been the previous year, and they had to wait until the beginning of July for their first number one single, 'It's All Over Now'. Such was the group's momentum, however, that their first album, *The Rolling Stones*, knocked *With The Beatles* off the top of the LP charts that spring, and on 20 November their next single, 'Little Red Rooster', entered the *NME* chart at number one, a feat hitherto reserved only for Elvis Presley and, more recently, the Beatles.[72] Written by the American blues singer Willie Dixon, 'Little Red Rooster' was a slow blues ballad, entirely unlike the beat numbers that dominated the charts. As one of the Stones later put it, 'the tempo made the track virtually undanceable', which made its success all the more impressive.[73]

Unlike most of the Beatles' competitors, the Rolling Stones were able to sustain and build upon their initial success. Their next five singles, 'The Last Time', '(I Can't Get No) Satisfaction', 'Get Off My Cloud', 'Nineteenth Nervous Breakdown' and 'Paint It Black', all testified to the versatility and maturation of their talents, as the Stones began to evolve into the most controversial rock band in the world. At the same time, their next three albums, *The Rolling Stones No. 2*, *Out of Our Heads* and *Aftermath*, reached first, second and first place in the charts, respectively; and in June 1965 they conquered the American charts with the iconic, snarling '(I Can't Get No) Satisfaction'. That October, when their next American album, *December's Children (and Everybody's)*, was advertised in Times Square with a giant billboard showing the Stones' portraits, taken by David Bailey, in a sixty-by-forty-foot blow-up, it was clear to all the world that the Rolling Stones had made it.[74]

Amid all the excitement and controversy of the Rolling Stones' rise to fame at home and abroad, one development, little noticed at the time, was to have profound consequences for the group. When Andrew Oldham walked into the Crawdaddy Club in April 1963, the Stones were still unquestionably Brian Jones's band. It was Jones who had put the group together, arranged the performances, selected the songs, collected the money, paid the bills and so on. But at almost exactly the point when the Stones started to become successful, Jones's importance began to decline. For one thing, he simply did not have the temperament or the constitution to survive the rigours of touring and playing full time. As early as August 1963, while the Stones were on their nationwide tour playing second fiddle to various Americans, Jones collapsed with nervous exhaustion and had to skip several dates. A week or so later he collapsed again, this time breaking out in a rash for good measure. His fellow-musicians noticed that he always looked tired and haggard, but assumed he was simply a hypochondriac. As one recalled, his 'illnesses became a band joke'.[75]

Jones's physical weakness was only one element in his gradual decline. In October 1963 the other Stones discovered that he was being paid a little extra for being the 'leader' of the band, and that he was insisting on being put up in better hotels than his colleagues. They immediately protested, and although from that moment they were all nominally equal, the momentum was clearly shifting towards Jagger and Richards. By 1964 Jagger, Richards and Oldham were all living together, with Jones on his own in Belgravia, and his position seemed to be crumbling by the week. Oldham would sometimes switch off Jones's microphone while he was singing, or fade out his instrument during playbacks, and although Jones knew that something was up, he was incapable of putting up any resistance. 'Brian would try to ingratiate himself by crawling first to Mick and then to Andrew, which didn't do any good,' recalled Bill Wyman. 'He should simply have been strong in himself.'[76] A stronger character might have been able to fight back, but since Jones was already extremely sensitive and insecure, this was never likely. Even as the Rolling Stones were taking their first steps towards international stardom, he had already begun the inexorable slide that would end in tragedy five years later.

More than any other group of the sixties, the Rolling Stones were the embodiment of pop music at its most controversial. In July 1963 the band provoked a brief furore when they made their television debut on ATV's Saturday night pop show *Thank Your Lucky Stars*. Even though they appeared at the bottom of the bill for little more than a minute and were dressed in their matching uniforms of checked jackets and smart slacks, the Stones still managed to offend enough viewers to jam the switchboard. 'It's disgusting that long-haired louts such as these should be allowed to appear on television,' wrote one disgruntled viewer. Another wrote to the band personally: 'The whole lot of you should be given a good bath, then all that hair should be cut off . . . I'm not against pop music when it's sung by a nice clean boy like Cliff Richard, but you are a disgrace. Your filthy appearance is likely to corrupt teenagers all over the country.'[77]

Both the Beatles and the Rolling Stones attracted considerable press comment because of the length of their hair, which carried connotations of effeminacy, dirtiness and dissidence. However, since the Beatles went out of their way to present themselves as friendly young men, they were never treated with anything like the vituperation that greeted the Stones. Rhythm and blues had no chart history before 1964: many older listeners had never heard anything like it, and it therefore sounded much more 'extreme' than the kind of music played by the Beatles. At the same time, because most rhythm and blues groups had rather bohemian roots, they affected a generally scruffy and rebellious style, with long hair and disorganised clothing, so it was easy for the press to present them as dangerous extremists from the very beginning.[78]

By the spring of 1964, even before they had scored their first number one, the Rolling Stones had become the favourite bogeymen of the national press. 'They look like boys whom any self-respecting mum would lock in the bathroom!' commented the *Daily Express* on 28 February, calling them 'five tough young London-based music makers with doorstep mouths, pallid cheeks and unkempt hair'.[79] A month later Maureen Cleave, the influential pop writer of the *Evening Standard* and the first major journalist to champion the Beatles, entered the fray:

> This horrible lot are not quite what they seem . . . they've done terrible things to the music scene, set it back, I would say, about eight years. Just

when we'd got our pop singers looking neat and tidy and, above all, *cheerful*, along come The Rolling Stones, looking almost like what we used to call beatniks . . . They've wrecked the image of the pop singer of the sixties . . . Girls stop and stare in the street, men shout things that are unrestrainedly rude, the Hilton Hotel shows them the door and so do many provincial pubs.[80]

A few days later *Melody Maker* ran the tongue-in-cheek headline 'WOULD YOU LET YOUR SISTER GO WITH A ROLLING STONE?' Maureen Cleave promptly borrowed the phrase for her next discussion of the group on 14 April, heavily emphasising their supposed sexual threat:

BUT WOULD YOU LET YOUR DAUGHTER MARRY ONE? Parents do not like The Rolling Stones. They do not want their sons to grow up like them; they do not want their daughters to marry them.

Never have the middle-class virtues of neatness, obedience and punctuality been so conspicuously lacking as they are in The Rolling Stones. The Rolling Stones are not the people you build empires with; they are not the people who always remember to wash their hands before lunch.[81]

Cleave's articles set the standard for the press treatment of the Rolling Stones, and in future no self-respecting journalist wrote about the band without mentioning the length of their hair, their dissolute morals and their general dirtiness and aggression. Even though Brian Jones was known to his fellow musicians as 'Mr Shampoo' because he washed his hair twice a day, he still came in for criticism, and the president of the National Federation of Hairdressers said that he looked 'as though he has got a feather duster on his head'.[82] Jones was having none of it. 'My hair is not a gimmick,' he angrily told *Melody Maker*. 'It doesn't strike me as dirty, scruffy or effeminate. To be honest, I think it looks good.'[83]

Mick Jagger, too, was a frequent target, and when he pleaded guilty in November 1964 to three minor traffic offences in Tettenhall, a middle-class suburb of Wolverhampton, his solicitor felt compelled to issue a long plea that the length of his client's hair should not count against him:

Put out of your minds the nonsense talked about these young men. They are not long-haired idiots but highly intelligent university men. The Duke of Marlborough had much longer hair than my client, and he won some famous battles. *His* hair was powdered, I think because of fleas. My client has no fleas! The Emperor Caesar Augustus was another with rather long hair. He won many great victories. Long hair is worn by barristers in court curled up at the ends . . .

This unhappy country suffers from a perennial disease called the balance of payments crisis and it needs every dollar it [can] earn. The Rolling Stones earn more dollars than many professional exporters.[84]

All of this publicity meant that by the beginning of 1965, the Rolling Stones were already household names, less for their music than for their controversial appearance and demeanour. This was the background to the most infamous incident of their early years, which took place on the evening of 18 March as they were driving home from a concert in Romford. After twenty minutes, the band's chauffeur-driven Daimler pulled into the forecourt of the Francis service station in Stratford, East London. To the horror of the manager, Charles Keeley, a 'shaggy-haired monster', later identified as Bill Wyman, approached him and asked 'in disgusting language' if he could use the toilet. Keeley refused, at which point the other Stones and various hangers-on joined the fray. Notable among them was Mick Jagger, who announced: 'We piss anywhere, man', and attempted to negotiate with the service station staff. Keeley then shouted: 'Get off my forecourt!', which provoked Brian Jones to dance around singing: 'Get off my foreskin!', and the episode finally ended with Wyman, Jagger and Jones urinating on the forecourt wall and then driving off in triumph in their Daimler.

Keeley, however, was not one to forgive and forget. Three months later the guilty parties appeared in court in East London facing a private prosecution. They were all convicted of 'insulting behaviour' liable to cause a breach of the peace and handed a very small fine; but in the eyes of their critics the incident proved that the Rolling Stones represented nothing but anarchy and rebellion.[85] As one Scottish magistrate put it that summer, they were 'complete morons [who] wear their hair down to their shoulders, wear filthy clothes and act like clowns'.[86] And the *News of the World*, later to become a bitter enemy of the band, spoke for millions when it declared that they were 'wallowing in a swill-tub of their own repulsiveness'.[87]

The Rolling Stones' image had been carefully cultivated by the group's manager to maximise their commercial appeal. Andrew Loog Oldham was well aware that it would be very difficult to compete with the Beatles on their own turf, and decided that the market needed 'a sort of anti-Beatles, something the kids could keep for themselves, something their parents could never, ever smile tolerantly on'.[88] From the end of 1963 onwards, therefore, he consciously set out to cast his boys as 'the group parents loved to hate ... dangerous, dirty and degenerate', and instructed them to 'be as nasty as they could wish to be'.[89] Indeed, Oldham was so fond of publicity that he made no secret of his strategy. 'If parents begin to like the Stones,' he told one interviewer, 'the teenagers who made that group will begin to feel they're losing them to older people and discard the group. I've made sure the Stones will not be liked too much by older people.'[90]

Clearly the Rolling Stones' reputation partly reflected their own rebelliousness, but this is nevertheless frequently exaggerated. In his book *The Teenage Revolution* (1965), the journalist Peter Laurie noted that 'off stage they are quiet and modest; and Mick Jagger, their leader [sic], is unusually friendly and intelligent'.[91] In fact, the latent conservatism of the Rolling Stones was one of their most striking characteristics. Although both Brian Jones and Keith Richards had been teenage tearaways, Wyman and Watts had held down steady jobs, while Jagger had been an economics student at one of the country's most prestigious institutions. When challenged about his long hair, Wyman even told his mother: 'Mum, it's only for about three years, and I'll get a nice car and a nice house, fully furnished, out of it.'[92]

Charlie Watts, meanwhile, showed little interest in the trappings of fame, and his mother was baffled by his association with a group like the Stones:

> He's always been a good boy. Never had any police knocking on the door or anything like that. And he's always been terribly kind to old people. He was always a neat dresser. That's why I get perturbed when they're called ugly and dirty. When he's home you can't get him out of the bathroom. People think he's moody. But he's not really. He's just quiet. He hates fuss and gossip.[93]

Even Keith Richards, later celebrated as the bad boy *par excellence*, had his conservative side. Not only was he a keen fan of the comedian Max Miller, he liked nothing more than to ape the style of an English country gentleman, especially in his beautiful Sussex mansion, Redlands. A dedicated bibliophile, he was later forced to cancel several concert dates after falling off a ladder while searching for Leonardo da Vinci's book on anatomy.[94] Like many of his fellow musicians, he was also a model of filial loyalty, always keeping in touch with his mother during tours and regularly sending her expensive presents. Every Friday night Charlie Watts, too, sent his mother her favourite coffee gateau.[95]

By the end of 1965 pop music had already evolved to an extent that would have seemed barely conceivable just a few years earlier. The popular performers of the early sixties, like Cliff Richard, Acker Bilk and Frank Ifield, had rapidly fallen from fashion, and a new direction was becoming clear in the confrontational stage presence and raucous sound of bands like the Kinks and the Animals. At the same time, the Rolling Stones had effectively redefined the cultural associations of pop music, moving the focus from love to sex and cultivating an uncompromising, even violent attitude. This both drew on their roots in the narcissistic pessimism of the blues tradition, and appealed to an older and more bohemian audience.[96] So while the Beatles' early hits had been sentimental and good-humoured, appealing to teenagers and adults alike, the songs of the Stones and their contemporaries were cynical and belligerent, appealing to disaffected adolescents. And while the Beatles had sung about innocent, idealised love affairs, the Animals sang about a whorehouse in New Orleans and the Stones projected an image of aggressive, predatory sexuality that often alarmed adult listeners.[97]

The challenge that now faced the Rolling Stones was exactly the same as that confronted by the Beatles after the triumph of their American tour in 1964: what next? New groups like the Yardbirds and the Who were already beginning to threaten their reputation as the country's foremost interpreters of the blues and its most aggressive pop stars, and it was far from impossible that, like the Shadows and the Tornados before them, the Rolling Stones would soon fall from favour. As so often in their career, they turned to their greatest rivals for inspiration.

In December 1965 the Beatles released their record tenth consecutive number one single, 'Day Tripper/We Can Work It Out', and in the *NME* end-of-year poll they retained their position in both the World and British Vocal Group categories, easily beating off the Stones and their lesser rivals.[98] That Christmas they also had Britain's number one album, *Rubber Soul*, a sign of things to come. It was the fruit of weeks of painstaking work in the studio, with each song a delicately constructed compilation of endless vocal, rhythm and instrumental tracks, put together with the latest technology by the group's producer, George Martin. *Rubber Soul*, said Martin, presented 'a new Beatles to the world', making albums that they hoped would be seen as 'art in their own right'.[99]

Once again the Beatles had left their rivals, not least the Rolling Stones, in their wake, and they looked forward to 1966 with renewed enthusiasm. 'What do we hope for in 1966?' wondered Paul McCartney during an interview. 'That's a tricky one. For everything to go smoothly and swing on, I suppose. For happiness. For health. For things to be just right.' And what about McCartney's own personal ambitions? 'I know I'd welcome a bit of peace and quiet now and again,' he said wistfully. 'Being so well-known can sometimes be a disadvantage! But you can't have everything, can you?'[100]

9

WOMEN! WIN MR HEATH!

> I was rather surprised to see Harold standing on the breakfast table performing a strange dance with the Inspector. 'Have a care,' I cried, 'you will overturn the Wheatipuffs!' Harold then uttered a word which I can only imagine he picked up from watching the television, leapt down from the table, and planted a kiss on my still rather inflamed nose. 'Eighteen per cent NOP lead, Gladys!' he cried, waving the *Daily Mail* in my face, 'so much for Edward Heath!', and he indicated with his finger and thumb the size of Mr Heath's standing in the eyes of the nation.
>
> 'Mrs Wilson's Diary', *Private Eye*, 26 November 1965

In May 1965, barely six months after the general election, the Conservatives had finally recaptured the lead over Labour in the opinion polls. In June they pulled almost 5 per cent clear, and by August, with the government beset by the latest sterling crisis, the gap reached 8 per cent, the largest Conservative lead for five years. Then, in September, there was a sudden and apparently decisive swing, as Labour not only recaptured the lead but soared almost 7 per cent clear. Just as Wilson's friends abroad had finally done him a good turn, so his enemies at home seemed suddenly to have shot themselves in the foot.[1]

The Conservatives had not taken well to life in exile, which was hardly surprising given that until October 1964 they had been in power for thirteen years. Sir Alec Douglas-Home's understated, patrician style seemed ill suited to the rigours of leading a party in opposition, and speculation about a possible successor was soon under way.[2] One old heavyweight was already shuffling off the stage: in January 1965, four days after Churchill's funeral, Rab Butler accepted the mastership of Trinity College, Cambridge, and a life peerage. Twice he had been the favourite to take over as Prime Minister; twice he had been thwarted by his own diffidence and the machinations of others. Instead he had the distinction of having served as Chancellor, Foreign Secretary and Home Secretary without ever getting his hands on the ultimate prize. 'I think I could have made quite a tolerable leader,' he wrote later that year, and indeed many historians regard him as the outstanding Prime Minister who never was.[3]

When Wilson announced on 26 June that he would not be calling a general election that year, many Conservatives thought that this was the moment for Home to step down so that a younger leader could have time to prepare for an election in 1966. The very next morning the *Sunday Express* ran a front-page exclusive claiming that a hundred Conservative MPs were involved in a 'bid to oust Sir Alec', and the pressure increased. Home probably could have stayed on if he had wanted, but he had lost his appetite for the fight. On 15 July an NOP poll found that voters thought Wilson was the more 'sincere' of the two leaders, and three days later the *Sunday Times* published an editorial entitled 'The Right Moment to Change', congratulating Home on having 'played the sort of captain's innings one used to see in county cricket before the war', but inviting him to hand over the captaincy.[4] On 22 July, at a meeting of the backbench 1922 Committee, he finally announced his resignation – although this was not quite the end of Sir Alec Douglas-Home in British politics.[5]

At the beginning of the year the Conservatives had finally overhauled their method of choosing a leader, and under the new system there would be a secret ballot of MPs to pick Home's successor. Three candidates eventually came forward: the expected front-runners, Reginald Maudling and Edward Heath, and a dark horse, Enoch Powell. Few observers gave Powell much of a chance; he had already resigned twice from the Cabinet and was seen as a rather intense and eccentric figure. His supporters tended to be younger members, keen for the party to adopt a more radical cutting edge. Indeed, his two most energetic campaigners, John Biffen and Nicholas Ridley, would later go on to become important figures in the rise of Thatcherism more than a decade later. At this stage, however, Powell's intentions were relatively modest. He did not expect to win, although he was disappointed to attract only as few votes as he did. 'I left my visiting card,' he said dryly a few years later.[6]

Maudling was the clear favourite. On 26 July, the day before the ballot, an NOP poll for the *Daily Mail* showed him leading Heath by 44 per cent to 28 per cent among the electorate in general, and by 48 per cent to 31 per cent among Conservative voters.[7] Both were seen as modernisers, and both were committed to Keynesian economics, the welfare state and the maintenance of full employment.[8] The election would therefore be fought on the grounds of style and personality. On the same day that the NOP poll appeared, the BBC devoted the *Panorama* programme to a profile of the three contenders. Maudling, apparently, was backed 'by those who back brain-power above energy, and judgement above drive ... Reggie is the man for those Conservatives who want the driver at the wheel to be steady, sound and shrewd.' This all made him sound a slightly boring choice, especially when set against Heath, who was portrayed as 'thrustful, pugnacious, aggressive ... the man for those Conservatives who think the party needs "a tiger in its tank"'.[9]

Although the two front-runners came from similar middle-class backgrounds and were both Oxford-educated scholarship boys, their images were entirely different. Maudling was seen as the more old-fashioned Establishment candidate; Heath was presented as a more modern, dynamic professional figure, a kind of Conservative answer to Harold Wilson.[10] Of the three potential candidates, Heath was the only one who had not been damaged in any way by the controversial leadership campaign of 1963, and he had steadily been gaining ground ever since.[11] After the election he was appointed Shadow Chancellor, which allowed him to get stuck into Wilson's economic misfortunes, while Maudling served as Shadow Foreign Secretary, which was by comparison something of a backwater.[12] Heath's aggressive displays in the Commons went down very well with the press, too. After one onslaught in November 1964 the *Guardian* had crowned him 'the hatchet man of the Opposition' and praised his 'jaunty but aggressive speech' which 'slashed at the Government, goaded Labour backbenchers to sustained anger and moved Mr George Brown in particular to positive fury'. It was 'astonishing', the paper said, to see how the hitherto worthy and solid Heath had become 'a new Heath with a vengeance – a blasting Heath'.[13]

Most observers agreed that Heath was a much more dynamic figure. *The Times* insisted that Britain needed 'a tough man to lead her', the *Mail* demanded 'a leader who is a man of action', and the *Daily Sketch* praised the 'fire in his belly'. Only two papers, the *Sunday Telegraph* and the *News of the World*, preferred his opponent.[14] Nevertheless, Maudling was extremely confident of victory as he looked forward to the ballot. His campaign strategy reflected his relaxed personality: he intended to treat his parliamentary colleagues as adults and to refrain from badgering them in a manner that would only annoy them. Heath, too, had adopted a strategy that reflected his personality: he had a tightly organised team of campaigners, who took care to contact every Conservative MP at least once and to make careful notes of their intentions and susceptibility to persuasion.[15] This was bound to impress those people who valued ambition and energy, while Maudling's approach ran the risk of looking complacent and was described by one of its own strategists as 'a total shambles'.[16] 'Heath really is a positive force – a leader,' noted the press baron Cecil King two days before the ballot, 'while dear Reggie, though very intelligent, does like a good lunch and parties that go on late into the night.'[17]

On the morning of 27 July the Conservative MPs filed into Committee Room 14 to cast their votes, and the result was announced that afternoon. Heath was sitting in a friend's office near by, talking nervously about his dreams for the country if he won. Maudling, as though determined to confirm everything others said about him, wandered amiably around the Commons' smoking room before heading off for lunch in the City. At two-fifteen he took a telephone call from Robert Carr, one of his supporters, who sadly reported that Powell had won 15 votes, Maudling 133 and Heath 150. Maudling had little choice but to concede. In public he remained as suave as ever: the journalist Alan Watkins bumped into him as he was returning to the Commons and later reported that, 'in his affable way', he had simply remarked: 'That was a turn-up for the book.'[18]

In his memoirs, however, Maudling admitted that the defeat came as 'a bitter blow'.[19] Enoch Powell remembered that he kept asking: 'What went wrong? Why did I lose?' In answer Powell pointed out that after the general election Maudling had immediately taken on three important directorships, one of them full-time, therefore bolstering the impression that essentially 'you weren't interested any longer'.[20] This was an underestimate. In the aftermath of their defeat in 1964 Heath had taken on just one directorship. Maudling had accumulated thirteen.[21]

At forty-nine, Edward Heath was the youngest Conservative leader in living memory. Like Harold Wilson, his elder by four months, he could point to a life of hard work and self-discipline. He had been born and brought up in Broadstairs, a Kentish seaside resort known for its quiet prosperity and middle-class respectability. His parents, like Wilson's, were intensely ambitious for their son and happy to make the necessary sacrifices for his advancement. And, again like Wilson, Heath had grown up in the sober and thrifty world where the skilled working class met the lower middle class. His father was an accomplished carpenter who ended up running his own business and was one of the most reliable contractors in the area. He worked hard and did well, and the young Heath wanted for very little.[22]

Growing up in Broadstairs, Teddy Heath was almost eerily perfect: always beautifully turned out, never one to join a gang or indulge in schoolboy high jinks, never even one to join the other boys for a game of marbles when he could be doing something more constructive. Even as a boy he was remarkably self-contained and focused, spending hours reading quietly in his bedroom. He had little time for team sports; only solitary activities like swimming and cycling attracted his interest. At home, the best armchair was reserved for him; he was excused from washing-up duties so that he could concentrate on his homework; and he was even bought his own piano so that he could practise at home. He was the classic spoiled prodigy who grows up with a broad streak of selfishness; later in life, in the words of his biographer John Campbell, 'he often seemed to take it for granted that everyone around him was there to do things for him'.[23] Perhaps only Heath could have called his dog 'Erg', after his own initials.[24]

Both Wilson and Heath were, in their different ways, grown-up school swots. However, while Wilson was the eternal Boy Scout, Heath was more the stereotypical head prefect. For all his eager enthusiasm, Wilson always had a breezy, cheeky side. By contrast, Heath was like some Spartan school captain from the pages of the *Boy's Own Paper*. At his grammar school, he conducted the school orchestra, was secretary of the debating society, served as a prefect and was unsparing in his pursuit of other boys whose dress and demeanour were not up to scratch. 'He thought that breaking a school rule amounted to disloyalty to the school,' one master recalled.[25] His final school report would leave most parents glowing with pleasure but most teenage boys cringing with embarrassment. 'I cannot speak too highly of the tremendous work he has done,' wrote his music teacher. 'He has been a help to me and an inspiration to the boys. As a conductor of choirs, both here and elsewhere, he has been outstanding; as a performer he has been successful; in orchestral work he has had splendid opportunities of widening his experience.' His headmaster went even further: 'The purity of his ideals, his loyalty to them and his sense of duty have made him outstanding among the boys who have helped to build the school. That his mental and moral worth may have the reward they deserve is my wish for him.'[26]

Like Wilson, Heath was a student at Oxford in the heady days of the late thirties. He won an organ scholarship to Balliol, the most prestigious, egalitarian and intellectually powerful of the colleges, before enlisting in the

Royal Artillery at the outbreak of war. Much of his college life was taken up with directing choirs, conducting orchestras and even composing.[27] But unlike Harold Wilson, he was indisputably one of the leading undergraduates of his generation, becoming president of the Balliol Junior Common Room, the Oxford Union, the Conservative Association and the nationwide Federation of University Conservative Associations as well as carrying out his musical duties and working for a solid second-class degree.[28] And unlike Wilson, he was good friends with the other rising stars of the time, like Denis Healey and Roy Jenkins. It was one of the ironies of post-war politics that two of Heath's most effective adversaries during his period as Conservative leader should be old friends from the same Oxford college.[29]

Perhaps the most important experiences of Heath's early life were his European journeys, first as a student and then as a soldier. In 1937 he visited southern Germany and was a guest at a Nazi rally in Nuremberg, where he heard a speech by Hitler and afterwards was invited to a party where he met Goebbels, Goering and Himmler, whom he found 'insignificant-looking', 'bulky and genial' and 'drooping', respectively.[30] He returned to Britain a passionate critic of appeasement, and the following summer went to Spain as a guest of the Republican government. This was his first experience of war, and nearly his last. On one occasion, a plane carrying him to Madrid came under fire from Nationalist batteries; a few days later his car was machine-gunned by a Nationalist plane; and then a bomb fell on his hotel in Barcelona.[31] Having lived to tell the tale, he enlisted in the army during the Second World War and fought his way through France and the Low Countries in 1944 and 1945. At one point he was told to organise the execution of a soldier guilty of rape and murder; the experience, he wrote later, heavily influenced his opposition to the death penalty as Tory leader.[32]

As a student Heath was unimpressed by both state socialism and the unrestrained free market, which, taking into account his Kentish lower-middle-class background, implied that he was a natural moderate, 'One Nation' Conservative.[33] While on leave during the war, however, he did have one unlikely meeting which could have propelled him into Labour politics. After visiting his parents one night, Heath was waiting in the station tearoom for the train back from London when he bumped into Roy Jenkins's father Arthur. Mr Jenkins explained that he was waiting for Clement Attlee, then the Deputy Prime Minister, who liked to 'get away from it all' after his late-night meetings with Churchill and would therefore arrange to 'have a quiet drink together in some unusual place'.

Shortly afterwards, Attlee arrived and sat down with us, quietly smoking his pipe. 'This', said Jenkins, 'is young Heath, who was at Oxford with Roy.' 'Oh,' said Attlee. 'He's now commanding a battery of guns near the Rhine,' continued Jenkins. 'Oh,' said Attlee again. 'From what he's been saying he's obviously still interested in politics.' 'Oh,' said Attlee, for the third time. 'I think he'll make a damn good politician,' said Jenkins, ploughing on. 'I think we ought to try to grab him as one of our candidates.' 'Oh,' said Attlee. At this point the notice for my train came up, and I bade them both good night. This was the nearest I ever came to becoming a Labour candidate.[34]

Instead, Heath was selected as the Conservative candidate for Bexley, in his native Kent. With its rows of semi-detached houses, its lower-middle-class professionals and skilled workers, it was the ideal seat for an ambitious Tory moderate.[35] Since he was himself an example of social mobility, Heath had an obvious appeal to voters who were about to enjoy the fruits of affluence. Even his accent, which never sounded quite right and was probably adopted when he first went up to Oxford, suggested the kind of striving and self-improvement that might appeal to Bexley voters.[36]

In February 1950 Heath narrowly won the seat and never looked back. In 1955 Sir Anthony Eden made him Chief Whip, an impressive promotion for a man still in his thirties, and he built up a close rapport with Eden's successor, Harold Macmillan. While Macmillan dealt with the broad sweep of politics, Heath handled the nuts and bolts of parliamentary management, and they made an excellent team.[37] Between 1961 and 1963 he oversaw Britain's bid to join the Common Market, and despite de Gaulle's veto, he was widely thought to have done an excellent job.[38] It was not surprising that Macmillan viewed him as one of the party's most promising rising stars, representing 'everything that is best in the new progressive modern Tory party'.[39]

Heath was a fairly conventional Conservative MP in all respects but one: he was a bachelor. By the mid-sixties, 95 per cent of men and 96 per cent of women under the age of forty-five were married, but not Edward Heath.[40] In a period when marriage was more popular than ever before or since, this was seen as both unusual and slightly suspicious. 'An unmarried person in this country is a social misfit, and is suspect,' declared the *Sunday Pictorial*.[41] Heath had never shown a great deal of interest in girls, but there is no evidence that he was homosexual. It is more likely, as his biographer carefully explains, that he simply suppressed his sexual urges in the single-minded pursuit of his career. But professional ambition is surely not the whole story;

repression, shyness or simple lack of interest must also have contributed in varying ways. Denis Healey once remembered that, one hot summer afternoon in 1938, he was strolling through the Balliol quadrangle with Heath when he mentioned that a mutual acquaintance was going off for the weekend with his girlfriend. 'Teddy looked at me in horror,' he recalled. '"You don't mean to say they are sleeping together?" he whispered. "I don't know. I suppose so," I replied. "Good heavens," said Teddy. "I can't imagine anyone in the Conservative Association doing that."'[42]

Heath was certainly never a flirt and was often shy around women, but he did have a girlfriend as a young man, a local girl called Kay Raven. Most of his friends expected him to marry her and were surprised when he never proposed. Eventually she married a former airman instead, and Heath later admitted that he had been 'saddened' by the news.[43] With this notable exception, he was never romantically linked to a woman and never seemed particularly bothered by his bachelorhood. In the first entry in her fictitious 'diary' after Heath became leader, Mrs Wilson asks Harold 'whether we couldn't get him round for the evening to play the Hammond Organ. I am sure he often feels lonely in the evenings.'[44]

On 6 August 1965 *Private Eye* greeted Heath's election to the Conservative leadership with an enticing competition:

WOMEN!
WIN MR. <u>HEATH</u>!

2nd PRIZE * A weekend with Mr Maudling
3rd PRIZE * A lifetime with Enoch Powell

* TOUGH
* ABRASIVE
* DYNAMIC
* Superbly Professional
* MODERNISING
* Grammar School
* RUTHLESS
* Silvery Grey Hair
* ABRASIVE
* Trains run on time

Just place the above in order of preference, snip and send to Lord Gnome, 22 Greek St., London W1.[45]

'Formidable: This Man of Incisive Action', read the headline in the *Daily Sketch*, which warned Wilson that he would 'have to face a bowler who has been chosen for one purpose – to get him out'.[46] He was, said the *Mirror*, 'a new kind of Tory leader – a classless professional politician who has fought his way to the top by guts, ability and political skill'.[47] Four different newspapers used the word 'abrasive', three called him 'tough', and there seemed no end to the profiles praising Heath's energy, classlessness and professionalism. 'Do you appreciate', one interviewer asked, 'that you are the first Tory leader with wall-to-wall carpeting?'[48]

Heath's treatment by the press was reminiscent of Harold Wilson's honeymoon two years earlier. On this occasion, however, the profiles, with their talk of his 'hard, direct stare', 'astonishing capacity for hard work' and even 'ruthless dieting', teetered on the brink of self-parody.[49] One feature in the *Observer Magazine* might almost have been a spoof:

> Ted Heath likes to gather people, younger people, around him. He summons them on the telephone. They come to breakfast with him at his chambers in the Albany.
>
> Like Kennedy he is very intelligent, but no intellectual. But he ruthlessly uses intellectuals and experts to advise him, to feed him with facts . . . it is part of the technique, the computer mind at work.[50]

This kind of coverage extended to Heath's associates, too. During the mid-sixties a new generation of well-educated, professional Conservative MPs was gradually replacing the old retired colonels and knights of the shires, and the likes of Geoffrey Howe, Norman St John Stevas and Terence Higgins were beginning to make their marks.[51] Heath's lieutenants were seen as champions of the breed. Peter Walker, Edward du Cann and David Howell posed for newspaper photographs in their 'senatorially furnished' London flats, often with a portable television or Space Age telephone in the picture to add the right air of 'efficiency'.[52] Just like Wilson and his allies in 1963 and 1964, these 'whizz kids' were presented as middle-class meritocrats who would drag Britain into the technological age. 'The party lines', said the *Spectator*, 'will never be the same again.'[53]

Heath confronted Wilson in the Commons for the first time on 2 August, putting the Conservative case in a debate of censure. Many observers thought that the ruthless, abrasive Tory 'hatchet man' would soon have his opponent on the ropes. They were to be cruelly disappointed.

Visibly nervous and trying to appear statesmanlike, Heath ploughed through the government's economic record in the stodgiest and dullest fashion. Benn commented that it was 'so dull and statistical and so full of quotes that he lost the House and bored us all'.[54] Crossman delightedly called it 'a pretty good flop', and dismissed Heath as 'a second-class orator . . . He was neither a tremendous attacking force nor a statesman, and there can't have been many Tories who didn't whisper under their breath, "My God, I see the point of Maudling now."'[55]

Wilson, meanwhile, was on his very best cheeky, quick-witted form. He sarcastically reminded the House that the debate was supposed to 'transform the political scene and electrify the Conservative party', and cleverly undermined Heath's speech by praising an earlier one by Maudling, his defeated rival, adding to Labour laughter: 'It was a great pity that he did not make it a fortnight earlier.' He ended the speech in supremely mischievous style, refuting Heath's criticism of the import surcharge by revealing that the Conservatives themselves had planned to do something similar had they been re-elected. Heath sprang to his feet, 'white-faced and goaded beyond endurance', said *The Times*, to try to deny the allegation, but time had run out, and Wilson had the last word: 'The Right Honourable Gentleman is afraid. We treat his censure motion with contempt.'[56]

The humiliation of Heath's debut as leader was the first of a long series of disappointing performances. He had been built up by the press into a merciless debating machine when in fact he was nothing of the kind, and the gulf between expectation and reality was so great that he could not avoid looking like a dud. Almost every time Heath confronted Wilson in the Commons he came off the loser, like a lumbering heavyweight outsmarted by a smaller, sharper opponent. Whenever he tried to draw the House's attention to some serious point, Wilson immediately undermined him by sarcastic remarks or patronising gibes. Whenever he tried to craft a grand phrase, it sounded leaden and laboured. Whenever he tried to make a joke, it fell flat. And when he had finished speaking, Wilson would inevitably rise to the despatch box with a condescending smile. 'If he can't do better than that . . .' he would begin; or: 'The Right Honourable Gentleman really must improve . . .' Of course, this only drove Heath further into fits of bad-tempered earnestness, delighting the Labour benches and embarrassing his own supporters.[57]

Heath's bad beginning was made worse by the fact that the 'jaunty', 'swinging' character that had been presented during the leadership election was obviously a myth. Trying to look statesmanlike, he ended up appearing aloof, awkward and arrogant, and plenty of Conservative MPs complained that they had elected a gruff, grumpy robot rather than the dynamic whizz-kid that had been advertised. The irony was that very few postwar politicians were less like a robot. Heath was not only passionately interested in classical music, but was an extremely talented musician of near-professional ability. And from the late sixties onwards he was also a highly accomplished yachtsman who captained his boat to victory in international competition. These interests were easily parodied by the press, but they placed him in a different league from the likes of Wilson and Margaret Thatcher, who had almost no interests outside politics. The obvious comparison was with his old Balliol friends Denis Healey and Roy Jenkins, both of whom liked to show off their cultural 'hinterland'. However, the fact that Heath was such a proficient musician and sailor surely sets him apart. His biographer suggests that he was the most versatile Prime Minister since Gladstone; it is hard to disagree.[58]

Heath's tragedy was that he was a terrible communicator, who never found the right way of selling his personality to the electorate or even to his own backbenchers. By the autumn of 1965, regularly trounced by Wilson in the Commons, he was beginning to look like a liability. Covering the Conservative Party conference for the *Spectator*, Alan Watkins wrote that 'in their less guarded moments' Heath's MPs were heard asking: 'Have we made a terrible mistake?'[59] Another problem was that, as a middle-class boy made good, Heath did not inspire the same kind of deference given to Macmillan and Home; his appeals to modernisation, rather than to tradition, did not fire up the Tory faithful.[60] When, at the end of the year, his party fell out over the issue of sanctions against the rebels in Rhodesia, he found himself powerless to control them. 'Heath is a pathetic figure,' remarked Benn in November, 'kicked this way and that, and is incapable of giving firm leadership.'[61]

Heath's nightmarish start was exacerbated by the opinion polls. When he took over, his party led by almost 8 per cent; a month later, after the electorate had had a good look at him, Labour were back in front by over 6 per cent. By December, thanks partly to the recovery of the pound, the government was eight points clear and set fair for re-election. Heath's personal approval rating, meanwhile, had fallen from 64 per cent to 43 per cent in six months.[62] As the position worsened, so he withdrew further into himself, shunning the Commons tearoom and protecting himself behind an outward show of grumpy defensiveness and a coterie of close advisers.[63]

The New Year brought more bad news. On 14 January the *Spectator* published a remarkably frank article by Heath's Commonwealth spokesman Angus Maude, entitled 'Winter of Tory Discontent'. 'The Conservative Party', said Maude, 'has completely lost effective political initiative. Its own supporters in the country are divided and deeply worried by this failure, while to the electorate at large the opposition has become a meaningless irrelevance.' The problem, he continued, was that the party stood for nothing: they were content 'to talk like technocrats' which would 'get them nowhere'.[64] Heath's response was immediate: he sacked Maude from his position in the Shadow Cabinet. But there could be no disguising the depths of his predicament as, week by week, Labour's lead stretched further into the distance.

One of Heath's misfortunes was that he was elected as a moderniser at precisely the point when the vogue for modernisation had already reached its peak. It is hard to imagine that voters were impressed by talk of 'dynamism', 'ruthlessness' and 'classlessness' when they had already been listening to such rhetoric from academics, commentators and Labour politicians for five years. And although Wilson had comfortably been able to fend off his rival's attacks, the stuttering start made by his own administration hardly testified to the virtues of modernisation.

To the casual observer in 1965 or 1966, there were plenty of ways in which the very look of Britain was becoming more 'modern'. Motorways, housing estates, high-rise tower blocks, new schools and hospitals, new cars on the roads, even new appliances in high-street shops: all of these suggested that the country was rapidly moving ahead, although they did not always meet with an enthusiastic reception. In many instances changes were made to bring Britain into line with her European neighbours in case of a successful application to join the Common Market. Following the report of the Worboys Committee in 1963, a new standardised system of road signage was introduced over the next four years, based largely on European models. A similar spirit of modernisation prevailed in the world of communications. Post Office planners had first experimented with postal codes in Norwich in 1959, but Croydon was the first area to receive its own permanent postcode in 1966, and the rest of the country then followed suit. In the same year 'all-figure numbering' replaced the old lettered telephone exchange system in six major cities, anticipating the nationwide introduction of telephone addresses made up entirely of numbers. Even time was not immune to the vogue for reform. In October 1968 the clocks were moved an hour forward to British Standard Time for a three-year trial, leading to darker mornings and lighter evenings. The innovation supposedly helped to reduce the numbers of accidents in the evenings, although farmers, builders and other workers complained that on winter mornings they were working in the dark, and the experiment was discontinued after 1971.[65]

The most obvious example of official enthusiasm for modernisation was the reform of the currency. The old system of pounds, half-crowns, florins, shillings and pence had been steadily evolving throughout the century: the production of farthings, for instance, had ended in 1956 because inflation had completely eroded their value. Most of Britain's competitors, however, used a decimal system, and in 1961 Harold Macmillan had established the Halsbury Committee to study the issue. The embrace of decimalisation was a classic example of the self-flagellating 'What's Wrong with Britain' spirit of the early sixties, and critics denounced the imperial currency as an insular, eccentric anachronism that was holding back British businesses. Decimalisation was also seen as an important step towards European integration. In 1963 the committee duly recommended, by four to two, the replacement of the currency by a decimal system, and the Wilson government subsequently seized on the issue as a perfect example of its commitment to modernisation.[66]

The decision to decimalise was taken by just two men, Callaghan and Wilson. In February 1966 the Chancellor mentioned to the Prime Minister that he could include the proposal in his forthcoming budget. Wilson simply nodded and said: 'Why not?'[67] It was extraordinary that such a historic change could be decided in a few seconds, but it was nonetheless typical of his style of government. On 24 February they took the scheme to the Cabinet, which approved the decision with barely any discussion at all.[68] Keen to look progressive in their turn, the Conservatives indicated that they would not oppose the reform, and attention then turned to the nature of the new system. The Bank of England were adamant that, to preserve the international reputation of sterling, the pound must be retained, and the Halsbury Committee had recommended a system of pounds, cents and half-cents. Most banks, industrialists, retailers and trade unions, however, supported a shilling system, with ten shillings as the basic unit. But the Bank of England won the day and the pound was retained. In 1968 five-pence and ten-pence pieces entered circulation as the first step towards decimalisation; in 1970 the half-crown was withdrawn; and in 1971 the threepence, the tanner and the ten-bob note, with all their historic associations, were finally swept away.[69]

By this point the limits of modernisation had already become clear. Indeed, as early as 1965 it was obvious that its rhetorical gimmickry had no real answer to the problems of the pound or Britain's declining international competitiveness. Having been all the rage in the early sixties, the talk of Jet Age modernisation was now looking unfashionable, clichéd and slightly ridiculous. In 1965 *Private Eye* published a caustic history of the 'synthetic faith' in White Heat, mocking the 'pallid young men [who] had found a comfortable high-minded faith in strutting about in the jack-boots of "dynamism", talking "tough" military jargon about "making breakthroughs", "blasting aside the cobwebs of reaction and complacency" and "getting Britain moving"'. The *Eye* identified one man in particular as the quintessential champion of modernisation: the Postmaster General, Anthony Wedgwood Benn, or 'Wedgie the Whizz'.[70]

Wedgie the Whizz was a classic example of patrician progressivism. His father, a Liberal MP and then a Labour minister, had been a leading Nonconformist campaigner for progressive causes, and Benn himself was educated at Westminster and Oxford. He entered Parliament as a fairly moderate figure in 1950 and became associated with the Gaitskellites. His biggest brush with fame came with his long battle to disclaim his title and claim his seat in the Commons, but despite its constitutional importance, this did not mark him out as particularly left-wing. As Wilson's trusted lieutenant, he had the reputation of a crew-cut, teetotal man of the centre, bright and presentable but not especially radical.[71] Like Wilson, he was something of a Boy Scout, full of wheezes and enthusiasms, but he also had a much stronger moralising streak. Crossman commented that he had 'a kind of Nonconformist self-righteousness about him which seems to come out even more strongly in office'.[72] Gaitskell thought that although 'talented in many ways', Benn had 'extraordinarily poor judgement'.[73] 'Nothing the matter with him,' was the typical judgement of Anthony Crosland, his old Oxford tutor and Cabinet colleague, 'except he's a bit cracked.'[74]

Throughout his career, Benn was notorious for his addiction to gadgets and innovations of any kind. Marcia Williams remarked on his 'almost childlike gift for seeing the excitement and the possibility of the science-fiction future we have so often been invited to look at'.[75] His appointment as Postmaster General gave him the opportunity to put the creed of technology into practice, from the Post Office Tower and colour television to the 'car radiophone' and his most famous scheme, the redesign of the postage stamp.

As the birthplace of the stamp, Britain was the only country not to have its national name on its stamps; instead, they always carried the symbol of the monarch's head.[76] Benn had decided that this must change, ostensibly for design reasons, but in reality because he considered it an affront to democratic principles. Reading his diaries, it is clear that he became completely obsessed by the issue. After various negotiations, in March 1965 he managed to obtain an audience with the Queen at which he gave a long lecture about stamp design and ended by getting down on the floor, spreading out his designs and passing various examples up to the monarch for her to inspect. This bizarre encounter left him 'feeling absolutely on top of the world' and convinced that his 'charm' had done the trick.[77] When he told Wilson about it the next day, however, the Prime Minister listened solemnly, perhaps trying not to laugh, and then simply asked: 'Did she get down on the floor with you?'[78]

It turned out that Benn's celebrations were premature. It was the Queen who had charmed him, rather than vice versa, and she was not going to give up her head without a fight. Wilson was not disposed to take issue with the monarch, and in October he had an official send Benn a letter advising him that the Queen was entitled to reject his advice, and forbidding him from commissioning any more headless stamps or showing them to the press.[79] Benn had to be dissuaded from making a personal appeal to the Queen, and in December he admitted that it was 'probably rather foolish of me to go on knocking my head against a brick wall'.[80] Wilson, he complained, wanted to be 'more royal than the Tory Party' and was therefore strengthening 'the reactionary elements in society'.[81] Still, even though he had lost the battle of the Queen's head, Benn felt that he had struck a blow for progress. Six months later, contemplating a set of stamps planned for February 1967, he told himself that 'even if we have to put a little gold head on each of those we shall have got back into the absolute lead in world stamp design. It is immensely satisfying.'[82]

Benn's problems with his stamps reflected the government's general inability to fulfil its promises of modernisation. One of the central institutions in the projected modernisation of Britain was the new Ministry of Technology, which, under the name of MinTech, was supposed to be a gleaming monument to government planning in the Space Age. The idea was that MinTech would maintain the infrastructure for government research and development, disseminate new technologies throughout business and industry, and support four important hi-tech industries: computers, machine tools, telecommunications and electronics.[83] However, the new department got off to a slow start, partly because of the problems of the economy but also because at its head Wilson had appointed Frank Cousins, the general secretary of the Transport and General Workers' Union.

Historians have not been kind to Cousins; he was a vain, painfully earnest character and an incompetent administrator who performed so badly in the Commons that he made Edward Heath look like Demosthenes.[84] He was obviously out of his depth, bewildered by what he saw as Wilson's conservative economic measures, and within months was talking about resignation.[85] To make matters worse, his junior minister was another unorthodox appointment, the scientist and novelist C. P. Snow, rather than a politician who knew what he was doing. Richard Marsh, who was sent to MinTech as parliamentary secretary to keep an eye on the two newcomers, complained that Cousins simply 'couldn't handle' the Commons, while Snow spent his days having lunch with industrialists and then going to sleep.[86] This ludicrous situation could not go on for long. Snow lasted barely a year, and in the summer of 1966 Cousins finally resigned, allowing MinTech to make a new start under a different minister, as we will see.[87]

MinTech was only one of two departments that Wilson had set up in 1964 specifically to handle the proposed modernisation of Britain, the other being the Department of Economic Affairs, or DEA. Its basic remit was to organise economic policy: while the day-to-day minutiae of economic management was to be left to the Treasury, the DEA would set out the long-term vision and coordinate its implementation across the country.[88] Its creation reflected the general enthusiasm for planning in the early sixties. Plenty of journalists and academics, as well as Labour politicians, argued that centralised planning represented the best chance of modernising Britain's economy and encouraging higher productivity. Even the Conservatives had feebly flirted with ideas of planning when establishing the National Economic Development Council in 1962.[89] However, Wilson wanted to go further. Labour's 1964 manifesto promised that the new DEA would set out 'the broad strategy for increasing investment [and] expanding exports', and, more importantly, would produce a 'National Plan' under which 'each industry will know both what is expected of it and what help it can expect'.[90]

Wilson explained that the head of the DEA would be 'the central and most important Minister on the home front', with the Chancellor relegated to a secondary position.[91] The position went to George Brown, who saw the DEA as 'the opening campaign of a major social revolution'. Its principal goal was to be 'economic expansion', and he hoped to set up a variety of planning boards, working to encourage rapid economic growth.[92] These were lofty objectives, and given Brown's notorious unreliability he might have seemed an implausible choice to fulfil them. However, unlike Cousins, he was widely considered to have made an impressive start to life in government. Crossman spoke for many when he wrote in February 1965 that there was 'no one more talented in the whole Cabinet or nicer or more loyal or more basically constructive'.[93] Given that Crossman had long distrusted Brown, his verdict was all the more impressive. 'We came into office full of doubts about George Brown,' he admitted. 'Actually, his leadership has been outstanding ... and there is no doubt that as First Secretary and Deputy Prime Minister he is absolutely dominant over poor old James Callaghan who trails along as number three.'[94]

Crossman's unusually generous assessment did not tell the whole story. Brown's first few weeks at the DEA were characterised by complete chaos. On his first morning he occupied the old Ministry of Defence buildings in Great George Street, only to find that they were largely unfurnished. Only one office had a table, a chair and a telephone, and Brown's first meetings took place with him in the chair and his officials either squashed together on the table or squatting on the floor. There were no typewriters and no departmental notepaper, and they only managed to get a copy of the economic brief for new ministers because his private secretary stole a copy from Callaghan's office.[95] Meanwhile, Brown's new parliamentary secretary, Bill Rodgers, had been given the wrong directions by Harold Wilson and was left wandering through the streets. In the end, humiliatingly, he had to go into the Treasury and ask a secretary for directions.

> She looked up and said, 'We haven't got any list of it here. Why do you want to know?' I said, 'I'm a minister.' 'Oh,' she said. 'Are you?' And she picked up the telephone and she rang someone and said, 'There's a gentleman here who says he is a minister in the Department of Economic Affairs. Where is it?'[96]

Most civil servants had been opposed to the creation of the DEA from the start. The Treasury naturally disliked any dilution of its responsibilities, and other officials warned Wilson that a new department would have an impossible job in trying to compete with the Treasury's entrenched power. There were no clear dividing lines between the two departments, and conflict was almost inevitable.[97] Callaghan, for obvious reasons, was extremely suspicious of the DEA and determined to protect his own position.[98] Brown's personal volatility did not make this uneasy relationship any smoother. On the first evening after his confirmation as First Secretary, he invited his closest allies over to his flat to celebrate. First to arrive was Anthony Crosland, who was to be his chief lieutenant at the DEA; he had brought his wife Susan. While Brown, dressed in his finest velvet smoking jacket, was cheerfully pouring the drinks, Crosland casually remarked that he had just been speaking to the new Chancellor about the division of functions between their two departments. At that, Brown stopped pouring, looked up and literally shrieked: '*Treason!*', his eyes popping almost out of his head with rage. '*Treason!* Back-stabber!' he shouted. 'I'll have to rethink the whole thing. How could any man *do* such a thing?'[99] When Roy Jenkins, Bill Rodgers and their wives arrived, they found Susan Crosland struggling to hold back tears while Brown and his number two were having a blazing row. It did not augur well for the new department.[100]

Oddly, after this unfortunate beginning, Brown and Crosland enjoyed fairly good relations, largely because the latter was one of the few people who would stand up to the First Secretary.[101] In general, however, Brown's relations with his officials were extraordinarily strained. He was a terrible bully, regularly upbraided senior officials in front of their colleagues, and several times attempted to sack his principal private secretary, Tom Caulcott, even though he did not have the power to do so. On one occasion Brown convinced himself that Caulcott had lied about a conversation with one of Wilson's officials, and forced the poor man to telephone Downing Street in front of him to prove his story. While Caulcott was talking, Brown paced angrily up and down, only stopping when he noticed that the official had sat down in his chair. 'He literally screamed, "Get out of my chair!"' Caulcott recalled. 'He had a sort of momentary vision that I was somehow taking over, and it was too much, it was more than he could take.'[102] Such were Brown's rages that Caulcott arranged with the Post Office for a bug to be placed on his private line, so that officials could listen to his calls and make sure that he was not disgracing himself. Another secret device was attached to the door of his office, so that whenever Brown left unexpectedly, as was his wont, Caulcott could send a junior official to tail him and report on his destination.[103]

By the spring of 1965 Brown was well on the way to accumulating a record of misconduct that made him unquestionably the worst-behaved minister of modern times. Most of his colleagues saw him as a Falstaffian figure: drunken rants and rages at official receptions were not uncommon, and he was notorious for kissing wives and secretaries with inappropriate enthusiasm.[104] On 31 May, after a meeting about Commonwealth trade links, Barbara Castle noted that Brown was 'offensively truculent' to everybody present. Later, Wilson told her that Brown had been as drunk 'as a coot', and she wondered if they 'couldn't get rid of him before he got us into real trouble'.[105] All in all, the various diaries for these early months list thirteen separate incidents when Brown was obviously drunk, and doubtless there were other occasions when his intoxication was better concealed.[106]

Brown's misbehaviour was mainly caused by his alcoholism, but a contributing factor was his enduring bitterness at having been defeated for the leadership by Harold Wilson. Brown sincerely believed that he deserved to have been Prime Minister, and every day's work was therefore a painful reminder that he had been beaten by, in his eyes, a much lesser man. He treated Wilson with aggressive contempt, even hatred, and made no effort to conceal the fact from their colleagues and civil servants. Wilson, meanwhile, was much more circumspect. Although Brown was spectacularly disloyal in private and public, the Prime Minister treated him with a mixture of scorn, pity, patience and even mild affection. With his advisers, Wilson used to joke about Brown's 'horny-handed' background and drinking habits, and they had a running joke about Marcia Williams hiding the key to the drinks cabinet whenever Brown visited No. 10.[107]

In later years Wilson was generous about Brown's undoubted political talents. At the time, however, he devoted hours if not entire days to dealing with his turbulent deputy. On 13 April 1965, for example, Brown had a drunken tantrum over a minor proposal to send 175 army reservists to Aden. As the Defence Secretary, Denis Healey, pointed out, these men were specifically paid for accepting such an eventuality, but Brown exploded:

> 'They'll never stand for it in Swadlincote,' he said. Swadlincote was a small village in his constituency, always quoted by George as a touchstone of

public opinion. 'There'll be revolution. The Government will fall.' And he resigned. Next morning only one newspaper even mentioned the call-up, and that in a single paragraph. George withdrew his resignation.[108]

What Healey did not know was that behind the scenes Brown had given Wilson a two-hour lecture on the subject, followed by various telephone calls demanding that Wilson cancel a trip to the United States and accept his resignation. Wilson simply ignored him, and after Brown had slept off his temper things continued as usual.[109] In fact Brown resigned, or threatened to resign, so many times that Marcia Williams kept a special file on the subject. One estimate has him 'leaving' the government seventeen times, a post-war record.[110]

Throughout this period, Brown was working on the National Plan, which he confidently anticipated would be the centrepiece of Labour's administration and was due to be published on 16 September 1965. In characteristic Brown fashion, the Plan was launched in circumstances of high farce. The night before its publication Brown was forced to drive over to meet an anxious delegation from the Federation of British Industry at a country house in Berkshire. At two in the morning they finally signed up to the Plan, and Brown ordered his driver to take him back to London with the only copy. An hour later the car broke down on a remote country road and Brown started shouting at the driver, who drew himself up and said haughtily: 'I'm a member of the Transport and General Workers' Union too, Mr Brown.' The DEA's director-general, Sir Donald McDougall, then disappeared to find a telephone box and order another car from the ministry, or at worst a taxi.

At this point Brown lost patience and flagged down a passing Mini, occupied by a young man with a red beard and his girlfriend, an attractive blonde in pink trousers. Abandoning his colleagues, Brown jumped into the back seat, clutching his Plan, and demanded to be driven to London. Amazingly, under the circumstances, the couple agreed to take him, and they shot off through the night, with Brown, hunched in the back, aggressively urging his bearded benefactor to drive more quickly because he was on urgent government business. When they arrived in Parliament Square, Brown was out of the car and dashing up the stairs to his office before it had completely stopped. The National Plan, however, was still on the back seat of the Mini as it pulled away into the distance, and by the time Brown realised his mistake it was too late. Fortunately enough, the bearded man returned it before the morning.[111]

The Plan was an extremely ambitious document. Its preamble promised to cover 'all aspects of the country's economic development for the next five years' and pledged to increase national output by 25 per cent by 1970, with an annual growth figure of 4 per cent. Productivity was to rise by some 3.4 per cent annually, and the volume of exports by 5.25 per cent, almost double the rate achieved in the past. All this would be implemented through a checklist of thirty-nine different initiatives, ranging from management training and education programmes to cuts in overseas defence spending.[112] Despite the rigours of the night before, Brown put in an excellent television performance to launch the Plan and earned high praise from the newspapers, which were clearly excited to be covering something of historic importance.[113]

Within Whitehall, however, few people thought that Brown's targets were realistically attainable. A host of Treasury economists tried to point out that dynamic growth could not simply be wished into existence.[114] The obvious flaw had already been pointed out to the Cabinet in August by Anthony Crosland, who was disturbed by the blatant contradiction between the Plan's lofty goals and the deflationary policy currently in operation to defend the pound:

> Tony Crosland . . . asked how we could talk about a plan based on a 4–percent average increase of production per year when we knew perfectly well that for the next eighteen months at least it wasn't going to rise by anything like that – in fact when the Government was actually cutting back production by its deflationary measures . . . He then went on, 'We are launched on deflation and I know I shall have to rewrite the whole of my chapter in George Brown's National Plan. It makes no sense any more.'[115]

The Plan could only work in conditions that favoured investment and expansion. But Wilson and Callaghan were determined to defend the value of sterling through regular bursts of deflation that made those conditions impossible. Wilson's refusal to acknowledge the obvious contradiction with the goals of the Plan was self-delusion masquerading as self-confidence. Only one of these policies could survive; not both.[116]

Callaghan's deflationary measures meant that the Plan was already out of date when it was published, and four days before its publication Brown told the Cabinet that growth was running at only 1 per cent or so, unemployment was expected to rise, and 'there was unfortunately no evidence of modernization' in industry.[117] Yet even without the problems of sterling, the National Plan would probably have failed. It was ludicrously ambitious, covering 'everything from the balance of payments, investment, pay, regional policy, through to detailed projections of output in individual industries'.[118] The growth targets had been chosen for political purposes, and the thirty-nine-point checklist had been cobbled together by asking different Whitehall departments what they fancied doing in the next few years. There was no detailed indication of how the economy would move towards its goals for 1970. Worse, there was no means of implementing the Plan's requirements and no machinery to make sure that the targets were met.[119] In the end its optimistic forecasts bore little relation to Labour's actual economic performance in office, and it was remembered only as an embarrassing monument to the inflated expectations of Wilson's early years.[120]

Having been supremely fashionable in the early sixties, planning as an economic strategy fell from grace with astonishing speed, and within a decade or so was regarded as a hubristic and antiquated relic of the past. The irony is that, in Britain at least, planning was never really tried. Taken together, the miserable industrial conditions of the mid-sixties and Wilson's restrictive economic policies meant that the Plan itself was never fully put into operation. But even if it had been, it was not a very good example of state planning. Indeed, all the talk of planning was really just another way of criticising the Tories for being backward and amateurish, and the commitments made by Wilson and Brown were more rhetorical than actual. As it turned out, they had raised expectations that they could not possibly satisfy.[121]

The failure of the National Plan was a severe blow to George Brown's prestige and to the future of his department. Brown partly blamed its collapse on the machinations of Callaghan and his Treasury officials, whose deflationary emphasis destroyed his hopes for growth.[122] In April 1965 Crossman wrote that 'in the Whitehall struggle the views of Jim Callaghan have prevailed and the views of George Brown have not'.[123] In truth the DEA, the great vehicle for the realisation of the New Britain, was probably doomed from the start.[124] Even if it had been run by someone more stable and hard-headed, success would still have proved elusive because the department had no institutional weight or direction. Many historians, like Brown, have blamed Harold Wilson for encouraging two different departments to run 'diametrically opposed policies' and never bringing himself properly to choose between them.[125] Wilson's euphemistic name for this was 'creative tension', but in failing to set out the proper responsibilities of the DEA or make a definitive choice between expansion and deflation, he ended up with a minimum of creativity and a great deal of tension. As his colleagues remarked, he was gradually losing interest in the whole modernisation project anyway, for by the end of 1965 he was spending more and more time on diplomatic issues like Vietnam and Rhodesia, neither of which seemed likely to produce great rewards.

Vietnam, Rhodesia, the ordeal of the pound, the disappointment of MinTech, the flawed ambitions of the National Plan: it was hardly a record to trumpet from the rooftops. In many of these cases Wilson could point to a difficult inheritance or mitigating circumstances, but after the heightened expectations of 1963 and 1964 it was not surprising that the murmurs of disappointment were growing ever louder. *Tribune*, the mouthpiece of the Labour left, was a good barometer of grass-roots dissatisfaction with the government. On 20 August 1965 one furious activist complained:

> Socialist principles have been tossed aside with almost indecent cynicism and casualness. Racial discrimination in Britain has been condoned and strengthened. American butchery in Vietnam has been actively supported and encouraged. Social welfare and economic development in Britain have been sacrificed to carry out a reactionary economic programme at the behest of international finance capital.

A month later the paper's education correspondent wrote to announce his resignation from the party. 'We are not right to view the Labour Party and its latter-day works as having anything to do with socialism,' he explained. 'They don't, they won't and it is time we faced up to it.'[126]

Much of the criticism was aimed at Wilson himself, the 'dynamic' leader who had been the focus of so many hopes in 1964. Cecil King, the chairman of the IPC news conglomerate that controlled the *Mirror*, the *Sun* and the *People*, had been an enthusiastic Labour supporter in the election campaign. By the middle of August 1965, however, King was complaining that the Prime Minister was simply 'a very short-term tactician, obsessed with the House of Commons', whose 'days look to be numbered'. He dismissed the government as 'a lacklustre lot' containing 'every hack in the business'.[127] 'Opinion in his party is increasingly critical,' King wrote at the end of the month, adding that 'he will finally be brought down by his inability to produce results. Government by gimmick is bound to fail even in the medium run.'[128]

King rarely spoke for anybody but himself, but even some of Wilson's closest collaborators were now beginning to voice similar sentiments. 'I felt what a humdrum Cabinet we are – a gang of competent politicians,' wrote Crossman after one meeting in September 1965. 'Once again Harold Wilson showed himself without a trace of vision.'[129] Tony Benn, so enthusiastic about the 'New Britain' two years previously, complained that Wilson seemed 'too cunning and crafty and smart, and to be somewhat lacking in principle'.[130] In February 1966 he spent an 'extremely unattractive' evening listening to Wilson's diagnosis of all his colleagues' personal weaknesses. 'My opinion of Harold is lower tonight than it has ever been before,' Benn wrote afterwards. 'He really is a manipulator who thinks that he can get out of everything by fixing somebody or something. Although his reputation is now riding high, I'm sure he will come a cropper one day when one of his fixes just doesn't come off.'[131]

And yet, for all the criticism, by the spring of 1966 Wilson had managed to hold the government together for eighteen draining months. In the opinion polls his approval rating had quickly recovered from its sharp decline of June 1965 and now stood at a very healthy 60 per cent or so.[132] His government had not only abolished prescription charges but implemented the largest ever increase, in real terms, in pensions and other social security benefits. These were considerable achievements, even if they came at a heavy financial cost.[133] And although some observers might question his principles, nobody doubted his resilience, his composure in a crisis, his ability to charm the House of Commons, to think on his feet, to rouse a party conference, to speak coolly and clearly to the nation on television.[134] The young minister Richard Marsh rightly commented that Wilson's ability to keep his fractious party together might be called 'two facedness' or 'trimming' by some, but it was nonetheless 'an essential and honourable skill'.[135] Denis Healey thought that Wilson's tactical skill since October 1964 had been 'brilliant'.[136] 'He's nothing but a shabby tactician,' one young MP remarked to Anthony Crosland. But Crosland was not so sure. 'Harold is a bastard,' he replied, 'but he's a genius.'[137]

Overall, as 1966 opened, Wilson could afford to shrug off the voices of criticism. The pound was stable at last, bank rate had been reduced, the economy was growing, unemployment remained low, and most importantly, the polls showed him at least 5 per cent ahead of the luckless

Heath.[138] On 1 February he invited his closest advisers to dinner in his Downing Street flat. While Mary looked after the food, they talked about the next election. Wilson had been reading a book about the American presidential election of 1964 and had decided that it was time to give up the old dynamic 'Kennedy' image in favour of something calmer and more reassuring. 'I am a doctor figure,' he said, repeating the phrase in case any of them had missed it.[139]

Later that month he finalised the decision they were all expecting: they would go to the country on the last day of March. In the opinion polls the government's lead was now up to 7 per cent and increasing. 'All set for the election,' wrote Crossman on 19 February. The mood was good. The Tories were 'beaten before they start'. 'Are there any snags we face?' he wondered. His answer was bleak:

> Yes, of course there are. The main trouble is that we haven't delivered the goods; the builders are not building the houses; the cost of living is still rising; the incomes policy isn't working; we haven't held back inflation; we haven't got production moving. We are going to the country now because we are facing every kind of difficulty and we anticipate that things are bound to get worse and we shall need a bigger majority with which to handle them.[140]

PART TWO

ENGLAND SWINGS

10

BRITAIN IN 1965

JACK HAY: It's a crying shame, I know. But they don't want to know about the balance of payments . . . You might say they're frigid about ideology, too. The only Marx they care about is linked with Spencer, not Engels.

Dennis Potter, *Vote, Vote, Vote for Nigel Barton* (1965)

On 9 November 1964 Secker & Warburg published *Late Call*, the latest novel by one of the most respected writers in Britain. Angus Wilson had been the deputy superintendent of the Reading Room of the British Museum until 1955, when the success of his early works prompted him to throw up his job and try his luck as a full-time writer. With novels like *Anglo-Saxon Attitudes* (1956) and *The Middle Age of Mrs Eliot* (1958), as well as several volumes of short stories, he had already established a reputation as a master of satire. Few British writers of the post-war decades were better able to reproduce the manners, values and speech patterns of the affluent society; few were so adept at pointing out the moral weaknesses of modern life, or the limits and contradictions of scientific optimism. The author of acclaimed critical studies of Dickens and Zola, Wilson was frequently hailed as their latter-day inheritor, a 'moral scourge' who emulated their social sweep and elaborate brushwork.[1] For Malcolm Bradbury, writing in the early seventies, Wilson was nothing less than 'the most developed and impressive novel-writer of his generation'.[2]

Like its predecessors, *Late Call* attracted plenty of admiring notices. The Sunday papers all gave it rave reviews, the *New Statesman* thought that it was a brilliant dissection of modern society, and Wilson's publisher assured him that he was 'a top novelist from egghead to pop levels'.[3] The novel is the story of Sylvia Calvert, a timid, self-effacing woman in her mid-sixties, recently retired as a seaside hotel manageress. In the opening chapters, she moves, along with her rather selfish invalid husband Arthur, to the New Town of Carshall, where they are to live with their widowed son, Harold, and his children. The stark contrast between Harold and Sylvia Calvert provides much of the satirical thrust of the novel, and around these two characters Wilson weaves an intricate tale of British life in the mid-sixties.

Harold, whose name obviously suggests parallels with both Macmillan and Wilson, is the personification of the liberal optimism of the sixties, brimming with faith in social engineering, technological progress and all things shiny and modern. As a comprehensive headmaster with a smart suburban home, he is the epitome of what the critic Bernard Bergonzi calls 'the *Observer*-ethos, with its naïve love of gadgets, doctrinaire progressiveness, would-be exotic eating habits, cultural status-seeking and neurotic concern to be with-it'.[4] 'We've got a new hopeful world here of uncrowded leisure-ful happy living,' he says at one point, referring to the New Town, of which he is inordinately proud.[5] Reprimanding his daughter Judy, whom he suspects of excessive county-set tendencies, he proudly declares: 'I think I'll belong to the modern world of electronic engineers and fabric design rather than pretend to gentility with family solicitors and private school headmasters'.[6]

Yet, despite his apparent broad-mindedness, Harold is actually inflexible, obsessive and thoroughly dislikeable. His technological enthusiasm is merely a shield for his obsessive insecurities. By contrast, his mother Sylvia, whom he teases for being reactionary and out of touch, is a much more attractive character. By describing the New Town through her eyes, Wilson exposes the hollowness of its classless pretensions. Rejecting Harold's high-brow enthusiasms, Sylvia takes refuge in the diversions of cheap mass culture: true crime books, romantic novels, popular biographies, and, above all, the television. One of Harold's less amiable neighbours, the local welfare officer, lectures her for 'living in other people's lives all the time . . . Queen Anne who's been dead for centuries and all that nonsense on television – unreal people, talking unreal twaddle!'[7] But at the end of the book it is Sylvia, not her son, who emerges as the stronger and more open-minded character. While Harold descends into neurotic angst, she rediscovers a sense of self buried since her youth. When Harold reacts angrily to the news that his son is homosexual, denouncing his 'abnormalities' and calling him 'a little whore', she is horrified by his lack of sympathy: 'I'm not staying to listen to any more. But I'll tell you this, if nobody else goes to stay with Ray, I shall. He's been a lovely boy to me.'[8]

As a part-time lecturer at the University of East Anglia, a new university on a purpose-built campus that first admitted students at the end of 1963, Wilson was already familiar with the new landscape of Britain in the mid-sixties. In the preparation of *Late Call* he also spent a lot of time researching the background to Carshall, his fictional New Town, visiting Harlow and Basildon as well as interviewing architects, planners and educationalists.[9] The picture of the New Towns that emerges from the book, however, is pretty unflattering. The fact that their greatest champion is Harold Calvert, easily the most self-centred and self-deluding character in the novel, tells its own story. Sylvia, meanwhile, likens Carshall to a prison: she reflects gloomily on 'its crowds of children on bicycles and kidicars and tricycles, its ton-up boys and girls in jeans, its endlessly houseproud young couples producing more and more kids ... its prams and arcades, and queues of teenagers for the Mecca, and churches like halls, and ten pin she didn't understand, and murals she could make nothing of'. Although at the end of the book she manages to reconcile herself to her new life, it is her first impression that lingers in the reader's memory.[10]

Although the New Towns are often seen as emblems of post-war modernity, their roots went back to the Edwardian idea of 'garden cities' like Letchworth (founded in 1903) and Welwyn Garden City (1920). However, the immediate impulse for the New Towns came from a series of wartime reports recommending the creation of new urban areas to relieve the overcrowded industrial conurbations. In 1946 the New Towns Act established fourteen such towns across the country. Eight – Stevenage, Crawley, Hemel Hempstead, Harlow, Hatfield, an expanded Welwyn Garden City, Basildon and Bracknell – formed part of a projected satellite ring around London, while the remaining six – Corby, Cwmbran, Newton Aycliffe, Peterlee, East Kilbride and Glenrothes – were designed to alleviate particular regional pressures.[11]

The New Towns of the late forties and fifties had a strong moralistic ethos, and to many commentators they seemed the architectural embodiment of the New Jerusalem that Labour had promised to build after the Second World War.[12] As early as 1953, however, they were coming under attack: the *Architectural Review* thought that their open 'prairie' style was a mistake, lending itself to the dreaded 'subtopia', and demanded higher-density housing in line with Brutalist architectural fashions.[13] But what the critics most disliked about the first New Towns was exactly what most ordinary people liked about them: their unpretentious, low-level landscapes. In Stevenage, for example, the residential neighbourhoods that radiated out from the new town centre generally consisted of quiet streets of terraced or semi-detached brick houses. Although it was the first pedestrian shopping centre in the country, the heart of Stevenage was low-rise, pragmatic and unexceptional: there was nothing to shock or excite the visitor. The highlight, a clock tower standing in an ornamental pool, was exactly the kind of thing that ordinary people quite liked and architectural critics utterly detested.[14]

By contrast, the town that supposedly represented the way ahead was very different. Cumbernauld was designed in 1955 to relieve the demographic pressure on Glasgow, especially in slum areas like the Gorbals, and its chief architect Hugh Wilson took the opportunity to break new ground.[15] Unlike the previous New Towns, Cumbernauld fully embraced the brave new world of the car, with plenty of ring roads but little provision for pedestrians, cyclists or public transport. Residential areas were easily accessible only by road; there were no pedestrian crossings or traffic lights; and travellers on foot had to make their way by a series of bridges or rather gloomy underpasses.[16]

Cumbernauld's highlight was the town centre, which Wilson had designed as a spectacular statement of intent: a single 'mega-structure', half a mile long, built on nine levels from car parks to penthouses. According to a plan unveiled at the end of 1962, Cumbernauld town centre would contain almost half a million square feet of shopping space, including an enormous supermarket, as well as 'cultural and recreational halls, an hotel, offices, banks, public houses, a church, a police station, a bus station and other constituents'. On the top storey would be terraced penthouses, decanting their inhabitants to their workplaces by day and the bowling alleys and cinemas of the centre by night. *The Times* explained that 'some rather revolutionary ideas were being considered' too, from '24-hour automatic vending of a wide range of household goods' to 'closed-circuit television' and floor-cleaning by 'automatic vacuum cleaning machines'.[17]

Yet, despite all the high hopes, Cumbernauld's fate was not a happy one. The design for the town and its centre proved too inflexible to cope with the eccentric patterns of everyday life. As a critic put it several years later, the sight of the vast central complex looming miserably over a 'moat of green fields' was both 'heroic' and 'slightly absurd'.[18] By the beginning of the twenty-first century it was regularly cited as one of the worst places to live in Britain, with even its own residents nominating the town centre for destruction in a television survey to find the most hated eyesore in the country.[19]

In the sixties, however, Hugh Wilson's plans met with enormous enthusiasm. The first wave of New Towns had not been enough to cope with the pressures of urban overpopulation, slum clearance and immigration, so the governments of the sixties became the midwives for a second wave: Skelmersdale (1961), Livingston (1962), Redditch, Runcorn and Washington (all 1964).[20] This time, following the example of Cumbernauld, far more emphasis was placed on the car, the town centres were much more ambitious, and there was a palpable sense of technological enthusiasm. In Runcorn, for example, planners designed the futuristic Shopping City, described by press reports as 'a modern ivory castle of self-cleaning ceramic tiles which are designed to stay white'. Shopping City was a veritable temple to the gleaming optimism of the sixties: newspaper reports waxed lyrical over 'the comfort and charm of the carpeted areas, furnished with excellently designed grey plastic chairs and round white sofas, the centres of which are full of shrubs and flowers', as well as 'the overall quality and taste of the terrazzo-floored malls and marble-faced walls'.[21]

Looking more like a set from *Doctor Who* than a typical British town centre, Shopping City would have fitted nicely into the futuristic landscape of another second-generation New Town, Washington, just outside Sunderland, where most houses had central heating, double glazing and cable television. So modern was Washington that its districts had numbers, not names: visitors arriving by car were directed not to Lambton or Ayton, but to District Seven. Predictably enough, the development corporation also had plans for a monorail system and a hovercraft service to the coast, but, equally unsurprisingly, these were never realised.[22]

The third and final wave of New Towns lasted from 1967 to 1970, and produced Peterborough, Northampton, Telford, Warrington and Central Lancashire New Town. The most successful product of this era, however, was Milton Keynes in Buckinghamshire, which was both the last New Town and the most ambitious.[23] It was established in 1967 as an American-style town based on a pattern of grid squares, with the emphasis on rapid mobility and, inevitably, on the car. More than any other New Town, it was a 'motorised town', with offices and workplaces dispersed around the periphery to avoid traffic congestion, while the town centre, a pseudo-American shopping mall, was positioned off-centre.[24] Even the parks and landscaping were designed on the grid-square principle, with a geometrical system of walkways and cycle paths.[25]

Yet, for all its overtones of urban modernisn, Milton Keynes was a classic example of the compromise between urban, suburban and rural that marked most of the British New Towns. The town centre's wide boulevards were lined with plane trees and given deliberately traditional names: Midsummer Boulevard, Secklow Gate, Saxon Gate, and so on. Even the roundabouts had names like North Saxon and North Witan. The Development Corporation constantly emphasised the green look of the town, and advertisements regularly trumpeted the lakes, fields and bridleways dividing one residential estate from another. Far from representing a new mode of urban living, Milton Keynes in fact marked the triumph of suburbia.[26]

Angus Wilson was not alone in spotting the fictional possibilities of New Town life. One of its first appearances in popular culture came in the radio serial *Mrs Dale's Diary*, which followed the lives of a fictional middle-class family in a quiet London suburb and attracted up to seven million listeners. In February 1962, trying to modernise the show, the producers moved the Dale family to Exton, a fictional New Town in East Anglia with a rather grittier feel. In time the show was renamed *The Dales*, and the two lead characters were recast to give them a more up-to-date feel. As in *Late Call*, the New Town was used as a kind of microcosm of modern Britain, with the Dales being forced to confront contemporary social issues, from cancer and illegitimacy to racism and homosexuality. As Bernard Levin remarked, the discovery of issues like these 'in the early days of the serial would have been about as likely as an acute attack of paedophilia by Dr Dale', but although the retooled programme did win back listeners, it did not survive the sixties, finally being wound up in April 1969.[27]

New Towns were also conspicuous on television. The extremely popular police serial *Z Cars*, for example, was set in 'Newtown', a working-class overspill estate just outside 'Seaport', the two communities being based on Kirkby and Liverpool respectively. 'Newtown', according to a preview in the *Radio Times*, brought together 'a mixed community, displaced from larger towns by slum clearance . . . and housed on an estate without amenities and without community feeling', and the programme's emphasis on social tensions, from teenage runaways and deranged murderers to racism and wife-beating, gave a typically unflattering portrait of life in the New Towns.[28]

They even came off badly in the fantasy adventures of the day. In Patrick McGoohan's surreal series *The Prisoner* (1967–8), the protagonist is trapped in the Village, an architecturally homogeneous place where the residents have numbers rather than names and are compelled to take part in various communal activities and entertainments by the sinister central planners. The Village has every conceivable amenity, including its own public transport, but has only one little shop rather than a full-scale Shopping City. Everything is standardised and bureaucratised, just like life in Angus Wilson's Carshall, and as in *Late Call*, the protagonist struggles to escape the cloying blanket of New Town life. *The Prisoner* bewildered audiences and critics alike by refusing to yield any very precise meaning, but since the programme was clearly designed as a satire on the homogenisation and alienation of contemporary life, the parallels with the alleged miseries of the New Towns were pretty obvious.[29]

By far the most prominent example of New Towns in the media, however, was the television soap opera *The Newcomers*, which was shown twice a week on BBC1 from 5 October 1965. Like *Z Cars* before it, *The Newcomers* was designed to explore contemporary social issues, and its creator wrote that he wanted to address the 'real problems of our time'.[30] The opening episodes introduce the Cooper family, who live in London but are moving to 'Angleton' in East Anglia, which, although not strictly speaking a New Town, has been designated as an 'expanded town'.* Ellis Cooper, the head of the household, works as a supervisor in a computer component factory, while his wife, Vivienne, is a fashion-conscious marriage counsellor, and very much a modern woman. They have three teenage children, who are perpetually in and out of trouble, and Vivienne's rather miserable widowed mother also lives with them, a set-up which directly parallels that in *Late Call*. The plot unsurprisingly shows how the Coopers struggle to adapt to their new life: Vivienne, for instance, succumbs to a bad case of depression, finding the whole experience alienating after the pleasures of London. The picture is not all bad, of course: the Coopers clearly enjoy their spacious new house and its country setting. But, as in *Late Call*, the overall impression of New Town life is less than favourable, and this set the tone for much of the BBC's coverage of suburban life in the decade that followed, especially in sitcoms like *The Good Life*, *Butterflies* and *The Fall and Rise of Reginald Perrin*.[31]

---

*Real expanded towns included Andover, Bletchley, Swindon, Basingstoke and Thetford, among others, where new housing estates were built to house overspill population, usually from London.

Although social critics and television producers insisted that life in the New Towns and suburbs of the sixties was dull and dehumanising, the reality was rather different. Surveys consistently found that most people who moved to New Towns, typically ambitious working-class couples, did so with great enthusiasm, and the move usually turned out to be a success, bringing new standards of privacy, security and comfort.[32] When the Ford family moved to Hemel Hempstead, for example, Mrs Ford walked into her new home on the first day and burst into tears. 'I wept simply because I was so happy,' she said: 'we had a garden for the children to run in . . . we had a house, a home of our own and we could shut the front door and we didn't have to worry about anybody.'[33] Another woman who moved to the same town recalled her joy at 'a completely new life', with a smart new kitchen, hot running water, 'green trees and sunshine'. 'After what we'd been through,' she said, reflecting on their years in the battered streets of North London, 'it was such a relief, it was like shedding an old overcoat.'[34]

Of course, there were plenty of teething troubles, and families often complained that the building of amenities lagged well behind the arrival of new residents.[35] Yet most people made allowances for a few initial problems, and the New Towns proved much more popular and successful than the other solution to the housing problems of the period: high-rise tower blocks. Time and again residents cited the same novelties and delights: space, greenery, security, privacy and, above all, freedom. One woman whose family arrived in Stevenage from Islington told an interviewer that she had never before had 'the luxury of a bath, hot water on tap and best of all in the children's eyes, our own stairs. They ran up and down them on that first day calling out "these are our stairs" and they all kept flushing the toilet.'[36]

Even in Cumbernauld, residents expressed great contentment at their move from the working-class slums of Glasgow. Eight out of ten respondents to a survey in 1968 said that they were satisfied with their new homes; more than seven out of ten said that they had 'bettered themselves' by moving; nine out of ten, defying the stereotypes, thought that their neighbours were friendly. 'Cumbernauld is a happy town,' reported *The Times*. 'The people are friendly, more of them have cars and telephones than Glaswegians do, there is no teenage problem and there are more than 100 clubs and societies in the community . . . So much for "new town blues"'.[37]

Although many of the New Towns had their fair share of social problems, the fate of Milton Keynes illustrates the wider picture. In the late sixties Buckinghamshire newspapers had lamented the arrival of a 'Little Los

Angeles', and in 1967 *New Society* had warned of the threat of the 'North Bucks Monster', 'a beast to be invited in by official capitulation to the motor car'.[38] A better prediction made in the same year came from a horse breeder at Shenley Lodge Farm, inside the area designated as the New Town, who named his two-year-old brown mare after the town and told reporters: 'I've a feeling we're going to be hearing a lot more about Milton Keynes.'[39] He was right. From Basildon and Corby to Peterlee and Telford, the general story of the New Towns was one of rapid and impressive growth, and from 1970 onwards, Milton Keynes was the fastest-growing urban area in Britain. What was more, polls and surveys overwhelmingly suggested that most people rather liked living there.[40]

Milton Keynes and the other New Towns thrived largely because they became associated with the affluence, mobility and ambition of the 1950s and 1960s. It should always be remembered that the real motor behind the social and cultural changes of the sixties was the steady growth of average weekly earnings, which rose by a staggering 130 per cent between 1955 and 1969. Since unemployment in the same period was little more than nominal, it is not surprising that many people later remembered the sixties as a time of enormous optimism, when each new year brought new rewards, new household goods, new clothes, new luxuries and new experiences.[41]

Money did make the world go round, although money itself was changing. Not only did the Wilson government decide to introduce a new decimal currency, but the Barclaycard, Britain's first credit card, was launched in June 1966, and Barclays installed the first British cash dispenser at their Enfield branch a year later.[42] It was a measure of the underlying optimism of the day that by 1966 sales on credit accounted for a tenth of all consumer spending: indeed, more than 40 per cent of all spending on cars, furniture, radios and appliances was based on credit.[43]

Shopping, too, had radically changed since the end of the Second World War. Although many older or working-class women, like Sylvia in *Late Call*, disliked chain stores and preferred going to local shops, the supermarkets were carrying all before them. In 1971, a survey found that two-thirds of housewives made regular trips to the supermarket. Instead of popping down to the local high street once a day, women were concentrating their shopping into one big trip to Sainsbury's or Tesco, usually at the weekend.[44] Even the retail price index, used to measure inflation since 1956, reflected the pace of modern consumerism and now included sliced bread, fish fingers, crisps, jeans, scooters and, from 1968, 'meals out'.[45] And it was no coincidence that the fastest-growing association of the decade was the Consumers' Association, with more members than either of the major political parties. In 1967, to mark the tenth anniversary of its foundation, the Association published a special edition of its magazine *Which?* devoted to washing machines, with contributions from both Edward Heath and Harold Wilson.[46]

For ordinary consumers, all of this meant not only more money in their pockets but fundamental changes in their way of life. Millions of people now owned their own homes or could realistically aspire to do so: between 1950 and 1970, nearly six million new houses were built across the nation, and home ownership almost doubled, from 27 per cent to 50 per cent of all households. With home ownership came a new ethos of domesticity, fitting neatly with the new emphasis on the family unit and the pursuit of leisure. In the same period the number of gardens more than doubled to 14 million; and 29 million people were reported to be regular gardeners. The number of cars on the roads, meanwhile, rose from 2.3 million to 11.5 million. Not for nothing was the Mini, designed for BMC in 1959 by Sir Alec Issigonis, 'the motoring icon of the Swinging Sixties'. It was small, efficient, fashionable and, above all, affordable: at less than five hundred pounds, it was deliberately built to appeal to affluent young couples and single women.[47]

As wallets became heavier, so horizons broadened. Even working-class families could now look forward to a weekend pottering around the garden, doing up the front room, going for a drive to the seaside, or simply lazing in front of their new television. Tastes and interests that were once reserved for a wealthy upper-middle-class elite, from colourful furnishings and fashionable dresses to foreign holidays and evenings out in an Italian restaurant, had now been opened up to millions of ordinary people.[48] Indeed, having been something of a luxury just a few decades before, the extended holiday was now part of the fabric of everyday life. By the beginning of the sixties, ninety-nine industrial companies out of a hundred gave their workers two weeks' paid leave, which most still chose to spend at one of the traditional coastal resorts.[49]

But holidays themselves were changing, as thousands of families abandoned the old resorts for caravans, coach tours and the Costa del Sol.[50] Caravanning, for example, was one of the great unheralded success stores of the sixties, representing a shift from collective to individual leisure.[51] The Caravan Club's membership figures doubled in the course of the decade, and the club ran two hundred different sites, mostly along the coast. By

1970, caravans accounted for almost a fifth of all holiday accommodation, and it was estimated a few years later that more than half of the entire population had been on a caravan holiday at some point.[52] What was more, in conjunction with touring holidays and day trips, caravanning opened up remote parts of the country to mass tourism, from the seaside towns of East Anglia to the fishing villages of the Pembrokeshire coast. Millions of people discovered the pleasures of Devon and Cornwall, which had formerly been relatively quiet, even exclusive destinations.[53] By 1969 *The Times* was even complaining that both counties were blighted by 'perennial summer traffic chaos', which would have been unthinkable just a few years before.[54]

The traditional seaside holiday, meanwhile, was in slow but undeniable retreat. Many people were repelled by the increasing pollution of the sea: in Blackpool, for example, millions of tonnes of raw sewage were pumped into the harbour, only to be swept towards the beach by the tide.[55] Even in Blackpool, the most successful of all seaside resorts, landladies renamed their boarding houses 'guest houses' to try to present a more modern image, and the president of the local hoteliers' association told an American reporter that they were 'trying to get rid of the aspidistra'.[56]

Holiday camps, too, were beginning to struggle. Butlin's tried to attract the lucrative teenage market in the early sixties and subsequently found themselves lumbered with a reputation for vandalism, gang violence and sexual immorality. They responded by segregating teenagers from families, hiring battalions of security men and organising chalet patrols to cut down on nocturnal misbehaviour, but family bookings declined nonetheless. Finally, in 1968, the camps banned single teenagers outright, but by then the damage had been done.[57] As Fred Pontin, who ran a rival chain, told the press, conventional holiday camps were 'dying on their feet'.[58]

What really worried the holiday-camp bosses was the new vogue for taking holidays abroad. The most popular overseas destination, by a considerable margin, was Spain. In a bid to attract foreign currency the Spanish dictator Francisco Franco had decided to turn parts of the country into a tourists' playground, beginning with the Balearic Islands and the southern and eastern coasts.[59] One pretty little village south of Valencia, for example, had fewer than three thousand inhabitants in 1957, most of whom made their money from fishing, farming or weaving. Just three years later, the same village was almost entirely unrecognisable. Benidorm had 300 new buildings, including 30 high-rise blocks of flats; it boasted 34 hotels, 4 cinemas and a string of luxury boutiques; and it attracted more than 30,000

British and German visitors during August and September alone.[60] 'Benidorm is a home from home for the English, with all the good and bad that implies,' one paper remarked in 1963; 'but a home with white sands and, by day, constant sunshine.'[61]

The success of package holidays abroad is often rather exaggerated. In 1966 they still accounted for less than 4 per cent of the total holidays taken by British families, and even in 1971 they accounted for just 8.4 per cent.[62] All the same, it was obvious that they represented the future. With the industry falling into the hands of a few powerful operators, British package deals were the cheapest in Europe, and by the beginning of the 1970s two weeks in Spain might cost as little as twenty pounds. Overcoming their doubts about foreign customs and dodgy food, more families were taking the plunge, while entire Spanish towns were being transformed into overseas branches of Blackpool or Bognor.[63] Addressing a heckler during the 1970 election campaign, George Brown pointed out that 'only a couple of years ago at the Labour Club in my constituency you'd have seen a poster advertising the annual outing. It used to be a day at Blackpool or New Brighton or Skegness. Where do you think people go now?' At that, the club secretary broke in and pointed out that at that very moment there was a poster outside carrying the details of the latest trip. 'We're going for a week to the Mediterranean,' he added proudly.[64]

In 1972 *Carry On Abroad* took the familiar comic team to the Spanish resort of Elsbels, a less than idyllic resort where, as the studio press release put it, 'electrical points explode alarmingly; taps don't work and when they are finally persuaded to function it is sand that comes out instead of water; the restaurant is invaded by clouds of mosquitoes; the wine is definitely "off" and so is the food, only more so'.[65] For many people, this doubtless struck a chord: there were plenty of tales of nightmarish delays, unfinished hotels, substandard rooms and the like.[66] Indeed, even though people were flocking in growing numbers to the Mediterranean resorts, many remained extremely nervous of what they would find. Middle-aged Englishmen could often be seen wearing a jacket and tie on the beach, peering warily at restaurant menus, and scouring the streets for newspapers from home. One woman later recalled that it took her a week to muster the courage to eat in a French restaurant, where she was dumbfounded to discover olive oil in her tomato salad. Another had to be restrained by a waiter in San Remo from chopping up her spaghetti with her fork and spoon, but his efforts were wasted because she was sick afterwards anyway.[67]

One famous anecdote about British holidaymakers abroad concerns a group of Derbyshire miners who went to the Adriatic with crates of their own beer and even hired a cook to come with them. On their return, however, the miners were quoted as saying that 'wine and spaghetti are not all bad', and thousands of other British tourists evidently agreed with them.[68] Drinking wine had for many years been seen as a 'faintly sinful display of luxury', but thanks in part to their experiences abroad, middle-class consumers soon adopted it back home. Annual wine consumption per head doubled between 1960 and 1970, and then more than doubled again in the following decade.[69] 'Wine's a Winner with Sunday Dinner' an advertisement told potential customers in 1964. 'Pay a compliment to your wife's cooking by bringing in a bottle of wine to have with your Sunday dinner. Wine will make it the meal of the week . . . The man in the shop will gladly help if you want advice.'[70]

The popularisation of wine was just one of several changes in British drinking habits in the fifties and sixties, reflecting the influence of foreign travel and the vogue for all things French and Italian. The rise of coffee, principally in the instant form of Nescafé, was another example; and a third was the increasing popularity of lager. At the beginning of the sixties, lager accounted for a mere 3 per cent of the British beer market, and some brewers' predictions that it would one day eclipse bitter seemed very far-fetched indeed. Unlike bitter and stout, though, it was easy to preserve in bottles and cans, which made it a more enticing commercial prospect. Brewers recognised that British drinkers, used to downing more liquid than their European neighbours, might find it difficult to cope with lager's additional strength, so they developed 'standard lagers' like Skol, Harp and Carling Black Label, with an alcoholic content of just 3 per cent or so. These were then marketed to the young as glamorous 'European' beers of the kind consumed by, say, Alain Delon or Brigitte Bardot.[71] Within a few years, lager was available in almost every pub in Britain. Three out of four English pubs sold Skol, while in Scotland, where lager's appeal was stronger, three out of four pubs offered draught lager and it accounted for almost 20 per cent of the beer market. 'The long-term trend is unmistakeable', commented *The Times* in 1967.[72] With its fashionable, youthful associations, lager was set fair for a profitable future.

While the sales of wine and lager seemed to mark a convergence of British and European tastes, there was an even more pronounced transformation in what people ate. Aspiring cooks had more money to spend, better equipment, and a greater choice of foodstuffs than ever before. Immigrants from Asia and the Caribbean brought new flavours with them, and Chinese takeaways and curry houses joined Berni Inns and Wimpy bars on high streets across the land.[73] Avocados, aubergines and courgettes were becoming increasingly familiar, while dinner-party guests were no longer surprised to be offered prawn cocktail or coq au vin from the hostess's new trolley, followed, no doubt, by the latest exotic cheese from the Continent.[74] Even in the run-down Nottingham district of St Ann's, researchers in the late sixties spotted a crowded Italian corner-shop, 'with its baskets of aubergines and green peppers outside, and inside a passing glimpse of pasta in every shape and size [and] bottles of cheap Chianti'.[75]

In many ways Britain was clearly becoming a more 'European' country in the sixties. More and more people drove German cars, took their holidays on the Spanish coast, drank French wine and copied the latest Italian fashions. But we should not go too far: people might eat avocados, but they still laughed at and looked down on their Continental neighbours. At a public forum on the Common Market, the Conservative politician John Hay admonished a questioner who had referred to 'Eyeties' and 'Froggies' with the words: 'We as a nation must not sneer at others who perhaps have not had the same chances as ourselves.'[76] And although, in *Late Call*, Harold Calvert is a great fan of Continental cuisine, his parents are much more suspicious. When Harold cooks a meal of goulash and 'apfelstrudel', his father refuses to touch it. 'You cook for me and I can't want anything better,' Arthur Calvert tells his wife. 'If they prefer a lot of greasy Eyetie mess, let them get on with it.'[77]

At first glance, the success of credit cards, caravans and foreign holidays bears out the common impression of the sixties as a period of unprecedented social change. Many contemporary commentators, especially left-wing critics like Richard Hoggart and Raymond Williams, thought that traditional working-class culture was being swept away by the tide of affluence. In his BBC play *Stand Up, Nigel Barton*, broadcast in December 1965, the television dramatist Dennis Potter showed how affluence, education and social mobility drove a wedge between the generations. Young Nigel, the protagonist, is a grammar-school boy who has made it to Oxford, while his father is a miner from a Northern pit village. As new opportunities present themselves to Nigel, so a chasm begins to open between him and his parents, who are left behind in the traditional world of the terraced street, the pub and the working men's club. His values are no longer theirs.[78]

What is more striking, however, about British tastes and habits in the age of affluence is that they changed so little, not so much. When people moved to Milton Keynes in the late sixties, surveys found that they overwhelmingly preferred their houses to present a traditional brick or white-rendered exterior; more colourful or experimental façades did not appeal to them.[79] Indeed, far from the bright lights of Swinging London, life seemed to go on much as before. In 1964 Geoffrey Moorhouse commented that East Anglia 'does not yet look as if it has changed much over the years'. As for the rural Midlands, he concluded:

> Very little seems to happen here that we get to hear of or that is worth making a song and dance about when we do. The only angry noises which have so far emerged from Ludlow in the sixties, for instance, arose from a suggestion that the cobblestones of Broad Street might be covered with tarmac and the rector's promise that he would encamp on them rather than let this happen . . . This feeling that nothing ever changes here, that whatever may be going on in the rest of the country this part of it will be smothered in blossom come next spring with no new developments in sight, produces its own satisfaction. Here there are people who seem not only to be living in the past but who are fairly wallowing in it.[80]

Moorhouse himself admitted that the idea that 'nothing ever changes here' was a little simplistic. Motorways, supermarkets, comprehensive schools and other innovations changed the landscape of the countryside just as they altered the rhythm of life in the cities and their suburbs. But it was certainly true that in many parts of the country change came only slowly or subtly. Across Scotland, Wales and Northern England, and perhaps even more in Northern Ireland, entire communities were still terrified of unemployment, and among the traditional manual working classes, cultural change was often less marked than in other sections of society. As the historian Steven Fielding puts it, 'while miners, of whom there were still half a million in 1960, enjoyed historically unprecedented standards of living, many remained in the same village, went to the same pubs and clubs, and worked in the same pit as their grandfathers'.[81]

Teenagers in Northern England felt themselves 'backward' or 'behind the times', precisely because change seemed so elusive. 'Everything reached Hull about five years after it reached everywhere else,' complained one woman, who had been a student in the Humberside metropolis. 'It was about 1967 and everywhere else girls were wearing mini-skirts, but in Hull I'm sure they'd never heard of them.'[82] And another woman who grew up in a village near Sunderland later told an interviewer:

> It took six months or more for anything fashionable to reach the North-East. London was well into minis, it was splashed everywhere that this revolution in dress had taken place, before any of it reached us . . . It was a long time before minis made it up North. In fact, I think it was about 1966 or 1967 before they reached our village. They may have worn them in Newcastle before that, but not in Sunderland.

'I don't think the Pill had even reached our village by the mid-sixties,' she added. 'I'd never even heard of a condom.'[83]

Anecdotes like these suggest that, for good or ill, the experience of the sixties was marked as much by continuity as by revolutionary change. When David Frost and Antony Jay examined the state of the nation in 1967, they questioned the idea that attitudes had 'changed utterly in the space of a few years.' 'The English are as reserved as ever they were,' they wrote, 'and anyone who doubts it is perfectly welcome to try to strike up a conversation with a stranger in a train, but he is advised to take a book on his journey, too.'[84] A year later, after a detailed investigation of daily life and habits in Huddersfield, Brian Jackson concluded that the old order had 'held its ground', not least because of the strong 'suspicion of the new and strange' that ran through working-class culture in West Yorkshire.[85] Brass bands, for instance, were still as prevalent as ever, with thirty-six of them competing for recruits within a fifteen-mile radius, and continued to attract new blood.[86] Crown Green bowls, meanwhile, was still staggeringly popular: Huddersfield alone had thirty-three different bowling clubs and five thousand regular bowlers, which meant that it was easily the most popular participatory sport in the area.[87]

And working men's clubs, too, retained their appeal, despite the competitive pressures of the television, the family and the car. They claimed some two million members at the end of the sixties, giving working-class men across the country somewhere to have a convivial pint and a chat. The clubs owed their success, though, to the fact that they gently moved with the times. When Jackson visited one club in Huddersfield on a Wednesday night, he saw two or three young men playing billiards, about twenty men drinking and chatting, and then, towards the end of the evening, a dozen or so 'wives and mothers'. Most clubs welcomed women by the end of the sixties; this was nothing to do with the advance of feminism, but simply a reflection of the prominence of women in the labour force and the new 'companionate' relationship between husbands and wives, and it helped to keep the clubs alive in the age of the affluent family.[88]

The apparent continuity of much of British life during the sixties was less a case of change having failed to reach provincial communities, and more one of ordinary people actively holding on to their familiar habits. Even politically, most people shrank from innovation: when Gallup asked Labour voters in October 1969 what they thought of the government's policies, 32 per cent believed they were 'too socialist', 32 per cent 'about right' and only 18 per cent 'not socialist enough'.[89] Another, more detailed survey of a thousand adults published in *New Society* the following month was even more revealing. Asked which changes of the sixties they were most pleased with, 51 per cent identified 'better old age pensions', followed by 18 per cent who cited the 'rising standard of living'. Asked which changes they most disliked, 26 per cent chose 'easier laws for homosexuality, divorce, abortion etc.', 23 per cent selected 'immigration of coloured people' and 23 per cent chose 'student unrest'. All social groups, rich and poor, young and old, agreed that there was 'too much publicity given to sex', that 'murderers ought to be hanged' and, by an enormous margin, that there were 'too many coloured immigrants in the country now'. The generation gap, meanwhile, appeared to be a myth. In a stunning refutation of the simplistic identification of young people with political progressivism, two-thirds of young people between sixteen and twenty-four agreed that hanging should be brought back, while hostility to coloured immigrants was even stronger among the young than among pensioners.[90]

The findings in *New Society* were far from unusual: as the sixties drew towards their close, other surveys produced similar results. In December 1969 NOP asked respondents: 'If you could pass one law, what would it be?' The biggest proportion, 26 per cent, chose the return of hanging, followed by 25 per cent who chose to bring back the birch, 5 per cent who wanted the government to tighten welfare benefits, and 5 per cent who wanted an immediate halt to immigration.[91] The fascinating thing about all these polls is that they showed very little difference between Labour and Conservative supporters or young and old. Almost all respondents, whatever their age, income or political affiliation, disliked immigration, the liberal reforms of the 'permissive society', student protest and the commercialisation of sex. What was more, young and old had strikingly similar ambitions for the 1970s: keeping prices and unemployment down, getting 'the country's economy sound' and improving children's education. This sits uneasily with the notion that young people constituted a revolutionary vanguard, that their views and values clashed with those of their parents, or that they were always the first to embrace change. But as the historian John Benson points out, 'the great majority of young people spent more time in their bedrooms or at church youth clubs than they did at rock festivals or on the football terraces'.[92]

Of course, it would be absurd to deny that the 1960s was an era of social and cultural change. Yet it is important to realise that the changes were often halting, fragmentary and bitterly contested. What is more, the effects of change were often manifested in ways that seem disappointingly mundane to writers who like to sneer at 'Middle England'.[93] Instead of tearing down established conventions and habits, the rollicking consumer growth, technological innovation and social mobility of the sixties often ultimately reinforced them. Foreign visitors had long remarked on the importance of the domestic household to an Englishman's sense of self; thanks to the combination of home ownership, rising wages and expanded leisure time, millions of men were now drawn into the arcane world of 'do-it-yourself', spending their weekends building and knocking down walls, putting up shelves and drilling holes in the wrong places.[94]

Indeed, DIY was one of the great success stories of the sixties, and probably tells us more about ordinary life than a thousand psychedelic records. Magazines like *Man about the House*, *Handyman* and *Homemaker* offered instructions to men who wanted to improve their domestic environment; the BBC's DIY expert Barry Bucknell received hundreds of letters from viewers impressed by his cheerful makeover programmes; and from 1957 onwards an annual DIY exhibition attracted tens of thousands of visitors.[95] As one magazine put it, what had begun as 'an economic necessity has now become a pleasurable pastime which brings profit to the pocket and self-satisfaction to many thousands'.[96]

But popular as DIY was, it did not come close to competing with the most widespread weekend pastime of all, gardening.[97] As a Cabinet report put it in May 1963, despite even the advance of the television, 'gardening is still the greatest British hobby'.[98] Indeed, television and gardening occasionally went hand in hand: from 1955, Percy Thrower presented the immensely popular

BBC show *Gardening Club*, before transferring to the equally successful *Gardener's World* in 1968. When Thrower first opened his own garden to the public, more than nine thousand people turned up and the police were forced to redirect local traffic.[99] Gardening was also an increasingly technological business, as was only appropriate in Harold Wilson's Britain. Flymo launched the battery-powered plastic hover-mower, inspired by the hovercraft, in 1965, and four years later the same company also introduced the world's first electric hover-mower. Chemical weedkillers, composts and plastic garden tools were all readily available from the local garden centre, itself an innovation reflecting the affluence of the day.[100]

Although the popularity of gardening owed much to the social and economic circumstances of the fifties and sixties, it was also widely interpreted as evidence of the underlying conservatism, individualism and domesticity of British life. For centuries, England had been presented as an idealised rural idyll, a 'little, local, gentler' world of common sense, good manners and rolling hills. Englishness itself was often defined in terms of garden metaphors, its people as strong and sturdy as oaks.[101] Since Britain was one of the most heavily urbanised and densely populated countries in Europe, this vision of national identity offered the perfect antidote to the realities of metropolitan and suburban life. When the patriotic historian Sir Arthur Bryant wrote that every Englishman dreamed of 'a rose garden and a cottage in the country', he was not altogether exaggerating.[102] A quarter of a century later, describing life in the industrial towns of the North, Richard Hoggart noted 'the persistence of the desire to grow things, in windowboxes and on patches of sour soil in back-yards', as well as in allotments and little gardens.[103]

Not for nothing did the new housing estates and suburbs of the sixties often adopt a kind of rustic ethos. The very word 'estate' conjured up an atmosphere of country gentility, while the names chosen for estates and individual houses – the Hawthorns, Rose View, Acacia Villas and so on – carried rural or floral connotations. Estate agents often placed great emphasis on the size, condition and privacy of the suburban garden, and there was an unspoken assumption that if a house had a big garden, it was more likely that the husband would spend his free time there rather than in the pub with his friends.[104] The New Towns, too, often cultivated a pseudo-rural appearance, and surveys of people who moved to Milton Keynes in the late sixties and seventies found that one of the principal attractions was the prospect of a sizeable suburban garden.[105]

Even the Beatles knew the importance of the English garden. Paul McCartney's father Jim was a dedicated gardener, filling their front garden with dahlias, snapdragons and a lavender hedge, and often sending his son off to collect horse manure for the soil. Eventually Jim became the secretary of the Speke Horticultural Society, and during his early teenage years young Paul often found himself ringing doorbells and asking people whether they would 'like to join the gardening club'. It was an unlikely but nonetheless appropriate way for the future Beatle to spend his formative years.[106]

For as the journalist Anthony Sampson wrote in his *New Anatomy of Britain* just after the end of the sixties, the newspapers might talk all they wanted about sex, drugs and rock and roll, but for millions of ordinary people the real pleasures of the time were very different:

> Britain is the greatest nation in Europe for handymen and potterers-about; it has the highest proportion of people who do their own wallpapering, painting, drilling and plumbing, and the highest proportion who buy second-hand cars. A broad picture unfolds of the British living a withdrawn and inarticulate life . . . mowing lawns and painting walls, pampering pets, listening to music, knitting and watching television . . .

'If one wanted a symbol of what distinguishes contemporary British life from that of other countries,' he concluded, 'it might well be the potting shed.'[107]

11

THE WILD ONES

A mother said: 'I asked him why he wanted to go to Brighton, and he said it would be good for his pimples to have a day in the sun. I told him his spots would go quicker if he got a haircut.'

The Times, 22 May 1964

Some people pick up their guitars and take Route 66. I took the M1.

Ray Davies, 1995

The Easter weekend of 1964 was one of the gloomiest that most people could ever remember. Rain poured down from slate-grey skies, and Easter Sunday, which fell on 29 March, was the coldest for eighty years. At the seaside resort of Clacton in Essex, spirits were low. For some years respectable working-class families from the capital had been taking their holidays elsewhere, and with every passing summer Clacton looked a little poorer, a little wearier, a little shabbier. It now attracted a very different group of visitors: bored teenagers from Essex and East London, with money in their pockets but not much to do. That Easter, there were hundreds of them in Clacton, wandering sullenly under the shopkeepers' stares or riding their scooters up and down the front. Rival gangs taunted one other across the beach; one or two stones were thrown; a couple of scuffles threatened to break out; and then the trouble started.[1]

The next day, Britain's best-selling newspaper, the *Mirror*, carried the story on its front page: 'The Wild Ones invaded a seaside town yesterday – 1,000 fighting, drinking, roaring, rampaging teenagers on scooters and motorcycles . . . Leather-jacketed youths and girls attacked people in the streets, turned over parked cars, broke into beach huts, smashed windows, and fought with rival gangs.'[2] No fewer than 97 people had been arrested after the fighting on the seafront, and the scuffles had caused an estimated £513 worth of damage. Two days later the paper reported that MPs were calling for 'stiffer penalties – including jail – to deal with the menace of the "Wild Ones". They made their demands as angry Clacton licked its wounds – inflicted by the hundreds of marauding teenagers who turned Easter there into a weekend of terror.'[3]

And that was not all. On 17 and 18 May, over the Whitsun holiday, the teenagers were back at the seaside. 'There was Dad asleep in a deckchair and Mum making sandcastles with the children,' said the *Express*, 'when the 1964 boys took over the beaches at Margate and Brighton yesterday and smeared the traditional postcard scene with blood and violence.'[4] At Bournemouth there were 56 arrests and £100 worth of damage; at Brighton there were 76 arrests and £400 worth of damage; and at Margate the police arrested 64 people and reported damage worth £250.[5] The next day the *Mirror* ran an enormous photograph of one teenager kicking another as he lay defenceless on Brighton beach. 'LIVING FOR KICKS' screamed the headline:

> They met on the beach at Brighton yesterday – the Mod and the Rocker. And the boot went in . . .
>
> There are no rules in the war between Mods and Rockers. And no mercy.
>
> The Mod kicked the Rocker in the face. And after the Rocker was able to lift his face, it was smeared with blood.
>
> This was just one moment of violence out of the many which flared in Brighton and Margate over the Whitsun holiday.

When the mayor of Margate suggested that the press were only encouraging more violence by drawing such lurid attention to it, the *Mirror* was furious.[6] 'If the Blinkers Brigade imagine that this newspaper is going to suppress the ugly activities of the lunatic fringe, they are going to think again,' thundered an editorial. 'There are matters more important, Mr Mayor, than a slump in the day's takings of a whelk stall in Margate. And the future of the youth of Britain is one of them.'[7]

Fears about adolescent misbehaviour had deep roots in British history. The very term 'hooligan' had been coined in 1898 after drunken working-class boys ran amok in London over the August holiday, and Victorian and Edwardian writers often worried about the 'problem of youth', using it as a kind of shorthand for their anxieties about industrialisation, urbanisation and social and cultural change.[8] In the late 1940s newspaper commentators had fulminated against the 'spivs' and 'wide boys' whom they blamed for the rising rates of burglary and theft. Similarly, in the 1950s there had been much anxiety about extravagantly dressed Teddy Boys armed with flick knives, 'juvenile delinquents' bent on terrorising their neighbours, and sexually precocious teenagers with more money than sense.[9] In his history of hooliganism Geoffrey Pearson goes even further back, noting the 'striking continuities' across the centuries: 'the same rituals of territorial dominance, trials of strength, gang fights, mockery against elders and authorities, and antagonism towards "outsiders"'.[10] There is no doubt, however, that the threat of groups like the Teddy Boys was greatly exaggerated by the popular press. Teenagers became 'folk devils' in the late fifties and sixties, not because they were all delinquents, but because they were ideal scapegoats for all the changes occurring in the affluent society. Teenagers in the sixties were iconic figures, not only because of what they did, but because they personified so many of the issues of the day, from the rise of mass entertainment to the new working-class prosperity. As a representative of modernity, energy, sexuality and ambition, the teenager may have captured the hopes of British society, but he also compounded its fears.[11]

Despite all the press excitement about Teddy Boys in the late fifties, the fashion for dressing in dapper Edwardian finery had begun to wane as early as 1955, and by the end of the decade there had emerged a new style by which affluent teenagers could proclaim their distinctiveness.[12] As early as 1959, in his novel *Absolute Beginners*, the writer Colin MacInnes was describing a teenage boy's 'modernist' appearance: 'College-boy crop hair with burned-in parting, neat white Italian rounded-collared shirt, short Roman jacket *very* tailored (two little vents, three buttons), no-turn-up narrow trousers with 17-inch bottoms absolute maximum, pointed-toe shoes, and a white mac lying folded by his side.' His 'chick', meanwhile, was dressed with similar attention to detail: 'Modern jazz boy's girl – short hemlines, seamless stockings, pointed-toed high-heeled stiletto shoes, crêpe nylon rattling petticoat, short blazer jacket, hair done up into the elfin style. Face pale – corpse colour with a dash of mauve, plenty of mascara.'[13]

This was a look that demanded immense care, time and, above all, money. It originated with affluent teenage children from middle-class London suburbs, many of whom liked to listen to jazz. This had long been the favoured music of grammar-school boys and students, and its aficionados came in two varieties: 'trad' fans who liked traditional jazz from the early part of the century; and 'modernists', who preferred the more intricate, experimental sounds of Charlie Parker or Miles Davis.[14] Modernist fans, or 'mods', were also associated with coffee bars, Continental fashions and a slight taste for literary bohemianism.[15] All of these things were markedly middle-class, and all suggested a certain style and sophistication, often identified with France and Italy, that set their admirers apart from the herd. As one writer puts it, Mod was all about 'catching the latest continental movies and hanging about coffee bars and jazz clubs in terrific togs wired up on amphetamines and trying terribly hard to look as if one weren't trying at all'.[16]

By 1964 or so this first incarnation of Mod had been overtaken by a second version, which was more closely associated with rhythm and blues music, Italian scooters, a hectic, amphetamine-fuelled social life, and, most of all, the latest fashions.[17] The typical second-wave Mod wore a smart shirt, a short, box-shaped jacket, narrow trousers and gleaming black boots, while his hair was cropped short in a neat 'Italian' or 'French' cut. Black and dark blue predominated, although towards the middle of the sixties some Mods began dressing in Fred Perry sports shirts and even cardigans. The whole point was to cultivate a look of 'effortless' Continental sophistication, like an idealised vision of Italian elegance somehow transported to suburban England.[18]

The Mod boom was excellent news for coffee bars and clubs. With no dependants and money jangling in their pockets, many young earners were extremely keen to spend their evenings out on the town. One Mod interviewed by the *Sunday Times* and somewhat incongruously called Denzil explained that in an average week he went out dancing every night to clubs like the Marquee and the Scene, with the exception of Thursdays, when he washed his hair.[19] This might sound a punishing and expensive routine but it was not necessarily exaggerated. Many Mods sustained themselves by swallowing amphetamine and barbiturate pills, which they nicknamed 'purple hearts'. 'They used to keep you going most of the night, but the only dodgy night was Sunday night because you were really tired then, so we'd take a handful and we'd be OK,' recalled one apprentice printer from Islington. His social routine was pretty exhausting:

> Monday was Tottenham Royal, Tuesday the Lyceum, Wednesday the Scene, or maybe stay in and wash your hair, Thursday Tottenham Royal again (because it was our own little hangout), then Friday night was 'Ready Steady Go' . . . Then after 'Ready Steady Go' you'd go on to the Scene later. Saturday and Sunday was either a party or the Tottenham Royal, then the next week you'd start again.[20]

Needless to say, the likes of the Tottenham Royal did very well out of all this. So, too, did Soho and West End clubs like the Marquee, the Flamingo, the Last Chance and the Roaring Twenties; and suburban clubs like the Goldhawk in Shepherd's Bush.[21] And although the Mod scene was generally associated with London, it was not confined to the capital. Liverpool, Birmingham and Newcastle all boasted Mod populations, but perhaps the largest concentration north of London was found in Glasgow, where they established a reputation for gang violence.[22] The monthly magazine *The Mod*, which had been founded at the beginning of 1964, was bombarded with letters from Scotland complaining about its London bias, and its editor was forced to apologise. 'We're always inclined to think that the girls and guys up there walk about in kilts saying "haggis" or "och" with every other word,' he admitted. 'It's not true. Seeing the photographs that they have been sending . . . I'd say that in some parts they are in fact just as much fashion mad go-ahead as we are in London.'[23]

Many commentators found it impossible to talk about the Mods without also mentioning their famous enemies, the Rockers. These were the successors to the 'Ton-up Boys' of the fifties, who were almost exclusively from working-class backgrounds. Ton-up Boys and Rockers took their inspiration from the United States, and especially from groups like the Hell's Angels, which they had seen in 'biker films' like *The Wild One* (1953). They wore black leather jackets, often with shiny metal studs, white T-shirts, tight blue jeans and cowboy boots. Unlike the Mods, the Rockers wore their hair long and greasy in the style of the late fifties; they also rode around on motorbikes rather than scooters, preferred cheap petrol station cafés to smart suburban coffee bars and listened to white rock and roll rather than black rhythm and blues. They were not interested in sophistication, more in projecting an image of aggressive masculinity, and since they harked back to the Teddy Boys and Ton-up Boys, they were usually seen as much less modern figures. Mods were both folk devils and fashionable trend-setters; Rockers were just folk devils.[24]

There was little love lost between the two groups, reflecting partly the usual gang rivalries of adolescence, but also the genuine class antipathy between their members. To the Mods, the Rockers were backward, primitive and uncouth; to the Rockers, the Mods were pretentious, precious and effeminate.[25] 'We hate and despise [the Rockers],' one seventeen-year-old Mod girl told the *Mirror*. 'They can join us if they like – or they can get out of the country. They've got a different attitude to life. Mods enjoy life: they like to dance. Rockers don't dance . . . they just listen to pop music.'

Reflecting on the recent violence, she mused that it was a way of getting people 'to take notice of us. The word gets around and it gets exciting and you go where you think the fights are going to be.'[26]

In fact most reports of the seaside violence were wildly exaggerated. Most of the teenagers at Clacton had come not to fight but to mooch around, vaguely hoping that they might meet some girls, and they were bored and aimless rather than crazed with bloodlust. Innocent families had not been trampled underfoot on the beaches; the weather was so cold and wet that the teenagers had the beaches to themselves.[27] 'There was no evidence of drink or drugs and no gang warfare,' insisted the *New Statesman*. 'Some of the charges, compared with the Easter headlines, seemed piffling: "stealing half a pint of petrol", "attempting to steal drinks from a drinks machine" (fined £20 for this), "obtaining credit to the amount of 7d by means of fraud other than false pretences" (an ice cream in fact).'[28] 'There was a lot of running around, a few slaps, a few got a good kicking and maybe a few lumps,' another young Mod recalled. 'It wasn't much more than that. You spent most of the day running around, you were knackered. You felt you'd been in a fight but often you hadn't.'[29]

All the same, the newspapers were determined to present the fighting as though it had been a latter-day medieval battle. The *Evening Standard* talked about 'Goths by the sea'; even more colourfully, the *Sheffield Star* described the Mods and Rockers as a 'marauding army of Vikings going through Europe massacring and plundering, living by slaughter and rapacity'.[30] The *Daily Express* called the culprits 'ill-conditioned odious louts'; the *Sketch* labelled them 'retarded vain young hot-blooded paycocks'; and the *Telegraph*, which specialised in withering denunciations of the teenage population, branded them 'grubby hordes of louts and sluts'.[31]

The most memorable reaction came from the Margate magistrate Dr George Simpson, who was evidently determined to make a name for himself. To Dr Simpson, the forty-four defendants who appeared before his court were 'miserable specimens', 'strutting hooligans', 'louts', 'dregs' and 'vermin' – and those were just the compliments. 'It is not likely', he said coldly, 'that the air of this town has ever been polluted by the hordes of hooligans, male and female, such as we have seen this weekend and of whom you are an example.' Announcing a string of extremely heavy fines and detention sentences, he told one defendant:

> These long-haired, mentally unstable, petty little hoodlums, these sawdust Caesars who can only find courage like rats, in hunting in packs,

came to Margate with the avowed intent of interfering with the life and property of its inhabitants. Insofar as the law gives us power, this court will not fail to use the prescribed penalties. It will, perhaps, discourage you, and others of your kidney who are infected with this vicious virus, that you will go to prison for three months.

To the press, Dr Simpson was the hero of the hour. On 19 May, beside a photograph of the gallant magistrate, the *Express* hailed this 'small man in a grey suit' as 'the Quiet Man who Rocks the Thugs'.[32]

But as *The Times* noted, far from being the 'dregs' of the East End, as was often claimed, many of the defendants came from 'respectable backgrounds'. The disturbances had 'jolted the complacency of fathers and mothers in middle-class suburbia', and in 'thousands of homes all over Britain anxious parents today are asking themselves where they have gone wrong'. Many parents wondered whether they had been 'over-indulgent': one father of a sixteen-year-old boy, for instance, decided he had been 'too easy-going, letting him do more or less as he likes. I am certainly going to tighten up now.' 'I can't understand what has gone wrong,' one New Town housewife, whose son had been arrested in Brighton, told an interviewer. 'We have given him everything and done everything we can to help him.' Many of those interviewed thought that magistrates should be able to order the birching of young offenders; others called for the return of National Service, a common theme in the sixties and seventies even though the rise in juvenile crime had started long before it was abolished. *The Times* pointed out that many of the 'wild ones' came from homes where both parents had jobs: the real culprits, it implied, were Britain's working mothers.[33]

Nine months after the battle of Clacton, a former Mod group called the Who scored their first hit single, 'I Can't Explain', a pounding expression of sexual frustration written by their guitarist, Pete Townshend. On entering the charts, it climbed very slowly, peaked at number ten, and then fell away, but it was enough to create a groundswell of interest. The tape of their next single, 'Anyway, Anyhow, Anywhere', was initially rejected by Decca executives who thought that it was 'defective'. In fact the band had deliberately used feedback to capture the nihilistic aggression of their live performances, and especially to evoke their habit of smashing their instruments. This time the single climbed more quickly, peaked at number ten again, and then fell back. An unexpected bonus was its selection as the new theme tune for

Ready, Steady, Go!, and this good luck led *Melody Maker* to announce that the Who were 'poised on the brink of a breakthrough'.[34]

The Who were also fortunate to be breaking into the charts at a time when public interest in pop music had never been more intense. The record market was booming; the press paid much more attention to the activities of pop stars than ever before; and pop music seemed to have acquired an entirely new cultural cachet. As one historian puts it, there had been a 'decisive shift' in the 'public imagery associated with pop music'. In the very early sixties pop had been seen as little more than a frivolous, fleeting form of entertainment for working-class teenagers, a peripheral cultural product far from the centre of British adult life. By 1965, however, it had become 'a symbolisation of style', linked to the worlds of fashion, photography and design, and associated with the luxury and decadence of Swinging London.[35]

Much of this change could be attributed to one group, the Beatles. The *NME* reported that when they returned to Liverpool in July 1964, 'having conquered America, Australia, Scandinavia and Hong Kong', they were greeted by a cheering crowd of some 150,000 people, lining their car's route to a reception at the Town Hall.[36] Even George Harrison told the *Daily Mail* that the adulation, both at home and abroad, was 'out of all proportion'.[37] 'The Beatles were no longer a teenage fad,' writes Philip Norman: 'they had become a national obsession . . . In Britain throughout 1964, their doings and sayings ran in all the papers every day like some wildly popular, all-embracing strip cartoon. They had become, like cartoon characters, an elemental silhouette in which all desires and fantasies could be lived and gratified.'[38]

The Beatles' cultural importance was well illustrated on 12 June 1965 by the great excitement surrounding the news that they had each been awarded the MBE. Even Harrison commented that he 'didn't think you got that sort of thing just for playing Rock and Roll music'.[39] Many conservative observers agreed with him. One military veteran, returning his own award in disgust, told the press that 'the Beatles' MBE reeks of mawkish, bizarre effrontery to our wartime endeavours'.[40] Harold Wilson's colleagues, too, were unimpressed. Barbara Castle recorded that in the Commons 'the reaction was wholly unfavourable, the word "gimmick" being prominent'.[41] Tony Benn, meanwhile, was appalled, seeing it as proof of Wilson's innate monarchism:

> The *Daily Mirror*'s headline was 'Now They've Got Into the Topmost Chart Of All'. But the plain truth is that the Beatles have done more for the royal family by accepting MBEs than the royal family have done for the

Beatles by giving them. Nobody goes to see the Beatles because they've got MBEs but the royal family love the idea that the honours list is popular, because it all helps to buttress them and indirectly their influence is used to strengthen all the forces of conservatism in society. I think Harold Wilson makes the most appalling mistake if he thinks that in this way he can buy popularity, for he is ultimately bolstering a force that is an enemy of his political stand.[42]

Even the readers of the *NME* were divided. 'In three years they have done more than a stuffy Civil Servant could hope to achieve in 100 years,' wrote one fan from London. 'It makes a mockery of the whole system, to award them medals just because they've won a million apiece,' wrote another reader from Cardiff. In an attempt to weigh all the competing arguments, the paper's editor agreed that it was 'incongruous to lump war heroes together with entertainers', but still condemned the 'snobbery' of Fleet Street. In any case, the Beatles were not merely 'entertainers': their music might well 'be regarded as culture by generations to come'. Above all, they were a rare British success story in an age of political and economic decline:

I think it's wrong to imply that they have earned their medals as dollar-earners . . . No, where The Beatles honestly and justifiably deserve their awards is in the field of prestige. Their efforts abroad to keep the Union Jack fluttering proudly have been far more successful than a regiment of diplomats and statesmen.

We may be regarded as a second-class power in politics, but at any rate we now lead the world in pop music![43]

Even at this stage in their career, with their names and faces familiar to hundreds of millions across the world, the Beatles' daily routine had not greatly changed since 1963. Like their competitors, they remained a touring outfit, winning teenage audiences by releasing singles and playing live concerts. Fame brought its problems: even to visit the shops or go to the cinema, Paul McCartney sometimes had to call the police so that he would be able to make it safely through the crowds.[44] And although they travelled the world, they saw surprisingly little. Their days were tightly regimented, their hotels guarded and even their meals specially prepared and brought to their rooms.[45] This was an extremely draining and claustrophobic lifestyle, and few people were able to stick the touring routine for long. No doubt this was at the back of Brian Epstein's mind in January 1965 when he told reporters that the Beatles had 'two or three more years at the top' before, like Tommy Steele or Cliff Richard before them, they became 'established [i.e., showbusiness] stars' or 'film stars'.[46]

The Beatles' dissatisfaction with their fans had been evident as early as the autumn of 1963, when their provincial concerts were almost completely ruined by screaming. Ringo commented that he wished the crowd would be quiet, 'but what can you do about it? The time to start worrying is when they don't make any noise.'[47] But the problem only worsened as the group became more successful. One fan who attended a Beatles concert in Hull later complained that she had 'never heard a single note':

> It was a continuous, deafening cacophony of screaming. To keep up that very high-pitched and very loud screaming for that long – it was well over an hour – is amazing. If you really fixed your eyes on the stage, you thought you knew which one was singing. I was obsessed with the Beatles, so I was very disappointed by this concert, because I'd really like to have heard them.[48]

This problem was not confined to the Beatles. Keith Richards remarked that when the Rolling Stones performed live, 'it was like they had the Battle of the Crimea [sic] going on, people gasping, tits hanging out, chicks choking, nurses running round with ambulances. We couldn't hear ourselves. It was impossible to play as a band onstage.'[49]

But there is no doubt that the Beatles had the worst of it. On their second American tour, in August 1964, they were driven straight from San Francisco airport into a protective iron cage, from which the police soon had to rescue them after a mob of screaming fans threatened to demolish the cage itself. Worse was to follow. In Dallas fans broke through police barricades and clambered onto the wings of the group's aeroplane, and at the hotel a terrified chambermaid was threatened with a knife until she revealed the number of the Beatles' suite. In Cleveland they had to be dragged offstage by security guards while mounted police lassoed two hundred besotted fans in a giant net. The daily routine was 'cops and sweat and jelly beans hailing in dream-like noise', writes the band's biographer; 'it was faces uglied by shrieking and biting fists; it was huge amphitheatres left littered with flashbulbs and hair rollers and buttons and badges and hundreds of pairs of knickers, wringing wet'.[50]

Yet despite the number one records and endless tours, the British press, incredibly, complained that the Beatles were *under*-exposed. As far as the papers were concerned, the Beatles were likely to remain famous for no more than two or three years, so they ought to wring as many stories out of them as possible. Most commentators agreed that teenage tastes were so fickle that any worthwhile pop group should be milking its success almost every day of the week. In April 1965, just a few months after 'I Feel Fine' had made it to number one, the *NME*'s Chris Hutchins wondered if the Beatles had left it too long until their next single. 'Is the group's career suffering by under-exposure?' he wondered. 'Should the Beatles make more records? Many fans are demanding they should. Should they go out of their way to appear on Britain's top prestige TV programme *Sunday Night at the London Palladium*?'[51]

Complaints like this were so frequent that in August Lennon and Harrison felt obliged to defend the group's record. 'If we go on like we've been doing – *Ready, Steady, Go, Top of the Pops, Lucky Stars* and so on – people are going to get fed up with us,' Lennon remarked. 'We need *less* exposure, not more,' Harrison agreed. 'At one time people just got sick of having us rammed down their throats. It was Beatles, Beatles, Beatles.'[52] What was more, they thought that the pressures of touring were inhibiting their musical development. Lennon commented that they had no chance 'to improvise or improve [our] style'. 'We don't progress,' Harrison added gloomily, 'because we play the same things every day, every time we play somewhere. The thing is, we used to improve at a much faster rate before we ever made records.'[53]

The group's solution was to exchange one cage for another. 'We now spend more time in the studios than ever before,' George Martin explained almost a year later. 'The Beatles have come to accept that recording is their way of life. They accept the voluntary imprisonment of being in the studios for as long as 14 hours on end.'[54] And as the Beatles gradually retreated within the walls of the studio, so their music increasingly began to reflect their own artistic aspirations rather than the expectations of the singles market.[55]

The songwriting partnership between Paul McCartney and John Lennon has long been the subject of intense speculation. But as Ian MacDonald, the foremost authority on their music, has shown, for most of their time in the Beatles they were a 'genuinely tight' unit. There were considerable differences in their personalities and musical styles, but their instincts were sufficiently similar to allow them to work closely together and to make memorable songs out of snippets that each 'happened to have lying around'. In MacDonald's words:

> Lennon knew that while McCartney could be superficial, he was also the better musician and melodist and, when pushed, could rival and sometimes surpass him as an expressive writer. Conversely, McCartney's diplomatic charm and mainstream instincts worked as a brake on Lennon's anarchic disruptions and aggressive sarcasm. It was an ideal match. They laughed at the same things, thought at the same speed, respected each other's talent, and knew that their unspoken urge to best and surprise each other was crucial to the continuing vitality of their music.[56]

In the years after the Beatles' separation the instinct of many commentators, and indeed of John Lennon himself, was to praise his contribution to their success while simultaneously denigrating that of McCartney. In 1994, for example, Lennon was posthumously inducted into the Rock 'n' Roll Hall of Fame in New York. McCartney, who generously attended the ceremony, had to wait another five years; Harrison another ten; and Ringo Starr has not yet been inducted at all. Not only was Lennon effectively beatified in the minds of many after his murder in 1980, but he was given credit for anything the Beatles did that was supposedly risky, dark or adventurous, while anything gentler or more populist was blamed on McCartney. As the latter's biographer puts it, 'everything remotely experimental or avant-garde is always attributed to John Lennon, including Paul's loop tapes and orchestral experiments on "A Day in the Life"'.[57]

What made the Beatles so successful, as MacDonald points out, was the fact that Lennon and McCartney were such a good team, with the crucial difference between them being that 'the former was basically a pessimist and the latter basically an optimist'.[58] Lennon's emphasis was on introspection and self-expression: his lyrics, for instance, tended to be 'allusive, moody affairs', and his music was rich in harmonies and dissonance. McCartney, meanwhile, was more of 'a natural melodist, a creator of tunes capable of existing apart from their harmony': he was a more energetic, fluent, elegant writer, which made it easy for critics to dismiss him as glib. And McCartney was also unquestionably the more natural musician, which was not surprising given that his father Jim had been the leader of a jazz band. In the group's early days McCartney had been so far ahead of the other Beatles that they had even wondered whether he was too good to play with them.[59]

Even in the mid-sixties McCartney remained far more musically ambitious than his colleagues: by 1966, for instance, he was not only an accomplished guitarist and drummer but was also taking private piano lessons.[60] McCartney was also a much more outgoing, empathetic and intellectually generous songwriter than Lennon, often writing about imaginary third parties in 'novelistic' songs like 'Eleanor Rigby' and 'Lovely Rita'. Lennon, however, later dismissed 'these stories about boring people doing boring things — being postmen and secretaries and writing home. I'm not interested in third-party songs. I like to write about me.'[61]

McCartney's boundless cultural curiosity also explains his enthusiasm for the avant-garde in the mid-1960s. At the time, he was living with the upper-class family of his girlfriend, the actress Jane Asher, at Wimpole Street, London, and thoroughly enjoying himself as a man-about-town. Lennon, by contrast, was stuck in a mock-Tudor mansion in the Weybridge commuter belt, sinking deeper into misery and self-pity as his marriage collapsed under the weight of his infidelities.[62] While Lennon contented himself with taking greater quantities of drugs or beating up his wife, McCartney was busily pursuing not only girls but a wide variety of artistic interests: as one account has it, 'he thirsted for new ideas and stimuli as potential new strings to his bow as an artist'. After Jane Asher played him the music of Vivaldi, for example, he decided that he wanted the string arrangement in 'Eleanor Rigby' to adopt a similar style; and in 'Penny Lane' he specifically requested a high baroque trumpet for the solo section after watching a televised performance of Bach's Brandenburg Concertos.[63]

McCartney's interest in avant-garde music seems to have begun during 1965, after he had fallen in with a highly educated, bohemian circle through his girlfriend's brother Peter. He was particularly fascinated by tape loops, and spent many happy hours running tapes backwards, making loops of guitars or voices, and playing them to his new friends over a bottle of wine.[64] Karlheinz Stockhausen, the controversial German serialist and electronic pioneer, was a particular favourite, but perhaps the biggest influence was the American experimental composer John Cage, who had shocked the musical world with his notorious composition for piano containing no notes at all.[65] McCartney quickly realised that he could incorporate similar elements into the Beatles' own productions, marking them out from their increasingly numerous competitors. 'I'm learning all the time,' he told an interviewer in 1966. 'You do, if you keep your eyes open. I find life is an education. I mean, nowadays I'm interested in the electronic music of people like Berio and Stockhausen. It opens your eyes and ears.'[66]

What also pushed the Beatles further towards musical experimentation was the pressure from their chart rivals. At home, groups like the Rolling Stones, the Kinks, the Animals and the Who had all accumulated significant fan bases and were developing their own distinctive styles. By the autumn of 1965 both the Stones and the Kinks were consistently producing songs that matched the Beatles' own releases, and with hard-hitting and innovative singles like '(I Can't Get No) Satisfaction' and 'See My Friend', they were even threatening to surpass them. As if that were not enough, the Beatles also faced serious musical competition from American rivals like the Beach Boys and Bob Dylan. Harrison admired Dylan's folk-blues musical style, while Lennon was so obsessed with copying him that the other Beatles took to teasing him about his 'Dylan cap'.[67]

In August 1964 the Beatles met the adenoidal American in New York, where he introduced them to cannabis. Previously, like the other British pop stars of the day, they had stuck to alcohol and Drinamyl pills, or 'purple hearts'.[68] Alcohol and amphetamines were not substances that encouraged great introspection; by contrast, cannabis lent itself to a mood of sensuality, soul-searching and vague spiritualism. This new emphasis was further strengthened when the Beatles began experimenting with the hallucinogen LSD in the spring of 1965. Rather incongruously, they had first come across it when Harrison and Lennon's drinks were spiked at a dinner party with their dentist.[69] Although McCartney and Starr, the more down-to-earth members of the band, were always rather suspicious, Lennon became a great fan. LSD suited his self-pitying, self-indulgent and pretentious personality, and his drug experiences clearly informed songs like 'Tomorrow Never Knows' (1966) and 'A Day in the Life' (1967).[70]

But the overall influence of drugs on the Beatles' career is probably exaggerated. They had been enormously successful before they ever took cannabis or LSD, and their success was largely attributable to their ambition, self-discipline and sheer talent rather than to their intermittent chemically induced moods. As thousands of their imitators were to discover, drugs were often the road to insufferable self-importance rather than genuine insight or commercial success. Despite all the tales of drug-fuelled excess, the Beatles generally 'avoided anything that would blur their musical awareness', and so almost never touched alcohol or LSD when they were recording.[71] McCartney recalled that they 'didn't want to be lying around unable to do anything', not least because it would antagonise George Martin and the sound engineers. 'I think most of our best stuff was done under reasonably sane circumstances,' he concluded, 'because it's not easy to think up all that stuff, and you've really just got to get the miracle take if you're stoned. It can be done, just sometimes, but it may be one in a hundred.'[72]

The Beatles had first began to break away from the conventions of the three-minute pop single as early as August 1964, when they began experimenting with sea shanties, nursery rhymes and folk ballads. Two months later Lennon deliberately used electric guitar feedback to open 'I Feel Fine', and other innovations included McCartney's overdriven guitar in 'What You're Doing' and the fade-in to 'Eight Days a Week'.[73] Perhaps most strikingly, in February 1965 they recorded 'Ticket to Ride', one of their first singles to mimic the amplified sound of a live performance.[74]

In addition to developing a heavier sound the Beatles were beginning to rethink the content of their songs. For their early singles they had been content to rehash the romantic clichés of the day, but by the end of 1965, when *Rubber Soul* was released in the United States, they had already moved on. Protest songs were becoming popular, but McCartney told the *NME* that the Beatles disliked them 'because we're not the preaching sort and in any case, we leave it to others to deliver messages of that kind'. Instead, he confided, 'we've written some funny songs — songs with jokes in. We think that comedy numbers are the next big thing after protest songs.'[75] He was undoubtedly thinking of the song they had been working on just the day before, 'Norwegian Wood', which was essentially a comic short story. So too was 'Drive My Car', which they had recorded a week previously.[76]

Like its predecessors, *Rubber Soul* made it to number one in the album charts. More importantly, it represented a musical breakthrough for the group, tying together the technical experiments that had begun the previous autumn with the whimsical lyrics of songs like 'Norwegian Wood'. All fourteen songs were original compositions, and they spanned an unprecedented variety of styles, from the pseudo-gospel of 'The Word' to the cabaret pastiche of 'Michelle'.[77] And unlike the pop albums that had preceded it, *Rubber Soul* was recognisably the fruit of long days in the studio playing with the possibilities of audio technology. It was, said the group's producer George Martin, the first Beatles album to stand as 'a bit of art in its own right' and 'an entity of its own', rather than as a mere 'collection of singles'.[78]

Rubber Soul was an album in which Martin's own role had never been more important. With his background in orchestral music and novelty records, his patient handling of his charges and his willingness to challenge convention, he was the perfect producer and a crucial member of the Beatles' team. In the summer of 1965, for example, when Paul McCartney was working on 'Yesterday', it was George Martin who gently suggested he add a string quartet, showed him how to voice the chords and booked the best classical musicians. It was still McCartney's song, of course, but it would not have been the same without the advice of his debonair mentor.[79] As the group's biographer Philip Norman puts it, Martin's importance in the Beatles' success simply 'cannot be over-emphasised'.[80]

The artistic success of Rubber Soul gives the lie to the frequent claim that the Beatles spent most of their career merely imitating American models, from the rock and roll stars of the 1950s to Bob Dylan or the Beach Boys. This is quite simply nonsense, ignoring both the Beatles' immensely varied musical output and their diverse influences. Although they were deeply interested in American music, they grew up, lived and worked in Britain, not in the United States. Their recording history makes little sense outside its British context, from the traditions of the music hall and the Goons to the bohemian scene of the fifties and the satire boom. And this context became more important, not less, as they grew more successful. In their early years, true, the Beatles had often imitated American rock and roll stars like Little Richard and Chuck Berry. After their retreat to the studio in the mid-1960s, however, these American heroes 'gave way to a kaleidoscopic *mélange* of local influences from the English fringe arts and the Anglo-European counterculture as well as from English folk music and music-hall'.[81] In this respect they were not so very different from many of their home-grown competitors. Even the Rolling Stones, whose music was obviously inspired by American blues, were never quite as pro-American as some critics imagine. 'I wouldn't live in America,' Mick Jagger told a reporter in October 1965. 'I don't like the country enough. I prefer England.' Perhaps unexpectedly, his major complaint was a culinary one. 'I don't like the food because menus lack variety,' Jagger explained. 'The transport cafes are better than the transport cafes in England but the good restaurants here are not anywhere near as good. All the food tastes pre-packed.'[82]

To many listeners, what was really striking about the Beatles' music after 1965 was its sheer imagination. More than any other group of the day, they were comfortable with different musical styles and genres.[83] As for their lyrics, as one critic later put it, they had 'a flair for cleverness without being artful or supercilious'. Often lines or single words carried associations beyond the song, and more literate listeners could often spot references to which teenage pop fans were oblivious.[84] When McCartney and Lennon were teenagers writing together in Liverpool, the former remembered, they would 'sit around giggling, just saying puns really', and discussing their admiration for the likes of Lewis Carroll, Robert Louis Stevenson, Edgar Allan Poe, Edward Lear, Kenneth Grahame and Richmal Crompton.[85] It was no accident, therefore, that nonsense and wordplay were constant features of the Beatles' output. Even 'Yesterday' originally began life as a nonsense song entitled 'Scrambled Eggs', celebrating the virtues of the omelette.[86]

This emphasis on wit and whimsy was closely related to another element of the Beatles' style: their theatricality. Rock and roll music in Britain had originally been seen as just another branch of the variety business, and early performers had regularly appeared on the same bill as stand-up comedians, dancers and even jugglers and animal acts. Tommy Steele, for example, sometimes performed after two young comedians, Frank and Bernie Winters, who helped him to polish his act, and by the early sixties he had become a popular variety performer in his own right.[87] The Beatles saw themselves as heirs, not challengers, to this tradition, and they enjoyed excellent relations with older showbusiness artists like Lionel Blair and Alma Cogan, at whose London parties they were regular guests.[88] But they owed their most important theatrical debt to the comedy of the music hall. Many commentators had been complaining for years that music-hall traditions were about to die out, stifled by the advent of the cinema and, above all, television. The playwright John Osborne, for instance, wrote in the preface to his play *The Entertainer* (1957) that music hall was 'dying, and with it, a significant part of England'.[89] By the late sixties most music halls had been closed down or converted into bingo halls: in one episode of *The Avengers*, the villains turn out to be a troupe of former music-hall stars aggrieved at the collapse of their livelihoods. But although the halls themselves had been closed, their traditions endured in seaside variety shows, Christmas pantomimes, plays by the likes of John Arden and Harold Pinter, the *Carry On* film comedies and television shows like *Sunday Night at the London Palladium* and *The Morecambe and Wise Show*.[90]

The Beatles' dependence on music-hall traditions is an excellent example of the underlying continuity of British cultural life during the twentieth century. Pop music appealed to exactly the same kind of people who had patronised the music halls in their late nineteenth-century heyday: working-class and lower-middle-class youngsters, living in towns and cities and having a spare bob or two in their pockets for a cheap evening's entertainment.[91] In the Beatles' case there was also a direct link. McCartney's father had once worked as a spotlight operator at the Liverpool Hippodrome and would play the old tunes on the piano when teaching young Paul how to sing.[92]

It was hardly surprising, then, that the Beatles should imitate the styles and cadences of music-hall comedy. Their most famous album, *Sgt. Pepper's Lonely Hearts Club Band* (1967), was steeped in music-hall traditions, and McCartney's song 'When I'm Sixty-Four' could almost have been a hit for George Formby. The group's taste for comic clowning, as demonstrated in dozens of press conferences and television appearances, was well known, but it was also far from unusual. Dave Dee, Dozy, Beaky, Mick and Tich, who had a string of Top Ten hits between 1965 and 1969, had a taste for dressing up in flamboyant costumes and liked to intersperse their concerts with comic routines and 'risqué patter'.[93] The Hollies recorded a tongue-in-cheek title song for the Peter Sellers comedy *After the Fox* (1966). And even the Jeff Beck Group would occasionally strike up 'Strangers in the Night' as a joke.[94]

The group that most closely matched the Beatles, both in their imagination and in their debt to native cultural traditions, was the Kinks. As we have seen, the group had been blacklisted by the American unions and were therefore unable to tour across the Atlantic, so their retreat into the studio was a matter of necessity as well as design. But, like the Beatles, the Kinks were self-consciously eclectic: Dave Davies later remarked that his band 'had an advantage over everybody [because] we had so many different ways of doing things'.[95] And, like the Beatles, the Kinks spent hours experimenting with new techniques. Ray Davies told *Melody Maker* that they were 'always looking, searching for new sounds'.[96] They were the first group, for example, to borrow from Indian music, incorporating a heavy, almost dreamy feedback drone into 'See My Friend' (1965), imitating the sound of the sitar. Pete Townshend, who was inspired to take the Who in a similar direction, later commented that it was 'far, far better than anything the Beatles ever did'.[97]

The Kinks were also theatrical to an extent that few other groups ever matched, even during the flamboyant psychedelic era. By the middle of the decade Ray Davies had told the *NME* that 'See My Friend' was about bisexuality and was generally cultivating an air of dandyish camp.[98] Despite his background in suburban Muswell Hill, he had also begun singing in the style of an aristocratic dilettante, most notably in 'Dedicated Follower of Fashion' and 'Sunny Afternoon' in 1966. Occasionally the band even played while dressed in foppish aristocratic regalia or bright red hunting gear, which made it easy for critics to dismiss them as whimsical oddities. As Charlie Gillett puts it, however, 'the records stood the test of time and served to inspire and influence other British writers to deal with the British way of life, sung and played in an English manner'.[99] Indeed, Englishness was absolutely central to the Kinks' self-image. Ray Davies explained that on 'Sunny Afternoon', for example, he adopted an upper-class accent because he 'didn't want to sound American. I was very conscious of sounding English.'[100]

Since the Kinks had little chance of breaking into the American market, they were free to wallow in their parochial Englishness. Ray Davies developed a lyrical style all his own, and instead of singing about sex and drugs, he would regale the listener with comic monologues, music-hall routines and quirky stories about the forgotten rhythms of English life: cracked ceilings and leaking kitchen sinks ('Dead End Street', 1966); 'fat old Uncle Charlie . . . outside a bed and breakfast in sunny Southend' ('Picture Book', 1968); and the 'last of the good old fashioned steam-powered trains' ('The Last of the Steam-Powered Trains', 1968).[101] In October 1967, for example, the Kinks reached number three with 'Autumn Almanac', which Davies described as a 'song about a contented little gardener'.[102] A paean to old-fashioned Englishness describing 'dew-soaked' hedges, 'tea and toasted, buttered currant buns', it explicitly rejected the internationalism fashionable in avant-garde circles:

> I like my football on a Saturday,
> Roast beef on Sundays, all right.
> I go to Blackpool for my holidays,
> Sit in the open sunlight.
>
> This is my street, and I'm never gonna leave it,
> And I'm always gonna stay here
> If I live to be ninety-nine,
> 'Cause all the people I meet
> Seem to come from my street

> And I can't get away,
> Because it's calling me – come on home –
> Hear it calling me – come on home [. . .]

In 1968 the Kinks' immersion in idealised Englishness reached its apotheosis with the appearance of *The Kinks Are the Village Green Preservation Society*. Released with terrible timing on exactly the same day as the Beatles' 'White Album', it was a commercial disaster, even though it was arguably much more imaginative and intelligent. Ray Davies now explicitly embraced the persona of an antediluvian relic in an age that celebrated change rather than continuity. 'I live in a museum, so I'm OK,' he sings in 'The Last of the Steam-Powered Trains', adding that 'all this peaceful living is driving me insane'. He later commented that the album was 'a culmination of all those years of being banned from America. I just wanted to do something English. I felt I just wanted to write something that, if we were never heard of again, this is where we came from. It was a final stand.'[103]

Although the Kinks fell from favour in the late sixties, they remained an excellent example of the kind of group that aspired to make an artistic statement rather than merely sell singles. After their initial breakthrough, most groups with art-school roots were keen to do something a bit more ambitious, and this explains why the pop music of the mid- and late sixties was so rich with 'eclecticism, self-referentiality, parody and pastiche'.[104] Ray Davies commented that 'without the bridge of art college, I don't think the rest would have happened'.[105] Similarly, Pete Townshend tried to incorporate the avant-garde poetry and theatre he had studied at Ealing into the Who's performances.[106] Copying the band's bassist John Entwhistle, he dressed in bright Union Jack jackets with badges and military medals, while Keith Moon wore Pop target-themed T-shirts and Roger Daltrey decorated his white sweater with geometrical patterns made from electrician's tape. Townshend explained to *Melody Maker* that they stood for 'pop art clothes, pop art music and pop art behaviour', whatever that meant. 'We live pop art,' he insisted.[107]

The Who's fascination with Pop Art illustrates the way in which the artists, designers, filmmakers and musicians of the mid-sixties borrowed from one another's work, so that, say, the paintings of Bridget Riley or the music of the Beatles had unexpected reverberations in completely different fields. But it was also a good example of what one writer calls the 'art school/fringe-theatre tradition in English pop'. Fantasy, artifice, frivolity and

'The final act in Britain's greatness': the funeral of Sir Winston Churchill, St Paul's Cathedral, 30 January 1965. *(Bettmann/Corbis)*

'We will campaign for the rapid modernisation of Britain.' The first edition of the *Sun*, 15 September 1964. *(Getty Images)*

Scouting for Boys: Harold Wilson on holiday in the Scilly Isles, 1965. *(Getty Images)*

James Callaghan in the Chancellor's office, April 1965. On his desk, a file is boldly marked 'Action', but critics charged him with hesitancy and half-measures. *(Getty Images)*

George Brown unveils the ill-fated National Plan, 16 September 1965. *(Getty Images)*

Harold Wilson meets the Beatles at the Variety Club showbusiness awards, March 1964. John Lennon looks typically polite and unassuming. *(Getty Images)*

Policemen struggle to hold back the crowds as the Beatles collect their MBEs from Buckingham Palace, 26 October 1965. *(Getty Images)*

British soldiers threaten a terrified Arab civilian during a demonstration in Crater, Aden, 1967. *(Getty Images)*

'I've heard of a special relationship, but this is ridiculous.' Gerald Scarfe's merciless cover for *Private Eye*, 30 April 1965.

The perils of the Space Age: the Cybermen invade London in an episode of
Doctor Who, 1968. *(BBC)*

'Nowhere else in England is there more excitement in the air.' Birmingham's new Bull Ring, circa 1965.
(Getty Images)

'One hundred per cent British': Diana Rigg and Patrick Macnee look splendid in their *Avengers* regalia, mid-sixties. *(TopFoto)*

Edwardian adventurer meets dolly bird: Gerald Harper and Juliet Harmer promote *Adam Adamant Lives!*, 1966. *(Getty Images)*

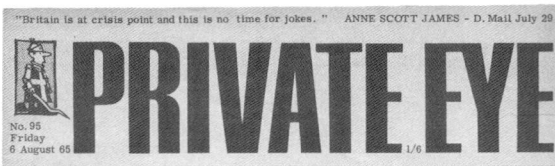

Private Eye greets 'the first Tory leader with wall-to-wall carpeting', 6 August 1965.

An unusually ebullient Edward Heath on his campaign plane, March 1966. Many Conservatives, however, blamed him for their second successive defeat. *(Getty Images)*

second to Barrabas'.[124] But when Lennon's comments were reprinted that summer in an American teenage magazine, all hell broke loose. Thirty-five American stations banned the Beatles' music; one town hired a tree-crushing machine to destroy the offending records; and bonfires of Beatles memorabilia blazed across the southern states.[125]

Lennon went to great pains to explain his remarks, repeatedly telling reporters that he was sorry for any offence. 'I can't express myself very well,' he told the *Washington Post*.

> That's my problem. I was just saying, in my illiterate way, what I had gleaned from a book I was reading . . . I'm more of a Christian now than ever I was. I don't go along with organised religion and the way that it has come about. I believe in God, but not as an old man in the sky. I believe that what Jesus and Mohammed and Buddha and all the rest said was right. It's just that the translations have gone wrong.[126]

Although the Beatles went ahead with their American tour, the furore over Lennon's comments meant that it began in a bitter mood. They were already tired of the routine of bland hotels and screaming crowds, and since it was practically impossible to reproduce their latest songs on stage, they were beginning to wonder why they bothered.[127] The American tour was shoddily organised: tickets were so expensive that many stadia were only half-full, there was too little time to rest, and the band played badly throughout. It hardly mattered – nobody could hear them anyway – but in the heat of the American summer they were tired and jittery. Everywhere they went they were surrounded by armed guards, while outside the arenas members of the Ku Klux Klan held demonstrations and burnings of their records. By the time that the Beatles arrived in California, they were determined that they would never put themselves through it again. 'They were really tired,' commented their local promoter. 'They were tired of their own music and they were tired of each other.'[128]

The last concert, in Candlestick Park in San Francisco, seemed a microcosm of all that had gone before. The night was cold and windy; the sound was rudimentary; and the audience consisted largely of teenage girls who screamed from start to finish and made it impossible for the Beatles to hear themselves playing. McCartney, who knew that the band were on the verge of disintegrating, asked a friend to tape the show on his cassette recorder, and just before one of the last numbers, all four members of the group excitement and disbelief. However, he admitted, he had 'also played it to Cilla [Black] . . . who just laughed!'[118]

Like the Beatles' previous albums, *Revolver* went straight to number one purely on the strength of its pre-orders.[119] Among their fellow musicians it was immediately recognised as a masterpiece. The jazz musician and critic George Melly commented that the Beatles had broken 'right through the conventions of popular song, let alone pop', and that pop had finally 'come of age'.[120] Like *Rubber Soul* before it, *Revolver* felt like a coherent creative work, but it went much further in musical experimentation and complexity. It was the first record that the Beatles had ever made that was simply impossible to reproduce live without the technological facilities of the studio. And more than any other record of the decade, it radically redrew the boundaries of pop music and established the standards that future musicians would struggle to meet.[121]

Despite the success of *Revolver*, however, the summer of 1966 was not very kind to the Beatles. At the end of June they had begun their latest world tour with a trip to their old stamping grounds in Hamburg, but from there it all began to go wrong. When they arrived in the Philippines, they accidentally missed a reception organised by Imelda Marcos, the extravagant wife of the local dictator. In revenge, the regime promptly withdrew all the group's security, and when the Beatles departed from Manila airport on 5 July they were physically harassed by customs officials and even punched, kicked and spat upon by security guards. In the end they were forced to run, as if for their lives, to their waiting aeroplane, with Filipino guards aiming blows at them as they passed. 'If I go back,' Harrison told the press afterwards, 'it will be with an H-bomb to drop on it.'[122]

Worse was to follow. By the time the Beatles arrived in the United States on 12 August, they had become engulfed in a storm surrounding Lennon's remark that Christianity was about to 'vanish and sink'. 'We're more popular than Jesus now,' he had told the *Evening Standard* in March 1965. 'I don't know which will go first – rock'n'roll or Christianity. Jesus was all right, but his disciples were thick and ordinary. It's them twisting it that ruins it for me.'[123]

In Britain, where religious passions were usually reserved for churches and private homes, his remarks passed almost unnoticed. Indeed, most people took them as a fairly accurate reflection of the long decline in church attendance figures, especially among the young. As one Church of England bishop pointed out, 'in the only popularity poll in Jesus's time, he came out surprise some of their fans. 'I supposed there's some won't like it,' he admitted, 'but if we tried to please everyone we'd never get started.'[113] Songs from the new album were gradually released to radio stations during the next month, increasing the anticipation for what was expected to be a radically new departure. Finally, on 5 August, a week after the World Cup Final at Wembley, *Revolver*, with its arresting black-and-white proto-psychedelic cover, reached the shops.[114] In separate interviews both Lennon and McCartney told the press, 'They'll never be able to copy this,' reflecting their shared satisfaction at the finished product.[115]

The music press clearly did not know what to make of it. The *NME*'s reviewer Allen Evans, for instance, commented that *Revolver* 'certainly has new sounds and new ideas', and his assessments of the individual songs betrayed his bewilderment:

> 'Eleanor Rigby' — a folksy ballad sung with a very clear diction by Paul McCartney, telling the wistful tale, complete with violins in backing, of Miss Rigby being buried with no-one there to see it and asking where do all the lonely people come from . . .
>
> 'Love You Too' is an Oriental-sounding piece, with George joining with Anil Bhagwat to play some sitar jangles, and George singing a Karma Sutra type lyric . . .
>
> 'Tomorrow Never Knows' is John's vocal, telling you to turn off your mind and relax and float downstream. But how can you relax with the electronic, outer-space noises; often sounding like seagulls? Even John's voice is weirdly fractured and given a far-away sound.[116]

In fact, 'Tomorrow Never Knows' was the fruit of Lennon's experiences on LSD and McCartney's experiments with tape loops. No other song in the Beatles' career had been more creatively assembled, and it exhibited almost every technical trick in their repertoire — tape loops, an Indian drone, automatic double-tracking, deliberate distortion of instruments and so on — woven together to create a mood of unprecedented mysticism and transcendence. In Ian MacDonald's judgement the Beatles had created 'a riveting blend of anarchy and awe, its loops crisscrossing in a random pattern of colliding circles . . . [I]n terms of textural innovation, [it] is to pop what Berlioz's *Symphonie fantastique* is to 19th-century orchestral music'.[117] McCartney proudly told the *NME* that when he had played the song to the Rolling Stones and the Who a few weeks before the album's release, they had 'visibly sat up' in irony all regularly cropped up in the records of the Beatles, the Kinks, the Rolling Stones and the Who, and were much more obvious in British popular music than in its American equivalent. British pop stars often came over as playful, witty and ironic, as in the Beatles' press conferences or the Kinks' fondness for dressing up. By contrast, their American counterparts generally strove for a kind of heroic earnestness that struck some listeners as profound and grown-up, but others as ponderous and pretentious.[108]

In any case, there is no doubt that the art-school emphasis on unorthodoxy and complexity was ideally suited to the extraordinary development of British pop music between 1964 and 1967. As one critic puts it, groups like the Beatles and the Kinks 'expanded many of the existing conventions of pop to the maximum'.[109] The enduring popularity of music from this era testifies to the sheer quality of their songwriting: in an age before the advent of synthesised drum-beats and ever heavier bass lines, the songs of the sixties reflected the influence of very different musical or even literary genres. At the same time, competing groups pushed one another to improve, musically and lyrically, and their close friendships and respect for one another's work were crucial factors in explaining their rapid artistic development.[110]

The key figures in all this, of course, remained the Beatles. In later years their music became so familiar that it was easy to forget just how fresh it had once seemed, and it is often tempting to downplay their achievement merely for the sake of appearing iconoclastic. But there is no doubt that at the time they were universally regarded as the most important pop group in the world; not only did their records easily outsell those of their competitors, but their rivals themselves frequently and frankly acknowledged the Beatles' pre-eminence.[111]

Thanks to the impact of *Rubber Soul*, the Beatles entered 1966 with a redoubled grip on their crown as the world's dominant group. After finishing the album, they had taken three months off, their longest break for almost four years, and spent their time relaxing on holiday and enjoying themselves in London. In April they began work on their next album, having been promised by EMI that they could take as long as they wanted. But, as so often, they were working under pressure from their rivals: in this case, McCartney was particularly concerned about the Beach Boys, who had just released their masterpiece, *Pet Sounds*. Although it was a commercial dud, McCartney thought that it was 'the album of all time', and was convinced that the Beatles would have to surpass everything they had ever done to match it.[112]

On 24 June McCartney warned an interviewer that the new album might retired to the back of the stage and posed for a photograph with their backs to the audience, 'because we knew that was the last show', said Harrison. When they had finished playing, they ran off the stage, and, as usual, were bundled into an armoured car for their own protection. A little later, as their plane took off for Los Angeles and then home, Harrison sipped a drink and said exhaustedly: 'Well, that's it. I'm finished. I'm not a Beatle any more.'[129]

12

DEDICATED FOLLOWERS OF FASHION

ADAM ADAMANT: Miss Jones, this masculine attire – is it part of the madness above? Some protective disguise, perhaps?
GEORGINA JONES: Hey, watch it! This gear cost me a bundle!
ADAM ADAMANT: 'This gear cost me a bundle' – that is some kind of code?

'A Vintage Year for Scoundrels', *Adam Adamant Lives!* (1966)

In Swinging London, whether you want to buy mauve hipsters or rent a man's chest wig for the weekend, the King's Road, Chelsea, is the place to look. They come in all shapes, sizes and sexes.

'Portrait of Brenda', *The Saint* (1969)

At the beginning of 1966 Pye Records announced the forthcoming release of a new 'humorous, catchy, sing-along number' by the Kinks.[1] 'Dedicated Follower of Fashion' was a scathing portrait of an affluent young shopper 'eagerly pursuing all the latest fads and trends,/'Cause he's a dedicated follower of fashion'. The single reached number two in the chart, an impressive achievement given its unconventional music-hall melody, affected vocal style and caustic vision of modern consumerism. Its timing, however, was perfect. The song's portrait of a trendy young thing, who 'flits from shop to shop just like a butterfly', evidently struck a chord with listeners, and the phrase 'dedicated follower of fashion' soon became familiar even to people who were no fans of the Kinks and had never heard the song.[2]

A few months later, reflecting on the cultural changes that had affected British life in the last few years, the young journalist Jonathan Aitken declared that 'the fashion revolution [was] the most significant influence on the mood and *mores* of the younger generation in Britain in the last decade', and had 'seized the threads of all the contemporary cults and woven them together in a strand that binds the entire younger generation with a new sense of identity and vitality'. As he saw it, the designers, photographers and models of the mid-sixties had become 'the new folk heroes and heroines of contemporary London'. They personified the values that Aitken associated with the 'swinging' scene: 'wealth, sex appeal, fame, youth, talent, novelty, and quick success', and they also embodied the 'new spirit' of Harold Wilson's Britain: democratic, dynamic and, above all, modern.[3]

In the public imagination no individual was more closely associated with the sensational success of the British fashion industry during the sixties than Mary Quant. Born in 1934, the skinny, serious-faced daughter of liberal Welsh schoolteachers, she had spent the early fifties studying fashion at Goldsmiths in London and there met her future husband, Alexander Plunket Greene. Through her relationship with Plunket Greene, Quant fell in with the so-called Chelsea Set, a raffish group of young, upper-class dandies who saw themselves as the successors to the Bright Young Things of the 1920s.[4] Although they dressed in outrageously colourful outfits and were animated by a vague spirit of rebellion, the members of the Chelsea Set were well-connected, well-educated and reasonably affluent; in Quant's words, they included 'painters, photographers, architects, writers, socialites, actors, con-men, superior tarts, racing drivers, gamblers and TV producers'.[5]

Although the Chelsea Set anticipated the incestuous social whirligig of Swinging London in the mid-sixties, very few people in the country at large had ever heard of them.[6] Ordinary mortals were generally excluded from their socially exclusive circle, and some of its members rarely ventured beyond the environs of Sloane Square. 'We were all very spoiled and very tiresome', recalled Simon Hodgson, a friend of the Quant crowd. 'Most of us were subsidised by our parents and our lives were built around going to parties and getting drunk and meeting gangsters . . . But we were really frightfully snobbish. Everyone had to be rich, funny or famous, or at least notorious.'[7]

While the great majority of the Chelsea Set never came close to national recognition, Mary Quant was destined to become one of the emblematic figures of British popular culture in the mid-1960s. Her first step towards stardom came in the autumn of 1955, when she and Plunket Greene opened their King's Road boutique, Bazaar.[8] At this stage the King's Road was a quiet local high street, full of bakers', greengrocers' and fishmongers', catering for the writers, actors and artists who lived nearby. Within a few years, however, it began to attract the attention of ambitious developers and retailers, and it proved the perfect location for their new business venture.[9] The plan, as Quant explained it to her partners, was to open 'a *bouillabaisse* of clothes and accessories ... sweaters, scarves, shifts, hats, jewellery, and peculiar odds and ends'.[10] Her own tastes were very different from the prevailing trends of the day, and she particularly disliked the swirling curves of the New Look that had taken hold in the late forties.[11] 'I hated the clothes the way they were,' she later explained. 'I wanted clothes that were much more for life, much more for real people, much more for being young and alive in.'[12]

On the day that Bazaar opened the only thing that Quant had been able to make in time was a pair of brightly coloured 'madhouse' pyjamas, but since the pyjamas were photographed by a journalist from *Harper's Bazaar* and then bought by an American clothier who wanted to sell copies across the Atlantic, this was not such a disaster after all. Indeed, Bazaar was an immediate success, and in the first week alone Quant took five times as much money as she had expected. In an era of high wages, economic growth and commercial expansion her courage had paid off.[13] Within a few months almost all the clothes were being made by Quant herself or her team of sewing-machinists, and the distinctive, bold 'Chelsea look' was beginning to capture the attention of the fashion editors. By the time Quant's second boutique, designed by Terence Conran, opened in Knightsbridge in 1957, she had already acquired a reputation for stylish informality.[14]

Like any good bohemian, Quant ignored convention, preferring to draw inspiration from children's clothes: pinafore dresses, short skirts, knickerbockers, knee socks and black stockings. She used fabrics like gingham, tartan and flannel that few other designers would touch; she converted cardigans into dresses, turned out trench-coats in PVC, and threw together startling combinations in polka dots and stripes. The Quant look was bright, neat and, above all, informal, very different from the intricate, flowery curves of established fashion. Her girls were not 'pretty'; they were 'kinky' or 'kooky'. The accent was on youth and ease, not on glamour; she wanted to make 'clothes to move and run and dance in'.[15]

In 1961 Quant decided to move into mass production, forming a limited company to sell her brand to other manufacturers. The fifties and sixties were a period of dramatic transformation in the fashion industry. American techniques of wholesaling, licensing and marketing were becoming increasingly popular, and a new organisation, the London Fashion House Group, was instrumental in arranging the London Fashion Weeks and a series of highly successful tours to Paris and New York.[16] Quant reaped enormous benefits from these new networks of design and commerce. In 1963 she launched the Mary Quant Ginger Group to sell her designs to an international mass market and signed a contract with J. C. Penney, one of the largest clothing chains in the United States, to market her label in its 1700 American branches. By 1966 she was turning out well over five hundred designs a year; her companies were raking in an annual income of more than six million pounds; the *Sunday Times* had given her an award for 'jolting England out of its conventional attitude towards clothes'; and she had been awarded the OBE.[17]

Quant saw herself as the herald of the new, democratic, 'swinging' age, in which her customers might be 'dukes' daughters, doctors' daughters or dockers' daughters'. 'Snobbery has gone out of fashion,' she claimed, 'and in our shops you will find duchesses jostling with typists to buy the same dresses.'[18] This kind of classless rhetoric was extremely popular among London's fashionable set in the middle of the 1960s, but in reality Bazaar was far from classless. A Quant pinafore dress featured in *Vogue* in 1960, for example, cost almost seventeen guineas, the equivalent of three weeks' wages for a girl working in an ordinary office. As one writer puts it, there is simply no evidence that Bazaar had 'a working-class customer base'.[19] The young Lesley Hornby, later Twiggy, was obsessed by fashion but never bought Quant's clothes. 'Bazaar in the King's Road', she later wrote, 'was for rich girls.' Dockers' daughters were rarely in evidence.[20]

Quant acknowledged that her success was partly a question of extremely good timing. Not only were clothes brighter and bolder, but consumers could afford to buy them on the basis of desire rather than need, carefully selecting their wardrobe to present a particular image. Women enjoyed unprecedented financial and social independence, and Quant tried to design clothes that they could put on 'first thing in the morning and still feel right at midnight; clothes that go happily to the office and equally happily out to dinner'.[21] 'I just happened to start when that "something in the air" was coming to the boil,' she wrote afterwards. 'The clothes I made happened to fit in exactly with the teenage trend, with pop records and expresso bars and jazz clubs.'[22]

As early as 1959 *Vogue* had commented that 'young' was becoming 'the persuasive adjective for all fashions, hairstyles, and ways of life', and even lower-middle-class girls from Neasden like Lesley Hornby could afford to follow the fashion pages.[23] There was simply much more interest in fashion, and especially fashion for the young, than ever before, and this helps to explain why Quant's designs captured so much attention. 'Suddenly someone had invented a style of dressing which we realised we had been wanting for ages,' explained the young *Daily Express* fashion writer Brigid Keenan. 'Comfortable, simple, no waists, good colours and simple fabrics. It gave anyone wearing them a sense of identity with youth, and adventure, and brightness.'[24]

Bazaar was only the first and best-known example of the boutiques of the late fifties and sixties.[25] The rise of the independent little boutique went hand in hand with the decline of the department store, which, with its rituals of telephone ordering, sluggish delivery and painstaking alterations, looked rather old hat to the new shoppers of the sixties.[26] Unlike the major clothing stores, boutiques were rarely situated on major thoroughfares, where rents were too high and leases too long. They had no staff hierarchies, and shoppers were free to browse in an informal atmosphere that emphasised cheapness, classlessness and, more than anything else, fun.[27] And by 1966 the financial rewards of running a successful boutique seemed almost limitless. The 'sartorial revolution', wrote Jonathan Aitken, had become an industrial institution, 'triumphant and unassailable', and at its pinnacle stood Mary Quant, international celebrity and 'Queen of Modern Fashion'.[28]

Quant was more than just a figurehead for the fashion boom of the early 1960s. She was largely responsible for what she called 'the Look', the bright, sharp style that dominated British boutiques until the hippy style took over in the late sixties.[29] In the late fifties the Look was really a cleaner version of the 'beatnik' appearance cultivated by art students across the country: pale faces, pouting lips, lank hair and heavy eye-shadow, carefully arranged to give the right impression of decadence and rebellion. Within a few years, however, this had evolved into a style more likely to appeal to ordinary office girls on provincial high streets, the 'dolly birds' of 1964 and 1965. Bohemian dissolution was out, replaced by a confident sense of youthfulness and modernity.[30] By the end of 1964 an aspiring dolly bird might spend the best part of an afternoon covering her eyelids with white powdered eye-shadow, attaching her long false eyelashes with glue, drawing black eyeliner around her sockets and beneath the false lashes, sketching a thin, black arch in place of her plucked eyebrows and, finally, applying her black waterproof mascara.[31] When Quant launched her own make-up range in 1966, her advertisements showed pale-faced models wearing 'Starkers' foundation cream, their heavily made-up eyes gazing sullenly into the camera.[32] 'The ideal now', she wrote, 'is to look as though you have a baby skin, untouched by cosmetics. Lipstick is kept to a pale gloss and the only area where you can go to town is round the eyes. There you can use the lot . . . eye-shadow, eye-liner, and lashings of mascara plus false eyelashes.'[33]

Close attention to the intricacies of black-and-white eye make-up was only one way in which the dolly bird of 1964 proclaimed her modernity and distanced herself from the adult fashions of the fifties. It was equally important, for instance, to have the right haircut. At the beginning of the decade it was still fashionable for a woman to force her hair into elaborate patterns through the ruthless application of curling tongs. Once again it was Quant who popularised a different style, developed by the ambitious young hairdresser Vidal Sassoon, who ran a fashionable salon on New Bond Street. In 1963 Quant asked him to come up with a new cut for the models in her next fashion show. As luck would have it, Sassoon already had an idea of 'the Shape', a carefully structured bob, short at the back and long at the sides. He agreed to try it out on Quant herself first. 'I'm going to cut the hair like you cut material,' he told her. 'No fuss. No ornamentation. Just a neat, clean, swinging line.'[34]

Quant's haircut became almost as famous as her clothes. 'At last hair is going to be hair again', one fashion commentator wrote in *Vogue*, before heading out to have a similar cut herself.[35] Twelve months after Mary Quant had walked out of Sassoon's salon, thousands of young women were copying the short, neat bob that they equated with the Look. Indeed, the 'Mary Quant' bob was among the most immediately recognisable features of the 'kinky', 'groovy', 'Mod' style associated with the period from 1963 to 1966.[36]

The overall effect of the Look was bold, clean and, above all, modern. Just like the inventors and architects who looked forward to building the new Jet Age Britain, Quant and her rivals were fired with a messianic faith in the future. In May 1962 *Vogue* called for 'space age clothes that can be launched to cram into suitcases, crush into narrow spaces for long journeys, and emerge at the end laboratory fresh'.[37] Within a few years, many trendier boutiques sold clothes that appeared better suited to a world of monorails, bubble cars and excursions to Venus than one of British Rail, Ford Anglias and Bognor Regis. Quant even tried to turn PVC into a fashion statement, bringing out a pioneering rainwear range in 1965. As she explained a year later, 'this super shiny man-made stuff' was the ideal material for an era in which science and technology were equated with style and modernity.[38]

The peak of Space Age fashion came that spring, when the British press enthusiastically reported the launch of André Courrèges' latest Paris collection, a clinical array of short skirts, gleaming boots and goggle-eyed sunglasses. The dominant colours were white and silver, occasionally broken by black stripes or polka dots; the clothes were cut in simple geometrical shapes; and even the models marched 'on and off like robots, giving themselves just enough time to display the clothes with quick, jerky movements'.[39] The *Observer* told its readers that Courrèges had invented the 'Clothes of the Future', which meant 'clothes for the space age: the age of action, freedom, and participation'. Older visions of feminine glamour and grace had been banished; instead, Courrèges emphasised youth, informality and freedom of movement. 'I don't make clothes for women who lead an unreal, pampered life,' the designer explained, 'but for girls who go shopping, run for buses.'[40]

Courrèges' Clothes of the Future attracted more attention than any other collection of the decade, and made an immediate popular impact. In July 1965, for example, *Queen* magazine advised its readers to dress in silver PVC, a material that fitted 'into current fashion like an astronaut into his capsule'.[41] Copywriters were quick to jump aboard the bandwagon: magazine advertisements for Lipsheens lipstick, for instance, showed the model Jill Kennington posing in a gleaming silver catsuit while pretending to work in a Space Age laboratory.[42] As the *Private Eye* journalist Christopher Booker remarked, walking through London in 1965 it was impossible to avoid seeing 'the shiny surfaces and violent colours of plastic PVC or the dazzling blacks and whites of Op Art'. What he called the 'Op Art Look' had become 'the craze of the summer, having spread in barely a year from avant-garde paintings on the walls of Mayfair art galleries to hats, handbags, furniture, wallpaper and even make-up'.[43]

The most influential champion of the Op look never actually existed. In 1964 the producers of *The Avengers* were forced to find a replacement for Honor Blackman, who had left the series to play Pussy Galore in *Goldfinger*. They settled on the twenty-seven-year-old Shakespearean actress Diana Rigg, and as part of their project to present the programme as modern, sophisticated and fashionable, they asked the designer John Bates to create a distinctive outfit for her new character. Out went Blackman's leather catsuits; in came the classic wardrobe of the mid-sixties – straight black-and-white dresses ending just above the knee, belted trousers, white stockings and white boots. In the autumn of 1965 Emma Peel was unveiled to the press as the ideal heroine for Harold Wilson's brave new Britain. As the show's publicist put it, she was 'a willowy, auburn-haired beauty with a sparkling wit who leads the streamlined life of an emancipated, jet-age woman, dressed in ultra-modern, man-tailored fashions'.[44] Almost every daily newspaper in Britain carried photographs of Diana Rigg in her *Avengers* regalia, and the *Daily Mail* explained that her clothes would be 'younger, gayer, [and] more feminine' than anything else on television. 'What with sensational outfits and television's hypnotic effect on the buying public,' its fashion editor commented, 'the Avengers clothes can't but be the success of the season.'[45]

Since *The Avengers* regularly appeared among the ten most popular programmes of the week, there could hardly be a better way to sell the Op look to millions of ordinary people.[46] But although Emma Peel inspired thousands of imitators, some women found that their efforts to copy her style did not always meet with the expected success. One woman recalled that her friend 'went to London and came back to Wales wearing white boots with cut-outs, like the Courrèges ones, and masses of eye make-up, including false eyelashes and painted-on eyelashes underneath, and white lipstick'. The interviewee was immediately determined to do the same. 'I went to London,' she remembered, 'and bought myself a white PVC mac with black buttons from Miss Selfridge.' However, when she returned to Wales, she discovered that her neighbours were not impressed by the look of the future. 'Everyone asked me where my crossing sign was,' she reported, 'because I looked like a lollipop lady.'[47]

One obvious reason for the success of the Emma Peel character was that she captured the confident, hedonistic spirit associated with the dolly birds of the mid-1960s. Like the teenager, the dolly bird was an invention of affluence, an emancipated female consumer with plenty of cash and an inexhaustible appetite for entertainment. The manager of one boutique in the King's Road reported that her customers were predominantly 'working-class girls' who spent 'between £6 and £10 a week' each. 'It must mean at least half their wages going on clothes,' she said in delighted amazement.[48] To sell records, clothes and cosmetics, advertisers increasingly played on the autonomy of working-class and lower-middle-class teenage girls, reminding them that they were living in a new era of cultural and economic independence. 'The real dynamo behind the teenage revolution', wrote Peter Laurie in 1965, 'is the anonymous adolescent girl from twelve to sixteen, nameless but irresistible'.[49]

'The real point about very short skirts, white lace stockings and pantomime boots', commented the *Guardian* in 1965, 'is that they separate the girls from the women.' The new fashions apparently proclaimed: 'I am young. Therefore I am different. I am special.'[50] While this reflected the values of an affluent, assertive teenage market, it also echoed the rhetoric of change and modernisation that was so common in the early sixties. And it suited the aesthetic tastes of designers like Mary Quant who were looking for a radical alternative to the fashions of the fifties. 'I grew up not wanting to grow up,' she explained. 'Growing up seemed terrible. It meant having candy-floss hair, stiletto heels, girdles and great boobs.'[51] She boasted that her clothes had 'abolished' middle age and 'perpetuated youth'.[52]

For the previous quarter-century, femininity and glamour had been established by emphasising the contrast between the narrow waistline and the projecting bust, but both disappeared underneath the boyish shifts of the Look. The perfect dolly bird, according to Barbara Hulanicki, the owner of Kensington's fashionable Biba boutique, had 'an upturned nose, rose cheeks, and a skinny body with long asparagus legs and tiny feet. She was square-shouldered and quite flat-chested.'[53] Asked in 1967 why 'fashion has virtually abolished the bust', Quant explained that it was 'a motherhood symbol', inappropriate for the era of youth and independence.[54] Instead, the fashionable designers of the mid-sixties deliberately cultivated an immature, even boyish appearance, and in the United States her designs were advertised as 'a little boy look, an almost gangling adolescent look'.[55] 'There was a time when every girl under twenty yearned to look like an experienced, sophisticated thirty,' Quant wrote in 1966. 'All this is in reverse with a vengeance now. Suddenly, every girl with a hope of getting away with it is aiming to look not only under voting age, but under the age of consent.'[56]

The word *dolly* had been originally been used three hundred years previously to describe a loose woman or prostitute.[57] The sexual identity of the dolly birds of the 1960s, however, was much less straightforward. According to Quant, the Look expressed their sexual independence, announcing: 'I'm dressed as a boy and I'm as good as a boy.'[58] But as several fashion historians point out, dolly birds did not really dress like young men of the same age. Instead, they looked more like undernourished waifs or innocent schoolgirls, 'under the age of consent', as Quant herself admitted. The point was to play on the self-conscious youthfulness of the teenage market and to create the maximum possible contrast with the mature, womanly look of the early fifties. Quant's pinafore dresses, thick black stockings and little white boots, for example, deliberately mimicked the styles of school uniforms, and she liked to tell the story that her 'skinny-ribbed sweaters' had been inspired by an incident when she had 'pulled on an eight-year-old boy's sweater for fun'.[59]

As far as Quant was concerned, this was all associated with what she saw as the sexual assertiveness of young women, who, thanks to the spread of contraception, were beginning to cast off their age-old anxieties about childbirth and motherhood. Women, she said enthusiastically, were now 'the sex in charge', and therefore her clothes were designed to 'lead the eye' towards the crotch:

> The way girls model clothes, the way they sit, sprawl or stand is all doing the same thing. It's not 'come hither', but it's provocative. She's standing there defiantly with her legs apart saying, 'I'm very sexy. I enjoy sex, I feel provocative, but you're going to have a job to get me. You've got to excite me and you've got to be jolly marvellous to attract me. I can't be bought, but if I want you, I'll have you.'[60]

There is no doubt that many young women in the early sixties did associate the designs of Quant and her contemporaries with their own sense of optimism and self-determination. But to many commentators in later years the Look suggested not so much the potential of female independence as its limits. The silver boots, mini-dress, exaggerated eye make-up, white lipstick, and clinging sweater added up to present an image of a baby-faced doll, not a mature, independent adult. As Jonathon Green puts it, this meant that there was 'a strange ambivalence' about the dolly birds, who presented an image of sexual vulnerability and compliance that 'seemed at times to be geared to the paedophiles'.[61] Contemporary newspaper reports often treated them as though they were merely one more entertaining spectacle to be seen on the streets of Swinging London, or even as though they were material luxuries to be consumed like any other. 'Young English girls take to sex as if it's candy and it's delicious,' wrote one delighted American reporter in 1965.[62]

By the last years of the sixties increasing numbers of women were becoming uncomfortable with what they saw as the infantilisation of young womanhood. Commenting on the ubiquity of the image of the pretty girl, on 'hoardings, cinema screens, televisions, newspapers, tins, packets, cartoons, bottles, all consecrated to the reigning deity, the female fetish,' one woman wrote: 'Her dominion must not be thought to entail the rule of women, for she is not a woman . . . For she is a doll: weeping, pouting or smiling, running or reclining, she is a doll. She is an idol, formed of the concatenation of lines and masses, signifying the lineaments of satisfied impotence.' She was, concluded Germaine Greer, a 'female eunuch'.[63]

Like pop music, fashion relied upon the allegiance of hundreds of thousands of loyal customers keen to keep up with the latest trends, especially through the pages of daily newspapers and glossy magazines. Between 1957 and 1967, annual spending on weekly and monthly publications went up from £46 million to over £80 million, an increase, in real terms, of almost a third.[64] By far the most successful were the so-called 'women's magazines' that had first taken off during the interwar years and placed a heavy emphasis on domesticity, femininity and consumerism.[65] As the ranks of affluent housewives swelled in the fifties and sixties, so their circulation and influence grew still further. In 1957 *Woman* was being read by one in every two women in Britain between the ages of sixteen and forty-four. Newspapers, struggling to prop up their advertising revenue after the launch of commercial television and eager to attract female readers, scurried to employ journalists giving the 'woman's angle', and even *The Times* launched a 'women's page', dispensing advice on fashion, cookery and childcare.[66]

By the beginning of the sixties five out of every six women read at least one magazine a week.[67] Women's magazines now concentrated more on the woman as consumer than the woman as housewife, and advertisers played a central role in determining the look and appeal of the magazine.[68] At the same time, younger readers were being wooed by a fresh wave of lifestyle magazines for the teenage market. Shopping was extremely important to teenagers and especially to adolescent girls, allowing them to find their niche within their own peer group, and reinforcing their sense of belonging to a specific youth culture.[69] Teenage magazines like *Romeo*, *Mirabelle*, *Valentine* and *Boyfriend* instructed them how to get on with their parents, how to manage their pocket money, how to choose the right clothes, how to stop their boyfriends from taking too many liberties, and so on.[70] They also ran dozens of small advertisements trumpeting the virtues of record players, jewellery, make-up and even credit facilities, and their stories often associated romantic success with economic activities like buying and listening to the latest records, choosing trendier clothes and going out to the dance hall.[71]

The most prominent magazine of this kind was *Honey*, which was launched in 1960. Designed to reflect the lives of modern girls in the Swinging Sixties, it was modelled on adult magazines like *Vogue* rather than on romantic weeklies like *Mirabelle* or *Valentine*. More than any other teenage magazine of the day it exploited the purchasing power of its readers, running lucrative advertisements for shampoo, soap, sweaters and stockings, and by 1964 its circulation had reached 140,000.[72] Its writers offered advice on how to emulate the Look, attract a boyfriend and choose a career, echoing the independent, self-confident tone associated with the dolly birds. They even toured the country offering advice on the modern lifestyle, while *Honey*-themed boutiques and hairdressers opened in more than a hundred stores around the country.[73] *Honey*'s readers were, according to the magazine's slogan, 'young, gay and going far'; the cover of the January 1965 issue asked them: 'How Far Will You Go? It's a Year for the Daring'.[74]

The most influential magazine of the early sixties, however, was neither a traditional women's magazine nor a teenage publication. In 1957 Jocelyn Stevens, a wealthy, twenty-five-year-old journalist, had bought the magazine *The Queen* for some £500,000. *The Queen* was a rather dusty, struggling society journal, but Stevens was determined to turn it into an irreverent, youthful magazine emblematic of the affluent society.[75] Under his leadership, the rebranded *Queen* ran profiles of 'New Thinkers' like Mary Quant and Terence Conran, launched satirical attacks on the aristocratic establishment, and generally embraced the modernising spirit of what it predicted would be 'the crazy Sixties'.[76]

Queen's greatest innovations, though, were photographic. The art editor, Mark Boxer, thought that the look and layout of the magazine were vital for establishing a youthful, fashionable identity, and recruited a young, upper-class photographer called Antony Armstrong-Jones, who was quickly winning a national reputation for his kinetic, informal style.[77] Among the general public, however, Armstrong-Jones's photographic talents were overshadowed by the identity of his wife. In 1960, taking the title Lord Snowdon, he had married the Queen's sister Princess Margaret, and for many people, his royal marriage transformed at a stroke the image of the professional photographer. 'No longer is the photographer a type of glorified plumber, answering to the beck and call of rich clients,' Jonathan Aitken explained:

> Almost overnight lensmen became invested with glamour and prestige. Advertisers grew more conscious of their talents and more generous with their cheques; the newspaper and magazine industry extended handsome verbal and photographic patronage; débutantes fought for jobs as

photographers' receptionists; Oxbridge graduates, Old Etonians and young peers of the realm flocked to join their ranks, and the bandwagon of fashion was well and truly rolling.[78]

The photographers who attracted most public attention in the sixties were those associated with fashion, advertising and consumerism. The biggest stars were three young men who became synonymous with Swinging London and the fashionable set of the mid-sixties. They were first introduced to a mass audience in Francis Wyndham's long article, 'The Model Makers', published in the *Sunday Times Colour Section* in May 1964:

> The London idea of style in the 1960s has been adjusted to a certain way of looking, which is to some extent the creation of three young men, all from the East End. These are the fashion photographers Brian Duffy, Terence Donovan, David Bailey. Between them, they make more than £100,000 a year, and they are usually accompanied by some of the most beautiful models in the world: they appear to lead enviable lives.[79]

Duffy, Donovan and Bailey were the first photographers to become celebrities in their own right. All three were young; all three were closely associated with the fashion boom; all three were innovative and aggressive; and all three made great play of their working-class London origins. The oldest was Duffy, who was also the quietest and the first to secure a staff contract with *Vogue*. He worked in a cavernous studio in Swiss Cottage, surrounded by champagne bottles, and was reported to have earned some £45,000 in 1966 alone.[80] Terence Donovan, meanwhile, was a much more ebullient character, a great bear of a man who loved drink, women and parties. As he later put it, he spent a fortune on 'rum, bum and the gramophone'.[81] The son of an East End lorry driver, he had left school at eleven with the intention of becoming a chef, but fell into photography instead and found a lucrative berth at Michael Heseltine's trendy society magazine *Town*.[82] He captured the reader's attention by photographing his models in the most striking surroundings imaginable: half-concealed in the doorways of the East End, for instance, or wreathed in steam in front of the hulking pipes and cooling towers of factories and gasworks. By the mid-sixties he was one of the most successful photographers in the country, with a Rolls-Royce and a six-room Mayfair pad. 'To come from the Mile End Road and have a million quid by using your loaf must be a great sensation,' he once remarked, 'and that's what I'm aiming for.'[83]

Donovan's gregarious style made him a natural favourite of models and interviewers alike, but even he was hard pressed to keep up with the youngest member of the trio. Born in 1938, David Bailey was the son of a tailor's cutter and grew up in East Ham, an unlikely upbringing for a man who was to become the glamorous personification of Swinging London. He first experimented with photography as a boy, as part of a deeper interest in birdwatching, but he really fell in love with the camera during his National Service in Singapore.[84] When he returned home, Bailey worked as a photographer's assistant and then quickly began to make his own way, setting himself up as a freelance photographer in April 1960 at the age of just twenty-two. One of his first newspaper commissions, an unusually informal image of the model Paulene Stone posing with a squirrel in the *Daily Express*, marked him out as an iconoclastic talent, and by the end of the year he had secured a staff contract with *Vogue*.[85]

Like Mary Quant, Bailey owed his success to timing as well as talent. The affluent society was in full swing, the fashion industry was booming, and the magazine world was in transition as established publications took on younger staff to beat back the challenge of *Queen*, *Town*, commercial television and the newspapers. Bailey himself was initially taken on by *Vogue* to work for its 'Young Ideas' section, which was designed to appeal to readers in their teens and twenties.[86] He played on his East End background, portraying himself as a new broom sweeping aside the old order. 'When I first went to work at *Vogue*,' he recalled, 'they used to pat me on the head and say, "Oh, doesn't he speak cute?" . . . Within nine months, the managing director was asking me if I'd mind moving my Rolls-Royce so he could get his Ford out. I used to savour those moments.'[87] As George Melly, one of his subjects, put it, he came over as 'uneducated but sophisticated; charming and louche; elegant but a bit grubby; the Pygmalion of the walking, talking dolly'.[88] Fashion, Bailey joked, allowed him to pursue his 'three main interests: photography, women and money'.[89]

By the beginning of 1965, Bailey, Donovan and Duffy, along with a handful of other photographers like Lewis Morley, John Cowan and Gered Mankowitz, were widely perceived as leading members of London's swinging set.[90] The fact that the new generation owed their income to fashion magazines and advertising agencies only added to their lustre. Bailey and Donovan were keen to play up to their image as conspicuous consumers: both drove Rolls-Royces, and neither was shy about listing his earnings and achievements.[91] As Melly put it, the photographer had become a 'pop hero', the incarnation of technical expertise, glamour and modernity, not unlike James Bond or Paul McCartney.[92] 'I think the photographer is one of the first completely modern people,' Bailey declared. 'He makes a fortune, he's always surrounded by beautiful girls, he travels a lot and he's always living off his nerves in a big-time world.'[93]

The photographers' relationships with women lay at the heart of their achievements and their notoriety. 'Before us,' Brian Duffy remarked, 'most fashion photographers were tall, middle-class and a bit camp. We are short, working-class and heterosexual.'[94] They made no effort to disguise their pleasure at directing and taking pictures of beautiful women, and Melly perceptively compared the photographer to 'the ultimate eye [in] an age increasingly obsessed with sexual voyeurism'.[95] Most photographers had one particular woman, a kind of muse, with whom they worked extremely closely. Terence Donovan, for instance, almost always worked with Celia Hammond, who later became his girlfriend, while John Cowan was famous for his partnership with Jill Kennington. The resulting intimacy allowed them to create a greater atmosphere of intensity, sexuality, even adventure. Indeed, Cowan's photographs of Kennington modelling furs in the Arctic Circle and sarongs in the Arabian desert, parachuting through the air, leaping off rooftops and generally flirting with danger became some of the most memorable and dynamic images of the decade.[96]

The most recognisable and the highest paid of all the models of the early sixties was Jean Shrimpton, who through her relationships with Bailey and the actor Terence Stamp became a household name and a symbol of the swinging era. For such a star of the sixties, Shrimpton's background was almost disappointingly conventional. Her father was a prosperous businessman in the building trade, and she grew up on the fringes of the Buckinghamshire county set. A striking, coltish brunette, she originally planned to become a secretary but eventually enrolled at the Lucie Clayton modelling school.[97] In 1960 she was shooting a cornflakes advertisement in the *Vogue* studio when Bailey popped in, caught a glimpse of her, and was immediately impressed.[98] A few weeks later he booked her for one of his own *Vogue* shoots; he then continued to book her, again and again; and within several months, despite the fact that Bailey was married and Shrimpton was still living with her parents, they were having an affair. Over the next two years or so they worked together almost every day and enjoyed unparalleled success.[99] As Shrimpton put it: 'I was the top model and Bailey was the top photographer. We made a formidable team.'[100]

Curiously for someone who became so closely identified with Swinging London, Shrimpton was an intensely shy woman who never enjoyed either the limelight or her chosen profession. 'I would very much have enjoyed being a gardener,' she wrote in her autobiography. 'It is still a puzzle to me that I ever became a model. I am an excessively private person and do not have the temperament for fame.'[101] Yet in many ways it was precisely this lack of interest in modelling that contributed to Shrimpton's appeal. In her private life she rarely made much of an effort to dress up; Bailey claimed that she 'looked like a bag lady'.[102] Where older models had been poised and glamorous, she had an accessible look that only added to her natural beauty and perfectly suited Bailey's innovative style. 'Jean had an appeal that was kind of democratic,' he explained. 'Everybody liked her. Culturally, she had no barriers. She wasn't the girl next door. She was the girl you wished lived next door.'[103]

This brisk informality was perfectly attuned to the cultural priorities of the early sixties, and as the decade progressed Shrimpton's star soared onwards and upwards. In 1962 she had her first *Vogue* cover; in 1963 *Glamour* made her their 'Model of the Year'; and *Elle* even dubbed her 'The Most Beautiful Girl in the World'. Millions of teenage boys wanted to meet 'the Shrimp', while millions of teenage girls wanted to *be* her: in suburban Neasden, for instance, Lesley Hornby 'idolised' her and had her pictures 'plastered all over [the] walls'.[104]

By the beginning of 1964, when the news of David Bailey's divorce made the front page of the *Daily Mail*, Shrimpton was a household name. Her face stared out from *Vogue* magazine covers on both sides of the Atlantic, yet she had never been more dissatisfied. Whereas Bailey enjoyed what she considered 'the creative role', her working life consisted of posing for photographs, 'constantly having to dress and undress' and 'sitting in front of a mirror putting on make-up'.[105] The pressure of spending all her time, day and night, with one man – Bailey – was too much. In the spring of 1964 their relationship collapsed. Shrimpton took up with the glamorous young actor Terence Stamp, and Bailey moved on to a new muse, the eighteen-year-old Sue Murray.[106]

By this point Shrimpton's career had reached the point where she could thrive quite easily without Bailey's patronage. She was selected as the first face of Yardley cosmetics; in May 1965 she made it on to the cover of the American current affairs magazine *Newsweek*; and at the end of the year she was offered a two-week promotional job in Melbourne, Australia, modelling a range of synthetic Orlon dresses at the Spring Racing Carnival. Her two-thousand-pound fee, partly funded by the Victoria Racing Club, was equivalent to at least a year's income for the average Australian; a year earlier, when the Beatles had toured Down Under, they had been paid just fifteen hundred pounds.[107]

When Shrimpton arrived at the Flemington racecourse for Derby Day on 30 October she was widely considered, in the words of the local *Sun News-Pictorial*, to be the 'most beautiful girl on earth'. What happened next turned her from an internationally famous fashion model into an unwitting symbol of social and cultural change. Two days later the paper's correspondent breathlessly told his readers:

> There she was, the world's highest paid fashion model, snubbing the iron-clad conventions of fashionable Flemington with a dress five inches above the knee, NO hat, NO gloves and NO stockings! For my money, she looked tremendous – but Flemington was not amused. Fashion-conscious Derby Day racegoers were horrified. 'Insulting' . . . 'a disgrace' . . . 'how dare she?' . . . ! If the skies had rained acid not a well-dressed woman there would have given The Shrimp an umbrella.[108]

Shrimpton had designed her sleeveless white shift dress herself from the Orlon fabric she had been given. It was a sweltering spring day, and she saw no need to wear stockings, despite the fact that her hemline ended several inches above the knee. The conservative matrons of Melbourne were appalled, but when the news reached London the newspapers were delighted, seeing an excellent opportunity to mock the stuffy sensibilities of the colonies. 'Surrounded by sober draped silks and floral nylons, ghastly tulle hats and fur stoles,' said one correspondent, 'she was like a petunia in an onion patch.'[109] Shrimpton herself was stunned by the furore. 'The trouble is they should never have asked me to come here in the first place,' she indignantly told the press. 'They wanted a mannequin, not a photographic model. I'm not interested in clothes and I hate people staring at me.'[110]

Shrimpton's appearance at the Melbourne racecourse made the front page of almost every newspaper in Britain, and is often considered to have marked the emergence of the mini-skirt. Strictly speaking, she had worn a mini-dress, not a mini-skirt, and she later admitted that it had only been so short 'because Orlon had been stingy with their fabric'.[111] And while her example certainly acted as an inspiration to thousands of women back home, designers had already been toying with mini-skirts for some time. In his famous Space Age collection in the spring, Courrèges had dressed his models in silver boots and mini-skirts, while both Mary Quant and John Bates had also been experimenting with shorter skirts and shift dresses.[112] In a cultural climate that equated style and sexual attractiveness with youth, frankness and modernity, it was no surprise that young women were keen to show off their legs, and the *Sunday Times*'s influential fashion correspondent Ernestine Carter had even dubbed 1963 the 'Year of the Leg'.[113]

The Shrimpton controversy, therefore, simply gave extra impetus to a trend that was already under way.[114] By the spring of 1966, mini-skirts were everywhere, and Quant, who was popularly credited with inventing the new garment, was delighted. 'It was young, liberated and exuberant,' she wrote three decades later, adding that it proclaimed: 'Look at me. Isn't life wonderful.'[115] Some women, however, felt that it only encouraged men to think of dolly birds as little more than sex objects. 'It made you look like a little toy girl,' one woman later insisted, 'just there to please men.'[116] But the tide was irresistible. As *Vogue* put it: 'Brevity is the soul of fashion.'[117]

The popularisation of the mini-skirt completed the stereotypical look of the Swinging Sixties. For many observers, the British fashion industry, which now employed some thirty thousand people, had never been more important. In the capital an estimated two thousand boutiques jostled for attention; in the King's Road alone armies of dolly birds tramped from Bazaar, the birthplace of the Look, to Just Looking, the ultimate Space Age boutique with its anodised aluminium shop front, taking in en route the likes of Forbidden Fruit, Through the Looking Glass, Blast Off and Clobber.[118] Boutiques were everywhere, their flamboyantly painted shop fronts giving way to bright, welcoming interiors ringing with the latest chart hits. Even Harrods, the department store most closely associated with old-fashioned values, belatedly set up its own Way In boutique in 1967.[119] 'The boutique bonanza is the new selling sound, the loud note at the retail level . . . 1965 fashion's lots-for-less beat,' the fashion editor of the *Daily Express* excitedly wrote. 'In the past year hundreds of boutiques have opened all over Britain. Lots of them in London . . . They are vulgar, brash, loud (literally – they find sales increase in direct ratio to the volume of the record player) and great fun.'[120]

Both admirers and detractors of the new youth culture saw the boutique as its temple. In Kingsley Amis's satirical novel *Girl, 20* (1971), the narrator's disdain for the values of the late sixties is rarely stronger than when he visits a trendy boutique:

Uncouth minstrelsy enveloped me again when I crossed the threshold of what I supposed was the boutique. A single room about the size of a squash court, but with a low ceiling, was illuminated by a faint daylight glow through thick curtains and by some objects that might have been electric-toaster elements fixed to the wall at head height. By their aid I was able to pick out a shirt-collar, a belt-buckle here, a leg, the back of a head there ... A rehoboam of deodorant would hardly have been enough to neutralise the miasma of surrounding bodies.[121]

But to their enthusiastic young customers, shopping in the boutiques had become 'an end in itself'. It represented a declaration of independence from the tastes and constraints of their elders; it gave them a place to meet like-minded people of a similar age; and it allowed them to participate in the bold new culture of fashion, pop music and conspicuous consumption.[122]

The heyday of the boutiques between 1964 and 1968 coincided with the triumph of a second wave of innovative young designers inspired by pioneers like Mary Quant. Fashion correspondents were keen to champion new British talent, and there were plenty of promising candidates, from Zandra Rhodes and Ossie Clark to Jean Muir, Gerald McCann and the double-act of Marion Foale and Sally Tuffin.[123] Foale and Tuffin were seen as the quintessential figureheads of the second wave. Their guiding principle was 'fun'. 'We didn't want to be chic,' they explained; 'we wanted to be ridiculous.'[124] In 1961 they found a studio in a dilapidated Soho back street, and the following year they opened their own boutique nearby.[125] The backwater they chose was called Carnaby Street, and within five years it would become one of the focal points of the boutique craze, 'the weekly Ascot for the mods and dolly birds', and the ultimate symbol of Swinging London.[126]

The unexpected rehabilitation of Carnaby Street was closely connected to the rapid transformation of men's fashion. Although convention confined the middle-class man to a heavy dark blue or grey suit, male dress had been edging towards greater colour and informality for the best part of half a century.[127] In an affluent society that placed a heavy emphasis on visual flair, young men were increasingly willing to expend considerable time and money on their appearance. Teddy Boys, Mods and Rockers were all immediately identifiable by their hairstyles and clothing, but ordinary men without any group allegiance were also spending more of their weekly wages on clothes. By the beginning of the 1960s the *Evening Standard* had even launched a weekly column, 'Mainly for Men', offering tips on fashion, grooming and general deportment.[128]

Just as in women's fashion, there were plenty of designers and entrepreneurs eager to take advantage of the vogue for more colourful male dress. A good example was Cecil Gee, an enterprising London tailor who pioneered the 'Italian look', a short, box-shaped jacket, worn with a dark, narrow tie and tight, tapered trousers: a self-consciously cosmopolitan style that anticipated the narrow Beatle suits and Mod jackets of the early sixties.[129] His closest competitor was John Michael, who opened his first shop on the King's Road in 1957. Michael's silk-lined grey suits and pink button-down-collared shirts were expensive, but to fashion-conscious young men at the beginning of the sixties, his boutique was a paradise of urban sophistication.[130]

Both Gee and Michael catered for moneyed, middle-class consumers rather than for the mass market. Their most celebrated rival, however, sold much cheaper clothes to a wider clientele. John Stephen, the 'King of Carnaby Street', was the son of a Glaswegian shopkeeper, and moved to London at nineteen to work as a tailor's clerk, before setting up his own boutique, His Clothes, on the western fringe of Soho.[131] One early customer recalled that the shop was full of 'fantastic daring colours [in] loads of different styles and fabrics . . . crammed into a little space with lots of good music coming from speakers on the wall'. Customers could try on whatever they liked, while the assistants were 'all very young and friendly and polite' – a refreshing change from the formality of most old-fashioned tailors.[132]

Stephen's clothes were casual, colourful and, crucially, cheap. They were produced in a hurry, and often fell apart pretty quickly, but they cost half as much as comparable garments from Cecil Gee or John Michael. In His Clothes a jacket might cost less than ten pounds, or a pair of trousers just three pounds, prices barely imaginable on the King's Road.[133] As in Pop Art or Space Age design, modernity and disposability went hand in hand, and in this general air of happy optimism, Stephen took the opportunity to experiment with flamboyant cravats, violently dyed trousers and the like. Although the Menswear Association initially dismissed him for selling 'the codswallop fashions of perverted peacocks', he soon began to worry that competitors were stealing his ideas.[134] Within a few years Austin Reed had opened fifty-six branches of its Cue chain, designed for the 'bachelor man about town' and selling brightly coloured shirts, flared trousers and suits for thirty pounds, which was less than a week's salary for many young white-collar workers. Jaeger weighed in with the Young Jaeger chain, and even eminently respectable department stores like Simpson's of Piccadilly opened their own men's boutiques.[135]

But John Stephen had little to fear, for his own success was nothing short of sensational. By 1962 he had opened three more London branches, and by 1967 he owned ten boutiques on Carnaby Street alone, fifteen more elsewhere in London, twenty-one in Europe and twenty-four in the United States. Stephen owned a flat in Jermyn Street, a seafront house in Brighton, a Rolls-Royce and an imported Cadillac. But like most icons of the swinging scene, he was keen to play up his proletarian credentials, calling himself 'a working-class boy at heart'. 'I can't think why I haven't got the OBE for services to the rag trade,' he joked to an interviewer. 'I've conquered London, now I'm conquering America, next it's the world.'[136]

It is easy to exaggerate the impact of fashion in the sixties. When Prudence Glynn, the fashion correspondent of *The Times*, wrote a piece on the women she had seen on the London Underground one day in August 1966, she pointed out that they had all been dressed in relatively sober, predictable clothes. Of the seventeen women in her compartment, ranging in age from mid-teens to mid-forties, '12 were wearing cardigans of some sort, 10 had chosen navy blue as their colour, and 13 were wearing sandals or sandal type shoes'. Almost all were wearing printed fabric dresses, and they all had fairly ordinary, even boring haircuts. Above all, 'there wasn't a mini-skirt in sight'. Most people, she concluded, were interested in being 'comfortable' rather than 'smart': hence the cardigans and sandals. Even the two youngest women, secretaries in their late teens, were carrying not the latest fashionable, expensive handbags or shoulder bags, but something much more mundane: the humble shopping bag.[137]

So why did fashion acquire such prominence? One answer is that it genuinely became more important in the sixties, not only because British designers enjoyed unprecedented commercial success abroad, but because people had more money to spend on increasingly colourful and aggressively marketed clothes. More importantly, however, fashion had become a powerful metaphor for wider social and cultural changes. Mary Quant put her finger on it when she told the *Guardian* that fashion 'reflects what is really in the air'.[138] The development of the affluent society, the growth of a consumer culture, the increasing assertiveness of teenagers, the changing role of women, the growing frankness about sex and the celebration of technology and innovation were all wrapped up in the British fashion boom of the early and mid-sixties.[139]

Meanwhile, two words above all epitomised the combination of creativity and commerce that had transformed British fashion and design. 'Carnaby Street', commented *Design* magazine in August 1966, 'has turned into one of those phrases that sets the adrenalin pumping into your bloodstream. It tends to make you feel either young, stylish and hyper-aware – or else, old, old and old.'[140] A ramshackle Soho backwater when Stephen had first opened His Clothes, the street and its surrounding alleys now teemed with fashionable establishments of one kind or another, from boutiques like Domino Male, Lord John and Lady Jane to art nouveau shoe-shops, the Cranks health-food bars and Gear, a patriotic knick-knack shop selling tatty Victorian memorabilia and jewellery.[141] With more than two dozen shops competing for the teenage market, Carnaby Street was generating a turnover of more than five million pounds a year.[142]

For the press, Carnaby Street was the ideal emblem of the Swinging Sixties, drenched in the 'pop sounds and op colours' that future generations would continue to associate with the era.[143] But contrary to popular myth, any visitors hoping to spot the stars would have done better to loiter elsewhere. 'Carnaby Street's customers are (to use an unfashionable expression) working class,' commented one contemporary guidebook. 'While they think nothing of spending a week's wages on a complete outfit, the class that shops on the King's Road will spend that sort of money on a *shirt*.'[144] Another journalist quipped that visiting the area meant a guest appearance in 'home movies made for untold numbers of housewives in New York and Texas'; it was 'the land of American Express and Diners' Club cards'.[145] 'The "in" group,' announced George Melly, 'wouldn't be seen dead in Carnaby Street.'[146]

But these voices were in a minority. To millions of people, not only in Britain but around the world, Carnaby Street was alive with the spirit of Swinging London. In the *Telegraph*'s new *Weekend* supplement John Crosby painted a glowing picture:

> On any twilight evening when the day's work is done, Carnaby Street pulses with slender young men in black tight pants that fit on the hips like ski pants, their tulip-like girlfriends on their arms, peering into the garishly lit windows at the burgundy coloured suede jackets with the slanted, pleated pockets – very hot stuff with the Mods right now . . .
>
> The impact of Carnaby Street is becoming worldwide. Tony Curtis wears Carnaby Street clothes. So do Peter Sellers and the Beatles.

For Crosby and his contemporaries, Carnaby Street was the heart of a broader phenomenon, linked to the worlds of art and design, pop music and film, sex, drugs and rock and roll. It was not merely the home of the miniskirt and the boutique but the hub of a social and cultural revolution. It was the central axis in 'the most exciting city in the world'.[147]

13

THE SWINGING CITY

> Journal of Ye Plague Year Nineteen Hundred and Sixty-Five
> A common conclusion was that the chief carriers of the pest appeared to be certain chronicles and journals which, allowed freely into the homes of rich and poor alike, do spread th'infection daily; these being glossy magazines and Coloured Sections. On contact with these vile effulgences, the reader eventually lapses into a kind of wild madness and a delusion that only the present time is of any importance and that he must present the right appearance to the world by donning strange garbs, filling his house with op-art tablecloths and drivelling his need for 'dynamic' Government.
>
> *Private Eye*, 1965

On the evening of 22 June 1966, just east of Piccadilly Circus, a new nightclub opened its doors for the first time. Packed into Sibylla's small, square basement, surrounded by gleaming glass walls and mirrors, a more glittering line-up of guests could hardly be imagined. All four Beatles were there, accompanied by their wives or girlfriends; so were Mick Jagger, Keith Richards and Brian Jones, David Bailey and Sue Murray, Terence Donovan and Celia Hammond, Mary Quant and Alexander Plunket Greene, Cathy McGowan, Michael Caine, Julie Christie and Andrew Loog Oldham. An interviewer asked one of the club's owners, the ambitious young property dealer Bruce Higham, whether the club's paid-up members would be upset to have been overlooked. Higham smiled and replied: 'I should think that they will say to each other, "If *I* wasn't asked, *then who was?*"'

Higham had planned Sibylla's a year earlier with two friends, the advertising copywriters Terence Howard and Kevin MacDonald. Their aim was to create 'the first Classic London Discothèque', and they had raised the money by appealing to their fashionable friends and contacts, whom Higham called 'the new boy network'. They were, he said, people who were doing things in finance, architecture, press, pop and films ... the kind of people the colour supplements write about ... the talented people, people who are good at something. It doesn't really matter *what* they're good at – photography, or modelling, or making love fantastically well three times a night. What they have is a kind of self-confidence, an awareness, which they transpose to their environment.

When it opened, Sibylla's was the most technologically advanced nightclub in Britain, serving hot spare ribs and cold champagne, the lighting modulated by dimmer switches, the volume and the 'emotional temperature' controlled by the model Marie-Lise Gres using an infrared panel. Meanwhile, the owners hired Alan Freeman as their first disc jockey. 'It was watching him sell that detergent on TV that convinced me,' Kevin MacDonald remarked. 'After all, I am an advertising man, and I *know*.' And they agreed on a fearsomely exclusive door policy to create the right air of exclusivity. 'After all, what is a good discothèque?' asked Bruce Higham. 'It's only successful if you can't get in.'[1]

As one socialite remarked before Sibylla's had even opened, it was 'a legend before its time'. And once it *had* opened, the club was an immediate success. After just a few months the owners turned down an offer for the club of four times what they had originally invested, and they also turned down a newspaper's offer of a thousand pounds for a mere glimpse of the membership list.[2] When, at the end of the summer, a journalist approached Kevin MacDonald for an interview, he found him in ebullient form:

This is Psychedelphia, man, it's all happening ... Sibylla's is the meeting ground for the new aristocracy, and by the new aristocracy I mean the current young meritocracy of style, taste and sensitivity. We've got everyone here [he clicked his fingers to emphasise the point], the top creative people [click], the top exporters [click], the top artists [click], the top social people [click] and the best of the P.Y.P.s [swingingese for pretty young people]. We're completely classless. We're completely integrated ... We've married up the hairy brigade – that's the East End kids like photographers and artists – with the smooth brigade, the debs, the aristos, the Guards officers. The result is just fantastic. It's the greatest, happiest, most swinging ball of the century, and I started it![3]

A few weeks later, on 15 October 1966, MacDonald killed himself by jumping off the top of a Chelsea building. Nobody ever found out why he had done it.

Fifteen years earlier, few would have predicted that London would soon play host to the 'most swinging ball of the century'. The drab, empty pubs and miserable tea-shops, the endless drizzle and tired, threadbare hotels captured the mood of a city that had been battered by the Luftwaffe and worn down by austerity.[4] Dingy, damp and dark, the city was a symbol of exhaustion and decline. For the literary journalist Cyril Connolly, it was

> the largest, saddest and dirtiest of great cities, with its miles of unpainted half-inhabited houses, its chopless chop-houses, its beerless pubs, its once vivid quarters losing all personality, its squares bereft of elegance, its dandies in exile, its antiquities in America, its shops full of junk, bunk and tomorrow, its crowds mooning round the stained green wicker of the cafeteria in their shabby raincoats, under a sky permanently dull and lowering like a metal dish-cover.[5]

But the reinvigoration of London was not long off. The capital's notoriously polluted air was beginning to improve as the Clean Air Act of 1956 imposed strict smoke controls to eliminate the hacking coughs associated with the annual winter smog.[6] And as the post-war governments invested in housing estates and New Towns like Harlow and Stevenage, so the capital became steadily less overcrowded. Between 1951 and 1971, London lost just under a tenth of its population, mostly from inner city boroughs like Tower Hamlets, Islington, Southwark and Hammersmith.[7] With families moving out of the city to build better lives in the suburbs, the character of London's population subtly began to change, becoming younger and more diverse. Manufacturing in the inner city was dying out, but there were plenty of jobs for white-collar office workers. Immigration brought thousands of Asian and West Indian newcomers, while young middle-class couples were buying cheap terraced houses in so-called 'inner suburbs' like Islington, Camden Town and Clapham. The deregulation of rents, the licence given to property developers and the growth of middle-class bohemianism all contributed to the gentrification of areas from Paddington to Camberwell.[8] Once dingy and drab, London was becoming distinctly fashionable, and culturally it was arguably more important than ever.

The BBC, the British Film Institute, the British Council, the Arts Council and the Independent Television Authority were all based in the capital, and when awarding grants the Arts Council tended to give London disproportionate attention. Among those who worked in the media and the arts, therefore, there was a strong sense that London was the only place to be.[9] In the novels and plays written by the rising literary stars of the 1950s, for example, London was almost always presented as a promised land of prosperity and opportunity.[10] In the cinematic adaptation of the New Wave novel *Billy Liar*, London is the destination for the swinging, liberated Julie Christie, while poor, self-deluding Billy stays in his provincial backwater. And in *Lucky Jim*, probably the most influential novel of the fifties, a move to London is part of Jim Dixon's ultimate reward, along with a new girlfriend and a new job. Having made good his escape from academic drudgery, he gleefully pronounces the names to himself: 'Bayswater, Knightsbridge, Notting Hill Gate, Pimlico, Belgrave Square, Wapping, Chelsea.' (Although: 'No, not Chelsea,' he immediately thinks, identifying it with his arch-enemy Bertrand Welch, and therefore with bohemian, pseudo-Gallic pretentiousness.)[11]

In his book *The Other England* (1964) the journalist Geoffrey Moorhouse tried to capture the experience of English life outside the capital. As he pointed out, London was not only 'at the front of the queue, sometimes it seems to be in a specially privileged queue of its own'. Its cachet was beyond question: even the National Coal Board had its headquarters in the city, despite the fact that the nearest significant coalfield was no closer than the Midlands. Moorhouse was hostile to the metropolitan bias of most of his colleagues, but even he admitted that London could not be ignored:

> It is four capitals rolled into one: the headquarters of politics and society, of industry and commerce. It is the one place in England which every Englishman feels he has to visit at some time unless he is to experience in greater and lesser degree a sense of loss, and it has no contenders for this title. It is the only place in England which can look every other one in the eye and say, of the innumerable things which an urban society marks as amenities and as the distinguishing marks of civilization, 'You Name It, We've Got It!' It is at the front of the queue for everything that is new in this line, for everything that seems exciting, for everything that is smart.[12]

'You Name It, We've Got It!' was an appropriate motto for London in the sixties. At the heart of what came to be known as 'Swinging London' was the association of cultural creativity and consumer affluence, or, more simply, style and shopping. As one journalist put it, the high salaries of the city's young men and women made them 'the richest group of consumer spenders in the country, pouring money into records, entertainments and extravagant clothes, and enabling them to afford motor-bikes and cars while still in their teens'.[13] In fact it was impossible to be a fashionable Londoner without money. 'Taste' and 'style', those values most closely associated with the swinging city, were luxuries, advertised by pop stars and models and sold by ambitious young designers and entrepreneurs. Not for nothing were the landmarks of Swinging London, its boutiques, salons, restaurants and discotheques, all associated with spending large quantities of money.[14] How, though, to decide what to buy? The answer was to consult that bible of the Swinging Sixties, the Sunday colour supplement.

The origins of the colour supplement lay in Fleet Street's desperation to maintain its steady advertising income. The newspapers had been badly hit by the advent of commercial television in 1955, which had seduced advertisers away from the print media. Within four years ITV's advertising revenue was greater than that of all of the Fleet Street newspapers combined, and between 1960 and 1962 no fewer than five national newspapers went out of circulation.[15] In 1961 the *Telegraph*'s owner Lord Hartwell, keen to improve his paper's image among younger readers, brought out a Sunday edition, which promptly began to siphon off readers from the *Sunday Times*. In response, the owner of the *Sunday Times*, the Canadian millionaire Roy Thomson, decided to launch the glossy *Colour Section*, the first British colour supplement.[16]

The consumerist credentials of the *Sunday Times Colour Section* were obvious from the very first edition, on 4 February 1962. David Bailey's cover photographs showed Jean Shrimpton modelling a grey flannel dress designed by Mary Quant, while a headline promised 'a new James Bond story by Ian Fleming'. Inside, much of the magazine was devoted to large advertisements and short profiles of 'People of the 60s', who included a sociologist from the London School of Economics, an industrialist, a footballer, the artist Peter Blake and, predictably, Mary Quant and Alexander Plunket Greene. There was also a grainy black-and-white 'photo-feature' devoted, rather incongruously, to the city of Lincoln, excitedly chronicling 'its jazz clubs, its art students, its coffee bars, its electronics factory, its go-ahead young repertory company and its dynamic young architect'.[17]

The *Colour Section* was a great success, and within nine months of its launch the *Sunday Times* had acquired 200,000 extra readers.[18] Advertising agencies were fighting for space in its glossy pages, and it was no great surprise that the *Sunday Telegraph* and the *Observer* followed suit in September 1964 with supplements of their own. All three had the same mixture of articles about art, design and fashion, stories of travel and adventure, and advertisements for the latest clothes, cars and gadgets.[19] It was no coincidence that the very first supplement had been launched with a Bond story; the point of these magazines was to tell the ordinary consumer how he or she, too, could have the lifestyle of a James Bond or an Emma Peel. As one of the *Sunday Times*'s writers later put it, the colour supplement was:

> a mirror and chronicler of suddenly stylish, affluent, double cream-gorging, 'swinging' Britain, [addressing] the economic future of Ecuador, the potential of a new cabinet minister, the direction of Parisian couture, the filming of the latest James Bond story, the durability of a French copper cooking pot, the most pristine shade of white emulsion paint [and] the authentication and true nature of any of the thousand-and-one new 'trends' which materialised each week.[20]

But for some critics, the colour supplements were emblematic of everything that was wrong with the affluent society. The columnist Bernard Levin thought they projected the impression that the British people 'lived in a haze of Drambuie, After Eight chocolates, Kosset carpets, Jaguar motor-cars, Swedish glass, Viyella blankets, Lanvin perfume and king-size cigarettes'.[21] *Private Eye*, always quick to puncture pomposity, ran a spoof extract from *About*, a kind of cross between the colour supplements and magazines like *Queen* and *Town*. Owned and edited by the 'daring, brilliant' property developer and aspiring politician Clive Brilliantine, who was clearly modelled on Michael Heseltine, *About* offered photo-journalism by Thornton Weeds, travel articles by Merryman Tube and poetry from the convicted murderer Harry Gash. It had a film column ('Vaguely Nouveau'), a round-up of the latest trendy restaurants ('the Bistro Lhasa' in the King's Road, with its 'fashionable Tibetan delicacies') and a 'brilliant, daring report' on the town of Slagville, to show 'how the other half of Britain lives . . . people who have, some of them, never even been to London. Not people like us. Urbane. Brilliant. Cosmopolitan. But the ordinary people of Britain . . . the other nine-tenths.'[22]

As *Private Eye*'s parody suggested, the ethos of the colour supplements was closely bound up with the cultural and economic revival of London. By the beginning of 1965 the Swinging London phenomenon was well under way. According to the historian Jerry White, its 'high summer' lasted from 1963 to 1967, 'its temples were the boutique and the discothèque . . . its high priests the pop star, the fashion designer, the model and the photographer; its emblems the miniskirt and the haircut'.[23] The rise of the Beatles, the popularity of Sean Connery and the celebrity of Jean Shrimpton were all interpreted as symbols of a national renaissance founded on entrepreneurship and meritocracy. Since this dovetailed nicely with Harold Wilson's vision of the New Britain, many writers happily borrowed his rhetoric in order to sell Swinging London to their readers. It was a world of 'youth', 'dynamism', 'vitality', 'excitement', 'elegance' and 'brilliance'; above all, it was 'new'. Its inhabitants were 'impatient', 'brisk', 'cool' and 'professional'. Even the Queen's brother-in-law Lord Snowdon was attributed with 'pure, high-octane nervous energy, rattling leisure into work and work into leisure'.[24]

Just as Harold Wilson eagerly sought to win the approval of his American counterparts, who supposedly knew more than anyone else about dynamism and vitality, so British newspapers were particularly keen to quote Americans announcing that London was now the international capital of youth. In one of the earliest of these pieces, which appeared in the *Telegraph*'s *Weekend* supplement in April 1965, the American writer John Crosby told his readers that London was 'The Most Exciting City in the World'. He opened his piece with an enthusiastic description of the capital's nightlife:

> In Soho, at the Ad Lib, the hottest and swingingest spot in town, the noise is deafening; the beat group is pounding out 'I Just Don't Know What to Do With Myself'; on the floor under the red and green and blue lights, a frenzy of the prettiest legs in the whole world belonging to models, au pair girls or just ordinary English girls, a gleam of pure joy on their pretty faces, dancing with the young bloods, the scruffy very hot-shot photographers like David Bailey or Terence Donovan, or a new pop singer – all vibrating with youth. At the corner table more or less permanently reserved for the Beatles (you'll always find at least one of them here when they're in town) Ringo proposes to Maureen (that's where he did it).

This, he said, was 'just a symptom, the outer and visible froth [of] a sort of English renaissance', founded on youth, classlessness, fashion and sex. 'London', Crosby concluded, 'is where the action is, as New York and then Paris were right after the war, as Rome was in the mid-Fifties. Now it's London — the gayest, most uninhibited, and — in a wholly new, very modern sense — most wholly elegant city in the world.'[25]

Crosby's article was so enthusiastic that it came very close to self-parody. And yet, at the time, it evidently struck a chord. Indeed, many British journalists took their lead from foreign contemporaries for whom the success of Mary Quant and the Beatles seemed to overturn the old stereotypes about stuffiness and reserve and to equate Britishness with youthful ambition. In September 1964, for instance, the French magazine *L'Express* ran a feature on the new London, and a year later the Spanish *Epoca* followed suit, describing 'the happiest and the most electric city in Europe'.[26] In the United States, meanwhile, the success of British designers, models and pop groups meant that there was a minor cult of all things English. The American country singer Roger Miller even had a Top Twenty hit on both sides of the Atlantic with his bouncy, if hideous, 'England Swings', a novelty single about 'bobbies on bicycles' and 'dapper men with derby hats and canes'.[27]

The most famous example of American enthusiasm for Swinging London was the cover story that appeared in *Time* magazine on 15 April 1966, entitled 'You Can Walk Across It on the Grass', a reference to the capital's many parks. According to its author, Piri Halasz, the story had been written to appeal to American tourists and was timed for the spring because 'Americans would be going to Europe and they would want a travel story telling them where to go'.[28] The cover design of that week's issue was a Pop collage of guitars, dolly birds, mini-skirts and Minis, and the headline proclaimed: 'London: The Swinging City'. Inside, the story was little different from Crosby's piece in the *Weekend Telegraph* a year earlier. In pursuit of their art, Halasz and her colleagues had undergone four days of 'the most concentrated swinging . . . that any group of individuals has ever enjoyed or suffered', and the article was constructed as a storyboard for an imaginary film about the city, moving from the nightclubs of the West End to the coffee bars of the King's Road. Like Crosby, Halasz devoted most of her attention to the 'new and surprising leadership community: economists, professors, actors, photographers, singers, admen, TV executives and writers — a swinging meritocracy'. And also like Crosby, she emphasised the supposed classlessness of the new London, juxtaposing the Rolling Stones,

Michael Caine and the Dirty Dick pub in Bishopsgate with the likes of Princess Margaret, the Changing of the Guard and the 'incredibly exclusive' Clermont Club in Berkeley Square.

> Ancient elegance and new opulence are all tangled up in a dazzling blur of op and pop. The city is alive with birds (girls) and beatles [sic], buzzing with minicars and telly stars, pulsing with half a dozen separate veins of excitement. The guards now change at Buckingham Palace to a Lennon and McCartney tune, and Prince Charles is firmly in the long-hair set. In Harold Wilson, Downing Street sports a Yorkshire accent, a working-class attitude and tolerance towards the young that includes Pop Singer 'Screaming' Lord Sutch, who ran against him on the Teen-Age Party ticket in the last election . . .
>
> In this century, every decade has had its city. Today, it is London, a city steeped in tradition, seized by change, liberated by affluence, graced by daffodils and anemones, so green with parks and squares that, as the saying goes, you can walk across it on the grass. In a decade dominated by youth, London has burst into bloom. It swings; it is the scene.[29]

Back in the United States, *Time*'s conservative readers hated the article. One disgruntled correspondent complained that *Time* had used 'a hell of a test by which to measure a city's greatness: its ability to appeal to the moronic fringe, the smart alecs and the social climbers'. 'You have managed to look decadence in the face without seeing it,' wrote another, adding that all the 'turned-on young men and women will burn out as quickly as a light bulb of British manufacture'.[30] Even a month later the magazine's letters page still burned with controversy. 'Visitors still find the same old dingy streets and grimy restaurants,' wrote one level-headed reader. 'Girls, except for women street cleaners, do not wear plastic suits.' However, the last word went to a young woman from the capital whose letter again came close to self-parody. 'As a dolly from the scene,' she wrote defiantly, 'I say cheers for your gear article on the swinging, switched-on city of London, and boo to all the American geese who call it humbug.'[31]

Swinging London is often described in terms of a particular group of people or state of mind, but it was also a specific place, or more precisely, a number of specific places. In its famous cover story on the Swinging City, *Time* even printed a map of central London, labelled 'The Scene', indicating where the most fashionable shops, restaurants, nightclubs and galleries were to be found. There was also a small inset map of the rest of Britain, which was evidently less interesting to American readers and consisted largely of 'Liverpool, the home of the Beatles' and an enormous arrow to indicate the surge of provincial talent into the capital. Piri Halasz later explained that it was 'written for a tourist who would want to take it along and read it'.[32]

By this point, American tourists, thanks to the falling costs of air travel, were arriving in London in greater numbers than ever. In 1960 the capital had received some one and a half million foreign visitors, but by the middle of the decade three million were arriving each year, drawn by the promise of fashion, theatre and pop music. Successive governments, desperate to attract foreign currency, ploughed more resources into the London tourist industry: in 1963 the London Tourist Board was set up, and by the end of the sixties the Wilson government offered generous grants for new hotels.[33] And just as the colour supplements acted as lifestyle guides for the affluent, so the London 'scene' acquired its own guidebooks for aspiring swingers, from *Len Deighton's London Dossier* to Hunter Davies's *The New London Spy: A Discreet Guide to the City's Pleasures*. Halasz herself published the *Swinger's Guide to London*, promising that it would introduce the visitor to 'the places where London's swingers meet, eat, hang out, join in, turn on and generally move'.[34]

According to the guidebooks, life in Swinging London revolved around a small number of exclusive shops, restaurants and nightclubs. Some boutiques, for instance, were much more exclusive than others, an example being Top Gear, a little shop on the King's Road run by the milliner James Wedge and the model Pat Booth. In addition to Wedge's hats, Top Gear sold prohibitively expensive clothes by the likes of Foale and Tuffin and Ossie Clark. The purchases came in painfully fashionable white bags with a bull's-eye design, and, according to legend, Mick Jagger kept accounts there for his girlfriends, which he would immediately terminate as soon as he had tired of them, obliging them to pay any remaining bills.[35]

Having worked up an appetite after a hard day at the likes of Top Gear, the trendy Londoner then moved on to the latest restaurant on the swinging circuit, perhaps the Trattoria Terrazza, which looked out on to Romilly Street in Soho and was considered the best place for spotting film stars and models. Italian style had been extremely fashionable in the late fifties and early sixties, and a taste for Italian cooking was still regarded as a mark of sophistication and superiority. The Trattoria was a favourite with the likes of Michael Caine and Terence Stamp, and the basement Positano Room, according to one account, was always crowded with 'film people, theatre people, pop people, hot young journalists, gorgeous models, photographers, fashion designers – everyone'. 'If you weren't in the film industry or some sort of personality,' recalled the head waiter, Alvaro Maccioni, 'I would not put you there. I ran it like a club.'[36]

In April 1966 Maccioni left to set up his own restaurant on the King's Road, Alvaro's, which soon overtook the Trattoria to become the most fashionable eating-place in the city. By the end of the year it was already making more than six thousand pounds a month and had acquired an enviable reputation. Jonathan Aitken noted that it was 'patronised by all the stars of the new and old aristocracy, [is] impossible to get into unless you know Alvaro personally, and as the ultimate gesture of restaurant one-upmanship, its telephone number is ex-directory'. Alvaro's visiting cards and matches even carried a picture of Maccioni with a finger to his lips and the caption: 'If you know who I am, don't say where I am'. The most important reason for his success, he said, was not the food but the atmosphere, for 'in London today you can almost choose the wanted customer – they are charming people. Honestly, I don't look at the pocket, I like nice people with a style in dressing and youth.'[37]

After dinner, the self-respecting trend-setter then moved on to one of London's new nightclubs. It is commonly thought that discotheques only arrived in the capital in the middle of the sixties, but this is not quite true. In the late fifties, expresso bars and jazz clubs like the famous 2–Is skiffle club in Old Compton Street had attracted hordes of teenagers and young couples, although they relied on live bands rather than records played by a disc jockey.[38] Real showbusiness types, meanwhile, frequented more exclusive Mayfair clubs like Annabel's, the Astor Club and the Blue Angel. Cabaret typically began some time after midnight: there was always a stand-up comedian, a couple of singers and perhaps a resident band, playing slightly old-fashioned dance tunes. These were distinctly superior establishments, catering for the wealthy and cultivating an atmosphere of Continental sophistication. Indeed, 'Montmartre in Mayfair, where you can shuffle or listen to the Don-Claude Quartet', hardly sounded like a place for the typical fun-loving teenager.[39]

The new discotheques of the mid-sixties were slightly different, with dancing taking priority over dinner. The tables even had their legs cut down so that the chicken-in-a-basket element felt more like a brief interlude before dancing, rather than the main event.[40] The most famous early example was the Saddle Room in Mayfair, which in 1962 George Melly described as 'the most fashionable discothèque in London'. He was not, however, impressed by 'all the flabby jowls and bottoms wobbling about on the dance-floor', commenting that when the Twist was 'danced by the young it is certainly immensely erotic, but danced, and danced badly, by the middle-aged it becomes obscene'. The Saddle Room not only attracted a middle-aged crowd but offered a rather uneasy mixture of faux-aristocratic nostalgia and trendy modernity. 'The décor is harness and hunting pictures and horse-box panelling,' Melly reported. 'The music all comes from a loud hi-fi gramophone . . . It is very crowded, everyone a little irritable.' Yet just inside the door was a notice announcing that the membership list was closed, which he interpreted as a sign of the Saddle Room's success.[41]

By the beginning of 1966 nightclubs that specialised in drinking and dancing, called discotheques to distinguish them from cabaret clubs, were all the rage.[42] The Bag o'Nails in Soho, for example, played live music by the likes of John Mayall's Bluesbreakers and was a particular favourite of Paul McCartney and his friends. It was there, in May 1967, that McCartney met the American photographer Linda Eastman, who was to become his wife and the co-founder of the much-maligned rock group Wings.[43] The Cromwellian in South Kensington, meanwhile, was a more salubrious establishment, with three floors offering dancing for 'the younger set', a bar for those who preferred to drink and chat, and an upstairs casino. Its manager described the customers as 'a lot of continental people, film extras, hairdressers, P.R.s, advertising people . . . [and] quite a few wrestlers'.[44]

By contrast, there were very few wrestlers at the Pickwick in Great Newport Street, which was designed in a style described as 'Victorian whimsy' and closely associated with showbusiness figures like John Barry, Terence Stamp and Michael Caine. One observer summed up its clientele as 'impresarios in a rustle of slub-silk suits and seven-year contracts [and] agents feeding their ulcers with bourbon, while their blonde-lamé clients try to persuade them out onto that press-clipping-sized floor'.[45]

The Pickwick was one of a triumvirate of discotheques that epitomised the spirit of Swinging London. The most famous and sophisticated was the Ad Lib Club, which opened in December 1963 and was reached by a tiny lift from an alleyway behind Leicester Square. The disc jockey wore a dinner jacket; the turntables were hidden inside a piano; the drinks were served in glass miniatures; the walls were hung with mirrors; and a vast window was installed looking proudly out across central London. 'For the pop stars, fashion photographers and young actors,' wrote George Melly in 1965, 'this must suggest a conquered world.'[46]

Although about three hundred people crammed into the Ad Lib penthouse every night to drink and dance, it was extremely difficult to become a member. As Barry Miles puts it, the Ad Lib was the first club 'aimed specifically at the rock 'n' roll crowd', with carefully selected music, very late hours and an atmosphere of free-wheeling tolerance.[47] In fact the music was so loud that the Ad Lib attracted endless complaints from neighbours, whose irritation at being unable to sleep outweighed any admiration they might have felt for the club's celebrated guests. A local milkman told the police that the music stopped only when he was getting up for work, while protests poured in from the priests at a neighbouring Catholic church. Eventually the Ad Lib's owners were compelled to spend some ten thousand pounds on sound-proofing, double-glazing and hotel costs for the disgruntled neighbours, while the manager twice ended up in court after ignoring a judicial order to keep the noise down.[48]

Probably no other establishment was more symbolic of Swinging London than the Ad Lib. Ringo Starr and George Harrison were reputed to have introduced the other Beatles to the club, and it was also a favourite of the Rolling Stones, David Bailey and Jean Shrimpton. Francis Wyndham, the *Sunday Times*'s resident expert on the swinging scene, wrote that it was 'not so much a nightclub, more a happening; an unselfconscious, spontaneous celebration of the new classless affluence'.[49] *Queen*'s Anthony Haden-Guest loftily described it as 'the chosen haven for the gilded mafia of the Pop scene, with its nightly Beatle or Stone, and the supporting fashion-photographers, satyrs in this urban Arcady'.[50] George Melly, meanwhile, enthused that it was 'dedicated to the triumph of style. It may be chic, non-committed and amoral, but it's also cool, tolerant and physically beautiful.'[51]

Unfortunately for the Ad Lib, fashion is fickle, and by the following spring the club's star was in terminal decline. A kitchen fire in the New Year forced the owners to switch the location to Leicester Square itself, and by the time they moved back to the penthouse, the swinging scene had moved on.[52] The beneficiary, and the third club in the swinging triumvirate, was the Scotch of St James's, hidden in an old stable yard in the heart of St James's. To gain admittance, members had to submit to a brief interview through a sliding panel in the thick wooden entrance door, although pop stars were welcomed by name and ushered in. The interior, rather oddly, was 'Scottish Baronial', with 'sporrans, swords and antlers in abundance', and the disc jockey was hidden inside a nineteenth-century coach next to the dance floor, playing American soul music so loud that conversation was virtually impossible.[53]

The Scotch of St James's was deliberately targeted at pop stars, and its regular guests included not only the Beatles and the Rolling Stones but the Animals, the Moody Blues and the Yardbirds. But whereas the Ad Lib had made a great fuss about its famous faces, its successor was rather more discreet. By 1966 many of the more successful musicians wanted to be left alone, and the manager, Rod Harrod, deliberately refrained from expansive banter. 'The groups can come here incognito,' the owner told George Melly. 'Nobody bothers them.' Indeed, Harrod admitted that he had once thrown somebody out for asking George Harrison for his autograph, and anyone else who bothered the stars was given similarly short shrift:

> He told me [wrote Melly] that a party of millionaires came down recently and wanted to sit at the table reserved for the Stones. Mick and Chrissie Shrimpton were there by themselves. There was plenty of room, but he wouldn't let the millionaires join them and they went away offended. He'd turned away perhaps £50 worth of business, but he knew he was right.

Yet Harrod still treated the biggest stars with special consideration. Their tables were placed slightly apart from the others, on a little platform raised just above the rest of the floor. 'The top groups were not to be bothered perhaps,' noted Melly, 'but very sensibly their presence was not allowed to pass unnoticed . . . The Scotch of St James's has struck a clever balance between privacy and adulation on their behalf. It's a trick every fashionable restaurant head-waiter has practised for decades.'[54]

One of the more unlikely members of the fashionable set was a young man called Maurice Micklewhite, the son of a charlady and a Billingsgate fish porter. Micklewhite grew up in South London during the Attlee years, and after deciding to become an actor took the name Michael Scott. However, there was already another actor with that name, so he was forced to change it again. By 1960, when Micklewhite appeared at the Royal Court in Harold Pinter's play *The Room*, he was calling himself Michael Caine, and from that point onwards his career began, slowly, to take off. However, it was not until he was thirty that Caine got his big break, the part of the upper-class Lieutenant Bromhead in the imperial epic *Zulu* (1964). Thereafter, other major roles rapidly followed, notably the leads in two distinctly fashionable British films, *The Ipcress File* (1965) and *Alfie* (1966).[55]

By 1965 Caine was considered one of the most promising actors in the country and a certain bet for international stardom. He was also a man of vision, telling an interviewer that he hoped to become a film producer. 'Perhaps it's my last vestiges of working-class chips,' he explained, 'but I'm a tremendously patriotic person and I care a great deal about how this country runs. The only resources we've got in this country are the brains of our young people, and what really annoys me now is that we're not using our own talent in films.' He even added that he was 'very keen on the new universities, and I'd like to start courses in film directing in places like Sussex. We can't go on muddling through missing good people all the time.'[56] In the next four decades he went on to appear in well over a hundred films, and he was eventually knighted in 2000 under his old name of Maurice Micklewhite. The film course at Sussex, however, never quite materialised.

Maurice Micklewhite's prominence in the swinging set was only partly down to his success as an actor. It also owed much to his friendship with a fellow-thespian, Terence Stamp, six years his junior. Like Micklewhite, Stamp was a Londoner, born in Bow and brought up in nearby Plaistow. After appearing together in a touring production of Willis Hall's play *The Long and the Short and the Tall*, the two men had become fast friends, and they ended up sharing a flat in Kensington. They were still living together when Stamp made his own great breakthrough in Peter Ustinov's film *Billy Budd* (1962), which won him an Oscar nomination and marked out him as a star to watch.[57]

Stamp was a much less prolific actor than his flatmate, and by the beginning of 1966 he had appeared in just two more films, neither of which was tremendously successful. In truth, his fame owed more to his looks, his reputation as a ladies' man, and, eventually, his girlfriend than it did to his films. Both Caine and Stamp were enthusiastic seducers, and the younger man soon overtook his mentor. In the late spring of 1964 he acquired a more permanent girlfriend, Jean Shrimpton, who had just left David Bailey and was at the height of her fame.* 'I suppose that was the final fantasy realised,' he

---

*Caine had already moved out into his own flat in Bayswater and was taken aback to find Stamp and Shrimpton on his doorstep expecting to be put up in the second bedroom. He did install them as requested, but there was evidently a misunderstanding about how long the lovers would be staying, and in the end Caine cancelled their newspaper subscriptions and invited them to leave.

said later. 'I had money, I became famous, and then I met the perfect sexual partner. I hadn't thought it out beyond that, not even in dreams.'[58]

Between 1964 and 1966, Stamp and Shrimpton were the undisputed golden couple of Swinging London. 'We made our appearances in [the] obligatory restaurants with clockwork regularity,' she wrote years afterwards. 'Terry and I were the young glamorous couple around town, on display each night with whoever he had invited to join us.' The men tended to do all the talking, and Shrimpton felt as though she were 'merely ornamental'.[59] Indeed, while his girlfriend was generally shy and retiring, Stamp was unusually keen to sing his own praises, telling the press that he was at the head of a new generation:

> People like me, we're the moderns. We wear elastic-sided boots and smoke Gauloises, we work hard and we play hard. We have no class and no prejudice. We're the new swinging Englishmen. And it's people like me that are spreading the word . . .
>
> There's a new kind of Englishman that I think the general public will be interested in. He's very masculine, very swinging, very aware, well-dressed and all that but with great physical and mental strength. He's the working-class boy with a few bob as opposed to the chinless wonder. French girls and American girls used to look on Englishmen as idiots because they only saw the ones that could afford to travel. Now they're seeing the new types and they think they're great.

'I would like to start a Terence Stamp trend,' he said modestly, 'but of course to do this I would have to be in a more important position than I am now.'[60]

Although Stamp and Shrimpton were the envy of millions of admirers, this admiration was largely misplaced. Shrimpton later claimed that all was not well in the bedroom, and, according to her memoirs, their time together was dominated by rows, resentment and general unhappiness.[61] Stamp wanted to live 'the film star life of grand restaurants, grand clothes, grand furniture and Being Seen', but Shrimpton preferred 'something more down to earth like a nice quiet evening together in front of the television'.[62] She did not enjoy life in the swinging set, later reminiscing that she 'would take my knitting to nightclubs because I was so bored. It used to make Stamp furious.'[63]

If anything, it is surprising that their relationship lasted so long. As one of his admirers puts it, Stamp was 'prone to weirdness', devoted to Royal Canadian Air Force exercises and a variety of peculiar fads that had him eating little but wheat-germ, yoghurt and carrots.[64] As the decade drew on, he became a vegetarian, gave up smoking, drinking and drugs, and took up fasting on Thursdays. During an interview with the *Daily Express* he sipped a cup of tea and honey and remarked gnomically that 'the best part of the flower becomes honey, and when I eat honey that flower becomes part of me'.[65] By the summer of 1967 Shrimpton could not stand it any more, and amid rumours of infidelities on both sides, she walked out. Stamp took the news extremely badly; at the same time, perhaps not entirely coincidentally, his film career ran aground, and in the end he disappeared to India in search of spiritual enlightenment.

While Jean Shrimpton was involved with David Bailey and Terence Stamp, her younger and more rebellious sister Chrissie was linked with an even more controversial character. In early 1963, the seventeen-year-old Chrissie had gone to watch a local blues group play at the Stars and Garter in Windsor, and ended up falling for the charismatic lead singer. Mick Jagger's parents were very taken with his girlfriend; on the other hand, Shrimpton's parents were less than impressed by the emaciated figure she brought home, although they were mollified when they found out that he was a student at the LSE. Jagger even told them that he hoped to marry Chrissie when he had finished his degree; he claimed to have his eye on a career in business or politics. But their relationship was volatile, to say the least. As we have seen, when Andrew Loog Oldham first met Jagger outside the Station Hotel a few days later, the singer was having a fight with Chrissie in an alley; and as time went on they became notorious for conducting loud and even violent rows in public.[66]

At first, the Shrimpton connection opened up new social opportunities for Jagger, notably friendships with the likes of David Bailey and Mary Quant that elevated him out of the narrow world of pop music and into the heart of the swinging set. During the early days of the relationship, he would drop copious references to Chrissie into his interviews with local reporters.[67] Later, however, he tried to play down her existence in case she alienated his female fans, and his resentment of her efforts to domesticate him were said to have inspired some of the Stones' more memorable songs of the mid-sixties. In the spring of 1966, for example, the Stones recorded two equally misogynistic songs in one marathon session. In 'Under My Thumb' Jagger brags about dominating the girl who once had him down, spitting out his scorn for the 'squirmin' dog' who has now had her day. And, if anything, 'Stupid Girl' goes even further, the lyrics heavy with resentment and hatred, the thick-lipped singer dripping with contempt for the girl he calls the 'sickest thing' in the world. In 'Stupid Girl', Jagger adds that he is 'sick and tired', full of disdain and doubt, and this was a pretty accurate reflection of his feelings towards Chrissie Shrimpton. On 18 December 1966, a few months after Jagger had started an affair with the elfin Marianne Faithfull, he and Chrissie had a final blazing argument in their Harley House flat. Shrimpton then took an overdose of sleeping pills, and this brought Jagger to her bedside at the Greenway Nursing Home in Hampstead, where he announced that he was leaving her. When the nursing home sent him the bill for her stay, he posted it back with the instructions that the patient herself would be paying. He also cancelled her credit accounts at Harrods and Fortnum and Mason and, on Christmas Eve, hired a van to remove her belongings from Harley House.[68]

Mick Jagger's relationships with Chrissie Shrimpton and Marianne Faithfull confirmed his place at the very centre of the small social network that made up Swinging London. As the *Evening Standard* put it, he was 'the most fashionable, modish man in London, the voice of today'.[69] His only real competitor was Paul McCartney, who had become a close friend.[70] Jagger was a regular visitor to McCartney's house in Cavendish Avenue, and they made sure that their singles were released several weeks apart, so that both groups would have a free run at the number one spot. Marianne Faithfull later remembered that 'Mick always had to come to his house, because he was Paul McCartney and you went to him. Paul never came to us.' She thought that 'there was always rivalry there. Not from Paul, none at all. Paul was oblivious, but there was something from Mick. It was good fun. It was like watching a game on the television.'[71]

Like Jagger, McCartney was beginning to spread his wings beyond the narrow confines of the pop world. By 1966 he had been occupying a little attic room in the Asher family home for three years. At the very height of the Beatles' success, he was basically part of an upper-class English family, taking recorder lessons in the music room from Jane's mother, playing word games at dinner with her fearsomely intelligent father and generally living the life of an old-fashioned gentleman of leisure. Through Jane he met Harold Pinter and Kenneth Tynan, among others, but this was hardly the gaudy world associated with the swinging city. Indeed, although McCartney and Asher were icons of fashionable London, the reality of their cosy, domesticated lifestyle would have horrified many of their more rebellious admirers.[72]

In December 1965 something rather odd appeared in London's bookshops. It was not a book, exactly; strictly speaking, it was a box. Inside *David Bailey's Box of Pin-ups* were thirty-six stiff sheets of card, each with a black-and-white portrait on one side and a short caption on the other. The box had been designed by Mark Boxer, the progenitor of the *Sunday Times Colour Section*, while the captions were written by Bailey's friend Francis Wyndham, whose introduction set the tone:

> Together, these 36 photographs make a statement not only about the man who took them, but also about London life in 1965. Many of the people here have gone all out for the immediate rewards of success: quick fame, quick money, quick sex – a brave thing to do. Glamour dates fast, and it is its ephemeral nature which both attracts Bailey and challenges him. He has tried to capture it on the wing, and his pin-ups have a heroic look: isolated, invulnerable, lost.[73]

Bailey's subjects reflected the values of Swinging London. Only four women made it into the thirty-six portraits: Jean and Chrissie Shrimpton, Celia Hammond and Sue Murray. Two of them had been Bailey's girlfriends, while all but Shrimpton minor were models. As for the men, all the familiar names were there: Lennon and McCartney, the Rolling Stones, Brian Epstein, Andrew Loog Oldham, Terence Stamp, Michael Caine, David Hockney, Vidal Sassoon and Brian Morris, the manager of the Ad Lib. All were photographed in the same stark style, and some of the pictures became classic icons of the period: Jagger smouldering beneath the furry hood of his parka; Lennon and McCartney, all in black, staring blankly into the void; Caine, hidden behind his thick glasses, an unlit cigarette dangling from his lips. All had the same hard, bleak edge; all had the same sense of unabashed arrogance. In a review in the *Observer* Malcolm Muggeridge remarked that the pictures were relics of the 'religion of narcissism, of which photographers such as Mr Bailey are high priests'.[74]

What made the *Box of Pin-ups* controversial was the inclusion of two particular photographs. The first was an image of the 'energetic' Lord Snowdon; the second was a group portrait of Charlie, Reggie and Ronnie Kray. The juxtaposition of the Queen's brother-in-law with a gang of East End thugs did not go down well with many critics, and Snowdon withdrew permission for Bailey to use his picture, thereby preventing him from publishing it in the United States.[75] By including the Krays in his *Box of Pin-ups*, Bailey was implicitly comparing them with glamorous stars like the Beatles; what was more, Francis Wyndham's caption was preposterously gushing, claiming that 'to be with them is to enter the atmosphere (laconic, lavish, dangerous) of an early Bogart movie, where life is reduced to its simplest terms yet remains ambiguous'. Wyndham later admitted that he had been 'very naïve'. Bailey, however, remained unrepentant. 'I know people will hate me for saying this,' he said later, 'but I like [them]. I suppose that's like saying I like Hitler.'[76]

The association between East End gangsters and Swinging London reflected a much broader enthusiasm for working-class culture that was rooted in the intellectual climate of the early sixties. Reacting against the Macmillan government and the alleged corruption of the Establishment, many commentators had embraced working-class culture as simple, honest and invigorating.[77] And by the middle of the sixties this rather patronising vision of working-class life had evolved to a point where it was fashionable, even 'swinging', to have proletarian roots. The young writer Margaret Forster, whose novel *Georgy Girl* was adapted into a film starring Alan Bates and Lynn Redgrave, admitted in 1966 that she was 'terribly pleased to be working-class because it's the most swinging thing to be now . . . a tremendous status symbol really'. She was 'very conscious of it', she added, 'because I know it's a good thing, and it makes me seem all the brighter and cleverer and more super to have come from the muck of the North. People are such comic inverted snobs nowadays.'[78]

A common explanation for the Swinging London phenomenon is that it represented the irresistible triumph of working-class values.[79] The erstwhile Maurice Micklewhite, for example, claimed in his autobiography that 'for the first time in British history, the young working class stood up for themselves and said, "We are here, this is our society and we are not going away. Join us, stay away, like us, hate us – do as you like. We don't care about your opinion any more."'[80] Yet although the affluence of the sixties and the expansion of entertainment did promote a few proletarian prodigies like Micklewhite and Bailey to unprecedented levels of wealth and status, the simplistic identification of Swinging London with working-class rebellion does not really stand up. After all, it is very unlikely that Micklewhite, an extremely well-paid and internationally renowned actor, was a typical representative of the British working classes.

For other observers, Swinging London was less an upsurge of proletarian energy than merely the latest aristocratic fad. By the middle of the decade both the Stones and the Beatles had been taken up by upper-class figures like the Old Etonian art dealer Robert Fraser, the Old Etonian antiques dealer Christopher Gibbs and the Guinness heir Tara Browne.[81] In 1965 the 'William Hickey' column in the *Daily Express*, which was usually devoted to chronicling the activities of debutantes and society hostesses, announced: 'There's no harm these days in knowing a Rolling Stone . . . some of their best friends, in fact, are fledglings from the upper classes.'[82] Marianne Faithfull later remarked that Mick Jagger would eagerly turn up to 'dinners given by any silly thing with a title and a castle. He was as smitten as any American millionaire in the movies.'[83] And Terence Stamp recalled his delight that 'some yobbo like me could get into the Saddle Room and dance with the Duchess of Bedford's daughter, and get hold of her, and get taken down to Woburn Abbey to hang out for a long weekend and have dinner in the Canaletto room with the Duke's sons!'[84]

Many commentators liked to think of Swinging London as another symbol of Harold Wilson's New Britain, a 'new class' forged in the white heat of popular culture and social mobility. In November 1963 the *Mirror*'s Noel Whitcombe described the Beatles as examples of 'a brand new race of artist', while four months later Marjorie Proops repeated that they were members of 'a whole new race'.[85] At the end of his survey of Swinging London Jonathan Aitken concluded that

> a completely new class has been formed, running parallel to the existing system . . . This class, and it is a very small one, consists of people who compete in fields where although birth and breeding may accelerate progress, success nevertheless ultimately depends on merit and talent alone . . . The class includes actors and public performers of all kinds, authors and journalists, TV men, dress designers, photogenes, pop singers and money makers in open markets, to name a few.* In short, all the people who are billed as belonging to the classless society or the new aristocracy belong in fact to this new group which, for want of a better terminology, can be called the 'talent' class.[86]

---

*Some of the young members of the 'talent' class identified by Aitken did go on to prominent careers: examples include Nigel Lawson, Leon Brittan, Peter Mayle, Melvyn Bragg, Norman Lamont, John Selwyn Gummer and Michael Winner.

Many of the swinging stars, however, denied that they made up a 'new class'. They preferred to think of themselves as class-*less*, which perhaps undermines Michael Caine's rhetoric about the working-class rebellion of the sixties. Terence Stamp, casting himself as the voice of a generation, explained that 'there was an absolute coming together', based on 'music and dancing'. The 'main thing', he added, 'was that there was suddenly access between the classes. Had the '60s not happened, I would never have been able to spend the night with a young countess because I would never have met her.'[87] George Melly agreed that 'the will to classlessness' was an important factor in the rise of youth culture.[88] And in their survey of the state of the nation, David Frost and Antony Jay announced that the 'ancient partitions' had been 'swept away':

> Mr Edward Heath takes over from the fourteenth Earl of Home: the clubs of St. James's yield to the coffee houses of Chelsea; Carnaby Street usurps Savile Row; Liverpudlian pop stars weekend at ducal castles; dukes go out to work; ancient universities welcome upstart sons of hobnailed workmen. The bad old system is smashed . . . The three great classes melt and mingle. And a new Britain is born.[89]

In reality, very few of the prominent characters of Swinging London were genuinely proletarian. The Beatles, for example, were lower middle class rather than working class. Lennon had been brought up in a mock-Tudor villa called Mendips; McCartney grew up in an aspirational, *Daily Express*-reading household; Harrison lived in a smart new council house where his parents could afford to lend him thirty pounds for his first guitar; and only Ringo Starr, the son of a barmaid and a bakery worker, grew up in anything resembling genuine poverty.[90] Indeed, although Bailey, Stamp and Caine could point to working-class roots, most of their friends came from distinctly privileged backgrounds. Robert Fraser and Andrew Loog Oldham were both public schoolboys, Julie Christie had been brought up on her father's tea plantation in India, and Marianne Faithfull was the daughter of a Viennese baroness.[91] Apart from a few celebrities, the guest list for the opening of Sibylla's was made up of Wodehousian names like Peregrine Elliot, Belinda Volpeliere, Kitty Gordon Hercy and Julian Ormsby-Gore. Far from being classless, clubs like Sibylla's were actually extremely exclusive, with that exclusivity being based less on talent or even wealth than, quite simply, on breeding.[92]

Stars like Jagger and McCartney were not routinely referred to as the 'new aristocracy' for nothing. As far as they were concerned, the point of being rich was to imitate the habits and values of the upper classes. Every member of the Beatles and the Rolling Stones bought his own elegant London residence or sprawling country house, from George Harrison's neo-Gothic pile outside Henley to Keith Richards' thatched mansion, complete with moat, in Sussex. When Bill Wyman moved into Gedding Hall in Suffolk, which had been built in 1480, he officially became Lord of the Manor of Gedding and Thormwood, a title which went nicely with his six bedrooms, three bathrooms and eight-car garage. One of the most unlikely lords of the manor in history, he was just thirty-two years old.[93]

Far from being revolutionary pioneers, the stars of Swinging London were not unlike the self-made industrialists of the nineteenth century. Not only did they associate with aristocrats, entrepreneurs and Old Etonians in exclusive London clubs, they eagerly snapped up vastly expensive country houses and city apartments of the kind once inhabited by peers of the realm. While most fiercely denied that they had ever lost touch with their modest roots, the actor Tom Courtenay was more honest, admitting in 1966 that he had 'nothing in common' with his working-class father. By contrast, he added:

> I'm getting to know quite a lot of upper-class people now, and I like them a lot. They're rather frightening, and very mysterious, but the ones I know have got a lot of attractive things about them — they're intelligent, cultured, sympathetic, and they've got a tremendous self-confidence about them . . . I'll never be one of them, yet I think I'll borrow some of their style when I set up in my own house. No, it's not snobbish imitation at all, I just admire a lot of things about the upper classes and I now can't find anything to admire about the working classes.[94]

Even Terence Stamp, with his East End roots and his ambition to be a 'new kind of Englishman', was not immune to the charms of upper-class life. In 1966 he delightedly moved into a set of rooms in Albany, an eighteenth-century mansion on Piccadilly divided into sixty bachelor flats. Since other famous residents had included Byron, Palmerston, Gladstone, T. S. Eliot, Graham Greene and Terence Rattigan, his new address rather belied his supposedly classless ambitions. When he moved in, his most famous neighbour was the leader of the Conservative Party.[95]

And far from being open and classless, the swinging scene was essentially the province of a self-satisfied elite. In some ways this tight, incestuous world was an advantage, fostering a spirit of cooperation between, say, Mary Quant, Terence Conran and Vidal Sassoon, or the Beatles and the Rolling Stones, and thereby creating a sense of synthesis between the worlds of art, music and fashion. But it is hard to deny that the swinging elite had simply replaced one form of snobbery with another. Caine later remembered that 'everybody was a success and you didn't know anybody who wasn't'.[96] But the model Celia Hammond was less enthusiastic. It was, she said, a 'closed set-up, a clique, hard to break into'.[97] The journalist Bernard Levin was even more damning. The swinging scene, he said, was full of 'pimps and agents and tenpercenters, whores and pedlars and actors, film-makers and playwrights and decorators'. It was the 'froth and scum' of a decadent, doomed society.[98]

In June 1966 the BBC began broadcasting a new adventure series that they hoped would capture the spirit of the Swinging Sixties. *Adam Adamant Lives!* followed the exploits of a gentleman adventurer from 1902 who has been frozen alive and is accidentally resuscitated by demolition workers in the heart of London in 1966. It was devised by Sydney Newman, the creator of *The Avengers* and *Doctor Who*, and his production team told their writers that the show must be swinging, with 'way-out stories and characterisation . . . design, lighting, sound and camera-work [that] must have panache [and] be continually inventive to supply the eye-jerking, the ear-fixing, the unexpected'.[99]

More than any other television show of the era, *Adam Adamant Lives!* was firmly rooted in the world of Swinging London. Adam (Gerald Harper) is a dashing, square-jawed hero with old-fashioned attitudes and an amusingly dated vocabulary, but his sidekick, Georgina Jones (Juliet Harmer) is a fashionable girl-about-town, described by reviewers as 'a breathless blonde dolly' and 'a chick in a mini-skirt who represents London as imagined by *Time* magazine'.[100] At first Adam is horrified by what Britain has become and is driven almost to madness by the sight of strip clubs, double-decker buses, mini-skirted girls and the like, but he soon gets used to it. It is not long before he, too, is driving a Mini and living it up in a penthouse apartment hidden above a multi-storey car park in the West End. As a supporting character confidently announces: 'This is London, 1966, the swinging city.'[101]

Adam Adamant Lives! never really took off with audiences, partly because they had seen it all before, but also because the BBC's timing was dreadful. By the summer of 1966 Chelsea and Carnaby Street were turning into tourist clichés, optimistic modernism was giving way to eclectic bohemianism, and journalists and readers alike were bored of anecdotes about discotheques and mini-skirts. *Queen* magazine complained: 'London? No, not more about London!' and commissioned an angry piece from the publisher Anthony Blond entitled 'Swingers: I Hate You'.[102] Even Piri Halasz thought that the myth had been oversold: when she visited London a few months after her *Time* cover story, she admitted to being 'horrified' at how it had been 'cheapened and vulgarised'.[103]

In truth, most people remained completely untouched by the swinging 'social revolution' that was supposed to be shattering the old boundaries and creating a new class. A poll published by the *Sunday Times* in the summer of 1966 suggested that the great majority were bored of hearing about 'miniskirts, pop music and bingo', and wanted the media to spend more time on serious issues like the state of the economy.[104] The historian Robert Murphy spoke for millions when he wrote that during the mid-sixties he was 'working as a filleter's labourer in a fish factory in Grimsby, and when I came down to London in 1968 it might still have been swinging but, living in cheap bed-sits with building workers and kitchen porters for neighbours, I hardly noticed'.[105] And soon even David Bailey turned against Swinging London, admitting that it was 'a very elitist thing [for] 2000 people living in London'.[106] Thirty years later, he told an interviewer that he had never liked it in the first place. 'It became a theme-park,' he said wearily. 'It wasn't real. It was all about money and manufacturing, and selling the American flag and the Union Jack as pop art symbols. There was no substance, really.'[107]

By the end of 1966 both the Ad Lib and the famous Cavern Club in Liverpool had closed down. Kevin MacDonald, the co-owner of Sibylla's, killed himself that October; two months later Tara Browne, the Guinness heir and friend of the Beatles, was killed in a car crash. With the government teetering and the economy in severe trouble, the optimism of 1964 and 1965 was rapidly ebbing away. It was just as well that *Private Eye*'s 'All-purpose Swinging England Titillation Supplement' had included the advice:

DECADENT ENGLAND

Note to editors
The Swinging England Supplement may be easily transformed into a Decadent England Supplement merely by simple reversal of key phrases, e.g. for

'The pound may be sinking, but down Chelsea way the mini-skirts are flying in a town that has suddenly become young at heart, etc.'
read
'The mini-skirts may be flying down Chelsea way, but the pound is sinking and London has become obsessed with juvenile trivia, etc.'[108]

And as 1966 drew on, with the optimism of two years before rapidly fading into history, the *Eye*'s advice on Decadent England seemed ever more appropriate. 'The revolution seems to have spent its force,' concluded the *Sunday Times* that August. At last it appeared that the 'Age of Pop' was 'Swinging to a Stop'.[109]

14

THE DAY IT ALL STOPPED

> All hail! The Conquering Hero comes
> Brave Harold Proud and Good
> The people wave and lift their thumbs
> To signify their mood.
> All hail George Brown, Jim Callaghan too
> Of thee we too would sing
> And Barbara Castle, splendid heroes who
> To Harold peculiar tributes bring.
> So through the corridors of fame
> Wise Harold's name shall sound
> And babes unborn shall lisp his name
> The Saviour of the £.
>
> 'Mrs Wilson's Diary', *Private Eye*, 15 April 1966

On 19 March 1966 Richard Crossman and his wife Anne drove up to Coventry for the formality of his nomination as the Labour candidate in the general election. 'We motored over in exquisite weather,' he wrote afterwards, 'and the atmosphere was as though Anne and I were getting married again, with the mayor and the town clerk having a drink with us and a great sense of ease and repose. Never have I known an election as easy as this one.'[1] The following morning, as they relaxed at their farm in Oxfordshire, Crossman sat in the spring sunshine and reflected on the campaign:

> A lovely day here, starting with a thick white fog and coming out into a cloudless blue sky and hot spring air. Steady, perfect electioneering weather. It really is getting like the autumn of 1959 when Gaitskell was fighting his valiant, hopeless campaign against Macmillan and the country had never had it so good and would have nothing said against him. All this week we have been fighting 1959 in reverse. Now it is we who are on top of the world, we who are the Government being given credit for

the weather, we who are letting wages rise faster than prices. The Tories can't find a way to break through the complacent acceptance by the electorate of super-Harold.[2]

A languid, almost lazy sense of inevitability hung over the election campaign. Barbara Castle thought that it was 'one of the most boring Election campaigns I have ever experienced' and felt that 'there was an air of unreality' about the whole thing.[3] With ten days to go, Labour's lead in the opinion polls was still in double figures and only one result looked likely. There hardly seemed any point in campaigning: when Gallup asked people whom they expected to win, almost 70 per cent said Labour and fewer than 16 per cent named the Tories.[4] Despite the disappointments of the last eighteen months, few voters had forgotten the setbacks of the Conservatives' last years in office and three times as many people blamed the Conservatives for Britain's economic difficulties as blamed their successors.[5] The Conservative campaign seemed listless and uninspired; party morale was low and the manifesto lacked any great theme.[6] Edward Heath fought a vigorous campaign, although his performances were still flat and unexciting, and he had to be fortified with half a bottle of champagne before press conferences. But he already knew that he had no hope of winning, and the highlight of his election was when a window on his aeroplane blew out and he saved a reporter from disappearing along with it.[7]

The central theme of the Labour campaign was summed up in its slogan: 'You _know_ LABOUR government works'.[8] Wilson told audiences that his new government had made a good start; now they needed a proper mandate to finish the job. As the title of the Labour manifesto put it, it was 'Time for Decision'.[9] As in 1964, Wilson ran a presidential campaign, and many commentators agreed that he was still Labour's foremost asset. But behind the scenes his advisers spent much of the campaign fighting among themselves. There were tantrums, shouting matches and sobbing fits; Marcia Williams hurled accusations of treachery and incompetence left and right; there was even, in a provincial railway station, a physical scuffle between two of the staff.[10]

And yet while all these battles raged in his entourage, Wilson himself rose above it all, concentrating on the polls, cool and confident of victory. To Wedgwood Benn, he explained that the public were 'not interested in politics and want to play tennis and clean their cars and leave things to the Government'. His electorate therefore 'wanted him to be the doctor who looked after the difficulties so that it could go on playing tennis'.[11] Meetings and rallies were quiet and good humoured, and there were few of the rowdy incidents that had marked the previous election. When Wilson spoke at the Birmingham Bull Ring, where Home had endured such an ordeal two years previously, all his skills were on show. For twenty minutes he worked the crowd into a frenzy, goading hecklers and cracking jokes, then, when the ITV camera lights blinked on to show that they were live, he suddenly lowered his voice and became the serious, mature statesman, carrying his message to the country in the face of his enemies. It was the performance of a talented campaigner at the top of his form.[12]

Election night, unlike in 1964, was an anti-climax. After the first few results it was clear that Labour were going to win their anticipated mandate, and in the end they took 48 per cent of the vote and 363 seats to the Conservatives' 42 per cent and 253 seats. They had picked up votes not only in their traditional industrial heartlands but in middle-class towns and suburbs, New Towns and cathedral cities, in Bristol, Croydon, Bedford, Exeter, York, Oxford and Cambridge. Wilson now had a parliamentary majority of ninety-seven and could take pride in his record as only the second Labour Prime Minister, after Attlee, to win two successive general elections.[13]

It was an unusually personal triumph, and given the parlous economic conditions Wilson had confronted during his short first term, it was an impressive achievement. The commentator Ernest Kay, who was close to Wilson, even suggested that since the Prime Minister was still a relatively young man by political standards, he might remain in power for at least two more terms, 'for at least sixteen years of consecutive rule. That will take him up to the end of 1980 and, even then, he will only be sixty-three.'[14] Marcia Williams revelled in the glow of victory, so different from the nail-biting tension of the last campaign:

> Now there were bouquets and gifts to welcome us back; congratulations and smiling faces on all sides. It was a most peculiar feeling suddenly to realise what it all meant; this was No. 10, Labour was in power, the power which the Labour Party had wanted for so long.
>
> We were utterly tired and exhausted on that first morning, as one always is after an election. What I remember most of all despite the weariness was climbing into the lift with Harold to go up to the second floor;

in answer to a query he looked at me most solemnly, saying in a very tired voice: 'Now we can have a rest from politics.' How wrong he was.[15]

In March 1966 James Callaghan had been looking forward to the next few years. Thanks to the American agreement of the previous autumn, the pound had been relatively untroubled by speculation for months, and the economy was still slowly growing. Unveiling his budget, he told the Commons that the economy was 'reasonably well poised' for expansion, with no likelihood of severe tax increases.[16] And yet when he returned to the Treasury after the election, he found 'long faces'. The forecasts were bleak. Not only was the balance of payments looking much worse than they had anticipated, but earnings were almost 10 per cent higher than they had been a year before, which suggested that the voluntary incomes policy agreed with the unions was not working. 'I was naturally put out,' Callaghan wrote afterwards, with grim understatement.[17]

On 12 May the regular Cabinet meeting was taken up with just one item: the prospect of a strike by the National Union of Seamen (NUS). The details of the dispute were extremely complicated, but in essence the seamen had fallen out with their employers over the question of working on Saturdays and Sundays, and as a result were demanding a reduction in the working week from fifty-six hours to forty hours, with weekend work to be paid as overtime. However, any strike would severely disrupt British maritime trade; and more importantly, the union's demands were the equivalent of a pay rise of 17 per cent. An NUS victory therefore threatened to undermine the voluntary incomes policy, which depended on a pay 'norm' of 3.5 per cent and had been requested by the Americans when they had bailed out the pound a year before. As Wilson told his colleagues, 'we had no choice: it was make or break for P[rices] and I[ncomes]'.[18] What was more, Wilson, Callaghan and Brown agreed that if they stood up to the seamen, it would earn them greater credibility in the eyes of international investors, and would therefore strengthen the position of the pound. On 15 May Wilson called the union's leaders into Downing Street and explained the situation to them. The following day the seamen, having been unmoved by his entreaties, walked out on strike. However, far from improving, the position of the pound immediately came under pressure, and the Bank of England had to step in to shore it up. International investors, it turned out, were more worried about the prospect of a long strike than they were impressed by the government's determination to stand firm.[19]

Addressing the nation on television on 19 May, Wilson explained that since the principles of sound economic management were at stake, 'our determination to insist on these principles when the cost is great will be taken by everyone at home and abroad as a proof of our determination to make that policy effective.' 'This is a challenge we did not seek,' he added, 'and do not want.'[20] Yet, as Crossman admitted, the Cabinet knew perfectly well that they could have 'a settlement at any time, since the employers were ready to put up the cash: it was the Government that was preventing the settlement'.[21] 'Cabinet felt that there was no alternative but to back George Brown and his prices and incomes policy,' he noted. 'We have got to be clear with ourselves that it is we, the Labour Cabinet, who have prevented the ship-owners from surrendering to the seamen, simply because a surrender would have made nonsense of the 3½-per-cent norm and given the men too big an increase. We are paying a very high price for George Brown and his policies.'[22]

On 20 June, frustrated by a month of fruitless negotiations, Wilson raised the stakes with a speech in the Commons that stunned his supporters and radically transformed his reputation on the Labour left. The strike had started, he said, as 'a natural democratic revolt', but it was now 'giving way, in the name of militancy, to pressures which are anything but democratic'. The fault, he said, lay with a

> tightly knit group of politically motivated men who, as the last General Election showed, utterly failed to secure acceptance of their views by the British electorate, but who are now determined to exercise back-stage pressures, forcing great hardship on the members of the union and their families, and endangering the security of the industry and the economic welfare of the nation . . . Some of them are now saying very blatantly that they are more concerned with harming the nation than with getting the justice we all want to see.[23]

Although Wilson never once used the word 'Communists', everybody knew what he meant. His information had obviously been provided by MI5, and most observers guessed that it came from wiretaps placed on the telephones of the NUS leaders. In one sense this was very clever politics, playing on public antipathy to Communism as well as weariness with the strike. Polls showed that 58 per cent agreed with him in blaming the Communists, and an overwhelming majority thought that Communists exploited industrial unrest.[24] Eight days later Wilson went even further, naming eight members of the NUS executive who were suspected of having associations with the Communist Party. The very next day the strike was called off.[25]

Wilson's handling of the dispute in the Commons appalled many of his own colleagues. Crossman reported 'consternation on the Labour back benches'.[26] Peter Shore thought it was 'completely bonkers'; Benn recorded that 'it made me sick and reminded me of McCarthyism'.[27] Although his remarks had helped to end the strike, Wilson was taking an enormous risk. Barely three months into his new administration, he had alienated a significant number of his backbenchers and undermined his own standing with the unions, who now saw him as another politician who did not understand their problems.[28] *Tribune* was roused to new heights of outrage, and its edition of 24 June led with a front-page denunciation of the government by Michael Foot:

> WHAT'S WRONG WITH OUR GOVERNMENT?
> The short answer is: plenty . . . No glimmer of a changed strategy, an enlarged vision, since the election . . . The Cabinet never sat down to consider how an intelligent and intelligible incomes policy could have been operated . . . Pathetic acceptance of the Tory legacy in defence and foreign policy . . . We and our Labour government share the guilt for the continuance of the infamy [of Vietnam].[29]

Even though the strike had been a victory for the government, it had come at an enormous cost. Across the country, activists, students and Labour sympathisers were bewildered and upset by Wilson's determination to defeat the seamen and his scathing attack on industrial militancy.[30] To make matters worse, the government's defence of its incomes policy had made no impression on the speculators, and the pound looked weaker than ever. 'It would be foolish to say that Harold is finished,' wrote a gloomy Benn, 'but the magic has definitely gone.'[31]

In the aftermath of the strike, Frank Cousins finally resigned from the Cabinet in opposition to the incomes policy.[32] More importantly, by the beginning of July sterling was coming under increasing pressure. Thanks to the strike, exports had fallen in the previous month by 20 per cent or so, and the monthly trade figures showed a loss of some £40 million. At the same time, the Bank of England was still haemorrhaging gold and currency reserves in an attempt to stave off the speculators. On 1 July the inner triumvirate of Wilson, Brown and Callaghan agreed that they could probably muddle through to the autumn without any need for drastic measures, but within a day or two this prediction was looking absurdly optimistic. Cousins's departure did not impress the markets, and at a press conference on 7 July the visiting French Prime Minister, Georges Pompidou, heavily implied that the pound should be devalued. From that moment onwards, confidence seemed to dissipate by the hour. Two days later the new Governor of the Bank of England, Sir Leslie O'Brien, warned Wilson and Callaghan that, yet again, the pound was in serious trouble. Domestic demand simply had to be cut to restore international confidence, and he specifically wanted them to raise bank rate by 1 per cent, introduce a new, and more severe, deflationary package, and announce a more rigorous prices and incomes policy. Ironically, this was precisely what Wilson's firm stand against the seamen's strike had been designed to avoid.[33]

The only other serious alternative for the government was devaluation, which Wilson had managed to keep off the agenda for the previous eighteen months. But this option had been gradually picking up adherents in recent months, partly because ministers who favoured entry into the Common Market recognised that it was a necessary first step towards Europe. The most important factor, however, was the growing sense of frustration at the interminable cycle of crises and cuts, which was preventing the government from enacting the kind of policies on which it had originally been elected. From this perspective, deflation was the way of conservatism and stagnation, while devaluation would allow the economy, with one great bound, to break free. This was a very simplistic argument, for to work properly devaluation would have to be accompanied by sweeping cuts to keep inflation down and release resources for export. But in the minds of an increasingly vocal group, including Crossman, Castle, Benn, Crosland and Jenkins, devaluation would at least end the constant battle to defend the pound. When, on 9 July, the *Observer* called for the floating of the pound, it spoke for a widening number of Labour MPs, from both left and right.[34]

The most important convert, though, was George Brown. His change of heart owed much to his frustration at the DEA, where his plans for dramatic economic growth had been inhibited by Callaghan's regular bursts of deflation. By his own recollection, he began to move towards devaluation in the late summer of 1965, sick of the 'deflationary shackles that were periodically clamped on the country'.[35] He even arranged a clandestine seminar that summer for himself, his officials and two sympathetic colleagues, Crosland and Jenkins, where they discussed the possibility of devaluation.[36] By the beginning of 1966, in his typically emotional way, he had convinced himself that devaluation was the only true path and that without it the government would fail. In the words of one historian, he had turned the issue into 'a holy war'.[37] On 1 July, with the government on the brink of its latest sterling crisis, he shared a glass or two of sherry with Callaghan and told him that his mind was made up for entry into the Common Market, in order to break the constant dependence on the Americans, and devaluation as soon as possible.[38]

On Monday, 11 July, while England's footballers were preparing for their opening match in the World Cup, Brown requested a meeting with Wilson and confidently announced that the long-running war between the Treasury and the DEA had at last been patched up. But from Wilson's point of view this was not good news at all. 'The Chancellor was now a devaluation convert, and had obviously been knocked off balance by the French,' he noted afterwards. 'George told me that Jim and he had jointly decided that we should have to devalue and that deflation would be necessary as an accompaniment.'[39] Only a month before Wilson had told Barbara Castle that Callaghan was 'getting too arrogant'. 'You ought to get rid of him,' she replied. Wilson had 'smiled a cunning smile', and said: 'The thought had occurred to me. But not a word to anyone.'[40] Now he had discovered his Chancellor in what looked like a rebellious alliance with Brown, and all his suspicions were confirmed.[41]

On the following day, Callaghan told his Cabinet colleagues that they were on the brink of the worst crisis yet. The pound had fallen to its lowest level since November 1964, while the economy was in an 'inflationary condition', with wages rising too quickly and rampant demands for imports. He was asking for cuts of £500 million in public spending, almost three times the amount slashed in the summer of 1965. Crossman intervened:

> I chipped in and said to the Chancellor, 'We came into office as socialists and the essence of a socialist policy is a shift from private to public expenditure. The public sector is not too big now – it's far too small. There can be no question of a cut-back.' At this point the Chancellor woke up and said that he must tell Cabinet frankly that he didn't know how we were going to get out of the mess. We had totally failed to reach our objectives, we were drifting into devaluation in the worst possible conditions and he didn't know how he could retain his position as Chancellor.[42]

This was not what Wilson wanted to hear; as one minister put it, the Prime Minister immediately moved to end the meeting 'rather like a policemen trying to get a blanket around a nude streaker'.[43] Later that day, he saw Brown and Callaghan and secured an agreement that they would wait until the end of the month before making a final decision either way. By then he would be back from a planned trip to Washington, and he was now pinning his hopes on prising some new deal from the Americans.[44]

At this point the situation was changing rapidly from day to day, and allegiances were shifting almost as quickly. On 13 July Brown again saw Wilson and insisted on an immediate devaluation of the pound. This left Wilson in a tricky spot, but he worked his way out of it brilliantly. First, he managed to mollify Brown by promising that if he returned from Washington without a deal, he would have a serious look at the devaluation option. More significantly, he managed to turn Brown against his supposed partner, Callaghan. Wilson knew that Brown shrank from severe deflationary measures, whereas Callaghan had already hinted that he might resign if they were not enacted. Here was the Prime Minister's opening to prise his two rivals apart, and he suggested to the emotional Brown that they join forces against Callaghan by demanding that the Chancellor postpone his cuts. It worked perfectly, as Wilson privately recorded afterwards:

> George agreed and said that as Leader and Deputy Leader we should link arms – and send for Jim and tell him what we had decided. We agreed that if Jim would not agree and insisted on resigning . . . we should accept the resignation and that I should take over the Treasury for three or four weeks, at the end of which George might become Chancellor.[45]

By any standards, Wilson had played his cards superbly. Brown had walked into the meeting as the spokesman for an alliance with Callaghan against Wilson. He walked out as part of an alliance with Wilson against Callaghan. While all this was going on, however, Callaghan himself was quietly thinking things over. He had already told Roy Jenkins that he was favouring devaluation, and even added that he was keen 'to get out of the Treasury, perhaps out of the Government altogether'.[46] He was tired of fighting the markets and the rest of his colleagues; in his own words, he was 'depressed and felt the need to talk'. That afternoon he had a long meeting with his main advisers, Nicky Kaldor and Robert Neild, as well as Sir William Armstrong. 'The floodgates opened and we talked without reserve,' he wrote afterwards. Finally, his mind was made up: they had to devalue. He ordered his officials to draw up the plans for devaluation at the end of the month and requested a meeting with Wilson to tell him the news.[47]

Having already just spent hours persuading Brown to abandon his partnership with the Chancellor, Wilson now poured his energies into persuading Callaghan to turn against Brown. Somehow he managed to convince him to settle for severe deflation, rather than devaluation, with the promise that he would announce the package himself so that Callaghan did not get all the blame. There was also a hint that, if Callaghan had had enough of the Treasury, he could expect a move to the Foreign Office in the next reshuffle.[48] This all proved enough to get the Chancellor back into line, and by the evening Wilson could congratulate himself on successfully having turned his two antagonists against each other. That night he was due to dine at the Guildhall in honour of Sir Robert Menzies, the former Prime Minister of Australia, and in a burst of renewed self-confidence Wilson decided to insert a new passage into his speech of welcome, throwing down the gauntlet to the 'moaning minnies':

> I believe there is a determination in this country to strengthen our economy. But the sell-Britain-short brigade seem to be incapable of looking beyond their noses. We met the shipping strike with determination, but when the cost to our reserves of one month of the seven-week strike was published we heard the wailings and moanings of short-run calculators. They did not see that this was a price worth paying for maintaining the vigour of the incomes policy and the fight for economic solvency.
>
> I give an assurance that the value of sterling will be maintained. We shall not shrink from further measures, however severe or unpopular, that may be necessary. Anyone who doubts our ability or resolve entirely misjudges the temper of the British people and the British Government.[49]

With these words he had made it impossible to turn back. Now the two issues, the direction of the economy and the leadership of Harold Wilson, were inextricably intertwined.

The Cabinet met again the following morning. The alliance between Callaghan and Brown was clearly at an end; indeed, the two men had had a blazing row in the early hours of the morning over the timing of any deflation package.[50] Wilson told his colleagues that there would be no immediate devaluation, that bank rate would be raised by 1 per cent, and that they would work out a tough deflationary package to be presented after he returned from Washington. Under pressure from his colleagues, who were worried that this would look as though he was going to the United States on a begging mission, he agreed to bring the package forward to the final week in July; but this left Brown furious, because it implied that they were not going to consider devaluation at all, whatever happened.

In the meantime Wilson addressed the Commons and explained that details of the cuts would be forthcoming in due course.[51] On the markets the flight from sterling continued; in Westminster and Fleet Street rumours were circulating that either Brown or Callaghan, depending on who was telling the story, was on the verge of resignation.[52] In the Commons tea room Barbara Castle bumped into Wilson, who was 'on the prowl':

> He told me there was a great plot on by George and Jim to get rid of him. 'You know what the game is: devalue and get into Europe. We've got to scotch it.' He said Jim was in a bad state – seeing too much of Cecil King and always under the influence of the last person who had talked to him. I said, 'You ought to get rid of him as Chancellor.' To which he replied, 'You know my views about that.'[53]

The next day, Friday, 15 July, the plates once again, almost incredibly, began to shift. Wilson's statement had achieved little, and Sir Leslie O'Brien reported that 'money was flowing out fast and . . . unless something drastic was done soon, they could say goodbye to the exchange rate of the pound'.[54] Callaghan and Wilson met that evening and agreed to bring the deflationary package forward to the following week, after Wilson had returned from a long-arranged trip to Moscow. Callaghan was now wavering again and Wilson had to steady his nerve. Brown, meanwhile, was in Durham, standing in for the Prime Minister at the annual Miners' Gala, the Labour movement's traditional celebration of working-class solidarity. When he received the telephone call telling him what had been decided, he exploded, accusing Wilson of breaking his word and making crucial decisions behind his back. If they did not devalue, Brown said threateningly, then he would walk out of the government and tell the world why.

Wilson suspected that he had been drinking and hoped that a good night's sleep would change his mind, but when they spoke again on

Saturday morning, just before Wilson was due to fly to Moscow, Brown was still fuming. Unfortunately, there was no time to persuade him; Wilson had already decided against cancelling his engagement in the Soviet capital, and by lunchtime he was at Heathrow, leaving behind a furious Brown in Durham, an ambivalent Callaghan in London, and a government in chaos.[55]

The next three days were the high point of the crisis and the centrepiece of the so-called 'July plot' against Wilson's leadership. The key figure was George Brown, who was understandably concerned that another bout of deflation would destroy the National Plan and mean that all his work at the DEA had been for nothing. But Brown also had more personal reasons for wanting to get rid of Wilson. He had never forgiven the Prime Minister for beating him to the leadership in 1963, and knew that under normal circumstances, Wilson would be in office until 1970 at the earliest, when Brown would be too old to replace him. His only chance for the top job was to force him out in a palace coup. But this was never very likely: too many of Brown's Cabinet colleagues had serious doubts about his reliability, and at this stage there seemed no alternative candidate. Nevertheless Wilson was already beginning to succumb to the obsessive mistrust that marked his later years, and to him it looked very much as though there was 'a great plot on by George and Jim' while he was away in Moscow.[56]

The weekend's negotiations proceeded with labyrinthine complexity. Brown was still up in Durham, where, according to one report, he had 'gone berserk'.[57] Callaghan was staying with friends on a farm in Sussex. Roy Jenkins, the Home Secretary, was at a party at the country house of Anne Fleming, the widow of James Bond's creator and former mistress of Hugh Gaitskell. Wilson later got it into his head that Fleming, perhaps because of her links with both Gaitskell and, more tenuously, the world of intrigue, had organised a 'meeting' of the plotters, but this was nonsense.[58] In fact Jenkins arrived at her country house late on Friday evening, and took a telephone call from Brown in Durham, during which the Deputy Prime Minister, still well oiled, announced his intention to resign.[59] He repeated this threat to Benn the following morning as they were both waiting to address the miners' parade. Benn replied that 'if he did this it would mean the end of the Government', but Brown was unrepentant. 'You may just as well make your speech under the same misery that I am going to make mine,' he said with grim satisfaction.[60]

Meanwhile, garbled reports of these goings-on were slowly filtering through to Wilson in Moscow. In the oppressive heat of a Russian summer he wandered around the Soviet trade fair and sat through interminable discussions about Vietnam in a dissatisfied daze, while young secretaries slipped him notes of the latest developments in London. Marcia Williams, who had flown out with him, lay in her Moscow apartment with a badly upset stomach, unable to help or advise him. On the Sunday he was handed a telegram from Brown reaffirming his intention to resign. Wilson immediately cabled back asking him to wait a few more days.[61] He was now sure that Brown had an organised cabal behind him, consisting of Jenkins and Crosland as well as a group of right-wing backbenchers from the Midlands including Roy Hattersley and Brian Walden. Jenkins by this point was back in London, deep in conference with Crosland and then with Brown. Callaghan's position was still unclear. Like Brown, he had telephoned Jenkins at Anne Fleming's house to discuss the situation, and on the Saturday he had sent his economic adviser Robert Neild to go and see Jenkins about the prospect of devaluation. However, Callaghan was not part of any conspiracy; he had no desire to see Brown as Prime Minister.[62]

The next day, Monday, 18 July, found Wilson still trapped impotently in Moscow while conspiracy swirled around the Palace of Westminster. Throughout the day the key players – Callaghan, Brown, Jenkins, Crosland, Crossman and Castle – continued, warily, to circle one another. 'Everything is beginning to slip into place,' recorded Castle, 'and I can see a major battle is on, highlighted by reports from Moscow, where Harold is having a very unproductive time, that the PM is in a tough mood and intends to drive his policy through.'[63]

Brown's position was shifting by the hour. At lunchtime he told Crossman that he had changed his mind about resigning and was determined to have it out with Wison.[64] But that evening Roy Jenkins had arranged to have dinner with him at his club, Brooks's. 'By ill chance,' Jenkins wrote later, 'I was late and Brown had been early. The welcoming Brooks's habit of serving drinks to waiting guests for once rebounded, for George by the time I had arrived had already managed to engage in several quarrels with casually present members, about which I had to write an abject letter of apology to the chairman of the managers.' More to the point, Brown had decided to resign after all and had completely given up on the idea of fighting Wilson.[65]

After dinner Brown returned to his room at the Commons, where he was joined by Barbara Castle later that night:

I found George brooding ominously in his vast room. He had drunk enough to be voluble, though not offensive . . . He knew he would lose, and then he would resign. I told him I thought he would win and he said, 'No, I can't win because a Cabinet can't sack the Prime Minister. You wouldn't have me for Leader, would you?' 'No,' emphatically. 'There you are then. Look, I'm not seeking allies. Let me make that clear. You asked to see me, not me you. But I'm not going to wear this. And you will side with him.' Just then Wedgie [Benn] put his head round the door and George waved him in. 'We've got to break with America, devalue and go into Europe.'

Castle told him that if he resigned, he would destroy the government. Brown, 'in a state of high excitement', said he planned to 'resign silently' and 'just fade out of the picture'. Castle insisted that they had enough votes in the Cabinet to overrule Wilson and force him to change the policy. But Brown was having none of it, and launched into an extraordinarily emotional tirade:

Frantically George said, 'He can't do that. He won't do that. Look,' pulling telegrams out of his pocket, 'this is what I sent him yesterday and this is his reply. He won't budge. He can't budge.' 'Why?' 'Because he is too deeply committed to Johnson. God knows what he has said to him. Back in 1964 he stopped me going to Washington. He went himself. What did he pledge? I don't know: that we wouldn't devalue and full support in the Far East. But both of those have got to go. We've got to turn down their money and pull out the troops: all of them . . . This is the decision we have got to make: break the commitment to America. You are left-wing and I am supposed to be right-wing, but I've been sickened by what we have had to do to defend America – what I've had to say at the dispatch box.' 'Vietnam?' 'Yes, Vietnam too. And I know what he'll say this time: let's go over this again, then he'll go to Washington and cook up some screwy little deal. I've had enough of it.'

Every time that Castle or Benn tried to calm him down, Brown shouted: 'Let me get a word in for a change', before resuming his rant. Finally, he whipped out yet another piece of paper, a private letter he had sent to Wilson a year before protesting against his endless deflationary policies. 'By last July I had had enough,' he said thickly. 'I could see there would be no end to it. Look, I'm not looking for allies. What I do, I'll do alone.'[66]

Harold Wilson flew back the following morning from a sweltering Moscow into 'a trough of physical dismalness, with leaden skies and pouring rain'.[67] Waiting for him at the airport was George Wigg, the Paymaster General and his chief bloodhound, who had kept his ear close to the ground for the last three days. As they drove into London through the rain, Wigg reported on his colleagues' treachery. Westminster was seething with speculation, Fleet Street was sharpening its knives, and the Cabinet was scheduled to meet late that afternoon. The Prime Minister was exhausted from the trip, the long flight and his own anxiety, but his legendary cunning did not desert him.[68]

That afternoon he saw Crossman and played it beautifully, not fighting him, not standing firm, but calmly and reasonably listening to his arguments and promising that they would discuss devaluation at the forthcoming meeting. 'I'm not adamant against devaluation,' he said disingenuously, 'but we shall have to get the pound stabilized first so that we can float from strength and not from weakness.' Perhaps, he told Crossman, they could think about devaluing in the spring of 1967, when the economy was in better shape. It worked perfectly: Crossman left thinking that he had won the argument, when in fact the meeting had been yet another example of Wilson's supreme tactical skill.[69]

At five, with rain still falling and gloomy shadows lengthening outside, the Cabinet assembled for the decisive meeting. Wilson opened with a long statement on the crisis and the available options. He admitted that more cuts might not work, but said that he still did not think it was time to devalue. Instead, he suggested that they introduce heavy cuts now and leave the question of devaluation until after his visit to Washington. 'As he droned on,' wrote Castle, 'no one would have guessed that a major political drama was being played out – one never does at Cabinet. I don't know whether it is a deliberate tactic on Harold's part or just that casual, low key manner of his, but I always feel at Cabinet as if I were in a cocoon, cut off from the vulgar realities of political conflict.'[70]

Crossman spoke next, putting the case for devaluation. Jenkins followed from the right, 'quietly but convincingly'. Then Douglas Jay, the Gaitskellite veteran at the Board of Trade, countered that devaluation had done little good back in 1949. 'Crosland swung the argument back our way,' Castle recorded, 'and it looked as if we were winning it.' Brown weighed in, passionate as ever. 'But then,' Castle wrote, 'one after another the "do nothing yet" brigade mowed us down.' All the ministers who dealt with foreign affairs, like Michael Stewart and Denis Healey, were strongly opposed, and most of the more obscure Cabinet ministers, the likes of Arthur Greenwood, Douglas Houghton and Willie Ross, backed Wilson. Callaghan said very little. Brown's open rebellion had left the Chancellor in an unexpectedly strong position, effectively arbitrating between his two most powerful colleagues. Ever since the collapse of his alliance with Brown on the preceding Thursday, he had been nursing his bitterness, and he had finally made up his mind to support the Prime Minister.[71]

The formal vote was seventeen against devaluation and only six in favour: Brown, Jenkins and Crosland from the right; Crossman, Castle and Benn from the left and centre. They might be impressive names, but there were only six of them, and their opponents included the Prime Minister, the Chancellor and the Foreign Secretary. Wilson gave a great sigh of relief and, in a sudden burst of candour, remarked that if the vote had gone the other way 'he would have had to consider his position'. Brown's face, however, was a picture of disappointment, and as Wilson ended the meeting after five gruelling hours, the First Secretary said quietly that he could not accept the decision and therefore was thinking of resigning.[72]

When they reconvened the following morning to finalise the details of the deflation package, it was still unclear whether Brown was going or not, because he was certainly there in person although visibly elsewhere in spirit. Wilson was determined that everything should be sorted out by two o'clock, when he wanted to give the details to the TUC, the CBI and the Commons. Most ministers had barely had time to look through the Treasury's proposed cuts. 'Nothing had been adequately prepared,' remarked Crossman. 'Nothing had been thought out properly. We were fixing things once again, horribly inefficiently, at the last moment.'[73] A famous example was the agreed limit of fifty pounds in foreign exchange for holidays abroad. Callaghan supposedly came up with the figure after leafing through some travel brochures in search of inspiration, and when one of the less affluent ministers said: 'Well, no one could possibly need more than that,' Wilson said briskly, 'Right, £50 then', leaving some of his richer colleagues staring at each other in horrified silence.[74]

That morning the newspapers had warned Wilson that there could be no room for error. 'Today is Britain's last opportunity to avoid economic defeat,' insisted *The Times*:

The present crisis is totally different in kind from those before. Britain has entered the latest period of stress without having recovered from the one before. The Government must show that they understand the implications of this change. Britain is no longer seen as poised uneasily on a knife edge, swaying back and forth between debit and credit sides. Britain now looks as if it has lost its balance. Today's measures must convince everyone that this loss is retrievable.[75]

Shortly after three, Wilson wearily hauled himself up from the government front bench to present the austerity package to the House. To 'gasps of disbelief and dismay', he grimly went through the details: cuts of £100 million from the overseas budget and £150 million in public investment; the foreign travel limit of £50; a 10 per cent increase in excise and petrol duties; another 10 per cent increase in surtax; heavy hire-purchase restrictions; and, harshest of all, a mandatory freeze on all wages and prices for six months, to be followed by another six months of 'severe restraint'.[76] As he dully worked his way through his notes, all eyes were on the bench beside him. Brown was not present. 'His vacant place', said *The Times*, 'was an almost unmistakeable demonstration of a deep disagreement.'[77]

In fact Brown's letter of resignation had reached Wilson an hour or so earlier, but the Prime Minister had decided to ignore it and had sent it back to him. He was determined that Brown's resignation should not ruin the financial package; his fear was that if the news leaked out, then the international bankers would lose their remaining shreds of confidence in the pound and it would all have been for nothing. Unfortunately, although Wilson sent George Wigg to try to argue Brown round, the news did get out, and in the early evening ITV interrupted *Coronation Street* with a newsflash that the Deputy Prime Minister was about to resign. At about this point, however, Brown yet again began to have second thoughts. His supporters on the backbenches were already rallying to his side, and his junior minister Bill Rodgers had drafted a petition to get him to stay, for which he eventually collected a hundred names.[78]

At exactly the same moment, Wilson's attitude changed, too. Having spent the last few days trying to persuade Brown to remain, he was now heartily sick of his turbulent deputy and decided that since the news was out, it hardly mattered now whether he stayed or not. He therefore told Wigg to change his approach and try to put Brown off staying, so that he would resign and they would be rid of him at last. This indeed resolved the situation, but with precisely the wrong result from Wilson's point of view. Having discovered that Wilson was quite happy to bid him farewell, Brown decided that he really did want to remain in office, and later that night he appeared on the steps of 10 Downing Street and announced to the flashbulbs of the press that he was going to stay. Inside, Wilson turned to an aide and muttered gloomily: 'That bugger isn't going to resign after all.'[79]

The sorry farce of Brown's non-resignation was only a temporary distraction from the real story of the day – the latest and most arresting dose of economic austerity. Wilson estimated that the cuts would reduce demand by more than £500 million, and *The Economist* called them 'perhaps the biggest deflationary package that any advanced industrial nation has imposed on itself since Keynesian economics began'.[80] In the City the reaction was largely positive: the cuts were seen as 'the first positive step towards economic realism', and American bankers praised 'a very strong package'. But there was no doubt that deflation of this magnitude was a bitter blow to the government's modernising aspirations, and an unmistakeable sign that the days of never having it so good were over. As *The Times* pointed out, the plan would only work if people found themselves 'with no more money to spend . . . Most of the goods they want to buy will be more expensive because of higher indirect taxation,' an editorial grimly predicted. 'They will be faced with the need for much stiffer hire purchase payments, and be unable to take refuge in expensive foreign holidays. The psychological shock should be great.' Not surprisingly, the same newspaper described Wilson's performance in the Commons as that of 'a tired man who would rather be somewhere else' and noted that 'there was no joy on the faces around him'.[81]

It is hard to see the government's performance in July 1966 as anything other than wretchedly incompetent. Wilson's ministers never had a clear sense of direction, never discussed alternative proposals and ended up being rushed into a hastily concocted package of cuts to meet a deadline that they themselves had imposed. At almost every turn the future of the economy was mixed up with petty personal jealousies. In later years this would come to be seen as 'the crucial turning point in the life of the government; the moment when the wrong direction was taken'.[82] Faced with overwhelming evidence that their deflationary policies were a failure, the Cabinet chose to administer yet another dose of deflation, albeit harsher than ever. Devaluation would have involved equally severe cuts, but at least it would have promised an end to the interminable stop–go cycle. Deflation alone, however, was not a long-term solution at all. The young Labour MP and future historian David Marquand later reflected that 1966, not 1964, was 'the real catastrophe'. 'There is no question', he told an interviewer, 'that they should have devalued in 1966.'[83]

Why did Wilson refuse to devalue in 1966? George Brown's explanation, that he was 'bound personally and irrevocably to President Johnson', does have something to it, but it is certainly not the whole story.[84] Wilson still believed that devaluation was the wrong option, and throughout the crisis he never wavered. He recognised, as Brown did not, that devaluation was no painless panacea: it would require savage cuts, would bring down the standard of living, and might well send shock waves through the international monetary system. As he saw it, there was going to be brutal deflation either way; the choice was whether to devalue the currency into the bargain. Since the consequences would be uncertain, this would be taking a reckless leap into the dark, something a careful, calculating politician should avoid at all costs.[85] But there were personal considerations, too. If Wilson agreed to devalue the pound, his own credibility would be badly damaged, not just in Washington but around his own Cabinet table and in the country. His faithful protégé Peter Shore reflected that Wilson was 'emotionally committed' to protecting the parity, and that it had become bound up with his own reputation, 'so that he couldn't even bring himself to discuss the matter after a certain time'.[86] But, each time that he rejected the devaluation option, the price of failure became even higher. 'It was like he was a general throwing new armies into the battle', noted David Marquand. 'Each new army he threw in made it harder for him to retreat.'[87]

Barely four months after winning a second successive general election, Wilson's government seemed to have thrown it all away in scenes of almost unimaginable chaos. The Prime Minister claimed that they had been 'blown off course' by the seamen's union, but as one usually sympathetic historian puts it, they had 'rather seemed rudderless and in danger of being totally destroyed through a mixture of incompetence and misadventure'.[88] In May Gallup had put Labour some 18 per cent ahead of Heath's Conservatives. Now, in the first poll to be published after the July crisis, the Tories had regained a narrow lead, reflecting a swing of enormous proportions. In the same period, the personal approval ratings of Wilson and Callaghan fell by 17 and 18 per cent respectively, while for the first time a majority of the public blamed Labour, not the Conservatives, for Britain's economic misery.[89]

Around the country, the morale of Labour's activists and supporters could hardly have sunk lower. Not for nothing did the *Observer* call 20 July 'The Day It All Stopped'.[90] Even in Whitehall, among the officials charged with doing their masters' bidding, there was a sense of shock and disillusionment. 'I can't remember a government discrediting itself so completely and quickly,' remarked one of Callaghan's closest Treasury aides, adding that 'if a dozen of the most brilliant men in the country had been charged with planning the worst possible mess they couldn't have done better'.[91]

Both Brown and Wilson came out of the July crisis as losers. Brown, with his conspicuous conspiring, his public sulk and his dramatic, late-night change of heart, could hardly have made himself look more ridiculous if he had tried. As he had feared, the July measures completely eviscerated his National Plan and his experiment with the DEA. There was no hope now of raising productivity by 25 per cent in five years, or indeed of any serious economic expansion at all. The idea of planning was widely discredited; the government's strategy was more a matter of muddling through and hoping that the cuts had done enough.[92]

All of this left Brown a humiliated figure in a pointless department. That this had taken its toll was obvious a week later, when he was considered to have disgraced himself by giving a remarkably feeble performance in a Commons debate on the economy. 'He was overwrought, overtired, and he spoke so slowly that he incited the Tories to interrupt him,' recorded Crossman.[93] Benn, too, thought that Brown had made 'the most awful gaffes'. Speaking to backbenchers afterwards, he found that they were 'completely shaken by it', because it seemed that even the leadership had lost heart.[94] The newspapers were unforgiving. The *Daily Express* suggested that Brown had been drunk, while the *Sunday Telegraph* ran an editorial denouncing his 'emotional and incoherent performance'. Edward Heath had called it 'the most embarrassing thing he had ever seen in his whole political life', but the *Telegraph* thought that was being 'over-charitable'. The headline of the editorial said it all: 'GO, MAN, GO'.[95]

Wilson, meanwhile, tried to represent the crisis as another example of his ministers' fortitude and resolution. In a televised address he admitted that the government had been 'driven off course', but in his best Churchillian style he told the public that this was 'a time for greatness':

We are under attack. This is your country and our country. We must work for it . . . One thing the crisis has done, it has focused the eyes of the world on us. This is our chance to show them what we are made of . . . We have got to show the world that we mean business, Anyone who wants to write us off entirely underestimates the resolve and determination of which we are capable.

I believe that what we have done today is what the country wants. I believe that all of us are ready to show we mean business and that when Britain is up against it we are at our best.[96]

Optimistic as ever, he privately insisted that Labour would soon be able to bounce back. 'You don't realize that I am not so unpopular as everybody thinks,' he told Crossman five days later. 'I was in Liverpool last weekend and I went to the Cavern, where the Beatles first played, to be present at its reopening and the whole place stood and cheered me. Each time I go down Downing Street now more people cheer me than ever before. It's quite untrue that the people are against me, it's only the journalists and Parliament.'[97]

Crossman was baffled by his leader's good cheer. 'Had he really lost his nerve inside,' he wondered, 'or was it that he had drawn a thick skin round himself? Or has he – as I tend to believe – a deep natural survival instinct which enables him to deceive himself as a protection against collapse? Because he really had a terrible press this last weekend.'[98] He was right: as the months progressed, it became increasingly clear that Wilson's reputation had undergone a dramatic transformation. Before the crisis he had enjoyed the image of a cool, hard-working statesman, perhaps given to the odd flight of fancy, but essentially a decent man. After the events of July, however, he looked 'devious, calculating and inconsistent, driven more by paranoia than by policy priorities'.[99]

The collapse of Wilson's reputation after July 1966 was best captured by an article that appeared the following month in *Private Eye*. Until the summer of 1966 the *Eye* had been markedly more hostile to the Conservatives than to Labour, a legacy of its origins in the last days of the Macmillan government, but as its editor Richard Ingrams later admitted, 'from then on the magazine's attacks on Wilson were as savage as any on the Tories'.[100] Two months before, a Ceylonese-born swindler called Dr Emil Savundra had fled the country when his latest concern, the Fire, Auto and Marine Insurance Company, collapsed leaving 45,000 unpaid claims and

400,000 customers without insurance.[101] By conflating the two stories, the *Eye* perfectly captured the growing disquiet at Wilson's perceived dishonesty, unreliability and sheer incompetence:

WILSUNDRA VANISHES!

Dr Harold Wilsundra ('Conman extraordinary') is now believed to be resting in a Colombo clinic following his sensational flight from Britain.

In a newspaper report published yesterday Wilsundra was quoted as saying 'I have done nothing illegal'.

SENSATION

Wilsundra's sudden departure to Ceylon coincided with the collapse of the firm 'New Britain Ltd' of which he was the managing director. Millions of innocent policy-holders were affected by the 'crash'.

COLLAPSE

Wilsundra, who had been involved in a number of exceptionally shady deals prior to his interest in 'New Britain', started the company in 1964.

In exchange for their votes millions of people were offered fantastic benefits. The company's prospectus contained references in glowing prose to increased wages, great new technological advances, the 'white heat of scientific revolution', 'dynamic purposeful government' and other high-sounding claims.

FRAUD

It is now realised that all such promises were nothing but a gigantic fraud perpetuated by an extremely plausible entrepreneur with but little understanding of money matters.

Wilsundra had taken to 'making trips abroad' to try to raise 'political capital to prop up the company', including an appeal to his Texan friend 'Loony Bins' Johnson, but to no avail. 'Now,' the account concluded sadly, 'Wilsundra has finally fled the country, while the Official Receiver investigates the company's accounts. At his palatial residence in the heart of London, Mrs Wilsundra said yesterday: "I cannot believe it. There must be a mistake."'[102]

Wilson's image was never the same again. He had lost the aura of invincibility that had sustained him since his elevation to the leadership, and, as his biographer puts it, he 'acquired the character, which he was never to lose, of a leader under siege'.[103] In the Commons the Shadow Chancellor Iain Macleod voiced the silent anxieties of many Labour members as well as the vocal sentiments of his fellow Tories when he remarked that 'as long as [Wilson] sits in this house, on whichever side he sits, we do not feel that we will be able to trust him again'.[104] Tony Benn, once the loyal speechwriter, now reflected that his 'regard and affection for Harold Wilson' were 'fast evaporating'. 'I do not think that Harold has a long-term vision of the sort of society we want to create,' he wrote sadly, 'and the short-term dodging at which he is adept . . . has no place in the developing strategy for the next four years.'[105] Even Richard Crossman, who considered himself one of Wilson's few friends in politics, reflected that he had seen 'the destruction of the Wilson myth in the public eye and, even more, in my private eye.' 'I suppose', he admitted bleakly, 'it is the most dramatic decline any modern PM has suffered.'[106]

15

THE FACE OF '66

> As I was leaving the room I suddenly thought of the 1966 World Cup and I said, 'By the way, you do know, Prime Minister, we've got the World Cup on our hands in 1966?' And he didn't know what it was. 'What's that?' he said.
>
> Denis Howell, interviewed in 1996

> Harold sat, or rather lay, in a relaxed attitude in front of the television set, an almost empty decanter of Wincarnis at his side. 'Ah, Mr O'Brien! Come in, come in. You are just in time to see a slow motion reconstruction of the North Korean winning goal. Watch carefully as Ooh Mai Kok heads it in the net with oriental aplomb.' 'When you have a moment, Prime Minister,' whispered the man of affairs, 'the state of the economy gives rise to alarm.' 'Nonsense, nonsense,' replied Harold, draining his cut glass goblet of Wincarnis at a draught, 'relax man and help yourself to a glass of this bottled sunshine. Ooh! Ah! Well shot!'
>
> 'Mrs Wilson's Diary', *Private Eye*, 22 July 1966

As a Neasden schoolgirl in the early sixties, Lesley Hornby enjoyed a relatively contented existence. Her father was a skilled carpenter at the Elstree film studios, and was the first man in their suburban street to buy a car and a television. He even gave his teenage daughter a few shillings a week in pocket money, which she supplemented by spending her Saturdays working at a local hairdresser's. Like many teenage girls in the early 1960s, Lesley was fascinated by fashion, loved wearing the latest styles, and dreamed of imitating her heroine, Jean Shrimpton. Sadly, it was obvious to everyone that she looked nothing like her.

At the beginning of 1966, when she was sixteen, Lesley stood barely five foot six inches tall and looked much younger than her years. She weighed just six and a half stones; her shoe size was four and her dress size six; and her bust, waist and hip measurements were 30, 22 and 32 inches respectively. She looked, in short, like a little waif, and at school the other girls used to call her 'Olive Oyl', because, with her stick-like legs and plastic Mod mackintosh flapping around her feet, she could easily have passed for the comic heroine from the *Popeye* cartoons.[1]

In March 1965 Lesley had started going out with a much older man whose brother worked in the barber's shop beneath her hairdressing salon. His name was Justin de Villeneuve*; he dressed in all the sharpest Mod fashions, drove a red Spitfire and helped to run a stall in the Chelsea antiques market.[2] It was one of Justin's friends, a former fashion photographer, who first suggested to Lesley that she should have a stab at a modelling career, even though she was far smaller and skinnier than the leading models of the day. In the autumn of 1965, after she had suffered various knock-backs, another friend recommended her to the editor of *Women's Mirror*, a new magazine aimed at the cheaper end of the market. This time her good looks made more of an impression and she was offered a year-long contract at nine pounds a week for beauty-shots and head-shots.[3]

One lucky break now followed another. At her very first shoot for *Women's Mirror*, Lesley was advised to get her hair restyled, and the magazine booked her a session at Leonard's, an exclusive salon in Mayfair whose proprietor had been trained by Vidal Sassoon. Leonard was very taken with his new client's beauty, and arranged for her to have some pictures taken at a nearby studio. The new haircut showed off Lesley's enormous doe-like eyes and slender neck, and Leonard proudly put the photos on the walls of his salon. A few days later the pictures were spotted by another of the hairdresser's customers, Deirdre McSharry, the fashion editor of the *Daily Express*. The next thing Lesley knew, she was off to Fleet Street for a brief interview and a photographic session. She was still only sixteen and was barely weeks into her fashion career, although she had already started using a kind of stage name, 'Twiggy', which had evolved from various teasing nicknames coined by Justin's brother. Finally, early on the morning of 23 February 1966, her father burst excitedly into Lesley's bedroom waving the latest edition of the *Express*. There, in the middle of the newspaper, was a huge close-up photograph of Lesley's elfin face, and above it a banner headline proclaiming 'Twiggy, the Cockney kid with the face to launch a thousand shapes' to be 'the Face of '66'.[4]

---

*Justin's real name was Nigel Davies; he was a bricklayer's son from Edmonton. 'Justin de Villeneuve' was his second stab at an alias: previously Nigel had tried the similarly laughable 'Christian de Forget'.

More than any other iconic figure of the period, Twiggy enjoyed what can genuinely be called overnight success. Despite her popularity with the newspapers, many major fashion photographers refused to use her because she was too small and 'amateurish'. But it was her everyday appeal, allied to her striking looks and fashionably skinny figure, which explains why Lesley Hornby became so successful so quickly. With her large eyes, long neck and flat chest, she was the very picture of the dolly bird of the mid-sixties.[5] One fashion writer said that she had 'the calm appraisal of a child or a Martian . . . [a] rare, strange creature, tranquil, composed, almost bloodless', while another described her as 'one half orphan of the storm, the other purely aesthetic'.[6]

All in all, Twiggy could hardly have come closer to Mary Quant's vision of the Look: 'childishly young, naively unsophisticated'.[7] Even at the height of her fame she still lived with her parents, calling herself a 'Cockney kid' who only wanted '£10 a week for spending money' so that she could 'buy all the records I want, the Stones, the Beatles and all'.[8] But she had a lot more money than that. Despite her youth and lack of formal training, Twiggy was quickly making fifteen guineas an hour – three times as much as other successful models, although still less than Jean Shrimpton, who could command twenty-five guineas. She also signed an exclusive deal to design and sell her own clothes as well as a contract with Yardley for a new range of eye make-up. Mattel paid her $40,000 to endorse their range of Twiggy dolls; Monsanto paid her £50,000 to model their new line of synthetic fabrics; and Twiggy Enterprises issued licences for T-shirts, stockings, handbags, board games and thermos flasks. There were even life-sized Twiggy waxwork dummies for shop windows, although the manufacturers decided to inflate her measurements because their clients felt that her bust was too small.[9]

Twiggy would never have enjoyed such international acclaim had it not been for the remarkable success of British fashion across the Atlantic earlier in the sixties. American journalists were often delighted by the contrast between their stereotypical image of old-fashioned aristocratic Britishness and the reality of modern, youthful, even daring creativity. *Life* magazine, for example, thought that Mary Quant's 'kooky styles' seemed 'wackier than they are because they come from England, stronghold of the court gown, the sturdy tweed and the furled umbrella'.[10] 'These Britishers have a massive onslaught of talent, charm and mint-new ideas,' commented

Women's Wear Daily. 'English chic is fiercely NOW . . . by the young for the young.'[11]

What really transformed the country's image among young people abroad was the success of the British Invasion. By 1966 it seemed that American youngsters would happily snap up anything, from records to cosmetics, bearing the label 'Made in England'.[12] Even Des Moines, Iowa, had the 'Westminster Disco', where fashionable male patrons might wear a Beatle cap from the Carnaby Street Boutique mail-order catalogue, a pair of Liverpool Flame bell-bottoms from the Brolly Male collection, some English Leather cologne, and, perhaps, a Royal Navy pea-coat with a pair of Ford Falcon 'action driving gloves'.[13] Even Yardley made a special 'Britannic scent' for the American market, a 'frisky-frilly fragrance full of tender flowers' called Oh! de London, as well as face powders with brushes called 'luv puffs' and face masks in Blimey Blue.[14]

Although we often think of the British Invasion as a conquest of the United States, British popular culture was scarcely less popular on the Continent. As we have seen, French teenagers had initially been slow to take to the Beatles, but they yielded eventually.[15] By May 1966 *L'Express* had been forced to acknowledge that Britain was the country where 'the wind of today blows most strongly', and it later admitted that 'Twiggy is the teenage idol of '66 as the "Shrimp" was the teenage idol of '65'. A few months later the same magazine conceded that, 'thanks to the Beatles [and] the Rolling Stones, England rules over international pop music; their young actors are the best in the world'.[16] The Italians, meanwhile, even found kind words for Britain's new fashion entrepreneurs. In March 1967 the magazine *Epoca* welcomed the arrival of Mary Quant, 'the queen of the miniskirt', and Twiggy, 'the doll with the freckles'. A month later, a cluster of boutiques 'in the Carnaby style' with names like 'Lord Kingsay', 'Lady Ellen' and 'Portofino Beach' opened in the Standa department store in Milan. 'The ground floor of the shop has been transformed into an exact copy of Carnaby Street,' reported *Ciao Amici*. 'Here you can dress yourself exactly like our friends from across the Channel . . . The sales girls are pretty and, needless to say, dressed in mini-skirts.'[17]

At the cinema, too, Britishness was the height of fashion. In December 1965, when *Thunderball* opened worldwide, James Bond reached the summit of his appeal. In West Germany a million tickets were sold within a week; in New York the film played around the clock, non-stop; and at the beginning of 1966 it was setting new records simultaneously in Britain, the

United States, Canada, Continental Europe, the Caribbean, South Africa, Japan and the Philippines. *Thunderball* was easily the biggest worldwide hit of 1966, and in the United States alone it sold almost sixty million tickets, which meant that, statistically, one in every four Americans had been to see it.[18]

But Britain's cinematic appeal transcended Bond himself. The prominence of British actors and actresses at the Academy Awards, the highlight of Hollywood's social calendar, was simply astounding. From 1964 to 1966, the likes of Richard Burton, Peter O'Toole, James Mason and Vanessa Redgrave chalked up a staggering twenty-eight acting nominations between them, including victories for Rex Harrison, Julie Andrews, Julie Christie and Paul Schofield.[19] Added to the international success of Mary Quant and Jean Shrimpton, John Lennon and Paul McCartney, Ian Fleming and Sean Connery, David Hockney and David Bailey, even Twiggy herself, all of this suggested that Britain was finally punching its weight again at a cultural level. As John Crosby told the readers of the *Telegraph*: 'Talent is getting to be Britain's greatest export commodity.'[20]

A few years before there had been great concern about the so-called Americanisation of British life, but by the mid-sixties that term had almost been forgotten. British popular culture had proved its durability, and there was a genuine sense that British artists and performers, not Americans, were setting the cultural pace. As the *New Musical Express* commented after the Beatles were awarded their MBEs, they had been far more effective than any politicians at keeping 'the Union Jack fluttering proudly', and thanks to their achievements 'we now lead the world in pop music!'[21] What was more, groups like the Beatles and the Kinks were explicitly drawing on native cultural traditions, from music-hall pastiches to songs about steam trains, and they proudly wore their Englishness as a badge of style and sophistication. After the Who returned from a tour of the United States, Pete Townshend told an interviewer that 'what made us first want to go to American and conquer it was being English. We didn't care a monkey's about the American dream or the American drug situation or about the dollars . . . It was 'cos we were English and we wanted to go to America and be English.' As Manfred Mann put it after another tour, the pop stars of the sixties were proud to be 'Union Jack conscious'.[22]

'Union Jack consciousness' seemed to be stronger in the mid-sixties than at any other time since the war. The flag itself, once a symbol of old-fashioned patriotism, almost overnight appeared to become an emblem of sophistication. When the Who turned themselves into a 'Pop Art band' in the summer of 1965, they began wearing jackets and T-shirts with Union Jacks or target symbols, and as lesser musicians and artists began copying their example, the national flag suddenly started to look like a symbol of modernity. Enterprising manufacturers churned out tens of thousands of Union Jack mugs, boutiques sold Union Jack T-shirts in Union Jack carrier bags, and eventually there were even Union Jack bikinis and knickers.[23] George Melly observed that the implicit irony shocked many American visitors, for whom the 'casual acceptance of the flag as a giggle' was simply incomprehensible.[24] But the commercialisation of the Union Jack was more than cynicism or parody: many of the pop stars of the sixties were genuinely patriotic and wanted to celebrate the fact that their culture 'led the Western world'. 'Ironic it may have been,' comments Richard Weight, 'but there was nothing trivial or unpatriotic about it.'[25]

As the summer of 1966 began, national optimism seemed to be running higher than ever. According to the press, Britain was a country not of grey skies and wet weekends, but of Minis and mini-skirts, boutiques and bistros, dolly birds and pop stars. Even outside the privileged enclaves of Swinging London, wages were high, the economy seemed to be booming, and every day brought new cultural triumphs. Everyone who wanted a job could find one, and in June the number of people out of work fell to a nominal level of 253,000.[26] The lyrics of the Kinks' single 'Sunny Afternoon', which topped the charts that month, could hardly have been more appropriate:

> And I love to live so pleasantly,
> Live this life of luxury,
> Lazing on a sunny afternoon.
> In the summertime . . .
> In the summertime . . .
> In the summertime . . .

But the summer was not over yet, and for millions of ordinary people an event that would come to define the year and even the decade was upon them: the eighth football World Cup.

As long as he could remember, Harold Wilson had been a fan of Huddersfield Town. When he was a boy, they became the first English team to be crowned League champions in three consecutive seasons, under their legendary manager Herbert Chapman. Everyone who lived near Huddersfield shared the joy of the team's victories, and Wilson's father took him to almost every home game for several years. He never lost his enthusiasm for the Terriers, and he counted himself a fan for the rest of his life.[27] But by the time he became Prime Minister Huddersfield Town were no longer one of the great teams of English football. They had never really been the same after Chapman left to manage the Arsenal in 1925, whom he built into a superb new side that attracted support from across the South of England – including, by a delicious coincidence, Wilson's future rival, the young Teddy Heath.[28]

The fact that both party leaders in the mid-sixties still described themselves as football fans, even if they rarely attended matches, illustrates the extent to which sport permeated British society. After establishing the Sports Council in 1965, Wilson insisted that sport was 'essential to Britain's economic and social development' and added that it had 'not been given adequate priority in the past'.[29] In fact, sport had been seen as a central component of the welfare state, and large amounts of public money were ploughed into outdoor leisure pursuits through bodies like the Arts Council and the National Parks Commission.[30] Unfortunately, the 1950s had been pretty depressing years for British sportsmen and spectators.[31] At the 1952 Olympics Britain's sporting men and women managed to win precisely one gold medal, for equestrian team jumping. Even four years later, when the team rallied to win a total of forty-five medals, Britain still finished seventh in the medals table, a disappointing position for a supposed great power.

As many commentators pointed out, Britain was crippled by the burden of its amateur past. The true sportsman was supposed to play for pleasure, not for money, and to care more about taking part than winning. Professional athletes were generally seen as nothing more than glorified manual labourers, and professional sport was certainly not a respectable career choice for middle-class youngsters.[32] Of course, this would hardly have mattered were it not for the fact that sporting achievement was widely treated as a barometer of the nation's health and international standing. By the late fifties plenty of commentators had embraced the idea that 'the physical performances of a country's chosen representatives [were] structurally linked to the more general state of that nation, particularly its health, stability and world position'. So, for many observers, Britain's sporting mediocrity was just one aspect of a general decline, taking in everything from the dwindling of its international influence to the travails of the nation's finances.[33]

Accounts of British sporting life in the sixties understandably give enormous attention to the three major national team sports: cricket, football and rugby union. Together with horseracing, these sports commanded more press and public attention than all the others combined and were often treated as reflections of national identity and character. But the sporting landscape was much more diverse than we often imagine, taking in everything from badminton to speedway.[34] By far the most popular participatory sport, in fact, was fishing, which claimed the allegiance of some three and a half million regular anglers by 1970.[35] Still, sports like angling were generally ignored by the media because they seemed to be steeped in 'a world of cap-shifting, head-scratching, and the odd involuntary click of false teeth'; crucially, they did not really appeal to the affluent young people who mattered to advertisers.[36]

In the first half of the twentieth century there had been no doubt about the identity of England's national sport: county cricket. By the mid-sixties, however, the game seemed to be in deep decline. Satirical attacks on the upper-class elite, the collapse of the Empire, and the new emphasis on social mobility, classlessness and technological change all combined to make cricket look irredeemably old fashioned. Professional salaries had patently failed to keep pace with the expansion of working-class affluence, and manual workers now earned more than cricketers.[37] The England team was in the middle of a long losing streak, and did not even play entertaining cricket, while the County Championship was plagued by unadventurous play and far too many draws. Although crowd numbers were in a long-term slump, the conservatism of the game's authorities meant that they disliked making 'commercialised' overtures to spectators. 'Cricket is not a circus,' insisted Sir Pelham Warner, the president of the MCC, 'and it would be far better that it should be driven back to the village green . . . than yield a jot to the petulant demands of the spectator.'[38]

The game that supplanted cricket as the national sport, in England at least, was association football. (In Wales, however, the national game was rugby union. The sixties were good years for the Welsh team, which was entering a golden age of flamboyant play and glorious results.) More than any other team sport, football inspired passionate loyalties, and in the grim conditions of the industrial city it provided a source of solidarity and pride.[39] Like cricket, however, it suffered from falling attendances. In the 1948–9 season the league clubs had sold more than 41 million tickets, but by the 1964–5 season numbers had fallen to just 28 million. This was part of the general decline of collective entertainment, comparable to the decline of the holiday camp and even the pub.[40] With money in their pockets, working-class men and women preferred to devote their time to their families and their homes; there were simply more kinds of leisure and entertainment to choose from; and, as marriage itself became a more companionable enterprise, celebrations of masculine solidarity became less important. What the market researcher Mark Abrams called 'the Home-Centred Society' was at hand.[41]

Football adapted more easily than cricket to this new environment for two main reasons. First, it was better suited to the expansion of the media. Football sold more papers than any other sport because it inspired more passionate loyalties.[42] It was also extremely well suited to television, the kinetic appearance of the game and ninety-minute length of matches being much more appropriate for the casual television viewer than the more sedate three- or five-day routine of cricket. Football was even used in the fifties to sell televisions to suspicious shoppers. 'When they are talking about the big match on TV,' ran one slogan, 'will you have to remain silent?'[43]

The success of football on television explains why it was so adept at appealing to the middle classes. Among the millions who watched the major games on television were plenty of middle-class families who would have shuddered at the thought of standing on a rain-swept terrace next to their social inferiors, but were quite happy to watch from the comfort of their living rooms. The most successful sides of the 1950s and 1960s – Wolves, Everton, Tottenham and Manchester United – began to attract supporters far from their local hinterlands, while little sides in the Third and Fourth Divisions began to struggle for support.[44] Finally, as the newspapers ran more and more stories about football, and especially about international competitions, the game became an ideal vehicle for expressions of national identity in Scotland, Wales and Northern Ireland as well as in England, and it became patriotic to follow the fortunes of the national team.[45]

There was little to cheer, however, in the first half of the sixties. In 1962 England made it to the World Cup finals in Chile, the only home nation to do so, but in the quarter-finals they meekly surrendered to Brazil and the magical Garrincha.[46] As in the fifties, the nation's finest had been found wanting on the international stage. 'We could not play better than any other country, after all,' wrote the journalist Arthur Hopcraft. 'Far from knowing all there was to be known about the game we found that we had been left years behind by it. We even looked old. Our shorts were longer, thicker, flappier than anyone else's, so that our players looked like Scoutmasters struggling to keep pace with the troop.'[47]

Yet although British football was generally weighed down by a sense of disappointment and decline, the World Cup did not mean much to the ordinary fan. To the press, competitions of this kind were much less important than their domestic equivalents: in 1960 a government report observed that Britain's 'problems in international sport are not generally understood because the public are rarely made aware of developments abroad until they are taken by surprise by the results'.[48]

The BBC had begun showing England's World Cup matches back in 1954, but at that point fewer than four million households had a television. Four years later, with nearly ten million televisions in use, both the BBC and ITV had carried the home nations' matches live.[49] But the World Cup was not yet the enormous ritual of passion and patriotism that it would become, and defeat was rarely seen as a national calamity. The next tournament, scheduled for 1966, would be held in England itself to mark the centenary of the Football Association, but the public were hardly bubbling with anticipation at the thought of another damp squib on home soil. When Wilson asked Denis Howell to be the country's first Minister of Sport in October 1964, Howell had to remind him that the World Cup was happening at all.

In October 1962 the FA appointed a new manager to take control of the England team. Alf Ramsey seemed the obvious man for the job. Born in 1920 in a farm cottage in Dagenham, he was the son of a hay and straw dealer and initially worked as an errand boy. During the Second World War he was playing a friendly football match for his infantry battalion when he was spotted by Southampton and converted into a Second Division fullback. After moving to Tottenham, he held down a regular international place for thirty-one games, playing in the infamous defeats by the United States in 1950 and Hungary in 1953. Never an especially skilful player, he succeeded through hard work and constant self-improvement, qualities he would later prize in others. In 1955 he assumed the manager's job at lowly Ipswich and took them from the Third Division to the First, and then, in their first top-flight season, to the League title. He was not, however, the FA's first choice. Only when the Burnley manager Jimmy Adamson turned down the job did they turn to Ramsey, who would be the first England manager allowed to pick the team himself.[50]

Ramsey was a classic example of the ambitions and insecurities of the affluent society. He was embarrassed by his modest background and liked to play it down whenever possible. When, in his early days as England manager, he was asked by a radio interviewer where his parents lived, he hesitantly replied: 'In Dagenham, I believe', as though they might in fact be living somewhere rather more well-to-do.[51] Throughout the 1950s he worked hard to push himself into the suburban middle class, adopting what he thought were 'respectable' attitudes and mannerisms. The most obvious example was his investment in regular elocution lessons in a futile attempt to banish his Essex accent.[52] Jimmy Greaves, one of his England players, later commented that 'Alf should have asked for his money back', and compared the result with Dick van Dyke's dreadful pseudo-Cockney performance in the film *Mary Poppins* (1964).[53]

Ramsey's dedication to self-improvement was typical of the man. Although he invited his players to call him Alf and liked to join in with their games, he often came across as painfully formal, even wearing a shirt and tie at breakfast. A common joke among the players was that he went to bed 'in a well-pressed suit'.[54] Arthur Hopcraft observed that although Ramsey's formality was 'an obsessive self-defence' rooted in social insecurity, 'his cold dignity is certainly not an act'.[55] When the young Leeds player Allan Clarke went on his first trip abroad with England, Ramsey noticed him laughing with his team-mates on the aeroplane. 'Enjoying yourself, Allan?' he asked casually. 'Yes, Alf. Great. Thank you,' the player replied enthusiastically. Ramsey stared at him for a second, and then said: 'You don't fucking enjoy yourself with me. Remember that.'[56]

Still, most of Ramsey's players viewed him with deep respect. He was unwaveringly loyal to them, and his faith was reciprocated.[57] Like most working-class men of his generation, he was also fiercely patriotic. 'I have three loves in my life,' he told the press. 'My wife, my country and football.' On another occasion he remarked: 'I believe in England and Englishness, as well as English football.'[58] He was utterly dedicated to the revival of the nation's footballing fortunes. In October 1962 he told John Arlott that England might 'do well' in the World Cup, and in August 1963 he went even further, telling the press: 'England will win the World Cup in 1966.' Given that the side had not progressed past the quarter-finals in any of the last four tournaments, this was an extraordinarily reckless prediction. But Ramsey was insistent: 'We have the ability, strength, character and, perhaps above all, players with the right temperament,' he told his sceptical audience. 'Such thoughts must be put to the public, and particularly to the players, so that confidence can be built up.'[59]

On 20 March 1966 the tournament got off to an unexpectedly colourful start when the World Cup itself was stolen from an exhibition at Westminster Central Hall. In the days that followed pages of newspaper coverage were devoted to the theft, ensuring enormous publicity for the competition. After a week the trophy was still nowhere to be found. Then, on the eighth day, a Thames bargeman, David Corbett, set out from his home in suburban South London to make a telephone call. He took his black-and-white mongrel dog, Pickles, with him, but their walk came to an unexpected halt when Pickles disappeared under a garden hedge and began tearing at a package hidden at the bottom. 'The dog drew my attention to it,' Corbett said afterwards. 'It was very tightly wrapped in newspaper. I could see it was some sort of statue. I pulled the bottom ends of the paper away and I could see the discs. Then as I tore more of the paper away, I saw the names Germany, Uruguay, Brazil. And being a football fan I knew it had been stolen. I jumped up and drove to the police station.' Corbett collected the three-thousand-pound reward, but Pickles got all the glory, winning a year's supply of free dog food and a medal from the Canine Defence League. He even made it on to the silver screen, appearing alongside Laurence Harvey, Eric Portman and two bulldogs in the swinging spoof *The Spy with a Cold Nose* (1966), and on his death in 1973 he was mourned as a national hero.[60]

On 11 July England kicked off against Uruguay as the lone British representatives, Scotland, Wales and Northern Ireland having been eliminated in the qualifying rounds. After ninety minutes of turgid football, however, the English players were lagging well behind Pickles in the race for national popularity. They had failed to score at Wembley for the first time since 1938, and although their opponents had been obdurate in defence, the newspapers were united in their scorn. The team had also manifestly failed to capture the imagination of the paying public: almost twenty thousand tickets went unsold, despite the fact that this was the opening game of the tournament and included a short ceremony and an appearance by the Queen.

Five days later, against Mexico, with the pressure building, England managed to score at last. First, Bobby Charlton, a survivor of the Munich air disaster and England's midfield talisman, hammered a thirty-yard drive past the Mexican goalkeeper; then, forty minutes later, the goalkeeper pushed out a shot by the quicksilver Jimmy Greaves to the feet of Roger Hunt, his hard-working strike partner, who accepted the simplest of opportunities.

England's third game, against France on 20 June, produced another 2–0 victory. Once again, the home team played poorly, even though the French were reduced to ten men by injury after just four minutes. Hunt scored a scrappy opening goal, the match degenerated into scuffles and stoppages, and finally, after the French had come close to equalising, their goalkeeper fumbled Hunt's weak header into his own net for the decisive second. England were through to the quarter-finals, but they could hardly have progressed in a less inspiring fashion.[61]

England's first three matches at the 1966 World Cup therefore belie the patriotic myths subsequently associated with the event. Only their decisive game against the French had sold out, and there had been a total of nearly thirty thousand empty seats at their first two games. Many press commentators explicitly drew unflattering comparisons with more exciting matches elsewhere: in Liverpool, for example, where Portugal and Hungary had both thrillingly beaten the reigning champions, Brazil; or in Middlesbrough, where the locals cheered themselves hoarse after the Italians were humbled by North Korea. Others complained about the physical aggression of England's play. In all three games Ramsey had picked the toothless Manchester United ball-winner Norbert 'Nobby' Stiles in midfield, and in the game against France Stiles came very close to being sent off. Such was the outcry that the FA even suggested that Stiles be dropped for the quarter-final, but Ramsey held firm. If Stiles went, he said, so would he. They both stayed.[62]

In other areas, however, Ramsey continued to dither. The back six was settled: Gordon Banks, perhaps the world's best goalkeeper; two reliable full-backs, Ray Wilson and George Cohen; the two central defenders, the lanky Jack Charlton and the elegant captain Bobby Moore; and Stiles, sweeping in front of them. Further forward, though, little was certain. Bobby Charlton was guaranteed one of the midfield places, but Ramsey found it hard to choose between the effervescent Alan Ball and the thoughtful Martin Peters alongside him. Up front, he had started with Greaves and Hunt in all three games. The latter, a reliable but unspectacular supporting act, had scored three goals and cemented his place in the team, but what of

Greaves? The most celebrated and prolific forward in England, he had failed to score and now had a shin injury that would rule him out of the quarter-final. As for the last place, Ramsey had picked three different wingers so far, and none had really impressed. For the next game, therefore, he scrapped his wingers, packed the midfield with four players – Stiles, Charlton, Ball and Peters – and for the first time in the tournament picked the powerful Geoff Hurst to replace Greaves up front.[63]

England's quarter-final against Argentina on 23 July, the day on which the Kinks' 'Sunny Afternoon' finally fell from the top of the charts, was when popular interest in the World Cup really began to simmer. Argentina were the first team that England genuinely feared: their players were technically superb, their tactics were patient and defensive, and in recent years their team had developed a ruthless, cynical streak to compete with their Brazilian neighbours. According to the popular press, they were no better than knife-wielding assassins, conforming to every stereotype of the cunning, dirty Latin American. Much of this, of course, was inspired by sheer anxiety that they would prove too good for England.[64] One fan later wrote that when he arrived at Wembley for the game, he had 'rarely experienced an atmosphere so full of self-righteous malevolence'.[65] And even Ramsey sent out his players with the words: 'Well, gentlemen, you know the sort of game you have on your hands this afternoon.'[66]

It was almost inevitable that the game would be an ugly occasion, full of fouls, dives, appeals to the referee and jeers from the crowd. Geoff Hurst complained that 'there was an air of cold, calculated hostility' about the Argentinians, who had clearly set out to frustrate their opponents, disrupting their rhythm with calculated fouls every time they approached the Argentine penalty area.[67] Their captain, the languid Antonio Rattin, was effectively running the game, directing the play of his own side and ruthlessly chopping down any English player who came within reach. A giant of a man, he overshadowed the fussy little West German referee Rudolf Kreitlein, constantly complaining and indicating his contempt with haughty, dismissive gestures.[68]

Had Rattin stuck to playing the game, there is every chance that Argentina would have won. They were a more gifted side, their tactics had blunted England's attack, and they were manifestly playing the better football. But in the thirty-sixth minute Kreitlein cautioned another Argentine player and Rattin was over him again, gesticulating and jabbing a forefinger in his face. The referee's patience finally snapped; he raised his right arm and pointed to the touchline. Rattin had been sent off. The crowd broke into cheers of delight; the Argentine players, however, furiously surrounded the referee, and for almost ten minutes confusion reigned. Officials and policemen struggled to restore order while the England players jogged vaguely about in the sun, bewildered by the turn of events. At length, Rattin was persuaded to go, and the game resumed. As so often, however, the ten men proceeded to play better football than ever. No English player seemed to have anything like the subtlety of the South Americans; it was like the defeats of the fifties all over again.

The difference was that this time Ramsey had given his team a spine of steel. The match was meandering towards extra time when, with fifteen minutes to go, Ray Wilson broke up an Argentine attack and eased the ball down the left wing to Martin Peters. Taking a moment to glance up, the West Ham midfielder whipped the ball into the penalty area, and there, with a prodigious leap, was his team-mate Geoff Hurst, whose glancing header sent it unerringly into the right-hand corner of the net to give England the only goal of the game. [69]

If the match itself was controversial, what followed was even worse. On the pitch George Cohen took off his shirt and was about to exchange it with an Argentine opponent when a furious Ramsey grabbed his arm and dragged him away. In the tunnel one Argentine player spat at an official, another urinated on the concrete wall, and the South Americans angrily hammered on the locked doors of the England changing room. An hour later Ramsey appeared before the television cameras. 'We have still to produce our best football,' he said angrily, 'and this best is not possible until we meet the right kind of opposition, and that is a team that comes out to play football, and not to act as animals.' He could hardly have chosen more insulting words: across Latin America, they were relentlessly repeated as a classic example of English arrogance and an insult to an entire continent. At the time it seemed an inconsequential fuss, but the Latin Americans would not forget, and four years later they would have their revenge.[70]

The press treated the victory over Argentina as a triumph for simple English pluck over foreign artifice and dirty tricks. But most people watching on television in Latin America and southern Europe sided with England's opponents. Many overseas commentators objected to the fact that England played all their games at Wembley, which meant that they were able to train and rest in one place, unlike every other team in the tournament. What was more, the choice of referees certainly appeared less than impartial. There were just five Latin American officials and three from southern Europe, compared with five from northern Europe, three from Scotland, Wales and Northern Ireland and no fewer than seven from England. In Argentina and elsewhere the consensus was that the tournament had been 'fixed' to favour the hosts.[71] Of course, there was no evidence of a deliberate conspiracy; on the other hand, there is no doubt that England exploited their home advantage for all it was worth – as would other host nations in years to come.

The semi-final was a much more sedate and sporting occasion, played in the cool of the next Wednesday evening. England's opponents, Portugal, had never before reached a World Cup semi-final, but their side was based on the Benfica team that had reached the final of the European Cup four times in five years. Their centre-forward, the powerful Eusebio, was not only the reigning European Footballer of the Year but the outstanding attacking player of the World Cup thus far. In the semi-final, however, he came up against the tenacious Nobby Stiles, who was delegated to mark him out of the game. With Eusebio stifled, Bobby Charlton hammered home two fulminating drives to put the hosts within reach of the final. The second goal was so good that even some of the Portuguese players offered him handshakes of congratulation, a refreshing change from the blood and thunder of the previous weekend. Three minutes from the end his brother Jack blocked a goal-bound shot with his hand and Eusebio slotted home the penalty. But soon afterwards the final whistle went, and England were into the final.[72]

England at large had now finally succumbed to what would later be called 'World Cup fever'. One journalist wrote that the tournament had released 'a communal exuberance which I think astonished ourselves more than our visitors', with inhibitions thrown off 'so that we became a gay, almost reckless people in our own streets'. People looked 'unashamedly delighted by life', he thought: no doubt the warm and sunny weather, as well as England's sporting progress, had much to do with it.[73] And, as though the tournament had been copied from the pages of the most sensational melodrama, England would play West Germany, of all nations, to decide the world championship.

In the minutes before the World Cup Final kicked off Jack Charlton found himself thinking how odd it was that 'for six years we had waged a war against Germany, now we were preparing to do battle on the football field'.[74] Yet it is easy to exaggerate the popular hostility to Britain's old adversaries. Hatred of the enemy during the Second World War was never quite as virulent as it had been during the First: alongside other stereotypes there persisted the image of Field Marshal Erwin Rommel, gallant and chivalrous, a 'good' German whom Hitler had forced to commit suicide. To many British observers, Germans of the Rommel type were not very different from themselves: serious, hard-working, honest and so on.[75]

Indeed, popular attitudes towards the Germans seem to have been more generous in the fifties and sixties than they were later on, when West Germany's economic miracle inspired British envy and resentment. In December 1954, when the West German football team travelled to London for the first Anglo-German match since the thirties, the war was never even mentioned, either by the players or the press.[76] Four years later, when the West German president made a state visit to Britain, he was warmly greeted by the Queen, who reminded her listeners that both she and her husband were descended from the union of Victoria and Albert.[77] And in 1962 the *Daily Mirror* ran a highly favourable article about the new Germans as part of a series on Britain's neighbours. They apparently worked hard, never went on strike and were rolling in money; their homes were 'spotless, shining, and not a thing out of place'; and their schools produced models of politeness and respectability. 'Everywhere I go I can see what they can tell US,' wrote the *Mirror*'s man in Bonn, 'but I keep wondering what we can tell THEM.'[78]

In the build-up to the World Cup Final, therefore, there was little of the jingoistic baiting that would be associated with future Anglo-German encounters. Nevertheless, some commentators could not resist reminding their readers about the two nations' recent history. In the *Sun* Peter Lorenzo remarked that 'as the Fatherland are embarrassingly aware, England have never lost to Germany – at soccer either'; the *Daily Mail*, meanwhile, joked that 'if the Germans beat us at Wembley this afternoon at our national sport, we can always point out to them that we have recently beaten them twice at theirs'.[79] In response, the German television commentator Werner Schneider commented that the English were like 'tin soldiers' for whom 'winning at football is treated like a victory in battle . . . Perhaps we have learned our lesson because of the Second World War. Perhaps we think more than other people of how mad this thinking is. You would expect this from countries who have nothing else . . . But in England it is strange and sad.'[80]

Although English columnists liked to imagine that their players were the neutrals' favourites, this was nothing more than self-delusion. Of the 400 million people who watched the final worldwide, the great majority were estimated to have supported West Germany.[81] Even the French sporting paper *L'Equipe* carried a cartoon showing Bobby Charlton and a vampiric Nobby Stiles driving a Rolls-Royce while referees dressed as British policemen hold back France, Argentina and other teams. 'Let us pass, please,' read the caption.[82] This was partly a question of perceived refereeing bias, and partly, some writers suggest, a backlash against the complacent arrogance associated with London in the summer of 1966. But it also reflected the fact that England were a deeply unexciting team. They had never scored more than two goals in a game, while their football had been aggressive, disciplined and tactically cautious. Boring football makes few friends.[83]

Meanwhile, Alf Ramsey was again facing a dilemma, since Jimmy Greaves had recovered from his shin injury and was now ready to play. Many fans thought that Greaves ought to be put straight back in the team: with his pace and skill, he would surely frighten the West German defence. As Ramsey saw it, however, Greaves looked badly out of luck, so restoring him would be an enormous gamble. What was more, England had unquestionably played better with Geoff Hurst in attack, not only because Hurst worked well with his West Ham colleagues but because his unselfish style suited the team's approach. Almost every international manager interviewed by the British media agreed that Hurst, not Greaves, should play. In truth, then, Hurst was the only sensible option, and he duly started up front.[84]

Walking into Wembley Stadium on the afternoon of Saturday, 30 July 1966, most observers were struck above all by the sea of Union Jack flags and the heavy air of tension.* 'It was impossible to define the atmosphere precisely but it was palpable, and it was unique,' wrote the *Observer*'s correspondent Hugh McIlvanney. 'It was like walking into an ordinary, familiar room and knowing instinctively that something vital and unbearably dramatic was happening, perhaps a matter of life and death. The people hurrying and jostling and laughing nervously inside had a flushed supercharged look, but if they were high it was with excitement.'[85]

---

*Note that the English fans waved the national flag of the United Kingdom, not the red-and-white flag of St George. The England team was automatically equated with Britain as a whole, even though many Welsh, Scottish and Irish observers had been praying for anything but an English victory.

In the bowels of the grand old stadium the England dressing room was packed with journalists, photographers and well-wishers; even half an hour before kick-off there were still a hundred people in the room. At a quarter to three, the England eleven lined up in the tunnel for the long walk onto the pitch. Ramsey passed along the line, giving a quiet word to every one of them: Banks, the goalkeeper; Cohen, Wilson, Jack Charlton and Moore in defence; Stiles, Bobby Charlton, Peters and Ball in midfield; Hunt and Hurst up front. And then the two teams emerged from the tunnel to the cheers and screams of more than ninety thousand people, to the national anthems, and to the match itself.

Most people were expecting a dour stalemate. Both teams were disciplined and hard-working; neither was particularly flamboyant in attack; and one goal might be enough to win it. In the opening exchanges England seemed weighed down by the burden of the occasion, and after twelve minutes the usually faultless Ray Wilson misdirected a clearing header. The ball fell to Helmut Haller on the edge of the English penalty area and the German midfielder scuffed a low shot beyond Banks's dive to silence the English fans and give his side the lead.

In a sense, the goal was exactly what England had needed: the shock liberated them from their fear, and they began to press forward in search of an equaliser. Just seven minutes later Bobby Moore strolled forward from defence and was felled by a trip from Wolfgang Overath. The referee blew for a foul; Moore looked to take a quick free kick, checked momentarily, and then floated the ball into the German area, where Hurst, unmarked, was gliding noiselessly from right to left. A second later he met his West Ham team-mate's cross with perfect timing, nodding it cleanly past the motionless German goalkeeper. At half-time the teams were still level, and Ramsey calmly told his players that they were doing well, 'but you can improve. And if you do that you will win the cup.'[86]

England began the second half with a spurt of energy that eventually petered out, and for fifteen minutes a kind of languor took hold. With around half an hour left the home team, sensing that they were fitter and stronger, began to increase the tempo again, but still they did not make any clear-cut chances. Then, with just thirteen minutes to go, Alan Ball's cross was tipped behind by the German goalkeeper, Hans Tilkowski, for a corner. Ball himself whipped the ball in, a German headed it out to the edge of the area, and the waiting Hurst controlled it and made to shoot. As the ball flew into the area, a German defender took a great flailing swipe and sliced it into the air, where it span back towards the goal – directly into the path of Martin Peters, who gleefully smashed it into the back of the net. And that, surely, was that.

In the last ten minutes, as West Germany pressed and the crowd roared their encouragement, England looked likely to hold on to their lead. The clock ticked on and the final whistle came ever closer. Now there were four minutes to go. The Germans attacked, Moore cleared, and Peters found Hunt unmarked on the half-way line. He ran free down the German left, closed in on the penalty area, and laid the ball off to the waiting Bobby Charlton, poised for the kill. But in his tired state, Hunt had slightly misjudged the pass. Charlton stumbled, scuffed his shot wide, and collapsed on the grass.

Two minutes later Wolfgang Overath shot at England's goal but missed the target. There was just a minute left now. The Germans heaved the ball forward one last time. Siggi Held and Jack Charlton jumped together and fell in a heap, and the referee blew for a German free-kick, just outside England's penalty area. Charlton complained bitterly, but Gottfried Dienst, the Swiss referee, ignored him. With seconds to go, Lothar Emmerich stepped back and hit the ball with all his force past the wall and into George Cohen, who deflected it downwards. As if in slow motion, with 90,000 people watching in frenzied excitement inside Wembley and 400 million glued to their television screens, the ball span loose to Held, who knocked it into the body of Karl-Heinz Schnellinger. Again the ball bounced down – this all in a matter of a second or two – falling past the scrambling Ray Wilson and towards the German defender Wolfgang Weber – and then, at last, Weber lunged, made contact, and scooped the ball past Gordon Banks for the most dramatic equaliser imaginable. The Germans ran to embrace the goalscorer; the English players stood stunned and empty. A few seconds later, Dienst blew the whistle for full-time.

In the moments that followed it was as though an exhausted calm had descended after the tempest. England's players were distraught, furious, horrified. Peters looked as if he could barely run another yard; Stiles was prostrate with cramp; Moore stood frowning at the turf. They had been so close, and yet somehow the Germans had dashed the cup from their lips. Ramsey walked quietly across the field towards them. He had warned his players at half-time that West Germany would never give up, but they had ignored him and paid the penalty. Even now, however, he stayed loyal to his men. 'Look at the Germans,' he told the exhausted circle around him. 'Just have a look at them. They can't live with you. Not through another half an hour. Not through extra time.' As the players struggled to their feet his final words rang in their ears: 'You've won the World Cup once. Now go out and win it again.'[87]

Extra time kicked off, and England applied themselves to the task once more. Up at Lilleshall, the FA's training camp in Shropshire, the warden could not bear the tension, taking his dog for a walk rather than watch the unfolding drama on television. In a merchant ship on the Indian Ocean the Charltons' brother Gordon walked out of the radio room and took refuge among the ship's roaring engines. But on the pitch at Wembley England's fitness was telling at last: 'The West Germans were as tired as us,' Ray Wilson later remembered. 'Both sides had their socks rolled down. Cramp was taking its grip. Our shorts and shirts were soaked and stained with perspiration. Yet with an incredible surge I sensed that we in the England team were rising to the occasion more completely than the opposition.'[88]

After ten minutes of extra time came the moment that would be debated for as long as people played football. Stiles knocked a long ball down the right for Alan Ball, the ginger dynamo who had worked tirelessly all afternoon. Outpacing his German marker, Ball collected the ball and whipped in a cross towards Hurst, who waited with his back to the goal on the edge of the penalty area. The West Ham striker controlled the ball instantly with his right foot, swivelled, and in one motion, as he began to fall, hammered it towards the German goal. It flew over Tilkowski, thundered against the crossbar and bounced down, on to the goal-line and then back up into the goalmouth, from where Weber headed it over the bar to safety.

Roger Hunt, the nearest English player to the action, had already raised his arms and yelled that the ball had crossed the line. Hurst, desperately exhausted, was now appealing too, while the German players were shouting that the whole of the ball had not crossed the line. 'Yes, yes, yes!' cried the BBC commentator Kenneth Wolstenholme. Then – 'No! No! The linesman says no! The linesman says no!' And there, standing with his flag raised, was Tofik Bakhramov, the famous 'Russian linesman', although he was actually from Azerbaijan. Dienst ran towards the touchline. The players waited. Then the linesman nodded, Dienst pointed towards the centre circle, and Wolstenholme exclaimed in delight: 'It's a goal!' Hurst's teammates ran to congratulate him, the Germans ran to complain, the crowd roared, and England were in the lead again.

Of course, the goal should never have been given. After years of replays, reconstructions and debate, it is clear that the whole of the ball did not cross the goal-line. As Bobby Moore later admitted, England 'won the World Cup on the best appeal of all time'. Still, even if the goal had not really been a goal, it was not an outrageously bad decision. Neither the referee nor the linesman had the benefit of television replays: as they saw it, the ball probably crossed the line. Although the Germans were rightly aggrieved, and Moore commented that he 'wouldn't have liked a goal like that to be given against England', it did go to the much fitter and more enterprising team; even if it had not been given, it is likely that England would have prevailed regardless.[89]

As it was, the stronger side had the lead again, and this time they never looked like relinquishing it. Yet as the match reached its conclusion, with millions of English fans chewing their nails and millions of fans around the world willing the Germans to pull off another comeback, the pressure built again. With just four minutes to go, the ball found its way to the weary Emmerich in a good position, but he stumbled and the chance was lost. With two minutes to go, Haller headed a long cross towards Uwe Seeler, who was inches away from steering it towards the goal. Then, as the seconds ticked away and the Germans poured forward in desperate search of the equaliser, Bobby Moore intercepted a cross near his own penalty spot, played a neat one–two to move out towards the England left, and saw Hurst, the hero of the hour, lurking unmarked near the half-way line. As he did so, Gottfried Dienst checked his watch and put the whistle to his lips. The English fans, anticipating the final whistle, let out a great roar of unutterable relief and joy. 'The referee looks at his watch,' Wolstenholme told the television audience, his voice only slightly betraying his excitement. 'Any second now.' As he was speaking, Moore, elegant as ever, lobbed a forty-yard pass into Hurst's path, giving him a free run towards the German goal – and at that moment three England fans, unable to contain their excitement, burst on to the field. 'And here comes Hurst. He's got—' began Wolstenholme, and then: 'Some people are on the pitch! They think it's all over!' Dienst waved for the players to continue, and Hurst, the man who had only come into the team two games before, the man whom many thought should be dropped for the final, the man who was about to enter sporting legend, ran wearily on, checked on the edge of the area, and lashed the ball as hard as he could. 'I whacked it,' he said later. 'I knew I would never hit a better shot so long as I lived. The feel, the sound of leather on leather were exactly right.' The ball flew into the left-hand corner of the net. 'It is now!' cried Wolstenholme. 'It's four!' And in that instant, Dienst blew for full-time. 'It's all over!' Wolstenholme exclaimed. 'England are the world champions!'[90]

'The scene that followed was unforgettable,' wrote Hugh McIlvanney. 'Stiles and Cohen collapsed in a tearful embrace on the ground, young Ball turned wild cartwheels and Bobby Charlton dropped to his knees, felled by emotion . . . Soon the players, who had forgotten the crippling weariness of a few minutes before, were hugging and laughing and crying with manager Alf Ramsey and the reserves.'[91] In fact, Ramsey himself remained on the bench for a few moments after the final whistle, as if stunned by the scale of his achievement. 'It was because I did not want to forget that I stayed as I did,' he said later. 'My pleasure was to see what was happening. I was looking at the players. Amazed at their reaction, getting so much enjoyment just out of watching them.'

As Bobby Moore walked towards the Royal Box to collect the trophy, Ramsey stepped forward and embraced him; then the captain climbed the long steps towards the balcony, where he wiped his dirty hands on the velvet front so as not to soil the Queen's lily-white gloves. After Moore had received the Jules Rimet trophy and raised it to the roar of the Wembley crowd, Ramsey was persuaded to pose with the cup he had promised to win three years before. At last, the England manager permitted himself what 'he clearly regarded as an excessively flamboyant gesture': he kissed the World Cup.[92]

It is often tempting to imagine that everyone in Britain celebrated England's World Cup victory as a national triumph to set alongside Trafalgar and Waterloo; but this would be wrong. Tens of millions of people had no interest in football and did not watch the game. What was more, even some who did like football wanted England to lose. 'Scottish reporters sat in a smouldering sulk in corners in the Press Centre in Kensington and insisted that they did not know what all the carry-on was about,' recorded Hugh McIlvanney.[93] One of Bobby Charlton's team-mates for Manchester United, the fiery Scottish striker Denis Law, refused to watch the match and spent the afternoon playing golf, but he was so anxious that he could barely play a single decent shot. As he walked off the eighteenth green he heard a great roar from the clubhouse and knew what it meant: 'England had won the World Cup. It was the blackest day of my life.'[94]

All the same, for many people, England's victory in the World Cup was the perfect ending to a hot, contented summer, stamped with the cultural self-confidence of Swinging London. 'When 93,000 people are in the grip of that peculiar emotion somewhere between laughter and tears,' commented the *Sunday Telegraph* the morning after the final, 'there can be no mistaking the message. England had won and the crowd loved them.'[95] And the laughter and tears were not confined to the crumbling terraces of Wembley. More than thirty-two million people had watched the match on television, outstripping even the audience for the Coronation thirteen years earlier.[96] In London in particular public joy was unconfined, inspiring the wildest celebrations since the end of the Second World War. Traffic ground to a standstill as cheering crowds blocked the streets and danced in the fountains of Trafalgar Square well into the small hours. 'It's like VE Night, election night and New Year's Eve rolled into one,' a spokesman for the AA told the press at midnight.[97]

Outside the Royal Gardens Hotel in Kensington, where the England team were due to arrive for the official banquet, more than six thousand people waving Union Jacks were held back by a cordon of policemen. Wilson, Callaghan and Brown, who had all watched the match at Wembley, arrived first to 'mixed cheers and good-natured boos'. Brown, true to his roots, described the game as a 'blinder' and remarked that it was 'a good job Ramsey picked three West Ham men'. Wilson, who had wanted to appear on television at half-time to offer his expert opinion, told reporters that it had been 'a marvellous game' and that he was 'shattered when it went into extra time'. Characteristically, he could not resist adding: 'I said before the game that it would be 2–1 in England's favour and I was only a minute out.'[98]

The applause that greeted their appearance was as nothing, however, to the clapping and chanting that greeted the England players and, of course, Pickles the dog, who had also been invited. Only one man was missing: Jimmy Greaves, once the team's star player and now almost their invisible man, who could not hide his distress at having been overlooked for the biggest game in England's sporting history. After the final whistle he simply packed his bags and walked away alone into the night, nursing a sense of sorrow that was to last for years.[99]

In the next morning's papers Greaves was almost entirely forgotten. Hurst was the man of the hour, but the real hero was the man who had dared to pick him. Alf Ramsey had endured months of criticism for his team's supposedly dour style of play. Now he was vindicated. Hugh

McIlvanney wrote that while some of the criticisms still seemed valid, 'they are now utterly unimportant. The achievement is tremendous and the only thing to do is applaud it.'[100] 'England's glory', agreed the *Telegraph*, 'was the result of the most patient, logical, painstaking, almost scientific assault on the trophy there has perhaps ever been – and primarily the work and imagination of one man.' It was 'the final, rewarding vindication for one who has unwaveringly pursued his own, often lonely convictions'.[101]

As the endless references to VE Night, the Coronation and even the relief of Mafeking made clear, England's triumph in the World Cup was invested by the press with exaggerated historical significance. By seeing off the French and the Argentinians, the Portuguese and the Germans, England had supposedly reversed years of decline to plant her foot once again on top of the world. 'Everyone now looks again to England to lead the world,' the FA secretary said proudly.[102] According to the *Sunday Express*:

> A blaze of Union Jacks waved, as people unashamedly gripped by emotion and patriotism danced, wept and hugged each other . . . What they will tell their grandchildren in the years to come is that it was English nerve and English heart and English stamina which finally overcame the tenacious resistance of [West Germany] . . . No one who saw this historic World Cup Final can deny England their 'finest hour'.[103]

Yet as many commentators noted, what made victory all the sweeter was that it came after two months of terrible economic and political news, culminating in Wilson's drastic austerity package and the six-month wage freeze. 'They have given all our hearts a lift,' remarked one columnist in the *Observer*. 'Pay may be frozen, but elation is boundless.'[104] The FA newsletter thought that Ramsey's men had given the whole nation a lead:

> [The victory] is indeed one of the few bright spots in the sombre economic situation which faces the country this Summer. We feel sure that many of our export industries will derive . . . a welcome boost from this success. The players who have made it possible worked hard and made many sacrifices. They have set an example of devotion and loyalty to the country which many others would do well to follow.[105]

Even Wilson's own ministers expressed similar sentiments. Richard Crossman rather fancifully hoped that England's triumph might mark a turning point in the government's fortunes. 'I must record a big change in Harold's personal position,' he noted after watching the game on television. It had been 'a tremendous help for him that we won the World Cup on Saturday':

> That may well mean that his luck, which deserted him after he had dealt with the seamen's strike, has really turned now. When I told Anne over lunch today that the World Cup could be a decisive factor in strengthening sterling she couldn't believe it. But I am sure it is. Our men showed real guts and the bankers, I suspect, will be influenced by this, and the position of the Government correspondingly strengthened.[106]

But England's victory in the World Cup Final felt less like the dawn of a new era and more like the last day of a long, lazy summer about to be swept away by the winds of autumn. The same newspapers that reported Hurst's glorious hat-trick also discussed the impact of Wilson's pay freeze and Brown's non-resignation. 'Britain on course for old-fashioned slump?' read one headline in the *Observer*, while an editorial warned that the country was suffering from 'a dangerous spasm of anxiety'.[107]

For Twiggy and Geoff Hurst, it was true, the events of 1966 had changed their lives for ever. The summer had been glorious, and the World Cup a magnificent exhibition of sporting prowess. But when the fans who had celebrated victory on Saturday evening awoke on Monday morning, the economic outlook was no brighter. 'Nothing had changed,' wrote Bernard Levin; 'nothing was better for England just because the World Cup had been won'.[108] And, contrary to Crossman's prediction, things were not about to get better; instead, they were soon to get much, much worse.

16

IS BRITAIN CIVILISED?

If it's the last thing I do, I'm going to destroy every fucking grammar school in England.

Anthony Crosland, 1965

Let us be on the side of those who want people to be free to live their own lives, to make their own mistakes, and to decide, in an adult way and provided they do not infringe the rights of others, the code by which they wish to live.

Roy Jenkins, *The Labour Case* (1959)

In 1967 Anthony Wedgwood Benn gave an exclusive interview in his office 'on the 413th floor of the gleaming new Technology Tower'. He had been promoted to the head of MinTech at the end of June 1966, and evidently still burned with enthusiasm for the white heat of the scientific revolution. Before the interview he asked for a 'minute's silence for prayer and meditation', and, to his guest's surprise, 'knelt on a small inflatable rubber model of a Hovercraft' before an illuminated mock-up of the Concorde prototype. After an uneasy minute had passed, Benn explained:

> Technology is to me a spiritual affair. It liberates the soul from the enslavement of the ordinary human world . . . I've been attacked by normally quite sensible people for my scheme to abolish all street names and addresses and replace them with a simple code of 54–digit numbers. But what they don't realise is that this simple idea would save the Post Office £57,000 million a year – because no one would send letters any more.

Adding that in future he preferred to be known as '01–346–2167', Benn explained that since he had grown up in a city, 'to me technology has always been a way of life. Just as a country boy might be fascinated by the birds and bees, I am obsessed by the mating habits of the Triumph Herald. When I was young I used to sit for hours, just watching the traffic lights change from red to green to amber and then back to red . . . green . . . amber . . . no left turn . . . red . . . green.' 'As he spoke,' wrote the interviewer, there was a sound 'of weird electric humming . . . the room darkened and coloured lights began to revolve around us', before 'white-coated technicians' emerged to carry away the minister. The interview was over.[1]

'Benn's HoverBritain', published in *Private Eye*, read more like an episode of *Doctor Who* or *The Avengers* than the transcript of a genuine political interview. But like all successful parodies, it had more than a ring of truth. While other members of Wilson's Cabinet, exhausted after three years of economic misery, were content to muddle wearily on, Benn, or 01–346–2167, retained his enthusiastic commitment to science and modernisation. MinTech was the ideal post for somebody who was still thrilled about the possibilities of technology, and Benn was delighted by his promotion. 'The announcement will be made on Sunday,' he noted on the night he was offered the job, 'and I am in the Cabinet with a chance to create a new department that can really change the face of Britain and its prospects for survival.'[2]

As the sceptical Bernard Levin put it, Benn flung himself into MinTech with all the enthusiasm 'of a newly enrolled Boy Scout demonstrating knot-tying to his indulgent parents'.[3] In a speech to the Institution of Mechanical Engineers in November 1966, the new minister praised his slightly bewildered audience for having launched what he called 'the British Revolution of 1966'. He explained that the technological changes of the last few years were, 'by any definition, revolutionary':

> Technology, through the agency of the motor car, and the roads and bridges over which it travels, is one of the major forces undermining the whole basis of local government and forcing us to think about better structures to replace it. The trade unions too are being changed as old crafts and skills are being replaced by new machines and techniques which call for a new response, new organisation and new ideas.[4]

But Benn's ebullience did not always go down well with his colleagues. On one occasion Richard Crossman called him 'an intellectually negligible whizz-kid'; on another he complained about 'the lack of success of the interventionist policies of Peter Shore and Tony Wedgwood Benn, young men who with carefree arrogance think they can enter the business world and help it to be more efficient'.[5]

The goals of MinTech under Benn were not much different from those under Frank Cousins: the promotion and dissemination of research and development, and support for hi-tech industries like computers, communications and electronics.[6] However, the department itself was changing, and under Benn it reached a peak of publicity and power. MinTech was the classic example of one of the 'super-ministries' of the late sixties, gigantic bureaucratic leviathans that employed tens of thousands and were supposed to bring a new centralised efficiency to British government. In 1967 it swallowed up the Ministry of Aviation, and two years later it absorbed the Ministry of Fuel and Power and what remained of the DEA, taking over responsibility for coal, electricity, oil and gas as well as the textile and chemical industries, regional policy and investment grants. By this point Benn commanded 'the biggest state-directed complex of scientific and industrial power in Europe'. His staff had swelled from 8000 to 39,000; he disbursed £400 million a year on aircraft, electronics and defence technology; and he administered 17 different government research establishments employing 22,000 scientists and engineers.[7]

Benn's vigour and enthusiasm meant that he was very well suited to his new position. However, the achievements of MinTech were less than impressive. One of its chief responsibilities was to encourage industrial mergers and acquisitions through the Industrial Reorganisation Corporation, on the premise that enormous, centralised companies had a better chance of competing in overseas markets. MinTech therefore encouraged not only the consolidation of the GEC empire through takeovers of AEI and English Electric, but the creation of British Leyland in 1968, which was formed by the merger of Leyland Motors with the British Motor Corporation.[8] Benn was very proud of his role in the birth of British Leyland; the government had offered a loan of £25 million to encourage the merger in the belief that it would represent a challenge to Renault and Volkswagen, and Benn described it at the time as 'a fantastic achievement'.[9]

Unfortunately, the hideous blunders and misfortunes of British Leyland over the next few years did not mark it out as a stunning success, and in many ways it exemplified MinTech's overall impact. The department's responsibilities were never really thought through, and it was never given the institutional means to achieve its goals; one writer even comments that by comparison the creation of the DEA was a 'model of clear-sighted planning', which is harsh indeed. Many of its activities consisted of 'encouragement' or 'oversight', which basically amounted to reading reports, making telephone calls and organising ministerial visits.[10] Even those historians who have tried to make a case for MinTech have been forced to admit that employers were 'surprisingly reluctant' to follow its advice. Many of its wheezes, in short, did not come off, and it did little to encourage the transformation of British technology and industry. Compared with the promises of 'dynamic action' and 'white heat' in 1964, its record was disappointing, to say the least.[11]

The underachievement of MinTech, like the collapse of the National Plan and the debacle of the DEA, is often taken as a symbol of the inevitable collapse of Labour's modernising ambitions during the course of the 1960s. It is certainly true that, where the economy and industry were concerned, Wilson's government had little success in realising the idealistic hopes of their first campaign. But this is not to say that Labour's project for the modernisation of Britain failed entirely. In other areas, notably education and the law, changes introduced at Westminster during the mid-sixties had profound effects, for better or for worse, on the lives of ordinary people across the country. Indeed, the government's legacy in these areas proved much more enduring, and much more controversial, than the abortive gimmicks of MinTech and the DEA.

The educational and legal reforms of the mid-sixties, often bundled together in discussions of the 'permissive society', are typically attributed to the two great friends and rising stars of the Gaitskellite right, Anthony Crosland and Roy Jenkins.

Crosland was two years the elder and perhaps the more likely to succeed, given his pedigree as the author of *The Future of Socialism*. He was brought up in North London in the puritanical religious environment of the Exclusive Brethren, an extremely austere branch of the Nonconformist Plymouth Brethren. Indeed, his background helps to explain why Crosland was such a curious mixture of egalitarian earnestness and rebellious misbehaviour. At Oxford he was famed for his socialist convictions and his exuberant socialising; during the war he fought in Italy and France; afterwards he returned to Oxford as a charismatic young don and then entered Parliament. The next few years testified to Crosland's turbulent personality: too much drink, too many affairs, divorce, the loss of his seat, the stunning success of *The Future of Socialism*, and finally a return to Parliament and a more settled life with his second wife, an American journalist. Devastated by Gaitskell's death in 1963, he found it difficult to adjust to life with Harold Wilson as leader. Nevertheless, Wilson could not overlook his talent, and promoted him to the Cabinet as Education Secretary in January 1965.[12]

Wilson's government is often remembered as one overburdened with academic distinctions and rampant egos, and Crosland was the classic example. His friend Alan Watkins summed him up as 'languid, insolent, socially fearless and often offensive', which was a combination that mesmerised some and repelled others.[13] Crosland was regarded as a risky dinner-party guest, since he would either be the star of the show or ruin it for everybody by dismissing the conversation as boring, refusing all attempts at small talk and openly insulting friends and strangers alike.[14] Rudeness to women was his forte, as the following story about a party in Kensington demonstrates:

> He wore shirt, trousers and a pair of carpet slippers. He was bored by the company and, though not particularly drunk, lay at full length on the floor, just outside the room which was serving as the ladies' cloakroom. Any lady wishing to retrieve her coat had to circumnavigate or stride across his recumbent form. A tall, plain and very shy girl did this with some difficulty, and reactivated the Minister in the process. The supine Crosland looked up, focused on her and announced: 'Hello, ugly face!' Later, in tears, the girl asked 'Who is that horrible man?' and was told 'That is Her Majesty's Secretary of State for Education.'[15]

Crosland's chief idiosyncrasy, however, was what his wife called his 'passionate love affair' with *Match of the Day*, which had started in August 1964. 'Any living soul he was likely to run into on a Saturday', she wrote, 'was alerted that on no account must the outcome of the match be revealed.' Crosland even refused to enter his own living room until some other member of the family had turned on the television and made sure the players were on the field. When he was forced to attend a social engagement on a Saturday night, he would brief his children to come in at the appointed time and say, 'The Prime Minister wants to talk to you', so that he could excuse himself and return an hour later. During the government's greatest crisis in November 1967, he took the telephone off the hook while the programme was on, so that idle chatter about the survival of the economy would not interrupt the game.[16]

Crosland's attitude to his new department was unconventional to say the least. Although this was the golden age of university expansion and the creation of the polytechnics, he openly admitted: 'I'm not frightfully interested in the universities.'[17] He was even less interested in the most innovative educational development of the decade, the creation of the 'University of the Air', or Open University, as it was eventually called. This is often seen as Harold Wilson's personal creation; indeed, Wilson later said that it was the achievement for which he would most like to be remembered.[18] However, Wilson did not dream it up himself: the idea was a typical modernising initiative of the early sixties, tossed around progressive circles as a way of reversing Britain's economic decline. In December 1961, for example, *The Economist* had called for 'Televarsities', explaining that 'a British Television University . . . might just conceivably do more than anything else to transform Britain's position in the world'.[19] Wilson thought that this was a terrific idea, both modernising and egalitarian; his biographer thinks that it became 'his pet scheme, almost a hobby'. He constantly reminded Callaghan not to cut its budget and even ended up battling his own Education Secretary, who thought that it was a complete waste of time.[20] Crosland was not alone: when the crucial White Paper was published in the spring of 1966, the *Times Educational Supplement* called it a 'pipe dream . . . just the sort of cosy scheme that shows the Socialists at their most endearing but impractical worst'.[21] Wilson pressed on regardless. In 1969 the government decided that the new university would be based in Britain's last and most ambitious New Town, and two years later it admitted its first undergraduates.[22]

Although, like Milton Keynes itself, the Open University was easily mocked, its success was indisputable. Since lectures were broadcast on television, usually late at night or early in the morning, its students were very different from the middle-class youngsters who attended other universities: there were more women, far more mature students, and more students from poor backgrounds. By the 1980s it was awarding more degrees than Oxford and Cambridge combined, and by the end of the century it was admitting more than 100,000 students a year and had one of the highest research ratings in the country. It was not merely Wilson's proudest achievement; it was one of the most popular and successful legacies of the sixties.[23]

One of the more controversial legacies of the decade, however, was the government's promotion of comprehensive education, which replaced Rab Butler's system of grammar schools, secondary moderns and selection through the eleven-plus. Crosland and Wilson had not dreamed up the comprehensive system in an afternoon: it was the result of years of discussion in educational and political circles. The eleven-plus was already in deep dispute when they came to power. As early as 1952 research found that with only limited private coaching, a child's results could be radically improved, and over the next decade a string of studies suggested that the examination was seriously flawed.[24]

For many critics, the flaws of the eleven-plus were indicative of the failings of the entire system. In 1960, about two out of three state-educated twelve-year-olds went to a secondary modern, with the rest at grammar schools or, more rarely, technical colleges. Most of the secondary-modern pupils were encouraged to leave at fourteen or fifteen, since they were considered to have no future in higher education, and almost none went on to university. By comparison, well over half of the grammar-school pupils were still in school at seventeen, and most of these went on to university.[25] Children in rural or poor inner-city areas were particularly ill served; for many, it was almost inevitable that they would fail to reach a grammar school.[26] In his memoirs Butler wrote that the conditions in grammar and secondary-modern schools should have been 'broadly equivalent'. Instead, as he recognised, 'a stigma of inferiority' had become attached to the secondary moderns, 'which lacked the facilities and academic prestige of the grammar schools'.[27] The average grammar school had three times the resources of the average secondary modern, and usually had the pick of the best teachers.[28] 'To have been consigned to the limbo of the secondary modern is to have failed disastrously,' wrote the journalist Peter Laurie, 'and very early in life.'[29]

The first true comprehensive, in the Lake District town of Windermere, predated Crosland's arrival at the Department of Education by twenty years. However, the post-war Labour government had been largely indifferent to the comprehensive ideal; many Labour local authorities took great pride in their grammar schools, and Labour politicians were often grammar-school products who spoke warmly of the educational opportunities they gave to bright working-class children.[30] By the time that Crosland took over, however, the move towards comprehensives was well under way. During the fifties pressure had been growing from a number of sources: left-wing theorists who argued that comprehensives would be a force for social egalitarianism; educationalists who criticised the flaws of the existing system; and, most importantly, middle-class parents who were frightened that the eleven-plus would condemn their children to a second-rate school. Many local education authorities began to develop their own comprehensive schemes, but these were generally rejected until 1962, when Macmillan appointed a new Education Secretary.[31]

This individual, often overshadowed by Crosland but no less important in his way, was Sir Edward Boyle, a liberal Conservative who made some of his Labour counterparts look positively reactionary.[32] When Boyle took up his new job, he immediately realised how popular the comprehensive ideal was. Of the 146 local education authorities, 90 had already adopted a comprehensive system or drawn up plans to do so. Contrary to popular myth, this was not a partisan issue. For example, the Leicestershire authority, controlled by the Tories, was already working on a comprehensive system, while the Leicester city authority, run by Labour, was fiercely clinging on to its grammar schools. Boyle approved the local authorities' comprehensive schemes, but he had no plans to impose a model system from the centre. By 1964, when he left office, one in ten pupils was educated in a comprehensive, more than ten times the proportion in 1951, but still a small minority.[33]

Crosland had been a supporter of the comprehensive system since the fifties. In *The Future of Socialism* he had argued that a Labour government should 'explicitly state a preference for the comprehensive principle, and should actively encourage local authorities . . . to be more audacious in experimenting with comprehensive schools'.[34] From the very beginning of his stint at the Department of Education, he consistently fought for the comprehensive system, not only on the grounds of egalitarianism and educational merit but on the persuasive basis that this was what parents wanted.[35] 'The pressure on the part of parents to get rid of the eleven-plus is very, very strong,' he told ITN in 1965. 'I think this is a tidal wave and that there has been a tremendous shift of sentiment.'[36]

That July, Crosland issued Circular 10/65, which 'requested' local authorities to submit plans for a transition to a comprehensive system in which pupils from different backgrounds would mix, 'gaining stimulus from the contacts and learning tolerance and understanding in the process'.[37] Despite plenty of complaints from the supporters of the grammar schools, Crosland was actually pushing at an open door. Most education authorities, after all, had already drawn up plans on similar lines, and by 1970 only eight were refusing to oblige. In 1966 the government announced that money for new buildings would be conditional on a local authority drawing up comprehensive plans, although there was plenty of leeway regarding the details of the chosen system.[38] By 1970 there were 1145 comprehensive schools, and the proportion of children in them had risen from one in ten to one in three.[39] Very few authorities, however, made much effort to create a genuine social mix. Sheffield experimented with the compulsory 'busing' of pupils across the city to schools outside their residential area, but this was badly received by many parents and did not catch on.[40]

In 1963 Wilson had promised that the grammar schools would be abolished 'over my dead body', and the standard defence for his change of heart was that comprehensives would mean 'a grammar-school education for all'. The paradox was that although opinion polls consistently showed a majority against the eleven-plus, the same polls also showed a majority for the retention of grammar schools. Although nobody had a good word for the secondary moderns, some local authorities as well as many parents were justifiably proud of their grammar schools and were horrified at the prospect of losing them in return for vague promises of a better and more just system. On the left, however, the comprehensive reforms were widely welcomed as a step towards greater equality.[41]

Wilson himself had sent his children to private schools, as did most of his ministers. C. P. Snow explained that 'if you are living in a prosperous home it is a mistake to educate your child differently from most of the people he knows socially'.[42] Wedgwood Benn was an exception: in 1964 he took his children out of their private schools and sent them to Holland Park Comprehensive, one of the best state schools in the country. Crosland's step-children made a similar journey, moving from St Paul's Girls to Holland Park a couple of years later.[43]

The destruction of the grammar schools was a project close to Crosland's heart. He had been educated himself at Highgate, a minor public school.[44] If he had attended a grammar school, like Wilson or Heath, or his friends and rivals Jenkins and Healey, then he might have been less keen to abolish an institution that had manifestly succeeded in propelling bright pupils from modest backgrounds to the highest places in the land. Unfortunately, as Wilson and Heath were well aware, there was nothing quite like the condescension of the public schoolboy for his grammar-school equivalent. After one meeting with the teachers' associations, Crosland bitterly told his wife: 'If it's the last thing I do, I'm going to destroy every fucking grammar school in England. And Wales. And Northern Ireland.' 'Why not Scotland?' she asked. 'Because their schools come under the Secretary of State for Scotland,' he said, laughing 'at his inability to destroy their grammar schools'.[45] As Ben Pimlott puts it, these are words that deserve 'to be chiselled in stone over the entrance to British education's hall of infamy'.[46]

The abolition of the eleven-plus and introduction of comprehensive schools remains one of the most controversial social legacies of the 1960s. At the time, however, the comprehensive reforms were not as contentious as is often imagined.* During the Wilson years spending on education rose steadily, and despite the destruction of the grammar schools, many of which became private institutions, Labour's education policy consistently drew strong support in the opinion polls.[47] Ironically, though, while comprehensive education is invariably associated with the Wilson government, the rate of comprehensive expansion reached its peak under the Conservative administration that followed. The politician who approved more schemes for comprehensive education and closed more grammar schools than any other was not Tony Crosland or even his Labour successor Ted Short. It was Margaret Thatcher.[48]

Throughout his time in Downing Street, Wilson was careful to balance one potential rival against another. The most obvious example was the 'creative tension' between Brown and Callaghan, but one rung further down the ladder, he had arranged an equally subtle balance between Crosland and his great friend Roy Jenkins. Both were charming, intelligent and extremely ambitious, and if they had ever united they would have made a powerful combination. But they never did; instead, they became fierce and suspicious competitors, each striving to inch further up the greasy pole than his rival.[49]

Like Crosland, Jenkins had been devastated by the death of Hugh Gaitskell, and even considered leaving politics for good. Showing all the tactical skill for which he was renowned, Wilson successfully persuaded him that he could expect a glittering future if he remained in the Commons.[50] In 1964 Wilson kept his promise and made him Minister of Aviation, and in January 1965 he offered him Education. Jenkins turned it down, giving the excuse that his children were at private schools, though the real reason was that he was not very interested in education. Nonetheless, when he heard that Crosland had accepted the job, he felt 'an inevitable stab of jealousy that I had surrendered my brief lead over this great friend but formidable rival'.[51] But Crosland's lead did not last for long. In December 1965 Wilson finally got rid of his first Home Secretary,

---

*However, see the discussion of the Black Papers in Chapter 27.

Sir Frank Soskice, who was widely seen as an accident-prone incompetent. Casting round for his successor, Wilson settled on his young Aviation Minister.[52]

Roy Jenkins's background made him hard to place in the conventional class hierarchy of post-war British society. His father had been a South Wales coalminer, but he had also been a Labour MP, a member of the party's National Executive and Clement Attlee's parliamentary private secretary. Although Jenkins had grown up in the South Wales coalfields, he was nevertheless used to the company of trade union leaders, Labour activists and senior party leaders.[53] The young Jenkins was therefore a curious figure, both proletarian and privileged. He followed the same path into politics as many of his rivals: grammar school, Oxford and a good war, followed in his case by a diversion into the City and a second career, almost a hobby, as a biographer. Despite being the son of a Welsh miner, he always carried himself with patrician hauteur. When one MP suggested to Aneurin Bevan, South Wales's most famous socialist, that Jenkins was lazy, Bevan replied: 'No boy from the valleys who has cultivated that accent could possibly be lazy!'[54]

Jenkins had begun moving into all the right circles at Balliol, where he had become friends with the likes of Heath, Healey and Crosland, and over the next few decades he acquired a reputation as the ultimate 'champagne socialist'. In this respect he took after his mother, who had been one of Pontypool society's 'gracious ladies'.[55] He was famous for his love of tennis and croquet, hardly working-class hobbies, and his friends included the likes of Mark Bonham Carter and Sir Ian Gilmour, future grandees of the Liberal and Conservative parties respectively, as well as Jacqueline Kennedy and her sister Princess Lee Radziwill, with whom he conducted a discreet affair.[56] One friend wrote of 'Jenkins the author, Jenkins the claret-lover, Jenkins the gourmet, Jenkins the clubman, Jenkins the socialite, Jenkins the cultivated liberal intellectual, Jenkins the holder of the Order of Merit and Jenkins the chancellor of Oxford University', noting that 'Jenkins the Member of Parliament', a canny and skilful politician, tended to be overlooked. As Harold Wilson put it, his new Home Secretary was widely seen as 'a socialite, not a socialist'.[57]

Jenkins arrived at the Home Office with a very clear agenda. In 1959 he had written a short book for Penguin entitled *The Labour Case*. One of the chapters, 'Is Britain Civilized?', identified three objectives for any Labour Home Secretary:

First, there is the need for the State to do less to restrict personal freedom. Secondly, there is the need for the State to do more to encourage the arts, to create towns which are worth living in, and to preserve a countryside which is worth looking at. Thirdly, there is the need, independently of the State, to create a climate of opinion which is favourable to gaiety, tolerance and beauty, and unfavourable to puritanical restriction, to petty-minded disapproval, to hypocrisy, and to a dreary, ugly pattern of life.[58]

This was all very reminiscent of his friend Crosland's talk in *The Future of Socialism* of 'personal freedom, happiness and cultural endeavour', but Jenkins was much more specific.[59] He described hanging as 'barbaric' and the laws prohibiting male homosexuality as 'brutal and unfair', and remarked they were merely illustrative of 'the gross restrictions of individual liberty which are in urgent need of removal'. Others included the censorship of the theatre by the Lord Chamberlain, the 'ridiculous' laws on gambling, licensing and Sunday observance, the divorce laws, the 'harsh and archaic' abortion laws, the treatment of suicide as a criminal offence, and the restrictions on immigration. He concluded:

Let us be on the side of those who want people to be free to live their own lives, to make their own mistakes, and to decide, in an adult way and provided they do not infringe the rights of others, the code by which they wish to live; and on the side too of experiment and brightness, of better buildings and better food, of better music (jazz as well as Bach) and better books, of fuller lives and greater freedom. In the long run these things will be more important than even the most perfect of economic policies.[60]

Jenkins admitted that if Labour were to gain office, 'a great deal would depend on the reforming zeal and liberal spirit of the man who became Home Secretary'. But with the right man in the post, the government would be well on the way to building what he called 'the civilized society'.[61] When, at the end of 1965, he got the chance to put his own principles into practice, he did not falter. The reforms that he had proposed in *The Labour Case* came to fruition, and by the end of the sixties capital punishment had been abolished, abortion, homosexuality and suicide were no longer criminal offences, the divorce laws had been eased, and the Lord Chamberlain no longer censored theatrical performances.

Many historians believe that these were the Labour government's most successful and enduring achievements, and they make up the emblematic 'permissive' legislation of the sixties, later to be denounced by conservatives of both parties. The commentator Peter Hitchens even argues that Jenkins revolutionised British social behaviour, 'from where and when we drank, to how long we stayed married, who we went to bed with and what sort of punishments we faced if we broke the law . . . [Jenkins] devised a programme which had more effect on the way that life is lived in this country than the thoughts of any other post-war politician, including Margaret Thatcher.'[62]

Jenkins was certainly very keen to preach the values of the civilised society, and he made sure that the reforms had the discreet backing of the Home Office. But there is no need to go over the top; after all, similar measures were being carried out in most other Western democracies during the same period, with equally controversial results. And although Jenkins and Labour later took the credit, or the blame, the story is rather more complicated. Each reform was introduced not as a government initiative but as a private member's bill; in each case the Commons voted according to private conscience rather than party policy; and in each case the bill faced plenty of opposition on both sides of the House. The government was careful not to become too closely associated with the liberal reforms; after all, Labour had been elected in 1964 and 1966 on platforms of technological modernisation, and their manifestos had made no mention of moral issues like hanging, homosexuality or abortion. As one historian puts it, 'the moral reforms were marginal to the central direction of the government, and were often seen as irrelevant by those who directed its strategy'.[63]

There is even a good case that the Labour leadership positively distrusted the so-called permissive agenda. In 1961 both Gaitskell and Wilson had rejected the idea of supporting the Wolfenden Committee's recommendations on homosexual law reform, Wilson even arguing that it 'would cost us six million votes'.[64] Wilson, Callaghan and Brown all subscribed to a fairly traditional moral code; all three were religious in a non-demonstrative way, and both Callaghan and Brown were on record as expressing their intense dislike of homosexuality. Wilson was more circumspect, but nonetheless Crossman recorded that as 'a perfectly sincere Sunday Methodist . . . he's against the legal reforms to deal with homosexuality or abortion'.[65]

This was not unusual in a Labour Party still inspired by Nonconformist earnestness. Most 'traditional', working-class Labour MPs, reflecting the values of their constituents, were extremely suspicious of social reform.

Surveys suggested that party activists in the Midlands, the North and Scotland were staunchly opposed to permissive legislation, while a proposal for a homosexual club in Burnley was thwarted by pressure from local Labour members. As one veteran activist put it, there could be no 'buggers' club' in Burnley.[66] When the young MP David Owen reported his views on social questions to his Plymouth constituency management committee, they provoked 'a trenchant exchange'. 'An older engine driver and stalwart in ASLEF got up after hearing my parliamentary report', Owen recalled, 'and said, "David, I accept that you're all in favour of abortion and that you support family allowances for unmarried mothers but I do draw the line at buggery." He was rather upset when the entire committee broke into uncontrollable laughter.'

However, such differences of opinion rarely hurt those MPs courageous enough to exercise their own conscience. 'They were decent, tolerant people in my constituency Labour Party,' Owen wrote, 'and they never tried to inhibit me from exercising my judgement on such questions, even if on occasion they felt the backlash in Plymouth pubs or even the Labour club.'[67]

The abolition of the death penalty, perhaps the most striking and important of all the reforms of the sixties, is a particularly good example of the complexities of the 'permissive' years. In 1959 Jenkins had deemed hanging 'barbaric and useless', and memorably called for the 'ghastly apparatus of the gallows' to be torn down for ever.[68] In disliking hanging he was not unique among Home Secretaries of the period. Rab Butler, one of his Conservative predecessors, had shut himself up for days when compelled to review capital cases before the sentences were carried out, and described the entire process as 'hideous'; indeed, by the end of his time at the Home Office he had been converted into a staunch opponent of capital punishment.[69] When the Commons debated the matter at the end of 1964, the last Conservative Home Secretary, Henry Brooke, amazed the House by revealing that he too had been converted into an opponent, and many bright young Tories joined their Labour counterparts to ensure that the death penalty was abolished for a trial period of five years. Jenkins, however, was not yet Home Secretary, so this most emblematic of sixties reforms had very little to do with him at all. And in December 1969, when the death penalty was permanently abolished by 343 votes to 185, he was no longer at the Home Office.[70]

What is remarkable about the abolition of the death penalty is that the MPs of all parties who supported it were completely disregarding the sentiments of their constituents. It would be easy to imagine that this was an issue on which there were clear lines between women and men, or, perhaps, young and old. But this was not the case. All the evidence suggests that the abolition of the death penalty offended every section of society, irrespective of age, gender, class or political sympathies. In 1964 opinion polls estimated public support for abolishing the rope to be no more than 23 per cent, and by June 1966, after the five-year suspension had started, this had fallen to 18 per cent. Throughout this period Jenkins and other MPs were bombarded with letters imploring them to bring back the rope.[71] Public support for hanging was never lower than 60 per cent, and at times, after particularly newsworthy crimes, it reached more than 80 per cent.[72] In the 1966 election Sidney Silverman, the chief abolitionist and Labour MP for Nelson and Colne, found himself opposed by an independent pro-hanging candidate as well as his more conventional adversaries. Defying all predictions, the independent won more than 5000 votes and 13 per cent of the total, which at the time was thought 'an outstanding performance by an individual candidate'.[73]

In this instance, then, Peter Hitchens's verdict that the abolition of hanging was 'a victory for the elite over the people' is pretty accurate. As one rather less impassioned historian puts it, as with many of the other permissive reforms, politicians were 'ignoring the wishes of the electorate and altering the law in a way directly opposed to the opinions and feelings of the vast majority of the British people'.[74]

This fits in well with the popular image of the mid-sixties as a period in which the Labour government, inspired by a new climate of liberalism and cultural freedom, ran ahead of public opinion by passing the legislation to create a permissive society. The historian Christie Davies, for example, suggests that this reflected a wider enthusiasm for 'technical rationality' and 'social engineering': in other words, a general confidence in the power of experts to bring about social change.[75] In his history of the sixties Arthur Marwick identifies a slightly different phenomenon, which he calls 'measured judgement': the exercise of authority by people of 'traditional enlightened and rational outlook who responded flexibly and tolerantly to counter-cultural demands'. This measured judgement, he argues, was one of the hallmarks of the era, and helps to explain why it was marked by permissiveness: 'striking changes in public and private morals and . . . a new frankness, openness and indeed honesty in personal relations and modes of expression'.[76]

At first glance, Roy Jenkins's period at the Home Office and the liberal reforms with which he was associated seem to bear out Marwick's argument. But on closer examination the permissive society is revealed as something of a myth. Certainly, as the example of hanging suggests, there was no popular consensus in favour of permissiveness. When *New Society* conducted its poll in November 1969 to test popular attitudes to the changes of the sixties, only 5 per cent nominated 'easier laws for homosexuality, divorce, abortion etc.' as their favourite development, compared with ten times as many who cited the increase in the state pension. When asked which change they most objected to, 'easier laws for homosexuality, divorce, abortion etc.' was comfortably the most common choice, with only immigration and student protest coming close. In both cases, Labour supporters proved to be more hostile to the reforms than their Tory counterparts, and in both cases, young people were no more liberal than their elders.[77]

At least as far as the transformation of public opinion is concerned, then, the concept of the permissive sixties makes little sense. What is more, most historians of British moral attitudes agree that the very idea of permissiveness is not very useful. Rather than being some great tidal wave of reform washing over the old bulwarks of repression, the reforms were piecemeal, limited and often contradictory. They did not all spring from some fount of 'measured judgement', but were the result of very different, decades-old pressures. Indeed, although popular myth places the reforms at the centre of the liberated Swinging Sixties, this obscures their true origins. Rather than being part of some permissive package, each reform was carefully presented on its own specific merits and was the result of a particular set of pressures. Opposition to the laws on homosexuality, for example, did not begin in the 1960s but in the 1890s. The campaign to reform the divorce laws dated from the 1910s, the birth-control movement from the 1920s, and the abortion campaign from the 1930s. There was no such thing as a single permissive lobby: it was quite normal for a progressive reformer – like, say, Shirley Williams, Leo Abse or Norman St John Stevas – to support the legalisation of homosexuality while simultaneously voting against the abortion reforms. And none of the reforms came about as a result of 'counter-cultural demands': the groups that pushed for the decriminalisation of homosexuality and abortion were made up of eminent politicians, writers and professionals, not guitar-toting students.[78]

Much of the discussion about Roy Jenkins and the permissive society, in other words, is founded upon misconceptions and half-truths. The reforms were the fruit of decades of earnest progressive campaigning, not of the youthful bohemianism of the late sixties. They were inspired not by a single spirit of permissive hedonism but by very different and sometimes contradictory pressures, both liberal and conservative, both secular and religious. Although they won support from liberal-minded Labour MPs in the Commons, they were never seen as an integral part of government policy and were almost never mentioned in the election campaigns of 1964, 1966 or 1970. There was certainly nothing 'socialist' about them, as conservative critics often like to think. A Conservative government would certainly have had greater difficulty in endorsing the reforms, for fear of alienating the backbenches and local activists, but a government led by moderates like Heath, Maudling and Macleod might not have found it impossible.

Beyond the walls of the Palace of Westminster there was no overnight revolution in attitudes and behaviour, and opinion polls consistently found strong public suspicion of, or even opposition to, the reforms of the late sixties. As we will see, this became linked in some conservative quarters to a generalised sense of national decadence and decline, and in many ways it was ultra-conservative critics like Mary Whitehouse and Malcolm Muggeridge, and later Margaret Thatcher and Norman Tebbit, who *invented* the idea of the permissive society, as a way of expressing their hostility to secularism, consumerism, the welfare state and other manifestations of post-war social change. But at the time there was little sense that these were important partisan issues: even the furore over the abolition of capital punishment made little difference to the government's public standing.

Jenkins himself continued to enjoy the reputation of an able and efficient Home Secretary; far from being a particularly controversial figure, he was seen as one of the government's most distinguished successes. Indeed, by August 1966 he was comfortably ahead of his great friend Crosland in the race to become the heir apparent of the old Gaitskellites. According to the newspapers, Jenkins was now the obvious successor should Wilson be forced from office or fall on his sword. 'Why the fuck don't I ever read about Crosland for PM?' the Education Secretary snapped at one of his friends. 'What the hell are you doing about it?'[79] The unofficial contest between the two rivals had never been more intense, and with Wilson's position looking shakier by the week, the moment of decision seemed at hand.

17

SOWING DRAGONS' TEETH

> The Six Counties, unlike their neighbours across the border, belong to the British Welfare State. They share, too, as they richly deserve, many of the fruits of the affluent society. The processes of modernization have been carried far and they are not halted. On the contrary, they are on the march.
>
> *The Times*, 12 April 1965

Early in 1967 three Labour MPs arrived in Northern Ireland for a brief fact-finding trip. They were chiefly interested in sectarian discrimination, electoral malpractice and the enduring problem of unemployment. Not surprising, their arrival did not go down well with the ruling Unionist Party, whose spokesmen called the visitors 'interfering and unwelcome', 'hostile and provocative' and 'anti-Ulster'. One of the visiting trio, Paul Rose, was the parliamentary private secretary to Barbara Castle, and when he returned to London he went to tell her what he had discovered: 'I remember her patting me on the head and saying, "Why is a young man like you concerned about Northern Ireland? What about Vietnam? What about Rhodesia?"' he recalled. 'I just looked at her with incomprehension and said, "You'll see when they start shooting each other."'[1]

The civil strife that broke out in Northern Ireland had two dimensions. On one level it was a product of its time, of economic depression, social and cultural anxieties, and the decisions of individual politicians and paramilitaries. But as many observers recognised, the so-called Troubles had deep roots in Irish history. This does not necessarily mean that they were the inevitable expression of some native predilection for sectarianism and violence. It does mean, however, that they would never have erupted as they did were it not for 'existing animosities and unresolved issues of nationality, religion, power and territorial rivalry'. There was much about the Troubles that was new; but at the same time they formed 'a new phase in a continuum of division'.[2]

The division of Ireland dates from the seventeenth century, when the province of Ulster was colonised by Scottish Presbyterian settlers who lorded it over their indigenous Catholic neighbours. By the dawn of the twentieth century the settlers' descendants had built a prosperous, industrialised economy based on linen, shipbuilding and heavy engineering, and despite the rise of Irish nationalism, most northern Protestants feared that separation from Britain would erode their success and standing. As one historian puts it, the working-class culture of the major northern city, Belfast, 'had more in common with Glasgow, Manchester or Bristol than with Dublin, Cork or Galway'.[3] Belfast even looked different from Catholic cities like Dublin or Cork: it was a 'red-bricked Mancunian look-alike set down in the Irish countryside'. The surrounding area, too, had little of the lush wildness of the south, but more of 'the neat fertility of the Scottish lowlands'. So, as one historian puts it, the controversy over Ireland's destiny was 'the external, political manifestation of a series of fundamental differences between the Catholic and Protestant traditions'.[4]

Throughout the opening decades of the twentieth century the Protestants of the six northern counties doggedly hung on to the union with Britain. In 1912 a group of Unionist politicians led by the iconic Sir Edward Carson drew up the Ulster Covenant, pledging to 'defend for ourselves and our children our cherished position of equal citizenship in the United Kingdom, and in using all means which may be found necessary to defeat the present conspiracy to set up a home rule parliament in Ireland'. Almost half a million people signed the covenant, and a hundred thousand men were enrolled in the Ulster Volunteer Force, ready for the day when Home Rule became a reality.[5] In the end, although much of the country was scarred by savage fighting between the IRA and the British in the years after the First World War, the Unionists got their way. Under the terms of the Anglo-Irish Treaty that ended the conflict, the six northern counties were partitioned from the rest of Ireland and given their own parliament at Stormont in Belfast. While the rest of Ireland became a Free State and then an independent Republic, these Protestant-dominated counties, controversially known as Ulster or Northern Ireland,* remained part of the United Kingdom.[6]

---

*Historically, Ulster was one of the four provinces of Ireland and was made up of nine counties. Three became part of the Irish Free State in 1922, while the other six remained in the United Kingdom. Unionists usually referred to their territory as 'Ulster', even though obviously this was not strictly accurate. Nationalists preferred 'the Six Counties', 'the Six County State' or 'the North of Ireland'. Almost everybody in mainland Britain simply called it 'Northern Ireland'.

The central fault line in the new state of Northern Ireland divided the Protestant, Unionist majority from the Catholic, nationalist minority. Despite their numerical majority, Unionists clung to their self-image as plucky frontiersmen, supported only half-heartedly by their British allies against the swarming menace of Irish Catholicism. To many British visitors they seemed a curious combination of warmth and conservatism: slogans like 'No Surrender' and 'Not an Inch' reflected their suspicious mentality. Siege and sacrifice were vital elements of Unionist identity. Many proudly traced their lineage to the Presbyterians who had struggled to build new lives three centuries before; similarly, many remembered the sacrifice of thousands of Ulster Volunteers in the carnage of the Somme. Unionist politicians warily eyed their southern counterparts across the new border, fearful that their little state would be swallowed up in a united Ireland. At the same time, they were always nervously glancing over their shoulders at their own nationalist minority, whom they regarded as 'the enemy within', potential traitors to a man and a 'Trojan horse for the IRA'.[7]

These fears were enshrined in the structure of the Northern Irish state. The institutions of law and order, for example, were almost completely dominated by Protestants. They outnumbered Catholics in the Royal Ulster Constabulary (RUC) by more than nine to one, while the heavily armed auxiliary security forces, known as the B Specials, were exclusively Protestant. Thanks to the Special Powers Act, the police were entitled to make arrests and searches without a warrant, intern suspects without trial and prohibit meetings and publications, although most of these provisions were rarely used. Civil servants, too, were overwhelmingly Protestant: a survey in 1943 found that in the fifty most senior posts there were no Catholics at all; in the six hundred middle-ranking positions there were only thirty-seven Catholics; and overall, Catholics in the civil service were outnumbered by about nine to one. There were no Catholics in the Stormont Cabinet; no Catholics in the top ranks of the RUC; and no Catholics at the head of major public commissions, institutions and the like.[8]

By contrast, the Orange Order, a fiercely anti-Catholic fraternal organisation with close links to the Unionist Party, played a central role in the new state. Orangemen were explicitly pledged to 'resist the ascendancy of [the Catholic] church' by any legal means, and they were prohibited from attending 'any act or ceremony of Popish worship'. Orange marches to celebrate the Glorious Revolution were an integral part of life in Northern

Ireland, but the impact of the Order went well beyond the marching season. The RUC had its own Orange lodge, while most of the members of the B Specials were Orangemen and some B Special units were even based in Orange halls. According to one account, 'membership was an indispensable condition of political advancement'. Unionist Party meetings were held in Orange halls, and the Order had the right to nominate members of the party's ruling council. All but three of the fifty-four Unionist Cabinet ministers between 1921 and 1969 were members of the Orange Order, while of the ninety-five Unionist backbench MPs in the same period, all but eight were Orangemen.[9] 'I have always said that I am an Orangeman first and a politician and member of this parliament afterwards,' insisted the first Northern Irish Prime Minister, James Craig. 'All I boast is that we are a Protestant Parliament and a Protestant State.'[10]

Although sectarianism in Ireland had a long history, there is no doubt that partition made it worse.[11] And for Catholics growing up in the 1940s and 1950s the discriminatory nature of the Northern Irish state was impossible to ignore. Entire businesses and even industries simply refused to employ Catholics, and the unemployment rate among Catholics was usually more than double that among Protestants.[12] One teenager growing up in County Londonderry, whose parents were from the south, later recalled:

> The two things that came across very clearly were, one, the almost apartheid nature of society. Though people, Protestant and Catholic, lived side by side literally, there was little contact between them. Secondly you learned very quickly from the other children at school that Catholics couldn't get jobs in a whole range of occupations. There was no point in applying for jobs under the local authorities or within the Northern Irish civil service, for example. Nor in a whole lot of private employments, the shipyard and the aircraft factory and so forth. That was just the inherited folklore of all the children around, they didn't bother applying for these jobs, they were just closed to them.[13]

The principle behind all this was not so much deliberate cruelty as political control.[14] The whole point of the Northern Irish state was to maintain the position of the Unionist community, the most glaring example being its electoral boundaries, which were ruthlessly redrawn to engineer the largest possible Unionist majority. County Antrim in the sixties had an estimated population of 274,000, of whom 66,000 were Catholics; but all seven of its parliamentary seats went to Unionists. The 41,000 predominantly Catholic voters of Mid-Down, meanwhile, elected just one MP – exactly the same representation as that given to the 7500 voters of Belfast's Dock division, who were Protestants.[15] Similar principles applied in local government, too. Only ratepayers, in other words the owners or tenants of houses and flats, or their spouses could vote in local government elections. Since Catholics were disproportionately poor and often lived with their parents or in shared accommodation, this meant that many could not vote. What was more, the electoral wards had been so blatantly gerrymandered that many Catholic areas still produced Protestant councils. In Counties Tyrone and Fermanagh, for instance, although Catholics enjoyed a narrow majority, Unionists controlled the councils, building homes and providing jobs for their own voters.[16]

The local government issue was particularly sensitive as Northern Ireland entered the sixties because it was closely associated with the issue of housing. As one observer put it, 'he who controlled the allocation of public authority housing effectively controlled the voting in that area'.[17] Like many other industrialised parts of the United Kingdom, the province badly needed new housing to replace its crumbling nineteenth-century tenements and to accommodate a young population keen to move out from under the wings of their parents. But since a couple renting a public authority house were entitled to two votes in the local elections, Unionist councillors were reluctant to build houses in Catholic-dominated areas. In 1963, for instance, the chairman of the Enniskillen housing committee freely admitted: 'We are not going to build houses in the [Catholic] South Ward and cut a rod to beat ourselves later on. We are going to see that the right people are put in these houses, and we are not going to apologise for it.'[18] Nationalist councillors were not always models of altruism either. In the early 1960s, 765 council houses were built by the nationalist council in the border town of Newry; only 22 went to Protestants.[19]

There is no doubt, however, that most housing discrimination was directed by Unionists to disenfranchise Catholic voters.[20] Derry was the most glaring example: as one senior Unionist admitted in 1968, it was 'a Roman Catholic and nationalist city [which] has for three or four decades been administered (and none too fairly administered) by a Protestant and Unionist majority secured by a manipulation of the ward boundaries for the sole purpose of maintaining Unionist control'.[21] As the Catholic population increased, the electoral boundaries were continually redrawn and Catholics were systematically excluded from municipal jobs and public housing. In 1965 Derry had a population of 36,000 Catholics and 18,000 Protestants. Thanks to the restrictive franchise, only 14,000 Catholics and 9000 Protestants were entitled to vote in local elections, which still left a Catholic majority. However, thanks to some wily gerrymandering, the council was controlled by the Unionists. As a result, 145 of Londonderry Corporation's 177 employees were Protestants, and while almost every Protestant family had their own home, there were some 2000 Catholics on the housing waiting list.[22] *The Times* was not far wrong when, after an investigation into discrimination in the city in 1967, it called the Catholic population 'Ulster's Second Class Citizens'.[23]

Most people in mainland Britain knew almost nothing about all this. Until the mid-sixties, Northern Ireland virtually never made it into British newspapers or news bulletins, usually being mentioned only in the context of a royal visit.[24] Since most people had little reason to visit the province, they probably never gave it a moment's thought. Successive governments showed no interest in getting involved in Northern Ireland's affairs: since the province had its own parliament, the thinking went, British politicians had no business fishing in what were doubtless murky and unfathomable waters.[25] Some senior figures in the Labour Party did begin to take a vague interest in the province at the end of the 1950s, and a backbench Campaign for Democracy in Ulster was launched in 1965, but most British politicians remained completely uninterested. As James Callaghan later put it: 'Most Members of Parliament knew less about it than we knew about our distant colonies on the far side of the earth.'[26]

In March 1966 the Cabinet Secretary warned Harold Wilson that there was a real danger of sectarian disturbances in Northern Ireland on the fiftieth anniversary of the Easter Rising, which many people saw as the beginning of the Irish struggle for independence. According to intelligence reports, the clandestine IRA still commanded the allegiance of 'some 3,000 trained members or supporters', who had been supplied with arms and ammunition from the Republic of Ireland and had been schooled in more than thirty 'training camps' south of the border.[27] Wilson took the threat seriously, and the Cabinet agreed to move an additional infantry battalion to Northern Ireland.[28]

In fact, the anniversary passed off without major incident. Although the intelligence reports represented an overdue corrective to the complacency of successive British governments, the IRA was far from being a serious threat. It had largely disintegrated since the 1920s, with many of its members returning to quiet civilian lives. A minority on both sides of the border continued to fight on for a united Ireland, but their numbers were few and their impact was extremely limited.[29] When, during the Second World War, a young activist tried to commandeer a car in Belfast for the use of the IRA, he discovered how far the organisation had fallen, even among the Catholic community, in credibility and public esteem. 'I want your car for the IRA,' the aspiring warrior demanded. 'Fuck off, you wee bastard,' came the reply, 'or I'll give you a toe up the arse.'[30]

In 1956 what was left of the IRA launched Operation Harvest, trying to carve out 'liberated areas' along the border between the Republic and the North, but it had no popular support and no momentum. Its great problem, put simply, was that most Irishmen no longer had any interest in fighting for the reunification of the island.[31] Both the Republic and the North adopted tough policies of interning suspects without trial to deal with the insurgency; eight IRA volunteers were killed, as well as six RUC officers, and within a year or two the operation had fizzled out. Apart from a few desultory raids on RUC posts, IRA activities came to a halt. In February 1962 a formal statement announced that the organisation had dumped its arms, demobilised its volunteers and approved 'the termination of "The Campaign of Resistance to British Occupation"'.[32] The organisation's new chief of staff, a bohemian Dubliner called Cathal Goulding, later explained that 'the notion that the IRA was going to rise up some day and free Ireland and get rid of the British was a ridiculous pipe-dream, for the simple reason that we never had the support of the people north and south to do it'.[33]

What was left of the IRA now turned to the politics of socialism. Instead of taking on the Protestants of the North in sectarian battle, Republicans would seek to build a united, Communist Ireland through political means. This meant a shift away from the old emphasis on revolutionary violence, and in 1968 the IRA even sold some of its weapons to the tiny Free Wales Army.[34] But the Marxism of this new IRA did not always go down well with its supporters. At heart most Republicans were culturally conservative Catholics who instinctively disliked Marxism as 'the ideology of the ungodly'.[35] Joe Cahill, a veteran campaigner who had spent years behind bars for murdering a policeman, left the movement in disgust in 1964. He later told an interviewer:

I had a feeling that ultra-left politics were taking over. As far as I was concerned, the main purpose of the IRA and Sinn Fein was to break the connection with England and get rid of the 'Brits' from Ireland. They'd gone completely political and the military side of things was being run down. The Republican Movement was being led off the true path of republicanism. Sooner or later there'd have to be a showdown. A split was inevitable.[36]

At the time, however, most observers assumed that the IRA had simply disintegrated, and the organisation barely surfaced during the Easter commemorations of 1966. 'I hadn't heard of the IRA,' recalled one Catholic woman from Belfast who later joined Sinn Fein. 'There was no IRA activity on the streets. Absolutely nothing. It was just part of history.' To the IRA veteran Billy McKee, meanwhile, the Easter commemorations were an exercise in nostalgia, little more. 'I believed that it was dead, completely dead,' he said. 'And it was, except in the minds of myself and other old republicans.'[37]

The other political vehicle for Catholic dissatisfaction in the 1950s and 1960s was Northern Ireland's small Nationalist Party, but this was not much more effective. Although Catholic votes sent a handful of Nationalist MPs to the Stormont parliament, they were generally seen as disorganised, old-fashioned conservatives from the rural north, and certainly no match for their Unionist opponents.[38] South of the border, meanwhile, most people were too busy with their own lives to give much thought to their fellow-Catholics in the North.[39] Irish politicians made all the right noises about building a united Ireland and righting the wrong of partition, but in practice they were rarely particularly interested in the affairs of the Six Counties. Indeed, nationalists were consistently snubbed and ignored by their southern brethren. In 1945 northern Nationalists were invited to the Irish presidential inauguration only after writing to complain that they had been forgotten, and in 1956 their leader's request to address the Dublin parliament was summarily turned down. The Irish Prime Minister, Seán Lemass, barely hid his contempt for them, commenting that 'the Catholics in the north were just as intractable as the Protestants', and after his retirement he went even further, observing that they merely wanted to 'get their foot on the throat of the Orangeman across the road'.[40]

All of this helped to create a sense of stasis as Northern Ireland entered the 1960s. Thanks to their unrepentant gerrymandering, the Unionist parliamentary majority appeared unthreatened, and since their opponents had almost no chance of success, they rarely bothered competing. In some seats like South Antrim, the Unionist majority was so large that for nine consecutive elections no alternative candidate came forward. The Prime Minister, Sir Basil Brooke, had served for almost twenty years and radical change of any kind seemed extremely unlikely. Most Catholics either did not vote at all or did so with a kind of resigned passivity, certain that it would do little good. Although they still suffered from discrimination in the workplace, the voting booth and the street, they were certainly not interested in violence or rebellion.

Indeed, to reduce the story of Northern Ireland in the fifties and sixties to a narrative of discrimination does it little justice. Despite the looming shadow of sectarianism, most of the social developments that marked life elsewhere in the United Kingdom were mirrored across the Irish Sea. The affluent society brought more cars and televisions, washing machines and fridges, record players and mini-skirts. The everyday aspirations and anxieties of the average Belfast postman were not so different from those of his counterparts in Birmingham, Swansea or Glasgow. Just as in England, Wales and Scotland, people in Northern Ireland laughed at Hancock and Steptoe, listened to Lennon and McCartney, thrilled to James Bond and *The Avengers*, shopped at Sainsbury's and Boots and dreamed about Jean Shrimpton and Terence Stamp. Many housing estates were mixed, and although Catholic and Protestant children went to different schools they often lived and played cheek by jowl. The IRA was a folk memory, nothing more.[41] According to opinion polls, Catholics were actually less likely than Protestants to contemplate violence to achieve their political aims.[42] And although most Northern Catholics still dreamed of a united Ireland, few saw it as a plausible short-term outcome. In 1966, one Irish journalist concluded: 'The plain fact about the North today is that the secret wish of most Northern Catholics is not for Union with the South (entailing a fall-off in social benefits) but for an end to discrimination and for a fairer share of the Northern spoils. The truth may be unpalatable to us in the South, but it has to be faced.'[43]

In March 1963 Sir Basil Brooke retired as Prime Minister of Northern Ireland. He was succeeded by Captain Terence O'Neill, a Unionist MP in his late forties who had spent seven years as the province's Finance Minister. O'Neill was from a wealthy Anglo-Irish family, had been educated at Eton and had served with distinction with the Irish Guards in the Second World War. As a young man he spent most of his time in London rather than in Northern Ireland. He settled permanently in the region only when he was in his early thirties, and would rather have been a Conservative MP at Westminster than a Unionist sitting at Stormont. Still, his patrician background and manner, as well as a reputation for technocratic competence, propelled him up the ladder, and in 1963 he was chosen as the new Unionist leader by the ageing grandees who dominated the party establishment.[44]

O'Neill took the helm at a time when all the talk, in Northern Ireland as on the mainland, was of modernisation. Like Harold Wilson and Edward Heath, he was seen as a hard-headed moderniser who would haul the country into the technological age. His priority was economic development. Northern Ireland's economy had been stagnating since the end of the war, as the industries that had made it so prosperous in the past struggled with international competition and fluctuating demand. In the course of the 1950s employment in textiles and agriculture had fallen by 40 per cent, and in the Belfast shipyards, which had always been Unionist strongholds, it had fallen by almost 60 per cent. By 1963 almost 10 per cent of the workforce were unemployed, a disturbingly high rate given that in the rest of Britain unemployment was little more than nominal. What was more, average weekly earnings in Northern Ireland were only 78 per cent of those elsewhere in the United Kingdom, and one in three houses had either no piped water or no flushing toilets.[45]

It was no coincidence that as the economy was struggling, a new party was challenging the Unionists from the left. The Northern Ireland Labour Party was non-denominational, appealing to both Catholics and Protestants on the grounds of economic interest, although it supported the Union and drew most of its support from former Unionists. Although gerrymandering undermined its electoral performance, it still won four seats in both 1958 and 1962, and in the latter election it managed to attract 26 per cent of the vote. The emergence of this new party was a serious problem for O'Neill. First, it threatened to drain off Protestant working-class support; second, it had friends in very high places, especially as across the water Harold Wilson was poised to win the 1964 general election. For Northern Ireland's new Prime Minister, therefore, economic and political reform was a matter of urgency.[46]

O'Neill set about his modernisation programme with gusto. He encouraged 'schemes to rationalize railways, build motorways, encourage growth points, clear slums, reorganize ministries, establish a new university, create a new city, and reach a concordat with the trade unions', and all the time he appealed to Westminster for more money to put these plans into effect. Between 1958 and 1969 public investment per head doubled, and the government ploughed new funds into roads, schools, vocational training and, most importantly, public housing. Indeed, by the end of the sixties public spending per head in Northern Ireland had overtaken that in England. Meanwhile, O'Neill lobbied hard to attract investment from multinational corporations, and the likes of Michelin, Ford, Goodyear and ICI were all lured to the province with promises of cheap labour and excellent working conditions.[47]

As O'Neill had hoped, the charge of the Northern Ireland Labour Party was blunted, but the modernisation programme created problems of its own. 'While development has been pouring in at one end,' commented one British correspondent, 'the plug has been out at the other.' Most of the new investment was concentrated in Belfast and the eastern counties; in the more rural and heavily Catholic western counties, and especially in the western city of Derry, unemployment remained stubbornly high. This was not necessarily O'Neill's fault, since most corporations were keener to invest in the more urbanised east with its better transport links to the British mainland. But in the context of sectarian and regional discrimination, it was hardly surprising that rural discontent was on the rise. 'People there,' explained *The Times*, 'are becoming convinced that the Stormont Government's plans are designed to deprive them of new industries.'[48]

Even in the Protestant east, too, there were murmurs of dissatisfaction. The new corporations were not very interested in Northern Ireland's sectarian traditions, and older Unionist industrialists – and, indeed, workers – were often dismayed to find that their prejudices and practices counted for little. As one writer puts it, 'the tradition of the discreet word in Orange or Freemason lodge was not given its customary due by young personnel managers in Courtauld's or Du Pont'.[49] Unionism was a conservative creed, but O'Neill's reforms seemed to be tearing up decades of history and tradition.

Although it is often seen as monolithic, the Unionist Party was really an alliance of different Protestant groups, cutting across regional and class boundaries. Appeals to the flag and the Orange drum usually silenced any discord, but within the Unionist tradition there was a profound difference between the 'working-class Protestant in, say, the Shankill Road district of

Belfast, and the Anglican mill-owner, landlord or textile baron who reigned on the upper reaches of the party'.[50] In this context O'Neill was in many ways the worst possible person to guide the Unionist community towards reform and modernisation. He was an Anglican, he spoke with an Old Etonian accent, and to all intents and purposes he came over as an aristocratic Englishman. Many Unionists were automatically suspicious of England and the English, reflecting not only their self-image as embattled settlers whose homeland was always likely to sell them short, but their background in the Scottish Nonconformist tradition. The future Unionist leader David Trimble spoke for many when he explained that they felt 'abandoned or misled by the natural leaders of society'. 'Terence O'Neill', he reflected, 'never spoke or behaved as if he was one of us.'[51]

What was more, O'Neill was famously devoid of the little political skills that make for good leadership. 'He lacked the common touch,' said one of his Cabinet colleagues. 'He found it difficult to communicate warmth and friendliness. I found him distant and uninspiring: I would not, I confess, have felt like dying in a ditch for him.' A Unionist journalist, meanwhile, called him 'a disaster. Every time you met him you would have to be introduced to him all over again, whereas Faulkner might not have seen you for a year but would instantly know you.'[52]

Brian Faulkner, O'Neill's chief rival within the Unionist community, was one of the central figures in Northern Irish politics in the 1960s and 1970s. Unlike O'Neill, he did not have a patrician background: his father had started out as a linen salesman before becoming a successful shirt manufacturer. Faulkner worked his way up the Unionist hierarchy through sheer ambition and enterprise, and in 1963 became O'Neill's Minister of Commerce, responsible for dealing with the major companies that they wanted to attract to Northern Ireland. But whereas O'Neill was seen as the representative of the landed gentry, Faulkner championed the rights of small businessmen and the Unionist middle classes, vigorously criticising government regulations and high taxes. And whereas O'Neill presented himself as a moderniser, Faulkner always identified himself with the hardline wing of the Unionist Party, championing the right of the Orange Order to march wherever it wanted and regularly warning of the dangers of Catholic nationalism.

In 1963 many observers felt that had there been a direct democratic election for the leadership of the party, Faulkner would have won. Instead, the grandees chose O'Neill, the safe pair of hands, while his rival was away in the United States. From this point onwards relations between the two men were far from easy. 'Faulkner always found O'Neill aloof and remote,' writes the historian Henry Patterson, 'and resented the aura of the "Big House" and the attendant snobberies which he considered had given O'Neill an unfair advantage.' Meanwhile, 'O'Neill formed the judgement that Faulkner was tricky, devious, and profoundly ambitious, and was seeking every opportunity to displace him'.[53]

As far as the Unionist rank and file were concerned, O'Neill's greatest failing was the sense that he could not be trusted to handle Northern Ireland's religious question, and was likely to sell them short at any moment. For some historians, this was a great misunderstanding. Roy Foster, for example, calls him 'an unconvincing liberal' and criticises 'the illusion that he stood for introducing civil rights reform'.[54] O'Neill's chief adviser Kenneth Bloomfield later insisted that he 'remained very fundamentally a Unionist', and had no 'grand design' to improve relations between Protestant and Catholic. He was interested, said Bloomfield, 'in economic development, not political reform'. And yet Bloomfield added that O'Neill 'hated the injustice towards the Catholics. After all he had served in the Irish Guards which were mixed.'[54]

Even if this was an exaggeration, O'Neill never exuded the same fear and hostility that characterised many Unionists' feelings towards their Catholic neighbours. He certainly looked down on Northern Ireland's Catholics, but, unlike many of his supporters, he was not frightened of them. As one observer puts it, 'he moved among the Roman Catholic population like some ancient lord, anxious to do the decent thing by his tenants'.[56] His attitude was best captured in a famous interview with the *Belfast Telegraph* in 1969, in which he managed to patronise all sides at once:

> It is frightfully hard to explain to Protestants that if you give Roman Catholics a good job and a good house, they will live like Protestants, because they will have neighbours with cars and television sets. They will refuse to have eighteen children; but if a Roman Catholic is jobless, and lives in the most ghastly hovel, he will rear eighteen children on national assistance. If you treat Roman Catholics with due consideration and kindness, they will live like Protestants in spite of the authoritative nature of their Church.[57]

O'Neill's determination to encourage Catholics to 'live like Protestants' did not make him many friends within the Unionist tradition. He made a point of visiting Catholic schools and posing for photographs with nuns, and then secretly invited the Irish Taoiseach, Seán Lemass, to visit Belfast on 14 January 1965. No Taoiseach had ever visited Stormont, and Lemass told O'Neill: 'I shall get into terrible trouble for this.' 'No, Mr Lemass,' replied O'Neill, 'it is I who will get into trouble for this.'[58] Yet at the time, this dramatic gesture of intent seemed to go down well. *The Times*, for instance, thought that 'a 40-year deadlock has been broken':

> The Catholic community welcome it. But it is not only they who approve it. A great many enlightened Unionists agree with the Prime Minister that over and above the necessity of trade and tourism, the issues of religion and the border must become less vibrant. There are, of course, the extremists . . . But there is also now a feeling that the fever is subsiding. There is no telling what consequences may flow from the changing atmosphere that has followed the breaking of the deadlock between north and south. They can only be for the good. Forty years is a long time, but as one non-religious man put it – 'there's no going back now'.[59]

But this optimism was misplaced, for there were those within the Unionist community who feared and despised O'Neill's conciliatory initiatives. The *Belfast Telegraph*, a strongly Unionist paper, was full of praise for the Prime Minister's 'bridge-building', but as one young Presbyterian minister put it: 'A bridge and a traitor are very much alike, for they both go over to the other side.'[60] The minister's name was Ian Paisley, and over the next four decades his would become one of the most immediately recognisable and controversial voices not only in Northern Ireland but throughout the British Isles.

Paisley's importance in the history of the Northern Irish conflict is hard to overstate. As Tim Pat Coogan puts it, with 'his husky oratory, raw sex appeal and powerful personality and physique', he was 'a dominant figure, bestriding the political landscape of Northern Ireland with the Bible in one hand and both eyes on the ballot box'.[61] Born in Armagh in 1926, Paisley was the son of a Unionist volunteer and trained as a minister, as had his father, before founding his own evangelical church in 1951. From this point onwards he became increasingly famous as 'the Big Man', the flamboyant, utterly uncompromising standard-bearer of militant Unionism and anti-Catholicism. 'Through Popery,' he wrote in 1967, 'the Devil has shut up the way to our inheritance. Priestcraft, superstition and papalism with all their attendant vices of murder, theft, immorality, lust and incest [have] blocked the way to the land of gospel liberty.'[62]

Although Paisley won most renown as a political figure, he was always animated by fierce religious conviction and by his belief in the literal truth of the Bible. Like the anti-Catholic preachers of the sixteenth and seventeenth centuries, he used ferocious sexual imagery to illustrate the wickedness of the Church of Rome, so that one hostile observer described him as 'the great pornographer'. After the moderator of the Scottish Presbyterian Church made a friendly visit to the Pope, for example, Paisley's newspaper, the *Protestant Telegraph*, ran the remarkable headline: 'The Church of Scotland drunk with the wine of the fornication with the Roman whore'. At his early prayer meetings he would regularly produce 'nuns' who had allegedly escaped from Catholic convents rather than surrender to the lascivious attentions of priests and other nuns. In the late sixties the *Protestant Telegraph* frequently ran stories like 'The Love Affairs of the Vatican', 'Priestly Murders Exposed'. and 'Children Tortured — Monks Turned Out as Sadists'.[63] One issue in April 1967 even claimed, quite preposterously, that members of Sinn Fein swore the following oath:

> These Protestant robbers and brutes, these unbelievers of our faith, will be driven like the swine they are into the sea by fire, the knife or the poison cup until we of the Catholic Faith and avowed supporters of all Sinn Fein action and principles clear these heretics from our land . . .
>
> At any cost we must work and seek, using any method of deception to gain our ends, towards the destruction of all Protestants and the advancement of the priesthood and the Catholic Faith until the Pope is complete ruler of the whole world.[64]

To many observers in mainland Britain, where anti-Catholicism had effectively died out, Paisley seemed a bizarre, loud-mouthed relic of the seventeenth century, and it was difficult to take him seriously. But to thousands of working-class and rural Northern Irish Protestants, anxious at the prospect of economic decline and social change, he spoke in recognisable, even reassuring cadences. His was the voice of righteousness and freedom, and in the turbulent years of the late sixties, more and more Unionists would be drawn to his call.[65]

Paisley first made the headlines after a series of antics that would have appeared laughable were it not for their serious political consequences. In 1956 he 'rescued' a fifteen-year-old Catholic girl, Maura Lyons, from the tyranny of Rome and proudly trumpeted his achievement to the press until a court ordered him to return her to her family and leave her alone. Three years later he was in trouble again after hurling a Bible at the liberal Methodist minister Donald Soper, who was on a tour of Northern Ireland. In 1962 he tried to disrupt the opening of the Second Vatican Council, and a year later, on the death of Pope John XXIII, he led a march to Ulster Hall in Belfast to protest against O'Neill's decision to lower the Union Jack as a mark of respect. Paisley furiously denounced the 'lying eulogies now being paid to the Roman anti-Christ' by 'the Iscariots of Ulster', assuring his listeners that the 'Romish man of sin is now in hell'.[66] One witness recalled hearing him describe 'the flames of hell at that moment licking around the dead Pope. It was so graphic and colourful that the audience could almost feel the flames and feel the heat. I will remember the horror till the day I die.'[67]

Paisley's anger at the lowering of the Union Jack in 1963 was as nothing compared with his fury at the sight of another flag during the Westminster general election campaign a year later. Sinn Fein's candidate for the constituency of West Belfast, Liam McMillen, had been interned during the IRA campaign of the late 1950s, and in the window of his election office off the Falls Road his workers had hung a large Irish tricolour. Under the terms of the Flags and Emblems Act this was technically illegal, but normally the police turned a blind eye, especially since the flag was unlikely to upset anybody living in the heavily Catholic vicinity. To Paisley, however, the flag was an affront. On 27 September he told a cheering crowd that should the RUC fail to take it down, he would march on the Falls Road himself. 'I don't accept that any part of Ulster is republican and I don't want to see the Tricolour flying here,' he insisted. 'I intend to see that the Union Jack flies everywhere and that it keeps flying.'[68] One of his supporters later explained: 'It was like flying the swastika in London during the Second World War. It represented something that was anathema to every Ulsterman. We had to get that flag down and maybe burn the place where it was flown. That was the idea. Nothing was going to stop me. Come hell or high water, that flag was going to burn!'[69]

Faced with the possibility of Paisley leading a march into the heart of Catholic West Belfast, the RUC decided to act. On 28 September a group of heavily armed constables broke down the office door with pickaxes, seized the flag and retreated through a crowd of jeering Republicans. Over the next few days the political temperature rose in West Belfast. Republican supporters, furious at the disappearance of their flag, were determined to restore it, and two days later serious fighting broke out between thousands of local men, armed with rotten vegetables, stones, petrol bombs and the occasional loaded gun, and several dozen armed RUC men. After a trolley-bus was set ablaze and petrol bombs were thrown into the armoured cars of RUC reinforcements, the police turned water cannons on the crowd to try to break up the fighting. Only in the early hours of the morning was order finally restored. The following evening, after more disturbances, hundreds of RUC men in military gear moved into the Falls Road and systematically drove the protesters off the streets. Fifty civilians were so badly hurt in the clashes that they were taken to hospital, along with eighteen RUC men. In the end the authorities and Sinn Fein came to a compromise, under which the rioting stopped and the police allowed them to display the tricolour openly that Sunday at a Republican parade.[70]

Images of the fighting – the worst in Belfast for thirty years – had been carried across the world by the press and television, and the seeds of Northern Ireland's subsequent reputation had already been sown. 'The display of violence', said *The Times*, 'will disappoint those optimists who thought religious and nationalist antagonism were dying away in Ulster . . . There is a sickening familiarity about these exchanges for all who remember the bitterness and savagery with which the orange and green vendetta has been pursued in the past.'[71] In Dublin an angry crowd marched on the British Embassy and hurled stones at the Irish police. The era of the petrol bomb and the water cannon was at hand.

Paisley himself had spent the crucial evening at a meeting outside City Hall, leading his supporters in prayers and giving his usual anti-Catholic performance. His personal responsibility for what had happened, though, was unquestionable. Three decades later, interviewed by a British journalist about the flag furore, he insisted that the display of the tricolour was 'an act of defiance and the IRA made it clear they were defying the law and thumbing their nose at the authorities'. But had he not provoked greater unrest? 'It was the only way you could move the jellyfish who were in government,' he said defiantly. 'It wasn't as if I was a lone voice crying in the wilderness. I was voicing the strong resentment of the Ulster people at the time.'[72] In a sense he was right. On 15 October the Unionist candidate Jim Kilfedder won West Belfast, which some commentators thought might go to an opposition candidate, with seven thousand more votes than his nearest rival. In his acceptance speech he thanked Paisley for his support, without which, he said, victory would not have been possible.[73]

Paisley's ability to express and exploit the fears of the Unionist community, which had been demonstrated so clearly in the autumn of 1964, was to become one of the determining factors in Northern Irish politics over the next four decades. As an orator with the knack of rousing his audience he was quite superb. Noel Docherty, a young printer and constable in the B Specials, described the appeal of Paisley's tub-thumping fundamentalism:

> He was forthright and he wasn't afraid. I saw him as a true disciple of Christ. He thundered the message forth in a way that brought joy to my heart and I was spellbound by his oratory . . . I felt this is a man that's doing the Lord's work and if he's going to do the Lord's work, then I'm going to do it with him. I saw him as a great Ulsterman and a second [Sir Edward] Carson.[74]

Billy Giles, a working-class lad from East Belfast who became a Loyalist paramilitary, told an interviewer that listening to Paisley had been one of the formative experiences of his youth: 'He was the man. I thought that whatever Paisley said was true. Being affected by Paisley is part of being a Protestant. We went to his rallies. Tens of thousands followed him, just to hear what he had to say. He was preaching about the situation as if it was the gospel or a biblical text and, because of our upbringing, we were a ready audience.[75]

Paisley would not have got where he did on rhetorical skill alone. It was his eye for the moment and his ability to exploit the anxieties of Northern Ireland's Protestant community that explains his rise to prominence in the mid-sixties. Far from being the 'pantomime demon' of his opponents' imaginings, he was the first Northern Irish politician to make the most of television and newspaper publicity, especially through the launch of the *Protestant Telegraph* in 1966.[76] Indeed, for most viewers in Northern Ireland, the lasting television image of the year was not Geoff Hurst blasting home his third goal in the World Cup Final, but 'the Big Man with the blazing eyes, wearing a Roman collar and a white raincoat, leading protesters into various street confrontations'.[77]

An obvious example was the controversy over the planned commemoration of the Easter Rising. Two months before the commemoration Paisley told a rally of his supporters that 'thirty thousand [visitors from the Republic] are going to invade this city. I want to say as hard as I can, we mean business. We are not going to be hammered into the ground.'[78] When the parade finally went ahead on 17 April 1966, he told another crowd that it represented 'murder, treason and sedition', and warned that Terence O'Neill, by allowing the event to proceed, was endorsing Catholic rebellion. 'Our forefathers suffered from bullets and bombs and won,' Paisley insisted. 'We will do the same.'[79]

On 6 June he organised a march of fifteen hundred people to the annual assembly of the Presbyterian Church in Belfast, protesting against its supposedly 'Romanising' tendencies, and in the ensuing confrontation with the RUC, 'bottles, bricks, rivets and stones' were hurled, the police drew their batons and charged the crowd, the Governor's wife collapsed in shock, and eight people were arrested.[80] Paisley himself was charged with unlawful assembly, and when he appeared in court a month later an estimated two thousand supporters turned up to cheer their champion and throw stones at the police. After refusing to sign a court order to keep the peace for two years, Paisley was sent to prison for three months. This 'martyr's crown' did the preacher no harm among the working-class Unionists to whom he was trying to appeal. Indeed, in the aftermath of his conviction, thousands of supporters rioted outside the gaol, hurling bottles, smashing shop windows and chanting 'Paisley, Paisley', before being repelled by riot police.[81]

Paisley's imprisonment was one of a number of signs in 1966 that, far from improving, the political situation in Northern Ireland was moving towards outright confrontation. After the Crumlin Road riots, O'Neill finally decided to crack down, prohibiting all marches in Belfast for three months and empowering the RUC to ban any meeting of more than three people. In a Stormont debate on law and order the Prime Minister observed that Paisley and his followers called themselves 'loyalists'; but to whom were they loyal? 'To the Queen, whose personal representative they revile? To the United Kingdom, in which their fellow citizens view their conduct with a mixture of ridicule and contempt? To Protestantism, many of whose leaders they have personally abused? I am not prepared to accept lectures on loyalty from such a source.'[82] But Paisley's movement had already acquired momentum. Not only were his church membership lists lengthening by the week, but his political organisation was attracting new recruits.[83]

At the beginning of 1966, together with his protégé Noel Docherty, Paisley had established the Ulster Constitution Defence Committee, a staunchly Protestant organisation which was pledged to 'take whatever steps it thinks fit' to maintain 'Northern Ireland as an integral part of the United Kingdom'. However, this was really a front for another organisation that Docherty had set up, the Ulster Protestant Volunteers (UPV). The whole point of the UPV was to be prepared for any IRA insurgency, for example at the Easter Rising commemorations, and also to show O'Neill that Paisley commanded the streets. Docherty later explained that he and Paisley planned to have 'divisions' or 'cells'

> all over Ulster – in every hamlet, every town and every major city . . . If we needed a demonstration, the support was already organized and sitting there. We could do it at the toss of a coin . . . Paisley was our leader. He was our saviour, our Moses, our champion prepared to resist to the death to oppose the Roman Catholic Church and ecumenism. O'Neill spelled the end of the Ulster we all knew. In a 'doomsday' situation, we felt that in some mystical way, the UPV was going to save Ulster.[84]

What Paisley did not know, however, although he surely must have suspected, was that Docherty also planned to set up a secret armed militia within the UPV. As B Specials, Docherty and his friends already had been issued with Webley pistols and Sten guns; so, he recalled,

> we thought, "Why not have our own – under the floorboard", and that's what we started to do . . . My idea was to have the [secret] cells made up mainly of 'Specials' so that at the snap of a finger or a secret code word we could have had a private army just like Carson did with the signing of the Covenant. So Paisley would have had his own private army and he'd have been a second Lord Carson. That was my idea.

Docherty and his allies spent the spring of 1966 collecting guns and gelignite for their private army. And through these endeavours they came into contact with another Loyalist faction, a hardline group which called itself the Ulster Volunteer Force (UVF) in honour of Carson's volunteers.[85]

The volunteers of 1912 had been drawn from all sectors of Protestant society and led by Northern Ireland's patrician Unionist grandees. But the new incarnation of the UVF was a very different organisation, appealing to a few dozen militant, working-class Protestants who would meet in shabby pubs near the Shankill Road to discuss their fears that O'Neill's reforms were going too far, too fast. Its most prominent early recruit and future commander was Gusty Spence, an incongruously genial character who worked in the declining Belfast shipyards and had learned his Loyalist politics from his father, one of Carson's original volunteers. Like the other men who re-established the UVF in 1965, Spence was a former soldier in the British army. But the UVF was more than a social club for army veterans and military hobbyists: it was explicitly dedicated to the battle against the IRA. As Spence later remembered, they simply did not believe reports that the IRA had disappeared, and in the tense climate of the mid-sixties they were convinced that they had to strike first in case they were taken by surprise. 'There was still a sense, like with the old Ulster Volunteers, that you were for the cause,' Spence said later. 'You would fight and die for it – yes, fight and die for the cause.'[86]

It was a measure of the fevered atmosphere in Belfast in the late spring of 1966 that, even though the Easter commemorations passed off without any significant attack from the IRA, Spence and his associates still went ahead with their rather disorganised and often drunken campaign of petrol bombings against Catholic schools, shops and other institutions. On the night of 7 May a UVF gang decided to target a Catholic-owned pub just off the Shankill Road, and shortly before eleven they threw a petrol bomb through what they thought was the pub window. They had got the wrong address: the bomb actually landed in the house next door, which was rented by Mrs Matilda Gould, a frail seventy-seven-year-old widow, and her son Samuel. As the house went up in flames, Mrs Gould was still struggling to get out of bed; seven weeks later she died of her burns. Her death, the first of what became known as the 'Troubles', was both an appalling crime and a tragic accident. Her killers were Protestants, not Catholics; and in a hideous irony they had murdered one of their own, because Mrs Gould was a Protestant herself.[87]

But the UVF had gone too far to step back now. Two weeks later the Belfast newspapers received a statement from the fictitious 'Captain William Johnson, Chief of Staff of the UVF':

> From this day, we declare war against the IRA and its splinter groups. Known IRA men will be executed mercilessly and without hesitation. Less extreme measures will be taken against anyone sheltering or helping them, but if they persist in giving them aid, then more extreme methods will be adopted . . .

> We solemnly warn the authorities to make no more speeches of appeasement. We are the heavily armed Protestants dedicated to this cause.[88]

On 27 May, five days after the release of their statement, a group of UVF men met in a Shankill pub and decided that their next target would be Leo Martin, a prominent Republican who was reputed to be involved with the IRA. Four men were sent off to the Falls Road, but they could find no sign of Martin. On their way back they bumped into a young engineering worker called John Patrick Scullion, who was wandering home from the pub and drunkenly singing Republican songs. They decided that he would have to do. Scullion, like so many victims of the Troubles, was 'an innocent Catholic who happened to be in the wrong place at the wrong time'. But murder in those days was not the regular occurrence it later became, and when Scullion's body was found the assumption was that he had fallen down drunk and somehow injured himself. Two weeks later he died in hospital, but only a week after that, when another threatening statement from 'Captain William Johnson' appeared in the press, did the police realise that Scullion had been the second innocent victim of the mounting violence.[89]

A month later the Troubles claimed their third casualty. On the evening of Saturday, 25 June three young Catholic barmen were working late in Belfast's city centre. At the end of their shift their manager, Andrew Kelly, suggested that they repair to the Malvern Arms off the Shankill Road, which he knew stayed open after hours. Although the men were Catholics, they had no qualms about drinking in a Protestant area, and the landlord knew Kelly, so when they knocked on the door of the Malvern Arms they were welcomed in. 'It was around midnight,' Kelly remembered. 'There was no problem at all. We had a drink and stayed in our own company. The bar was quite busy that particular night.' What they did not know, however, was that three of their fellow-drinkers were members of the UVF, who had just given up on yet another attempt to find Leo Martin. One of these men was Gusty Spence. Another was Hugh McClean, who later told the police:

> The conversation came up about the religion of these fellows. Spence asked the company if they would be Catholics . . . Spence then went up to the bar beside the four lads to buy a drink. When he returned to our table, he said, 'I've been listening to their conversation and they are four IRA men.' We had some more drinks . . . Spence said, 'These are IRA men, they will have to go.'[90]

After almost two hours the four young Catholics made to leave the Malvern Arms, with eighteen-year-old Peter Ward leading the way. As soon as they got outside there was a sudden series of sharp bangs. Andrew Kelly recalled:

> Somebody gave a signal to start shooting. Peter Ward was hit first. Apparently the bullet went in through the fifth rib and came out through the ninth. He was dead when he hit the ground. I was shot too and dropped down but they kept on shooting at me. There were four gunmen. They didn't say anything. All I remember are the flashes and the shooting.

It was a miracle that three out of the four survived. But even as they were being taken to hospital, Ward's mother was waiting at home for her teenage son to return. She knew that he was likely to stay out late, but as the hours ticked by she became increasingly nervous. Finally, there came the knock at the door: it was her local priest, who said he had some bad news. Later she told a journalist: 'They shot at Peter and Peter fell. It was the UVF shot him and he was shot for nothing, just because he was a Roman Catholic. My Peter had nothing against any religion. He worked with everybody, Catholics and Protestants. Everybody was Peter's friend. He never had no enemies.' Andrew Kelly was similarly bewildered by the attack. 'I don't know why they did it,' he said. 'We were ordinary working people with no IRA connections. We were shot just because we were Catholics.'[91]

Three men – Spence, McClean and Robert Williamson – were convicted of the murder of Peter Ward and sent to prison for almost twenty years. To the vast majority of people in Northern Ireland, both Protestant and Catholic, all three of the summer murders had been deeply shocking, especially as violent crime was virtually unknown in the province. In mainland Britain, however, such was the public indifference to Irish affairs that they barely made it into the newspapers. Since the autumn of 1964 Harold Wilson's ministers had showed no sign of intervening in the politics of Northern Ireland, and at this crucial juncture in the history of the province Wilson and his senior colleagues were completely distracted by the wretched state of the pound and by their own internal faction-fighting. All that Wilson himself could think about was the seamen's strike; he had no time to spare for the affairs of what still seemed a remote outpost of the United Kingdom.[92]

On 28 June, three days after the murder of Peter Ward, Terence O'Neill cut short a trip to France, where he had been commemorating the sacrifice of the original Ulster Volunteers at the Battle of the Somme. In the House of Commons at Stormont he warned that public safety was under threat from 'a very dangerous conspiracy prepared at any time to use murder as a weapon'. There was no connection at all, he said, between the 'authentic and original UVF' and their latter-day successors, 'between men who were ready to die for the country on the fields of France and a sordid conspiracy of criminals prepared to take up arms against unprotected fellow citizens. No: this organization now takes its proper place alongside the Irish Republican Army in the schedule of illegal bodies.' And he offered a bleak warning: 'We stand at the crossroads. One way is the road to progress which has been opening up before us with all its promise of a richer and fuller life for all our people. The other way is a return to the pointless violence and civil strife of earlier years. We must not let anyone push us down that road.'[93]

In London *The Times* praised O'Neill's courage in banning the UVF and remained optimistic about the future. 'One of the happier aspects of Northern Irish politics', claimed an editorial column, 'has been the recent tendency in public life to move away from inflammatory appeals to religious bigotry. On these grounds it is possible to hope that the events of the past week may cause a revulsion in Ulster great enough to move the province nearer to tolerance.'[94] But in Northern Ireland's capital the *Belfast Telegraph* observed:

> Violence has been smouldering in Belfast and district for weeks past, and the point has been reached at which a united effort is called for to prevent crazy people leading the province on a path to self-destruction. No longer may any Protestant wonder where his loyalties lie. They lie on the side of law and order and public decency. They can have nothing to do with those who have been sowing dragons' teeth, and can see how terrible the harvest can be. Ulster is in danger of being thrown back into a dark past by sectarian forces which have long been winked at by many who should know better.[95]

It was an altogether more depressing verdict; but, as events were to prove, it was also a more prescient one.

18

THE YORKSHIRE WALTER MITTY

Ship me somewheres east of Suez, where the best is like the worst,
Where there aren't no Ten Commandments an' a man can raise a thirst;
For the temple-bells are callin', an' it's there that I would be —
By the old Moulmein Pagoda, looking lazy at the sea . . .

Rudyard Kipling, 'Mandalay' (1890)

As the summer of 1966 wore on, it was clear that Harold Wilson's reputation had been severely damaged by the events of June and July. According to the polls, at least four in ten voters were dissatisfied with his performance as Prime Minister, and the criticism from the backbenches and the constituencies showed no sign of abating.[1] Wilson's response was to plan a Cabinet reshuffle. As was becoming clear, summer reshuffles were his favourite way of keeping both his critics and his ministers on their toes.[2] The latest instalment, on the night of 10 August, was particularly important because the administration clearly needed a fresh start. The most important change affected George Brown, whose enthusiasm for the DEA had evaporated since the announcement of the July measures. He swapped jobs with Michael Stewart and therefore became Foreign Secretary. Given Brown's temperament and track record, an office demanding diplomatic sensitivity might not have seemed the obvious destination. Tony Benn recorded that it was 'a great surprise . . . Nobody can make out the reason for the change.'[3]

Wilson's motives were purely tactical. In a private memorandum he admitted that the Cabinet changes 'were designed to solve problems highlighted by the [July] crisis and also to close gates to further political manoeuvring'.[4] The chief problem was James Callaghan's new self-assertiveness, which had manifested itself in the Chancellor's confident forecasts to friends that he would soon be exchanging the burden of the Treasury for the Foreign Office.[5] This infuriated Wilson, who had no desire to be seen 'taking orders from one of my colleagues', and, as he recalled in his memoirs, he therefore decided to do precisely the opposite.[6] 'What I have done this time,' Wilson told his confidants, 'is to surround myself with friends and isolate Callaghan. When people see the result of what I have done they will realize that he has been defeated. Only he doesn't realize it yet.'[7] Twelve months later he admitted to Richard Crossman that his plan had been 'to increase my crown princes from two to six. That was the point of my reshuffle . . . Now I've got seven potential Chancellors and I've knocked out the situation where Jenkins was the only alternative to Callaghan.'[8]

Wilson's increasing suspicion of Callaghan, which was hardly the model for a working relationship between a Prime Minister and his Chancellor, was illustrative of the general mood of the government in the months that followed the July crisis. Indeed, in the aftermath of the reshuffle Callaghan saw Wilson several times and threatened to resign if he were not publicly recognised as the third man in the government, and unless Wilson confirmed the precedence of the Treasury over the DEA. At the same time the Chancellor began to prepare the ground for a possible leadership challenge, assembling a small cabal of junior ministers and strengthening his alliance with Anthony Crosland.[9]

This sort of behaviour was rapidly becoming the rule rather than the exception. Even a cursory glance at the Crossman or Castle diaries from July 1966 onwards reveals an almost unbelievable succession of tantrums, feuds and plots, real and imagined. Richard Marsh, the Minister of Power and a newcomer to the Cabinet, later wrote that he had 'never worked among a group of people who disliked and distrusted each other quite as much as that band of brothers'.[10] In August, for instance, Castle told Crossman that since other cabals were already forming, 'we had better have one of our own. We should be suspected of one anyway. Two or three of us ought to meet more often.'[11] Rather than worrying about the Conservatives, the government's senior ministers were spending more and more time bickering among themselves and jockeying for position should Wilson fall. By January 1968 the situation was so bad that Castle admitted that they spent 'three-quarters of our time in these personal pro and anti intrigues instead of getting down to real jobs'.[12]

The endless plotting from 1966 onwards owed a great deal to the fact that Wilson's own reputation among his colleagues had never been lower. His policy of 'creative tension' had not only failed to deliver the right economic results but had also left him with a very unhappy government.[13] In

December 1966 Crossman remarked to Jenkins that it would be nice to have a clearer vision of their 'long-term plan in Rhodesia'. The Home Secretary replied: 'I'd give anything for evidence that we have a long-term plan for any part of this Government's policy, thank you, Dick.' Crossman agreed that Wilson had no 'vision of a future for his country', no idea of 'long-term economic objectives' and a set of 'extremely conventional' moral values. 'His main aim is to stay in office,' he wrote gloomily. 'That's the real thing and for that purpose he will use almost any trick or gimmick if he can only do it.'[14] Other ministers were even more cutting. Denis Healey thought that Wilson had 'no sense of direction' and 'a capacity for self-delusion which made Walter Mitty appear unimaginative'.[15] And Crosland complained that 'one hasn't the faintest idea whether the bastard means what he says even at the moment he speaks it'.[16]

Many of Wilson's colleagues had always looked down on him as a suburban arriviste, but there was considerable truth in these new complaints. As the months went by, Wilson's optimistic pronouncements did have something of Walter Mitty about them, and his boundless self-confidence led more than one observer to liken him to Mr Toad. After the July crisis, he also appeared to spend inordinate amounts of time moving his ministers to and fro on some imaginary chessboard. The young MP David Marquand was not alone when he wrote of 'the disloyalty and distrust, the leaking and counter-leaking . . . that seemed to spread like some mysterious virus from the Prime Minister to his colleagues'.[17]

This was not simply a question of temperament. In July 1966 Wilson had become convinced, with some justification, that his colleagues were plotting against him, and he never recaptured the breezy self-assurance that had previously been his hallmark. That autumn he muttered angrily to Barbara Castle about 'Ministers who went a-whoring with society hostesses':

> 'Mrs Ian Fleming is another one,' he said darkly. 'If any of you knew your job you would find out who attended that weekend meeting at her place last July when I was in Moscow. And if you were there, Barbara, I will accept your resignation now.' He said he knew what the plot was – to make Jim Callaghan Prime Minister, Roy Jenkins Chancellor, and form a Coalition Government.[18]

Other confidants were given variants of the same rather paranoid story, with Callaghan and Jenkins always identified as the chief conspirators. 'He is convinced that a deliberate plot was conceived to get rid of him', observed Benn. 'He sees it operating like this: Roy Jenkins and his gang decided to get rid of George Brown and make Jim Callaghan No. 2, with a view to getting Roy in as No. 1.'[19]

As if the growing atmosphere of discord and distrust were not enough, the government also had to cope with the consequences of the July measures. In public Wilson exuded an almost preposterous sense of enthusiasm, telling his party conference that the savage cuts gave them 'a once-and-for-all opportunity to break the whole miserable cycle we inherited'. Instead of being 'a rejection of expansion', he said, 'they create an opportunity to continued expansion'.[20] In reality, the deflation package would work only if, as *The Times* had put it, ordinary people had 'no more money to spend'.[21] By November 1966 this was precisely what was happening, and the balance of trade figures showed a marked improvement for the last quarter of the year. However, this was hardly good news for the government's popularity. Production had slowed, high street spending was falling and more than 500,000 people were on the dole. Callaghan argued that the government needed to be even more stringent, and warned that unemployment might need to go higher to forestall another sterling crisis. He also persuaded his colleagues to agree to yet more cuts in public spending, so they decided to raise the charges for school meals and reduce the free milk given to schoolchildren.[22]

These measures took an inevitable toll on the government's political standing. Throughout 1967 polls consistently put the Conservatives five or six points ahead, and the government chalked up a truly wretched record in local elections and parliamentary by-elections. In March the Tories won Glasgow Pollock after a sensational performance by the Scottish Nationalists ate into the Labour vote. In September Labour lost Cambridge and West Walthamstow on swings of 9 and 18 per cent respectively. In November they lost Leicester South-West to the Tories on a 17 per cent swing and Hamilton to the Scottish Nationalists, who had not even run a candidate in 1966, and managed to finish third in Derbyshire South-West. These abysmal performances looked even worse because there was no precedent for humiliation on such a scale. Over its six years Attlee's government had never lost a single by-election, while throughout thirteen years the Conservatives had lost just ten. Now Wilson's government seemed to be shedding seats at the drop of a hat. The local election results were even worse, with Labour losing control of London (for the first time since the

1930s), Bristol, Cardiff, Leeds, Liverpool, Manchester, Newcastle, Nottingham and Wolverhampton. Across the country, the party had not been in such bad shape for thirty years.[23]

Oddly enough, despite the terrible election results, both Wilson and Callaghan still felt that they had grounds for optimism. The harsh July measures appeared to have done the trick, they were close to repaying their loans, and the Chancellor expected the balance of payments for 1967 to be an improvement on previous years. Slowly they began to ease off the brakes: bank rate was steadily reduced, and in the Cabinet there was some discussion of increasing public spending again to try to win back the hearts of the voters. In his annual budget speech in April Callaghan told the Commons that he expected a balance of payments surplus for 1967, a revival of consumer demand and a growth rate approaching 3 per cent. 'We are back on course,' the Chancellor said confidently. 'The ship is picking up speed. The economy is moving. Every seaman knows the command at such a moment. "Steady as she goes".'[24]

At midnight on 31 July 1966, the day after England's footballers were crowned world champions at Wembley, the Colonial Office finally ceased to exist. Founded in 1854, it had once been one of the great departments of state, and at its peak had been the heart of an empire that spanned the globe and controlled the lives of hundreds of millions beneath the British flag. Now, in the words of the *Sunday Telegraph*, 'the greatest imperial responsibility in history' was at an end.[25]

Although Britain's imperial mission, apart from a few loose ends here and there, was now a thing of the past, this did not mean that Her Majesty's Government had given up on the idea that Britain was a world power. Six months earlier the government had published a Defence White Paper reaffirming its commitment to Asia and the Far East and promising to 'maintain a military presence in this area'. Although the White Paper announced some small cuts, it kept open the possibility that Britain might stay in Asia for years to come.[26]

This was consistent with the Wilson government's general approach to foreign affairs. Keen to present himself as a good patriot and a reliable ally, Wilson had no wish to be seen rushing to tear up a hundred years of history. His first two Foreign Secretaries, Patrick Gordon Walker and Michael Stewart, were both similarly committed to the Cold War and to the so-called special relationship with the United States, and his Defence Secretary,

Denis Healey, was a robust intellectual bruiser who had been a Communist at Oxford but had since recanted. 'Hurricane' Healey, as the newspapers nicknamed him, was an intellectual heavyweight and a staunch Cold Warrior. He had even written articles for the *New Republic*, a liberal, anti-Communist American journal, under the Orwellian nom de plume 'Blair Winston'.[27]

Although in 1964 Labour had promised to give up Britain's supposedly independent nuclear deterrent, Wilson and Healey completely ignored this commitment and went ahead with the purchase of Polaris, a nuclear submarine system that Macmillan had ordered from the Americans. This was not a result of American pressure; in fact, the Americans urged them to transfer the Polaris fleet to NATO and give up on the illusion of British nuclear independence. It was more a question of the government's desire to appear strong and patriotic in foreign affairs, a corollary of which was Wilson's sentimental vision of Britain as a moral leader in the developing world.[28] As he told a meeting of the Parliamentary Labour Party in June 1966, 'though he was prepared to withdraw and reduce the number of troops East of Suez he would never deny Britain the role of a world power'.[29]

The phrase 'East of Suez', irresistibly reminiscent of the high days of empire, is from Kipling's poem 'Mandalay'. Although the British presence in the Far East had declined considerably since Kipling's day, when Labour took office in 1964 there were still more British troops east of Suez than in Germany. The biggest British base was in Singapore, with another important installation at Aden for operations in Africa and the Middle East. There were also smaller bases in Bahrain, Borneo, on Ascension Island and in the Maldives; there were military garrisons guarding Hong Kong and Gibraltar; and there were British bases on Malta and Cyprus.[30]

Wilson's reluctance to wind up these commitments was not simply a matter of a 'respectability complex', as some of his critics thought.[31] True, he liked the sense of tradition that came with Britain's world role, he hoped to assert Labour's credentials as a patriotic party of government, and he wanted to honour Britain's commitments to the Americans. But there also appeared to be good military and diplomatic reasons for Britain to keep its foothold in the East, especially since China appeared to be growing both stronger and more volatile. In South Vietnam American forces were bogged down in a brutal war against Communist guerrillas; to the south, British troops were engaged in a bloody campaign to defend Malaysia from

Indonesian invasion; and in southern Arabia British servicemen were facing a terrorist campaign in the streets of Aden.[32] In this context Wilson had no intention of bringing the soldiers home. At the beginning of 1966, when Castle and Crossman asked him about the continued military presence East of Suez, he 'argued passionately that we didn't want to become a "little England"', and insisted 'that we must have a military capability in that area in order to influence the US. It would be wrong to leave the field clear for a clash between the US and China.'[33]

In August 1966 the 'Confrontation' between British and Indonesian troops in Borneo finally came to an end, with the Indonesians reluctantly accepting the existing Malaysian border.[34] The end of hostilities inevitably brought renewed questions about Britain's military presence in the Far East. By this point left-wing backbenchers and some Cabinet ministers were also putting pressure on Wilson and Healey to slash overseas defence spending in order to take some heat off the pound. As early as January 1965 Crossman had complained that ministers were expected to make severe cuts in domestic expenditure even though Britain was still paying an enormous bill for its bases in Hong King, Singapore, Aden and so on.[35] The July crisis only made it more likely that the last vestiges of world power would eventually be scrapped, and by the party conference in the autumn, when there were impassioned calls for defence cuts, the question was no longer whether Britain should leave, but when.[36] Indeed, Wilson himself later admitted that hanging on East of Suez had been one of his worst mistakes, 'and it took a lot of hard facts to convert me. Others of my colleagues, left-wing and pro-European alike, were wiser in their perceptions.'[37]

As Healey points out in his autobiography, given Britain's commitment to Malaysia and Singapore, it would have been highly dishonourable to have pulled out immediately on taking office in 1964.[38] But the financial pressures inevitably took their toll, and after toying with various contingency plans, Healey reluctantly released a radical White Paper to the press in July 1967.[39] British troops would be pulled out of Malaysia, Singapore and the Persian Gulf within ten years, leaving in the Far East just a naval amphibious force and the garrison at Hong Kong. Resources would instead be concentrated on Europe and the North Atlantic alliance; as the White Paper itself admitted, Britain would 'cease to play a worldwide military role . . . We shall increasingly become a European power.'[40] At the time, the announcement was presented as just another modification to British defence policy, and drew surprisingly little press comment. This was good news for Wilson, who knew that the public generally shared his vague, sentimental attachment to East of Suez, and had no wish to be seen as an unpatriotic cost-cutter.[41] But, in Ponting's words, the White Paper was 'an important milestone', marking the end of Britain's history as a major international military power.[42] Many ministers recognised that they had taken a historic and irreversible step. Benn thought that it was 'the death knell of the British Empire east of Suez'. 'East of Suez', observed Barbara Castle, 'is dead'.[43]

Unfortunately, winding up Britain's world role was not quite as simple as that. In Aden, for example, Wilson's government took on an unenviable inheritance. Apart from a splendid setting in a large natural harbour around the crater of an extinct volcano, the South Arabian port was important for two reasons. First, it was a valuable centre for shipping, trade and oil storage; second, it was the perfect location for a military base in a part of the world of increasing strategic significance. In 1963 the Macmillan government had persuaded the feudal sheikhs of the Yemeni hinterland, which covered some 120,000 square miles of desert and mountains, to form the Federation of South Arabia, and had then cajoled the Adenis into joining it. However, this arrangement proved a disaster. The sparsely populated tribal sheikhdoms had little in common with Aden itself, a concrete cauldron of more than 200,000 urbanised and politically aware Arabs. By the time that Wilson and Healey took over responsibility for its affairs the city was paralysed by strikes, while the Marxist National Liberation Front (NLF) had embarked on a bloody campaign of urban guerrilla warfare to try to force a British withdrawal.[44]

Over the next two years, the situation in Aden steadily deteriorated. In 1964 there had been 36 terrorist attacks; in 1965 there were 286; and in 1966 there were 480.[45] One British serviceman later recalled a night when he had been on guard duty at the British base:

> During the evening a steward from the Officers' Mess came out with lemon juice for us and was generally convivial. He was a local Arab and seemed quite happy in his work. I finished at midnight, went down to the armoury to hand in my whistle, rifle and ammunition and was on the way to my billet when there was a tremendous explosion.
>
> The following day I found out that the Arab steward had been wiring up a bomb under the main dining table, timed to explode in the morning, hoping to kill the AOC, Air Vice Marshal Johnnie Johnson and Admiral Le Fanu, when the bomb went off prematurely, blowing him to pieces.[46]

The British troops present were unable to deal with the insurgency. The loyalties of the local police were extremely suspect; arms circulated freely; and attempts to negotiate a political settlement never got anywhere. As the Cabinet Secretary told Wilson in June 1965, the 'ludicrous position' was that 'we are anxious to grant independence as soon as possible but cannot get the people concerned even to discuss the sort of independence they would like to have'.[47] At the end of 1965, after the NLF murdered the Federal Speaker, Britain reverted to direct rule over the colony, but this was obviously no long-term solution. As a visiting minister reported in November, Aden's economy was in ruins, the political system was shattered almost beyond repair, and if Britain wanted to retain the military base, it would have to spend untold millions on maintenance and security. In the circumstances Aden was an obvious place to make savings, and Healey set a target of withdrawal by January 1968.[48]

But pulling out of Aden was not an easy business. In January 1967, alarmed at the increasing numbers of bombings, the British army took over responsibility for internal security, but in the dusty, crowded streets of the city this seemed only to alienate the local population. From the spring onwards there were hundreds of attacks a month, and efforts to negotiate were further frustrated by the appearance of a second nationalist organisation, the Front for the Liberation of South Yemen, which was fighting a bitter struggle of its own against the NLF. By March the date for withdrawal had been advanced to the end of 1967, and the collapse of law and order was well illustrated a month later when the members of a visiting UN delegation were forced to take refuge in their hotel from a mob of angry demonstrators. In the fighting that followed, eight rioters were shot dead and eighteen British soldiers were injured.[49]

Britain's worst day in Aden came on 20 June. It began when a mutiny broke out at the turbulent and ill-disciplined South Arabian Army barracks on the edge of the city, and in the confusion local security forces opened fire on a passing British army lorry, killing eight soldiers and wounding eight more. A group of Adeni policemen then burst into a nearby British camp, shooting an officer, two policemen and a public works employee, before reinforcements arrived to restore order. Word of these events spread to the crowded inner-city district of Crater, and in particular to the barracks of the Armed Police, a local paramilitary organisation which promptly staged a mutiny of its own. They took to the rooftops and opened fire on a passing British Land-Rover patrol, killing seven of the eight soldiers and setting their vehicles on fire. Another patrol then came under attack in its turn; the commanding officer, a Lieutenant Davis, took cover with three of his men while sending the rest of the patrol back for help. Davis and his men were never seen again, and their bodies were never recovered. In the meantime British reinforcements were pinned down by fire from the Armed Police barracks, and finally it was decided to leave the missing men behind, pull all the troops out of Crater and seal off the area.[50]

The violence of 20 June was graphically covered by the British newspapers and television bulletins, and it was widely seen as a national humiliation. The patrols attacked in Crater had contained men from the Argyll and Sutherland Highlanders, who had only just begun their tour of duty in the city, and their commanding officer, Lieutenant-Colonel Colin Mitchell, was furious that he was unable to recover the bodies of his men. Instead, for some two weeks 'rebel flags flew unmolested', in the words of *The Times*, with British troops stationed uneasily on the edges of the district.[51] Within the Argylls there was constant muttering against the politicians who had forbidden them from avenging their comrades, and there was a particular animus against the garrison commander, a staff officer from Whitehall. Mitchell, an aggressive and outspoken officer who had served in Korea, Palestine and Borneo, also had a flair for public relations, which ensured that the Argylls' resentments were regularly aired in British reports.

Eventually, two weeks after the initial mutiny, Crater was retaken. To the displeasure of the Argylls, the plan was for a gradual, three-stage operation, rather than the forthright, sweeping attack they would have preferred, and there was considerable controversy when Mitchell ignored his orders and sent his men streaming into the heart of the city, proudly marching in to the skirl of the bagpipes playing 'Scotland the Brave' in the grandest imperial style.[52] At home, the press loved it. 'Mad Mitch' was 'The Man of the Hour', who had restored British honour over the obstructions of his pettifogging, bureaucratic superiors. As one British woman working in the city later put it:

> When the Arabs took Crater it was a very upsetting time . . . It was a very low time for the Army, but life went on and it seemed to be accepted that we would let the Arabs hold Crater until we moved out. Then one morning I woke up to hear a loud wailing noise, the bagpipes . . . I am a Scot and there was no mistaking it. Over the radio later that day we

heard that the Argyll and Sutherland Highlanders had marched into Crater. 'Mad Mitch' and his men restored our faith in all things British and it did wonders for our morale.[53]

At a time when British public life seemed desperately short of heroes, Mitchell perfectly fitted the bill. Ordered to 'play it cool' by his superiors, who were worried about the effect of his melodramatics on the local population, his response was to appear on British television and tell the audience: 'They know that if they start any trouble again with us, we will blow their bloody heads off.'[54]

For all his popularity with British audiences, Mad Mitch was denied the decoration for his part in retaking Crater that many thought should have been his due. He left the army a couple of years later and became something of a champion for people who felt that the Wilson government was letting Britain down. When the Ministry of Defence announced plans to abolish the Argylls in a forthcoming reorganisation, he denounced the 'disgraceful decision made by thousands of paper tigers in Whitehall' and organised a 'Save the Argylls' petition. In the end the regiment was saved, although Mitchell himself came in for criticism in the House of Commons from Labour back-benchers who accused him of indiscipline and exceeding his orders in Aden. In 1970 he stood for election as the Conservative candidate for West Aberdeenshire, and won.[55]

By this time, however, the British presence in Aden was no more than a memory. Mad Mitch's heroics could not disguise the fact that the end was near; in the Yemeni protectorates the sheikhs were abandoned to defeat by nationalist guerrillas, and by the late summer of 1967 most British troops had been pulled back to Aden itself. In October ministers decided to bring the withdrawal date even further forward; as Crossman put it, 'chaos will rule after we've gone, and there'll be one major commitment cut, thank God!'[56] On 29 November the last British troops sailed out of the city to the sound of gunfire as the competing local factions struggled for supremacy. In the end the NLF won an easy victory, and the transfer of power to the new one-party People's Republic of South Yemen was surprisingly painless.

It was hard to look back with any pride at Britain's disengagement from Aden. True, the decision to cut and run meant that British troops did not become bogged down in a bloody quagmire, like their American counterparts in Vietnam, but many observers felt ashamed to have abandoned Britain's local allies to a repressive Marxist regime. In the absence of more troops and money, however, it is hard to see what Wilson's government could have done differently, and the straitened economic circumstances of 1966 and 1967 meant that they were glad to abandon such a difficult commitment.[57]

The challenge in Rhodesia was rather different. By the middle of 1966 it was quite clear that Ian Smith's regime had dug in for the long haul, and Wilson's hopes for a 'quick kill' had completely evaporated. The much-heralded sanctions had been less than effective, since the Rhodesian economy was still chugging along and oil was clearly reaching the rebels from Mozambique and South Africa. With the sanctions having failed, the only reason to maintain them was as a statement of moral contempt. As long as the Rhodesians were getting their supplies of oil, they could hold out indefinitely. The sanctions might have worked if they had also been applied to South Africa and perhaps Portugal but, given the fragility of the balance of payments, British officials wanted to see more trade with South Africa, not less. Unpalatable as it might have seemed to some of Wilson's critics, there simply was no easy way to bring the Smith regime to heel.[58]

Wilson therefore wearily returned to the negotiating table. At the beginning of December 1966, under the intense gaze of the world's media, he flew to meet Smith on board HMS *Tiger*, cruising off the coast of Gibraltar. This theatrical venue was very much to Wilson's liking, but the Rhodesians enjoyed it rather less, since many of them fell violently ill and relied on seasickness pills to keep their dignity intact. Although the two leaders agreed on a complicated package of Rhodesian concessions, Smith promptly turned it down as soon as he got back home, and Wilson was left looking rather foolish.[59] A few days later Cecil King observed:

> The whole thing was very humiliating for Wilson, who had planned this Churchillian conference on a cruiser. It was to have been a profound secret — only to be revealed when success was announced. In fact, this whole build-up only accentuated the failure. There is one advantage in going so far to meet Smith, and that is that Wilson can fairly claim that he tried very hard.[60]

After the debacle of the *Tiger* talks, matters carried on much as before, with the Rhodesians blithely evading the sanctions and the British vainly protesting that the measures would work eventually. Two years later Wilson decided to have another go, and in October 1968 he and Smith were reunited on another warship, HMS *Fearless*, although the boat was anchored this time to avoid more problems with Rhodesian seasickness. The talks dragged on for five days, but the result was the same. This was probably just as well, because during the negotiations Wilson had made concessions on the question of majority rule that would have horrified many of his Cabinet colleagues.[61] But when Smith returned home he once again made it clear that there was no common ground. In March 1970 the Rhodesian Front threw off the remaining ties to Britain and declared Rhodesia a sovereign republic based on the principle of white rule. Only in 1979, after a long guerrilla war against black nationalists, was the regime finally forced to give in.

In truth, Wilson had been wasting his time. The Rhodesian regime never gave any sign of accepting a settlement that promised black majority rule, so his attempts at personal diplomacy were always doomed to fail. Only military invasion could realistically have reversed UDI, but it would have been enormously expensive and could have provoked a wider war with South Africa. As one historian puts it, 'it simply was not worth running such grave risks, especially when all long-term analyses suggested UDI would eventually fail anyway'.[62] But Wilson took the blame for Britain's palpable loss of credibility on the world stage and growing unpopularity in the newly independent states of the Commonwealth. Indeed, there could hardly have been a more obvious and embarrassing symbol of the British government's fading reputation, military weakness and international impotence than its failure to control its own colonists.[63]

During Wilson's talks with the Rhodesians, he always took care to keep the White House informed of the latest developments.[64] While he needed American support for sanctions, they wanted him to stand firm in support of the war in Vietnam, which was provoking fierce anger in British radical circles. Wilson knew that if he publicly condemned the war, he would be jeopardising American cooperation over Rhodesia as well as the stability of the pound and the survival of the Atlantic alliance. On the other hand, he was coming under growing pressure at home to take a moral stand against the war. 'We can't kick our creditors in the balls,' he angrily protested to Frank Cousins after the latter had appealed to him to denounce the conflict. 'Why not?' Cousins asked.[65]

Although Wilson was often portrayed by his critics as President Johnson's grovelling lickspittle, their relationship was much less comfortable than many people imagined. 'I suppose I'll have that little creep camping on my doorstep again!' Johnson remarked when he heard that Wilson had called the 1966 election.[66] Yet although there was certainly no great rapport between the two men, and Johnson never concealed his irritation at Wilson's endless twisting and cadging, they did generally manage to get on quite well. Johnson sympathised with Wilson over his domestic troubles and recognised why the British leader felt unable to support him more fully in Vietnam; indeed, after one meeting the President told an adviser, 'I really do like that man.' In retirement he even invited Wilson to come and stay at his ranch in Texas, which hardly suggests great mutual antipathy.[67]

The slightly awkward nature of their relationship, however, occasionally resulted in some bizarre moments when one man went completely over the top in praising the other. The most famous example was in July 1966, when Wilson went to Washington at the end of a two-month period in which he had been badly bruised by the seamen's strike and the brutal cuts imposed to support the pound. Nevertheless, he arrived in the American capital in predictably cheerful form; the *Washington Post* reported that he was 'in his best bulldog mood', and the *Sunday Telegraph* called him 'cocky, cheeky, ebullient . . . as if he had just arrived hot foot from some tremendous victory'.[68]

In this mood Wilson proceeded to a lunch Johnson had organised in his honour, where the President delivered an encomium that was variously described as 'unexpected', 'extraordinary' and 'miraculous'. After opening with a few references to Shakespeare, Milton and Nelson, Johnson solemnly declared:

> England is blessed with gallant and hardy leadership. In you, Sir, England has a man of mettle, a new Churchill in her hour of crisis.
> She is blessed with a leader whose own enterprise and courage will show the way. Your firmness and leadership have inspired us deeply in the traditions of the great men of Britain.[69]

In any context this would have been lavish praise; in the circumstances it sounded like sarcasm. The general reaction of the British press was so derisive that Johnson later demanded to know what he had said that was so controversial. As Anthony Howard put it in the *Observer*, Wilson 'came in looking like an impoverished Mayor of Toytown and went out with all the swagger of a Tamburlaine'.[70] 'Recollected in tranquillity,' wrote the

Telegraph's correspondent Peregrine Worsthorne, 'it makes the flesh creep, and it is difficult to know whether to be more shocked by the Texan's assumption that Britain could be conned in this way, or by Mr Wilson's fantastic failure to dissociate himself and his colleagues from these grotesque analogies.'[71]

Ever since the Second World War the United States had occupied an uneasy place in the affections of the Labour Party. On the right of the party there was considerable, even obsessive, admiration for all things American, the assumption being that the United States was more progressive, equal, free and ambitious than Britain. On the left, however, there was still a wide streak of hostility towards a country associated with immaturity, aggression and materialism. Labour's election victories had brought a new generation to the backbenches and, paradoxically, the size of his majority created fresh problems for Wilson. His parliamentary managers operated an extremely lax regime, which meant that the new intake had few qualms about voting against the government. In March 1967, after sixty-two MPs abstained on the government's White Paper on defence, Wilson made an ill-judged remark that although every dog was allowed one bite, if it became a habit then the dog's owner might think twice about renewing its licence. The outcry was immediate. 'It was very insulting to imply that we were all dogs and he was our trainer,' wrote Benn.[72] But it was indicative of the worsening relations between Wilson and his own backbenchers. 'How's your handicap, Harold?' asked the Pakistani president after the 1966 election, while practising his putting on the Chequers carpet. Without missing a beat, Wilson replied: 'Up from 3 to 97.'[73]

The Vietnam War did not really become a serious issue until after the 1966 election. In June American bombers struck at the major North Vietnamese cities of Hanoi and Haiphong, and the outcry forced Wilson to admit his 'regret' that the Americans had acted in this way. Even this anodyne statement had been cleared with the White House beforehand.[74] But to many of his backbenchers, and to growing numbers of students and radical activists, Wilson's support for the war was worse than a mistake: it was a crime. There was nothing he could do to appease his critics: in their eyes the war was morally wrong, and therefore he should put his calculations aside and take a stand.[75]

It was not only the radical left that opposed the war. By the summer of 1966 only one in three Britons supported it, and almost half thought that the Americans should immediately withdraw their troops from Vietnam.

More disturbingly for Wilson, more than four in ten voters also thought that Britain was wrong to back American policy.[76] Although opposition to the war was later associated with the young and above all with students, these numbers clearly included many people who were neither. However, many historians tend to overstate the depth and importance of British opposition to the war. Polls consistently found that, unlike students, ordinary voters did not care very much about foreign affairs and were much more concerned about the economy, the cost of living, immigration and crime. Foreign affairs played no significant role in the general elections of the sixties and seventies. The paradox is that although popular images of the sixties often refer to mass protests against the Vietnam War, it was simply not an issue that greatly concerned the majority.[77]

The great nightmare for many Labour activists was that one day Wilson would announce that as a gesture of solidarity with their American allies, he had decided to send a detachment of troops to South Vietnam. Britain did provide aid of other kinds, such as providing covert help with intelligence and communications, training American officers in jungle warfare, supplying them with naval and airborne weapons, and allowing them to use the port facilities at Hong Kong. However, Wilson never committed a single regular soldier to the war and it was testament to his tactical skill that he still managed to keep on good terms with the Americans. In April 1967 Johnson told him that Britain's financial troubles would be over if he sent just two brigades. Given the state of the pound and his reliance on the special relationship in other areas, it would have been understandable if Wilson had given in, but he declined the President's offer. At the time he was under intense pressure from domestic critics who attacked him for being too supportive of the war; most modern historians, however, recognise that his refusal to send British soldiers to their deaths in Vietnam was one of his most significant achievements as Prime Minister.[78] 'Enormous efforts were made by the Foreign Office, the Treasury, the Americans to get Britain wholly to identify with the war and express this with a military presence,' observed Peter Shore two decades later. 'Harold did give support, but he never sent a single soldier.'[79]

In an attempt to win over his critics at home, Wilson devoted considerable energy to the search for a peace deal in Vietnam. He believed that he was the one international politician trusted in both Washington and Moscow, and therefore saw himself as an 'honest broker', although it was never clear that anybody else agreed with him.[80] In June 1965 he came up with an intricate scheme whereby four Commonwealth Prime Ministers, led by Wilson himself, would embark on a sort of grand tour of the relevant capitals in search of a compromise. As soon as the Americans agreed to the plan, however, the North Vietnamese promptly rejected it.[81] Wilson's colleagues were bemused that, with so many domestic challenges to face, he chose to devote so much time to these enterprises. Crossman, for instance, complained that the Commonwealth scheme was 'yet another of his stunts'.[82]

Despite the failure of the Commonwealth peace initiative, Wilson, rather incredibly, still believed that he could find the road to peace in Vietnam, and schemes came and went with depressing frequency. The low point came in February 1967, when the Soviet Prime Minister Alexei Kosygin visited London and Wilson decided that he would use their meetings to produce his great breakthrough. He secured American backing for his negotiations, although Johnson was extremely dubious whether anything would come of them, and the Americans sent over a senior official, Chester Cooper, to act as an intermediary. However, after Wilson had spent a great deal of time getting Kosygin to agree to a plan approved by the Americans, he was mortified to learn from Cooper that Johnson had changed his mind and wanted much tougher terms.

This was the prelude to a sequence of events ludicrous even by the standards of Wilson's government. Kosygin, thinking that they had an agreement, was about to board a sleeper train to Scotland when a Downing Street secretary dashed on to the platform to hand him the text of the revised peace proposal. Meanwhile, at No. 10, Wilson was 'beside himself with fury and frustration', and Cooper later recalled that in two decades of diplomatic life he 'had never seen anyone quite so angry'. As soon as George Brown heard the news he unleashed a barrage of abuse against Wilson, accusing him of self-deluding incompetence, and, to Cooper's embarrassment, Wilson then completely lost his temper. 'Wilson and Brown just went at each other, it was just terrible', Cooper remembered. 'Brown accused Wilson of being too premature; and that time and time again during these discussions Wilson didn't inform Brown as to what was going on; Brown on at least three occasions resigned as Foreign Minister.'[83] Wilson later explained that he was so frustrated because he had been convinced that his great diplomatic coup was at hand, but this was a preposterous claim.[84] 'Wilson is wrong,' Cooper commented after reading his memoirs. 'He didn't have peace within his grasp, he was always overly optimistic about it.'[85] The best indication of the Americans' attitude to all this was captured by a telephone conversation between Cooper and Walt Rostow, one of Johnson's chief foreign policy advisers. Cooper complained that both he and Wilson had been misled. 'Well,' said Rostow coldly, 'we don't give a goddamn about you, and we don't give a goddamn about Wilson.'[86]

Once again, it was hard to understand how Wilson managed to delude himself into spending so much time on an initiative that was never likely to succeed. The fact was that the Americans neither needed nor particularly wanted Wilson's help in finding a solution to the Vietnamese stalemate, and Johnson never set much store by the various British peace wheezes.[87] As the President well knew, a serious peace initiative would come through Soviet mediation, if at all, rather than through the unlikely and fractious diplomatic double act of Wilson and Brown.[88] The only real result of these schemes was that, taken in conjunction with Wilson's regular bulletins about the imminent collapse of the Rhodesian regime, the recovery of the economy and other prospective joys, they confirmed the caricature of the 'Yorkshire Walter Mitty'.[89] Edmund Dell's verdict is not entirely unfair:

> The time and effort expended on his excursions into international diplomacy were more likely to make him a laughing stock than win him a reputation for statesmanship. When, as he frequently did, he informed the House of his latest conversation with President Johnson, his critics would wonder whether there had, in fact, been anyone listening at the other end of the telephone. There is no evidence, however, that the performance of his government would have been improved if domestic policy had enjoyed more of his attention.[90]

After 1967 Wilson's interest in bringing peace to Vietnam distinctly cooled. The British government continued to lend public support to the American war efforts, while occasionally distancing itself from particular military offensives.[91] The Prime Minister, though, had little room for manoeuvre. If he had condemned the war, the White House would have taken no notice and the consequences for Britain could well have been severe. If the Americans had withdrawn their support for the pound, there would have been unhappy consequences for public spending on things like pensions, housing, health, education and even student grants.[92] As Ben Pimlott points out, few of the critics who blamed him 'simultaneously for helping the Americans abroad, and not doing more to help the poor at home, ever came to terms with the bleakness of the choice'.[93]

Wilson's conduct of British foreign policy after August 1966 was made rather more complicated by the presence at the Foreign Office of an increasingly turbulent George Brown. At one of his first official functions, a Commonwealth Prime Ministers' conference, Brown was observed by Barbara Castle 'rolling around sozzled' and complaining about his new job. 'I hate it,' he told her disconsolately. 'I didn't want it. It was an order: this or I go.'[94] As the months went by, Brown proved so unreliable that Wilson felt compelled to run foreign policy himself, and where sensitive issues like Rhodesia and Vietnam were concerned, he endeavoured to involve his Foreign Secretary as little as possible.[95]

Brown's extraordinary period at the Foreign Office got off to an appropriate start when, on his very first day, he came in through the wrong door, missed the crowds of photographers waiting at the main entrance, and therefore had to go back and start all over again.[96] This set the tone for a performance as Foreign Secretary that was so supremely ill-judged that it generated a host of anecdotes unmatched in post-war political history. Every morning Brown's private office assembled to hear the latest gossip, and one of them later recalled that if the Foreign Secretary had been at a function the previous evening and no stories had been received, 'there would be a certain anxiety – perhaps he had done something so awful that no-one dared tell us'.[97] Incidents that would have destroyed the careers of lesser politicians were, in Brown's case, merely part of the daily routine, and his officials were forced to accustom themselves to his characteristic mix of tantrums, minor sexual harassments and drunken outrages of all kinds.

One overseas excursion that went down in Whitehall legend was Brown's behaviour at a banquet held in his honour by the Belgian government in 1967. Brown's staff had been keeping a close eye on him, although he seemed happy enough 'conducting a boisterous conversation with the Prime Minister and the Foreign Minister'. But then, as one of his officials recalled, Brown made his move:

> Just as the party was breaking up, we noticed to our horror that George was not in his place. We saw him at the main door leading out of the dining room, and he was waving his arms in the air and saying 'Wait! I have something to say!' I thought, oh God, this is going to be terrible, and it was.

> We rushed over to him just as he was saying, 'While you have all been wining and dining here tonight, who's been defending Europe? I'll tell you who's been defending Europe – the British Army. And where, you may ask, are the soldiers of the Belgian Army tonight? I'll tell you where the soldiers of the Belgian Army are. They're in the brothels of Brussels!'
>
> We tried to grab his arm, and someone said, 'Come on, George, we're off – the party's over,' and we got him out of the room. But by that time the Belgians, who'd been shifting uncomfortably from one foot to another during this extraordinary outburst, were all absolutely frozen with embarrassment.

For any other politician, this would have been action enough for one night, but not for Brown. Returning to the British Embassy, he installed himself in the sitting room of the Ambassador, Sir Roderick Barclay, and complained: 'There's no fire in this room. I'm cold. I want a fire and I want a large whisky and soda.'

> Roddie got up and went over to the drinks tray and poured George a whisky and soda. George said, 'Fire, I want a fire.' The Ambassador said, 'I'm terribly sorry, Secretary of State, but it's getting on for midnight, all the servants have gone, so it would be rather difficult.' 'Where's your wife?' asked George. 'Well, she's in bed as she normally is at this time.' 'Get her up,' he said. So poor Lady Barclay had to come down and lay a fire. What an extraordinary day: it started badly, and ended worse.[98]

On another sortie abroad Brown told an ambassador's wife that she was too 'old and unfashionable' to represent Britain. Then there was the occasion he accidentally ate a bowl of artificial grapes while on a visit to the United Nations, or the time he dismissed Valéry Giscard d'Estaing as a 'Frog'.[99] However, perhaps the most famous Brown anecdote is possibly apocryphal, and certainly several different versions circulated within the Foreign Office. The story had Brown visiting a Latin American capital city, perhaps Brasilia, for trade talks and then being invited to a diplomatic reception for a delegation from Peru. According to one eyewitness, Brown had already knocked back a few drinks and was 'much the worse for wear'. He was driven through an extremely stormy night towards the reception, his progress being slowed by the rain and heavy traffic, and finally arrived to discover a lavish party in full swing:

It was really beautiful – I think only the Latin Americans still do it that way: all the military were in full dress uniform, and the ambassadors were in court dress. Sumptuous is the word, and sparkling. As we entered, George made a bee-line for this gorgeously crimson-clad figure, and said, 'Excuse me, but may I have the pleasure of this dance?'

There was a terrible silence for a moment before the guest, who knew who he was, replied, 'There are three reasons, Mr Brown, why I will not dance with you. The first, I fear, is that you've had a little too much to drink. The second is that this is not, as you seem to suppose, a waltz the orchestra is playing but the Peruvian national anthem, for which you should be standing to attention. And the third reason why we may not dance, Mr Brown, is that I am the Cardinal Archbishop of Lima.'[100]

When Brown was not busy on the Brazilian dance floor, his energies were devoted to the cause of European integration, which had been close to his heart for two decades. Britain, he thought, faced a historic choice between, on the one hand, association with the United States and maintenance of her world role, and on the other, entry into the Common Market and withdrawal from East of Suez.[101] His views fitted in well with a growing feeling among young officials in the Foreign Office that Europe was both more interesting than the Commonwealth and held out the prospect of greater international influence. British diplomats had for many years been suspicious, even dismissive, of the six Common Market countries. But now, having taken into account the relative successes of the Continental economies, the Foreign Office was on the verge of a Damascene conversion.[102]

Meanwhile, Wilson's own views were also beginning to shift. Withdrawal from East of Suez inevitably implied that a world role was out of the question; the choice apparently lay between relative isolation as a satellite of the United States or association with Britain's chief trading partners. Wilson's move towards the Common Market was therefore partly a belated recognition of the realities of diplomatic strategy and international trade. At the same time, the Commonwealth was becoming increasing fractious, business leaders were pushing for closer links with Britain's neighbours, and Edward Heath was threatening to turn the European issue into the Tories' pet project. Finally, Wilson hoped that European entry would dispel the impression of disappointment and drift that had marked his government's activities in so many other areas. Just like Macmillan in the early sixties, he saw it as a bold statement of purpose that would transform his personal standing and the fortunes of his administration. Macmillan's bid had ended in tears after President de Gaulle's veto in January 1963. Wilson, of course, was hoping for a different result.[103]

It is often suggested that the decision to go for European entry was a result of the crisis of July 1966, but in fact Wilson's mind had probably been made up months beforehand.[104] He did not outline his plans to the Cabinet, however, until 22 October, when he summoned them to Chequers for a day-long meeting. Some ministers, like Healey and Castle, were opposed to another bid for entry; others, like Callaghan and Crossman, were wobblers; the majority, spearheaded by the enthusiastic Brown and Jenkins, were in favour. Keen not to lose any of the sceptics, Wilson moved towards a decision by stealth. They never discussed the principle of European integration, but concentrated on the practicalities in particular areas, and Wilson's tactical skill ensured that when the application was finally made, not one senior figure resigned from his Cabinet.[105]

As in the early sixties, the major obstacle to British entry was the French President Charles de Gaulle. Wilson was confident that he could persuade de Gaulle to change his mind, but others were not so sure. Healey and Crossman both predicted that de Gaulle would once again veto Britain's application, and in July Cecil King, whose journalists were bringing pessimistic reports from the Continent, recorded that the French had 'made it clear that there is no prospect of admitting Britain to the Common Market at this stage. They are not convinced that the Government means business, and there is no question of us joining while we are so deeply in hock to the Americans.'[106]

Wilson told his ministers that he had thought of a way to allay these fears: 'a tour round Europe by George Brown and himself to visit the chief capitals and try to clarify the doubtful issues'. Crossman recorded that this 'gimmicky' scheme left him 'disconcerted and surprised', and he quietly suggested that it might be better to leave the negotiating to professional diplomats. 'I am a professional,' Wilson insisted defiantly. 'I *am* professional, Dick.'[107]

The 'Probe', as it was officially known, began in Rome on 15 January 1967 and continued, on and off, for two months. With the notable exceptions of Wilson and Brown themselves, observers generally agreed that it was a complete waste of time. Hugh Young calls it 'the acme of Wilsonian politics': 'It applied to Europe several of the defining traits of this remarkable leader. It put on show his fascination with tactics, his professional vanity, his impressionable mind, the grandeur of his self-confidence, his refusal to acknowledge the realities of international power. It was at times comical, at others almost calamitous.'[108]

The most important meeting was that with de Gaulle in Paris on 24 January. Brown was on his worst form, affectionately calling the proud French head of state 'Charlie', and, at a reception at the British Embassy, publicly unleashing a string of loud and foul-mouthed insults at the ambassador's wife. On the flight home he wandered into the secretarial quarters and amused himself by trying to chat up the girls.[109] Meanwhile, Wilson, having set out to win round de Gaulle, seemed only to have converted himself into the country's greatest champion of the Common Market. He had been hesitant before; now he was positively evangelical. On his return he delightedly told the Cabinet that de Gaulle had been greatly impressed by his rendition of the statistics of British grain production. Healey asked how the President had communicated his interest. Slightly bemused, Wilson replied that de Gaulle had listened in rapt silence. 'Perhaps he was bored,' said Healey, to ill-concealed snorts of laughter.[110]

At home, Wilson's bid to join the Common Market faced remarkably little opposition. Heath and the Conservatives had already proclaimed themselves in favour; the City and most businessmen were strong supporters; and every major newspaper, with the exception of the *Daily Express*, favoured the application.[111] Wilson's chief negotiator, Lord Chalfont, assured the Council of Europe that public support for entry was running high. '[The] New Britain', he said, 'is not Little England', and he waxed lyrical about the European sentiments of 'our bankers, our artists, our university lecturers, our doctors and other professional men', not to mention 'the young people of Britain':

> I hope no one will be deceived by the trivialities of Carnaby Street and much of 'Swinging London'. Behind all this there is, rising in my country, a generation of young men and women, tired of humbug, angry with social inequality, sickened by war, and resolved to do something about it. To these young people the future that lies within . . . the European idea is as exciting as anything that has happened in the long and vivid history of Britain.[112]

This was rubbish, of course. A few artists, doctors and university lecturers might have been excited at the thought of European entry, but most people were almost completely indifferent. In May 1967, after Wilson had concluded his Probe, he announced the beginning of a 'Great Debate' at home. The next issue of *Private Eye* caught the general feeling with one of its typically irreverent covers. 'COMMON MARKET: THE GREAT DEBATE BEGINS' read the caption, above a photograph of a group of solid citizens fast asleep in the park.[113] Opinion polls suggested that there was no real consensus one way or the other, and they fluctuated as wildly as the country's financial fortunes. At first there appeared to be a strong majority in favour of entry, but support steadily declined as the decade went on. In July 1966, after the seamen's strike and the sterling crisis, seven out of ten voters supported joining the Common Market. In April 1967, however, after Wilson had finished his Probe, only four in ten were in favour. By the end of the sixties this had fallen to a feeble two in ten.[114]

Meanwhile, Wilson himself had returned from his Probe full of enthusiasm for Britain's European destiny. At the end of April the Cabinet approved a formal application, and a few days later the Commons overwhelmingly endorsed the bid.[115] When Crossman asked him how he saw Britain's chances, Wilson was confident of success. 'Well,' he mused, 'perhaps in the last resort I shall have to see General de Gaulle alone and spell out to him the real alternatives. Either we come right in, I must say, or we are hostile members of an American bloc.' Crossman was appalled. 'Harold's illusions of grandeur scare me stiff,' he confided in his diary. 'If he tries to talk to de Gaulle in this particular way it won't come off any better than his "straight talks" with LBJ when he thought he was speaking on equal terms.'[116]

Crossman's fears seemed to be justified when, on 16 May, de Gaulle told reporters that Britain would be welcome only when 'this great people, so magnificently gifted with ability and courage, should on their own behalf and for themselves achieve a profound economic and political transformation which could allow them to join the Six Continentals'.[117] However, Wilson's balloon was not punctured so easily.[118] In a private letter to Brown he described the French President as a 'lonely old man . . . slightly saddened by the obvious sense of failure and, to use his own word, impotence that I believe he now feels'. De Gaulle, he thought, might be opposed to British entry, 'but if we keep firmly beating at the door . . . I am not sure that he any longer has the strength to keep us out'.[119]

When Wilson returned from Paris, he had commissioned an expensive set of patience cards with the Cross of Lorraine printed on the back, which he intended to give to de Gaulle as a present at their next meeting. But there was no next meeting. On 27 November de Gaulle once again vetoed Britain's application to join the Common Market. The rebuff could hardly have been more humiliating for the government, or for Wilson personally, and in the circumstances the gift was hardly appropriate. Two years later, after de Gaulle's retirement, it was decided to send the cards as a present for his eightieth birthday, but he died, while playing patience, just forty-eight hours before the big day.[120]

As so often, cruel reality had intruded on Wilson's boyish hopes. The Common Market application did have some positive repercussions: as in the early sixties, Britain's negotiators had made a good impression on their European counterparts, and it had been another important step on the road that led, at last, to entry in 1973. But from Wilson's point of view the entire exercise had been an embarrassing failure to set beside his negotiations over Rhodesia or Vietnam. To his critics, he looked less like a professional statesman, sailing proudly on the high seas of international diplomacy, and more like a self-deluding fantasist, paddling out in his little dinghy towards inevitable disaster.[121]

PART THREE

THE END OF ILLUSIONS

19

CARRY ON ENGLAND

SIR JAMES BOND: It's depressing that the words 'secret agent' have become synonymous with 'sex maniac'. Incidentally, where is my namesake?
HADLEY: We've had to take him off the board, sir; he's now doing television.

Casino Royale (1967)

On the afternoon of 9 July 1968, the Queen arrived at the South Bank to open the new Hayward Art Gallery. The opening ceremony was one of the grandest cultural events of the year, teeming with 'museum directors, art dealers and pundits', and, one report commented wryly, 'even a sprinkling of artists'.[1] Like its neighbours on the South Bank, the building was a temple to the concrete fashions of the day. The architecture critic of *The Times* drew attention to its 'somewhat aggressive informality of style', but nevertheless thought that it was 'agreeably picturesque'; many ordinary visitors, however, thought that there was quite enough concrete on the South Bank already.[2] But the opening exhibition, devoted to the French painter Henri Matisse, was a triumph, drawing rave reviews in the press and attracting two thousand visitors a day, comparable only to the lure of the Henry Moore exhibition across the river at the Tate.

'Both of these magnificent exhibitions', commented *The Times* a few weeks later, 'have been organized by the Arts Council.'[3] To anybody who followed the arts in Britain during the sixties, this would have come as no surprise. The chairman of the Arts Council, Arnold Goodman, had a close relationship with the Wilson government and helped to support a network of regional cultural groups as well as programmes of touring exhibitions, concerts and performances. Although some commentators deplored state subsidies for the arts, the opening of the Hayward had been almost entirely attributable to Arts Council sponsorship, and there was an undeniable sense that the arts were at last being taken seriously in the corridors of power.

Thanks to the expansion of leisure, earnings and higher education, as well as the sponsorship of successive governments, the sixties were years of new opportunities and booming audiences. The Royal Ballet was regarded as perhaps the best dance company in the world; the Royal Opera and English National Opera were performing longer seasons than ever; and, thanks to the likes of Benjamin Britten, Michael Tippett and Peter Maxwell Davies, British classical music enjoyed an excellent international reputation. More books were being published than ever before, and any complete list of novelists and poets active in the sixties would be both long and impressive, including established talents like Kingsley Amis, John Betjeman, Anthony Burgess, William Golding, Graham Greene, Philip Larkin, Doris Lessing, Iris Murdoch and Anthony Powell, as well as rising stars like J. G. Ballard, A. S. Byatt, Margaret Drabble, John Fowles and Ted Hughes.[4]

An excellent example of the cultural efflorescence of the sixties, and one often cited by historians, was the theatre. The threat of censorship by the Lord Chancellor was finally lifted in 1968, and this coincided with an impressive surge in theatrical talent. The young meteors of the fifties, like John Osborne and Arnold Wesker, had now been joined by a 'second wave' of creativity from Alan Ayckbourn and David Mercer to Joe Orton and Tom Stoppard.[5] Not for nothing did the American magazine *Life* comment in May 1966 that 'London's excitement draws famous, adventurous directors'; it even added that the National Theatre, which was then just three years old and based at the Old Vic, was 'already the finest and most versatile acting company in the world'.[6]

Under the direction of Laurence Olivier, rather eccentrically assisted by the critic Kenneth Tynan, the National Theatre almost immediately won an international reputation for daring and accomplishment. In its first few seasons, its company included the likes of Robert Stephens, Frank Finlay, Joan Plowright, Albert Finney, Maggie Smith, Michael Gambon and Derek Jacobi, a collection of young talent unmatched anywhere in the world.[7] Early productions like *Othello* and *The Royal Hunt of the Sun* (both 1964) were spectacular critical and commercial successes. Olivier's performance in *Othello* was judged by the Italian director Franco Zeffirelli to be 'an anthology of everything that has been discovered about acting in the last three centuries', while the *New Statesman* concluded: 'We have seen history'.[8] *The Royal Hunt of the Sun*, meanwhile, was considered one of the most ingenious productions of modern times, using all the resources of the theatre to tell the story of the conquistadors. Bernard Levin, writing in the *Daily Mail*, called it 'the finest new play I have ever seen'.[9]

Yet, despite the success of the National Theatre, as well as the Royal Shakespeare Company and other companies up and down the country, the great names of British theatre in the sixties were not ones that aroused great devotion or even recognition on the streets of Dudley or Dundee. The theatre was still something of a minority interest for the wealthy and well educated, as indeed were the ballet, the opera, classical music and the fine arts. In Angus Wilson's novel *Late Call*, Sylvia Calvert goes to see a school production of John Osborne's play *Look Back in Anger*, directed by her ever-trendy son Harold. She finds it hard to follow: 'she couldn't quite get what sort of people they were; the room was so shabby and yet they talked so well'; she is shocked by the violence of the language; and she notes that in the audience 'there were glum, disapproving faces'.[10]

In reality there were far more Sylvias than Harolds. Most avant-garde plays of the early sixties did not go down very well with audiences, and many were forced to close early because of poor box-office receipts. In general, theatregoers stuck to the tried and trusted, like comedies, detective stories and musicals. *Oliver!* ran for a staggering 2618 performances from June 1960, while *Charlie Girl*, which opened in December 1965, clocked up 2202 unbroken performances over more than five years. By comparison, the likes of Harold Pinter or John Osborne appealed to a minority of a minority.[11] When the aspiring Labour politician Roy Hattersley went to see a production of *Look Back in Anger* at the Chesterfield Repertory Theatre, 'there was not an angry young man in the house. Indeed, the only emotion expressed all evening was the rapture which followed an announcement made by Jimmy Porter after the final curtain came down. "Don't forget, folks. We've got something special for you next week – Agatha Christie's *Murder on the Orient Express*."'[12]

Since most writers about the sixties like to emphasise innovation, rebellion and nonconformity, the enduring success of things like *Murder on the Orient Express* is a source of some frustration to them, if they mention it at all. Discussing what he calls 'the masses', Jonathon Green condescendingly remarks that 'their real tastes remained predictable and grimly banal', an assertion which wilts before any serious enquiry.[13] There was no single, homogeneous audience: as John Russell Taylor wrote in 1971, British culture appealed to 'an infinitude of smaller, more specialized, more choosy publics'.[14] This is not to say that there was no common culture: thanks to the improved mobility and communications of the post-war years, people in different areas did share similar tastes, whether for football or *The Forsyte Saga*, easy listening or Alistair MacLean.[15] But there was so much variety that to talk of popular culture as 'predictable and banal' is simply absurd. What was predictable about the Beatles, or *Doctor Who*, or Larkin's poetry, or *Monty Python's Flying Circus*?

The most popular and influential source of entertainment in the late sixties, of course, was the television. Such was the impact of the new medium that by 1967 nine in ten households had a television set. The only homes without one were those suffering from either 'extreme deprivation or self-conscious intellectualism'.[16] In the same year the BBC proudly estimated that on an average day more than half of the population watched one of their programmes, with millions more preferring the more populist fare on ITV.[17] According to another survey, a staggering 97 per cent of British adults watched at least twelve hours of television a week, encompassing everything from news programmes and documentaries to game shows, football and science fiction.[18] As one middle-class viewer later put it, the living room 'became the television room . . . and everything started to give way to television'.[19]

As an essentially private, domesticated form of entertainment, the television was superbly suited for the affluent, 'home-centred' society. All the same, its appeal might have been expected to wane as its initial novelty value began to wear off, and this put more pressure on the BBC and ITV to develop more exciting programmes, from *The Prisoner* to *Monty Python*. The biggest innovation, however, was the introduction of colour in July 1967. The BBC's engineers had been working on the project for some time, but when they learned that the French were planning to begin colour broadcasts in the autumn, they moved their own date forward to the second week of Wimbledon, which was an excellent showcase for the new medium.[20] Over the next few months the BBC showed just five hours of colour a week, including classical concerts and football matches. Most regular programmes, however, were still made in black and white. Only in January 1970, for instance, did *Doctor Who* switch to colour.[21] But the take-up was much better than many people had expected. By 1972, more than one and a half million colour sets were in use, and by 1978 there were more than eleven million.[22]

In the late fifties many intellectuals had been alarmed by the enormous success of ITV, with its commercials, American imports and cheap game shows. But by the end of the sixties there were far fewer complaints. Thanks to the fierce competition between the BBC and ITV, producers and directors were regularly reaching new levels of accomplishment, and some of the programmes of the late sixties drew lavish praise. In May 1964, for example, BBC2 showed what was then considered the finest factual programme ever made, a documentary history of *The Great War*. Three years later the same channel surpassed itself with Kenneth Clark's series about the history of art, *Civilisation*. The day before the final episode was due to be shown, *The Times* even devoted its main leader to the success of the series, commenting that the BBC had 'shown what can be done when the sights are set high and kept high'.[23] Still, like the great achievements of the theatre in the sixties, *Civilisation* was essentially a minority pleasure: it drew much smaller audiences than, say, *Steptoe and Son* or *The Black and White Minstrel Show*.[24]

The most distinctive television genre of the sixties was the semi-fantastic adventure series. According to one estimate, between 1959 and 1974 there were thirty-two different series based on the adventures of spies, sleuths and secret agents, some of which proved very successful indeed. *Danger Man* ran from 1960 to 1967, *The Saint* from 1962 to 1969, and, most successful of all, *The Avengers* chalked up 161 episodes between 1961 and 1969. Other series, like *The Champions* and *Department S*, were more ephemeral but they were still fondly remembered more than three decades later. Unlike some of the films of the period, they were not merely weak imitations of the Bond extravaganzas; indeed, the likes of *Danger Man* and *The Avengers* began well before the cinematic release of *Dr No*. Nevertheless, especially in the later sixties, the influence of Bond became ever more apparent, not only in their design and editing, but in their plots and themes.[25]

In general, these series were carefully balanced between psychological realism, science fiction and fantasy. Like the Bond films, they wallowed in patriotism, modernity and consumerism, taking in exotic locations, bizarre villains and stunning girls along the way.[26] Many critics felt that they gave too much emphasis to fine living at the expense of character and content: the *Sunday Telegraph* complained that *The Saint* was 'glossy British rubbish with Roger Moore, who looks like an ad for after-shave', while the *Daily Mail* remarked that the heroes in *The Champions* looked like 'characters in the commercials when they've got hold of the right laxative or hair shampoo'.[27] *The Avengers* even featured costumes by designers like John Bates and Pierre Cardin, and was the first British television series to employ an 'exploitation manager' to sell product placement. Certainly the two heroes seemed to enjoy an existence of conspicuous luxury, spending their days drinking champagne in elegant London flats and driving their expensive cars, a Lotus Élan and a vintage Bentley, to and from their various adventures.[28]

The ITV series *The Saint*, staring Roger Moore as the dashing Simon Templer, was a particularly striking example of the link between the secret agent and the affluent society. Templer owns a mews house in London and an apartment in New York; he drives a white Volvo sports car, stays in the most luxurious foreign hotels and generally wallows in 'a fantasy of high living and expensive consumption'.[29] This evidently struck a chord with audiences all over the world: *The Saint* was sold to more than eighty countries, turning Moore into an international star. Critics often dismissed him as little more than a walking eyebrow, but as Virginia Ironside wryly pointed out in the *Daily Mail*, he was ideal for the part:

> He has excellent eyebrows that operate independently and give him a range of expression from quizzical to puzzled to amused to mildly surprised . . . He also has astonishing hair, so much of it that you can count each individual strand, and that never gets out of place even after the most strenuous fight. He never goes to bed with girls (at least, we never see it), and he is so gentlemanly about money you wonder how he can afford to run his smart sports car. Of his kind of hero, he is one of the smoothest and the best.[30]

It was no surprise that when Sean Connery finally handed in his licence to kill, Moore was selected as the new James Bond, with splendid results.

A far better series than *The Saint*, however, was *The Avengers*, which was the first British show to be shown at peak time on an American network. At its height it was regularly watched by thirty million viewers in seventy countries.[31] Its ethos, like that of the Bond films, was a combination of patriotic traditionalism and swinging modernity. The male lead, John Steed (Patrick Macnee), is a debonair gentleman adventurer, a former military officer and the self-confessed 'black sheep' of an aristocratic family. Although he wears Pierre Cardin suits, his ubiquitous bowler hat and umbrella reflect his reassuringly old-fashioned tastes. The show's publicity notes explained:

> In his tastes and character he embodies tradition and the qualities that people overseas have come to associate with the British way of life –

gracious living, a London house full of family heirlooms and handsome antiques, a cultivated appreciation of food, wine, horseflesh and pretty women, proficiency at ancient and gentlemanly sports such as fencing, archery and polo, exquisite tailoring, a high-handed way with underlings and an endearing eccentricity which manifests itself in such preferences as driving a vintage Bentley convertible and fighting with swordstick, rolled umbrella or any handy implement rather than the more obvious weapons such as guns.[32]

By contrast, Steed's female partners were much more modern figures. Until 1964 his principal companion was Cathy Gale, played by Honor Blackman and described by the *TV Times* as a woman of 'great beauty and intelligence, noted for her wide knowledge and wider acquaintances – and a passion for wearing leather clothes'.[33] The character's other notable feature was her judo expertise, which, together with her anthropology degree and witty self-confidence, made her much more independent and self-consciously modern than the Bond girls. ABC's publicity put her at the forefront of 'the new international fashion in women who dress and fight like men as well as enjoying the more conventional privileges of emancipation'. Her replacement, Emma Peel (Diana Rigg), was another modern heroine, dressed in the latest Op fashions and supposedly leading 'the streamlined life of an emancipated, jet-age woman'. And, like Cathy, Emma can handle herself in a fight since she is a dab hand at karate. She also publishes articles in scientific journals and is easily Steed's equal in courage and repartee.[34]

The Avengers tended to skirt around controversial contemporary issues, preferring to take refuge in a careful blend of nostalgia and modernity. On the one hand, it revelled in eccentric traditions, from steam trains and gentlemen's clubs to Steed's bowler hat and umbrella; on the other, it enthusiastically embraced the white heat of Harold Wilson's technological revolution, from laboratories and power stations to Emma Peel's swinging mini-skirts. This idealised, exaggerated Britishness was partly designed for the American market, but it also played well with domestic audiences. The managing director of ABC boasted that *The Avengers* was 'one hundred per cent British in conception, content, casting and style', while the series's most accomplished writer, Brian Clemens, described it as 'a never-never world ... the England of "Is there honey still for tea?" that people imagine existed even if it didn't'.[35]

By the time *The Avengers* switched to colour in 1967, its ethos was becoming increasingly surreal. Its designers were clearly inspired by Pop Art, with bright primary colours used for the sets and costumes, and the action was shot in an increasingly comic-book fashion. The plots, too, became ever more bizarre: a marriage bureau is merely the front for an organisation of assassins; a concentration camp is hidden inside a luxury hotel; a satellite-tracking station is concealed beneath a golf course; a group of dead fraudsters are found alive and well underneath a funeral parlour. Indeed, *The Avengers* went so far into the realms of pastiche that many critics regard it as a 'camp' or even 'post-modern' programme.[36] George Melly, for example, thought with its 'sexual ambivalence', 'balletic' violence and 'poetic and absurd' plots, *The Avengers* was 'the most consistently intelligent use of the pop camp tradition'.[37]

While television thrived during the sixties, the same could not be said of British cinema. In 1950 British audiences had been the most reliable and enthusiastic in the world. But as more people were able to afford their own homes, so they preferred to spend their money on domestic improvements, appliances and household goods. At the same time, as women went out to work, so the attendance at afternoon matinées dwindled. Since the rise of the television cut even deeper into film attendance, it was no surprise that these were wretched years for the film industry.[38] By 1970 many people never went at all, audiences were made up of teenagers and film fanatics, and thousands of cinemas had been demolished or converted into bingo halls.[39]

This background of decline explains the feverish enthusiasm for novelty and fantasy in the cinema of the mid-sixties. The outstanding cinematic success story of the day was the James Bond series, which peaked between 1964 and 1966 with *Goldfinger* and *Thunderball*, both of which broke box-office records wherever they played.[40] Portrayed with wry charm by the unknown Scottish actor Sean Connery, Bond was the ideal role model for the Swinging Sixties, a classless hero moving through a world of foreign travel, consumer luxuries and disposable pleasures. Like Harold Wilson, Bond looked 'towards the future rather than the past . . . the very model of the tough abrasive professionalism that was allegedly destined to lead Britain into the modern, no illusion, no holds-barred post-imperialist-age'. He was the ideal hero not only for Wilson's meritocratic New Britain, but for the supposedly liberated audiences of Swinging London.[41]

The American studio responsible for the Bond films, United Artists, had cannily established a London division in 1961, hoping to take advantage of cheap British production costs. They were also responsible for two of the other influential films of the period, *Tom Jones* (1963) and *A Hard Day's Night* (1964). Despite being superficially very different — an adaptation of an eighteenth-century comic novel, and a musical about the Beatles — both deliberately broke with the gritty, even depressing realism of the British New Wave of the late fifties, and both pioneered the distinctive, hyperactive cinematic style of the mid-sixties. While *Tom Jones* boasted plenty of slapstick, silent film captions and asides to the camera, *A Hard Day's Night* experimented with surrealistic dream sequences, freeze-frame close-ups and deliberately jerky editing.[42] And both were enormously successful. *A Hard Day's Night* broke all records for a pop musical, while *Tom Jones* won four Academy Awards and, having cost just $350,000, raked in an estimated $40 million.[43]

All things British were suddenly extremely attractive to American producers, and by 1965 Hollywood seemed to have decamped to London en masse. In 1964 two out of every three British releases had been made with American money; by 1966 it was three out of four; and by 1967 it was more like nine out of ten.[44] All of this money went into trying to reproduce the success of *Goldfinger* and *Tom Jones*, and over the next few years the British film industry churned out a series of increasingly gaudy, flamboyant and irreverent films. *The Knack*, *The Ipcress File*, *What's New, Pussycat?*, *Darling* and *Help!* all came out in 1965; the trend continued with *Alfie*, *Georgy Girl* and *Modesty Blaise* in 1966; and *Blow-Up*, *Here We Go Round the Mulberry Bush*, *Far from the Madding Crowd* and *Smashing Time* were released in 1967. All of these films were aimed at young audiences; all placed a heavy emphasis on fantasy and flair; and all were closely linked with the mood and milieu of Swinging London. The influence of the Bond films was palpable not only in their subject matter, but in their appearance. As one historian puts it, 'form was all. They revelled in bright colours, flip dialogue, spectacular stunts, speed, style and sensation.'[45]

Style and sensation were central to the cinema of the Swinging Sixties. Comedies like *The Knack*, *What's New, Pussycat?* and *Alfie* trumpeted their freedom from cinematic conventions through devices like rapid cutting, exaggerated slapstick and deliberately histrionic acting.[46] They were also notable for their obsession with sex, which allowed directors to create an atmosphere of fun-loving bawdiness and appeal to an audience in their teens and twenties. The most striking example was *What's New, Pussycat?*, another United Artists picture, which boasted the talents of Peter O'Toole, Peter Sellers and a host of other fashionable names from Ursula Andress to

Woody Allen.[47] O'Toole plays a fashion editor who has become addicted to sexual conquest, while Sellers, in one of his most extravagant performances, plays a deranged Viennese psychiatrist in a velvet suit and a ludicrous wig. Crammed with visual jokes, dreadful puns and double entendres, and culminating in an incoherent go-kart chase outside a French chateau, the film was not well received by the critics. The *Sunday Telegraph* thought that it had 'all the pace, wit, thrills, inventiveness and sheer high-spirits of a Bank Holiday traffic jam', while American critics called it 'salacious', 'leering' and 'over-sexed'. However, the emphasis on sexual comedy and the promise of exaggerated performances by Sellers and O'Toole clearly appealed to audiences, and by the end of 1965 *What's New, Pussycat?* was one of the most successful films of the year.[48]

Six months later Philip French spoke for growing numbers of his colleagues when he complained that British films 'looked increasingly as if they had been made under the personal supervision of the Regius Professor of Applied Camp at the Royal College of Art'.[49] The obvious contemporary example, which had been released at the end of May, was *Modesty Blaise*, based on a popular comic strip about a jewel thief and starring the ultra-fashionable Terence Stamp and Monica Vitti. As one critic wrote in the *Monthly Film Bulletin*: 'If a social historian were faced with the task of citing the film most representative of the age, *Modesty Blaise* would be a strong candidate.'[50]

Modesty Blaise was an expensive spy spoof at a time when Bondmania was at its height. It wallowed in luxury and consumption, it was full of Pop Art designs and Op Art costumes, and it was shot and edited in a deliberately madcap manner. And it was a disaster, with an unfathomable plot, incredible situations and an uneven tone lurching from heavy-handed seriousness to exaggerated slapstick. The film had cost almost ten times as much to make as the likes of *The Knack* and *Darling*, but most critics found it at best irritating and at worst unwatchable. When it was first shown at the Cannes Film Festival, *Modesty Blaise* was booed by the audience, while *The Times* commented that it was 'less a spoof than a limp-wristed kind of fairy tale, utterly cluttered up with homosexual malice, artsy gift-shop décor and the same old gagging gadgetry on which the Bondmen have patents pending'.[51]

The disaster of *Modesty Blaise* was the first sign that the bubble was about to burst. In the spring of 1967 yet another Swinging London film, Michelangelo Antonioni's cerebral *Blow-Up*, fared equally poorly with the critics. Although Antonioni had tried to make a film about the alienation of modern life, press releases bragged about his attention to 'the world of fashion, dolly girls, pop groups, beat clubs, models, parties and above all, the "in" photographers who more than anyone have promoted the city's new image'.[52] But most reviewers were left distinctly unimpressed. In *The Times* John Russell Taylor remarked that *Blow-Up* was 'ideally a film to talk about at smart parties, but when the party is over, disappointingly little remains'. Many reviewers admitted that their dislike of *Blow-Up* was rooted in their boredom with Swinging London and everything associated with it.[53] As Alexander Walker puts it, Antonioni's timing was terrible. The swinging scene had been done to death, and now most people were 'heartily sick of it'.[54]

By the end of 1967 the British film industry was in serious trouble. Pictures that might have done well a year or two earlier, like *Far from the Madding Crowd* and *Smashing Time*, were now dismissed as tired clichés.[55] The more serious problem, however, was that Hollywood was about to pull the plug. Between 1966 and 1970 almost every major American studio lost hundreds of millions of dollars thanks to their investment in disastrous British-made pictures, from *Star!* and *Goodbye, Mr Chips* (both 1968) to *Dr Doolittle* and *Battle of Britain* (both 1969). As one Paramount executive put it, 'when the money began to vanish' the American studios simply packed up and went home.[56] From the British point of view, this was an utter catastrophe. The domestic film industry had become almost entirely dependent on Hollywood's largesse, and when the investment dried up, so did the opportunities. By 1970 only 97 British-funded films were produced in Britain; by 1975 it was 81; and by 1980 it was down to a pitiful 31, the lowest rate of production since the Edwardian era.[57]

There were few mourners for the cinema of the Swinging Sixties. When Penelope Houston looked back on the decade at the end of 1970, she remarked that most British films had felt like yet 'another jaded party, dragging exhaustedly on into the night in its bedraggled fancy dress surrounded by its odds and ends of boutique bric-a-brac, and deaf to the ambulance sirens coming louder up the street'.[58] Film historians have tended to agree with her.[59] Jeffrey Richards, for example, deplores the 'hedonistic self-indulgence', 'increasingly frenzied saturnalia', and 'flamboyant, unrealistic decorativeness' that typified the era, and points out that its films lasted much less well than their supposedly boring predecessors of the forties and fifties.[60] And it is telling that the British cinema of the sixties did not produce a single director who could be ranked alongside the cream of his international contemporaries. There was no British equivalent of Federico Fellini, Akira Kurosawa or Ingmar Bergman, and there was certainly no successor to Alfred Hitchcock and David Lean.[61]

The disasters of the mid-sixties meant that by the end of the decade the British film industry was reduced to formulaic low-budget horror films and bawdy comedies. Both genres had originally emerged during the late fifties, when producers were eagerly hunting for novelties to lure audiences away from their living rooms and back to the cinema. At the time, the chief censor John Trevelyan encouraged a new climate of relative lenience, which provided a further boost to the general spirit of daring and innovation. The studios not only had the freedom to turn out gritty, realistic films like *Room at the Top* and *Saturday Night and Sunday Morning*, but felt able to push the boundaries a little further in their ostensibly 'popular' output, too.

The obvious example was the experience of the Hammer studio, which until the late fifties had been known for low-budget and fairly obscure comedies and thrillers. In 1955 the studio had an unexpected hit with *The Quatermass Xperiment*, an adaptation of the BBC's successful science-fiction series, and from this point onwards Hammer began to concentrate on pictures that articulated similar themes: resentment and distrust of authority, fear of science and technology, individual alienation and social disintegration.[62] Since these issues were usually explored in the context of an extremely exciting, sensationalist narrative, it is not surprising that Hammer's approach paid off. In 1957 the studio had its first major hit with *The Curse of Frankenstein*, which cost just £65,000 to make but recouped £300,000 in Britain, £500,000 in Japan and more than £1 million in the United States. This adaptation of Mary Shelley's Gothic novel established the template for subsequent Hammer horror films, boasting a severe, rationalist protagonist, played by Peter Cushing, who epitomises the frigid arrogance of modern science.[63]

Critics regularly deplored the appeal of the Hammer pictures, largely because they broke with the established conventions of cinematic taste and ignored the strictures of down-to-earth realism to which many film reviewers clung. *The Times*, for example, thought that *The Curse of Frankenstein* would attract viewers with 'a morbid taste for the revolting' and argued that 'the world has supped full enough of horror'.[64] 'The accent [is] on blood, blood and more blood', the same paper's critic lamented when discussing *Kiss of the Vampire* in 1964.[65] Audiences, on the other hand, clearly enjoyed Hammer's films, which cost little to make but usually generated a handsome profit. In an era when cinema audiences often consisted almost entirely of teenagers, Hammer had precisely the right blend of suspense and sensation.[66]

But this is not to say their horror films offered nothing more than escapist thrills. According to film historians like Marcia Landy, newspaper critics were wrong to dismiss the Hammer pictures out of hand. In fact, they reflected everything from contemporary panics about sex and violence to fears of the dehumanising effects of technology or the decline of traditional values in the affluent society. Authority is usually suspect: scientists are deranged or malign; aristocrats are degenerate and corrupt; institutions are riddled with vice. Revealingly, the two famous villains of the Hammer pictures, Peter Cushing and Christopher Lee, both spoke with a clipped upper-middle-class accent and appeared thoroughly patrician. Both men, whether playing Dr Frankenstein, Dracula or some other evildoer, were well suited to appear as representatives of knowledge, money and power – all of which, in the world of Hammer horror, carried sinister associations.[67]

Yet, however much the Hammer films functioned as criticisms of science, technology and the affluent society, their appeal was really based on sensuality and suspense. Older horror films had been content to dwell in the shadows, but thanks to the development of colour and the greater lenience of the censor, Hammer were able to indulge themselves, draping their narratives in deep, sensuous reds and purples. Sex was a vital element in Hammer's success, quite explicitly so in later films like *The Vampire Lovers* (1970), *Lust for a Vampire* (1971) and *Dracula AD 1972*.[68] Many commentators think that this reflected contemporary fears about changing gender roles and rampant female sexuality: one critic, for example, suggests that 'carnal desire is presented as dangerous', and that 'it is only with the destruction of monstrous or deviant sexuality that social order and normality can be reinstated'.[69]

This is all very well, but there is no doubt that what really pulled in the audiences, especially the teenage boys who most admired the Hammer pictures, was the promise of naked female flesh. In a more permissive cinematic climate, sex and sensuality were ideal ways to attract a young audience, especially as television broadcasters were much more constrained. This largely explains the success of the other British genre that survived into the 1970s: the low-budget farce, epitomised above all by the work of the director Gerald Thomas and the producer Peter Rogers.

Thomas and Rogers's *Carry On* series, which began in 1958, went through various incarnations, and the first entries, like *Carry On Sergeant* and *Carry On Nurse*, were much less risqué than their successors. These early films were generally set in public institutions, and embodied a cheerful spirit of resistance to authority. Their cheeky working-class heroes find their pleasure inhibited by middle-class bureaucrats; they rebel, often in a cack-handed fashion; and at the end of the film the characters unite in some collective enterprise, whether carrying out their own hospital operation, undermining a school inspection or capturing a gang of robbers. These early films were therefore very similar to other comedies of the era, notably the Boulting brothers' satires *Private's Progress* (1956) and *I'm All Right Jack* (1959), the four *St Trinian's* films (1954–66) and the films of Norman Wisdom, who forever subverts upper-class politeness and pomposity. All of them held up patrician authority figures to general ridicule, and all of them celebrated the plucky individual at the expense of the intrusive post-war state.[70]

It was not until 1963, when Talbot Rothwell took over the writing duties, that the *Carry On* series descended into outright bawdiness. From this point onwards, whether the films were parodying box-office hits or merely satirising the National Health Service, they were essentially bawdy farces, drawing their characters and situations from music-hall traditions and seaside postcards. As one historian puts it, their audiences were immersed in 'a world of fat ladies and overflowing bosoms, nervous honeymoon couples and randy jack-the-lads, chamber pots and bedpans'. And although the *Carry On* films would not have been possible without the new indulgence of the censor, they nevertheless represented a revival of old comic conventions, occupying 'territory mapped out in the 1930s and 1940s by the likes of Frank Randle and Max Miller'.[71] In place of refinement, education and elevation they promised 'sexuality, physicality, fun'; in a world where sexual conventions seemed to be under threat, they sought refuge in the traditional vulgarity of masculine working-class humour.[72]

In 1968 John Russell Taylor recalled a recent conversation with a French film buff who wanted 'to see a film which represents all that is most reliable and permanent in popular British taste'. 'There could only be one answer to that,' Taylor observed: *Carry On Doctor*. The comedy, he wrote, was firmly rooted in the traditions of Donald McGill's seaside postcards, 'more scatological and anatomical than sexual':

> There is much play with bed-pans, chamber pots, enemas and the like, and the injuries which bring characters into the hospital are likely to be banal without any noticeable eroticism. Sex, of course, does pop up from time to time, but only in the form of entirely harmless verbal doodling: most of the sexual jokes consist of *double entendres* which could easily be

converted into McGill postcards, thus: Doctor (considering a leg in plaster): 'It's high time you had it off.' Patient (eyeing pretty young woman in next ward): 'I've just been thinking the same.'

What was really striking, as Taylor recognised, was that this kind of humour still resonated in 'what we are always being told is a wholly immoral, liberated, permissive society'. The jokes, he pointed out, 'all turn on the assumption that if someone says "bum" out loud the walls will fall down. Ludicrous in 1968. Or is it? Millions of filmgoers prove that it is not, and that, permissive society or not, the old taboos continue as much in force as ever.'[73]

Although cultural critics regularly complained that commercial television and lowbrow films were eroding the intellectual fibre of the nation, if book sales are any guide, people were reading more than at any time in history. Record numbers of different books were being produced, too, rising from 25,000 titles in 1961 to 33,000 in 1970.[74] According to surveys, women read much more than men, the latter preferring to spend their free time in the garden or watching television, and the professional classes read at least twice as many books, per person, as the working classes.[75] But the sensational success of public libraries meant that more books were available to all, regardless of sex, income, age or education. The Public Libraries Act of 1964 compelled local authorities to provide 'a comprehensive and efficient service', and over the course of the sixties spending on public libraries more than doubled. As a consequence, borrowing increased dramatically: whereas in 1959 libraries had issued 397 million books, by 1970 they were issuing more than 600 million.[76]

What really changed the face of publishing and reading in the sixties was the rise of the paperback. Until 1960 or so, when writers and readers thought of books they thought of hardbacks, and since hardbacks were expensive, readers tended to borrow them from the library. Paperbacks had been around for a long time, but only with the advent of new technology in the fifties did they really become respectable. What one writer calls 'the democracy of cheaper books' was at hand.[77] Mills and Boon led the way, switching from hardbacks to paperbacks at the beginning of the sixties.[78] Other publishers then followed suit, and by 1970 readers were buying almost ninety million paperbacks a year, accounting for 40 per cent of all publishing revenue.[79]

The market leaders were still Penguin, who bravely abandoned their old colour-coded system in favour of Art Nouveau, Pop Art and even photographic covers designed to shock and intrigue. The new covers were an excellent way of freshening up the company's image, and they helped to account for Penguin's sensational success over the course of the sixties. In 1960 there had been some 6000 Penguin paperbacks in print; ten years later there were more than 37,000, accounting for almost a third of all paperback sales. But Penguin's dominance did not go unchallenged. Pan, in particular, were not far behind, with around 20 million sales a year to Penguin's 29 million. Pan also boasted the outstanding publishing phenomenon of the sixties, Ian Fleming's James Bond thrillers, which appealed through a blend of patriotism, consumerism, travel and sexual freedom. Of the first eighteen books to sell a million copies in Britain, no fewer than ten were Bond titles.[80]

Fleming's biggest rival was Alistair MacLean, who was well on his way to becoming, by the late seventies, the bestselling British novelist of all time. A Scottish schoolteacher who had served in the Royal Navy during the Second World War, he burst into the publishing scene in 1955 with *HMS Ulysses*, which sold a record 250,000 hardback copies in six months. His books were much more old-fashioned than the Bond stories, being unashamed tales of patriotic derring-do, usually populated by male casts in enclosed naval surroundings. Sex and luxury, the two staples of Bond's adventures, were almost entirely absent: MacLean's protagonists were morally rigorous heroes in the old imperial mould, appealing above all to conservative, middle-aged male readers. Year after year another MacLean book topped the bestseller lists, from *Fear Is the Key* and *Ice Station Zebra* to *Where Eagles Dare* and *Force 10 from Navarone*, and no fewer than eighteen of them sold more than a million copies.[81]

While men eagerly devoured the latest Fleming or MacLean, millions of women rushed to buy the latest bestseller by Georgette Heyer, Agatha Christie or Barbara Cartland, in descending order of sophistication. Christie's detective thrillers appealed to men too, of course, although romantic fiction was overwhelmingly a female genre. In 1967, for example, Mills and Boon had a mailing list of 9000 names, of which only two were male. But what all these books had in common was that they promised escapist thrills without greatly challenging the reader's assumptions and values.[82] Not all readers, however, liked them, and the sheer variety of bestsellers in the sixties gives the lie to claims that popular culture in general was predictable or banal. Penguin's biggest sellers, for example, included *Lady*

Chatterley's Lover, Animal Farm, Room at the Top and even *The Odyssey*.[83] And as John Sutherland points out, W. H. Smith's bestseller lists for the sixties contained plenty of surprises, from Giuseppe Tomasi di Lampedusa's novel *The Leopard* to Graham Greene's *The Comedians*, and from Iris Murdoch's *The Nice and the Good* to J. R. R. Tolkien's *The Lord of the Rings*.[84]

The obvious implication of all this is that popular tastes in the sixties were at once more diverse and more conservative than is often imagined. A similar picture emerges if we look at popular music. Although nostalgic accounts of the sixties present the period as the 'pop decade', the importance of pop music is often overstated. It mattered a great deal to many teenagers, of course, and many social commentators cast John Lennon and Mick Jagger as personifications of cultural change. But often overlooked is the fact that the music market peaked in about 1964 and then began to decline. By 1966 singles sales had fallen back to the level of the mid-fifties; and by the end of the decade they were well below even that. By 1969 only one single and one album were being sold in Britain per person each year.[85]

In later years the teenagers of the sixties often remembered their formative years as the decade of the Beatles and the Rolling Stones. This is true up to a point, in that these characters monopolised the attention of the press, but, again, it is easily overstated. Although the Beatles were, by general consent, the most influential pop outfit of the time, they nevertheless alienated much of their original audience when they moved to a more psychedelic style after 1965. When their improvised film *Magical Mystery Tour* was shown on BBC1 on Boxing Day in 1967 it received a staggeringly hostile reception. The *Mirror* called it 'piffle' and 'nonsense', the *Express* termed it 'rubbish', the *Mail* labelled it 'appalling', and the *Daily Sketch* thought that 'whoever authorised the showing of the film on BBC1 should be condemned to a year squatting at the feet of the Maharishi Mahesh Yogi'.[86] Irate viewers besieged the BBC switchboard to complain, and as one critic told his readers: 'It's been a long day's night since any TV show took the hammering that this Beatles fantasy received by telephone and in print'.[87] Even Paul McCartney admitted that 'if you look at it from the point of view of good Boxing Day entertainment, we goofed, really'.[88]

The dreadful reception of *Magical Mystery Tour* illustrates the fact that, for all their successes, the Beatles were never universally or unconditionally popular. Plenty of people hated them; millions more, probably a majority, were generally indifferent to them and their music. And the more the

Beatles departed from their conservative image of 1963, the more people disliked them. Even in the *NME* readers' letters expressed their disapproval of the band's bohemian turn. One reader from Belfast lamented 'their new "arty" image' and complained that 'Strawberry Fields Forever' was 'pseudo-intellectual, electronic claptrap'. Another wrote that it was 'impossible to compare [their old] songs like "And I Love Her" and "Yesterday" with the way-out rubbish on the *Sgt. Pepper* disc'. And a third, commenting on the single 'Hello Goodbye/I Am the Walrus', called it 'the biggest load of rubbish I have ever heard'. 'If this is progressive,' he added, 'then the pop scene must be going backwards . . . No doubt the Beatles' reputation will carry this one up the chart, but it is sickening to see Lennon and McCartney wasting their time on this drivel.'[89]

The limits of the Beatles' popular appeal were never more apparent than in February 1967, when, to the horror of their admirers, 'Penny Lane/Strawberry Fields Forever' was beaten to the number one spot by Engelbert Humperdinck's rousing ballad 'Release Me'. Although this is often cited as one of the great injustices of the sixties, the fact is that Humperdinck clearly appealed to a large swath of the population, almost certainly including many people who did not buy singles. Like some musical Alistair MacLean, he enjoyed enormous success because he offered older listeners something familiar, comfortable and undemanding. Indeed, although teenagers overwhelmingly preferred pop music to any other kind, the same was not true of their elders. Show tunes, light classical music, jazz and cabaret music all thrived during the sixties, appealing to middle-aged listeners because of their associations with affluence, sophistication, glamour and romance. It was no accident that the most successful chart act of the sixties was not the Beatles, but Cliff Richard.[90]

Even the appeal of Cliff, though, paled by comparison with one of the unlikeliest cultural success stories of the decade: the musical soundtrack. As one writer puts it, the most popular group of the sixties was not the Beatles or the Stones, but 'Soundtrack, featuring Original Cast'. The most popular Beatles' album, *Please Please Me*, spent forty-three weeks in the Top Ten. By comparison, the soundtrack of the American musical *South Pacific* spent forty-six weeks at *number one*, and more than three years in the Top Ten. Yet even this was dwarfed by the outstanding musical product of the sixties, Rodgers and Hammerstein's *The Sound of Music*. The two versions of this phenomenally successful musical – a Broadway recording from 1960 and the film soundtrack of 1965 – remained in the Top Ten of the album chart for more than five years, and the film soundtrack held the number one spot for a staggering 69 weeks. By October 1968, *The Sound of Music* had sold more than two million copies in Britain alone.[91]

With more than seventeen million sales worldwide by 1975, *The Sound of Music* easily outdistanced the Beatles' leading album, *Abbey Road*, which sold just nine million. Indeed, it even sold more copies than the Beatles' two most popular albums combined, while other musical soundtracks chalked up sales figures that easily eclipsed any pop or rock record of the sixties. Cinema audiences, too, adored *The Sound of Music*, and for five consecutive years Gallup polls found that it was Britain's favourite film.[92] As the historian Dave Harker observes, it was clearly the most popular musical work of the period, not only in Britain but throughout the English-speaking world.[93]

The success of *The Sound of Music* reinforces the point that there was much more to British cultural life in the sixties than soft drugs and long hair. It appealed to middle-aged and elderly listeners as well as to teenagers and children, and it projected a familiar, even conservative vision of the world, based on romantic love and family life. In a period of change it offered a sense of reassurance and stability, not only in its plot but also in its musical style. These are not values appreciated by most people who write about popular music, and this explains why they ignore it. But these were the values of millions of British record-buyers in the Swinging Sixties, and this explains why they bought it.

20

THE POUND IN YOUR POCKET

> Nobody knows what Harold Wilson's doing now, and nobody will know until he's done it. Well, I'd rather have him than Ted Heath. I'd sooner have Labour than the Tories, but I don't like either of them really. None of them seem to me to be doing as much as they could for the real benefit of the people. We want a party of truth, whether it's Communist, Catholic, Tory or anything.
>
> John Lennon, 19 May 1967

Harold Wilson had always prided himself on his good relationship with the press. From the beginning, he liked to call journalists by their Christian names, regularly saw them for briefings and general chit-chat, and even had them round to Downing Street for drinks and a quiet word. He knew how important the media had been in building up his image in 1963 and 1964, and he keenly studied the newspapers for evidence of his changing reputation. At night he would take the first editions of the next day's papers up to bed; then, over the breakfast table, he would read the later editions of the same newspapers. No Prime Minister since the war had a better idea of what each paper and each columnist could be expected to say about a particular issue.[1]

The corollary of this was that when Wilson's relationship with the press began to sour, he took it very hard. By the middle of 1967, hurt by the gathering tide of criticism, he was developing something of a persecution complex and saw some correspondents, notably Nora Beloff of the *Observer*, as personal enemies bent on his destruction. Barbara Castle noted that in May 1967 Wilson was 'writhing with annoyance at *The Times*', which had drawn attention to the opposition of a few dozen backbenchers to his Common Market plans. When he threatened to cut off *The Times*' correspondents, Castle was horrified. 'Frankly, I think Harold is getting quite pathological about the press,' she recorded.

I think, too, that we get a pretty fair press as a Government — and pointed out how well the press had treated me departmentally. Other members of the Cabinet tried to persuade him that the line he proposed would be unwise, but he kept brooding over the fact that one commentator had called him a con man. Pressed for more details as to how he would operate his embargo, he switched to another tack and spat out that it was time some members of the Cabinet stopped talking to our enemies like Nora Beloff (again!) and feeding them with material designed to destroy him.[2]

As Wilson's fortunes declined, so he became even more concerned about his treatment in the newspapers. Time and again he spent Cabinet meetings complaining that his ministers were leaking stories 'in the deliberate pursuit of personal political ambition'. His colleagues, however, rarely took any notice; indeed, most of them thought that he set far too much store by the newspapers. As Castle put it, his frequent harangues left most of them 'bored to tears'.[3]

Wilson's reputation had begun to slide after the crisis of July 1966, but its descent gathered speed in the course of the following year. In the spring he became bogged down in the so-called D-Notice Affair, a bizarrely trivial row with the *Daily Express*, the civil service and the world in general about the media's attitude to national security. Wilson thought that the *Express* had broken the 'Defence Notice' agreement, under which newspapers would kill stories that were deemed detrimental to national security. Why he became so caught up in this ridiculous business is something of a mystery: one biographer suggests that it was a case of displacement, 'a preoccupation with something unimportant because of the weight of real burdens'.[4] 'He is going off his rocker,' Barbara Castle gloomily remarked to Crossman. 'Think of the time he has wasted on this stupid issue,' the latter replied, 'instead of concentrating on key things like the economic situation. The Government is a total failure.'[5]

Other observers were equally harsh, and in the aftermath of the affair the relationship between Wilson and the newspapers became spectacularly bad. The newspaper magnate Cecil King, writing on 25 June, thought that the row had 'brought down on him the condemnation of all the newspapers and has made him look a fool . . . The result is the worst press any PM has had in my day.' As he pointed out, 'to unite the entire British press corps behind the *Express* is quite a feat . . . and press contempt for Wilson is not likely to evaporate'.[6]

*

The Downing Street celebrations of Wilson's thousandth day in office, in July 1967, were distinctly less exuberant than the tributes that had greeted his hundredth. Rhodesia, Vietnam and the saga of the Common Market made sorry reading, but perhaps even more depressing was the fact that, as always, the government's prospects for recovery rested on the economy. The previous month Jim Callaghan had felt sufficiently confident to announce that 'a period of controlled growth and expansion' was at hand.[7] In fact, expansion was never really on the agenda. The Treasury's original estimates for 1967 had predicted a mild surplus in the balance of payments, but by the early summer, partly because of the disruption caused by the Arab-Israeli Six-Day War, they were hastily revising their forecasts. In August they predicted a heavy deficit for 1967 of over £300 million, with worse to come in 1968. It appeared that the harsh measures of July 1966 had not worked as well as Wilson and Callaghan had hoped, and there seemed little prospect of new loans to fight off fresh attacks on sterling.[8] In the meantime unemployment had almost doubled in twelve months, and the jobless total for July 1967 was the highest summer figure since the war. It was not a pretty picture.[9]

In public Wilson and Callaghan were adamant that devaluing the pound to try to break out of the cycle would be a disaster. In official circles, however, opinion was shifting. By the middle of 1967 the champions of devaluation included not only influential ministers like Jenkins, Crosland and Crossman, but the entire staff of the DEA, Wilson's economic advisers Thomas Balogh and Nicky Kaldor, Callaghan's economic adviser Robert Neild and his senior civil servant Sir William Armstrong. The Chancellor's future son-in-law, Peter Jay, was a passionate advocate of devaluation and, as financial editor of *The Times* from April 1967, frequently used its columns to advance his case.[10]

Even Wilson himself seemed to be flirting with the idea, at least in private. At dinner with his chief courtiers in July 1967, he suddenly declared that it was time to 'talk about the subject we all know is there though we never talk about it: devaluation. I should like to hear your views.' After a 'stunned silence' Balogh and Castle put the case in favour of floating the pound. Wilson nodded, and replied calmly:

> I don't rule out devaluation . . . But I don't think we should devalue from weakness – nor from strength. There was a point earlier this year when people wanted us to do it and I considered it. But the trouble is that, once you have done it deliberately and you float, people say to themselves that there is no reason why the pound should not fall further still. When I do

it, I want to do it for political not economic reasons . . . This must be a political issue when it comes: we devalue to defend our independence.

The Six-Day War, he mused, might have been an opportunity: he could have 'gone on TV' and blamed 'these Arabs, Nasser and all that'. Or he could have blamed Johnson and the escalation of the Vietnam War. Instead, as his listeners knew, he had done nothing.[11]

If Wilson had not been prepared to devalue in 1964 or 1966, when the pressure had been at its greatest, he was hardly likely to do so in the early months of 1967, when he was confident of recovery. Many Treasury officials, as well as Callaghan, still believed that the inflation and austerity measures that would accompany devaluation, not to mention its unpredictable effect on the world economy, would be much more damaging than the current policy.[12] The problem was that as summer turned to autumn the economic picture was as bleak as ever, and no alternative strategy presented itself. Wilson's plan was therefore that they could somehow muddle through, administering the occasional dose of deflation, until 1970 or 1971. If they managed to build up a small balance of payments surplus, then they might be able to relax the brakes in the run-up to the next election, cutting unemployment and reviving the spirit of consumer confidence that had so often benefited his Conservative predecessors. Three years earlier he had decried 'the defeatist stop–go cycle'; now he was pinning his hopes on it.[13]

On 8 September, addressing a crowd of supporters at Newport, Wilson acknowledged that the last year had been much tougher than many people had been used to, but promised that 'a turning point' was in sight:

> For three years, the Government, industry and the people have shown their determination to pay our way. We have pursued this objective ruthlessly, regardless of political popularity. We have had to ask for efforts and for sacrifices — for hardships, even, and we have not yet seen the end of the hardship which may be necessary, although the measures which made it necessary are bringing us through.[14]

Just a few weeks before, he had taken personal command of the ailing DEA in the hope of exercising a stronger influence on economic affairs. His protégé Peter Shore was promoted to the role of Secretary of State at the DEA, but his Cabinet colleagues knew that Shore was basically a front man. Crossman told the Prime Minister: 'He's despised by his fellow members of

Cabinet, he's hopeless in the House of Commons and he can't put your policy to the TUC and the CBI.'[15] Wilson, however, rather fancied the idea of using Shore to run the department himself. 'If I can't run the economy well through DEA I'm no good,' he told Crossman. 'I was trained for this job and I've taken the powers to run the economy.'[16]

The events of the next few weeks made a mockery of Wilson's optimism. On 18 September, after a series of local internecine disputes, thousands of dockers walked out, and the vital ports of Liverpool, Manchester, Hull and eventually London fell silent. Goods for export piled up uselessly on the quaysides, and when the latest trade figures were published a few weeks later they showed a severe deficit: £52 million for September, and then a record £107 million for October. Taken in conjunction with the news of the government's bad beatings in Cambridge and West Walthamstow, they inspired little confidence in Wilson's sense of direction.[17] What was worse, if speculators started selling sterling, then the Bank of England could not resist for long. Its reserves had already been taking the strain of speculation for twelve months, and the prospects for more loans were uninspiring since Britain was already struggling to pay off its outstanding debts to the International Monetary Fund. Callaghan increased bank rate by 0.5 per cent, but it did no good. By the end of October investors were rushing to sell sterling, and as the following month opened the pound had fallen to its lowest level for fifteen years.[18]

With sterling under intense pressure, any sign of weakness or uncertainty on the part of the government might conceivably be the trigger for the final avalanche. It was therefore unfortunate that the latest financial crisis coincided with a fresh outbreak of misbehaviour in the Foreign Office, where George Brown was facing intense press criticism. Cecil King, whose patience with Wilson's government appeared finally to have run out, had already ordered the *Mirror* to prepare a campaign against Wilson's ministers, and the paper began by picking on the Foreign Secretary.[19]

Brown's run of bad behaviour in the autumn of 1967 was spectacular even by his own standards. On 22 September he had been photographed at a party on board the *Queen Mary*, then moored in New York, at which he had been doing a dance called the 'frug' (a sort of lewd, stationary waddle) with a buxom American public relations consultant. This was not in itself grounds for controversy, but one particular photograph seemed to show the diminutive Brown peering down the front of his partner's low-cut gown. The *Daily Express* promptly ran the picture on its front page, and Brown was so upset that he offered Wilson his resignation, which, as usual, was turned down.

The sequel took place ten days later at the Labour Party conference in Scarborough, where photographers had been instructed to get a similar picture of Brown disgracing himself on the dance floor. As soon as the Foreign Secretary appeared at the party agents' ball with his wife, he found himself bombarded by the flashes of camera bulbs, and after a short and undignified scuffle he withdrew to the hotel, angrily protesting: 'They would not let me dance with my wife. There ought to be some limit. It ought to be stopped.'[20] The press were delighted, of course, but Brown's colleagues were not impressed. Wilson commented that 'George was being more crazy than usual', while Castle lamented his 'unseemly brawl with the press, shouting at them about how he was being persecuted by photographers and saying, "This is on the record." His poor wife Sophie had stood on the stairs wringing her hands and saying over and over again, "He *isn't* drunk."'[21]

Brown's resentment at the press now began to boil over. On 30 October, at a Foreign Office reception, he spotted Cecil King's son Michael and proceeded to deliver a barrage of drunken insults about his father, culminating in a rant 'about his being Foreign Secretary, being in charge, no one was going to push him around'.[22] Later that night, Harold Wilson had an unexpected telephone call from Brown. He had just had a blazing row with Sophie, he said emotionally; he could not carry on in office any longer, and wanted to resign. Wilson, in a characteristic display of the personal kindness for which he was renowned, suggested that Brown should come over to talk 'as a friend', and the latter agreed. But while Wilson was waiting for his errant Foreign Secretary to arrive he had an unanticipated visitor: Sophie Brown. As he later recorded, she said 'that George was on his way to see me, walking, that I must not take any notice of his desire to resign, that they had just had a family tiff and that these things do happen in every family'. Sophie then left and Brown himself arrived, sober again and immensely miserable.

To Wilson's astonishment and no doubt mild embarrassment, his old rival now embarked upon a painfully frank monologue about his family life, his marriage and his general unhappiness. 'For years he had had this problem with Sophie,' Wilson noted, 'that basically Sophie did not like this life, had an inferiority complex, but that secondly Sophie was highly suspicious about his relations with [his secretary]'. Wilson listened quietly and made reassuring noises at the right moments, but Brown was in full flow and impossible to stop. The strain was too much, he said; his married life was a disaster, the press were always on his back, he was not sleeping and he must resign. 'I went over the ground very fully and sympathetically,' Wilson's account continues, 'mainly asking questions about Sophie, about whether their family could help, or any of Sophie's friends, or Mary [Wilson].' Brown answered in the negative: he wanted to leave home, but it was impossible to walk out while he was still in office because of the suffocating attention of the press. So he was determined to resign. Wilson again urged him 'not to go on this', and finally persuaded Brown to go home and try to get some sleep. The next morning Brown sent him a note thanking him for his sympathy but repeating his intention to leave. When they met on the front bench that afternoon Wilson quietly asked how things were. 'Exactly the same,' Brown replied.[23]

That night, Brown was due to speak at a dinner at the Savoy given by Lord Thomson of Fleet, the Canadian owner of *The Times* and the *Sunday Times*, which had criticised his performance at both the DEA and the Foreign Office. The other guests included fifty American businessmen and an impressive selection of the great and the good: the founder of the BBC, Lord Reith; the philanthropist Paul Getty; the government's scientific adviser, Sir Solly Zuckerman; the chairman of the British Motor Corporation, Sir Donald Stokes; and an assortment of former ambassadors, field marshals and Foreign Office grandees. A more distinguished audience could hardly be imagined, and in his current mood Brown would have been well advised to skip the event entirely. Instead, he sat brooding at the top table while Thomson began his laboured introduction with a joke that if Brown wanted to live until he was a hundred, he had been advised by his doctor to give up smoking, drinking and women. He might not live to be a hundred, the joke ran, but in the circumstances it would certainly feel like he had. 'Perhaps Lord Thomson deserved to be punished for telling such a poor joke,' writes Brown's biographer, 'but he was not to realise that retribution would arrive so swiftly.'[24]

'I think you made the most of your opportunity,' Brown began, glaring with undisguised hatred at the man who had just introduced him. 'The only thing I will say in response is that you are the only man I have ever known who actually cheated me.' Thomson, desperately hoping this was another joke, tried feebly to interject. But Brown was having none of it:

> I am not telling a joke. I am being absolutely serious. You actually once gave me your bond and broke it. My dear Roy, I think everybody here

who has heard the jokes you have presumed to tell about me should know you broke your word . . .

I understand the *Sunday Times* is somehow in your control. If I may say so, my dear Roy, we would be much happier if you would *exercise* a little control . . .

Now I don't really mind and I don't think any of us in the government really mind. All I tell you is that you are doing – your papers are doing – a very great disservice to this country . . . I don't want any misunderstanding. I am your guest. But I must make this quite clear. I think you are overdoing it, and I think it is about time you stopped . . . Some of us are concerned about the country. Some of us think it is about time we stopped giving the Russians a head start on what we are doing, and – my dear Roy – I ask you and the *Sunday Times* to take this into account and for God's sake, stop.

As soon as he had finished, Brown was besieged by reporters asking for clarification of his thoughts about Thomson's alleged perfidy. The American guests watched in disbelief as Brown, clutching a large glass of white wine, proceeded to quarrel, loudly and furiously, with the assembled journalists for a full quarter of an hour. Above the general hubbub, bizarre snippets of Brown's rant floated across the room, apparently at random:

Will you just shut up for a second? I am answering a bloody question. Can I just answer one question before I get another? My speech runs to 64 pages – just print that . . . Will you shut up? I broke no bloody rules at all. If you break them, I will know where I am, *d'accord*? You are free to break any rules. If you break them, I am perfectly free to break them too.

One of the Foreign Secretary's officials began pulling at Brown's arm to try to drag him away, but the aide was impatiently brushed aside. Brown announced that he had decided to sever all relations with the press for ever, and ordered the journalists to put down their pencils. When a reporter from the *Express* failed to do so, Brown snatched it angrily from his hand. The *Express* man said that Brown would be the only loser from all this: 'If you do not speak to the Press, you do not speak to the country.' Brown seized his hand and held it tight. '*Quiet*,' he shouted. 'Let's hear this. You said it – the man from the *Express* has said it. Now let them all hear it. If I do not talk to the Press – *what?*' The reporter repeated his remark. Brown nodded. 'That is it. The man from the *Express* has said it. So be it.'[25]

Disastrously, Brown's remarks had been recorded on tape, and the next day the story made every radio and television news bulletin. *The Times* called for him to resign or be sacked, describing his position as 'insupportable' and his conduct as 'too erratic, too bizarre, too damaging and too consistently offensive'.[26] While reading the morning papers, Crossman switched on the eight o'clock news and

> heard the recording of George Brown's astonishing scene at the Savoy, where he really misbehaved himself in public. This is intolerable, I felt, and I took up the phone and rang up Harold and told him what had happened. He'd read something in the press but he hadn't heard the radio and he said quickly, 'Don't say any more. I'll act on this. This is it but don't say a damn thing to anybody.' And he rang off.[27]

However, Wilson did not sack Brown. One reason was that it would look as though he was giving in to the newspapers' attacks on the Foreign Secretary. But, perhaps more importantly, Wilson also knew that to dismiss Brown after their emotional conversation two nights before would be a cruel betrayal. A more ruthless politician might have struck, but Wilson was never a cold-blooded butcher. Instead, while the press pushed for Brown's resignation, the Prime Minister did nothing. 'He's got to go, but not straightaway,' he told Crossman on 3 November. 'Nobody realizes what an awful time I've had with him.' Still, he wanted Crossman to prepare the ground, just in case. 'I want you to do something,' he added. 'See Jimmy Margach [of the *Sunday Times*, ironically] and tell him that the Cabinet is against George.'[28]

In the end, Brown was saved by the economic crisis that was soon to engulf the government. The delicate position of sterling meant that Wilson was reluctant to take any action that might upset the markets, and in the turmoil of the following month Brown's behaviour at the Savoy was temporarily forgotten. This gave him the chance to perpetrate one further outrage a few days later, which some connoisseurs thought was among his best; indeed, his biographer calls it 'one of the most monumental and embarrassing scenes which any of Brown's associates can remember'.[29]

The debacle in question was a reception for President Sunay of Turkey on

7 November, which had been organised by Bob Mellish, the Minister of Works and a former docker. Brown rolled up having already been to a party at the Soviet Embassy to commemorate the fiftieth anniversary of the October Revolution, and proceeded to down three large gin and tonics. From this point onwards, as Mellish later put it, 'he began to behave like an absolute shit'.[30] Brown opened his speech of welcome by emotionally congratulating the Turkish President on being married to 'the most beautiful woman in the world'. Unfortunately, as all the assembled guests could see, Madame Sunay was singularly unattractive, and an embarrassed silence descended over the gathering. If Brown's officials had provided him with a text, he never even glanced at it; instead, he gazed around the room, caught sight of an appalled Mellish, and embarked on a violent harangue against the Catholic Church, to which Mellish belonged. This somehow led him into a discussion of the dispute in the docks between the Transport and General Workers' Union and the National Amalgamated Stevedores and Dockers' Union. The rather tenuous link was that the latter had once been a Catholic union, and Brown therefore thought that Mellish should do something about it. This whole impassioned outburst was translated to the bemused Turkish President, who was, of course, neither a Catholic nor a connoisseur of dockland politics. Eventually a troupe of dancers from the Royal Ballet School was summoned to provide alternative entertainment. Staring at the dancers in angry disbelief, Brown turned to the stunned Sunay and said loudly: 'You don't want to listen to this bullshit. Let's go and have a drink.'[31]

In other circumstances this latest misdemeanour might have cost Brown his job, but Wilson and his senior ministers were preoccupied by more serious problems. The first days of November brought no respite from the intense pressure on the pound: investors were still rushing to sell, and the Bank of England's reserves were running dangerously low. On the afternoon of 2 November the Chancellor was handed a 'top secret' packet from Sir Alec Cairncross, the head of the Economic Section. Cairncross had been one of the strongest opponents of devaluation, so, as Callaghan later wrote,

> it had a profound effect on me when I opened the packet and found it contained a personal and pessimistic typed memorandum on the outlook, together with a covering, handwritten letter from him for my eyes alone. In this, he said that, having started with the conviction that I was right to try as hard as possible to solve our problems without devaluing,

he had after long consideration changed his mind and was now a 'convert to devaluation'.

'If it cannot be avoided,' Cairncross added, 'the sooner it is over and done with, the better'. Callaghan was deeply shaken: he folded the letter and put it in his breast pocket, where, he admitted, 'it stayed, burning a hole, throughout the rest of the day and long into the night'.[32]

The two men met privately the following morning, and Cairncross repeated his gloomy tidings. The trade figures had been much worse than they had hoped, and with Britain already indebted to the tune of more than £1500 million, there was no chance of further loans to stave off the pressure. Cairncross knew that devaluation would mean the complete repudiation of government policy and almost certainly the end of Callaghan's command of the Treasury. He asked if Callaghan was managing to sleep, and the Chancellor replied that he was. Now that the end had come, he was facing it with resigned equanimity. 'He gave no sign', wrote Cairncross, 'of worry or perturbation. His demeanour was that of a man who has thought it through, come to a firm conclusion, and is incapable of being ruffled.'[33]

The next morning, Saturday, 4 November, Callaghan walked from 11 Downing Street through the little passage that led to the Prime Minister's rooms next door, to tell Wilson the bad news:

> The two of us sat alone in the quiet Cabinet Room looking out onto Horseguards Parade. Everything was peaceful. People were strolling through St James's Park on their Saturday pursuits. No one out there had any idea of the welter of emotions I felt. My mind went back to a similar Saturday morning three years before, when the three of us had held our first discussion and decided against devaluation. I felt that the three years of struggle had been of no avail.
>
> Harold sensed my feelings and was kindness itself. As soon as I had told him of my change of heart, I felt relief to have shared my anxieties. He was encouraging and I came away reinforced in my decision and ready to set in motion the necessary action. It is a common experience that whatever doubts and terrors assail us in making up our minds, once a decision is reached a calm descends.[34]

But this was not the end of the affair. Devaluation would take at least a week to prepare, and in the meantime both men still hoped that something would turn up to save them. Over the next few days the Chancellor strove desperately to drum up a loan. At a meeting of the Cabinet's Steering Committee on Economic Policy, he even told his fellow ministers that devaluation would be 'a disaster . . . a political catastrophe as well as an economic one'. Since he already knew the likely outcome, he could hardly have enjoyed pronouncing these words.[35]

Wilson, meanwhile, had come up with one of his characteristic schemes to put off the day of reckoning. His plan was to fly to Washington, under the pretext of discussing the war in Vietnam, and give President Johnson an ultimatum that if the Americans did not come up with a massive loan, then Britain would be forced not only to devalue but to pull her troops out of West Germany, Singapore and her other overseas bases. Cold water was poured on this rather fanciful scheme by, of all people, George Brown, who doubted whether anybody would believe the Vietnam story or whether the US Congress would approve financial assistance obtained by such dubious means. Wilson's officials then devised an even wilder scheme involving the Prime Minister and his wife flying to see their son Robin, then studying in Boston, on 'family business', and popping in to blackmail Johnson on the way. This, too, was abandoned. On 9 November they finally agreed to send a telegram to Washington floating the loan idea, but nobody held out much hope of success.[36]

In the days that followed there was nothing to do but wait. On the evening of Saturday, 11 November, Callaghan and Brown went round to 10 Downing Street to discuss the situation. Wilson was still for putting off devaluation at all costs; Callaghan hoped it might somehow be postponed until the next budget; Brown was in favour, but thought that an immediate surrender would smack of haste and panic. At this point Wilson handed round some drinks, the atmosphere became less formal, and, as Pimlott puts it, the three rivals turned, 'with the camaraderie of old prize-fighters', to political gossip. Brown, who was putting away brandy as though the world's supply were running out and beginning to stumble over his words, took the opportunity to swear his undying loyalty to Wilson, but warned him that the press did not believe a word he said any more. Understandably rather taken aback by this, Wilson managed to change the subject to the possibility of setting up an Inner Cabinet of senior figures, and the three men then spent a happy hour or so traducing their colleagues. Wilson was interested to see the extent of 'Jim's venom' when Roy Jenkins's name was mentioned; evidently the Chancellor saw Jenkins as his main rival for the succession. Brown, meanwhile, was becoming increasingly overexcited as the drinks continued to flow, and, unbelievable as it may seem, one of Wilson's officials entered with a message that Thomas Balogh was working late nearby 'and would we keep our voices down'. 'Later,' added Wilson, 'I heard that Thomas had asked who was that woman in there. The woman was in fact George screaming.'

As the night wore on and the drinks continued to flow, the conversation became increasingly unguarded. Brown drunkenly repeated to Wilson that 'he was not a candidate for the succession'. The Prime Minister replied rather defensively that at the moment there was no vacancy. 'Quite,' put in Callaghan, adding rather disingenuously that for his part 'he had reached the limit of his ambitions – an elementary school boy who had become Chancellor'. Wilson, swilling back his whisky, liked that idea. 'Wasn't it interesting', he asked them, 'that the Inner Inner Cabinet consisted of three ex-elementary school boys, the first time in British history?' Brown's mind, however, was still on the succession question, as Wilson recorded:

> They then started talking about what would happen if I got under a bus. I said that I had no intention of so doing and that I thought this was very morbid. George was too excited to be put off . . . [and] asked Jim if he would stand if I did get under a bus. Jim said yes. And George said who did he think would stand against him, because George would not. Jim said, Roy. George was anxious to know whether Jim thought he could beat Roy and sharply reminded Jim that if he didn't this would be Jim's second defeat, and . . . then he couldn't run again. I called them to order, wanting to sum up the meeting, and protesting my health and virility.

At last Callaghan got to his feet for the short walk home to bed. 'As Jim was going,' Wilson noted, 'George asked if he could stay behind and speak to me.' When the door had closed behind the retreating Chancellor, Brown turned to Wilson and said thickly: 'Do not trust Jim, he is after your job.' Then Brown, too, was gone. 'I had learnt a great deal about human nature' was Wilson's verdict on an extraordinary evening.[37]

On the following Monday Wilson and Callaghan anxiously waited for the reply from Washington. 'Well, we are for it,' Callaghan privately told Crossman, 'unless we get the right answers this morning. This time the bankers' terms will be unacceptable.'[38] The answer came that evening, while the Prime Minister and his Chancellor were preparing for the Lord Mayor's banquet at the Guildhall. It was negative.

Just after eleven that night, Callaghan noted, they met again, still in their evening finery, and *decided finally*. Devaluation was planned for 18 November, with $2.40 the probable rate. The next day Callaghan and his officials worked out a tentative deflationary package to accompany the announcement, and he then briefed a small group of senior ministers. Denis Healey, whose Ministry of Defence would bear the brunt of the cuts, was absolutely furious. Callaghan, he said, had 'misdirected' the economy for three years, and he wondered 'why anyone should trust him or believe his forecasts after what he has dragged the party through'.[39]

On 16 November the Cabinet assembled as normal, but before they could start Wilson quietly said that the Chancellor had an important statement to make:

> We all stiffened and Jim began heavily, 'I have decided that the pound must be devalued. If Cabinet agrees, the necessary machinery will be set in motion and devaluation will be announced on Saturday. This is the unhappiest day of my life.' We all sat very still.
>
> He then elaborated on the recent run on the pound. We could arrange another massive loan, but the thought of going through the whole process again was sickening. He and the PM therefore recommended 14.3 percent devaluation. This was the only alternative to further deflation, which would be intolerable . . . In conclusion he said, 'This is the most agonizing reappraisal I have ever had to do and I will not pretend that it is anything but a failure of our policies.[40]

Wilson, as usual, tried to make the best of things. It was 'a setback', he admitted, but people in the Labour Party would at least feel that 'we have broken free'. He reminded ministers that their discussion was top secret, and to avoid alarming the markets they had to make sure that their meeting did not drag on longer than usual. Callaghan therefore began reading aloud the details of his cuts package. 'When he'd finished I blew up,' Crossman recalled. 'I said I'd never seen business done in such a deplorable way. Roy Jenkins backed me up.' Wilson tartly pointed out that the last time the pound had been devalued, in 1949, the Cabinet had not even been forewarned; Crossman should be grateful to have been given any notice at all.[41]

Although the decision had already been taken, there would be a delay of three days before it was formally announced on Saturday evening. As Roy Jenkins put it, 'this stately delay had a disastrous effect'.[42] During the

Cabinet meeting word reached Callaghan that a Labour backbencher, Robert Sheldon, was planning to ask the Chancellor about reports that the government was negotiating a new deal with the central banks. Unwisely, Callaghan was sent to the Commons to waffle through an answer without telling a direct lie about the forthcoming devaluation. In the event he muddled through for about ten minutes, during which he never said that devaluation was on the cards, but never denied it either. It was a disaster. 'We're going to lose a lot of money through Jim's answer yesterday – the whole operation is going as badly as it could,' Crossman angrily told Wilson the following morning.[43] Guessing that a change was on the way, the speculators were rushing to sell their sterling holdings at the higher value of $2.80, and in just two days the foreign exchange reserves haemorrhaged a staggering $1.5 billion. Not for nothing was Sheldon's enquiry later called 'the most expensive question in British parliamentary history'.[44]

The announcement that Britain was devaluing the pound to $2.40 was made just after nine on the evening of Saturday, 18 November, its timing carefully planned in order to cheat the following day's newspapers.[45] The accompanying cuts programme raised bank rate from 6.5 to 8 per cent, imposed hire-purchase restrictions and higher Corporation Tax, and slashed about £400 million in the expected rate of growth of public spending. However savage these cuts might appear, many observers thought them inadequate: if devaluation was to work properly, it needed to be accompanied by more severe deflation to free resources for the production of exports.[46]

Perhaps the only way that devaluation could have been averted in the life of the Wilson government is if, at the very beginning, Callaghan had imposed a really stern bout of deflation, with much higher tax increases and more severe spending cuts. To critics like Edmund Dell, Callaghan's failure was that he never had the guts to implement the tough measures necessary to save the pound.[47] However, this is a very harsh and slightly unrealistic verdict. As Richard Holt points out, although Callaghan was 'just not tough enough . . . it would have been surprising if the Chancellor had been tougher, and it is surely unreasonable to blame a Labour Chancellor of the 1960s for thinking like a Labour politician of the 1960s'.[48] Callaghan's tragedy was that his political identity, and the social commitments of the government of which he was a part, made it impossible for him to contemplate the kind of brutal deflation that might have averted devaluation. Indeed, even a Conservative government of the era would probably have baulked at that kind of austerity, and certainly the likes of Macmillan and Maudling would have considered it unthinkable. Nevertheless, few observers thought that this mitigated Callaghan's failure at the Treasury, and even he looked back on it as a pretty inglorious episode. Many press commentators remarked that he had clearly been out of his depth, and the verdict of history has not, in general, been any kinder.[49]

Callaghan handed in his resignation on the day that devaluation was announced, although Wilson persuaded him to stay on at the Treasury for a few days before moving to another senior post in the Cabinet.[50] This meant that it was Callaghan, battered and bruised, who presented the deflationary package to the Commons on Monday, 20 November and wound up the subsequent debate two days later. In the circumstances, he did so well that his comeback was already under way within days of his greatest failure. Crossman, never a great admirer, still admitted that the initial statement was 'one of the best parliamentary performances I've ever heard'.[51] And in the debate Callaghan was even better. Wilson had given an aggressive, partisan speech the day before, but the outgoing Chancellor adopted a much more successful approach:

> He gave us an informal chat followed by a kind of appeal from a retiring Cincinnatus. It was a deliberate consensus speech, modelled very much on the style of Anthony Eden, and he managed to make everyone in the House feel he was being appealed to individually. Up till then it had been a slap-bang party political debate. Jim put party aside and spoke as though he was above the dust of battle. He showed himself superior to the rough-and-tumble of the party knockabout of the previous two days. I had wanted Harold to do this but in his speech he had remained the party politician. Jim had then seized his opportunity.[52]

The press, which guessed that this was to be Callaghan's swansong, was full of praise. For *The Times*, 'there was something in the sombreness and gravity of his manner that profoundly impressed the House'; while the *People* called him 'the Tories' favourite Socialist'.[53] Barbara Castle could barely bring herself to record that he 'had the Tories almost eating out of his hand and our people gave him a great ovation too'. She thought that 'the more sophisticated of us could see his ploy standing out as obvious as the Albert Memorial'. Thomas Balogh told her that he had never seen 'the knife put more deliberately into a leader's back', and he 'almost spat out the word "Casca"'.[54]

For all his misery at the Treasury, Callaghan had consistently been the government's most popular minister, and he managed to emerge from the devaluation crisis with his popularity intact.[55] His reputation was strengthened by the contrast with Wilson, whom Crossman had found strangely 'full of optimism because of the wonderful response he'd had from all over the world to his courageous decision'.[56] But when Crossman saw the notes for Wilson's planned broadcast to the nation, he thought them 'ghastly – all about the wicked speculators who had been disloyal and made life intolerable and have driven us off the pound'. He suggested that Wilson should just 'admit the defeat' and then go on to talk about the future. 'Dick, you like admitting defeats,' Wilson replied, 'but I never do that kind of thing.'[57]

Wilson's broadcast had been scheduled for Sunday, 19 November at six, rather than late on Saturday night, because his advisers were confident that he would make a good impression and wanted to make sure that as many people were watching as possible.[58] Crossman and three other ministers were at Windsor Castle for a Privy Council meeting with the Queen, and they arranged to hold it early so they could watch the speech:

> We got our business done in record time and she immediately said to me, 'Well, we must get along the passage to the television room,' and we practically ran along that great corridor which George III constructed and which the royal children bicycle up and down. Then suddenly she turned sharp left into a little sitting-room and there by a great big coal-fire and a great big television-set we watched Harold performing on the screen. She sat us on her sofa and summoned me to sit beside her while the others got down into comfortable chairs and it wasn't until some minutes after we had started watching that I realized that she and I were in some difficulty. What on earth were we to say to each other when the broadcast finished?[59]

On the screen, watched not only by Crossman and the Queen but also by millions of his fellow-countrymen, Wilson was explaining precisely what devaluation would mean for the nation. Even after a few sentences it was clear that he had no intention of admitting defeat, as his friend had urged. As so often, he was falling back on Churchillian rhetoric; but as his biographer points out, while it might have been appropriate to conjure up the spirit of Dunkirk, 'Wilson seemed to be announcing El Alamein, or Trafalgar'. For three years he had been arguing that devaluation would be a national defeat, 'the economic equivalent of a plague or a war'; now that it had finally taken place, he was expected to react with the gravity and solemnity the situation demanded.[60] Instead, he appeared to be in a 'strange mood of post-battle elation', as he announced:

> Our decision to devalue attacks our problem at the root and that is why the international monetary community have rallied round with a display of formidable strength to back the operation . . .
>
> Tonight we must face the new situation. First, what this means. From now the pound abroad is worth 14 per cent or so less in terms of other currencies. That does not mean, of course, that the pound here in Britain, in your pocket or purse or in your bank, has been devalued. What it does mean is that we shall now be able to sell more goods abroad on a competitive basis. This is a tremendous opportunity for all our exporters, and for many who have not yet started to sell their goods overseas. But it will also mean that the goods that we buy from abroad will be dearer, and so for many of these goods it will be cheaper to buy British.

He predicted that as imports became more expensive, so 'industrial production will go up', and there would be 'more work' and 'more jobs in the development areas'. Prices would be higher, and there would be harsh cuts in public spending, but there was no reason for despair:

> Devaluation has been a hard decision, and some of its consequences will themselves be hard for a time. But now the decision has been taken, all of us, together, must now make a success of it. We must take with both hands the opportunity that has now been presented to us . . .
>
> As I have said, we have the chance now to break out from the straitjacket of these past years.
>
> We are on our own now.
>
> It means – Britain first.[61]

When Wilson's final words had died away there was 'a long, long silence' in the Windsor Castle sitting room. Finally the Queen said, almost under her breath: 'Of course it's extraordinarily difficult to make that kind of speech.' Crossman began to make a 'a polite noise', but before he could finish Patrick Gordon Walker boomed in enthusiastically: 'Oh, a wonderful performance.' 'She couldn't say "yes",' recorded Crossman, so 'I got her on to foot-and-mouth disease.'[62]

The Prime Minister's jaunty tone had not been put on for the occasion. It was classic Wilson, the same 'interminable self-defeating optimism' that Crossman regularly bemoaned and that Castle had warned 'could be fatal' just a few weeks earlier.[63] Unfortunately, he had badly misjudged his audience. Having argued for years that devaluation would be a severe blow to the ordinary British consumer, Wilson now seemed to be arguing that it was a great national victory. His denial that 'the pound here in Britain, in your pocket or purse or in your bank, has been devalued' sounded like the twisting evasion of a glib, dishonest politician, and laid him open to mockery as the man who had managed to devalue sterling without devaluing 'the pound in your pocket'. His allies were horrified: Barbara Castle noted 'a feeling abroad that he was too complacent by half', while Crossman thought that he had been 'a bloody fool'.[64]

Wilson himself was bewildered by the hostile reaction. In later years he tried to argue that it had not been his fault, that the optimistic phrases had been suggested by Crossman or the civil service, and that his words had been twisted by the newspapers and the Conservatives. But, as Pimlott notes, this missed the point. The 'pound in your pocket' fiasco illustrated just how much Wilson's image had changed since 1964, and the words became a catchphrase, forever hung around his neck to illustrate his supposed slipperiness. Brown's drunken words of a week before had been right: the brutal reality was that nobody any longer believed a word he said.[65]

On 27 November President de Gaulle announced his veto of Britain's bid to join the Common Market. November had been a truly horrendous month for the government, with terrible trade figures, record losses in the reserves, the collapse of Wilson's European aspirations and, above all, devaluation. According to the Gallup polls, public opinion on the rights and wrongs of devaluation was pretty evenly divided, although a slight majority agreed with the Conservative leader Edward Heath that it had been a 'defeat for Britain'. Almost nine voters out of ten expected the cost of living to rise, and four out of ten planned to cut down on their personal spending. Nearly two in ten would be spending less at Christmas; one in ten said that they were giving up their plans to buy a new car, and a similar proportion claimed that they were abandoning plans for a foreign holiday or purchases for the home.[66] Labour's standing in the opinion polls, already perilous, now reached depths unknown since polling began. In December 1967 only 21 per cent of the electorate approved of the government's record, while no fewer than 64 per cent expressed disapproval. The Conservatives, who had been eight points ahead in October, now found themselves an enormous 18.5 per cent clear of their rivals.[67]

Few people shared Wilson's confidence that they could 'break out of the straitjacket'; most expected a grim, tough slog. But Wilson's irrepressible spirit kept him upright; and almost alone among his ministers, he still believed that he could turn things around. 'I can do whatever I like now,' he remarked to James Margach of the *Sunday Times*. 'Don't you see, devaluation has made me the most powerful Prime Minister since Walpole.'[68] In a reassuring note to Wilson's father, his faithful secretary reflected his optimism. 'It has been a very bad week for the PM,' Marcia Williams wrote. 'It is bad enough to fight the enemy in front, but when you have to look over your shoulder the whole time as well, as you can guess, this is very tiring and bad for the nerves . . . However, I think everything is now under control, though it is going to be hard going for some time.[96]'

21

I WAS LORD KITCHENER'S VALET

CLAIR: May I compliment you on your exquisite *ensemble*? I always said the Victorian look would be back.
ADAM ADAMANT: It was always my hope, sir.

'To Set a Deadly Fashion', *Adam Adamant Lives!* (1966)

The taxi turned left and took them along a row of shops. Here, among climbing plants, lumps of driftwood, and heaps of pebbles, pairs of velvet trousers were displayed on dummies that finished abruptly just above the waist; faceless busts in what looked a bit like bronze wore shorts of ribbed corduroy, flashed gigantic wristwatches, had their necks encircled by flowing scarves evidently made out of somebody's auntie's summer dress.

Kingsley Amis, *I Want It Now* (1968)

On 11 November 1966 the *Daily Mirror* hit the news-stands with an exclusive interview with two of the Beatles. This was something of a coup, because since the debacle of their world tour earlier that summer, the band had been very quiet indeed. In August their last single, 'Yellow Submarine/ Eleanor Rigby', had topped the chart as expected, but the A-side, sung by Ringo Starr, was more a comic novelty song than a pop classic. Their ground-breaking album *Revolver*, which had reached the top of the LP chart in the same month, had since been displaced by the soundtrack of *The Sound of Music*, the commercial juggernaut that had been released more than a year before. What had become of the Beatles in the meantime was a matter of increasing speculation and, for their fans, deep concern, with rumours circulating that George Harrison, sick of life in the limelight, had left the group.

Harrison's dissatisfaction with his role in the Beatles, where he felt stifled by the predominance of Lennon and McCartney, was quite genuine, but since the chaotic American tour he had reconsidered his half-serious decision to leave. Having fallen in love with Indian music, he had recently spent six weeks in Bombay learning to play the sitar and had returned a more serious, ambitious and thoughtful individual. He nodded when John Lennon told the *Mirror*'s interviewer that there was 'no great mystery about the long, long silence of the Beatles'. 'We've been resting and thinking,' Harrison added in agreement.

> It gave us a chance to re-assess things. After all, we've had four years doing what everybody else wanted us to do. Now we're doing what we want to do. But whatever we do, it has got to be real and progressive. Everything we've done so far has been rubbish as I see it today. Other people may like what we've been doing, but we're not kidding ourselves. It doesn't mean a thing to what we want to do now.

'George is being a bit blunt,' Lennon interjected hastily. 'You can always look back and say what you've done before was rubbish, especially in comparison with what you're doing today. It was all vital at the time, even if it looks daft when you see things differently later on.'[1]

Two weeks later all four Beatles reassembled in the familiar surroundings of the Abbey Road studios to begin work on their latest album. As always, they keenly felt the pressure from their competitors, especially as other groups had followed their lead in moving the focus from the three-minute single to the album, which was now seen as the 'natural format for an idiom bursting its commercial and creative limits'.[2] The Rolling Stones, the Beach Boys and Bob Dylan had all released impressive new albums in the last few months, and the Beatles were determined not to rest on the laurels they had been awarded for *Revolver*. Paul McCartney told the *NME* that their days of touring were definitively over, since the music they now wanted to make was impossible to reproduce on stage. 'We feel that only through recording do people listen to us, so that is our most important form of communication,' he explained. 'We have always changed our style as we went along and we've never been frightened to develop and change . . . We take as much time as we want on a track, until we get it to our satisfaction.'[3]

Yet there was a strong sense in the autumn of 1966 that the Beatles had gone about as far as they could as a recording outfit. All of them were tired of life as international pop stars: their road manager Neil Aspinall told the press that they were 'not even the Beatles anymore' but merely 'four very different, four incredibly wealthy men, who have lives of their own to lead [and] come together now to record as sort of a hobby'.[4] Even McCartney, the most dedicated member of the band, had sought escape that autumn by driving through France sporting a false moustache, and had found it enormously reinvigorating. On the flight home from a safari in Kenya, just before recording was about to start, he wondered whether there might be a lesson there. He later recalled:

> I got this idea. I thought, Let's not be ourselves. Let's develop alter egos so we're not having to project an image which we know. It would be much more free. What would really be interesting would be to actually take on the personas of this different band . . . I thought we can run this philosophy through the whole album with this alter-ego band, it won't be us making all that sound, it won't be the Beatles, it'll be this other band, so we'll be able to lose our identities in this.[5]

McCartney explained the idea to his fellow Beatles when they met at Abbey Road, and although Lennon had his doubts, they agreed to go along with it.[6] The attraction was that it freed the Beatles from their pop-star image and allowed them to indulge their new enthusiasm for studio experimentation. Indeed, their rediscovered commitment was such that the sessions for their new album went on and on until April 1967.[7] The very first song they recorded, John Lennon's hallucinogenic pastoral 'Strawberry Fields Forever', devoured no fewer than fifty-five hours of studio time. Released as a single alongside 'Penny Lane' in February 1967, it offered an intriguing foretaste of the new album; as Ian MacDonald remarks, it 'extended the range of studio techniques developed on *Revolver*, opening up possibilities for pop which, given sufficient invention, could result in unprecedented sound-images'.[8] George Martin, the band's inventive producer, commented that it marked 'the major change in the boys' lives', seeing them embark on a 'highly imaginative' phase in which they came close to 'complete tone poem imagery . . . like a modern Debussy'.[9]

As the Beatles extended their range, however, they were beginning to move away from the mass audience that had supported them since 1963. The new single was their first since October 1962 to fall short of the top of the chart, being beaten to the number one spot by Engelbert Humperdinck, a bombastic balladeer from the East Midlands. Humperdinck's single 'Release Me' was a conventional love song, unlike either 'Strawberry Fields Forever' or 'Penny Lane', and its greater success hinted at the enduring conservatism of much of the pop audience. And as recording dragged on into the spring of 1967 and the music became 'more and more avant-garde', Martin became concerned that his charges had maybe gone too far. 'I was beginning to wonder whether we were being a little over-the-top,' he later remembered, 'and a little bit, maybe, pretentious. There was a slight niggle of worry. I thought, "Is the public ready for this yet?"'[10]

As it turned out, his fears were groundless. When *Sgt. Pepper's Lonely Hearts Club Band* was released at the beginning of June 1967, it shot to the top of the LP chart, and it remained in one of the top two places, alternating with *The Sound of Music*, until February 1968. In *The Times* the theatre critic Kenneth Tynan hyperbolically praised *Sgt. Pepper* as 'a decisive moment in the history of western civilization', while other upmarket publications followed suit. The *Times Literary Supplement* described the lyrics as a 'barometer for our times'; the *New York Review of Books* hailed a 'new and golden Renaissance of Song'; and the American magazine *Newsweek* called it 'the Beatles' *Waste Land*', after the poem by T. S. Eliot.[11]

However, although most of the Beatles' fellow musicians were similarly awestruck, this acclaim was far from universal, and although many histories of the Beatles and the sixties insist that the record was 'almost everywhere immediately accepted as a cultural milestone', this is not entirely true.[12] For one thing, the millions of people who preferred to buy *The Sound of Music* instead were extremely unlikely to be impressed by McCartney and Lennon's new style; for another, less intellectually ambitious reviewers, who were more likely to influence and reflect the opinions of the Beatles' ordinary fans, registered not excitement and ecstasy but simple bafflement at the band's new turn. The *NME*, for example, had already registered its bewilderment in its review of 'Strawberry Fields Forever' in February, with one reviewer describing it as 'unusual and way-out' and admitting: 'Quite honestly, I don't really know what to make of it.'[13] The same paper's review of *Sgt. Pepper* a few months later carried the headline 'Something different to get the brain working', and the writer, Allen Evans, wondered whether the album was really 'worth the five months it took to make'. Puzzlement was the order of the day and many of the comments on individual songs were almost laughably literal. 'Lucy in the Sky with Diamonds', for instance, was apparently 'about a girl and a pier, with its electric lights', while Harrison's Indian experiment 'Within You, Without You' was described simply as 'weird'.[14] A very different paper, the *Daily Mail*, took a similar line:

> What's happened to the Beatles? It's now around four years since [they] happened, and, since the early days of 1963, the Beatles have changed

completely. They rose as heroes of a social revolution. They were everybody's next-door neighbours. The boys whom everybody could identify with. Now, four years later, they have isolated themselves, not only personally, but also musically. They have become contemplative, secretive, exclusive and excluded.[15]

Sgt. Pepper's Lonely Hearts Club Band remains probably the most discussed pop album of all time. It is frequently described as a 'drug album', but this does it little justice. As in the recording sessions for *Revolver*, the Beatles avoided taking anything stronger than cannabis while they were working, and the only member of the group regularly taking LSD at any time was John Lennon.[16] This is not to deny that drugs played a part, particularly in the composition of hallucinogenic songs like 'Strawberry Fields Forever', but their influence is probably overrated. 'Lucy in the Sky with Diamonds', for instance, is often rather tiresomely identified as a song about LSD, when in fact the title was borrowed from a drawing by Lennon's four-year-old son Julian and the imagery was inspired by the fiction of Lewis Carroll.[17]

Indeed, as with *Rubber Soul* and *Revolver*, other influences were arguably more important. George Martin was once again a central figure, stretching the technological resources of the studio to the limit, mixing in radio clips and tape collages, booking classical musicians and patiently showing the Beatles how their musical fantasies could become reality. It was Martin who arranged the clarinets for McCartney's vaudevillian love song 'When I'm Sixty-Four'; it was Martin who devised the fairground sound on 'Being for the Benefit of Mr Kite'; and it was Martin who booked and conducted the symphony orchestra that played in the album's most imaginative song, 'A Day in the Life'.[18] His influence was so strong that many reviewers called *Sgt. Pepper* 'George Martin's finest album', provoking McCartney to an uncharacteristic outburst of discontent. 'We'd put our heart and soul into it, all this work,' he said later, 'and not to detract from George . . . but he couldn't have made this album with Gerry and the Pacemakers, so it's not just George Martin.'[19] McCartney was right, of course; but at the same time it is hard to imagine the Beatles being quite so successful with a less imaginative or courageous producer.

For many contemporary listeners, *Sgt. Pepper's Lonely Hearts Club Band* was an extraordinary, often confusing, experience, with its continuous stream of sound, its studio banter, steam organs, sitars and even farmyard barking, and its combination of cartoonish psychedelia, circus vaudeville, driving rock music and gentle ballads. But although it is often treated as a revolutionary breakthrough, its themes and influences were actually pretty similar to those of *Revolver*. Like the earlier album, it was a collage of different musical genres, from Edwardian brass bands and American blues to Indian rhythms and experimental tape loops; and the lyrics reflected a similarly wide range of interests, from the sights and sounds of a Northern childhood to the dilemmas of youth in the late 1960s.[20] The strongest motif, of course, was that of the late Victorian or Edwardian music hall, which furnished the inspiration for the Beatles' corporate alter ego, Sergeant Pepper's Lonely Hearts Club Band. We have already seen how deeply the Beatles, as well as rivals like the Kinks, drew on the traditions of nineteenth-century variety, and in songs like 'Being for the Benefit of Mr Kite' and 'When I'm Sixty-Four' their enthusiasm reached its peak, with the former even being set in a Victorian fairground.[21] The album's famous cover, designed by the whimsical collagist Peter Blake, captured the same spirit of Victorian revivalism and English nostalgia. The original idea was McCartney's, and he came up with various drawings of the Beatles in Victorian costumes, posing before a floral clock in a municipal park. This evolved into the final image of the group in bright bandsmen's uniforms standing with the massed ranks of their cultural heroes behind a colourful flower bed, which was arranged and photographed by Blake and his wife, the American artist Jann Haworth.

The Beatles' choice of heroes was typically revealing. John Lennon plumped for the Marquis de Sade, Edgar Allen Poe and Oscar Wilde, as well as Christ and Hitler, who were both removed before the final photograph. George Harrison's list consisted of nothing but Indian gurus; McCartney's selection ran all the way from Karlheinz Stockhausen to Fred Astaire; and Ringo Starr said that he would happily go along with whoever the others chose. Blake himself added a few extra faces, and the result was an image that perfectly captured the Beatles' characteristic blend of experiment, whimsy and nostalgia.[22]

It was the ideal cover for an album that rapidly assumed the status of a classic. *Sgt. Pepper's Lonely Hearts Club Band* set the seal on the Beatles' achievement since 1963, rounding off an unprecedented triumvirate of chart-topping, ground-breaking albums. In later years it became fashionable to decry it and insist that *Rubber Soul* and *Revolver* were better, fresher records, but this was not how the Beatles' rivals perceived it at the time. In the United States bands like the Byrds and Jefferson Airplane listened to the new album in a state of 'almost religious awe', stunned by the Beatles' musical sophistication and sheer courage in reinventing themselves in such daring, gaudy fashion.[23] Yet again the group had proved that, for musical range, lyrical dexterity and cultural awareness, they were simply unmatchable. Other people might be better at doing one thing; none were so good at doing so many things. As their foremost critic puts it, the Beatles had, in the last of their three great albums, created the 'imperishable popular art of its time'.[24]

Like so many of the Beatles' cultural innovations, *Sgt. Pepper* was superbly timed. By the beginning of June 1967 Mods and Rockers had disappeared from the headlines, technological optimism was in full retreat, and the press had discovered a new phenomenon, 'flower power'. This was originally an American, and specifically Californian, phenomenon, drawing inspiration from the movements for black civil rights and against the Vietnam War, and reflecting the frustrated moralising of American students in an age of economic abundance. As student numbers swelled, cannabis use became more common and discontent about the war in Vietnam increased, many young Americans began to adopt the style and values associated with bohemian beatniks. The slogan of this movement was 'peace and love', in explicit contrast to the brutality of the war in South-East Asia, and young protesters brandished flowers to demonstrate their gentle intentions and closeness to nature. This reputedly inspired the poet Allen Ginsberg to coin the phrase 'flower power' in 1965, and within two years American youth culture had become suffused with images of flowers, dancing children, smiling girls and so on.[25]

Although the Beatles' latest album both reflected and shaped the perception of 1967 as the 'Summer of Love', the development of flower power in fact marked a diminution in the international influence of British youth culture. Between 1964 and 1966 Mods, mop-tops and mini-skirts had been all the rage overseas, but now the focus had moved back towards the United States and to hippies, acid rock and political protest. At the same time British pop groups began to loosen their grip on the American singles charts. Successful singles now celebrated not the bobbies and buses of Swinging London but the flower children of San Francisco, the Californian city that epitomised protest, bohemianism and the drug subculture. Although the Beatles and the Rolling Stones remained enormously popular – more popular, indeed, than any other groups of the day – they were also extremely familiar, and many American fans were more excited by the overtly drug-influenced, counter-cultural style of West Coast bands like the Byrds, the Doors, Jefferson Airplane and the Grateful Dead.

The swing of the pendulum away from Britain was well illustrated by the use of slang. In 1965 and 1966 American teenagers often affected linguistic mannerisms copied from the Beatles, describing things as 'fab' or 'gear', for instance. By contrast, the word that best summed up the spirit of the late sixties was identifiably American, and derived from the words 'hip' and 'hipster', originally used by black Americans to indicate style and sex appeal, and then by writers like Norman Mailer to describe white Americans who imitated black culture. By the end of 1965 this had evolved into 'hippy', used by San Francisco newspapers and magazines to describe the swelling ranks of young bohemians. In July 1967 the word received the ultimate endorsement: a cover story in *Time* magazine, discussing 'The Hippies'.[26]

Hippies are often described simply as drop-outs, but this is not quite right. Most people who looked and acted like hippies, wearing hippy clothing and using hippy slang, continued to hold down regular jobs. Although most hippies insisted that their movement was something entirely new, being a hippy was not ultimately all that different from being a Teddy Boy, a Mod or a Rocker in earlier periods. It was a label adopted by young people for leisure purposes, denoting a certain style of dress, vocabulary and behaviour at evenings and weekends. Hippies dressed in a self-consciously eclectic, shabby way, deliberately flouting the conventions of adult fashion; as one later explained, the point was to avoid looking 'nice', 'pretty' or 'bourgeois'.[27] They took drugs, especially cannabis and LSD; they venerated nature; they affected a childish innocence; and they were fascinated by all things 'Oriental', from Indian religions to North African designs. But genuine, hard-core, full-time hippies were very few in number. Even in the United States, the heartland of hippy culture, there were no more than 200,000, and in Britain their numbers were far smaller.[28] As Philip Norman puts it, '"Love" and "Peace", the hippy watchwords' were possible only for 'the very young and the very rich', and there were no more than a few dozen hippy communes in the entire country.[29]

Most young people did not drop out and were very feeble or occasional hippies, but many copied hippy dress and habits. As one young bohemian put it, they were 'fellow travellers', wearing their hair long and sporting jeans at the weekends, but cheerfully going back to work on Monday mornings.[30] The significance of flower power therefore depended on the diffusion of its fashions and values outwards, into the broader youth culture of the late sixties. It became a form of consumerism: at Gandalf's Garden, a King's Road boutique named after the wizard in *The Lord of the Rings*, shoppers could pick up handmade pottery, clothes and leather goods, as well as health foods and books about drugs and mysticism.[31]

By the beginning of 1967 many people in the British fashion and pop music scenes were adopting the idiom of American hippies. 'There are sparrows and fountains and roses in my head,' the disc jockey John Peel told his readers in the *International Times* in May 1967. 'Sometimes I don't have enough time to think of loving you. That is very wrong.'[32] Dozens, if not hundreds, of groups produced records with sleeves decorated in bright, floral patterns and whimsical or childish titles like 'Dandelion', 'See Emily Play', 'Love and Beauty', 'A Day in My Mind's Mind', and even 'The Town of Tuxley Toymaker'.[33]

In December 1966, a new nightclub had opened at the Blarney, an Irish dance club in a capacious basement on Tottenham Court Road. UFO was said to be the 'epitome of hipness', presenting concerts, poetry readings, erotic plays, juggling acts and displays of underground magazines.[34] Drugs were in plentiful supply, and many visitors felt that they heightened the transcendental experience of the UFO light-shows, for which the club was famous. The whole experience was supposed to be 'psychedelic', awakening the subconscious and prompting visions of a world beyond the mundane. The psychedelic vogue clearly had a lot to do with the increasing popularity of drugs, especially LSD, and it was not limited to UFO: other clubs, like the Electric Garden and Middle Earth, tried for similar effects in 1967 and 1968. It also required a new kind of soundtrack, breaking with the conventions of the three-minute single and trying to foster a sense of drug-fuelled transcendentalism.[35]

Psychedelic music set out to evoke the dilation of the senses experienced through LSD 'acid trips'. Its songs abandoned traditional structures for lengthy, often self-indulgent improvisation, while its lyrics were self-consciously 'spiritual' and 'meaningful'. An obvious bestselling example was Procul Harum's single 'A Whiter Shade of Pale', which included an introduction based on Bach and some magnificently pretentious lyrics:

> We skipped the light fandango,
> Turned cart-wheels across the floor.

I was feeling kind of sea-sick,
But the crowd called out for more.

With references to 'sixteen Vestal virgins', people 'wandering through playing cards', mermaids taking 'Neptune for a ride' and so on, this was typical psychedelic stuff, anticipating the lyrical excesses of progressive rock in the early 1970s. To someone who had just swallowed LSD and was staring at a barrage of lights in a darkened club, however, sentences like 'If music be the food of love, then laughter is its queen' evidently meant a great deal.[36]

By far the most successful psychedelic outfit was the band that played on UFO's first five evenings. After the Pink Floyd made their debut in October 1966, *Melody Maker* commented that 'the group's trip into outer-space sounds promised very interesting things to come', and so indeed it proved.[37] In the same month they played at the launch party for the underground magazine *International Times*, although the reviewer felt that they were being overshadowed by their light show and 'very groovy picture slides'.[38] In fact Pink Floyd (who dropped the definite article early in 1967) were extremely well positioned to take advantage of the trends of the late sixties. Unlike almost every other group of the day, they showed no interest in the American blues tradition; instead, they were a genuinely experimental, middle-class band. Of their four founding members, Roger Waters, Nick Mason and Rick Wright had met as architecture students at the Regent Street Polytechnic, while Syd Barrett, a friend of Waters from the Cambridge High School for Boys, had studied briefly at Camberwell Art School.[39] More than any other group of their day, Pink Floyd were keen to embrace new media, especially light shows, and were associated with overtly 'thoughtful' or 'poetic' lyrics. They were, in other words, the quintessential example of art-school music.[40]

The success of Pink Floyd was a very good illustration of the fragmented way in which the look and sound of the hippy subculture gradually filtered into British culture as a whole. Since most young people never went near clubs like UFO, Pink Floyd's audience tended to be disproportionately affluent and well educated.[41] When the group played before middle-class metropolitan audiences, they were applauded and idolised; when they ventured out to provincial halls and discotheques, however, they were 'bottled and spat upon'.[42] That said, although most hippy bands eventually sank without trace, Pink Floyd were notable for reaching out beyond their small coterie of bohemian fans. Their first two singles, 'Arnold Layne' and 'See Emily Play', reached numbers twenty and six in April and June 1967 respectively, but afterwards they concentrated on the album market, which was much more lucrative and appealed to older audiences who were more likely to appreciate their mystical lyrics. One footnote to their enormous commercial success in the seventies, however, was that by then Pink Floyd had lost their brilliant lead singer Syd Barrett, whose excessive consumption of LSD and other drugs probably contributed to the psychological problems that drove him into retirement.[43]

Barrett's enthusiastic drug consumption was by no means unusual. Even the Beatles were now widely identified with drugs, a remarkable turnaround from their early days in the spotlight. In 1963 the *Daily Mirror* had described them as the 'super clean' boys who preferred 'tea and cakes' to alcohol.[44] Now they struck many middle-aged observers as distinctly weird. In June 1967 McCartney publicly admitted that he had taken LSD four times, adding that it had 'opened his eyes' and allowed him to tap the 'hidden part' of his brain. This revelation cemented the general belief that the band had 'changed completely', and the *Daily Mail* spoke for many when it denounced him as 'an irresponsible idiot'.[45]

On one hand, the Beatles' transformation into Britain's most famous hippies lost them the support of much of the press and many conservative onlookers. Yet, on the other, it allowed them to maintain their popularity among younger listeners, for whom the band's evolution was a sign that they were still at the cutting edge of popular culture. 'Having achieved world-wide fame by singing pleasant, hummable numbers,' wondered an interviewer from the *NME*, 'don't they feel they may be too far ahead of the record-buyers?' Harrison disagreed. 'People are very aware of what's going on around them nowadays,' he explained. 'They think for themselves and I don't think we can ever be accused of under-estimating the intelligence of our fans.' Lennon concurred. 'The people who bought our records in the past must realise we couldn't go on making the same type for ever,' he insisted. 'We must change and I believe people know this.'[46]

In some ways the Beatles' association with the hippy counterculture can be overstated. Far from dropping out, they continued to work extremely hard in the studio, and they always retained a healthy scepticism towards the solemn excesses of the bohemian underground. The band's natural sarcasm and irony meant that even in their most self-important phase they still found it hard to take the counterculture entirely seriously. When George Harrison visited San Francisco in 1967, he found not a paradise of spiritual enlightenment, peace and love but 'a load of horrible, spotty drop-out kids on drugs'.[47] Yet at the same time, hippy fashions, bohemian attitudes and Eastern mysticism probably all owed their rapid popularity to their endorsement by the Beatles. More than any other cultural figures of the sixties, indeed, they were responsible for popularising values previously reserved for a peripheral clique, from pacifism and Buddhism to meditation and marijuana.[48]

Pondering the success of the Beatles in 1969, George Melly remarked that 'alone in pop, with the possible exception of the Kinks', they seemed 'at their happiest when celebrating the past'. There was certainly a good deal of truth in this: even Sergeant Pepper himself, we are told, began to play 'twenty years ago today', and much of *Sgt. Pepper's Lonely Hearts Club Band* evokes the fading memories of circuses, music halls and terraced streets.[49] This emphasis on nostalgia helped to distinguish the Beatles and the Kinks from their American counterparts while linking them with British creative artists in other genres, from fiction and poetry to the theatre and television, whose gaze was similarly fixed on the past.

Nostalgia was one of the most powerful forces in post-war British culture, which was hardly surprising, given the collapse of the empire and all the talk about national political and economic decline. Britain's leading literary figures often seemed to be obsessed by the past: as the critic D. J. Taylor puts it, 'the whole tendency of the post-war novel, a few disagreeable projections excepted, is retrospective'.[50] L. P. Hartley's classic novel *The Go-Between* (1955), for instance, begins with the famous line 'The past is a foreign country: they do things differently there', and is entirely concerned with the relationship between the past and the present.[51] Similarly, Angus Wilson wrote academic studies of the nineteenth-century realists Dickens and Zola, and in three of his novels cast an eye back to the prelapsarian world of Edwardian England.[52] Other writers, from Kingsley Amis and Anthony Powell to Alan Sillitoe and Margaret Drabble, betrayed similar preoccupations with a lost world of simplicity and innocence, and the enormous success of the BBC's adaptation of John Galsworthy's *The Forsyte Saga* (1967–8) showed that nostalgia fascinated the masses as well as the intellectuals.[53]

The Forsyte Saga was shown on BBC2 in twenty-six episodes from January 1967, and immediately proved a popular sensation. Indeed, with a cast including Kenneth More, Eric Porter, Nyree Dawn Porter and Susan Hampshire, the series could hardly fail. On the strength of the first episode alone one critic hailed it as 'a great adventure in British television [and] a delight to viewers'.[54] But although the first run was a triumph, attracting adoring reviews and audiences of six million, it did not please everybody. Irate viewers complained that a prestigious series of this kind should be shown on BBC1, where everybody could see it. As one correspondent put it, 'the elderly, the ill and the impecunious', who could not afford a new set capable of receiving BBC2, were being treated as 'second-class citizens' by being excluded from the *Forsyte* phenomenon.[55] In the autumn of 1968, therefore, the series was repeated on BBC1. This time the sensation was even greater. Eighteen million people – a third of the population – tuned in every Sunday evening, and there was a mild furore when several churches altered the times of their evening services to allow their worshippers to watch it.[56]

Yet some highbrow critics despised the series and deplored its popular success. The writer Paul Scott took a swipe at Galsworthy's 'mediocrity', while the new professor of poetry at Oxford, Roy Fuller, devoted part of his inaugural lecture to an attack on the 'philistine' appeal of a writer who had been 'discredited forty years ago'.[57] The critic Henry Raynor, who described the programme as '*Coronation Street* for the middle class', thought its characters were essentially shallow, 'unchanged' by events, reflecting 'the surface of experience without experience'.[58] This rather woolly analysis drew a furious response from viewers who disliked Raynor's patronising tone. 'This is an example of how critics tend to become quite divorced from the opinion of ordinary people,' wrote one man from Dorset, who noted that all the people he had met 'in the last six months have thoroughly enjoyed the Saga'.[59] As a plumber put it, 'once you switch on, you are glued to your set until it is finished'.[60] The angriest and most revealing response of all, however, came from a Mr Boydell of Leeds:

> Henry Raynor condemns the Forsyte Saga for being a glorified soap opera, and in so doing condemns the 17 million viewers who have enjoyed it.
>
> Why shouldn't we enjoy it?
>
> We are sick to death of living in a world where we are exhorted to be different from what we are by critics and politicians. We are tired of having a guilty conscience if we are luckier than our neighbours and of trying to take the burdens of Vietnam and Biafra on our shoulders.
>
> Above all, we are sick of the sight and sound of scruffy teenagers and students and kitchen sink drama!

> No wonder we are happy to escape for 45 minutes each week into a world of elegance and good manners and to enjoy watching the superb acting of Margaret Tyzack and Eric Porter.[61]

Although the nostalgic tendency in British culture had deep roots, it clearly gathered strength towards the end of the sixties.[62] Instead of throwing themselves into the pursuit of futuristic modernity, artists and designers began to turn back towards Britain's imperial past and 'self-conscious historical revivalism'.[63] This was partly a commercially driven backlash: consumers were growing tired of shiny plastic, and in truth there had always been a healthy market for historical revivalism. But it also reflected a wider reaction against the very idea of modernity, especially as the utopian hopes of the early sixties lost their appeal. The ecology and conservation movements, which gathered momentum in the late sixties as reactions to the excesses of scientific planning, deliberately looked back to the supposedly simpler world of the past. Conservationists in particular sought to preserve Britain's nineteenth-century architectural heritage, not unlike the Kinks, who sang about protecting 'Tudor houses, antique tables and billiards' from the ravages of progress.[64]

Like the Kinks and the Beatles, plenty of other artists, bored of Pop and Op, looked to the Victorian and Edwardian eras for inspiration. From the mid-sixties onwards, fabric and wallpaper manufacturers began to produce self-consciously revivalist designs, and in May 1966 a trade magazine reported that the recent vogue for 'Victorian flower designs' had 'blossomed into bold, vigorously designed prints reflecting the current preoccupation with Art Nouveau and Geometrics, in vivid Byzantine colours'.[65] Art Nouveau was all the rage in the late sixties, partly because designers were influenced by popular retrospective exhibitions on Alphons Mucha and Aubrey Beardsley in 1963 and 1966, and partly because its lavish excesses seemed such a perfect fit with the psychedelic spirit of youth culture.[66] Advertisements for Art Nouveau wallpapers, for example, showed them in the context of plastic chairs and trendy lamps, and were clearly aimed at young people.[67] By the end of the sixties the bold colours of late Victorian art had effectively conquered the world of fabric design, and through the seventies designs based on the work of artists like Beardsley and William Morris propelled Laura Ashley to international success.[68]

Victorianism was a powerful force not merely in design but in much of the culture of the late sixties, not least because it allowed artists to return to the days when Britain had been an unquestionably great power. Indeed, bearing in mind the success of *Sgt. Pepper* and *The Forsyte Saga*, as well as the vogue for wearing cast-off British imperial uniforms, it was not always easy to tell the late 1960s from the late 1860s. In 1969, for example, John Fowles published *The French Lieutenant's Woman*, one of the most imaginative and influential English novels of the period, which was set in 1867. Fowles's novel paid homage to the respectable conventions of Victorian England while showing how they were being undermined by Darwin, Marx and the Pre-Raphaelites. Similarly, it was both a nostalgic work of psychological realism and a distinctly 'postmodern' novel, in which the narrator draws explicit parallels with the world of the 1960s and even appears as a character in his own book.[69]

Fowles's ironic juxtaposition of old and new was not so different from that of the Beatles in *Sgt. Pepper*, or, indeed, that of thousands of ordinary people in their own households. No self-respecting bohemian in the late sixties would have been seen dead in a modern suburban home; instead, they preferred to live in renovated Victorian cottages, stuffed with a random array of gaudy Space-Age gadgets and fading historicist furnishings. As the interior decorator David Hicks told the readers of the *Sun*, the fashionable homeowner should have a television set, 'covered with Perspex so that you can see all the works', surrounded by 'things like penny-farthing bicycles, and those old GPO red wicker delivery barrows', a bizarre combination of flashy modernity and battered junk.[70]

Overt eclecticism of this kind epitomised the 'hippy look', which was summed up by the *Mirror*'s fashion correspondent Felicity Green as 'baubles, bangles, beads and bells'.[71] As Elizabeth Wilson puts it:

> Hair, which had been short, lacquered and straight, became long and curly, for both sexes. Sleeves which had been tight and shortish became long, gathered, flowing. Bell-bottomed trousers widened until they looked like skirts, and skirts which had been short and straight sank to the floor. Jackets were suddenly flowery, eighteenth-century, and brocade and velvet bloomed. Scarves, a garment unknown either to the mods or Mary Quant, were festooned in twos, threes, fours around the throat, to sink floating to the knees. Collars got larger and longer, like rabbits' ears. Make-up became first naturalistic, then vampishly exaggerated.[72]

As with the wider culture of revivalism, the hippy look can easily be interpreted as a reaction against the sharp lines of scientific optimism. Where Mary Quant and the dolly birds had emphasised stark geometric precision, younger designers like Ossie Clark and Celia Birtwell preferred flowing curves and floral patterns, creating an impression of lush Victorian neo-romanticism.[73] Certainly by 1967 or so it was clear that the Mod look was distinctly old hat and that trendy young things were wearing rather more dishevelled and self-consciously bohemian outfits. 'Suddenly,' announced the *Daily Sketch* in July 1967, 'happiness is flower-shaped.' The 'in' things, apparently, were 'Indian jackets and dresses, kimonos, Victorian dresses, elaborately patterned, beaded and flowing twenties and thirties dresses, bell-bottomed trousers and brocade waistcoats. Plus, of course, those beads, bells — and flowers.'[74]

Although aspiring hippies prided themselves on their eclecticism, they nevertheless wore a kind of uniform, just like the Mods before them. In place of mini-skirts, many young women wore maxi-dresses and maxi-coats stretching down to their ankles. Since these garments covered up the female figure, they had the right cultural connotations for the age of women's liberation. Many women even wore trousers, usually in denim or corduroy, which was in itself a radical break with the tradition that men and women wore entirely different things below the waist. The woman who wore trousers, rather like the woman who had worn a mini-skirt a few years before, implicitly proclaimed her independence from the old stereotypes, so it was hardly surprising that the sight of women in trousers continued to offend older men for the next decade or so.[75] The trousers in question were usually flared bell-bottoms, a striking contrast with the narrow drainpipes of the late fifties and early sixties. One trendy young thing later reflected that he had worn 'flared trousers so big that your shoes disappeared . . . I used to shop at Lawrence Corner, the Army surplus place. They had the best loons in the world, proper ex-sailor's trousers that they dyed in psychedelic colours, and other bits of naval kit like square-necked shirts and sweaters.'[76] Bell-bottomed trousers were themselves a nineteenth-century invention, designed for Royal Navy sailors who wanted to roll up their trouser legs while working on deck, and, like many of the trends of the late sixties, they had rather ironic military connotations. What one writer calls the 'playful subversion of vintage military uniforms' was one of the more striking fashions of the period, reflecting the exaggerated patriotism of pop iconography in the middle of the decade. As early as *A Hard Day's Night* (1964), the Beatles had delighted in dressing up in a variety of uniforms, and of course they were at it again on the cover of *Sgt. Pepper's Lonely Hearts Club Band*.

Thanks largely to the Beatles, uniforms were extremely fashionable by 1967, and the best place to buy them was at I Was Lord Kitchener's Valet, a painfully trendy boutique on the Portobello Road, which overflowed with Union Jacks and imperial memorabilia.[77] In July 1967 an advertisement promised drill tunics, authentic 'naval bell-bottoms', 'Continental police capes', capes lined with silk and velvet, and even pilot's sunglasses from the Second World War.[78] The shop became so well known that there was even a reference to it in an episode of *The Avengers*: when Steed attends a party in military fancy dress another character murmurs: 'Kitchener's Valet?'[79]

To avoid looking too militaristic at a time when many youngsters were concerned about the Vietnam War, many men wore these outfits with beards and moustaches. In the fifties and early sixties facial hair had been seen as slightly deviant, identified by, say, the heroes of Kingsley Amis's novels as an unmistakeable sign of bohemian pretentiousness, but this only made it all the more attractive to the younger generation. Facial hair was also a reassuring indicator of masculinity, making up for the 'feminisation' of men who wore bright, floral or even lacy shirts, flowery scarves and shaggy coats.[80] By the time of the launch party for *Sgt. Pepper*, for example, Lennon, Starr and especially Harrison all sported luxuriant moustaches and thick whiskers, while McCartney, although still clean-shaven, nevertheless had impressively long hair. All four experimented with beards over the next few years, often with slightly comical results.

Such was the Beatles' influence over the young that by the end of 1967 advertisements were offering teenagers the chance to become hirsute overnight. Under the headline 'Make the scene with these fantastic new raves!', Paul White Productions presented its 'False Sidepieces' and 'False Moustache' — adding, rather intriguingly, 'as seen on TV!' For just 19s 6d, young men could 'send now for these great false sideburns, made in authentic crepe hair'. Apparently the 'Edwardian style' sideburns were 'so realistic [they are] almost undetectable [and] can be used time and time again'. Customers were advised to 'send [a] small cutting of your hair for colour and matching. Your shade will be matched as near as possible.' Fixative glue, however, was extra.[81]

Like other fashions before it, the hippy look depended on the influence of pop stars and the commercial expertise of a string of boutiques, of which I Was Lord Kitchener's Valet was a typical example. Another was Hung on

You, a large basement decorated with William Morris prints just off the King's Road. When a journalist visited the shop towards the end of 1966, he encountered two assistants, the man clad in 'a lace shirt and orange trousers too tight for him to move without appearing to be suffering from arthritis', and the woman in 'a mini-skirt so short it would not even have afforded decent coverage over a pigmy's buttocks' and a 'transparent smock through which it was easy to see that she was wearing no other garment of any kind'. Despite their striking appearance, the assistants were hampered by the fact that the shelves were bare of products of any kind. Customers were supposed to request specific items, which were then brought out of a back room, a rather whimsical arrangement that never caught on.[82] Other visitors were more fortunate to arrive when the clothes were actually put out for inspection: *Vogue*, for example, reported that 'the strains of Bob Dylan float up past cupboards groaning with satin stripe shirts and racks heavy with jackets and trousers in ravishing pin stripes, blue, grey and marmalade'.[83]

The most striking hippy boutique was Granny Takes a Trip, owned by Nigel Waymouth, a former medical journalist on the fringes of the bohemian underground. Waymouth was more interested in the shop's appearance than in its bank balance, which was a recipe for disaster, although for a short time it was patronised by the likes of the Beatles and the Rolling Stones. He later explained:

> The shop definitely had an intimidating quality, a mystique. It was not a friendly shop. We were spearheading a movement, not consciously in a political way, but certainly style-wise. We were trying to break away. We weren't following designer traditions. The shop was part of that, trying to establish a look for people of the underground culture. Our customers were debs, gays, pop people, and both sexes. It was completely androgynous, we had only one changing room and the clothes were mixed on the rail.[84]

As Waymouth admitted at the time, the ethos of Granny Takes a Trip was all about 'playing out fantasies in real life'. When Jonathan Aitken visited the store for his research into Swinging London, he reported that it appeared to be 'run by bizarre eccentrics for bizarre eccentrics'. The exterior on the King's Road often changed to suit the whims of the proprietors: sometimes it was emblazoned with a grinning sun; sometimes it displayed a massive image of Sitting Bull; once it was even adorned with the front half of a Dodge car, which was welded to the wall as though it had crashed through. What never changed, however, was the rather precious slogan above the door: 'One should either be a work of art or wear a work of art.' Inside were mounds of mini-skirts, gold-rimmed sunglasses, floral ties, velveteen trousers and yellow suede jackets, while behind them were racks of Victorian bustles, Boer War helmets, Ottoman fezzes, Charleston dresses and Chicago gangster suits, as well as shelves of 'blown up photographs of Edwardian chorus girls at £2 each, antique swords, glass walking sticks, Victorian feather boas, an early gramophone [and] everything that would seem totally out-dated and absurd'. Picking one's way through this vast accumulation of junk was a difficult business, since it was so dark that Aitken could barely tell 'the difference between a flapper dress and a trouser suit', although by his own admission he was distracted by the 'Edwardian peep-show photo-machine, where one can look at slides of naked ladies'.[85]

Even Granny Takes a Trip paled into obscurity when set alongside the most successful boutique of the late sixties, Biba. This was the brainchild of Barbara Hulanicki, who had been born to Polish parents before moving to London in the late 1940s, studying at Brighton Art College and becoming a fashion illustrator for the likes of *Vogue*, *The Times* and the *Express*. Since Biba is often compared with Habitat as an emblematic enterprise of the sixties, it was fitting that it opened in similar circumstances and in the same year. Hulanicki had long nurtured ambitions of designing and selling her own clothes, and in May 1964 the *Daily Mirror* advertised her pink gingham dress as a readers' offer for twenty-five shillings. Demand was such that the paper reputedly received orders worth some £14,000, and Biba's Postal Boutique immediately took off.[86]

In September 1964 Hulanicki opened her first store in an old chemist's shop on Abingdon Road, Kensington, and it proved an overnight success. Unlike Mary Quant's shop Bazaar, Biba did not present an appearance of slick modernity, retaining the dilapidated exterior of the building and cultivating the air of 'an Eastern souk', with navy-blue painted walls, plum William Morris curtains, old bronze lamps and an antique Dutch wardrobe. Although the boutique was originally supposed to be a sideline to Hulanicki's booming mail-order business, its unusual pseudo-Oriental atmosphere immediately pulled in the crowds.[87] Twiggy described it as 'like no shop I had ever seen', with 'clothes hanging off wooden hat stands and wicker baskets filled with T-shirts like vests with shoe-lace necks'. There were no shop assistants, she remembered, just 'young girls with long blonde hair wandering about', replacing discarded clothes on the hat stands 'and taking the money in a big old-fashioned cash register'.[88]

The enormous success of Biba was due partly to the atmosphere of the store itself and partly, of course, to the clothes. In October 1965 Hulanicki told the *Telegraph*: 'I love old things. Modern things are so cold. I need things that are lived.' These were, according to the newspaper, 'baffling words for such a "with-it" designer', but they accurately foreshadowed the tastes of the late sixties.[89] Shunning the bright primary colours and black-and-white Op patterns beloved of other designers, Hulanicki preferred richer, darker tones: 'prune, aubergine, sage, dull duck egg blue, dirty cyclamen, sepia, cream, brick dust, and *bois de rose*', an array of shades of brown and maroon that anticipated the styles of the seventies.[90] By the time that Biba moved to a bigger store in 1966, this look had become even more exaggerated, and the new shop, a temple to *fin-de-siècle* extravagance, was stuffed with huge felt hats, feather boas, sweeping Victorian evening dresses and yards of crêpe, silk and satin. The aim was not to look clean and modern but decadent, sinister, even 'vampiric'.[91] As one customer put it, Biba cultivated 'a sort of lasciviousness, a sort of voluptuousness'; it sold 'clothes for the sinful and *louche*'.[92]

Biba was famous for its celebrity customers, from Cathy McGowan and Julie Christie to Marianne Faithfull and Brigitte Bardot. Unlike many boutiques, however, it was genuinely democratic. Bazaar, according to Twiggy, was for 'rich girls', but Biba, which she visited many times before her rise to fame, 'was for anyone'.[93] Hulanicki told an interviewer that she tried to 'keep everything as cheap as possible, about half the price of everywhere else'. Most dresses cost no more than £2.10s or so, with scarves, belts and the like priced at just a few shillings each. Even the most expensive items in the shop, like the maxi-coats, cost about seven pounds, which was much cheaper than the average garment in Hung on You or Granny Takes a Trip.[94] 'In 1966,' recalled the *Vogue* journalist Georgina Howell, 'for £15, the price of a Mary Quant party dress, you could walk out of Biba in a new coat, dress, shoes, petticoat and hat.'[95]

More than any other institution of the sixties, Biba was a shrine to the new spending power of youth, with services held on Saturdays. When the shop moved into Kensington Church Street at the end of 1966, one journalist reported that 'an estimated 3,000 dolly birds each week push through the heavy Victorian wood and brass doors, intent on dissipating their last shillings on the tempting sartorial baubles of the Aladdin's cave that lies within'. An office girl who earned just thirteen pounds a week admitted that she spent more than half of it at Biba every Saturday. Another said that she worked three nights a week as a waitress, on top of her day job, so that she could spend six pounds a week at Biba. A third estimated that she spent 'half my wages' at the store, although she admitted that 'if I come here and I see something I really like and can't quite afford, I just nick it'.[96] A shop assistant later recalled:

> Every Saturday it was madness. It was an amazing atmosphere, there were hundreds of girls milling around the shop. You just couldn't move. The changing rooms were knee-deep in clothes. Nobody put anything back. All the clothes were so cheap, you wore them one week and threw them away the next. That didn't stop lots of the gear being pinched. Hardly anybody came in without buying something or taking it. It was so chaotic, there were bags everywhere. Once the morning's takings were handed over to one of the customers in a bag, instead of her feather boa. Nobody noticed at the time.[97]

All of this 'madness' only added to Biba's appeal. By the beginning of 1967 it was reputed to have the highest turnover per square foot of any shop in the world.[98] Two years later Biba moved into even bigger premises, an old warehouse in Kensington High Street with Egyptian columns, marble floors, stained-glass windows and wood-panelled walls. This new store enjoyed even more success, attracting an estimated 100,000 customers a week and 30,000 on Saturdays alone, and claiming a turnover of more than £200 per square foot, four times that of the average department store.[99]

Biba was now more than a store. It was the quintessential brand of the late sixties and early seventies, producing cosmetics, shoes and boots, clothes for men and children, and even wallpaper and home furnishings. However, as in any good tragedy, the signs of disaster were already apparent. Shoplifting was a chronic problem and an illustration of the disorganisation at the heart of the store. On the opening day of the Church Street store in 1966, Hulanicki lost 103 pairs of earrings, 78 pairs of sunglasses and 'God knows what else', and in an average week she prosecuted about a dozen shoplifters, although many others doubtless went undetected.[100] Biba's democratic ethos also meant that it never greatly impressed the fashion writers, who treated it with the same condescending scorn that they lavished on the tourist traps of Carnaby Street. The clothes were cheap but they were also made in a hurry, and standards were not always high. Hulanicki herself wrote of an 'uncomfortable Biba smock that itched' and 'long skinny sleeves ... so tight they hindered the circulation'.[101] But the real problem was overambition. In 1973 Biba moved to its biggest location yet, the former Derry and Toms department store in Kensington, which was converted into seven storeys of Art Deco luxury. Hulanicki and her business partners had spent nearly £4 million buying the premises and £1 million on the conversion, and it certainly showed: there was a food hall, a concert hall, a rooftop garden, a marbled restaurant serving fifteen hundred meals a day on black china, and so on. This 'Big Biba' was the first new department store in London since the Second World War, but despite the opulent splendour it was a fiasco, being simply too large to run properly and haemorrhaging money. Just two years after it had opened Hulanicki's partners pulled the plug.[102]

Like almost every other boutique of the late sixties, Biba did not survive the transition to the harsher commercial environment of the mid-1970s. Indeed, it is striking that despite all the attention often given to the boutiques of Swinging London, their story was ultimately one of excessive ambition, insufficient capital and commercial disaster. As early as 1966 fifty fashion businesses were filing for bankruptcy every month, and as the economic picture darkened at the turn of the decade the culture of the boutiques disintegrated. The eclecticism of the hippy look was always relatively difficult to maintain without time and money, and in any case most high-street chains had now adapted to the needs of the younger market, using their efficient design, distribution and marketing networks to produce similar clothes for lower prices. Even Barbara Hulanicki, who had prided herself on the cheapness of her products, found that in the last days of Biba she could walk down the road and find very similar designs at C&A for half the price.[103]

Only one boutique really survived the journey into the cut-throat world of the seventies and eighties. In 1967 the first Laura Ashley shop opened in Kensington, just down the road from Biba, and was similarly immersed in Victorian revivalism and the spirit of William Morris. The ethos of Laura Ashley was much gentler and more restrained, but in the long run that was its great strength. By the late seventies it would come to seem the very incarnation of middle-class conservatism, appealing to young and old alike, striving for a timeless appeal rather than trying to ride the winds of fashion. Few people remarked on the irony that, more than any other establishment on the British high street, it was Laura Ashley that preserved the look of the late sixties.[104]

22

HEAVENS ABOVE!

> *Honest to God* is certainly the most helpful Christian theology that I've ever come across and I'm sure millions of others feel the same.
>
> Tony Benn's diary, 13 May 1963

> You won't find any of the Stones going around praying, see us in church or reading the Bible. We're atheists and not ashamed to admit it. When you get to know us, we're pretty good guys at heart. People who go to church just for the sake of it, to keep up appearances and smile at the vicar, are idiots. Those who go because they believe in God's faith, that's fine. We'll leave religion to the dedicated.
>
> Keith Richards, 1965

On 24 August 1967 the four members of the Beatles pushed their way through the crowds into the Park Lane Hilton for a most unusual lecture. The speaker was the Maharishi Mahesh Yogi, a self-professed Indian holy man with a grey beard, long robes and bunches of flowers. He had studied transcendental meditation for thirteen years in the Himalayas, and thanks to a highly developed public relations operation already had some 250 worldwide meditation centres and 10,000 British converts.[1] None of his followers, however, were as famous as the Beatles. After the Hilton lecture they were granted a brief audience with the great man. 'You have created a magic wand in your name,' he told them. 'Wave it so that it will move in the proper direction.'[2]

Amazingly, the Beatles were so impressed by all this that they agreed to go the following day to a course for the 'spiritually regenerated' in the unlikely surroundings of University College, Bangor. This was the first journey the Beatles had made without Brian Epstein or their road managers, and Lennon compared it to 'going somewhere without your trousers', although they were travelling with their wives and girlfriends, and had persuaded Mick Jagger and Marianne Faithfull to accompany them. When the party left Paddington Station the following morning they were waved off by a horde of journalists as well as the usual mob of screaming fans, and spent the journey crammed into one first-class train compartment, afraid to venture to the toilet for fear of being molested by the general public. Meanwhile, further down the train, the Maharishi occupied his own first-class compartment, squatting on a sheet draped over the British Rail upholstery.[3]

On arrival in Bangor, the passengers disembarked to the sound of teenage screaming. Amusingly enough, the Maharishi assumed that the crowds were there for him, not for the Beatles. His famous guests had to sleep in the same drab college bedrooms as the three hundred other meditation students who were on the same course, and a telling moment of farce ensued when they all went out for a Chinese meal in Bangor and discovered at the end that none of them, despite their millions, had enough money to pay the bill. Eventually, a sheepish Harrison pulled off his sandal, levered open the sole and produced a wad of ten-pound notes.[4]

The course itself was rather mysterious, all flowers and mantras, but the Maharishi was canny enough to organise a press conference for the massed journalists camped outside the college. On the second day, however, while his guests were strolling around the grounds, their reverie was broken by a telephone call bringing the most horrendous news: Brian Epstein, the man who had managed the Beatles since their days of obscurity in Liverpool, had been found dead after a drug overdose.

Even though Epstein's influence had been on the wane, his death came as an unexpected and shattering shock to his former charges. They were 'desolate', noted a sympathetic Marianne Faithfull: 'it was as if a part of them had died'. But when the Beatles went in to see the Maharishi and told him that they had to return to London, he appeared completely unmoved. Faithfull was struck by how impassively he took their terrible news: 'He gave them the classic Indian thing, which is, "There was a death in the family. There are many families, there is one family. Brian Epstein has moved on. He doesn't need you any more, and you don't need him. He was like a father to you but now he is gone, and now I am your father. I'll look after you all now." I was appalled.'[5]

Although the sixties are often seen as a secular, even post-religious, age, in few decades of the twentieth century were religious issues so hotly and enthusiastically debated. In 1963, when the Beatles first stormed into the charts, one of the most popular British films of the year directly addressed the subject of religion in the affluent society. The comedy *Heavens Above!* was notable for a wonderful performance by Peter Sellers, who plays an idealistic, progressive clergyman, forever clasping and unclasping his hands, smiling naively but serenely, his accent poised between the provincial lower middle class and church training college. One priest even told Sellers that it was 'very convincing, very moving'.[6] As the critic Raymond Durgnat puts it:

> A gesture of quietly clasping his hands is half old-style pious resignation, half new-style happy-clappy. The mad gleam in his eye coexists with quiet cunning. You never know if his next remark will be naively archaic, or wildly trendy, or uncomfortably acute. He is an ever-surprising mixture: buoyantly unselfish, a creeping Jesus, instinctively non-snobbish, invincibly self-righteous.[7]

The appeal of *Heavens Above!* rested on the fact that Sellers was playing such an instantly recognisable stereotype. Throughout the late fifties and early sixties there were several infamous examples of Anglican vicars striving desperately to appear culturally relevant, and few caricatures were as laughable as the 'trendy vicar'. The Bishop of Coventry told the *Observer* that he was looking forward to 'experiments in "new-look worship"', while his provost even described the city's new cathedral as 'a gigantic visual aid'.[8] One East End example, the Reverend William Shergold, established a bikers' youth club and dressed in black leather, making him an easy target for the cartoonists who imagined motorbikes charging down the church aisles to the sound of the prayer 'Oh Gawd in Heaven, bless this Norton 650'.[9]

Appearing in a televised BBC discussion with the singer Adam Faith in 1962, the Archbishop of York, Donald Coggan, took great pains to present himself as a modern churchman. 'I'm one of those who feel that sex is a thoroughly good thing, implanted by God,' he explained. 'I'm not one of those who belong to the generation who thought it was a sort of smutty thing that you only talk about hush-hush.' Although Faith appeared unconvinced, Coggan insisted that he was 'all for' rewriting the classic hymns so that the young could understand them. 'All youngsters should think out a faith strong enough for this life and for the world to come,' he went on. 'Religion is jolly relevant to this life.'[10] It was hardly surprising that a spoof soon appeared in the form of a *Guardian* piece by Michael Frayn purporting to be the thoughts of the Bishop of Twicester (pronounced

'Twister'). 'You see', wrote the fictitious Bishop, 'religion isn't just a narrow set of dos and don'ts, or a lot of abstract doctrine and long-winded ritual. It's – well, it's taking a girl to the pictures. It's doing the ton on your motorbike. It's rocking and rolling.'[11]

The most controversial progressive churchman of the sixties was Dr John Robinson, a former Cambridge theology lecturer and, from 1959, Suffragan Bishop of Woolwich. Robinson was a member of the Labour Party, a founder of Christian CND and an outspoken opponent of apartheid, as well as a spokesman for the ordination of women and a translator of the *New English Bible*.[12] His first stint in the limelight came at the *Lady Chatterley's Lover* trial in 1960, where he claimed that D. H. Lawrence was trying to 'portray the sex relationship as something essentially sacred . . . as in a real sense an act of holy communion'. Asked whether the novel was 'a book which in your view Christians ought to read', he replied, confidently: 'Yes, I think it is.'[13] This exchange unsurprisingly found its way into the newspapers, and Robinson earned himself a rebuke from the Archbishop of Canterbury, who commented that Robinson's appearance in the courtroom had been 'a cause of offence to many ordinary Christians'.[14] Robinson, however, was unapologetic. A week later he wrote in the *Observer* that Lawrence's ideas about 'the sacredness of sex' fitted quite well into Christian teaching, and that the Church had 'an unhappy record in this matter, for which it has to make amends'.[15]

But this controversy was as nothing compared with the furore that greeted Robinson's book, *Honest to God*, in March 1963. Two days before publication Robinson summarised his arguments in an inflammatory article for the *Observer* entitled 'Our Image of God Must Go', although this was not a title he had chosen himself. Christianity, he explained, had reached a turning point. If it was to survive, 'it must be relevant to modern secular man, not just to the dwindling number of the religious'. Modern man, he said, had 'become increasingly non-religious', and the churches 'deplored this as the great defection from God'. But Robinson disagreed: modern man was actually 'coming of age'.

> For good or ill he is putting the religious world-view behind him as childish and pre-scientific . . . I believe that Christians must go through the agonising process in this generation of detaching themselves from this idol. For to Twentieth Century man the 'old man in the sky' and the whole supernaturalist scheme seem as fanciful as the man in the moon.[16]

In *Honest to God* Robinson developed this argument in greater depth. The idea of a 'God who is literally or physically "up there"' was, he said, 'more of a hindrance than a help'. He even thought that 'we should do well to give up using the word "God" for a generation, so impregnated has it become with a way of thinking we may have to discard if the Gospel is to signify anything'.[17] God, he went on, is not 'another Being *at all*' but 'the depths of your life . . . what you take seriously without any reservation'.[18] And where morality was concerned, he was even more iconoclastic. Nothing, he said, 'can of itself always be labelled as "wrong"', despite the strictures of the Bible and the Church. Instead, the only imperative was to follow the path of love, depending on the situation. As a sympathetic churchman later put it: 'Our moral decisions must be guided by the actual relationships between the persons concerned at a particular time in a particular situation, and compassion for persons overrides all law. The only intrinsic evil is lack of love.'[19]

Even though Robinson had already floated these controversial views in the *Observer*, the entire print run of *Honest to God*, some six thousand copies, was snapped up within days of publication. Within a year the book had sold over 300,000 copies, an unprecedented amount for a theological text, and the publishers also brought out a companion volume of essays and reaction.[20] Although Robinson had his defenders, many of his fellow churchmen were bitterly hostile to the arguments in *Honest to God*. 'It is not every day that a bishop goes on record as apparently denying almost every Christian doctrine of the Church in which he holds office,' remarked the *Church Times*.[21] The Bishop of Bristol accused Robinson of 'irresponsibility in publishing his book', while the Bishop of Pontefract claimed that *Honest to God* was a 'dangerous book likely to disturb the faith of more people than it will stimulate'. The Bishop of Llandaff, however, replied that the book asked sensible questions about some important issues, 'and when we try to answer them we find the bishop's answers so often ring true more than our own'.[22]

Many of the more traditional members of the Church of England, as well as conservative commentators in the national press, were appalled by the popularity of *Honest to God*, and regarded Robinson as little better than an atheist doing a very poor impersonation of a bishop. T. E. Utley, writing in the *Sunday Telegraph*, thought it a shame that only a protracted prosecution for heresy could remove Robinson from his post when he was so clearly damaging the cause of the Church.[23] Bernard Levin recorded:

An energetic Scottish lady cried out that 'A bishop who writes a book like this should be stripped to his socks', and inked in the enchanting picture she thus conjured up by adding: 'If the Archbishop of Canterbury doesn't unfrock him, I and the women of England will'; alas, she never made good her threat, so the public debagging of a bishop, a spectacle which would surely have attracted spectators of all shades of religious opinion and of none, never took place.[24]

The success of *Honest to God* makes sense only in a wider social and cultural context. Robinson was already a contentious public figure after his appearance in the *Lady Chatterley* trial, and he profited from the fact that he was the first Anglican theologian to bring the fashionable religious ideas of European thinkers to a domestic audience. Virtually nothing in *Honest to God* was original, with Robinson's ideas generally being borrowed from the likes of Dietrich Bonhoeffer, Rudolf Bultmann and Paul Tillich. More importantly, the book appeared at a particularly auspicious moment. The late fifties and early sixties had been a period of intense moral debate, as existing values were challenged by affluence, mobility and modernity. Discussions about teenage delinquency and sexual misconduct reflected wider concerns about morality and social identity, and a book like *Honest to God* was well placed to exploit them.[25] It was also very well timed because established religion in Britain was thought to be under unprecedented threat. Robinson himself insisted: 'If Christianity is to survive, let alone to recapture "secular" man, there is no time to lose.'[26] Two months before his book was published Monica Furlong had written in the *Guardian* that 'the best thing about being a Christian at the moment is that organized religion has collapsed . . . It is common knowledge that the foundations have shivered, that there are cracks a mile wide in the walls.'[27]

Indeed, there does seem to have been a sense in the early sixties that the foundations of British Christianity were finally crumbling under the harsh lights of modernity. Bryan Forbes's popular film *Whistle Down the Wind* (1961), for example, tells the story of three Lancashire children who mistake an escaped convict for the returned Christ. The established Church is depicted as mediocre and irrelevant: at one point a girl is looking for the vicar, who, engrossed in a detective novel, tries to avoid her. When she does find him, he answers with entirely false warmth, getting her name wrong in the process. At the same time the film is permeated by a sense of sadness. Although it mocks the pretensions of religion, it does so mournfully, and when in the final scene the police arrest the children's Christ and take him off in handcuffs, we have the impression that their naive but touching innocence has been destroyed.[28]

A similar atmosphere of melancholy pervaded much contemporary literature. In 'Church-Going', for example, written in July 1954, Philip Larkin describes a visit to a dusty, empty church, heavy with 'a tense, musty, unignorable silence'. He wonders what will become of churches when they 'fall completely out of use': will they be let 'rent-free to rain and sheep', perhaps, or avoided as 'unlucky places'?[29] In John Betjeman's poems, meanwhile, there are plenty of references to crumbling, half-empty 'country churches old and pale', 'plaintive bells' echoing down silent country lanes, and so on.[30] And there is an even stronger sense of pain, isolation and doubt, of man left alone in a godless world, in the verse of the Welsh poet R. S. Thomas. In his poem 'In Church' (1966) he imagines a lone worshipper kneeling in the silence and gloom of an empty church:

> There is no other sound
> In the darkness but the sound of a man
> Breathing, testing his faith
> On emptiness, nailing his questions
> One by one to an untenanted cross.[31]

The sense of decline that pervaded British Christianity in the sixties was all the more striking because just ten years earlier, many people had been predicting a religious revival. Opinion polls in the mid-1950s suggested that at least seven out of ten people believed in God; an estimated one in four people went regularly to church, with perhaps half that number going every week; and half of all families sent their children to Sunday school.[32] The established churches reported increases in ordinations, confirmations and general attendance; the readership of the *Church Times* reached its highest level since 1900; and the 1958 Lambeth Conference confirmed Anglicanism's place among the major religions of the world.[33] What was more, for a short time, Anglicanism was culturally respectable again, its appeal bolstered by the intellectual credibility of prominent worshippers like C.S. Lewis, John Betjeman and Dorothy L. Sayers.[34] Indeed, as the researchers Peter Wimlott and Michael Young found in the London suburb of Woodford, the local church was in some ways a quintessential middle-class club, a way of meeting new neighbours and mixing with the right sort. For many, perhaps most people, church-going was a similar social ritual to attending a Women's Institute or Conservative Association meeting, a matter of appearing in one's best clothes and listening to worthy speeches.[35]

And yet Willmott and Young also noted that 'even among the middle class in Woodford, regular weekly church-going is the practice of only a minority'.[36] In truth, the churches were steadily losing their hold on the hearts and minds of their British congregations. Throughout the twentieth century, the faster that affluence and social mobility increased, the faster religious affiliation dwindled.[37] By the beginning of the sixties decades of gradual decline had left barely one in ten people going to church every week. Congregations were predominantly middle class, and there were far more women than men. Just under half the population were irregular churchgoers, attending perhaps once or twice a year at Christmas, Easter and special occasions, but only by the loosest possible definition could they be called 'practising Christians'. Around two in five people, meanwhile, never set foot in a church, except perhaps to attend marriages or funerals.[38] By 1970 organised religion was in an even more parlous state, with fewer than two in a hundred adolescent boys being confirmed in the Church of England, while fewer than 50 per cent of babies were even baptised.[39] Whatever indicator is taken, the same picture emerges: a steady fall until 1960, then a sudden collapse. Even the involvement of the Church in the management of death was undermined, as more people chose to have their funeral organised in a crematorium by professional funeral directors, rather than in a parish church by the local vicar.[40]

The Church of England was not the only religious institution to suffer in the post-war decades. At the beginning of the sixties just under two million people were members of a Nonconformist sect, of which the Methodists and Baptists were most popular, and five million more were Catholics.[41] The Nonconformists had an especially bad time of it, and as the appeal of traditional working-class thrift and rigour declined their numbers fell by as much as a third.[42] For Roman Catholicism, however, it was a different story. Most Catholics were of Irish working-class origin and were concentrated in big cities and ports like London and Liverpool.[43] Not only were they slow to abandon their religious habits, but their numbers were swelled in the sixties by further immigration from both parts of Ireland. The Catholic Church had also jealously guarded its place in the classroom, and Catholic schools therefore represented a seductive alternative for parents distrustful of ordinary state secondary education.[44] By the end of the sixties, with a Catholic Director General of the BBC, a Catholic editor of *The Times*, and a Catholic General Secretary of the TUC, it was easy to forget how potent anti-Catholicism had once been in mainland British life.[45]

There are many explanations for the decline of Protestant church membership in the 1960s. As people became more affluent, so they began to reconsider the values of their parents. As they benefited from advances in medical science, so their longing for spiritual security decreased. As social clubs and organisations of all kinds proliferated, so the parish church exercised less of a pull; as people moved around the country, so they lost their connection with their local vicar. Christianity was also a declining force in the nation's schools: after the 1944 Education Act many Anglican schools had been converted into ordinary state schools, and in the following twenty-five years the number of English Protestant church schools fell by three-quarters. At the same time the decline of religious instruction in schools meant that children grew up without the religious vocabulary that their parents, whatever their beliefs, had automatically shared.[46] As the theologian Adrian Hastings puts it, the 'advancing secular consensus of middle England in the Sixties owed a great deal to the educational choices made in the 1940s'.[47]

One other explanation might be that people were actually put off, rather than attracted, by the new progressive trend epitomised by John Robinson and his admirers. Many Protestant churchmen, alarmed at their inability to reverse the long decline, concluded that 'relevance was the order of the day'. According to Grace Davie, the churches, besotted like so many other institutions by the 'desire to be modern', consequently 'looked to the secular world for a lead and borrowed, in some cases rather uncritically, both its ideas and forms of expression'. It was in this period, for example, that liberal churchmen first began wielding guitars, introducing handclapping into the Anglican rite and generally conducting themselves like frustrated pop singers, a tactic that failed to attract many new parishioners and often alienated those still loyal to the Church of England.[48]

From the early sixties onwards, fictional vicars on film and television, as in *Heavens Above!*, *All Gas and Gaiters* and *Dad's Army*, were portrayed as comically naive and incompetent figures, cut off from worldly realities and laughably inept in their attempts to appear modern.[49] Indeed, when the church hierarchy supported the legislative reforms on homosexuality, abortion and divorce in the late sixties, it often earned the opprobrium of sections of the public. Michael Ramsey, the gentle Archbishop of Canterbury, publicly opposed the death penalty, endorsed both divorce and abortion, reached out to the Methodists and the Catholics and allowed the ordination of women in Hong Kong, all positions which horrified some of the more conservative members of the Church and provoked a stream of furious letters from ordinary parishioners.[50]

For some observers, the decline of organised religion was part of a broader, long-term repudiation of supernatural authority. Bryan Wilson, for example, wrote in 1969 that 'religion – seen as a way of thinking, as the performance of particular practices, and as the institutionalization and organization of these patterns of thought and action – has lost influence'.[51] Similarly, Callum Brown claims that people 'started to reject the role of religion in their lives', turning against the idea of faith itself in an overwhelming 'secularisation' of British society.[52]

But the collapse of churchgoing did not necessarily mean that religion 'as a way of thinking' was in retreat. Other observers, like David Martin, in *Religion in Secular Society* (1966), and Harvey Cox, in *The Seduction of the Spirit* (1974), thought that man's spiritual urge was constant, and that religious belief was being expressed in new ways.[53] A survey in 1947 had found that while only 50 per cent of people believed in the Virgin Birth, the divinity of Christ and life after death, the great majority did believe in God, and only one in twenty was a firm atheist.[54] These figures remained fairly constant throughout the next forty years or so, with just under half of the population believing in an afterlife and three-quarters believing in God, with the majority of the rest undecided.[55] This is what Grace Davie calls 'believing without belonging': while participation fell out of fashion, belief remained constant. Indeed, over the course of the century 'belonging' in general lost its attraction: clubs, trade unions, political parties and churches all lost members as life became individualised, domesticated and increasingly private. Rather than becoming 'secularised', then, most people simply became 'unchurched'.[56]

Despite frequent claims to the contrary, therefore, Britain in the sixties was not a secular or 'post-religious' society. Older generations were still bound together by their knowledge of the popular hymns that they had sung in churches and schools, on ships and battlefields and at football or rugby matches.[57] The great commercial success of the *New English Bible*, the first part of which was published in 1961, indicated that Christianity still meant a great deal to many people.[58] And although the Church of England

and the other Protestant churches were dwindling in terms of attendance, they still commanded the instinctive cultural allegiance of millions who attended only once or twice a year or even not at all: perhaps thirty million people in all.[59] Most people lacked any sophisticated religious world-view, but instead shared a hazy belief in God and an intuitive loyalty to the Church of their parents. Davie quotes a memorable exchange from one academic survey in Islington in the late sixties:

'Do you believe in God?'
'Yes.'
'Do you believe in a God who can change the course of events on earth?'
'No, just the ordinary one.'[60]

The most notorious example of the persistence of the spiritual impulse in the 1960s was the vogue for superstitions, cults and Eastern religions, with the Beatles, as we have seen, at the forefront. This was not a new phenomenon: mesmerism and spiritualism had been popular in the late nineteenth and early twentieth centuries, and the Orient and the occult feature heavily in the novels of both Arthur Conan Doyle and Agatha Christie. In bohemian or artistic circles all things Oriental had the lure of the mysterious, the glamorous, even the forbidden. Indeed, intellectual fascination with the supposedly exotic, elaborate East ran deep, from *The Moonstone* and *The Mikado* to *Kim* and carpets. And after the Second World War the greater ease of international communications and travel meant that Eastern influences were stronger than ever, while the increasing affluence of the middle classes meant that they could aspire to the same fashionable Oriental affectations as their social superiors.[61]

Eastern values were often depicted in popular culture as impenetrably strange and yet also closer both to nature and to the supernatural, representing a primitive but powerful spiritualism absent in the materialistic, rationalist societies of the West. In the early Hammer horror film *The Abominable Snowman* (1957), for example, a group of Himalayan explorers led by Peter Cushing ignore the advice of a kindly lama and head off to search for the Yeti, with disastrous results. The British are crude, selfish, unimaginative and violent; the Tibetans are mystical, gentle people, full of simple wisdom. As one film historian puts it, 'the culture of the East is now seen as offering a corrective to that of the West'.[62] This was very similar to the appeal of Oriental religions in the sixties. From Buddhism to transcendental meditation, they gave an implicit rebuke to the materialism of the affluent society, and answered the spiritual yearnings of those who found established Christianity unappealing but were drawn by the lure of the supposed exoticism and simplicity of the East.

In Agatha Christie's detective novel *Endless Night* (1967), a surprisingly successful stab at updating her style for a contemporary readership, one young man complains:

> They wanted me to go steady with a nice girl, save money, get married to her and then settle down to a nice steady job. Day after day, year after year, world without end, amen. Not for yours truly! There must be something better than that. Not just all this tame security, the good old welfare state limping along in its half-baked way! Surely, I thought, in a world where man has been able to put satellites in the sky and where men talk big about visiting the stars, there must be *something* that rouses you, that's worth while searching all over the world to find![63]

For many similarly disaffected young Britons in the sixties, the solution to all this existential doubt lay in India, or rather in their romanticised image of mysticism, drugs and spiritual enlightenment. The 'hippy trail', with its promise of sunshine and opium, lured hundreds of wealthy British students on a trek from Turkey to Nepal, to the mingled amusement and irritation of the local peoples.[64] However, this appealed only to a small, affluent minority. Much more popular, and less expensive, was the internal journey towards enlightenment, of a kind practised by bohemians for decades. The mode of expression had changed, of course, since the pre-war years, when George Orwell had grumbled about the faddishness of the 'fruit-juice drinker, nudist, sandal-wearer, sex-maniac, Quaker, "Nature Cure" quack, pacifist and feminist'. Still, in the sixties sex and sandals were still *de rigueur* for the self-respecting bohemian, although fruit juice was no longer considered quite so exotic.[65]

One of the more controversial religious phenomena of the sixties was the rise of Indian gurus like the Maharishi. 'Never was it easier to gain a reputation as a seer,' wrote Bernard Levin; 'never was a following more rapidly and readily acquired. Teachers, prophets, sibyls, oracles, mystagogues, avatars, haruspices and mullahs roamed the land, gathering flocks about them as easily as holy men in nineteenth-century Russia.'[66] There were plenty of notorious examples. The 'Awakener', one Meher Baba, kept a vow of silence from 1925 until his death in 1969 and made a great impression on Pete Townshend and the rest of the Who. Rather more disturbingly, there was the Bhagwan Shree Rajneesh, whose gospel of unbridled sexual excess had by the early eighties attracted 200,000 orange-robed devotees worldwide, swelling the Bhagwan's coffers and allowing him to indulge his obsession with Rolls-Royces until his American commune fell apart amid various lurid allegations of murder, lust and embezzlement.[67]

By far the most fashionable Indian guru, of course, was the Maharishi Mahesh Yogi, whose association with the Beatles propelled him into the headlines. The band first became interested in India during the filming of *Help!* in April 1965, when George Harrison was greatly taken with a group of sitar-playing musicians. That October he persuaded Lennon and McCartney to let him play the sitar on the track 'Norwegian Wood'.[68] In the autumn of 1966 he visited India with his wife Patti Boyd, and spent six weeks practising with Ravi Shankar and generally immersed himself in Eastern mysticism. When he returned to Britain Harrison 'practised day and night, sitting on the floor in his Indian smock in his Esher home', listening to tapes of Shankar's instructions.[69] After complaints from some fans about his 'Arabic-sounding guitar', he insisted: 'I won't stop playing it if you, or anyone else tells me it's unfashionable. I don't care what people say.'[70]

Despite the tragedy that had cut short the Beatles' expedition to Bangor, they were still fascinated by the Maharishi, who offered them something so different from the usual weary round of interviews, concerts and recording. In February 1968 they embarked on perhaps their strangest journey of all, flying to his idyllic retreat in the foothills above the Ganges at Rishikesh, with their wives and friends in tow.[71] This time they wore Indian clothes: the women were in saris and the men, who also grew beards, in tunics and loose trousers, to which John Lennon added a turban. They were housed in a row of stone cottages and ate communal vegetarian meals in an open dining room. Ringo Starr, wary of foreign food, had brought a suitcase full of baked beans with him, but he did not enjoy the routine and left with his wife Maureen after ten days.[72]

The others – George and Patti Harrison, John and Cynthia Lennon, Paul McCartney and Jane Asher, as well as the actress Mia Farrow, the folk singer Donovan and various other associates – stuck it out for rather longer. However, although they wrote forty songs between them, and enjoyed the simplicity and exoticism of the location, they found the routine of the camp extremely restrictive. Very quickly their natural irreverence began to assert itself, and the Maharishi almost caught McCartney and Donovan smoking an illicit cigarette behind the lecture hall. McCartney later recalled that they saw it 'as a tourist thing. "Eh, you got any of them snake charmers, then, Swami? Can you do the Indian rope trick?" ... We were just Liverpool lads,' he wryly recalled. 'Let's face it, this was not the intercontinental Afro-Asian study group; this was not a group of anthropologists.'[73]

McCartney left after nine weeks, reasonably satisfied with the experience. The others remained, but Lennon was becoming restless, and there were allegations that the Maharishi had been making overtures to some of the women. At last Lennon led a revolt against the guru, marching into his quarters one morning and announcing that they were off home. When the startled Maharishi asked why, Lennon acidly retorted: 'You're the cosmic one. You ought to know.'[74] Taxis were called, and the British party roared off towards the airport, although when Lennon's cab broke down he became convinced that the Maharishi was wreaking some sort of supernatural vengeance. Insecure as ever, he had entertained high hopes of the Maharishi, and his disappointment, expressed in the bitter song 'Sexy Sadie' that he wrote during his final hours in Rishikesh, was therefore all the greater.[75] Even George Harrison, who never lost his affection for Indian culture, became disillusioned. 'The thing is, we just went off him,' he admitted in June 1968. 'I'm not against spreading the word of meditation – I still believe in it just as deeply as I ever did – but he started to go about it the wrong way and make the whole thing seem a drag.'[76]

Even though the Beatles' association with the Maharishi was short-lived, many other young Britons were eager to follow their lead. Buddhism and Hinduism, transcendental meditation, spiritualism, black magic and unconventional superstitions of all kinds were briefly fashionable among bohemians and bright young things. This was still a minority taste confined to the well educated and wealthy; transcendental meditation was never especially popular in the back streets of Bolton. It was, however, given great publicity, largely thanks to the involvement of the Beatles, and conservative observers saw spurious Oriental cults as a symbol of the degeneracy of modern culture. When the novelist Anthony Powell published *Hearing Secret Harmonies* (1975), the last volume of his sequence *A Dance to the Music of Time*, and set in the late sixties, he devoted great attention to the fictional 'Harmony' cult, led by the sinister Scorpio Murtlock. One of the cult members is 'dressed in a blue robe, somewhat more ultramarine in shade, a coin-like object hanging from his neck too, hair in ringlets to the shoulder, with the addition of a Chinese magician's moustache': not so far removed, then, from the appearance of the Beatles themselves in their psychedelic phase.[77]

With its frequent references to mystics, clairvoyants, card-readings and planchette boards, Powell's work illustrates the importance of religious and spiritual ideas throughout British culture in the fifties and sixties. Although the newspapers tended to concentrate on realist fiction by the likes of Kingsley Amis and John Braine, many other writers, reflecting the experience of the Second World War and their fears of nuclear holocaust, preferred to emphasise themes of mysticism, madness and evil. By far the most commercially successful were the Inklings, a group of conservative Catholic and High Anglican Oxford dons who wrote between the late 1920s and the late 1960s. Their most famous members were J. R. R. Tolkien and C. S. Lewis, who were both disillusioned by the politics of the welfare state and the style of most contemporary literature.[78] Both poured their energies into fantasy cycles: Lewis wrote the Narnia stories for children, while Tolkien published *The Hobbit* and *The Lord of the Rings* and worked on an enormous cycle of Middle-Earth myths, composed for his own amusement and never published during his lifetime.

The Lord of the Rings was actually written during the 1940s and published in the following decade, but its popularity reached its peak during the late sixties, when American students embraced it as a mystical alternative to modern values. This was not a development that greatly pleased the book's very reserved and conservative author.[79] But no other book had a comparable appeal to students, protesters and romantics in the late sixties, and no other book managed so successfully to tap the growing discontent with science and technology, or so powerfully to affirm the value of the individual as opposed to the machine. And there could be no argument with Tolkien's sales. By 1968 more than three million copies of *The Lord of the Rings* had been sold across the world, and by the early seventies the paperback edition was selling 100,000 copies a year in Britain alone. By the end of that decade *The Lord of the Rings* had sold more than eight million copies in eighteen different languages, and it was estimated that only one book – the Bible – had sold more copies.[80] All in all, the impact of the book was simply staggering: on top of all the sales, it also inspired thousands of imitations, and was consistently nominated by the British public as the 'book of the century'.[81]

Although *The Lord of the Rings* is often seen as a deeply nostalgic book, its appeal was also rooted in its modernity. It was a work of fantasy, of course, but it used the genre to face the challenges of the century head-on. Like many other contemporary writers, from Orwell to Golding, Tolkien had experienced war at first hand, fighting in the trenches of the Somme. And like many of his contemporaries he was deeply intrigued by issues of evil and power, reflecting not only his conservative Catholicism but the traumas of the Second World War.[82] In *The Lord of the Rings*, for instance, evil is often associated with mechanisation, conformity and technology, while the central device of the Ring of Power reflects Tolkien's belief that there was 'something wrong, something irreducibly evil in the nature of humanity'.[83] An obvious comparison is the work of another popular fantasy pioneer, Mervyn Peake, who had served as an artillery gunner during the war and saw the horrors of Belsen at first hand. In Peake's case the traumas of the conflict found their way into his claustrophobic, doom-laden *Gormenghast* trilogy (1946–59), with its rotten, crumbling castle and crooked, nightmarish characters. It was no coincidence that, like *The Lord of the Rings*, Peake's books experienced their greatest commercial success in the late sixties, the era of flower power, student protest and the Vietnam War.[84]

Although the likes of Kingsley Amis and Philip Larkin insisted that writers should concentrate on the concrete experiences of ordinary people, British literature in the sixties was rich in fables and religious imagery. The novels of Iris Murdoch, for instance, frequently made references to myths and magic rituals, reflecting her interest in violence, mental anguish and repressed sexuality.[85] These brooding undercurrents, or 'dark gods', as Murdoch calls them in *A Severed Head* (1961), could also be found in the work of writers from William Golding and Anthony Burgess to Doris Lessing and Angela Carter.[86] And a new generation of poets, like A. Alvarez, Ted Hughes and Sylvia Plath, explored similar themes of aggression and insanity, often expressed through animal imagery.[87]

On the British stage, too, Harold Pinter's plays, like *The Room* (1957), *The Birthday Party* (1958) and *The Caretaker* (1960), combined dark comedy with references to interrogations, violence and madness.[88] A common theme in Pinter's work is the invasion of domestic territory by mysterious intruders, partly an expression of the author's fears as a Jewish boy during the war. Both *The Room* and *The Birthday Party* begin with the mundane ritual of breakfast, creating an impression of quiet domesticity that is soon undermined by the arrival of unexpected newcomers.[89] There is a constant atmosphere of 'palpable and imperceptible threats': the audience are never allowed to feel comfortable, the true identities of the characters are rarely explained, and the action takes place in a closed, claustrophobic world of basements and gas ovens, where the characters fight for territory and the stage becomes a prison.[90] Pinter was not alone: surveying the new playwrights of the sixties, John Russell Taylor remarked that 'again and again' they were drawn to 'such subjects as child murder, sex murder, rape, homosexuality, transvestism, religious mania, power mania, sadism [and] masochism'.[91] Indeed, over the course of the decade violence and evil were two of the thematic mainstays of British theatre, from Peter Hall's *The Wars of the Roses* cycle at the RSC to Peter Brook's pioneering *King Lear* and *Marat/Sade* at the Aldwych.[92]

Perhaps the most obvious instance of a contemporary writer who used religious imagery to illustrate the issue of evil was William Golding, especially in his novels *Lord of the Flies* (1954), *The Inheritors* (1955) and *The Spire* (1964). In *Lord of the Flies*, his first and most famous work, Golding shows how a group of boys marooned on a desert island rapidly regress into savagery, superstition and murder. The obvious implication is that beneath the thin veneer of civilisation, man is inherently violent and evil, and Golding admitted that he wanted to explore 'the fallen nature of man', an allusion to the Christian doctrine of original sin.[93] In both cases the obvious implication is that the horrors of the twentieth century are rooted in the essential cruelty of human nature. Just as in the Book of Genesis, man is inherently sinful, doomed to savagery and evil.[94]

Similarly, in Pinter's *The Caretaker* the tramp Davies tries to play the two brothers Mick and Aston off against each other, so that he can lay claim to part of their house for himself. The animalistic nature of this contest, in which violence is barely suppressed beneath superficial courtesy, finally breaks through in Mick's triumphant tirade:

> What a strange man you are. Aren't you? You're really strange. Ever since you came into this house there's been nothing but trouble. Honest, I can't take nothing you say at face value. Every word you speak is open to any number of different interpretations. Most of what you say is lies. You're violent, you're erratic, you're just completely unpredictable. You're nothing else but a wild animal, when you come down to it, you're a barbarian.[95]

The idea of man as a wild animal clearly reflected the horrors that men had inflicted on one another in two world wars, the Holocaust and innumerable massacres since the dawn of the century. Plenty of people wondered how such atrocities could possibly have happened, while thousands more struggled to come to terms with the looming menace of nuclear annihilation. All of this helps to explain why books like *Honest to God*, *Lord of the Flies* and *The Lord of the Rings* were commercial successes during the sixties. It also explains one of the unlikelier publishing success stories of the period: the vogue for popular anthropology. Not only did this exploit the consumer's fascination for reading about his own behaviour; it tried to provide explanations for human cruelty. The Austrian geneticist Konrad Lorenz, for example, argued in *On Aggression* (1966) that, like animal behaviour in the wild, human behaviour was genetically determined: man had no free will to choose his own course, because biology had chosen it for him.[96] Other authorities agreed: hence the titles of books like *The Territorial Imperative* (Robert Ardrey, 1966) and *Human Aggression* (Antony Storr, 1968).[97]

The most successful anthropological text of all was published in 1967 by Desmond Morris, an academic zoologist and sometime presenter of Granada Television's *Zootime*. The tremendous impact of *The Naked Ape*, which sold millions of copies worldwide within a few years of its publication, undoubtedly owed something to Morris's reputation from his television appearances.[98] More importantly, however, it depended on his willingness to shock and challenge his readers. The book famously begins:

> There are one hundred and ninety-three living species of monkeys and apes. One hundred and ninety-two of them are covered with hair. The exception is a naked ape, self-named *Homo sapiens*. This unusual and highly successful species spends a great deal of time examining his higher motives and an equal amount of time studiously ignoring his fundamental ones. He is proud that he has the biggest brain of all the primates, but attempts to conceal the fact that he also has the biggest penis, preferring to accord this honour falsely to the mighty gorilla. He is an intensely vocal, acutely exploratory, over-crowded ape, and it is high time we examined his basic behaviour.
>
> I am a zoologist and the naked ape is an animal.[99]

Morris's central premise is that man is merely an animal, governed by the same basic desires as other primates. There is no biological difference between the men who hunted with primitive axes and the men who orbited the earth, for 'behind the façade of modern city life there is still the same old naked ape'.[100] Man remains 'very much a primate', and violence is an inherent and biologically sensible part of the human condition.[101] As for God, there is no such thing. Gods do not 'exist in tangible form' and have obviously been 'invented' to 'keep the group under control'.[102] In a passage that displeased many religious readers, Morris explains:

> Religion has also given rise to a great deal of unnecessary suffering and misery, wherever it has become over-formalised in its application, and whenever the professional 'assistants' of the god figures have been unable to resist the temptation to borrow a little of his power and use it themselves. But despite its chequered history it is a feature of our social life that we cannot do without.

For modern man, 'experience and understanding' were the new gods, schools and universities the new religious centres, and 'libraries, museums, art galleries, theatres, concert halls and sports arenas are our places of communal worship. At home we worship with our books, newspapers, magazines, radios and television sets.'[103]

The longest chapter of *The Naked Ape*, and probably the one that most people read first, concerns sex, and Morris here is no less uncompromising. Not only does man have the biggest penis of all the primates but he is 'the sexiest primate alive'.[104] Morris goes on to describe sexual contact in close detail: there are several explicit paragraphs discussing 'kissing, licking and sucking' before we get to copulation, all of which no doubt titillated and appalled its readers in equal measure. Sex is natural and healthy; sexual repression is not. We have changed the way we sit, the way we groom ourselves, even the way we smell, to disguise our own sexuality, using commercial deodorant as an 'anti-sexual' control to suppress our natural odour. But, says Morris, 'the naked ape's evolution as a highly sexed primate can only take so much of this treatment. Its biological nature keeps on rebelling.' Monogamy is unnatural: 'the pair-bonding mechanism' frequently breaks down, and more basic sexual urges inevitably emerge.[105] Promiscuity, infidelity and adultery are therefore biologically natural, while pornography is 'comparatively harmless and may actually help our species', allowing us to satisfy our sexual curiosity without embarking on relationships that might threaten the pair-bond.[106]

In an especially provocative passage Morris even explains that homosexuality is comparable with devoting one's life to God:

> As a zoologist I cannot discuss sexual 'peculiarities' in the usual moralistic way . . . If certain sexual patterns interfere with reproductive success, then they can genuinely be referred to as biologically unsound. Such groups as monks, nuns, long-term spinsters and bachelors and permanent homosexuals are all, in a reproductive sense, aberrant. Society has bred them, but they have failed to return the compliment. Equally, however, it should be realised that an active homosexual is no more reproductively aberrant than a monk.

Meanwhile, even 'the most bizarre elaboration of sexual performance' should be applauded if it encourages copulation, fertilisation and breeding.[107] Yet on the other hand, contraception and abortion should also be welcomed, since they will prevent overcrowding and take the edge off the struggle for resources that lies at the heart of human violence. Indeed, 'the best solution for ensuring world peace is the widespread promotion of contraception or abortion'.[108]

Perhaps the most revealing aspect of the *Naked Ape* phenomenon was the simple fact of the book's success. Morris made enough money from it to retire to Malta and spend five years painting, writing and leading a life of scholarly leisure. Even its serialisation in the *Sunday Mirror* was considered the leading 'circulation builder' of the year.[109] This success suggests that moral attitudes were less dogmatic than we often imagine: even if people held firm views on religion and sex, they were not necessarily averse to reading books that challenged them.

For, if Morris's conclusions were generally accepted, the consequences would be extremely far reaching. Promiscuity, contraception and state-provided abortions would all become quite normal, while, most shocking of all, open homosexuality would be considered no more unusual than becoming a monk or a nun. All of these things, surely, were quite unimaginable. And yet, as some observers saw it, Britain was already heading towards precisely that kind of future – the future promised by perhaps the most controversial legacy of the 1960s, the sexual revolution.

23

LOVE WITHOUT FEAR

London is now widely alleged to be the sexiest city in the world, the mecca of permissiveness, promiscuity and perversion. These are strong words, but they have been well earned.

Jonathan Aitken, *The Young Meteors* (1967)

A not uncommon experience for a young Englishman is to sit on a sofa with his girl friend in the half darkness while she tells him she has found a shop that sells the most revealing black mini-skirt with slits up the side, really fab, with a white see-through skinny sweater with a hole in the middle and a plunging neckline, and some super fishnet stockings, and a frothy lace petticoat with an op-art silk lining. Inexpressibly intrigued, he attempts to kiss her. And gets his face slapped.

David Frost and Antony Jay, *To England with Love* (1967)

In March 1967 the young playwright Joe Orton was chatting to his lover Kenneth Halliwell when the subject turned to sex and rebellion. Orton thought that subverting the sexual conformity of society was the best way to challenge the staid, conservative establishment. 'It's the only way to smash up the wretched civilization,' he insisted. Later, while recording the conversation in his diary, he mused: 'Yes. Sex is the only way to infuriate them. Much more fucking and they'll be screaming hysterics in next to no time.'[1] But Orton never had the chance to see if he would be proved right. Five months later, at the age of just thirty-four, he was dead, his skull shattered with a hammer by the jealous Halliwell, who then killed himself with an overdose.[2]

In a sense, Orton was right: few things infuriated people during the sixties as much as sex. The principles of sexual morality and behaviour were bitterly disputed throughout the twentieth century, and as the historian Jeffrey Weeks explains, sexuality 'assumed major symbolic importance as a target of social intervention and organisation'. So while sex remained the most private of activities, it was nevertheless one of the activities to which moral codes were most stringently applied. At the beginning of the 1950s, for example, it was commonly accepted that the state had the right to regulate sexual behaviour. Sex within marriage was natural and even praiseworthy; sex outside marriage was immoral but not illegal. Sex between two unmarried adults was lamentable; sex between two unmarried teenagers was outrageous. Sex between two women was legal; sex between two men was not. But as in Orton's own plays *Entertaining Mr Sloane* (1964) and *Loot* (1965), what was said or written about sexual behaviour was often very different from what went on. 'People would talk,' says a character in the very last line of *Loot*. 'We must keep up appearances.'[3]

As Orton recognised, the power of sexual morality lay in its being taken extremely seriously. Even a satirical challenge could have wider repercussions, threatening the existing social hierarchy. And this, according to many historians, is precisely what happened in Britain during the 1960s: a 'sexual revolution', after which British society was never the same again. One popular account calls it 'the most sensational lifestyle change of the sixties'.[4] In his history of the bohemian counterculture Jonathon Green quotes plenty of people who argue that sexual liberation was an essential characteristic of the period: the dean of the counterculture John Hopkins, for instance, told him that 'undoubtedly there was a sexual revolution'.[5] Even Arthur Marwick, who hesitates to endorse the idea of a sexual revolution, believes that 'Victorianism was finally laid to rest', whatever that means.[6]

The conventional account of the sexual revolution is relatively simple. Until the sixties, sexual attitudes were supposedly marked by unflinching conservatism, repression and reserve. Green writes that the 'moral world of 1950s Britain, at least as far as the statute book was concerned, was barely altered from that of a century earlier', and explains that it was marked by 'tawdry prejudices', 'tedious fulminations' and an 'overriding terror of almost literally unspeakable, but hugely potent horrors'.[7] But during the sixties a new challenge was laid down with unprecedented frankness and enthusiasm, and afterwards British sexual attitudes were irrevocably transformed. Heroic liberals cast out the repressive Victorian laws that regulated sexual behaviour. Thanks to the revolutionary appearance of the Pill, millions of women gained control of their own fertility for the first time. Young people rejected the antiquated values of their parents and embraced the spirit of free love. People had sex more often, with more people and in more interesting ways. As Mary Whitehouse put it some years later, 'pre-marital sex, abortion on demand [and] homosexuality' were rampant, and a new generation emerged who saw 'sex as the great liberator, and self-control and self-denial as the only sins'. The old moral codes crumbled; a new hedonism prevailed; and Britain was never the same again.[8]

Even at first glance the stereotypical version of the sexual revolution raises more questions than it answers. If nothing else, it rests on very little hard evidence. After all, sexual behaviour and attitudes are extraordinarily difficult to measure. As Hera Cook notes, those people keenest to talk about their sexual exploits tended to lead the most uninhibited and unusual lives, making it harder for historians to recapture the experience of the silent majority.[9] Many people were and are reluctant to discuss their sex lives and moral attitudes. Even when they do, people are liable either to feel guilty about their feelings and therefore to give what they think are 'normal' answers, or, out of insecurity, to boast about their conquests and misadventures. The history of sex, then, is peculiarly vulnerable to distortion. And, not surprisingly, the conventional myths of the sexual revolution, when examined closely, turn out to be deeply misleading.

According to the conventional accounts of the sexual revolution, the period before the beginning of the 1960s was one of stagnation and repression. As one writer puts it, the transformation of the sixties liberated both men and women from 'the cloying stranglehold of marriage, family and domesticity which had characterised the 1950s'.[10] The English, one student activist later claimed, 'were dead. They didn't talk about what they felt, they didn't do what they felt, everybody was compartmentalised.'[11] And in the words of Noël Annan, British reticence meant that these were 'not years of innocence, but years of ignorance', resulting in illegitimate births, illegal abortions, shotgun marriages and disastrous relationships.[12]

In some respects this account does ring true. There is no doubt that before the sixties most people received no sexual education at all. Since nakedness and sexual curiosity were both considered 'rude', parents and children were inhibited from discussing such matters: according to one survey, fewer than one in ten people in the late 1940s had received any sex education from their parents.[13] The critic Richard Hoggart noted that most working-class people exhibited 'a great shyness about some aspects of sex'. 'Even today,' he wrote in 1958, 'few working-class parents seem to tell their children anything about sex. They know they will quickly pick it up from the street-corner.' Men might joke about sexual matters with their friends, but they shrank from discussing them sensibly with their families, and parents were 'likely to be greatly upset if they find their children talking or acting "dirty"'.[14] As late as 1965 the psychologist Michael Schofield reported that two-thirds of the boys he interviewed, and one-third of the girls, had never had any sex advice from their parents. 'I can't ask my mother anything,' explained one girl. 'She just looks at me dubiously and says, "What do you want to know for?" She thinks I'm growing up too fast.' 'The only advice I got', said another, 'was from my dad when he said, "keep your legs crossed and say no".'[15]

In affluent middle-class families, just as in working-class ones, politeness and reserve were the rule, and sex was never mentioned except in the most bloodcurdling terms. An example was the Amis household in the 1930s, where, according to Kingsley, his father 'neither directly nor indirectly offered me any enlightenment at any stage about sex, with the exception of a short course of harangues about what happened, in some detail, to boys who played with themselves. Every ejaculation (although my father put it differently, I am sure) thinned the blood and the victim eventually fell into helpless insanity.'[16] Finally, when Kingsley was sixteen, his mother said: 'Well, I suppose by now you know all there is to know about marriage and so on,' to which he replied: 'Yes, I think so, Mum.'[17]

In many cases this culture of ignorance meant that couples' wedding nights were rather arduous occasions. One South London woman, for instance, found that she 'didn't know what to do' and was told by her angry husband that she had 'got the rhythm all wrong'. She gave up in despair and thought: 'Sod this, I want to go home.'[18] Another woman found that sex was 'a disaster' and kept making excuses to avoid it: after bursting into tears in front of her mother when she returned from her honeymoon she was sent off to a Harley Street specialist who succeeded in arousing her with a series of plastic devices and then concluded triumphantly: 'There's nothing wrong with you, you just need to tell your husband to touch and arouse you before he makes love, then it won't hurt.'[19] A third woman was so used to thinking of sex as dirty that 'it still seemed wrong' and she 'tensed up so much that we couldn't do anything'.[20]

It is also true that until the sixties the British saw themselves as much more sexually reserved than their European neighbours. Whereas Frenchmen and Italians were hot-blooded sexual animals, the British were gentlemanly and reticent. In *How to Be an Alien* (1946), the Hungarian émigré George Mikes's comic study of the British character, the chapter on sex consisted of a single sentence: 'Continental people have sex life; the English have hot-water bottles.'[21]

All the same, the usual story of stuffiness and conservatism seems much too clichéd to be credible. Even during the first years of the twentieth century there had been a wide gulf between people's self-image and their behaviour. As the historian Paul Ferris notes, illegitimacy, prostitution and venereal disease were all extremely common in the 1910s and 1920s.[22] And it is quite untrue that British women were paragons of virtue who never dreamed of having sex before marriage. A survey of six thousand women published in 1956 by Eustace Chesser, a Harley Street doctor, suggested that nearly one in five married women born before 1904 had engaged in premarital sex, rising to one in three among those born during the following decade. As for women born between 1924 and 1934, nearly half admitted that they had had sex before marriage. Since there had been no comparable increase in illegitimate births, the implication was that they or their partners had been using contraceptives.[23]

All of this hints at a rather more complicated picture than the standard narrative. Ross McKibbin points out that over the course of British history there is a 'clear relationship between sexual permissiveness and income levels'.[24] Rising incomes brought with them a greater willingness to experiment sexually, to condone sex before marriage and to use contraception. Indeed, relatively cheap methods of birth control had been widely available for decades from barbers' shops, chemists' and mail-order companies.[25] Effective diaphragms were available from 1918, and contraceptive jelly from 1932, while the sales of vulcanised rubber sheaths rocketed during the interwar decades. Marie Stopes sold hundreds of thousands of copies of her advice manuals, while even the Church of England's Lambeth Conference voted in 1930 to allow the use of contraception where there was a 'clearly felt obligation to limit or avoid parenthood'.[26] By visiting the right barber's shop or chemist's or answering newspaper advertisements, a man with ten shillings in his pocket could quite easily have bought one of Stopes's books and a packet of twelve 'French letters', and still had enough change for a good-quality diaphragm. That many men did not was as much a matter of habit and morality as of availability.[27]

In this context the developments of the sixties look less like a revolution and more like the latest stage in a long period of development. As early as the thirties, according to Ferris, Britain was 'drifting away from the ideals of continence and chastity', but he admits that 'the ideals had never been more than declarations of intent' anyway.[28] Well before the *Lady Chatterley* trial and the Profumo scandal, women's magazines were discreetly addressing sexual issues. The likes of *Woman's Own*, *Woman's Illustrated* and *Housewife* dispensed sexual advice in their 'agony-aunt' columns, recommending booklets on family planning and gently addressing common marital problems. The housewife, it was implied, would satisfy her husband only if she were just as proficient in the bedroom as she was in the kitchen.[29] For many women, however, this was more easily said than done: since most women had little or no sex education, they were often woefully uninformed about their own bodies, let alone the one beside them. It was 'often news to them that they might at all share the sex enjoyment of their husbands.'[30]

Salvation lay in the enormously popular sex manuals of the post-war years, the sales of which belie the myth that sex was simply never discussed before the 1960s. Sexual textbooks were a thriving market, and some husbands were even reputed to keep them by the bedside in case they needed to look up some complicated manoeuvre in a hurry.[31] The decline of the extended family, the growth of mass consumerism and the increasing popularity of domestic pleasures all put pressure on middle-class couples to work towards a mutually satisfying and enriching marriage. And since the Second World War had badly damaged many family relationships and brought increased rates of infidelity, illegitimacy and divorce, the happy marriage was vigorously advertised as the cornerstone of adult life, the key to independence, respectability and success.[32]

The most popular sex manual before the sixties was *Love Without Fear: A Plain Guide to Sex Technique for Every Married Adult*, written by Eustace Chesser and published in 1941. 'Do not begin your marriage with a rape,' begins the chapter on honeymoons. Foreplay was recommended, and different procedures were tactfully described with the suggestion that both partners wash themselves before getting down to business. The book cost just six shillings, and it was distributed somewhat clandestinely through mail order and in backstreet shops. Nevertheless, in its first ten years it sold an extraordinary 720,000 copies, and by 1964 no fewer than three million copies had disappeared from the shelves.[33] Its success illustrated the links between commercialism and sexual frankness. In an economy based on mass consumption, sex was a big seller, and commercial publishers were bright enough to exploit a potential market.[34]

The demand for Chesser's manual also suggested that couples felt great pressure to make a sexual success of their marriages. Middle-class couples in particular were beginning to talk more freely about their relationships, largely because they were being encouraged to see marriage as a joint partnership.[35] This meant the gradual abandonment of the old notion of a man's conjugal 'rights', or the expectation of sex whenever he felt like it. However, the concept of conjugal rights died out more slowly in working-class areas than among the more affluent, and in many cases it survived for decades. Wives considered it their duty to service their husbands, but a good husband was one who 'wouldn't trouble you at all'.[36] One woman from Scunthorpe, for example, a mother of six, remembered that when her husband returned every night from the pub at eleven, there would follow a predictable routine:

> When I heard footsteps I'd blow the lamp out and pretend to be asleep. He would come home full of romance and full of beer and start mauling me. I just wanted to sleep and it used to cause no end of trouble if I refused him . . . It was a duty, a horrible duty to me, I didn't like it . . . you'd be looking at the cracks in the ceiling thinking, 'Oh that crack could do with filling in, that could do with a bit of whitewashing.' It was no fun, it was just nasty, dirty and degrading.[37]

A builder from Salford admitted that he felt like 'the lord and master' inside the bedroom. 'I would expect sex when I wanted it, when I felt like it, whether she'd worked hard all day, whether the kids had been difficult, it made no difference to me,' he explained. 'I wanted sex so I had it.'[38]

Many men assumed that their wife's sexual role was purely passive. This way of thinking, however, had taken a powerful knock during the war, when widespread female infidelity suggested that British women were no less sexually demanding than their men.[39] In the fifties and sixties, with millions of couples struggling to readjust to married life, social commentators recognised that marriage was 'a tough job' requiring compromise and effort, and mutual sexual satisfaction was seen as an integral part of a successful partnership.[40] The Marriage Guidance Council, for instance, published the booklet *How to Treat a Young Wife*, which explained that a loving husband should try to develop the sexual potential of his young bride. By the late 1960s the booklet was being published under the more direct title *Sex in Marriage*, and had sold over half a million copies. The ideal, as one marriage expert explained, was 'satisfying orgasm for both. Simultaneous orgasm is a desirable ideal.'[41]

Several other successful manuals of the period were aimed specifically at newly married women. In *The Sexual Responsibility of Women* (1957), Maxine Davies explained that a wife must give her husband's sexual nature 'full attention for a long time in order to understand it with her reflexes as well as her brains'. A successful sexual relationship was her responsibility, not his, and required intensive concentration.[42] By contrast, in *The Power of Surrender* (1959), which sold over a million copies, Dr Marie Robinson argued that 'the act of surrender' was crucial to a woman's fulfilment. She described satisfaction as 'a tremendous surging physical ecstasy in the yielding itself, in the feeling of being the passive instrument of another person, of being stretched out supinely beneath him, taken up will-lessly by his passion as leaves are swept up before the wind'.[43]

Both manuals reflected an increasing frankness about sexual behaviour that pre-dated the supposedly revolutionary events of the 1960s. But like all the manuals of the day, they were written specifically for the marital bedroom: sex before or outside marriage was a very different matter. As we have seen, one survey revealed that nearly half of the women born between 1924 and 1934 admitted that they had engaged in pre-marital intercourse, so it is simply a myth that people did not have sex before marriage. However, this does not mean that they thought it was morally right; in fact it seems likely that many people behaved in ways that they themselves believed were wrong. There is plenty of evidence that even in the supposedly tedious, terrified 1950s many people could not resist breaking their own moral codes. More than 25 per cent of the volunteers interviewed by Geoffrey Gorer in 1950, for example, admitted to having had a sexual relationship before or outside marriage.[44] In another survey of English women in 1955 Eustace Chesser concluded than more than four out of ten married woman had lost their virginity before their wedding day, with one in five having had sex before her eighteenth birthday.[45] Whatever the potential flaws of these surveys, they do suggest a general trend, and they tally with the evidence of sexual behaviour a little earlier. Overall, it is likely that during the fifties at least half of the adult population had engaged in sex before marriage, and perhaps one in three marriages were hurried, shotgun affairs to legitimise an unexpected pregnancy, as depicted in Stan Barstow's novel *A Kind of Loving* (1960).[46]

The obvious conclusion is that many people were simply unable to keep to their high standards. So while censorship kept sexual references out of films and novels, millions of readers still bought advice manuals; and while most people told researchers that women should remain virgins until their wedding night, between a third and a half of British women had sex before marriage. The onus was on the woman to retain her honour, but it was only natural for a man to try to seduce her. One South London woman, for instance, recalled that she nearly yielded several times to her future husband while they were courting in the 1950s:

> It wasn't for lack of trying on his part that we didn't do it. It was never say die. Whether we were in the pictures or if he was walking me home, he'd try and get his old boy out, he even did it once in the front room when my mum had gone out to make a cup of tea. I never did it though, you just didn't then. I wanted to save myself for my wedding night.[47]

When Richard Hoggart worked on a building site during his university holidays, the revelation that he was a virgin stunned his fellow bricklayers. They thereafter viewed him, he said, 'in a friendly way, as less than a man, as another kind of monk, dedicated to books rather than to religion'.[48] Indeed, it was not very difficult for willing young men to gain sexual experience. Even before the war Mass Observation researchers in Bolton had found seven couples entwined in one street and five in another. Late at night, they suggested, almost every street had a couple enjoying a 'knee-trembler' against a wall. In Blackpool, which had a reputation as a sexual playground, in one night on the beach the observers found more than two hundred couples engaged in 'petting, feeling and masturbating one another'.[49]

Since it takes two to tango, evidently not all girls were determined to remain pure before marriage. A survey of life in York in 1951 came up with the example of 'Miss T', a twenty-four-year-old, unmarried shop girl, who liked to smoke, drink and bet on horses, loved dancing and 'going round the shops', and had no interest whatsoever in religion. Miss T was 'very attractive', the report noted, 'without being particularly good-looking', and led 'an active sexual life', casually explaining to the researchers: 'I don't see any harm in it. I always have one steady lover and it doesn't hurt him if I have an occasional fellow besides.' Of course, Miss T is just one example, but all the evidence suggests that she was not all that unusual, even in the supposedly puritanical days of the 1950s.[50]

Sexual morality before the sixties was clearly much more complicated than the stereotypes suggest. There was no uniform experience, even within particular groups, and real life was messier than the moralistic ideals of the time. Few people who walked the five-mile stretch in London between Soho and Queensway, for example, could have doubted that prostitution was still a thriving trade, with an estimated three thousand women on the streets.[51]

During the preparations for the Festival of Britain and the Coronation in the early 1950s the authorities worried that tourists might be harassed by London streetwalkers, and there was talk of London becoming 'the vice capital of the world', even though there were actually fewer prostitutes in the fifties than there had been before the war.[52] According to Sir John Wolfenden, 'there was increasing public concern at what was regarded as the growing shamelessness of prostitutes, in the streets of London and some other big cities . . . Besides breaking the law they were, by flaunting themselves and pestering passers-by, causing an intolerable degree of embarrassment and giving visitors a deplorable impression of London's immorality.'[53]

Prostitution became a public issue because it represented a challenge to the ordered world of marriage that experts were at such pains to promote after the war. The prostitute was a symbol not only of public disorder, but of unchecked female sexuality, and was therefore seen as a threat to social stability.[54] Local councils and moral pressure groups, as well as some senior policemen, demanded a tougher line on streetwalkers. So although the number of prostitutes was actually falling, convictions for street offences rose from about two thousand during the early 1940s to nearly twelve thousand by 1955.[55] Meanwhile, there was a similar panic about homosexuality; and, as with prostitution, there was a striking increase in the number of convictions for sodomy and gross indecency. Homosexuality was seen as a threat to the new emphasis on mutually fulfilling married love, and while prostitution was associated with immigration, homosexuality carried overtones of subversion and treason.[56]

In April 1954, responding to pressure from moral activists and sections of the Church of England, the government appointed an interdepartmental committee under Sir John Wolfenden to examine the treatment of homosexuals and prostitutes under the law. Wolfenden, the vice-chancellor of the University of Reading, was a Nonconformist Yorkshireman and a committed believer in the sanctity of marriage. He could barely bring himself to use the words 'homosexual' and 'prostitute', and therefore called them 'Huntleys' and 'Palmers' instead.[57] While he was preparing the committee's report, Wolfenden became increasingly worried about the conduct of his son Jeremy, who made no secret of his louche, homosexual lifestyle.

Eventually, alarmed at the prospect of a scandal that would engulf the report, Wolfenden senior sent his son a letter:

> Dear Jeremy,
> I have only two requests to make of you at the moment.
> 1.) That we stay out of each other's way for the time being;
> 2.) That you wear rather less make-up.[58]

In September 1957 the Wolfenden Report was published at last. The committee lamented 'the general loosening of moral standards' since the war, and mourned 'the emotional insecurity, community instability and weakening of the family' in modern Britain.[59] Wolfenden and his colleagues thought that the laws governing prostitution should be tightened, and that penalties for the prostitutes themselves should be increased. However, they argued that homosexual behaviour between two consenting adults should no longer be considered a crime. This did not mean that they approved of homosexuality. Wolfenden explained that their goal was 'the preservation of public order and decency'. Cracking down on prostitutes would remove their 'obtrusive presence', but 'private morality or immorality was a private affair', and nothing to do with the courts. So 'while steps should be taken to clear the streets of soliciting prostitutes, the behaviour of consenting male adults in private was their affair and not the law's'.[60]

The implication of the Report was that although the state should still regulate public sexual behaviour, it should stay out of private morality, including homosexuality. So while the report reflected the moral anxieties of the fifties, it dealt with them in a novel way, suggesting that the state had no place suppressing private vice.[61] This principle lay behind much of the 'permissive' legislation of the sixties. As the law lord Patrick Devlin pointed out, the implication was that 'an established morality' enforced by law was no longer to be the basis of national unity and social order. Like many more conservative observers, Devlin warned that progressive reform might only bring moral and social collapse. For if homosexuality was to be permitted, then why not any number of other practices?[62]

As it turned out, the Wolfenden Report's recommendations to decriminalise homosexuality were simply ignored. Most conservative newspapers were extremely critical of the Committee's conclusions, while the *Sunday Express* even called the report the 'Pansies' Charter'.[63] The recommendations about prostitution, however, were quickly written into law. The Street

Offences Act (1959) drove prostitutes off the streets and into the greasy back rooms of cheap hotels and shady brothels. Instead of soliciting in public, prostitutes in the following decades advertised their services by leaving cards in shop windows, promising 'French lessons', 'correction' and other services.[64]

The reaction to the Wolfenden Report illustrates the complexity of sexual attitudes at the dawn of the 1960s. Many people, especially in the older generation, clearly deplored the increasing frankness of recent years and worried that the evolution of public morals would bring social disaster. When the Commons debated the report in November 1958 the Conservative member for Bromsgrove, James Dance, likened homosexuals to 'Teddy cosh boys', and complained that 'too many people are looking into the mind of the homosexual rather than considering the repugnance that is caused to millions of decent people all over the country'. He warned his audience that 'it was the condoning of these offences which led to the fall of Nazi Germany. Yes, that is perfectly true. I believe that here at home, if these offences are allowed to continue unchecked, our moral standards will be lowered.'[65]

For Dance, rising crime and sexual excess were all part of the same phenomenon, and well before the tide of permissive legislation in the late sixties moral conservatives of his stripe were arguing that 'old ladies' and 'millions of decent people' were being ignored in favour of undeserving deviants and criminals. Dance later became a close associate of Mary Whitehouse in the struggle to 'clean up' television. As we will see, this was only the most obvious example of the conservative reaction against the perceived lawlessness, obscenity and secularisation of the modern world.[66]

As Britain entered the sixties, conservatives like James Dance were particularly disturbed by the increasing prominence of teenage sexuality, which was often mixed up with the ongoing panic about juvenile delinquency. This had a symbolic resonance, since teenagers were often seen as representatives of social change, but it also had a solid basis in fact. Young people were maturing earlier, thanks to improvements in their health and diet. In the late nineteenth century girls began menstruating at seventeen, and boys reached their physical peak at about twenty-three, but by the 1960s the equivalent ages were thirteen and seventeen respectively.[67] Children in their early teens were becoming sexually aware at an age that surprised many observers; one recalled that the 'council estate girls' all wore lipstick and stockings and had boyfriends at thirteen.[68] As the *Mirror* put it, 'Our Children Are Changing.'[69]

Teenage promiscuity is a central part of the legend of the Swinging Sixties. Brian Masters, for example, claims that teenagers in the sixties were 'the first generation since the war to decide that the mysteries of sex should be explored and discoveries made for the sheer fun of it. People copulated on the slightest pretext after an acquaintance of some minutes. Sexual partners were snapped up and discarded without ceremony, provided that they had the newly-available contraceptive pill in their pocket or hand-bag.'[70] Like many other writers, Masters believes that this permissiveness depended upon the ground-breaking introduction of the Pill, so that, in the elegant words of one sixties veteran, 'it was safe for everybody to fuck from about 1962 onwards'.[71] 'The years between 1965 and 1969 were when the sexual revolution began in Britain,' claim Miriam Akhtar and Steve Humphries. 'The pace of change was astonishing – and the Pill made it all possible.'[72]

However, the revolutionary impact of the contraceptive pill is often wildly exaggerated. The fact is that the most common method of birth control in the sixties was still the condom, available in packets of three from a barber, a chemist or even a specialist 'rubber shop' for a couple of shillings. By the beginning of the sixties condoms were cheaper and thinner than ever and, above all, were pre-lubricated, which explains their rapidly growing appeal.[73] Far from representing a rebellion against authority, birth control was even beginning to acquire an air of respectability. In 1958, for instance, the Church of England proclaimed that contraception was 'a right and important factor in Christian family life and should be the result of positive choice before God'.[74] In 1963 the Consumers' Association decided to test everything from condoms and caps to jellies and creams, publishing the results in a special *Which?* magazine supplement.[75] Two years later Boots agreed to stock rubber condoms for the first time and in 1966 the Royal College of Obstetricians and Gynaecologists finally gave birth control its official approval.[76]

The contraceptive pill was first tested by the American biologist Gregory Pincus in the mid-1950s. By the end of the decade British newspapers were reporting the imminent arrival of the 'life tablet', 'no-baby drug' or 'free-love formula', and doctors first prescribed the Pill in January 1961. They were besieged by enquiries from women keen to try out the new invention, and by the summer of the following year about 150,000 women were taking it, rising to an estimated 480,000 in 1964.[77] These figures might be superficially impressive, but they are nowhere near large enough to bear out the common claim that the Pill was a major cause of the sexual revolution. During the mid-sixties the Pill was simply not a factor in the lives of most British women. Geoffrey Gorer found in 1969 that less than one in five married couples under forty-five used it, and those women who did take it tended to be young and unusually affluent. As for those having sex outside marriage, he found that the condom was 'practically the only birth-control device used'. Of the one hundred unmarried women in his sample, only four were taking the Pill, and one of those was for purely medical reasons.[78] Another survey of women in 1970 concluded that fewer than one in ten single women had ever used the Pill.[79]

The explanation for this is that access to the Pill was tightly restricted. The existing network of Family Planning Association clinics catered for married couples, so young single women had nowhere to go until the introduction of the first Brook clinic in 1964, which accepted unmarried girls as young as sixteen. The Brook clinics, founded by a wealthy birth control campaigner, were controversial precisely because they did not take account of marital status, and in 1966, when the fourth clinic was opened in Birmingham, the local branch of the BMA complained that these 'teenage sex clinics' were 'undercutting the whole basis of family medicine'.[80] In the long run, however, they played a decisive role in shaping public opinion and providing birth control for young women.[81]

By contrast, only after the Family Planning Act of 1967 did the state commit itself to family planning, and even then the decision to establish a clinic was left to local authorities. Most of the new clinics were run by the Family Planning Association, and not until 1970, threatened by the success of the Brook clinics, did the FPA change its rules about seeing unmarried women. Only at the very end of the sixties, therefore, did the Pill really take off as a common method of birth control, and only in the following decade did many women gain access to it for the first time. It certainly had an enormous impact on British sexual behaviour, but in the seventies and eighties, not in the sixties.[82]

If the legend of the Pill fails to stand up to examination, the other myths of the sexual revolution fare little better. Brian Masters, of course, suggests that by the end of the sixties, 'people copulated on the slightest pretext after an acquaintance of some minutes', which seems rather unlikely given their behaviour just a few years before.[83] Another observer even claimed during the mid-seventies that 'intercourse is practised where previously a kiss might have been appropriate', a development that would surely justify being called a revolution.[84] But all of this looks highly suspicious. If wild and abandoned sexual relations suddenly became the norm, why did marriage reach such unprecedented levels of popularity? By the end of the sixties, 95 per cent of men and 96 per cent of women under the age of forty-five were married, while young couples were getting married younger than had their parents.[85] In 1946 the average age of marriage for a bride had been twenty-five; in 1970 it fell below twenty-three. This was not merely down to social pressure: modern couples had been sexually mature for longer, and many now had the means to set up an independent household straight away. Thanks to these early marriages and the new affluence of the day, there was also a bulge in the birth rate, which rose to a peak of 18.8 births per 1000 in 1964. All of this, of course, does not necessarily imply that people were more sexually active; but it does imply a consistent belief in the institutions of marriage and the family.[86]

There are plenty of anecdotes attesting to the debauchery of sexual behaviour in the Swinging Sixties. One young man who worked at Butlin's during the summers told a journalist that he 'became sickened, it was so totally available', although not, of course, until after he had personally sampled the depravity on offer.[87] An actor in his early twenties told Jonathan Aitken that in London 'the chicks are so cool about sex. At a party you can come up to someone and say within a couple of minutes of meeting her, "How about coming back to my place?" There'll be no messing about, if she likes you she says, "Sure, let's go."'[88] Or there was the young mother in her twenties, a computer programmer with two children, who admitted to an interviewer in 1968: 'When Tom is away what I do frequently want, and I admit this, is a quick screw . . . I need a screw every so often and I like to have it and get it over with a cheerio.'[89]

But stories like these are not exactly representative, and it is ultimately more illuminating to look at more rigorous, statistical evidence. Of course, surveys and statistics are never wholly reliable either, but they are surely more authoritative than the recollections of self-selected sixties veterans. The two major surveys of sexual attitudes and behaviour in the sixties were Michael Schofield's book *The Sexual Behaviour of Young People* (1965), which was based on interviews with two thousand teenagers aged between thirteen and nineteen, and Geoffrey Gorer's analysis of *Sex and Marriage in England Today* (1971), which took a similarly large sample of men and women, all between the ages of sixteen and forty-five. Between them, these two surveys give a good impression of English sexual behaviour in the mid-sixties, covering a range from adolescence to middle age.

Both Schofield and Gorer agreed that promiscuity and moral decay were wildly exaggerated. Schofield's survey, for example, found that most teenagers were still virgins at nineteen. Only one in three boys and one in six girls between seventeen and nineteen had ever had sex. These figures might appear high to those for whom all teenage sexual activity was deplorable, but, as Schofield noted, 'when contrasted with the recurring outcry about teenage immorality, these figures may seem low'.[90] As for younger teenagers, sexual experience was very rare: only 6 per cent of the fifteen-year-old boys and 2 per cent of the fifteen-year-old girls had already lost their virginity.[91] In almost all cases the first experience of sex had been with a regular boyfriend or girlfriend: this was not random promiscuity, but sex with a steady partner. Of the sexually experienced girls, for example, only 18 per cent had ever had more than three partners, which means that, at most, a mere two in a hundred of the entire female sample could be called promiscuous. Among the boys, meanwhile, only one in ten had made love with more than three girls. As Schofield concluded: 'These results suggest that promiscuity, although it exists, is not a prominent feature of teenage sexual behaviour.'[92]

Schofield's survey tells us about teenagers in 1964, so it might be that the real change came too late for his research to pick it up. But Gorer's research, which was carried out in 1969, reached very similar conclusions. Among his married interviewees, one in four men and two in three women had been virgins on their wedding day, figures that were not radically different from those for earlier periods.[93] Gorer observed that although the importance of virginity to both sexes was still 'remarkably high', attitudes to pre-marital experience had relaxed since 1950. Majorities of both women and men thought that there was some benefit in a young man gaining experience: 'once married he can please his wife more if he has had experience', as one young housewife put it. However, although more than half the men thought that it was reasonable for women to be experienced too, only a third of the female interviewees agreed. 'It's not so good for a woman to have experience; she can learn from her husband,' said the wife of a station foreman.[94]

All in all, as the questions ranged over issues from love and fidelity to contraception and homosexuality, the picture that emerged was of a settled, conservative people, a little more tolerant of extra-marital sex than in 1950, but not much. Gorer noted, for example, that the most important influence on people's behaviour was religious observance: those who went regularly to church were much more likely to have led quiet lives and to have begun married life as virgins.[95] Most married couples had sex once or twice a week, but those who had sex less often were much more numerous than those who had sex more frequently. Most of his unmarried interviewees, meanwhile, never had sex, and only a few had it more than once a week.[96] There was no evidence, meanwhile, that young people were more active than their elders. In fact, since young people were more likely to be unmarried, the implication was that in fact they were having sex considerably less often. Far from being especially wanton, then, most young people led extremely boring sex lives; far from storming the barricades of moral repression, most of them spent their evenings in front of the television.[97]

Moral attitudes also remained remarkably constant during the sixties. Schofield's team found that most teenagers were very shy about discussing sexual matters: one boy thought it was inappropriate to be interviewed in a church hall; another was only happy to discuss masturbation if a euphemism was used; and one girl refused to be interviewed at home because she 'would have felt funny'.[98] Indeed, Schofield's researchers often encountered very different reactions from the ones they expected. Asked whether she had ever been in love, one girl solemnly replied: 'Only with my dog.' On another occasion an interviewer, wearing a white raincoat, was mistaken for a local child molester and was 'hustled into the police station'. In yet another bizarre incident a boy hid from the interviewer in the belief that he was a policeman investigating the boy's role in a recent burglary. The boy's grandmother, who was watching in bewilderment, concluded that the interviewer must be a child molester and reported him to the police.[99]

Schofield's findings tallied with other reports of teenagers in the sixties, whose behaviour was apparently characterised more by embarrassment, shyness and 'insecurity' than by exuberant promiscuity.[100] In general, he wrote, they wanted to be 'better than their parents, but not so very different'. Three out of four teenagers agreed that 'people should realize that their greatest loyalty is to their family', while more than half thought that parents should actually be stricter with their children. Although they were at a supposedly rebellious age, most of the girls thought that teenagers should not venture out in the evening without telling their parents where they were going, and most agreed that they would rather ask their parents for advice than their friends. On some issues, their attitudes were even 'more restrictive than many of their parents'. For example, the vast majority opposed divorce reform, and one of the biggest majorities of all agreed that 'teenagers have sex thrown at them all the time from advertisements, films and TV'. Half of the boys, meanwhile, and a third of the girls, thought that 'all homosexuals should be severely punished'. If there was a new permissive consensus among the young, then, it was very well disguised.[101]

Of course, this does not mean that there were no changes at all. Since the turn of the century, sexual relations outside marriage had steadily become more acceptable. Schofield found that one in three boys and one in four girls approved of pre-marital sex, while another survey found that sixth-formers in 1970 were much more tolerant of sex before marriage than their predecessors had been in 1963.[102] But generally, the picture that emerges is not one of sexual revolution, but of underlying continuity and conservatism. Schofield observed that although a significant minority of teenagers had sexual experience, very few were genuinely promiscuous, and there was no evidence of moral disintegration.

Five years later, Gorer concluded that only 11 per cent of the unmarried population, usually young men, were even relatively promiscuous, having had three or more sexual partners.[103] He estimated that of the English population aged between sixteen and forty-five, about a tenth could be called 'licentious', in other words extremely permissive, and about twice as many could be termed 'censorious'. The rest, 'who do not get over-excited about the idea of sex in either direction', were floating somewhere in between, their values uncertain or ambiguous.[104] 'England', he concluded, 'still appears to be a very chaste society.'[105]

For one particular group, however, the late sixties did bring a tremendous change. Since the Macmillan government had declined to follow the advice of the 'Pansies' Charter', all forms of physical love between two men were still technically illegal. Homosexuality was still popularly regarded as evidence of moral degradation, a psychological disorder or a debilitating illness. In 1958, the psychologist Clifford Allen had declared that it derived from 'immaturity and lack of emotional development', and a year later Eustace Chesser agreed: 'the invert', he said, 'has not grown up'.[106] Most men with homosexual feelings probably struggled to suppress them and tried to live a supposedly 'normal' heterosexual life. One Cambridge graduate, engaged to a woman for whom he had strong affection but no physical longing, went

'This is London, the swinging city': *Time*, April 1966. *(Getty Images)*

Dedicated followers of fashion: the Kinks in the television studio, mid-sixties. *(Getty Images)*

Mary Quant, the 'Queen of Modern Fashion', 1965. *(Getty Images)*

Jean Shrimpton and Terence Stamp, the golden couple of Swinging London, 1965. *(Rex Features)*

A model poses outside Biba, the emblematic boutique of the late sixties. By 1967 it was rumoured to have the highest turnover of any shop in Britain. *(Rex Features)*

A sunny afternoon on Carnaby Street, 1967. *(TopFoto)*

Twiggy, the 'Face of '66'. *(Getty Images)*

'Everyone now looks again to England to lead the world.' Alf Ramsey's triumphant players salute the Wembley faithful, 30 July 1966. *(Getty Images)*

The rise and fall of Swinging London: from the high jinks of *Modesty Blaise* (1966) and *Blow-Up* (1967) to the violence of *A Clockwork Orange* (1971). *(Kobal Collection)*

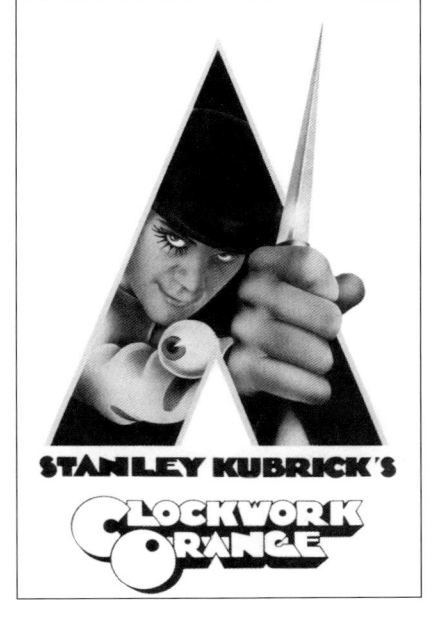

'What's happened to the Beatles?' The Fab Four at their psychedelic peak, 1967. *(Rex Features)*

With political troubles mounting, Maharishi Wilson announces his retreat to Bangor: Stanley Franklin in the *Daily Mirror*, 2 October 1967.

The Rolling Stones saunter through Green Park, January 1967. Keith Richards and Brian Jones are extravagantly attired, to say the least. *(Getty Images)*

Beauty and the beast: Anita Pallenberg and Mick Jagger on the set of *Performance*, 1968. Meanwhile, her jealous boyfriend Keith Richards was waiting outside in the car. *(Getty Images)*

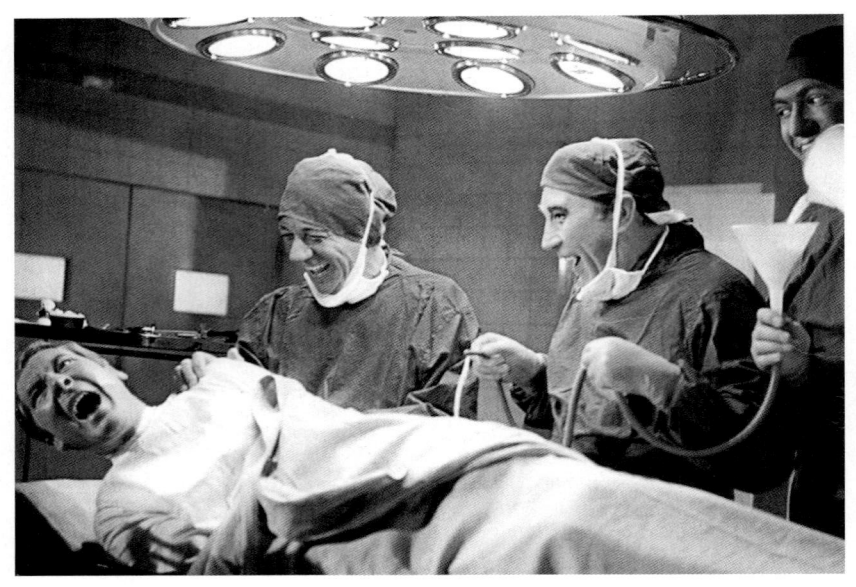

No laughing matter: Kenneth Williams, Sid James and the team explore the funny side of the NHS in *Carry On Doctor* (1968).

'A vision of hell': Michael Caine takes his revenge in the final scenes of *Get Carter* (1971), filmed on a desolate beach outside the New Town of Peterlee. *(Rex Features)*

I can only suppose that the opponents of this Bill will be afraid that their imagination will be tormented by visions of what will be going on elsewhere. Surely, if that is so, that is their own private misfortune, and no reason for imposing their personal standards of taste and morality on the minority of their fellow citizens who can find sexual satisfaction only in relations with their own sex.[119]

The bill became law on 27 July 1967 and society did not disintegrate as George Brown had feared. However, the new law did not apply to Scotland or Northern Ireland. The Secretary of State for Scotland, Willie Ross, told Roy Jenkins that opposition was 'substantially stronger' north of Hadrian's Wall, and after an intense campaign by newspapers and church leaders against the 'sin of Sodom', the Scots were exempted. Only in 1980 did homosexual behaviour become legal in Scotland, while Northern Ireland had to wait another two years after that.[120]

For homosexual men in England and Wales, the Sexual Offences Act 1967 was, of course, a tremendous advance. Although prejudice against them was still widespread, they no longer went in fear of police raids and prosecution and were finally free to conduct their private lives as they chose. There was, as Brian Masters puts it, 'quiet relief' rather than strident rejoicing, but it was genuine relief, all the same.[121] Lord Arran, a sick man who had been instrumental in pushing the reform through but was bombarded with hate mail and abuse from his critics, observed that 'perhaps a million human beings will be able to live in greater peace', and described it as 'an awesome and marvellous thing'. But he reminded the Lords that 'no amount of legislation will prevent homosexuals from being the subject of dislike and derision, or at best of pity. We shall always, I fear, resent the odd man out. That is their burden for all time, and they must shoulder it like men — for men they are.'[122]

More than any other reform of the sixties, the legalisation of homosexual behaviour challenged the moral status quo, but contrary to the expectations of Joe Orton, Patrick Devlin and James Dance, society did not fall apart. So why all the fuss? The answer is that sex worked as shorthand for other, more general anxieties about morality, modernity, social change and national decline. Because sex was discussed more frankly and often in the sixties, partly as a result of the expansion of the commercial media, it served as a convenient symbol for the grievances of the insecure and the ambitions of

British merchant seamen were forbidden from engaging in homosexual acts with each other, they were free to have sex with male passengers or, indeed with seamen from foreign fleets.

When the bill was introduced in July 1966 it still attracted intense criticism, and provoked excited debates in both Houses. Abse argued that since society was becoming more indulgent towards extra-marital sex, it was hardly fair to deny such tolerance to homosexuals. As it stood, he said, the law 'leaves the homosexual feeling that he is almost a selected minority specially chosen for persecution'. Within the wider community he sees increasingly permissive attitudes, he sees more permissive attitudes adopted to fornication and adultery. He sees franker and often salacious advertisements on the screen and television.' At the same time, Abse took great care to stress that he did not condone homosexual sex between older men and teenagers. 'No one, he said, was condoning 'homosexual conduct which can affect young people in their formative years'. David Owen, another bright young Labour reformer, noted that 'no Hon. Member, whatever viewpoint he or she put forward, has condoned homosexual behaviour'. Perhaps the most important element of the bill, for Owen, was that it would 'stamp out corruption of youth and minors'.[117]

Opponents of the bill took two rather different positions. Some argued that homosexuality was simply immoral and ought to be suppressed by law; others, however, warned that reform would inevitably lead to the corruption of the young. George Brown, who often liked to cast himself as a representative of working-class common sense, was bitterly opposed to reform. Arguing with a group of colleagues, he insisted:

This is how Rome came down. And I care deeply about it – in opposition to most of my Church. Don't think teenagers are able to evaluate your liberal ideas. You will have a totally disorganized, indecent and unpleasant society. You must have rules! We've gone too damned far on sex already. I don't regard any sex as pleasant. It's pretty undignified and I've always thought so.[118]

However, after a nail-biting last reading on the night of 3 July 1967, the Commons finally approved the bill, with a hundred supporters having stayed up all night to move the closure and keep it alive. During its final passage through the Lords there were the usual feisty exchanges, with Baroness Wootton mocking the assembled bishops and peers who opposed it:

Times calling for reform of the law, among them Lord Attlee, A. J. Ayer, Isaiah Berlin, Cecil Day-Lewis, J. B. Priestley, Bertrand Russell, A. J. P. Taylor and Angus Wilson, as well as the Bishops of Birmingham and Exeter.[112] This group formed the nucleus of the Homosexual Law Reform Society, which ceaselessly badgered newspapers and MPs for a change in the law. Throughout the mid-sixties the campaign inspired an apparently endless series of unsuccessful bills in both Houses of Parliament, with the House of Lords, where members had no need to fear the wrath of their constituents, generally in the vanguard of reform. Indeed, it was the Upper House that, in October 1965, first declared in favour of reform.[113]

The work of the Homosexual Law Reform Society in the mid-sixties reflected a general trend. Religious objections to homosexuality, for example, were certainly weaker in the sixties than ever before. The Bishops of Bristol, London and St Albans joined their colleagues from Birmingham and Exeter in publicly supporting reform of the law, and in 1963 the Friends' Home Service Committee published a pamphlet entitled *Towards a Quaker View of Sex* which insisted that 'homosexual affection can be as selfless as heterosexual affection . . . we cannot see that it is in some way morally worse'.[114]

Perhaps the crucial change was the decline in the number of people thinking that homosexuality was a sin. Most now viewed it as a disease or a disorder, suggesting a general shift from revulsion towards condescension. Since Britain in the mid-sixties was a society with enormous respect for science and scientists, it was not surprising that most people thought that a medical problem should be treated rather than punished. In 1963, for instance, an opinion poll found that 93 per cent of respondents thought that homosexuals were ill and needed medical treatment; at the same time almost two-thirds agreed that they should be free of legal persecution.[115]

The prime movers in the reform of the homosexuality laws were the liberal peer Lord Arran and the maverick Labour MP Leo Abse, a colourful South Wales solicitor and well-known proponent of liberal causes.[116] Abse was also a pragmatist, careful not to push too much for fear of alienating the sixty or so Conservative members whom he knew to be sympathetic. He made concessions to the government on both the age of consent, which was fixed at twenty-one rather than sixteen, and, curiously, on the issue of merchant seamen, who were exempted from the terms of the act. Interestingly, though, the clause exempting merchant seamen was very badly worded, so while to see a doctor because he was worried that he 'had fantasies about men not women'. The doctor asked him a few questions, and then explained reassuringly: 'Well, if you're not an artist and you're not effeminate, you can't be homosexual.' Only years later did the man come clean to his wife.[107]

In general, public attitudes to homosexuality were still extremely hostile. According to Gorer's research, the most common reaction was 'revulsion', voiced by one in four men and women, while others muttered 'don't like it', 'not understandable, odd' or 'mentally ill, sick'.[108] 'I can't put words strong enough; utter contempt; would drown the lot of them,' said a cemetery foreman in his late thirties. 'Disgusting; they want shooting,' insisted the middle-aged wife of an electrical engineer. However, a minority, roughly three in ten women and almost two in ten men, were a little more tolerant, opting for 'pity' rather than hostility. 'I just think it's very sad for them,' said one woman in her twenties. 'I am at a loss with this one; it is some form of illness and more to be pitied than anything else,' explained a heating engineer.[109]

One important shift was that younger respondents tended to be more tolerant than their elders. Gorer suggested that tolerance of homosexuality went hand in hand with more liberal sexual attitudes in general, so that those who think of sex as enjoyable, as fun, are more likely to be tolerant of the idea of homosexuality, or sorry for the pleasure homosexuals are losing'. Since young people were becoming increasingly tolerant of sex outside marriage, it seemed plausible that in future they would also become more indulgent towards homosexuality.[110] However, it is worth remembering that about one in three people aged between sixteen and twenty-four was still extremely hostile. Many young people were just as offended by homosexuality as were their parents. One woman student later recalled: 'When my boyfriend found out that his flatmate at university was gay he went ballistic. Kicked him out, refused to speak to him ever again, the works. It was terrible.' Others, however, simply did not understand what homosexuality was: 'I had never heard of a homosexual, had no idea what the word meant, until I was eighteen,' said another woman. 'Then when I saw some men with umbrellas, I thought, oh, they must be homosexual. I'd never seen a man with an umbrella before.'[111]

Although homosexuality remained taboo in many parts of the country, it did find defenders in high places. In fact, in some upper-middle-class circles, homosexuals were not only tolerated but openly defended. In March 1938 thirty-three eminent political and cultural figures signed a letter to *The*

the optimistic. Too many historians of the sixties have been eager to listen to the anecdotes of a promiscuous minority, or to mistake rhetoric for reality, and have ignored the simple fact that sex for many people in the sixties was not very different from how it had been in the fifties, or even the thirties. Far from being eroded by affluence, the old conventions seemed alive and well. And far from being an age of near-universal promiscuity, the sixties were really an age of near-universal marriage.[123]

This does not mean, of course, that the changes associated with the sixties were entirely fictional. In October 1967 the novelist Margaret Drabble wrote that Britain faced 'the certainty of a sexual revolution', in which the institutions of marriage and parenthood would be profoundly altered by the spread of effective contraception.[124] 'There has undoubtedly been a revolution in sexual attitudes over recent years,' announced an editorial in *The Times* four years later, 'and there is a good deal of evidence to suggest a corresponding revolution in sexual behaviour.' Pre-marital and extra-marital sex had steadily increased since the beginning of the century; birth control was cheaper, easier and more respectable; homosexuality was gradually becoming tolerated; and, in general, attitudes were unquestionably loosening.[125]

In September 1969 the press discovered that during the summer, Reginald Maudling's daughter Caroline had given birth to a baby girl as a result of a brief affair. Two months after the baby's birth, she had then married a South African businessman – not the father of her daughter. Ten years earlier, this would have been regarded as a matter for secrecy and shame. But both the Maudlings and the newspapers treated the story as 'an old-fashioned romantic drama with a happy ending'. 'The world is changing and mainly for the better, I think,' Maudling remarked. 'We do not comment on our children's affairs. All we are concerned about is their happiness.'[126] The reaction of one evening paper summed up the new tolerant spirit:

> How splendidly Mr and Mrs Maudling have faced a test that is a nightmare to many a parent. How different their love and loyalty from the attitude, still common, of 'Go, and never darken my doors again.' They make it quite clear that they are proud of their daughter and delighted with their first grandchild. Long may they all live to bring each other such family joy.[127]

Yet, despite the experience of Caroline Maudling, for millions of people the sexual revolution of the sixties was little more than an illusion. As one survey of public attitudes concluded, people might like sex, but very few thought that it was the 'be-all and end-all of life'.[128] The frankness and indulgence that are often associated with the decade were long-standing trends connected with secularisation, urbanisation and affluence, and had been anticipated as far back as the 1920s. Young people were increasingly tolerant of sex before or outside marriage, but millions of people had been having extra-marital sexual relations for decades anyway. A tiny minority of young, wealthy Britons enjoyed a lifestyle that explicitly defied the morality of their elders, but not until the 1970s and 1980s would the institutions of marriage and the family come under serious attack. During the supposedly radical sixties, the majority of Britain's fifty million people led quiet and somewhat dull sex lives, with one or two sexual partners over a lifetime, and soon settled down to a cheerfully humdrum married life during which they might have sex twice a week until their dotage. For most people, the sexual revolution happened in the newspapers, not the bedroom.[129]

24

THE ARCTIC WINTER OF THE TREASURY

> A beastly year by most standards; good riddance . . . The Government's economic policy collapsed into shambles. The worst peacetime freeze and squeeze, imposed in July 1966, proved to be of no avail. In the end it was to be devaluation plus stagnation plus the highest level of unemployment for 27 years.
>
> *The Times*, 29 December 1967

> Runners from our back benches kept bringing us reports of great scenes going on in the tea-room, where George was apparently holding court and announcing at the top of his voice that he had had enough of this 'bloody Government'. What on earth was the matter with him now?
>
> Barbara Castle's diary, 14 March 1968

On 17 November 1967 Harold Wilson wrote to President Johnson explaining why he had taken the decision to devalue the pound. 'Each of us, I suppose,' he mused, 'must at times have suffered the misery of an abscess which breaks out, is temporarily healed, then breaks out again. Each of us has shrunk from having the tooth pulled out. But when we finally decide to do so, the feeling of relief is not merely an illusion. The removal of a certain poison from the system purges the whole system itself.'[1] Wilson's satisfaction that he had at last pulled his 'aching tooth' was characteristic of the man. Nine days later his confidant Dick Crossman wrote that the Prime Minister was 'settling down after the shock and feeling that everything is OK and he's on top of the world. His resilience, his bounce, his india-rubber quality which are a tremendous strength but also a drawback!'[2]

But despite the Prime Minister's ostentatious good cheer, as 1967 drew to a close the mood of his ministerial colleagues could hardly have been gloomier. With the devaluation of the pound, all their hopes for economic growth and modernisation had finally been swept away. 'We felt our legs kicked from under us,' reflected one junior minister, Edward Short:

'everything we believed in had been destroyed.'[3] Their survival in government seemed extremely unlikely: ten days after devaluation Gallup put the Conservatives almost 18 per cent clear in the opinion polls, their biggest lead since the war.[4] Even Crossman, one of Wilson's most loyal ministers, despite his penchant for gossip, was 'extremely depressed' and thought that 'we were coming to the end of Harold's premiership'.[5] On 31 December, he noted despondently in his diary:

> The Government has failed more abysmally than any Government since 1931. In Macmillan's case, after all, it was after six years of fantastic success as Supermac. But in Harold's case the failure consists of tearing away the magic and revealing that he's really been failing ever since he entered No. 10. We have simply not succeeded and this feeling has been getting into my bones.[6]

The first problem that confronted Wilson in the aftermath of the devaluation crisis was the balance of his reshuffled Cabinet. In an odd way the debacle had brought about a rapprochement with his outgoing Chancellor and close rival, Jim Callaghan, who wrote later of Wilson's 'personal consideration and kindness' during the long nights of November.[7] Despite his perceived failure at the Treasury he was rewarded with another top job, that of Home Secretary.[8] This was a post far better suited to the talents of 'PC Jim', the former parliamentary consultant for the Police Federation, and it was one he took on with relish. Unlike Roy Jenkins, Callaghan was not interested in building a reputation for progressivism, and was determined to reflect what he saw as the ordinary, decent values of Labour's working-class electorate. 'I haven't got a liberal image to maintain like my predecessor,' he told Crossman. 'I'm going to be a simple Home Secretary.'[9] After just a few months Jenkins was already complaining that his successor was 'the most reactionary Home Secretary . . . for some time'.[10] Not surprisingly, they had a dreadful personal relationship. The young David Owen, who admired both of them, wrote that while 'Roy thought Jim was unintelligent and philistine', 'Jim thought Roy arrogant and effete'.[11] Wilson knew that since one would never support the other for the leadership, his position might be safer than it looked.[12]

In the meantime he had to find a new Chancellor. Callaghan had already recommended his ideal successor, the current President of the Board of Trade, Anthony Crosland.[13] Immediately after the devaluation announcement

Callaghan told Crosland that he should become Chancellor 'in about a week or so', since 'the odds on this are 95:5'. In the next few days the normally laid back Crosland could hardly contain his excitement; he even began planning how he would sort out his domestic arrangements at 11 Downing Street. The shock was therefore all the greater when, on 30 November, he heard that the new Chancellor was to be his old friend and bitter rival, Roy Jenkins.[14]

Jenkins's elevation to the Treasury came as a surprise not only to Crosland and Callaghan but to the new Chancellor himself. Jenkins suspected that personal factors might have had something to do with it: while Crosland always looked down on Wilson, Jenkins enjoyed chatting to him about 'railway timetables or *Wisden*-like political records'. At the same time, Jenkins was a much more successful performer in the Commons, and he also had a much more enthusiastic following on the right of the Labour Party. The result, as Jenkins himself put it, was that Wilson decided 'that the best hope for safety and stability was that he and I should be bound together, if not by hoops of steel, at least by bonds of mutual self-interest'.[15]

But while his unexpected promotion meant that Jenkins was unquestionably the second man in the government, it destroyed his relationship with his closest political friend. Having for years seen himself as the senior partner, Crosland was now forced to accept that Jenkins had taken a decisive lead in their private race to the top. The resulting coolness between the two stars of the right was excellent news for Wilson, meaning that they would never join forces against him. For Crosland, however, it remained a source of deep bitterness and disappointment.[16]

Jenkins's first priority was to deal with the legacy of devaluation, making sure that domestic economic demand was constrained so that resources could be released for exports. Meanwhile, the government's attention was distracted by an enormous row over arms sales to South Africa. Before taking office Wilson had promised that his government would not sell arms to the apartheid regime, and this pledge had been kept, although the pressure of the balance of payments deficit meant that the government strongly encouraged other exports. As the economic pressures worsened, however, some ministers began to question the arms embargo, and when the South Africans placed an order in the summer of 1967 for more than £100 million of British arms and equipment, the government did not immediately turn them down. Wilson hinted to George Brown that a more flexible interpretation of the arms moratorium might be in order, and Brown sent the South African Foreign Minister a 'nod and a wink letter', implying that a deal could be on the cards.[17] In September, however, the issue came to a Cabinet committee meeting, and Wilson, worried about upsetting his backbenchers, changed his mind. This greatly annoyed Brown, who, as always, was looking for an opportunity to fall out with Wilson.[18] When the issue came up again, in early December, the discussion was more heated than ever, and since it looked as though Wilson was going to be overruled by his own Cabinet committee on foreign policy, he insisted that it should go to a vote of the full Cabinet.[19]

By this point, of course, the government had been forced into devaluation and was still in the depths of despair. This meant that instead of being considered on its merits alone, the South African issue became confused with bigger questions of Wilson's leadership, his standing with his colleagues, and the balance of power within a divided Cabinet. Many ministers, especially those on the right, like Brown, Denis Healey, Callaghan and Crosland, felt that the government simply had to accept all export orders, irrespective of any ethical considerations. At the same time, they recognised that Wilson's prestige was at an all-time low; if he were overruled on this issue so soon after devaluation, it might be destroyed completely. If Wilson were forced to change his policy, then it would be obvious that he could no longer control his own government; in that case he might well be forced out. As Healey later put it, the crisis that unfolded was 'about far more than South African arms; it was about Harold Wilson's style of government'.[20]

Always suspicious of his more ambitious colleagues, Wilson had been cultivating a sense of injustice and insecurity ever since the summer of 1966. When, on 11 December, he heard that Callaghan had remarked in an after-dinner speech that he was in favour of lifting the South African arms embargo, he leapt to the conclusion that this was the opening shot in an organised rebellion by his right-wing ministers.[21] His response was typically cunning. The day after Callaghan's speech, the Chief Whip organised a backbench motion expressing support for the arms embargo, and on 13 December Wilson enlisted the support of Barbara Castle, whose opposition to the segregationist regimes in South Africa and Rhodesia was well known. 'I know you never leak but perhaps you can be persuaded in a good cause,' he began. 'Barbara, I'm in a real spot over South Africa . . . They are not going to trap me on this, which is what they are trying to do.' If necessary, he said grimly, he would resign and invite the parliamentary party to decide the issue:

And when we went to them on this they'd re-elect me again and then I should really be in control. George may resign on this: good, I've been looking for a chance to get rid of him. Now I wouldn't mind it being known that George and Denis are behind this move. Let the Party be mobilized. And I wouldn't mind getting a letter from junior Ministers saying they won't stand for a change of policy. But remember, none of this must be traced back to me.[22]

Wilson also made sure to keep the newspapers well informed. 'I'm taking on the briefing of the press myself,' he told Crossman defiantly. 'This time I'm damn well going to get the result I want.'[23]

Brown was in Brussels while all this was going on, and, to make matter worse, his flight home was delayed because of heavy fog. By the time he got back, on the morning of 15 December, Wilson's emissaries had done their work, and the newspapers were pointing the finger at Brown as the instigator of the entire South African controversy. Unsurprisingly, the Foreign Secretary was not a happy man. 'George is back,' wrote Barbara Castle. 'As we streamed into the Cabinet room I heard him say to Denis Healey, "It's getting worse and worse." It was soon clear that he was determined to pick a fight.'[24]

At the very beginning of the meeting Brown insisted on telling the entire Cabinet the unexpurgated history of the South African arms discussions, as well as launching a 'thunderous' denunciation of Wilson's press campaign against him. 'The knives were really out,' Castle observed, 'and the atmosphere was nastier than I have ever known in Cabinet.' Crossman described it as 'an hour and a half of mutual abuse' while Healey wrote that it had been 'the most unpleasant meeting I have ever attended'. Wilson angrily responded that Brown and Callaghan had 'stirred up' the whole controversy and that the parliamentary party had 'risen in its wrath of its own accord'. After the most bitter debate that any of them could remember, Wilson tried to sum up that the Cabinet was eleven to seven against lifting the embargo, but Brown immediately snapped: 'Some of us can count and we don't make it out that way.' Embarrassed and stung, Wilson retreated, and the meeting finally broke up with an agreement to postpone the decision until the New Year and a general consensus that there must be no more leaks to the newspapers.[25]

From Wilson's point of view, the Cabinet meeting had been a humiliating experience. As always, however, he was one move ahead of his opponents, and was confidently expecting them, in Crossman's words, 'to destroy themselves'.[26] So it turned out: over the weekend the newspapers were full of what Castle called 'the most astonishing anti-Harold campaign I have ever read', obviously 'based on an organized leak' from Brown's office.[27] Brown and his allies evidently felt that they had no choice but to put their own version of events to the press, but they were clearly breaching the no-leaking pact agreed at Cabinet. That all of this was going on at all was extraordinary enough; as Crossman remarked, there was surely no precedent for 'a Cabinet opposition publishing their dissent in the press so flagrantly and openly'.[28] Even more extraordinarily, however, this was precisely what Wilson had intended. 'It is all going very well,' he said cheerfully. 'This time George has over-reached himself. I am just ringing to say: no counter-briefing. George and his friends must have no alibi.'[29]

The denouement came on the following Monday, 18 December. Wilson's allies were livid at Brown's press campaign against him; even the normally mild-mannered Benn said that he wanted 'these buggers to eat dirt, make them accept unconditional surrender'.[30] The Prime Minister called a special Cabinet meeting that morning to discuss South Africa, and he was in fighting form. 'I have never seen him so grim and white,' noted Castle, 'whether from fear or deliberate anger it was difficult to tell. For twenty minutes he dilated on the press stories: their uniformity, their unscrupulous bias against himself. This was character assassination of the most overt kind designed to make his position in the House impossible and clearly coming from within Cabinet.'[31]

Brown, meanwhile, sat silent and downcast, like a prefect admonished by his headmaster. 'I've never heard anybody publicly scourged as George Brown was scourged by Harold this morning,' recorded Crossman with a combination of admiration and pity. 'When he had finished there was total silence. George Brown never said a word in reply, nor did any of the others.'[32] Brown had been completely crushed, and his colleagues knew it. 'While George and Denis sat utterly silent,' Castle wrote gleefully, 'one person after another said that the only issue now was the position of the Prime Minister. The credibility of the Government depended on his credibility and Cabinet must be ready to restore it. And so it was agreed. The statement that afternoon should include a categoric decision: no arms to South Africa.'[33]

Wilson read the statement that afternoon in the Commons, to great cheers from his backbenchers. He was so flushed with victory that, at a

Christmas drinks party for the lobby correspondents that evening, he could not resist boasting about his triumph, even giving them the highlights of that morning's Cabinet meeting. As the watching Crossman later remarked, this was curious behaviour from someone who supposedly abhorred leaks to the press.[34]

But although, in the short term, Wilson had won a notable victory, the South African arms controversy took a severe toll on both his government and his reputation. His relationship with Brown, always extremely rocky, was now damaged beyond repair.[35] In a wider context the controversy had exposed as never before the bitter rivalries at the heart of the government. What was worse, it was one in which Wilson himself had played an active part, whipping up a campaign in the press against senior ministers in his own Cabinet. With the humiliating devaluation of the pound so fresh in the memory, it was not surprising that many ministers began, quite seriously, to contemplate a change of leadership. Denis Healey, who later admitted that he had been wrong to consider selling arms to the apartheid regime, nevertheless concluded that the government 'never really recovered its balance or its unity' after the South African controversy. In the weeks and months that followed he began to hear 'increasing talk both inside the Labour Party and outside about trying to find another leader'.[36]

While his Cabinet colleagues were busy tearing themselves apart in the South African arms controversy, Roy Jenkins was grimly contemplating what he called 'the long dark Arctic winter of the Treasury'. To work properly, devaluation had to be accompanied by a severe dose of deflation, which meant not only higher taxes but cuts in government spending. Although Callaghan had pushed through a deflationary package in November, it soon became painfully clear that this was wholly inadequate. In their desire to soften the blow on their hard-working electorate, Wilson's ministers had blunted the impact of devaluation.[37]

On taking office, Jenkins resisted calls to push through a second wave of cuts immediately, telling the Commons: 'We do not want to dig a hole and leave it empty.' Instead he preferred to wait until the New Year, which turned out to be a very unwise decision. 'I ought to have been shovelling earth out like mad from the moment of my appointment,' he later admitted in his memoirs.[38] As a consequence, December saw one last 'spree of anticipatory buying', which did the balance of payments no good at all.[39] Indeed, as the winter wore on, the new Chancellor realised that he had taken on a frighteningly difficult responsibility. One cold night, he remembered, he sat up in bed reading a Treasury paper which predicted that if the pound was forced to float on the exchange markets before the large sterling balances held by the old colonies had been settled, its value would collapse completely. The 'British standard of living would crash to perdition', he realised, 'and it would be mainly my responsibility'. That night he slept only fitfully and woke early, which became the pattern over the next few weeks, when he would wake at five and lie in bed until seven, 'contemplating the prospect with apprehension and gloom'.[40]

Jenkins began discussing the new round of cuts with Wilson during December 1967.[41] A few days after the end of the South Africa row, the Chancellor warned his colleagues that devaluation had been 'completely unsuccessful', since none of the lost reserves had been recouped, and 'we are losing even more day by day. Even at its reduced level the pound has to be sustained.' He wanted at least £800 million slashed from the public sector, as well as tax increases in the next Budget to take the total deflationary impact beyond £1 billion. He had four particular areas in mind. First, he wanted a postponement of the planned raising of the school-leaving age; second, he wanted to reintroduce prescription charges; third, he demanded complete withdrawal from East of Suez; and finally, he wanted to cancel the order for the American F-111 aircraft.[42]

Jenkins' proposals did not go down well with his colleagues, and he managed to get his way only after a gruelling marathon of Cabinet meetings in the New Year, lasting a total of thirty-two hours. He later estimated that he spoke for at least eight hours and was 'unable to take my eye off the ball during the remaining twenty-four'.[43] Each of his four main targets proved, for various reasons, intensely controversial. George Brown and Denis Healey in particular were thoroughly uncooperative. Both assembled great teams of officials to plead their case in front of Jenkins, and, as the Chancellor later put it, stood up for Britain's world role 'with an attachment to imperial commitments worthy of a conclave of Joseph Chamberlain, Kitchener of Khartoum and George Nathaniel Curzon'. Brown, he thought, 'let through the most shafts of reason', although there was 'a good deal of banging of the table'.[44] Healey, however, was fiercely aggressive, calling the defence cuts 'mad' and 'crazy'. 'His language was full of f. . . this and f. . . that,' wrote a disapproving Tony Benn.[45]

Since the wounds of devaluation and the South African controversy had yet to heal, it was not surprising that the debates over Jenkins's cuts resulted in several memorably bitter exchanges. George Brown was particularly upset about the postponement of the raising of the school-leaving age to sixteen, which had been promised in the last two election manifestos. Since Brown was a working-class boy made good, he took state secondary education far more seriously than many of his patrician or middle-class colleagues. When the wealthy Education Secretary, Patrick Gordon Walker, said that he would prefer the postponement rather than cuts to university funding, Brown exploded:

> *Brown*: I want a straight answer to a straight question. If you had to choose between these 400,000 fifteen year olds and university students, which would you help?
> *Gordon Walker*: If I had to make such a choice, I suppose I'd help university students.
> *Brown*: May God forgive you. You send *your* children to university and you would put the interests of the school kids below that of the universities.[46]

'It took some time to restore order,' noted Benn; meanwhile, Gordon Walker sat 'speechless and obviously trembling'. However, since most of the Cabinet had middle-class backgrounds and had been educated at Oxford or Cambridge, Brown lost the day, and the Cabinet voted for the postponement. Indeed, Crossman even thought that Brown's speech had been 'unpleasantly class-conscious', a revealing point for a self-described socialist to have made.[47]

The second great row took place a few days later, on 12 January. This time the focus was on foreign policy and defence. Brown had just returned from a draining series of talks in Washington and announced that 'relations with the US are now critical'. The Americans were extremely displeased by the proposal to withdraw immediately from the Far East and to scrap the F-111 order. Indeed, their Secretary of State, Dean Rusk, had mockingly asked Brown: 'Why don't you act like Britain?' This had evidently left Brown 'deeply upset' and he admitted that afterwards he had felt 'physically sick' and was too shaken to speak to his own officials.[48] 'There isn't any straight answer to that [question],' he added to his Cabinet colleagues. 'We've not gone pacifist: we've gone straight neutralist.'[49] But Jenkins was not about to give ground. As he reminded his colleagues, the trade gap in the last months of 1967 had been just as bad as at the end of 1964, so they were 'not merely back to square one but back to square zero'.[50]

The debate now turned to the F-111, at which point Healey began a characteristically belligerent rearguard action in defence of his favourite project. Brown had already told the Cabinet that President Johnson was threatening to retaliate if they cancelled the F-111 deal. For once, Wilson was having none of it, and even made vague threats of 'countermeasures that we could take against the Americans'. After Brown and Healey had talked themselves into exhaustion the Cabinet voted by eleven to nine in favour of Jenkins's proposals. The Chancellor had got his way not only on domestic spending but on defence, too.[51] As they wearily rose from the table, Brown remarked to nobody in particular: 'Well, I shall be resigning.' Since they were all used to such threats by now, nobody took him seriously.[52]

When Wilson announced the package of cuts to the nation on 16 January, they amounted to some £716 million shorn from public spending.[53] Most ministers recognised the desperate need for deflation, but none of them liked it. 'It was a shattering experience to do this,' recorded Benn, 'because it is an irreversible decision which will affect the future of this country over the next ten or fifteen years and probably for ever.'[54] What was more, in the bitter, perfervid atmosphere of January 1968, the deep jealousies were more obvious than ever. As Benn put it, 'the character of the people concerned did come out':

> Denis behaved with enormous courage and dignity in the face of a shattering blow, quite as great for him as devaluation was for Jim Callaghan; George Brown was emotional, sensational and immensely powerful in personality; Crosland rather niggling; Jim Callaghan trying to be weighty but without substance; Harold never quite equal to the occasion. I don't know what it is about Harold, but he always falls two or three points below par. Roy was very effective: I must say my opinion of Roy rose – I don't regard him as having any principles but today in argument, getting all that he wanted from his colleagues, he was very impressive.[55]

A note that Brown pushed across the table to Healey while Crossman was lecturing them about the school-leaving age nicely captured the general mood of Wilson's government. 'I am fed up with this Jesuitical bastard,' it read. 'By Christ, if I have to go, I'll roast him unashamedly.'[56]

In some circles the announcement of the cuts provoked outrage and despair, especially the decision to accelerate Britain's withdrawal from East of Suez. Healey gloomily told the Commons that 'this is the end of two centuries of British history, an era which covers some of the brightest pages and some of the darkest, in the story of our people'.[57] Many observers agreed that there was something depressingly shabby about giving up the trappings of world power in order to save money. In John le Carré's novel *A Small Town in Germany*, published later that year, a disillusioned British diplomat observes that they have been 'making a great number of cuts . . . It's all the rage in London these days. They throw things away and call it economy.'[58] Most famously, in January 1969, Philip Larkin wrote his sarcastic 'Homage to a Government':

> Next year we are to bring the soldiers home
> For lack of money, and it is all right.
> Places they guarded, or kept orderly,
> Must guard themselves, and keep themselves orderly.
> We want the money for ourselves at home
> Instead of working. And this is all right.

'Our children will not know it's a different country', Larkin concludes. 'All we can hope to leave them now is money.'[59]

The cuts also marked a new low in the supposedly special relationship with the United States. Dean Rusk's cutting question to George Brown accurately captured the Americans' impatience with their impecunious allies, while Wilson's refusals to bow to Johnson's pressure over the F-111 hinted at a new defiance in Downing Street. There was no longer any pretence that Britain might send troops to fight in Vietnam; nor was there any illusion that the British would continue to hold the line in the Middle East and South-East Asia against the spread of international Communism.[60] In Washington Rusk reported that 'the US and UK are working on fewer real problems' and that 'the concept of Atlantic co-operation could replace the special relationship'. The British 'do not have the resources, the backup or the hardware to deal with any big world problem', added the Secretary of Defense. 'They are no longer a powerful ally of ours because they cannot afford the cost of an adequate defense effort.'[61]

Wilson was due to visit Washington in February 1968, and in preparation for his talks with Johnson the State Department prepared a special report entitled 'What Now for Britain?' which made depressing reading. Wilson's political standing was considered to be 'at an extreme low', while his country had 'few friends and no future course that promises success'. Britain, the report concluded, had 'never cut a less impressive figure in Washington's eyes'.[62] When Wilson arrived in Washington the New York Metropolitan baritone Robert Merrill, who was scheduled to perform in his honour at the White House, was ordered by American officials to drop 'I've Got Plenty of Nuthin'' and 'The Road to Mandalay' from his repertoire in case he appeared to be making fun of the Prime Minister's recent tribulations.[63]

Wilson returned home to a grinding battle to shore up the beleaguered pound. Those observers who had put great faith in devaluation as the answer to all Britain's economic problems were sorely disappointed, for in the early months of 1968 the grim statistics continued to pour into the Treasury. To Jenkins, it seemed that his 'long dark Arctic winter' was without end. 'We were always near to the edge of the cliff,' he wrote later, 'with any gust of wind, or sudden stone in the path, or inattention to the steering, liable to send us over.'[64]

At the beginning of March the abyss seemed closer than ever, with the pressure compounded this time by the weakness of the dollar, which was being undermined by the cost of the Vietnam War. As investors lost their confidence in the dollar, so they moved to sell their sterling holdings, as well as their dollars, in order to invest in gold, which was thought to be safer. In the first week of the month the Bank of England reported to Jenkins that they were suffering heavy losses from their currency reserves, including the disappearance of $250 million on successive Fridays.[65] Cecil King, one of the directors of the Bank, recorded that they were 'living from day to day' and coming ever 'nearer the brink'.[66] This pessimism was shared by most of the Chancellor's own advisers. They had assumed that the shock treatment represented by devaluation would bring some respite from the constant pressure; now that devaluation had apparently failed, there seemed to be no hope for stability or recovery.[67] Sir Alec Cairncross, for instance, thought that the situation 'was more frightening than in the run-up to devaluation, perhaps more than any crisis in the last twenty years'.[68] Jenkins himself, when briefing Crossman on the situation at the beginning of the month, 'could hardly have been gloomier'. 'If confidence in the pound is not restored,' he explained, 'there could be a second devaluation within three months and in that case the Government won't survive.'[69]

This latest sterling crisis, the most serious yet, approached its peak on the afternoon of 14 March. Jenkins, who had been at a routine Cabinet meeting, returned to the Treasury and heard the deeply troubling news that 'the Americans were going to take some drastic action during the day'. His advisers reported that 'any American action would create shock waves which could submerge us within twenty-four hours. Sterling had become so exposed and our reserves so nearly exhausted that we were almost bound to be driven off the $2.40 rate.' In other words, Britain would be forced into a second, utterly humiliating devaluation, with horrendous consequences for the domestic economy. In a state of deep depression, Jenkins told Wilson the news. As so often, the Prime Minister reacted 'with fatalistic calm'.

For the rest of the day the Chancellor waited for the news from Washington, and just before eleven that night the word came. The Americans wanted Britain to close the London gold market, which would give them time to organise a major economic conference that weekend in order to relieve the pressure on the dollar. Jenkins and his advisers decided to accede to the American request, but with a cunning twist of their own. Not only would they shut down the gold market, they would use this as an excuse to close the London foreign exchange market and proclaim a four-day Bank Holiday, in order to buy some time for the beleaguered pound. With this agreed, Jenkins disappeared down the connecting corridor to No. 10, where Wilson was waiting to hear what the Treasury had decided.[70]

By this time it was getting on for midnight, and the various actors in the drama were already shattered. None of them, however, could possibly have imagined the extraordinary events that were in store. Wilson agreed to the plan and began making arrangements for an immediate meeting of the Privy Council, which would proclaim a bank holiday. For this he needed a third minister to make up the quorum, with the Queen and her private secretary being the other participants. Wilson had already told Callaghan about the growing currency crisis, and he had tried to tell Brown, too, but the Foreign Secretary could not be found. Wilson sent officials to locate him, but deep down he was worried that the excitable Brown might, through some outbreak of melodramatic misbehaviour, undermine the whole delicate exercise. When word reached him that Brown had been spotted but 'was only "so-so" when last seen', Wilson called off the search.[71]

Brown had actually been in the Commons for most of the evening, and was in a typically erratic mood. Walking through the division lobby at ten o'clock, he had cheekily unbuttoned the back of Barbara Castle's blouse, grinning 'like a schoolboy' and giving the impression 'almost of euphoria'. Later, chatting loudly to her on the government bench, he complained of feeling tired, and emotionally remarked that 'we were getting old . . . getting bloody well near to sixty, although it took some realizing'. He seemed to her 'emotion-intoxicated rather than drunk'.[72]

While Brown was chattering away on the front bench, Wilson had enlisted his protégé Peter Shore to come to the Privy Council. As they made the journey up to Buckingham Palace just after midnight, it became obvious to Jenkins that Shore 'had not the slightest idea why we were going . . . He had in the most literal sense come along for the ride.' The meeting passed off rapidly and successfully, with the Queen in extremely chatty form despite the late hour, and Wilson was driven back to Downing Street.[73] But by now Brown had found out about the meeting, and he was absolutely furious. As far as he was concerned, Wilson had deliberately excluded him from a vital meeting on which depended the survival of the government; what was worse, he had taken Shore, the Prime Minister's glorified 'office boy', instead.[74]

All of Brown's pent-up resentments against Wilson now came to a head. He shot out of his office in the Commons and immediately rounded up as many Cabinet ministers as he could find, including Stewart, Crosland and Benn, none of whom knew what was going on. What followed, as Benn records, was typically histrionic:

> While we were all sitting there, George picked up the phone and got through to Harold and exploded. He shouted at Harold and said it was intolerable and there were a lot of discontented Ministers. All we could hear at our end was George saying, 'Will you let me speak, Christ, Christ, will – you – let – me – speak,' and so on. Then we heard George say, 'Now don't say that: don't say in my condition. That may have been true some other nights, but not tonight. *Don't say in my condition.*' It was obvious that Harold was saying he had tried to contact him, but that George was drunk. I don't know whether or not he was drunk, because you can't always tell.
>
> George continued to shout at him and Harold must have asked, 'Who's over there?' George told him and Harold said he had no right to call an irregular meeting of Cabinet Ministers, a cabal and so on.

After this bizarre shouting match, Michael Stewart, normally one of the Prime Minister's most loyal allies, told Wilson that they all wanted an immediate meeting to discuss the situation. Brown tried to insist that Wilson come to the Commons, but the latter was adamant that he was going nowhere; if they wanted a meeting, they must come to Downing Street.[75]

From Wilson's point of view, of course, all of this was extremely disturbing. It appeared to be what he had always dreaded most: a 'cabal' of Cabinet ministers, led by one of his oldest rivals.[76] By this stage he had summoned Jenkins from the Treasury for support. 'About ten minutes later,' the Chancellor subsequently recalled, 'they all trooped into No. 10.' Wilson then asked Jenkins to explain 'what we had done and why', and to their relief the assembled ministers rapidly accepted his explanation. Crosland, evidently still in his ongoing anti-Jenkins sulk, continued to make 'rather sour complaints about lack of consultation'. The star of the show, however, was Brown, who promptly exploded into 'a great deal of incoherent shouting'.[77] He had thrown tantrums before, of course, but on this occasion, he surpassed himself:

> George shouted and Harold insisted he had tried to phone him and George said, 'I don't believe it.'
> Harold said, 'I tried for an hour and a quarter.'
> 'I do not believe it.'
> Harold got rattled and rather irritated and said, 'I am not going to be called a liar.'

As his colleagues looked on in mute horror, Brown simply carried on with his tirade, angrier and angrier, so that, even if he was not drunk, as Benn put it, 'he was certainly behaving as if he were'.[78] Finally he got to his feet, 'very red in the face', and shouted: 'You know you've done wrong . . . You made a colossal blunder and you tried to put the blame on me,' adding, for good measure, that it was 'not the first you have made'.[79] Richard Marsh recalled that Brown walked around the Cabinet table 'and stood breathing flame and fury down Harold Wilson's neck. It looked as if he was about to hit him.'[80] But the blow never fell; instead, Brown 'shrieked and bellowed abuse', before turning and dashing out of the room, slamming the door violently behind him.[81]

Even by the standards of Harold Wilson's government, this was an incredible scene to have unfolded in the Cabinet Room of 10 Downing Street. Wilson was visibly shaken, and in the horrified silence that followed he said angrily that Brown 'would have to apologise or go'. Shore tried to pacify him: 'You did very well until you lost your temper with George. Just calm down.' Jenkins, meanwhile, simply looked on inscrutably. He was 'very detached and strong and rather impressive,' Benn noted. 'He's got his eye on the main chance and he thinks Harold will destroy himself and he, Roy, will then take over.'[82]

At this point a telephone call came through from Crossman, who was still at the House of Commons, reporting that news of the Privy Council meeting had come through, the backbenchers had worked themselves into a lather and someone urgently needed to make a statement to the Commons. Castle, who was with him, observed that the House was 'like a live thing, the Tories twisting and snarling and ready to spring at our throats'. By the time Wilson and Jenkins arrived, at three o'clock in the morning, it was even worse. 'You could feel the anxiety on the benches behind us and a scarcely controlled exultation on the other side,' she wrote. 'This time you could sense them saying to themselves, "It's a kill."'[83]

All things considered, Wilson and Jenkins handled the situation perfectly, both men projecting a reassuring sense of steadiness that belied the excitement of the previous few hours. Jenkins calmly explained that 'the crisis which is closing the banks tomorrow is an American one and not ours'. With that, 'the pressure and anxiety and anticipation slipped out of the chamber like air out of a balloon'. Every time he sat down after answering a question, Wilson patted him on the back 'with an exuberance of bonhomie', while the only sign of the Chancellor's tension, according to Castle, was his 'funny little habit of fingering his buttock every time he stands up'.[84]

Yet, although the House was packed to hear the statement, one prominent figure was absent from the government front bench. 'George sat ostentatiously on the Back Benches,' recorded Benn, 'and said he was now a Back Bencher.'[85] Since he had not officially resigned, Brown's position was not entirely clear, but he was evidently still in a rebellious mood. Castle heard reports of 'great scenes going on in the tea-room, where George was apparently holding court and announcing at the top of his voice that he had had enough of this "bloody Government"'.[86] 'Is George Brown resigning?' one young Tory backbencher asked a policeman in the corridor behind the Speaker's chair. 'I don't know, sir,' the policeman replied, 'but I've just heard him tell Ray Gunter he'll never serve under that bloody little man again.'[87] Of course, Brown had resigned before – on dozens of occasions – but he had never done so in the middle of the House of Commons. 'He behaved so disgracefully,' thought Benn, 'that under no circumstances should Harold take him back as Foreign Secretary.'[88]

When the Cabinet met the following morning Brown was once again conspicuous by his absence. After a long discussion of the economic situation, the conversation turned to Brown. Marsh 'wanted to know whether we had a Foreign Secretary'. Wilson replied that 'George was asleep' and that he alone would decide questions of resignation or non-resignation.[89] Afterwards, he interrogated a couple of ministers about Brown's antics in the Commons, which had been curtailed only when a group of backbenchers managed to corner the wayward Foreign Secretary in the tearoom and forced him to go home. Since more than a hundred MPs had heard Brown hurling some 'choice epithets' in Wilson's direction, the Prime Minister had the latitude to do whatever he wanted. He had manifestly had enough of his turbulent deputy: only if Brown sent a grovelling apology would he have a chance of staying on.[90]

Brown, meanwhile, was at home, waiting for the inevitable telephone call asking him to return. But by five o'clock, no call had come. His friend Bill Rodgers urged him to telephone Wilson to apologise and retract his resignation. 'I can't,' Brown said, with a combination of misery and pride. 'You've got to,' Rodgers insisted.[91] Eventually, Brown wrote out a brief letter of resignation, which reached Wilson at six o'clock. The letter vaguely alluded to 'the way this Government is run and the manner in which we reach our decisions', and ended with Brown's suggestion that they 'part company'.[92] Even now Wilson gave Brown a last chance to change his mind before losing patience, sending off a letter to accept his resignation and offering Michael Stewart the chance to become Foreign Secretary for a second time. Meanwhile, in his Carlton Gardens flat, Brown was feeling extremely sorry for himself, 'pacing up and down ... drinking heavily and getting steadily more drunk, all the time railing against the Prime Minister'. Somehow he still expected Wilson to have him back; when, at last, his resignation was accepted, the news came as a terrible shock.[93]

Brown had failed to resign so many times since 1964 that many observers thought that he would always be there when the dust cleared. Instead, he was gone.[94] What was really surprising, given his record of misbehaviour, was that it had taken so long for Wilson to get rid of him. Yet Brown's talents were beyond doubt. A year earlier *The Times* had called him 'a remarkable man with some of the qualities and all of the courage of a great statesman'.[95] Even Crossman, one of his bitterest enemies in the government, reflected that he had been 'the most attractive member of Cabinet, certainly the most gifted, certainly the most imaginative, possessing a mind which has a sense for the evidence buried in the documents or in a speech and which can smell it out'. The tragedy, however, was that his 'increasing drunkenness and rudeness' made him 'pretty unbearable'. Crossman concluded that he was always 'a bit of a Jekyll and Hyde and the good part has always been extraordinarily nice and talented . . . But on Thursday night he suddenly blew up and Hyde appeared shouting and screaming round the lobbies like a hysterical barrow-boy.'[96] Benn, too, praised his 'extraordinary intellect, courage and ability', but added the crucial caveat: 'his instability is such that it is impossible to have him in Government'.[97]

The collapse of Brown's public reputation was illustrated by the fact that once he had resigned, his name almost completely disappeared from the newspapers. His former supporters regrouped around the likes of Jenkins and Healey; in 1970 he lost his parliamentary seat; and in 1976 he left the Labour Party. After various embarrassing drunken mishaps, he became a great admirer of Margaret Thatcher, left his wife for a secretary half his age, and died of liver failure in 1985.[98] Tragically, but perhaps appropriately, Brown's most enduring legacy was a phrase originally coined by *Private Eye* as a euphemism for his drunkenness: 'tired and emotional'.[99]

Brown's resignation actually distracted public attention from what was potentially a much more serious problem for the government. Jenkins bluntly admitted that had it not been for the bank holiday, 'we could have had a catastrophic run on the pound leading to a second devaluation'.[100] On the Sunday after Brown's departure the Chancellor told a group of senior ministers that the reserves were so depleted that if the pound were to float freely, it might sink from $2.40 to as low as $1.50. If the worst happened when the markets opened the following day, then Britain would have to default on its debts of some £4 billion to the sterling area and various former colonies. Their contingency plan, 'Brutus', made for depressing reading. The pound would no longer be an international reserve currency; in the eyes of the world Britain would become a 'pariah state'; and at home the country would be 'plunged into a siege economy and domestic austerity' that would certainly bring down the government. Other implications included an immediate increase in domestic unemployment, the withdrawal of British troops and diplomats from overseas, a 15 per cent cutback on imports and the prohibition of imported luxuries like strawberries, avocados and fine wines.[101] Months later the Treasury came up with an alternative to this siege-economy plan, 'Hecuba', which provided for massive domestic deflation, including deep public spending cuts, crippling tax increases and a freeze on wages.[102] Both plans were equally terrifying, and thankfully neither was ever put into effect. Thanks to a four-billion-dollar credit package from Washington, the pound just survived the opening of the markets on the Monday morning.[103]

For Jenkins, however, the trial was not quite over. The very next day, 19 March, he presented his first Budget to the House, speaking for over two hours with a painful headache that had only slightly been eased by 'a fair amount' of wine at lunchtime.[104] He offered yet another exercise in austerity, but this time the medicine tasted worse than ever. Selective Employment Tax was increased by 50 per cent; betting tax was doubled; duties on wine, spirits, tobacco and petrol all went up; and there was a special one-off levy on all incomes over three thousand pounds a year. In total, Jenkins was raising taxation by a staggering £923 million, more than double the previous record tax increase, even in wartime.[105]

It was an indication of just how close the government had come to disaster that when Jenkins presented his bleak measures to the Cabinet, they were accepted with virtually no opposition at all. And it was a sign of the Chancellor's growing reputation that even his left-wing colleagues were impressed with his speech. Crossman called it 'a tremendous performance', and Castle noted that 'its brilliance is proved by the fact that the most swingeing Budget in history left our people positively exultant'.[106] Even his Conservative opponent, Iain Macleod, admired the 'lucid elegance' with which Jenkins presented his unpleasant news.[107] Somehow, Jenkins had come through his arctic ordeal with his reputation enhanced; and now, as winter gave way to spring, he turned his eyes to the leadership.

25

PLAY POWER

When I got to university in 1966 there was a television set in the basement of my hall of residence. I very much wanted to watch *Top of the Pops* and *Doctor Who* but had a suspicion this would be regarded as desperately uncool. So that first week I didn't tell anyone where I was going and snuck quietly down the stairs to watch *Top of the Pops*. My progress was halted halfway by the seething mass of humanity gathered to do just that. I learned that you had to arrive at least half an hour earlier to guarantee a seat.

Former student, interviewed in the late 1990s

In America, the rock 'n' roll bands have gotten very political. They express themselves very directly about the Vietnam War. But when I come home to England, everything is completely different, so quiet and peaceful.

Mick Jagger, 28 October 1968

In the spring of 1968 one of Cheltenham College's most distinguished old boys returned to begin work on his new film. Lindsay Anderson had cut his teeth in the days of Free Cinema and the New Wave at the end of the fifties, but despite his fierce radicalism he admitted to having 'very fond memories of my schooldays'. He explained to Cheltenham's headmaster, David Ashcroft, that it was going to be 'a poetic, humorous view of life seen through the eyes of the boys . . . a bit like *Tom Brown's Schooldays*'. This all sounded harmless enough, and Anderson's crew set to work. Throughout the months of filming, the director always took care to treat the school staff, and especially the headmaster, with complete courtesy. Then, one day, while he was chatting to David Ashcroft about his happy days as a schoolboy, the headmaster suddenly broke in. 'You know, Lindsay,' he said with a mild smile, 'I do know what's going on.'[1]

As the headmaster had always suspected, Anderson's film was far from an affectionate boarding-school comedy. The script, a savage satire written by two former boarders at Tonbridge, had been circulating around British film circles for years but had found no takers until Anderson read it in 1966. Every studio turned it down, an executive at the Crown Film Unit suggested that the authors should be 'horse-whipped', and the producer Lord Brabourne called it the most 'evil and perverted' script that he had ever read. At last, Paramount agreed to put up the necessary finance, and the film was on.[2]

If . . . is set in a particularly brutal example of the British public-school system, where the sadistic 'whips' flog their juniors, loyalty and conformity are enforced through military training, and a general spirit of authoritarian brutality holds sway. But for Anderson, who carefully blended naturalistic realism and free-wheeling fantasy to stretch the limits of cinematic narrative, the film was also a scathing portrait of Britain in the late sixties. When the fictional school's liberal headmaster lectures his sixth-formers, his words parody the political rhetoric of the day:

> College is a symbol of many things, integrity in public life, high standards in the television and entertainment worlds, huge sacrifice in Britain's wars . . . Education in Britain is a nubile Cinderella, sparsely clad and much interfered with. Britain today is a power-house of ideas, experiments, imagination, on everything from pop music to pig breeding, from atom power stations to mini-skirts, and that's the challenge we've got to meet.[3]

But for all the pieties about change, both the school and the country are animated by conservatism, not reform. At the school's Founder's Day the boys are addressed by the retired General Denson, who complains that 'it is fashionable to belittle tradition'. People talk about freedom, he says dismissively, 'but we won't stay free unless we are ready to fight. And you won't be any good as fighters unless you know something about discipline.' His speech ends: 'I know the world has changed a great deal in the past fifty years. But England, our England, doesn't change so easily. And back here in college today I feel, and it makes me jolly proud, that there is still a tradition here, which has not changed and by God it isn't going to change.' This is the cue for the famous attack on the chapel led by Travis (Malcolm McDowell), whose little band of dissidents, armed with machine-guns and grenades, opens fire on the assembled staff, parents and pupils. In the final scenes General Denson enthusiastically leads a counter-attack while the headmaster, the voice of the liberal consensus, falls with a bullet between the eyes. An elderly woman in a floral hat, the very picture of English middle-class respectability, seizes a machine-gun and turns it on the insurgents, screaming: 'Bastards! Bastards!' Finally, Travis turns his own machine-gun towards the camera and fires, bringing the audience directly into the fray.[4]

The timing of *If . . .*'s release could scarcely have been better. While Anderson and his cast were shooting in Cheltenham, television bulletins were carrying the latest news from the United States, where the streets were full of students protesting against the Vietnam War. Just across the Channel, too, France appeared to be going through its own version of the film's final scenes. In May hundreds of thousands of students threw up barricades and battled riot policemen in the centre of Paris, and by the end of the month they had been joined by millions of workers who occupied their factories or walked out on strike. Although President de Gaulle eventually managed to regain control, there was a palpable sense of revolutionary change, especially among students, radicals and their bohemian sympathisers. Similar protests in West Germany, Italy and Mexico, as well as the short-lived hopes of the Prague Spring in Czechoslovakia, meant that many people came to believe in 1968 as a year of change, the year of youth and revolution.

When *If . . .* received its premiere at the end of the year, therefore, it could hardly fail to strike a chord. Many radicals naturally saw it as a powerful forecast of the revolution to come, but even the mainstream press recognised its merits. The *New Statesman* called it 'a masterpiece'; the *Daily Telegraph* praised its 'inventive and well organized satire'; even the *Daily Mail*, so often the voice of populist conservatism, declared that the film's effect was 'to make you rock with laughter and then send you away for some very serious thinking'.[5] 'The whole film', said *The Times*, 'is a rich, complex, obscure metaphor of the way we live now, the tone of the times.'[6]

Although *If . . .* was a commercial success, it was hardly the kind of film likely to appeal to the vast majority of cinemagoers, and it was comfortably less popular than *The Jungle Book* and *Oliver!*, the two biggest hits at the British box office in 1968. It appealed above all to the kind of people who welcomed the news of the demonstrations in France and who hoped for similar events in Britain, people who saw themselves as members of the 'underground', the 'counter-culture' or the 'alternative society'.

The roots of this 'alternative society' went back a decade or more. Many of its most prominent figures had been students in the 1950s, often at Oxford and Cambridge or at art colleges. They were keen on American beat writing and the French existentialists; they disliked National Service and what they saw as the conservatism of British culture in the post-war years; they were attracted to jazz, impenetrable poetry, coffee bars, duffel coats, art-house films and CND marches.[7] They were not confined to London and the old universities: thanks to the art-school diaspora, there were little bohemian scenes in the unlikeliest places. Sheila Rowbotham, a teenage girl in Leeds in the late fifties, recalled seeing French films in the local art-house cinema, listening to modern jazz in a little club, 'drinking Nescafe, quoting Baudelaire and Shelley, and debating Bertrand Russell and Sartre'.[8]

The crucial thing about all this was that it remained the province of a very small middle-class minority. Devotees of the bohemian scene liked to pretend that they were building an alternative society, but they were able to do so because they generally came from an upper-middle-class, moneyed background, which explains why they rarely worried about getting jobs, paying the bills and the kinds of concerns that bothered most of their contemporaries. This scene was not in any way representative of the great majority of British youngsters in the sixties, most of whom were far more interested in, say, pop music, football and Jean Shrimpton than in jazz, poetry and Jean-Paul Sartre.[9]

Poetry, for example, had a very powerful appeal to a highly educated minority of young people, but simply repelled most of the rest. The most popular poet in the country, and probably the only one of whom most people had heard, was John Betjeman, whose nostalgic love of country churches, teddy bears and tea shops was hardly likely to appeal to the avant-garde inhabitants of the alternative society. Instead, their cultural tastes were best captured by one particular moment: the International Festival of Poetry, held at the Royal Albert Hall on 11 June 1965.

Organised to coincide with a visit to Britain by Allen Ginsberg, who was joined on stage by a vast array of poets from all over the world, the festival was later remembered as a seminal moment in the evolution of the alternative society. According to one account, it made visible 'a hunger for poetry as part of a wider counterculture', appealing to a 'community that was summoned up in its thousands'. Most poetry readings pulled in an audience of a few dozen at most, but the Albert Hall event attracted some seven thousand people, many drawn by a preview on the BBC evening news, others by word of mouth within the bohemian community.[10] Jim Haynes, the founder of the Traverse Theatre in Edinburgh and one of the most prominent figures in the British counter-culture, remembered reflecting: 'God, I thought it was just me and a few friends, but *this* many ... That was the revelation of the evening. There were lots of people out there like us.'[11]

But although many historians of the sixties pay a great deal of attention to the International Poetry Festival, it is one of those cultural events of the decade that, from a wider perspective, seem much less important. Seven thousand people was indeed an enormous attendance by the standards of poetry readings; on the other hand, it was still considerably smaller than the typical crowd for a Second Division football match. To the proverbial man on the Clapham omnibus, the poetry surely sounded like the most impenetrable piffle, and to many millions of people the event meant absolutely nothing. What was more, it had not even been a very good reading: much of the poetry was lost in the cavernous emptiness of the Albert Hall; the whole thing appeared to have been badly organised; and there was a general air of drunkenness and anarchy.[12] Even Barry Miles, a stalwart champion of avant-garde poetry, thought that much of it was 'awful bullshit and made the whole thing so boring'. It was 'a dreadful reading,' he admitted, 'one of the worst poetry readings ever'.[13]

Despite the inadequacy of the poetry, the Albert Hall reading remained the most famous example of the counter-cultural 'happenings' of the midsixties: unorthodox and often improvised celebrations of avant-garde culture, appealing to a young, highly educated minority and frequently fuelled by alcohol or drugs. Strictly speaking, happenings were theatrical events inspired by Dadaist art, Antonin Artaud's grotesque 'theatre of cruelty' and the artistic experiments of Abstract Expressionism, but there was never a clear distinction between a proper, organised happening and a random outpouring of iconoclastic energy. The first recorded British happening, for example, took place at a writers' conference in Edinburgh in August 1963 and featured a naked female art student being wheeled around a conference hall in a wheelbarrow to the skirl of the bagpipes. This rather preposterous occasion nevertheless provoked outrage in the press and resulted in the cancellation of the following year's conference, and the same pattern of provocation and reaction typified most subsequent happenings.[14]

In retrospect many happenings look like deliberate attempts to provoke the Lord Chamberlain, who until 1968 was responsible for theatrical censorship. In June 1964, for example, a group of experimental actors staged a happening at a small theatre in London. Their producer, Michael White, later described the scene:

The event started with painted girl happeners parcelling the audience in long rolls of white news print. Immersed in this sea of paper, the onlookers were then sprinkled with detergent powder while Carolee went about spraying cheap perfume everywhere... Various tableaux unfolded before the entranced audience. A girl had a picture of the Pope projected on her bottom. More girls were painted, slapped about with wet fish and strings of sausages, parcelled up in polythene bags. Two schoolgirls flogged a policeman. It was sensational, I suppose. But many of the performances were very evocative and effective.

The pursuit of art came to a sudden halt, however, when the door flew open and the theatre's enraged caretaker burst into the auditorium, furious that the performers had left a tap running in the dressing room. 'Since he was also standing alongside me most people took it for part of the show,' wrote White. 'Peter Brook went up to him and said: "I think you're the best thing in the entire evening, a most interesting performance."'[15]

No doubt many such anecdotes were embellished in the telling, but there is still something striking about the sheer earnestness with which many aspiring artists embraced ridiculousness of this kind. This particular happening was, perhaps predictably, French in inspiration, and formed part of the 'International Festival of Free Exhibition' mounted by Jean-Jacques Lebel. Other Lebel eccentricities included the spectacle of a footballer incarcerated in a cardboard box; this was, he claimed with deep solemnity, a 'sociodramatic event' which had 'important analogies with disciplines such as Buddhism, Vedanta and Samkhya Yoga, which strip away the illusory world of "form" and "name"'.[16]

Lebel's contemporaries included the Austrian 'action artist' Hermann Nitsch, whose work *21st Action* was staged at St Bride's Institute in September 1966. One onlooker reported:

> The carcass of a lamb was ritually paraded, nailed, hit, manhandled. Its entrails were produced, offered to the audience: one performer put them inside his trousers and pulled them out by his fly buttons. Simulated blood was poured over the carcass and a film projected onto it. This showed a penis, with a cord attached to it, moving from side to side. Every now and then there was a cacophony of shouting, stamping, banging and trumpeting.

Among the audience were several bewildered police officers, who were unconvinced by the artistic pretensions of the piece and charged its producers with mounting 'an exhibition of a lewd, indecent and disgusting nature'.[17] It was probably just as well that they missed a performance by one of Nitsch's Austrian collaborators a few years later in Vienna, where he 'cut himself in the thigh with a razor, urinated into a glass and drank it, rubbed himself with excrement, and began to masturbate while singing the Austrian national anthem'.[18]

Happenings made up only part of the colourful mosaic of bohemian life in the mid-sixties. In their attempt to build the alternative society, some of its members tried to set up institutions untainted by the conformity of the 'straight' world: the aforementioned Traverse Theatre in Edinburgh; the Arts Lab in Covent Garden, which offered cheap food and strange films; the Free School in Notting Hill, purportedly a venue for impromptu classes but more often a place to dabble with drugs and have sex with strangers; and even an Anti-University in the East End. Some of these, like the Traverse, were more successful than others, but in general they tried to project a sense of hedonism, camaraderie and, above all, the rejection of middle-class convention.

One particularly noteworthy establishment was Indica, a little bookshop and art gallery in St James's, founded by Barry Miles and his friend John Dunbar, a Cambridge-educated bohemian and former husband of Marianne Faithfull. Miles and Dunbar bridged the gap between the avant-garde rebels and the rock stars of the day, principally through their friendship with Paul McCartney, who helped to put up the shop's bookshelves, drew its flyers and designed its wrapping paper. Later, when Indica ran into difficulties, he lent his friends several thousand pounds to pay their creditors. Almost none of this made it into the newspapers, which explains why McCartney was still seen as the most conservative of the Beatles, despite the fact that he was more deeply immersed in the world of the counter-culture than almost any other British pop musician of the period.[19]

Even the most far-sighted ventures of the alternative society often ran into difficulties, largely because good intentions and enthusiastic drug-taking did not always make for prudent financial management. At the end of 1968 Indica's owners finally gave up the struggle against penury and shoplifting, and the enterprise went into liquidation with debts of five hundred pounds, which would have been much greater had it not been for McCartney's generosity.[20] Another example was the Macrobiotic Restaurant, which opened in a Holland Park basement in February 1967, selling felafel, brown rice and vegetables in an atmosphere of tolerance, nonconformity and marijuana smoke. 'People wrote out their own chits for what they'd had,' the organiser later recalled; 'someone would watch the till and take their money. It was very trusting.' However, he soon found that this system was unlikely to pay the bills. One night he discovered that while he had sold twenty-four slices of apple crumble, only one had been paid for. 'So after that,' he remembered wistfully, 'we went onto a slightly more structured basis.'[21]

As well as a host of clubs, bookshops and restaurants, the bohemian scene also boasted its own newspaper, the *International Times*, or *IT*. This first appeared in October 1966, at about the point when the alternative society was becoming strongly politicised as a result of the campaign against the Vietnam War. Although *IT* drew on a long tradition of anarchic pamphlets and highbrow 'little magazines', it was unmistakeably a product of its time, dependent on the expansion of the student market. Like all magazines, it relied on advertising, but by 1966 its founders, a group of avant-garde figures including Jim Haynes and Barry Miles, were justifiably confident of attracting interest from record companies and from the organisers of various fashionable or counter-cultural happenings.[22]

IT's launch party at the Roundhouse Theatre attracted the likes of Paul McCartney, Michelangelo Antonioni and Monica Vitti, with a groundbreaking psychedelic light show and live music from the Soft Machine and the Pink Floyd. 'The audience was drowned in noise and colour', according to one account; 'those who were not already drunk, stoned on pot or tripping on LSD found themselves transported into the magical atmosphere of an opium dream'.[23] Like the poetry festival at the Albert Hall a year earlier, this was a central moment in the history of the alternative society. As one bohemian partygoer later put it:

> All these little groups from all over London were massing together ... at this *IT* thing they were actually rubbing up against each other, sharing joints, talking frantically about turning on the world. Everyone had made plans of various kinds and they all babbled away furiously about either electrifying the skies so that messages of love and peace could be beamed off the clouds, or turning European universities into a vast

library of worthwhile information and so on. It all seemed like jolly good fun and a good idea at the time.[24]

Unlike many of the American underground newspapers with which it is often compared, *IT* took itself very seriously indeed, with solemn articles on drugs, sexual liberation and avant-garde theatre. By the middle of 1968 its circulation was at least forty thousand a fortnight, mainly in London and the major English university towns.[25] But this was only a brief peak, after which it went into rapid decline. In August the founders of *IT* were ousted by a group of younger contributors who wanted a more aggressive tone reflecting the spirit of the barricades, rather than earnest tributes to avant-garde poetry. In October 1969 there was a second office coup, and by this stage any pretence of coherent organisation had completely disappeared.[26] The music editor later recalled that 'the business management of *IT* was a joke', while it was 'distributed in a very haphazard and piecemeal way'. It was also hard to attract decent contributors because, he recalled, 'sometimes we got paid in money and drugs and sometimes just in drugs. Sometimes we didn't get paid at all.'[27]

By 1973 *IT* had effectively collapsed, which for an underground publication was pretty much par for the course. With unreliable advertising revenue, small readerships and extremely disputatious writers, most alternative newspapers survived for no more than two or three years. In March 1968, for example, the radical activist Tariq Ali had launched *Black Dwarf* as an attempt to bridge the gap between the counter-culture and the far left, but two years later he resigned to found the International Marxist Group's paper *Red Mole*. Another offshoot of *Black Dwarf*, entitled *Idiot International*, lasted until 1971, while the British edition of *Rolling Stone* was relaunched as *Friends* in 1969 and went into liquidation in 1971 before resurfacing as *Frendz*. The only survivor was *Time Out*, which began as an underground listings magazine before embracing the 'straight' world as well.[28] At the time many young bohemians blamed the censorship laws or the hostility of the authorities, but it is hard to see how, given the constant infighting and the changing winds of cultural fashion, many of these publications could have survived anyway. One editor of *Frendz* remembered 'four years of appalling messes, typographical horrors, pages that were so dense they were illegible', and concluded that it was 'a miracle that people read very much of it'.[29]

Perhaps the greatest problem for magazines like *IT*, *Black Dwarf* and *Friends* was that they reflected the narrow interests of a very incestuous and self-absorbed social scene. The disc jockey John Peel, who moved on the fringes of this world, told an interviewer that it was 'terribly small, and very, very localised'.[30] Even *IT*, which purported to be 'international', was, in the words of its music editor, 'like a village scandal sheet, a parish pump'.[31] Indeed, although most bohemians despised the glitz and glamour of Swinging London, the two worlds were actually very similar. Both made a great fuss about classlessness, but both were generally affluent and upper middle class. As one hippy later explained:

> You could bum around without doing any work and then you'd think, 'Shit! I'd like to go to Morocco so I'd better get a job for a few weeks' and the job was there to be had. Whenever you wanted to work, there was a job there . . .
>
> You had a good time, you rejected the whole philosophy you were brought up on . . . You just did things because you wanted to do them. Some people did worry, but not in our world.[32]

These sentiments hardly reflected the feelings of most young people in Britain in the late sixties. Many bohemians, however, were oblivious to the realities of ordinary life because they moved in such a narrow, closed world. To take one example, Nigel Waymouth, the founder of the boutique Granny Takes a Trip, had grown up in the same part of North London as John Dunbar, who befriended Barry Miles and Jane Asher's brother Peter and through them came to know Paul McCartney and John Lennon. Dunbar was even at the same Cambridge college as Waymouth's best friend. 'The whole thing is so incestuous,' Waymouth admitted. 'People know each other through people and that's just how it went on.'[33]

While many people disliked the solipsism of the underground, others were outraged by its explicit sexism, which was often much more blatant than in the supposedly reactionary 'straight' world. This was 'the seedy side of the underground: arrogant, ignorant and prejudiced', wrote Sheila Rowbotham, who worked on *Black Dwarf* before becoming a central figure in the new feminism of the seventies.[34] As another account puts it, building the counter-cultural utopia was 'a boy's game. Women were lovers, secretaries, tea-makers, but co-revolutionaries only when they behaved like the boys.'[35] Girls, said one female art student, were expected to sit quietly in the corner, 'rolling joints . . . nodding your head . . . You were there really for fucks and domesticity.'[36]

Above all, most ordinary people stood almost no chance of being accepted into the alternative society. Jonathan Park, who rather incongruously kept up a job as a structural engineer while helping to organise an 'alternative' show for children at the Roundhouse, greatly disliked what he called its 'social callousness'. 'The elitism meant that I was always an outsider,' he commented later. 'I had no starry nature, no wild wit or gift of the gab, lots of money or leather trousers.'[37] Sheila Rowbotham, too, thought that the alternative society was scarred by social hierarchies, 'sanctimony and pride'.[38] And Jonathan Park's wife Cheryl recalled that newcomers were accepted only if they were 'beautiful' or were 'able to take lots of drugs or able to get lots of drugs':

> And that elitism took the whole movement over and the people who could afford to carry on living like that did, and the rest dwindled away. There was no working class in the underground because nobody did any work . . . You didn't *have* to be an intellectual and you didn't *have* to be rich, but you had to have something that you could contribute to be one of the 'beautiful people'. If you were an ordinary person who lived in some suburb, you had no chance at all.[39]

The movement to which the counter-culture was most closely related was the so-called New Left. Although the British New Left is often confused with its American and Continental counterparts, it had very different roots. In 1956, after the revelation of Stalin's atrocities and the Soviet invasion of Hungary, one in four members of the little British Communist Party had walked out, and a small, highly educated group congregated around the *New Left Review*, the principal vehicle for what consequently became known as the New Left.[40]

As its origins might suggest, the New Left partly defined itself in opposition to the old, 'official', Stalinist left, but it was also fiercely critical of the affluent society, the political consensus of the fifties, and the pragmatism of the Labour Party under Gaitskell and Wilson. New Leftists shared a vision of 'participatory democracy', a kind of socialism that paid as much attention to culture, the environment and the workplace as it did to economic management, and which gave ordinary people a feeling of power and self- determination. And books like Raymond Williams's pioneering work of cultural studies *Culture and Society 1780–1950* (1958) and E. P. Thompson's *The Making of the English Working Class* (1963) focused not on party politics, but on work, family life and sexual relations, which were all examined in the light of Marxist ideas about 'alienation'.[41]

Although the New Left talked a great deal about the plight of ordinary people, the irony was that it never really appealed to those it sought to defend. Most of its writings, with the exception of a few classic works, were didactic, abstract and often rather impenetrable. Outside the academy, meanwhile, its influence and visibility were extremely small and even most Labour supporters were probably unaware that it existed. In the words of the Marxist historian Eric Hobsbawm, 'in practical terms these "New Lefts", although intellectually productive, were negligible', producing 'neither new parties of the left . . . nor lasting new organizations of significance . . . nor even individual national leaders'.[42]

In the universities and cultural institutions, however, it was a different story. For a time, both the Institute of Contemporary Arts and the British Film Institute looked like bastions of middle-class Marxism, and a new wave of intellectual periodicals like *Screen*, *Radical Philosophy*, *Radical Science Journal* and *Working Papers in Cultural Studies* betrayed the influence of New Left thinkers like Raymond Williams, Ralph Miliband and Stuart Hall.[43] These went hand in hand with a proliferation of new left-wing sects, from the Solidarity Group (founded in 1960) and the International Socialists (1962) to the International Marxist Group and the Institute of Workers' Control (both 1968), reflecting radical dissatisfaction with the record of the Wilson government and appealing to Britain's growing numbers of students and graduates.[44]

At first glance, the New Left and the counter-culture appeared to have very little in common. New Leftists tended to be earnest academics, happiest when reading about Marxist philosophy or nineteenth-century history, while most hippies were more comfortable in a world of drugs, psychedelic music and free love. E. P. Thompson thought that the counter-culture was a form of 'psychic self-mutilation . . . self-absorbed, self-inflating and self-dramatising'.[45] The radical director and theatre critic Charles Marowitz wrote scornfully in the *Guardian* about the 'fraternal mysticism' to be found in the underground, 'devoid of taste and sinew', with 'all the charms of a Labrador puppy slobbering over the fingers of a disinterested master'. London's hippies, he argued, were 'not only drop-outs but . . . "cop-outs" – people who equate mind-erasure with the dissolution of social problems'. They had 'a political naiveté', Marowitz concluded, 'which may be adorable in the abstract, but is infuriating to those who battle the same enemies with conviction and a thorough understanding of who and what they are up against'.[46]

What brought the New Left and the counter-culture together, however, was their shared opposition to the war in Vietnam.[47] By the beginning of 1967 a sizeable section of the Labour electorate, including students, young activists, old CND supporters, pacifists and other radicals, regarded 'the war as an obscenity and Britain's complicity as unforgivable'.[48] On university campuses and in avant-garde circles Wilson and his ministers were seen as 'not merely wrong, but contemptible'. Just before Christmas 1966 the Prime Minister was even stripped of his honorary presidency of the Cambridge University Labour Club. In the universities feelings ran so high that few visiting ministers avoided the welcoming chants of 'Murderer!' or 'Fascist pig!'[49] In the same year the Royal Shakespeare Company even mounted a collaborative production called *US*, telling the story of the Vietnam War through the eyes of a British journalist sent to cover it. In the final scene the actress Glenda Jackson turned on the audience, accusing them of moral cowardice and calling for the bloodshed to be brought home so that napalm would fall on suburban English lawns. The play drew a lot of attention, but the reviews were truly appalling: the critic Hilary Spurling spoke for many when she denounced its 'hysterical clowning, self-righteous belligerence and mawkish attempts at solemnity'.[50]

The British campaign against the war in Vietnam was obviously a descendant of old progressive traditions, appealing to what Michael Frayn called 'the Britain of the radical middle-classes – the do-gooders; the readers of the *News Chronicle*, the *Guardian* and the *Observer*; the signers of petitions; the backbone of the BBC'.[51] But it was also strongly influenced by similar movements on the Continent, where Vietnam had become a convenient symbol of broader radical grievances. 'Internationalism' meant a great deal to British activists, partly because it reflected their upper-middle-class origins, but also because it lifted them above the parochial concerns of boring old Britain.[52] In a sense, politics and culture *were* more international in the late sixties, thanks to the development of telecommunications, the availability of cheap air travel and the popularity of Mediterranean food and American films. But this is often rather overstated: native cultural traditions died hard. 'People began to think they ought to be more American and people really believed they were actually following that idea,' commented Mark Boyle of the psychedelic group the Soft Machine. 'Which was wrong, because we weren't.'[53]

Many people copied the style of American protest movements because they thought they were fashionable, and this explains why American practices, like calling authority figures 'pigs' and 'fascists', appeared in Britain in the late sixties. In the United States this kind of language reflected the genuine social tensions of the day and the fevered debate over the Vietnam War; in Britain, however, it sounded trite and incongruous. Sue Miles thought her contemporaries were 'all copying American culture', and admitted: 'We were not pushed by any major issues. There was no draft, you could piss around in England quite a lot.' 'As far as much of the counter-culture was concerned, the leading edge of what was happening was in the United States,' remarked the activist and historian Robin Blackburn. 'The Vietnam War, however much one might demonstrate against it here, was theirs.'[54]

All of this meant that the British peace movement of the late sixties was a peculiar hybrid, speaking in a language borrowed both from the New Left and from the counter-culture. Its first major organisation, the British Council for Peace in Vietnam, was formed in April 1965, and that autumn the first small-scale demonstrations took place outside the American Embassy in Grosvenor Square.[55] Most marchers were very similar kinds of people to those who had participated in the CND marches of the late fifties. Indeed, often they were *exactly* the same people: students, educated progressives, radical activists and so on, with a sprinkling of trade unionists. Although opinion polls consistently showed wide public opposition to the Vietnam War, the movement did not really appeal to the electorate at large. Ordinary voters were more interested in more immediate economic issues, and when the *Guardian* leader-writer and KGB 'agent of influence' Richard Gott decided to stand as an anti-war protest candidate in the Hull North by-election in January 1966 he attracted a pitiful 253 votes.[56]

The peace movement was never likely to attract mass support for the simple reason that most people simply did not care enough about a war in which they were not directly involved. When Sheila Rowbotham held open-air meetings on behalf of the Vietnam Solidarity Campaign, she was disappointed to find that the 'local working-class shoppers' of Hackney were almost completely indifferent.[57] What was more, it often seemed that the somewhat bizarre style of the movement could have had been deliberately designed to alienate working-class opinion. In 1965, for example, the Cavern Club hosted a 'multi-media anti-nuclear extravaganza' devised by the local poet Adrian Henri. 'At the end of a four-minute countdown the lights went out and a false ceiling made of paper came down on people's heads, to the most deafening noise we could devise,' he explained. 'The cloakroom girls screamed and hid under the counter. In the darkness and confusion, strange mutant figures moved.'[58] This was all very well, but it was unlikely to convince most ordinary Liverpudlians that they ought to devote their weekends to marching against the bomb.

Nor were they impressed by another son of the city, John Lennon, whose efforts on behalf of the anti-war movement struck many commentators as grossly self-indulgent. On 25 March 1969, for example, at the beginning of his honeymoon with Yoko Ono, Lennon announced his latest 'move for peace'. Brandishing a stack of envelopes, he told a press conference: 'Yoko and I plan to send one of these envelopes containing two acorns to the head of state of every country in the world. We want them to plant them for peace.'[59] Popular bewilderment at Lennon's antics, however, was well captured by his humiliating live appearance on ITV's *Today* show a few days later. The mood of the studio audience was less than sympathetic. 'What's beautiful about acorns?' one man asked. 'The acorn is a symbol of growth and, if you plant it, the tree will grow,' Lennon replied. 'But if you bomb it, it won't.' Unimpressed, the man shouted back: 'I think you're a bit of a nutter!' Another man described Lennon's scheme as 'the biggest piece of rubbish that I've heard this year', and, referring to the couple's notorious 'bed-in' for peace during their honeymoon, he went on to suggest that 'if you stayed there much longer, I think it would be better for everybody'. Evidently shocked by the applause that greeted these remarks, Lennon suggested that his antagonist 'look in the mirror before you get insulting'. 'I'm sure I don't mind looking in the mirror,' the man replied to more laughter, 'because I see something better than looking at you!'[60]

The peace movement reached its peak in 1968, when two demonstrations outside the American Embassy in Grosvenor Square attracted unprecedented national attention. Both were organised by the Vietnam Solidarity Campaign, which tried to straddle the gap between the radical left and the counter-culture. Dominated by Trotskyists, the VSC was not, strictly speaking, a 'peace' movement, since its own pamphlets proclaimed that it was 'committed to the victory' of the North Vietnamese Communists and their guerrilla allies. Its chief spokesman was Tariq Ali, a charismatic young Pakistani activist in his mid-twenties who had been president of the Oxford Union. To his admirers, Ali was courageous, charming and inspirational, the voice of a generation; to his critics, he was little more than a professional rabble-rouser, denounced by James Callaghan as 'a spoilt rich playboy'.[61]

Ali was much to the fore on 17 March 1968, when some 25,000 people, most in their late teens and twenties, assembled in Trafalgar Square for the march towards the American Embassy. This was Britain's biggest anti-war march so far, and the Metropolitan Police were ready for them. When the march reached Grosvenor Square, the mood rapidly turned ugly: fighting broke out between the police and the demonstrators, and ranks of mounted policemen charged the tightly packed crowd. Many accounts blame the police, who clearly despised their middle-class antagonists and certainly seem to have been heavy-handed. On the other hand, some demonstrators were obviously spoiling for a fight and were delighted to be given the opportunity.[62] A photographer for *IT* magazine described the scene:

> When the police started to charge with their horses and really lay into people and beat the shit out of them there was one girl that was shouting and screaming back at them and then about five police really laid into her and really kicked her on the ground and then they pulled back. I have photographs, one, two, three and four pictures, where the crowd surrounds one policeman that did not get away and they really laid into him and beat him to the ground.[63]

Still, compared with what was going on across the Atlantic and the Channel, this was pretty small-scale stuff. The police did not use tear gas or bullets, and the violence was hardly comparable with that in Paris a couple of months later.[64] As far as the press were concerned, however, it had been an appalling exhibition of the dangers of radicalism. 'This kind of thing has to be stopped,' declared the *Daily Mail*, while both the left-leaning *Sun* and conservative *Telegraph* suggested that demonstrations of this kind ought to be banned.[65] More scuffles the following month, outside the offices of a right-wing German press group, only confirmed the impression that the protesters were a thoroughly bad lot. *The Times* complained that they saw violence as 'a means of self-expression', while the *Observer* declared that they were 'like a highbrow version of football hooliganism'.[66]

The next major demonstration was scheduled for 27 October, and since the intervening months had been ones of bloodshed across the Western world, it was not surprising that many people were seriously worried about the consequences. Six weeks beforehand *The Times* warned its readers that 'a small army of militant extremists', armed with Molotov cocktails and 'a small arsenal of weapons', had developed a 'plan to seize control of certain highly sensitive installations and buildings in Central London'.[67] The authorities immediately denied the story and *The Times* backed down, but nonetheless the rumours continued. The Conservative home affairs spokesman Quintin Hogg advised James Callaghan that he should shut down all the capital's mainline stations, turn back all buses bound for London, and hold the Guards regiments ready in their barracks to retake the streets.[68] Another Conservative MP, appropriately called Tom Iremonger, called in the Commons for 'alien militant agitators' (clearly meaning Tariq Ali) to be deported, adding that 'the British people are fed up with being trampled underfoot by foreign scum'.[69]

On the day of the march itself, more than a hundred policemen were sent to guard Broadcasting House, while the BBC sent duplicate tapes of its programmes to Birmingham, just in case their buildings were occupied by the long-haired hordes.[70] The *People* advised its readers to maintain a 'stiff upper lip', citing the example of the local Lyons Corner House, which intended to stay open regardless. 'If we didn't stop our service for the Germans,' said a Lyons spokesman, 'why should we stop for our own people?' 'Whatever happens,' said the *People*'s editorial, no doubt speaking for millions of anxious readers, 'the HORSES must not get hurt.'[71]

In the event, the horses emerged unscathed. Split by sectarian bickering, the peace movement came up with two competing routes for the march: about thirty thousand people walked peacefully to listen to speeches in Hyde Park, while a smaller, more aggressive group of some five thousand confronted the police in Grosvenor Square. But the predicted violence never erupted; there were only a few minor injuries, and a mere handful of arrests.[72] 'Police Win Battle of Grosvenor Square' read the next day's headline in *The Times*, while the *Mirror* revelled in 'The Day the Police Were Wonderful'.[73]

As far as public opinion was concerned, Jim Callaghan was the hero of the day, and that night he made his way down to Grosvenor Square to congratulate the police. When the Cabinet met two days later he was heartily praised.[74] 'Jim's real strength was that he wasn't rattled and that he took police advice not to have troops in readiness,' recorded Richard Crossman. 'He deserved our congratulations because he would have got all the curses if after all the demonstration had turned violent. No doubt it has added even more to his strength, building him up as the only alternative to Harold Wilson.'[75]

Perhaps the most extraordinary thing about the British movement against the Vietnam War was the speed with which it disappeared. In October 1968 thousands of young people had marched through London, but then most of them simply went home. Although the American war dragged on for another five years, vocal protest in Britain ran out of steam. In some cases left-wing activists were distracted by the emergence of more salient issues, notably industrial conflict and Northern Ireland, but many thousands seem simply to have lost interest as soon as 1968 ended and revolution went out of fashion.

Of all the social groups who had been associated with the alternative society and the peace movement, the most visible were the students. Their numbers had been steadily rising since the fifties as successive governments pumped more money into the university system. In 1962 some 216,000 people had been enrolled at British universities; by 1965 there were almost 310,000, and the total continued to rise. Students had hitherto made up only a tiny fraction of the population in their late teens and early twenties; now, one in ten young people of that age attended university. Until the mid-sixties British students had a reputation for conservatism and quiescence, but the first signs of unrest surfaced at the London School of Economics in the autumn of 1966. It was no accident that the first disturbances took place at the LSE. Its students were generally extremely bright and well educated: the great majority were from private or grammar schools, their school results had been exceptionally good, and their academic interests meant that they were more politicised than most student bodies.[76]

The catalyst was the appointment of a new director, Walter Adams, who had previously been the principal of University College, Rhodesia, and who was therefore condemned by the LSE's student union as an accessory to racism. On 31 January 1967 student activists called a 'Stop Adams' meeting in the Old Theatre, but when a crowd of students arrived they found the outgoing director, Sir Sydney Caine, waiting for them with various officials and porters. In the ensuing mêlée one of the porters, the sixty-four-year-old Edward Poole, slipped and suffered a severe heart attack. The student organisers then tried to break up the crowd, but instead the protesters forced their way into the theatre, one of them punching Caine, who was attending to the stricken porter. Moments later Caine climbed onto the stage and said tremblingly: 'The man has now died. Does that satisfy you?' Incredibly, the crowd shouted back: 'No!' In the next few minutes, however, as the news sunk in, the students began to disperse.

In the aftermath of Poole's death the university authorities decided to suspend two particularly militant students, provoking a wave of strikes, sit-ins and marches which culminated in a parade of a thousand students down Fleet Street carrying placards, banners and, of course, flowers. However, their militant fervour did not survive the temptations of hearth and home, and during the Easter holidays the LSE governors and the student union managed to come to a compromise.[77] But although the LSE stayed relatively quiet after Easter 1967, the protest bug now appeared to have spread to other institutions across the country. Over the next year or so there were sit-ins and marches everywhere from the universities of Essex and Leicester to the Regent Street Polytechnic and the Holborn College of Law and Commerce.[78]

At the end of May 1968 two hundred students occupied the administrative wing of the University of Hull in protest against their final examinations, which were then in progress. As the International Socialist Group explained, instead of offering the students 'the kingdom of the mind', examinations were 'a crude quantification' leading to 'money and militarism, poverty and police forces'.[79] By this stage sit-ins were news, and *Black Dwarf* sent Sheila Rowbotham north to investigate:

> Everyone is smiling at each other, food appears from nowhere. People give it to each other. The Commissions which have been created move into operation. Blankets, food, toothbrushes are collected from the halls with incredible efficiency. There is total participation – no referring, no deferring. Each student is himself. The organization. No them. Messages, donations, visits from staff and townspeople who support the sit-in. The sit-in becomes a celebration. Everyone is dancing, talking, grinning, giving their food away. Everyone IS.[80]

Whether the 'townspeople' of Hull were really flocking to support the students seems extremely unlikely. In any case, the students eventually ran out of steam; the summer holidays came and, after a few concessions, the authorities effectively won the day.[81]

One of the bitterest confrontations came not at a university but at the Hornsey College of Art in North London, and ran from 28 May to 8 July 1968. Here the students occupied the main building and demanded a complete revision of the way art was taught, including an 'open system whereby all individual demands can be taken into account'. Entry requirements and graded assessment were to be abolished; subjects should be 'set up in response to the need of an individual or group of individuals at any moment'; and there should be 'complete freedom of individual or group research at any time with or without tutorial assistance'. As at other institutions, the activists won support from radical younger lecturers; but, also as at other institutions, after making a handful of concessions on issues like student representation on college committees, the authorities ultimately prevailed.[82] And, as elsewhere, the reaction of the local community was less than supportive. The *Wood Green, Southgate and Palmers Green Weekly Herald* offered perhaps the best glimpse of public opinion in an extraordinarily uncompromising editorial column:

> [A] bunch of crackpots, here in Haringey, or in Grosvenor Square, or Berlin, or Mexico, can never overthrow an established system . . . They may dislike having to conform to a system in which they are required to study, and follow set programmes, and take examinations or their equivalents; and acknowledge that in doing so they are through the indulgence of others preparing themselves for a lifetime of earning . . .
>
> The system is ours. We the ordinary people, the nine-to-five, Monday to Friday, semi-detached, suburban wage-earners, we are the system. We are not victims of it. We are not slaves to it. We are it, and we like it. Does any bunch of twopenny-halfpenny kids think they can turn us upside down? They'll learn.[83]

The attitude of the national press, meanwhile, was not much more favourable. The *Telegraph* even called student protesters 'pretentious adolescents, generally of small intellectual ability'.[84] Most reports found that working-class sentiment was extremely hostile, and Gallup found that only 15 per cent sympathised with the students' grievances about the universities.[85] Indeed, the *Sunday Telegraph* was not far off the mark when it spoke of an 'almost vindictive hostility to the student population'.[86]

In January 1969 the LSE returned to the headlines. Although Walter Adams had taken up his post, his links with Rhodesia continued to provoke student unrest. When a new sit-in was thwarted by specially installed fire doors and iron gates, the protesters simply battered them down with pickaxes and sledgehammers. The police hauled a number of the insurgents off to Bow Street magistrates' court, which unsurprisingly provoked fresh demonstrations, and Adams finally decided to close down the LSE. In the meantime some students decamped to the University of London's student union building, where they received informal classes from sympathetic younger lecturers. Eventually the LSE reopened, but when the authorities sacked two lecturers for abetting the demolition of the gates, protests broke out once more. The student union voted to boycott lectures, some 'academic assassins' were singled out for harassment, and the senior common room was occupied for a second time. The LSE appeared utterly ungovernable. And then, as elsewhere, the protests simply and suddenly ran out of steam. The University of London's academic board found in favour of the authorities; the sacked lecturers went on their way; the students grudgingly settled back down to work; and by the summer of 1969 the whole thing seemed to have blown over.[87]

The new disturbances at the LSE won the students few friends in the press, the Commons or the country. Although the students made a great deal of fuss, they achieved very few of their stated goals. Indeed, most sit-ins ground to a halt fairly quickly, for the simple reason that they were difficult to sustain. Not only were there mundane practical problems, like the difficulty of sleeping, washing and changing one's clothes, but many participants inevitably lost interest after a few days' sitting around.[88] Some protests were frankly preposterous: a 'revolutionary festival' at Essex in February 1969, for example, was nothing short of a shambles. According to *New Society*, 'a car was set on fire and a student and a mathematics professor struggled over possession of a hosepipe'. Nearby wall slogans, painted in imitation of the famous Parisian slogans of May 1968, proclaimed 'Revolt or fester', 'The shit heap is smouldering', and, rather bizarrely, 'Don't just stand there – wank'.[89]

As the dramatic overseas events of 1968 began to fade from the memory, student protest lost its cachet, and by the end of the decade it had fallen from fashion completely. In the winter of 1969–70 an attempt to rekindle the fire at Warwick proved a very damp squib indeed. 'This week an open university was declared at a poorly attended teach-in,' one student wrote to *Black Dwarf*. 'Irrelevant speeches were delivered to an apathetic audience. Already many students had left on vacation and all that was left was the small band of militant organisers, and some hundred or so students who were waiting for the trendy music from London . . . The only possible outcome is further disillusion.'[90]

Despite the anxieties of the press, there was no comparison between the rather ineffectual protests in Britain and the much larger, more important student movements in the United States, France and West Germany. Surveys consistently found that British students were simply not very interested in protesting.[91] As Marwick puts it, most students, far from being revolutionary firebrands, were 'docile' and 'hard-working'.[92] A poll of students at Leeds, six months after a sit-in opposing a visit by a right-wing Conservative MP, found that 86 per cent described student politics as 'boring', while 63 per cent said that they had opposed the sit-in.[93] Even at the LSE there was plenty of evidence that students were much more conservative than was generally imagined. A careful survey of students' attitudes during the troubles of 1967 found that six out of ten had taken no part in the protests at all, while fewer than one in ten had managed to stick to the sit-in for more than four days. Although they wanted a say in matters like the running of the library and discipline, only 13 per cent thought they ought to have a say in appointing the LSE's director and only 9 per cent wanted a role in academic appointments. They were reformers, not revolutionaries.[94] A year later, after the disturbances had broken out again, the *Guardian* interviewed a group of students and found them surprisingly pragmatic. One first-year economist thought the protests were 'futile'; another said they were 'pointless'. Of course, the newspaper could have quoted more radical voices; however, the moderates were comfortably in the majority. 'I have got examinations in a fortnight,' said a third student, speaking for hundreds of his fellows. 'That is more important to me.'[95]

In 1969 a survey published in *Encounter* found that four out of five British students were glad to be at their institution, while three out of four proclaimed themselves content with university life.[96] Despite the flaws and inequities of the education system, British students really were 'better treated than anywhere else in the world'. Tuition was free and almost all living costs were covered by the state grant. Teacher–student ratios were extremely low, and whereas most Continental students were compelled to sit through tedious recitals in overcrowded lecture theatres, many British students were taught in small classes and seminars. In other words, they had much less to complain about than most of their overseas counterparts. What was more, during the late sixties most universities responded to student pressure by mildly relaxing their rules and admitting student representatives to university committees, most of which were pretty tedious anyway. From this perspective, therefore, the fact that British students were much less active than their Continental and American counterparts hardly seems surprising at all.[97]

After 1968 the counter-culture, the new radicalism and student protest all began to fade from the headlines. For many figures in the bohemian underground the end finally came when the editors of the magazine *Oz* were hauled into court on obscenity charges. An underground magazine that had moved from Australia to London, *Oz* captured better than any other publication the irreverent, mischievous, often wildly self-indulgent style of the counter-culture. However, in April 1970 it overstepped the mark with a 'School Kids Issue', largely produced by middle-class adolescents who fancied themselves as radical journalists and had responded to an advertisement for new blood. The real problem was the cover, which showed a naked black girl in eight different erotic poses, featuring not only the use of sex toys but the participation of other girls and even some sort of creature that might be a rat or a lizard.

The police, clearly looking for an opportunity to teach the editors a lesson, promptly pounced, raiding the *Oz* offices on 8 June, ten days before the general election. The case did not come to trial until the following summer, and it was widely seen as a trial not only of the magazine's three editors but of the entire counter-culture. The three were found guilty on all counts except conspiracy, and each was given a prison sentence, while the magazine's Australian founder, Richard Neville, was also sentenced to deportation. These sentences, which many commentators felt were excessively harsh, were reversed on appeal, but the symbolic importance of the trial was captured by the fact that while the editors were being held in prison their long hair was forcibly cut off by the warders. The system, it seemed, had won after all.[98]

For many of the young people who had participated in events like the Albert Hall poetry reading, the Grosvenor Square marches and the occupation of the LSE, the late sixties would always remain a lost golden age of liberation, romance and political possibility. 'We had a great time, listened to good music, wore a uniform of our own invention, played like children among the drugs and light-shows, fucked copiously, took to the streets, and seriously frightened the horses in Grosvenor Square,' wrote Jenny Diski thirty years later, 'and all the while felt righteous, that we were blowing away the dust of the world.' Yet, as Diski also recognised, propping up all this apparent disaffection was the bedrock of social and economic security. 'The underlying promise', she noted, 'was that after we dropped out, we would be able to drop back in again, get in the work, education and stability that we had thrown up in the name of getting it right.' This explains why youngsters from poorer backgrounds, who had so much more to fear and to lose, were less likely to join the alternative society. And it explains why young people were less likely to be drawn to overt rebellion in the more insecure, economically threatening times that followed in the 1970s and 1980s.[99]

For some historians, what really stands out about the events of 1968 is the contrast between the parochial, small-scale events in Britain and the genuine upheaval and bloodshed in, say, France and the United States. As the American political economist Albert Hirschmann points out, the '1968 Revolution' never happened in Britain, which made it exceptional among the major countries of the Western world.[100] But this is easy to explain. For one thing, it is not really true that there was a single international '1968 Revolution' that broke out throughout the rest of the Western world. Despite the mood of international revolutionary excitement, the events that unfolded in the United States, France and West Germany were motivated by different local causes and took very different paths. In other words, the British were not necessarily missing out on something that everybody else was going through. Indeed, bearing in mind its self-conscious traditions of conservatism and pragmatism, the relatively comfortable conditions in its universities, the rather gloomy stability of its political life and the long continuity of its institutions, it is hardly surprising that Britain did not witness vast protests to compare with, say, the events in Paris in May 1968.[101]

In the summer of 1968 the activist and art teacher Jeff Nuttall wrote the preface to his forthcoming history of the counter-culture. 'The plain obvious fact', he insisted, 'is that between the autumn of '67 when I completed this manuscript, and the summer of '68 when I am writing this preface, young people under various pretexts made war on their elders, and their elders made war on them. The war continues.'[102] But this was nonsense. The vast majority of young people did not make war on anybody; instead, they spent their days at work and their evenings watching television. Hippies, radicals and drop-outs were never more than a tiny minority, and working young people were even less likely than students to be drawn to the radical left.[103] Surveys consistently described them as 'conventional' and 'realistic' in their political attitudes and voting behaviour, and a study in *Political Quarterly* in 1969 described the young as 'conformist, conservative and respectable'.[104]

Most young people were extremely unlikely to respond to appeals from those whom they saw as privileged and self-indulgent, especially as these appeals were often couched in terms that repelled the majority of ordinary people. Nuttall's vision of the alternative society, for example, ran as follows:

> The spread of an ego-dissolving delirium wherein a tribal telepathic understanding could grow up among men . . . to cultivate aesthetic perception in the face of utilitarian perception, to reinstate the metalled road as a silken ribbon . . . to outflank police, educationalists, moralists through whom the death machine is maintained . . . [to allow] people to fuck freely and guiltlessly, dance wildly and wear fancy dress all the time. To eradicate . . . the pauline lie . . . that people neither shit, piss nor fuck . . . to reinstate a sense of health and beauty pertaining to the genitals and the arsehole.[105]

Even less likely to appeal to the average citizen were the views of Richard Neville, as expressed in his manifesto *Play Power* (1970). Neville explained that in the ideal alternative society 'a generous girl will "put on a queue" behind the sand dunes for a seemingly unlimited line-up of young men', and elsewhere in the book he enthused about the pleasures of a 'hurricane fuck [with] a cherubic 14-year-old girl from a nearby London comprehensive school'. The politics of the future, he said, would be 'the politics of play: the international, equi-sexual, inter-racial survival strategy for the future. The laughing-gas to counteract tomorrow's Mac. Onwards to the Eighties, Motherfuckers.'[106]

For many readers, and probably the vast majority of young people in the sixties, let alone their elders, this was both bewildering and offensive. After Neville was convicted of obscenity in the *Oz* trial, the *Telegraph*'s editorial column had no sympathy:

> Without the protection of the law, which they so obscenely abuse, how long would these drop-outs survive, for the most part so manifestly weak and weedy as they are? Many of them, incidentally, including two of the *Oz* defenders, wear spectacles – a visible mark of their dependence on the normal world they despise, as ludicrous in its way as false teeth in the mouth of a noble savage.[107]

The *Telegraph*, admittedly, was a conservative newspaper, and plenty of commentators felt that the *Oz* defendants had been victimised. But, bearing in mind the evidence of the opinion polls, there is little doubt that it spoke for the majority of the British public, both young and old. Far from being a caricature, the genteel old lady with her machine-gun at the end of *If*. . . had pretty well captured the feelings of 'the ordinary people, the nine-to-five,

Monday to Friday, semi-detached, suburban wage-earners'. Even John Osborne, the famous 'angry young man' of the late fifties, described the counter-culture as 'uninteresting and ugly'. 'I don't know any students and I certainly would not like to see a Negro minority taking over this country,' he said defiantly. 'I know this sounds very Blimpish — the prospect of rule by instant rabble doesn't appeal to me either.'[108]

The ultimate question is whether any of this really mattered. Despite the publicity that attended the rise and fall of the hippy movement and the fighting in Grosvenor Square, they made little difference to the lives of most ordinary people. Arthur Marwick argues that the various counter-cultural movements 'permeated and transformed' mainstream culture, but it is very hard to point to any substantive changes that came about as a result.[109] Richard Trench, who was recruited to the ranks of the underground as a schoolboy and became an activist at Essex, later commented that the counter-culture had 'almost no effect at all'. Perhaps its only legacy, he mused, was that it became more respectable for middle-class people 'to get jobs like being a wheelwright, or a furniture restorer in Norfolk'. Otherwise, he said, 'I can't think of anything in this country that wouldn't have come anyway.'[110]

Sexual frankness, feminism, the ecology movement and so on pre-dated the counter-culture of the sixties, and were the result of deeper social and cultural changes reaching back for decades or more. In terms of electoral politics the New Left, the counter-culture and even the movement against the Vietnam War were completely irrelevant: there is no evidence that they made the slightest difference to how most people thought about politics, or to how they voted in 1970.[111] As one bohemian veteran, Christopher Logue, later commented, 'it was rather pretentious and silly in some ways . . . kids in the playground'. Like many commentators, he remarked on the fact that the counter-culture seemed 'intellectually flat and unadventurous', certainly when compared with the avant-garde scene of the late 1950s. 'There was no "alternative society",' he said scornfully. 'It was playtime.'[112] And by the end of the sixties, on the brink of a new decade of inflation, terrorism and industrial unrest, playtime was over.

26

SYMPATHY FOR THE DEVIL

> I don't think Mike takes drugs. But if they have been having a lark they will have to take the consequences.
>
> Eva Jagger, *Sunday Telegraph*, 19 February 1967
>
> I'm not rebelling against anything! I never rebelled against my parents.
>
> Mick Jagger, 1968

At seven-thirty on the evening of Sunday, 12 February 1967, Keith Richards was looking forward to a quiet evening in front of the television. He had spent the weekend at Redlands, his magnificent thatched country house in West Sussex, surrounded by eight friends who had driven down from London for a short break. That day they had been out walking and larking about on the beach, and now Richards and his friends were enjoying a roaring fire, an old gangster film and a few Bob Dylan records. Upstairs Marianne Faithfull was running a warm bath, and in the kitchen the art dealer Robert Fraser's Moroccan manservant was preparing a buffet supper. It was a lazy, laid-back Sunday evening, and nothing seemed likely to spoil it.[1]

At that moment, to the guests' astonishment, a face unexpectedly appeared at the drawing-room window. Richards wearily sighed and said that there must be 'a little old lady' outside, no doubt hunting for autographs. But then there was an almighty knocking at the front door, and Richards reluctantly hauled himself up from his armchair to answer it. Opening the door revealed not a little old lady but the imposing, uniformed figure of Chief Inspector Gordon Dineley of the West Sussex Police, surrounded by constables, who announced that, pursuant to the Dangerous Drugs Act of 1965, he had a warrant to search the premises. It later emerged that the police had been tipped off earlier that day by executives of the *News of the World*, who had an informant within the household.

The police search of Redlands went ahead with surprising calm and good grace on both sides. Many of the policemen had never seen such decadence, from the half-timbered walls and Moroccan curtains to the large television set and state-of-the-art stereo speakers. 'Redlands gave us a bit of a shock,' remembered PC Don Rambridge. 'From the outside it's a beautiful house – Olde Worlde, half-beamed. Then you go inside and it's decorated in mauves and blacks, all the beams painted like that. It turned out to be a real raver's place. It really hurt looking at the inside.'

All of the constables knew of the Stones' reputation as loutish bad boys, although Richards himself was known in the neighbourhood as a polite young man. 'They all had long hair and the way-out language,' Rambridge recalled. 'Alien to our way of life, of course.' Still, the police treated their suspects with impeccable courtesy throughout. They were clearly amused by the fact that Marianne Faithfull, having taken off her muddy clothes before her bath, was wrapped in an enormous fur rug. But when the rug slipped, whether by accident or design, to reveal her naked body, the constables kept their cool. 'She wasn't anything to look at anyway,' said Rambridge dismissively. 'She was obviously a drop-out type.'[2]

Most of the guests were confident they had nothing to fear. Although they had all taken drugs the previous evening or earlier in the day, they did not have any lying around. But this confidence was misplaced. Cannabis was found on one of the guests, an American drug pusher nicknamed Acid King David, while upstairs one policeman found Italian amphetamine capsules in the pocket of Mick Jagger's green velvet jacket. These actually belonged to Faithfull, but Jagger gallantly said they were his, adding that they had been prescribed by his doctor. Back in the drawing room, Richards was calmly answering all the inspector's questions and asked if his men could avoid treading on the expensive North African cushions. When cautioned that if any drugs were found on the premises he would be liable for prosecution, Richards said sardonically: 'I see. They pin it all on me.'[3]

The guest who had most to fear was Robert Fraser, whose pockets contained a lump of hashish, a handful of amphetamines and, far more seriously, a carved wooden box containing twenty-four white heroin tablets. As Fraser knew, possession of heroin carried a mandatory prison sentence. In the agonising minutes while the police were searching his friends he managed to shake the pills into his trouser pocket, in the vain hope that they would not be noticed. Unfortunately, Constable Rambridge spotted traces of white powder in the box and asked him to turn out his pockets. In silent despair Fraser handed over the pills, which Rambridge then passed to his senior officer, Sergeant Stanley Cudmore. They looked, Cudmore said thoughtfully, like heroin. 'Definitely not,' Fraser replied. Struggling to keep the desperation out of his voice, he explained that he was diabetic and the tablets were insulin pills. He had been affable and cooperative throughout, as 'good as gold', in Rambridge's words, and his Old Etonian manner clearly impressed the policemen. After a second's pause, and to Fraser's unutterable relief and joy, Cudmore nodded and handed back the pills. Then he hesitated, said slowly, 'I'd better keep just one back for analysis', and stretched out his hand. 'At that moment,' Fraser reflected, 'I knew I'd had it.'[4]

When the *News of the World* broke the news that the police had raided 'a secluded country house near the south coast' and confiscated drugs from 'several [unnamed] stars', many readers would have immediately guessed the culprits.[5] In fact, the Rolling Stones often led much more conservative lives than people imagined, with Jagger the man-about-town and friend of the aristocracy, and Richards the bibliophile and war-film buff in his Sussex manor house. But the Stones' public image had long since passed beyond their control, and, like the Beatles, they had become symbols of something that went far beyond pop music, personifying the social and cultural changes of the late sixties. As one writer puts it, they had become 'wasted emblems of decadent hedonism . . . transgressive, outlawish and on the edge, outraging everything respectable and safe'.[6]

As always, the Rolling Stones' major challenge was to keep pace with the Beatles, who generally seemed a step ahead when it came to anticipating the latest musical trends. Although *Aftermath* had become their third chart-topping album in 1966, it was still some way short of *Rubber Soul* or *Revolver*. Even Brian Jones admitted that the Stones' music was 'not very original'.[7] Most of his colleagues thought that the solution was to cut loose from their blues roots, and for over a year Jagger and Richards had been trying to reposition the Stones as a more eclectic outfit. It was not obvious, however, that they would be able to maintain their success. 'Everything in the Rolling Stones' garden is very nice at present,' commented *Melody Maker*:

> But despite their height of appeal, they haven't got the staying power of the Beatles. Because of changes in taste in popular music, the Stones cannot hope for lasting popularity. The very nature of their music

precludes drastic change . . . It is difficult to see or discover which direction they are challenging in. Where do they go from here?[8]

In January 1967 the Stones' next album, *Between the Buttons*, peaked at number three, the poorest performance by any of their LPs so far. As the band's biographer remarks, it was clearly produced in a state of artistic exhaustion, 'in which lack of ideas combined with over-production to produce a curious, limply echoing effect, like a Vaudeville show in an almost empty hall'.[9] When the Beatles released *Sgt. Pepper's Lonely Hearts Club Band* a few months later the Stones' effort looked like even more of a damp squib. That summer, their inferiority complex had never been more obvious. In July the Beatles had a number one hit with 'All You Need Is Love'; a month later the Stones released 'We Love You', an embarrassingly slavish imitation that washed up at number eight and was their least successful single since November 1963.[10]

The Rolling Stones' recording efforts in the summer of 1967 were severely hindered by the fact that their three chief musicians, Jagger, Richards and Jones, were all facing drugs charges and the possibility of imprisonment. At this stage, though, most of the Stones were not particularly excessive drug users. Wyman and Watts were both almost completely indifferent to the drug culture of the time and were nicknamed 'the straightest rhythm section in rock 'n' roll'.[11] Even Jagger and Marianne Faithfull, despite their fondness for cannabis and LSD, were shocked by Robert Fraser's heroin habit.[12] Keith Richards, however, had taken to drugs much more enthusiastically, partly as a way of dealing with the pressures and insecurities of fame, and ended the sixties well on the way to heroin addiction. But Jones was a more serious case. The most ostentatious and flamboyant member of the band, he meandered through London in 'frock coats, flowing scarves and floppy-brimmed hats'. Yet, despite his sartorial self-confidence, Jones was more insecure than ever. As early as 1965 he was regularly drinking two bottles of whisky a day, as well as taking handfuls of pills, and visitors to his home often saw enormous lumps of hashish openly lying around.[13]

Although it is impossible to know for certain how many people experimented with drugs in the late sixties, there is no doubt that between the late 1950s and the early 1970s there was a steep rise in drug use and addiction. People had always taken drugs, of course, from laudanum in the nineteenth century to cocaine in the 1920s, but these were always minority tastes. In the late fifties and early sixties the drug issue still appeared largely insignificant. There was no black market for drugs, and therefore no problem with drug dealers or criminal drug rings. Heroin addiction, for example, was almost completely unknown, with only ten new cases a year nationally.[14] Cannabis use, meanwhile, was a minority pursuit reserved for West Indian immigrants and a few white bohemians.[15]

This picture began to change as more middle-class youngsters were drawn to black culture and especially black music, and through them to the exotic appeal of drugs. In 1960 there were 235 cannabis convictions; in 1964, 544; in 1967, 2393; and in 1970, 7520.[16] As Jonathon Green comments, these figures also reflect the booming police interest in drugs, epitomised by the foundation in the mid-sixties of special drug squads.[17] Drugs had become a symbolic issue, associated with other anxieties about the sexual precocity and supposed delinquency of the young, the decay of traditional structures under the impact of affluence, and the influence of immigrant communities. In 1964, for example, a Home Office report noted that in Notting Hill 'heroin and hemp were said to be available and coloured men were associating with white girls'. Young people, the report observed, were 'in serious moral danger . . . It requires a strong character and a secure home background with understanding parents to avoid contamination once the young person has entered the club world.'[18]

But there was a reality behind the moral panic. Home Office figures showed that the number of teenagers registered as heroin, cocaine or opium addicts tripled between 1964 and 1965, and by the late sixties heroin addiction in Britain was growing at the fastest rate in the world.[19] Thanks to the economic growth and consumerism of the fifties and sixties, teenagers and young adults had unprecedented spending power and leisure time; and thanks to the improvement of international transport and communications, drugs like cannabis and cocaine were being imported much more easily from overseas. In other words, the potential market for chemical stimulants was bigger than ever and dealers were able to supply it. The obvious example in the early sixties was the popularity among the Mods of purple hearts, which were perfectly legal until the government passed the Drugs (Prevention of Misuse) Act in 1964.[20]

From 1966 or so, amphetamines lost their fashionable cachet to cannabis and LSD. Cannabis was associated with immigrants and therefore with black music, and it was also popularised by the likes of the Beatles and the Rolling

Stones as a harmless relaxant that would help users to embrace peace and love. It was readily obtainable overseas, notably in North Africa, and packets were easily smuggled through Customs and then sold on the street for about seven pounds an ounce in 1966.[21] Exactly how many people used it is impossible to say with any certainty. The Wootton Committee, which met in 1968, guessed that there might be anything from 30,000 to 300,000 users, while Arthur Marwick gives a probably inflated estimate of one to two million. In some circles, especially among students and in the pop music industry, dope-smoking was clearly quite common by 1970, and it was regularly celebrated in songs and illustrations of the time. As Green says, it was 'as much symbolic and gestural as purely self-indulgent', so the simple act of lighting a joint was enough to make the user look 'an outsider, a subversive, a rebel'.[22]

The use of LSD seems to have been much less common, although accurate figures are even harder to establish. Like cannabis, it had subversive associations as well as an artistic cachet: embarking on an acid trip was a way of proclaiming one's emancipation from the mundane world of mortgages, Margate and Mary Whitehouse.[23] A typical tab of LSD in the late sixties was about six times stronger than in later decades, and since the drug induces colourful illusions and fantasies, often culminating in synaesthesia (the neurological mixing of the senses), it was not surprising that the typical acid trip was an extraordinarily intense experience. Even Jonathan Aitken, who took acid under clinical supervision as part of an experiment for the *Evening Standard*, testified to the power of the drug. Six hours after taking it, he was shouting wildly:

> I see rivers running with blood . . . I am flying over the continents of the world . . . black men are fighting brown men who are fighting yellow men who are fighting white men . . . Blood is everywhere . . .
>
> I know more about myself too, and resolve all kinds of doubts about my future . . . but it's the future of the world that's so terrible . . . I know I am seeing into the future . . . I have seen something no one else has.

The trip, he wrote later, had been 'grim and terrifying . . . one experience I shall never want to repeat'.[24]

Others shared his opinion: John Peel, for example, thought that taking LSD 'was rather like going to Stratford-on-Avon: once you'd done it I didn't see any need to do it again'.[25] As Ian MacDonald puts it, taking LSD in such large doses was akin to 'gambling with sanity itself', because the drug's impact on the brain was impossible to predict and the results might include 'beatific visions, pleasantly dotty distortions of normal perception, paranoia, hellish hallucinations, even mental annihilation'.[26] In some cases the psychological effects could be devastating: the mental breakdown of Syd Barrett, the leading light in Pink Floyd in the late sixties, was a case in point.[27]

Even though the true figures of how many people smoked cannabis and took LSD in the late sixties will never be known, it is safe to say that they were nowhere near the most popular recreational drugs in Britain at the time, being easily outstripped by alcohol, tobacco and caffeine. Both the government and the overwhelming body of public opinion, however, drew a firm distinction between different kinds of drugs. Like LSD and amphetamines, cannabis was prohibited under a succession of Drugs Acts passed by both Conservative and Labour governments in the course of the sixties. And the Home Secretary James Callaghan was certainly no friend to drug users, seeing them as dangerous influences on the young. In January 1969 he had no qualms in dismissing the Wootton Committee's recommendation that cannabis be legalised. To enthusiastic applause from both his own trade union MPs and the Conservative benches, he declared his intention 'to call a halt to the rising tide of permissiveness', which he called 'one of the most unlikeable words that has been invented in recent years'. In this respect, as in so many others, Callaghan was simply reflecting public opinion.[28]

Public anxieties about drugs and moral corruption, as well as the excited prurience of the newspapers, meant that the Redlands raid was a front-page story. Several hundred Rolling Stones fans were camped outside the courthouse in Chichester for the first day of hearings on 27 June 1967, and the ensuing trial received enormous publicity. Richards was charged with allowing his home to be used for the purpose of smoking cannabis, Jagger with the unlawful possession of amphetamines, and Fraser with the possession of amphetamines and, far more seriously, heroin. The defendants knew that they were being tried as much for their notoriety as for their specific offences. Since the Rolling Stones had wilfully cultivated a rebellious image, many people assumed they were guilty before the trial had even begun and looked forward to their inevitable punishment.

For Jagger, Richards and Fraser, the trial went about as badly as they could have imagined. The presiding chairman of the Quarter Sessions, a retired naval commander called Leslie Block, was clearly unsympathetic from the beginning, while the jury of eleven local men and one woman showed no inclination towards leniency. Fraser pleaded guilty on the first day. Jagger, meanwhile, claimed that his Knightsbridge doctor had given him verbal permission to take amphetamines in case of stress or emergency. Although the doctor confirmed the story, this was not considered a formal prescription, and Block therefore directed the jury to find him guilty. Fraser and Jagger were then handcuffed and carted off to Lewes Prison for the next couple of nights while they waited for the verdict on Richards.

On the face of it, Richards's offence was minor, but his appearance on the stand was by far the most sensational. It was during his trial, for example, that the police revealed that they had found Marianne Faithfull naked except for the famous rug, an apparently irrelevant revelation that infuriated Richards's counsel because it fostered an impression of general depravity.* Richards himself claimed that he had no idea that anyone was smoking cannabis and would never have allowed such behaviour to take place. Asked by the prosecuting counsel whether he thought it was 'normal' for Faithfull to be lounging around in nothing but a rug, he replied dismissively: 'We are not old men. We are not worried about petty morals.' This did little to commend him to the jury, who took just over an hour to find him guilty. Jagger and Fraser were then hauled into the dock beside him to hear Justice Block read the sentences: twelve months in prison and five hundred pounds costs for Richards; six months and two hundred pounds for Fraser; three months and one hundred pounds for Jagger.[29]

All three of the defendants took the announcement of the sentences very hard. Richards stared furiously ahead; Fraser blew out his cheeks in despair; Jagger put his head in his hands and was visibly distressed as he was taken down.[30] Outside the courtroom hundreds of fans screamed in horror when they heard the news, and that evening a small crowd held an all-night protest vigil at Piccadilly Circus, to no great effect. Their heroes, meanwhile, were already behind bars: Richards and Fraser in Wormwood Scrubs, and Jagger in Brixton Prison. This was hardly a pleasant experience, but Richards and Jagger were both out by the following evening after paying a total of seven thousand pounds bail, pending appeal. They were immediately driven to an impromptu press conference at a pub in Soho, where both men remarked that they had been well treated during their very brief stint inside. 'The other prisoners were

---

*This then evolved into the entirely erroneous rumour that they had actually discovered her entwined with Jagger, who was supposedly eating a Mars Bar from between her legs.

great,' said Richards, while Jagger reflected that they had been 'very kind and helpful'. Fraser, however, had been refused bail. In the newspaper storm that followed the unfortunate art dealer was rather overlooked, and even some historians occasionally forget that there were three defendants, not two.[31]

For the press, the whole Redlands affair was enormously exciting. 'The dreamlike world of pop music came down to earth when Jagger and Richards swapped their millionaire homes for prison cells,' commented the *Mirror*. 'Each of the Stones is worth at least £250,000, so Jagger and Richards can afford to take a rest. Even an involuntary one.'[32] Yet, at the same time, many commentators thought that the defendants had been extremely harshly treated and that the judge had paid too much attention to lurid reports of their decadent lifestyle. As the *Evening Standard* remarked, the treatment of Jagger and Fraser during the trial itself, when they had been handcuffed to their police guards, had surely been 'an unnecessary humiliation'. 'Are the two really considered dangerous criminals liable to make trouble unless they are manacled?' an editorial asked disbelievingly.[33]

The *Evening Standard*'s disapproval of the defendants' treatment belies the common interpretation of the Redlands affair as some sort of 'conspiracy' by a monolithic Establishment. In later years the Stones themselves claimed that they had been singled out as scapegoats for the permissive society. 'This is why we got busted,' Richards said. 'They saw us as a threat.'[34] Marianne Faithfull agreed, writing that 'by the beginning of 1967, there were highly placed people in Her Majesty's government who actually saw us as enemies of the state'.[35] But this is ridiculous. For one thing, the Rolling Stones, with their country houses, antique firearms and expensive libraries, posed far less of a threat to British life than they liked to think. For another, there was no such thing as a single, united Establishment directing the affairs of politicians, policemen and judges. What was more, Wilson's ministers manifestly had much better things to worry about than the supposed depravity of the Rolling Stones. Indeed, far from the institutions of the upper classes being directed *against* the Stones, it was *The Times*, on 1 July, that made the biggest fuss about the severity of their sentences.

When Mick Jagger opened Britain's most prestigious newspaper the morning after his release, he was amazed to see that its first leader, written by the paper's bookish editor William Rees-Mogg, was given over to his case. Under the headline 'WHO BREAKS A BUTTERFLY ON A WHEEL?' Rees-Mogg pointed out that Jagger had been caught with only four pills, fewer than one would expect of a 'pusher of drugs' or an addict. Above all, he felt that the singer had suffered unduly because of the 'primitive' attitudes of people who thought that he had 'got what was coming to him':

> They resent the anarchic quality of the Rolling Stones' performances, dislike their songs, dislike their influence on teenagers and broadly suspect them of decadence, a word used by Miss Monica Furlong in the *Daily Mail*.
>
> As a sociological concern this may be reasonable enough, and at an emotional level it is very understandable, but it has nothing at all to do with the case. One has to ask a different question: has Mr Jagger received the same treatment as he would have received if he had not been a famous figure, with all the criticism and resentment his celebrity has aroused? If a promising undergraduate had come back from a summer visit to Italy with four pep pills in his pocket, would it have been thought right to ruin his career by sending him to prison for three months? Would it also have been thought necessary to display him handcuffed to the public?

In short, Jagger must be 'treated exactly the same as anyone else, no better and no worse . . . There must remain a suspicion in this case that Mr Jagger received a more severe sentence than would have been thought proper for any purely anonymous young man.'[36]

Rees-Mogg's editorial reflected a widespread feeling among liberal commentators and legal experts that the three Redlands defendants had been unfairly treated. The very next day the *Sunday Times* ran a similar if less celebrated editorial, and its commentator Hugo Young wrote that Jagger had been sentenced 'to appease the lust for social revenge'.[37] There was evidently some truth in this: a few months later, speaking at the annual dinner of the Horsham Ploughing and Agricultural Society, Justice Block boasted that 'we did our best, your fellow countrymen and I, and my fellow magistrates, to cut these Stones down to size'.[38] But far from Block being the voice of a repressive Establishment, he was roundly condemned by newspapers and politicians alike for joking about a past case, and one Labour MP even threatened to refer his performance to the Lord Chancellor.[39]

The really striking thing about the Redlands case is that it was the general public, not the supposed Establishment, who wanted to see the Stones behind bars. It is simply untrue that, as Bill Wyman claims, 'public opinion was genuinely angry with the convictions and the severity of the sentences'.[40] Polls consistently indicated that most people sided with Block, rather than with the three defendants. A few days after the two Rolling Stones' sentences were quashed by the Court of Appeal, Gallup found that 88 per cent of the population, both young and old, thought that dealing in soft drugs should be a criminal offence, while 77 per cent thought that smoking cannabis should also be a crime. The same poll also suggested that only one in four young people thought that Jagger's sentence had been 'too severe', while the remainder felt it was reasonable enough. When Mick Jagger was interviewed on *World in Action* on 31 July, the programme began with the stunning statistic that in another survey more than eight out of ten young people thought that he deserved his prison sentence.[41] Writing in the *Evening News*, Charles Curran spoke for millions of his countrymen:

> I hold that people who break the law ought to be punished. The law that Jagger and Richards broke is not a trifle, either. For it seeks to prevent people from using dangerous drugs for fun . . . Look at Jagger and Richards. Each of them is a millionaire at twenty-three. How does it come about that they are so rich? Their wealth flows from the fact that they are manufactured pieces of wish-fulfilment . . . Their lives tend to represent, in reality, what their admirers' are in fantasy. So long as the pop idol sticks to bawling and wailing – well, we can put up with that. But once he starts to add drugs to his drivel, society must take immediate note of it.[42]

Just like the Profumo trial in the summer of 1963, the Redlands case crystallised existing anxieties about the pace of social and cultural change, allowing the newspapers to bemoan the ills of a society sinking under the weight of sexual licence and moral corruption. Like Stephen Ward and Christine Keeler before them, Jagger and Richards had become emblems of affluence and permissiveness, representing all that many conservative observers hated most about Britain in the sixties.

As for Robert Fraser, he was forced to serve out four months in Wormwood Scrubs. Jagger and Richards both frequently wrote to him in prison. 'We went to see Maharishi Yogi this weekend who really showed us some nice things,' wrote Jagger, '[and] it would be great to go to India when you return. I'm sure we could have a groovy time. We're just doing our album now . . . Everything will be so much more beautiful when you come back, there will be so many things to do. I'm sure you've thought of a million things so we'll put them together.'[43]

The album on which Jagger and the rest of the Stones were working in the summer of 1967 was supposed to be their answer to *Sgt. Pepper's Lonely Hearts Club Band*, but the group were clearly struggling to adapt to the psychedelic style of the day. They listened repeatedly to songs like 'Lucy in the Sky with Diamonds' and 'A Day in the Life' to try to dredge up some inspiration, while Jagger and Richards 'cudgelled their brains for incandescent imagery and riffs that would have the mesmeric power of Hindu mantras'.[44] Finally, after a long delay, *Their Satanic Majesties Request* was released on 12 December, in time for the Christmas rush. In the United States alone, advance orders came to some two million dollars, and the sense of expectation was enormous.[45]

Unfortunately, the result was a complete fiasco. The *NME* predicted that 'critics will call this album everything from "brilliant" to "nonsense"'. In fact, nobody called it brilliant while almost everybody thought that it was nonsense.[46] The Rolling Stones were extremely ill suited to recording psychedelic whimsy, and the album came over as a weak pastiche of the Beatles' last production. According to one American critic, it was so bad that it 'puts the status of the Rolling Stones in jeopardy'.[47] Even the Stones themselves agreed. Just six months later Mick Jagger admitted that the group's recent records 'were so strange, they just weren't any good. They were great to do once, but we couldn't bear listening to them more than six times.'[48]

The failure of *Their Satanic Majesties Request* was a turning point in the career of the Rolling Stones. Nursing their wounds, they fell back on the love of American blues that had brought them together in the first place. 'Jumping Jack Flash', which reached number one in May 1968, was a return to the pounding, aggressive style that had made their name four years before, only this time they seemed more snarling and sardonic than ever. The following December the album *Beggars' Banquet* banished the tinkling whimsicality of 1967 and replaced it with the much more austere and compelling sound of songs like 'Sympathy for the Devil' and 'Street Fighting Man'.[49] 'The Stones have returned,' wrote Jann Wenner in *Rolling Stone*, 'and they are bringing back rock 'n' roll with them. Their new album will mark a point in the short history of rock and roll: the formal end of all the pretentious, non-musical, boring, insignificant, self-conscious and worthless stuff that has been tolerated during the past year.'[50]

Beggars' Banquet reflected a wider backlash against the gaudy excesses of flower power. Instead of reaching for the heavens, many musicians at the end of the sixties preferred to return to their roots in American blues and country music.[51] And as the pop stars of the mid-sixties reached their late twenties with their financial security assured, they became less obsessed with winning over teenage audiences. For the first time, ideas of formal aesthetic merit began to percolate through the world of pop music, with some performers, like the virtuoso guitarists Eric Clapton, Jimi Hendrix and Jeff Beck, more interested in setting new standards of musical ability than in reaching a mass audience.[52] Until the late sixties, pop had appealed overwhelmingly to teenagers, which explains why almost all the performers tended to be in their late teens or early twenties. Hit singles by the likes of Elvis Presley, the Beatles or the Rolling Stones had been marketed to the young and provided a soundtrack to their adolescence. The lyrics were not terribly important, and most listeners were probably content simply to hum along while doing something else. At the end of the decade, however, much of this audience had grown up and wanted something rather more stimulating. At the same time, their adolescent favourites had grown up, too, and studio technology had developed to the point where they could indulge their artistic ambitions. Instead of punching out disposable three-minute singles, the likes of McCartney and Lennon and Jagger and Richards, wanted to use the new multi-track technology to produce 'serious' albums that would stand the test of time. They were no longer content to be stars; they now saw themselves as artists.[53]

In the early days of pop, groups had concentrated on singles for the obvious reason that their listeners could more easily afford a 45rpm single than an LP. Now that their audience had grown up, they switched their attention to albums. In 1964 singles had outsold albums by three to one; four years later the two formats were neck and neck, selling forty-nine million units each.[54] The singles market had already entered its long, deep decline, and since albums were more expensive and more profitable, it made commercial sense for self-consciously serious groups like Cream and Pink Floyd to concentrate on an older audience. Bill Wyman even admitted that the Stones had put their energies into *Beggars' Banquet* because they feared the implications of a 'sales slump' in the singles market.[55]

The new distinction between the singles and albums markets went hand in hand with another new distinction, between two kinds of popular music. Although there had been various kinds of pop music in the late fifties and early sixties, there was still a sense that, say, Cilla Black and the Rolling Stones both inhabited the same world. Between about 1967 and 1969, however, a gulf opened between pop on the one hand, and so-called rock on the other. The former was catchy and commercial, designed for the radio and the singles charts, but its detractors saw it as trivial and insubstantial. Rock, on the other hand, was meant to be authentic and artistic, and appeared on albums, not singles. Rock was worthy but difficult; pop was cheerful but trite. Rock appealed to adults, pop to teenagers. 'Rock was not only a thousand watts louder,' writes Philip Norman; 'it was also a thousand times more serious.'[56]

As Charlie Gillett points out, this simplistic pop–rock dichotomy was manufactured to serve the commercial interests of musicians who wanted to exaggerate the differences between teenage and adult tastes so that they could tap the adult market.[57] And yet it did capture a genuine divergence in tastes in the late sixties: the difference between those people who preferred the early Beatles records, for example, and those who were more impressed by self-consciously artistic albums like *Revolver* and *Sgt. Pepper*. The approximate moment when this distinction first became apparent – 1967 – was the year of the Redlands raid and *Sgt. Pepper*, but it was also the year when Pink Floyd released their first album, when the first outdoor rock festival took place in California, and when *Rolling Stone* magazine was founded in San Francisco, all of which acknowledged the significance of an older and more demanding audience. From this point onwards, some groups – not only the Beatles and their more controversial rivals, but also the likes of Cream, Pink Floyd and Deep Purple – began to take themselves very seriously indeed.[58]

At the same time rock music was also louder and more aggressive than anything that had gone before. The quintessential example was Led Zeppelin, a band that evolved out of the 'back to basics' blues revival of 1968. Led Zeppelin were both a typical progressive rock band, recording protracted songs inspired by *The Lord of the Rings*, and a prototypical 'heavy metal' outfit, seeking to overwhelm audiences through sheer volume and violence. They were doggedly uncommercial, declining to issue press releases or group photographs, shunning television and radio appearances and even refusing to release any singles. Yet, despite or probably because of this, they were also 'among the most commercially successful groups in the entire history of popular music', producing six albums in six years, each of which sold more than two million copies. In 1975, all six Led Zeppelin albums held places in the American Top 200 album chart, an achievement without precedent in musical history.[59]

Yet unlike the Beatles or the Rolling Stones, Led Zeppelin made their millions without having any impact on the singles chart, without winning any great press attention, and without winning the hearts of the teenage audience. They appealed to affluent, middle-class, male students rather than working-class schoolgirls; they sang about mystical knights and queens rather than the girl next door; and they sold albums, not singles. Their very success was a dramatic illustration of how much popular music and youth culture had changed since the Beatles' breakthrough back in 1963.[60]

Despite the Rolling Stones' revival in 1968, a cancer was eating away at the heart of the group. Ever since the day that they had signed with Andrew Loog Oldham the Stones had been moving further and further away from the vision of their founder, Brian Jones. As early as the autumn of 1963 Oldham had begun to push Jones aside, elevating Mick Jagger and Keith Richards as the chief songwriters and creative dynamos of the band. Since Jones was already psychologically insecure and physically fragile, he reacted badly to his relegation. By 1964 he was well on his way towards paranoia: when a friend found him standing in a hotel corridor with his ear to the door of the band's room, Jones whispered: 'They're talking about me. Go in and find out what they're saying.'[61]

Over the next four years, Jones's mental state declined almost as quickly as his standing within the group. In the spring of 1965 he moved into a fashionable cottage in Chelsea, living out his fantasy of being a successful pop star, but the veneer of Regency furnishings and expensive gadgets barely concealed the unhappy reality of 'dirty tins [and] old, encrusted milk bottles'.[62] He continued to mistreat women, stringing along and beating up an endless series of girlfriends, and by 1966 he was nervously swallowing handfuls of pills, often without knowing exactly what they were.[63] That March, he disappeared for a few days before returning to the studio in no condition to play. Andrew Loog Oldham unsympathetically recalled that Jones 'was beyond feeling shame or hurt. Grey to the gills, ready to explode in mind and body, he clutched his guitar like a life-preserver, though life was hard to find. He just lay in a pathetic foetal position on the floor, draining the life out of the room.'[64]

The central figure in Jones's life at this point was Anita Pallenberg, an Italian-born model who came from a wealthy, artistic family and spoke four languages fluently. Although Pallenberg was stunningly attractive, she also had a mesmeric, self-destructive quality that some observers half-seriously attributed to her fascination with witchcraft.[65] In any case, she was certainly a bad influence on someone as insecure as Brian Jones. Through 1966 each encouraged the other to take increasing numbers of drugs, and when Pallenberg was not photographing her lover indulging his peculiar fondness for setting fire to Dinky cars and toy trains, she was dressing him in Nazi uniforms, laying into him with a whip during their protracted bedroom sessions, or nursing him through the aftermath of a nightmarish LSD trip. By the late summer of that year, their relationship had degenerated into occasional bouts of fisticuffs, and the following spring it finally descended into disaster.[66]

In March 1967 the couple set off on holiday, driving through France towards Spain and Morocco. In Toulon Jones developed pneumonia and insisted that he would catch up later, leaving Pallenberg with Keith Richards, who needed a break from the pressure of the impending Redlands trial. By the time the travellers reached Valencia they had become lovers, and when Jones finally joined them in Marrakech the tension was unbearable. Day after day went by with Richards and Pallenberg staring intently at each other across the swimming pool, while by night Jones took out his frustration by beating her black and blue or forcing her into orgies with Berber prostitutes. Finally, worried for Pallenberg's health, Richards bundled her into the back of his car and drove off in the direction of Spain and safety, leaving Jones alone in the hotel.[67]

Losing his girlfriend to his own colleague was an enormous blow to Jones's fragile self-esteem, and many people thought that he came close to collapse in the weeks that followed. 'However badly he treated Anita,' commented Wyman, 'he loved her and her embrace of a man he had thought was a mate was heartbreaking. He leaned increasingly on drink, LSD and marijuana to help him through; he was obviously shattered.' To other friends, Jones tearfully complained: 'They took my music; they took my band; and now they've taken my love.'[68] Richards, however, had little sympathy. 'I don't think honestly that you'll find anyone who liked Brian,' he remarked years later. 'There was extra hassles between Brian and me because I took his old lady. You know, he enjoyed beating chicks up. Not a likeable guy. And we all tried at certain times to get on with him but then he'd shit on you.'[69]

With the loss of Pallenberg, Jones's decline gathered pace. On 10 May 1967 the police raided his flat and seized eleven different items, including hashish, methedrine and cocaine. Sitting forlornly among his Moroccan cushions, Jones weakly complained that the cocaine was 'not my scene. No man, no man, I am not a junkie. That is not mine at all.' The following morning he made a brief appearance at a magistrates' court in an uncanny replay of the Redlands pre-trial hearing, which had just taken place two hours' drive to the south. 'Please don't worry. Don't jump to nasty conclusions and don't judge me too harshly,' he reassured his parents in a telegram later that day.[70]

Beneath the apparent calm, however, Jones was falling apart, spending day after day in a self-pitying stupor. He was, writes the Stones' biographer, 'a haunted and a haunting sight', his face 'puffy and sick-pale'.[71] By the time that Jagger and Richards were standing trial in Sussex, Jones was addicted to daily doses of brandy, barbiturates and LSD, and was also regularly visiting a Harley Street psychiatrist. At one point he was persuaded to spend three weeks at a private clinic in Hampshire, where the chief psychiatrist noted that he was 'anxious, considerably depressed, perhaps even suicidal . . . He has not a great deal of confidence in himself. He is not sure of his identity as a person. He is still trying to grow up in many ways.'[72]

It was a measure of Jones's eclipse that when his own case came to trial, on 30 October 1967, there was far less press interest than there had been in the Redlands case, and there were very few fans outside the London courtroom. After Jones's psychiatrists testified in his defence, the chairman of the magistrates remarked that he had been 'moved' by Jones's plight, but still thought that he ought to be setting a better example, and sentenced him to nine months' imprisonment. But Jones spent only one night in prison, albeit a frightening and lonely one, being released on bail the very next day, pending appeal.[73] As before, the facts of the case make a mockery of the idea that the Establishment was out to get the Rolling Stones. The press generally agreed that the sentence had been too harsh, with the *Daily Sketch* commenting that it was 'as likely to turn a pop star into a martyr as to deter his fans'. As in the Redlands case, the Court of Appeal struck down the prison sentence, placing Jones on probation for three years.[74]

One condition of Jones's probation was that he must continue to receive psychiatric treatment, and to anyone who read the newspapers the extent of his collapse was now painfully clear. The defence lawyer explained that the musician had a 'fragile mental make-up', while his psychiatrist described him as an 'extremely frightened young man'.[75] But Jones made little effort to alter his lifestyle, and in May 1968 the police raided his flat once again, confiscating a small quantity of cannabis resin. Jones's anguished courtroom performance again made a strong impression on the chairman of the court, Reginald Seaton, the same man who had presided at his last trial. Far from being eager to punish the Stones, Seaton went out of his way to show clemency, delivering a summing-up that leaned heavily towards the defendant and handing him only a small fine. 'You really must watch your step and keep clear of this stuff,' he wearily told a relieved Jones. 'For goodness' sake don't get into trouble again. If you do, there will be some real trouble.'[76]

The end was not far away now. For much of 1968 Jones had been no more than a semi-detached member of the Rolling Stones, spending weeks on end in Morocco indulging his new enthusiasm for North African music.[77] His colleagues, too, were spending less and less time working together, partly because their American business manager, Allen Klein, had dragged them into a bewildering series of legal battles.[78] In the meantime Jagger had decided to reinvent himself as a screen idol, beginning with Donald Cammell's film *Performance*, the tale of a gangster on the run who falls into the decadent, drug-addled world of a rock star and his two girlfriends. Filming began in July 1968 and continued until the autumn, complicated by the consumption on set of vast quantities of drugs and the palpable sexual frisson between Jagger and his co-star Anita Pallenberg, who was playing his enigmatic mistress.[79]

While the two were filming on location in a Knightsbridge mansion, Keith Richards sat outside in the car, smouldering with jealousy. He was furious with Pallenberg and Jagger, who spent their working days rolling round naked for the benefit of the cameras, and he positively detested the film's bohemian director. Time did not mellow his attitude. 'That film was probably the best work Cammell ever did,' the guitarist mused later, 'except for shooting himself [in 1996]. I did kind of like Donald, but I found him a vicious manipulator of people, a selfish bastard . . . He was a failed director. He shot himself because he realized who he was.'[80]

When *Performance* was finally released in the summer of 1970, its themes of decadence and death seemed peculiarly appropriate, because the story of the Rolling Stones themselves had taken a decisive turn. At the beginning of 1969 the band had begun planning a major American tour to pay off the crippling tax and legal bills incurred by a dispute with Andrew Loog Oldham, who had drifted away two years before. With two drug convictions, however, Brian Jones had no chance of getting an American work permit. Since he was little more than a dead weight anyway, the Stones simply had no choice but to get rid of him.

In the circumstances it was more of a mercy killing than an execution. Even Jagger and Richards recognised that their old friend was seriously troubled, and therefore went out of their way to make it appear more of an amicable split than a sacking. One evening late in May 1969 the two men, accompanied by Charlie Watts, drove down to Jones's new Sussex estate, Cotchford Farm, which had once belonged to A. A. Milne and was stuffed with relics of Christopher Robin and Winnie the Pooh. For the sake of appearances, they pretended that it was merely a temporary measure, while Jones, for his part, pretended that he was happy to leave. They agreed to put out a disingenuous statement to the press, and then the three visitors drove away. When they had gone, Jones went into his kitchen, rested his head on the wooden table, and wept.[81]

Over the next few weeks he talked enthusiastically about his plans to set up a new blues band. He had not given up drink and drugs, and he was still an anxious, restless character, but he did seem to have calmed down a little from the paranoid excesses of recent years. On Wednesday, 2 July, he spent the hazy summer's day at Cotchford Farm with his latest girlfriend, a Swede in her early twenties called Anna Wohlin. The air was thick with pollen, and the asthmatic Jones carried his inhaler everywhere with him, wheezing and puffing as he wandered about the house. That evening he relaxed with Anna in front of the television, drinking slowly but steadily, until they headed over to the swimming pool shortly after ten. There they were joined by Frank Thorogood, a builder who was doing some work for Jones at the farm and was staying with his own girlfriend in a little flat above the garage. Lazing by the pool in the warm night air, the four of them polished off a bottle of brandy, a bottle of vodka and a half-bottle of whisky, which Jones supplemented, as was his custom, with a handful of amphetamine pills. At around midnight the two men dived into the pool for a brief swim and it was there, a short while later, that the accident happened.

The news of Jones's death reached the press just after three in the morning of Thursday, 3 July. The following Monday, when the inquest was held at East Grinstead, all three witnesses stated that they had gone into the house for a few minutes, leaving Jones splashing happily in the pool. When they returned, he was lying face down at the bottom, completely still. Their drunken and disorganised attempts at artificial respiration, as well as the subsequent attentions of an ambulance crew, proved futile, and by the time the police arrived he had been pronounced dead. A pathologist reported that Jones's liver had been twice the usual size, bloated by drink and drug abuse. His heart, too, was abnormally distended, and tests unsurprisingly revealed substantial quantities of alcohol and amphetamines in his bloodstream. Death was due to drowning 'associated with alcohol, drugs and severe liver degeneration'.[82]

Despite the wild conspiracy theories to the contrary, this is by far the most plausible explanation for Brian Jones's death. It is hardly likely that he would choose to kill himself at the end of such a pleasant evening, and claims that groups from the Mafia to the Rolling Stones themselves had him murdered are simply laughable. Thirty years later rumours surfaced that the late Frank Thorogood had confessed to killing Jones, either in drunken horseplay or because they had fallen out over the building work at the farm. Of course, it is possible that Thorogood killed Jones, but since there is no hard evidence that he did, and no proof of the famous confession, there is no good reason to question the coroner's verdict.[83] When Anna Wohlin broke her thirty-year silence to publish a sensationalist and often inaccurate book entitled *The Murder of Brian Jones*, his former comrade Charlie Watts was suitably scathing:

> All that about Brian being knocked off is rubbish. I know a lot of people would have willingly knocked him off, but it didn't happen. Brian was just very weak. He was asthmatic, unhealthy. The stuff he took – uppers, downers, leapers, bleepers, whatever they were were too strong for his body. He couldn't take it. And his swimming pool was about 70 degrees or something – it used to shimmer with heat. You'd drive down there on a spring morning and the heat would be rising off the top. And he got in there, and I suppose it was like getting into a warm bath, and he fell asleep. And that's how he died.[84]

Jones was not a victim of the sixties, as is often claimed. If any explanation beyond that of simple accident is necessary, it is that he was a victim of his own demons, his self-confidence eroded by chronic insecurity and his physical health undermined by drink and drugs. His funeral, held on 10 July in his home town of Cheltenham, was attended by his distraught parents, grieving sister and a host of friends from London's bohemian scene, as well as Bill Wyman and Charlie Watts. Mick Jagger and Marianne Faithfull had just left for Australia, but they sent a large wreath. Keith Richards and Anita Pallenberg stayed away.[85]

While the funeral was a serious, sombre occasion, the Rolling Stones' tribute to their founder, which took place five days earlier, had a very different flavour. Almost three weeks before Jones's death, the four remaining members of the Stones had unveiled his replacement, Mick Taylor, a prodigious young guitarist from Welwyn Garden City. Taylor was scheduled to make his debut in a free concert in Hyde Park on Saturday, 5 July, which would guarantee enormous public exposure.[86] When the news came of Jones's death, most of the arrangements had already been made: a special souvenir edition of the *Evening Standard*, six Granada television crews, an armoured personnel carrier to transport the band to the stage, even Jagger's stage outfit from the Mr Fish boutique. At Charlie Watts's suggestion, therefore, the band decided to go ahead and perform, 'as a memorial to Brian'.[87]

The Hyde Park concert is generally hailed as one of the great set pieces of the sixties, so in the interests of balance it is well worth putting the event in context: the estimated 250,000 people who crowded into the park on that searing afternoon might have amounted to a vast crowd by the standards of pop concerts, but they looked pretty puny when set alongside the 20 million or so who preferred entertainment like *The Black and White Minstrel Show*. Nevertheless, the Rolling Stones' travails had turned them into universally recognised symbols of cultural change, and the concert therefore attracted an enormous amount of press attention. By eleven in the morning, more than twenty thousand fans were already there, bathing in the Serpentine or eating ice creams in the bright sunshine by the water's edge, policed not only by the London constabulary but by a gang of surprisingly gentle Hell's Angels engaged by the Stones' promoters. Two hours later the supporting acts began playing to the swelling but nevertheless orderly crowd. At around three o'clock the armoured personnel carrier set off from the Rolling Stones' Park Lane hotel, followed by a mobile camera crew, rather like a team coach embarking for the FA Cup Final.[88]

When the Stones finally arrived on stage Mick Jagger immediately made his way to the microphone to address the crowd. He cut an extremely striking figure: as Philip Norman remarks, 'no one could have expected him to take the stage in lipstick, rouge and eye-shadow, and wearing a white, frilly garment which, for all the white vest and bell-bottoms visible beneath, still resembled nothing so much as a little girl's party dress'.[89] The addition of a leather dog-collar and wooden crucifix completed Jagger's extraordinary get-up, and as he began to speak the crowd fell silent, though whether in respect or in shock remains unclear.

'Now listen, will you just cool it for a minute,' he began, 'because I would really like to say something about Brian . . . about how we feel about him just going when we didn't expect him to.' He then produced a volume of poems by Shelley, and began to read the thirty-ninth stanza from 'Adonais', the poet's elegy on the death of John Keats:

> Peace, peace! he is not dead, he doth not sleep,
> He hath not awaken'd from the dream of life;
> 'Tis we, who lost in stormy visions, keep
> With phantoms an unprofitable strife
> And in mad trance strike with our spirit's knife
> Invulnerable nothings . . .

And so he continued, his hoarse voice carried across the park by the public address system, until he turned to a new page and the fifty-second stanza:

> The One remains, the many change and pass;
> Heaven's light forever shines, Earth's shadows fly;
> Life, like a dome of many-colour'd glass,
> Stains the white radiance of Eternity,
> Until Death tramples it to fragments. – Die!
> If thou would be that which thou dost seek!
> Follow where all is fled!

As Shelley's words died away, the Stones' stagehands shook several brown cardboard boxes towards the crowd, releasing hundreds of white butterflies into the air. It was a suitably arresting visual image with which to end the tribute. Conservationists, however, objected that many of the butterflies must have suffocated in the cramped boxes, and London's gardeners complained for weeks that they had caused terrible damage to their plants.[90]

It was always going to be hard for the Rolling Stones to live up to expectations, but on that hot Saturday afternoon they fell quite remarkably short. The band had not played together in public for more than a year, and it showed. Although Jagger kept screaming 'Tempo!' at his musicians, the result was, in Norman's view, 'possibly the Stones' worst musical performance ever'. The audience seemed not to notice, or at least care, and the concert duly went down as another triumph for the self-proclaimed 'greatest rock and roll band in the world'.[91] Yet there was no doubt that the death of Brian Jones had badly shaken the Rolling Stones: just three days later Marianne Faithfull took an overdose of sleeping pills, enough to kill three people, and was only saved by the prompt attentions of Mick Jagger and an Australian doctor.

The premature death of their founding member robbed the Stones of the naive exuberance that had underpinned the stage violence of their career. Fame was no barrier to suffering, and what had once been a game now seemed painfully real. Exactly five months after the Hyde Park concert they gave another free concert at the Altamont Raceway, a stock-car track forty miles south of San Francisco. Once again they hired Hell's Angels to provide security, but the Californian bikers were vicious semi-criminal gangs, very different from their English equivalents. Instead of the Hyde Park sunshine, there was grey, gloomy half-light. The organisation was shambolic, there were nowhere enough toilets or medical tents, and the whole event seemed awash with impure drugs supplied by local crime syndicates. Even before the Stones took the stage, fights had broken out in the audience, with the Hell's Angels indiscriminately beating bystanders with specially weighted sawn-off pool cues. After two other bands had effectively fled the stage, the Stones finally appeared, although Jagger had already been struck in the face by a drug-crazed fan and was still shaken. When he began singing 'Sympathy for the Devil' the Hell's Angels went berserk before his eyes, wildly beating at the audience with their cues. In the general confusion, and with Jagger pleading vainly for calm, a frightened black teenager, Meredith Hunter, produced a long-barrelled revolver before the Hell's Angels descended, stabbing and kicking him to death. All the time, Jagger stood impotently on the stage, dressed in his extravagant devil's cape, his satanic pretensions exposed while genuine, fatal violence raged beneath him.[92]

Altamont, Bill Wyman wrote later, was 'rock 'n' roll's Armageddon. It was a heartbreaking end to the epochal sixties.'[93] As the band's overcrowded helicopter carried the frightened musicians back to San Francisco, they were still unaware that four people had died – two young fans run over by a car, and one who had drowned in a drainage ditch, as well as Hunter. But all the glittering fantasies of musical stardom could not keep out the chill of reality. A band once synonymous with the carefree pleasures of Swinging London had now become a byword for violence and death – not the stage Satanism of 'Sympathy for the Devil', but the real thing.

Altamont that cold December evening seemed a world away from Hyde

Park in the July sunshine, or the lush decadence of Redlands, or the smart sophistication of Jagger's bachelor pad. Above all, it seemed a world away from the sweaty good humour of the Crawdaddy Club in Richmond, or the childishly grubby flat that Jagger and Richards had shared with their friend Brian Jones in Edith Grove in the winter of 1963, back in the days when they had just been three anonymous aspiring musicians, living off stolen potatoes, giggling together in the freezing cold and dreaming of making a living by playing the blues.

27

WHY LUCKY JIM TURNED RIGHT

> Oh, fuck the Beatles. I'd like to push my bum into John L's face for forty-eight hours or so, as a protest against all the war and violence in the world.
>
> Kingsley Amis, letter to Philip Larkin, 19 April 1969

> I throw out a challenge. Men and women who believe in the decent way of life step forward and say so. Provoke the newspapers and the BBC to show where they stand. Let it clearly be seen that all that is immoral and 'sick' in our society is not to be tolerated, let our leaders in all walks of life speak out before it is too late.
>
> Dr S. E. Ellison, letter to *The Times*, 11 October 1969

At six o'clock on the morning of 7 October 1965 a shaken young man called David Smith telephoned Hyde police station, Greater Manchester, with an incredible story. Just a few hours before, he and his wife had been entertaining her sister, Myra Hindley, at their home in the suburb of Gorton. At about midnight Smith walked her home, where she invited him to collect some miniature wine bottles. At this point the evening took a very unexpected turn. Smith was standing alone in the kitchen, reading the labels on the bottles, when suddenly he heard 'a scream, a very loud and long one, very shrill', and then he heard Myra shouting: 'Dave, help me!'

Smith ran into the living room, and there he saw Hindley's boyfriend, Ian Brady, standing over a 'rag doll', an axe in his hand. In the next moment Smith realised that it was not a rag doll at all, but the body of a young man, and before his disbelieving eyes Brady brought down the axe again and again on the man's skull. Finally, he wrapped a wire around his victim's neck and pulled it tight, muttering 'You dirty bastard' as he did so. At last the body stopped moving, and Brady looked up at the watching Hindley. 'That's it,' he said. 'That's the messiest yet.'[1]

The murder of Edward Evans was not the first crime carried out by Ian

Brady and Myra Hindley. They had already sexually abused and killed at least four children from the Manchester area and buried their bodies on Saddleworth Moor, where they then posed for photographs. If this were not horrendous enough, they had also made a tape recording of the murder of one little girl, which was played in court during their trial in the spring of 1966.[2] Their crimes were the most shocking and disturbing in Britain for decades, and had an immediate impact on public opinion. The novelist Pamela Hansford Johnson wondered whether the Moors murders might be an indictment of an entire society in which moral standards had been eroded by affluence, secularisation and permissiveness. In her book on the case, *On Iniquity* (1967), she suggested that the trial had exposed 'the results of total permissiveness'. 'A wound in the flesh of our society had cracked open,' she wrote, 'we looked into it, and we smelled its sepsis.'[3]

Like many other commentators at the time, Johnson was struck by the fact that Ian Brady owned and admired the works of the Marquis de Sade. Brady and Hindley, she suggested, were not just deranged aberrations, but products of a permissive society in which pornographic writing acted as a spur to impressionable young minds. Other observers disagreed: the literary editor of the *Sunday Times*, for instance, objected that 'the appetites of Brady are formed long before any books can have influenced them'.[4] But Johnson's argument clearly struck a chord in a society worried about the decline of traditional moral values.[5] 'The time has come', said the *Spectator* in May 1966, 'to call a halt to the restless belief that change itself is the only ultimate good, and to seek instead a period of social and intellectual stability during which we can once again put down roots and gather strength.'[6] Even five years later many commentators cited the case as an example of the costs of the permissive society. 'If anyone says that people are not corrupted by what they read,' insisted the Conservative party chairman, Peter Thomas, in 1971, 'I suggest they read the history of the Moors murders.'[7]

More than any other event of the mid-sixties, the Moors murders raised the possibility of a link between moral permissiveness and violent crime. This was not necessarily a fanciful connection, for censorship had indeed been relaxed, and there was no doubt that crime had recently increased. In 1955 there had been fewer than 6000 violent crimes against the person, but by 1960 there were more than 11,000, and by 1969 more than 21,000. A string of particularly newsworthy offences helped to keep public attention focused on the issue: the

Moors murders themselves, the Great Train Robbery (1963), the Shepherd's Bush police murders (1966) and the arrest of the Kray brothers (1969).[8]

Very few historians believe that there was a direct causal link between permissiveness and crime. It is much more likely that both resulted from other social developments: affluence, mobility, urbanisation and so on. Nonetheless, for cultural or political conservatives, the increase in crime and the growth of obscenity appeared to be two aspects of the same phenomenon: the moral and political decline of Britain from the settled, orderly society that they believed it had been before the war. And unsurprisingly, since much of this anxiety was bound up with ideas about sexuality and personal morality, critics were most concerned about the institution of the family.

This had long been the focus of considerable anxiety for reformers of all kinds. It was seen as peculiarly vulnerable to social change, threatened by everything from promiscuity and generational conflict to rising crime and high taxation.[9] Novels and films of the early fifties often showed the family under siege: in melodramas like *The Holly and the Ivy* (1952) and *Hobson's Choice* (1954), domestic life is threatened by arguments between the generations, alcoholism, illegitimacy, loneliness and snobbery.[10] Later in the decade a wave of 'social problem' films like *No Trees in the Street* and *Violent Playground* (both 1958) suggested that the materialism of the affluent society was undermining domestic happiness and decent behaviour. And by the early sixties producers had hit on a new way of expressing the same themes, based on the confrontation between a middle-aged man, representing the old ways, and a sexually precocious teenager, representing the new. There were plenty of mediocre examples, but perhaps the most revealing was *Term of Trial*, which starred Laurence Olivier.[11]

Olivier plays Graham Weir, a discontented, alcoholic schoolteacher in a shabby inner-city secondary modern, sick of his loveless marriage, the petty jealousies of his colleagues and the rebellious indifference of his pupils. He befriends a bright, attractive fifteen-year-old girl (played by Sarah Miles in her first screen role) who falls in love with him. On a school trip to Paris, she comes to his room, and although he tries to defuse this awkward situation with gentle sympathy, his temper finally snaps. Before he knows it, she has accused him of indecent assault, which comes as an enormous shock to such a sensitive, idealistic man. At the trial that inevitably follows, the girl admits her deception and Weir is acquitted. But the film ends in an extremely downbeat way. His friends and colleagues still think he was guilty, while his wife threatens to abandon him. In the final scene she packs her bags to leave, but then tells him that she will stay if he admits that he abused the girl after all. Against all his principles, a broken Weir lies that he did. He has saved his marriage, but he has sacrificed his integrity. In an aggressive, cynical world his basic decency is simply out of touch.[12]

The most striking scene in *Term of Trial* comes just before Weir's trial, when he wanders distractedly through the streets of the city, seeing everywhere the debased images of materialism and promiscuity. Teenagers in a coffee bar dance to a jukebox; youths peer into shop windows full of glamour magazines; students and immigrants slouch outside the door of a record shop; even the local cinema is showing *The Ape's Revenge*, illustrated with a gaudy poster showing a woman with a sword through her breast. 'Everywhere he goes he is reminded of "sex",' explained a studio press release. 'It thrusts itself at him from the lurid covers of books: "sexy" songs reach him over the radio, and half-naked women peer at him from outside cinemas.'[13] At his trial Weir launches an impassioned attack on modern values:

> It is exquisite irony that I should be condemned by a society which presumes itself more moral than I, a society endlessly titillating itself with dirty books and newspapers and advertising and television and the work of cynical and indifferent minds. I must be condemned by them for walking round with a child in a foreign city; I must be condemned for smacking her lightly to lessen the pain at the end of her pathetic infatuation. What I felt for her was the love of an unworthy man for a quality — innocence, tenderness, love — the thing God gives us before the filth of the world begins to cover it up. But it was love, not the filth you mean.[14]

Term of Trial was released in the summer of 1962, well before the pornography boom or the permissive reforms of the late sixties. Even at this early stage, plenty of people agreed with Weir's verdict that the country was run by 'cynical and indifferent minds' determined to drown the old values under a tide of 'dirty books and newspapers and advertising and television'. For conservatives, it seemed that one outrage led almost inexorably to the next. In 1959 the Obscene Publications Act had relaxed the law on literary censorship, allowing 'literary merit' to be taken into consideration. The very next year Penguin Books were acquitted in the famous *Lady Chatterley's Lover* trial.[15] And in 1965, when discussing censorship on the late-night show *BBC-3*, the critic Kenneth Tynan won the dubious distinction of being the first person to use the word 'fuck' on television, provoking a predictable storm. Hundreds of viewers angrily telephoned the BBC, while one commentator in the *Daily Express* considered that Tynan had committed 'the bloodiest outrage' he had ever known. Five motions attacking Tynan and the BBC were listed on the Commons order paper, supported by over a hundred Members from both sides of the House, and Harold Wilson was called upon to defuse the issue by wryly promising never to use the word in his own television appearances.[16]

What was even more disturbing to many people, however, was the spread of pornography. By the late sixties no visitor to Soho could miss the garish signs for strip-clubs, peep-shows and private cinema clubs showing explicit films.[17] Clubs like these prospered because of the increased consumer spending of the day, the trend for greater sexual frankness and, above all, the legacy of the Wolfenden Committee, which had driven prostitution indoors in the late fifties and replaced streetwalking with an underworld of clubs and call-girls. One entrepreneur who made money from the resulting strip-club boom was Paul Raymond, a former variety-show clairvoyant who opened his famous Raymond's Revuebar, a glitzy private club, in Soho in 1957. He was occasionally fined for shows that went too far, but no doubt his supernatural powers meant that he always knew what was coming.[18]

Although pornography had been illegal since 1857, it was always available to those with the right contacts and the money to afford expensive imported publications from Paris.[19] In the 1950s it was cheaper and easier to buy than ever, thanks to tumbling printing costs, inexpensive foreign travel and increasing middle-class prosperity. By 1952 the Home Office had identified thousands of illicit paperbacks and 16mm films, as well four hundred prohibited magazines, from *Razzle* and *Eyeful* to *Jigger*, *Titty* and *Oomph*. If detected by the police, these materials were confiscated and burned, but those importing and buying them faced no penalty, and human nature being what it is, it was impossible to stifle demand.[20]

When the new Obscene Publications Act was passed in 1959, its provisions were so vaguely worded that it became much harder to prosecute those who sold pornographic materials. At the same time, increasing sexual openness as well as the growth of more serious crimes meant that the police often had little time or inclination to worry about dirty magazines. As John Sutherland puts it, the act created 'a vast new "legitimate" market – but no geared up British mass production to exploit it'.[21] American and Scandinavian publications filled the gap until the appearance in 1964 of the glossy home-grown magazine *Penthouse*, followed in 1966 by *Mayfair* and *Fiesta*. By the end of the sixties at least fifty Soho sex shops sold pornography of various kinds to their overwhelmingly male customers.[22] Thanks to the corruption of the Metropolitan Police's own Obscene Publications Squad, entrepreneurs were able to trade with complete impunity, filling their windows with magazines and neon signs. Only in the 1970s did it emerge that the so-called Dirty Squad was running Soho 'like a fiefdom, with a business efficiency which the Kray Gang might have envied'.[23]

For many people, the spread of obscenity was one of the more regrettable by-products of the affluent society. Many critics argued that it would inevitably corrupt the morals of the nation, and like the contemporary debates about homosexuality, abortion and teenage sexuality, the discussion about obscenity was overshadowed by fears of general national decline. 'If *Mayfair* sells half a million,' commented one writer in the *Spectator*, 'then we must be a nation of masturbators.'[24] Pamela Hansford Johnson, meanwhile, argued that the 'new freedom' promised during the sixties meant merely the 'freedom to revel, through all kinds of mass-media, in violence, in pornography, in sado-masochism . . . The walls of the police storerooms are almost bulging outwards with the pressure of tons and tons of dirty books – the ones still within the scope of the law.'[25] Few politicians, however, associated themselves with the issue: for most aspiring Westminster heavyweights, there were much more pressing issues to worry about.

One morning in March 1963 at the secondary modern school in Madeley, Shropshire, a group of fourth-year girls accosted their senior mistress, Mary Whitehouse. Mrs Whitehouse took their sex education lessons, and she was appalled to hear that on the previous evening the television programme *Meeting Point* had hosted a discussion about sex before marriage. 'I know what's right now, miss,' one of the girls said confidently. 'I know now I mustn't have intercourse until I'm engaged.' Whitehouse was horrified, for she had taught them that any sexual contact before marriage, engaged or not, was entirely wrong. It never occurred to her that they might be winding her up.

Worse was to follow. A couple of months later Mrs Whitehouse reprimanded three girls and two boys who had, according to their classmates, been 'doing things they shouldn't do' in emulation of Christine Keeler and Mandy Rice-Davies. 'Well, miss,' the ringleader explained, 'we watched them talking about girls on TV and it looked as if it was easy and see how well they done out of it miss, so we thought we'd try.'

Not long afterwards came the last straw. One evening a distressed mother told Mrs Whitehouse that her daughter had 'gone off with a boy'. The miscreant had apparently been watching a play on television, and then, the mother said, 'when it got to the sexy part I could see her getting redder and redder in the face, she was so worked up. Then she got up and ran straight out of the house and went off with this boy.'[26]

This was the background to Mary Whitehouse's long battle against what she saw as the permissive society. Born in Warwickshire in 1910, she had trained as a teacher and worked in a school just outside Wolverhampton. There she met and fell in love with a married man sixteen years her senior, although, she said, 'there was no misbehaving'.[27] Eventually Mary broke off the relationship, but the episode left her in great emotional turmoil, made worse by the news that her parents had separated. Consequently, at the age of twenty-five, she turned to religion, joining the Wolverhampton branch of Moral Rearmament. Founded by an American evangelist, this movement demanded 'Absolute Honesty, Absolute Purity, Absolute Unselfishness and Absolute Love'. The purpose of Moral Rearmament, according to its founder, was 'the remaking of the world. We remake people; nations are remade.'[28] Certainly Mary seems to have found in Moral Rearmament the solace she craved: it was there that she met her future husband Ernest Whitehouse, and in 1940 they were married.[29]

Ernest Whitehouse worked for his father's flourishing manufacturing business, and made enough money for Mary to give up work and raise a family.[30] For the next twenty years, then, she was a housewife. But she was not, as she often claimed, an 'ordinary' housewife like millions of others. Unlike most housewives, she was confident and familiar with the media. At the Queen's accession in 1952, she wrote to the BBC with suggestions on how people could help the new monarch in her duties, and she even delivered a talk during the special Coronation edition of *Woman's Hour*.[31] She was also exceptionally religious. Every day began with a Bible reading in bed, after which she would complete a series of physical exercises and then have a formal morning prayer, all before breakfast.[32] Unlike most women of her age, she was completely convinced of the presence of the divine in her life. Her work, she wrote, was about 'fulfilling God's purpose'; she had 'day by day, a sense of meaning and a sense of faith that God was in [it]'.[33]

In the summer of 1963, worried that her children were being 'won over to a sub-Christian concept of living', Whitehouse began to write angry letters to the BBC.[34] On 27 January 1964 she announced the launch of the

Clean-Up TV Campaign, in collaboration with her friend Norah Buckland, the wife of a Staffordshire vicar and a fellow member of Moral Rearmament. 'We women of Britain believe in a Christian way of life,' began their manifesto, which urged women to 'fight for the right to bring up our own children in the truths of the Christian faith, and to protect our homes from the exhibitions of violence'. From the outset their target was the BBC, which they accused of peddling 'the propaganda of disbelief, doubt and dirt' as well as 'promiscuity, infidelity and drinking'. Instead, they argued, the BBC should be broadcasting programmes that 'encourage and sustain faith in God and bring Him back to the heart of our family and national life'.[35]

On 5 May 1964 Clean-Up TV held its first public meeting at Birmingham Town Hall. Seventy-three coachloads of people filled the hall to capacity, and the BBC sent a camera crew to record this gathering of its critics. 'Most of the audience', wrote one observer, 'were middle-aged women.' All but five of the twenty-seven speakers were women, too, and almost all shared the view that television was corrupting the morals of the nation. There were messages of support from the Mothers' Union, the Catholic Women's Organisation, the Women's Institute, the Townswomen's Guild and all manner of church and youth groups. 'In view of the terrifying increase in promiscuity and its attendant horrors,' read a telegram to the Queen drafted by Buckland and Whitehouse, 'we are desperately anxious to banish from our homes and theatres those who seek to demoralize and corrupt our young people.' By the end of the evening it was evident that Clean-Up TV was up and running. 'There are those who will find it easy to laugh at the women who were here tonight,' commented an article in *The Times*; but the scoffers little knew whom they were dealing with.[36]

For Mary Whitehouse, the argument about television was really an argument about a bigger issue, namely the apparent erosion of Christian values by modern consumerism and mass culture. She picked on the BBC because it was seen as the pre-eminent national cultural institution, 'an additional established church', as one writer puts it.[37] But she was not the first to do so. There were clear links between Clean-Up TV and Moral Rearmament, from which she drew friends and supporters. Indeed, Moral Rearmament campaigners had been complaining for years that the BBC, especially in its factual programmes, was 'a corrupting influence' and 'a spiritual sewer [that] flows out into the homes of Britain'.[38] Whitehouse told audiences that people watched BBC programmes 'at the risk of serious damage to their morals, their patriotism, their discipline and their family life'.[39] A report prepared for the Birmingham meeting listed the 'objectionable' features of recent BBC programming: 'sexy innuendoes, suggestive clothing and behaviour; cruelty, sadism and unnecessary violence; no regret for wrong-doing; blasphemy and the presentation of religion in a poor light; excessive drinking and foul language; undermining respect for law and order; unduly harrowing and depressing themes', and so on.[40]

In the spring of 1965 Whitehouse and Buckland decided to replace Clean-Up TV with a new organisation that would speak for the entire television audience and would work harder at influencing BBC executives. They also decided to tone down some of the fierce evangelical rhetoric in order to attract more supporters. The new group was the National Viewers' and Listeners' Association (NVALA) and its preliminary meetings were attended by, among others, the Bishop of Hereford, a representative of the Catholic Archbishop of Westminster, a Methodist representative, six Members of Parliament, the chief constable of Lincolnshire and various other officials.[41] During the next few years few programmes escaped its scrutiny, and even escapist fantasies were not immune. Whitehouse was especially critical of *Doctor Who*, which she solemnly attacked for its reliance on 'strangulation – by hand, by claw, by obscene vegetable matter'.* This was perhaps her greatest weakness: very few programmes, however innocuous, passed muster. Had she concentrated on a handful of genuinely controversial productions, she might have wielded greater influence. But many people who shared some of her anxieties were undoubtedly put off because she appeared so extreme.[42]

The BBC, not surprisingly, were intensely suspicious of Mary Whitehouse from the beginning. An internal report on the Birmingham Town Hall meeting described it as 'comical' but also 'sinister' and 'menacing'.[43] However, she exercised no real influence over programming or policy in the sixties; indeed, programmes rapidly became more controversial and sexually explicit, not less. In a letter to the *Church Times* in August 1964 one senior official insisted that 'serious and creative writers of this generation must be free to write about society and its problems as they see them'.[44] This was an opinion shared by the BBC's liberal Director General, Hugh Carleton Greene, who detested his conservative critics. After retiring as Director

---

*This was probably a reference to the Krynoid, a carnivorous plant from outer space that attacked Tom Baker in 1976. Although frightening, it was probably not a great threat to the morals of the nation.

General in 1969 he took the curious decision to hang in his home a full-frontal nude painting of Mary Whitehouse with no fewer than five breasts. According to some accounts, he would occasionally amuse himself by throwing darts at it, squealing with pleasure at every strike.[45]

Greene was not the only person who thoroughly disliked Mary Whitehouse. She was bombarded with hundreds of threatening telephone calls and letters, and attempts were made to lure her sons to orgies on the pretext that they were Christmas parties.[46] The Conservative backbencher Sir Gerald Nabarro told a television audience that she was 'a hypocritical old bitch'.[47] On the other hand, she also had her defenders, especially within Nabarro's own party. In 1974 Sir Keith Joseph hailed 'that admirable woman, Mary Whitehouse', and called her 'a shining example of what one person can do single-handedly when inspired by faith and compassion'. She even claimed an endorsement from the unlikely figure of Mick Jagger, whom she had met on a television panel. 'He said he expected me to be the wrong kind of person,' she confided, 'and, well, I wasn't at all – and he felt we had a rapport.'[48]

As many observers remarked at the time, the NVALA was a militantly anti-radical movement, opposed to what Whitehouse called 'the secular/humanist/Marxist philosophy'.[49] Her husband Ernest told an interviewer that what had first disturbed them was the 'pressure from the left-wing [to] destroy the Christian faith', and a family friend observed that their 'dread of communism really surprised me'.[50] This no doubt owed much to the influence of Moral Rearmament, which was fiercely anti-Communist, and it is hard to imagine a similar dread among many other Shropshire housewives.[51] Whitehouse insisted that there was a deliberate Communist conspiracy to undermine British morality. 'The enemies of the West', she said in 1965, 'saw that Britain was the kingpin of Western civilisation; she had proved herself unbeatable on the field of battle because of her faith and her character. If Britain was to be destroyed, those things must be undercut.'[52] She even hinted that the BBC itself had fallen under the control of Communist agents. 'They've infiltrated the trade unions,' she explained. 'Why does anyone still believe they haven't infiltrated broadcasting?'[53]

Other commentators, however, argued that the NVALA was essentially a religious movement. Whitehouse herself thought that during the early sixties 'religion, the idea of God, Christianity in particular, were very much under attack'.[54] She was bewildered by her lack of support from the Church of England, and blamed 'soft permissives' and 'left-wing humanists'.[55]

According to one account, her object was 'to recolonise social life for God', turning Britain into 'a cross between a wet Sunday in Wales and eternal *Songs of Praise*'.[56] Indeed, to many observers, her campaign looked like a kind of religious revival, opposed not only to homosexuality, abortion and divorce, but to liberalism, humanism and moral flexibility. In this sense it was not unlike American religious conservatism during the same period, rooted in small towns and the countryside, deeply informed by anti-Communism, and bitterly resentful of the dismissive indifference of educated elitists like Hugh Carleton Greene and his colleagues at the BBC.[57]

More than any other individual, Mary Whitehouse popularised the issues of permissiveness and moral corruption, and she was undoubtedly one of the best-known and most controversial women of the sixties and seventies. In some ways she anticipated the appeal of Margaret Thatcher, another dutiful mother from the provincial English lower middle class, steeped in Protestant values, dedicated to the family and driven by a sense of her own rectitude and righteousness. Both called for a return to traditional values, both believed that the country was on the path of corruption and decline, and both rejected the liberalism they associated with the permissive society.[58] Most of the groups associated with the NVALA reflected the interests of Conservative, middle-class England: at the first meeting of the Viewers' and Listeners' Council in March 1968, the speakers included the chief constable of Lincolnshire, the president of Stoke-on-Trent's Rotary Club, a representative of the president of the Magistrates' Association and the vice-chairman of the Cheshire Women's Institute.[59] As Whitehouse herself put it, there was 'a growing revulsion among these people, and a desire to dissociate themselves from Swinging London'.[60]

The similarities with Margaret Thatcher suggest that Whitehouse was much more than an evangelical revivalist. Her attack on the permissive society was also a reaction to many of the major political and social changes since the end of the war: the creation of the welfare state, the growth of consumerism, the rise of the working classes, the militancy of the unions and so on. Like Thatcher, she appealed to middle-class households who felt threatened by socialism and social change, and who worried that their values were being eroded by collectivism and permissiveness. Unlike the leading politicians of the sixties, she was not prepared to accept economic materialism and cultural liberalism as acceptable national goals. Instead, she presented a world-view based on zealous anti-radicalism and moralistic Christian rigour, and informed by a powerful sense of loss and nostalgia. As Jeffrey

Weeks notes, she was 'far from being a crank'; she was a portent of the future.[61]

At the first NVALA convention the principal speaker had been the Conservative backbencher William Deedes. At the second, in May 1967, the main speaker was the journalist Malcolm Muggeridge, and he did not disappoint his audience:

> I am absolutely convinced that our civilisation will rush down the Gadarene slope which others have slipped down before, if we adhere to the notion that the image of life is not God but pigs in a trough. If life is pigs in a trough ... then of course it does not matter much what you show on TV. If that were life, if *Till Death Us Do Part* is life, I cannot see that there would be anything to do but to commit suicide.[62]

As one watching journalist remarked, Muggeridge's appearance at the NVALA convention would have been 'widely welcomed by connoisseurs of strange events and weird juxtapositions'.[63] By any standards, he was a pretty extraordinary character. A former Marxist who had changed his mind after visiting the Soviet Union in the thirties, he had been the editor of *Punch*, had courted controversy by publicly mocking the monarchy in the mid-1950s, and had become one of the most prominent television interviewers in the country, famous for his clowning behaviour as well as his sardonic wit. And as a legendary drinker, smoker and womaniser, he had few peers, once organising a threesome with Kingsley Amis and George Orwell's widow Sonia that passed off disastrously in the bedroom but ended with a lavish breakfast at the Waldorf Hotel.[64]

What many of his friends did not know, and what gradually became evident during the sixties, was that Muggeridge also had a deep sense of spiritual longing. After spending an evening drinking with friends, he would sit at home reading the works of Christian mystics until the small hours.[65] By the early sixties, surrounded by conspicuous consumption, he was becoming a fierce critic of modernity and materialism, opposed to 'wealth, ambition, celebrity, sexual liberation'.[66] Like his great hero St Augustine, he converted to Christianity and began transforming himself from libertine to ascetic. He became a vegetarian, gave up smoking, and delightedly told interviewers that he had given up sex.[67] By 1965 the days of orgies were long gone. Sex, Muggeridge wrote, was ultimately 'a trivial dream of pleasure which itself soon dissolves into the solitude and despair of self-gratification'.[68]

In November 1966 he was elected rector of Edinburgh University, a ceremonial position in which he was supposed to represent the interests of the students to the university authorities.[69] It was a fairly meaningless accolade, but when Muggeridge was formally invested on 16 February 1967 he used the occasion to launch a sensational assault on both the university system and the values of modern Britain. He complained that the government was bent on 'raising the school age, multiplying and enlarging our universities, increasing public expenditure on education until juvenile delinquency, beats and drug-addicts and general intimations of illiteracy multiply so alarmingly that, at last, the whole process is called into question'. If this were not enough, he predicted that 'permissive morality' would soon come into question, too:

> When birth pills are handed out with free orange juice, and consenting adults wear special ties and blazers, and abortion and divorce – those two contemporary panaceas for all matrimonial ills – are freely available on the public health, then at last, with the suicide rate up to Scandinavian proportions and the psychiatric wards bursting at the seams, it will be realized that this path, even from the shallow point of view of the pursuit of happiness, is a disastrous cul-de-sac.[70]

Unsurprisingly, this did not go down well with the students, and within a few months the rector had irreparably fallen out with his electors over drugs and contraception. By the beginning of 1968 the university magazine *Student* was pressing him to resign, and it even printed a cartoon showing Muggeridge as a rotting skull with worms crawling into his sockets. Anyone who knew Muggeridge was well aware that he was unlikely to give in, but his response surpassed even his own iconoclastic standards. He was already due to deliver the annual rectorial address from the pulpit of St Giles's, the High Kirk of Edinburgh, on 14 January 1968, and when the day came, the cathedral was packed with an expectant crowd that included representatives from Fleet Street and a television crew from the BBC, all eager to hear his reaction.[71]

Muggeridge, as usual, did not disappoint. He gave not an address but a sermon, and began by comparing modern Britain to the last days of the Roman Empire, which he called an age of fantasy, materialism and spiritual decay. Then he turned on his critics, 'the students in this university', whom he called 'the ultimate beneficiaries in our welfare system'. They were 'supposed to be the spearhead of progress', and he would welcome any sign of 'rebelliousness or refusal to accept the ways and values of our run-down, spiritually impoverished way of life . . . up to and including blowing up this magnificent edifice in which we now sit'. But he detected no such signs: they were too busy wallowing in the detritus of the affluent society.

> How sad, how macabre and funny it is that all they put forward should be a demand for pot and pills. It is the most tenth-rate form of indulgence ever known. It is the resort of any old slobbering debauchee anywhere in the world at any time – 'dope and bed'. The feeling raised in me is not so much disapproval as contempt. This, as you may imagine, makes it difficult, indeed impossible, for me as rector to fulfil my function.[72]

As he stepped down from the pulpit, Muggeridge also relinquished his post, the first rector ever to do so.[73] Even when the student union voted to support his reinstatement – a hint that the students were more conservative than many people imagined – he refused to heed them, but continued on his long, lonely march towards greater conservatism and, eventually, Catholicism.[74]

Both Mary Whitehouse and Malcolm Muggeridge presented themselves as champions of moral conservatism and religious reaction, so it was no surprise that they both became prominent supporters of the Nationwide Festival of Light in September 1971. This event was the brainchild of Peter Hill, an evangelical Baptist missionary, who planned a campaign to 'alert Britain to the dangers of moral pollution which are now eroding the moral fibre of this once great nation'. Muggeridge enthusiastically lent his backing to 'a wonderful and heartening occasion' that would halt the 'slide into decadence and godlessness', while other supporters included various bishops, the anti-pornography campaigner Lord Longford and the housewives' favourite, Cliff Richard.[75]

The campaign began badly, however, when demonstrators disrupted a meeting in London and eighty people were forcibly ejected after heckling Muggeridge's address.[76] Similar disruptions also marred the festival's main event, a rally in Trafalgar Square on 25 September, at which members of the Gay Liberation Front threw stink bombs at the speakers. Muggeridge, Whitehouse and their colleagues were undeterred, however, and regarded the demonstration as a great success, although the attendance of thirty thousand was less than half what they had earlier predicted. The overtly evangelical flavour of the occasion no doubt deterred many people who otherwise shared their views on obscenity, drugs and permissiveness, and the campaign soon fizzled out.[77]

The Festival of Light was just one of many campaigns in the late sixties and early seventies that tried to resist the sexual licence and moral decay associated with the permissive society. In October 1969 Dr S. E. Ellison, a GP from London, wrote to *The Times* suggesting that a group be 'formed to resist the destructive and demoralizing trends in our present community':

> There is increasing evidence that the stability of the traditional British way of life is threatened. Venereal disease is increasing. Termination of pregnancy is increasing. Drug addiction is increasing. Smoking is increasing. Gambling is increasing. All being examples of anti-social behaviour . . .
>
> This tide of immorality, self-deception, and insatiable appetite for all that is worthless, must be resisted by an even stronger group in the community who do not wish to see this country destroyed by a sickness as dangerous and as virulent as the plague.[78]

Ellison received more than two hundred letters of support, and two years later he was part of a group of doctors and educationalists who founded the Responsible Society, dedicated to encouraging 'a responsible and balanced attitude towards sexual behaviour' and fighting 'the commercialization and trivialization of sex'.[79] Its most prominent supporter was Pamela Hansford Johnson, who praised the growth of 'greater frankness and tolerance' during the sixties but warned that 'commercial sex-exploiters and "progressive" protagonists of sexual anarchy' were undermining social stability. The initiative attracted considerable praise in the press, including an admiring editorial in *The Times*, but it was operating in a very crowded market. It never came close to matching the appeal of the NVALA, not least because its more moderate approach was less attractive to potential recruits.[80]

Of all the anti-permissive campaigns, perhaps the most famous example was Lord Longford's Commission on Pornography, convened in the early summer of 1971 by the elderly Labour peer. Longford was a Catholic convert, a sentimental idealist and a dogged advocate of unpopular causes like penal reform, as well as one of Muggeridge's oldest and closest friends. He had been completely unaware of the existence of pornography until 1970, when it came as such a shock to him that he immediately decided to destroy it. In April 1971 he initiated a debate in the House of Lords about the 'incipient menace of pornography in Great Britain' and prepared for the occasion by visiting a strip-club, the Soho Stokehole, as well as sitting through 'an exhausting course of prurient films' and visiting a 'sex supermarket'.[81] This was only a taste of what was to come. In May he released the names of an extraordinary collection of people who had agreed to join his inquiry into pornography, including six peers, an archbishop, three bishops and three professors, as well as Jimmy Savile, Cliff Richard and, inevitably, Malcolm Muggeridge.[82]

The commission was supposed to examine the link between pornography and sexual violence, and Longford's approach to the problem was unconventional, to say the least. In August he took five other commission members, including the future jumper model Gyles Brandreth, to Copenhagen to investigate Denmark's obscenity laws. The trip kicked off with a visit to two sex shows, in which women were paired with men, other women and animals. Unsurprisingly, Longford found it all too much and lasted only five minutes in the first club, walking out in disgust with the manager trailing behind him saying, 'But sir, you have not seen the intercourse. We have intercourse later in the programme.' The second club was even worse. Here, according to an amused reporter, 'a half naked girl thrust a whip into Lord Longford's hand and invited him to flagellate her. He declined and after she had playfully mauled him by thrusting the whip around his neck and pulling violently on it, he got up and left.' By contrast, his colleagues stuck it out rather longer, and disagreed with Longford's verdict that this kind of thing was likely to encourage sexual violence. Brandreth even announced that he would like to see the Danish laws introduced back home.[83] This all made for splendid newspaper copy, but it also made it hard to take Longford seriously. When his report finally came out the following year many people could not banish the image of the elderly peer being strangled with a whip in the strip-clubs of Copenhagen.[84]

One of the more unlikely members of the Commission on Pornography was the novelist Kingsley Amis, who knew a good deal about the subject and privately thought that Longford was a 'fucking fool'.[85] But Amis, too, found much to dislike in the cultural climate of the late sixties, and in his own way he also anticipated the conservative reaction of the seventies and after.

As an adolescent, Amis had been a Communist, like Muggeridge, and when he rose to prominence in the 1950s he was still a strong Labour supporter.[86] In 1957, however, he wrote a pamphlet on socialism in which he declared that the best political motive was 'self-interest' and attacked 'the professional espouser of causes, the do-gooder, the archetypal social worker'.[87] By 1960 his relationship with the party had reached 'the name-calling and walking-out stage', and in 1964 he voted Labour for the last time.[88]

In 1967, utterly disillusioned by the Wilson government, Amis wrote an article for the *Sunday Telegraph* entitled 'Why Lucky Jim Turned Right', and followed it up with a pamphlet for the Conservative Political Centre called 'Lucky Jim's Politics'. He had abandoned Labour, he said, because he hated idealism, and had converted to 'grudging toleration of the Conservative Party because it is the party of non-politics, of resistance to politics'. He thought that the 'evils of life [were] ineradicable by political means, and that attempts to eradicate them are disastrous'. He was sick of progressive education, sick of socialist improvement and sick of the appeasement of Communism abroad; above all, he was sick of the whole 'abortion–divorce–homosexuality–censorship–racialism–marijuana package'.[89]

Amis was not the only prominent writer who advertised his contempt for the Wilson government. His best friend Philip Larkin, the most accomplished poet in the country, similarly prided himself on being an ordinary chap from the provincial middle classes rather than a stuck-up liberal highbrow. Larkin regularly dashed off letters to his friends dripping with contempt for trade unionists, immigrants, students and socialists of all kinds.[90] 'Fuck the lot of them, I say,' he wrote to Amis in 1969, 'the decimal-loving, nigger-loving, army-cutting, abortion-promoting, murderer-pardoning, daylight-hating ponces, to hell with them, the worst government that I can remember.' There was an element of self-caricature in all this, but at the same time it did reflect Larkin's genuine displeasure at the apparent leftward tilt of national life. 'England is going down generally!' he wrote to his elderly mother in 1970. 'It was shown recently that one child in eight born now is of immigrant parents. Cheerful outlook, isn't it? Another fifty years and it'll be like living in bloody India – tigers prowling about, elephants too, shouldn't wonder. We'll both be dead.'[91]

Other writers of the same generation shared this discontent at the social and cultural developments of the late sixties. The poet Donald Davie, who taught English at Essex before leaving for the United States, admitted: 'I detect in myself much the same drift to the Right that Amis admits to, and I don't apologise for it any more than he does.'[92] He had no need to, for by the late sixties plenty of middle-aged writers agreed with him. Some of them even used to meet for regular 'Fascist lunches' at Bertorelli's restaurant in Charlotte Street, among them the historian Robert Conquest, the novelists John Braine and Anthony Powell, and of course Amis himself.[93] Larkin, meanwhile, contented himself by sending his friends instructions on 'How to Win the Next Election', to be sung to the tune of 'Lillibullero':

> Prison for strikers,
> Bring back the cat,
> Kick out the niggers,
> What about that?
>   (Cho: niggers, niggers, etc.)
>
> Trade with the Empire,
> Ban the obscene,
> Lock up the Commies –
> God save the Queen!
>   (Cho: Commies, Commies, etc.)[94]

One factor pushing Amis and his friends to the right was the war in Vietnam, which they saw as a vital crusade against international Communism.[95] In a symposium of twenty-three British intellectuals in 1968, only Amis and Conquest supported the war, and Amis even demanded the immediate mobilisation of British troops to help the Americans.[96] Even without the war in Vietnam, however, it is likely that they would have moved rightwards, pushed by their fierce contempt for idealism and populism. The fashionable intellectual values of the late 1960s, which emphasised sensation and spirituality, were very different from the pragmatic detachment they had celebrated in the fifties, while their moral values were affronted by what they saw as the excesses of the permissive society. Both Amis and Larkin had been brought up in reserved, middle-class households in the twenties and thirties, and although they often defied their parents' values, they still respected them. Amis, for example, was a womaniser, but he did not regard promiscuity as an inherently good thing; and even though he owned pornography himself, he still joined Longford's commission.*

Like Larkin and Davie, Amis was appalled by the expansion of higher education, and he consistently argued that 'more will mean worse'.[97] Even in *Lucky Jim* there is a scene where two lecturers discuss the increasing pressure to 'chuck Firsts around like teaching diplomas and push every bugger who can write his name through the Pass courses'.[98] While Anthony Crosland was arguing passionately for greater egalitarianism and opportunity in higher education, Amis insisted that 'there must be an elite, and there can't be equality'.[99] In April 1965 he wrote mockingly to the *Observer*:

> Perhaps only you could have published a whole article on university failures that laid no weight on the almost invariable cause of failure: *insufficient ability*, or, alternatively, *excessive stupidity*.
>
> I was glad to learn from you, however, that as many as 14 per cent of people do fail. Evidently not all standards have been fully lowered everywhere yet. But your fashionable brand of sentimental mercy will hasten the process.[100]

The education reforms of the sixties were instrumental in pushing a considerable number of older intellectuals towards the anti-permissive right. To the likes of Amis and Davie, Labour's commitment to comprehensive schools and polytechnics was probably the single most unattractive feature of modern political life. Two men who agreed were C. B. Cox and A. E. Dyson, both university lecturers in English and the founders of the literary magazine *Critical Quarterly*. Cox and Dyson were lower-middle-class men who had won scholarships to Cambridge and regularly voted Labour. The former, a committed Christian, had even campaigned for Labour during the 1966 election. Dyson, meanwhile, had been a vocal member of the

---

*Amis also had personal reasons for opposing the Wilson government. In 1957 he had a bitter row with Anthony Crosland at a party when the two men drunkenly wrestled for control of the record player. It was Crosland's machine, but the records belonged to Amis. On another occasion, Amis was outraged when Tony Benn, a teetotaller, turned up uninvited to one of his parties and then refused all offers of alcohol. In his memoirs, Amis recorded that he realised then that Benn was 'a cunt'.

Homosexual Law Reform Society and had organised the famous letter to *The Times* in 1958 calling for the decriminalisation of male homosexuality. They also edited *Critical Survey*, a periodical aimed at teachers of English, and in March 1969 they devoted a special issue to a discussion of progressive education, comprehensive schools, the expansion of universities and student unrest. They called it their 'Black Paper'.[101]

The essays in the first Black Paper had two common themes: first, that educational standards were falling; and, second, that a misguided egalitarianism was undermining British education and culture. The issue had an apocalyptic tone, with talk of 'the progressive collapse of education', 'anarchy becoming fashionable' and the rejection of 'discipline and work'.[102] Cox insisted that the Black Paper was politically non-partisan, but the introductory essay was by the Conservative right-winger Angus Maude. Meanwhile, the new Education Secretary, Ted Short, was furious, and rather wildly claimed that the publication of the Black Paper was 'one of the blackest days for education for the past hundred years [and] the crisis of the century'.[103] Delighted at the ensuing publicity, Cox and Dyson published four more Black Papers over the next six years, all attacking comprehensive education, the collapse of standards, and progressive methods of teaching. Within the Labour Party and in the pages of liberal newspapers like the *Observer* and the *Guardian*, the authors were regarded as 'fascists' who were trying to destroy opportunity and equality; but in the columns of Conservative newspapers and among the Tory rank and file, they were heroes.[104]

It is not really true that the Black Papers were written by 'right-wing' academics, as Arthur Marwick claims. Just like Amis, their most famous contributor, Cox and Dyson were former Labour activists who saw themselves as enlightened liberals and educational pioneers. They had even marched behind the banners of CND, and Cox had sent his own children to a 'progressive' primary school, with disastrous results.[105] As one historian puts it, the Black Papers represented 'a scream of pain against a growing anti-examination, pro-egalitarian culture in education, of dismay at the apparent destruction of authority in universities and secondary schools'.[106] The controversy also reflected the increasing politicisation of education. The introduction of 'progressive' teaching methods, often based on play rather than instruction, alarmed many parents who worried that their children were being used as guinea-pigs in some hare-brained Hampstead experiment. What was more, the abolition of grammar schools and the introduction of comprehensives not only provoked a rift between reformers and traditionalists within the Conservative Party but antagonised middle-class parents who might otherwise have voted Labour.[107]

Thanks to the introduction of comprehensives, education became one of the most divisive political issues in the country from the early seventies onwards, and it was crucial in alienating former Labour supporters like Cox and Amis. Education was also the area in which arguments about the cultural legacy of the sixties were most obviously politicised. Even though student disturbances in Britain were pretty minor compared with those elsewhere, they became a symbol linking the indulgence of idealistic socialist ministers with the degenerate promiscuity of modern consumer culture. In this context they provided a link between the moralistic outrage of Whitehouse and Muggeridge, on the one hand, and the rebellion of former Labour supporters like Cox and Amis, on the other. This all amounted to both a cultural and a political critique, a reaction against falling moral standards as well as a denunciation of Labour's social engineering. It would provide excellent ammunition for a new generation of Conservatives in the years to come.

Between denouncing the government and contributing to the Black Papers, Kingsley Amis also found the time to continue his literary career. By the end of the decade he was the leading exponent of what D. J. Taylor calls 'the anti-1960s novel', a savage social satire attacking the liberal values associated with the period.[108]

Amis's first novel along these lines was *I Want It Now* (1968), the very title of which expresses the impatient self-indulgence that he associated with the late sixties. The central character is a shallow television interviewer who falls in love with a promiscuous but unsatisfied society girl, providing an excuse for Amis to satirise fashionable liberalism and social snobbery. At one point the hero hosts a television discussion about cultural freedom with a theatrical producer and a novelist, both of whom agree that Soviet writers are 'significantly freer' under Communism than British writers are under capitalism.[109] On another occasion he glances at a newspaper, and sees the headlines '*Export Gap Widens — Britain Loses £22m Arms Order — Textile Strike Spreads — Malta: Agreement Hopes Fade — Two Shipyards To Close — Ceylon Britons Told To Quit — England Follow-on in Sydney Test*'. 'The forces of progress', he thinks, 'were really gaining ground at last'.[110]

Three years later Amis published *Girl, 20*, which has a good claim to be his funniest book. Its narrator, Douglas Yandell, is a music critic and a good friend of the eminent conductor and composer Sir Roy Vandervane, a quintessential middle-aged progressive desperately trying to 'arse-creep youth'. Vandervane takes a dreadful seventeen-year-old mistress, drags Douglas around a succession of hideous boutiques and nightclubs, and finally completely disgraces himself by performing the ludicrous piece 'Elevations 9' on stage with a rock band called Pigs Out.[111] This performance, which forms the climax to the novel, takes place at a giant disused tramway depot before an audience of around a thousand people. Only 'here and there' can Douglas see 'an ordinary human being: journalist, performer's parent or ill-instructed queer'. Around him there is 'a prevailing hairiness', and one member of Pigs Out is likened to 'a degenerate descendant of Charles II'. On stage he can just make out some 'jerking anthropoid figures with musical instruments or microphones in their grasp, and surrounded in depth by enough electronic equipment to mount a limited thermonuclear strike'. All in all, 'it smelt of tennis shoes, hair and melting insulation, and was fearfully hot'.[112]

Plenty of other writers shared Amis's concerns about the direction of modern life, from A. S. Byatt and Piers Paul Read to Simon Raven and Malcolm Bradbury.[113] Perhaps the outstanding example of anti-permissive satire, though, is Anthony Powell's *Hearing Secret Harmonies* (1975), the final volume of *A Dance to the Music of Time*. Indeed, *Hearing Secret Harmonies* presents one of the most ludicrous spectacles in the anti-sixties novel, when the despicable Kenneth Widmerpool, a recurring figure in the cycle, transforms himself from a Labour peer and the chancellor of a new university into 'Ken', an absurd polo-necked apologist for student revolution. In a nice parody of the 'radical chic' of the late sixties Widmerpool even disrupts a prize-giving ceremony by publicly condemning 'the wrongness of the way we live, the wrongness of marriage, the wrongness of money, the wrongness of education, the wrongness of government, the wrongness of the manner we treat kids like these'. He finally ends up a wretched member of the 'Harmony' commune, chanting meaningless mantras and prancing about in blue robes.[114] Curiously, Lord Longford later claimed to have been one of the models for Powell's grotesque comic character, although the novelist himself denied it.[115]

In chronicling Widmerpool's decline and fall with such savage relish, Powell, like his friends Amis and Muggeridge, was also presenting an implicit indictment of the values of the permissive sixties. All three, despite their obvious differences, agreed that the liberal legislation and sexual frankness of the decade had gone too far. This was also the conclusion of the first influential non-fiction accounts of the era: Christopher Booker's *The Neophiliacs* (1969) and Bernard Levin's *The Pendulum Years* (1970). Both men had made their names during the satire boom of the early sixties, but both thought that cultural change had run out of control. Levin argued that the sixties had been 'a credulous age, perhaps the most credulous ever', a decade of fads and fashions, wild excesses and political inertia, during which Britain became 'diseased' and 'dazed'.[116] Booker, a close friend of Muggeridge and a fellow Christian convert, thought that Britain had 'lost an empire and any serious purpose'. The country was living out hollow fantasies of social engineering and cultural enthusiasm, a 'nightmare' in which the dreamers were doomed to catastrophe.[117] As he later explained:

> In the flashing lights and blaring cacophony of the discotheques, in the four-letter words and displays of nudity, in the drug obsessions, the 'love festivals', the cults, the crazes, the dazzling patterns of Op Art and the infantile playthings of Pop, the children of the Sixties sought to shake, deafen, blind and drug themselves into the 'ultimate experience' on a scale never before seen – until there was almost nowhere further to go.[118]

In the years to come, both Levin and Booker, like other critics of permissiveness, became great admirers of Margaret Thatcher. This was no coincidence: their interpretation of recent history had an obvious appeal to the Thatcherites of the late 1970s and 1980s. By presenting the sixties as a decade of excess, self-indulgence and national decline, the Conservatives hit on a deceptively simple explanation for Britain's woes that could easily be blamed on Harold Wilson and the Labour Party. But they did not invent the anti-permissive case, and its appeal transcended partisan boundaries. The reaction against the changes of the sixties was clearly under way as early as 1962, when Laurence Olivier lambasted 'dirty books and newspapers and advertising and television' in *Term of Trial*. Plenty of working-class Labour voters agreed that liberalism had gone too far, and plenty of ordinary people preferred the bluff cultural conservatism of 'PC' Jim Callaghan to the elegant liberalism of Roy Jenkins.

Of course, the anti-permissive version of the sixties was a caricature, exaggerating the changes of the period at the expense of the continuities, presenting a vision of decadence and excess that often bore little relation to the mundane realities of daily life. All the same, modern writers like Jonathon Green, who dismisses with casual superiority the 'invincible ignorance' and 'ripe hypocrisy' of Mary Whitehouse and her supporters, are missing the point.[119] Whitehouse, Muggeridge, Amis and the others spoke for millions of people who felt frightened or threatened by social and cultural change. These millions of people were unhappy that British power was so clearly in decline, felt let down by the Wilson government, and worried that the country they loved was changing beyond recognition. They were troubled that while church attendance was falling, the figures for divorce, abortion, delinquency and violent crime were all on the rise. They saw the sixties not as years of liberation, but as an age of anxiety. And in the decade to come they would find their champion — a middle-aged, middle-class grocer's daughter from Grantham.

PART FOUR

I'M BACKING BRITAIN

28

THE OTHER ENGLAND

Governments! What do they care about us? We don't belong to the great future. We're not teenagers . . . We ought to be bloody dead.

Angus Wilson, *Late Call* (1964)

'What exactly is it, sir, that you're going to do?'
   'Oh,' said Dr Branom, his cold stetho going all down my back, 'it's quite simple, really. We just show you some films.'
   'Films? I said. I could hardly believe my ookos, brothers, as you may well understand. 'You mean,' I said, 'it will be just like going to the pictures?'
   'They'll be special films,' said Dr Branom. 'Very special films.'

Anthony Burgess, *A Clockwork Orange* (1962)

On the evening of Wednesday, 16 November 1966, six million people tuned in to BBC1 to watch the latest instalment of *The Wednesday Play*. Created two years earlier by the BBC's head of drama Sydney Newman, the series was designed to persuade audiences 'that the working man was a fit subject for drama, and not just a comic foil in middle-class manners'.[1] Newman was convinced that 'great art has to stem from, and its essence must come out of, the period in which it is created'.[2] To the BBC board of governors, he explained:

> Pre-marital intercourse has increased enormously since World War II; homosexuality and abortion have become subjects for parliamentary debate and legal concern. The Labour Party is totally responsible and so are the unions, the divorce rate has gone up, the relations between management and labour, parent and child, worshipper and minister, England and the World — all these are food for the hungry and aware playwright.[3]

In *The Wednesday Play* Newman had created a mirror for the social changes of the sixties. Writers like Nell Dunn, Dennis Potter and Michael Hastings seized the opportunity to tackle controversial subjects like abortion, class antagonism, political corruption and colonial repression. To some critics, notably the anti-permissive campaigner Mary Whitehouse, this all smacked of immorality; to others, however, the series marked a high point in British television drama, and the high viewing figures of between six and ten million reflected the public's keen interest in the latest plays. Newman insisted that his writers and directors have almost complete freedom to develop their own ideas. 'I said I want you to concentrate on the turning points of British society,' he later recalled. 'I gave them the money and left them alone. And so *Cathy Come Home* and *Up the Junction* – all those real breakthroughs.'[4]

For many viewers who tuned in to BBC1 that night, the latest *Wednesday Play* was the most affecting programme they had ever seen on television. Written by the radical playwright Jeremy Sandford, produced by Tony Garnett and directed with naturalistic insight by the young Ken Loach, *Cathy Come Home* traces the descent of a young working-class family into poverty, homelessness and separation. Cathy (played by Carol White) is a young Northern girl who moves to London and marries Reg (Ray Brooks), a local lorry driver. The couple have three young children and live happily in a modern flat, but after Reg has an accident at work and loses his job, their implacable decline begins. Forced out of their home, they move to an overcrowded tenement, then to shabby shared lodgings, a dirty caravan site, a derelict house and finally a grim hostel for the homeless. Here Reg is separated from his wife and child, and gradually he loses interest in paying their way. As a result, Cathy and her children are thrown on to the streets; they have nowhere to go, and in the heartbreaking final scene, filmed with hidden cameras in front of stunned passers-by, Cathy's children are taken from her by unsympathetic social workers.[5]

More than any other television programme of the period, *Cathy Come Home* struck a chord with its audience. '[It] has shown us how heedless we can be, and how heartless some of us are,' commented an editorial in the *Guardian*.[6] *The Times*, meanwhile, thought that it was 'not so much a documentary, rather more of a tract', but nevertheless found it 'infinitely moving'.[7] Few people, said the paper's television critic, could have watched 'without being deeply moved, whether by compassion or anger – even by disbelief . . . Television, with its mass audience and searching camera, can perhaps be a more powerful medium than any to force people to see the truth. There must, however, be enough truth or verisimilitude to be convincing – not that I would cast doubt on the credentials of this protesting study of human despair.'[8]

'Truth' and 'verisimilitude' were exactly what the young, Oxford-educated Ken Loach had been looking for, and it was his emphasis on documentary realism that gave the programme its charge. Drawing on the techniques of the New Wave films of the early sixties, Loach used hand-held cameras, outdoor locations and grainy 16mm film stock. His actors, often improvising, spoke with regional accents and in overlapping mumbles; the soundtrack was broken up with snippets of anonymous voices and street noise; and documentary-style statistics, commentaries and 'viewpoints' were woven into the story.[9] Although few viewers are likely to have thought that *Cathy Come Home* was a genuine documentary, nonetheless there was clearly some doubt whether it was 'a story based directly on a real incident, or . . . a construction developed from a range of research materials'.[10] This was exactly what Loach wanted. 'We were very anxious', he said later, 'for our plays not to be considered dramas but as continuations of the news.'[11]

With *Cathy Come Home*, Loach and his producer Tony Garnett had hoped to provoke a public reaction, and they were not disappointed. Television was superbly suited to foster debate because, as Garnett remarked, 'so many people are watching at the same moment and might go to work the next morning having experienced the same thing'.[12] But *Cathy Come Home* also owed its place in television history to sheer coincidence. Two weeks after the broadcast, on 1 December 1966, five charitable housing bodies launched a long-planned fundraising campaign to build and convert housing for the homeless. Initially its focus was on the four most severely afflicted cities – London, Birmingham, Liverpool and Glasgow – but eventually Shelter became a genuinely nationwide campaign.[13]

Despite the myths to the contrary, the two events were not connected. The first director of Shelter, Des Wilson, later admitted that he had missed *Cathy Come Home* because he was working late on the launch.[14] Yet there is no doubt that the impact of the play created additional publicity for his campaign, and Shelter's timing was superb. As public enthusiasm for the glitter of Swinging London began to wane, so the newspapers began to pay more attention to the darker side of life in the sixties. The *Guardian*, for example, noted that people had 'had their consciences badly shaken about homelessness in Britain', while *The Times* noted that 'the public conscience finds it unacceptable that in a relatively wealthy society so much bad housing is allowed to stand, that so many people live in unhealthy hovels, that so many live in hopeless overcrowding'.[15]

As Shelter's own advertisements explained, in January 1966 more than 12,000 people had seen in the New Year in a hostel for the homeless, while 4000 children had been taken into care because their families were homeless, and another 7000 were in care because they had been abandoned.[16] These were the 'officially homeless', but there were also the 'hidden homeless': 'thousands more families [who] are either so overcrowded or live in such conditions that they cannot reasonably be regarded as having a home'. One example was a house in Church Road, Birmingham, occupied by twenty-seven people, with one family to a room, sharing one toilet, two cold-water taps, and the company of innumerable rats. There were no central government figures for homelessness, but, according to Shelter's founder, the Reverend Bruce Kenrick, three million families were living 'in slums, in near-slums, or in grossly overcrowded conditions'. In the next decade, he predicted, 'the frustration caused by bad housing will be one reason why young children will become embittered, perhaps delinquent teenagers; why many young couples will find their marriages breaking under the strain of overcrowding; and why many old people will end their days in great unhappiness with one gas ring, a cold water tap, and a lavatory shared by up to twenty others'.[17]

Shelter's success belies the popular image of the mid-sixties as hedonistic, permissive and self-indulgent. It was during this period that academics, politicians and commentators began paying attention to the casualties of modern British society: the poor, the unemployed, the mentally disabled, the sick, the elderly and so on. Two years previously the journalist and travel writer Geoffrey Moorhouse had published his Penguin book *The Other England*, a survey of life outside London and the Home Counties.[18] This was the England of the Birmingham car workers who 'spend their days doing a repetitive job alongside a conveyor belt, the most deadly dull thing imaginable'.[19] It was the England of Openshaw, Lancashire, 'bisected by its stagnant canal, shaken by the passage of its arterial traffic, cross-hatched by its rows of Victorian cave-dwellings', where families lived without baths, toilets or hot running water.[20] And it was the England of South Yorkshire, with its slag heaps and furnaces, its forges and foundries, its 'acres of dilapidated homes . . . where some people inhale what must surely be the foulest air in England'.[21]

As the Wilson government floundered, commentators turned their attention from Britain's supposed economic potential to its enduring social problems. In the fifties politicians and academics had generally assumed that poverty and unemployment had been eliminated from British life.[22] But ten years later a new generation argued that their predecessors had been too complacent. According to sociologists like Richard Titmuss, Brian Abel-Smith and Peter Townsend, inequality and deprivation were still integral parts of British life. By revising the definition of the poverty line to an income below 140 per cent of supplementary benefit, they found that 14 per cent of the population, or 7.5 million people, were living in poverty, including more than 2 million children. Half a million children, meanwhile, were living in households where their father was earning less than if he had simply stayed at home and taken government benefits. When Abel-Smith and Townsend published their findings in *The Poor and the Poorest* in December 1965, it became an unlikely bestseller, 'tapping the seasonal market in goodwill' and raising popular awareness of the poverty beneath the veneer of the Swinging Sixties.[23] As one historian puts it, 'the poor family, and the poor working family, were about to be reborn as a political issue'.[24]

In all the talk about the new classlessness of the swinging era it was easy to forget just how unequal British society was. Between 1965 and 1975, the bottom 80 per cent of the population owned just over 10 per cent of the nation's wealth.[25] It was true that, for most people, life had improved considerably since the fifties, and there is no ignoring the impact of higher wages, home-ownership, televisions, kitchen appliances and so on. But for many others, life was not so cosy. Cassie McConachy, a teenage mother whose life uncannily mirrored that of Jeremy Sandford's Cathy, left her husband after he beat her, but her parents refused to take her in:

> I had a boy in nappies and I was pregnant and I just stuffed everything in the pram and took off . . . I went to several places, but when they saw me with a baby and looking like I had no money they didn't want to know. It was hard at the best of times getting a place when you had a baby. So I ended up on King's Cross station and I slept there for a week. I was regularly kicked out and I'd just walk around pushing the baby. My biggest fear was having my son taken into care away from me.

Fortunately, the authority figures in Cassie's story were more benign than those in *Cathy Come Home*:

> In the second week a kind policeman let me sleep in the waiting room and brought me sandwiches and a flask of coffee every night. And he paid for me to stay in a bed and breakfast place and told me about a hostel for the homeless. I was so grateful to him. Mind you, the hostel was hell, they treated you like a prisoner, you were totally institutionalized, but at least I was off the streets.[26]

Even for those who did have homes, life was often far from easy. As late as the mid-sixties, more than three million urban homes lacked bathrooms and hot running water, and for people living in cheap rented housing, conditions were frequently appalling. In 1963 Birmingham and Manchester estimated that they still had 70,000 and 80,000 slums respectively.[27] Indeed, the West Midlands in general struck Geoffrey Moorhouse as particularly depressing:

> Take a bus from West Bromwich to Wolverhampton by way of Wednesbury and Bilston, and there is nothing to be seen which would induce anyone to go and live there unless he had to. Where the decrepit buildings of the Industrial Revolution peter out, bleak and gritty housing estates have been allowed to sprawl with here and there patches of waste ground full of broken glass, fractured brick, garbage, and willowherb . . . It is a picture of desolation . . . a place to make you weep.[28]

The most detailed study of poverty in the late sixties was published in 1970 by two left-leaning academics at the University of Nottingham, Ken Coates and Richard Silburn. They focused on the nearby area of St Ann's, 'a typical late Victorian, working-class, city-centre neighbourhood in acute decline'. Although they strongly sympathised with its inhabitants, they clearly found this corner of the East Midlands a bleak and miserable place, 'with dingy buildings and bleak factories and warehouses, functionally austere chapels, a host of second-hand shops stacked out with shabby, cast-off goods; overhung through the winter by a damp pall of smoke'. St Ann's, they concluded, was dominated by 'hopelessness, in which the sense that things are inexorably running down weighs constantly on every decision, and inhibits many positive responses to make and mend'.[29]

As Coates and Silburn discovered, conditions in St Ann's had barely changed for decades. The cobbled streets were 'dirty and litter-strewn . . . the gutters ankle-deep in debris, and the pavements and roadways covered in a thin layer of rubbish'.[30] Inside, the houses were invariably infested by dirt, damp and vermin. In one house the floorboards in an upstairs bedroom were so rotten that a leg of the bed protruded through the ceiling below. In another the lady of the house reported that when she was making the bed 'my foot went right through the floor, and there I sat, hollering for help, with my leg waving about through the living-room ceiling'.[31] Bricks and woodwork were often rotten; walls were sodden with damp; chimneys and toilets were collapsing; cellars were full of water; cockroaches, mice and rats were everywhere. As the bricks rotted, so the sewers collapsed, blocking the drains and flooding the streets, so that not only were cellars 'filled with evil-smelling effluent' but entire back yards were 'overrun with sewage'.[32]

As the researchers recognised, if it was unpleasant for them to visit St Ann's, it was infinitely worse for people to live there. Wages were extremely low, and those in work generally depended upon 'crucifyingly long hours of regular overtime' merely to make ends meet.[33] Unlike millions of their more fortunate countrymen, the breadwinners of St Ann's returned to an environment in which a genuinely private life was completely impossible.

> Nothing is personal, unless it is whispered . . . If you want to go to the lavatory, you meet your neighbours in the yard. If you want to make love you may well feel it discreet to listen for your neighbour's snores before you start the bed-springs rattling . . . All of these deprivations add up. Their sum is backbreaking toil and hardship. And these pains are concentrated in houses that are too small, too densely concentrated together; houses that are in various stages of dilapidation and decay; houses that lack the basic amenities taken for granted by most people. You get dirty in St Ann's quite easily, but it is hard to get clean. It is often damp. It is often cold. It is never easy to make it dry and warm. Any one of these drawbacks would, on its own, constitute at least a serious irritation, but a combination of all of them, compounded in so many cases by material poverty, becomes well-nigh intolerable . . . Damp, cold, rot, decrepitude are as 'natural' in St Ann's as is the smoky atmosphere: for all most people know, they have been sent by Providence, and must be endured.[34]

One of the more depressing aspects of the Nottingham survey was that the poorest people in the area were pensioners, whose financial problems were compounded by loneliness, illness and frailty.[35] Few accounts of the

1960s have much to say about the old, even though there were eight million elderly people in Britain at the end of the decade and their numbers were increasing. At the time, most commentators ignored almost all the population who were over sixty. 'Continually the problems of young people, their education, their music, their drugs and their violence are surveyed, analysed, discussed and reported on,' wrote one journalist in 1971. 'They clamour for attention and they have the energy to make themselves heard. Youth, high in spending power and loud of voice, has become a cult and its words and slang have become part of our language. Old age, its antithesis, is not news.'[36]

The author of these words was Jack Shaw, a young man who in 1970 had co-written a series of reports on the plight of the elderly for the *Sheffield Star*. Shaw argued that the elderly had been 'neglected by society, their final years grim and cheerless'. They did not march or demonstrate; it was as though they were politically voiceless, and that made them all the more reliant on the goodwill of others. But 'in the vigour of our youth', he wrote, 'we prefer not to think that one day we too could be plagued with the stiffness of arthritic joints, that senility could befuddle our minds and that infirmity might make us dependent on others for our daily needs'. So 'we hide from the harsher realities of old age – realities that our society is too busy, or too selfish, or too preoccupied to give the needs of the elderly their rightful place in the order of priorities'.[37]

The *Star*'s campaign had begun with a telephone call on 1 January 1970, when the newspaper was asked if it 'could get anything done' for an old woman living in a nearby council tenement. She lived 'in conditions which, without exaggeration, can be described as horrifying', and the case, said Shaw, 'exemplified the depths to which an old person can sink through loneliness, senility and neglect'. When the *Star*'s reporters first arrived at the woman's flat, they were appalled by what they saw:

> She was found slumped in a broken, urine-saturated armchair in front of an empty firegrate. The day was bitterly cold and she had no fuel for the fire and no other means of heating. Nor had she any food. She gazed from blank, uncaring eyes and gave all the appearance of waiting for death to overtake her.
>
> Her person was filthy, face and hands showing embedded dirt. Her hair was lousy and her clothing foul rags. There was no change of underwear or winter clothing in the flat and it was obvious she had not changed the clothing she wore for a very long time.

> Her three-roomed flat was in a disgusting condition, its walls covered in soot and dirt, streaked with excreta and hung with cobwebs . . . [The living room] was a gloomy, stale-smelling place and every stick of furniture was thick with dust and grime. There were no carpets and the floor was encrusted with coal dust . . .
>
> The lavatory, outside on the landing, was too foul to use and the coal-bunker beside it was bare of even a scraping of coal.[38]

The *Star*'s reporters immediately borrowed some coal for the fire, made the woman some soup and called for an ambulance to take her to an old people's home. But she had been lucky. Many thousands of elderly people in Sheffield were living in similar conditions, and the newspaper could not intervene to save all of them. Across the nation, meanwhile, there were millions more. According to Help the Aged, some 350,000 nationwide lived without a bathroom, a kitchen or an indoor toilet; 2 million had access to an outside toilet only; 1.5 million lived on their own; and 300,000 were in 'urgent need of flats with some sort of supervision'.[39] The weekly state pension in 1970 was £5 for a single person and £8 2s for a married couple, which, as Shaw pointed out, was 'miserably inadequate and totally indefensible'.[40] And although Sheffield had twenty publicly provided residential homes, this meant only one space for every seventy-one pensioners in the city.[41] As a consequence, thousands of people were daily afflicted by 'physical disability, mental infirmity, loneliness, poverty and inadequate housing', all at precisely the time of life when they were most vulnerable.[42]

Life for the elderly in the 1960s was not all doom and gloom. More affluent pensioners were able to contemplate trips to the seaside or to European destinations organised by companies like Saga, which launched the extremely successful Saga Club in 1966. Many chose to retire to the sunnier climes of the South Coast, making new homes in the ageing seaside resorts that they had visited in younger days.[43] But even for pensioners in more comfortable surroundings life could be hard. In an era of increasing mobility and home-ownership children often moved away from their parents, leaving them to fend for themselves.[44] In a survey of the London suburb of Woodford at the beginning of the sixties, researchers heard plenty of complaints about infirmity, ill health, loneliness and depression. 'I just can't seem to walk any more, the ground seems to come up,' remarked one widow in her eighties. 'There's only one thing I want and that's a little happiness.' Another octogenarian said sadly: 'I can't dig the garden any more or mow the grass. I get so horribly breathless. I feel so frustrated.'[45] As one of the Woodford pensioners mournfully put it: 'Life isn't really much fun when you get old.'[46]

One of Jack Shaw's colleagues at the *Star*, a young reporter called Danny Gallagher, spent two weeks living with 'Mr C', a seventy-three-year-old pensioner in a two-up, two-down Victorian terrace. For Mr C, 'life was a series of long, uneventful days'. He spent much of his time lost in thought, sitting in front of the gas fire and gazing at his collection of angling trophies. 'I have also seen him stretched out on his bed for hours on end,' Gallagher wrote, 'just staring at the ceiling. His eyes were focused there, but his thoughts were not.' Every day was the same, 'so uneventful that it seemed interminable. Nothing happened, and it happened all the time.'[47]

At first the journalist looked on his fortnight as

> a prison sentence and was anxiously awaiting the time when I would be free. But then I realized that, although I was to live this life of seclusion for only a short period, he and the many pensioners like him would experience nothing else for the rest of their lives. It was a frightening thought. The most depressing thing was sitting looking out of the window at the people hurrying past. There was at most six feet between us but it might just as well have been six miles. The old man was all too well aware that his daily routine was simple and repetitive and twice I saw him break down and weep at the futility of it all.

When the two weeks were up Gallagher gratefully returned to the life of the young. But, as he recognised, Mr C was far from exceptional. This was the reality for millions of Britons in the sixties, and it was the reality that awaited millions of their younger fellows in the years to come. As Gallagher admitted, he had caught a glimpse of 'what lies at the end of the road'.[48]

As 1967 drew to a close there was a palpable sense that the optimism and glamour of the mid-sixties had disappeared. There was, wrote Christopher Booker, 'an underlying shift in the national mood', crystallised by the humiliating devaluation of the pound.[49] The press had long since tired of running stories about the triumphs of scientific planning, the pleasures of Swinging London and the joys of affluence. The politicians who had once been heralds of optimism had now become harbingers of woe; the tower blocks that had once been icons of modernity were now seen as symbols of decay; even the pop stars who had once epitomised youth and freedom seemed to be spending more time in the courtroom than the studio. For many commentators it was as though, after the intoxication of the swinging years, the country was paying the price for its pleasures. In Booker's words, there was 'a distinct and widespread mood of aftermath, of exhaustion, even of reaction'.[50]

The idea that Britain was in deep decline did not suddenly spring out of nowhere in the aftermath of devaluation. It had always been there, as long as anyone could remember, rooted in nineteenth-century debates about the future of the Empire, the plight of the cities and the health of the race. After the election of Harold Wilson in 1964 it had temporarily gone out of fashion; but the anxieties about national decline, the performance of the economy and the impact of affluence were always there, less public than before but simmering away nevertheless. Even while the Swinging London fad was at its height, some observers pointed out that the pound was under constant attack, the economy was lurching from deflation to devaluation, and the nation's diplomatic prestige had rarely been lower. In June 1966 the London correspondent of the *New York Times* told his readers that the British people, lost in the 'selfish' pursuit of material gratification, were heading down the road towards 'economic perdition'. 'The atmosphere in London can be almost eerie in its quality of relentless frivolity,' wrote Anthony Lewis. 'There can rarely have been a greater contrast between a country's objective situation and the mood of its people.'[51]

By the end of 1967 the pendulum had swung to the opposite extreme. To anyone who read newspaper editorials, the country seemed to be trapped in a downward spiral of economic failure, cultural decadence and public pessimism. In *To England with Love* (1967), David Frost and Antony Jay's good-humoured survey of the state of the nation, the authors parodied the orthodoxy of the day:

> Ruin and misery the pundit sees as he gazes upon his England. Huge debts, inefficient industries, antiquated unions, uncompetitive management, inadequate exports, depleted reserves, severely restrained wages, congested roads, decaying cities, irresponsible adolescents, irreligious clerics, escaped convicts, television addicts, short-sighted bureaucrats and myopic politicians. All trying to support the crumbling ruins of a derelict empire with an inadequate army, a doubtful currency and a Royal Mint with a hole in the middle.[52]

'Can anyone doubt', asked the Conservative grandee Quintin Hogg, 'that we are a people that has lost its way? Can anyone deny that the British people is in the act of destroying itself: and will surely do so if we go on as at present?'[53]

On 28 December 1967 five typists at Colt Ventilation and Heating Ltd, a firm based in Surbiton, decided that they had had enough. Valerie White, Joan Southwell, Christine French, Carol Fry and Brenda Mumford were all aged between fifteen and twenty-one and could barely remember a time when the economy had not been booming. Now that things seemed to be unravelling, they decided that everyone should be doing their bit, just like their parents during the war. The following day the girls wrote to the firm's marketing director offering to work an extra half an hour, during their daily tea-break, for free. Not wanting to look a gift horse in the mouth, their bosses accepted the offer and then realised that it might make excellent publicity, and within a few days the national press had got hold of the story.[54]

By New Year's Day the news had made the front page of *The Times*, which reported that the scheme was becoming a 'national movement'. Most of Colt Ventilation and Heating's 750 workers agreed to give up half an hour too, as did the managing directors, Alan and Jerome O'Hea. 'Overall the policy will mean an immediate 7 per cent rise in productivity,' the firm's marketing director, Frederick Price, told the press. 'Think if that was the same all over the country . . . I think this is the way to solve the country's problems.' Colt's bosses planned to write to no fewer than thirty thousand employers across the country 'inviting them to join the scheme', with a 'clearing house at Surbiton so that companies can get information', and the famous typists were already drafting telegrams to be sent to the three party leaders, as well as the Archbishops of Canterbury and Westminster and the senior officials of the TUC. According to Alan O'Hea, the plan was 'to catch the imagination of young and old'. To make the point, he intended to issue 100,000 Union Jack badges with the motto 'I'm Backing Britain'.[55]

Even though the first week of January 1968 was rather slow for news, it was nevertheless striking how quickly the 'I'm Backing Britain' campaign took off. Within just two days the Surbiton typists had received three thousand letters, telegrams and telephone calls, and the firm's public relations officer had to start work an hour and a half early to deal with all the enquiries.[56] One telegram came from Prince Philip, who described their initiative as 'the most heartening news I heard in 1967', and added: 'If we go into 1968 with that spirit we shall certainly lick all our problems and put this country well on its feet again.'[57] The Bishop of Southwark told his congregation that 'spending five minutes on your tea-break instead of half an hour would go a long way towards solving the country's economic problems'.[58] Even Harold Wilson, who might have considered the scheme an implicit criticism of his government's record, sent a telegram of support, congratulating the typists 'on their initiative', their 'public spirit' and their commitment 'to increase the competitiveness of Britain'.[59]

By the following week 'I'm Backing Britain' had become a national sensation, with hundreds of companies falling over one another in their haste to sign up to the campaign. At Grimston Electrical Tools in Ashford, Kent, for example, a hundred employees volunteered to work an extra half-hour a day with no pay, while a Blackpool firm of estate agents sent the Treasury a cheque for five hundred pounds, and a chain of department stores in the East Midlands announced a 5 per cent cut in prices. Some of these initiatives admittedly seemed rather gimmicky. Staffordshire Potteries, for example, produced 2500 'I'm Backing Britain' coffee mugs a week, decorated with the Union Jack. More incongruously, the songwriters Tony Hatch and Jackie Trent wrote an excruciating hit for Bruce Forsyth:

> I'm backing Britain,
> Yes, I'm backing Britain,
> We're all backing Britain.
> The feeling is growing,
> So let's keep it going,
> The good times are blowing our way![60]

Nevertheless, 'I'm Backing Britain' made an impact at Westminster, where most politicians were quick to scramble aboard. As an editorial in *The Times* commented, the campaign's alleged economic promise actually mattered less than its vague, defiant patriotism: it was so successful because it 'spontaneously associates personal economic effort with the national cause'. It was also, the newspaper explained, 'a popular surge of frustration against the restraints, inhibitions and plain sloth which have handicapped Britain's trading performance for so long'.[61] It caught the public mood, especially among the Conservative middle classes, because it represented a bold response to the devaluation of sterling and the growing sense of national decline. And it clearly appealed to Harold Wilson's old Boy Scout's instincts, too. On 9 January, the Prime Minister announced that he was 'backing

Britain', and urged consumers to 'buy a British product' wherever possible. There had been, he said, 'too much knocking of Britain and Britain's achievements – in Britain and, more seriously, out of Britain . . . Now the message is that self, and individual self-seeking, must give place to the task of putting Britain first.'[62]

Edward Heath also went out of his way to praise the movement, calling it 'a fine example of the spirit needed in this country today'.[63] This was not surprising, given that the campaign tapped a vein of popular patriotism and that Colt's managing directors were Conservative supporters and friends of Heath's front-bench ally John Boyd-Carpenter.[64] But this praise did not go down well with all his colleagues. Enoch Powell was still a member of Heath's team in January 1968, albeit an increasingly semi-detached and waspish one, but he despised the populist gimmickry of 'I'm Backing Britain'. It would be better renamed 'Help Brainwash Britain', he suggested, adding that it was 'not only ineffably silly, but positively dangerous'. As he pointed out, if British exports were still uncompetitive abroad, then the Surbiton typists could have 'no tea-break at all for perpetuity' but it would make no difference to the balance of payments or the health of the economy.[65]

But the most vociferous critics of the campaign were the leaders of the trade unions, who were understandably suspicious of a scheme to get people to do extra work for nothing.[66] Clive Jenkins, Britain's leading white-collar union leader, called it 'economic illiteracy', and reminded journalists that more than half a million people were unable to find jobs at all.[67] Will Paynter, the general secretary of the National Union of Mineworkers, was even more scathing. 'I back Britain,' he said, 'but I back solutions that are socialist in character. I regard the working of overtime, whether free or paid for, in much the same way as I regard piece work in industry – as a device by employers and management to hide inefficiency.'[68]

The unions' opposition to 'I'm Backing Britain' was most striking in Hampshire, where the Portsmouth branch of the Amalgamated Engineering Union banned its members from taking part. The story caught the attention of the press because among those members were two hundred workers at Colt's factory in Havant, who were proud of their firm's role in the campaign. 'Virtually everyone plans to work the extra time for nothing and some are even prepared to leave the union if necessary,' their shop steward, Harry Tyler, explained. 'People who were against the campaign have completely reversed their views because of the union attitude. No one likes being told what to do with their free time by the union.'[69] When the Havant workers turned up half an hour early for work, the union cracked down, hauling its shop stewards before a closed tribunal and suspending them from their posts. The unions' pressure paid off. By the middle of February even the previously steadfast Harry Tyler had given up on the scheme, and although Colt tried to shrug off the embarrassment, the campaign's momentum stumbled and never recovered.[70]

The acrimonious failure of 'I'm Backing Britain' seemed emblematic of the national mood as Britain entered the last years of the sixties. There was no longer a market for giddy optimism: instead, everyone, from newspaper columnists and novelists to television playwrights and film directors, seemed more interested in what was wrong with Britain, not what was right.

In some ways this was nothing new. Decline and degradation had long been a popular theme in literature, reflecting the dissolution of the Empire, the nightmares of the Cold War, the dangers of technology and the sense that highbrow culture was threatened by the spread of consumerism.[71] Science-fiction writers like John Wyndham, Brian Aldiss and John Christopher explored themes of alienation, invasion and disaster, while in the hands of novelists as diverse as Kingsley Amis, William Golding and Anthony Burgess modern Britain emerged as a gloomy, nostalgic society, devoid of idealism or hope.[72] In Burgess's novel *The Right to an Answer* (1960), for example, Britain is a grim, trivial place, crazed with sexual frustration and besotted by the television. Its values are summed up by his sardonic description of an old country pub, decaying in the midst of the affluent society:

> The Black Swan stood in a pocket of decaying village, the dirty speck around which the pearly suburb had woven itself. The village had shrunk to less than an acre. It was like a tiny reservation for aborigines. From the filthy windows imbeciles leered down at the weed-patches; cocks crowed all day; little girls of an earlier age shnockled over stained half-eaten apples; all the boys seemed to have cleft palates. Still, it seemed to me far healthier than the surrounding suburb. Who shall describe their glory, those semi-detacheds with the pebble-dash all over the blind-end walls, the tiny gates which you could step over, the god-wottery in the toy gardens?[73]

Nowhere was this new pessimism more obvious than in the film industry. The swinging comedies of the mid-sixties had failed to reverse the long-term decline of British film: by the end of the decade attendances were in free-fall and hundreds of cinemas were scheduled for demolition. As the American studios withdrew their investment, domestic production dried up; even cheap, cheerful perennials like the *Carry Ons* and Hammer horror films would not survive the 1970s.[74] In this atmosphere it was hardly surprising that the cinema mirrored the gathering gloom of the era. The transition to the despondency of the early seventies was particularly well captured by two films shot in the final months of 1970, both of which, in their very different ways, explored the 'other England' of pessimism, disillusionment and decay. The first looked back to Britain's crumbling terraced streets, the streets of *The Poor and the Poorest* and *Cathy Come Home*; the second gazed ahead to a future of soulless modernist estates, drugs and authoritarianism. Both were violent; both were controversial; both anticipated a coming decade of economic unrest, political fragmentation and everyday brutality.

In 1968 Ted Lewis, a budding thriller-writer from Humberside, had published his second novel, a bleak tale of corruption and revenge. *Jack's Return Home* is set in Scunthorpe and tells the story of Jack Carter, a professional gangster who comes home from London to avenge the death of his brother. Carter discovers that his family has been mixed up in a grubby world of provincial crime, gambling and pornography. As one account has it:

> The starkness of the prose is matched by the bleakness of the moral and behavioural world it describes. It is a parallel world of duplicity, conspiracy, egotism and sudden death that sucks in and entraps its participants, and it festers beneath the surface of even a small provincial town. In this world, the centres of power are difficult to locate, and the course of justice is rerouted by secret and venal relationships . . . The Humberside of *Jack's Return Home* – and, by implication, much of the rest of the country – harbours an undiagnosed sickness.[75]

At the beginning of 1970 work began on a cinematic version of *Jack's Return Home*, directed by Mike Hodges, a young man who had spent much of the sixties shooting arts documentaries for ITV. Hodges liked the unrelenting pessimism of the book, and recognised that it suited the national mood.[76] He saw himself as 'a surgeon opening up a cancer patient, [removing] every article of sickness and [revealing] it for what it is'. As he later told an interviewer, *Get Carter* was 'about observing the social structures and the deprivation of the country from which the character comes'. Humberside, however, looked too affluent to have the right effect, so Hodges searched for locations further north. 'We pressed on and came to Newcastle,' he recalled later. 'The visual drama of the place took my breath away. Seeing the great bridges crossing the Tyne, the waterfront, the terraced houses stepped up each side of the deep valley, I knew that Jack was home.'[77]

Newcastle was the ideal location for *Get Carter*: a dark stone city set in a deep valley, its terraced streets sloping down towards the North Sea beneath grey, glowering skies. Few cities in Britain, and certainly none in England, felt more remote from the gaiety and the glitter of Swinging London. Hodges and his cameramen shot *Get Carter* as though it were a documentary about everyday life in Newcastle at the end of the sixties, with derelict, crumbling locations and realistic, shabby interiors, often filmed in shadow and twilight. The contrast was all the greater because Carter was played by Michael Caine, one of the icons of the swinging era. When he disembarks from the train and goes into the crowded North Eastern pub, the camera cuts from the suspicious faces of the local drinkers to Carter, the alien with his black overcoat and adopted London accent, asking for his pint 'in a thin glass'. It is as though he is entering a different world, even a different time. Neither the local drinkers nor the barmen were actors, and it was no accident that the scene, and much of the rest of the film, had the feel of a 'realistic' social documentary, an exploration of the forgotten world of the working-class North.[78]

Few places better captured the spirit of the 'other England' than the depressed shipyards and factories along the banks of the Tyne. When Geoffrey Moorhouse visited the area at the beginning of 1964, he noted that unemployment was 7 per cent, more than treble the national average, and it remained unusually high for the remainder of the decade. 'The North-east has more poverty than any other part of England,' he wrote; 'there are more places in it which look as though they are wasting away than anywhere else in the country.' The Saturday second-hand market held in the shadow of the Tyne Bridge struck him as particularly depressing:

> Everything offered here has seen better days. The shoppers mostly look as if they haven't. There is a high proportion of varicose veins, small mutilations, and disfiguring birthmarks among those who inspect the cracked shoe leather whose shape has been determined by somebody else's bunions, pick and choose from indistinguishably shabby dresses,

and finally purchase chipped pushchairs with wheels that have lost their tyres. On this slope on Saturday mornings the musty taint of poverty is in the air.[79]

In nearby Sunderland nine out of ten families in privately owned houses had no indoor toilet, three-quarters had no bath, and half did not even have *cold* running water.[80] Similarly, in Jarrow there were 'acres of slums, as frightful as anything else in the country, with doors from which the paint had long since peeled off, windows with odd panes missing and pieces of cardboard put in their place to keep out the wind'. The whole place, Moorhouse thought, looked 'as if Doomsday has already been and gone'.[81] It was not surprising that when Edward Heath drove through the area in February 1969 he remarked to a friend: 'If I lived here I wouldn't vote for Harold Wilson. And I wouldn't vote for myself, either.' Who, his friend asked, would he vote for? 'Robespierre,' Heath replied.[82] As for Michael Caine, he noted that he had 'seen poverty in different parts of the world that had made my own childhood look quite privileged, but I had never witnessed misery like this in my own country'.[83] Safely back in London, he told a Geordie friend: 'I've always gone on about this working-class image I've got and so on; but now I've been to Newcastle I realize I'm middle-class.'[84]

For many critics, Newcastle itself was the real star of *Get Carter*. In the words of the film historian Steve Chibnall, it is 'virtually a necropolis, a cheerless city of coffins and hearses where the locals are suspicious and hostile'. Hodges, he writes, 'uses the bleak industrial landscape of Tyneside to express an oppressive sense of dereliction and a poverty of the soul, contrasting the belching chimneys and grimy terraces with the tawdry glamour of the bingo and dance hall and the uncompromising concrete slabs that pass for redevelopment'.[85] Newcastle was particularly well suited to illustrate this 'poverty of the soul' because, in addition to being one of the most deprived cities in Britain, it was one of the most corrupt. The leader of the council, the Labour politician T. Dan Smith, ran the city as a personal fiefdom and was convinced that through ruthless redevelopment it could be turned into a North Sea rival to 'Venice, Athens, Florence and Rome'. His instrument was Wilfred Burns, a controversial town planning expert who epitomised the belief of many modernist planners that they knew, far better than ordinary people, what was good for them. Burns described the inhabitants of Newcastle's slums as 'almost a separate race of people', and freely admitted that forcing them into tower blocks would have 'a devastating effect' on their community. 'But, one might argue, this is a good thing when we are dealing with people who have no initiative and civic pride,' he insisted. 'The task, surely, is to break up such groupings, even though the people seem to be satisfied with their miserable environment.'[86]

Smith talked a great deal about turning Newcastle into 'the Brasilia of the North', a 'city free and beautiful' and the 'outstanding provincial city in the country'.[87] He did not mention, however, that he stood to gain from the modernist project. Smith happened to be the chairman of the Northern Economic Planning Council, a consultant for the Peterlee Development Corporation, a public relations consultant for the Crudens building company and a consultant for the famously corrupt architect John Poulson, who specialised in cheap modular housing and had contracts all over the North of England. Poulson made sure that Smith was financially rewarded at a rate of fifteen pounds per unit of local authority housing, which added up to hundreds of thousands of pounds, and after both men were imprisoned for corruption in the mid-1970s there were allegations that Smith had pocketed money from others, too.[88]

The corruption of Smith's Newcastle was the ideal background for the plot of *Get Carter*, which focuses on the web of connections between local businesses, gambling, crime and pornography. The chief embodiment of the evil at the city's heart is the gangland boss Cyril Kinnear, played with silky menace by the dramatist John Osborne. His business empire partly rests on the production of pornographic films, which he then supplies to gangsters in London, and Carter discovers that his own niece has been roped into appearing in them. 'The corruption of [Carter's niece] by pornographers', writes one critic, 'is also a metaphor for a much more general malaise affecting urban Britain at the end of the 1960s.' Mike Hodges explained that '*Carter* wasn't just about pornographic films – it extended to local councils and building controls, undercurrents which eventually proved true with T. Dan Smith and Poulson.'[89]

This wider corruption includes Carter himself, who is, after all, a gangster and a killer, and it ensures that the film has a downbeat, depressing tone. Carter takes his revenge in bloody fashion: he coldly plunges a knife into the neck of his old friend Albert; he throws the slot-machine magnate Brumby from the top of his own multi-storey car park; he brutally strips his late brother's mistress and injects her with a fatal dose of heroin; he forces whisky down the throat of his arch-enemy Eric before crushing his skull with a rifle-butt. The final scenes are suitably desolate, filmed on a windswept beach near the New Town of Peterlee, littered with rusting debris beneath the shadows of cable-cars carrying slag to be dumped in the North Sea. Hodges thought that it was 'a sort of graveyard', and fittingly it is here that Carter too meets his end. In the director's own words, which could easily describe the entire film, the denouement on the beach is 'a vision of hell'.[90]

Grim, gloomy and gritty, *Get Carter* was an altogether pessimistic epitaph for the 1960s, capturing both a particular mood and a striking sense of place: Newcastle, the embodiment of the 'other England'. A similar sense of place was evident in another film shot just a few weeks later, this time in the Thamesmead estate in South-East London. Like *Get Carter*, Stanley Kubrick's controversial adaptation of *A Clockwork Orange* used a particular location to stand as the physical incarnation of violence, degradation and despair. But whereas *Get Carter* had been set in a naturalistic working-class North where the old ways died hard, *A Clockwork Orange* presented the unfamiliar Britain of the near future, showing how the utopian hopes of the scientific revolution had curdled into the dystopia of the 1970s and beyond.

In May 1962 the young writer Anthony Burgess had published a short novel entitled *A Clockwork Orange*, which sold fewer than four thousand copies and attracted some pretty lukewarm reviews. Burgess claimed that it had been inspired by two incidents in his own life. The first, and more harrowing, was an attack on his pregnant wife in 1944 by four American servicemen, which caused her to lose the baby, prevented her from ever having children and drove her to the brink of suicide. The second was a trip that Burgess made to Leningrad in 1961, where he observed the phenomenon of *Stilyagi*, or 'Style Boys', disaffected young Russian hooligans whose aggression seemed rooted in their social and cultural exclusion. Together these incidents sharpened the novelist's interest in violence and the problem of evil, and he decided 'to create a kind of young hooligan who bestrode the Iron Curtain and spoke an argot compounded of the two most powerful political languages in the world – Anglo-American and Russian'.[91]

This was the genesis of Burgess's famous fifteen-year-old hero Alex, who lives in the violent post-apocalyptic society of an imaginary Britain in the 1970s and speaks in 'Nadsat', an invented street slang combining elements of English, Russian, Romany and Cockney rhyming slang:

> 'What's it going to be then, eh?'
>
> There was me, that is Alex, and my three droogs, that is Pete, Georgie, and Dim, Dim being really Dim, and we sat in the Korova Milkbar making up our rassoodocks what to do with the evening, a flip dark chill winter bastard though dry. The Korova Milkbar was a milk-plus mesto, and you may, O my brothers, have forgotten what these mestos were like, things changing so skorry these days and everybody very quick to forget, newspapers not being read much neither. Well, what they sold there was milk plus something else.[92]

In the decaying world of the early 1970s Alex spends his days listening to classical music, especially Beethoven, and indulging in 'ultra-violence' and 'the old in-out-in-out'. After a string of particularly brutal attacks he is sent to prison, where he becomes the subject of an experimental aversion therapy which makes him incapable of violence. However, one unanticipated side-effect is that he can no longer listen to his beloved 'Ludwig van', and neither can he defend himself when his old victims attack him. Embarrassed by the political furore, the government reverses his conditioning and Alex is free to enjoy 'the glorious Ninth of Ludwig van' again – as well as the violence and debauchery that had been denied him. In the final chapter, omitted from the film and the American edition of the novel, an older Alex renounces hooliganism in favour of the prospect of marriage and fatherhood, discovering, to his own disbelief, that he is 'growing up'.

Burgess later explained that the title of the book came from the Cockney phrase 'as queer [odd] as a clockwork orange', but he also admitted playing on the Malay word for a man, *orang*.[93] His point is that violence and evil are natural and necessary parts of the human condition: when Alex is conditioned, he is no longer free to choose between good and evil, and his humanity is therefore diminished. The state can punish him for choosing evil, but when scientists intervene to remove his free will, they destroy all that is good in Alex (his love of classical music) and reduce him to a mere mechanical man, or 'clockwork orange'.[94]

But to many readers, and especially to the audiences who flocked to Kubrick's film adaptation, what was really striking about *A Clockwork Orange* was its extremely convincing and pessimistic vision of the future. The Britain of *A Clockwork Orange* is a vision of modernity gone to the bad. Its inhabitants live in soulless concrete estates: Alex himself comes from Municipal Flatblock 18A, between Kingsley Avenue and Wilsonsway. In the newspaper he reads about 'ultra-violence and bank robberies and strikes and footballers making everybody paralytic with fright by threatening not to play next Saturday if they did not get higher wages . . . more space-trips and bigger stereo TV screens and offers of free packets of soapflakes in exchange for the labels on soup-tins'.[95] Outside, vicious hooligans and corrupt policemen fight for control of the streets; rape and violence are common; drugs are readily available; and the fabric of society itself seems to be tearing apart. A remote, ruthless government struggles to maintain order by brainwashing its criminals. When this fails it throws its dissidents and political opponents into prison.[96]

Stanley Kubrick filmed *A Clockwork Orange* over the winter of 1970 and 1971, which accounts for the grey, bleak look of the film, not unlike that of *Get Carter*. In search of the Britain of the future he took his crew to the new modernist housing estate at Thamesmead. This was a monument to the ambitions of post-war planning. It had been built on the Erith marshlands east of Woolwich, and the original plan, published in 1966, envisaged a bright new riverside community of some sixty thousand people. The site seemed an odd, even foolhardy choice, since the marshes had to be drained, the peat soil was less than ideal for supporting new buildings, and there was a risk of pollution from the nearby sewage works. However, the Greater London Council was fully committed to the scheme, and work began in January 1967. In accordance with the fashion of the day the new housing was built in clusters of concrete tower blocks arranged around an artificial lake and connected by elevated walkways, with car parks and garages hidden beneath the flats. The name of the estate was chosen after a competition in the capital's *Evening News*.[97]

However, the bad news very quickly outweighed the good. Although the first residents, the Gooch family, moved into their 'luxury, three-bedroomed maisonette' in June 1968, they remained the only inhabitants until 1969. More than ten thousand people joined them over the next few years, drawn by the GLC's optimistic publicity, but by the beginning of the seventies the critics were gathering. Like so many other developments of the period, Thamesmead appeared to have been constructed with little thought for the surrounding environment or the young families who lived there. Many of the flats had terrible trouble with leaks and condensation; parents complained about the lack of play areas for their children; and, as one resident put it, the smell of the sewage works was 'strong enough to peel paint at ten paces'. By 1974 only twelve thousand people had elected to move into

Thamesmead's tower blocks, even though there was space for thirty thousand, and there were rumours that it had become a dumping ground for difficult tenants from other boroughs. Like many other contemporary estates, Thamesmead fell victim to vandalism, petty crime and a general sense of alienation. It was the ideal setting for Kubrick's nightmarish vision of Britain in the future.[98]

The miserable fate that awaited Thamesmead was not much worse than that which awaited Kubrick's film itself. By 1971, when it finally went on general release, the controversies surrounding other violent and explicit films like *The Devils*, *Straw Dogs* and *Get Carter* meant that the newspapers were keen to pounce on anything that smacked of sex and violence. Although most reviewers recognised the film's artistic merits, the tabloid press treated it as little more than an incitement to rape and murder. 'If a couple of nuns were raped in Berwick-upon-Tweed,' Burgess mournfully recalled, 'I would always get a telephone call.'[99]

In 1973, when a teenager beat a tramp to death in Oxfordshire after seeing the film, the howls of protests finally convinced Kubrick to withdraw *A Clockwork Orange* from circulation, partly because he was worried about his own safety. It was not shown again in Britain for over a quarter of a century. But in a sense that hardly mattered, for if people wanted to see Burgess's nightmarish vision of Britain in the seventies and eighties, they needed only to look around.[100]

29

STREETS IN THE SKY

It's a dump. An absolute dump. I've come out of a dump into a super-dump.

Resident of Park Hill, Sheffield, interviewed c. 1967

CLENT: You know how efficient our civilisation is, thanks to the direction of the great world computer . . . On the land that was once used to grow the food we needed, we built up-to-date living units to house the ever-increasing population . . . So the amount of growing plants on the planet was reduced to an absolute minimum.
THE DOCTOR: No plants, no carbon dioxide.
CLENT: Then suddenly, one year, there was no spring.

'The Ice Warriors', *Doctor Who* (1967)

On the morning of 16 May 1968 Mrs Ivy Hodge, a fifty-six-year-old cake decorator, was up early in her little flat on the eighteenth floor of a new council tower block in Newham, East London. Just before six, she filled her kettle with water for a cup of tea, rested it on the hob of her cooker and lit the gas. At that moment, an almighty explosion ripped through the flat, blasting through the four flats above, tearing out her load-bearing walls and punching each living room down on top of the one below, all the way to the bottom floor. In just a few seconds, the entire corner section of the building was gone.

Incredibly, Ivy Hodge herself survived the gas explosion that devastated the Ronan Point block that morning. Since it was so early, most of the neighbouring families were in bed rather than in their living rooms, so only four people were killed. All the same, the explosion came as a spectacular and appalling shock. On the seventh floor James Chambers and his wife Beatrice, both in their sixties, were fast asleep when their 'bedroom wall fell away with a terrible ripping sound':

We found ourselves staring out over London. Our heads were only a matter of 2ft from the 80ft drop. The room filled with dust and showers of debris and furniture were plunging past us.

Suddenly we heard screams. I think it must have been someone falling with the debris. I grabbed my wife and we got out of the flat as soon as we could . . . I thought the whole place was going to collapse. The staircase of the building was crowded with people. We must be the luckiest couple in the block. I am really surprised we are alive.[1]

In Clever Road dozens of terrified families milled around in their pyjamas and dressing gowns. Above them clouds of dust drifted down from the scarred, shattered building, where, noted one reporter, 'dressing tables, electric fires, chairs and sofas were left perched on the remains of some of the floors'.[2]

At the time of the explosion the Ronan Point block had been open for less than two months. It was one of four council blocks in a two-million-pound slum clearance contract awarded by Newham council to the Taylor-Woodrow-Anglian building firm. More than 200 feet tall and containing 110 flats, it was a classic example of the 'system-built' high-rise blocks so popular in the fifties and sixties. Instead of being hand-built, brick by brick, like the houses of the past, it had been assembled from pre-fabricated concrete panels, hoisted into position by cranes and then bolted together. For many observers, Ronan Point was a symbol of the new possibilities of technology and engineering, offering the chance of a comfortable new life to hundreds of council tenants.[3]

The explosion on 16 May, however, deeply shook public confidence in this brave new world of high-rise living. Investigators found that the joints within the structure had been filled not with concrete but with rainsodden newspapers, and instead of resting on a solid bed of mortar, the walls were only supported by two levelling bolts per panel, which had led the load-bearing panels to crack under the strain.[4] Although the government immediately ordered the removal of gas installations from similar towers, public unease could not easily be assuaged.[5] 'Most of us are waiting to be rehoused, but we certainly do not want to go into these skyscraper flats,' said one Newham man. Another resident told interviewers that she had 'lost two friends in the disaster. My mind is made up – I'm not interested in moving into those flats.'[6] But when the residents of the Beckton ward demanded a meeting with local officials to discuss their opposition to high-rise housing, the area's Labour MP, council officials and councillors all refused to attend. Only one lonely Labour councillor turned up, spending the evening listening miserably to two hundred furious residents. Their efforts were useless: in the end they were all compelled to move into high-rise flats after all.[7]

For many observers at the end of the sixties, the tragedy of Ronan Point was a spectacular indictment of the utopian modernism that had inspired British city planning since the Second World War. Modernist principles dominated the major architectural schools, and almost every architect in the country took his lead from the Swiss pioneer Le Corbusier, unquestionably the most influential urban planner in the world. Famous for his faith in order and centralisation, Le Corbusier rejected what he saw as the bourgeois prejudices of the ordinary person. 'The design of cities', he once remarked, was 'too important to be left to the citizens'. Convinced that the new world of industry and urbanism needed a radical new approach, he argued that the house was 'a machine for living in', while, 'to save itself, every great city must rebuild its centre'.[8] Yet in Britain, as in much of Europe, Le Corbusier's ideas enjoyed enormous prestige. He was widely regarded as the prophet of a better society, who would sweep away the old city, with its haphazard eccentricities and festering slums, and replace it with an ordered landscape of towers, avenues and walkways.[9]

Modernism in planning went hand in hand with the so-called Brutalist movement in architecture, which was motivated by similar socialist political principles. Brutalist designers like Peter and Alison Smithson were fiercely critical of the nostalgic, almost dainty cosiness that they felt had inhibited British architecture for too long. Instead they preferred a more austere, aggressive style, with simple structures and clean surfaces, often exposing the framework of the building, and relying above all on the strength and simplicity of concrete. Brutalism was a supremely modern and self-confident movement, dismissing the legacy of the past and projecting a grandiose, egalitarian, scientific future.[10] Its most notorious exponent was the patrician Hungarian-born architect Ernö Goldfinger, who lived in an uncompromising concrete-framed cottage in Hampstead that he had designed himself, infuriating his wealthy neighbours. The novelist Ian Fleming took such exception to Goldfinger's home that he used his surname for one of James Bond's most evil adversaries. When Goldfinger consulted his lawyers Fleming threatened to rename the character 'Goldprick', and the case never came to court.

Goldfinger was a superbly villainous figurehead for the new architectural radicalism. A self-proclaimed Marxist, he nevertheless wore suits from Savile Row and handmade shoes from St James's, adopted an outstandingly arrogant and domineering manner and regularly dismissed assistants for being too light-hearted.[11] His most famous creations – the Department of Health offices at Elephant and Castle, the twenty-seven-storey Balfron Tower in Poplar and the Trellick Tower in North Kensington – were typical not only of the man but of the moment. To their admirers, they were radical, striking and progressive. To their detractors, they were concrete eyesores that ignored their surroundings and crushed the spirit of the individual. The conservative philosopher Roger Scruton, for example, commented that the forbidding concrete appearance of Trellick Tower revealed its architect's 'contemptuous conception of life's values'.[12]

Like the other architects of the day, Goldfinger benefited from social and economic circumstance as well as from the prevailing intellectual climate. From the late forties onwards, successive governments had embarked on an enormous public spending spree, not only clearing the old Victorian slums but pouring money into schools, hospitals and universities, New Towns, renovated city centres and the like. All of this, of course, meant more patronage and increased opportunities for young architects and designers. Instead of experimenting on paper, they could now turn their ideas into reality. The first major public building erected in Britain after the war, Basil Spence's new cathedral in Coventry, begun in 1956, was a sign of things to come. With contributions from the likes of Jacob Epstein and Graham Sutherland, it was a striking concrete and steel creation, breaking with tradition and shocking many older observers. When it was consecrated in 1962, Spence was bombarded with hundreds of abusive letters, but the crowds of tourists queuing to get in testified to its impact.[13] As Bernard Levin put it, the cathedral was 'a boundary-stone that marks the divide between one age and another'.[14]

Coventry Cathedral was just one of dozens of public buildings built during the late 1950s and 1960s that seemed to bear out Harold Wilson's vision of a New Britain of 'roaring progress' and 'scientific invention'. As in interior and industrial design, architects like Spence and Denys Lasdun often emphasised clean lines and geometric shapes, from the tubular telephone kiosks at Manchester airport to the vast cylindrical tower of Birmingham's

Rotunda, from the hexagonal blocks of the Sunderland Civic Centre to the cascading ziggurats of the University of East Anglia.[15] University buildings in particular captured the optimistic spirit of architectural modernism. Lasdun's dramatic and much-copied concrete terraces at UEA were matched by similarly striking buildings elsewhere, not least Spence's brick and concrete designs for the new University of Sussex and the system-built campuses at York and Essex.[16]

Modernism's ambitions, however, went well beyond a few new buildings on university campuses. During the fifties town planners had adopted a policy of 'gentle modernisation', accommodating modern traffic and commercial requirements while retaining the traditional features of the British town. By the early sixties, however, the vogue was for much more radical change.[17] Planners like Colin Buchanan, in his seminal report *Traffic in Towns* (1963), argued that, as the volume of traffic increased, British cities needed a profound reconstruction to cope with the pressure.[18] Buchanan thought that this represented a wonderful opportunity for planners and architects, suggesting that 'a vigorous programme of modernising our cities, conceived as a whole and carried on in the public eye, would touch a chord of pride in the British people and help to give them that economic and spiritual lift of which they stand in need'.[19]

Buchanan's recommendations tallied perfectly with the modernising spirit of the early sixties, and local planners were quick to take advantage. By the turn of the decade many town and city centres had become rather shabby and threadbare, congested with traffic and increasingly old-fashioned. For many local authorities, the obvious solution was to encourage private development, but the drawback was that the developers, motivated by profit, had little time for aesthetics or tradition. Vast office blocks, most notoriously the Centre Point building in London, were erected with scant consideration for their surrounding area. In Bristol a system-built concrete garage and office block were put up within a hundred yards of a seventeenth-century theatre and an eighteenth-century coaching inn. In Bath the historic Georgian core was overshadowed by a stunningly insensitive concrete megastructure that combined a hotel and a multi-storey car park.[20] Even when local authorities themselves took charge of redevelopment the emphasis remained the same. Conservative and Labour planners alike agreed that 'smart typists and skilled young workers will not put up with Victorian by-law streets any longer', and insisted that modernity must sweep away the relics of the past.[21]

By 1965 no fewer than five hundred different redevelopment schemes were under consideration across the country. Streets that had endured for centuries were dismissed as 'medieval cart tracks', while enormous motorways and flyovers were welcomed as 'an exciting new element' that would inject the right spirit of 'movement' and vitality.[22] In 1964 Geoffrey Moorhouse reported on the depressing situation in Gloucester, another historic cathedral city:

> It is almost as if they were desperately trying to suppress history here. A bleak row of shops has taken the place of St Michael's demolished nave in the city centre. Other towns may leave their redundant churches to moulder gracefully but here they pull them down . . . The same drastic surgery goes for secular buildings in Gloucester. Some of the remaining half-timbered houses in the city have been chopped down to make way for the redevelopment of the Westgate area alongside the cathedral. In Southgate Street a whole group of scheduled buildings is likely to meet the same fate to make room for high-density car-parking facilities. 'Obsolescent property' they call such buildings here and summon the bulldozers before anyone can contradict them.[23]

Other examples were not hard to find, from the ugly, congested redevelopment of the Elephant and Castle area in London to the glass, steel and aluminium vaults of the Brunel Centre in Swindon.[24] Some schemes were so grandiose that they never got off the ground, like Pilkington Glass's plan to construct a massive glass ceiling over eighty-three acres of Soho, on top of which would be built six enormous twenty-five-storey tower blocks, more than doubling the population of the West End.[25] Yet other Brutalist megastructures did make it off the page, like Patrick Hodgkinson's Brunswick Centre in Bloomsbury, which contained almost six hundred flats, shops, a supermarket, a cinema and an underground car park, all within one uncompromising tiered structure.[26] Perhaps the most controversial concrete monolith, however, was Owen Luder's Tricorn shopping centre in Portsmouth. Luder claimed that it was modelled on an Arab kasbah and called it his 'Market in the Sky', but most local people loathed it. Opening the building in 1966, even the Lord Mayor of Portsmouth described it as 'horrible'. After just ten years it was struggling to attract retailers, and in 2001 it was voted 'Britain's most hated building'. Three years later, bowing to local pressure, the government allowed it to be demolished.[27]

The most notorious case of insensitive town planning was the wholesale redevelopment of Birmingham city centre. Although Birmingham suffered extensive damage during the Second World War, it remained one of the finest Victorian cities in Europe. Local politicians were proud of its reputation as England's second city, and this explains why they threw themselves so enthusiastically into the task of modernisation. In 1957 work began on an inner ring road budgeted at £25 million, and this was followed by a major redevelopment of the city centre for a cool £40 million and the erection of a new Bull Ring centre for a further £5 million. 'Nowhere else in England', wrote the normally judicious Geoffrey Moorhouse, 'is there more excitement in the air.'

> No other major city has yet identified its problems, tackled them and made more progress towards solving them than Birmingham. Not even in London is there so much adventure in what is being done . . .
>
> Turn down New Street and at the bottom you walk straight out of the nineteenth century into the mid-twentieth. Or should it be the twenty-first? Better still, plod on into the Bull Ring, which at the moment is the centre of this transformation, and stand with your back to St Martin's church. Then look up. The sky is cut across by a great horizontal slab of concrete, embellished at one end with a fierce symbolic taurus in metal. This is the new Bull Ring market . . . Behind it and towering above it is a cylindrical office block, the Rotunda, all glass and concrete frame. No one ever thought of making one of those in England before . . . This is Birmingham moving forward.[28]

Just a few years later Birmingham's profusion of concrete towers, ramps and flyovers, its grim, rain-swept concrete market and its choked, bewildering rings of dual carriageways, would seem horribly misguided. One journalist who grew up nearby wrote that being surrounded by concrete Brutalism was 'like having a depressive but not totally unlovable older brother who was always there – inert, sullen and communicating only a barely scrutable sarcasm'.[29] Yet in 1964 the relatively conservative Moorhouse praised its 'forward movement' and predicted that the Bull Ring and Rotunda would 'show up' the skyscrapers and 'cigar boxes' of London. Birmingham, he said, needed only to demolish the Victorian slums at the fringes of the city centre, then it could 'start talking about itself with justification as the most go-ahead city in Europe'.[30]

*

Birmingham was not the only city that drew Geoffrey Moorhouse's praise during his travels. In South Yorkshire, too, he was impressed by the audacity of the planners. 'As you look down on Sheffield now from the Pennine rim,' he wrote, 'you see new towering blocks standing like beacons upon the small peaks of the city, escarpments of masonry following the contours around the bowl of land.' In particular, he was much taken by 'the enormous cliff-dwelling at Park Hill . . . Here each level has been provided with a sort of street in mid air, with the front doors opening on to it, where children can play and their parents are thrown together as much as they were along the old terrace streets on the ground.'[31]

Park Hill was one of the iconic new housing projects of the sixties, a spectacular demonstration of the power of modern architecture to transform the everyday environment. It was built between 1957 and 1961 by the architects Jack Lynn and Ivor Smith, and was designed to house families from Sheffield's Victorian slums. According to Roy Hattersley, the chairman of the Housing Committee while Park Hill was being built, the model was Le Corbusier's Unité d'Habitation in Marseille, a vast housing megastructure generally regarded as the peak of post-war utopianism.[32] Park Hill was arguably even more striking, looming, said *The Times*, 'like the curtain wall of a grim Welsh castle' above the city.[33] In an attempt to stave off the alienation associated with high-rise buildings, Lynn and Smith had come up with the concept of 'streets in the sky': broad stone decks and walkways stretching the entire length of the thirteen-storey complex. Most front doors opened directly on to the deck, which was also wide enough to accommodate milk floats every morning. The point, as Moorhouse noted, was to recapture the intimate feel of the 'old terrace streets' that had been destroyed along with the slums.[34]

Although critics of the high-rise buildings of the sixties often seem to think that they were put up out of sheer arrogance and spite, the planners who constructed them believed, often with good reason, that they were offering people a far better life than that they had known in the slums.[35] In the late forties and early fifties the Labour and Conservative governments had been keen to move people out of tenements and into purpose-built housing estates, generally made up of cheap cottages in a fairly traditional style.[36] During the Macmillan years, however, the government seemed to lose interest, and by the time Wilson took office the pressure to put more money into public housing had become irresistible. Cities like Birmingham, Liverpool and Glasgow were badly overcrowded already: in Glasgow 48,000 families were living at more than two people per room. Thanks to the bulge in the birth rate and the phenomenon of mass immigration from overseas, most experts expected a large population increase during the next couple of decades, and clearly people would need somewhere to live.[37]

During the 1964 election Labour promised more investment in public housing, and public housing approvals and slum clearance programmes shot up during the mid-sixties.[38] In just two years, the number of new council houses built per year rose from 119,000 to 142,000, while during the 1966 campaign Wilson and his Housing Minister, Dick Crossman, promised to build half a million houses a year by 1970. In fact they fell well short: housing completions peaked at 368,000 a year in 1967 and then fell after the devaluation of the pound. Furthermore, most of these were in the private sector, and council-house building under Wilson never reached the heights of the early fifties.[39]

The new houses of the Wilson era were infamous, however, because so many of them were located in huge high-rise tower blocks. These buildings had first become fashionable in the mid-fifties, when the Conservative government saw them as a cheap and spectacular alternative to housing estates and started paying higher subsidies for taller blocks.[40] The high-rise principle also owed much to the influence of Le Corbusier and his disciples, who dominated the Royal Institute of British Architects and determined the editorial policy of the *Architectural Review*, the country's foremost journal on the subject.[41] Then there was the more general vogue for all things technological, which meant that politicians, commentators and even ordinary voters regarded high-rise buildings as progressive and optimistic. Potential problems with materials like concrete and glass, or with the design of the new buildings, were dismissed out of hand: the assumption was that technology held all the answers.[42]

Perhaps even more important, however, was the widespread horror at the disappearance of green fields beneath more and more housing estates. One of the benefits of high-rise buildings, rarely acknowledged by their critics, is that they helped to curtail urban sprawl and to protect the countryside from further encroachment. Many progressive-minded planners were desperate to halt the advance of what they called 'subtopia', and high-rise buildings within the cities seemed the obvious answer.[43] What was more, most suburban and rural voters disliked the growth of New Towns and housing estates and wanted to protect the integrity of the countryside.[44] The Birmingham press, for example, regularly demanded action to stop the city's growth and preserve the green belt around it. The *Evening Dispatch* called for 'really high building . . . tall towers 20, 30 or 40 storeys high to release more space for sweeping parklands in the new Birmingham', while the *Birmingham Gazette* thundered: 'OCTOPUS – Where will it all end – this creeping rash that is pushing the countryside further and further from our doors? While there's still time – stop it!'[45]

The other crucial factor was the pressure from construction firms themselves. Such was the demand for new buildings, as well as the limited labour and capital resources, that firms could effectively dictate to and extract concessions from politicians and officials.[46] 'I always had a particular feeling', said one Labour planning committee chairman, 'that I mustn't antagonise Big Business.'[47] Just seven companies – Wimpy, Concrete, Laing, Wates, Taylor Woodrow, Camus and Crudens – dominated the market and set the agenda, and they presented themselves as public servants rather than profit-makers.[48] They worked hard to cultivate local politicians. Birmingham's chief architect remembered one occasion when Harry Watton, the Labour council leader known as 'Little Caesar', went with his officials to see the opening of a new system-built block in Kidderminster:

> To get to the block we passed through a marquee which was rolling in whisky, brandy and so on, so by the time they got to the block they thought it was marvellous – they wanted to change over the whole [housing] programme [to tower blocks]. As we were leaving Harry Watton suddenly said: 'Right! We'll take five blocks' – just as if he was buying bags of sweets. 'We'll have five of them and stick them on X' – some site he'd remembered we were just starting on.[49]

Sometimes this largesse crossed the line into naked corruption. While T. Dan Smith was pocketing back-handers from John Poulson, Alan Maudsley, Birmingham's chief architect between 1966 and 1973, reached an arrangement with the local firm Ebury and Sharp, appointing them to carry out work for the city in return for lavish bribes. Maudsley and Sharp played golf together, drank at their local Conservative club, and were well known to be in cahoots: if anything, their association was so blatant that it was astonishing they were not discovered sooner.[50]

By the early seventies Britain boasted a total of almost 440,000 high-rise flats, radically redrawing the look of countless towns and cities across the country.[51] Greater London accounted for almost half of all the high-rise buildings in England and Wales, with 9400 flats in Southwark, 8600 in Westminster and 8300 in Islington. Outside the capital, the great old Victorian cities led the way. Birmingham, where tower blocks were unusually popular, boasted some 24,000 flats, Liverpool had 19,200 and Leeds 11,900. In each case high-rise flats accounted for a fifth of all the council properties in the city. Even smaller towns leapt aboard the bandwagon: in Wolverhampton, for example, the 3700 flats built during the sixties made an enormous impression on the skyline.[52] Any self-respecting industrial town, it seemed, needed its own concrete pillars glowering on the horizon, like 'staggering emblems of municipal decisiveness'.[53]

But the greatest exponents of high-rise living were to be found north of the border. Glasgow's planners had been converted to the virtues of system-built towers back in the early fifties, and massive slab blocks became the city's new trademark. Between 1961 and 1968, 75 per cent of Glasgow's new public housing consisted of high-rise flats, and the city's architects prided themselves on building bigger and taller blocks than anywhere else. On 28 October 1966 they unveiled their supreme achievement, the Red Road flats, costing more than nine million pounds and reaching thirty-one storeys high. At the time they were said to be the tallest flats in Europe.[54]

In 1967 the staff of the *Architectural Review* were planning a special issue on housing design. One of the assistants suggested that they should get some evidence of exactly what sort of homes ordinary people wanted. The journal's editor, Hubert de Cronin Hastings, a great fan of the new look, stared at him in astonishment. 'But we *know* what should be done!' he said dismissively.[55]

As it turned out, Hastings was quite wrong. All the evidence of dozens of surveys carried out in the sixties and seventies suggests that people resented having to live in a building that looked like a multi-storey car park, and they frequently compared tower blocks to schools, prisons and even concentration camps. By contrast, they much preferred smaller, lower buildings, decorated with bright, cheerful colours, surrounded by grass and trees, and built using traditional materials like wood and brick – precisely the kind of buildings, in fact, that modern architects dismissed as old-fashioned.[56] As the urban historian Peter Hall puts it, the basic problem was that the new order had been 'laid down on people without regard to their preferences, ways of life, or plain idiosyncrasies; laid down, further, by architects who – as the media delighted to discover — themselves invariably lived in charming Victorian villas'.[57]*

The tale of one particular estate illustrates the wider story. In 1961, hoping to rejuvenate a run-down area of West Ham, planners came up with a scheme to build two tall blocks to house a mixture of single people, couples and families. Work on the estate finished in the autumn of 1966, and the *Newham Recorder* captured the optimism with which locals greeted the new buildings. 'The 22 storey skyscrapers which form Barnwood Court are flanked on one side by dockland and on the other by factories,' the newspaper explained. 'The nearest shops are an eight-pence bus ride away and places of entertainment even further. But the residents of the airy, ultra-modern homes do not mind. They are determined to make it a little self-contained community and provide their own entertainment.'[58]

At the end of January 1968 the architects and councillors responsible for Barnwood Court were awarded a prize from the Civic Trust in recognition of their efforts. But by this time the mood had already turned sour, and the tenants' association greeted the news with derision. Many of the little shops at the base of the towers remained unoccupied; nearby roadworks had been abandoned without being finished; and going into the block entrances, said the chairman of the association, was 'like going into a prison yard'. Residents complained that the towers suffered from vandalism, with lift control panels being ripped off, pram sheds destroyed and doors kicked in. The windows in the community centre had been smashed by teenagers so many times that they had finally been replaced by sheets of corrugated iron, presenting an ugly and forbidding appearance. 'It can't go on like this,' the chairman told the press.[59]

But it did. In April 1968 BBC2's *Man Alive* series broadcast a documentary on the flats and the tenants' complaints, showing how the problems stemmed as much from the behaviour of the residents themselves, who had never adjusted to their new lives, as it did from the flaws of the buildings. For the next few years arguments continued to rage: in February 1969 there were complaints about the estate's electrical safety, while in March 1970 the council decided that the gas supply was too dangerous and converted the blocks to electricity. By this stage, less than four years after their grand opening, the flats already looked 'the worse for wear'. Residents even talked

---

*In fairness, though, it should be noted that Ernö Goldfinger moved into his Balfron Tower for two months to prove that it was perfectly habitable. Then he moved back to Hampstead.

darkly about ghosts in the basement, all of which added to the general atmosphere of frustration and despair. A decade later the estate was 'running to seed at an accelerating rate, with only a pub and a battered community centre by way of amenities'.[60] Finally, thirty years after it had been built, the experiment was abandoned, and the towers disappeared beneath the lavish Britannia Village redevelopment, a very different vision of urban renewal.

For many people the story of Barnwood Court was depressingly familiar. By the beginning of the 1970s newspapers were regularly carrying stories about the nightmarish experience of living in a tower block. A survey for the Department of the Environment in 1973 found that high-rise residents suffered more health problems since they were less inclined to go out and take exercise, while older women and young children often suffered from respiratory infections.[61] The elderly, the infirm and the disabled all lived in terror of the lifts breaking down, leaving them stranded with no access to shops and amenities. One woman in Sheffield who suffered from multiple sclerosis, for example, was forced to call the police when the lifts broke down so that they could carry her wheelchair up to the twelfth floor.[62] Six out of ten residents complained at the lack of a garden, more than three out of ten said they were ashamed of their building, and half said they would move, given the chance. This was hardly the brave new world of which the planners had dreamed. Above all, researchers found that most people would have greatly preferred to live in their own house, rather than a flat, which many people regarded as distinctly inferior and not really a home in the traditional sense.[63]

The biggest problems, however, afflicted families with children. In tower blocks children could no longer wander out into the yard, as they had done in the Victorian terraces, and were confronted by a row of blank doors rather than a bustling street of doorsteps and windows. Shut up inside a cramped flat, unable to play in the fresh air, they often became bored and irritated, creating more problems for their parents and neighbours.[64] To make matters worse, families with three or more children had a high priority on local authority housing lists, and most tower blocks therefore contained a disproportionate number of teenagers. Not surprisingly, high-rise blocks became synonymous with vandalism and juvenile delinquency: with few amenities and no access to green space, adolescents often genuinely had nothing better to do.[65]

If all this were not enough, the high-rise project suffered from serious structural and economic problems. Even grandiose modernist projects like the Brunswick Centre and Trellick Tower worked better on the page than in reality because their architects seemed not to have taken account of the weather. In Britain's climate, so much damper than the weather in Le Corbusier's Marseille, their sheer concrete walls rapidly became stained, growing lichen and even stalactites and suppurations.[66] Most tower blocks had been built quickly and on the cheap, and they were never given the funding, amenities or attention necessary to make them work.[67] Many had been so incompetently put together that the cost of maintenance and repairs soared beyond the planners' wildest imaginings.[68] On one Portsmouth estate workers found that water had leaked behind the concrete cladding panels, badly weakening the load-carrying floors and walls. To repair just two blocks cost the local authority a cool £1.5 million. And in a survey of sixty local authorities at the end of the seventies Sutherland Lyall found that they had been forced to put new cladding on blocks that were barely a decade old, repair structural cracks in towers that were barely five years old, and, almost everywhere, repair leaking walls and roofs – all of which cost at least £200 million.[69]

In October 1965, in 'sheets of rain' and 'driving wind', Richard Crossman arrived in Wigan to open a new housing block. 'It was an enormous cube of flats of very poor quality,' he wrote gloomily. 'The houses are of an appalling dimness and dullness, and I am afraid that they have built a Wigan that in 2000 will look just as bad as the old 1880 Wigan looks in the eyes of the 1960s.'[70]

Later that year John le Carré published *The Looking-Glass War*, a depressing tale of administrative incompetence, botched espionage and national decline. In one marvellously resonant scene two disillusioned officials go to break the news of an agent's death to his wife. To their surprise, the men find that she lives in a new tower block, a world very different from the fantasies of the James Bond films:

> They stood at the top of a rise. It was a wretched place. The road led downward into a line of dingy, eyeless houses; above them rose a single block of flats: Roxburgh Gardens. A string of lights shone on to the glazed tiles, dividing and re-dividing the whole structure into cells. It was a large building, very ugly in its way, the beginning of a new world, and at its feet lay the black rubble of the old: crumbling, oily houses, haunted by sad faces which moved through the rain like driftwood in a forgotten harbour.

Inside, the atmosphere is no better: 'a concrete entrance . . . a flight of rubberized steps . . . The air smelt of food and that liquid soap they give in railway lavatories. On the heavy stucco wall a hand-painted notice discouraged noise. Somewhere a wireless played.' In the agent's flat they find a 'pallid rag of a girl not above ten years old', left alone while her mother is at work. She takes a message and accepts a clumsy gift of ten shillings; then she closes the door, 'leaving them on that damned staircase with the wireless playing dreamy music'.[71]

By the late sixties more and more people were beginning to share le Carré's evident dissatisfaction at the 'new world' of architectural modernism. Brutalism and utopian modernity were no longer in fashion; instead, designers were glorying in nostalgia. The vernacular tradition, which had always retained its popularity with the general public, was now respectable again, and conservation had become the vogue. Magazines like *Design* urged architects to show more consideration for the environmental ramifications of their work. Rather than rushing to clear their Victorian slums, local authorities were becoming interested in preserving and renovating them, while planners were beginning to think about the virtues of the individual and the eclectic.[72]

Some Brutalists held on to their concrete dreams: one contributor to *Architect and Building News* called for buildings 'to move further beyond the 30 or 40 storeys into the hundred storeys'.[73] But the tide had turned. The Ronan Point disaster had alienated public opinion, but the decisive factor was probably the devaluation of the pound at the end of 1967 and the biting public spending cuts that followed. In August 1968 the Ministry of Housing announced that it intended to discourage the building of more tower blocks. Angrily denying that people disliked his buildings, an agitated Ernö Goldfinger told the press that he was 'appalled' by their 'ridiculous attitude that will put us back 30 years'.[74] His protests were in vain, and by the early seventies the high-rise experiment had been abandoned.[75]

The modernisation of the British landscape did not go unchallenged, even in the sixties. The literary critic F. R. Leavis, for example, was one of the first public figures to complain about the demolition of the Victorian streets of the East End and the destruction of much of Dickens's London.[76] Viscount Esher, the president of the Royal Institute of Architects, consistently argued for conservation as a counter-weight to modernist idealism, and his efforts to preserve York's medieval centre endured as a model of common sense and sensitivity.[77] And Ian Nairn, probably the best architectural writer of his generation, regularly flayed the excesses of urban redevelopment and asserted that 'every time that somebody hurts a landscape or a townscape he is being loveless and stupid and arrogant'.[78] In February 1966 he issued the first major challenge to the redevelopers in an *Observer* article headlined 'Stop the Architects Now'. 'The outstanding and appalling fact about modern British architecture', he insisted, 'is that it is just not good enough. It is not standing up to use or climate, either in single buildings or the whole environment.'[79]

The most famous critic of the architectural new wave, however, was a poet. It is hard to overstate John Betjeman's popularity during the fifties and sixties: a reassuring, even cuddly figure, he wrote brisk, witty poems that ordinary people could enjoy, and his *Collected Poems* (1958) sold a staggering 100,000 copies, elevating him to a level of popularity unprecedented since Kipling's day. He had first published on architecture before the war, and was well known as a champion of the Victorians, a furious critic of reckless modernity, and an outspoken voice of common sense. In 1948 his poem 'The Town Clerk's Vision' presented a prescient vision of the future, all 'glass and polished steel', with Devon and Cornwall renamed South-West Areas One and Two:

> Hamlets which fail to pass the planners' test
> Will be demolished. We'll rebuild the rest
> To look like Welwyn mixed with Middle West.
> All fields we'll turn to sports grounds, lit at night
> From concrete standards by fluorescent light:
> And all over the land, instead of trees,
> Clean poles and wire will whisper in the breeze.[80]

In subsequent years plenty of Betjeman's poems poured scorn on the idealistic ambitions of the 'age of progress'.[81] Perhaps his most scathing indictment of modernisation came in 'Inexpensive Progress', published in 1966:

> Let no provincial High Street
> Which might be your or my street
> Look as it used to do,
> But let the chain stores place here

> Their miles of black glass facia
> And traffic thunder through.
> And if there is some scenery,
> Some unpretentious greenery,
> Surviving anywhere,
> It does not need protecting
> For soon we'll be erecting
> A Power Station there.
> When all our roads are lighted
> By concrete monsters sited
> Like gallows overhead,
> Bathed in the yellow vomit
> Each monster belches from it,
> We'll know that we are dead.[82]

But Betjeman did not confine his protests to his collections: he delivered regular homilies on the BBC, wrote for newspapers and magazines, and organised campaigns to save notable Victorian buildings. When developers threatened to demolish St Pancras Station, probably the finest example of nineteenth-century Gothic architecture in the world, Betjeman placed himself at the head of the campaign to save it, and it was his voice that carried most influence with the general public.[83]

Betjeman's horror at the advance of progress was echoed by innumerable other writers and artists. Fears of technological idealism had always been present in British popular culture, but they gathered momentum from the mid-sixties onwards. The thalidomide scandal of 1961–2, when it turned out that the sedative given to pregnant women was responsible for hundreds of deformed babies, came as a great shock to people who liked to trust their scientists, but perhaps the decisive event was the *Torrey Canyon* disaster in March 1967.[84] The *Torrey Canyon* was the world's first supertanker, an enormous 120,000-tonne ship which ran aground off the Scilly Isles, spilling thousands of tonnes of crude oil into the sea. Over a hundred miles of the English coastline were contaminated and fifteen thousand seabirds killed, and for many people the disaster served as a warning of the perils of progress.[85] Even Tony Benn recorded that there had 'never been a monster accident like it and it began to make people wonder more publicly about technology and mergers and economic growth'.[86]

In the wake of the *Torrey Canyon* disaster, the devaluation of the pound, the bombing of Vietnam and the Ronan Point explosion, technology and modernisation suddenly looked distinctly unfashionable. Even plastic, now seen as 'the symbol of sterility and capitalist degeneration', had lost its charms.[87] In February 1970 the BBC began showing *Doomwatch*, a thriller series devised by Gerry Davis and Kit Pedler, the creators of the Cybermen in *Doctor Who*. The plot followed the Department for the Observation and Measurement of Science, a government agency established to protect the nation from the abuses of progress, and *Doomwatch* was widely seen as the first 'green' television drama, attracting almost twelve million viewers. Among various dangers faced by its heroes were 'wonder drugs', toxic waste, nuclear weapons, man-made viruses, animal experimentation, genetic mutation and embryo research, all testifying to the prescience of the show's creators.[88]

Science fiction had been extremely popular since the fifties because its themes – discontent with contemporary society, national degeneration, the alienation of the individual and the final destruction of mankind – seemed to fit so well with the mood of the Cold War, the Atomic Age and the Space Race. Writers like John Wyndham, Brian Aldiss and John Christopher commanded large and loyal readerships addicted to stories of alien invasions, floods, famines and nuclear disasters.[89] And throughout the sixties more literary writers explored the dangers of technological idealism, painting elaborate dystopian portraits of Britain in the near future. In 1960, for example, L. P. Hartley published *Facial Justice*, the story of a bleak, egalitarian England after the Third World War. The post-holocaust weather is 'a uniform, perpetual March', in keeping with an authoritarian society where individuality and idiosyncrasy are suppressed by law. In Hartley's Britain the state enforces 'Economic Justice', 'Social Justice' and 'Facial Justice' – the latter involving plastic surgery to stop pretty girls getting ahead through their good looks.[90]

Anthony Burgess called *Facial Justice* 'a brilliant projection of tendencies already apparent in the post-war British welfare state', and it is likely that he drew inspiration from it when writing his two dystopian fables, *A Clockwork Orange* and *The Wanting Seed* (1962). Although the latter is much less well-known, it is arguably even darker as a depiction of the future. It describes a Britain where Greater London sprawls as far as Lowestoft, Bournemouth and even Birmingham. Migrants from the provinces 'had, it was said, no need to move; they merely had to wait'.[91] The country is now so overpopulated that the government enforces contraception by law and encourages infanticide. Ambitious young men are advised to become homosexuals to win preferment: 'It's Sapiens to be Homo' reads the message on a propaganda poster.[92] With so little space, citizens live in tiny flats in enormous tower blocks, tens or hundreds of storeys high. As the novel continues, the population pressure becomes so great that people are reduced to eating one another for sustenance, while the government organises a military campaign in the west of Ireland, directly modelled on the offensives of the Great War, to try to kill off as many people as possible. 'I cannot foresee the highly schematic world of *The Wanting Seed* as ever coming to birth,' Burgess wrote later, 'but I think some aspects of it . . . are already with us.'[93]

In Burgess's novels, as in those of other writers, from Harold Pinter and Ted Hughes to Iris Murdoch and Angela Carter, the pleasures of Swinging London and the bright hopes of the scientific revolution were notable by their absence. Instead of serving as metaphors for progress and idealism, New Towns and tower blocks instead signalled the onset of decline and dystopia.[94] The poet Roy Fisher's sequence *City* (1962) presents what one critic calls 'a Vorticist nightmare of disused and corroded industrial machinery, blank walls, shut factories and somnambulant semi-humans'. Fisher's city is Eliot's Waste Land made concrete; its inhabitants have been reduced to machines, while 'the gaping office block of night/Shudders into the deep sky overhead'.[95] It is not unlike the urban landscapes in the work of J. G. Ballard, whose novels *Crash* (1973), *Concrete Island* (1974) and *High Rise* (1975) revealed his fascination with the dehumanising consequences of the modern technological environment. In the dystopian *High Rise*, a tower block becomes a metaphor for society: the tenants divide themselves into classes depending on the location of their flats, fight for territory and control of the lifts and end up murdering and eating one another.[96]

But the most popular example of a writer whose work reflected the backlash against technological modernism was a very different character. As we have seen, J. R. R. Tolkien wrote *The Lord of the Rings* during the 1940s and 1950s, but enjoyed his greatest acclaim during the 1960s and 1970s. Like so many other writers, he disliked the advance of machinery, computers, science and commercialism. In *The Hobbit*, we discover that 'wheels and engines and explosions' always delighted the goblins, while in *The Two Towers*, the evil Saruman is described as having 'a mind of metal and wheels, and he does not care for growing things, except as far as they serve him for the moment'.[97] Similarly, in Tolkien's friend C. S. Lewis's fantasy *The Last Battle* (1956), the villains' plans for Narnia involve a new order of 'roads and big cities and schools and offices and whips and muzzles and saddles and cages and kennels and prisons': a modern, mechanical world, imposed on a pastoral utopia.[98] It was hardly surprising that both Tolkien and Lewis enjoyed their greatest commercial success and literary respectability at the end of the sixties, when science, technology and modernity itself were coming into question.[99]

Le Corbusier drowned in August 1965 after swimming in the sea off the French Riviera. He died too early to see his ideas repudiated and the modernist project falling into disrepute. Just a year later the journalist Barbara Ward published *Spaceship Earth*, which was destined to become the manifesto for a new movement. Ward asked her readers to imagine the planet as a tiny, delicate capsule, floating in space, and housing 'a single, vulnerable human community . . . The most rational way of seeing the human race today is to see it as the ship's crew of a single spaceship . . . This space voyage is totally precarious. We depend upon a little envelope of soil and a rather large envelope of atmosphere for life itself. And both can be contaminated and destroyed.'[100]

Spaceship Earth was superbly timed. In the United States Rachel Carson's investigative report into the horrific effects of chemical pollution, *Silent Spring* (1962), had already caused a considerable stir, and when the book was released in Britain a year later it was welcomed as 'a social study, eloquent, sincere – and alarming'.[101] As miles of fields and farmland disappeared beneath motorways, housing estates and tower blocks, people were beginning to question the post-war emphasis on economic growth and scientific progress. For some commentators, the nightmarish future predicted by Anthony Burgess in *The Wanting Seed* was too close for comfort. In 1964 demographic forecasts suggested that the British population would reach more than seventy-four million in 2001, putting more pressure on space and resources.[102]

After several weeks of correspondence in the *Observer* and *New Scientist*, a group of liberal activists decided to do something about it. On 17 March 1966 they announced the foundation of the Conservation Society, dedicated to fighting 'against the menace of decreasing standards of life due to population pressure . . . the threat to wildlife, interference with existing areas of unspoilt coastline, the spoiling of historic cities, pressure to apply chemical methods of food production and control before they are properly tested'.[103] The first effective environmentalist organisation in Britain, it was extremely conservative compared with those that came afterwards, but it nevertheless heralded the beginning of a new era. Eleven new journals dedicated to conservation and the environment were founded in the next few years, as well as more than a thousand different pressure groups and organisations. Even groups like the Ramblers' Association saw their membership double between 1965 and 1973.[104]

By the end of the sixties very few people were still talking about building a brave new world in glass and concrete. Politicians were rightly wary of the popular backlash against motorways, tower blocks and megastructures, while many architects and designers had become more interested in conservationism, revivalism and the burgeoning craft movement. Plastic and nylon were out; wood and wool were in. At the dawn of the seventies designers looked to the legacy of the past, not the possibilities of the future. The optimism of the modern movement, it seemed, had gone the way of the *Torrey Canyon* and Ronan Point.[105]

30

WILSON MUST GO

'I draw your attention to today's *Mirror*,' said the voice. 'I have spoken. Let the people tremble. My car is at the door, and I will take up residence later in the day at Number Ten. The eagles are flying high.' 'Is that you, Mr King?' I queried, recognising the speaker's Wykehamist tones and fleshy chuckle. 'Cut out the Mister,' replied the Press Lord, 'my destiny is accomplished. I am the seven-eyed Beast of the Apocalypse.'

'Mrs Wilson's Diary', *Private Eye*, 24 May 1968

Everybody sits in the armchair and says Harold Wilson did this and Harold Wilson did that . . . but it's our fault, not Harold Wilson's.

John Lennon, *New Musical Express*, 21 June 1969

With Roy Jenkins's first Budget in March 1968, there came a brief breathing space for Harold Wilson's exhausted ministers. They had stumbled through one of the worst six-month periods in modern political history, from the dock strike, devaluation and de Gaulle's veto to the South African arms debate, the gold crisis and the resignation of George Brown. Wilson himself had kept his cool amid the storm, and Jenkins wrote later that 'he had been very steady' when the economic news was at its worst.[1] But there was no disguising the fact that the government had suffered a collapse in popularity and prestige virtually unknown in living memory. In the local elections in May Labour lost control of Sheffield and Sunderland for the first time since the war, and were left with just four London boroughs out of thirty-two.[2] Only one in five people said that they would support the party at the next election. Asked if they were satisfied with the government's record, a pitiful 19 per cent replied in the affirmative, with a record 69 per cent pronouncing themselves dissatisfied. No government had been so widely disliked and despised since polling began.[3]

Wilson himself bore the brunt of the popular backlash against his government. Public satisfaction with his performance as Prime Minister had itself suffered a record collapse, from 69 per cent in May 1966 to a mere 27 per cent in May 1968. Even the wooden and widely mocked Edward Heath now led him in public esteem.[4] Among the public at large, it was increasingly common to view him as little more than a jumped-up charlatan who offered no hope for the future. The Conservatives regularly called him a 'cheat', a 'twister' or a 'fraud', because they knew that many voters, of whatever political persuasion, agreed.[5] The gimmicks and affectations that had once stood Wilson in such good stead, marking him out as modern and innovative, now looked hollow or even ludicrous, and even his awards to celebrities like the Beatles, David Frost and Violet Carson (*Coronation Street*'s Ena Sharples) drew as much ridicule as praise.[6] Within his own party many people genuinely hated him. The victories of 1964 and 1966 had brought a new generation of left-wingers into the parliamentary party who cared nothing about the old battles of the forties and fifties and were impatient for an aggressive programme of socialist transformation: to them, the Prime Minister was little more than a reactionary stooge.[7]

In intellectual circles, too, Wilson's name was mud. In 1968 the young journalist Paul Foot published *The Politics of Harold Wilson*, arguing that Wilson had 'reversed or abandoned' every single promise with which he had come into office:

> Racialist minorities in Southern Africa have been appeased. The American Government, with his support, have trebled their fire-power in Vietnam. Programmes for overseas aid, housing, hospital building, school building, a minimum incomes guarantee have been abandoned or slashed. Even the existing welfare services – free health prescriptions, free school milk in secondary schools, sick pay in the first week off work – have been trimmed, or threatened with trimming.[8]

Foot's analysis went down well with the so-called 'New Left' of radical young intellectuals. In the same year one group of writers and academics published a *May Day Manifesto*, attacking Wilson as the spokesman for 'a new capitalist consolidation' and the defender of 'the system of economic and social power'. The manifesto was drafted by the cultural theorist Raymond Williams and the historian E. P. Thompson, both Marxists, but their hopes that it would act as a rallying cry to a generation of students and activists came to nothing.[9]

Wilson himself was not really bothered by the criticism of a handful of intellectuals. He was, however, much more concerned about his treatment by the press. *Private Eye*, for example, had been attacking him relentlessly since the middle of 1966. When the fraudulent financier Emil Savundra came to trial in 1968 the *Eye* once again conflated his crimes with Wilson's performance as Prime Minister:

> Posing variously as an economist, a socialist, a pragmatist and a statesman, Wilsundra has conned, conned and conned again till the public has ceased to care. Never before has such a gigantic hoax been perpetrated by such a small man. But now his promises have come home to roost and you see him before you in the dock . . .
>
> To call this man a liar is to flatter him. Lying calls for a degree of subtlety and determination, qualities which are only too plainly lacking in the accused. You will be told by my ignorant friend that the accused is not in full possession of his faculties. My case will be that he has never had any faculties apart from the ability to deceive himself and others with fantasies, myths and the hopeless promises of fairy tale utopias.[10]

By this point the *Eye*'s treatment of Wilson was far from unusual. For five years the fashion had been to praise his modest tastes, quick wit and emphasis on modernisation; not any more. Journalists who had once written gushing articles about Wilson and the New Britain now allowed their admiration to curdle into contempt. There were no more chatty telephone calls and drinks parties; the lobby system of off-the-record briefings effectively collapsed, and Wilson took to confiding in a so-called 'White Commonwealth' of friendly reporters, which had the effect of further alienating all the rest.[11] Wilson and his allies often liked to think there was a press conspiracy against them, but as Ben Pimlott argues, 'it was simply a state of mind. The assumption that Wilson was weak, two-faced, morally corrupt – with hints of other, darker, forms of corruption – became so pervasive that it did not need a plot to back it up.'[12]

Wilson's colleagues often remarked on his unquenchable cheerfulness, but he had always taken his relationship with the press extremely seriously, and when the newspapers turned against him he became, in Barbara Castle's words, 'quite pathological' in his bitterness and hatred.[13] When Joe Haines, a new press secretary, joined his team in 1969 he found that Wilson was simply obsessed with his newspaper coverage. 'He devoured every word of the political columns,' Haines wrote later. 'He recalled every wound, every jibe, every inaccuracy which was ever penned against him. By the time I got in each morning, he had read every newspaper and would fire questions and judgements at me as soon as I sat down to talk.' Yet at the same time, 'his hatred of the press knew few bounds, perhaps because he loved it so much and had been jilted'.[14]

Television, and in particular the BBC, was not immune from Wilson's growing suspicions. As early as November 1965, he complained that the Corporation gave Labour fewer ministerial broadcasts than they had allowed Macmillan and Home, although he was made to look rather foolish when Heath pointed out that most of the last government's broadcasts had been 'exhortations to post early for Christmas'.[15] The definitive turning point, however, came during the 1966 campaign, when Wilson again asked the BBC to change the schedules on polling day. Hugh Carleton Greene refused to delay *The Man from UNCLE* as Wilson had requested, and in consequence the Prime Minister decided to teach the BBC 'a lesson they won't forget in a hurry' by refusing to give them a victory interview on the train back to London. The BBC had the last laugh, however. They arranged for Desmond Wilcox, who had just joined them from ITV, to meet Wilson on the Euston platform. Since Wilcox was not wearing his BBC badge, the Prime Minister allowed himself to be interviewed. When he found out the truth, of course, he was even angrier.[16]

In the years that followed Wilson became convinced that the BBC was out to get him.[17] In fact there was no evidence of genuine bias: the truth was that in 1963 Wilson had become used to extremely favourable treatment, and he took it hard when the Corporation insisted on reporting the bad as well as the good. On one occasion he even complained that the disc jockeys on Radio One read out 'news items with an anti-Labour slant' before embarking on what Crossman called 'an extraordinary outburst about the wicked political bias of the BBC compared with the honesty of commercial television'.[18] His solution was to appoint a man from independent television, the former Conservative minister Charles Hill, as the new BBC chairman in 1967, but unfortunately this scheme backfired when Hill 'went native' and refused to take his instructions from Downing Street.[19]

The low point came the following year, when Wilson threatened to sue the BBC, and Hill personally, for libel. He had been provoked by a joke on a comedy programme in April 1968, which ran as follows:

> You know how you can always tell when someone is lying – there are always unconscious bits of body language which give him away every

time he tells a whopper. It might be a nervous tic near his eye, or his hand may go up to touch his face, or a vein in his neck might stand out. But what's the tell-tale sign with Harold Wilson? What's the piece of body language to look for to tell if he's lying? [*Pause*] When you see his lips move.

Only after a tense summit with Hill did Wilson abandon his threat of legal action, but the bitterness lingered. At the end of 1969 Wilson summoned the chairman and Director General to Downing Street, where he complained of 'endemic bias' in the Corporation.[20] Nothing that Hill said could possibly appease him. In February 1970, for example, Tony Benn sat through another twenty-minute Wilson rant 'about the bias of the BBC against him personally; he remembered everything that had ever happened over the years. How badly he'd been treated by *Woman's Hour*, how Heath had been given more time on *Panorama*, etc.'[21]

This all added up to what his colleagues were beginning to call Wilson's 'paranoia', although in the circumstances, surrounded by intemperate critics and ambitious rivals, he had good reason to fear the knife in the dark. 'The trouble is that Harold is very paranoid and I think he is, in a sense, creating the very thing he is afraid of,' remarked Benn in April 1968, 'namely a plot against himself. He just lives in fear of the day when four senior Ministers will come to him and say they won't serve under his leadership.'[22] The principal target of the Prime Minister's suspicions, however, was Roy Jenkins, the man of the moment. At a Cabinet meeting in June Wilson's anxiety finally boiled over and he suddenly unleashed a furious rant about a recent string of ministerial indiscretions, ending with the ominous words:

> I know where a great part of the leaking and backbiting comes from. It arises from the ambitions of one member of the Cabinet to sit in my place. But I can tell him this: if he ever does sit in my place he will find that the difficulties which have been created by the present atmosphere in the Cabinet are such that life will be as intolerable for him as it is for me.

Everybody knew that he was talking about Jenkins, and the Chancellor insisted on staying behind to have it out with his accuser. Jenkins was entirely innocent of the leak in question, and told Wilson that 'personal relations had become intolerable because of his method of conducting business, and I had pretty well had enough of it'. Typically, Wilson's anger almost immediately melted away, and he wearily replied: 'Well you may find this an intolerable Cabinet to sit in, but I can tell you that you cannot be any more miserable about it, or find it any more intolerable, than I do to preside over it.'[23]

Later that day Wilson had a visit from Crossman, who bluntly told him that he had made 'a false accusation', which showed 'how ridiculous you are to expect a conspiracy'.

> 'I'm not wrong to expect a conspiracy,' he said, 'I've had them in the past. It just happens not to be so in this case but it's given me the opportunity to dress the Cabinet down.' 'No it hasn't, Harold,' I said. 'It's given you the opportunity to reveal once again to Cabinet your persecution mania and how obsessed you are by these suspicions of an inner conspiracy. Instead of assuming that it came from the Opposition you always assume it came from your closest friends.' 'Of course,' he said. 'Who else could it have come from?'

Nevertheless, when Wilson saw Jenkins again the following evening he apologised and promised to set the record straight. Mollified, the Chancellor accepted his apology, and then, for the first time, Wilson raised the question of the succession. 'He said that it would obviously be mine,' Jenkins recorded, 'and that he did not intend to stay too long as Prime Minister. We cemented the atmosphere with about twenty minutes' conversation on nineteenth-century railways, and then concluded the meeting.'[24]

Wilson had good reason to beware Jenkins and his allies. Until the end of 1967 he had successfully played off one 'crown prince' against another, but now Brown was gone and Callaghan was in the doldrums, so Jenkins stood alone as the likely successor. He was younger than Wilson, more urbane and sophisticated, a powerful figure in the Cabinet and an excellent speaker with an eager parliamentary following. Crossman called him 'the only possibility' to replace Wilson, and Jenkins himself wrote later that 'there was no alternative to Wilson in 1968 except for me'.[25] His strength in the government was such that when Wilson decided to ask Barbara Castle to reinvigorate the DEA, Jenkins smoothly vetoed it, telling Wilson 'that he was going to jolly well run the show on the economic side without a rival'.[26]

Like any genuine crown prince, Jenkins commanded the loyalty of a growing number of courtiers, some disaffected with the compromises of the old regime, others simply ambitious for preferment under a younger leader.[27] Jenkins himself described his supporters as 'a dedicated group of commandos, waiting as it were with their faces blackened for the opportunity to launch a Dieppe raid against the forces of opportunism [i.e., Wilson]'. Their leaders on the backbenches, Christopher Mayhew, Austen Albu and the recently sacked Patrick Gordon Walker, had even compiled lists of more than a hundred supporters in order to persuade the Chancellor to strike.[28] In addition, Jenkins had the active support of a group of junior ministers within the government itself, generally younger men on the right of the party like Jack Diamond, Dick Taverne and Bill Rodgers.[29]

By the beginning of May the huntsmen were beginning to scent blood. 'With a little luck we might be able to oust the Prime Minister in about June, July,' one of the conspirators, the young MP David Owen, wrote to his American girlfriend. 'It certainly will be difficult but something has to be done – there are signs that he is developing mild paranoia apart from everything else.' A week or so later he wrote again, explaining that 'there can be no doubt now that the Prime Minister must be removed'.[30]

On 27 May Gordon Walker told Jenkins that he had put together an elaborate system of 'dissident cells' on the backbenches, as well as a commanding 'inner group' of nine or ten MPs who would coordinate the revolt. The Chancellor, impressed almost despite himself, came up with a couple of names from within the Cabinet, including, interestingly, the ever-Machiavellian Crossman, who could always be counted on for duplicity of some kind.[31] On 17 June Gordon Walker called a meeting in Roy Hattersley's office where the chief plotters drew up a definitive list of 120 or so potential rebels. 'The Conspiracy is now in full swing,' Gordon Walker excitedly wrote in his diary, noting that even the chairman of the parliamentary labour party, Douglas Houghton, was 'wholly for removal of Harold and ready to act'. Both Gordon Walker and Houghton were for striking now; all they needed was the signal from Jenkins.

But the Chancellor hesitated. On 4 July he called Gordon Walker into his office and urged him to be careful. 'Roy Jenkins thought better not move now,' Gordon Walker noted. 'He wanted to be consulted and might advise against action – but otherwise, would leave it to us. He clearly did not want to be implicated in actually launching an action.' The momentum faltered; some of the conspirators agreed that it was better to wait than to move too soon; and two weeks later plans for a parliamentary coup were finally shelved until the autumn.[32]

The chance to strike for the premiership comes to very few men and very rarely, so when it does, it is best seized with both hands. Such a chance was unquestionably presented to Jenkins in the spring of 1968, but he did not take it. 'Wilson could have been toppled by Roy and Roy now knows it,' Rodgers remarked later.[33] Why, then, did Jenkins fail to move? His own explanation, given in his memoirs, was that his attention was monopolised at the crucial moment by the burdens of the Treasury; what was more, he always wondered whether he would enjoy being Prime Minister, and thought he lacked the ruthless, focused ambition necessary to seize the supreme political prize.[34] Of course, this is rather self-serving, and Jenkins's colleagues certainly thought that he was very ambitious indeed. 'He was never satisfied with second place in any field,' wrote Denis Healey; 'he always wanted to be top.'[35] David Marquand later argued that 'Roy was too ambitious, not insufficiently ambitious . . . He never thought it was the right moment; he always thought it was too risky.'[36] Jenkins knew that if he bid for the leadership and lost, then his career might suffer a terminal setback; so he waited. Revealingly, he once remarked to Healey: 'I will never be caught with a dagger in my hand unless it is already smoking with my enemy's blood.' He was so close to the premiership that he could almost reach out and touch it, but his fear of moving too soon and missing the prize that seemed certain to be his prevented him from taking the decisive step.[37]

One of Wilson's fiercest backbench critics was the eccentric Labour right-winger Desmond Donnelly, who regularly compared him with Neville Chamberlain and claimed that, thanks to his 'supine vacillation', Britain was sliding towards disaster.[38] In one slashing attack published in 1968 Donnelly even claimed that 'Wilson and his clique' did not care 'about Britain's interests, about pledges, about allies', but only about 'staying in their own little offices'. Wilson, he explained, was the British equivalent of the brilliant but unscrupulous Pierre Laval, who had served as the French Prime Minister in the pro-Nazi Vichy government.[39]

Donnelly was an obscure, unreliable figure with no following in the Commons or the country, so it was easy for Wilson to ignore his abuse. But in his fervent hatred Donnelly was certainly not alone. As Wilson's biographer puts it, by 1968 'a strange collective revulsion [had begun] to take effect . . . directed against the man whom rich and powerful people decided was the incubus of the nation's ills'. In City boardrooms and around Home Counties dining tables, where his tax increases were beginning to bite, Wilson was 'now regarded with a new and peculiarly virulent form of loathing'. He was not merely incompetent, this 'semi-seditious chatter' ran; he was a traitor, deliberately undermining the nation's economic and moral well-being at the behest of Moscow.[40]

The most sensational example of this kind of 'Wilson-must-go' talk was found on the fringes of the intelligence community and the extreme right, a twilight world of rumours and half-truths, where a small number of rogue MI5 officers got it into their heads that Wilson was a Soviet agent propelled into Downing Street in order to betray the Western alliance. This was an utterly preposterous story with no factual basis, but nevertheless the insinuations continued to swirl around Fleet Street, never quite surfacing in the press, but never quite going away either. In the early 1970s they became the basis for the so-called 'Wilson plot', cooked up by the MI5 officer Peter Wright, a handful of his friends and various deluded right-wing journalists and businessmen. This was a campaign of dirty tricks designed to undermine the Labour leader, but given that he managed to win two successive general elections in that time and left politics at a date of his choosing, the plot was an abject failure.[41]

What was far more worrying, as far as Wilson was concerned, was the talk of establishing a coalition government with someone else at the helm. This was an option regularly discussed in the City and on Fleet Street, reflecting contemporary fears that the country was heading for an economic crisis similar in scale to that of 1931, when the Labour government of Ramsay MacDonald had been replaced with a National Government. The editorial column of *The Times*, too, frequently pondered whether a coalition might be the answer to Britain's misfortunes.[42] Most of these imaginative scenarios involved a National Government of moderate Conservatives and Labour right-wingers, led by a centrist Prime Minister like Maudling, Jenkins or Healey. Jenkins himself told Healey in the autumn of 1968 that if sterling collapsed, 'Britain's only hope' lay in a partnership between Maudling and Healey, which would have been an intriguing alliance between two powerful intellects, one renowned for emollient indolence, the other for boisterous rudeness.[43] Another Cabinet colleague, the impressionable Tony Benn, was even more worried that 'the City could be planning a coup against the Government'.[44] But Benn was not necessarily being fanciful, for in February 1968 he had spent an uncomfortable lunch at the headquarters of the *Daily Mirror*, listening as the chairman of the IPC media group, Cecil King, explained his plans for 'a Coalition Government'.[45]

As a director of the Bank of England and the chairman of IPC and the

Reed Paper Group, Cecil King was one of the most impressive and influential newspapermen in the country. The International Publishing Company was the biggest publishing organisation in the world, controlling the *Daily Mirror*, the *Sunday Mirror*, the *People* and the *Sun*, as well as the *Daily Record* and the *Sunday Mail* in Scotland, and hundreds of magazines, journals and book divisions. The *Daily Mirror* building in Holborn, a giant, eighteen-storey glass tower, was the most extravagant newspaper headquarters in Europe.[46] King's suite was described by one observer as 'fit not merely for a King but an emperor': it was dominated by an eight-foot octagonal desk, flanked by two eighteenth-century Italian tables and surrounded by Persian carpets, Anatolian prayer mats and shelves of antique books. It even had its own coal fire, ventilated by a special chimney, and in many ways resembled the villain's inner sanctum in a particularly imaginative James Bond film. And every night, nine floors below, the basement presses thundered out five million copies of the *Mirror*, easily the biggest-selling daily newspaper in the country.[47]

Not for nothing did Cecil King see himself as one of the most powerful men in Britain. His uncle, Alfred Harmsworth, later Viscount Northcliffe, had founded the *Daily Mail* and the *Daily Mirror*, brought down the Asquith government, directed the official propaganda in the First World War and finally succumbed to megalomania after trying to run Lloyd George's government for him. Northcliffe's younger brother Harold, Viscount Rothermere, was not far behind, controlling the Associated Newspapers group, dabbling in right-wing politics in the inter-war years, and keeping up the family reputation for autocratic management and political interference.[48]

King grew up determined to emulate the great press barons who had established his family's reputation. A huge man, six foot four inches tall and weighing eighteen stones, he was also a rather peculiar one. He was deeply reserved and found human contact extremely difficult, but he was utterly obsessed by sex, even telling his first wife that he would like to sleep with at least a dozen women a year.[49] 'Greatness' was another of his obsessions, and he believed that society progressed through the ruthless imposition of order by great men, notably his uncles and, naturally, himself.[50] His prestige was based on his control of the *Daily Mirror*, which he ran in tandem with the paper's brilliant populist editor, Hugh Cudlipp. With an estimated fifteen million readers a day, the *Mirror* was simply the most important publication in the country. It had no obvious competitor for the working-class market, was closely associated with the Labour Party and had perfected a heady blend of 'bite-sized news, crime, sensationalism, astrology, sentiment, social conscience and sex'.[51] As Roy Jenkins later explained, 'it combined radical chic with immense popular success', and it was hard to exaggerate just how much the *Mirror* mattered to him and his colleagues.[52]

King had enthusiastically backed Labour in 1964, and even drove around London during the campaign with a red flag inscribed with the message 'Vote Labour' fluttering from the bonnet of his Rolls-Royce.[53] It did not take long, however, for the relationship to go sour. King was desperate for a hereditary peerage to match those given to Northcliffe and Rothermere, but what he really wanted was an earldom, so that he would outrank them. Wilson told him that he had decided to award no hereditary peerages, although King was welcome to a life barony if he wanted it. Outraged, King turned it down. A life barony for a great man like himself was an insult, and he privately wrote Wilson off as a mediocre trickster who would lead the country into 'a frightful mess' and simply had to go.[54]

Since Wilson and his Labour colleagues had no wish to antagonise the *Mirror*, they spent a great deal of effort trying to win round the furious press baron. But although the *Mirror* endorsed Labour again in 1966, King was not easily appeased. He had fallen under the influence of a second wife, the musician Ruth Railton, who appears to have been a spectacularly unpleasant woman, 'jealous, merciless, fiercely manipulative and an inveterate liar and fantasist'.[55] Most of his friends thought that King was never the same after he married her: he had always been an autocrat, but now, under Ruth's influence, he became even more arrogant and determined to flex his muscles in the world of politics. Hugh Cudlipp and his colleagues tried to restrain him, but by the mid-sixties they were aware that he was 'well on his way' to megalomania.[56] Ruth was not joking in 1964 when she rather incoherently wrote in her diary: 'We must have LEADERS. The world has never gone through such a difficult time. Europe could again be 72 years old – standing man to man to White House Moscow & China but the one man is CHK.'[57]

As early as June 1966 King had written to Wilson telling him that 'people are talking of a British de Gaulle or National Government', and urging him to purge his Cabinet and adopt a fiercely pro-European, anti-inflationary tack. As Cudlipp noted, this missive was received in Downing Street 'with the same enthusiasm with which a guest at an early sixteenth-century feast would accept a chocolate meringue from Lucrezia Borgia'.[58] King, however, was convinced that disaster beckoned unless he could assemble some sort of

National Government. For the next two years he spent much of his time 'ceaselessly expressing his misgivings to Wilson's own Cabinet Ministers, overtly encouraging disloyalty and disillusion among the Prime Minister's entourage, stopping short only of advocating open revolt'.[59]

By August 1967 King was recording that 'the whole world seems to be sliding downhill' and that economic collapse, anarchy and revolution were just around the corner.[60] With the mildly bemused Cudlipp, he spent Saturday mornings drafting his ideal administration, originally a 'National' or 'Coalition' government, but eventually, and more dramatically, an 'Emergency' one. The list of potential ministers, mostly businessmen and moderate politicians, was kept in the top-left-hand drawer of one of King's baroque tables.[61] Cudlipp later remembered that the only uncertainty was 'whether the new regime would send for Cecil Harmsworth King or King send for the new regime; what was certain was that the moment was near at hand'.[62]

Far from concocting his scheme in absolute secrecy, King operated with staggering indiscretion. In February 1967 he suggested to Roy Jenkins that they ought to have 'a National Government under some other name', but noted that Jenkins 'did not fancy the idea'.[63] In May he sent Edward Heath a private letter warning that 'if we are to save our democratic institutions something drastic will have to be done' and recommending a government with 'people from outside who do command public respect'.[64] King even asked Dick Crossman if he would be interested in serving as the figurehead for a coalition government, a highly inappropriate choice which indicated just how far his plans diverged from reality.[65] And in February 1968, dining with the *Mirror*'s Paris bureau staff, he told them that he expected Wilson to be replaced with a coalition Cabinet in which King himself would play a leading role. 'Timing is vital,' he explained. 'He has to go, but I have to time everything with great care.'[66]

When Benn came to have lunch with him that month, King was in expansive form. Wilson and Heath, he said, would be 'swept away' by the coming crisis, and Jenkins, too, would 'go down in the crash'. Callaghan was 'ruled out' because of devaluation. So Denis Healey, he thought, was the man to lead the 'emergency' coalition. As his visitor left, King added ominously: 'There may well be a larger part for you to play.' Benn was absolutely horrified, and thought that King must be 'slightly unbalanced', but noted that 'if it was true that this was being said in the City and to him, it was almost certain this was getting abroad and therefore the confidence problem was very serious ... The entire weight of IPC would be thrown against Wilson in favour of a coalition and probably in favour of Denis Healey as well.' That evening Benn rang Wilson and told him exactly what had happened. 'Harold was rather agitated and excited', he wrote, 'and said that Cecil King was mad – a view with which I would not really disagree'.[67]

Unlike most madmen who talk of toppling the government and rescuing the country from disaster, King controlled the world's biggest publishing company and the country's bestselling newspaper. At various times he had lunched privately with almost every senior minister in the Cabinet and his list of powerful contacts was second to none. At the beginning of May he decided that the time had come to act. His first and most extraordinary step was to arrange a meeting with the man whom he hoped would serve as the figurehead for his coup: Earl Mountbatten of Burma, the former Supreme Allied Commander in South-East Asia, the last Viceroy of India, and the former First Sea Lord and Chief of the Defence Staff. Ambitious, energetic and exceedingly vain, Mountbatten was the Queen's second cousin and Prince Philip's uncle, and could hardly have been better connected. He was also on friendly terms with Cudlipp, who had first sounded him out at King's request in July 1967.[68] In April 1968 they met again and Mountbatten did not immediately dismiss the *Mirror* editor's overtures. Like many men of his background, he was dismayed by the government's performance under Harold Wilson and wanted to see Britain great again. Indeed, he told Cudlipp that he had been thinking along similar lines:

> Important people, leaders of industry and others, approach me increasingly saying something must be done. Of course, I agree that we can't go on like this. But I am 67, and I'm a relative of the Queen: my usefulness is limited: this is a job for younger men, and obviously talent and administrative ability which does not exist in Parliament must be harnessed.

Mountbatten suggested that Barbara Castle, whom he greatly admired, should be approached to rally the nation in this dark hour. Cudlipp thought that this was a ridiculous idea and explained that Castle would simply tell Wilson all about their plans. Instead, he explained, King was 'thinking along the lines of an Emergency Administration or Emergency Government' led by Denis Healey. Mountbatten then thought of some more names of his own. How about Lord Beeching, he suggested; perhaps a few senior civil servants; a handful of businessmen; and some respected politicians like Jenkins, Maudling and Sir Alec Douglas-Home? This was precisely what Cudlipp had wanted to hear, and so they agreed to talk again:

> Mountbatten suggested a 'private meeting of some sort: what did I think?'
> H. C. 'I think it is important you take no personal initiative of any sort. You should wait until you are approached.'
> M. 'I certainly don't want to appear to be advocating or supporting any notion of a Right Wing dictatorship – or any nonsense of that sort. But like some other people I am deeply concerned about the future of their country.'[69]

On 8 May Cudlipp and King drove out to Mountbatten's country house, Broadlands, for the great meeting. A fourth man, Mountbatten's close friend Sir Solly Zuckerman, the government's chief scientific adviser, was due to join them a little later.[70] King opened with his usual gloomy prediction that 'the Government would disintegrate, there would be bloodshed in the streets, the armed forces would be involved . . . People would be looking to somebody like Lord Mountbatten as the titular head of a new administration, somebody renowned as a leader of men who would be capable, backed by the best brains and administrators in the land, to restore public confidence.'[71] Mountbatten, as before, was intrigued, but hesitated to commit himself. King recorded his reply:

> Mountbatten said that he had been lunching at the Horse Guards and that morale in the armed forces had never been so low. He said that the Queen was receiving an unprecedented number of petitions, all of which have to be passed on to the Home Office. According to Dickie, she is desperately worried over the whole situation. He is obviously close to her and she is spending this weekend at Broadlands. He asked if I thought there was anything he should do. My theme was that there was a stage in the future when the Crown would have to intervene: there might be a stage when the armed forces were important. Dickie should keep himself out of public view so as to have clean hands if either emergency should arise in the future.[72]

By this time Zuckerman had turned up, and since he had a better grasp of political reality than either Mountbatten or King, he reacted with horror. 'This is rank treachery,' he exclaimed. 'All this talk of machine guns at street corners is appalling. I am a public servant and will have nothing further to do with it. Nor should you, Dickie.' Then he walked out.[73]

In the stunned silence that followed Mountbatten evidently came to his senses, telling his visitors that Zuckerman was right and the scheme was 'simply not on'. King and Cudlipp were shown out a few moments later. That night Mountbatten recorded that he had been listening to a lot of 'dangerous nonsense', and when he encountered Zuckerman the following day he remarked 'that he greatly regretted that he had ever consented to the meeting'. A month later he saw Cudlipp again and told him that he had reported the entire conversation to the Queen.[74]

King brushed off the loss of his figurehead as though it had never happened. The very next day, preparing for the inevitable crisis, he sent his resignation to the Court of the Bank of England and instructed Cudlipp to prepare the IPC newspapers for the day of reckoning. That night the results of the local elections came through: more horrendous news for Labour. But when the readers of the *Mirror*, the *Sun* and the *Daily Record* awoke the following morning, Friday, 10 May, they found that the front page of their newspapers carried the photograph not of a crestfallen Wilson but of a determined King, illustrating an apocalyptic editorial that the IPC chairman had written himself:

ENOUGH IS ENOUGH

By Cecil H. King
Chairman of the International
Publishing Corporation

The results of the local elections are fully confirming the verdicts of the opinion polls and of the Dudley by-election.

Mr Wilson and his Government have lost all credibility: all authority.

The Government which was voted into office with so much goodwill only three and a half years ago has revealed itself as lacking in foresight, in administrative ability, in political sensitivity, and in integrity. Mr Wilson seems to be a brilliant Parliamentary tactician and nothing more . . .

We can now look back nearly twenty-five years to the

end of the war and see that this country under both Tory and Labour administrations has not made the recovery or the progress made by others, notably the defeated Japanese, Germans and Italians.

We have suffered from a lack of leadership and from an unwillingness by successive Prime Ministers to make any serious attempt to mobilise the talent that is available in this once great country of ours . . .

We are now threatened by the greatest financial crisis in our history. It is not to be removed by lies about our reserves, but only by a fresh start under a fresh leader.

It is up to the Parliamentary Labour Party to give us that leader – and soon.[75]

The first that anyone outside the *Mirror* knew of King's broadside had been at midnight, when news of the editorial was announced on the special television bulletins covering the local elections. Alastair Burnet, the editor of *The Economist*, explained to the watching audience that 'perhaps the biggest loss which Mr Wilson, at any rate, has sustained tonight is the loss of the *Daily Mirror* and Mr Cecil King'.[76] The following morning, however, Wilson shrugged off the attack. 'It's a free country, it's a free press, long may it remain so,' he told reporters. 'I hope that newspaper proprietors will always be as free to find as much space in their newspapers.'[77] Most Labour MPs, who naturally disliked being lectured by a press baron, rallied to their leader, and even King himself noted that the other newspapers were 'pretty hostile'. His reference to 'lies about our reserves' was particularly controversial: sterling suffered a steep fall as foreign investors reacted to the news.[78]

In the days that followed it became embarrassingly clear that King's attack had backfired. Northcliffe had tried and failed to dominate Lloyd George; a decade later Rothermere had tried and failed to topple Stanley Baldwin. Now King appeared to be following in their footsteps. That weekend almost every newspaper except those in the IPC stable devoted acres of column inches to the story, and none of them could find a good word for King. *The Times* commented that his 'diatribe' [was] more likely to close the ranks of Labour MPs behind the Prime Minister'; the *Observer* thought that Wilson looked 'a straightforward character by the side of the devious Mr King'; while the *Sunday Express* called King a 'fool' and an 'ass' who 'babbled, and said nothing coherent because he didn't know anything'. Most observers agreed that King was suffering from 'a hereditary family condition'.[79] The cover of the next issue of *Private Eye* even carried a statement by 'Cecil Harmsworth Gnome', illustrated with a picture of Napoleon. 'A new Prime Minister is needed to lead the nation on the road to recovery' read a caption parodying King's message to the nation. 'It is not for me, a mere lunatic, to suggest who that man should be. Suffice it to say he should be none other than myself.'[80]

The scornful press reaction to the *Mirror*'s editorial ensured that it was a disaster not for Wilson, but for King. Instead of preparing the ground for a dramatic constitutional coup, he had, in Crossman's words, 'provided the positive factor required for rebuilding Harold's reputation'.[81] At the same time he had thoroughly horrified the journalists of the IPC group, who prided themselves on their close relationship with the government and were terrified that Labour voters might now desert the *Mirror*. King's fellow directors were already seriously worried about his commitment to their newspapers, and his autocratic manner went down badly with younger colleagues. His attack on Wilson offered them the perfect excuse for bringing his reign to an end.[82]

Early on the morning of 30 May King was summarily dismissed as chairman of IPC and replaced, ironically, with Hugh Cudlipp.[83] With typical egotism, King telephoned the BBC and ITN himself to break the news and arrange an unrepentant appearance on the evening bulletins.[84] 'I was stabbed in the back for my views,' he insisted to the *Sunday Express*, 'but I will not retract a single one. Harold Wilson is leading this country into a financial crisis and he must go. I was fired because I wrote that, but what I said will come true, mark my words.'[85]

Although King's machinations had come to nothing and Jenkins's conspirators had sheathed their daggers, the government's position remained extremely precarious. In July the Chancellor was forced to call for another £300 million in public spending cuts, reducing Benn almost to tears at the thought of losing £3 million from his MinTech budget.[86] Still the pound teetered on the brink; almost every month there seemed to be another sterling crisis. In October a poor set of trade figures heaped fresh pressure on the currency. Part of the problem was that the West German Deutschmark was clearly undervalued, and Wilson and Jenkins became involved in an almighty row with their counterparts in Bonn, who refused to consider revaluing it. On 22 November Jenkins was forced to introduce yet another austerity package, including higher duties on petrol, cigarettes and spirits, increased purchase tax, hire-purchase controls and 'import deposits', a scheme whereby importers had to deposit with the government a sum equal to half the value of whatever they wanted to import. The result of all this was that, although the pound was saved, the domestic economy sank further into the doldrums, and gloom continued to envelop Wilson's ministers.[87]

This febrile atmosphere was well illustrated by an incident on 5 December, when the City was unaccountably swept by rumours that first Jenkins and then Wilson had resigned. Before the two men could issue their denials, the markets were thrown into a panic and a cool $100 million disappeared in the ensuing struggle to prop up the pound. Jenkins spent the weekend pursued by the press across the North of England, where he was on a brief speaking tour, but since he had not resigned he had nothing to tell them. The markets, however, remained exceedingly jittery. Four days later, during a Cabinet meeting, Jenkins heard that another $100 million had been lost in forty minutes and that sterling was 'very near to disaster'. By the time that he had got over to the Treasury the losses had reached $200 million and he discovered they had 'practically nothing left'. But then, while the Chancellor was nervously having lunch, the market 'in some mysterious way' picked up and the rate dramatically improved.[88] In such circumstances it was hardly surprising that Jenkins keenly welcomed the end of the year. More than £1400 million had been spent in 1968 to keep sterling afloat; as Jenkins well knew, the government could not survive another year like it.[89]

Throughout all this time the public mood remained fiercely anti-Labour. Edward Heath and the Conservative Party had spent much of 1968 arguing among themselves about immigration, as we will see, but nonetheless they remained comfortably ahead in the opinion polls. After the December sterling crisis Labour sank even further behind: Gallup polls taken at the end of the year put the Conservatives more than 25 per cent clear.[90] By now, ordinary voters were clearly tired of the government's promises that things were bound to improve. Asked how they had been affected by four years of Wilson's government, almost half of the sample thought that they were 'worse off'.[91] Only 28 per cent were satisfied with Wilson's performance as Prime Minister; only 18 per cent thought that his economic policies were likely to succeed; only 17 per cent approved of his government's record to date.[92]

Elsewhere, 1968 had been a year of political turmoil and social upheaval: riots and assassinations in the United States; student rebellion in France;

bombings in West Germany; massacres in Mexico City; bloodshed in Saigon and Prague. But for Britain, it had been another year of gloom, of economic austerity and a limping, bloodied government. Few people thought that 1969 would be much better.

In the midst of all his economic and political difficulties, Harold Wilson had begun planning a new strategy that would prove the government's mettle and lift them out of the doldrums. Still smarting from the effect of the seamen's strike in July 1966, he was beginning to wonder whether industrial relations might offer the answer.[93] As early as March 1967 he had quarrelled with his backbench 'trade union group' about the need for a statutory prices and incomes policy to control wage inflation. He even told Crossman that he was tempted by 'the idea of forming a Labour Party independent of the unions, like the American Democratic Party'. Crossman countered that the only way to deal with the unions was 'if he'd taken over the job and run it himself'. 'Ah,' Wilson replied, 'Barbara Castle could have done it.'[94]

A year later, with the twin problems of unofficial strikes and soaring pay claims uppermost in his mind, Wilson began to think more seriously about moving Castle from Transport, where she had been a great success, to sort out the unions.[95] On 29 March he confided to Crossman his plans for a 'Wilson Government Mark II', giving Castle a brief to bring the unions under control. 'Barbara is to be the new inspiration,' he explained: 'she'll spark the new model. Tell her today when you see her at lunch but don't tell her any more. She'll spark the whole difference by taking over relations with the trade unions.'[96] Of course Crossman immediately told her the whole story. 'The thought terrifies me,' she reflected that evening. But 'someone had got to do it so I might as well have a shot'.[97]

Three days later Wilson appointed Castle as the new First Secretary of State at the Department of Employment and Productivity. Crossman gushed that she was now 'the biggest personality in the Government . . . a natural number two and if she weren't a woman she would be a natural number one: she could quite conceivably be the first woman Prime Minister'.[98] As Castle herself recognised, the future of the government was resting on her shoulders:

Well, I am in the thick of it now, for better or worse – probably worse. I am under no illusions that I may be committing political suicide. I have at last moved from the periphery of the whirlwind into its very heart . . . My fan mail has been growing, and I am about to change all that for the very focal point of unpopularity. And yet I know I couldn't do anything else. If I go down in disaster as I may, at least I shall have been an adult before I die.[99]

31

BACK BRITAIN, NOT BLACK BRITAIN

NIGEL: Well, of course, it is our policy to look closely at the immigration bill . . . But you must understand we don't intend to exclude people merely on the grounds of their colour alone. There's no place for the second-class citizen in Britain.
HOUSEWIFE: That's what my Ronnie says. They should stay in their own places, shouldn't they?

Dennis Potter, *Vote, Vote, Vote for Nigel Barton* (1965)

'London? . . . You-all got trouble there. Real bad trouble.'
'Trouble?' Ronnie visualized the abolition of expense accounts, the appointment of George Brown as Chancellor of the Exchequer. 'What's happened?'
'What's happened? You-all have got all these coloured people coming in all the time from the Caribbean and India and Pakistan . . . and you-all are not doing one damn thing about it.'

Kingsley Amis, *I Want It Now* (1968)

On 22 July 1965 the BBC's *Comedy Playhouse* introduced audiences to a character who would become synonymous with television in the sixties. Johnny Speight's play *Till Death Us Do Part* followed a working-class East End family, the Ramseys, who live in a terraced house in the shabby streets of Wapping. The head of the family, superbly played by Warren Mitchell, is the irascible Alf, a staunch supporter of the monarchy and the Conservative Party who ceaselessly inveighs against left-wingers, do-gooders, 'darkies' and 'wogs'. Strong stuff this may have been, but the play was written, performed and produced with all the crackling intensity of kitchen-sink drama, and proved a tremendous success. More than eight million people tuned in to watch, and BBC audience research produced an appreciation rating of 67, bettered in that slot only by the pilot episode of *Steptoe and Son*. And, like *Steptoe*, Speight's new creation was destined for great things.[1]

The first full series of *Till Death Us Do Part* began on BBC1 in June 1966, with only two changes. The family was renamed Garnett, to avoid any confusion with the England football manager, and the actress playing Alf's wife dropped out to be replaced by the magnificently phlegmatic Dandy Nichols. Once again, it was a great success. Just five weeks into the series the show had toppled *Coronation Street* from the top of the ratings; by February 1967 the audience had reached more than sixteen million; and an extended edition the next month drew a stunning eighteen million viewers.[2] For five more series, running until the end of 1975, *Till Death Us Do Part* regularly attracted the highest viewing figures of the week.[3]

Till Death Us Do Part was not merely popular but extremely controversial. Alf Garnett's reactionary tirades set new standards for vulgar and aggressive language on television. The 'bloody coons', he insists, are undermining the nation's moral fibre and social fabric, and should be sent back to 'their own countries'. In one notable rant he explains:

Before the war started we was experimenting . . . trying to solve the black question . . . trying to breed 'em smaller. Ideal for chimney sweeping – even have five of 'em sitting under the bonnet of your car pedalling it. An' that's what we was doing, experimenting like you do with your dogs . . . Miniature blacks would have been a very handy size to have about the house. I mean, you'd only need a dog kennel or a little shed to put 'em in, and they'd have been very handy nipping about the house cleaning out the ashtrays, peeling potatoes, and all them sort of little woman's jobs. It would have put an end to this question of women's lib too, wouldn't it?[4]

Speight and Mitchell always insisted that they wanted people to be repelled by Alf Garnett rather than to empathise with him.[5] But he was such a compelling character that often the audience could not help but laugh along with his reactionary flights of fancy. Since the programme was broadcast with a laughter track, it is obvious that audiences often laughed more at his racist jokes than at his inevitable comeuppance. Indeed, as most critics agreed, the series owed much of its appeal to the fact that there were plenty of genuine Alf Garnetts in real life. The *Mirror* observed that it was 'compulsive watching for millions – even for those unfortunate ones who relished this confirmation of their own intolerance, unable to see the parody behind prejudice', while *The Times* agreed that, 'alas, it is terribly true'.[6]

'Who, then, is this Alf Garnett and what is he?' asked Peter Worsley in the *Financial Times*:

Why, he's the rampaging, howling embodiment of all the most vulgar and odious prejudices that slop about in the bilges of the national mind. Whatever hidden hates, irrational fears and superseded loyalties stand in the way of our slow stumble towards a more civilised society, Alf Garnett is the living, blaspheming expression of them. He is everything most hateful about our national character – xenophobic, illiberal, racist, anti-semitic, toadying, authoritarian. He's a flogger, a hanger, a censor, a know-all and a Mister-Always-Right. He is a positive anthology of unconsidered bigotry.[7]

Alf Garnett's views, said Milton Shulman in the *Evening Standard*, 'can be seen and heard most days in most pubs, factories and boardrooms in the land . . . Fortunately, there are few of us who possess all of Alf's bulging portmanteau of hates and prejudices. But it is only the saint among us who does not share at least one.'[8]

Of all Alf Garnett's prejudices, by far the most controversial was his racism. The very presence of more than half a million 'coons' in Britain, as he saw it, was an affront to his patriotism and a clear sign of national decline. And although few people were as outspoken as Alf Garnett, there is little doubt that many agreed with him. Casual racism was present at all levels of British society in the sixties, from Conservative politicians who felt that the newcomers could never be assimilated to working-class Labour voters who resented the competition for jobs and housing. In jokes, comedy sketches, private conversations and even electoral campaigns racial prejudice regularly reared its head.[9]

Of course, many of the immigrants who had arrived during the 1950s and early 1960s encountered tolerance and friendliness, too. Institutions like the National Council for Civil Liberties and the Institute for Race Relations, publications like the *Guardian* and *The Economist*, and liberal politicians on both sides of the Commons prided themselves on their welcoming attitudes.[10] But, in general, most white reactions were much more ambiguous. A survey in Manchester found that, while white patients were perfectly happy to have a black or Asian doctor, their friendliness and respect seemed to vanish once they were outside the surgery. 'I can take them or leave them the same as anybody else, you know,' said one Liverpool taxi driver. 'I don't mind having a drink with a coloured chap. I've met some very nice coloured people but with regard to intermarriage, I think I'd draw the line there.'[11] In a survey carried out in North London in 1965 two out of five people said that they were acquainted with black or Asian immigrants, one in five objected to working alongside them, and half said they would refuse to live next door to them. Nine out of ten, meanwhile, said they disapproved of mixed marriages.[12]

Racial prejudice had complicated roots and causes. Partly it reflected cultural factors, from what people were taught in schools to what they saw on television and read in their library books. Partly it was based on realistic anxieties about the intensified competition for jobs and houses, or on cultural conflicts with the newcomers. And partly it reflected class resentment: liberal politicians and commentators usually lived in areas far too expensive for most immigrants, whereas poorer working-class voters had to compete with them. Racism did not exist in a vacuum: it was based on old ideas of British imperial predominance, and by the late sixties it had become interwoven with broader anxieties about cultural change and national decline.[13]

Although the late sixties are often seen as the peak of anti-immigrant sentiment in Britain, the era of mass immigration had actually ended some time before. Thanks to the Commonwealth Immigrants Act of 1962, only migrants with employment contracts or specific skills, or the dependants of immigrants who had already settled in Britain, were allowed in. For much of the rest of the decade, emigrants easily outnumbered immigrants, as more people left an apparently gloomy, declining Britain for a new life in Australia, Canada, New Zealand or South Africa.[14] But far from weakening over the course of the sixties, racial resentments seem rather to have hardened, reflecting popular anxiety at national decline as well as simple prejudice. 'We were very kind to them when they first came,' said one Birmingham shopkeeper, 'but now I just get in my car at the weekends and drive to where I cannot see a black face. Some of them are very decent folk, but others have this inferiority complex and they try to make up for it. They are rude and cheeky.'[15] In poll after poll conducted between 1964 and 1974 at least eight out of ten people thought that too many blacks were entering Britain – even though successive governments had imposed tight curbs on immigration.[16]

Newcomers from the Caribbean, India, Pakistan and elsewhere often had to face everyday discrimination and, in some cases, violence. The Nottingham and Notting Hill riots of 1958, in which white working-class mobs had attacked local black residents, had provoked horror and hand-wringing in equal measure, but they did not mark the end of racial violence in Britain. In August 1961, for example, hundreds of whites went on the rampage in

Middlesbrough, chanting, 'Let's get a wog'. Two years later, after a customer was killed in a fight in a Chinese restaurant in St Helen's, Chinese-owned properties in the town were burned and ransacked, provoking further racist incidents as far away as Birmingham.[17]

On a more mundane level, landladies regularly refused to let rooms to West Indians and Asians, British Rail porters were said to operate an unofficial colour bar, and the Bristol Omnibus Company explicitly refused to employ black drivers or bus conductors. Throughout housing, employment and public services, there persisted 'racial discrimination varying in extent from the massive to the substantial'.[18] It was hardly surprising that when one researcher examined the West Indian community in Nottingham towards the end of the decade he found a deep sense of disappointment: 'I never knew there was so much colour bar . . . I thought the people of Britain would be good and affectionate – now most of them are against us . . . I did not know I was coloured until the English told me so . . . I expected people to be nice – it's like a slap in the face.'[19]

During the fifties and early sixties the politics of race had been surprisingly muted. Such was the need for cheap labour, and so entrenched was the idea of common imperial citizenship, that few prominent politicians associated themselves with anti-immigrant resentment. But from the mid-fifties onwards a small group of Conservative backbenchers, notably Sir Cyril Osborne, the intemperate MP for Louth, had begun to argue for greater controls on the grounds of alleged disease, prostitution and crime. In 1958 Osborne broke down in tears when his Conservative colleagues refused to take any notice of his predictions of racial disaster, and he angrily told the press that it was 'time someone spoke out for the white man in this country'.[20] Three years later he informed the *Daily Telegraph* that unless immigration was stopped, the white population would soon be outnumbered, and Britain would 'cease to be a European nation and become a mixed Afro-Asian society'.[21]

At the time Osborne was regarded as something of an eccentric, but he was not alone. The controversial Conservative backbencher Sir Gerald Nabarro* once asked a live radio audience: 'How would you feel if your

---

*Nabarro was easily one of the most colourful politicians of the era, although he never held ministerial office. When asked to write his own obituary for the *Daily Telegraph*, he began: 'A splendid moustache, a deep resonant voice, a remarkable memory were among the characteristics of this notorious man.'

daughter wanted to marry a big buck nigger with the prospect of coffee-coloured grandchildren?'[22] This was not a partisan issue: several Labour parliamentarians also shared Osborne's fears. George Rogers and James Harrison, who represented the areas afflicted by race riots in 1958, both demanded greater immigration controls.[23] And in 1963, in the West London suburb of Southall, where thousands of Punjabis had settled in the fifties and property values were falling, a local residents' association was formed to campaign against the newcomers. Among other things, it demanded segregated schools and encouraged estate agents to sell to whites only.[24] Their 'whole way of life', according to the association, was 'threatened and endangered by a flood of immigrants who are generally illiterate, dirty, and completely unsuited and unused to our way of life. They overcrowd their properties to an alarming degree, create slums, endanger public health, and subject their neighbours to a life of misery, annoyance, abuse and bitterness.'[25]

The appearance of the Southall Residents' Association was an ominous sign of things to come. For the first time, ordinary white citizens had organised their own anti-immigrant campaign, reflecting not only deep-seated prejudice but genuine anxieties about cultural conflict, competition for housing and tumbling property prices. At the time, however, no major political figure lent them his support. Even though Southall had a higher immigrant population than any other suburban area in Britain, and even though it had been among the first to have its own organised nativist movement, it virtually disappeared from the national headlines after 1963. Instead, the geographical focus of the debate over race and immigration moved north – to the Midlands.

The fifties had been relatively good years for the industrial towns of the West Midlands. Thanks to the high worldwide demand for British exports, the engineering and manufacturing firms of Birmingham, Wolverhampton and the Black Country were booming.[26] But at the same time the potential workforce was beginning to dwindle as affluent workers moved to the suburbs, so there was plenty of demand for cheap, unskilled labour.[27] 'More workers must be found,' announced Wolverhampton's *Express and Star* in January 1956. 'Where? The new recruits to British industry must come, it seems, from abroad, from the colonies, Eire and from the continent.'[28]

This was precisely what happened. Between 1953 and 1958, the West Indian population of Wolverhampton doubled from 1500 to 3000, and in Birmingham it swelled from 8000 to 30,000.[29] In the years that followed immigrant workers continued to pour into the area, so by 1966 Wolverhampton had a higher concentration of recent immigrants than anywhere else outside London. Pakistanis worked as labourers in the factories; Indians toiled in the furnaces, foundries and rolling mills.[30] One of the attractions of Wolverhampton, however, was that rents were cheap. Parts of the town were badly run down, and it was in these decrepit areas that immigrants found affordable housing. As more immigrants arrived, so house prices began to fall, and anxious white residents moved out towards the suburbs. The consequence was that 'whole streets, then whole districts, turned black', and since these were the dingiest areas of the town, it was easy for critics to blame the newcomers.[31]

At first there was no real sense of discontent or resentment. In 1956 the pro-Conservative *Express and Star* welcomed a new contingent of West Indians as 'British citizens [with] a perfect right to come here and try to earn a living ... Many are better behaved than some of their white cousins in this country and have proved themselves industrious workers.'[32] Correspondents generally praised their new neighbours as 'very friendly' and hard-working: one local trade unionist wrote that any illusions about their stamina and commitment had been banished when he watched them 'alongside our own workers'.[33] The town's medical officer admitted that he was 'surprised and pleased how minor a problem the immigrants present', and thought that some were 'above the standard of our own people'.[34]

This is not to deny that racial tensions existed: the Scala Ballroom in the town centre, for example, operated an explicit colour bar, and there were rumours of housing discrimination on suburban estates. But, as one observer put it, any resentment was 'kept very much below the surface and was of little or no political significance'. The town's leading politicians, notably the Conservatives' young meteor Enoch Powell, the MP for Wolverhampton South-West, generally supported the principle of immigration and gave no support to its critics. Powell's Labour opponent in the 1959 election even said that he had been 'impressed by [Powell's] refusal to get involved' in the immigration debate.[35]

By the beginning of the sixties, however, there were already hints of the controversy to come. In 1961 grass-roots activists founded the Birmingham Immigration Control Association, an organisation that received considerable publicity thanks to the support of backbenchers like Cyril Osborne.[36] In neighbouring Wolverhampton, too, pressure was growing. As Clem Jones, the editor of the *Express and Star*, later recalled, there was a growing feeling that greater immigration would push down property prices, frightening homeowners who had worked and saved to buy their own little terraced house. Since most immigrants were young single men, there were also predictable clashes over loud music, exuberant parties and sexual misbehaviour.[37] But the campaign appeared to make little headway. When activists visited Enoch Powell in 1961, they received a frosty welcome. 'He was all for the immigrants,' recalled one disgruntled welder. 'We had a lot of examples of the dirty filthy habits of immigrants which we could prove, and we asked him to act on them – or at least make a fuss about them . . . [But] we didn't get any satisfaction from him.'[38]

Anti-immigrant resentment ran strongest in the dilapidated industrial town of Smethwick, situated in the heart of the Black Country between Birmingham and Wolverhampton. At the beginning of 1964, its population of 70,000 people included between 5000 and 7000 recent immigrants, the highest concentration in any county borough in England. Smethwick was a pretty gloomy place, where many white inhabitants viewed the newcomers with suspicion and distaste. Most pubs excluded black drinkers from their lounge bars, and some barbers even refused to cut their hair. To make matters worse, the town was badly in need of good council housing, and many white residents complained that they were missing out thanks to the influx of immigrants. In response, local Conservatives argued that tenants and applicants should be given priority if they had lived in Smethwick for ten years or more, effectively excluding the newcomers.[39]

The local paper, the *Smethwick Telephone*, took a fiercely anti-immigrant line, devoting dozens of columns in 1963 alone to the alleged depredations of the newcomers. Its most frequent critic of immigration was Peter Griffiths, a local headmaster and leader of the Conservative group on the borough council, who regularly tried to show that 'Labour were the immigrants' friends, or were supported by them'.[40] Griffiths had been selected as the Conservative parliamentary candidate in 1964, and local observers thought that Patrick Gordon Walker, the town's liberal-minded, patrician Labour MP, faced an uphill struggle to defend his slim majority.[41]

Immigration barely featured in the national campaign, but as *The Times* noted, it was 'possibly the only issue which is really capable of arousing deep-seated political passions of old-fashioned intensity'. Public opinion was both ambiguous and divided, disconcerting senior politicians of both parties, for 'on this subject there is a great gulf fixed between the ordinary man in the street and the leaders of public opinion in Parliament, the churches, the intelligentsia, and the press'.[42] This gulf would consume the candidacy of Patrick Gordon Walker. In the first week of the campaign stickers were plastered across the Black Country with the message 'Vote Labour for More Nigger-type Neighbours'.[43] A fortnight later, more posters appeared carrying the slogan 'If you want a nigger neighbour, vote Liberal or Labour'. Canvassers spread rumours that 'Gordon Walker's daughters married black men', 'Gordon Walker sold his house at Smethwick to the blacks' and 'because most of the blacks have leprosy, they are building two secret leper hospitals in the town'.[44] The tide appeared to be with Peter Griffiths. He was 'an ideal MP', one reader wrote to the *Express and Star*, because he was 'not afraid to speak his mind on coloured immigrants'.[45]

When the votes were counted, Griffiths beat Gordon Walker by 1174 votes. Across the country, there had been a swing of more than 3 per cent to Labour; in Smethwick there was a swing of more than 7 per cent to the Conservatives. In his victory speech Griffiths denied that he had exploited the race issue, but nevertheless demanded that all immigration be halted for five years. In a rare public flash of emotion Harold Wilson called the result 'a disgrace to British democracy', and angrily dismissed Griffiths as a 'parliamentary leper'.[46] But the new Prime Minister and his colleagues were well aware that plenty of working-class voters shared Griffiths's views. 'Ever since the Smethwick election,' noted Dick Crossman in February 1965, 'it has been quite clear that immigration can be the greatest political vote loser for the Labour Party if one seems to be permitting a flood of immigrants to come in and blight the central area of our cities.'[47]

While Peter Griffiths was settling into the House of Commons, one of his neighbours in the West Midlands was pondering broader questions about the future of Conservatism. Although he had spent little time as a Cabinet minister, Enoch Powell had already established a reputation as one of the most fearsome intellectuals in his party. Once a brilliant young scholar of Greek, he had made his name in the Conservative Research Department after the war before entering Parliament and rapidly rising through the ranks. A man of almost obsessive passions, from the poetry of Housman to the thrill of the hunt, he had resigned from the government in 1958, appalled by what he saw as Macmillan's reckless expenditure. After returning two years later as Minister of Health, he promptly walked out again at the end of 1963, this time because he had pledged not to serve under Sir Alec Douglas-Home. Powell prided himself on his remorseless, logical intellect, but in fact his austere demeanour concealed the spirit of a nineteenth-century romantic, seething with messianic fervour.[48] As the *Sunday Express* put it in April 1965, he had 'the taut, pale face of a missionary, and the zealous energy of a man who is not afraid of the stake'.[49]

The odd thing about Powell, as his friend Iain Macleod commented, was that he did not 'fit into any political slot. He is just Enoch Powell.' On many social and cultural issues, like homosexual law reform and the abolition of the death penalty, Powell was a staunch liberal.[50] But on economic issues, he was gradually moving further to the right. The Macmillan and Home governments, he thought, had been wrong to go along with the vogue for planning and intervention; instead, they should have left the economy to the laws of 'supply and demand, working through the market'.[51] This was an extremely unfashionable case to be making in 1964: most people thought that free-market economics was a discredited nineteenth-century relic. But Powell drew succour from his links with the emerging Institute of Economic Affairs (IEA), a new think-tank devoted to laissez-faire and monetarist economics. The IEA was generally opposed to the post-war Keynesian consensus, the welfare state and economic intervention, and from about 1965 onwards its association with Powell became very close indeed. Both the man and the organisation were to play crucial roles on Britain's road to Thatcherism.[52]

Like many of his colleagues, Powell was frustrated by Edward Heath's performance as leader, and he was particularly disgruntled by Heath's reluctance to embrace a more radical, free-market agenda. At the same time Powell himself seems to have changed, taking on the mantle of a missionary bringing the truth to the masses. 'He ceased to have the ability to laugh with you, let alone laugh at himself' noted his colleague Robert Carr. 'He seemed steadily to be taking himself so much more seriously. There was no give and take. It was all or nothing.'[53] In meetings Powell sat silent and brooding while his colleagues spoke, and by the beginning of 1966 he was tending to direct his fire more at his own side than at the government. To Heath, this was unpardonable, and between the two men the breach widened still further.[54]

When the Conservatives suffered their second successive election defeat in 1966 Powell felt that his attitude had been vindicated. For Heath, however, the result was a bad blow. Not only was his standing with the public very low, but after barely two years of his leadership his own backbenchers were restless. His aloofness was legendary: he often seemed incapable of making small talk with his colleagues, and he had a reputation for inviting people over to his flat and then neglecting to provide them with food and drink.[55] The real problem was Heath's extreme social awkwardness, which often came over as sheer rudeness. He inspired genuine loyalty in some of his younger colleagues, and in private he was known for his deadpan, teasing sense of humour; but this never came over on television, or in the House of Commons.[56]

Heath's one consolation during the travails of the mid-sixties was his discovery of sailing. In the summer of 1966 he started taking lessons in his home town of Broadstairs, and quite unexpectedly found that he was exceptionally good at it.[57] Sailing appealed to his competitive, methodical instincts, while providing a bracing outlet from the pressures of politics. As his biographer puts it, in commissioning his boats, picking his crew, devising their racing strategy and taking the helm, Heath 'displayed leadership of the highest order'. Within just a few years this enthusiastic amateur had made a demonstrable impact on the sailing world, bringing unprecedented publicity to the sport and setting high standards of boat design, strategy and all-round professionalism. His sailing interests were regularly mocked by both his colleagues and newspaper commentators, but in an age of one-track career politicians, they gave him an unusual sporting hinterland.[58]

Unfortunately for Heath, his expertise on the water was not matched by any great advances on land. Throughout the remainder of the sixties, he was widely perceived as charmless and wooden, and his personal poll ratings lagged well behind those of his party. In February 1967 his popularity fell to an all-time low of just 24 per cent, by far the worst rating recorded by any leader of the Conservative Party.[59] That October *Panorama* ran a stunningly caustic profile of the struggling Heath, showing him opening a new Conservative Club. 'He tried very hard like a sensitive man in a butcher's shop to conceal a faint nausea,' ran the commentary as Heath struggled to pull the first pint, 'still pasting on a grin, laughing a little too determinedly at all the fleshy cordiality.' The programme then cut to the studio, where Heath had been grimly watching the film. 'Mr Heath, how low does your personal rating from your own supporters have to go before you consider yourself a liability to the Party you lead?' asked Robin Day. In reply, Heath muttered that 'popularity isn't everything'. The very next evening, on ITN, he faced a similar question: 'Mr Heath, are you at all worried by your total failure to make a breakthrough as Tory leader?' 'No,' Heath said gloomily.[60]

While Heath was floundering, Powell was moving closer to outright rebellion. In April 1966 he declared that the Conservative Party needed some 'harsh, fierce destructive words, aimed in defiance and contempt at men and policies we detest', and demanded complete 'liberty to question and propose'. He even called his programme 'Words not Action', mocking Heath's campaign slogan in 1966, 'Action not Words'.[61] Just a week later Heath called him in and told him that if he wanted to stay in the Shadow Cabinet, he would have to toe the line. The two men came to an awkward arrangement, although Powell still believed that he had the right to say whatever he wanted about anything and everything. By the end of the year it was as though his compact with Heath had never happened.[62]

During the fifties and early sixties Powell had not been very interested in immigration, and his public comments on the subject were usually pretty bland. During the 1964 election he even wrote a piece for the Wolverhampton *Express and Star*, calling for greater racial tolerance and integration. 'I have set and always will set my face like flint', he wrote, 'against making any difference between one citizen of this country and another on the grounds of his origin.'[63] However, in an article for the *Sunday Telegraph* after the election, he took a new line, standing up for the people of Smethwick and insisting that immigration should be a 'live and real' issue, not a 'taboo':

> It is not colour prejudiced or racially intolerant to say that only if substantial further addition to our immigrant population is now prevented, will it be properly possible to assimilate the immigrants who are already here, which in turn is the only way to avoid the evils of the colour question . . . A politician who says these things – in the Black Country or elsewhere – does no more than his duty.[64]

Over the next couple of years Powell repeatedly returned to the same theme, but because he was also voicing unorthodox opinions on other subjects, too, it took time for his views to sink in. In April 1965, for example, he argued that the time had come for the 'virtual termination of net immigration', and even suggested that since many immigrants found their life in Britain 'a misery', 'we should open the door in the reverse direction and encourage a backward flow'.[65] A month later, he told a meeting of Tory activists that Commonwealth immigrants and their dependants should be treated just like 'aliens' from any other country. This made him the first senior politician to suggest removing the right of families to join immigrants already in Britain, and marked a decisive move to the right on the immigration question.[66]

Powell always insisted that he was merely reflecting the views of his Wolverhampton constituents, who were fed up with being swamped by newcomers from foreign lands. It is certainly true that Wolverhampton was not a very happy place during the mid-sixties. The town's manufacturing industries were suffering, unemployment was climbing, and the streets were looking increasingly tired and threadbare. According to one estimate, one in twenty of the borough's 262,000 inhabitants had recently arrived from overseas, and it is hardly surprising that racial tensions were on the rise.[67] In the summer of 1965, for example, local Conservatives drew attention to recent reports suggesting that the immigrant birth rate was eight times higher than that of the indigenous population, and that immigrants accounted for almost a quarter of all births in Wolverhampton.[68] Powell himself frequently alluded to these findings in order to justify his own hardened line on the subject.[69]

In fact, he was being rather disingenuous. Immigration was not the only issue that interested his constituents. The leader of the Conservative group on Wolverhampton Corporation told Paul Foot that it had not been a major issue until Powell took it up. He even thought that the amount of 'public concern about immigration' before 1965 was 'negligible, infinitesimal, I would say'.[70] Indeed, even though Powell always claimed that he was simply speaking up for the common people of Wolverhampton, it is striking how little immigration seemed to matter to his electorate. Right-wing pressure groups and nakedly racist organisations completely failed to make any headway, immigration barely featured in the election campaign of 1966, and in Smethwick Peter Griffiths lost the seat he had won two years earlier.[71]

As Foot argues, Powell's self-image as a tribune of the plebs, the mouthpiece of the Molineux crowd, was enormously misleading. He never had a reputation for being very interested in local issues, he was rarely mentioned by the local paper and he infrequently mentioned Wolverhampton in his Commons speeches. He spent most of his time in his elegant house in South Eaton Place, Belgravia, which could hardly be more different from the homes of the constituents whose views he claimed to reflect. His self-ascribed image 'as a man of the people, living and understanding their problems from association with them, was new and entirely false'.[72]

Why, then, did Powell take up the immigration issue? One explanation is that it allowed him to whip up support among ordinary voters in the country, to reposition himself on the right of the party, and to distinguish himself from Heath and senior Tory moderates like Maudling and Macleod. On the other hand, Powell had never been interested in personal advancement for its own sake, and even his critics generally agreed that he was a man of principle – too much principle, some thought – so it is hard to see ambition as the main factor. A much more convincing explanation is that he was motivated by his intense patriotism, which often came close to nineteenth-century nationalism. In Powell's view national identity was built on the long continuity of England's history, culture and institutions. It was based on the 'continuous life of a united people in its island home', on Parliament and the monarchy. But this romantic vision could not encompass newcomers from very different cultures, because in Powell's view they had no stake in English history, and could never properly be assimilated.[73] Contrary to myth, he fiercely rejected the idea that 'one race is inherently superior to another', so in this sense he was not a racist. But on the other hand, he argued that if racism meant 'being conscious of the differences between men and nations, and from that, races, then we are all racialists'.[74]

By early 1967 Powell was convinced that it was his duty to champion the anti-immigration case, at all times and in all places, regardless of the consequences. He told Heath that in Wolverhampton he had seen 'an ominous deterioration, which is taking the form not of discrimination by white against coloured but of insolence by coloured against white and corresponding fearfulness on the part of white'. Given Powell's reputation as a linguist, his choice of words – 'ominous', 'insolence' – could hardly have been an accident. It not only smacked of the worst kind of racial snobbery but showed how far he had already moved towards the rhetorical excesses that would bring the final breach.[75]

Throughout the summer and autumn of 1967 Powell continued to return to the subject of immigration. Public attention had redoubled as it became clear that thousands of Asians living in Kenya were being forced out of the newly independent country, and would inevitably look to Britain for help.[76] According to the newspapers, this tide of refugees threatened to become a deluge, and there were warnings that the influx might reach some fifty thousand people a year. This was the cue for Powell, in tandem with the former Tory minister Duncan Sandys, to launch a campaign to 'turn off the tap'. Sandys insisted that 'the breeding of millions of half-caste children would merely produce a generation of misfits and create increased tension'.[77] Powell's rhetoric was more considered, but by October 1967 he was openly declaring that racial difference was 'an undeniable truth' and that immigrants who were 'not fitting in' should 'return to the country where they belong'.[78] On 7 December he insisted that immigration had to stop, and added that 'no amount of misrepresentation, abuse or unpopularity is going to prevent the Tory party, my colleagues and myself from voicing the dictates of common sense'.[79]

The furore over the Kenyan Asians exemplified the increasing intensity of the immigration debate in the second half of the 1960s. As the economy struggled and national self-confidence began to slide, so many working-class whites, frightened for their livelihoods and angry at rising prices, began to look for scapegoats. Alf Garnett was not the only person who blamed immigrants for Britain's national decline. There were widespread rumours about West Indians and Asians harassing white women, urinating in the streets, dallying with prostitutes, using violence to evict white tenants, holding lavish all-night parties and so on.[80] All of this was made worse by the news from the United States, where every summer seemed to bring bloody race riots to the cities and the Black Power movement was in full cry. No less an expert than Mick Jagger told an interviewer that immigration was going to 'break up' British society. 'Because they just are different and they do act differently and they don't live the same, not even if they were born here they don't,' he explained in the spring of 1968. 'I mean, why should they? They don't, they just don't, and it breaks up the society.'[81]

All of these anxieties played into the hands of the racist far right. Organisations like the British Ku Klux Klan, the English Rights Association and the Racial Preservation Society began to pick up recruits, while the press reported increasing violence against immigrants and their families.[82] In February 1967 activists founded the National Front, which drew on an underground heritage of British fascism and placed a heavy emphasis on the immigration issue. The National Front was most popular in areas where it could exploit existing anti-immigrant sentiment, and it probably owed most to the example of groups like the Southall Residents' Association and the Birmingham Immigration Control Association. By 1969, so the party claimed, membership enquiries had reached some 180 a week.[83]

This rising pressure helps to explain why, faced with the prospect of the arrival of the Kenyan Asians, the government decided to invalidate the refugees' passports and prevent a mass flight to Britain. Only 1500 Kenyan Asians would be allowed in each year, a strikingly strict quota given that there were already 7000 waiting for their papers to come. This was an intensely controversial measure and it was certainly discriminatory, since it left a loophole for passport holders with parents or grandparents born in Britain, who were bound to be white.[84] The legislation was prepared by Roy Jenkins, rather belying his liberal reputation, but by the time the issue came to the boil he had been replaced at the Home Office by James Callaghan.[85] Although Callaghan was no racist, he took his image as the champion of the common man very seriously and thought that government policy ought to reflect public opinion. He was determined to force through the Commonwealth Immigrants Bill, even though it attracted fierce criticism from middle-class activists and the liberal newspapers.[86] *The Times*, for example, called it 'the most shameful measure' that a Labour government had ever introduced, while the *Spectator* thought that it was 'one of the most immoral pieces of legislation to have emerged from any British Parliament'.[87] Crossman recorded that Callaghan had 'the air of a man whose mind was made up. He wasn't going to tolerate this bloody liberalism. He was going to stop this nonsense, as the public was demanding and as the Party was demanding. He would do it come what may and anybody who opposed him was a sentimental jackass.'[88]

On 1 March 1968 the bill went through. Not surprisingly, few historians have anything good to say about it: the government not only broke its solemn contract with the holders of British passports but clearly discriminated against a vulnerable group of non-white refugees.[89] But, as Crossman observed, it did Callaghan's image no harm at all, since he seemed to be 'standing up for Britain against the Africans, [and] saying "No more bloody immigrants whatever happens." . . . On immigration, on everything you see, there is Jim Callaghan, sensible, constructive, sturdy, thoroughly English, doing his job, a big man who could keep the movement going even when it is defeated and gets rid of Harold Wilson.'[90]

A few weeks after the Commonwealth Immigrants Bill had become law, attention turned to the government's new Race Relations Bill, which prohibited discrimination in housing, employment and commercial services. The Conservatives were deeply divided over the proposals, just as they were over immigration. Within the Shadow Cabinet 'One Nation' liberals like Quintin Hogg and Iain Macleod backed the bill, while more right-wing figures, notably Powell, were against it. At a meeting on 10 April, Heath and Hogg reached a compromise position: the Tories would vote against the second reading of the bill, tabling a 'reasoned amendment' that pointed out specific weaknesses instead of opposing the general principle. The meeting broke up amid great cordiality, and the Conservative high command congratulated themselves on their compromise.

Powell, though, had not spoken at all during the discussion, but sat sunken and brooding. His colleagues knew that he had been speaking out with growing vehemence on immigration, but they assumed that his silence meant that he agreed with the party line. They were wrong. Powell thought that they 'simply had not understood' the issues, and instead of resting over the Easter break he began to plan a speech that he hoped would change the debate for good.[91]

At lunchtime on Saturday, 20 April 1968, Powell walked into the Midland Hotel, Birmingham, to address the annual meeting of the West Midlands Conservative Political Centre. His speech had been carefully prepared, but instead of releasing it to the press through Conservative Central Office, as was the norm, he circulated it himself through the West Midlands group. Powell was determined to have his say at last, free from the collegiate constraints of the Shadow Cabinet. His wife Pam, who typed the text, said later that she thought it was 'just a good speech, a forceful speech'. Powell himself knew that it was more than that. A few days before he had told his friend Clem Jones, the editor of the *Express and Star*, that the speech would '"fizz" like a rocket; but whereas all rockets fall to earth, this one is going to stay up'.[92]

Powell began by remarking that true statesmanship lay in facing up to difficult challenges rather than ducking them. A few weeks before, he said, he had been chatting to a working-class constituent. He recounted the man's words: 'If I had the money to go, I wouldn't stay in this country . . . I have three children, all of them been through grammar school and two of them married now, with family. I shan't be satisfied till I have seen them all settled overseas. In this country in fifteen or twenty years' time the black man will have the whip hand over the white man.' Powell recognised that this story would probably provoke uproar:

> I can already hear the chorus of execration. How dare I say such a horrible thing? How dare I stir up trouble and inflame feelings by repeating such a conversation? The answer is that I do not have the right not to do so. Here is a decent, ordinary fellow Englishman, who in broad daylight in my own town says to me, his Member of Parliament, that this country will not be worth living in for his children. I simply do not have the right to shrug my shoulders and think about something else. What he is

saying, thousands and hundreds of thousands are saying and thinking — not throughout Great Britain, perhaps, but in the areas that are already undergoing the total transformation to which there is no parallel in a thousand years of English history.

Powell quoted the official predictions from the Registrar General's office, which projected that immigrants and their children would make up some three million people by the end of the 1980s. By 2000, he predicted, they might be 'five to seven million, approximately one-tenth of the whole population'.* These people represented an 'alien element', and it was the task of government to cut their numbers by putting a stop to immigration and 'promoting the maximum possible outflow'. Then his voice took on a harder, more passionate tone:

> It almost passes belief that at this moment twenty or thirty additional immigrant children are arriving from overseas in Wolverhampton alone every week — and that means fifteen or twenty additional families a decade or two hence.
> Those whom the gods wish to destroy, they first make mad. We must be mad, literally mad, as a nation to be permitting the annual inflow of some 50,000 dependants, who are for the most part the material of the future growth of the immigrant-descended population. It is like watching a nation busily engaged in heaping up its own funeral pyre.

There must be no 'second-class citizens', Powell said, but that did not mean that 'the immigrant and his descendants should be elevated into a privileged or special class', or that the ordinary citizen 'should be denied his right to discriminate in the management of his own affairs'. Indeed, he added angrily, many native-born Britons had now become 'strangers in their own country'. They found 'their wives unable to obtain hospital beds in childbirth, their children unable to obtain school places, their homes and neighbourhoods changed beyond recognition, their plans and prospects for the future defeated'. At work, their employers 'hesitated to apply to the immigrant worker the standards of discipline and competence required of the native-born worker'. And now, in the Race Relations Bill, they were

---

*At the time some saw this as disgraceful scaremongering, but Powell's prediction was out by only 2 per cent or so.

faced with a 'one-way privilege' to be established by the government, 'enacted to give the stranger, the disgruntled and the *agent provocateur* the power to pillory them for their private actions'.

'Those without direct experience', Powell continued, could hardly understand the 'sense of being a persecuted minority which is growing among ordinary English people in [some] areas of the country'. So he proposed to read a letter from a woman who lived in Northumberland, describing an incident in his own Wolverhampton constituency. According to his correspondent, the story concerned an elderly woman running a boarding house 'in a respectable street'. In 1960 'a Negro' had moved into an empty house, and eventually every other property in the street had been 'taken over' by immigrants. The old lady's white lodgers moved out and she was left alone, terrified of assault. Black families tried to rent rooms in her house, but she always refused.

> She is becoming afraid to go out. Windows are broken. She finds excreta pushed through her letterbox. When she goes to the shops, she is followed by children, charming, wide-grinning piccaninnies. They cannot speak English, but one word they know. 'Racialist', they chant. When the new Race Relations Bill is passed, this woman is convinced she will go to prison. And is she so wrong? I begin to wonder.

When the speech was quoted in days to come commentators often forgot that these were not Powell's words but those of the woman from Northumberland. But the words of the peroration were Powell's, and they were controversial enough:

> Like the Roman, I seem to see 'the River Tiber foaming with much blood'. That tragic and intractable phenomenon which we watch with horror on the other side of the Atlantic but which there is interwoven with the history and existence of the States itself, is coming upon us here by our own volition and our own neglect. Indeed, it has all but come. In numerical terms, it will be of American proportions long before the end of the century. Only resolute and urgent action will avert it even now. Whether there will be the public will to demand and obtain that action, I do not know. All I know is that to see, and not to speak, would be the great betrayal.[93]

Powell never himself used the phrase by which the speech came to be known – 'rivers of blood' – but was quoting from Virgil. However, he knew that it would have a dramatic impact, hence his remark about 'sending up a rocket'. As both the sympathetic Simon Heffer and the hostile Paul Foot point out, it was the tone of the speech, with its letters and anecdotes, that really struck his contemporaries.[94] Powell chose to repeat these stories because they suited his argument, not because a politician is duty-bound to read out whatever his constituents tell him. What was more, Powell's story about the old lady, the 'excreta' and the 'piccaninnies' seemed to have been borrowed directly from the stock racist fables of the far right. Although newspapers sent reporters to discover the woman in question, she was never found, and probably never existed.[95] Very similar anecdotes were circulated in the late sixties by the National Front, the British National Party and others: it was the kind of story that most councillors and MPs regularly dismissed as extremist rabble-rousing. By repeating it, Powell confirmed 'the ugliest fears of people who knew nothing of immigration problems'.[96]

This was not the first time Powell embraced the racist urban myths of the day. Two months earlier he had alluded to a little girl in Wolverhampton who was the only white child in her class. Again, newspapers searched in vain for the school in question, and Powell finally admitted that no such class existed. Now he seemed to have fallen, yet again, for the propaganda of the National Front. Even his closest admirers thought that repeating the story about the old lady was a serious mistake. Yet Powell was famous for his precise use of language, and almost certainly included it because he knew it would have an enormous impact. The same applies to his comment about the Tiber 'foaming with much blood'. Had he left it in the original Latin, the effect would have been muted. Instead he offered a deliberately emotive translation, and in doing so he sealed his political fate.[97]

In Birmingham Powell's speech met with enthusiastic applause. Elsewhere the reaction was very different. Quintin Hogg, the Tories' spokesman on home affairs, had been out walking in the Lake District, and switched on the evening news to see footage of what appeared to be an extraordinarily inflammatory address. He rapidly decided that Powell had to go, and he was joined by Iain Macleod, Robert Carr and Sir Edward Boyle. 'Enoch's gone mad and hates the blacks,' observed Macleod, who had been a close friend and ally in their younger days.[98] All of them felt that Powell had betrayed their trust, and many also thought that he had gone out of his way to stir up racial antagonism. Heath had no choice. On the following morning he began telephoning his Shadow Cabinet colleagues to prepare them for the inevitable news. That night he spoke to

Powell and told him that he had been sacked. It was the last conversation they would ever have.[99]

After he had sacked Powell Heath released a statement explaining that he thought the speech 'racialist in tone and liable to exacerbate racial tensions'. Most of the newspapers agreed with him. Under the headline 'An Evil Speech', *The Times* called Powell's words 'racialist', 'disgraceful' and 'shameful'. It was 'calculated to inflame hatred between the races', and was 'the first time that a serious British politician [had] appealed to racial hatred, in this direct way, in our post-war history'.[100] The *Mirror*, meanwhile, thought that if Powell's sentiments 'were merely the ravings of a sick hysteric they would excite only pity' and feared that he had 'given the green light to the prejudiced and the psychopaths'.[101] At Westminster the general consensus was that Powell had gone too far. Barbara Castle melodramatically recorded her 'intense depression' that he had 'taken the lid off Pandora's box'. Race relations in Britain, she thought, 'would never be the same again . . . I believe he has helped to make a race war, not only in Britain but perhaps in the world, inevitable.'[102]

However, away from the Commons and the liberal press, Powell's words met with firm approval. The *News of the World* predicted that 'most people in this country will agree with him', and concluded its report with the words: 'WE CAN TAKE NO MORE COLOURED PEOPLE. TO DO SO, AS MR POWELL SAYS, IS MADNESS'.[103] On Monday morning the offices of the *Express and Star* in Wolverhampton were deluged with letters in Powell's favour. Clem Jones was so appalled by Powell's 'old lady' story that he immediately broke off their friendship. But in many parts of the Black Country Powell was regarded as a hero, and every day that week Jones received 'ten, fifteen or twenty mail bags full of readers' letters' backing their local MP.[104] When he invited his readers to send in their views on a postcard, he received 35,000 backing Powell and virtually none against him.[105] In the town of Bilston fifty workers at a boiler factory staged an impromptu strike in Powell's favour, and shop stewards at a large engineering works in Wednesbury began a petition for his reinstatement.[106] Contemporary opinion polls make it clear that Powell also enjoyed enormous support in the country at large. At the end of April a Gallup poll found that 74 per cent agreed with what he had said, with only 15 per cent disagreeing. Seven out of ten thought that Heath had been wrong to sack him, and more than eight out of ten wanted stricter immigration controls.[107]

This was not simply a matter of racism. Powell's appeal was based on a kind of patriotic populism, playing on the voters' resentment towards the politicians who seemed to have let them down. The *Guardian*'s commentator Peter Jenkins astutely suggested that Powell attracted support because he exploited the feeling that 'the politicians are conspiring against the people, that the country is led by men who have no idea about what interests or frightens the ordinary people in the backstreets of Wolverhampton'. Powell's appeal was therefore 'anti-political', which allowed him to mobilise working-class Labour voters disappointed by Wilson's record.[108] Dick Crossman, for one, agreed. He recorded that Powell was 'a fanatic, a bizarre conservative extremist', who appealed to 'the real Labour core, the illiterate industrial proletariat, who have turned up in strength and revolted against the literate'.[109]

The revolt Crossman had in mind was the famous march of the East End dockers. On 23 April, as the Commons was preparing to vote on the Race Relations Bill, more than a thousand dockers converged on the Palace of Westminster carrying placards that read 'Don't Knock Enoch' and 'Back Britain, Not Black Britain'. Three hundred of them made their way into the building, where they cornered the Labour MPs Peter Shore and Ian Mikardo and caused general havoc. That these men were habitual Labour voters made their rebellion all the more striking, and, to the government, all the more alarming. The following day, six hundred more voted to hold a one-day strike at St Katharine's Docks, while the national press carried reports from the West Midlands, Derbyshire, Southampton, Norwich and Reading of more wildcat strikes supporting Powell.[110]

By this point, Powell had received more than 20,000 letters, largely in his favour, and the Post Office had to assign him a special van to make several daily deliveries. 'How dare Mr Heath sack you for your courage?' asked one supporter. 'Believe me, sir, you have not only support from the Midlands but all the country. Good luck sir, in your efforts to save the country.' By the beginning of May Powell had received more than 43,000 letters and 700 telegrams. Only four of the telegrams and 800 of the letters disagreed with him.[111]

Powell always denied that he was a racist, but he insisted that racial and cultural differences made it impossible for native-born Britons and immigrants to live together in harmony. In July he told an interviewer that it was simply a question of numbers: 'Do I object to one coloured person in this country? No. To 100? No. To 1,000? No. To a million? A query. To five million? Definitely.'[112]

Yet whatever the nuances of Powell's views, most immigrants regarded him as an implacable enemy, and there is little doubt that genuine racists drew comfort from his stand. On 30 April a West Indian christening party in Wolverhampton was broken up by white youths wielding knives and shouting, 'Powell, Powell'. Wade Crooks, a grandfather who needed eight stitches after being slashed over one eye, remarked afterwards that he had lived in Wolverhampton 'since 1955 and nothing like this has happened before. I am shattered.' His local Labour councillor, meanwhile, insisted that 'this is the first case of an attack on coloured people here since the Powell speech, and I feel Mr Powell is responsible'.[113]

A poll for *Panorama* at the end of the year found that only 8 per cent of immigrants said they had encountered more abuse since Powell's speech, so its effect is probably often exaggerated. But there were still numerous stories of similar attacks across the country, especially in London and the West Midlands. 'Paki-bashing', as it was called, was on the rise anyway in the late sixties, and it is likely that gangs chanted Powell's name because they thought it would give them some sort of legitimacy.[114] But he was not always quick to condemn such incidents, which only strengthened the case of those who blamed him for the rise in racism. In January 1969 David Frost asked him to condemn a gang who had beaten up an Indian student while chanting, 'We want Enoch'. 'I am not going to start condemning the behaviour of people who are condemned by their own actions,' Powell said dismissively. 'It is not for a politician to be a preacher.'[115]

For Powell's old colleagues in the Conservative Shadow Cabinet, the furore over immigration proved excruciatingly difficult to handle. Heath's postbag was full of critical, even threatening letters, while a short tour of the Midlands brought heckling and unrest.[116] Throughout the next two years the Tory leader's image in the country remained astoundingly bad. He regularly lagged as many as 20 percentage points behind his party, and polls showed that barely one in three voters thought him an effective leader.[117] By sacking Powell he had turned him into a martyr, 'the hero alike of the patriotic white working class represented by the marching dockers and of the new suburban middle class grumbling at the golf club'. Powell now stood as a focus for opposition within the Conservative Party, a plausible leader-in-waiting should Heath go down to a second successive defeat at Wilson's hands.[118]

Meanwhile, Powell never repudiated his Birmingham speech, but tacked even further to the right. In November 1968, for example, he suggested the creation of a 'Ministry of Repatriation' with the urgent task of organising voluntary repatriation before England sank into inter-racial bloodshed.[119] Once again his remarks drew bitter condemnation. *The Times* called them 'evil', and concluded that 'he is hostile to coloured people in Britain, that he is afraid of them, and that they have reason to be afraid of him'. Heath condemned what he called racial 'character assassination', which led, he said, to 'tyranny', while Wilson denounced Powell's ideas as 'utterly evil'.[120]

In liberal circles at Westminster and beyond Powell was now well on the way to becoming a pariah. A few mavericks and intellectuals, some from the left, like Michael Foot and Tony Benn, still respected him. When most MPs were shunning Powell, Foot went out of his way to show his comradeship, slapping him on the back in the Commons library and asking after his family.[121] But many senior Conservatives regarded him as little more than a deranged embarrassment. Iain Macleod, the Shadow Chancellor who had once been Powell's closest political ally, effectively cut off all relations with him and ended their friendship.[122] Meanwhile, students and radical groups saw him as their archenemy: when Powell spoke in Oxford in January 1969 around a thousand protesters fought with policemen in an attempt to storm the venue.[123]

Powell's heresy was not limited to immigration. Liberated from the flimsy shackles of party loyalty, he began to sketch out much of the ideology that would later be called Thatcherism. By the autumn of 1968 he was already calling for 'a shake-up, a shock, a revolution even', which would involve dismantling the post-war welfare state, selling off the major state-owned corporations and reorganising industry and commerce on unashamedly 'capitalist' lines. And at the party conference in October he presented a plan to slash the basic rate of income tax by half while cutting public spending by almost £3000 million.[124]

This breathtakingly radical agenda borrowed from the ideas of neo-liberal thinkers like Friedrich Hayek and Milton Friedman, as well as from the stream of policy papers and economic proposals coming out of the IEA and other small New Right think-tanks.[125] But few other Conservatives showed much inclination to turn themselves into proto-Thatcherites, and most senior figures were still attached to so-called Butskellism – low unemployment, the welfare state and gentle state intervention. Within the Palace of Westminster, Powell's was a voice crying in the wilderness.[126]

To the relief of hundreds of thousands of new British citizens, Enoch Powell's vision of 'the River Tiber foaming with much blood' never became a reality. It is certainly true that racial violence appeared to be on the rise in the late sixties, but this was probably a reflection of the cultural gloom and economic turmoil of the day rather than a reaction to Powell's rhetoric itself. The rise of the 'skinhead' phenomenon in working-class urban areas, which was a gritty, anti-romantic riposte to middle-class flower power, brought with it a new cult of masculine violence manifested both in football hooliganism and in 'Paki-bashing'.[127] In April 1970 a Pakistani porter called Tosir Ali was stabbed to death a few days after a skinhead rampage in the East End, but although prejudice, discrimination and racist assaults continued, this did not mark the beginning of a bloody 'race war'.[128]

Powell's apocalyptic prediction of disaster remains the most notorious speech by any British politician of the sixties. To his detractors, 'he had made racialism respectable, and had helped engineer a climate in which some people in Britain, purely on account of the colour of their skin, felt they had to live in fear'.[129] Even if Powell is exonerated of racism, there is little doubt that he had conducted himself with striking insensitivity towards an extremely vulnerable group. He became 'a rallying point for most of the hostility and rage we encountered, a shorthand for hatred and contempt,' wrote the black journalist Mike Phillips. '"I'm with Enoch," they said, or "they should let Enoch sort you lot out," and that was enough.'[130]

But it may be that to reduce Powell's career to one issue misses his lasting importance. What observers called 'Powellism' – a blend of intense patriotism, neo-liberal economics, cultural conservatism and populist rhetoric – seemed heretical, even eccentric, in the late sixties, but ten years later it became government policy. As his biographer puts it, 'his effect on the thinking of others', from ministers to voters, outstripped that of almost all his colleagues in post-war politics. Powell did not invent the ideology of the New Right single-handedly, but he gave it respectability and brought it into the mainstream. Not for nothing did Margaret Thatcher cite him as one of her two greatest influences.[131]

The irony was that in allowing himself to be sidetracked by immigration, Powell attracted such opprobrium that his hopes of national leadership were effectively destroyed. His friend Michael Foot thought that if he had steered clear of the issue, Powell would have succeeded to the Tory leadership in place of Margaret Thatcher. 'It was a tragedy for Enoch,' he wrote, 'and a tragedy for the rest of us too.'[132] Millions of people clearly agreed. In the spring of 1969 a Gallup poll found that Powell was the single most admired man in the country, while more than three decades later a BBC poll to find the greatest Britons of all time placed him just outside the top fifty.[133] The paradox of Powell's career was that no name on the list occasioned greater controversy or greater opposition. For millions of white working-class voters resentful of the social changes of the sixties, he would forever be a hero who said what he thought and dared to defy the establishment. But for millions of black and Asian Britons, his name would forever live in infamy, as Alf Garnett's favourite politician.

32

DESPERATE HOUSEWIVES

What is a Mum?
A Mum lives with a Dad and 2.4 children in a rented house where the neighbours notice her washing on the line. A Mum relies on secret ingredients and instant cake-mixes. She has kids with dirty teeth who regularly shout, 'Don't forget the Fruit Gums, Mum.'

That Was The Week That Was (1963)

We want to drive buses, play football, use beer mugs not glasses. We want men to take the pill. We do not want to be brought with bottles or invited as wives. We do not want to be wrapped up in cellophane or sent off to make the tea or shuffled in to the social committee. But these are only little things. Revolutions are about little things. Little things which happen to you all the time, every day, wherever you go, all your life.

Sheila Rowbotham, *Black Dwarf*, 10 January 1969

In the autumn of 1965 John Schlesinger's new film *Darling* was released to a tremendous critical reception and, eventually, a blizzard of awards. As one reviewer put it, the film was 'mercilessly observant and sleekly accomplished', a triumph of 'dazzlingly accurate' social commentary.[1] It follows the exploits of Diana Scott (Julie Christie), a beautiful, ambitious and self-possessed London model known to everyone as 'Darling', who has affairs with a series of men, from a television interviewer to an advertising executive and, ultimately, a wealthy Italian prince. Diana is glamorous and self-confident, but she is also materialistic and feckless. Unlike most women in films of the sixties, she is sexually assertive, seducing her boyfriends rather than the other way around. And whereas the hero of, say, *Alfie* is interested in sex for its own sake, Diana is different. Sex for her is about power, which explains why *Darling* is often seen as a landmark in the cinematic depiction of female sexuality. Instead of being vulnerable and innocent, Diana is avaricious and manipulative, working her way sexually through a string of older men to get what she wants, and using her looks to push her way to the top.²

It was no coincidence that the '*Darling* girl' became a key figure in the cinema of the mid-sixties. She was defined as 'an unpredictable, spontaneous, emotionally honest, sexually active young woman', and by concentrating on this kind of character, the studios hoped to attract young female audiences who saw their own musical and fashion tastes reflected in the lives of the characters.³ Dolly birds and swinging girls were largely defined by the clothes they bought, the records they listened to, the hairstyles they adopted and so on, and in *Darling*, too, Diana's career is bound up with modern consumerism. Her first real break is when she appears on television; she is the darling of the newspapers and the fashion magazines; her looks advertise everything from charities to chocolate. The men in her life devote themselves to making and selling images, whether on television or in advertising, and even her best friend is a magazine photographer, an extremely fashionable job in 1965, and one closely associated with commerce and the power of the image.⁴

For all her gorgeous good looks and carefree demeanour, however, Diana is clearly meant to embody the vices, not the virtues, of the affluent society.⁵ As Schlesinger explained to the *Daily Mail*, the film was an indictment of material greed in the modern world. 'What this film is about is the loneliness that Diana's life must lead to,' he said. 'The emotional coldness that descends upon her in the end is the real danger.'⁶ And yet, like *Room at the Top* and *Alfie*, the film never unequivocally condemns its protagonist. Christie, who won an Academy Award for her performance, was convinced that the film's appeal was rooted in its central character, not a role model, admittedly, but an embodiment of the new economic and cultural self-confidence of British women:

> Here was a woman who didn't want to get married, didn't want to have children like those other kitchen-sink heroines: no, Darling wanted to have *everything*. Of course at the time, this was seen as greedy promiscuity and she had to be punished for it. But there was an element of possibility for women, of a new way of living, which is why the film was a success.⁷

At the beginning of the 1950s, most married men and women generally lived separate lives. A wife was expected to concentrate on her duties as a mother and homemaker, while it fell to her husband to earn enough money for the family to live in the expected style.[8] Most observers agreed that the most inflexible separation was found in isolated industrial areas: one survey of a mining village in Yorkshire found that husband and wife lived 'separate, and in a sense, secret lives', with the woman being regarded as decidedly inferior.[9] As Richard Hoggart noted in *The Uses of Literacy*, a wife conducted her social life 'over the washing-line, at the corner-shop, visiting relatives at a moderate distance occasionally, and perhaps now and again going with her husband to his pub or club. He has his pub or club, his work, his football matches. The friends of either at all these places may well not know what the inside of their house is like, may never have "stepped across the threshold".'[10]

In their survey of suburban Woodford in 1959 Peter Willmott and Michael Young noted that the life of a girl after school followed a predetermined path: 'Daughter follows mother in her main occupations of child-rearing and housekeeping.'[11] In both working-class and middle-class households little girls were groomed to be housewives and mothers. Although universal free education represented a great opportunity for girls, many people agreed with the eminent educationalist John Newsom, who wrote that their teachers should not aim 'to iron out their differences from men, to reduce them to neuters, but to teach girls how to grow into women and to relearn the graces which so many have forgotten in the last thirty years'.[12] In 1963 he recommended that girls' education should follow 'broad themes of home making, to include not only material and practical provision but the whole field of personal relations in courtship, in marriage, and within the family'. Needlework, for instance, was a good idea: 'as young married women they will soon be responsible for buying clothes for the family and furnishings for the home: they will need some foundation of taste, and an eye for finished workmanship and quality in materials, fashion and design'.[13]

Like many other educationalists of the day, Newsom argued that 'the influence of women on events is exerted primarily in their role as wives and mothers'.[14] 'Almost all intelligent women', he claimed, agreed that motherhood was 'the essentially feminine function in society'. He even thought that women teachers were 'involuntary virgins', doomed to lives of 'drab and distressing spinsterhood'.[15] Many women agreed with him. In 1961 Monica Dickens told the readers of *Woman's Own* that women were 'born to love, born to be partners to the opposite sex . . . and that is the most important thing they can do in life . . . to be wives and mothers, to fix their hearts on one man and to love and care for him with all the bounteous unselfishness that love can inspire'.[16]

Throughout the 1950s and into the 1960s most married women described themselves as 'housewives'. The work of the housewife was organised around an unchanging routine: washing on Mondays, ironing on Tuesdays, dusting and polishing on Wednesdays and Thursdays, shopping on Fridays, and a combination of cooking and washing-up on Sundays. It was not easy: the housewife's day, according to a survey in 1957, began just after seven in the morning with breakfast and often ended only at ten in the evening.[17] 'It is a hard life,' wrote Richard Hoggart, 'in which it is assumed that the mother will be "at it" from getting up to going to bed: she will cook, mend, scrub, wash, see to the children, shop, and satisfy her husband's desires.' According to Hoggart, most working-class wives in the North of England thought that it was unnatural for a husband to help around the home, 'and would not want him to do too much of that kind of thing for fear he is thought womanish'. In many cases, he observed, 'a wife would not only "never dream" of having his help with the washing, but does not feel that she can "'ave the washing around" when he is at home'.[18]

The role of the housewife had been evolving for decades, in line with broader social and economic developments. In the 1930s, for example, a new range of women's magazines like *Woman's Own* and *Women's Illustrated* appealed to a new kind of housewife: the young, middle-class woman without servants, who was cooking and cleaning for herself and liked to think of her work as a craft or profession in its own right.[19] From the thirties onwards, the modern housewife was presented as young, stylish and efficient, effortlessly controlling the new technological appliances of the consumer society. She was not only a wife and mother but a consumer. 'It is not an exaggeration to say that woman as purchaser holds the future standard of living in this country in her hands,' explained John Newsom. 'If she buys in ignorance then our national standards will deteriorate.'[120]

Throughout the fifties and sixties advertisers trying to sell household appliances appealed predominantly to women. Innovations like the electric cooker and the washing machine made an enormous difference to the lives of most housewives, bringing a welcome breath of freedom. According to one advertising executive, companies 'should emphasize that the appliances free [the housewife] to have more time with her children and to be a better mother'. Kenwood appliances were sold with the slogan 'Your servant, Madam', while advertisements for the Mercury vacuum cleaner proclaimed:

'Drudgery's out!' and those for the Colston Classic dishwasher advised women: 'You may be beautiful but a Colston is in better shape to be a dishwasher.'[21] Similarly, convenience foods were marketed not merely as cheap but as time-saving, meaning that a woman would have more time to tidy the house, smarten herself up and even pursue her own interests before her husband returned home.[22] 'I wanted desperately to do things outside the home,' recalled one woman. 'I was always trying to think of short cuts to the housework, to get out and stimulate my own interests, and that's where the washing machine, the Hoover, etc., really came into their own.'[23]

In 1964 Harry Hopkins declared that the kitchen had been transformed from the emblem of 'woman's subjugation' into 'the shining badge of her triumph'. It was, he explained, 'the temple of those twin symbols of the new life, the refrigerator and the washing machine', as well as 'the heart of the feminine dream', full of 'gadgetry, whirring and wires'.[24] In the age of the technological revolution the new feminine ideal was the 'kitchen goddess', the glamorous mistress of her technological environment. The economic journalist Norman Macrae even claimed that the 'solicitor's wife with three children and no mother's help in Wimbledon' and the 'steel-worker's wife with the same size of family in Middlesbrough' led very similar lives. 'Each', he explained, 'has the same modern equipment in her kitchen and vacuum-cleaner cupboard.'[25] Furthermore, he added, the modern housewife was also supremely sexy. Who could not 'look out upon the housewives' tight trousers on motorbike pillions and family side cars on a summer Saturday morning rolling along the road to Brighton, and fail to feel a great and surging sense of poetry welling up within him at the sight of them'?[26]

Although the role of the housewife was often dismissed by subsequent generations as trivial and unsatisfying, this is not necessarily true. Housework, as one historian has recently argued, was 'of major economic, social and cultural importance', providing the context in which families ate, slept, entertained and socialised. The skills of the housewife helped to determine the social status of her family: the way she prepared her food, wore her clothes and maintained the house all 'provided the means by which the family presented itself to the world'.[27]

How women themselves felt about being housewives, however, was a different matter. At the beginning of the fifties a survey in the *Manchester Guardian* had suggested a very mixed picture. Two out of five women said they were happy at home and did not want a job; on the other hand, half of the sample admitted that they were often bored.[28] Most women, though, simply accepted their lot. 'Your husband went out to work,' said one, 'and you looked after him and had his meal ready when he got home and you never thought of working unless you were very hard up and went cleaning or did dressmaking . . . Working hard had been one part of your life, and then you married, and gave it up, and made the home for your husband and family.'[29]

Indeed, many women were proud of their efforts. 'I tried to be a perfect housewife,' one Manchester woman later recalled. 'I did try my very best, I kept it clean and I put good food on the table.'[30] A teacher from Rotherham, who had carried on working after her marriage, agreed that the housewife was a professional technician in her own right:

> I was mistress in my kitchen and that is how I liked it. I did everything. I knew where everything was. My kitchen was like a very, very efficient workshop. Roland, my husband, never came into the kitchen, so I did all the cooking, all the preparation, all the washing up. He didn't know the first thing about the washing machine, he didn't know the first thing about ironing, and he didn't know the first thing about the cooker. It was my ambition to run the house to the best of my ability. Being a housewife was a twenty-four hour job so I allotted myself an additional two evenings a week to my home.[31]

But some women did not feel the same way. Many bright and ambitious women, having shone at school, found domestic life extremely dull. One housewife living on a new housing estate near Bedford, for instance, missed her husband and longed 'to rush out into the road and have a sensible conversation with an adult'.[32] Another admitted that she was 'fighting like mad to get out of the bloody kitchen . . . I felt domestic life was perfectly terrible. I nearly went mad with it. It's soul-destroying spending all day alone cleaning and only having conversations with people aged under six.'[33] By the early 1960s liberal newspapers like the *Observer* and the *Guardian* were regularly printing stories about desperate housewives. And it was a letter to the *Guardian* from a frustrated woman in 1962 that became the germ of the National Housewives' Register, a mutual support network that organised talks and coffee mornings in an effort to make housewives feel less isolated.[34]

In 1959 the *Financial Times* confidently observed that 'at the age when men are making their way up the ladder, most women are bringing up their families'.[35] This was not quite true: in fact, millions of British women had already taken the decisive step over the threshold from the home into the office. As contraception became more available and the birth rate fell, so women were released from 'the wheel of childbearing' and had the opportunity to pursue their own careers.[36] Even during the thirties, a period of high unemployment in many areas, it was noticeable that more women were going out to work than ever before. During the war almost all single women were called up to 'work for victory', and millions of married women voluntarily joined them.[37] And after the war, despite the rhetoric of educationalists like John Newsom, the pattern continued. Women were having fewer children and were living longer, making them an attractive and cheap source of labour in an expanding economy.[38] The biggest change, however, was the collapse of the marriage bar, the unwritten rule that a woman would leave her job as soon as she got married. One in five married women was working in 1951; ten years later the equivalent figure was one in three; by 1972 it was almost one in two.[39] As Arthur Marwick notes, the opportunities for women in Britain were much greater than in countries like France or Italy, and by the 1990s three-quarters of all British women were working outside the home.[40]

Women were only paid a fraction of what men earned: in 1958, according to one calculation, a woman would be paid less than two-thirds of what a man received for doing the same job.[41] In the late fifties both the civil service and the state education system began introducing equal salaries for men and women, but not all employers followed their lead, and even at the end of the sixties many women were still paid far less than their male equivalents.[42] Furthermore, government research suggested that most women were employed in unskilled jobs with little scope for promotion or self-improvement, so there was a 'serious waste of women's talents'.[43] Only certain careers were considered suitable for women. In the late fifties and early sixties the Bodley Head published a series of books called 'Careers for Girls': titles included *Air Hostess Ann*, *Pam Stevens Secretary*, *Jill Kennedy Telephonist* and *Sheila Burton Dental Assistant*. In each book the heroine begins her job dedicated and enthusiastic, sure that she wants to pursue a career and not be trapped into marriage, but romance usually prevails. Only in the 'doctor' and 'teacher' volumes does the heroine continue working after marriage. In the case of the doctor, though, she moves into public health, explaining to her beloved: 'I'd be free in the evenings to get your meals.'[44]

For many men, the appearance of women in the workplace was unsettling and even deplorable. 'No woman works as well in a trade or profession as does a man,' one disgruntled Surrey man wrote to the *Picture Post*, adding that 'most women enter business with their ambitions fixed on achieving independence in a kitchen as some lucky man's wife'.[45] During the fifties most childcare experts argued that an intimate relationship between mother and child was essential for the child to be a healthy and useful member of society. John Bowlby, for example, famously insisted that the 'mother of young children is not free, or at least should not be free, to earn'.[46] At the time, this was considered quite a progressive position. By holding up the ideal of the family and emphasising the importance of maternal love, Bowlby was breaking with the authoritarianism and reserve of the past.[47] But his argument also provided the opponents of working mothers with a powerful intellectual rationale, and women were often blamed for juvenile delinquency. Working mothers were apparently selfish and unnatural, putting their own ambitions above the needs of their children and the interests of society. Even though a social study in 1962 concluded that the children of working mothers were no more unruly or ill behaved than those of domestic housewives, the myth took a long time to disappear.[48]

The distrust of modern women was a common theme in British life and letters during the late fifties and sixties. Social critics who were suspicious of modern mass culture often identified it with women and feminine values, not least because women appeared to have gained so much from the technological advances of the affluent society. As the critic D. E. Cooper put it, the New Wave writers of the late fifties projected the idea of an 'effeminate society', steeped in 'pettiness, snobbery, flippancy, voluptuousness, superficiality, materialism'.[49]

A more light-hearted analysis of the relationship between modern women, consumerism and social change appears in the film *Battle of the Sexes* (1960). The story follows the fortunes of a little Scottish tartan business, struggling to defend the old ways against Mrs Angela Barrows (Constance Cummings), a dreadful American 'industrial consultant', and a divorcee. The firm does business from its ramshackle old headquarters, a Dickensian house stuffed with ledgers, scrolls and quills. Mrs Barrows, a modern woman with no respect for tradition, wants to sweep all this away and bring in furnishings befitting the sixties: pot plants and cacti, Anglepoise table lamps, abstract paintings, efficiency charts and tables. The resistance is led by the family's faithful old chief clerk (an unusually subdued Peter Sellers) and at last her modernising schemes are defeated. The portrait of the late paternalistic owner is restored to its rightful place, and Angela Barrows bursts into sobs: 'man's greatest hazard — a woman's tears', as the film caustically remarks.[50]

Many men continued to resent the idea of wives going out to work. One in three husbands interviewed in 1965 still disliked the idea, and 6 per cent felt that a woman's place was in the home.[51] Women's magazines, so quick to extol the virtues of the kitchen goddess, were slow to endorse the trend of women in the workplace. Monica Dickens explained to her *Woman's Own* readers in 1961:

> Ask any man if he'd rather his wife worked or stayed at home and see what he says; he would rather she stayed at home and looked after his children, and was waiting for him with a decent meal and a sympathetic ear when he got home from work . . . You can't have deep and safe happiness in marriage and the exciting independence of a career as well.[52]

Even a woman's own children might put pressure on her to stay at home. One little boy later recalled 'being truly mortified' when his mother went out to work, 'because she wasn't at home to look after me like other mothers', and he would 'sit in the bus stop, age five, waiting for her to come home every night'.[53] We do not know how his mother felt, but it takes little imagination to guess that the sight of her child waiting miserably for her in the dusk could not have been a completely happy one.

The transformation of the British woman was unquestionably one of the most important social changes of the century. One of the results was that the conventional patronising view of women, which presented them as intellectually weak, unreliable and oversensitive, was no longer sustainable. Even the producers of the James Bond films constantly insisted that their heroines were independent women from the modern world. The director Terence Young told an interviewer that they were 'women of the nuclear age, freer and able to make love when they want to without worrying about it'. This vision of modern femininity obviously owed a great deal to male fantasies, but at the time it also represented a radical break with the passive cinematic women of the fifties. The lead actress of *Thunderball* (1965), the French beauty queen Claudine Auger, claimed that her character was 'the ultimate in modern, emancipated woman', and said of the Bond girls in general: 'They can live without a man doing everything for them because they are independent. They like to decide their future destinies for themselves. They are highly sexual – but only with men worth their loving. They are free, you see, completely free.'[54]

Despite the stereotype of the passive little wife, the kitchen goddess of the fifties and sixties was expected to play an active part in the physical relationship of marriage, as skilful and effective in the bedroom as she was in the kitchen. As the infidelity and illegitimacy of the Second World War had made clear, women had sexual needs and desires of their own, and organisations like the Marriage Guidance Council put a greater emphasis on female sexual pleasure than had ever been contemplated by a government agency.[55] When in 1948 the Council's secretary advised that the goal was 'satisfying orgasm for both', he was giving unprecedented official sanction to female sexuality.[56] Since the growing popularity of birth control sidestepped the inevitability of pregnancy and childbirth, it focused attention on the purely pleasurable aspect of sex, and the female body became increasingly identified with eroticism rather than reproduction.[57]

At the same time the ideal of marriage itself was evolving into a genuine partnership between husband and wife. 'In the modern marriage, both partners choose each other freely as persons,' explained the textbook *The Family and Marriage in Britain* (1966). 'Both are of equal status and expect to have an equal share in taking decisions and in pursuing their sometimes mutual, sometimes separate and diverse, tastes and interests.'[58] Although most commentators focused on the transformation of the traditional housewife, the evolving role of the modern husband also reflected the impact of affluence and cultural change. In 1961 the sociologist Ferdynand Zweig wrote that the 'stern, bullying, dominating and self-assertive father . . . is fast disappearing, and the new image of a benevolent, friendly and brotherly father is emerging'.[59] In comfortable middle-class communities like Woodford, where couples had often moved away from their parents, husbands were more likely to push against traditional gender divisions. Willmott and Young noted that in place of the stereotypical working-class husband, 'forcing a trial of unwanted babies on his wife, has come the man who wheels the pram on Sunday mornings'. One man, they reported, 'washes up the dishes every night and lays the breakfast for the morning'. Another admitted: 'On Sunday mornings I usually hoover around for her while she does a bit of washing'. A third polished the floors and made the beds at weekends.[60]

In 1971 Geoffrey Gorer described such new arrangements as 'symmetrical marriage', based on 'an ideal of equality, of husband and wife doing everything together, of minimal separation of interests or pursuits outside working hours'. When he asked his interviewees which qualities made for a happy marriage, he found that the most common choice was 'comradeship', defined by respondents as 'doing things together', 'togetherness' or 'communication'.[61] Younger people were particularly likely to emphasise equality and common interests. 'Give and take. Getting along together and the sharing of pleasures together,' explained a builder's wife. 'You have to work together to keep it happy,' declared a self-employed building contractor. 'It can be hard work; you must all give [things] up. You have to have give-and-take; it is not all romance and roses.'[62]

Unfortunately, many marriages strayed a long way from the path of romance and roses. Divorce, still uncommon, was regarded as a social stigma: one girl who grew up during the sixties remembered feeling so 'embarrassed and ashamed' by her parents' divorce that she kept it hidden even from her best friends for eight years, never inviting school friends back to the house in case they found out.[63] The existing legislation, which required proof of some 'matrimonial offence' before a divorce could be granted, was plainly inadequate for the modern world. In 1963 the Labour MP Leo Abse introduced an unsuccessful bill permitting divorce after seven years of separation, and three years later, a church commission advocated using 'irremediable marriage breakdown' as the basis for divorce, rather than heaping all the blame on to one partner.[64]

It took the Divorce Reform Act of 1969, one of the last liberal reforms of the Wilson era, to end the emphasis on guilt and fault. From 1971, the sole grounds for divorce were that 'the marriage has broken down irretrievably'. Furthermore, the Matrimonial Property Act of 1970 recognised for the first time that a wife's work, whether inside or outside the home, made a financial contribution to married life that must be taken into account when dividing up the property, which meant that divorce was no longer a financial disaster for women.[65] By this point Britain already had the highest divorce rate of any country in Europe, and within a year the rate had doubled to some 100,000 annually. In 1965 there had been just 2.8 divorces per 1000 married adults in England and Wales; by 1975 there were 9.6; by 1980 there were 12. Within twenty years of the change in the law, the annual number of divorces lagged only slightly behind the number of marriages.[66]

The reform of the divorce laws reflected the changing role of women and the transformation of marriage from an unequal contract into a romantic partnership based on affection and companionship. Divorce reform recognised women as equal partners in marriage, and it gave them nominal parity within the home. It was one of several developments in the sixties that illustrated the growing independence and assertiveness of ordinary women. The development of birth control, for example, gave women power over their own fertility: no longer would their health be at the mercy of the lusts of their husbands.

More controversially, the legalisation of abortion in 1967 gave women the feeling that they controlled their own lives and bodies, so that pregnancy need not be a life-changing disaster. Until this point, abortion had been technically illegal, although historians agree that there were at least 100,000 'back-street' abortions and self-induced miscarriages a year in the decades beforehand. Indeed, Diana Gittens even suggests that abortion was the most common form of birth control for the unskilled working class.[67] Self-induced miscarriages, carried out in the cramped confines of the working-class household, were particularly nasty affairs. One woman later recalled watching her mother induce a miscarriage 'by means of gin, quinine, jumping down the stairs and similar traditional methods . . . The foetus, raw and bloody looking, "came away" to flop on the floor when she was in the kitchen.'[68]

This was obviously a traumatic and dangerous business, but the alternative was no better, since back-street abortions were just as unreliable and sometimes fatal. Between 1958 and 1960 eighty-two women lost their lives after undergoing an abortion, while thousands more were hospitalised or left permanently damaged after the operation went wrong.[69] Some abortionists were competent gynaecologists and anaesthetists, others were little better than semi-qualified quacks, but most found it a lucrative business. One girl had a cheap forty-pound abortion arranged by her boyfriend, who had blithely been giving her pills and claiming they were contraceptives. Both were too naive to realise what was coming, and had arranged to go out for the evening after the abortion. Instead, the girl spent more than a day lying on sheets of newspaper in a dirty, empty flat somewhere in London. The doctor had taken the money, induced labour with a saline injection and then simply disappeared. The girl was in excruciating pain and later had to be treated in hospital. 'The abortion was the changing point of my life,' she later recalled. 'I hated my body because it had done this to me, plus men as well, because it was all their fault.'[70]

After Paul Ferris published an exposé of the abortion industry in 1966 he was bombarded with dozens of letters asking for help and advice. It was a depressing litany of misery: 'I am an unmarried teacher of twenty-three yrs and my career will be shattered'; 'I am just about on the verge of panic'; 'I am in a terrible state'; 'I am eighteen and need now to save, not me particularly but my family, the shame and ignominy of it all.' The writers were usually frightened, isolated young women from small towns and suburbs, and Ferris did his best to give them the necessary information. 'A name, an address, a phone number would give admission to the network,' he wrote later.[71] But for girls living at home in a provincial town, the abortion network often seemed a distant impossibility. 'Your choices', as Mary Ingham puts it, 'were to have it adopted; keep it, as an unmarried mother – not a very enviable option, as it ruined your marriage prospects – or hastily get married.'[72] For many girls whose pregnancy had led to a rift with their parents, adoption was often the only possibility. About forty thousand women a year found their way to the austere surroundings of a church-run mother and baby home, where after childbirth the babies were taken away for adoption.[73]

The moral complexities of the abortion issue meant that it always remained a controversial subject, although it was nowhere near as contentious in Britain as it was in some Catholic countries or in the United States. For thousands of women, however, the Abortion Act of 1967 undoubtedly represented liberation from a dangerous and miserable plight. This particular reform was based on decades of campaigning by women's groups and pro-abortion organisations, and there had already been several unsuccessful bills in 1953, 1961, 1965 and 1966.[74] The event that most swayed public opinion towards reform was probably the thalidomide disaster at the beginning of the sixties, when pregnant women taking the tranquilliser started giving birth to deformed children. In May 1962, six months after the drug had been withdrawn, the Ministry of Health instructed medical officers to take 'every possible effort' to prevent the births of the deformed babies. As several commentators pointed out, it seemed hypocritical to permit abortions in this case but no other, and by 1965 polls suggested that more than seven out of ten people supported reform.[75]

As in the campaigns to liberalise homosexuality and divorce, Anglican churchmen were in the vanguard of the struggle to legalise abortion. In 1965 the Church Assembly's Board for Social Responsibility declared that it could be justified if 'there was a threat to the mother's life or well-being', taking the latter to include 'the life and well-being of the family'.[76] Two years later the young Liberal MP David Steel introduced a bill that, with government support, became the Abortion Act, under which an abortion merely needed the approval of two doctors satisfied of its medical or psychological necessity. Private clinics rapidly appeared across the country, the price of an abortion plummeted, and it was even possible to have one, albeit after waiting six weeks or so, through the National Health Service.[77] Although the number of abortions naturally increased, there is no evidence that the legislation encouraged promiscuity, despite the conservative folk myth to the contrary. In fact, a survey in 1972 of unmarried women who had had an abortion suggested that most were naive and sexually inexperienced, and that their pregnancy resulted from an unexpected or unplanned loss of control rather than wilful self-indulgence.[78]

While new opportunities in the labour market, the popularity of birth control and the reform of the divorce and abortion laws were giving women more personal freedom in the sixties, there was very little talk of feminism. The women's movement that had fought for the vote was widely believed to have disappeared. Modern women were kitchen goddesses; feminists were dusty, old-fashioned harridans. 'Today, the spirit of the old pioneers is so dead it seems a miracle that it ever existed,' wrote Jill Craigie in the *Evening Standard*. The future Labour MP Shirley Williams, the daughter of the legendary campaigner Vera Brittain, admitted that she was 'not a feminist . . . but that's a matter of generations I think, don't you?'[79] And the young Sheila Rowbotham, later a prominent campaigner for women's rights, thought that feminists were 'shadowy figures in long old-fashioned clothes who were somehow connected with headmistresses who said you shouldn't wear high heels and make-up. It was all very prim and stiff and mainly concerned with keeping you away from boys.'[80]

One of the most remarkable things about the decline of feminism was that it had become such a dirty word on the left, where it was seen as divisive, self-indulgent and irredeemably middle class. In 1969 one delegate at the Labour Women's Conference demanded to know 'what was the matter with women today'. Why, she wondered, were they all demanding equal opportunities and equal pay? 'They did not deserve to be mothers,' the minutes recorded. 'If they could not sacrifice five years for their children before the children went to school they did not know what they were missing. They were missing the relationship between child and mother. It was no wonder there were so many child delinquents when that relationship was missing. Forget about the money . . . and stay at home until the children go to school.'[81]

In February 1968 Barbara Castle, undoubtedly the most powerful female politician in the country, was asked to speak to the TUC to mark the fiftieth anniversary of female suffrage, but she found the whole thing 'agony'. 'It's time we stopped thinking in [these] women *v.* men terms,' she wrote afterwards. 'As long as we are so sexually conscious about our work we will never really get ourselves "assimilated", any more than the immigrants will.'[82] In later years Castle rarely had a good word for the women's liberation movement. 'I had a mind as well as a vagina,' she wrote caustically, 'and I did not see why the latter should dominate – there are too many interesting things in life.' As for the invention of terms like 'Ms' and 'chairperson', she was utterly scathing, commenting: 'I don't give a damn if I am called "chairman" so long as I am in charge.'[83]

All the same, although feminism itself had fallen from fashion, women were challenging the old gender stereotypes in a way that anticipated the 'women's lib' campaigns of the seventies. In 1963 an examination of young people in working-class Sheffield noted

> the signs that some girls are tending towards more independence in their dealings with men, and that they will not be content to sign over their lives to their husbands on marriage . . . They are determined to remain smart and in control of events after they have married; they are not prepared to be bowed down with lots of children, and they will expect their husbands to take a fuller share than their fathers in the running of the home.[84]

However, many young women resented the expectations that accompanied more liberal attitudes to pre-marital sex. In Kingsley Amis's novel *Take a Girl Like You* (1960), which draws heavily on the author's own experiences, the heroine Jenny Bunn is torn between her caddish boyfriend Patrick, who is always pressing her to have sex with him, and her 'old Bible-class ideas'. At one point Jenny muses that what Patrick calls being 'frank, free, and open' means nothing more than 'in practice a frank, free, and open (and immediate and often repeated) scuttle into bed with some man; to tell them all to drop dead, however frankly, freely and openly, did not count as that'.[85] In other words, a 'progressive' attitude to pre-marital sex is merely an excuse for a man to get whatever he wants, regardless of the woman's own scruples. Near the end of the book Patrick ends the argument by deflowering Jenny after she has passed out drunk at a party, and although the two are finally reconciled, the incident leaves a very bitter taste in the mouth.[86]

The lesson of *Take a Girl Like You* was that so-called 'free love' was not always the blessing it appeared, and so it proved for many young women in the counter-culture of the late sixties, where sexual self-indulgence was seen as an act of rebellion against bourgeois imperialism.[87] The reminiscences of their male counterparts do not always make very pleasant reading. 'Getting emotionally involved was not good form; you had to be detached,' one recalled. 'Once I learnt that, I was very successful.'[88] In his egregious manifesto *Play Power* (1970) the underground journalist Richard Neville explained his rationale for bedding endless 'chicks': 'If the attraction is only biological, nothing is lost except a few million spermatozoa, and both parties continue their separate ways.'[89] 'Chicks' were led to feel that they were being conservative or boring by refusing the attentions of their male contemporaries. One female hanger-on later observed that 'it was paradise for men in their late twenties: all these willing girls. But the trouble with the willing girls was that a lot of the time they were willing not because they particularly fancied the people concerned but because they felt they ought to.'[90]

Obviously what went on in the bohemian underground only affected a tiny minority of people, although among them were prominent feminist writers of the seventies like Germaine Greer, Rosie Boycott and Sheila Rowbotham.[91] But there is anecdotal evidence that similar attitudes prevailed elsewhere, too. One Derbyshire man recalled of the late sixties: 'It was all lust . . . Once I'd had sex that were it. After that I'd drop her because I'd had what I wanted. It was a case of hop on and hop off . . . You just got stuck in and enjoyed yourself.'[92] Although most young people led surprisingly chaste sex lives, the more promiscuous among them did not always look back on the experience with great fondness. One woman reflected that although she thought she was 'breaking all the taboos . . . we had our own taboos and one of them was we couldn't talk about our problems or admit to being unhappy'. She was 'unfulfilled', she said sadly; she rarely 'had an orgasm, because the men were so selfish'; but she lacked 'the confidence to say, "No, that's not right, I don't want to do that."'[93]

It was not surprising that many bright young women despised the sexual politics of the counter-culture, and this sense of dissatisfaction inspired some of the most outspoken voices of the women's movement of the following decade. As early as 1966 the radical journal *New Left Review* ran an article by the feminist writer Juliet Mitchell, while three years later Sheila Rowbotham proclaimed in *Black Dwarf* that 1969 would be 'The Year of the Militant Woman'. For these women, feminism was the natural reaction to their experiences in the subculture of bohemian London.[94] As Rosie Boycott observed, the underground scene

> pretended to be an alternative [but] it wasn't providing an alternative for women. It was providing an alternative for men in that there were no problems about screwing around or being who you wanted. You were still able to do it on a chauvinist level and there was still a power game going on in that women were typists, men were the bosses, men were the ones who decided what wages people got, whether people had jobs. Women were dependent on men.[95]

By the end of 1969 there were about seventy 'women's lib' groups across the country, and their efforts were complemented by the prominence of outspoken women in other fields, from Doris Lessing and Iris Murdoch to Vanessa Redgrave and Barbara Castle.[96] The new feminism of the seventies owed much to these women, but it also drew on the efforts of other, little-known women in the late sixties: the fishermen's wives who campaigned in Hull for improved safety at sea; the sewing-machinists at the Dagenham Ford plant who went on strike for equal terms with men; and the London bus conductresses who demanded the opportunity to drive the buses. Their struggles, and those of women within the trade union movement, helped to draw attention to women's issues and prepare the ground for the Equal Pay Act of 1970.[97] Even at this stage, however, women's issues were still not considered particularly newsworthy. The Equal Pay Act sailed through the Commons with no opposition, and polls showed that a majority of both men and women supported it. But at the final reading the Commons chamber was almost completely empty, and most newspapers afforded it barely a paragraph or two. In later years this would change.[98]

Although the women's liberation movement did not really get under way in Britain until the early seventies, three moments in 1970 hinted at what was to follow. First, in February, there was the first National Women's Conference, held at Ruskin College, Oxford, at which more than five hundred women demanded equal pay, free contraception and abortion, and twenty-four-hour childcare. Most of the delegates, according to reports, were 'young women, many of them students with long flowing hair, trousers and maxi-coats', although 'here and there were middle-aged mothers and housewives from council estates'.[99] It was 'very exciting', recalled one delegate. 'You thought, "This is the first time anybody's noticed this and, by God . . . it's going to be different tomorrow."'[100] Then, in October, there appeared the seminal feminist manifesto of the seventies, Germaine Greer's bestselling polemic *The Female Eunuch*, a sparkling argument for female liberation from stereotyping, passivity and male condescension.[101] Finally, the following month, came the rather more farcical scenes at the Miss World contest at the Albert Hall, during which concealed agitators, encouraged by the freelance protester Peter Hain, attacked the bewildered host, Bob Hope, with flour, smoke bombs and general abuse.[102] Oddly enough, thanks to the enormous publicity it received, the Miss World affair probably did most to bring feminism to the attention of the general public, although not all women approved of it. 'I do not think women should ever achieve equal rights. I do not want to,' declared Miss World, from Grenada. 'I still like a gentleman to hold a chair back for me.'[103] Prince Charles, meanwhile, had his own explanation for the Miss World protesters. 'Basically,' he mused, 'I think it is because they want to be men.'[104]

At the end of the sixties feminism was still regarded by most people as a 'minority obsession' or 'extremist nonsense'.[105] But this should not detract from the fact that the era brought enormous changes to the lives of millions of ordinary women. They were implicated in all the major social trends of the period, from the increasingly flexible nature of work and the technological transformation of the household to the liberalisation of divorce and the legalisation of abortion. By having smaller families, expanding into the workforce and asserting their equal status with men, women participated in British national life as never before.

A girl of sixteen in 1970 was far more likely to remain in education than a similar sixteen-year-old in 1956. She was more likely to pursue her own intellectual and cultural interests for as long as she liked, to marry when and whom she wanted, to have children when and if she wanted, and, above all, to choose whether she remained at home as a housewife or pursued her own career. These were not small advances, and they had a profound effect on the way men saw women and women saw themselves. If we are looking for a genuine revolution in the sixties, then perhaps this was it: a revolution with its roots deep in British social history, but a revolution nonetheless.

33

IN PLACE OF STRIFE

As we watched in horrified silence, a number of highly polished boots descended the stairs, and Mr Victor Feather stood before us, nervously twisting his cloth cap in his large hands. 'Excuse me, Sir, coming in when you're having your tea, like, but me and t'lads have put our heads together as you might say, and come up with certain proposals.'

'Mrs Wilson's Diary', *Private Eye*, 6 June 1969

Sooner or later the government of the day will have to take on the trades union movement – and win.

Cecil King's diary, 25 June 1969

On Tuesday, 9 April 1968 Barbara Castle walked into the Cabinet Room at 10 Downing Street and had 'a bit of a shock'. Instead of being allocated her usual seat, down at the bottom corner of the table where she could doodle to her heart's content, she had been placed right in the middle, opposite the Prime Minister. The change was a symbol of her new status at the heart of Harold Wilson's government. Now that 'planned, purposive growth' had been blown away by devaluation, Wilson hoped to show that his government could stand up to the unions and end the plague of wildcat strikes. With her high reputation on the backbenches and on the left of the Labour Party, as well as her excellent record at the Department of Transport, Castle seemed the ideal choice to accomplish his latest grand design.[1]

As the only woman in Wilson's Cabinet, Castle was bound to stand out, but her fiery, flirtatious personality only added to her fame. She came from a typical Northern radical family, steeped in political activism and the Social Gospel.[2] After spells as a Labour councillor and a journalist on the *Daily Mirror*, she was elected MP for Blackburn in the landslide of 1945, and rapidly acquired a reputation as a rising star of the left. She had close relationships with a number of Labour colleagues, notably Michael Foot, but one of her most enduring alliances was her bond with the young Harold Wilson. Both had worked their way from provincial Yorkshire to grammar school, Oxford and Westminster, both were ambitious and industrious, and both resented the social snobbery of the Hampstead set on the party's right. Wilson, with his quicksilver mind and parliamentary wit, was always the senior partner, but as he advanced, so Castle followed in his wake.[3]

As a non-driving Transport Minister, Castle had introduced breathalysers, compulsory seatbelts and the seventy-miles-an-hour speed limit; nevertheless by the beginning of 1968 she was probably the most popular minister in the government.[4] She was 'a star', wrote one of her junior ministers, Roy Hattersley; but that meant 'she possessed all a star's disadvantages as well as a star's virtues'. She approached every issue with the same 'frenzied excitement', even when cool detachment might have been more appropriate.[5] In Cabinet she happily flirted and giggled with her colleagues, but she also irritated them with long monologues about their failure to live up to her socialist principles. And crucially, although she was a 'party animal' to her fingertips, she had few close friends in the Cabinet and had never bothered to cultivate her own following in the Commons. She might have been the most popular minister in the government, but as she bent her mind to the thorny issue of union reform, she had remarkably few reliable allies.[6]

More than eight million men and two million women belonged to a trade union in the late sixties, encompassing everything from coal-miners and train-drivers to actors and footballers. Contrary to myth, industrial relations in Britain since the Second World War had been rather good, and in 1964 the Conservatives' election propaganda boasted that they had kept strike levels lower than in any other major Western country except West Germany.[7] By this point, however, employers were already complaining about the frequency of unofficial, 'wildcat' strikes that were hard to predict or prevent. This new wave of disputes, often provoked by internecine feuds or rivalries between different groups of workers, did not attract much sympathy from the general public: as early as 1959 *The Times* had condemned the 'little bullies and petty Napoleons' on the shop floor.[8] And as unofficial strikes continued, so the image of the unions became increasingly tarnished: polls showed support for them falling, and increasing numbers of people cited industrial unrest as one of Britain's major economic problems.[9]

Although Wilson was well aware of this rising public disaffection with the unions, he was initially reluctant to contemplate government intervention. Not only were the unions the major financial backers of the Labour Party, but they controlled the party conference and had a powerful influence on the National Executive. Their relationship with the Wilson government, however, was less than smooth. In an attempt to keep inflation under control and impress the international bankers, Wilson and Brown had initially adopted a voluntary incomes policy. Even though this was pretty toothless, it still irritated the union leaders, who thought that the government had no business telling them what their members should earn. In any case, it was a fiasco. Even though Brown had stipulated an annual wage increase of 3.5 per cent, many unions chose to ignore him, and by the summer of 1966 wages were rising by more than three times the recommended rate.[10]

At this point, following the seamen's strike and the July sterling crisis, Wilson imposed a mandatory six-month wage freeze, to be followed by another six months of severe restraint. To many union leaders, the virtual prohibition of collective bargaining by a Labour government came as a staggering betrayal.[11] At a National Executive Committee meeting in February 1967 the union members warned that 'the traditional relationship between the two sides of the [Labour] movement would crack if the Government persisted in its policy'.[12] And once the freeze had ended, incomes were soon soaring ahead of government guidelines: in the twelve months after April 1968 wages rose by around 5 per cent and real annual earnings by 7 per cent. 'Incomes policy has broken down and to the most alarming extent,' commented *The Economist*, adding that 'employers, convinced that inflation is inevitable, are falling over themselves . . . to grant large wage increases'.[13]

As if this were not enough, Wilson was becoming increasingly worried about the rising levels of strikes. Since 1966, industrial disputes had become steadily more common, consuming the energies of more workers and swallowing up more working days. Although Britain's strike record was still better than those of, say, the United States, France or even Japan, more than 90 per cent of disputes were unofficial affairs, often in flagrant breach of the unions' own regulations.[14] After one meeting with the 'top brass of British Leyland', Castle recorded that they were obsessed by 'unofficial strikes in the motorcar industry . . . and who can blame them?'[15]

The situation took a decisive turn for the worse in 1968. Every year since 1962, fewer than 3 million working days had been lost to strikes, but in 1968 some 4.7 million days were lost. In the first eight months alone, more days were lost to industrial action than in all but four years since 1945.[16] The newspapers were full of reports of wildcat strikes, sit-ins and go-slows, and, according to the Conservative press, the fault lay with a handful of extreme shop stewards, whose irresponsibility endangered the health of the economy. 'Anyone with the impression that 1968 is having more than its fair share of labour disputes is absolutely right,' announced *The Times*, calling it 'The Year of the Strike'.[17]

As Wilson himself had suggested in 1966, the Communist Party and other Marxist groups wielded a disproportionate influence in some unions. As the militant anti-Communism of the 1950s had begun to recede, many unions had relaxed their rules on Communist participation. Indeed, a considerable number of radical shop stewards belonged to the Liaison Committee for the Defence of Trade Unions, which was basically a Communist front organisation. Perhaps more importantly, a new generation of union leaders, like Bill Kendall, Alan Fisher and Ray Buckton, were eager to dispel the rather cosy, bureaucratic flavour of their predecessors. And in 1968 the two largest unions in the country, the Transport and General Workers and the Amalgamated Engineering Union, fell into the hands of perceived radicals, Jack Jones and Hugh Scanlon.[18]

However, economic insecurity, rather than Marxist passion, is the most obvious and compelling explanation for the strikes of the late sixties. As *The Economist*'s labour correspondent Stephen Milligan pointed out, inflation was probably the single biggest spur to union militancy, since it frightened workers into thinking that their earnings were falling behind rising prices. Even workers who won handsome annual wage increases thought that they were losing out when they read in the newspapers that others were also winning hefty pay awards.[19]

To make matters worse, the Wilson government had raised taxes to pay for its spending commitments, and as Callaghan and Jenkins applied repeated doses of severe deflation to protect the pound many people felt that their own economic progress had stalled or even slipped into reverse. Between 1967 and 1969, average real take-home pay remained exactly static, since rising wages were cancelled out by rising prices and higher taxes, which hit lower-middle-class and working-class workers especially hard. The paradox was that expectations had never been greater, thanks to the unprecedented spread of television and advertising, so the average worker's ambitions far outstripped his earnings. It was hardly surprising, therefore, that skilled craftsmen, public sector employees and others looked to the unions to protect them, and 'militancy slowly percolated through the spectrum of moderation'.[20]

Still, it is worth remembering that the economic importance of industrial unrest has probably been exaggerated. Even in the late sixties, the amount of working time lost to strikes was far less than that lost to illness.[21] Wilson's economic adviser Andrew Graham argued that of the five billion days worked every year, just five million, or 0.1 per cent, were lost to strikes. Even when he trebled this to allow for their knock-on effect, the impact on productivity and competitiveness was almost wholly insignificant.[22] Strikes might have exacerbated Britain's competitive problems in the seventies, but they did not cause them. There were more strikes in France or Italy than in Britain between 1965 and 1974, and far from industrial unrest being a 'British disease', it was an international phenomenon, affecting every major developed nation in Europe as the world economy ran aground.[23]

But even though the economic impact of strikes was exaggerated, they still represented, and were viewed as, a serious political problem. Conservative newspapers treated industrial unrest as though it were a national calamity, and although many people sympathised with the strikers, there were also plenty who found them irritating, subversive or unpatriotic. In April 1968 the Conservatives proposed a radical new legal framework for industrial relations, and just a few weeks later a royal commission under Lord Donovan recommended that the government establish a Commission for Industrial Relations that would prod the unions into reforming themselves.[24] Together, the Conservative plan and the Donovan Report constituted an irresistible spur to action, and Wilson and Castle recognised that they had to come up with something in reply. As the *Sunday Telegraph* put it, Castle had 'to steal Mr Heath's thunder and to save Mr Wilson's bacon, all in the same tumultuous breath, in time for the next election'.[25]

Castle was already convinced that the unions had to change. The long battles over prices and incomes left her tired and bitter, and soon after taking up her new job she had 'realized how facile are some of the remedies which the Left peddles: as though interfering with a market economy . . . were as easy as voting a decision in Cabinet'. She even recorded that she was sickened by '*Tribune*'s constant propaganda to the effect that every wage claim is sacrosanct and every industrial dispute noble. They are just not prepared to pay the price of economic independence.'[26] As Castle's biographer puts it, a 'heady sense of martyrdom' was already creeping into her diaries as she contemplated the task ahead.[27]

By the autumn of 1968 Castle believed that the government needed to take firm action to reform industrial relations. The newspapers were full of the shop stewards' latest excesses, this time at the Girling brake factory in Cheshire. Girling supplied crucial components to most of the car industry, but the factory had been plagued by fifty-seven separate disputes in eighteen months. On 11 November, after a member of one union turned on an oil valve that supposedly should be touched only by a member of a rival union, twenty-two machine-setters walked out on strike. The dispute dragged on for four weeks, and as the car industry ground to a halt, more than five thousand workers were laid off at other plants. As the commentator Peter Jenkins put it, it was the kind of strike 'which most exasperated the public and caused foreign financiers to despair of Britain ever solving her economic problems'.[28]

On 15 November Castle took her officials away for the weekend to the Civil Service training college at Sunningdale, Berkshire, and thrashed out a tentative programme of action.[29] Some observers, like Roy Hattersley, worried that they were heading for confrontation with the unions, but Castle's course was set. It was, she wrote afterwards, 'a fabulously successful weekend. We can all see our way on Donovan quite clearly now. We agreed that we would never get anything positive out of the TUC and that the Government would have to risk taking a lead.'[30] By the end of the month she had the first draft of what was to become the most famous and controversial White Paper in British political history.[31]

Castle's White Paper adopted an explicitly interventionist tone, insisting on the need for radical change to preserve the spirit of free collective bargaining in a changing industrial climate. First, the Employment Secretary would have the discretionary power to order a strike ballot if there seemed to be a serious threat to the national economic interest. Second, in unofficial disputes the government could order strikers to return to work for a 'cooling off' period of twenty-eight days. Third, the government could refer inter-union disputes to an Industrial Board, which would hand down a legally binding decision. All of this was backed up with unprecedented 'penal clauses': if the unions refused to comply with the Board's recommendations, they would face heavy financial penalties; and if they then refused to pay up, the obvious implication was that their officials would go to prison.[32]

When the first draft of the White Paper landed on Wilson's desk at the beginning of December it came as a very welcome tonic after months of awful trade figures and by-election disasters.[33] Terrified of leaks to the press, the Prime Minister planned to keep it close to his chest, telling only a few Cabinet colleagues before the grand unveiling in the New Year. As usual, this conspiracy of silence lasted no more than a week before the *Guardian* ran a front-page exclusive based on a leak from Roy Jenkins's office. Castle then decided, in a kind of damage-limitation exercise, to hold a series of briefings for leading trade unionists, explaining what the White Paper entailed. This went predictably badly: union leaders like Frank Cousins, Jack Jones and Hugh Scanlon were hardly likely to welcome the prospect of government intervention, and they promptly leaked even more details to the newspapers. All of this meant that before most of the Cabinet had even laid eyes on the White Paper it had already provoked a fierce debate in the Labour movement and the press.[34] But Castle remained optimistic that she could steer the proposals through the Cabinet and the Commons. 'She and Harold have got themselves into the mood of saying that if they can get this through Cabinet on Friday,' wrote Dick Crossman, 'there will be no difficulty in handling it, but I have the gravest doubts, I must admit.'[35]

When the Cabinet met to discuss Castle's White Paper on 3 January things did not go entirely to plan. The meeting dragged on for six hours, and it was clear that Wilson and Castle had miscalculated. Many ministers were disgruntled that they had not been told about the proposals earlier, while others were worried that they would alienate the party's rank and file.[36] Ominously, the opposition cut across conventional left–right boundaries, and even his supporters were unimpressed by Wilson's apparent duplicity in putting the package together. In the end, the Cabinet was so clearly divided that it took a series of further meetings over the next eleven days before Wilson and Castle were able to command a majority for the bill.[37]

The White Paper was finally published on 16 January. It now had a catchy but singularly inapposite title, *In Place of Strife*, suggested by Castle's husband Ted the morning before publication.[38] Although the left-wing newspapers were largely hostile, the proposals drew praise from *The Economist* and the *Financial Times*, both of which were usually very critical of the government.[39] The reaction among the general public was even better news for the beleaguered government. According to Gallup, 73 per cent of voters approved of government intervention in unofficial strikes, 69 per cent supported financial penalties for unions that ignored the Industrial Board, 63 per cent liked the idea of a secret ballot, and 61 per cent backed the proposed 'cooling-off' period.[40] Most Labour voters supported the initiative, and most Labour MPs at least agreed that government action was necessary. Even rank-and-file union members, according to a later poll, supported most of Castle's innovations by a wide margin.[41]

The real challenge for Wilson and Castle, however, was winning over the union bosses. Jack Jones thought that the unions owed the Labour government nothing, and should simply look after their own interests.[42] His fellow militant Hugh Scanlon was an intense Marxist, described as 'the personification of hard-line trade unionism', so there was clearly little chance of concessions from him, either.[43] The incoming head of the TUC, Victor Feather, was a rather more attractive character, 'cheerful, extrovert, energetically practical and amenable'. Unfortunately for the government, though, he nursed a long-running animus towards Barbara Castle, whom he had known as a young radical in Bradford. In 1931 she had elbowed him out of a reporting assignment at the Labour Party conference, and he had never forgotten it. Industrial correspondents and civil servants alike knew that 'he hated her with a vehemence that went far beyond the irritation she regularly caused'. 'I knew that girl when she had dirty knickers,' he used to mutter grimly.[44]

The union leaders' first reactions to *In Place of Strife* were not promising. Both Jones and Scanlon had worked their way up from the shop floor, and both recognised that although unofficial strikes implicitly challenged their own leadership, they were an effective way for their men to get what they wanted.[45] Both the TGWU and the AEU therefore asked their sponsored MPs to vote against Castle's bill.[46] Feather, meanwhile, was convinced that Wilson was 'doing the wrong thing for the wrong (political) reasons'. From an early stage, he reached out to allies in the senior echelons of the Labour Party, notably the chairman of the Parliamentary Labour Party, Douglas Houghton, and the Home Secretary, James Callaghan.[47]

Castle had long suspected that Callaghan was likely to make trouble. She was exactly the kind of Oxford-educated intellectual whom he resented and despised, while she thought he was an overrated working-class bully.[48] She also knew that he was extremely close to the union leaders: in September 1968, after he had passed on a message about incomes policy, she wrote: 'I don't trust that man further than the end of my nose.'[49] Unhappily for her, Callaghan was determined to flex his muscles again after the humiliation of the devaluation crisis. He made much of his humble origins, presenting himself as 'the one who knows what the chaps in the unions think' and the 'Keeper of the Cloth Cap'.[50] As Crossman observed, the Home Secretary was clearly out to tap popular disapproval of 'middle-class intellectuals' and put 'himself forward as the spokesman of the conservative working man'.[51]

Callaghan's opposition to *In Place of Strife* was founded as much on conviction as ambition. He was implacably opposed to legal penalties for the unions, since he thought that they should have complete freedom to bargain on behalf of the working classes. His contacts in the unions warned him that, in any case, they would make it impossible for the legislation to pass.[52] On top of all this, Callaghan recognised that the controversy offered him a wonderful opportunity to secure the loyalty of the unions in a leadership election. Commentators and interviewers rarely noted that, belying his reputation for ordinariness, Callaghan was one of the Commons' most accomplished chess players, familiar with such stratagems as the Ruy Lopez and the Sicilian Defence.[53] 'Behind the glad-hand charm, behind the beaming visage of Sunny Jim,' wrote the *Guardian*'s Peter Jenkins, was a 'cat-like speed of claw'. Even as the Cabinet voted to support Castle's plan, Callaghan readied himself to strike.[54]

It did not take long for *In Place of Strife* to run into trouble. When Castle arrived for the first meeting on the subject with backbenchers she encountered 'almost non-stop objections to the three proposals they dislike most: the strike ballot, the conciliation pause and the attachment of wages, especially the latter'. She thought that it was 'astonishing how much furore' they had created, a sure sign that she had misread the mood of the parliamentary party.[55]

It was her bad luck that in February 1969 one of the bitterest industrial disputes for years broke out at the Ford Motor Company. Ford's managers had just agreed a pioneering deal with the leaders of fifteen unions represented at their plants. In return for a pledge to scrap all unofficial strikes, the company offered a handsome pay rise, larger holiday bonuses and other benefits. This looked like the ideal formula to bring peace to a troubled industry, but against the advice of their leaders the shop stewards promptly rejected it and ordered their men out. The TGWU and AEU then completely reversed their position and decided to support their rebellious shop stewards. An interim court injunction decided in favour of Ford, but the unions simply ignored it, and the strike spread.[56] *The Times* thought that the unions must have a 'death wish ... almost as if they were trying to demonstrate that they are not able to run themselves properly or to play a constructive or even honourable part in collective bargaining'.[57] Wilson himself commented that the strike gave 'powerful support' to the case for *In Place of Strife*. It was not a remark that endeared him to the unions, and their determination to destroy his bill only grew as a result.[58]

Discussing *In Place of Strife* on television towards the end of January, Wilson had remarked: 'We have got to do what is right and go on regardless of unpopularity.'[59] But as the unions began to flex their muscles, many Labour MPs wondered whether the bill was really worth fighting for. Tony Crosland remarked that 'around the country nobody has read "In Place of Strife", and they just think Wilson has got a massive trade union bug in him and that Barbara has gone bonkers'.[60] Indeed, the legislation's timing was even worse than it first appeared, since it coincided with Wilson's ham-fisted attempt to reform the House of Lords, which collapsed in the spring of 1969. At the beginning of March Crossman even recorded that party discipline had frayed so badly that they 'might have to go for an autumn election because we have disintegrated'. The backbenchers, he observed, had decided to be 'difficult' on just about everything, throwing Wilson's entire programme into doubt.[61]

At this point, sensing Wilson's weakness, Callaghan made his move. On 26 March the party's National Executive Committee met to approve Castle's programme. To her anger and astonishment, as fifteen of her colleagues lifted their hands in opposition, Callaghan ostentatiously raised his own to join them. For a senior Cabinet minister to repudiate his own government's policies was simply extraordinary, and in the febrile atmosphere of the day it looked as though he was finally launching his leadership challenge. On the telephone to Wilson that afternoon, Castle made it clear that she had had enough. He should send Callaghan a letter, she insisted, reading: 'Dear Jim, As you are no longer prepared to defend Government policy in public, I assume you have resigned.' Wilson rather feebly replied that he could not sack Callaghan immediately because he was about to fly off to Lagos for a Commonwealth conference. However, he promised that he would 'be very tough about it when I get back'. Castle knew from long experience what to expect from Wilson's promises. 'I'll believe that', she noted sardonically, 'when it happens.'[62]

On the evening of 2 April Wilson flew back into London. The newspapers were full of the 'showdown' he was expected to have with Callaghan at the next day's Cabinet meeting, and many commentators expected that the Home Secretary would have to resign. 'Mr Callaghan is now very plainly the leader of the internal opposition in the government,' declared *The Economist*. 'If Mr Wilson and Mrs Castle falter now, they will be inviting Mr Callaghan's friends to take over.'[63] That night, Wilson stayed up late drinking brandy with Castle and Jenkins, telling them 'how roughly he was going to denounce Callaghan in front of his colleagues for his gross disloyalty'.[64] Both his allies therefore anticipated fireworks in the morning, and the tension was further increased when, as the moment approached, Callaghan strolled in ten minutes late, apparently oblivious to the drama of the occasion. 'He really is a cool one!' thought Castle, as she looked forward to the great showdown.

And then, of course, it simply never happened. Callaghan's colleagues agreed that he had behaved disgracefully, but instead of laying down the law to his errant Home Secretary, Wilson appeared content to let everyone else do the talking. Castle thought that she had 'never seen him so weak-kneed'. Tony Benn, meanwhile, recorded that Wilson 'allowed Jim to get away with an explanation that was simply not true' and concluded: 'I am afraid Jim is winning.' Yet the very next day the Cabinet were astonished to read in the papers that Wilson had administered a thorough 'dressing down'. All of them knew what had happened: he had 'clearly compensated to the lobby for what he had failed to do in Cabinet', bragging that he had kicked Callaghan into line when in fact he had done no such thing. Benn was not the only minister to be appalled by this ludicrously childish behaviour, and thought that it revealed 'what a very small man he is'.[65]

Trying to bring the whole mess to a swift conclusion, Wilson agreed with Castle, Jenkins and Crossman that they should go for a 'short, sharp' bill, instead of waiting until the autumn, as they had planned.[66] On 11 April, however, the TUC representatives arrived in Downing Street for their long-awaited meeting with Wilson, and it went even worse than Castle had feared. Vic Feather and his colleagues had already heard rumours of the change of timing, but Wilson denied that he had made up his mind. At the end he told them that if the TUC wanted the government to abandon *In Place of Strife*, they should come up with 'an alternative plan which was equally urgent and equally effective'. Feather spotted his opportunity, and even repeated the words back to Wilson for confirmation. After all his promises that the government would never waver, Wilson had unexpectedly opened the door to precisely the kind of compromise the unions wanted.[67]

Meanwhile, the plans for the new interim bill went ahead in virtual secrecy. Four days later, presenting his latest Budget to the Commons, Roy Jenkins stunned the Labour benches with the news that the government had decided 'to implement without delay . . . some of the more important provisions incorporated in the White Paper *In Place of Strife*'. 'Moans of pain' came from the backbenches, while cheers rang out from the Conservative side of the House. The following afternoon Castle confirmed that they were going to legislate immediately, bringing in the controversial 'conciliation pause' and government intervention in inter-union disputes, both backed up by the threat of penal sanctions.[68]

Furious that Wilson had misled them about his timing, the TUC insisted that they would not accept the new legislation, but the Prime Minister was in unusually combative form, telling his backbenchers that it was 'essential to our economic recovery' and that 'there can be no going back on that'.[69] The very next day *Tribune* appeared with the banner headline 'The Maddest Scene in Modern History' above an excoriating attack on *In Place of Strife* by Castle's old friend Michael Foot. 'Harold Wilson and the Labour Cabinet', wrote Foot, 'are heading for the rocks', thanks to their disastrous decision 'to declare war on the trade unions'. He insisted that 'the only way to save the Labour movement' was for everyone in it 'to make it as clear as possible that the anti-trade union legislation will not be tolerated'. He ended on an ominous note: 'Only after that shall we be able to pick up the pieces. The choice about the time when we can start upon that fruitful work of construction rests with the Cabinet and the party's leaders, whoever they may turn out to be.'[70]

By the end of the following week, Wilson's allies sensed that he was close to breaking. 'He is in danger of total disintegration,' Castle told Crossman on 27 April. Almost despite himself, Crossman agreed:

> Total disintegration! There is nothing of him left as a leader and a leftist. He is just a figure posturing there in the middle without any drive except to stay Prime Minister as long as he can. The other thing which I suspect has now begun to happen . . . is that he assumes that we can't win the next election. I noticed that in Cabinet this week he twice spoke on the assumption that the Tories would be taking over in the 1970s, whereas he has been scrupulously careful to avoid such talk in the past.[71]

Two days later they went over to Downing Street to mull over the worsening parliamentary situation. Wilson told them that he had decided to have an Inner Cabinet of seven ministers, from which Callaghan would be excluded, and that he was planning to sack the liberal Chief Whip, John Silkin, who had manifestly lost control of the Labour backbenchers. When

Castle asked about his replacement, Wilson replied vaguely that 'it hasn't really got as far as that yet'.[72] But just a few hours later Castle heard that a new Chief Whip had been appointed. It was Bob Mellish, a working-class disciplinarian from the East End. She could hardly have been more disappointed. Not only did she dislike Mellish intensely, but she knew he would impose a tough parliamentary regime that could easily alienate her old associates on the left and jeopardise her cherished bill. Perhaps even more infuriating, however, was the fact that Wilson had deliberately kept her in the dark. Anger rose in her, she recorded, 'coldly and massively. So *this* was what Harold had been hinting at this morning. He had known what announcement he was about to make and he hadn't even the courtesy to tell us.'

That evening, she poured out all her frustrations to the sympathetic Crossman. She had had enough of Wilson's secretive style of leadership, and felt completely humiliated by her treatment. 'I'm through with Harold now,' she raged, sounding like an abandoned royal mistress. 'Henceforth I dedicate myself to his destruction. I'm going to write the sort of letter on which he ought to ask for my resignation.'[73] The letter reached Downing Street later that night:

Dear Harold,
Nothing that has happened in 4½ years has made me as angry as this. To me it is inconceivable that a Prime Minister should call on a colleague to pilot the most controversial Bill of our whole Parliament through the House and then switch Parliamentary pilots in the middle of it without even telling her. I still simply cannot believe that you knew what you knew this morning and had not the courtesy to take me into your confidence. This is indeed the 'manner of government' of which others [i.e., George Brown] have complained. I must warn you that faith can never be the same again and that if the strategy is to railroad my Bill through Parliament on a Healey-type regime of reactionary discipline, I will have no part of it.
Yours, Barbara[74]

Tucked up in bed at home, Castle told her husband that if Wilson rang — as he shortly did — he was to say that she was not yet there, and might not be coming home at all.[75]

Terrified that his closest allies were deserting him, Wilson finally got through to Crossman instead. 'I have never in my life heard him so frightened,' Crossman noted in his diary. He too believed that Wilson had behaved abominably. 'It is exactly this kind of conduct', he observed, 'that makes Harold an intolerable, mean leader. When he does this he is a timid, awful little man.'[76]

The next morning Wilson persuaded Castle to come and see him in Downing Street, where he made a feeble effort to mollify her, promising that he was still committed to pushing through *In Place of Strife* by persuasion rather than bullying. Castle then went off and 'bought three new dresses to steady my morale', although she noted that she was 'now really frightened at Harold's state'. This was not simply melodramatic exaggeration, for the following day Wilson missed a Cabinet meeting for the first and only time during his premiership. The word was that he had a stomach upset, but Castle thought that he had finally cracked under the pressure, and Crossman suspected that he had been drinking.[77] Later that day the two of them went round to see him. It was clear that the backbench rebellions, the leadership speculation and, above all, the rebellion of his friends had finally taken their toll, and Crossman recorded the extraordinary, pathetic scene:

> Harold was frightened and unhappy, unsure of himself, needing his friends. The great india-rubber, unbreakable, undepressable Prime Minister was crumpled in his chair. It was a touching evening for Barbara and me. We sat with him as old friends who wanted to help. Mind you, he had been spending the previous night boozing with the industrial correspondents, claiming that he had a stomach upset when he really had a hangover, but we saw at last that he was injured, broken, his confidence gone, unhappy, wanting help.

Wilson weakly admitted that he was going to have Callaghan in his Inner Cabinet after all. He tried to claim that he had wanted him in all along, but Crossman noted that this 'was quite untrue because he had said the opposite'. But Crossman felt too sorry for the stricken Prime Minister to be angry with him:

> I don't think Harold is lying in these things, and I don't think I blame him, except for once again changing his mind, twisting and turning and saying different things to different people. Barbara and I sat beside him and she said, 'My God, we want to help you, Harold. Why do you sit alone

Devaluation hits the streets of London, 19 November 1967. *(Hulton-Deutsch Collection/Corbis)*

James Callaghan produces his devalued currency, but the mini-skirted Britannia looks distinctly unimpressed: Cummings in the *Daily Express*, 20 November 1967.

'I'm Backing Britain': A patriotic onlooker waits for Roy Jenkins to leave Downing Street on Budget Day, March 1968. *(Getty Images)*

Captain Mainwaring (Arthur Lowe) leads the nation's favourite platoon into action in a publicity shot for *Dad's Army*, 1970. *(Getty Images)*

Fighting the good fight against 'decadence and godlessness': Mary Whitehouse sings a duet with Judy Mackenzie at the Festival of Light, September 1971. *(Getty Images)*

Linda Marshall, an evacuee from Ronan Point, admires the view from her new home, 1969. The council had installed her in another high-rise flat, this time on the nineteenth floor of a block in Canning Town. *(Getty Images)*

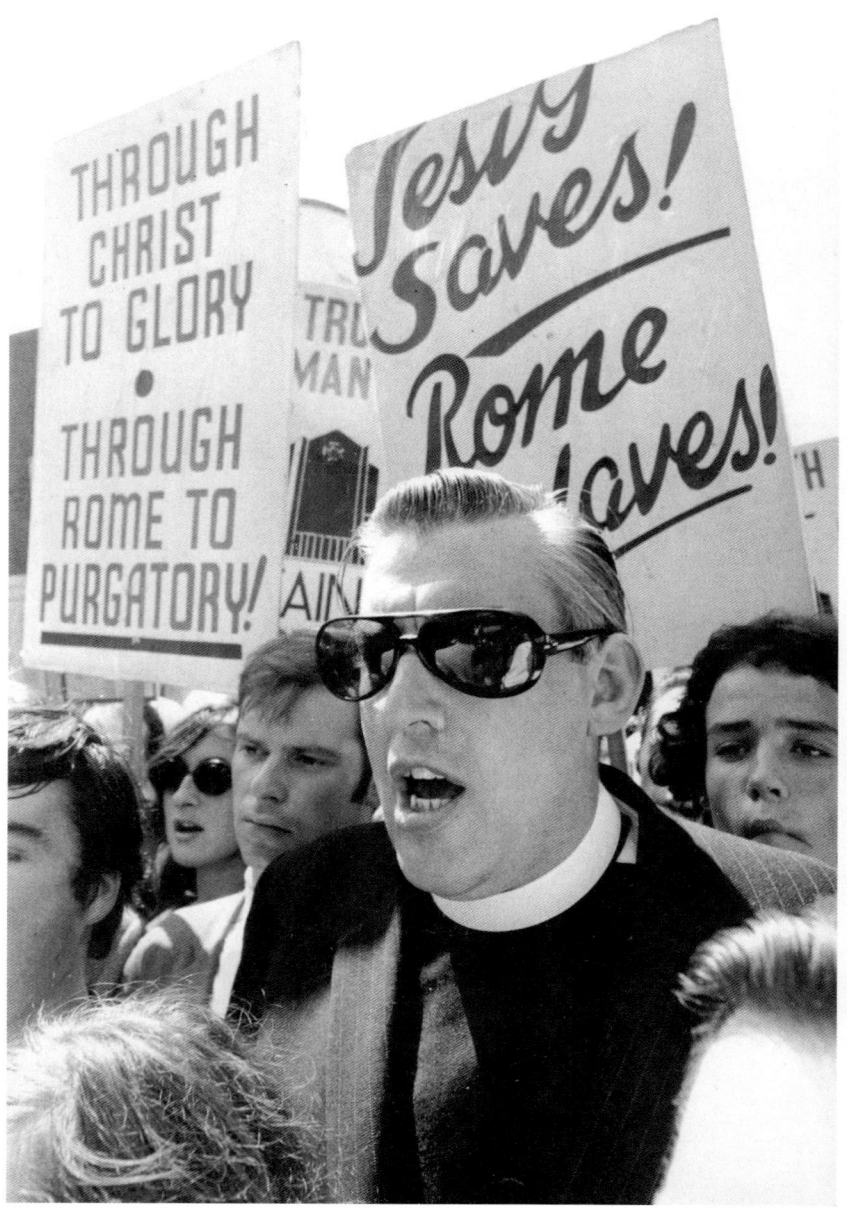

'Jesus saves! Rome enslaves!' Ian Paisley leads a demonstration outside Canterbury Cathedral, 1970. He was objecting to the first Catholic mass to be held there for four hundred years. *(Getty Images)*

Armed with petrol bombs, Catholic youngsters take on the RUC in the Battle of the Bogside, 12 August 1969. *(Getty Images)*

The sign of things to come: local children taunt an army patrol in Belfast, July 1970. *(Getty Images)*

A typically cheerful family Christmas at the Garnett household, 1966. *(Getty Images)*

'Powell for PM': the immigration debate spills on to the streets, May 1968. *(Getty Images)*

'I am under no illusions that I may be committing political suicide.' Barbara Castle addresses the Labour Party conference, October 1968. She was already hard at work on what would become *In Place of Strife*. *(Getty Images)*

'There's many a slip twixt ball and t' Cup.' Two days after England's defeat in the World Cup quarter-final, Labour's manager addresses his players: Emmwood in the *Daily Mail*, 16 June 1970.

'Do you want a better tomorrow?' Edward Heath looks forward to the new dawn of the 1970s. *(Bettmann/Corbis)*

in No. 10 with Marcia and Gerald Kaufman and these minions? Why not be intimate and have things out with your friends? . . . If you have to have Jim in the inner Cabinet, all right, but do also have your friends . . . We all want to help you and we want to put you back.[78]

Wilson's situation, as his friends recognised, was desperate. In the last three months or so, he had managed to alienate not only the unions but dozens of his backbenchers and even some of his closest colleagues. A deep sense of disillusionment and defeatism hung over Westminster as April turned to May. Crossman disconsolately recorded that 'not only have the trade unions written the Government off as finished and as a mere prelude to a Tory Government but most of the members of the Parliamentary Party itself are just fighting to keep up their morale. Deep underneath they know they can't win next time.'[79] The government itself seemed to have collapsed into near anarchy, with the Home Secretary in open revolt and other ministers united only by their contempt for Harold Wilson. As Wilson's biographer puts it, 'private venom against the Prime Minister became a form of group therapy'.[80] Tony Crosland even remarked that Wilson's 'unspeakable nature is one of the great facts of our political life'.[81]

Wilson never came closer to collapse than in that first week of May 1969. Across the Labour Party, he was widely dismissed as a failure; he was the least popular Prime Minister since Neville Chamberlain; and his government appeared to have lost its way completely. On 2 May the main headline in *The Times* announced: 'Attempt to replace Mr Wilson may be imminent'. According to the story, a 'coup of former Ministers and some backbenchers' was already under way, with more than thirty dissidents poised to strike. The report even quoted one insider to the effect that as many as a hundred MPs were 'party to the manoeuvres to manipulate a senior Minister, presumably Mr Callaghan, into Mr Wilson's place as Prime Minister'.[82] This was more than the usual political gossip. With Wilson's position crumbling by the hour, both Callaghan and Jenkins were widely expected to challenge for the leadership. For many observers, the real question was not whether Wilson would go, but which of them would replace him. Callaghan had more support across the ideological spectrum, but he did not yet have a well-drilled team working on his behalf; Jenkins did. Indeed, although the newspapers identified Callaghan as the chief conspirator working to unseat Wilson, the real plotters were working for Jenkins.[83]

Having come extremely close to launching a leadership challenge in the spring of 1968, the Jenkins camp were determined not to let Wilson escape this time. At the beginning of May 1969, a group of conspirators led by Patrick Gordon Walker, Bill Rodgers and John Mackintosh drew up a list of sixty MPs who were prepared to request a special meeting of the party to discuss the leadership. Forty more were ready to vote against Wilson in a secret ballot if a meeting could be arranged. Of these hundred dissidents, twenty were already members of Wilson's government, while many others were part of the 1966 intake, with good reason to fear for their seats at the next election.[84] On 7 May the chief plotters met and decided that in the next few days they should 'launch a move to get rid of HW. No better chance would ever occur.' They wanted twelve senior MPs to sign a letter to Douglas Houghton, the chairman of the parliamentary party, calling for an end to factional strife. This would be the cue for Houghton to call a general meeting of the party, at which they would move a vote of no confidence in Wilson and then begin work on Jenkins's leadership campaign.[85]

Wilson knew perfectly well what was happening, which explains why he had been so terrified at the thought of Castle's resignation. His great fear was that the Callaghan and Jenkins supporters would join forces to trigger a leadership contest, which was precisely what Jenkins's team were planning. In the meantime, buoyed by the assurances of support from Castle and Crossman, Wilson made a typically defiant speech at a May Day rally in the Royal Festival Hall. 'May I say, for the benefit of those who have been carried away by the gossip of the last few days, that I know what is going on,' he said solemnly. There was an audible intake of breath, and his audience waited for the inevitable revelation of treachery. '*I* am going on,' he then said, to a great roar of relief and laughter. 'Your Government is going on. Your Government is going on to build on the achievements of which you are proud and I am proud. And our Government is going to win.'[86]

But far from calming the leadership speculation, Wilson's speech only inflamed it, and over the next few days the Prime Minister's future remained the lead story in the newspapers. Rumours swept the lobbies of the Commons that a challenge was imminent, and on 7 May Houghton launched a biting public attack on *In Place of Strife* and the government's bullying tactics. For a moment, it looked as though the game might be up for Wilson. But in a curious way the speech backfired. Houghton was thought to be operating on behalf of Callaghan, but his intervention seemed so obviously disloyal that it probably did more harm than good to the Home

Secretary's cause. The very next day Jenkins, who was always nervous of moving too soon and ruining his own chances, ordered his troops to hold their fire. Worried that Callaghan might beat him to the ultimate prize, the Chancellor preferred to prop up Wilson for a little longer rather than clear the way for his own bitter rival.[87]

Yet again, Wilson had been saved by the inability of his foes to work together. In the end Callaghan and Jenkins disliked each other so much that they cancelled each other out. Jenkins, though, was probably right to hesitate, for if Wilson had been toppled in the spring of 1969 Callaghan was in the stronger position to succeed him. Instead, the great survivor lived to fight another day, and in the months that followed Jenkins was to be found among Wilson's strongest supporters, not out of any lack of ambition of his own, but because he was so keen to stop Callaghan.[88]

Somehow, like a latter-day Houdini, Harold Wilson had wriggled free once again. He even had the pleasure of seeing Callaghan humiliated at last. On 8 May the Cabinet were again arguing about the Industrial Relations Bill when suddenly Crossman broke into a 'furious attack', accusing the Home Secretary of having organised Houghton's speech the day before:

> Some people believed they could get us off the hook by ditching Harold and finding another leader. That was obviously why Houghton had made the speech . . . It wasn't a spontaneous speech, but deliberately calculated, written out and given to the press . . . But the plotters had better realize that it wouldn't work: 'four of the inner heart of the Cabinet couldn't and wouldn't serve' under the supplanter.
>
> 'I detest those rats who are leaving our sinking ship to climb on to another sinking ship,' he concluded. 'We have got to sink or swim together.'

At this, Callaghan, who knew that Crossman was talking about him, was unable to resist muttering: 'Not sink or swim, sink or sink.' Crossman immediately pounced: 'Why can't you resign if you think like that? Get out, Jim, get out.' Clearly stunned by the ferocity of the attack, Callaghan mumbled miserably: 'Of course, if my colleagues want me to resign, I'm prepared to go if they insist on my going.' 'Why don't you go? Get out!' repeated Crossman. 'We all sat electrified,' Barbara Castle recorded, 'till Harold intervened soothingly. "We don't want you to go. We want you to stay and be convinced." Nonetheless I could see [Harold] was secretly delighted.'

Crossman, too, was pleased at the result. Callaghan 'had been punctured', he noted afterwards. 'He hadn't responded, he had crawled and it was quite a moment.'[89]

Although his position seemed safe, Wilson was still faced with the intractable problem of *In Place of Strife*. He could hardly abandon it after all they had been through, but at the same time the way ahead remained difficult and dangerous. On 13 May he removed Callaghan from the new Inner Cabinet after being persuaded by Jenkins and Crossman that the Home Secretary was operating as a spy for the TUC.[90] The unions, however, were not dismissed so easily. Just a few hours after the great Cabinet row between Crossman and Callaghan the Inner Cabinet had privately agreed that their position was simply too weak to push the bill through immediately. Instead, they would wait for the unions to come up with their own proposals, and then negotiate a compromise. When the TUC plan appeared on 12 May, however, it fell a long way short of what Wilson and Castle thought acceptable. It allowed for the TUC to intervene in unofficial and inter-union disputes, but only in an advisory capacity, and it ruled out government intervention or penal sanctions.[91]

Wilson and Castle now embarked on a bewildering series of negotiations with the union leaders.[92] Yet, even as the talks dragged on, support for the bill was steadily evaporating. The trade unions were implacable in their opposition, while the new Chief Whip rapidly found that about 150 union-sponsored Labour MPs were likely to vote against the bill when it came to the crunch. Even Castle herself was beginning to have doubts, and on 22 May they were confirmed when some of the bill's consistent supporters in Cabinet, like Peter Shore and Tony Benn, voiced their anxiety at the continuing stalemate.[93] Wilson, however, was determined to fight on. 'Brinkmanship is essential,' he told his closest colleagues; 'we have to push it right up to the edge.'[94] With Castle, he was more honest:

> He astonished me by saying that he didn't see how we could get a settlement with the TUC, but he and I were now too committed to back down. He therefore intended to make this an issue of confidence in *him*, and if we were defeated, he would stand down from the leadership. The Government would drag on for a time and he could use the issue devastatingly against Heath. He clearly visualized that it wouldn't be long before he staged a comeback.[95]

Wilson's private sentiments made it all the more extraordinary that, just two days later, he allowed Castle and Crossman to disappear on a Mediterranean cruise on Sir Charles Forte's luxury yacht. Castle's own biographer describes this as 'one of the strangest decisions of her political career', especially since Forte was a well-known critic of trade unionism. But Wilson was all in favour of the jaunt, so, on 23 May, the Castle and Crossman families set off for Naples, accompanied by Gino, the head waiter from the Café Royal. Castle's officials thought that the trip was 'absolutely inexplicable', and both ministers feebly tried to keep the holiday a secret from their colleagues and the press.

This utterly bizarre interlude was made even odder by the fact that Wilson insisted on preparing a special code to use for radio messages to the yacht. At first he asked Roy Hattersley to draw up codenames, but when Hattersley suggested 'Gloriana' for Castle, Wilson decided to do the job himself. He called himself 'Eagle', Castle 'Peacock' and Crossman 'Owl', and then devised codenames for the other major players, too. Jenkins was a measly 'Starling' and Callaghan a dismissive 'Sparrow'; Vic Feather was 'Rhino', Jack Jones 'Horse' and Hugh Scanlon 'Bear'. The TUC General Council was the 'Zoo', the penal sanctions were 'teeth', so, naturally, the TUC's rival proposals were 'false teeth'. Should there be a crisis, the message for Castle to return would be 'Aunty has mumps'. Unfortunately, the codenames were never used because communications with the yacht proved impossible. Rumour had it that Crossman had sabotaged the radio.[96]

On 1 June Castle flew back to Chequers for a weekend of secret talks with the three senior union leaders, Feather, Jones and Scanlon. She later recalled that 'the atmosphere was positively jovial from the start', and over brandy in the long gallery they settled down to a frank discussion of the issues. Scanlon said bluntly that 'the question isn't whether our scheme works or your scheme works. It is the fact that our people won't accept Government intervention.' He added that even the TUC's proposals were unlikely to work, because individual union leaders would not allow anybody else a say in settling inter-union disputes. In other words, all the concessions that the unions had made so far were merely designed to ruin the government's own legislative plan.

Castle asked: 'Is it penal powers you are against, or legislation? Because the penal powers need never operate if the TUC delivers the goods.' 'Legislation,' Scanlon replied, adding that even if the bill made it through the Commons, they would continue to fight it afterwards by demonstrations, strikes and unrelenting pressure. At this, as Castle recalled, Wilson spoke up: '"If you say that, Hughie," said Harold very quietly, very conversationally, "then you are claiming to be the Government. I will never consent to preside over a Government that is not allowed to govern. And let us get one thing clear: that means we can't have a Labour Government for I am the only person who can lead a Labour Government."' 'We accept that', 'None of us has ever said anything else', they chorused. 'Well,' continued Wilson, 'there are two types of Prime Minister I have made up my mind I will never be: one is a Ramsay MacDonald and the second is a Dubček.* Get your tanks off my lawn, Hughie!'[97]

Unsurprisingly, the discussions got nowhere, and by midnight Castle had retired to bed. The next morning, she went to see Wilson in his Chequers bedroom where, in the best Churchillian tradition, he was breakfasting in bed. 'It's about as black as can be' was his greeting. 'Those two only want the TUC proposals in order to avoid legislation, not because they believe in them.'[98] But the government could hardly break off negotiations, because they needed to convince their restless backbenchers that they had done everything possible to reach a compromise. Rather amazingly, Castle then flew back to Naples to resume her holiday, telling herself that she needed a rest and leaving Wilson to hold the fort.

At Castle's first meeting after her return, an Inner Cabinet session on 8 June, the mood was bleak. While Wilson explained what had happened at Chequers and Crossman fell asleep, she felt 'surprised at how depressed they all seemed'. Both Healey and Jenkins gloomily admitted that the TUC was winning the battle for public opinion. A furious Castle 'began to lose patience with them':

> The history of the Government in the past few months had been one of capitulation – and much good it had done us. The only way to win victories was to stand up to pressures. We could win here, too, if only the PLP didn't lose its nerve. 'The PLP *has* lost its nerve,' chipped in Dick and then went on to warn Harold that, if he and I faced them with a showdown over this, Harold's position would be at risk and they would opt for a Government under Callaghan.

---

*Alexander Dubček, the reformist leader of the Czechoslovakian Communists, had been deposed by a Soviet invasion in August 1968, which explains Wilson's reference to tanks on the lawn.

Slowly but surely, Castle could sense her colleagues' resolution draining away. Michael Stewart passed her a note saying that 'anyone who lets you down at this stage is a prize shit', but for the first time Jenkins was looking 'shifty', and other supporters were beginning to wobble.[99]

Wilson himself was now exhausted by the endless rounds of beer and sandwiches with the union leaders. 'Harold looked tired and drawn,' one TUC negotiator reported afterwards. 'There was something the matter with his right eye. It was dropping and showing too much white which is a sign of mental fatigue. At one point he said, "Well, that sounds all right to me . . ." but Barbara nudged him. At another point he said, "I'm bewildered by all this."'[100] Castle, too, was running out of enthusiasm. On 9 June she looked on powerlessly as Wilson admitted that they might drop the penal clauses if the TUC agreed to toughen up its own sanctions. The next day the *Guardian* reported that Roy Jenkins was thinking of abandoning the bill, and she speculated that he 'now saw a chance of snatching the leadership' by posing as an advocate of compromise. By now Castle's health had buckled under the strain: for three days she was overwhelmed by sickness and could barely eat, but somehow she forced herself to keep going.[101]

The tension finally came to a head on Tuesday, 17 June, which Castle described as 'the most traumatic day of my political life'. When the Inner Cabinet met that morning it was clear that both Jenkins and Crossman were wobbling badly, and of the senior ministers, only Michael Stewart was still a strong supporter of the bill. Mellish, the Chief Whip, delivered a pessimistic verdict on the parliamentary party, warning Wilson that 'you won't get it through the House . . . if the TUC rejects it'. All of this meant that the high command then had to go into a full Cabinet meeting 'disunited and unprepared', as Castle put it. Wilson explained the situation, and then, Castle wrote, 'one after another, the vultures moved in on us': first Crossman, then Crosland, Callaghan and Richard Marsh. Mellish repeated his belief that without an accommodation with the unions the backbenchers would never support the bill. For many ministers, his intervention was decisive: if they could not get the bill through, then they simply had to compromise. To Wilson's undisguised fury, his support immediately began to crumble, with many ministers prefacing their remarks with the words: 'In view of what the Chief Whip has said . . .' The most remarkable speech came from Peter Shore, who was usually seen as Wilson's lapdog. 'He threw all of his weight against us,' Castle noted, 'and for once he was impressive . . . What was I most concerned with? Winning a victory over the TUC or reducing the number of damaging strikes?' Like many other ministers, Shore chose to believe the TUC's promises, and argued that accepting them meant 'an enormous advance', not surrender. Unlike Wilson and Castle, of course, he had not heard Jones and Scanlon dismiss them as mere window-dressing.[102]

At lunchtime they broke for a couple of hours, and in private Jenkins told Castle that 'he no longer thought the fight was worth the cost'. This was perhaps the key betrayal: without the Chancellor at their side, Wilson and Castle looked shrill and isolated. When the Cabinet reassembled it was clear that *In Place of Strife* was doomed. Crossman thought that 'it was the most devastating Cabinet meeting I have attended'. Wilson wanted to tell the TUC that they must alter their rules or the penal clauses would be made law, but he was outvoted by sixteen to five. Instead, the Cabinet agreed that he and Castle should be given a free hand to negotiate with the unions in the morning, but that they could no longer threaten them with the penal clauses.

For Wilson, the humiliation could hardly have been greater. During the last half-hour he had put away three double brandies, and finally he lost his patience completely. 'You're soft, you're cowardly, you're lily-livered,' he shouted contemptuously, adding that his colleagues were 'abandoning your Cabinet commitments because they are unpopular ... You can't deny me this.'[103] Never before had he lost his cool in front of his ministers in this way, 'striking out in all directions, like a wounded animal', as his biographer puts it.[104] Jenkins thought that although Wilson 'sounded fairly unhinged', he still had 'a touch of King Lear-like nobility'.[105] Crossman called it 'a terrible exhibition in which the PM was rasped, irritated and thoroughly demoralized, really shouting I won't, I can't, you can't do this to me, terribly painful because he expressed a loathing, a spite and a resentment which is quite outside his usual character ... He was a little man, for the first time dragged down on our level.'[106] Summing up the events of the day, Tony Benn commented that Wilson had shown himself 'a small man with no sense of history and as somebody really without leadership qualities. My opinion of Harold Wilson, if I haven't set it down in my diary recently, is very low indeed.'[107]

On the morning of 18 June Wilson and Castle went into their last meeting with the TUC in the dining room at No. 10. By late afternoon the entire Cabinet had assembled downstairs, waiting anxiously for news. Both Callaghan and Jenkins had spent the morning making contingency plans for a leadership election should Wilson resign. They had been wasting their time, though, for at long last, through the door of the Cabinet Room, appeared Wilson and Castle. 'We have a settlement,' Wilson said happily, and the entire room burst into spontaneous applause. Benn recorded that Wilson acted as though 'he had pulled it off again and this was his great achievement and nobody felt disposed to disagree with him at that particular moment'.[108] 'Then we had a series of odious little speeches,' noted Crossman, with Callaghan 'soft-soaping' and promising that nobody would work harder than him to win the election. 'We hardly waited to listen to him,' Castle recalled, 'and hurried out to the press conference, oozing contempt for the cowards from every pore.'[109]

Hugh Scanlon had come up with the face-saving formula, based on the unions' own 'Bridlington Agreement', which allowed the TUC to intervene when one union poached another's members. Instead of accepting a change in their rules, the unions gave a 'solemn and binding undertaking' to follow its advice in unofficial strikes.[110] In a live broadcast to the nation Wilson insisted that he was 'in no doubt about their determination to carry out this undertaking'.[111] If so, he was in a very small minority. As numerous Labour MPs admitted to the press, the settlement looked like 'a charade' designed to conceal the fact that the government had surrendered.[112] Even Wilson's own colleagues found it hard to take the 'solemn and binding' pledge seriously: the weekend's papers were full of leaks from Cabinet ministers admitting the deal was largely a public-relations stunt.[113]

In almost every newspaper in Britain the verdict was the same: 'Surrender'. In a sense Wilson only had himself to blame: having insisted time and again that the government simply had to turn *In Place of Strife* into law, he could hardly complain when the papers pointed out how far he had retreated.[114] The blow fell hardest of all on Barbara Castle, who had put nine months' work into her efforts to reform the unions . Watching the assembled Labour MPs cheering news of the deal, she 'felt deflated to the point of tears'.[115] Her reputation in the Labour movement was irreparably tarnished, and her career never recovered. Although she remained part of the Labour high command into the seventies, it was as a kind of sentimental favourite rather than as a genuine powerbroker. 'Poor Barbara,' Wilson remarked to one of his officials. 'She hangs around like someone with a still-born child. She can't believe it's dead.'[116]

Roy Jenkins, whose last-minute abandonment of *In Place of Strife* had been one of the crucial reasons for its failure, later wrote that its defeat was 'a sad story from which [Wilson] and Barbara Castle emerged with more credit than the rest of us'.[117] If the bill had passed, curbing unofficial strikes, curtailing the power of the shop stewards and cutting off the drive towards greater militancy, then the traumas of the future – the Conservatives' controversial Industrial Relations Act, the three-day week, the Winter of Discontent and the Thatcher government's battle against the miners – might have been averted. Indeed, one of the ironies of the story was that if the Conservatives had promised to support *In Place of Strife*, they might have been spared the awful turmoil that greeted their own legislation in the early seventies. Instead, Heath denounced the bill for not going far enough. He would have done better to lend Wilson a hand, for in the long term, the unions' victory only sharpened their appetite for confrontation – as the Conservative leader would soon discover.[118]

Just two weeks after the final settlement Crossman recorded that the government had 'completely lost control' of the unions, with 'a rash of unofficial strikes – dock strikes, Leyland strikes, GPO and National Health Service threats'.[119] Indeed, 1969 proved to be a terrible year for industrial unrest. Almost 7 million working days were lost to strikes, up from what had once seemed an enormous 4.7 million in 1968, and the total continued to grow in the years that followed, reaching a record 23.8 million days in the industrial anarchy of 1972.[120] Even Jim Callaghan admitted that the unions never made their own reforms effective. It was perhaps the greatest irony of all that the Keeper of the Cloth Cap, who had done so much to help the unions defeat the bill, would himself be brought down by their excesses ten years later.[121]

If Harold Wilson's supporters still had any illusions about his leadership skills, they were utterly blown away by the fate of *In Place of Strife*. Although he had shown admirable resolution under pressure, he had nevertheless made a string of tactical errors and had ultimately been defeated by his own ministers.[122] It was no surprise that he appeared, in Crossman's words, 'even more conspiratorial, even more persecuted and even more devastatingly isolated' than ever.[123] Benn recorded that he 'just felt contempt for him', and that any lingering respect had long since disappeared: 'I just feel that Harold is finished.'[124]

Although Wilson had talked about resigning if the Cabinet defied him over *In Place of Strife*, he had no real intention of surrendering his grip on power.[125] A month later David Frost asked him on television what he would like his obituaries to say. 'I'd like them to say that in the hardest times, we kept our nerve, showed that we'd got guts, didn't get pushed from one side to the other and went right on to the end of building up Britain's economic strength,' Wilson replied.[126] As always, he was full of plans for the future, telling friends 'how, when the crisis was over, he would get rid of the lily-livered people, how Callaghan would have to go and that Jenkins was a coward'.[127]

In the short term the undisputed winner from the whole debacle was Callaghan. His performance at the Home Office was one of the government's few widely acknowledged successes in the late sixties: whether handling the demonstrations in Grosvenor Square, pushing through race relations legislation or articulating public anxieties about student protest and drug abuse, he cut a reassuring and impressive figure.[128] As we shall see, even his handling of the growing chaos in Northern Ireland struck most observers as firm, judicious and sure-footed. When Jenkins sneered at his great rival's intelligence, Crossman countered that he was 'a wonderful political personality, easily the most accomplished politician in the Labour Party, and I think he is quite able as well'.[129] Even Wilson, almost despite himself, was impressed with Callaghan's performance in Northern Ireland, and in December 1969 the *Guardian* named him as its 'Politician of the Year'.[130]

Meanwhile, Callaghan's rival was still struggling to sort out the mess he had left behind at the Treasury. Jenkins's priority was to build a surplus on the balance of payments to avoid another sterling crisis.[131] To do this, he needed to keep up the regime of severe deflation, stifling consumer demand at home and obviously inhibiting Labour's chances of clawing their way back in the opinion polls. For a long time, however, his measures seemed to be falling some way short. In February 1969 a new set of poor trade figures triggered yet another sterling crisis and more deflationary medicine, and some ministers wondered whether they would ever find their way out of the woods. However, in his April Budget Jenkins turned the screw further by raising taxes by £340 million, and, although the Conservatives complained that he had been insufficiently severe, this eventually did the trick. The trade figures for May and June showed significant improvement, and by the late summer Jenkins was feeling decidedly optimistic.[132]

Yet, while the balance of payments was steadily improving, another, potentially more corrosive economic problem was on the horizon. On 23 October the Cabinet heard the depressing news:

> Then we had Barbara, who had to admit that the whole industrial field is in complete anarchy, with strikes in the motor-car industry, the whole

of the coal mines on strike, including the prosperous fields, and now this madness affecting the nurses, who are steaming up at their conference at Harrogate. We find this unrest and disarray everywhere in the public service, firemen, dustmen, local government officers. Barbara reported that everything was out of control.

Strikes were a worry, of course, but the real danger was inflation. Since the government had given up on statutory controls, they had no real answer to the surge of pay claims that ran through industry in the second half of 1969. Over the course of the year wage increases were nearly 8 per cent higher than in 1968, and by the end of 1970 inflation was running at some 6.4 per cent.[134]

The historian Nicholas Woodward lists seven different factors that contributed to the surging inflation of the late sixties, from the Vietnam War and the rise in global commodity prices to the aspirations of the consumer society and the impatience of the affluent young. Workers often had genuine grievances rooted in the industrial changes of the era, and looked for higher wages to make up for them. And as we have seen, many low-paid workers, frightened that they were falling behind their neighbours, resented the pay restraint of the mid-sixties, and therefore sought handsome wage increases when the opportunity came. But the Wilson government also bears direct responsibility. The failure of *In Place of Strife* meant that there was no effective check on industrial disputes, while the government's credit with the unions stood at an all-time low. The union leaders had little inclination to restrain the militants on the shop floor, and in the second half of 1969 there came a great wave of pay claims and strikes by workers who felt that their standard of living was slipping thanks to the government's deflationary policies.[135]

At this crucial moment Wilson and his ministers consciously decided that a little inflation was no bad thing. They knew that an election was imminent: if wages seemed to be rising rapidly in the months beforehand, then they would be able to exploit the resulting sense of well-being. In November Jenkins privately remarked that he would be quite happy with a general increase of 6 per cent, and in the next few months the government made no real effort to stifle the soaring pay claims.[136] However, in January and February 1970 some public sector pay settlements reached 12 per cent, and over the course of the year wages and salaries rose 13 per cent above their levels of the previous year.[137]

In his Budget speech that spring, Jenkins warned that 'if serious inflation gets a grip it will be very difficult to shake it off'.[138] But less complacent observers thought that it had already taken hold. 'Mr Jenkins', said *The Times* the following day, 'is already staring into the face of runaway inflation.'[139] On 21 April the economist Michael Shanks predicted that inflation was likely 'to grow more acute during the 1970s . . . What is happening now in the United Kingdom on the wage front is an indication of how dangerous it can be for governments to slacken the reins, however inefficiently they may appear to have grasped them previously.'[140] Nine days later, Lord Shawcross, a former Labour President of the Board of Trade, declared that the next government would be forced to take 'the most disagreeable measures' to prevent a disastrous inflationary surge. 'Seven or eight months ago I was ridiculed for saying we seemed in for a period of runaway inflation,' he remarked gloomily. 'Nobody doubts that now.'[141]

34

CHILDREN OF WRATH

We then settled down to discuss the Ulster situation . . . Cledwyn Hughes said, 'It's a pity that the Catholics and Protestants can't cooperate a bit more at the religious level.'

Tony Benn's diary, 19 August 1969

'I'm pleading with you, Jim. Send in the army.' And I'll never forget his reply. 'Gerry,' he says, 'I can get the army in but it's going to be a devil of a job to get it out.'

Gerry Fitt, interviewed in 1992

By the late 1960s, Terence O'Neill's project for the modernisation of Northern Ireland was running into severe difficulties. The new industries he had attracted to the province were overwhelmingly based in the Protestant east, not in the rural, Catholic west, and unemployment was still disproportionately high in Catholic areas like the city of Derry.[1] '[Londonderry] is losing prosperity fast,' reported *The Times*. 'The sickness is recognizable – it has the face of a dying man.' A group of unemployed dockers told the paper's reporter that 'Derry was suffering because being a Catholic majority city, discrimination was being practised against it'. Even one Protestant man thought that 'there seemed to be a deliberate plot in Belfast to draw investment away from the dangers of nationalism in Derry'. The local people were angry, the article concluded, 'because they can see no other reason why the town of Londonderry is being left to die'.[2]

Although O'Neill's reforms had alienated many people within the Protestant community, plenty of Catholics argued that he had gone nowhere near far enough. A new generation of politicians and activists, representing the affluent Catholic middle class, were already pushing for faster changes. Gerry Fitt, for example, was elected to Westminster for the Republican Labour Party in 1966. A clubbable ex-seaman from West Belfast, he immediately made an impact, courting publicity and winning friends in the bar of the House of Commons. John Hume, meanwhile, was a Derry schoolteacher who had been drawn into politics after the government refused to build Northern Ireland's second university in his home town. And Austin Currie was an outspoken young Nationalist MP who forced his way on to the front pages by loudly protesting against housing discrimination in County Tyrone. All three were unimpressed by O'Neill's record of slow, grudging reform, and all three were determined that Catholics should be second-class citizens no longer.[3]

All three men were also linked to the growing movement for Catholic civil rights, which was formalised in January 1967 by the foundation of the Northern Ireland Civil Rights Association, or NICRA. Modelled on the civil rights movement in the United States, NICRA never really exercised any strong authority: instead, individual groups organised their own meetings and marches to push for an end to anti-Catholic sectarianism. To many observers in mainland Britain, their demands seemed reasonable enough: legislation to prohibit discrimination; fairer electoral boundaries and housing allocation; the disbanding of the B Specials; and, above all, the principle of 'one man, one vote', so that every adult could vote in local government elections.[4]

However, although NICRA won generally sympathetic treatment in the British press, Unionist politicians consistently described it as a front for the IRA. The hard-line Home Affairs Minister William Craig insisted that it was 'the beginning of a republican campaign organized entirely by the IRA', exploiting gullible activists as part of a deliberate 'threat to the state'.[5] It is tempting to dismiss this as mere sectarian scaremongering, but historians now agree that although the civil rights movement was 'based on perfectly reasonable demands for fairer treatment for Catholics', there *was* an indisputable link with what remained of the IRA. Indeed, John Hume refused to join the association because he was concerned that it might be a front for more extreme organisations. As the organisation's most authoritative historian points out, Craig's prejudiced verdict was not so wide of the mark: the IRA did create the civil rights movement, and 'did so with the explicit intention of bringing down the Northern Ireland state'.[6]

NICRA was a product of the IRA's move towards the Marxist left under the leadership of Cathal Goulding. In 1964 IRA members had established a series of Wolfe Tone societies across Ireland, north and south. These were 'radical republican discussion groups' designed to 'foster republicanism by educating the masses in their cultural and political heritage'.[7] It was from the Wolfe Tone Society in Dublin, for instance, that the idea of a civil rights campaign first emerged. And for the Republican intellectuals active in the Wolfe Tone societies, like Roy Johnston and Desmond Greaves, the whole point was to undermine Unionism. Wolfe Tone literature explained that Northern Ireland was based on 'an artificially fostered sectarianism, an anti-Catholic prejudice and bigotry which has become identified with the state system'. Once this was dismantled there would be no reason for the Northern Irish state to continue, and Protestants and Catholics would effectively join hands and walk together into a bright, united future.[8]

This mish-mash of Irish nationalism and second-hand Marxism convinced Goulding and his IRA colleagues to pour their energies into a civil rights movement that would press for peaceful change. Their influence was greatly downplayed at the time, and NICRA was presented as a non-sectarian movement working for fairness and justice. But Goulding himself said later that 'the Army Council of the IRA set up NICRA, it and the Communist Party together', and even Gerry Adams admitted that the civil rights campaigns were 'the creation of the republican leadership'.[9] When NICRA was formally established in Belfast on 29 January 1967 there were two prominent Wolfe Tone representatives on the thirteen-man committee, as well as Liam McMillen, a member of the IRA. As Richard English puts it, there was 'a direct, causal, practical and ideological connection between the 1960s IRA and the civil rights initiative'.[10]

Yet the civil rights movement was more than simply a front for the IRA. A grass-roots Campaign for Social Justice had been established back in 1964, before the Wolfe Tone societies set to work, and the movement soon acquired a momentum of its own. A wide range of local groups and individuals threw themselves into the campaign in the late sixties, inspired by the examples of the American civil rights movement, the Prague Spring and the student demonstrations on the Continent. Most ordinary activists were not out to overthrow the state, but merely wanted to push for electoral reforms, fair housing allocation and so on. Although a few Marxists and Republicans actively welcomed conflict and instability, most activists had much more moderate objectives. In other words, Unionist politicians who thought that the IRA had 'infiltrated' the movement had things 'the wrong way around'. The truth was that the IRA had set up the movement only for it to be taken over by thousands of people with a very different vision: non-violent, non-sectarian, and designed to reform the Northern state rather than dismantle it completely.[11]

The tragedy of the civil rights movement was that, however reasonable its objectives, it emerged at an extremely tense moment in Northern Ireland's post-war history. Thanks to the economic troubles of the early sixties, the dislocating effect of O'Neill's reforms and, above all, the agitation of Ian Paisley and the violence of the UVF, suspicion and anxiety were running high among the Unionist community. Since the civil rights movement concentrated on the plight of Northern Ireland's Catholics, arguing that they were treated as 'second-class citizens', this implied that the Protestants were 'first-class', living it up at their neighbours' expense. But this was very far from the truth. Most working-class Protestants faced similar problems of unemployment, low wages and decaying housing, and they deeply resented the suggestion that they were enjoying a life of luxury based on exploitation and bigotry.[12] 'Our housing was the same as our Catholic next-door neighbour – two-up and two-down with an outside toilet,' said one Paisley supporter. 'It irks me when I hear about the disadvantages that the Catholics had and the agenda for equality that they go on about now.' Asked if he was a 'first-class citizen', he replied angrily: 'Absolutely not. There was no difference.'[13]

For many working-class Protestants, the civil rights movement was yet another threat in an increasingly insecure world. As they saw it, their livelihoods and families were under pressure from the travails of heavy industry and from the machinations of conspiratorial Catholics. In this climate the moderate Unionism of Terence O'Neill was much less appealing than the blood-and-thunder oratory of Ian Paisley, with his simple moral verities and appeals to sectarian tradition. As the preacher denounced Stormont for selling out to Catholic conspiracies, so many Unionist politicians, worried about losing the support of working-class Protestants, took greater pains to emphasise their own opposition to change. As one account puts it, Paisley 'did not create the fundamentalist and uncompromising strand in Unionism', but he exploited it to the full, and in doing so made O'Neill's position increasingly precarious.[14]

O'Neill had never been a great favourite of the Unionist rank and file. Many younger working-class Protestants were unimpressed by his brand of patrician, 'big house' politics, which went down well with wealthy farmers but seemed to offer few remedies for their own daily anxieties. 'We were election fodder,' one told Peter Taylor:

> They'd come down every four or five years with 'kick the Pope' bands and we were happy enough to cheer them on. They'd wave their Union Jacks

and flags at us and wind up my parents and people like that. At the end of the night, we went back to our ghettos and they went back to their big houses. Then we didn't see them for another four or five years.[15]

By 1967 some branches of the Orange Order had openly turned against O'Neill. At that year's marches activists distributed leaflets attacking his 'tottering leadership', while Unionist politicians who backed him were heckled and manhandled. Even O'Neill himself was now careful where and when he spoke: a year later he was pelted with eggs and flour at a party meeting in Belfast after visiting a Catholic convent school a few days before.[16]

At a local level, too, the temperature was rising. John Beresford Ash, a descendant of one of the four oldest Protestant families in Northern Ireland and the owner of an imposing country house just outside Derry, was a typical example of a 'big house' Unionist. Like O'Neill, he had gone to Eton and served in the British army before returning home in the late fifties. In the old days his word would have been respected by the local Unionist community, but when he told them that they would have to make concessions or face serious disturbances, he was simply ignored or told to keep quiet. His kind of patrician, conservative politics was on the way out. The politics of wrath was on the way in.[17]

While tensions were simmering in Northern Ireland, the British government might have been a million miles away. Even after the violence of 1966 and the opening of the civil rights campaign, Irish affairs barely impinged on Westminster or Fleet Street.[18] According to one estimate, until the very end of the sixties the House of Commons discussed Northern Ireland for an average of two hours *a year*, while the government virtually ignored the province altogether.[19] As James Callaghan later explained, the government's position 'very sensibly [was that] we are not going to get involved in this when we are not welcomed by the Northern Ireland government'.[20]

Throughout the crucial period from 1964 until 1969, Wilson was distracted by what appeared to be more immediate and pressing issues. When he relaxed with Marcia Williams, Barbara Castle or Richard Crossman over a late-night Scotch, he almost never mentioned Northern Ireland.[21] His Home Secretaries took a similar line. Roy Jenkins 'caused near despair' among civil rights campaigners by refusing to take any meaningful action to encourage reform and reconciliation. For Terence O'Neill, it was 1966 – the year of the Easter Rising commemorations, the imprisonment of Ian Paisley and the first murders by the UVF — that 'made [the Troubles] inevitable', but while all this was going on Jenkins did nothing.[22]

But it is a myth that the Troubles were inevitable: as one of O'Neill's senior officials later put it, there were 'half a dozen things' that could have been done differently, from electoral reform to the abolition of housing discrimination. O'Neill failed to act because he was frightened of losing the streets to Paisley and of being repudiated by his own party. Jenkins and Wilson failed to act, meanwhile, because they were distracted, because they thought that Northern Ireland was best left alone, and because they were fatally complacent. Although he had talked a good game before moving to the Home Office, Jenkins showed little interest in Irish affairs once he had settled in and never even bothered to visit the province.[23]

Even when Jenkins switched jobs with Callaghan at the end of 1967 a similar sense of complacency prevailed. At the Home Office the affairs of the province were still considered part of the 'general department', a kind of dumping ground for issues that did not fit in anywhere else, where they sat alongside such crucial national questions as British Summer Time, London cabs, the protection of birds and the administration of pubs in Carlisle.[24] In the Labour Party at large, too, Northern Ireland remained a pretty obscure subject: most MPs and activists were much more worried about the tribulations of the economy and the personal rivalries at the heart of the Wilson government. At the party conference in 1968 Northern Ireland was not even on the agenda.[25]

If any Home Secretary of the sixties deserves criticism for complacency and inaction, it is probably Jenkins rather than Callaghan. But it is nevertheless revealing that even now Northern Ireland was so far from the centre of British political attention. Callaghan later commented sadly that he 'should have taken action to press the Stormont government to do things', but that at the time he thought 'it was not, given the surrounding circumstances, politically possible to do it'. 'It took a crisis,' he said, to persuade the British government to act. But by their earlier failure to act, they had brought that crisis upon themselves.[26]

On 24 August 1968 almost four thousand people marched from the village of Coalisland to the town of Dungannon, County Tyrone, in Northern Ireland's first major civil rights demonstration. For many observers, who associated the idea of marching with Unionist ritual, the sight of Catholics marching in the street was something of a shock. Contrary to the predictions of some hard-liners, however, the march passed off without any serious violence, although a counter-demonstration organised by Ian Paisley's supporters hinted at the potential for sectarian conflict.[27]

Buoyed by the success of the march, NICRA scheduled another demonstration for Derry on 5 October. The route, from the Protestant Waterside district across Craigavon Bridge, through the old city walls and into the heart of the city, had been devised by a radical group within the civil rights movement, who were hoping to provoke violent repression and thereby attract international attention. As Tim Pat Coogan puts it, it appeared almost deliberately inflammatory, 'as though Hamas had paraded through Jerusalem's Holy Places and concluded with a rally at the Wailing Wall'. William Craig promptly announced that the march would be banned, and most NICRA moderates agreed that it should be postponed to another date. Around four hundred local activists, however, turned up in Duke Street at the appointed hour, ready to march for their rights.[28]

Although the first sectarian killings had come two years before, that autumn day in Derry really brought home the potential disaster that awaited the people of Northern Ireland. Two cordons of RUC policemen assembled at either end of Duke Street, trapping the marchers between them, and after five minutes of speeches the police moved forward to clear the streets by force. Those demonstrators who managed to escape from the hail of blows ran towards Craigavon Bridge, where a police water cannon pushed them back towards the RUC batons. Men, women and children were indiscriminately hacked to the ground, including prominent Catholic politicians like Austin Currie and Gerry Fitt. All of this was captured on film by an enterprising Irish journalist, and images of the violence were shown repeatedly in both Dublin and London.[29] Fitt was keen to let the world's media see what had happened to him, as he later explained:

> A sergeant grabbed me and pulled my coat down over my shoulders to prevent me raising my arms. Two other policemen held me as I was batoned on the head. I could feel the blood coursing down my neck and on to my shirt. As I fell to my knees I was roughly grabbed and thrown into a police van. At the police station I was shown into a room with a filthy wash basin and told to clean up but I was not interested in that. I wanted the outside world to see the blood which was still flowing strongly down my face.[30]

Derry was the worst possible place for such a clash to occur. More than any other city it suffered from economic recession and sectarian discrimination; more than any other city it symbolised the imbalances and injustices of Northern Irish society. Anger and resentment were running higher there than anywhere else, and if the civil rights movement had a nucleus, it was in Derry.[31] But the reckless violence of the RUC had only made matters much worse. Over the next few days hundreds of youths from the Catholic Bogside district hurled stones and petrol bombs at riot policemen, while there were peaceful demonstrations in Catholic areas of Belfast and other, smaller towns. The civil rights movement immediately acquired unprecedented credibility, and in the weeks that followed 'marches, sit-ins, demonstrations, protests and court appearances became almost daily occurrences'.[32] As Niall Ó Dochartaigh puts it, 'a state which had for decades seemed implacable and stern to its opponents [now seemed] desperately unstable and insecure'.[33]

In the aftermath of the violence in Derry, Terence O'Neill recognised that something had to give.[34] On 14 October he told his colleagues that although there were 'anti-partitionist agitators' at work, 'can any of us truthfully say in the confines of this room that the minority has no grievance calling for remedy?' If they did not act, then Harold Wilson would. 'Are we ready, and would we be wise to face up to this?' he asked. 'We would have a very hard job to sell concessions to our people: but in this critical moment may this not be our duty?' Ominously, however, not all of his colleagues agreed with him. William Craig spoke for many hardliners when he warned of 'disastrous political repercussions' if they introduced electoral reforms, and disagreed that 'Wilson should be allowed to tell them how to act'. British intervention, he said defiantly, 'would provoke a constitutional crisis and a massive uprising in the loyalist community'.[35]

On 4 November Northern Ireland's beleaguered Prime Minister, accompanied by the fractious William Craig and Brian Faulkner, arrived at 10 Downing Street for what has been described as 'a mauling' by Wilson and Callaghan. Wilson kicked off by reminding his visitors that they were economically dependent on Westminster and warned that unless they pushed through immediate reforms, he would be tempted to cut off some of their subsidies. Callaghan added that 'if there was any thought of just stringing the UK government along it had better be forgotten'. After the Home Secretary had listed a series of overdue reforms, Wilson concluded with the explicit threat that if Stormont did not behave accordingly, 'they would feel compelled to propose a radical course involving the complete liquidation of all financial agreements with Northern Ireland'. This was pretty strong stuff, throwing O'Neill and his colleagues completely on to the back foot. O'Neill complained that he was doing as much as he could: indeed, he had already gone so far that Loyalist extremists had threatened his life. Craig said that local government reform would take at least three years, defended the RUC and insisted that the IRA were to blame for the current tension. Wilson and Callaghan, however, were having none of it.[36]

In the end O'Neill persuaded his colleagues that they had to keep the British government happy. On 22 November he announced a five-point package: the establishment of a Londonderry Development Commission; the appointment of an ombudsman to whom citizens could appeal; limited voting reforms; a new system of housing allocation; and a future review of the Special Powers Act.[37] As one *Belfast Telegraph* journalist commented, the Catholics had won more in the forty-eight days since Derry than they had in the past forty-seven years.[38]

Yet, for O'Neill personally, it was a disaster. A few years or even a few months earlier, the programme would probably have appeased the frustrations of the Catholic community; now it seemed like too little, too late. In Unionist circles, meanwhile, it went down very badly. By apparently 'giving in' to the civil rights movement, O'Neill had confirmed everything that Paisley and his supporters had ever said about him. The loyalty of his own colleagues, always grudging and fragile, was beginning to crack. At the beginning of December, Craig told a Unionist rally that the civil rights movement was 'nonsense', being inspired by 'our old traditional enemy exploiting the situation'. When O'Neill told the Stormont parliament that he regretted his colleague's tone, Craig promptly gave the same speech again a few days later.[39]

Exhausted by the effort to control his own ministers, O'Neill finally decided to go over their heads. On 9 December 1968 both the BBC and UTV broke into their normal evening schedules to bring a live message from the Prime Minister himself. On screen the viewers saw a tired, strained man, speaking with obvious sincerity in a last-ditch attempt to forestall the tempest:

> Ulster stands at the crossroads. I believe you know me well enough by now to appreciate that I am not a man given to extravagant language. But I must say to you this evening that our conduct over the coming

days and weeks will decide our future. And as we face this situation, I would be failing in my duty to you as your Prime Minister if I did not put the issues, calmly and clearly, before you all . . . The time has come for the people as a whole to speak in a clear voice.

O'Neill then defended his goal of promoting a 'programme of change to secure a united and harmonious community', and warned that if Stormont failed to move, the British government might 'act over our heads'. 'Where would our Constitution be then?' he asked grimly. 'What shred of self-respect would be left to us? If we allowed others to solve our problems because we had not the guts – let me use a plain word – the guts to face up to them, we would be utterly shamed.'

To those Unionists who contemplated following Rhodesia into rebellion, O'Neill's message was stark. 'These people are not merely extremists,' he said witheringly. 'They are lunatics . . . They are not loyalists but disloyalists: disloyal to Britain, disloyal to the Constitution, disloyal to the Crown, disloyal – if they are in public life – to the solemn oaths they have sworn to Her Majesty the Queen.' To the civil rights movement, meanwhile, his message was equally clear:

> Perhaps you are not entirely satisfied, but this is a democracy, and I ask you now with all sincerity to call your people off the streets and allow an atmosphere favourable to change to develop. You are Ulstermen yourselves. You know we are all of us stubborn people, who will not be pushed too far. I believe that most of you want change, not revolution. Your voice has been heard, and clearly heard. Your duty now is to play your part in taking the heat out of the situation before blood is shed.

Gazing earnestly into the camera, in closing, O'Neill asked his listeners what kind of Ulster they wanted. 'A happy and respected Province, in good standing with the rest of the United Kingdom? Or a place continually torn apart by riots and demonstrations, and regarded by the rest of Britain as a political outcast?' He ended with a heartfelt appeal:

> Please weigh well all that is at stake, and make your voice heard in whatever way you think best, so that we may know the views not of the few but of the many. For this is truly a time of decision, and in your silence all that we have built up could be lost. I pray that you will reflect carefully

and decide wisely. And I ask all our Christian people, whatever their denomination, to attend their places of worship on Sunday next to pray for the peace and harmony of our country.[40]

O'Neill's eloquence and courage made an immediate impression on his audience. When Craig commented that the Prime Minister had gone too far, O'Neill immediately sacked him from the government, and the very next day the parliamentary party backed his decision by twenty-nine votes to nil, with four abstentions. In Derry civil rights campaigners announced that they would suspend all demonstrations for a month in a gesture of goodwill, and in Dublin the *Sunday Independent* named O'Neill its 'Man of the Year'. The *Belfast Telegraph*, meanwhile, launched an 'I'm Backing O'Neill' campaign, with a petition that was eventually signed by some 150,000 people, more than one in ten of the province's entire population.[41]

Yet O'Neill himself knew that this fleeting optimism was almost certainly misplaced. He had missed the opportunity to push through sweeping reforms when passions were cooler, and not only had he failed to appease the grievances of the Catholic minority, he had failed to persuade his own Unionist supporters.[42] The Wilson government, too, had been guilty of fatal complacency, allowing the situation to drift towards anarchy without summoning the necessary interest to intervene. Had they acted earlier, making it clear that financial aid was dependent on reform, Wilson's ministers might have averted the violence to come.[43] And instead of ending sectarianism, the emergence of the civil rights movement in the summer of 1968 had simply exacerbated it, raising tempers and 'unintentionally [helping] to produce a descent into awful and lasting violence'.[44]

O'Neill's tragedy was that he had acted too late. On Christmas Eve, two weeks after his 'Crossroads' speech, he wrote a prescient letter to his private secretary, Kenneth Bloomfield:

My Dear K,
What a year! I fear 1969 will be worse – or that portion of which we may survive. The one thing I cannot foresee in 1969 is Peace. As I look in the glass darkly I see demonstrations, counter-demonstrations, meetings, rows and general misery. In such an atmosphere of hatred would one in fact wish to continue this job, I doubt it. The only solution, direct rule from London, will of course never materialise and so we shall drift from crisis to crisis.[45]

On the first day of 1969 several dozen young civil rights campaigners began a march from Belfast to Derry. They were members of People's Democracy (PD), a radical faction of the civil rights movement, and had ignored the advice of other groups to give O'Neill more time. One of the marchers, a twenty-one-year-old psychology student called Bernadette Devlin, later explained that their aim was 'to break the truce, to relaunch the civil rights movement as a mass movement, and to show people that O'Neill was, in fact, offering them nothing'.[46]

Devlin and her fellow PD marchers knew that this was a risky strategy, because violence was in the air. On 30 November police roadblocks had prevented Ian Paisley's supporters from attacking a civil rights march in Armagh, which was just as well because the Paisley faction had been armed with at least two revolvers and more than two hundred other weapons, including sharpened pipes, bill-hooks and scythes.[47] Yet the PD activists welcomed the prospect of bloodshed, because they thought it would dramatise their cause to a television audience and expose the violent nature of the Northern Irish state. 'We knew we wouldn't finish the march without getting molested,' said Devlin. 'What we really wanted to do was pull the carpet off the floor to show the dirt that was under it, so that we could sweep it up.'[48]

Just as had been predicted, the march ended in tears. On the evening of 3 January, Paisley held a religious rally in Derry's Guildhall while his supporters fought with Catholic demonstrators and policemen outside. By this point the PD marchers were just outside the city, and the police told them not to go any further in case they provoked a riot. Next morning, however, the marchers went ahead, tramping on until they reached Burntollet Bridge, a few miles from Derry. Here they were briefly halted by the police. Then, suddenly, as Devlin and her fellow-marchers began moving again, 'a curtain of bricks and boulders and bottles brought the march to a halt'. 'From the lanes,' she recalled, 'burst hordes of screaming people wielding planks of wood, bottles, laths, iron bars, crowbars, cudgels studded with nails, and they waded into the march beating hell out of everybody.'[49]

According to eyewitness reports, most of the attackers, who wore white armbands to identify themselves, were off-duty B Specials and members of various Unionist factions. The police made little effort to intervene or to arrest the malefactors, even 'standing around chatting and smoking quite happily' with them afterwards. Many of the marchers were badly bloodied and battered, and the brutal scenes were inevitably shown on British and

Irish television that evening.[50] To make matters worse, later that night a mob of drunken policemen charged into the Catholic Bogside area, smashing windows and laying into any unfortunate residents they could find. The next day the first barricades went up, erected by angry Catholics to prevent any further attacks by the supposed representatives of law and order.[51]

Since the PD marchers explicitly welcomed violence, some of their fellow campaigners were less than sympathetic.[52] Even those Republican intellectuals who had been behind the civil rights movement in the first place deplored the 'coat-trailing' antics of their successors.[53] Indeed, the PD march and its bloody culmination illustrate the point that although the Troubles drew on the historic legacy of sectarianism, they were also created by the decisions of particular groups and individuals who could have chosen different paths. For in the long run the beneficiaries were the extremists who stood to gain from greater polarisation, hatred and violence: on the Protestant side Paisley and his acolytes; on the Catholic side the more extreme members of the IRA. Sean MacStiofain, a hardliner who was to become the first chief of staff of the Provisional IRA, later commented that only the 'courage and foresight' of Devlin and her fellow-marchers had staved off the prospect of peaceful reform under Terence O'Neill, which would have been a bitter blow for the IRA. Their 'daring action', he said, had 'effectively ended O'Neill's chances of political survival' and opened the way for the politics of the gun.[54]

For many observers, the violence at Burntollet Bridge was a spectacular lesson that Northern Ireland's internal tensions were beyond easy resolution. For many Protestants, the fighting only increased their anxiety that they were friendless and beleaguered. Among Catholics, however, there was understandable outrage that the marchers had been subjected to such sickening violence. On the mainland, Northern Ireland was front-page news again, with most papers thinking that the outlook was grim. A long editorial in the *New Statesman* observed that if O'Neill could not 'deliver the goods' on reform, then Wilson would have to intervene. British military intervention to secure order, the editorial commented, still seemed a melodramatic prospect, but 'people are likely to be killed in Ulster if things get worse . . . how many will have to be killed before the idea of mobilising British soldiers seems less laughable?'[55]

For O'Neill, Burntollet was the beginning of the end. On 5 January he condemned the march as a 'foolhardy and irresponsible undertaking', but ten days later he set up the Cameron Commission to examine the surge of sectarian violence.[56] Many Unionists disliked even the idea of a commission, since they feared that it would recommend more reforms, and on 24 January they found a prominent champion when O'Neill's deputy, Brian Faulkner, resigned from the government. Faulkner's departure was largely a question of ambition; he had never forgiven O'Neill for beating him to the premiership, and was convinced that he could better articulate the anxieties of Unionism. With critics calling for him to step down, O'Neill now felt compelled to gamble everything. On 3 February, to the great surprise of most political observers, he announced that a general election would be held in three weeks' time.[57]

In Britain O'Neill's gamble was widely seen, in the words of the *Spectator*, as a 'leap in the dark'.[58] Crossman thought that it was all 'very exciting because O'Neill is the man we are relying on in Northern Ireland to do our job for us' and hoped that he would 'smash the old-fashioned people and enable Ulster to go forward'. However, if O'Neill failed, then 'we shall have to do something about it'. Crossman already had an inkling of what they might do, recording that Callaghan had told him 'in the greatest secrecy, that he had to work out the plan for a take-over of Government in Northern Ireland if the government were in danger of collapsing'.[59] In fact, as early as the autumn of 1968 Callaghan's officials had begun working on a contingency plan to send troops to Northern Ireland, including provisions to suspend the Stormont parliament and impose direct rule from London. But this was a nightmare scenario: like Crossman, other ministers hoped that somehow O'Neill would pull it off.[60]

The election campaign was extraordinarily bitter. Paisley had been sent to prison for three months after the Armagh disturbances at the end of November 1968, but having raised the money to pay a heavy bail bond, he was free to challenge O'Neill in his Bannside constituency. For three weeks he tramped through the streets, followed by flute bands and drummers, denouncing 'the traitor' who would soon be crushed beneath 'the marching feet of the Protestants'.[61] When the votes were counted O'Neill held on to his seat, but his party was deeply divided. Only in the more prosperous and overwhelmingly Protestant areas around Belfast did the reformers attract wholehearted support: in working-class areas their standing was not high at all.[62] The longer the campaign went on, the more the momentum of the 'Crossroads' speech seemed to ebb away.[63]

For most British observers, it was the worst possible result: unclear, indecisive and indicative of Northern Ireland's deep divisions. O'Neill no longer led a united party, and the Unionists seemed to be shifting towards hard-line politicians like Craig and Faulkner.[64] *The Times* predicted that it might spell the end for O'Neill's leadership, while other commentators were beginning to contemplate direct British intervention. Yet again, however, the turmoil in Northern Ireland took second place to more parochial considerations. Wilson was a beleaguered man in the late winter and spring of 1969, his attention dominated by the conflict with the trade unions and the threat to his leadership from Callaghan. While the province slipped further towards disaster, his mind was elsewhere.[65]

For O'Neill, meanwhile, the end was not long delayed. On 30 March, while the Prime Minister was waiting for a vote of confidence from the Ulster Unionist Council, a bomb went off at the Castlereagh electricity substation, plunging much of Belfast into darkness. O'Neill mobilised a thousand B Specials to guard Northern Ireland's power and water installations, but it was no good, and more bombs went off at water pipelines, reservoirs and electricity stations throughout the next month. By 26 April much of Belfast was without water and special trucks had to be sent through the streets carrying emergency water supplies to people who could not reach stand-pipes.[66]

According to Paisley's *Protestant Telegraph*, the 'sheer professionalism' of the bombing campaign proved that it was the handiwork of the IRA. In reality, the bombs had been planted by members of the Loyalist Ulster Volunteer Force, working in collusion with Paisley's own Ulster Protestant Volunteers. But as the UVF had expected, in the anxious atmosphere of April 1969 most Unionists blamed the IRA – and Terence O'Neill. 'The plan', said Gusty Spence, 'was simply to give the impression that O'Neill with all his liberality was perhaps responsible for the IRA taking liberties. It was carefully planned to bring down O'Neill so that a new leadership would take over.'[67]

On 28 April, having forced through electoral reform at last, O'Neill gave up his long struggle and resigned the premiership. On television that night he admitted sadly that 'old fears, old prejudices and old loyalties' had been too strong for him. In Loyalist areas celebratory bonfires burned long into the night. Many historians remark on the flaws that prevented O'Neill from reaching out to his own community: the patrician manner, the clipped Old Etonian accent, the habits and values of the 'big house'. And it is easy to exaggerate his commitment to reform: at the beginning of his premiership O'Neill had been more interested in economic modernisation than in undoing the legacy of discrimination. But given what had gone before, and what would come afterwards, it would be unfair to judge him too harshly. Caught between renascent nationalism and intransigent Unionism in an era of economic insecurity, O'Neill was the wrong man trying to do the right thing at the wrong time. Perhaps the *Irish News*, in a surprisingly generous political obituary, put it best: 'The judgement of history will certainly be kinder to him than to his predecessors, who did nothing at all to bridge the chasm that divides our society and which Unionism of the anti-O'Neill variety still seems unwilling to attempt. At least Mr O'Neill tried.'[68]

O'Neill's final act as leader of the Unionist Party was to cast the deciding vote that handed the premiership to his distant relative, James Chichester-Clarke. A Londonderry farmer and a former major in the Irish Guards, Chichester-Clarke was yet another politician from the 'big house' tradition. Wooden and worthy, he was hardly an inspiring leader, and Paisley greeted his elevation with the observation that he had already 'brought down a captain and could bring down a major as well'.[69]

Chichester-Clarke inherited an increasingly febrile situation. In Derry, where sectarian violence had been almost unknown before 1968, every week seemed to bring more bad news. Sectarian attacks on quiet streets late at night were becoming increasingly common, with victims ordered to state their name and religion and brutally beaten if they gave the wrong answers.[70] A few days before O'Neill's resignation a group of RUC policemen had beaten to death Samuel Devenney, a Bogside taxi driver, and thirty thousand people attended his funeral in a silent demonstration against 'police brutality'.[71] Meanwhile, in a by-election on 17 April, Bernadette Devlin had dramatically wrested the Mid-Ulster seat at Westminster from the Ulster Unionists. The extent to which the British press understood Northern Ireland can be gauged from the coverage of Devlin's election. 'She's Bernadette, she's 21, she's an MP, she's swinging', announced the *Express*, while the *Mirror* called her 'The Honourable Swinging Member for the marchers'. The youngest MP for half a century, she made an immediate impact on the British press when she gave a passionate maiden speech insisting that 'there can be no justice while there is a Unionist Party, because while there is a Unionist Party they will by their gerrymandering control Northern Ireland'. She suggested that Wilson 'consider the possibility of abolishing Stormont and ruling from Westminster'.[72]

Degree by degree, the temperature was rising, yet still Wilson and Callaghan hesitated to act. On 12 July, after the traditional Orange parades,

Derry was convulsed by three consecutive days of looting. On the weekend of 2 and 3 August there was more rioting, this time in Belfast, where Loyalist mobs ordered Catholic families to 'get out or be burned out' of the mixed Crumlin Road neighbourhood, while Republican gangs issued similar orders to Protestant families in the Hooker Street area. The next major scheduled event was the traditional march of the Apprentice Boys of Derry, when fifteen thousand Orangemen would commemorate the relief of the city by Protestant troops in August 1689. Given the feverish mood of the city, 'it was clear to any politician with even the most rudimentary knowledge of recent events that serious trouble was inevitable'.[73]

Nevertheless Chichester-Clarke was very unlikely to prohibit the march. If he did, many rank-and-file Unionists, as well as Paisley, would immediately accuse him of appeasing the IRA. Wilson's government, however, did not have the same excuse. Several Labour backbenchers urged Callaghan to stop the march going ahead, and even Wilson himself, by his own recollection, thought that they ought to ban it.[74] But Callaghan's voice prevailed. According to some reports, his officials had already warned him that the RUC did not have the resources to stop the Apprentice Boys from marching, and he was also worried that prohibiting the march would inflame Unionist opinion and make life intolerable for Chichester-Clarke. Callaghan was not stupid, and knew that there was a serious risk that the parade would end in violence. But in the aftermath of the collapse of *In Place of Strife* he was in expansive form, enjoying flexing his muscles around the Cabinet table. He had not banned the Grosvenor Square march in October 1968, either, and that had turned out well enough. Even at this late hour, he thought that Stormont, not Westminster, should have the decisive word.[75] 'The problems of Northern Ireland', he told a delegation of Labour backbenchers on 31 July, 'should be solved within Northern Ireland, without any outside intervention.'[76]

Despite the Home Secretary's apparent confidence, most neutral observers were dreading the Apprentice Boys' march. In Derry itself a Citizens' Defence Association was set up under the leadership of Sean Keenan, a grizzled IRA veteran, with street committees to orchestrate the defence of the Bogside and plans to build barricades at strategic junctions. Catholics should defend themselves, Keenan said, with 'sticks, stones and the good old petrol bomb', although at this point he ruled out using firearms.[77] In the days leading up to the parade, tens of thousands of empty milk bottles went missing in the Bogside as its residents prepared to defend themselves with petrol bombs. The night before the parade, barricades went up in the Bogside, while in the Protestant Fountain district celebratory bonfires blazed in the dark. Almost everybody anticipated trouble.[78]

With tempers high even before the march had begun, it was hardly surprising that it went about as badly as possible. While the Apprentice Boys were forming up on the city walls at lunchtime, a few of them lobbed handfuls of pennies down at the hostile Catholic crowds watching from the Bogside below. By early afternoon the first scuffles were already under way as young Catholics threw nails and stones at the RUC men guarding the barricades set up to keep the two sides apart. By four o'clock the Apprentice Boys themselves had come under attack and had broken ranks to fight back. By five the RUC barricades had been torn down completely. In a desperate attempt to regain control the police ordered a baton charge into the Bogside, but they were walking directly into the arms of the Derry Citizens' Defence Association. As the police charged forwards, supported by a small mob of stone-throwing Apprentice Boys and Protestant youths, they were met by a stream of petrol bombs from the roof of the high-rise Rossville Flats, which overlooked the area. In the general chaos RUC officers called for a water cannon to disperse their assailants, but by the time it had been prepared many of the surrounding homes and shops were already ablaze.

By nightfall the disturbances had taken on the quality of a full-scale pitched battle, with casualties to match. In one police unit from County Down, for example, forty-three out of fifty-nine officers had been injured, and RUC officers were desperately calling for reinforcements. For the first time they asked for permission to use CS gas, but even this proved ineffective. The gas failed to reach the petrol bombers on top of the Rossville Flats, but 'hung in the air like smog, saturating the narrow streets, invading the tightly packed homes, racking lungs, damaging eyes, wreaking havoc on the old'. Wreathed in gas, illuminated by blazing buildings, throbbing with shouts and screams, the Bogside had become a battlefield.[79]

Although Northern Ireland had seen its fair share of riots before, the 'Battle of the Bogside' was different. Never before had the state so obviously lost control of its own territory; never before had the province seemed closer to civil war. As dawn broke on 13 August the Bogside was still under siege, with the RUC holding a line across the top of Rossville Street, at the entrance to the neighbourhood, but with the entire community mobilised against them. In the back streets emergency first-aid stations treated civilian casualties, while in the little terraced houses women and children were hard at work making petrol bombs to be taken to the front line.[80]

For many young Catholics, the battle was an invigorating act of self-defence against the invading forces of the Unionist state. Tony Miller, a fifteen-year-old who later joined the IRA, explained:

> I was throwing stones, petrol bombs, bottles, everything. You name it. I remember having a serious hatred for the RUC at the time and just wanting to sort of take revenge because you saw people getting battered and choked with CS gas. I was on top of Rossville Flats with a full view of everything that was going on. There were hundreds of people below and you had a perfect view. On top of the flats was a thing constructed by the Bogside people at the time. It was like a huge catapult. We could put the petrol bombs on it and shoot the petrol right onto the spot where the RUC were actually congregating . . . It was a powerful feeling, like you were fighting an armed force. That was my first conflict with the RUC.[81]

On the other side, too, passions ran high as the normal conventions of life disintegrated. One British reporter wrote that what really shocked him was not 'the RUC's stoning or petrol-bombing', but 'their hate . . . matching that of the Catholics. The obscenities, the threats, the religious tauntings – and all coming from a peace-keeping force.'[82] Many of Londonderry's Protestants, however, saw the RUC as their only defence against a Republican uprising. Gregory Campbell, a teenager who worked in the city centre, made an excuse to leave his shop and go down 'to help the police'. 'What I saw was an insurrection,' he told the journalist Peter Taylor. 'I saw groups of people defying law and order . . . and the police were the bulwark against them . . . I felt then that they needed all the help they could get.' Asked what was going through his mind while he was throwing stones from behind the RUC line, Campbell explained his feelings in terms that would have struck a chord with thousands of other working-class Unionists:

> I felt these people are trying to destroy Northern Ireland. They are marching for rights that I don't have. They're saying that I'm preventing them from getting the rights and now they're trying to destroy the country. I felt I had to do something and it was all I could do at that stage and it was just about bordering on what was morally acceptable for me to do.

But unlike many other young men, both Protestant and Catholic, who became drawn into the violence, Gregory Campbell did not join a paramilitary organisation. His refusal to do so, on what he said were 'moral grounds', illustrates the point that individuals were not compelled to become terrorists because of deep historical forces. They did have a choice.[83]

By the end of the second day the RUC were still camped at the entrance to the Bogside, where the air was thick with smoke and dozens of shops and homes still burned. 'Derry is in a state of war' read one hastily produced 'newsletter' that circulated in the back streets, carrying reports from the 'battlefronts' and instructions for making and using petrol bombs. Civil war was no longer an unlikely fantasy; on the streets of Derry it was nightmarish reality. The Citizens' Defence Association issued a public appeal for 'every able-bodied man in Ireland' to come and help in the fighting, and many Catholics even hoped that the army of the Republic of Ireland might come to their rescue.[84]

The Irish government had gone to great efforts to avoid being sucked into the growing chaos in the North. Although Irish newspapers covered the civil rights marches in great detail, the government appeared content to let the British sort out the mess.[85] The Battle of the Bogside made an enormous impression on public opinion in the Republic, however, and many senior figures within the government were convinced that they had to take action. Some hard-line ministers like Neil Blaney and Charles Haughey, who had murky links to the Republican movement, even urged the despatch of Irish troops into Derry, risking armed clashes with the RUC and even the British. Thankfully for all concerned, this was never likely, but they did persuade the Taoiseach, Jack Lynch, to deliver on the evening of 13 August a television address drafted and approved by his colleagues.[86]

A former hurling star, Lynch was a consensual, pipe-smoking politician, and his mild reputation gave his words added authority. Stormont, he said, was 'no longer in control of the situation'. Indeed, the events in Derry were 'the inevitable outcome of the policies pursued for decades by successive Stormont Governments'. It was clear, he added, 'that the Irish Government can no longer stand by and see innocent people injured and perhaps worse.' He had therefore ordered the Irish army to set up 'field hospitals' along the border, where injured Catholics could receive treatment. He insisted that the RUC was no longer 'an impartial police force' and urged Britain to accept an international peace-keeping force in Northern Ireland. Finally, he assured his audiences that 'the re-unification of the national territory can provide the only permanent solution for the problem', and pledged to enter early negotiations with the British to 'review the present constitutional position of the Six Counties of Northern Ireland'.[87]

Like so many interventions in Northern Ireland's history, Jack Lynch's speech had a very different effect from that anticipated by the well-meaning Corkonian. In Derry itself many Catholics assumed that the Irish army was about to relieve the city, while Protestants feared that their worst nightmare, a full-scale Irish invasion, was upon them. In the hours following the speech several hundred Protestants from other areas poured towards the Bogside, massing behind the RUC lines in preparation for what they thought would be a titanic battle to the death. Even Callaghan, who had finally decided to break off his holiday, wondered whether the field hospitals might be 'a blind for further [Irish] troop movements', and asked his officials whether British units should be sent to the border, just in case.[88]

Meanwhile, the situation in the streets of Derry became steadily worse. A crowd of furious Protestants managed to break through the RUC lines, but by the time they came to blows with the Catholic defenders, they had become generally intermingled with the RUC men supposedly keeping them back. In the general confusion, with more Catholics streaming into the streets to repel the invaders, an RUC constable fired into the crowd, wounding two or three people. This was the first time that firearms had been used in the battle, and behind the front lines a group of young men confronted Sean Keenan and insisted that he must yield control to armed Republicans who would be better able to resist the forces of the state. With rumours swirling around that mysterious men from the south had offered the Catholics 200 rifles and 100,000 rounds of ammunition, it was an ominous moment, illustrating the potential for armed paramilitaries to exploit a volatile situation.[89]

To make matters worse, news came that night that fighting had also broken out in Belfast, Armagh, Newry and elsewhere. In the capital Catholic crowds laid siege to an RUC station near the Falls Road, and wild rumours of violence spread through the Protestant community. One youngster recalled:

> In those days it was the word of the jungle where rumours spread very quickly ... I remember Protestants at that time making petrol bombs and getting ready for an attack that they believed would come on the Thursday night from the Falls. We were kids and we were watching the

older ones and everybody seemed to be excited. Everybody was involved – the whole community. Basins of water were set out and doors left open for people to run into. Everybody was bracing themselves for what they believed was going to be a massive attack from nationalists on the Falls Road in order for them to spread the violence and therefore help other nationalists in the Bogside.[90]

By the time that the violence entered its third day, Thursday, 14 August, Northern Ireland seemed on the brink of full-scale civil war. In Derry the RUC had finally managed to persuade the Protestant rioters to withdraw from the Bogside; the battle between the police and the Catholic community went on. Fighting continued throughout the morning, and in the afternoon a fresh wave of sectarian violence broke out in the city centre. At around four o'clock, with the police utterly exhausted, the call went out for a general mobilisation of the B Specials, which was greeted with delight by many Protestants. As evening approached the B Specials, armed with sticks and pickaxe handles, began to form up on the city walls and at the edge of the Protestant Fountain district, ready to launch a decisive assault, backed by the RUC and a mob of Protestant sympathisers, into the Bogside.[91]

In Belfast the situation was even worse. After scuffles between Protestants and Catholics on the borders between their areas, hundreds of rioters broke into the Catholic areas, bent on destruction. In Conway Street they set light to fifty Catholic houses; in Bombay Street they burned more than half the houses; in Percy Street a mob of some two hundred Protestants hurled petrol bombs into the Catholic school and neighbouring houses. While all this was going on, the RUC had been drawn into gun battles with a handful of IRA men determined to protect Catholic areas at all costs. Near Divis Flats, the police opened fire with machine-guns mounted on armoured cars, shooting dead a nine-year-old Catholic schoolboy called Patrick Rooney, who was in bed when the bullets ripped through the wall and into his head. The IRA veterans were not shy of using their weapons either, firing down at the Protestant rioters in Divis Street and wounding at least eight of them. One IRA man, armed with a Thompson submachine-gun, established himself on top of the Catholic school and opened fire over the heads of the Protestant mob, forcing them to fall back.[92]

Belfast that night looked like a vision of the apocalypse: houses and shops ablaze, petrol bombs streaking through the sky, the sound of gunfire, sirens and screaming, everywhere men and women shouting and running. In just two days seven people had been shot dead: two by the IRA, one by Loyalists and four by the RUC or B Specials. Across Northern Ireland as a whole, the violence officially claimed at least 750 other casualties, although the reluctance of Catholics to visit state hospitals means that the true figure was probably much higher. Almost two hundred homes – the majority of them Catholic – had been destroyed, and a hundred more required major repairs. And, according to one estimate, some 1800 families, most of whom were Catholics, had been forced to flee their homes, piling their belongings into cars and trucks for the drive south, where the Irish authorities had established makeshift camps to cope with the influx of refugees.[93]

On the mainland millions of ordinary British citizens watched in horror as the violence unfolded on their television screens. 'Ulster is on the edge of civil war,' warned *The Economist* on 16 August.[94] To many viewers watching the evening news, it was simply inconceivable that riot and destruction on such a scale could take place in a part of the United Kingdom where people listened to the Beatles, tuned in to *Coronation Street* and shopped at Sainsbury's. 'This was not just on our doorstep,' Wilson told the BBC. 'This is in our house.'[95]

Although Jack Lynch had gone out of his way to discourage the deployment of British troops, requests for military intervention had begun to come in earlier that day. John Hume, for instance, told reporters that to stop more lives being lost, 'the Westminster government must intervene at once and take control'.[96] The next day, taking refuge in a bookmaker's office from the fighting in Belfast, Gerry Fitt was surrounded by a small crowd of Catholics 'pulling my coat, screaming and shouting that they were going to be murdered in their beds and begging, begging me to get the army in'. As he later recalled:

> I quietened them all down and said, 'Look, before I lift the telephone and ring Jim Callaghan, what do you want me to say? You're all asking me to get the army in?' And they all said yes. So I picked up the phone and rang him. I said, 'I'm pleading with you, Jim. Send in the army.' And I'll never forget his reply. 'Gerry,' he says, 'I can get the army in but it's going to be a devil of a job to get it out.'[97]

This is a good story; perhaps a little too good to be true. Yet there is no doubt that Callaghan came under enormous pressure on 13 and 14 August to deploy the army. Even Bernadette Devlin, later a ferocious critic of the British military presence in Ireland, telephoned Roy Hattersley and emotionally told him that 'Catholics would be slaughtered' if the government did not send troops at once.[98]

The decisive request came from Stormont, where Chichester-Clarke and his colleagues at last recognised that the situation had deteriorated beyond their control. Late on the afternoon of 14 August they asked the Home Office to deploy troops on the streets of Derry. Callaghan was actually on an aeroplane flying back from Cornwall, where he had been discussing the situation with Wilson, when the call came through on the radio-telephone. 'Permission granted,' he scribbled, and handed the note to the RAF navigator. At five that afternoon, just as the B Specials were preparing to launch their attack into the Bogside, the 1st Battalion of the Prince of Wales's Own Regiment of Yorkshire appeared at the head of the street, marching smartly down to replace the exhausted RUC forces at the edge of the district. Almost as soon as they had arrived the fighting died down: the very sight of heavily armed British personnel patrolling the streets was enough to douse the passions of the last week, and a fragile peace descended.

In Belfast, however, the fighting continued into the morning of 15 August. By dawn the local police commanders knew that they had lost control, and in the fearful climate of the day they convinced themselves that some sort of IRA offensive was imminent. By midday a petition for military intervention had reached Stormont, and at around lunchtime Chichester-Clarke made a formal request to Callaghan, who was by now back in London. Callaghan again gave the go-ahead, and by six o'clock 250 soldiers of the 1st Royal Regiment of Wales were marching towards the Springfield Road police station, where they established their headquarters.[99]

As in Derry, the arrival of the troops brought an uneasy end to the violence, and in London it seemed that Callaghan had saved the day. The Home Secretary was buoyant, enjoying the sensation of wielding power and still revelling in the excitement of the last few days. When Crossman had dinner with him that night, Callaghan was in excellent form, 'big and burly and happy'. 'By God,' he remarked in a sudden burst of enthusiasm, 'it's much more fun being Home Secretary than the Chancellor. This is what I like doing, taking decisions.'[100]

The decision to send British troops into Belfast and Derry was one of the pivotal moments in the history of Northern Ireland. In later years some critics came to see it as an act of imperialist aggression, but this is certainly not how it was viewed at the time. Throughout the crisis, Callaghan had been extremely reluctant to intervene; looking back, he described the decision to deploy troops as 'the last thing we wanted to do . . . We held off until the last possible moment until we were being begged by the Catholics of Northern Ireland to send them in. What an irony of history, that it was they who begged us, and I understand why. Their lives were in danger and we had to respond.'[101]

Like their political masters, the British troops who marched on to the streets of Belfast and Derry had no inkling of what was to come. Northern Ireland was not a particularly glamorous or dangerous posting; it was viewed simply as a brief exercise in peace-keeping before the politicians inevitably sorted everything out. The commanding officer, General Sir Ian Freeland, even remarked that he was greatly looking forward to his new responsibilities because Northern Ireland offered such excellent opportunities for shooting and fishing.[102]

Above all, the soldiers were struck by the warmth of their reception. One young lance-corporal who drove into Derry on 14 August recalled being 'clapped and cheered' as the Bogside residents shouted: 'We're glad to see you. Thanks for coming. Thanks for saving us.'[103] In Belfast, too, soldiers were amazed by the friendliness of the Catholic residents. 'I felt like a knight in shining armour,' one said afterwards. 'Kids were following you everywhere. Tea? There was too much tea – and buns and sandwiches . . . The reception was fantastic.' Even many Republicans welcomed the arrival of the troops, seeing them as their protection against Protestant attack. Brendan Hughes, the future commander of the IRA in Belfast, remembered 'people bringing tea to them at the corner of our street and my father objecting'. But his father, a staunch Republican, was in a small minority: almost all observers commented on the warm relations between the troops and the Catholics in the late summer of 1969.[104]

On 27 August Callaghan arrived in Northern Ireland to see the situation for himself. At this stage the British were still seen as the protectors of the Catholics, and many Unionists viewed their presence with mixed feelings at best. 'This was our own army coming in,' one young man recalled, 'and it felt as though we were being invaded by them.'[105] This explains why Callaghan encountered little warmth from the Unionist community, while in the Bogside hundreds of Catholic residents cheered when he crossed the white lines drawn to indicate 'no go' areas. For many Catholics he cut an impressive figure, clearly restating the British government's commitment to reform and equality.[106] Yet perhaps the most telling exchange came in an uneasy forty-minute summit with Ian Paisley. 'You know, Dr Paisley,' Callaghan said mildly at one point, 'we are all the children of God.' Paisley stared back at him. 'No, we are not, Mr Callaghan,' he said firmly. 'We are the children of wrath.'[107]

In a sense Paisley was right. By the autumn of 1969 the fear and mistrust that had been building up for years were too strong to be swept away by a few thousand British troops drinking tea on the streets of Belfast. In the capital, as in Derry, the violence of August had left enduring scars: ugly makeshift barricades of burned-out cars, discarded furniture and sheets of corrugated iron. 'Free Derry', patrolled by Republican vigilantes, still endured behind a specially erected 'peace line' that cut off the Bogside from the rest of the city.[108] Indeed, throughout the Catholic community, there ran a deep vein of anguish and bitterness after the riots of August. To many working-class Catholics in Belfast and Derry, the lesson was clear: the Unionist state was beyond redemption, and they must arm themselves in preparation for the battle to come.[109]

Yet on the other side, too, there festered a deep resentment. On 10 October the British government announced that the RUC was to be disarmed and the controversial B Specials replaced with a new Ulster Defence Regiment under British army control.[110] That night, fierce rioting erupted on the Shankill Road and the RUC were forced to call in British army units to repel Protestant petrol-bombers. The so-called 'Battle of the Shankill' raged for almost three days, and television viewers were treated to the bewildering spectacle of British forces being attacked by mobs waving Union Jacks and chanting 'Englishmen go home'. In the confusion two local men, George Dickie and Herbert Howe, were killed by army bullets; one RUC constable, Victor Arbuckle, was shot and killed by a UVF sniper. There was a grim irony in the fact that the first policeman to be killed in the Troubles had been murdered not by the IRA but by a Loyalist gunman.[111]

As the end of 1969 approached, the commanders of the British army in Derry launched a 'hearts and minds' campaign, through which they hoped to cement the good relationship between the troops and the Catholic residents. Many young Catholics were beginning to tire of the constant checkpoints and curfews, the competition for girls and seats in the pubs, the restrictions on where and when they could walk down their own streets.[112]

The hearts and minds campaign was therefore designed to revive the honeymoon atmosphere of August. There were two specially organised boys' clubs, attracting hundreds of visitors; there were hiking, canoeing and keep-fit classes for children; there was an indoor football match between soldiers and girls from the Bogside; there was a free New Year's Eve dance. One soldier dressed as Father Christmas and visited the city's department store; others helped with the Meals on Wheels scheme or visited patients in the local hospital.

In January the campaign reached its highest point with the marriage of a British soldier to a local girl, who had been born in a village just across the international border in County Donegal. The wedding took place in her home village; the groom wore his full military uniform, but had converted to Catholicism just before the big day. It seemed the ideal way to celebrate a new era of goodwill and harmony, a romantic union of the youth of Britain and Ireland, burying the hatreds of the past. But it was merely a brief moment of sunshine before the storm finally descended.[113]

35

THE CARNIVAL IS OVER

> Sir, Thinking of strange reversals of fortune: Could it be that Harold Wilson is 2–nil up with 20 minutes to play?
> Yours faithfully,
> Peter Grosvenor
>
> *The Times*, 18 June 1970

On Boxing Day 1969, in the sparkling sunshine of an Australian summer, seventy-nine yachts cruised out of Sydney Harbour for one of the world's classic ocean races. One of the smaller competitors in the annual race to Hobart, Tasmania, some 640 miles away, was *Morning Cloud*, the boat owned and skippered by the leader of the Conservative Party.

For Edward Heath, who was still a novice in the world of ocean racing, the race was an exhilarating challenge but an enormous risk. If he made a mess of it, he would be a laughing stock on every front page back home. But he was determined to compete in the race, if nothing else because he wanted to prove a point to his hosts. A few months before, visiting Sydney to talk to past winners of the race, Heath had been irritated by their belief that 'Britain was pretty well down and out, unable to meet her obligations economically, politically or militarily, and largely populated by long-haired lay-abouts and ne'er-do-wells . . . It seemed to me that if we could take out a boat and a crew who could beat them in their own waters, we might do something to change that depressing view of Britain.'[1]

Four days and six hours after *Morning Cloud* had left Sydney Harbour, Heath had the satisfaction of bringing his boat home as the first British winner of the race since 1945. The British, he commented afterwards, were 'not quite such a decadent people after all'.[2] In Downing Street Harold Wilson was almost speechless with envy. But Richard Crossman, in his diary, took his hat off to the reborn Tory leader:

I suppose there is one other thing that, as a party, we have to admit – the new enthusiasm, courage and drive of Ted Heath, who rather gallantly went out to Australia and won the first prize in the great Sydney–Hobart yacht race. He's back again with his cup, and this week he showed real courage in standing up to an even more provocative racial speech by Enoch Powell. Ted dismissed him as inhuman and made it clear that he'll have nothing to do with Powell. I would say Heath has reached his nadir and is now on the way up.[3]

A few weeks later the newly self-confident Heath assembled his Shadow Cabinet at the Selsdon Park Hotel in Surrey to hammer out their policies for the forthcoming election. In the newspapers the conference was treated as though it marked a major new step in Conservative thinking. According to *The Times*, the party's five principal proposals would be tax cuts, trade union reform, higher pensions, immigration controls and a heavy emphasis on law and order. 'In giving such priority to law enforcement the Tories are catching a popular wind,' a leader column explained. 'People are deeply anxious and angry about the mounting crime rate and the increasing resort to violence, both as a means of political persuasion and for its own sake without apparent purpose at all.'[4] *The Economist*, meanwhile, called its lead story 'The Stainless Steel Tories', splashing a photograph of the Shadow Cabinet on the cover with the caption 'The Hard Men'.[5]

The man who really propelled Selsdon into the national consciousness, however, was Harold Wilson. Keen to stamp out Heath's personal revival before it gathered pace, Wilson told a Labour rally on 7 February that the Tories' reactionary programme was best understood as the product of 'Selsdon Man' – a reference to famous anthropological discoveries like 'Piltdown Man' and meant to imply that Heath would take Britain back to the Stone Age. 'Selsdon Man', Wilson explained, 'is not just a lurch to the right, it is an atavistic desire to reverse the course of 25 years of social revolution. What they are planning is a wanton, calculated and deliberate return to greater inequality [and a] brutal onslaught on the standard of life for the great majority of people.' Heath would replace 'the compassionate society with the ruthless, pushing society . . . His message to the rest is: you're out on your own.'[6]

In later years some historians would see the Selsdon affair as the point when Heath steered his party towards a radical, proto-Thatcherite course, which he later abandoned in government. But this is rather misleading.

Heath had planned the Selsdon weekend as a private 'brainstorming' session, not as a media event, and was surprised to find journalists milling around the hotel.[7] What was more, the idea that the Conservative Party had suddenly lurched to the right was a myth invented by Wilson and the press. The discussions followed a pretty vague and predictable line, and on matters from the economy and housing to education and social security there was nothing to suggest a radical new agenda. As one historian puts it, all the talk of Selsdon Man actually 'gave Heath's vague policy proposals a coherence they had previously lacked'.[8]

But in the long term the furore did neither Wilson nor Heath any good. The former's dazzling rhetoric ultimately backfired: it made Heath look more ruthless and consistent than he really was, and it only bolstered the Conservatives' appeal to voters worried about crime, inflation and industrial unrest.[9] Yet for Heath, too, the Selsdon label turned out to be deeply damaging. As his biographer notes, 'he went along with it, smiling nervously, content after all his trials to ride the wave wherever it took him'. On the one hand, he alarmed the moderate trade union leaders whose support he would need if he ever gained power; on the other, he raised unrealistic expectations among a generation of young, right-wing Conservatives. Despite Wilson's warnings, Heath was still a creature of the post-war consensus, attached to full employment and government activism. But he had allowed himself 'to be thought to have more radical intentions than in fact he had. He ended up between two stools, convincingly neither one thing nor the other: a fierce bark, with no real intention to bite.'[10] In the years to come this would cost him dear.

A few months before the Selsdon furore, on 8 September 1969, Roy Jenkins had been opening an exporters' exhibition at Earl's Court when the latest trade figures arrived from the Treasury. It was the news of which he had long dreamed, but which he had feared would never come. British exports had surged from £602 million in July to £662 million in August, and at long last the pound was back in the black.[11] By December, after years of yawning deficits, the balance of payments was showing a surplus of £440 million. At a stroke, Britain's economic prospects and the government's electoral fortunes seemed to have been transformed.[12]

When Wilson rose to address the Labour Party conference in Brighton on 30 September, he was back to the form of 1963. He was 'floating blissfully on a cloud richly lined with last month's trade figures', commented *The Times*, which thought the speech his best since he had become Prime Minister. His opening jibes at Edward Heath were 'classical music hall at its finest', and for much of the speech he returned to the theme that had served him so well almost exactly six years before. The Labour government, he boasted, had put his rhetoric about 'white heat' into practice. From New Towns to carbon fibres, from nuclear reactors to hovercraft, from jet engines to satellite stations, Britain was leading the world:

> We are creating a Britain of which we can be proud. And the world knows it. The world's tourists are coming here in their millions . . .
>
> Month after month, the Tories have been painting the picture of a Britain down in the dumps . . . But that isn't the Britain that really exists. It isn't the Britain that these hundreds of thousands of tourists have been coming here to look at. They have been coming here because to them Britain – yes, Britain with a Labour Government – is an exciting place.[13]

The audience loved it, giving him the longest standing ovation of his premiership, and the newspapers had rarely been kinder. 'A resounding success,' said the *Telegraph*, while the *Guardian* praised 'Mr Wilson the pragmatist, Mr Wilson the moralist, and Mr Wilson the music-hall comedian'.[14] 'The delegates rose to cheer the Prime Minister,' reported *The Times*, 'and the platform shone and beamed upon him like so many glow-worms round a candle.'[15]

In August 1969, in the aftermath of *In Place of Strife*, Wilson's personal approval rating had reached rock bottom. Now there was a palpable new mood. Within just two months his approval rating had climbed by 17 per cent, putting him well ahead of Edward Heath, and his party was within just 2 per cent points of the Conservatives. It was one of the most rapid and impressive comebacks in modern political history, and it left Wilson's colleagues astonished and delighted. Even though the Tories clung on to their narrow lead through the winter, most observers thought that, given the new sense of optimism, as well as the handsome pay awards being handed out to public sector workers, Labour now stood a great chance of winning the election.[16]

Six years before, when an unpopular Conservative government had been clawing its way back in the opinion polls, Reginald Maudling had unveiled his famous 'dash for growth', engineering a short economic boom that brought the Tories within a whisker of victory. Now many of Wilson's ministers thought that the time had come for Jenkins to 'do a Maudling'.[17]

Between the summer of 1969 and the spring of 1970, the Cabinet discussed the issue again and again. Barbara Castle argued that they should 'show our people some results in their lives of the last three years' tough policy', calling for a package of 'vote winners' and 'morale boosters'.[18] Crossman recommended 'a real sloshing working-class Budget', with tax cuts and spending plans adding up to between £400 million and £600 million. 'People had waited a long time,' he said, 'and they were entitled to it.'[19]

But Roy Jenkins had no desire to engineer a short-term election boom. His Treasury advisers, he recalled, were 'somewhat obsessed by 1964 guilt', and regularly recommended the virtues of continued austerity. In any case, he had 'sweated too hard to turn the balance of payments . . . to be willing to put it at risk by a give-away Budget', which he regarded as 'a vulgar piece of economic management below the level of political sophistication of the British electorate'.[20] 'I would rather lose the Election than jeopardize our economic success,' he piously told the Cabinet in February 1970.[21]

On 14 April Jenkins presented his Budget to the Commons. As *The Times* remarked, it was 'an economist's Budget', and 'one of the more cautious of economists at that'. Instead of 'doing a Maudling', the Chancellor made few changes, except for higher personal allowances to ease the tax burden on the low paid.[22] As even Wilson recognised, after the Conservatives' naked bribery in 1959 and 1964, it was no bad thing for the government to look responsible just before an election.[23] 'We have now invested so much political capital in his strategy, we had better stick with it,' wrote Barbara Castle, who nevertheless noted that her husband, a Labour councillor, thought 'there wasn't a vote in it'.[24] The press reaction, however, was almost wholly favourable, and even the Conservatives seemed nonplussed by Jenkins's rectitude.[25]

Most importantly, the public seemed to like it. Exactly a week later Harold Wilson awoke in a Glasgow hotel, where he was staying before a speech to the Scottish TUC in Oban. As he was leaving the hotel somebody handed him a copy of the *Scottish Daily Express*. 'GOOD MORNING MR WILSON,' read the front-page headline: 'LABOUR TAKES THE LEAD'.[26] Jenkins, too, was away from London, staying in Dublin on the first morning of a much-deserved holiday. The British papers had arrived early, and as he looked at the front pages he discovered 'the most extraordinary and encouraging news'. For the first time in three years the *Daily Express*'s Harris poll showed Labour in the lead, while Gallup found that Jenkins's Budget was the most popular since 1955. Only R. A. Butler had ever enjoyed a higher approval rating as Chancellor.[27] The next morning brought more good news, as Marplan predicted a Labour majority of twenty seats in the next election. 'In the wake of the Chancellor of the Exchequer's neutral Budget,' wrote *The Times*'s political correspondent, 'the long sustained Tory lead over Labour has completely disappeared.'[28]

The crucial question now was timing. Wilson could call an early election, probably in June, or hold on until the autumn, when his standing in the polls might have improved even further but wage inflation might be running out of control. At a Chequers strategy meeting he warned his colleagues that 'one of the problems was the World Cup. If it wasn't for that, he would favour the end of June, and was now trying to find out at what time of day the match was played, because he thought this was a determining factor.' Many of his ministers thought that they should go for an early election. 'First half of June,' said Healey. 'Have our battle plan for June: delay if necessary,' said Benn. 'As soon as we think we can win,' said Callaghan, 'subject to the World Cup.' Wilson summed up with his own thoughts:

> Now autumn 1970 is the obvious date but that meant the Tories would pile up their propaganda and be ready for us and, again, the World Cup was crucial. The longer we go on, he said, the greater is the danger of our balance of payments being undermined. The Tories are well organized and from early June until September . . . there could be strikes, endless hazards, he said, and clearly his mind was moving to June.

'The risk of June is the World Cup,' reiterated Crossman, 'the risk of October is rising prices.'[29] A month later Wilson raised the subject again. 'There was really only one election date,' he explained, 'the third week in June . . . Wage inflation is continuing and in the country there is a wild sense of unreality, far worse than in 1966, when we got in before things busted and wage inflation won us the election. This time people fear that boom will be followed by bust and we may as well get in first.'[30]

The deciding factor was the local elections on 9 May, which were far better for the government than anyone had dared to imagine. Labour took a sensational 443 seats, and Wilson was said to be 'purring like a Persian cat'.[31] Three days later Gallup put the government 7 per cent ahead, and when the Inner Cabinet met on 14 May all five polling organisations gave Labour a comfortable lead. The swing to Labour since 1969 had been the biggest in any twelve-month period since polling began, and Wilson's ministers found it hard to contain their optimism. The Prime Minister announced that his mind was made up: they would go to the country on 18 June, and he expected 'a majority of over twenty'. One by one, his ministers agreed. 'No one demurred,' recorded Castle. 'In fact we began planning as if it were all settled, but Harold wasn't going to let us dodge sharing responsibility.' 'Everyone agreed?' he asked. 'Right: then no-one will be able to claim the virtue of hindsight.'[32]

While Wilson and his ministers were calculating when they would go to the country, the attention of much of the press was focused elsewhere. Since the spring of 1963 the Beatles had been synonymous with British youth culture. Their tours of the United States, Australia and the Far East had been reported at home like triumphant imperial campaigns; their hairstyles, dress and even vocabulary were imitated across the world; and their records had won admiration and envy from Liverpool to Los Angeles.

'Looking back, I think [Harold] was right to give the Beatles their MBEs,' reflected Crossman on the first day of 1970. 'How respectable they look now, how neat their hair-cuts and their dark blue suits, compared to the hippies of five years later.'[33] Indeed, since 1965 the Beatles had become increasingly controversial figures, flirting with harder drugs, talking earnestly about Eastern religions and deliberately alienating many of their older admirers. 'Every week we read something bad about The Beatles in the Press,' the *New Musical Express* commented gloomily in March 1969, listing the rumours of financial mismanagement, internal rows and disputes with girlfriends. 'But far outweighing all these things is the fact that their talent is acclaimed worldwide at a time when Britain is stifling any talent she may have by excessive taxation and minimal encouragement financially for new ideas.'[34]

Yet by this point it was already clear that the Beatles could not keep it up for much longer. Partly this was a question of changing taste: audiences and journalists alike were constantly looking for new faces and innovative sounds. But it was also the simple fact of advancing years. As pop musicians grew older, they became less inclined to spend weeks cloistered in the studio; and as they grew rich, they began to contemplate a life of leisure.[35] After recording *Sgt. Pepper's Lonely Hearts Club Band*, the Beatles found it increasingly difficult to muster much enthusiasm for more studio sessions, and in records like *Magical Mystery Tour* (1967) a palpable carelessness, even laziness, was beginning to creep in.[36]

To make matters worse, the group had also become bogged down in a string of unsuccessful non-musical ventures, often at the behest of their friends and hangers-on. The Apple boutique on Baker Street lasted barely six months, while Apple Corps, the conglomerate they had established to oversee their various business interests, was an utter shambles, notable only for the enormous drink and drugs bills incurred by its staff and its wretched history of mismanagement and theft.[37] In January 1969 Lennon admitted to an interviewer that 'if it carries on like this, all of us will be broke in the next six months'.[38] At last, in desperation, the Beatles hired the Rolling Stones' ruthless accountant Allen Klein, who promptly sacked almost all of Apple's staff, including many of the group's oldest friends, and renegotiated their contract with EMI.[39] At a press conference, Harrison explained that they had 'had enough of being screwed by people, right down the line'. 'People say the Beatles have changed,' Ringo Starr put in plaintively, 'because of the Maharishi and drugs and things. But, basically, we are still the same.'[40]

In spite of Ringo's protestations, though, they *had* changed. Like so many pop musicians before them, the Beatles were losing interest in what had once brought them such success. Lennon, for example, had changed a good deal since the early sixties, his insecurities compounded by an uncontrollable drug intake. Where once he had been caustically self-deprecating, he now came over as pious and pretentious. He dropped LSD as casually as he had once smoked a cigarette, and unsurprisingly was a 'mental wreck', psychologically addicted to his increasingly traumatic acid trips.[41]

During the studio sessions for the Beatles' next album, Lennon insisted on being accompanied by his new lover, the Japanese artist Yoko Ono, and it was clear that he valued her opinion much more than those of his old collaborators. Under Ono's influence, he wrote songs that were harsher in tone and content, deliberately alienating the listener, and he made it clear that he thought little of McCartney's more melodious efforts.[42] Despite some ecstatic early reviews, the resulting double album, *The Beatles* (generally known as the 'White Album'), released in November 1968, was a disorganised, sprawling mess. With typical good sense, George Martin had advised his charges to release just a single album of their best work, but it was entirely characteristic of the Beatles' mood at the end of 1968 that they would not, or could not, listen to him.[43]

Over the next year or so the Beatles disintegrated. Harrison had long since tired of the pressures of fame: always a moody man, he simmered with resentment at his subordinate position in the band. Starr, slightly bewildered by the group's transformation into apostles of peace and love, was still reassuringly down-to-earth, but was more interested in his new career as a comic actor. Above all, Lennon seemed lost in bitter, sanctimonious self-regard, and devoted more and more time to 'bed-ins' and 'bag-ins' for peace with Yoko Ono, whom he married in March 1969.

The only person still committed to the Beatles, therefore, was Paul McCartney. Always more emollient than Lennon, he was confused by his old partner's cold contempt, and lay awake at night wondering how he could revive the spirit of the old days.[44] To the others, however, McCartney often came over as a kind of schoolmaster, forever nagging them to turn up at the studio on time. Starr had already left the band for ten days in August 1968, but by the New Year the tension was almost intolerable.[45] On 10 January, sick of being lectured by McCartney, Harrison announced that he was leaving and walked out of the studio. Five days later he returned, on the condition that they abandon McCartney's cherished plan for a live performance. Although the band managed to complete their 'Get Back' studio sessions, they clearly could not survive for much longer.[46]

In the end, though, it was John Lennon who broke up the Beatles. Completely devoted to Yoko Ono, he admitted that 'as soon as I met her, that was the end of the boys'.[47] She came to almost every studio session, sitting silently behind him in the corner, her ghostly face staring blankly at him as he played. Many of his friends thought that Ono brought out Lennon's very worst qualities, exacerbating his already considerable egotism and self-absorption, but he would not hear a word against her.[48] During the recording sessions for *Abbey Road* in the late summer of 1969, his heroin-fuelled behaviour was more unpredictable than ever. Twice he and McCartney came close to blows; once he even took a swing at the latter's wife Linda. On another occasion an equally violent argument erupted when Ono stole one of Harrison's chocolate digestives.[49]

In September, when the band were signing their latest American contracts, Lennon confided that he had no intention of making any more Beatles records, but planned merely to pocket the money. Over the next few months his old colleagues played for time, hoping that he would change his mind, but there was no going back. 'John's in love with Yoko and he's no longer in love with the three of us,' McCartney later told the *Evening Standard*. 'I started the band. I disbanded it,' Lennon explained. 'It's as simple as that.'[50]

On 10 April 1970, giving an interview to promote his first solo album, McCartney finally admitted that the Beatles were never going to work together again. 'PAUL IS QUITTING THE BEATLES' screamed the front page of the *Daily Mirror*, which was rather ironic since McCartney, more than anyone, had wanted them to carry on.[51] Besieged by reporters, the group's press officer admitted that it was a 'sad day':

> We live day to day here, and we live with events, but we sometimes look back to the days when we were younger. When we were all on the road together . . . While the four of them are alive, then there is still The Beatles . . . Many pop groups have broken up, but The Beatles are not a pop group, they are an abstraction, a repository for many things . . . If The Beatles is alive as an idea, The Beatles is alive, then, all four Beatles will respond to that idea, at some time or other and will become Beatles again.[52]

But a final twist made it very unlikely that the band would ever become Beatles again. On 8 May Apple released the 'Get Back' material as the album *Let It Be*, which turned out to be the ultimate slap in the face for McCartney. In his absence, Lennon had called in the American producer Phil Spector to remix McCartney's ballad 'The Long and Winding Road', adding an orchestra and a female chorus and completely altering the effect. In the circumstances it looked like a last act of spite. McCartney reluctantly decided to free himself from the shackles of Apple, and in February 1971 he filed a writ in the High Court to dissolve the Beatles' partnership.[53]

The Beatles had come an unimaginably long way since the Woolton church fête in July 1957. Nobody could have guessed that the journey would be so long and so successful, or that it would end in such sadness and recrimination. Between 1963 and 1967 the Beatles had completely reshaped the contours of popular music, not only redefining what pop music could be but constantly challenging the tastes of their audience. No other British group had so many chart hits, appealed to audiences for so long, or experimented so much while still producing bestselling songs. No other group drew on so many different sources of inspiration, from classical music and folk songs to nursery rhymes and sea shanties. No other group were so sensitive to their cultural context, popularising everything from mysticism to moustaches, and no group better reflected the fashions of the day. Above all, no other group better captured the sound and the spirit of the sixties.

Back in December 1963 the music critic of *The Times*, William Mann, had been the first classical expert to take the Beatles seriously. Now, writing the day after McCartney's revelation, Mann reflected that their 'image and influence on pop culture in the last ten years' had been simply unsurpassed. What 'lifted them above every pop group in the world', he wrote, 'was the composing partnership of John Lennon and Paul McCartney'.[54] Even four decades later few would disagree. As Ian MacDonald remarks, nobody competing with them in 1963 could possibly have imagined what kind of records they would be making just a few years later. 'Other groups shadowed this revolution,' he writes, 'but no other songwriting/record-making set-up outstripped Lennon–McCartney in terms of consistency of quality or sheer aural fantasy. They were, and remain, the measure of popular music in their time – and, by genealogical descent, of music in our time, too.'[55]

The separation of the Beatles meant that for a generation of pop music fans, the spring of 1970 would always mark the end of an era. By contrast, Harold Wilson was confident that his own 'great adventure', which had begun in the autumn drizzle of 1964, would be continuing unbroken into the seventies. On 18 May he announced that the general election would be held exactly a month later, and he clearly expected to win it. Interviewed on the evening news, puffing his pipe in the Downing Street garden, he looked the very picture of confidence and contentment. Roy Hattersley, who watched the broadcast, remembered that 'at one point – just as he was mentioning the years of peace and prosperity which lay ahead – a bird, which I thought to be a lark, could clearly be heard opening its heart to heaven somewhere over Whitehall'.[56]

On the day that Wilson announced the election date, polls showed Labour 2 per cent clear of their rivals, and almost everybody outside Edward Heath's inner circle expected the gap to widen. The Tories, said *The Economist*, faced 'the apparent certainty of humiliating defeat'.[57] In the *Sunday Times* James Margach wrote that he had 'never seen a party plunged more suddenly and irrationally into such black despair'.[58] Meanwhile, after so many months of hard slog, press criticism and appalling ratings, Labour's exhilaration was palpable. 'The position is extremely good,' recorded Tony Benn, 'far better than we dreamed possible.'[59] Wilson was already mentally sketching out his plans for the next few years. Jenkins would go to the Foreign Office and Healey to the Treasury, while Wilson himself would remain at No. 10 until June 1973, breaking Asquith's twentieth-century record for survival at the top. For a man who had endured so much criticism, it was a happy thought.[60]

It was a lazy, hazy, sunny campaign. The first *Private Eye* cover of the contest featured photographs of the two leaders. 'You've never had it so good', says Wilson, while his bachelor rival adds: 'And I've never had it!'[61] The weather was extraordinarily fine, and for the entire four-week period most of the country had no rain at all, just endless, dreamy blue skies. Few people could remember a summer month like it: in the first week of June, for example, there were three consecutive days of fourteen-hour sunshine. Children splashed around in fountains; teenagers listened to Mungo Jerry's timely hit 'In the Summertime'; couples strolled contentedly down high streets, debating whether to invest in a new colour television for Wimbledon and the World Cup. Many people cheerfully told researchers that they were more interested in the football than in the election.[62]

Not everybody, of course, was obsessed with the forthcoming World Cup in Mexico. Domestic football attendances were in long-term decline, and hooliganism was already becoming a problem, even though it was not until later in the 1970s that it really grabbed the headlines.[63] All the same, millions of people still followed football through the newspapers or on television. The quality of the domestic game seemed to have reached a post-war peak: not only had Celtic and Manchester United won the European Cup, but Leeds, Newcastle, Arsenal and Manchester City had all picked up other European trophies. Star players earned handsome salaries, attracted admiring press profiles and were used to promote a vast range of consumer luxuries. George Best, the impish winger from Northern Ireland who played for Manchester United, was even nicknamed the 'fifth Beatle' for his extravagant skills, shaggy hair and all-round star quality.[64]

In 1970, as in 1966, only one of the home nations would take part in the finals of the World Cup. Since 1966, England had played thirty-six games and lost just four, a record unmatched by any other team in the world.* Most experts agreed that their starting eleven was stronger than ever. The spine of the team – Banks and Moore at the back, Charlton, Peters and Ball in midfield, Hurst up front – lacked nothing in experience or accomplishment, while Alf Ramsey, who had been knighted in 1967, could call on an impressive list of younger players to accompany them, from Terry Cooper and

---

*Scottish fans will immediately recall that among these games was their famous 3–2 victory at Wembley in 1967, a result that, for many Scots, implied that they were the real world champions.

Keith Newton as marauding full-backs to Alan Mullery in central midfield and Francis Lee in attack. As one World Cup preview put it, they had 'team spirit, temperament, discipline and iron will-to-win', all of which meant that they flew to Mexico as one of a handful of favourites to lift the trophy.[65] But as the England squad assembled at Heathrow, Ramsey fought shy of extravagant predictions. 'We'll be a hard team to beat,' he told the press. 'It will take a great team to beat us. If we are not successful, the responsibility is mine.'[66]

Although England's first game would not kick off for almost a month, it was hard to exaggerate the excitement with which millions of fans back home looked forward to their latest international adventure. The ninth World Cup finals marked the triumph of transcontinental satellite broadcasting, beaming live colour pictures from Mexico City and Guadalajara into the living rooms of Huddersfield and Hull. More than 600 million people across the globe were expected to tune in for the tournament, and thanks to the commercial importance of the affluent audiences of Western Europe, the timetable had been arranged to suit their viewing habits. The BBC alone were devoting almost eighty hours to the football: on match days viewers could watch an hour-long breakfast show, a ninety-minute lunchtime edition of *World Cup Grandstand*, a teatime match preview and five hours of match coverage in the evening.[67]

Television coverage, however, was only one example of the World Cup's commercial reach that summer. Almost every major newspaper offered a wallchart or souvenir poster, while fans could collect sticker albums, magazines, hats and even mock-silver coins bearing the heads of the England players, free with four-star petrol from Esso filling stations. The most striking commercial spin-off from the tournament, however, was the England squad's official song, 'Back Home', which spent an impressive sixteen weeks in the singles charts. It was an indication of the enthusiasm with which many people looked forward to the World Cup that within two weeks of its release it had climbed to number three, and on 16 May it reached the top spot, where it remained for another three weeks.[68]

Just as in 1966, the build-up to the tournament was marked by allegations of theft, but this time the England captain was the apparent culprit. 'BOBBY MOORE HELD AS THIEF' read the headline in the London *Evening News* as commuters made their way home on 26 May. According to news reports, Moore had been detained in the Colombian capital Bogotá, where he and his team-mates had just played two warm-up games, on suspicion of stealing a diamond-and-emerald-studded bracelet. For the next four days Harold

Wilson and Edward Heath were compelled to yield the headlines to Moore and the case of the missing bracelet. The England captain steadfastly protested his innocence, and even though he was no saint, very few people thought that he would have done something so reckless. On the other hand, Moore's team-mates later admitted that there had been plenty of pranks during the tour. Just a few days before, in Mexico, a watch had gone missing after a jewellery salesman visited the team hotel, and the England players had all chipped in to pay for it. Moore's authorised biographer suggests, probably rightly, that the captain took the blame for a moment of stupidity by one of the younger players. In any case, Moore did not have too long to worry. On 27 May a formal hearing revealed gaping inconsistencies in various witnesses' stories, and the following morning the judge informed Moore that he was free to rejoin his team-mates.[69]

Back home, Wilson had been following the case with close attention. On the day that the news of Moore's arrest broke, the Prime Minister personally cabled the president of the Football Association to assure him that the government were doing everything they could to secure the captain's release. He even offered to telephone the President of Colombia and ask him to speed up the judicial proceedings so that Moore would be available for England's first match.[70] Wilson's interest in the case was partly inspired, of course, by his own electoral considerations. Since 18 May he had been conducting a notably laid-back campaign, adopting the style of 'a stage personality who could share old jokes with his fans'.[71] Keen to draw a veil over the controversies of the last few years, he seemed bored by ideological arguments and policy proposals. A cartoon in the *Daily Express* showed him posing in the guises of Walpole (with the caption 'Let sleeping dogs lie!'); Baldwin ('Safety first!'); and Macmillan ('You've never had it so good!').[72]

With consummate effrontery, the Labour leader now identified himself with Stanley Baldwin, a Conservative Prime Minister famous for his cheerful, nostalgic inactivity. Like Baldwin, Wilson presented himself as a sort of kindly uncle, puffing gently on his pipe, indifferent to passion and partisanship.[73] He even borrowed the slogan used by Baldwin and the National Government in 1931. 'We're really asking for a doctor's mandate,' he told his Inner Cabinet just before the campaign began. 'We're the best doctors the country's got.'[74] 'He has dispensed with practically all policy and there is no party manifesto because there are no serious commitments at all,' noted Crossman three weeks later. 'In that sense we are fighting a Stanley Baldwin, "Trust my Harold" election, or a "Doctor's Mandate" election.'[75]

On the campaign trail Wilson was in the form of his life. Borrowing the methods of an American presidential candidate, he staged a series of spontaneous walkabouts, happily exchanging pleasantries with excited passers-by. His train or car took him from constituency to constituency, and each time Wilson would cheerfully climb out, his wife at his side, and banter with the waiting crowds. 'You don't want a speech from me,' he would begin, to cheers of contradiction from his audience. 'It's great to have a summer election. I'll allow you ten minutes off your canvassing so you can see me on TV tonight.' And indeed, night after night, the television news showed an affable, suntanned Prime Minister in his shirtsleeves among the voters, brushing aside the hecklers with practised ease.[76]

While Wilson himself worked the crowds, his colleagues contented themselves with mere cameo appearances. The only Labour candidate who threatened to steal his thunder was, not unpredictably, George Brown, whose exile to the backbenches had not moderated his behaviour. Brown knew that, because of boundary changes, he was certain to lose his seat at Belper, so instead he devoted himself to Labour candidates up and down the country, addressing two hundred meetings in just two weeks. With all inhibitions gone, he was free to enjoy himself. In Sheffield he told one disgruntled student, to roars from his audience, 'I don't suppose you ever worked in your life. Come here, give me your name and address and I'll give you a job labouring tomorrow.' In Norfolk, when a pretty girl shouted, 'Never!' during the impassioned climax to his speech, Brown broke off and said with mock solemnity, 'My dear girl, there are some big words which little girls should not use, and "never" is one of them.'[77]

Perhaps Brown's most remarkable meeting came on 3 June, when he was addressing a meeting in Colchester. After a 'stormy half-hour' during which he had been persistently heckled by students from the University of Essex, he found himself surrounded by an angry mob complaining about Vietnam. As he reached the end of the aisle a scuffle broke out. 'I left one long-haired young man who had been shoving me about in no uncertain fashion very surprised indeed,' Brown wrote gleefully, 'when he found himself lying on the floor as a result of the accidental collision of his chin with my fist.' The extraordinary thing about this was not so much that Brown had punched a student to the ground, but the fact that the journalists covering his tour had joined in alongside him. 'All of them,' he reflected, 'without a moment's pause, went into physical combat on our behalf.' It was somehow a gloriously appropriate way for Brown to bow out of electoral politics: as expected, he lost his seat, and never returned to the House of Commons.[78]

For the pressmen travelling with Edward Heath there were no such pugilistic diversions. 'Covering Heath's campaign', one of them remarked, 'is like covering El Salvador in the World Cup.'[79] Since the Salvadorans lost all three of their matches without scoring a goal, this was even worse than it sounded. For all the efforts of his advisers, Heath still sounded more like an ill-tempered accountant than a world statesman, with none of Wilson's wit or warmth. At his first walkabout, in Edinburgh, he 'accosted shoppers in the manner of an orderly officer asking his men if there were any complaints' and then, after half an hour, turned to his aides and said loudly: 'I think that is enough for them, don't you?'[80] The political editor of the *Daily Mail*, meanwhile, remembered seeing Heath disembarking from his private plane on a blazing afternoon 'and being offered a pint of ice-cold lager by an honest British workman who had been disturbed whilst digging a trench at the airport'. Heath's advisers, who thought that this would make a good clip for the news, had put the workman up to it. But Heath simply 'looked into the lenses of the assembled television cameras and said, "No thank you very much, I had a cup of tea on the plane."'[81]

Heath's strategy was to target working-class housewives, who were thought to have suffered most from the price rises of the last few years. He hammered away at the issue of inflation, insisting that it hurt 'those least able to protect themselves' as well as the ordinary housewife. 'There may be an overseas balance of payments surplus,' he declared, 'but there are precious few housewives who have a surplus on their housekeeping accounts . . . Is it any wonder that housewives keep telling me that they are having to cut down on the family's weekly joint, getting cheaper meat, smaller cuts or that they are having to buy standard eggs from the supermarket instead of large ones and to make the children's shoes go on a little longer?'[82] None of this seemed to do any good, however, and on all sides there was a growing sense that the battle was over. Wilson reminded his advisers that 'there was too much complacency about and that we should none of us take anything for granted'.[83] But most senior Tories had privately given up hope, and were already making plans for the leadership campaign to come.[84]

Heath's most controversial rival, meanwhile, was vigorously campaigning in the West Midlands for his own brand of Conservative radicalism, calling for free-market economics and drastic tax cuts. Enoch Powell was rarely out of the headlines, and for several days he was even the lead story. On 3 June Tony Benn accused him of 'filthy obscene racialist propaganda', and warned that 'the flag hoisted at Wolverhampton is beginning to look like the one that fluttered over Dachau and Belsen'.[85] Even people who abhorred Powell's views felt that Benn had gone too far, and Harold Wilson was furious.[86] Both sides came in for severe press criticism. 'Dial Wedgwood Benn for computerised hate', said the *Daily Sketch*, while the *News of the World* asked: 'HAS ENOCH GONE MAD?'[87] And yet, surprisingly and reassuringly, immigration barely featured in the campaign. Even in the West Midlands most Conservative candidates, with a couple of exceptions, downplayed the subject. There was no Smethwick in 1970, and to the relief of almost everybody, the nascent National Front performed abysmally, not even making any impact in Wolverhampton.[88]

Benn's attack on Powell was also notable because it briefly drove the football off the front pages. Although Bobby Moore had been released, the papers had certainly not lost their interest in the World Cup, and the likes of the *Mirror*, the *Sketch* and the *Sun* devoted just as much time to it as they did to the election.[89] With television coverage running into the early mornings, millions of people seemed unable to talk about anything else.[90] After a laboured victory over Romania, England faced the flamboyant Brazilians on 7 June, a much more challenging fixture in the blazing, hundred-degree Mexican heat. In the event England played superbly, relying on their teamwork and their much-heralded defence. In the first half Gordon Banks justified his reputation as the world's best goalkeeper with a breathtaking save from Pelé, and in the second Moore pulled off an equally famous interception, spiriting the ball away from the dangerous Jairzinho as he bore down on the English goal. It was Jairzinho, however, who scored the only goal of an engrossing encounter. Afterwards, some Labour politicians claimed that Ted Heath took pleasure in England's defeat, a suggestion bitterly refuted by the self-proclaimed Arsenal fan.[91]

'WEEP FOR ENGLAND'S GLORY BOYS' read the headline in the next day's *Sun*. But there was no need for tears: England could still qualify for the next round, and their players confidently predicted that they would gain revenge over the Brazilians in the final.[92] Three days later an England side containing a mixture of reserves and old hands beat Czechoslovakia by a single goal. The path to the final was now clear: a meeting with the old enemies, West Germany, in León; then the semi-final in Mexico City, probably against the Italians. The day after the semi-final was Election Day, so that would take people's minds off the football. Then, on the following Sunday, would come the final.

On the day of the England–Czechoslovakia game Tony Benn, no football fan, noted that two polls put Labour 7 per cent clear, which meant 'a substantial Labour victory of 100 seats perhaps'.[93] Two days later Saturday's papers brought even better news: according to NOP, Labour now led by a staggering 12.5 per cent, an astonishing turnaround from just a year before. When Heath heard the news from a journalist he could barely believe it. 'I was watching Mr Heath's eyes,' another reporter wrote. 'They glazed and watered slightly with a brief spasm of misery and despair, then the mask was put back. One saw the ambition of a lifetime temporarily shattered.'[94]

For most observers, the NOP poll effectively ended the election as a contest. On the same day the *Spectator*'s political commentator George Gale paid tribute to Harold Wilson, who had bestridden the election 'like a cosy pet and cuddly toy Goliath':

> His cool, his calm, his confidence is like nothing I have ever seen from a Prime Minister (or Opposition Leader) fighting an election . . . He looks ahead with pleasure, secretly telling himself, I think, that now, now will come the time, now that the economic problem of the balance of payments is manageable, now, now when he has won thrice over, will be the chance to change the place, to make the country different, to be a great Prime Minister.[95]

Crossman thought that it had been 'one of the easiest campaigns I've known', reminding him of 1959, when Macmillan had coasted to re-election on the back of booming consumer confidence and high-street sales. He appreciated the delicious irony that Wilson, who had struck such a chord by campaigning against the Macmillan administration, was now poised for an election hat-trick by borrowing his old foe's style:

> As in 1959, the Opposition are fighting a fine weather mood and a sense of complacency, yet I have to record that we can't say the electorate has never had it so good. Macmillan could point to five years of economic expansion and a tremendous rise in living standards, five years of Tory easy-going. We have given them three years of hell and high taxes. They've seen the failure of devaluation and felt the soaring cost of living. Yet Harold Wilson is running the election in this Macmillan-like way and

he has suddenly found that the mood is on our side and that people are good-humouredly willing to accept another six years of Labour Government.[96]

Crossman dictated that entry on Sunday, 14 June, while resting on his farm from the rigours of the campaign. It was yet another gloriously sunny day, and millions of people were looking forward to the evening's match between England and West Germany. At home it was still warm and light as the two teams walked on to the pitch in the Guanajuato Stadium, León. As in the World Cup Final of four years before, West Germany wore white and England red, but this time the atmosphere was very different. With England widely perceived as arrogant imperialists who played boring football, most of the 32,000 supporters were cheering for the Germans. Like the thirty million people watching on television in Britain, they immediately spotted that something was different as the England team made their entrance. Gordon Banks, the talismanic goalkeeper, was missing, struck down by a bout of diarrhoea. Even so, there was was little for alarm. His replacement, Peter Bonetti of Chelsea, was a perfectly capable shot-stopper who had already won six caps. 'Peter had always been a good goalkeeper,' remarked Alex Stepney, the squad's third goalkeeper. 'There were no worries about that.'[97]

For the first half-hour of the game, it was England, the world champions, who dictated the pace. For perhaps the first time in the tournament, they were playing in a style that justified their status as favourites, knocking the ball about with pace and ambition, the red tide coming ever closer to Sepp Maier's goal. Then, after thirty-one minutes, the pressure told. Surging forward from his right-back position, Keith Newton carried the ball down the touchline and clipped in a cross to the edge of the area, from where Alan Mullery delightedly smacked a half-volley into the German net. It was no more than England deserved, and better was to follow. After fifty minutes Newton broke forward once more on the right and whipped the ball into the area, where Martin Peters bundled it over the line. Two goals to the good, England already had one foot in the semi-finals, and the BBC's commentator David Coleman could barely contain his confidence.[98]

Then, with twenty-two minutes left, West Germany got the break they needed. On the touchline, Alf Ramsey had already decided to rest Bobby Charlton's weary legs and ordered Manchester City's all-action midfielder Colin Bell to prepare for the fray. Seconds later, Franz Beckenbauer ran on to the ball midway inside the English half, sidestepped a challenge and hit a weak, low shot towards Bonetti's goal. The Chelsea goalkeeper dropped to his right to catch the ball, but it bobbled agonisingly under his grasp and trickled into the net. Suddenly, as if from nowhere, West Germany were back in the game, and almost unnoticed, Bell came on for the inspirational Charlton. Moments later the German striker Gerd Müller wriggled free and hammered a shot towards the English goal, only for Bonetti, at point-blank range, to throw himself in the way. 'If Banks got the OBE, Bonetti will be knighted,' a relieved Coleman gasped to the audience. 'What a *great save*.'

As the clock ticked down England's red line began to withdraw ever closer to their own goal. There were just ten minutes left now and, sensing their opponents' exhaustion, West Germany poured forward. A minute later the ball was hoisted into the England area and was only partially cleared to Schnellinger on the German left. In came the cross, arcing over the red shirts of the England defence towards the back post, and there the veteran German forward Uwe Seeler half-jumped, half-fell to meet it, flicking the ball over the motionless Bonetti and into the far corner of the net. 'Seeler, a goal,' yelled a horrified Coleman. 'And England are letting this go. England are now struggling in a match they never looked like losing.'

At ninety minutes the whistle blew. Just as in 1966 the score was 2–2; just as in 1966 West Germany had clawed their way back from the dead. The heat was stifling now, and instead of staying proudly on their feet, the red-shirted England players slumped prostrate on the turf. Their defenders were clearly exhausted, and when the game restarted a few moments later it was the Germans who pressed forward. Yet neither side scored in the first period of extra time, and a coin toss was looming to decide the semi-finalist. Then, three minutes into the second period, Grabowski ran at Cooper again, outpaced his man and sent the ball spinning over into the area – too far, it seemed. As the ball dropped, however, the left-winger Löhr was waiting, and he headed it back towards the penalty spot. And there, darting in between the floundering Labone and Moore, was Müller, spinning in the air, volleying the ball gleefully into the net. Bonetti barely moved.

There were still twelve minutes for England, somehow, to fight their way back. Colin Bell broke into the penalty area and was clearly pulled down by Beckenbauer. The English players screamed for the penalty; the referee remained unmoved. Minute after minute ticked relentlessly by. England pressed forward. Mullery hammered the ball over. Ball shot wide. There was just one minute left, and Newton's desperate long-range shot was tipped over. 'Surely this must be England's last chance,' said Coleman as the corner came in. Mullery drove the ball over the bar. Then the referee blew his whistle, and it was all over. 'Germany have beaten England,' said Coleman, 'and gained revenge for 1966.' In a bizarre echo of those famous scenes from four years earlier, there was another pitch invasion, but this time it was led by a gaggle of fat men in Alpine hats blowing plastic bugles. One of them trailed a banner in the Mexican breeze: 'This is revenge for the Wembley robbery of 1966.'[99]

In the dressing room after the game the England players sat in stunned, tearful silence. Ramsey, to his credit, kept his famous stiff upper lip, shaking each player by the hand and telling them: 'You've done me proud, you've done yourselves proud, you didn't deserve that.' Talking to a BBC reporter a few minutes later, he said blankly: 'They took advantage of our mistakes ... Good luck to the Germans. Good luck to them in the next round.'[100] But there was no disguising his disappointment. Boarding the flight home two days later, he told the *Daily Express* that he knew 'the players I have with me now are good enough to have won the championship. They are still the champions in my eyes. I appreciate that the people at home are sick over elimination. Believe me, nobody – and I mean nobody – feels it as badly as I do.'[101]

The morning after the match most of the papers praised England's courage and deplored their bad luck.[102] Harold Wilson, who had watched the game, telephoned Ramsey in León and offered his commiserations, adding that he should be proud of a 'magnificent performance'.[103] Like most of his colleagues, the Prime Minister had expected England to advance to the semi-final, which would be played the evening before polling day. Now the team was out and millions of fans had ripped up their wallcharts in disappointment. In later years more than one Labour minister would point to the match as a pivotal moment in the election campaign. Roy Jenkins, who heard the news after a rally in Edinburgh, remembered that he 'had heard Wilson propound a theory of almost mystical symbiosis between the fortunes of the Labour Party and the England football eleven'. That theory was about to be put to the test.[104]

Monday, 15 June began with the release of new government statistics showing that strike levels were increasing, but the major development of the day came at noon, when the Board of Trade released the latest trade figures. After all Jenkins's hard work to build up a surplus in the balance of payments, the visible trade balance for May showed a deficit of £31 million.

Jenkins had known for a week or so that the figures would look bad, but this was clearly a gift to the Tories.[105]

Heath immediately pounced, reiterating his belief that this was 'the housewife's election' and insisting that the figures illustrated Labour's mishandling of the economy.[106] Jenkins countered that the figures were an aberration, distorted by the government's purchase of two Boeing jumbo jets worth £18.5 million, as well as a dock strike in Southampton and a month of 'erratically low' exports. The Conservatives, said the Chancellor, were 'desperately clutching at any straw they can find, and a pretty thin straw this one is . . . If the Tories, in their hopeless and divided plight, believe that they can escape from defeat on the wings of a couple of jumbo jets they will believe anything – just as they will now say anything to hide their growing sense of hopelessness.'[107]

But Jenkins was rather more worried about the impact of the trade figures than he was letting on, as were some of his colleagues. '[Heath] made a really big issue of them, saying there was a big economic crisis and that we had misled the public,' noted Benn. 'This was the first real breakthrough by Heath. He has concentrated in effect simply on two things – prices and the economic situation . . . These twin themes are the ones that are beginning to get through.' But although Benn had caught the jitters, Wilson remained calm, telling him that evening that 'there was nothing to worry about'. 'He sounded as if he was just composing himself for another Election triumph,' Benn recorded.[108]

By the following morning it seemed that the combination of Wilson's insouciance and Jenkins's scorn had done the trick. Although the press treated the trade figures as the major story of the final days, most commentators agreed that Labour were still set for victory. The *Sunday Times* predicted that Wilson was 'headed straight back towards 10 Downing Street, probably with an increased majority'; the *Financial Times* forecast a Labour 'majority of 40 or 50 seats'; and the *Evening Standard* announced that 'Labour will certainly win'.[109] Polls showed that more than two out of three voters, regardless of their own preferences, expected Wilson to win.[110] On Wednesday, 17 June, the last day of campaigning, *The Times* announced that 'a Labour victory is a near-certainty and a landslide victory a considerable possibility'.[111]

The two parties had made their final televised appeals on Monday and Tuesday evening. First, on 15 June, came the Conservatives, with a professional broadcast designed to promote their leader as a man of courage. Hand-held cameras followed the shirtsleeved Heath through the summer crowds, interspersed with images from his childhood, while a narrator explained how the Tory leader had defied his critics. The picture cut to *Morning Cloud*, flashing through the water to win the Sydney–Hobart race. 'I see no point in competing', said Heath, 'unless you are determined to win.' Then the film switched back to the campaign trail, showing Heath surrounded by cheering supporters, while the narrator described him as 'not an easy man to know, but when they know him, people feel he is a man worth knowing. A man to trust.' Finally, the picture cut to Heath himself, behind his desk, speaking earnestly into the camera:

> I well remember being driven to the boat for the start of the Sydney–Hobart race. There was a bright blue sky with the sun beating down over the glorious harbour. And I said to the young Australian driver: 'What confidence there is here, what's it all about?' And without batting an eyelid, he said: 'Well, you see, everyone here knows that tomorrow will be better than today.'
>
> Nobody in this country would say that. Not these days. And yet, why not? . . . We may be a small island. We're not a small people . . . Do you think we should settle for second rate? I think we should enter a race to win . . . Do you want a better tomorrow? That's what I want and that's what I will work for with all my strength and with all my heart. I give you my word and I will keep my word.[112]

Wilson followed suit the following evening with a broadcast that cut in similar fashion between images of cheering crowds and footage of the Prime Minister behind a desk. But whereas Heath had been driven and determined, Wilson strove to come over as friendly and reassuring. 'It has been like this all over the country,' he said after discussing his large audiences, 'because people everywhere are feeling a new confidence.' He insisted that 'no Prime Minister this century has fought an election against such a background of economic strength as we have got today', and hammered away at the Conservatives' warnings of economic crisis. His broadcast concluded on an upbeat note: 'The socialism I believe in means above all using all our resources for making Britain a better place to live in . . . a great country, tolerant and compassionate . . . admired and respected throughout the world because it combines stability with change.' Yet even Wilson's own advisers thought that he had been much less effective than his rival, sounding complacent where Heath had been stirring. BBC audience research and

Conservative private polls found that voters had been much more impressed by Heath. Even so, the consensus was that the broadcasts would have little impact on the result.[113]

In the last days, the coverage of Heath's brave but seemingly futile campaign became almost elegiac in tone. 'Witnessing Heath's electoral ordeal has been painful,' wrote George Gale, who noted his fellow journalists' 'sorrowful admiration' for the Conservative leader's 'wounded dignity'.[114] *The Times* thought that Heath had shown 'strength of character in what seems certain, or almost certain, to be defeat, and for that he is more respected and with more real affection than at any previous time in his leadership'.[115] 'As a sheer slugging political infighter, Mr Heath at last came good in the last week of the campaign,' agreed *The Economist*. But his new vigour in press conferences and town centres had come far too late: 'He looked so good at all this that some strong men among his colleagues nearly wept that he had not started in this mood three weeks before.'[116]

Indeed, senior Tories were already preparing for life under a new leader. On Sunday evening, while England's footballers were crashing out of the World Cup, a small group of elder statesmen had met for dinner and agreed that Heath must resign the morning after the election. To prevent Enoch Powell from taking over, they decided that Sir Alec Douglas-Home should make a brief comeback as a unifying figure before handing over to a younger man. Willie Whitelaw, Heath's Chief Whip, agreed to drive to Home's ancestral seat at the Hirsel on the Friday afternoon to confirm the arrangements. Heath knew none of this, of course: touchingly, he presumed that Whitelaw would be spending Friday with him in Downing Street to 'help choose the government when we have won'.[117]

As Election Day dawned, it was clear that Thursday, 18 June was going to be another glorious summer's day. Roy Jenkins reflected that 'it was as perfect a day as could be imagined for a summer election [with] not a cloud in the Birmingham sky from early morning to sunset'.[118] Voters streamed to their local polling stations in the sunshine, many of them teenagers, who, for the first time, could vote as soon as they had turned eighteen. Harold Wilson spent the day in his Huyton constituency, touring the housing estates, shaking hands with voters, and shooing away the crowds of children who gathered in the windless heat. At lunchtime he repaired to a local pub for steak and chips before resuming his tour; then, as in 1964 and 1966, he retreated to the Adelphi Hotel in Liverpool.[119]

Hundreds of miles to the south in Bexley, Edward Heath was also touring the polling stations in his shirtsleeves. At lunchtime he had an unexpected visit from Peter Carrington, the Conservative leader in the Lords, who had been delegated to hand over the metaphorical revolver. After congratulating him on the campaign, Carrington gently told Heath that if they lost, he would be expected to step down. Heath took the news with typically gruff equanimity. He already knew that if the polls were right, his leadership was over.[120]

For Wilson's exhausted ministers, Election Day felt like the end of a long battle against chance and circumstance. In Birmingham Roy Jenkins, always nervous before the count, idled away the last hours with his wife and children discussing what it would be like to be Foreign Secretary, and wondered whether they would spend their weekends at the Foreign Secretary's official country residence at Dorneywood.[121] In Liverpool Marcia Williams was organising a party for the journalists who had followed Wilson's national tour. The mood, she recalled, was 'rushed but good-humoured', and 'everyone seemed to be optimistic'. The *Observer*'s political correspondent, Nora Beloff, told Williams that she had already written her piece explaining Labour's victory. A couple of hours later she went up to join Wilson, his wife and closest advisers in his suite, where they confidently prepared to watch the results.[122]

While Wilson was settling down in front of the television, his old friend Richard Crossman was in the Police Hall, Coventry, preparing for his count. All day Crossman had been worried that Labour voters were simply not coming out, and now he felt that 'something was going badly wrong'. The Labour agent came over and said quietly that the first boxes were giving them only a slight lead, '3000 votes to 2000, 4000 to 2000, not at all the proportion we expected'.[123]

Then, just after 11.15 p.m., came the first result, from Guildford: a swing of more than 5 per cent to the Conservatives. Suddenly, almost without anyone having time to stop and think, the entire picture had changed. In Liverpool Wilson caught Marcia Williams's eye and gave a slight grimace. They both knew that unless Guildford turned out to be an aberration, they were in trouble. The next two results soon followed, and showed a similar swing. Williams telephoned Downing Street and told the secretaries to start packing. There was no need: they had heard the results and knew what they meant.[124] In Bristol Tony Benn drew the same conclusions. 'It was quite clear that we were out,' he noted. 'In a fraction of a second, one went from a pretty confident belief in victory to absolute certainty of defeat.'[125]

It was the most unexpected General Election result in modern political history. With 46 per cent of the vote, the Conservatives won 330 seats, while Labour took 43 per cent and 288 seats; the Liberals accounted for just 6 seats, and nationalist parties took another 6. Clearly the polls had been mistaken, but this should not have been a great surprise: in 1966, too, the opinion polls had exaggerated Labour's lead by between 1 and 4 per cent. This time, the likeliest explanation for the error is that the polls simply failed to pick up a very late swing towards the Conservatives. According to the exit polls, more than one in ten voters had made up their minds how to vote during the campaign itself, and, unnoticed by the press commentators and the daily polls, most of them had gone for Heath.[126]

After the event, Labour politicians came up with plenty of excuses for their defeat. Many felt that if the election had been held earlier, before England's World Cup exit and the disappointing trade figures, they would have won comfortably. Jenkins, for example, wondered how different British political history would have been if the election had been held just seven days earlier.[127] Others, like Crossman, blamed Wilson for running a 'comfy, complacent' campaign.[128] But Wilson's defeat was no fluke. Ever since the devaluation of the pound, Labour had been haemorrhaging support among working-class and older women, the famous housewives of Tory rhetoric, especially in the South-East and the West Midlands.[129] Wilson's tentative recovery since the autumn of 1969 had been far too flimsy to withstand the rigours of a long election campaign or the shock of the most recent trade figures. After all, given the government's economic record since 1966, especially when compared with Wilson's soaring promises, it was hard for voters to have much confidence in its future performance.[130]

In later years historians would bitterly dispute the legacy of Wilson's government between 1964 and 1970. To many, in the words of Kenneth Morgan, it seems 'a paradigm of economic failure, social indirection and political paralysis . . . [and] a major reference point in charting the inadequacies of British democratic socialism as a programme for power.'[131] David Marquand, too, suggests that 'few modern British governments have disappointed their supporters more thoroughly', and describes the Wilson years as 'an era of lost innocence, of hopes betrayed'.[132]

Yet in many ways Wilson and his colleagues have been maligned. For all the fuss at the time about their economic record, in historical terms it was not all that bad. Unemployment never rose above 2.7 per cent; inflation for much of the sixties remained below 4 per cent; and annual economic growth never dipped below 1.8 per cent. By the standards of, say, the 1970s and the 1980s, these are pretty impressive figures.[133] Living standards generally improved, while spending on health, education, research, transport, social security and housing went up by an annual average of more than 6 per cent between 1964 and 1970.[134] In its commitment to social services and public welfare, the Wilson government put together a record unmatched by any subsequent administration, and the mid-sixties are justifiably seen as the 'golden age' of the welfare state.[135] Liberals argued that the government's legal reforms, too, had made Britain a more civilised society. When Wilson left office in 1970, homosexuality was no longer a criminal offence, unhappy marriages could easily be dissolved, women could legally end unwanted pregnancies, overt racial discrimination was punishable by law, and the state no longer executed criminals. In foreign affairs, meanwhile, Wilson and his ministers managed to extricate themselves from the Far East without great bloodshed or disaster, and performed miracles to avoid being dragged into the Vietnam War, an achievement which was all the more impressive given Britain's economic dependence on the United States.

Yet, whatever historians might say in retrospect, at the time, and for years afterwards, Wilson's administration was seen as a failure. Both on the left and the right critics listed a string of broken pledges, mockingly quoting the extravagant, exaggerated promises of 1964.[136] Most Labour activists felt embarrassed by their government's record, conscious that since 1966 it had drifted without direction from one crisis to the next. Clive Ponting, for instance, writes of the government's 'hypocrisy' in foreign affairs and its 'lost opportunities and broken promises' at home. Like many other commentators, he has little time for the decision to defend the pound in 1964 and 1966, the insistence upon the 'special relationship' with the United States, the shambolic economic management, the undisciplined factionalism, and, above all, Wilson's endless short-term twisting. Not for nothing is Ponting's book entitled *Breach of Promise*.[137]

To many observers at the time, the government was simply a mess, and most people knew whom to blame. In many ways the election of 1970 was an 'unpopularity contest'; but for most of the late sixties, nobody in Britain had been less popular than Harold Wilson.[138] He was undoubtedly a highly intelligent, industrious and cool-headed politician, and, unlike some of his colleagues, he was also a strikingly kind and decent man. But Edmund Dell is perhaps only a little harsh when he paraphrases Tacitus's remark about the Emperor Galba: 'Everyone would have considered Wilson capable of occupying the office of Prime Minister, if only he had never held it.'[139]

Wilson returned to Downing Street shortly after dawn on the morning of Friday, 19 June, a year and a day after the deal with the TUC that had destroyed *In Place of Strife*. 'It was a beautiful day again, with a lovely sunrise,' remembered Marcia Williams. 'Outside No. 10 the street was deserted, except for two solitary workmen clearing away the traces of what had clearly been a crowd the night before.'[140] Once inside, Harold and Mary started packing their personal belongings. Their two sons, Robin and Giles, had dropped in to help, and as they loaded their things into trunks and tea-chests, they listened again and again to the Seekers' record 'The Carnival Is Over'.[141]

A few hours later Roy Jenkins arrived, having endured a humiliating railway journey down from Birmingham, surrounded by quietly delighted businessmen. He noted that Wilson looked 'appallingly battered, but he was wholly calm and unrecriminating'. 'Well, there it is,' Wilson said. Jenkins thought him 'rather impressive, and the occasion moving'.[142] Later that afternoon they held a brief meeting with a handful of Cabinet ministers who had returned to London and braved the mocking crowds outside. None of them had much to say. At the end Benn produced his beloved movie camera and asked if he could shoot some pictures of Wilson sitting in the Cabinet Room for the last time. It was, thought Jenkins, 'a climax of embarrassed bathos'.[143]

After a last, brief trip to Buckingham Palace, Wilson left Downing Street by the garden gate at about five that evening, his arm around his wife, while their sons loaded their suitcases, books and blankets into two blue Minis.[144] For the moment, they had nowhere to live, but Heath had generously offered them the use of Chequers for the weekend while they found their feet.[145] In Downing Street Marcia Williams supervised the last of the office packing, and looked on reluctantly as the new incumbent arrived:

> We heard the cheers in Downing Street and saw the Garden Girls, the Civil Service typists, rushing from the basement in high excitement to see him in the front hall, and we heard the staff clapping as he entered. As I finally went through the garden entrance, I could see him in the Cabinet Room. With him, giving him his first briefing as Prime Minister, were the

same civil servants who had been serving Harold a few hours before. The King was dead, long live the King.[146]

For Teddy Heath, the earnest schoolboy prodigy from Broadstairs, it was the sweetest of moments. Alone among his colleagues, he had believed that he could win, and at last he had been vindicated. His aide Douglas Hurd, who had accompanied Heath in the car back to London early that morning, remembered that his leader never seemed surprised by his staggering good news. And as the press recognised, it had been an unusually personal victory, won, said one reporter, by a 'leader who was doubted and who conquered against the most daunting psychological odds'.[147] 'Well done, Ted Heath,' gushed the *Sun*, which had actually endorsed Wilson. 'The British love to see an outsider come surging up to pass the favourite.'[148] 'Let there be no mistake,' said the *Express*, 'the Tory victory was won by the Prime Minister's own guts and leadership.'[149] 'Only one man won this election,' concluded *The Economist*, 'and that man is Mr Heath.'[150]

At three in the morning Heath made it back to his flat in Albany, where he received a congratulatory telephone call from Willie Whitelaw. It was the only time that this most self-controlled of men allowed his feelings to break through: as Whitelaw offered earnest congratulations, Heath was so choked with emotion that he could barely speak.[151] He slept until noon, when his housekeeper awoke him with a cup of tea and the news that a man called Nixon had been ringing all morning to offer his congratulations. At seven that evening came the moment that, rather like Wilson before him, Heath had been dreaming of since he was a boy: the drive to the Palace, the audience with the Queen, the invitation to form a government. Then came the journey to Downing Street, the cheers and chants of the crowds, and his first words as Prime Minister, spoken before the world's press from the steps of No. 10. 'This Government', he promised, 'will be at the service of all the people the whole time. Our purpose is not to divide but to unite and, where there are differences, to bring reconciliation.'[152]

That evening, Heath and Whitelaw got down to business. Over hastily arranged coffee and sandwiches, they drew up their new team, and during the next twenty-four hours a picture gradually emerged of the government that would take Britain into the brighter, better world of the 1970s. Most reports focused on the big names: the new Chancellor, Iain Macleod; the new Home Secretary, Reginald Maudling; and especially the Foreign Secretary, Sir Alec Douglas-Home, making a comeback of his own after the travails of 1964.

But one newspaper preferred to concentrate on another, rather more obscure name. For the *Finchley Press*, the only real story was the appointment of the area's local MP to the post of Education Secretary, her first taste of Cabinet office. The paper's interviewer even wondered whether she would like to be Britain's first female Prime Minister. Despite the social and cultural changes of the sixties, she thought it was too soon. 'No,' Margaret Thatcher replied, 'there will never be a woman Prime Minister in my lifetime – the male population is too prejudiced.'[153]

EPILOGUE

At twenty past eight on the evening of Wednesday, 31 July 1968, in a small town on the South Coast, a lavish and convivial dinner was winding towards its conclusion. To cheerful applause from his guests, the chairman introduced the guest of honour, 'a man of many parts – banker, soldier, magistrate, alderman and secretary of the Rotary Club – a good fellow all round'. Clambering to his feet in front of a large Union Jack, the rotund little figure of George Mainwaring spoke for the first time on British television:

> Mr Chairman, Mr Town Clerk, ladies and gentlemen. When I was first invited to be guest of honour tonight at the launching of Walmington-on-Sea's 'I'm Backing Britain' campaign, I accepted without hesitation. After all, *I* have *always* backed Britain. I got into the habit of it in 1940, but *then* we *all* backed Britain. It was the darkest hour in our history: the odds were absurdly against us, but young and old, we stood there, defiant, determined to survive, to recover, and finally to *win*! The news was desperate, but our spirits were always high.

With that, the picture dissolved, Bud Flanagan's famous theme song began, and seven million viewers settled down to the very first episode of BBC1's latest situation comedy, *Dad's Army*. Half an hour later, with Britain at the mercy of the Nazis, Captain Mainwaring had assembled his men – Sergeant Wilson, Corporal Jones, and Privates Frazer, Godfrey, Walker and Pike – and had announced his intention to turn them into 'ruthless killers'. The episode ended with another oration by the redoubtable little man:

> Remember, men, we have one invaluable weapon on our side: we have an unbreakable spirit to win. A bulldog tenacity that will help us to hang on

while there's breath left in our bodies. You don't get *that* with Gestapos and jackboots! You get that by being British! So come on, Adolf: we're ready for you![1]

Of all the cultural success stories of the late sixties, *Dad's Army* was not only one of the most unexpected, but one of the most enduring. Few people had guessed that this mild-mannered comedy about the wartime Home Guard, written by David Croft and Jimmy Perry, would be such an enormous hit. During rehearsals, the actor John Le Mesurier, who played the languid Sergeant Wilson, told his friend Barry Took that his new series was 'a disaster'. 'I really can't tell you,' he went on, 'oh, it's absolutely *appalling*, it can't *possibly* work, no, no, my dear boy, it's an absolute *disaster!*'[2]

He could hardly have been more wrong. An audience figure of more than seven million represented an encouraging start, but there was even better news from the critics, who almost unanimously enjoyed the programme. In the *Sunday Telegraph* Philip Purser thought that the characterisations had been 'maturing over a dozen years and in some of the greatest cellars in comedy', while in the *Observer* Tom Stoppard wrote that *Dad's Army* was 'liable to bring a smile and a tear to every lover of England and Ealing'.[3] The *Daily Express* even predicted that it would become 'a classic comedy series', appealing to young and old alike. 'Give me a week or two and I'll tell you whether this is really comedy's finest half-hour,' wrote the newspaper's television critic, Ron Boyle. 'All I say now is that the possibilities are tremendous.'[4]

Although there were many enduring and memorable television series in the late sixties, from *Till Death Us Do Part* to *Monty Python's Flying Circus*, few matched the enormous and steadily increasing popularity of *Dad's Army*. At the end of 1968 the show had more than eight million viewers; by the end of 1972, its regular audience numbered more than sixteen million. *Dad's Army* won British Academy awards, Writers' Guild of Great Britain awards, a special Variety Club award and even the Ivor Novello award for its theme song. Its cultural sweep included a feature film, a West End musical, a comic strip, activity books, annuals, board games and bubble bath, and its stars appeared in everything from variety shows to advertisements.[5] When the series finally came to an end in 1977 the *Guardian* mourned its passing with the comment that it had 'given us finer farces, straighter faces, richer characterisation and a good deal more social observation than most of the more pretentious dramas, and always kept us guessing which would turn up next'.[6]

The continuing appeal of *Dad's Army*, hardly the most fashionable of television programmes, is hard to exaggerate. Of the iconic series that began in the 1960s, only *Coronation Street* and *Doctor Who* matched its enduring popularity with ordinary viewers. Even thirty years after the series began, repeats of the most popular episodes attracted more than ten million viewers; the famous 'Don't tell him, Pike!' scene was often voted the funniest in television history; and several polls found that the series remained the nation's favourite comedy.[7] In 2000 the British Film Institute placed the show thirteenth in its list of the best television programmes of the twentieth century, observing that 'purely in terms of its sustained popularity the show is without equal'.[8]

Dad's Army might seem an incongruous monument to the culture of the 1960s, but just as much as any of the Beatles' records or the trendy films of Swinging London, it captured the spirit of the age. Rather than appealing to a small group of well-educated, wealthy young people, it reached out to millions of ordinary families from the South Coast to the Highlands: young and old, rich and poor, men and women. It formed part of a new common culture diffused across the United Kingdom through the mass media. It benefited from the new technology of the day, switching from black and white to colour at the end of 1969, but its gaze was fixed firmly on the past. It celebrated a lost era of austerity and collective endeavour, but its appeal depended on the domestication of leisure and the new individualism of the affluent society.

The *Dad's Army* phenomenon would never have been possible had it not been for the changes of the fifties and sixties. Like so many other national institutions, the BBC encouraged a spirit of adventure and enquiry, so that a comedy series poking fun at the record of the Home Guard, which might have seemed too close to the bone fifteen years before, now seemed perfectly acceptable. The technological advances of the time meant that cheap televisions were delivered to high streets the length and breadth of the country, while, thanks to virtually full employment and rising wages, millions of middle-class and working-class Britons were able to invest in their own private entertainment and instruction. In just over a decade the popularity of the television and other household appliances had utterly transformed everyday life. Men now stayed at home to watch programmes like *Dad's Army* when they would once have gone out to the pub with their workmates; women, liberated from hours of housework by the invention of cheap labour-saving devices, now felt free to put their feet up in front of the screen.

Yet the success of *Dad's Army* also hints at the serious limitations of what some historians still insist on calling the 'cultural revolution' of the sixties. Indeed, its enormous popularity is hard to understand without reassessing the clichés associated with the era. The delight with which audiences greeted the squabbles between the petit-bourgeois Captain Mainwaring and the patrician Sergeant Wilson suggests that, for all the waffle in the mid-sixties about the 'classless society' and the 'new class' of 'swinging Englishmen', class distinctions still meant a great deal to most people. Similarly, for all the talk about the new morality and the sexual revolution, it was remarkable that the most popular comedy series on British television contained very few references to sex and no major female characters, and projected a distinctly old-fashioned moral code, leavened by the good-humoured tolerance associated with the national character.

Although the sixties is often seen as a period of utopian optimism, the culture of the time, from the albums of the Beatles and the Kinks to the poems of Philip Larkin and the novels of John Fowles, was suffused with a powerful sense of nostalgia. Like the Ealing comedies of the fifties, *Dad's Army* looked back to a kinder, simpler age of neighbourhood corner shops and village banter, a settled, orderly society untroubled by the corrosive effects of modernity.[9] It was no accident that the first episode opened with George Mainwaring's address to the local 'I'm Backing Britain' campaign in 1968. For millions of viewers, whatever their politics, the story of Britain since the mid-sixties had been one of moral decay and economic decline. According to Mainwaring himself, the country needed not the spirit of 1968 but the spirit of 1940, what one historian calls 'shared effort and sacrifice, common purpose and good neighbourliness and justified struggle against a wicked enemy'.[10] And even amid the hurly-burly of the late sixties and seventies, millions of people shared the old-fashioned vision of England lovingly described by Sergeant Wilson:

> Every day, I walk up the high street to work, and, as I pass those little shops, a nice, friendly, *warm* atmosphere seems to come wafting out – I mean, even from that *dreadful* fellow Hodges's greengrocer's – and then I stroll on a little bit further and I pass Frazer's funeral parlour, and then before I cross the road to come to the bank there's Jones's butcher's shop – white tiles all gleaming and shining, and old Jones standing there with his straw hat on and wearing his striped apron, and giving me a cheery wave – and do you know, sir, it sort of, I don't know, it sort of sets me up for the day. I feel it's my time, you see.[11]

Class consciousness, cultural conservatism, a deep sense of nostalgia: these are not values that we readily associate with the sixties. It would be absurd to deny that things changed during the era: it was only thanks to the unprecedented consumer affluence and technical innovation of the day, after all, that people could even watch programmes like *Dad's Army*. But most of the changes associated with the period, from working-class affluence and the changing role of women to mass immigration and permissive reform, actually had their roots in earlier periods of British history.

It is true that by 1964 the pace of change had greatly increased, thanks largely to the economic boom of the day. But although popular accounts of the era concentrate on the small group of affluent, self-confident young people who welcomed change, millions of others clung firmly to what they knew and loved. Perhaps an editorial in *New Society*, referring to the magazine's famous survey of social attitudes at the end of the decade, best captures the ambiguity of public opinion:

> Shouldn't one talk of the Cautious Sixties, rather than the Swinging Sixties? Hardly any of the obsessions of the metropolitan mass media rate favourably; some of them don't even rate strongly. You emerge with the very strong impression that if the 1960s meant anything special to most people in Britain it was because they got, during them, a better chance to lead a not-too-poor, not-too-insecure life . . . Despite the way the 1960s have often been portrayed, this has not become a wildly changed country; people are not that keen on being disturbed.[12]

This sounds very like the British people described by George Orwell back in 1941: 'a nation of flower-lovers, but also a nation of stamp-collectors, pigeon-fanciers, amateur carpenters, coupon-snippers, darts-players, crossword-puzzle fans'. Yet Orwell had also observed that 'in Slough, Dagenham, Barnet, Letchworth, Hayes . . . the old pattern is changing into something new'. In these 'vast new wildernesses of glass and brick' he discerned a new world of council houses, concrete roads and swimming pools, 'a rather restless, cultureless life, centring around tinned food, *Picture Post*, the radio and the internal combustion engine'. He even foresaw the coming of Harold Wilson's scientific revolution, a world of technicians, airmen, mechanics and chemists, 'a civilization in which children grow up with an intimate knowledge of magnetoes and in complete ignorance of the Bible'.

In this world of technological progress and cultural revolution the nostalgic vision of *Dad's Army* was supposed to have been swept away. But the sixties are best understood not as a dramatic turning point, interrupting the course of the nation's history and sending it off in a radically new direction, but rather as a stage in a long evolution stretching back into the forgotten past. The national characteristics that Orwell recorded in 1941 – the 'mild knobby faces . . . bad teeth and gentle manners', the 'horror of abstract thought', the 'love of flowers', the 'addiction to hobbies and spare-time occupations' – still distinguished British life in 1970. And despite the innovations of draught lager and foreign holidays, Britain was still marked by its 'abhorrence of foreign habits', since most people still laughed at foreigners, refused to learn their languages, and looked askance at schemes promoting European unity. 'Their old-fashioned outlook, their graded snobberies, their mixture of bawdiness and hypocrisy, their extreme gentleness, their deeply moral attitude to life': all of these things endured.

For, as Orwell understood, the continuity of national history was much stronger and more resilient than the transient whims of fashion. For all the Minis and mini-skirts, the sex, drugs and rock and roll, Britain in 1970 was still fundamentally the same country it had been twenty, thirty or a hundred years before. National character, Orwell wrote, is 'continuous, it stretches into the future and the past, there is something in it that persists, as in a living creature. What can the England of 1940 have in common with the England of 1840? But then, what have you in common with the child of five whose photograph your mother keeps in the mantelpiece? Nothing, except that you happen to be the same person.'

> The Stock Exchange will be pulled down, the horse plough will give way to the tractor, the country houses will be turned into children's holiday camps, the Eton and Harrow match will be forgotten, but England will still be England, an everlasting animal stretching into the future and the past, and, like all living things, having the power to change out of all recognition and yet remain the same.[13]

THE END

NOTES

Documentary references beginning PREM, T and so on are taken from papers at the National Archives in Kew.

References to 'Benn diary' are taken from Tony Benn, *Out of the Wilderness: Diaries, 1963–67* (London, 1987) and *Office Without Power: Diaries 1968–72* (London, 1988).

References to 'Castle diary' are from Barbara Castle, *The Castle Diaries, 1964–70* (London, 1984).

References to 'Crossman diary' are from Richard Crossman, *The Diaries of a Cabinet Minister: Volume 1: Minister of Housing, 1964–66* (London, 1975), *Volume 2: Lord President of the Council and Leader of the House of Commons, 1966–68* (London, 1976), and *Volume 3: Secretary of State for Social Services, 1968–70* (London, 1977).

References to 'King diary' are from Cecil King, *The Cecil King Diary, 1965–1970* (London, 1972).

PREFACE

1 *Daily Express*, 25 January 1965; *The Times*, 25 January 1965.
2 Richard Crossman diary, 30 January 1965.
3 Jonathan Dimbleby, *Richard Dimbleby: A Biography* (London, 1975), p. 384.
4 *The Times*, 1 February 1965.
5 Quoted in Richard Weight, *Patriots: National Identity in Britain 1940–2000* (London, 2002), p. 455.
6 Bernard Levin, *The Pendulum Years: Britain and the Sixties* (revised edition: London, 1977), p. 403.
7 Weight, *Patriots*, pp. 455–456.
8 *The Times*, 1 February 1965.
9 *Daily Express*, 1 February 1965.
10 Dimbleby, *Richard Dimbleby*, p. 386.
11 Levin, *The Pendulum Years*, p. 403.
12 Crossman diary, 30 January 1965.
13 *Observer*, 31 January 1965.
14 George Orwell, *The Road to Wigan Pier* (Harmondsworth, 1962), p. 140.

Part One

1 LET'S GO WITH LABOUR

1. Ben Pimlott, *Harold Wilson* (London, 1992), p. 302.
2. *The Times*, 2 October 1963; Pimlott, *Harold Wilson*, pp. 302–304; Philip Ziegler, *Wilson: The Authorised Life* (London, 1993), pp. 143–144.
3. *The Times*, 2 October 1963.
4. *Tribune*, 4 October 1963, quoted in Steven Fielding, '"White Heat" and White Collars: The Evolution of "Wilsonism"', in Richard Coopey, Steven Fielding and Nick Tiratsoo, eds, *The Wilson Governments 1964–1970* (London, 1993), p. 29.
5. *Guardian*, 2 October 1963.
6. *Daily Herald*, 2 October 1963.
7. Quoted in Stuart Laing, *Representations of Working-Class Life 1957–1964* (Basingstoke, 1986), p. 64.
8. See Pimlott, *Harold Wilson*, pp. 266–269.
9. *Daily Express*, 8 November 1962.
10. Anthony King and Robert J. Wybrow, eds, *British Political Opinion 1937–2000: The Gallup Polls* (London, 2001), p. 7.
11. *Daily Telegraph*, 19 May 1963.
12. *Observer*, 17 February 1963.
13. King and Wybrow, eds, *British Political Opinion*, pp. 205, 211.
14. King and Wybrow, eds, *British Political Opinion*, p. 27.
15. Anthony Howard and Richard West, *The Making of the Prime Minister* (London, 1965), p. 130; Fielding, '"White Heat" and White Collars', pp. 36–37; Austin Mitchell and David Wienir, eds, *Last Time: Labour's Lessons from the Sixties* (London, 1997), pp. 38–40.
16. Howard and West, *The Making of the Prime Minister*, pp. 130–131; Fielding, '"White Heat" and White Collars', p. 37; Steven Fielding, *The Labour Governments 1964–1970: Volume 1: Labour and Cultural Change* (Manchester, 2003), pp. 75–76.
17. Marcia Williams interviewed in Mitchell and Wienir, eds, *Last Time*, pp. 40–41. See also Lawrence Black, '"The Bitterest Enemies of Communism": Labour Revisionists, Atlanticism and the Cold War', *Contemporary British History* 15: 3, Autumn 2001, pp. 38–40.
18. In March 1961, for example, the *Observer* published two long articles celebrating the supposed 'dynamism' and 'change' of Kennedy's 'New Frontier': see *Observer*, 19 and 26 March 1961; Paul Foot, *The Politics of Harold Wilson* (Harmondsworth, 1968), pp. 13–14; Black, '"The Bitterest Enemies of Communism"', p. 37.
19. Pimlott, *Harold Wilson*, pp. 283–284.
20. Christopher Booker, *The Neophiliacs: The Revolution in English Life in the Fifties and Sixties* (revised edition: London, 1992), p. 252.

21 Pimlott, *Harold Wilson*, p. 270; Ziegler, *Wilson*, p. 155.
22 Benn diary, 28 September 1964; and see also the entries for 27 March 1963, 21 May 1963 and 23 January 1964.
23 Benn diary, 3 December 1963.
24 Benn diary, 23 January 1964.
25 Benn diary, 17 December 1964.
26 Speech at Birmingham, 19 January 1964, reprinted in Harold Wilson, *The New Britain: Labour's Plan* (Harmondsworth, 1964), p. 10; see also the verbatim extracts in Howard and West, *The Making of the Prime Minister*, pp. 115–116; and Ziegler, *Wilson*, p. 144.
27 Crossman diary, 22 June 1963.
28 Quoted in Ziegler, *Wilson*, p. 145.
29 John Harris quoted in Ziegler, *Wilson*, p. 150.
30 Benn diary, 14 and 18 October 1963.
31 *Observer*, 16 September 1962.
32 Noël Annan, *Our Age: The Generation That Made Post-War Britain* (London, 1990), p. 557; Humphrey Carpenter, *That Was Satire That Was: The Satire Boom of the 1960s* (London, 2000), pp. 275–276.
33 Lord Home, *The Way the Wind Blows: An Autobiography* (London, 1976), p. 203; Michael Cockerell, *Live from Number 10: The Inside Story of Prime Ministers and Television* (London, 1988), pp. 104–105.
34 Ziegler, *Wilson*, p. 153.
35 Quoted in Kevin Jefferys, *Retreat from New Jerusalem: British Politics, 1951–64* (London, 1997), p. 195.
36 PREM 11/5006, 'My Philosophy', 30 December 1963. For two different interpretations of this memorandum, see Ian Gilmour and Mark Garnett, *Whatever Happened to the Tories: The Conservatives since 1945* (London, 1997), pp. 210–211; Peter Hennessy, *The Prime Minister: The Office and Its Holders since 1945* (London, 2000), pp. 284–285.
37 Gilmour and Garnett, *Whatever Happened to the Tories*, p. 210.
38 See Sir Alec Douglas-Home, *Peaceful Change* (London, 1964), p. 25.
39 Speech at Swansea, 20 January 1964, reprinted in Douglas-Home, *Peaceful Change*, pp. 59–66.
40 Howard and West, *The Making of the Prime Minister*, pp. 116–117.
41 Speech at Newcastle, 2 March 1964, reprinted in Douglas-Home, *Peaceful Change*, p. 69.
42 Douglas-Home, *Peaceful Change*, p. 98.
43 Speech at Newcastle, 2 March 1964, reprinted in Douglas-Home, *Peaceful Change*, p. 68; Howard and West, *The Making of the Prime Minister*, p. 120.
44 John Campbell, *Edward Heath: A Biography* (London, 1993), pp. 150–151; Richard Cockett, *Thinking the Unthinkable: Think-Tanks and the Economic Counter-Revolution, 1931–1983* (London, 1995), pp. 145–146; D. R. Thorpe, *Alec Douglas-Home* (London, 1996), pp. 355–356.
45 Thorpe, *Alec Douglas-Home*, pp. 356–357; Edward Heath, *The Course of My Life: My Autobiography* (London, 1998), p. 263.
46 Campbell, *Edward Heath*, pp. 152–153; Gilmour and Garnett, *Whatever Happened to the Tories*, pp. 207–208.

47 Home later told interviewers that the RPM controversy had cost the Conservatives several seats in the general election: see Hennessy, *The Prime Minister*, pp. 280–281. But there is little doubt that the measure itself was a success: the small shopkeepers did not immediately go to the wall, commerce continued to thrive, and the affair suggested that the Conservatives did take modernisation seriously after all. See David Butler and Anthony King, *The British General Election of 1964* (London, 1965), p. 23; Campbell, *Edward Heath*, pp. 155–157; Thorpe, *Alec Douglas-Home*, pp. 357–358.
48 Thorpe, *Alec Douglas-Home*, p. 320.
49 Howard and West, *The Making of the Prime Minister*, p. 115.
50 Jefferys, *Retreat from New Jerusalem*, pp. 185–189; King and Wybrow, eds, *British Political Opinion*, p. 187.
51 *The Times*, 19 February 1964; Howard and West, *The Making of the Prime Minister*, pp. 123–124; Thorpe, *Alec Douglas-Home*, p. 353.
52 Thorpe, *Alec Douglas-Home*, pp. 353–355.
53 Howard and West, *The Making of the Prime Minister*, pp. 135–136; Jefferys, *Retreat from New Jerusalem*, p. 187.
54 Benn diary, 6 July 1964.
55 See Howard and West, *The Making of the Prime Minister*, p. 128.
56 King and Wybrow, eds, *British Political Opinion*, pp. 167–168.
57 King and Wybrow, eds, *British Political Opinion*, p. 8.
58 Cockerell, *Live from Number 10*, p. 103.
59 Howard and West, *The Making of the Prime Minister*, pp. 142–143; Clive Ponting, *Breach of Promise: Labour in Power 1964–1970* (London, 1990), p. 15.
60 Quoted in Cockerell, *Live from Number 10*, p. 100.
61 *Let's Go with Labour for the New Britain: The Labour Party's Manifesto for the 1964 General Election* (London, 1964).
62 *Let's Go with Labour for the New Britain*, *passim*; Howard and West, *The Making of the Prime Minister*, pp. 138–139.
63 *Prosperity with a Purpose: The 1964 Conservative Party General Election Manifesto* (London, 1964).
64 Howard and West, *The Making of the Prime Minister*, p. 136.
65 Butler and King, *The British General Election of 1964*, p. 113; Thorpe, *Alec Douglas-Home*, p. 366.
66 Grace Wyndham Goldie quoted in Cockerell, *Live from Number 10*, p. 105.
67 Sir Robin Day, *Grand Inquisitor: Memoirs* (London, 1989), p. 221.
68 Dick Taverne interviewed in Mitchell and Wienir, eds, *Last Time*, p. 66.
69 Quoted in John Lawton, *1963: Five Hundred Days* (London, 1992), p. 307.
70 Howard and West, *The Making of the Prime Minister*, p. 220.
71 Anthony Howard, *Crossman: The Pursuit of Power* (London, 1990), p. 264.
72 *The Times*, 9 October 1964; Anthony Howard interviewed in Mitchell and Wienir, eds, *Last Time*, pp. 35–36.
73 Pimlott, *Harold Wilson*, pp. 314–315.
74 Crossman diary, 7 November 1964.
75 Howard and West, *The Making of the Prime Minister*, pp. 172–174.

76 Howard and West, *The Making of the Prime Minister*, p. 204.
77 Howard and West, *The Making of the Prime Minister*, p. 195.
78 Roy Hattersley, *Who Goes Home? Scenes from a Political Life* (London, 1995), pp. 40–41.
79 On the Bull Ring debacle, see Howard and West, *The Making of the Prime Minister*, pp. 194–195; Thorpe, *Alec Douglas-Home*, p. 368.
80 Home, *The Way the Wind Blows*, pp. 214–215; see also Cockerell, *Live from Number 10*, p. 107; Gilmour and Garnett, *Whatever Happened to the Tories*, p. 213; Hennessy, *The Prime Minister*, p. 276.
81 *Daily Express*, 9 October 1964.
82 Howard and West, *The Making of the Prime Minister*, p. 226; Pimlott, *Harold Wilson*, p. 317.
83 Cockerell, *Live from Number 10*, p. 107; Asa Briggs, *The History of Broadcasting in the United Kingdom: Volume V: Competition* (Oxford, 1995), pp. 447–448.
84 Thorpe, *Alec Douglas-Home*, pp. 372–373.
85 Pimlott, *Harold Wilson*, p. 318; see also Howard and West, *The Making of the Prime Minister*, pp. 226–234.
86 Howard and West, *The Making of the Prime Minister*, p. 225.
87 Howard and West, *The Making of the Prime Minister*, pp. 236–237; Pimlott, *Harold Wilson*, p. 318.
88 Howard and West, *The Making of the Prime Minister*, p. 225.
89 Butler and King, *The British General Election of 1964*, pp. 357–358; Jefferys, *Retreat from New Jerusalem*, pp. 191–195; Fielding, *Labour and Cultural Change*, p. 79.
90 As argued in Alan Sked and Chris Cook, *Post-War Britain: A Political History* (second edition: London, 1984), pp. 194–195.
91 Sked and Cook, *Post-War Britain*, p. 195; Peter Clarke, *Hope and Glory: Britain 1900–1990* (London, 1996), pp. 295–296.
92 See, for instance, John Barnes, 'What if the Conservatives Had Won in 1964?', in Duncan Brack and Iain Dale, eds, *Prime Minister Portillo, and Other Things That Never Happened* (London, 2003), pp. 121–138.
93 Thorpe, *Alec Douglas-Home*, p. 299.
94 Alistair Horne, *Macmillan 1957–1986: Volume II of the Official Biography* (London, 1989), p. 582.
95 Thorpe, *Alec Douglas-Home*, p. 373.
96 Sir Derek Mitchell quoted in Pimlott, *Harold Wilson*, p. 324.
97 Reginald Maudling, *Memoirs* (London, 1978), p. 132.
98 Howard and West, *The Making of the Prime Minister*, p. 239.
99 Michael Pinto-Duschinsky, 'Bread and Circuses? The Conservatives in Office, 1951–1964', in Vernon Bogdanor and Robert Skidelsky, eds, *The Age of Affluence* (London, 1970), p. 55; Peter Oppenheimer, 'Muddling Through: The Economy, 1951–1964', in Bogdanor and Skidelsky, eds, *The Age of Affluence*, pp. 137–138.
100 For hostile verdicts on the Conservative legacy, see Pinto-Duschinsky, 'Bread and Circuses?', pp. 57–58; Sked and Cook, *Post-War Britain*, pp. 197–198; Jefferys, *Retreat from New Jerusalem*, pp. 6–7, 197–200.
101 Benn diary, 16 October 1964.
102 Quotations from *Let's Go with Labour for the New Britain*.

103 Howard and West, *The Making of the Prime Minister*, p. 237.

104 Ziegler, *Wilson*, p. 163.

2 THE TEN FACES OF HAROLD

1 Ben Pimlott, *The Queen: A Biography of Elizabeth II* (London, 1997), p. 342; see also Howard and West, *The Making of the Prime Minister*, pp. 237–239.

2 Harold Wilson, *The Labour Government 1964–1970: A Personal Record* (London, 1971), p. 22.

3 Pimlott, *The Queen*, pp. 342–343.

4 Quoted in Pimlott, *Harold Wilson*, p. 524.

5 Pimlott, *Harold Wilson*, p. 42; Ziegler, *Wilson*, p. 18.

6 Ziegler, *Wilson*, p. 18; Pimlott, *Harold Wilson*, pp. 49–50.

7 Paul Foot, *Harold Wilson*, p. 31.

8 Pimlott, *Harold Wilson*, p. 122.

9 Pimlott, *Harold Wilson*, p. 11; on his family background in general, see Pimlott, *Harold Wilson*, pp. 3–20; Ziegler, *Wilson*, pp. 1–13.

10 Ziegler, *Wilson*, p. 5; Pimlott, *Harold Wilson*, pp. 15, 23.

11 Pimlott, *Harold Wilson*, p. 16.

12 Pimlott, *Harold Wilson*, pp. 11–13; Ziegler, *Wilson*, pp. 5–6.

13 Ziegler, *Wilson*, p. 6.

14 Crossman diary, 16 April 1968.

15 Ziegler, *Wilson*, p. 14.

16 Pimlott, *Harold Wilson*, p. 51; Ziegler, *Wilson*, p. 20.

17 *The Listener*, 29 October 1964.

18 Pimlott, *Harold Wilson*, p. 50.

19 Ziegler, *Wilson*, p. 22.

20 Kenneth O. Morgan, *Labour People: Leaders and Lieutenants, Hardie to Kinnock* (revised edition: London, 1992), p. 247.

21 Pimlott, *Harold Wilson*, p. 53; Ziegler, *Wilson*, p. 16.

22 Pimlott, *Harold Wilson*, pp. 53–54.

23 Pimlott, *Harold Wilson*, pp. 29–33.

24 Benn diary, 2 November 1965.

25 Pimlott, *Harold Wilson*, p. 78. On Wilson's work for Beveridge and during the war, see Pimlott, *Harold Wilson*, pp. 60–91.

26 Pimlott, *Harold Wilson*, pp. 96–97, 105.

27 On the devaluation disagreement, see Pimlott, *Harold Wilson*, pp. 139–143.

28 Gaitskell diary, 1 February 1950, quoted in Pimlott, *Harold Wilson*, p. 152.

29 See Ziegler, *Wilson*, pp. 60–61.

31 Joe Haines, *Glimmers of Twilight: Harold Wilson in Decline* (London, 2003), xiii–xiv.

31 Marcia Falkender, *Downing Street in Perspective* (London, 1983), p. 194.

32 Ziegler, *Wilson*, xi.

33 John Cole, *As It Seemed to Me: Political Memoirs* (London, 1995), p. 47.

34 See David Walker, 'The First Wilson Governments, 1964–1970', in Peter Hennessy and Anthony Seldon, eds, *Ruling Performance: British Governments from Attlee to Thatcher* (Oxford, 1987), pp. 188–189; Ziegler, *Wilson*, p. 42.

35 See Lord Wigg, *George Wigg* (London, 1972), p. 313.
36 Pimlott, *Harold Wilson*, p. 165; Ziegler, *Wilson*, pp. 87–88.
37 Morgan, *Labour People*, p. 251.
38 Crossman diary, 18 December 1958.
39 Quoted in Christopher Booker, *The Seventies: Portrait of a Decade* (Harmondsworth, 1980), p. 114. Booker himself had written the text for the cartoon.
40 *Daily Mail*, 19 June 1964.
41 Quotations from Ziegler, *Wilson*, p. 43.
42 Henry Kissinger, *The White House Years* (London, 1979), p. 92.
43 Harold Macmillan, *Riding the Storm, 1956–59* (London, 1971), p. 48; Ziegler, *Wilson*, pp. 110–111.
44 Quoted in Ziegler, *Wilson*, p. 45.
45 Castle diary, 21 September 1967.
46 Crossman diary, 22 September 1965.
47 See George Brown, *In My Way: The Political Memoirs of Lord George-Brown* (Harmondsworth, 1972), pp. 17–40; Peter Paterson, *Tired and Emotional: The Life of Lord George-Brown* (London, 1993), pp. 1–56.
48 Crossman diary, 17 March 1968.
49 Paterson, *Tired and Emotional*, p. 1.
50 Ben Pimlott, ed., *The Political Diary of Hugh Dalton 1918–40, 1945–60* (London, 1986), pp. 700, 686–687.
51 Crossman diary, 17 March 1968.
52 Paterson, *Tired and Emotional*, p. 115.
53 Paterson, *Tired and Emotional*, p. 40.
54 Dickson Mabon interviewed in Mitchell and Wienir, eds, *Last Time*, pp. 25–26.
55 Crossman diary, 30 May 1960.
56 Quoted in Pimlott, *Harold Wilson*, p. 177.
57 Pimlott, *Harold Wilson*, p. 213.
58 Letter quoted in Ziegler, *Wilson*, p. 128.
59 Benn diary, 18 January 1963.
60 Susan Crosland, *Tony Crosland* (London, 1983), pp. 115–116; Giles Radice, *Friends and Rivals: Crosland, Jenkins and Healey* (London, 2002), pp. 124–125.
61 Kenneth O. Morgan, *Callaghan: A Life* (Oxford, 1997), pp. 181–183.
62 Howard and West, *The Making of the Prime Minister*, p. 28.
63 Pimlott, *Harold Wilson*, p. 259.
64 See Ziegler, *Wilson*, pp. 134–135.
65 Howard and West, *The Making of the Prime Minister*, pp. 31–37; Paterson, *Tired and Emotional*, pp. 129–131.
66 Quoted in Andrew Roth, *Sir Harold Wilson: The Yorkshire Walter Mitty* (London, 1977), p. 271.
67 Crossman diary, 15 February 1963.
68 Cole, *As It Seemed to Me*, p. 24.
69 Rodgers interviewed in Mitchell and Wienir, eds, *Last Time*, p. 23.
70 *Financial Times*, 15 February 1963.
71 Ziegler, *Wilson*, p. 137.

72 Harold Macmillan, *At the End of the Day, 1959–1961* (London, 1973), p. 396.
73 Quoted in Ziegler, *Wilson*, p. 141.
74 See Pimlott, *Harold Wilson*, pp. 263–264; Ziegler, *Wilson*, pp. 140–141.
75 Crossman diary, 12 March 1963.
76 See Ponting, *Breach of Promise*, pp. 16–17; Pimlott, *Harold Wilson*, pp. 326–328; Ziegler, *Wilson*, pp. 170–179.
77 Richard Holt, *Second Amongst Equals: Chancellors of the Exchequer since the Second World War* (London, 2001), p. 107.
78 James Callaghan, *Time and Chance* (London, 1987), pp. 24–25; Morgan, *Callaghan*, pp. 14–15.
79 Callaghan, *Time and Chance*, p. 29.
80 See Morgan, *Callaghan*, pp. 3–5, 55–56.
81 Morgan, *Callaghan*, pp. 10, 17–18, 29.
82 Morgan, *Callaghan*, pp. 65–66.
83 Morgan, *Callaghan*, pp. 108, 164.
84 See Edmund Dell, *The Chancellors: A History of the Chancellors of the Exchequer, 1945–90* (London, 1996), p. 305.
85 Morgan, *Callaghan*, pp. 174–176.
86 Dell, *The Chancellors*, p. 305.
87 Morgan, *Labour People*, p. 266.
88 Morgan, *Callaghan*, pp. 114–116, 134; Pimlott, *Harold Wilson*, pp. 332–333.
89 See Pimlott, *Harold Wilson*, p. 329.
90 Paterson, *Tired and Emotional*, pp. 147–150, quoting the recollections of Milton Shulman.
91 Paterson, *Tired and Emotional*, pp. 150–151.
92 Crossman diary, 2 December 1963; Benn diary, 22 and 23 November 1963.
93 Paterson, *Tired and Emotional*, pp. 152–154.
94 *People*, 1 December 1963.
95 Letters quoted in Paterson, *Tired and Emotional*, pp. 158–159. There are plenty more examples.
96 Benn diary, 8 September 1964.
97 Ziegler, *Wilson*, p. 178.
98 Pimlott, *Harold Wilson*, p. 337.
99 See Howard, *Crossman*, passim.
100 David Marquand, *The Progressive Dilemma: From Lloyd George to Blair* (second edition: London, 1999), p. 139.
101 Crossman diary, 8 February 1963.
102 Cole, *As It Seemed to Me*, p. 64.
103 Pimlott, *Harold Wilson*, p. 335.
104 Crossman diary, entries from 11 to 18 May 1965; and see also Howard, *Crossman*, pp. 270–271.
105 Roy Jenkins, *Portraits and Miniatures: Selected Writings* (London, 1993), p. 254.
106 See David Childs, *Britain since 1945: A Political History* (London, 1979), p. 162; Denis Healey, *The Time of My Life* (London, 1989), p. 345.
107 Richard Ingrams, ed., *The Life and Times of Private Eye* (London, 1971), p. 21.

108 Edmund Dell, *A Strange Eventful History: Democratic Socialism in Britain* (London, 2000), pp. 311, 324; see also Dell interviewed in Mitchell and Wienir, eds, *Last Time*, pp. 30, 46, 85.
109 Ponting, *Breach of Promise*, p. 16.
110 Healey, *The Time of My Life*, p. 252.
111 Tony Benn interviewed in Mitchell and Wienir, eds, *Last Time*, p. 79.
112 Healey, *The Time of My Life*, p. 252.
113 Marcia Williams interviewed in Mitchell and Wienir, eds, *Last Time*, pp. 112–113.
114 Pimlott, *Harold Wilson*, p. 338.
115 Stephen Dorril and Robin Ramsay, *Smear! Wilson and the Secret State* (London, 1992), pp. 72–77; Ziegler, *Wilson*, p. 183; Pimlott, *Harold Wilson*, p. 340.
116 See Dorril and Ramsay, *Smear!*, pp. 66–71; Pimlott, *Harold Wilson*, p. 340; Ziegler, *Wilson*, p. 178.
117 See Dorril and Ramsay, *Smear!*, pp. 73–74; Pimlott, *Harold Wilson*, p. 339; Ziegler, *Wilson*, pp. 93–94; on Balogh and planning, see Jim Tomlinson, *The Labour Governments 1964–70: Volume 3: Economic Policy* (Manchester, 2004), p. 73.
118 Pimlott, *Harold Wilson*, pp. 199–200; Ziegler, *Wilson*, pp. 118–119.
119 Pimlott, *Harold Wilson*, p. 204.
120 Joe Haines, *The Politics of Power: The Inside Story of Life at No. 10* (London, 1977), p. 158.
121 Ziegler, *Wilson*, pp. 120, 182.
122 Ponting, *Breach of Promise*, p. 18.
123 Pimlott, *Harold Wilson*, p. 206.
124 Dorril and Ramsay, *Smear!*, pp. 44–48; Pimlott, *Harold Wilson*, pp. 209–210.
125 Ziegler, *Wilson*, p. 119.
126 See Marcia Williams, *Inside Number 10* (London, 1975), p. 28.
127 Pimlott, *Harold Wilson*, pp. 342–344.
128 See Pimlott, *Harold Wilson*, pp. 344–345.
129 Benn diary, 2 November 1965.
130 Pimlott, *Harold Wilson*, p. 346.
131 Pimlott, *Harold Wilson*, p. 325.
132 Crossman diary, 17 March 1966.
133 See the collected entries in Richard Ingrams and John Wells, *Mrs Wilson's Diaries* (London, 1966) and *Mrs Wilson's Second Diary* (London, 1966).
134 Ingrams and Wells, *Mrs Wilson's Second Diary*, p. 3.
135 Crossman diary, 3 January 1965; on Wilson's cronies, see Pimlott, *Harold Wilson*, pp. 669–670, 707–709.
136 Ziegler, *Wilson*, p. 166.
137 Crossman diary, 26 May 1965.
138 Crossman diary, 17 March 1965.
139 Castle diary, 3 May 1966.
140 Castle diary, 19 April 1966.
141 Crossman diary, 22 September 1965.
142 Callaghan, *Time and Chance*, pp. 184–185.
143 Williams, *Inside Number 10*, pp. 107–108.
144 Crossman diary, 9 November 1964.

145 Pimlott, *Harold Wilson*, pp. 521–522.
146 Williams, *Inside Number 10*, p. 64.
147 Ziegler, *Wilson*, pp. 166–167.
148 Crossman diary, 4 April 1970.
149 Pimlott, *Harold Wilson*, pp. 33–35.
150 Ziegler, *Wilson*, pp. 196–197.
151 Castle diary, 21 June 1965.
152 Quoted in Morgan, *Callaghan*, p. 229.
153 Quoted in Cockerell, *Live from Number 10*, p. 100.
154 See Andrew Alexander and Alan Watkins, *The Making of the Prime Minister 1970* (London, 1970), pp. 121, 144; Ponting, *Breach of Promise*, p. 19.
155 See Dickson Mabon interviewed in Mitchell and Wienir, eds, *Last Time*, pp. 176–177.
156 Denis Healey interviewed in Mitchell and Wienir, eds, *Last Time*, p. 122.
157 Pimlott, *Harold Wilson*, p. 355.
158 Pimlott, *Harold Wilson*, p. 356.
159 James Margach, *The Anatomy of Power* (London, 1979), p. 5.

3 THE SPACE AGE

1 Jennifer Harris, Sarah Hyde and Greg Smith, *1966 and All That* (London, 1986), p. 153; *Guardian*, 10 November 2001.
2 Benn diary, 15 July and 8 October 1965; 'Pillars of Society 6: Wedgie the Whizz', in Ingrams, ed., *The Life and Times of Private Eye*, p. 119.
3 Benn diary, 17 May 1966.
4 Benn diary, 15 July 1965.
5 On the revolving restaurant, see <http://www.lightstraw.co.uk/ate/main/postofficetower/t60.html>, a website entirely devoted to the history of the tower.
6 'Benn's HoverBritain', in Ingrams, ed., *The Life and Times of Private Eye*, p. 151.
7 See David J. Howe and Stephen James Walker, *Doctor Who: The Television Companion* (London, 1998), pp. 93–96.
8 Sean Topham, *Where's My Space Age? The Rise and Fall of Futuristic Design* (Munich, 2003), pp. 8–12.
9 Morris, 'Technology 1930–55', in Gary Day, ed., *Literature and Culture in Modern Britain: Volume 2: 1930–1955* (London, 1997), p. 238; Arthur Marwick, *British Society since 1945* (Harmondsworth, 1982), pp. 24–25.
10 See Marwick, *British Society since 1945*, pp. 95–98; Annan, *Our Age* pp. 379–382; Kenneth O. Morgan, *The People's Peace: British History since 1945* (second edition: Oxford, 1999), pp. 108–109.
11 Morris, 'Technology 1930–55', pp. 244–245; T. I. Williams, *A Short History of Twentieth Century Technology* (Oxford, 1982), pp. 356–357.
12 Anthony Sampson, *Anatomy of Britain* (London, 1962), pp. 462–463.
13 See Georgina Ferry, *A Computer Called LEO: Lyons Teashops and the World's First Office Computer* (London, 2003).
14 Booker, *The Seventies*, p. 7; and see Arthur Marwick, *The Sixties* (Oxford, 1998), pp. 249–250.

15 *Daily Mirror*, 27 June 1955; and see also the editions for the remainder of the week.
16 Sampson, *Anatomy of Britain*, p. 463.
17 James Chapman, *Saints and Avengers: British Adventure Series of the 1960s* (London, 2002), pp. 83–84.
18 See Howe and Walker, *Doctor Who*, pp. 93–96, 141–162.
19 Howe and Walker, *Doctor Who*, p. 105; Gary Gillatt, *Doctor Who from A to Z* (London, 1998), p. 108.
20 Quoted in Nicholas Timmins, *The Five Giants: A Biography of the Welfare State* (London, 1995), p. 156.
21 Weight, *Patriots*, p. 236.
22 Marwick, *The Sixties*, pp. 248–249.
23 Morgan, *The People's Peace*, p. 233. Hailsham bitterly refutes the suggestion that he was an unsuitable figure: see Lord Hailsham, *A Sparrow's Flight: The Memoirs of Lord Hailsham of St Marylebone* (London, 1990), p. 325.
24 Weight, *Patriots*, p. 236.
25 Michael Shanks, *The Stagnant Society* (Harmondsworth, 1961); Sampson, *Anatomy of Britain*; Anthony Hartley, *A State of England* (London, 1963); Nicholas Davenport, *The Split Society* (London, 1964). On the 'modernisation' debate in the early sixties, see Pimlott, *Harold Wilson*, pp. 299–301; Jefferys, *Retreat from New Jerusalem*, pp. 122–128; Jim Tomlinson, *The Politics of Decline: Understanding Post-War Britain* (Harlow, 2000), pp. 21–23; Rodney Lowe and Neil Rollings, 'Modernising Britain, 1957–64: A Classic Case of Centralisation and Fragmentation?', in R. A. W. Rhodes, ed., *Transforming British Government, Volume 1: Changing Institutions* (London, 2000).
26 Tomlinson, *The Politics of Decline*, p. 25.
27 See Bernard Bergonzi, *Wartime and Aftermath: English Literature and Its Background, 1939–1960* (Oxford, 1993), pp. 122–123; Randall Stevenson, *The British Novel since the Thirties* (London, 1986), pp. 136–137.
28 See C. P. Snow, *The Two Cultures* (Cambridge, 1993), *passim*; and for contrasting recent analyses, see Roger Kimball, 'The Two Cultures Today', *New Criterion* 12: 6, February 1994; Geoffrey Wheatcroft, 'Two Cultures at Forty', *Prospect*, May 2002.
29 Kimball, 'The Two Cultures Today'.
30 The lecture is reprinted as 'The Two Cultures: The Significance of C. P. Snow' in F. R. Leavis, *Nor Shall My Sword: Discourses on Pluralism, Compassion, and Social Hope* (New York, 1972).
31 Quoted in Kimball, 'The Two Cultures Today'.
32 Martin Wiener, *English Culture and the Decline of the Industrial Spirit 1850–1980* (Cambridge, 1981); Correlli Barnett, *The Audit of War: The Illusion and Reality of Britain as a Great Power* (London, 1986).
33 See Tomlinson, *The Politics of Decline*, pp. 21–26.
34 Quotations from Foot, *The Politics of Harold Wilson*, p. 149.
35 *Scotsman*, 26 November 1957, quoted in Pimlott, *Harold Wilson*, p. 217.
36 See Ziegler, *Wilson*, p. 112.
37 Quoted in David Horner, 'The Road to Scarborough: Wilson, Labour and the Scientific Revolution', in Coopey, Fielding and Tiratsoo, eds, *The Wilson Governments 1964–1970*, p. 57.

38 Mark Abrams and Richard Rose, *Must Labour Lose?* (Harmondsworth, 1960), pp. 47–58; see also Vernon Bogdanor, 'The Labour Party in Opposition, 1951–1964', in Bogdanor and Skidelsky, eds, *The Age of Affluence*, pp. 95–96; Kevin Jefferys, *Retreat from New Jerusalem*, pp. 156–159.
39 Abrams and Rose, *Must Labour Lose?*, p. 53.
40 Fielding, '"White Heat" and White Collars', p. 31; Fielding, *Labour and Cultural Change*, p. 66.
41 Kevin Jefferys, *Anthony Crosland* (London, 1999), pp. 60–61.
42 See Bogdanor, 'The Labour Party in Opposition', pp. 88–89; Marquand, *The Progressive Dilemma*, pp. 166–178; Edmund Dell, *A Strange Eventful History*, pp. 251–281; Jefferys, *Anthony Crosland*, ch. 7.
43 Anthony Crosland, *The Future of Socialism* (London, 1956), pp. 97, 99.
44 Crosland, *The Future of Socialism*, pp. 285–286.
45 Crosland, *The Future of Socialism*, pp. 520–524.
46 Booker, *The Neophiliacs*, p. 141.
47 Morgan, *Labour People*, pp. 236–237; Fielding, *Labour and Cultural Change*, p. 76; Tomlinson, *Economic Policy*, pp. 72–75.
48 Dilwyn Porter, 'Downhill All the Way: Thirteen Tory Years 1951–1964', in Coopey, Fielding and Tiratsoo, eds, *The Wilson Governments 1964–1970*, p. 10.
49 Pimlott, *Harold Wilson*, pp. 274–275.
50 Ziegler, *Wilson*, pp. 142–143.
51 *The Times*, 4 June 1963; *Sunday Times*, 21 July 1963.
52 Fielding, '"White Heat" and White Collars', p. 44; Tomlinson, *The Politics of Decline*, p. 37.
53 *The Economist*, 20 June 1964.
54 See Booker, *The Neophiliacs*, pp. 229–230.
55 Fielding, '"White Heat" and White Collars', p. 40.
56 Sampson, *Anatomy of Britain*, pp. 509–510.
57 Godfrey Hodgson, *In Our Time: America from World War II to Nixon* (New York, 1976), p. 6.
58 Eric Hobsbawm, *Age of Extremes: The Short Twentieth Century 1914–1991* (London, 1994), pp. 264–265; Marwick, *The Sixties*, p. 248.
59 Harry Hopkins, *The New Look: A Social History of the Forties and Fifties in Britain* (London, 1964), p. 385.
60 *Daily Express*, 5 October 1957.
61 Roger Sabin, *Adult Comics: An Introduction* (London, 1993), pp. 25–26; Ross McKibbin, *Classes and Cultures: England, 1918–1951* (Oxford, 1998), p. 498.
62 Topham, *Where's My Space Age?*, p. 25.
63 Advertisements reprinted in Topham, *Where's My Space Age?*, pp. 12, 36–37.
64 Lesley Jackson, *The Sixties: Decade of Design Revolution* (London, 1998), p. 37.
65 Booker, *The Neophiliacs*, p. 158.
66 Booker, *The Neophiliacs*, p. 158.
67 *Encounter*, April 1961.
68 Twiggy, *Twiggy: An Autobiography* (London, 1976), p. 27.
69 For the 'utopian years', see 'Introduction', in David Alan Mellor and Laurent

Gervereau, eds, *The Sixties: Britain and France, 1962–1973: The Utopian Years* (London, 1997), pp. 7–8.
70 *Queen*, 15 September 1959.
71 *The Economist*, 26 December 1959.
72 *Sun*, 15 September 1964.
73 Ruth Dudley Edwards, *Newspapermen: Hugh Cudlipp, Cecil Harmsworth King and the Glory Days of Fleet Street* (London, 2003), pp. 305, 326; Roy Greenslade, *Press Gang: How Newspapers Make Profits from Propaganda* (London, 2004), pp. 154–155.
74 Greenslade, *Press Gang*, pp. 155–156.
75 Laing, *Representations of Working-Class Life 1957–1964*, pp. 21–22; Dudley Edwards, *Newspapermen*, pp. 327–328.
76 Booker, *The Neophiliacs*, p. 247.
77 *Sun*, 15 September 1964.
78 Booker, *The Neophiliacs*, p. 248.
79 Benn diary, 15 September 1964.
80 Dudley Edwards, *Newspapermen*, pp. 328, 412–414; Greenslade, *Press Gang*, pp. 157–158, 214–216.
81 *The Times*, 2 October 1963.
82 Dell, *A Strange Eventful History*, pp. 309–310.
83 *Spectator*, 11 October 1963.
84 See Foot, *The Politics of Harold Wilson*, pp. 135–138; J. F. Wright, *Britain in the Age of Economic Management: An Economic History since 1939* (Oxford, 1979), pp. 57–58; Pimlott, *Harold Wilson*, pp. 304–305; Tomlinson, *Economic Policy*, pp. 73, 194–195.
85 Bogdanor, 'The Labour Party in Opposition, 1951–1964', pp. 109–111.
86 Edmund Dell punctures their assumptions with merciless aplomb: see *A Strange Eventful History*, pp. 260–278.
87 Arthur Koestler, ed., *Suicide of a Nation? An Enquiry into the State of Britain Today* (London, 1963), pp. 39–50.

4 THIS IS TOMORROW

1 *Guardian*, 22 December 2001.
2 Jackson, *The Sixties*, pp. 47–49.
3 See Aitken, *The Young Meteors*, pp. 218–219; Jackson, *The Sixties*, pp. 46–49.
4 Deborah S. Ryan, *The Ideal Home through the 20th Century* (London, 1997), pp. 123–124.
5 Ryan, *The Ideal Home through the 20th Century*, pp. 112–116.
6 Jackson, *The Sixties*, pp. 14–15. For more comprehensive coverage, see Lesley Jackson, *The New Look: Design in the Fifties* (London, 1991) and Lesley Jackson, *Contemporary: Architecture and Interiors of the 1950s* (London, 1998).
7 Robert Hewison, *In Anger: Culture in the Cold War, 1945–60* (London, 1981), p. 49.
8 Michael Frayn, 'Festival', in Michael Sissons and Philip French, eds, *Age of Austerity* (Oxford, 1986), pp. 305–328; Paul Addison, *Now the War is Over: A Social History of Britain 1945–51* (London, 1985), pp. 197–201; Becky Conekin, '"Here is the Modern World Itself": The Festival of Britain's Representations of the Future"', in Becky E. Conekin, Frank Mort and Chris Waters, eds, *Moments of Modernity: Reconstructing Britain 1945–1964* (London, 1999), pp. 228–246; Hopkins, *The New Look*, pp. 268–277;

Weight, *Patriots*, pp. 191–204; Becky E. Conekin, *The Autobiography of a Nation: The 1951 Festival of Britain* (Manchester, 2003).
9. Conekin, '"Here is the Modern World Itself"', pp. 228–230.
10. Weight, *Patriots*, pp. 200–201.
11. Quoted in Conekin, '"Here is the Modern World Itself"', p. 238.
12. Conekin, '"Here is the Modern World Itself"', p. 245.
13. Conekin, '"Here is the Modern World Itself"', pp. 236–238.
14. John Heskett, 'Industrial Design', in Boris Ford, ed., *The Cambridge Cultural History of Britain, Volume 9: Modern Britain* (London, 1992), pp. 294–295.
15. Advertisement reprinted in Juliet Gardiner, *From the Bomb to the Beatles* (London, 1999), p. 89.
16. Gardiner, *From the Bomb to the Beatles*, p. 88.
17. See Hopkins, *The New Look*, pp. 329–330; Peter Lewis, *The Fifties* (London, 1978), p. 187; Gardiner, *From the Bomb to the Beatles*, pp. 89–90.
18. Unknown interviewee quoted in Alison Pressley, *The Best of Times: Growing up in Britain in the 1950s* (London, 1999), p. 11.
19. Heskett, 'Industrial Design', pp. 297–298; Miriam Akhtar and Steve Humphries, *The Fifties and Sixties: A Lifestyle Revolution* (London, 2001), p. 121.
20. Jackson, *The Sixties*, p. 17; Gardiner, *From the Bomb to the Beatles*, p. 89.
21. Heskett, 'Industrial Design', pp. 299–301; Philippe Garner, *Sixties Design* (Cologne, 1996), p. 24.
22. George Melly, *Revolt into Style* (Oxford, 1989), p. 146.
23. Robert Hewison, *Too Much: Art and Society in the Sixties 1960–75* (London, 1986), p. 63; Simon Frith and Howard Horne, *Art into Pop* (London, 1987), pp. 74–75, 81; Marwick, *The Sixties*, p. 57; Shawn Levy, *Ready, Steady, Go! Swinging London and the Invention of Cool* (London, 2002), pp. 114–115. Notable pop musicians of the sixties who studied at art schools included John Lennon, Paul McCartney, Ray Davies, Keith Richards and Pete Townshend, as well as a host of lesser lights.
24. Jackson, *The Sixties*, p. 147.
25. Lewis, *The Fifties*, pp. 192–193; Peter Fuller, 'The Visual Arts', in Ford, ed., *Modern Britain*, pp. 106–107.
26. Quoted in Harriet Vyner, *Groovy Bob: The Life and Times of Robert Fraser* (London, 2001), p. 122.
27. On This is Tomorrow and Hamilton's work, see Robert Hughes, *The Shock of the New: Art and the Century of Change* (revised edition: London, 1991), pp. 342–344; Thomas Crow, *The Rise of the Sixties: American and European Art in the Era of Dissent 1955–1969* (London, 1996), pp. 44–47; David Masters, 'British Art', in Clive Bloom and Gary Day, eds, *Literature and Culture in Modern Britain: Volume 3: 1956–1999* (London, 2000), pp. 209–210; Chris Stephens and Katharine Stout, 'This Was Tomorrow', in Chris Stephens and Katharine Stout, eds, *Art and the 60s: This Was Tomorrow* (London, 2004), pp. 10–12.
28. Stephens and Stout, 'This Was Tomorrow', p. 11.
29. Letter dated 16 January 1957, reprinted in Richard Hamilton, *Collected Words: 1953–1982* (London, 1982), p. 28.
30. See Fuller, 'The Visual Arts', p. 107; Hewison, *In Anger*, pp. 190–191; Hewison, *Too Much*, pp. 41–42; Crow, *The Rise of the Sixties*, pp. 39–43.

31 Garner, *Sixties Design*, p. 54.
32 Aitken, *The Young Meteors*, p. 198.
33 Quoted in *Independent*, 1 October 2001.
34 Quoted in Hewison, *Too Much*, p. 50.
35 This comparison is implicitly made in Hewison, *In Anger*, pp. 140–141.
36 Hughes, *The Shock of the New*, p. 342.
37 Quoted in Vyner, *Groovy Bob*, p. 79.
38 Stephens and Stout, 'This Was Tomorrow', p. 17. For a much less admiring account, see Fuller, 'The Visual Arts', p. 111ff.
39 Hewison, *Too Much*, p. 50; Stephens and Stout, 'This Was Tomorrow', p. 28.
40 See Stephens and Stout, 'This Was Tomorrow', pp. 19–24.
41 On Blake, see Hewison, *Too Much*, p. 44; Masters, 'British Art', p. 211; Stephens and Stout, 'This Was Tomorrow', p. 13.
42 Hewison, *Too Much*, p. 50; Marwick, *The Sixties*, pp. 324–325; and see Peter Webb, *Portrait of David Hockney* (London, 1990); David Hockney, *That's the Way I See It* (London, 1999).
43 Aitken, *The Young Meteors*, p. 199.
44 *Independent*, 25 May 2002.
45 *Sunday Times Colour Section*, 26 January 1964.
46 Quoted in Fuller, 'The Visual Arts', p. 135.
47 Aitken, *The Young Meteors*, p. 191.
48 Hewison, *In Anger*, p. 187; Hewison, *Too Much*, pp. 53–54; Stephens and Stout, 'This Was Tomorrow', pp. 28–29.
49 Vyner, *Groovy Bob*, pp. 1–70. For a contemporary profile of Fraser, see Aitken, *The Young Meteors*, pp. 192–193.
50 See Vyner, *Groovy Bob*, pp. 98–157.
51 Vyner, *Groovy Bob*, p. 70.
52 Aitken, *The Young Meteors*, p. 192.
53 Paul Moorhouse, ed., *Bridget Riley* (London, 2003), and see Jackson, *The Sixties*, p. 89; Stephens and Stout, 'This Was Tomorrow', p. 34.
54 See the interview in Aitken, *The Young Meteors*, pp. 196–197.
55 Crow, *The Rise of the Sixties*, p. 111; Stephens and Stout, 'This Was Tomorrow', p. 34.
56 Hewison, *Too Much*, p. 48; Crow, *The Rise of the Sixties*, pp. 111–112.
57 See Garner, *Sixties Design*, pp. 74–80; Jackson, *The Sixties*, pp. 90–92.
58 Preface to Dennis Young and Barbara Young, *Furniture in Britain Today* (London, 1964), quoted in Garner, *Sixties Design*, p. 20.
59 See Jackson, *The Sixties*, p. 57; much of what follows is based on Lesley Jackson's magisterial survey of design in the 1960s.
60 Jackson, *The Sixties*, p. 58.
61 See Jackson, *The Sixties*, pp. 58–121.
62 On Grange's lighter, see Whiteley, 'Shaping the Sixties', in Harris, Hyde and Smith, eds, *1966 and All That*, pp. 28–29.
63 Jackson, *The Sixties*, p. 139.
64 Ryan, *The Ideal Home through the 20th Century*, p. 133.
65 Quoted in Whiteley, 'Shaping the Sixties', p. 16.

66 Advertisement reprinted in Akhtar and Humphries, *The Fifties and Sixties*, p. 119.
67 Jim Shaw quoted in Akhtar and Humphries, *The Fifties and Sixties*, p. 119.
68 Jackson, *The Sixties*, pp. 30–32; Topham, *Where's My Space Age?*, pp. 61–63.
69 Quoted in Topham, *Where's My Space Age?*, p. 100.
70 Jackson, *The Sixties*, pp. 73, 200–201; Nigel Cawthorne, *Sixties Source Book: A Visual Guide to the Style of a Decade* (London, 1998), p. 108.
71 Ryan, *The Ideal Home through the 20th Century*, p. 137.
72 Quotations from Jackson, *The Sixties*, pp. 36–37.
73 Gardiner, *From the Bomb to the Beatles*, p. 88.
74 Jackson, *The Sixties*, p. 36.
75 'Laura', in Cecile Landau, ed., *Growing up in the Sixties* (London, 1991), p. 5.
76 'Julia', in Landau, ed., *Growing up in the Sixties*, p. 93.
77 Akhtar and Humphries, *The Fifties and Sixties*, p. 118.
78 Alan A. Jackson, *The Middle Classes 1900–1950* (Nairn, 1991), p. 63.
79 Jackson, *The Middle Classes*, p. 68.
80 David Butler and Michael Pinto-Duschinsky, *The British General Election of 1970* (London, 1971), p. 26; Sked and Cook, *Post-War Britain*, pp. 251–252; Timmins, *The Five Giants*, p. 268.
81 Ken Coates and Richard Silburn, *Poverty: The Forgotten Englishmen* (Harmondsworth, 1970), p. 60.
82 Aitken, *The Young Meteors*, pp. 216–217.
83 Lesley Jackson gives the examples of Terence Conran, Mary Quant and Peter Murdoch: see Jackson, *The Sixties*, pp. 145–147
84 Jackson, *The Sixties*, p. 35.
85 Jackson, *The Sixties*, p. 49.
86 *Independent*, 19 February 2004.
87 On Habitat, see Jackson, *The Sixties*, pp. 46–49; Gardiner, *From the Bomb to the Beatles*, pp. 139–140; Jennifer Harris, Sarah Hyde and Greg Smith, 'New Trends in Shopping and Selling', in Harris, Hyde and Smith, eds, *1966 and All That*, pp. 57–58.
88 See Jackson, *The Sixties*, pp. 35, 46–52.

5 THE HUNDRED DAYS

1 Callaghan, *Time and Chance*, p. 162.
2 T 171/758, 'General Briefing for the Chancellor', 16 October 1964; and see Dell, *The Chancellors*, p. 310; Morgan, *Callaghan*, p. 203.
3 Sir Alec Cairncross, *Managing the British Economy in the 1960s: A Treasury Perspective* (London, 1996), p. 92.
4 Jack Diamond interviewed in Mitchell and Wienir, eds, *Last Time*, pp. 100, 149–150.
5 Maudling, *Memoirs*, pp. 105–122; Lewis Baston, *Reggie: The Life of Reginald Maudling* (London, 2004), pp. 192–195.
6 Richard Lamb, *The Macmillan Years 1957–1963: The Unfolding Truth* (London, 1995), pp. 100–101; Dell, *The Chancellors*, pp. 297–299; Baston, *Reggie*, pp. 233–244.
7 Hansard, 14 April 1964; Baston, *Reggie*, pp. 225–228.
8 Baston, *Reggie*, pp. 228–229; and see Morgan, *Callaghan*, p. 188.
9 Gilmour and Garnett, *Whatever Happened to the Tories*, p. 211.

10 Quoted in Morgan, *Callaghan*, p. 193.
11 T 171/755, 'The Economic Situation', 12 October 1964; see also Baston, *Reggie*, pp. 229–230.
12 Callaghan, *Time and Chance*, pp. 154–155.
13 See the accounts in Callaghan, *Time and Chance*, p. 162, and Cole, *As It Seemed to Me*, p. 83.
14 Callaghan, *Time and Chance*, p. 163.
15 See Callaghan, *Time and Chance*, pp. 168–169; Ponting, *Breach of Promise*, pp. 66–68; Dell, *The Chancellors*, pp. 321–324; Morgan, *Callaghan*, pp. 214–215.
16 Anthony Crosland, *Socialism Now* (London, 1975) p. 18.
17 Dell, *The Chancellors*, p. 315.
18 See, for instance, Nicholas Woodward, 'Labour's Economic Performance, 1964–1970', in Coopey, Fielding and Tiratsoo, eds, *The Wilson Governments 1964–1970*, p. 82; Dell, *The Chancellors*, pp. 310–315.
19 Callaghan, *Time and Chance*, pp. 159–160.
20 Crossman diary, 24 November 1964.
21 Pimlott, *Harold Wilson*, p. 351.
22 Paterson, *Tired and Emotional*, p. 183.
23 Quoted in Peter Hennessy, *Muddling Through: Power, Politics and the Quality of Government in Postwar Britain* (London, 1996), p. 251.
24 Dell, *The Chancellors*, p. 315.
25 T 171/758, 'Devaluation', 15 October 1964; see also Ponting, *Breach of Promise*, pp. 64–65; Morgan, *Callaghan*, p. 213; Tomlinson, *Economic Policy*, p. 49.
26 Morgan, *Callaghan*, p. 212.
27 Ponting, *Breach of Promise*, p. 65.
28 See Woodward, 'Labour's Economic Performance', pp. 82–83, and Tomlinson, *Economic Policy*, p. 223: these are the leading analyses of Labour's economic record.
29 Quotations from Ziegler, *Wilson*, p. 191.
30 See Pimlott, *Harold Wilson*, pp. 352–354.
31 Barbara Castle interviewed in Mitchell and Wienir, eds, *Last Time*, p. 152.
32 S. Crosland, *Tony Crosland*, p. 128; Bill Rodgers interviewed in Mitchell and Wienir, eds, *Last Time*, p. 145.
33 Hansard, 4 and 8 April 1963.
34 See Woodward, 'Labour's Economic Performance', pp. 78–79; Morgan, *Callaghan*, pp. 204–205; Tomlinson, *Economic Policy*, p. 14.
35 Crossman diary, 22 October 1964.
36 See Ponting, *Breach of Promise*, pp. 66–67; Pimlott, *Harold Wilson*, p. 352; Dell, *The Chancellors*, pp. 321–322; Morgan, *Callaghan*, pp. 213–214.
37 Ponting, *Breach of Promise*, p. 68; Morgan, *Callaghan*, pp. 214–215.
38 Cairncross, *Managing the British Economy in the 1960s*, p. 97; *Guardian*, quoted in Morgan, *Callaghan*, p. 215.
39 See Dell, *The Chancellors*, p. 323; Morgan, *Callaghan*, p. 215.
40 *The Times*, 21 November 1964.
41 Woodward, 'Labour's Economic Performance', pp. 80–83; Dell, *The Chancellors*, pp. 310–346; Holt, *Second Amongst Equals*, pp. 236–237. Both Dell and Holt point out that

since ministers were dependent on the advice given them by civil servants, the Treasury has to shoulder some of the blame.

42 Dell, *The Chancellors*, p. 306.
43 Callaghan, *Time and Chance*, p. 167.
44 Crossman diary, 24 November 1964.
45 Crossman diary, 23 November 1964.
46 Callaghan, *Time and Chance*, p. 168; and see Pimlott, *Harold Wilson*, p. 353.
47 Pimlott, *Harold Wilson*, p. 354.
48 Crossman diary, 13 December 1964.
49 Ponting, *Breach of Promise*, p. 70.
50 See PREM 13/237, 24 November 1964; and the accounts in Wilson, *The Labour Government*, pp. 37–38; Callaghan, *Time and Chance*, pp. 174–175; Morgan, *Callaghan*, p. 216.
51 Ponting, *Breach of Promise*, p. 71; Morgan, *Callaghan*, pp. 216–217.
52 Foot, *The Politics of Harold Wilson*, p. 154. Foot notes that in 1961 Wilson had announced that he had 'always deprecated . . . in crisis after crisis, appeals to the Dunkirk spirit', because when facing economic problems, 'it is the long haul, not the inspired spirit, that we need'. He would have done well to have taken his own advice.
53 Crossman diary, 12 December 1964.
54 Quoted in Ponting, *Breach of Promise*, p. 72.
55 Crossman diary, 3 January 1965.
56 Benn diary, 14 January 1965.
57 Robert Pearce, 'Introduction', in Patrick Gordon Walker, *Political Diaries 1932–71* (ed. Robert Pearce: London, 1991), pp. 45–46.
58 Edward Pearce, *Denis Healey: A Life in Our Times* (London, 2002), pp. 269–270.
59 King and Wybrow, eds, *British Political Opinion*, p. 9.
60 Williams, *Inside Number 10*, p. 44.
61 Castle diary, 26 January 1965; Crossman diary, 26 January 1965.
62 Crossman diary, 21 January 1965.
63 Castle diary, 10 February 1965.
64 Castle diary, 28 January 1965.
65 Ponting, *Breach of Promise*, p. 73.
66 See Callaghan, *Time and Chance*, pp. 180–182; Morgan, *Callaghan*, pp. 220–221.
67 Tomlinson, *Economic Policy*, p. 51.
68 Ponting, *Breach of Promise*, pp. 30–31; Pimlott, *Harold Wilson*, pp. 357–359.
69 Pimlott, *Harold Wilson*, p. 359.
70 Castle diary, 3 June 1965.
71 Morgan, *Callaghan*, pp. 222–226.
72 Wilson, *The Labour Government*, p. 32.
73 Wilson, *The Labour Government*, p. 126.
74 Dell, *A Strange Eventful History*, pp. 334–335.
75 Cairncross diary, 22 May 1965, quoted in Hennessy, *The Prime Minister*, p. 286.
76 Crossman diary, 20 and 27 July 1965.
77 Castle diary, 27 July 1965; see also Ponting, *Breach of Promise*, pp. 77–79.

78 Dell, *The Chancellors*, p. 328.
79 Crossman diary, 28 July 1965.
80 Crossman diary, 5 August 1965.
81 Robert J. Wybrow, *Britain Speaks Out, 1937–87: A Social History as Seen through the Gallup Data* (London, 1989), p. 75; King and Wybrow, eds, *British Political Opinion*, p. 187.
82 Crossman diary, 5 August 1965.

6 INTRODUCING THE TURDS

1 Levy, *Ready, Steady, Go!*, pp. 127–128; 'Ready, Steady, Go!' in Colin Larkin, ed., *The Virgin Encyclopedia of Sixties Music* (London, 1997), pp. 366–367.
2 Philip Norman, *The Stones* (London, 1993), p. 86.
3 Twiggy, *Twiggy: An Autobiography*, p. 17.
4 Twiggy, *Twiggy: An Autobiography*, pp. 17–18.
5 Melly, *Revolt into Style*, pp. 187–188; Iain Chambers, *Urban Rhythms: Pop Music and Popular Culture* (Basingstoke, 1985), p. 76.
6 Mark Abrams, *The Teenage Consumer* (London, 1959), pp. 13–14; Mark Abrams, *Teenage Consumer Spending in 1959* (London, 1961), pp. 4–5.
7 Abrams, *Teenage Consumer Spending in 1959*, pp. 4–5.
8 John Davis, *Youth and the Condition of Britain: Images of Adolescent Conflict* (London, 1990), p. 166.
9 See Sandbrook, *Never Had It So Good*, ch. 13; and Andrew Blake, 'Popular Music since the 1950s', in Clive Bloom and Gary Day, eds, *Literature and Culture in Modern Britain: Volume 3: 1956–1999* (London, 2000), p. 227; Melly, *Revolt into Style*, pp. 56–57; Adam Clayson, *Beat Merchants: The Origins, History, Impact and Rock Legacy of the 1960s British Pop Groups* (London, 1995), p. 46; Davis, *Youth and the Condition of Britain*, p. 165.
10 See Philip Norman, *Shout! The True Story of the Beatles* (London, 1981), pp. 203–204.
11 See Sandbrook, *Never Had It So Good*, chs 13 and 19; and among thousands of books on the Beatles, Norman, *Shout!*; Ian MacDonald, *Revolution in the Head* (revised edition: London, 1997).
12 On the simple fact of musical increase, see Paul Griffiths, 'Music', in Ford, ed., *Modern Britain*, p. 49.
13 Booker, *The Neophiliacs*, p. 233.
14 *Daily Mirror*, 2 October 1963.
15 Peter Laurie, *The Teenage Revolution* (London, 1965), p. 63.
16 Laurie, *The Teenage Revolution*, p. 72.
17 Briggs, *Competition*, pp. 502–515.
18 Norman, *The Stones*, pp. 119–120; Briggs, *Competition*, pp. 565–566.
19 Chambers, *Urban Rhythms*, p. 15.
20 Ian MacDonald, *The People's Music* (London, 2003), pp. 71–72, 197–198.
21 MacDonald, *The People's Music*, p. 192.
22 *Melody Maker*, 5 May 1956; *Daily Mail*, 5 September 1956.
23 *Daily Mirror*, 10 September 1963; *Evening Standard*, 17 October 1963; *Daily Mirror*, 6 November 1963.
24 *New Statesman*, 28 February 1964.
25 Lawton, *1963*, p. 116.

26 *The Times*, 27 December 1963.
27 'Introducing the Turds', in Ingrams, ed., *The Life and Times of Private Eye*, p. 111.
28 *New Musical Express*, 3 January 1964.
29 Norman, *Shout!*, p. 195.
30 MacDonald, *The People's Music*, p. 45.
31 James Miller, *Flowers in the Dustbin: The Rise of Rock and Roll, 1947–1977* (New York, 1999), pp. 212–213.
32 Barry Miles, *The Beatles Diary: Volume 1: The Beatles Years* (London, 2001), pp. 126–127; Norman, *Shout!*, pp. 206–207.
33 See MacDonald, *Revolution in the Head*, pp. 56–57, 88–89.
34 Quoted in Keith Badman, *The Beatles off the Record: Outrageous Opinions and Unrehearsed Interviews* (London, 2001), p. 78.
35 Norman, *Shout!*, p. 211; Badman, *The Beatles off the Record*, p. 79.
36 Norman, *Shout!*, p. 213.
37 Quoted in Badman, *The Beatles off the Record*, pp. 80–81.
38 The Beatles, *The Beatles Anthology* (New York, 2000), p. 116.
39 Quoted in Badman, *The Beatles off the Record*, p. 85.
40 See Norman, *Shout!*, pp. 221–222; Badman, *The Beatles off the Record*, pp. 85–86.
41 *New Musical Express*, 14 February 1964; Norman, *Shout!*, pp. 217–218; Miles, *The Beatles Diary*, pp. 131–132.
42 *Washington Post*, 10 February 1964; and for more press coverage, see Norman, *Shout!*, pp. 217–218.
43 Quoted in Tony Palmer, *All You Need is Love: The Story of Popular Music* (London, 1977), p. 222.
44 Norman, *Shout!*, p. 220.
45 Dave Harker, 'Still Crazy after All These Years: What *Was* Popular Music in the 1960s?', in Bart Moore-Gilbert and John Seed, eds, *Cultural Revolution? The Challenge of the Arts in the 1960s* (London, 1992), p. 238; Clayson, *Beat Merchants*, p. 186; Levy, *Ready, Steady, Go!*, p. 140.
46 *Daily Mirror*, 8 February 1964.
47 Badman, *The Beatles off the Record*, p. 88.
48 Laurie, *The Teenage Revolution*, p. 23.
49 Lawton, *1963*, p. 115.
50 Clayson, *Beat Merchants*, p. 185.
51 Jane Stern and Michael Stern, *Sixties People* (New York, 1990), p. 141.
52 Peter Leslie, *Fab: The Anatomy of a Phenomenon* (London, 1965), p. 179.
53 *New Musical Express*, 31 July 1964.
54 Charlie Gillett, *The Sound of the City: The Rise of Rock and Roll* (London, 1983), p. 283.
55 Levy, *Ready, Steady, Go!*, p. 152; MacDonald, *Revolution in the Head*, p. 90.
56 See MacDonald, *Revolution in the Head*, p. 90.
57 See Norman, *The Stones*, p. 120.
58 Clayson, *Beat Merchants*, p. 187.
59 See 'Herman's Hermits', in Larkin, ed., *The Virgin Encyclopedia of Sixties Music*, p. 234; Clayson, *Beat Merchants*, p. 188.
60 Quoted in Booker, *The Neophiliacs*, p. 233.

61 Norman, *Shout!*, pp. 204–205; Clayson, *Beat Merchants*, p. 133; *Daily Mirror*, 8 January 1964; *Daily Mail*, 9 January 1964.
62 Clayson, *Beat Merchants*, p. 188; and see 'Dave Clark Five', in Larkin, ed., *The Virgin Encyclopedia of Sixties Music*, pp. 114–115.
63 See Jon Savage, *The Kinks: The Official Biography* (London, 1984), pp. 7–8; see also Ray Davies' fascinating, if peculiar, autobiography, *X-Ray: The Unauthorized Autobiography* (London, 1996).
64 Nick Hasted, 'Ready, Steady, Kinks', *Uncut*, September 2004, p. 51.
65 For instance, see Savage, *The Kinks*, pp. 32–34; Hasted, 'Ready, Steady, Kinks,' p. 52; 'The Kinks', in Larkin, ed., *The Virgin Encyclopedia of Sixties Music*, pp. 266–268.
66 Savage. *The Kinks*, p. 29.
67 Hasted, 'Ready, Steady, Kinks', p. 51; Savage, *The Kinks*, p. 34.
68 Hasted, 'Ready, Steady, Kinks', p. 54.
69 Hasted, 'Ready, Steady, Kinks', p. 48; Savage, *The Kinks*, pp. 42–43.
70 Savage, *The Kinks*, p. 38.
71 See Gillett, *The Sound of the City*, pp. 276–277.
72 Savage, *The Kinks*, p. 38.
73 Leslie, *Fab*, p. 178.
74 *New Musical Express*, 15 July 1964.
75 *New Musical Express*, 2 December 1964.
76 MacDonald, *Revolution in the Head*, p. 340.
77 Ian MacDonald, *The People's Music* (London, 2003), viii–ix.

7 SPECIAL RELATIONS

1 Crossman diary, 11 December 1964.
2 See Black, '"The Bitterest Enemies of Communism"', pp. 38–40; Peter Jones, *America and the Labour Party: The Special Relationship at Work* (London, 1997).
3 Chris Wrigley, 'Now You See It, Now You Don't: Harold Wilson and Labour's Foreign Policy 1964–70', in Coopey, Fielding and Tiratsoo, eds, *The Wilson Governments 1964–1970*, p. 121; Ponting, *Breach of Promise*, pp. 42–43.
4 Quoted in John W. Young, *The Labour Governments 1964–70: Volume 2: International Policy* (Manchester, 2003), pp. 19–20.
5 Dean Rusk to President Johnson, 24 October 1964, quoted in Ponting, *Breach of Promise*, p. 44.
6 Walter Heller to President Johnson, 30 March 1965, quoted in Ponting, *Breach of Promise*, pp. 45–46.
7 Roy Jenkins, *A Life at the Centre* (London, 1992), p. 248; Young, *International Policy*, p. 6.
8 Benn diary, 27 September 1965. The tortoise–hare analogy is borrowed from the title of an essay on Stewart and Douglas Jay in Marquand, *The Progressive Dilemma*, pp. 147–154.
9 Pimlott, *Harold Wilson*, pp. 334–335.
10 See Dorril and Ramsay, *Smear!*, pp. 165–166, which goes so far as to call Stewart the CIA's 'agent of influence' in the Cabinet; and see also Wrigley, 'Now You See It, Now You Don't', p. 129; Pimlott, *Harold Wilson*, pp. 334–335; Young, *International Policy*, p. 6.

11 Pimlott, *Harold Wilson*, p. 366.
12 Young, *International Policy*, pp. 71–72.
13 See Anthony Short, *The Communist Insurrection in Malaya, 1948–1960* (London, 1975); Matthew Jones, *Conflict and Confrontation in South East Asia, 1961–1965: Britain, the United States, Indonesia and the Creation of Malaysia* (Cambridge, 2001).
14 Jones, *Conflict and Confrontation in South East Asia*, p. 304; Young, *International Policy*, p. 74.
15 Wilson, *The Labour Government*, p. 80.
16 Sked and Cook, *Post-War Britain*, p. 209.
17 Hansard, 19 July 1965.
18 For example, see Pimlott, *Harold Wilson*, p. 394; Young, *International Policy*, pp. 70, 81–82.
19 Simon Heffer, *Like the Roman: The Life of Enoch Powell* (London, 1998), pp. 405–406.
20 Heffer, *Like the Roman*, p. 405.
21 Quoted in Wrigley, 'Now You See It, Now You Don't', p. 128.
22 Bundy to Johnson, 28 July 1965, quoted in Ponting, *Breach of Promise*, p. 50; Ziegler, *Wilson*, p. 205.
23 King diary, 5 August 1965.
24 Ponting, *Breach of Promise*, pp. 79–80.
25 Quotations from Ponting, *Breach of Promise*, pp. 50–52. Originally the Americans had wanted a freeze on wages and prices, but Wilson and Callaghan managed to bargain them down to a statutory incomes policy on the grounds that a wage–price freeze was politically impossible.
26 See Castle diary, 31 August and 1 September 1965; Crossman diary, 1 September 1965.
27 Ponting, *Breach of Promise*, pp. 81–82.
28 Bundy to Johnson, 10 September 1965, quoted in Ponting, *Breach of Promise*, p. 53.
29 See Ponting, *Breach of Promise*, pp. 82–83.
30 See the discussions in Ponting, *Breach of Promise*, pp. 40–60; Pimlott, *Harold Wilson*, p. 386; Ziegler, *Wilson*, pp. 205–206.
31 Crossman diary, 12 September 1965.
32 Castle diary, 11 February 1966.
33 Crossman diary, 14 February 1966.
34 Tomlinson, *Economic Policy*, p. 53.
35 Robin Renwick, *Fighting with Allies* (London, 1996), p. 200; Young, *International Policy*, p. 41.
36 As suggested in Ponting, *Breach of Promise*, pp. 53–60.
37 *Private Eye*, 30 April 1965.
38 Ponting, *Breach of Promise*, p. 141.
39 Lawrence James, *The Rise and Fall of the British Empire* (London, 1994), p. 619.
40 *Sun*, 15 November 1965.
41 *New Statesman*, 10 May 1963.
42 Pimlott, *Harold Wilson*, pp. 366–368; James, *The Rise and Fall of the British Empire*, p. 618; Denis Judd, *Empire: The British Imperial Experience from 1765 to the Present* (London, 1996), pp. 373–374.
43 Ponting, *Breach of Promise*, p. 144.
44 Pimlott, *Harold Wilson*, pp. 367–368.

45 Ponting, *Breach of Promise*, pp. 147–148.
46 Castle diary, 7 October 1965.
47 Crossman diary, 21 October 1965; Pimlott, *Harold Wilson*, pp. 368–369.
48 Wilson, *The Labour Government*, pp. 200–201, 216; Pimlott, *Harold Wilson*, pp. 370–371.
49 Pimlott, *Harold Wilson*, p. 371.
50 Ken Flower, *Serving Secretly: An Intelligence Chief on Record: Rhodesia to Zimbabwe, 1964–1981* (London, 1987), pp. 51–52.
51 Pimlott, *Harold Wilson*, p. 372.
52 Castle diary, 11 November 1965.
53 Benn diary, 11 November 1965.
54 Hansard, 11 November 1965.
55 Crossman diary, 9 December 1965.
56 Castle diary, 28 November 1966.
57 Healey, *The Time of My Life*, p. 332.
58 Castle diary, 28 November 1966; Pimlott, *Harold Wilson*, p. 373.
59 Crossman diary, 26 October 1965.
60 Pimlott, *Harold Wilson*, pp. 374–375; Campbell, *Edward Heath*, pp. 204–205.
61 *Sunday Telegraph*, 17 October 1965.
62 King diary, 8 December 1965.
63 Ingrams and Wells, *Mrs Wilson's Second Diary*, pp. 17–18.
64 Crossman diary, 23 December 1965.
65 Benn diary, 23 November 1965.
66 King and Wybrow, eds, *British Political Opinion*, p. 9; on Wilson's obsession with Rhodesia, see also Pimlott, *Harold Wilson*, pp. 380–381; Ziegler, *Wilson*, p. 219.
67 Ponting, *Breach of Promise*, pp. 152–156; Pimlott, *Harold Wilson*, pp. 375–376.
68 Crossman diary, 18 November 1965.
69 Crossman diary, 28 November 1965.
70 Ponting, *Breach of Promise*, pp. 156–157; Pimlott, *Harold Wilson*, pp. 375–376.
71 King diary, 24 December 1965.
72 Castle diary, 3 January 1966.
73 Pimlott, *Harold Wilson*, p. 377.
74 *Sun*, 6 January 1966; Pimlott, *Harold Wilson*, p. 379.
75 Young, *International Policy*, p. 174.
76 Pimlott, *Harold Wilson*, p. 378.
77 Pimlott, *Harold Wilson*, p. 380; Young, *International Policy*, p. 174.

8 ENTER THE STONES

1 George Melly quoted in Andrew Loog Oldham, *Stoned* (London, 2001), p. 192.
2 Oldham, *Stoned*, pp. 1–184; and see also Norman, *The Stones*, pp. 72–76.
3 Oldham, *Stoned*, p. 184.
4 Oldham, *Stoned*, p. 186.
5 Oldham, *Stoned*, p. 190.
6 As argued in MacDonald, *Revolution in the Head*, pp. 255–256.
7 Palmer, *All You Need is Love*, p. 158; and see Gillett, *The Sound of the City*, pp. 122–168; Miller, *Flowers in the Dustbin*, pp. 34–39.

8 On the influence of Muddy Waters and Howlin' Wolf, see Gillett, *The Sound of the City*, pp. 136–138, 147–149; Chambers, *Urban Rhythms*, p. 66.
9 Miller, *Flowers in the Dustbin*, pp. 34–39, 72.
10 Clayson, *Beat Merchants*, p. 23. Poor Ted Heath was initially famous in his own right before becoming arguably even more famous for *not* being the 'other' Ted Heath – sailor, conductor, politician and curmudgeon.
11 Clayson, *Beat Merchants*, pp. 149–150; Gillett, *The Sound of the City*, p. 260; Norman, *The Stones*, p. 42.
12 Bill Wyman, with Ray Coleman, *Stone Alone: The Story of a Rock 'n' Roll Band* (London, 1991), pp. 104–105.
13 Wyman, *Stone Alone*, pp. 103–104; Norman, *The Stones*, pp. 42–44; Tony Bacon, *London Live: From the Yardbirds to Pink Floyd to the Sex Pistols* (London, 1999), pp. 24, 46.
14 Norman, *The Stones*, p. 43; and see 'Alexis Korner', in Larkin, ed., *The Virgin Encyclopedia of Sixties Music*, p. 271.
15 Wyman, *Stone Alone*, pp. 106–107; Norman, *The Stones*, pp. 43–45; Bacon, *London Live*, pp. 48–49.
16 Quoted in Bacon, *London Live*, p. 49; and see Gillett, *The Sound of the City*, p. 261.
17 Clayson, *Beat Merchants*, pp. 151–152.
18 Chambers, *Urban Rhythms*, p. 69.
19 Leslie, *Fab*, pp. 184–185.
20 Chambers, *Urban Rhythms*, p. 69.
21 Frith and Horne, *Art into Pop*, p. 80.
22 Clayson, *Beat Merchants*, p. 45; Frith and Horne, *Art into Pop*, p. 73.
23 Quoted in Alison Pressley, *Changing Times: Being Young in Britain in the '60s* (London, 2000), p. 33.
24 Frith and Horne, *Art into Pop*, pp. 81, 86.
25 Tom Hibbert, 'Animal Tracks: Newcastle's Brand of Powerhouse Blues', online at <www.rocksbackpages.com>.
26 See Gillett, *The Sound of the City*, p. 271; 'The Animals', in Larkin, ed., *The Virgin Encyclopedia of Sixties Music*, p. 15.
27 Norman, *Shout!*, p. 257.
28 *New Musical Express*, 12 February 1966; Clayson, *Beat Merchants*, p. 160.
29 *New Musical Express*, 28 May 1966.
30 Quoted in Gillett, *The Sound of the City*, p. 272.
31 Mark Paytress, *The Rolling Stones off the Record* (London, 2003), p. 10; and see Norman, *The Stones*, pp. 38–39.
32 Norman, *The Stones*, p. 38.
33 See Norman, *The Stones*, pp. 26–28.
34 Norman, *The Stones*, pp. 32–34.
35 Paytress, *The Rolling Stones off the Record*, p. 5; Norman, *The Stones*, p. 40.
36 Norman, *The Stones*, pp. 47–48; Wyman, *Stone Alone*, p. 94.
37 Norman, *The Stones*, pp. 49–50.
38 Wyman, *Stone Alone*, p. 100.
39 Quoted in Wyman, *Stone Alone*, p. 129.
40 Wyman, *Stone Alone*, p. 377.

41 See Norman, *The Stones*, p. 49; Wyman, *Stone Alone*, p. 97.
42 Wyman, *Stone Alone*, p. 92.
43 Norman, *The Stones*, pp. 50–53.
44 Wyman, *Stone Alone*, p. 120.
45 *Jazz News*, 11 July 1962; and see Norman, *The Stones*, pp. 52–53; Wyman, *Stone Alone*, pp. 122–123; Paytress, *The Rolling Stones off the Record*, pp. 13–17.
46 Wyman, *Stone Alone*, pp. 91–92. The band began life as the Rollin' Stones but even in their first year occasionally performed as the Rolling Stones. They finally adopted the latter name in the summer of 1963 at the behest of Oldham.
47 Norman, *The Stones*, pp. 58–59.
48 Norman, *The Stones*, pp. 57, 62.
49 Wyman, *Stone Alone*, pp. 129, 134–135; Norman, *The Stones*, p. 62.
50 See Wyman, *Stone Alone*, pp. 1–132. Wyman's book, ghost-written by the journalist Ray Coleman, is by far the most reliable autobiography by a member of any of the leading groups of the sixties, and an invaluable source on the evolution of the Rolling Stones.
51 Wyman, *Stone Alone*, pp. 89–91.
52 Wyman, *Stone Alone*, pp. 203–204.
53 Norman, *The Stones*, p. 64; Wyman, *Stone Alone*, pp. 107–108, 138.
54 See Norman, *The Stones*, pp. 158–159; Wyman, *Stone Alone*, p. 211.
55 Norman, *The Stones*, pp. 66–67; Wyman, *Stone Alone*, pp. 143–148.
56 Vic Johnson quoted in Wyman, *Stone Alone*, pp. 145–146.
57 *Richmond and Twickenham Times*, 13 April 1963. The article is reprinted in Paytress, *The Rolling Stones off the Record*, pp. 23–24.
58 Wyman, *Stone Alone*, pp. 153–154.
59 Wyman, *Stone Alone*, p. 206.
60 Wyman; *Stone Alone*, p. 187; and see Norman, *The Stones*, p. 77; Wyman, *Stone Alone*, pp. 156–157.
61 Oldham, *Stoned*, pp. 210–212; and see Norman, *The Stones*, pp. 78–82.
62 Oldham, *Stoned*, pp. 222–223.
63 Wyman, *Stone Alone*, p. 160; on Stewart as the band's conscience, see Wyman, *Stone Alone*, p. 27.
64 Wyman, *Stone Alone*, p. 163; Norman, p. 83.
65 John Douglas quoted in Oldham, *Stoned*, p. 207.
66 *Record Mirror*, 11 May 1963; Norman, *The Stones*, p. 71.
67 Quoted in Paytress, *The Rolling Stones off the Record*, pp. 30–31.
68 Wyman, *Stone Alone*, p. 196.
69 Wyman, *Stone Alone*, p. 186.
70 *New Musical Express*, 20 December 1963.
71 Quoted in Wyman, *Stone Alone*, p. 214.
72 See Norman, *The Stones*, pp. 92–111.
73 Wyman, *Stone Alone*, pp. 334–335.
74 See Norman, *The Stones*, pp. 112–142.
75 Wyman, *Stone Alone*, pp. 176–177.
76 Wyman, *Stone Alone*, p. 212, and see also pp. 189, 204–205.

77 Letters quoted in Paytress, *The Rolling Stones off the Record*, pp. 33–34; on *Thank Your Lucky Stars*, see Norman, *The Stones*, pp. 83–84.
78 See Chambers, *Urban Rhythms*, p. 67.
79 *Daily Express*, 28 February 1964.
80 *Evening Standard*, 21 March 1964.
81 *Evening Standard*, 14 April 1964.
82 Stuart Hylton, *Magical History Tour: The 1960s Revisited* (Stroud, 2000), p. 7; Norman, *The Stones*, p. 96.
83 *Melody Maker*, 28 March 1964.
84 Norman, *The Stones*, p. 133; Paytress, *The Rolling Stones off the Record*, p. 77.
85 On the garage affair, see Norman, *The Stones*, pp. 131–132; Wyman, *Stone Alone*, pp. 363–366.
86 Wyman, *Stone Alone*, p. 389.
87 *News of the World*, 1 November 1964.
88 MacDonald, *The People's Music*, p. 52.
89 Oldham, *Stoned*, pp. 293–294.
90 Wyman, *Stone Alone*, p. 229.
91 Laurie, *The Teenage Revolution*, p. 84.
92 Wyman, *Stone Alone*, p. 230.
93 Wyman, *Stone Alone*, p. 249.
94 *Independent on Sunday*, 14 December 2003.
95 Norman, *The Stones*, p. 99.
96 Chambers, *Urban Rhythms*, p. 67; and see Gillett, *The Sound of the City*, pp. 268–270.
97 Chambers, *Urban Rhythms*, p. 68.
98 *New Musical Express*, 10 December 1965.
99 Badman, *The Beatles off the Record*, p. 188; and see Norman, *Shout!*, p. 252.
100 *New Musical Express*, 31 December 1965.

9 WOMEN! WIN MR HEATH!

1 King and Wybrow, eds, *British Political Opinion*, p. 9.
2 Gilmour and Garnett, *Whatever Happened to the Tories*, pp. 215–216.
3 Anthony Howard, *RAB: The Life of R. A. Butler* (London, 1987), pp. 338–340, 370.
4 *Sunday Times*, 18 July 1965.
5 See Thorpe, *Alec Douglas-Home*, pp. 378–387.
6 Heffer, *Like the Roman*, pp. 384–385.
7 *Daily Mail*, 26 July 1965; Baston, *Reggie*, pp. 254–255.
8 There is a good analysis in Robert Shepherd, *Iain Macleod: A Biography* (London, 1994), pp. 402–403.
9 Quoted in Campbell, *Edward Heath*, p. 178.
10 See Campbell, *Edward Heath*, pp. 178–180.
11 As argued in Campbell, *Edward Heath*, pp. 139–140.
12 Campbell, *Edward Heath*, pp. 168–169.
13 *Guardian*, 10 November 1964.
14 Quotations from Campbell, *Edward Heath*, p. 182.
15 Campbell, *Edward Heath*, p. 181.

16 Baston, *Reggie*, pp. 256–257.
17 King diary, 25 July 1965.
18 Alan Watkins, *A Short Walk down Fleet Street* (London, 2001), p. 75.
19 Maudling, *Memoirs*, p. 134.
20 Heffer, *Like the Roman*, p. 385.
21 Campbell, *Edward Heath*, p. 167; Baston, *Reggie*, pp. 247–252.
22 Heath, *The Course of My Life*, pp. 1–13; Campbell, *Edward Heath*, pp. 3–6.
23 Campbell, *Edward Heath*, pp. 7–8.
24 Andrew Roth, *Heath and the Heathmen* (London, 1972), p. 21; Campbell, *Edward Heath*, pp. 10–11.
25 Margaret Laing, *Edward Heath, Prime Minister* (London, 1972), p. 34; see also Heath, *The Course of My Life*, pp. 13–22.
26 *Evening Standard*, 28 July 1965; and see also Campbell, *Edward Heath*, p. 14.
27 Campbell, *Edward Heath*, p. 23.
28 Campbell, *Edward Heath*, p. 38.
29 Healey, *The Time of My Life*, pp. 26–28; Heath, *The Course of My Life*, p. 47.
30 Heath, *The Course of My Life*, pp. 42–44.
31 Heath, *The Course of My Life*, pp. 52–56.
32 Heath, *The Course of My Life*, p. 103.
33 Heath, *The Course of My Life*, p. 33.
34 Heath, *The Course of My Life*, p. 101.
35 Campbell, *Edward Heath*, p. 60.
36 As suggested in Campbell, *Edward Heath*, p. 18.
37 Campbell, *Edward Heath*, pp. 71–107.
38 Campbell, *Edward Heath*, pp. 132–133.
39 Campbell, *Edward Heath*, p. 106.
40 Cate Haste, *Rules of Desire: Sex in Britain: World War I to the Present* (London, 1994), p. 151.
41 *Sunday Pictorial*, 16 August 1953.
42 Healey, *The Time of My Life*, p. 32.
43 Heath, *The Course of My Life*, pp. 12–13; Campbell, *Edward Heath*, pp. 53–56.
44 *Private Eye*, 6 August 1965.
45 *Private Eye*, 6 August 1965.
46 *Daily Sketch*, 28 July 1965.
47 *Daily Mirror*, 28 July 1965.
48 Quotations from Booker, *The Neophiliacs*, pp. 27–28.
49 Booker, *The Neophiliacs*, p. 28.
50 *Observer Magazine*, 10 October 1965.
51 See Shepherd, *Iain Macleod*, pp. 387–388.
52 Booker, *The Neophiliacs*, p. 28.
53 *Spectator*, 30 July 1965.
54 Benn diary, 2 August 1965.
55 Crossman diary, 2 August 1965.
56 Hansard, 2 August 1965; Campbell, *Edward Heath*, pp. 191–192.
57 Campbell, *Edward Heath*, p. 193.

58 Campbell, *Edward Heath*, pp. xv, 255. Churchill, with his writing, painting and bricklaying, is his obvious twentieth-century rival. However, Churchill's books have not worn terribly well and his painting and bricklaying were not of professional or international class. Heath's seamanship undoubtedly was, while as a musician he was about as good as an amateur can conceivably be.

69 *Spectator*, 15 October 1965.

60 Campbell, *Edward Heath*, pp. 199–200.

61 Benn diary, 23 November 1965; on the Tories and Rhodesia, see Campbell, *Edward Heath*, pp. 204–205.

62 King and Wybrow, eds, *British Political Opinion*, pp. 9, 205–206.

63 Campbell, *Edward Heath*, pp. 200–201.

64 *Spectator*, 14 January 1966.

65 See Levin, *The Pendulum Years*, p. 190.

66 Weight, *Patriots*, pp. 486–487.

67 Morgan, *Callaghan*, p. 235.

68 Benn diary, 24 February 1966.

69 Oppenheimer, 'Muddling Through', p. 129; Shepherd, *Iain Macleod*, pp. 433–434; Morgan, *Callaghan*, p. 235.

70 'Pillars of Society 6: Wedgie the Whizz', in Ingrams, ed., *The Life and Times of Private Eye*, p. 119.

71 See Morgan, *Labour People*, pp. 303–304.

72 Crossman diary, 24 May 1965.

73 Gaitskell diary, late July 1956, quoted in Philip M. Williams, *Hugh Gaitskell* (Oxford, 1982), p. 279.

74 S. Crosland, *Tony Crosland*, p. 204.

75 Williams, *Inside Number 10*, p. 255.

76 Pimlott, *The Queen*, pp. 362–363.

77 Benn diary, 10 March 1965.

78 Benn diary, 11 March 1965.

79 Benn diary, 14 October and 2 November 1965; see also Pimlott, *The Queen*, pp. 365–366.

80 Benn diary, 17 December 1965.

81 Benn diary, 31 December 1965.

82 Benn diary, 15 June 1966.

83 On the origins of MinTech see Horner, 'The Road to Scarborough', pp. 48–71; Richard Coopey, 'Industrial Policy in the White Heat of the Scientific Revolution', in Coopey, Fielding and Tiratsoo, eds, *The Wilson Governments 1964–1970*, pp. 108–110; Woodward, 'Labour's Economic Performance', p. 87.

84 Quoted in Booker, *The Neophiliacs*, p. 283.

85 Crossman diary, 10 May 1965.

86 Richard Marsh interviewed in Mitchell and Wienir, eds, *Last Time*, p. 108.

87 On Cousins and Snow at MinTech, see Ponting, *Breach of Promise*, pp. 35, 270; Ziegler, *Wilson*, p. 172.

88 Tomlinson, *Economic Policy*, p. 75.

89 Sampson, *Anatomy of Britain*, p. 281; Nigel Harris, *Competition and the Corporate State:*

British Conservatives, the State and Industry, 1945–1964 (London, 1972), p. 157; Childs, *Britain since 1945*, pp. 138–139; Jefferys, *Retreat from New Jerusalem*, p. 125; Dell, *A Strange Eventful History*, pp. 82–96.

90 Ponting, *Breach of Promise*, pp. 108–109; Pimlott, *Harold Wilson*, pp. 278–280; Woodward, 'Labour's Economic Performance', p. 86; Tomlinson, *Economic Policy*, pp. 70–75; *Let's Go with Labour for the New Britain*.
91 Pimlott, *Harold Wilson*, p. 280.
92 Brown, *In My Way*, pp. 87, 93, 110.
93 Crossman diary, 18 February 1965; on Brown's high reputation, see Ponting, *Breach of Promise*, p. 33.
94 Crossman diary, 3 January 1965.
95 Brown, *In My Way*, p. 91; Ponting, *Breach of Promise*, p. 110.
96 Bill Rodgers interviewed in Mitchell and Wienir, eds, *Last Time*, pp. 89–90.
97 See Dell, *The Chancellors*, pp. 307–309.
98 Morgan, *Callaghan*, p. 186.
99 S. Crosland, *Tony Crosland*, p. 127.
100 Jenkins, *A Life at the Centre*, pp. 156–157.
101 Radice, *Friends and Rivals*, p. 139.
102 Quoted in Paterson, *Tired and Emotional*, pp. 174–175.
103 Paterson, *Tired and Emotional*, p. 169.
104 Pimlott, *Harold Wilson*, p. 329.
105 Castle diary, 31 May 1965.
106 As counted by Ponting, *Breach of Promise*, p. 34.
107 Pimlott, *Harold Wilson*, pp. 330–331.
108 Healey, *The Time of My Life*, p. 298.
109 Castle diary, 13 April 1965; Wilson, *The Labour Government*, p. 94.
110 Hennessy, *The Prime Minister*, p. 300. Hennessy suggests that Brown may have been beaten on the Conservative side by the Marquess of Salisbury's record in the 1950s.
111 Brown, *In My Way*, p. 99; Paterson, *Tired and Emotional*, p. 180. The latter is a much better version, although some details – the beard, the pink trousers, the Plan on the back seat, and so on – may have become slightly embellished over time.
112 Ponting, *Breach of Promise*, pp. 112–113.
113 Pimlott, *Harold Wilson*, pp. 360–362.
114 Pimlott, *Harold Wilson*, p. 362; Hennessy, *The Prime Minister*, p. 304.
115 Crossman diary, 3 August 1965.
116 See Pimlott, *Harold Wilson*, pp. 362–364.
117 Crossman diary, 12 September 1965; see also Tomlinson, *Economic Policy*, p. 88.
118 Tomlinson, *Economic Policy*, p. 75.
119 See Ponting, *Breach of Promise*, pp. 113–114; Dell, *The Chancellors*, p. 331; Tomlinson, *Economic Policy*, pp. 75, 88.
120 For a comparison of the National Plan's forecasts and actual performance, see Ponting, *Breach of Promise*, p. 118.
121 Tomlinson, *Economic Policy*, pp. 88–89; and see also Pimlott, *Harold Wilson*, p. 364, which comes to a similar conclusion.

122 Brown, *In My Way*, p. 104.
123 Crossman diary, 18 April 1965.
124 Dell, *The Chancellors*, p. 309.
125 Brown, *In My Way*, p. 104; see Ponting, *Breach of Promise*, pp. 109–112.
126 *Tribune*, 20 August and 24 September 1965, quoted in Foot, *The Politics of Harold Wilson*, p. 308.
127 King diary, 15 August 1965.
128 King diary, 30 August 1965.
129 Crossman diary, 12 September 1965.
130 Benn diary, 13 March 1966.
131 Benn diary, 20 February 1966.
132 King and Wybrow, eds, *British Political Opinion*, pp. 9, 187–188.
133 Timmins, *The Five Giants*, pp. 217, 225.
134 See Ziegler, *Wilson*, p. 189; Radice, *Friends and Rivals*, p. 134.
135 Richard Marsh, *Off the Rails* (London, 1978), pp. 94–95.
136 Quoted in Hennessy, *Muddling Through*, p. 255.
137 S. Crosland, *Tony Crosland*, p. 172.
138 On the sense of economic optimism, see Morgan, *Callaghan*, pp. 226–230.
139 Crossman diary, 1 February 1966.
140 Crossman diary, 19 February 1966.

Part Two

10 BRITAIN IN 1965

1 Malcolm Bradbury, *The Modern British Novel* (London, 1993), p. 308; see also Margaret Drabble, *Angus Wilson: A Biography* (London, 1996), pp. 335–343; Graham Martin, 'Anthony Powell and Angus Wilson', in Boris Ford, ed., *The New Pelican Guide to English Literature: Volume 8: From Orwell to Naipaul* (revised edition: London, 1998), pp. 184–199; Stevenson, *The British Novel since the Thirties*, p. 136.
2 Malcolm Bradbury, *Possibilities: Essays on the State of the Novel* (London, 1972), p. 211.
3 Drabble, *Angus Wilson*, p. 341.
4 Bernard Bergonzi, *The Situation of the Novel* (London, 1970), p. 158.
5 Angus Wilson, *Late Call* (London, 1964), p. 157: on Harold as the personification of the New Town ethos, see Mark Clapson, *Invincible Green Suburbs, Brave New Towns* (Manchester, 1998), p. 144.
6 Wilson, *Late Call*, p. 67.
7 Wilson, *Late Call*, p. 180.
8 Wilson, *Late Call*, p. 298. On the character of Sylvia and the resolution of the novel, see Martin, 'Anthony Powell and Angus Wilson', pp. 195–197; Bergonzi, *The Situation of the Novel*, p. 158; Stevenson, *The British Novel since the Thirties*, p. 134.
9 See Drabble, *Angus Wilson*, pp. 312–315, 322–323, 337.
10 Wilson, *Late Call*, pp. 143–144.
11 Paul Addison, *Now the War is Over*, p. 79; Andrew Saint, 'The New Towns', in Ford, ed., *Modern Britain*, pp. 147–149; Clapson, *Invincible Green Suburbs, Brave New Towns*, p. 45.

12 Saint, 'The New Towns', p. 147.
13 Saint, 'The New Towns', p. 150.
14 Saint, 'The New Towns', pp. 154–155, and see <http://www.stevenage.gov.uk/about/history/index.htm>.
15 *The Times*, 27 July 1955; Gordon E. Cherry, *Town Planning in Britain since 1900: The Rise and Fall of the Planning Ideal* (Oxford, 1996), pp. 151–152.
16 Saint, 'The New Towns', pp. 150–151; Joseph Rykwert, 'Architecture', in Ford, ed., *Modern Britain*, p. 268.
17 *The Times*, 30 November 1962.
18 Rykwert, 'Architecture', p. 268.
19 *The Times*, 21 February 2005.
20 Cherry, *Town Planning in Britain*, pp. 151–153; Clapson, *Invincible Green Suburbs, Brave New Towns*, p. 45.
21 *The Times*, 4 May 1972.
22 *The Times*, 4 January 1967, 23 February 1970.
23 Mark Clapson, *A Social History of Milton Keynes: Middle England/Edge City* (London, 2004), pp. xi, 37.
24 Rykwert, 'Architecture', p. 273; Clapson, *A Social History of Milton Keynes*, pp. 2, 40–41.
25 Clapson, *A Social History of Milton Keynes*, pp. 45–46.
26 See Clapson, *A Social History of Milton Keynes*, pp. 54, 58, 65.
27 Levin, *The Pendulum Years*, pp. 330–331; *The Times*, 30 January 1969; Briggs, *Competition*, p. 335.
28 *Radio Times*, 28 December 1961; see Stuart Laing, 'Banging in Some Reality: The Original Z-Cars', in John Corner, ed., *Popular Television in Britain* (London, 1991), pp. 127–134; Stuart Laing, *Representations of Working-Class Life*, pp. 169–181; Sandbrook, *Never Had It So Good*, pp. 379–382.
29 On *The Prisoner*, see Chapman, *Saints and Avengers*, pp. 49–51.
30 Briggs, *Competition*, p. 338.
31 See Clapson, *Invincible Green Suburbs, Brave New Towns*, pp. 9. 141; Jeff Evans, *The Penguin TV Companion* (second edition: London, 2003), pp. 515–516.
32 Clapson, *Invincible Green Suburbs, Brave New Towns*, p. 49.
33 Addison, *Now the War is Over*, p. 83.
34 Gina Spreckley quoted in Akhtar and Humphries, *The Fifties and Sixties*, p. 61.
35 See Akhtar and Humphries, *The Fifties and Sixties*, pp. 59–60.
36 Quoted in Clapson, *Invincible Green Suburbs, Brave New Towns*, p. 100.
37 *The Times*, 10 September 1968.
38 Clapson, *A Social History of Milton Keynes*, pp. 71–3; *New Society*, 19 January 1967.
39 *North Bucks Times*, 1 February 1967, quoted in Clapson, *A Social History of Milton Keynes*, p. 64.
40 See Clapson, *Invincible Green Suburbs, Brave New Towns*, pp. 45–47; Clapson, *A Social History of Milton Keynes*, pp. 112, 168.
41 Marwick, *British Society since 1945*, p. 118.
42 Hylton, *Magical History Tour*, p. 38.
43 John Benson, *The Rise of Consumer Society in Britain 1880–1980* (London, 1994), p. 41.
44 See Rosemary Scott, *The Female Consumer* (London, 1976); Benson, *The Rise of*

Consumer Society, pp. 69, 192.
45 *Independent*, 18 March 2003.
46 See Lawrence Black, '*Which?*craft in Post-War Britain: The Consumers' Association and the Politics of Affluence', *Albion* 36: 1, Spring 2004, pp. 52–66.
47 See Akhtar and Humphries, *The Fifties and Sixties*, pp. 160–161.
48 On the democratisation of style, see Jackson, *The Sixties*, p. 36.
49 Hopkins, *The New Look*, p. 430; Miriam Akhtar and Steve Humphries, *Some Liked It Hot: The British on Holiday at Home and Abroad* (London, 2000), pp. 10–53; Sandbrook, *Never Had It So Good*, pp. 123–125.
50 Clayson, *Beat Merchants*, p. 86; Weight, *Patriots*, p. 507.
51 Akhtar and Humphries, *Some Liked It Hot*, pp. 7–8; Benson, *The Rise of Consumer Society*, pp. 94, 171.
52 Benson, *The Rise of Consumer Society*, p. 89; Akhtar and Humphries, *Some Liked It Hot*, pp. 73ff.
53 Jeffrey Hill, *Sport, Leisure and Culture in Twentieth-Century Britain* (London, 2002), p. 83; Akhtar and Humphries, *Some Liked It Hot*, pp. 34–35.
54 *The Times*, 1 and 8 February 1969.
55 Akhtar and Humphries, *Some Liked It Hot*, pp. 24–25.
56 *New York Times*, 28 December 1969.
57 Akhtar and Humphries, *Some Liked It Hot*, pp. 46–49.
58 *The Times*, 13 July 1967.
59 On the first package holidays, see Akhtar and Humphries, *Some Liked It Hot*, pp. 105–106; Benson, *The Rise of Consumer Society*, p. 42; and on Horizon in particular, Roger Bray and Vladimir Raitz, *Flight to the Sun: The Story of the Holiday Revolution* (London, 2000).
60 Akhtar and Humphries, *Some Liked It Hot*, pp. 109–10.
61 *The Times*, 2 November 1963.
62 Benson, *The Rise of Consumer Society*, p. 88.
63 Akhtar and Humphries, *Some Liked It Hot*, pp. 32–33, 111–113; Hill, *Sport, Leisure and Culture in Twentieth-Century Britain*, p. 82.
64 Brown, *In My Way*, p. 263.
65 Undated press release, reproduced online at <http://www.carryonline.com/carry/PressRelease-CarryOnAbroad.html>.
66 Akhtar and Humphries, *Some Liked It Hot*, pp. 116–117. See also the BBC2 documentary *The Way We Travelled*, broadcast 17 July 2003.
67 Akhtar and Humphries, *Some Liked It Hot*, pp. 95–97.
68 Hopkins, *The New Look*, p. 463.
69 Weight, *Patriots*, p. 652.
70 *Daily Mail*, 16 October 1964.
71 See *The Times*, 31 May 1961.
72 *The Times*, 9 December 1967.
73 See Sandbrook, *Never Had It So Good*, pp. 128–130, 302–305.
74 See Akhtar and Humphries, *The Fifties and Sixties*, pp. 101–107.
75 Coates and Silburn, *Poverty*, pp. 95–6.
76 David Frost and Antony Jay, *To England with Love* (London, 1967), pp. 52–3.
77 Wilson, *Late Call*, pp. 74–75, 97.

78 Humphrey Carpenter, *Dennis Potter: A Biography* (London, 1999), pp. 164–172; Sandbrook, *Never Had It So Good*, pp. 170–174.
79 Clapson, *Invincible Green Suburbs, Brave New Towns*, pp. 104–105.
80 Geoffrey Moorhouse *Britain in the Sixties: The Other England* (Harmondsworth, 1964), pp. 70, 55.
81 Fielding, *Labour and Cultural Change*, p. 8.
82 'Susan', in Landau, *Growing up in Sixties*, p. 135.
83 'Joan', in Landau, *Growing up in the Sixties*, pp. 34, 37.
84 Frost and Jay, *To England with Love*, pp. 11, 13.
85 Brian Jackson, *Working-Class Community* (Harmondsworth, 1972), p. 169.
86 Jackson, *Working-Class Community*, p. 22.
87 Jackson, *Working-Class Community*, p. 106.
88 Jackson, *Working-Class Community*, pp. 47, 64–65, 70–71.
89 Nick Tiratsoo, 'Labour and its Critics: The Case of the May Day Manifesto Group', in Coopey, Fielding and Tiratsoo, eds *The Wilson Governments*, p. 172.
90 *New Society*, 27 November 1969.
91 Tiratsoo, 'Labour and its Critics', p. 172.
92 Benson, *The Rise of Consumer Society*, p. 168.
93 See, for example, Jonathon Green, *Days in the Life: Voices from the English Underground, 1961–1971* (London, 1998), vi; Jonathon Green, *All Dressed up: The Sixties and the Counter-Culture* (London, 1999), p. 86.
94 McKibbin, *Classes and Cultures*, pp. 84–85.
95 Gardiner, *From the Bomb to the Beatles*, p. 95; Akhtar and Humphries, *The Fifties and Sixties*, pp. 118–121.
96 See Frost and Jay, *To England with Love*, pp. 70–71; the magazine quotation is from Akhtar and Humphries, *The Fifties and Sixties*, p. 121.
97 Weight, *Patriots*, p. 323.
98 CAB 21/4965, 'Recreational Trends in Britain', May 1963.
99 See *Gardener's World* and *Gardening Club*, in Evans, *The Penguin TV Companion*, pp. 280–281; Akhtar and Humphries, *The Fifties and Sixties*, pp. 122–123.
100 See Akhtar and Humphries, *The Fifties and Sixties*, pp. 122–123.
101 Wiener, *English Culture and the Decline of the Industrial Spirit*, p. 49; Robert Colls, *Identity of England* (London, 2002), pp. 203–207.
102 Arthur Bryant, *The National Character* (London, 1934) pp. 22–23.
103 Richard Hoggart, *The Uses of Literacy* (Harmondsworth, 1958), p. 327.
104 See Paul Oliver, 'Great Expectations: Suburban Values and the Role of the Media', in Paul Oliver, Ian Davis and Ian Bentley, eds, *Dunroamin: The Suburban Semi and Its Enemies* (London, 1981), p. 134; Clapson, *Invincible Green Suburbs, Brave New Towns*, pp. 35, 103.
105 Clapson, *A Social History of Milton Keynes*, p. 114.
106 Barry Miles, *Paul McCartney: Many Years From Now* (London, 1997), p. 8.
107 Anthony Sampson, *The New Anatomy of Britain* (London, 1971), p. 427.

11 THE WILD ONES

1 Stanley Cohen, *Folk Devils and Moral Panics: The Creation of the Mods and Rockers* (London, 1972), pp. 29, 195–196.

2. *Daily Mirror*, 30 March 1964.
3. *Daily Mirror*, 1 April 1964.
4. *Daily Express*, 19 May 1964.
5. Cohen, *Folk Devils and Moral Panics*, p. 37
6. For the mayor's comments, see *The Times*, 20 May 1964.
7. *Daily Mirror*, 20 May 1964.
8. Davis, *Youth and the Condition of Britain*, pp. 44–49.
9. See Sandbrook, *Never Had It So Good*, ch. 12.
10. Geoffrey Pearson, *Hooligan: A History of Respectable Fears* (London, 1983), p. 202.
11. See Cohen, *Folk Devils and Moral Panics*, passim; Iain Chambers, *Popular Culture: The Metropolitan Experience* (London, 1986), pp. 41–42.
12. Paul Rock and Stanley Cohen, 'The Teddy Boy', in Bogdanor and Skidelsky, eds, *The Age of Affluence*, pp. 308–309; Davis, *Youth and the Condition of Britain*, pp. 147, 164.
13. Colin MacInnes, *Absolute Beginners* (London, 1980), pp. 62–63.
14. See Humphrey Lyttleton, *I Play as I Please* (London, 1954), pp. 116–125; Jim Goldbolt, *A History of Jazz in Britain, 1919–50* (London, 1984), esp. ch. 12; Chambers, *Urban Rhythms*, p. 48; Gillett, *The Sound of the City*, pp. 258–259.
15. See Nik Cohn, 'Mods', in Paolo Hewitt, ed., *The Sharper Word: A Mod Anthology* (second edition: London, 2002), pp. 137–8; Melly, *Revolt into Style*, p. 24.
16. Levy, *Ready, Steady, Go!*, p. 121.
17. Levy, *Ready, Steady, Go!*, pp. 121–123.
18. On Mod at its peak, see Richard Barnes, *Mods!* (London, 1989); Terry Rawlings, *Mod: A Very British Phenomenon* (London, 2000).
19. Quoted in Harry Shapiro, 'London's Speeding', in Hewitt, ed., *The Sharper Word*, p. 55.
20. Steve Humphries and John Taylor, *The Making of Modern London, 1945–1985* (London, 1986), p. 48.
21. Shapiro, 'London's Speeding', p. 58; Jonathon Green, *All Dressed up*, pp. 42–43.
22. George Marshall, 'Spirit of '69', in Hewitt, ed., *The Sharper Word*, p. 155.
23. *The Mod*, November 1964, quoted in Weight, *Patriots*, p. 392.
24. Nik Cohn, 'Yellow Socks Are Out', in Hewitt, ed., *The Sharper Word*, p. 19; Laurie, *The Teenage Revolution*, p. 25; Green, *All Dressed up*, p. 45; Davis, *Youth and the Condition of Britain*, pp. 187–189.
25. Jamie Mandelkau, *Buttons: The Making of a President* (London, 1971), p. 21.
26. Quoted in Leslie, *Fab*, p. 153.
27. Cohen, *Folk Devils and Moral Panics*, pp. 32, 151.
28. *New Statesman*, 1 May 1964.
29. Terry Shanahan quoted in Akhtar and Humphries, *The Fifties and Sixties*, p. 51.
30. *Evening Standard*, 18 May 1964; *Sheffield Star*, 18 May 1964, both quoted in Cohen, *Folk Devils and Moral Panics*, pp. 51–52.
31. Quotations from Cohen, *Folk Devils and Moral Panics*, p. 55.
32. *Daily Express*, 19 and 20 May 1964; Cohen, *Folk Devils and Moral Panics*, pp. 108–110. For a slightly different version of Dr Simpson's remarks, see *The Times*, 19 May 1964.
33. *The Times*, 22 May 1964.
34. Andrew Motion, *The Lamberts: George, Constant and Kit* (London, 1986), pp. 313–318.

35 Chambers, *Urban Rhythms*, p. 57.
36 *New Musical Express*, 17 July 1964.
37 *Daily Mail*, 20 April 1964.
38 Norman, *Shout!*, pp. 227–228.
39 Norman, *Shout!*, pp. 238–239.
40 Quoted in *Observer*, 19 November 2000.
41 Castle diary, 15 June 1965.
42 Benn diary, 13 June 1965.
43 *New Musical Express*, 25 June 1965.
44 Levy, *Ready, Steady, Go!*, p. 199.
45 Clayson, *Beat Merchants*, p. 230.
46 Badman, *The Beatles off the Record*, p. 137.
47 *Melody Maker*, 9 November 1963.
48 Quoted in Pressley, *Changing Times*, p. 41.
49 Wyman, *Stone Alone*, p. 260.
50 Norman, *Shout!*, p. 232.
51 *New Musical Express*, 2 April 1965.
52 *New Musical Express*, 6 August 1965.
53 Interview on 30 July 1965, quoted in Badman, *The Beatles off the Record*, p. 163.
54 *New Musical Express*, 17 June 1966.
55 MacDonald, *The People's Music*, p. 44.
56 MacDonald, *Revolution in the Head*, p. 329.
57 Miles, *Paul McCartney*, x. On the myth of Lennonism, see MacDonald, *Revolution in the Head*, p. 330 and *passim*; Miles, *Paul McCartney*, pp. 283–284, 586.
58 MacDonald, *The People's Music*, p. 47.
59 MacDonald, *Revolution in the Head*, pp. 11–12.
60 Norman, *Shout!*, pp. 32–33.
61 MacDonald, *Revolution in the Head*, p. 211.
62 Norman, *Shout!*, p. 235; Miles, *Paul McCartney*, pp. 101–128; MacDonald, *Revolution in the Head*, p. 136.
63 MacDonald, *The People's Music*, pp. 92–93.
64 Miles, *Paul McCartney*, pp. 219–221.
65 Miles, *Paul McCartney*, pp. 221, 237.
66 *New Musical Express*, 24 June 1966.
67 Norman, *Shout!*, pp. 257–258; MacDonald, *Revolution in the Head*, pp. 144–145.
68 See Miller, *Flowers in the Dustbin*, pp. 226–227; Miles, *Paul McCartney*, pp. 187–189; Badman, *The Beatles off the Record*, pp. 119–120.
69 Badman, *The Beatles off the Record*, pp. 146–7.
70 See MacDonald, *Revolution in the Head*, pp. 164–170, 201–205.
71 Miles, *Paul McCartney*, p. 191.
72 Miles, *Paul McCartney*, pp. 192–193.
73 MacDonald, *Revolution in the Head*, pp. 110–111, 118–122.
74 MacDonald, *Revolution in the Head*, pp. 122, 136–138.
75 *New Musical Express*, 22 October 1965.
76 See MacDonald, *Revolution in the Head*, pp. 144–148.

77 Miller, *Flowers in the Dustbin*, p. 229.
78 Badman, *The Beatles off the Record*, p. 188.
79 See McCartney's recollections of recording 'Yesterday' in Miles, *Paul McCartney*, pp. 205–207.
80 Norman, *Shout!*, p. 250.
81 MacDonald, *Revolution in the Head*, xiii. MacDonald's discussion of the Beatles' influences is quite superb and this section owes a great deal to his work.
82 Paytress, *The Rolling Stones off the Record*, p. 101.
83 See Allan F. Moore, 'The Brilliant Career of *Sgt. Pepper*', in Anthony Aldgate, James Chapman and Arthur Marwick, eds, *Windows on the Sixties: Exploring Key Texts of Media and Culture* (London, 2000), p. 141.
84 Tim Riley, 'For the Beatles: Notes on their Achievement', *Popular Music* 6: 3, 1987, p. 269.
85 Miles, *Paul McCartney*, p. 45.
86 The original lyrics are reprinted in Badman, *The Beatles off the Record*, pp. 165–166.
87 Palmer, *All You Need is Love*, pp. 213–214.
88 Miles, *Paul McCartney*, pp. 137–138.
89 John Osborne, *The Entertainer* (London, 1957), p. 7.
90 See Stephen Lacey, *British Realist Theatre: The New Wave in Context, 1956–1965* (London, 1995), pp. 125, 129.
91 See Bacon, *London Live*, p. 10.
92 Palmer, *All You Need is Love*, p. 225; Miles, *Paul McCartney*, p. 23.
93 'Dave Dee, Dozy, Beaky, Mick and Tich', in Larkin, ed., *The Virgin Encyclopedia of Sixties Music*, p. 141.
94 Clayson, *Beat Merchants*, p. 140.
95 Hasted, 'Ready, Steady, Kinks', p. 56.
96 *Melody Maker*, 22 August 1964.
97 Savage, *The Kinks*, pp. 57–58. The Kinks' song pre-dated 'Norwegian Wood', on which George Harrison played a sitar for the first time, by about two months.
98 Savage, *The Kinks*, p. 60.
99 Gillett, *The Sound of the City*, pp. 276–277.
100 Savage, *The Kinks*, p. 71.
101 See Clayson, *Beat Merchants*, p. 207.
102 Savage, *The Kinks*, p. 96.
103 Hasted, 'Ready, Steady, Kinks', p. 60.
104 Frith and Horne, *Art into Pop*, pp. 81, 86; MacDonald, *Revolution in the Head*, xiii–xv.
105 Quoted in Hasted, 'Ready, Steady, Kinks', p. 50.
106 Frith and Horne, *Art into Pop*, p. 101; Motion, *The Lamberts*, pp. 301–302.
107 Dave Marsh, *Before I Get Old: The Story of the Who* (New York, 1983), p. 170; Frith and Horne, *Art into Pop*, p. 101; Motion, *The Lamberts*, p. 314.
108 MacDonald, *Revolution in the Head*, xv.
109 Chambers, *Urban Rhythms*, p. 99.
110 See MacDonald, *Revolution in the Head*, pp. 337–342.
111 MacDonald, *Revolution in the Head*, pp. 335–336.

112 Miles, *Paul McCartney*, pp. 280–281; MacDonald, *Revolution in the Head*, pp. 164, 189–190.
113 *New Musical Express*, 24 June 1966.
114 See MacDonald, *Revolution in the Head*, p. 170.
115 Badman, *The Beatles off the Record*, p. 222.
116 *New Musical Express*, 27 July 1966.
117 MacDonald, *Revolution in the Head*, pp. 168–169.
118 *New Musical Express*, 24 June 1966.
119 Norman, *Shout!*, pp. 262–263.
120 Melly, *Revolt into Style*, pp. 84–85.
121 There is an excellent discussion of its significance in MacDonald, *The People's Music*, pp. 96–98.
122 Norman, *Shout!*, pp. 256–257; Badman, *The Beatles off the Record*, pp. 218–219.
123 *Evening Standard*, 4 March 1966.
124 Quoted in Weight, *Patriots*, p. 451.
125 Norman, *Shout!*, p. 259.
126 *New Musical Express*, 19 August 1966; Badman, *The Beatles off the Record*, pp. 232–234.
127 See Badman, *The Beatles off the Record*, p. 202.
128 Norman, *Shout!*, pp. 260–261; Badman, *The Beatles off the Record*, pp. 244–245.
129 Badman, *The Beatles off the Record*, pp. 244–245.

12 DEDICATED FOLLOWERS OF FASHION

1 Press release, undated [early 1966], online at <http://kinks.it.rit.edu/images/friis-PressDedicated.jpg>.
2 Savage, *The Kinks*, pp. 64–65.
3 Aitken, *The Young Meteors*, pp. 34–36.
4 Mary Quant, *Quant by Quant* (London, 1967), pp. 7–38; Melly, *Revolt into Style*, pp. 163–165; Levy, *Ready, Steady Go!*, pp. 47–49.
5 Quant, *Quant by Quant*, p. 41.
6 Davis, *Youth and the Condition of Britain*, pp. 178–179.
7 Quoted in Levy, *Ready, Steady, Go!*, p. 49.
8 Quant, *Quant by Quant*, pp. 40–45.
9 Ernestine Carter, *Mary Quant's London* (London, 1973), p. 4; Lewis, *The Fifties*, pp. 204–205; Oldham, *Stoned*, pp. 90–96; Max Décharné, *King's Road: The Rise and Fall of the Hippest Street in the World* (London, 2005).
10 Quant, *Quant by Quant*, p. 41.
11 Pearson Phillips, 'The New Look', in Sissons and French, eds, *Age of Austerity*, pp. 115–136; Hopkins, *The New Look*, pp. 95–96.
12 Quoted in Akhtar and Humphries, *The Fifties and Sixties*, pp. 39–40.
13 Quant, *Quant by Quant*, pp. 46–47; Levy, *Ready, Steady, Go!*, pp. 52–53.
14 Quant, *Quant by Quant*, pp. 48–49, 91–92.
15 Marnie Fogg, *Boutique: A '60s Cultural Phenomenon* (London, 2003), p. 26.
16 Roma Fairley, *A Bomb in the Collection: Fashion with the Lid off* (Brighton, 1969), p. 51.
17 Quant, *Quant by Quant*, pp. 117–120; Carter, *Mary Quant's London*, p. 6; Levy, *Ready, Steady, Go!*, pp. 53–54, 213; Fogg, *Boutique*, p. 26.

18 Quant, *Quant by Quant*, p. 80.
19 Fogg, *Boutique*, pp. 22–23.
20 Twiggy Lawson with Penelope Dening, *Twiggy in Black and White: An Autobiography* (London, 1997), p. 42.
21 Quant, *Quant by Quant*, p. 115.
22 Quant, *Quant by Quant*, p. 79.
23 Georgina Howell, *In Vogue* (London, 1975), p. 278.
24 Quoted in Aitken, *The Young Meteors*, p. 14.
25 See Fogg, *Boutique*, p. 7.
26 Elizabeth Wilson, *Adorned in Dreams: Fashion and Modernity* (London, 1995), p. 152.
26 Fogg, *Boutique*, pp. 14–17.
28 Aitken, *The Young Meteors*, p. 13.
29 Quant, *Quant by Quant*, p. 161.
30 Wilson, *Adorned in Dreams*, p. 112.
31 See Moureen Nolan and Roma Singleton, 'Mini-Renaissance', in Sara Maitland, ed., *Very Heaven: Looking Back at the 1960s* (London, 1988), p. 23.
32 Advertisements reprinted in Barbara Bernard, *Fashion in the 60s* (London, 1978), pp. 14 and 76; see also Levy, *Ready, Steady, Go!*, pp. 211–212.
33 Quant, *Quant by Quant*, p. 161.
34 Vidal Sassoon, *I'm Sorry I Kept You Waiting, Madam* (London, 1967), pp. 120–121; Levy, *Ready, Steady, Go!*, pp. 35–47.
35 Quoted in Levy, *Ready, Steady, Go!*, p. 37.
36 On the slang used to describe the Look, see Quant, *Quant by Quant*, p. 79.
37 Whiteley, 'Shaping the Sixties', p. 27.
38 Quant, *Quant by Quant*, pp. 138–139.
39 *Observer*, 7 March 1965; and see Topham, *Where's My Space Age?*, pp. 75–76.
40 *Observer*, 7 March 1965.
41 *Queen*, 14 July 1965.
42 Advertisement reprinted in Garner, *Sixties Design*, p. 106.
43 Booker, *The Neophiliacs*, p. 17.
44 James Chapman, '*The Avengers*: Television and Popular Culture during the "High Sixties"', in Aldgate, Marwick and Chapman, eds, *Windows on the Sixties*, p. 54; Bernard, *Fashion in the 60s*, p. 30; Fogg, *Boutique*, pp. 36–38.
45 *Daily Mail*, 27 September 1965.
46 See Chapman, *Saints and Avengers*, pp. 74–75.
47 Unknown interviewee, quoted in Pressley, *Changing Times*, p. 23.
48 Quoted in Aitken, *The Young Meteors*, p. 34.
49 Laurie, *The Teenage Revolution*, p. 151.
50 *Guardian*, 4 December 1965.
51 Quoted in Levy, *Ready, Steady, Go!*, p. 51.
52 Aitken, *The Young Meteors*, p. 13; Lewis, *The Fifties*, p. 204.
53 Quoted in Jackson, *The Sixties*, p. 42.
54 *Guardian*, 10 October 1967.
55 Carter, *Mary Quant's London*, p. 10; Bernard, *Fashion in the 60s*, p. 38.
56 Quant, *Quant by Quant*, p. 161.

57 Green, *All Dressed Up*, p. 76.
58 Quant, *Quant by Quant*, p. 157.
59 Quant, *Quant by Quant*, pp. 157–158.
60 *Guardian*, 10 October 1967.
61 Green, *All Dressed up*, p. 76.
62 *Weekend Telegraph*, 16 April 1965.
63 Germaine Greer, *The Female Eunuch* (London, 1993), pp. 68–69.
64 Stuart Laing, 'The Production of Literature', in Alan Sinfield, ed., *Society and Literature 1945–1970* (London, 1983), p. 129.
65 Jackson, *The Middle Classes 1900–1950*, p. 117; McKibbin, *Classes and Cultures*, p. 508.
66 Hopkins, *The New Look*, pp. 328, 336.
67 Sheila Rowbotham, *A Century of Women: The History of Women in Britain and the United States* (London, 1999), p. 297.
68 See Fogg, *Boutique*, p. 92.
69 Benson, *The Rise of Consumer Society*, p. 168.
70 Penny Tinkler, 'Girlhood and Growing up', in Ina Zweiniger-Bargielowska, ed., *Women in Twentieth-Century Britain* (Harlow, 2001), pp. 46–47.
71 Laurie, *The Teenage Revolution*, p. 62.
72 Laurie, *The Teenage Revolution*, p. 63.
73 Fogg, *Boutique*, pp. 92–95.
74 *Honey*, January 1965.
75 Aitken, *The Young Meteors*, pp. 63–65.
76 Booker, *The Neophiliacs*, pp. 43–44.
77 Martin Harrison, *Young Meteors: British Photojournalism, 1957–1965* (London, 1998), pp. 14–16, 56–58; Aitken, *The Young Meteors*, pp. 37–38; Levy, *Ready, Steady, Go!*, pp. 21–22.
78 Aitken, *The Young Meteors*, pp. 36, 39.
79 *Sunday Times Colour Magazine*, 10 May 1964.
80 Aitken, *The Young Meteors*, p. 42.
81 Levy, *Ready, Steady, Go!*, p. 32.
82 Harrison, *Young Meteors*, p. 58.
83 Aitken, *The Young Meteors*, pp. 41–42.
84 Levy, *Ready, Steady, Go!*, pp. 16–19; Harrison, *Young Meteors*, p. 97.
85 Aitken, *The Young Meteors*, p. 40; Levy, *Ready, Steady, Go!*, pp. 20–22.
86 Levy, *Ready, Steady, Go!*, p. 21; Harrison, *Young Meteors*, pp. 97–98.
87 Transcript of interview by Charles Gandee of *Talk* magazine, online at <http://www.pdnonline.com/legends/bailey/interview01.shtml>.
88 Melly, *Revolt into Style*, p. 160.
89 Quoted in Levy, *Ready, Steady, Go!*, p. 27.
90 *Sunday Times Colour Magazine*, 10 May 1964.
91 George Melly, quoted in Levy, *Ready, Steady, Go!*, p. 28.
92 Melly, *Revolt into Style*, p. 160.
93 Quoted in Aitken, *The Young Meteors*, p. 58.
94 Quoted in Alexander Walker, *Hollywood, England: The British Film Industry in the Sixties* (London, 1974), p. 293.
95 Melly, *Revolt into Style*, p. 162.

96 On Kennington and Cowan, see *Independent on Sunday*, 9 June 2002; David Alan Mellor, 'Realism, Satire, Blow-ups: Photography and the Cult of Social Modernisation', in Stephens and Stout, eds, *Art and the 60s*, p. 85. See also the interviews with Kennington on the BBC2 documentary *The Real Blow-Up*, broadcast 10 August 2002.
97 Jean Shrimpton, *The Truth About Modelling* (London, 1965), pp. 12–153; Jean Shrimpton, with Unity Hall, *An Autobiography* (London, 1990), pp. 7–42.
98 Levy, *Ready, Steady, Go!*, p. 29.
99 Aitken, *The Young Meteors*, p. 40; Shrimpton, *An Autobiography*, pp. 45–78.
100 Shrimpton, *An Autobiography*, p. 60.
101 Shrimpton, *An Autobiography*, p. 5.
102 Levy, *Ready, Steady, Go!*, p. 30.
103 *Vogue*, November 1999.
104 Lawson, *Twiggy in Black and White*, p. 5.
105 Shrimpton, *An Autobiography*, pp. 71–72.
106 Shrimpton, *An Autobiography*, pp. 77–83.
107 *Newsweek*, 10 May 1965; Shrimpton, *An Autobiography*, p. 106; 'Jean Shrimpton in Melbourne', unattributed essay, online at 'Milesago: Australasian Music and Popular Culture, 1964–1975', <http://www.milesago.com/Features/shrimpton.htm>.
108 *Melbourne Sun News-Pictorial*, 1 November 1965.
109 'Jean Shrimpton in Melbourne'.
110 Shrimpton, *An Autobiography*, p. 109.
111 Shrimpton, *An Autobiography*, pp. 106–107, 109.
112 Fogg, *Boutique*, pp. 32–38.
113 Quoted in Marwick, *The Sixties*, p. 66.
114 'Jean Shrimpton in Melbourne'.
115 Mary Quant, 'The Miniskirt', in John Mitchinson, ed., *British Greats* (London, 2000), p. 139.
116 Unknown interviewee, quoted in Pressley, *Changing Times*, p. 107.
117 Booker, *The Neophiliacs*, p. 294; Levy, *Ready, Steady, Go!*, p. 209.
118 Aitken, *The Young Meteors*, pp. 13, 18; Levy, *Ready, Steady, Go!*, p. 219.
119 Jackson, *The Sixties*, p. 37.
120 Quoted in Fogg, *Boutique*, p. 53.
121 Kingsley Amis, *Girl, 20* (London, 1971), p. 134.
122 See Jackson, *The Sixties*, pp. 35–37.
123 Aitken, *The Young Meteors*, p. 15; Whiteley, 'Shaping the Sixties', p. 19; Wilson, *Adorned in Dreams*, p. 174.
124 Quoted in Bernard, *Fashion in the 60s*, p. 16.
125 Fogg, *Boutique*, p. 31.
126 Aitken, *The Young Meteors*, p. 25.
127 Hopkins, *The New Look*, p. 315; Jackson, *The Middle Classes*, pp. 153–167.
128 Tony King, quoted in Oldham, *Stoned*, p. 153; Marwick, *The Sixties*, pp. 429–430.
129 Nik Cohn, 'Yellow Socks Are Out', pp. 17–19; Melly, *Revolt into Style*, p. 167.
130 See Oldham, *Stoned*, p. 77.

131 Aitken, *The Young Meteors*, pp. 26–27; Levy, *Ready, Steady, Go!*, pp. 116–118; Fogg, *Boutique*, p. 67.
132 Richard Barnes, 'Mods', in Hewitt, ed. *The Sharper Word*, pp. 27–28.
133 Nik Cohn, 'Carnaby Street', in Hewitt, ed. *The Sharper Word*, p. 35; Brian Masters, *The Swinging Sixties* (London, 1985), p. 22.
134 Quoted in Levy, *Ready, Steady, Go!*, p. 225.
135 Fogg, *Boutique*, p. 68.
136 Quoted in Aitken, *The Young Meteors*, p. 27.
137 *The Times*, 16 September 1966.
138 *Guardian*, 10 October 1967.
139 Aitken, *The Young Meteors*, p. 35.
140 *Design*, August 1966.
141 See Aitken, *The Young Meteors*, p. 28.
142 Fogg, *Boutique*, p. 64; Levy, *Ready, Steady, Go!*, p. 225.
143 Aitken, *The Young Meteors*, p. 28.
144 Quoted in Levy, *Ready, Steady, Go!*, p. 218.
145 Levy, *Ready, Steady, Go!*, pp. 223–225; Aitken, *The Young Meteors*, p. 26.
146 Levy, *Ready, Steady, Go!*, pp. 223–225.
147 *Weekend Telegraph*, 16 April 1965.

13 THE SWINGING CITY

1 Anthony Haden-Guest, 'Dancing Chic to Chic', *Queen*, June 1966, reprinted in Nicholas Coleridge and Stephen Quinn, eds, *The Sixties in Queen* (London, 1997), pp. 160–163; this also reprints the original guest list.
2 Levy, *Ready, Steady, Go!*, pp. 247–248.
3 Aitken, *The Young Meteors*, pp. 270–271. Clicking and swingingese in original.
4 Jerry White, *London in the Twentieth Century* (London, 2002), p. 60.
5 *Horizon*, April 1947; and see Hewison, *In Anger*, p. 14; Stevenson, *The British Novel since the Thirties*, p. 116.
6 Akhtar and Humphries, *The Fifties and Sixties*, p. 73.
7 White, *London in the Twentieth Century*, p. 59.
8 White, *London in the Twentieth Century*, pp. 64–65.
9 Krishan Kumar, 'The Nationalisation of British Culture', in Stanley Hoffman and Patrick Kitromilides, eds, *Culture and Society in Contemporary Europe* (London, 1981), p. 126.
10 Lacey, *British Realist Theatre*, p. 80; D. J. Taylor, *After the War: The Novel and England since 1945* (London, 1993), p. 70.
11 Kingsley Amis, *Lucky Jim* (London, 1954), p. 250.
12 Moorhouse, *The Other England*, pp. 19–21.
13 Aitken, *The Young Meteors*, p. 296.
14 Jackson, *The Sixties*, p. 36.
15 Lewis, *The Fifties*, p. 229; Briggs, *Competition*, p. 184.
16 Whiteley, 'Shaping the Sixties', p. 25; Harrison, *Young Meteors*, pp. 72–78; Greenslade, *Press Gang*, pp. 147–148.
17 *Sunday Times*, 4 February 1962. The description of the article about Lincoln is from

Booker, *The Neophiliacs*, pp. 47–48; the cover of the magazine is analysed in detail in Mellor, 'Realism, Satire, Blow-ups', pp. 78–79.
18 Aitken, *The Young Meteors*, p. 66.
19 Whiteley, 'Shaping the Sixties', p. 25; Greenslade, *Press Gang*, pp. 152–153.
20 Philip Norman, *Everyone's Gone to the Moon* (London, 1995), p. 22.
21 Levin, *The Pendulum Years*, pp. 185–186.
22 Reprinted in Ingrams, ed., *The Life and Times of Private Eye*, pp. 30–35.
23 White, *London in the Twentieth Century*, p. 345.
24 Booker, *The Neophiliacs*, pp. 20–21.
25 *Weekend Telegraph*, 16 April 1965.
26 *L'Express*, September 1964; *Epoca*, November 1965; both quoted in White, *London in the Twentieth Century*, p. 341.
27 Levy, *Ready, Steady, Go!*, p. 229.
28 Levy, *Ready, Steady, Go!*, p. 226.
29 *Time*, 15 April 1966.
30 *Time*, 22 April 1966.
31 *Time*, 6 May 1966.
32 *Time*, 15 April 1966; Levy, *Ready, Steady, Go!*, p. 227.
33 White, *London in the Twentieth Century*, p. 212.
34 Len Deighton, ed., *Len Deighton's London Dossier* (London, 1967); Hunter Davies, ed., *The New London Spy: A Discreet Guide to the City's Pleasures* (London, 1967); Karl F. Dallas, *Swinging London: A Guide to Where the Action Is* (London, 1967); Piri Halasz, *A Swinger's Guide to London* (New York, 1967).
35 Fogg, *Boutique*, pp. 14, 44–48.
36 Levy, *Ready, Steady, Go!*, pp. 156–157. Levy's use of 'everyone' is revealing.
37 Aitken, *The Young Meteors*, pp. 162–163; and see Levy, *Ready, Steady, Go!*, p. 222.
38 See Sandbrook, *Never Had It So Good*, pp. 131–133, 442–444.
39 Quoted in Miles, *Paul McCartney*, pp. 129–130.
40 White, *London in the Twentieth Century*, p. 346.
41 Melly, *Revolt into Style*, pp. 66–67.
42 See Haden-Guest, 'Dancing Chic to Chic', p. 162.
43 Miles, *Paul McCartney*, pp. 140–142.
44 Melly, *Revolt into Style*, pp. 111–112.
45 Haden-Guest, 'Dancing Chic to Chic', p. 162.
46 Melly, *Revolt into Style*, pp. 106–107; and see Levy, *Ready, Steady, Go!*, pp. 158–162.
47 Miles, *Paul McCartney*, pp. 132–133.
48 Levy, *Ready, Steady, Go!*, p. 161.
49 Quoted in Booker, *The Neophiliacs*, p. 25.
50 Haden-Guest, 'Dancing Chic to Chic', p. 162.
51 Melly, *Revolt into Style*, pp. 107–108.
52 Haden-Guest, 'Dancing Chic to Chic', p. 162; Levy, *Ready, Steady, Go!*, p. 162.
53 Melly, *Revolt into Style*, p. 109; Andrew Loog Oldham, *2Stoned* (London, 2003), pp. 255–256.
54 Melly, *Revolt into Style*, p. 110.
55 See Michael Caine, *What's It All About? The Autobiography* (London, 1992).

56 Aitken, *The Young Meteors*, pp. 238–239.
57 See Levy, *Ready, Steady, Go!*, pp. 56–65.
58 Shrimpton, *An Autobiography*, pp. 73–82; Levy, *Ready, Steady, Go!*, pp. 164–165.
59 Shrimpton, *An Autobiography*, p. 89.
60 Quoted in Levy, *Ready, Steady, Go!*, p. 66.
61 See Shrimpton, *An Autobiography*, p. 85 ff.
62 Shrimpton, *An Autobiography*, p. 111.
63 *Observer*, 15 July 2001.
64 Levy, *Ready, Steady, Go!*, p. 168; Shrimpton, *An Autobiography*, pp. 92–93.
65 Levin, *The Pendulum Years*, p. 34.
66 Norman, *The Stones*, pp. 98–99; Levy, *Ready, Steady, Go!*, p. 193.
67 Norman, *The Stones*, p. 99.
68 Wyman, *Stone Alone*, p. 468; Levy, *Ready, Steady, Go!*, pp. 205–206.
69 *Evening Standard*, 4 February 1966.
70 Norman, *Shout!*, pp. 270–271.
71 Quoted in Miles, *Paul McCartney*, p. 261.
72 On McCartney, Asher and life at Wimpole Street, see Miles, *Paul McCartney*, pp. 101–128, a very detailed account.
73 David Bailey, 'Introduction', in *David Bailey's Box of Pin-Ups* (London, 1965); on the launch of the book, see Hewison, *Too Much*, p. 74; Levy, *Ready, Steady, Go!*, p. 174.
74 *Observer*, 12 December 1965. On the narcissism of the *Box of Pin-Ups*, see also Booker, *The Neophiliacs*, pp. 24–25; Hewison, *Too Much*, pp. 74–75. On Bailey's innovative use of stark white lighting, see Mellor, 'Realism, Satire, Blow-ups', p. 83.
75 See, for example, *Sunday Express*, 19 December 1965.
76 Levy, *Ready, Steady, Go!*, p. 176.
77 See Sandbrook *Never Had It So Good*, chs 6 and 14–17.
78 Quoted in Aitken, *The Young Meteors*, p. 264.
79 See, for example, Masters, *The Swinging Sixties*, pp. 26–27.
80 Caine, *What's It All About?*, p. 159.
81 See Norman, *The Stones*, pp. 124–126; Miles, *Paul McCartney*, pp. 243–248; Vyner, *Groovy Bob*, pp. 99–199.
82 Quoted in Norman, *The Stones*, p. 124.
83 Levy, *Ready, Steady, Go!*, p. 202.
84 Levy, *Ready, Steady, Go!*, p. 68.
85 *Daily Mirror*, 5 November 1963, 5 March 1964; and see Davis, *Youth and the Condition of Britain*, pp. 196–197.
86 Aitken, *The Young Meteors*, pp. 272–273.
87 Levy, *Ready, Steady, Go!*, p. 23.
88 Melly, *Revolt into Style*, p. 17.
89 Frost and Jay, *To England with Love*, p. 85.
90 See Norman, *Shout!*, pp. 6, 15–16, 40–43.
91 See Booker, *The Neophiliacs*, p. 20.
92 The guest list is reprinted in Coleridge and Quinn, eds, *The Sixties in Queen*, pp. 161–162.
93 Wyman, *Stone Alone*, pp. 590–591, 603.

94 Quoted in Aitken, *The Young Meteors*, p. 266.
95 Levy, *Ready, Steady, Go!*, pp. 309–310.
96 Quoted in Eddi Fiegel, *John Barry: A Sixties Theme* (London, 2001), p. 133.
97 Speaking on *The Real Blow-Up* (BBC2, 10 August 2002).
98 Levin, *The Pendulum Years*, p. 358.
99 Quoted in Chapman, *Saints and Avengers*, p. 138.
100 *Daily Mail*, 5 August and 25 June 1966.
101 Briggs, *Competition*, p. 425; Chapman, *Saints and Avengers*, pp. 141–148.
102 Quoted in Levy, *Ready, Steady, Go!*, p. 230.
103 Levy, *Ready, Steady, Go!*, pp. 250–251.
104 Booker, *The Neophiliacs*, p. 298.
105 Robert Murphy, *Sixties British Cinema* (London, 1992), p. 4.
106 Levy, *Ready, Steady, Go!*, p. 353.
107 Transcript of interview by Charles Gandee of *Talk* magazine, online at <http://www.pdnonline.com/legends/bailey/interview01.shtml>.
108 Reprinted in Ingrams, ed., *The Life and Times of Private Eye*, pp. 134–135.
109 Quoted in Harris, Hyde and Smith, eds, *1966 and All That*, p. 45.

14 THE DAY IT ALL STOPPED

1 Crossman diary, 19 March 1966.
2 Crossman diary, 20 March 1966.
3 Castle diary, 4 April 1966.
4 King and Wybrow, eds, *British Political Opinion*, p. 27.
5 See King and Wybrow, eds, *British Political Opinion*, pp. 55–57; Ponting, *Breach of Promise*, p. 160.
6 See Shepherd, *Iain Macleod*, pp. 419–421.
7 Heath, *The Course of My Life*, pp. 281–282; Campbell, *Edward Heath*, pp. 209–211.
8 On the slogan, see Marcia Williams interview in Mitchell and Wienir, eds, *Last Time*, pp. 189–190.
9 *The Times*, 1 March 1966.
10 David Butler and Anthony King, *The British General Election of 1966* (London, 1966), p. 130; Pimlott, *Harold Wilson*, p. 398; Ziegler, *Wilson*, p. 246.
11 Benn diary, 7 and 21 June 1966.
12 Ziegler, *Wilson*, pp. 244, 247; Pimlott, *Harold Wilson*, pp. 396–399.
13 Ponting, *Breach of Promise*, p. 161; Pimlott, *Harold Wilson*, p. 400; Clarke, *Hope and Glory*, p. 302.
14 Ernest Kay, *Pragmatic Premier* (London, 1967), p. 233.
15 Williams, *Inside Number 10*, p. 85.
16 Hansard, 1 March 1966.
17 Callaghan, *Time and Chance*, p. 193; Ponting, *Breach of Promise*, pp. 184–185.
18 Castle diary, 12 May 1966; Ponting, *Breach of Promise*, pp. 186–187; Pimlott, *Harold Wilson*, p. 405.
19 See the narrative in Ponting, *Breach of Promise*, pp. 187–188.
20 Quoted in Wilson, *The Labour Government*, p. 300.
21 Crossman diary, 26 May 1966.

NOTES

22 Crossman diary, 19 May 1966.
23 Hansard, 20 June 1966.
24 Richard Clutterbuck, *Britain in Agony: The Growth of Political Violence* (London, 1978), pp. 34–35.
25 Pimlott, *Harold Wilson*, pp. 407–408.
26 Crossman diary, 21 June 1966.
27 Benn diary, 20 and 28 June 1966.
28 Pimlott, *Harold Wilson*, pp. 407–408.
29 *Tribune*, 24 June 1966.
30 See, for instance, the recollections of one idealistic young activist in Sheila Rowbotham, *Promise of a Dream: Remembering the Sixties* (London, 2000), p. 114.
31 Benn diary, 14 June 1966.
32 Pimlott, *Harold Wilson*, pp. 409–410.
33 Ponting, *Breach of Promise*, pp. 188–190; Pimlott, *Harold Wilson*, pp. 414–415.
34 *Observer*, 9 July 1966; and see Pimlott, *Harold Wilson*, pp. 413–414; Morgan, *Callaghan*, p. 242.
35 Brown, *In My Way*, p. 105.
36 Paterson, *Tired and Emotional*, p. 185.
37 Pimlott, *Harold Wilson*, p. 414.
38 Morgan, *Callaghan*, p. 242.
39 Harold Wilson, 'The Economic Crisis of July/August 1966', 9 August 1966, quoted in Pimlott, *Harold Wilson*, p. 415. This document is Wilson's private memorandum of the crisis, held in the Wilson family papers.
40 Castle diary, 14 June 1966.
41 Pimlott, *Harold Wilson*, p. 415.
42 Crossman diary, 13 July 1966; Morgan, *Callaghan*, p. 241.
43 Jenkins, *A Life at the Centre*, p. 191.
44 Pimlott, *Harold Wilson*, pp. 416–417.
45 Wilson, 'The Economic Crisis', quoted in Pimlott, *Harold Wilson*, p. 418.
46 Jenkins, *A Life at the Centre*, p. 191.
47 Callaghan, *Time and Chance*, p. 198.
48 Ponting, *Breach of Promise*, p. 193; Pimlott, *Harold Wilson*, pp. 417–418.
49 Quoted in Foot, *The Politics of Harold Wilson*, p. 179.
50 See Morgan, *Callaghan*, p. 243.
51 Castle diary, 14 July 1966.
52 Ponting, *Breach of Promise*, p. 194; Pimlott, *Harold Wilson*, pp. 418–419; Morgan, *Callaghan*, p. 243.
53 Castle diary, 14 July 1966.
54 King diary, 18 July 1966.
55 Pimlott, *Harold Wilson*, pp. 420–421; Morgan, *Callaghan*, pp. 243–244.
56 This follows the argument in Ponting, *Breach of Promise*, pp. 192–193.
57 Jenkins, *A Life at the Centre*, p. 192.
58 Castle diary, 6 October 1966.
59 Jenkins, *A Life at the Centre*, pp. 192–193.
60 Benn diary, 16 July 1966.

61 Pimlott, *Harold Wilson*, p. 421.
62 Jenkins, *A Life at the Centre*, pp. 193–194; Morgan, *Callaghan*, pp. 244–245.
63 Castle diary, 18 July 1966.
64 Crossman diary, 18 July 1966.
65 Jenkins, *A Life at the Centre*, p. 194.
66 Castle diary, 18 July 1966; Benn diary, 18 July 1966.
67 Jenkins, *A Life at the Centre*, p. 194.
68 Pimlott, *Harold Wilson*, pp. 424–425.
69 Crossman diary, 19 July 1966.
70 Castle diary, 19 July 1966.
71 Castle diary, 19 July 1966; Crossman diary, 19 July 1966; Pimlott, *Harold Wilson*, pp. 424–425; Morgan, *Callaghan*, p. 245.
72 Benn diary, 19 July 1966.
73 Crossman diary, 20 July 1966.
74 Alexander and Watkins, *The Making of the Prime Minister 1970*, p. 22; Ponting, *Breach of Promise*, pp. 198–199.
75 *The Times*, 20 July 1966.
76 Hansard, 20 July 1966; Alexander and Watkins, *The Making of the Prime Minister 1970*, p. 21; Ponting, *Breach of Promise*, p. 199; Dell, *The Chancellors*, p. 337.
77 *The Times*, 21 July 1966.
78 Pimlott, *Harold Wilson*, pp. 425–426.
79 Pimlott, *Harold Wilson*, pp. 426–427.
80 *The Economist*, 23 July 1966.
81 *The Times*, 21 July 1966.
82 Ponting, *Breach of Promise*, p. 200.
83 David Marquand interviewed in Mitchell and Wienir, eds, *Last Time*, pp. 198–199.
84 Crossman diary, 18 July 1966. Clive Ponting also makes a great deal of the American connection: see Ponting, *Breach of Promise*, pp. 54–56, 191–192.
85 Wilson, *The Labour Government*, p. 6; Pimlott, *Harold Wilson*, pp. 410–412.
86 Quoted in Phillip Whitehead, *The Writing on the Wall: Britain in the Seventies* (London, 1985), p. 7.
87 Marquand interviewed in Mitchell and Wienir, eds, *Last Time*, p. 199.
88 Morgan, *Callaghan*, p. 247.
89 Data from Alexander and Watkins, *The Making of the Prime Minister 1970*, p. 23; Wybrow, *Britain Speaks Out*, p. 79; King and Wybrow, ed., *British Political Opinion*, p. 188.
90 *Observer*, 24 July 1966.
91 Ian Bancroft quoted in Hennessy, *The Prime Minister*, p. 286.
92 Pimlott, *Harold Wilson*, pp. 363–364, 428–430.
93 Crossman diary, 27 July 1966.
94 Benn diary, 27 July 1966.
95 *Sunday Telegraph*, 31 July 1966.
96 *The Times*, 21 July 1966.
97 Crossman diary, 26 July 1966.
98 Crossman diary, 26 July 1966.

99 Morgan, *Callaghan*, p. 247.
100 'Introduction' in Ingrams, ed., *The Life and Times of Private Eye*, p. 19.
101 See Willi Frischauer, *David Frost: A Biography* (London, 1971), pp. 135–136; Hylton, *Magical History Tour*, pp. 167–169.
102 Ingrams, ed., *The Life and Times of Private Eye*, p. 140.
103 Pimlott, *Harold Wilson*, p. 404.
104 Hansard, 27 July 1966.
105 Benn diary, 18 July 1966.
106 Crossman diary, 24 July 1966.

15 THE FACE OF '66

1 Twiggy, *Twiggy on Twiggy* (London, 1976), pp. 7–27; Lawson, *Twiggy in Black and White*, pp. 18–41.
2 Twiggy, *Twiggy on Twiggy*, pp. 28–35; Lawson, *Twiggy in Black and White*, pp. 47–50.
3 Twiggy, *Twiggy on Twiggy*, pp. 36–39; Lawson, *Twiggy in Black and White*, pp. 54–56.
4 Twiggy, *Twiggy on Twiggy*, pp. 42–43; Lawson, *Twiggy in Black and White*, pp. 60–61.
5 Bernard, *Fashion in the 60s*, p. 64.
6 Quoted in Lawson, *Twiggy in Black and White*, p. 72.
7 Quant, *Quant by Quant*, p. 161.
8 Quoted in Aitken, *The Young Meteors*, pp. 52–53.
9 Aitken, *The Young Meteors*, pp. 51–53; Levy, *Ready, Steady, Go!*, p. 241.
10 *Life*, 5 December 1960.
11 Quoted in Quant, *Quant by Quant*, p. 105.
12 Levy, *Ready, Steady, Go!*, p. 152; MacDonald, *Revolution in the Head*, p. 90.
13 Stern and Stern, *Sixties People*, pp. 123–124.
14 Stern and Stern, *Sixties People*, pp. 139–140.
15 Marwick, *The Sixties*, p. 461.
16 Marwick, *The Sixties*, pp. 465–466.
17 Marwick, *The Sixties*, p. 468.
18 John Cork and Bruce Scivally, *James Bond: The Legacy* (London, 2002), p. 87.
19 See <http://www.oscars.org/awardsdatabase/index.html>.
20 *Weekend Telegraph*, 16 April 1965.
21 *New Musical Express*, 25 June 1965.
22 Quoted in Weight, *Patriots*, p. 393.
23 See Whiteley, 'Shaping the Sixties', p. 24.
24 Melly, *Revolt into Style*, p. 148.
25 Weight, *Patriots*, p. 393.
26 Harris, Hyde and Smith, eds, *1966 and All That*, pp. 43–49.
27 Pimlott, *Harold Wilson*, pp. 15, 26; Ziegler, *Wilson*, pp. 7–8.
28 Heath, *The Course of My Life*, p. 10.
29 Martin Polley, *Moving the Goalposts: A History of Sport and Society since 1945* (London, 1998), p. 21.
30 Polley, *Moving the Goalposts*, p. 17.
31 Brian Glanville, 'Britain against the Rest', in Sissons and French, eds, *Age of Austerity*, p. 153.

32 See Richard Holt, *Sport and the British: A Modern History* (Oxford, 1990), p. 306; Polley, *Moving the Goalposts*, pp. 18, 45.
33 Polley, *Moving the Goalposts*, pp. 35, 42.
34 Holt, *Sport and the British*, p. 193; Polley, *Moving the Goalposts*, p. 10.
35 McKibbin, *Classes and Cultures*, pp. 356–357.
36 Holt, *Sport and the British*, p. 193.
37 Mike Cronin and Richard Holt, 'The Imperial Game in Crisis' in Stuart Ward, ed., *British Culture and the End of Empire* (Manchester, 2001), pp. 112, 115–117; Holt, *Sport and the British*, p. 292.
38 Cronin and Holt, 'The Imperial Game in Crisis', pp. 119–20; Holt, *Sport and the British*, pp. 286–7.
39 Holt, *Sport and the British*, pp. 160–172.
40 Polley, *Moving the Goalposts*, p. 70; Weight, *Patriots*, p. 254.
41 *The Listener*, 26 November 1959; Polley, *Moving the Goalposts*, pp. 69–70, 130.
42 See Holt, *Sport and the British*, p. 309.
43 Holt, *Sport and the British*, pp. 313–315.
44 See Arthur Hopcraft, *The Football Man: People and Passions in Soccer* (Harmondsworth, 1971), p. 43.
45 Weight, *Patriots*, p. 262.
46 Brian Glanville, *The Story of the World Cup* (London, 1993), pp. 118–124; Jimmy Greaves and Norman Giller, *Don't Shoot the Manager: The Revealing Story of England's Soccer Bosses* (London, 1997), pp. 19–20; David Downing, *The Best of Enemies: England v Germany, A Century of Football Rivalry* (London, 2000), pp. 94–95.
47 Hopcraft, *The Football Man*, p. 185.
48 Central Council of Physical Recreation, *Sport and the Community* (London, 1960), pp. 80–81.
49 Glanville, *The Story of the World Cup*, pp. 68–69; Roger Hutchinson, *It Is Now! The Real Story of England's 1966 World Cup Triumph* (Edinburgh, 1995), p. 47.
50 Greaves and Giller, *Don't Shoot the Manager*, pp. 40–44; Hutchinson, *It is Now!*, pp. 19–43, 59.
51 Hutchinson, *It is Now!*, p. 21.
52 Hutchinson, *It is Now!*, pp. 37, 71.
53 Greaves and Giller, *Don't Shoot the Manager*, p. 40.
54 Greaves and Giller, *Don't Shoot the Manager*, pp. 42–43.
55 Hopcraft, *The Football Man*, p. 115.
56 Hutchinson, *It is Now!*, p. 70.
57 See Glanville, *The Story of the World Cup*, p. 134; Greaves and Giller, *Don't Shoot The Manager*, pp. 38–39.
58 Quoted in Weight, *Patriots*, p. 459.
59 Hutchinson, *It is Now!*, pp. 13–14.
60 Hutchinson, *It is Now!*, p. 108; and see <http://www.fifaworldcup.com>.
61 See Hutchinson, *It is Now!*, pp. 133–150.
62 Hutchinson, *It is Now!*, pp. 146–148.
63 See Glanville, *The Story of the World Cup*, pp. 135–137; Hutchinson, *It is Now!*, pp. 148–153.

64 Glanville, *The Story of the World Cup*, pp. 140, 146; Hutchinson, *It is Now!*, pp. 153–154.
65 Downing, *The Best of Enemies*, p. 108.
66 Quoted in Hutchinson, *It is Now!*, p. 154.
67 Quoted in Hutchinson, *It is Now!*, p. 156.
68 Glanville, *The Story of the World Cup*, p. 148.
69 See Glanville, *The Story of the World Cup*, p. 148; Hutchinson, *It is Now!*, pp. 159–160.
70 *The Times*, 24 July 1966; Hutchinson, *It is Now!*, pp. 160–161.
71 Hutchinson, *It is Now!*, p. 129.
72 See Hutchinson, *It is Now!*, pp. 165–75.
73 Hopcraft, *The Football Man*, p. 187.
74 Quoted in Hutchinson, *It is Now!*, p. 179.
75 Raymond Durgnat, *A Mirror for England: British Movies from Austerity to Affluence* (London, 1970), p. 102; Downing, *The Best of Enemies*, pp. 58–59.
76 Downing, *The Best of Enemies*, p. 75.
77 Downing, *The Best of Enemies*, p. 89.
78 Quoted in Downing, *The Best of Enemies*, pp. 89–90.
79 Downing, *The Best of Enemies*, p. 110; *Daily Mail*, 30 July 1966.
80 *Observer*, 31 July 1966.
81 The figure is from *Sunday Telegraph*, 31 July 1966.
82 *Observer*, 31 July 1966.
83 Hutchinson, *It is Now!*, pp. 180–181.
84 See Hutchinson, *It is Now!*, pp. 183–187.
85 Hugh McIlvanney, *McIlvanney on Football* (Edinburgh, 1994), p. 153.
86 Quoted in Hutchinson, *It is Now!*, p. 193.
87 Quoted in Hutchinson, *It is Now!*, pp. 195–196.
88 Quoted in Hutchinson, *It is Now!*, pp. 196–197.
89 Hutchinson, *It is Now!*, pp. 198–199; Downing, *The Best of Enemies*, pp. 115–116.
90 Quoted in Hutchinson, *It is Now!*, pp. 200–201.
91 *Observer*, 31 July 1966.
92 Hopcraft, *The Football Man*, p. 115.
93 *Observer*, 31 July 1966.
94 Quoted in Hutchinson, *It is Now!*, p. 203.
95 *Sunday Telegraph*, 31 July 1966.
96 See 'Britain's Most Watched TV: The 1960s', online at <http://www.bfi.org.uk/features/mostwatched/1960s.html>; Briggs, *Competition*, p. 593.
97 *Sunday Telegraph*, 31 July 1966.
98 *Observer*, 31 July 1966.
99 Hutchinson, *It is Now!*, p. 205.
100 *Observer*, 31 July 1966.
101 *Sunday Telegraph*, 31 July 1966.
102 *Sun*, 1 August 1966.
103 *Sunday Express*, 31 July 1966.
104 *Observer*, 31 July 1966.
105 Quoted in Weight, *Patriots*, p. 462.
106 Crossman diary, 31 July 1966.

107 *Observer*, 31 July 1966.
108 Levin, *The Pendulum Years*, p. 233.

16 IS BRITAIN CIVILISED?

1 'Benn's HoverBritain', in Ingrams, ed., *The Life and Times of Private Eye*, p. 151.
2 Benn diary, 30 June 1966.
3 Levin, *The Pendulum Years*, p. 179.
4 Speech to the Institution of Mechanical Engineers, 17 November 1966, reprinted in Tony Benn, *Out of the Wilderness: Diaries, 1963–67* (London, 1987), pp. 553–554.
5 Crossman diary, 12 October 1969 and 11 May 1968.
6 Woodward, 'Labour's Economic Performance', p. 87; Coopey, 'Industrial Policy in the White Heat of the Scientific Revolution', pp. 108–110.
7 Coopey, 'Industrial Policy in the White Heat of the Scientific Revolution', pp. 103, 112.
8 See Ponting, *Breach of Promise*, pp. 272–273; Dell, *A Strange Eventful History*, pp. 364–365; Tomlinson, *Economic Policy*, p. 112.
9 Benn diary, 17 January 1968.
10 See Ponting, *Breach of Promise*, pp. 270–271, a very scathing account.
11 Coopey, 'Industrial Policy in the White Heat of the Scientific Revolution', pp. 117–118, 120; see also Woodward, 'Labour's Economic Performance', p. 87; Pimlott, *Harold Wilson*, p. 527; Ponting, *Breach of Promise*, p. 280.
12 For Crosland's life until 1965, see S. Crosland, *Tony Crosland*, pp. 3–140.
13 Watkins, *A Short Walk down Fleet Street*, p. 79.
14 See Jenkins, *A Life at the Centre*, p. 103; Jefferys, *Anthony Crosland*, p. 53.
15 Recounted in Paul Johnson, ed., *The Oxford Book of Political Anecdotes* (Oxford, 1989), p. 240.
16 S. Crosland, *Tony Crosland*, pp. 153, 186.
17 S. Crosland, *Tony Crosland*, p. 147.
18 Pimlott, *Harold Wilson*, pp. 513–514.
19 *The Economist*, 16 December 1961.
20 Pimlott, *Harold Wilson*, p. 514.
21 *Times Educational Supplement*, 4 March 1966, quoted in Briggs, *Competition*, pp. 498–499.
22 Clapson, *A Social History of Milton Keynes*, p. 85.
23 See Ponting, *Breach of Promise*, pp. 133–134; Pimlott, *Harold Wilson*, p. 515; Clarke, *Hope and Glory*, p. 290.
24 Peter Calvocoressi, *The British Experience 1945–75* (Harmondsworth, 1978), pp. 157–158; Childs, *Britain since 1945*, p. 149; Timmins, *The Five Giants*, pp. 238–239.
25 Sampson, *Anatomy of Britain*, p. 184.
26 McKibbin, *Classes and Cultures*, p. 227.
27 R. A. Butler, *The Art of the Possible: The Memoirs of Lord Butler* (Harmondsworth, 1973), pp. 124–125.
28 Barnett, *The Audit of War*, p. 302.
29 Laurie, *The Teenage Revolution*, p. 141.
30 Timmins, *The Five Giants*, pp. 153–154.
31 Timmins, *The Five Giants*, pp. 239–240; Simon Gunn and Rachel Bell, *Middle Classes: Their Rise and Sprawl* (London, 2003), pp. 169–170.

32 *Sunday Times*, 9 September 1962.
33 Timmins, *The Five Giants*, pp. 240–241; Clarke, *Hope and Glory*, p. 285.
34 Crosland, *The Future of Socialism*, pp. 204–206.
35 See Jefferys, *Anthony Crosland*, ch. 12.
36 Quoted in Gunn and Bell, *Middle Classes*, p. 170.
37 Timmins, *The Five Giants*, pp. 238, 242.
38 Timmins, *The Five Giants*, p. 243.
39 Calvocoressi, *The British Experience*, p. 158; Timmins, *The Five Giants*, p. 243.
40 Gunn and Bell, *Middle Classes*, p. 173.
41 Timmins, *The Five Giants*, pp. 242–243.
42 Quoted in Gunn and Bell, *Middle Classes*, p. 172.
43 S. Crosland, *Tony Crosland*, pp. 146–147.
44 S. Crosland, *Tony Crosland*, p. 149.
45 S. Crosland, *Tony Crosland*, p. 148.
46 Pimlott, *Harold Wilson*, p. 512.
47 See Timmins, *The Five Giants*, pp. 269–273.
48 On Thatcher and the comprehensives, see Timmins, *The Five Giants*, pp. 298–299; John Campbell, *Margaret Thatcher: Volume 1: The Grocer's Daughter* (London, 2000), pp. 222–228.
49 On Wilson's balances, see Pimlott, *Harold Wilson*, pp. 402–403.
50 Jenkins, *A Life at the Centre*, pp. 149–151.
51 Jenkins, *A Life at the Centre*, pp. 170–171.
52 Jenkins, *A Life at the Centre*, pp. 176–177.
53 Jenkins, *A Life at the Centre*, pp. 22–23.
54 Quoted in Greg Rosen, 'What if Labour had won in 1970?', in Brack and Dale, eds, *Prime Minister Portillo*, p. 159.
55 See Jenkins, *A Life at the Centre*, pp. 8–9.
56 Radice, *Friends and Rivals*, p. 157.
57 Marquand, *The Progressive Dilemma*, pp. 189–190.
58 Roy Jenkins, *The Labour Case* (Harmondsworth, 1959), p. 135.
59 See Crosland, *The Future of Socialism*, pp. 520–524.
60 Jenkins, *The Labour Case*, pp. 136, 146.
61 Jenkins, *The Labour Case*, p. 140.
62 Peter Hitchens, *The Abolition of Britain* (revised edition: London, 2000), p. 304.
63 See Jeffrey Weeks, *Sex, Politics and Society: The Regulation of Sexuality since 1800* (second edition: London, 1989), pp. 266–267.
64 Peter Thompson, 'Labour's "Gannex conscience"? Politics and Popular Attitudes in the "Permissive Society"', in Coopey, Fielding and Tiratsoo, eds, *The Wilson Governments*, p. 139.
65 Crossman diary, 11 December 1966; David Walker, 'The First Wilson Governments, 1964–1970', in Hennessy and Seldon, eds, *Ruling Performance*, p. 191; Morgan, *Callaghan*, pp. 319–321
66 Thompson, 'Labour's "Gannex Conscience"?', pp. 139–141; Weeks, *Sex, Politics and Society*, pp. 266–267.
67 David Owen, *Time to Declare* (London, 1992), p. 104.

68 Jenkins, *The Labour Case*, p. 136.
69 Butler, *The Art of the Possible*, pp. 203–204.
70 Hitchens, *The Abolition of Britain*, pp. 310–311; Morgan, *Callaghan*, p. 297.
71 Christie Davies, *Permissive Britain: Social Change in the Sixties and Seventies* (London, 1975), p. 41; Thompson, 'Labour's "Gannex Conscience"?', p. 143.
72 Davies, *Permissive Britain*, p. 41.
73 See Jenkins, *A Life at the Centre*, pp. 199–200.
74 Hitchens, *The Abolition of Britain*, p. 314; Davies, *Permissive Britain*, pp. 42–44.
75 Davies, *Permissive Britain*, p. 39.
76 Marwick, *The Sixties*, pp. 13, 18.
77 *New Society*, 27 November 1969. See Chapter 10 for more of the poll's findings.
78 Weeks, *Sex, Politics and Society*, pp. 264, 266–267.
79 Jefferys, *Anthony Crosland*, p. 119.

17 SOWING DRAGONS' TEETH

1 Quoted in Peter Taylor, *Provos: The IRA and Sinn Fein* (revised edition: London, 1998), p. 32.
2 David McKittrick and David McVea, *Making Sense of the Troubles* (London, 2001), p. 1.
3 John Lynch, *A Tale of Three Cities: Comparative Studies in Working-Class Life* (Basingstoke, 1998), p. 1.
4 Tim Pat Coogan, *The Troubles: Ireland's Ordeal 1966–1996 and the Search for Peace* (London, 1996), p. 15.
5 Coogan, *The Troubles*, pp. 17–18.
6 Coogan, *The Troubles*, pp. 25–27.
7 Peter Taylor, *Loyalists* (London, 2000), pp. 13–28. For a sympathetic portrait of the Unionist mentality, see Ruth Dudley Edwards, *The Faithful Tribe: An Intimate Portrait of the Loyal Institutions* (London, 2000).
8 McKittrick and McVea, *Making Sense of the Troubles*, p. 11.
9 McKittrick and McVea, *Making Sense of the Troubles*, pp. 13–14.
10 Coogan, *The Troubles*, p. 41; McKittrick and McVea, *Making Sense of the Troubles*, p. 13. This is often misquoted as 'a Protestant Parliament for a Protestant people'.
11 See Richard English, *Armed Struggle: The History of the IRA* (London, 2004), p. 66; Thomas Hennessey, *Dividing Ireland: World War One and Partition* (London, 1998), *passim*.
12 McKittrick and McVea, *Making Sense of the Troubles*, p. 12.
13 Coogan, *The Troubles*, pp. 32–33.
14 Coogan, *The Troubles*, p. 34.
15 Coogan, *The Troubles*, p. 37.
16 Taylor, *Provos*, pp. 30–31; McKittrick and McVea, *Making Sense of the Troubles*, p. 8.
17 Austin Currie quoted in Coogan, *The Troubles*, pp. 34–5.
18 McKittrick and McVea, *Making Sense of the Troubles*, p. 13.
19 Taylor, *Provos*, p. 31.
20 For the most authoritative discussions of this issue, see David Smith and Gerald Chambers, *Inequality in Northern Ireland* (Oxford, 1991), p. 368 and *passim*; John Whyte, *Interpreting Northern Ireland* (Oxford, 1991), esp. pp. 64, 168.

21 Quoted in McKittrick and McVea, *Making Sense of the Troubles*, pp. 8–9.
22 Coogan, *The Troubles*, pp. 34, 38.
23 *The Times*, 24 April 1967.
24 Greenslade, *Press Gang*, p. 236.
25 McKittrick and McVea, *Making Sense of the Troubles*, pp. 24–25; and see Peter Rose, *How the Troubles Came to Northern Ireland* (London, 2001), pp. 1–10.
26 James Callaghan, *A House Divided* (London, 1973), p. 117; see also Coogan, *The Troubles*, pp. 39–40; Rose, *How the Troubles Came*, pp. 11–30.
27 PREM 13/980, Sir Burke Trend to Wilson, 24 March 1966; Sir Frank Soskice to Wilson, 4 April 1966.
28 Rose, *How the Troubles Came*, pp. 18–19.
29 See English, *Armed Struggle*, pp. 42–78.
30 Paddy Devlin quoted in English, *Armed Struggle*, p. 68.
31 English, *Armed Struggle*, p. 76.
32 Tim Pat Coogan, *The IRA* (London, 1995), p. 418; English, *Armed Struggle*, pp. 72–6.
33 Quoted in Taylor, *Provos*, p. 22.
34 English, *Armed Struggle*, pp. 82–84, 90.
35 On Catholicism and the IRA, see English, *Armed Struggle*, pp. 25–26, 130–132.
36 Quoted in Taylor, *Provos*, p. 24.
37 Quotations from Taylor, *Provos*, pp. 28–29.
38 Coogan, *The Troubles*, pp. 33–34; McKittrick and McVea, *Making Sense of the Troubles*, p. 18.
39 Michael Collins, *The Path to Freedom* (Cork, 1968), p. 79.
40 Quotations from McKittrick and McVea, *Making Sense of the Troubles*, pp. 20–21.
41 See Taylor, *Provos*, p. 33 and *passim*.
42 McKittrick and McVea, *Making Sense of the Troubles*, pp. 17–22.
43 Tim Pat Coogan, *Ireland since the Rising* (London, 1966), p. 317.
44 See Marc Mulholland, 'O'Neill, Terence Marne, Baron O'Neill of the Maine (1914–1990)', *Oxford Dictionary of National Biography* (Oxford, 2004), online at <http://www.oxforddnb.com/view/article/39857>; McKittrick and McVea, *Making Sense of the Troubles*, pp. 27–28.
45 Coogan, *The Troubles*, pp. 46–47.
46 McKittrick and McVea, *Making Sense of the Troubles*, pp. 28–29; Rose, *How the Troubles Came*, pp. 42–44.
47 Mulholland, 'O'Neill, Terence', <http://www.oxforddnb.com/view/article/39857>; Coogan, *The Troubles*, p. 47.
48 *The Times*, 12 April 1965.
49 Coogan, *The Troubles*, p. 48.
50 Coogan, *The Troubles*, p. 41.
51 Quoted in Coogan, *The Troubles*, p. 45.
52 Quotations in McKittrick and McVea, *Making Sense of the Troubles*, pp. 32–33.
53 Henry Patterson, 'Faulkner, (Arthur) Brian Deane, Baron Faulkner of Downpatrick (1921–1977)', *Oxford Dictionary of National Biography*, online at <http://www.oxforddnb.com/ view/article/31096>; and see David Bleakley,

Faulkner: *Conflict and Consensus in Irish Politics* (London, 1974), *passim*; Coogan, *The Troubles*, pp. 44–5.
54 Roy Foster, *Modern Ireland 1600–1972* (London, 1989), p. 585.
55 Quoted in Rose, *How the Troubles Came*, pp. 42–43.
56 Bleakley, *Faulkner*, pp. 40–41.
57 *Belfast Telegraph*, 10 May 1969.
58 McKittrick and McVea, *Making Sense of the Troubles*, pp. 30–31.
59 *The Times*, 12 April 1965.
60 McKittrick and McVea, *Making Sense of the Troubles*, pp. 30–31.
61 Coogan, *The Troubles*, p. 53.
62 *Protestant Telegraph*, 4 January 1967, quoted in Coogan, *The Troubles*, p. 53.
63 *Protestant Telegraph*, 10 August 1968, 30 November 1966 and 22 March 1969, quoted in Coogan, *The Troubles*, pp. 54–55.
64 Quoted in Coogan, *The Troubles*, p. 55.
65 See Ed Molony and Andy Pollak, *Paisley* (Dublin, 1986).
66 Molony and Pollak, *Paisley*, p. 111.
67 Bob Cooper quoted in Coogan, *The Troubles*, p. 54.
68 Patrick Marrinan, *Paisley: Man of Wrath* (Tralee, 1973), pp. 82–84.
69 Quoted in Taylor, *Loyalists*, p. 32.
70 *The Times*, 1 and 5 October 1964; Andrew Boyd, *Holy War in Belfast* (Tralee, 1969), ch. 11, online at <http://cain.ulst.ac.uk/othelem/docs/boyd69.htm>; Coogan, *The Troubles*, pp. 56–57; Taylor, *Loyalists*, pp. 32–33.
71 *The Times*, 3 October 1964.
72 Taylor, *Loyalists*, p. 33.
73 Rose, *How the Troubles Came*, p. 15.
74 Quoted in Taylor, *Loyalists*, pp. 30–31.
75 Quoted in Taylor, *Loyalists*, p. 2.
76 McKittrick and McVea, *Making Sense of the Troubles*, pp. 31, 33–34.
77 Coogan, *The Troubles*, p. 59.
78 Marrinan, *Paisley: Man of Wrath*, p. 90.
79 *The Times*, 18 April 1966; Marrinan, *Paisley: Man of Wrath*, p. 92.
80 *The Times*, 7 June 1966.
81 *The Times*, 19, 20, 21 and 25 July 1966; Coogan, *The Troubles*, pp. 53–54.
82 *The Times*, 16 June 1966.
83 Coogan, *The Troubles*, p. 56.
84 Quoted in Taylor, *Loyalists*, pp. 36–37.
85 Taylor, *Loyalists*, p. 36.
86 Quoted in Taylor, *Loyalists*, pp. 33–34.
87 Taylor, *Loyalists*, p. 40.
88 David Boulton, *The UVF 1966–73* (Dublin, 1973), p. 40.
89 Taylor, *Loyalists*, p. 41.
90 Quoted in Boulton, *The UVF 1966–73*, pp. 49–50.
91 The narrative of Ward's death and quotes are from Taylor, *Loyalists*, pp. 41–43.
92 See Rose, *How the Troubles Came*, pp. 30, 48, 59–60, 68–69.
93 *The Times*, 29 June 1966.

18 THE YORKSHIRE WALTER MITTY

94 *The Times*, 29 June 1966.
95 Quoted in McKittrick and McVea, *Making Sense of the Troubles*, pp. 35–36.

1 See King and Wybrow, eds, *British Political Opinion*, p. 188.
2 Pearce, *Denis Healey*, p. 370; Hennessy, *The Prime Minister*, p. 310.
3 Benn diary, 10 August 1966.
4 Harold Wilson, 'The Economic Crisis of July/August 1966', 9 August 1966, quoted in Pimlott, *Harold Wilson*, p. 437.
5 Callaghan, *Time and Chance*, p. 202.
6 Wilson, *The Labour Government*, p. 352.
7 Crossman diary, 10 September 1966.
8 Pimlott, *Harold Wilson*, pp. 489, 437.
9 Morgan, *Callaghan*, pp. 249–250.
10 Marsh, *Off the Rails*, p. 89.
11 Castle diary, 3 August 1966.
12 Castle diary, 25 January 1968.
13 Pimlott, *Harold Wilson*, pp. 402–403.
14 Crossman diary, 8 and 11 December 1966.
15 Healey, *The Time of My Life*, pp. 331, 334.
16 S. Crosland, *Tony Crosland*, p. 184.
17 Marquand, *The Progressive Dilemma*, p. 161.
18 Castle diary, entry for 29 September to 7 October 1966.
19 Benn diary, 6 August 1966.
20 Quoted in Ponting, *Breach of Promise*, p. 203.
21 *The Times*, 21 July 1966.
22 Woodward, 'Labour's Economic Performance, 1964–1970', p. 81; Ponting, *Breach of Promise*, pp. 284–286; Dell, *The Chancellors*, p. 339; Tomlinson, *Economic Policy*, p. 139.
23 Ponting, *Breach of Promise*, pp. 168–170.
24 Hansard, 11 April 1967; Callaghan, *Time and Chance*, pp. 211–212; Ponting, *Breach of Promise*, p. 288; Pimlott, *Harold Wilson*, p. 466; Dell, *The Chancellors*, p. 340.
25 *Sunday Telegraph*, 31 July 1966.
26 Ponting, *Breach of Promise*, p. 101; Young, *International Policy*, p. 45.
27 Healey, *The Time of My Life*, pp. 123, 297; on the Cold War commitments of the Labour right, see also Jeffrey Pickering, 'Politics and "Black Tuesday": Shifting Power in the Cabinet and the Decision to Withdraw from East of Suez, November 1967–January 1968', *Twentieth Century British History*, 13: 2, 2002, pp. 147–148.
28 Ponting, *Breach of Promise*, pp. 92–94; Pimlott, *Harold Wilson*, pp. 382–384, 433–434.
29 Crossman diary, 15 June 1966.
30 Healey, *The Time of My Life*, p. 278.
31 Tom Nairn quoted in Pimlott, *Harold Wilson*, pp. 382–383.
32 See John Darwin, *Britain and Decolonisation: The Retreat from Empire in the Post-War World* (London, 1988), p. 287; Young, *International Policy*, pp. 36–37; Pimlott, *Harold Wilson*, p. 383; Pearce, *Denis Healey*, p. 300.
33 Castle diary, 14 February 1966.

34 Healey, *The Time of My Life*, pp. 284–290; see also Pearce, *Denis Healey*, pp. 317–324; Young, *International Policy*, pp. 66–74; and two excellent studies of the conflict: John Subritzky, *Confronting Sukarno: British, American, Australian and New Zealand Diplomacy in the Malaysian–Indonesian Confrontation, 1961–5* (London, 2000); Jones, *Conflict and Confrontation in South East Asia*.

35 Crossman diary, 3 January 1965.

36 See Pearce, *Denis Healey*, pp. 329–330.

37 Wilson, *The Labour Government*, p. 243

38 Healey, *The Time of My Life*, p. 300.

39 Subritzky, *Confronting Sukarno*, pp. 199–201; Ponting, *Breach of Promise*, pp. 103–104; Pearce, *Denis Healey*, pp. 330–335; Saki Dockrill, *Britain's Withdrawal from East of Suez: The Choice between Europe and the World?* (London, 2002), pp. 148–151; Young, *International Policy*, pp. 42–48.

40 Pearce, *Denis Healey*, pp. 335–336; Young, *International Policy*, pp. 48–49.

41 See Pickering, 'Politics and "Black Tuesday"', p. 150.

42 Ponting, *Breach of Promise*, p. 105.

43 Quotations in Young, *International Policy*, pp. 48–49.

44 Healey, *The Time of My Life*, p. 231; and see Childs, *Britain since 1945*, pp. 113–114; Young, *International Policy*, pp. 89–91.

45 Young, *International Policy*, pp. 92–93.

46 Charles Carruthers interviewed in Robin Neillands, *A Fighting Retreat: The British Empire 1947–97* (London, 1996), p. 361.

47 Quoted in Young, *International Policy*, p. 91.

48 Healey, *The Time of My Life*, p. 284; Young, *International Policy*, p. 93.

49 Pearce, *Denis Healey*, pp. 315–316; Neillands, *A Fighting Retreat*, pp. 389–390; Young, *International Policy*, p. 95.

50 Neillands, *A Fighting Retreat*, pp. 391–395.

51 *The Times*, 17 July 1968.

52 See *The Times*, 17 July 1968; Neillands, *A Fighting Retreat*, pp. 395–399.

53 Linda Wood interviewed in Neillands, *A Fighting Retreat*, pp. 398–399.

54 Neillands, *A Fighting Retreat*, p. 399.

55 *The Times*, 1 October 1968.

56 Crossman diary, 30 October 1967; Young, *International Policy*, p. 96.

57 On Britain's legacy in Aden, see Young, *International Policy*, pp. 97–98.

58 Pimlott, *Harold Wilson*, pp. 457–458.

59 Ponting, *Breach of Promise*, pp. 242–244; Pimlott, *Harold Wilson*, pp. 450–451.

60 King diary, 11 December 1966.

61 Ponting, *Breach of Promise*, pp. 246–248; Pimlott, *Harold Wilson*, pp. 453–454; Ziegler, *Wilson*, p. 320.

62 Young, *International Policy*, pp. 186–187; see also the conclusion in Ponting, *Breach of Promise*, p. 255.

63 See Pimlott, *Harold Wilson*, p. 381.

64 Ponting, *Breach of Promise*, pp. 46–47.

65 Ziegler, *Wilson*, pp. 228–229.

66 Quoted in Ziegler, *Wilson*, p. 324.

67 See Sylvia Ellis, 'Lyndon Johnson, Harold Wilson and the Vietnam War,' in Jonathan Hollowell, ed., *Twentieth-Century Anglo-American Relations* (Basingstoke, 2001) pp. 184–187, 192–200.
68 *Washington Post*, 30 July 1966; *Sunday Telegraph*, 31 July 1966.
69 *Daily Telegraph*, 30 July 1966.
70 *Observer*, 31 July 1966.
71 *Sunday Telegraph*, 31 July 1966.
72 Benn diary, 2 March 1967.
73 Quoted in Pimlott, *Harold Wilson*, pp. 400–401.
74 Young, *International Policy*, p. 75.
75 Pimlott, *Harold Wilson*, pp. 392, 394.
76 King and Wybrow, eds, *British Political Opinion*, pp. 328–329; see also C. J. Bartlett, *The Special Relationship: A Political History of Anglo-American Relations since 1945* (London, 1992), pp. 114–115.
77 Young, *International Policy*, p. 18.
78 Young, *International Policy*, p. 77.
79 Quoted in Pimlott, *Harold Wilson*, p. 389.
80 Pimlott, *Harold Wilson*, p. 389.
81 See Ponting, *Breach of Promise*, pp. 221–222.
82 Crossman diary, 18 and 20 June 1965.
83 Chester L. Cooper, *The Lost Crusade: The Full Story of US Involvement in Vietnam from Roosevelt to Nixon* (London, 1980), p. 362; see also Ponting, *Breach of Promise*, pp. 223–226; Pimlott, *Harold Wilson*, pp. 460–463.
84 See the Crossman and Castle diary entries for 14 February 1967.
85 Oral history interview with Chester L. Cooper, Oral History Collection, Lyndon Baines Johnson Library, Austin, Texas.
86 Cooper, *The Lost Crusade*, p. 365
87 See Cooper oral history interview.
88 Pimlott, *Harold Wilson*, p. 464.
89 From the title of Andrew Roth's controversial biography, *Sir Harold Wilson: The Yorkshire Walter Mitty* (London, 1977).
90 Dell, *A Strange Eventful History*, p. 355.
91 Ponting, *Breach of Promise*, p. 220.
92 Young, *International Policy*, p. 82.
93 Pimlott, *Harold Wilson*, p. 394.
94 Castle diary, 8 September 1966.
95 See Young, *International Policy*, pp. 6–7.
96 Brown, *In My Way*, pp. 117–118.
97 Quoted in Paterson, *Tired and Emotional*, p. 206.
98 Paterson, *Tired and Emotional*, p. 214.
99 See Paterson, *Tired and Emotional*, pp. 212, 213, 215.
100 Quoted in Paterson, *Tired and Emotional*, pp. 215–216; for an alternative version, with the object of Brown's affections identified as the Archbishop of Montevideo, see Owen, *Time to Declare*, p. 102.
101 See Castle diary, 18 July 1966.

102 Hugo Young, *This Blessed Plot: Britain and Europe from Churchill to Blair* (London, 1998), pp. 172–181.
103 Pimlott, *Harold Wilson*, p. 435; Young, *This Blessed Plot*, p. 188; Morgan, *Callaghan*, pp. 234–235; Young, *International Policy*, p. 146.
104 See King diary, 20 January and 19 April 1966; Young, *This Blessed Plot*, p. 186.
105 Ponting, *Breach of Promise*, p. 213; Pimlott, *Harold Wilson*, pp. 437–438.
106 King diary, 5 July 1966.
107 Crossman diary, 22 October 1966; Young, *This Blessed Plot*, p. 196.
108 Young, *This Blessed Plot*, pp. 191–192.
109 Pimlott, *Harold Wilson*, p. 439; Young, *This Blessed Plot*, p. 192.
110 Pimlott, *Harold Wilson*, pp. 439–440; Jay, *Change and Fortune*, p. 371.
111 Young, *This Blessed Plot*, p. 197; Young, *International Policy*, p. 149.
112 Weight, *Patriots*, pp. 466–467.
113 *Private Eye*, 12 May 1967.
114 Gallup polls cited in Butler and Pinto-Duschinsky, *The British General Election of 1970*, p. 17.
115 Pimlott, *Harold Wilson*, p. 440; Weight, *Patriots*, p. 466.
116 Crossman diary, 21 April 1967.
117 Pimlott, *Harold Wilson*, pp. 440–441.
118 See Castle diary, 22 June 1967.
119 Wilson to Brown, 21 June 1967, quoted in Ziegler, *Wilson*, p. 335.
120 Ziegler, *Wilson*, p. 335.
121 See Pimlott, *Harold Wilson*, p. 442.

Part Three

19 CARRY ON ENGLAND

1 *The Times*, 10 July 1968.
2 *The Times*, 6 June 1968.
3 *The Times*, 7 August 1968.
4 See Hewison, *Too Much*, pp. 226–228 and *passim*; for an excellent survey of literature after 1960, see Patricia Waugh, *Harvest of the Sixties: English Literature and Its Background, 1960–1990* (Oxford, 1995).
5 See John Russell Taylor, *The Second Wave: British Drama of the Sixties* (London, 1978); Dominic Shellard, *British Theatre Since the War* (London, 1999), pp. 119ff.
6 *Life*, 29 May 1966.
7 Shellard, *British Theatre since the War*, pp. 101–102.
8 Tim Goodwin, *Britain's Royal National Theatre* (London, 1988), p. 32; Peter Lewis, *The National: A Dream Made Concrete* (London, 1990), p. 17.
9 Quoted in Goodwin, *Britain's Royal National Theatre*, p. 33.
10 Wilson, *Late Call*, pp. 154–156.
11 Sandbrook, *Never Had It So Good*, pp. 184–185; '*Oliver!*' and '*Charlie Girl*', in Larkin, ed., *The Virgin Encyclopedia of Sixties Music*, pp. 331, 107–108.
12 Hattersley, *Who Goes Home?*, p. 24.

13 Green, *All Dressed Up*, p. 86.
14 Taylor, *The Second Wave*, p. 12.
15 See Colls, *Identity of England*, p. 306. This was a striking contrast with the heterogeneous cultural landscape before the 1930s or so, as described in McKibbin, *Classes and Cultures*.
16 Holt, *Sport and the British*, p. 316.
17 Briggs, *Competition*, p. 593.
18 See Michael Young and Peter Willmott, *The Symmetrical Family: Study of Work and Leisure in the London Region* (London, 1973).
19 Tim O'Sullivan, 'Television Memories and Cultures of Viewing, 1950–1965', in Corner, ed., *Popular Television in Britain*, p. 167.
20 *Sunday Mirror*, 2 July 1967; Briggs, *Competition*, pp. 856–857.
21 Briggs, *Competition*, p. 858.
22 Briggs, *Competition*, p. 848.
23 *The Times*, 17 May 1969.
24 Briggs, *Competition*, pp. 612–614.
25 See Chapman, *Saints and Avengers*, pp. 1–15: this is the definitive study of the British adventure series of the 1960s.
26 David Buxton, *From The Avengers to Miami Vice: Form and Ideology in Television Series* (Manchester, 1990), p. 92; Chapman, *Saints and Avengers*, pp. 13–14.
27 *Sunday Telegraph*, 19 October 1969; *Daily Mail*, 27 November 1969.
28 Chapman, *Saints and Avengers*, p. 86.
29 Chapman, *Saints and Avengers*, p. 111; and see also Colin Watson, *Snobbery with Violence: English Crime Stories and Their Audience* (London, 1987), p. 22.
30 *Daily Mail*, 15 October 1970, quoted in Chapman, *Saints and Avengers*, pp. 113–114.
31 James Chapman, '*The Avengers*: Television and Popular Culture during the "High Sixties"', in Aldgate, Chapman and Marwick, eds, *Windows on the Sixties*, pp. 37–38; Chapman, *Saints and Avengers*, pp. 52–99.
32 Quoted in Chapman, '*The Avengers*: Television and Popular Culture', p. 51; see also Chapman, *Saints and Avengers*, pp. 61–62.
33 *TV Times*, 20 September 1963.
34 Chapman, *Saints and Avengers*, pp. 63–65.
35 Chapman, *Saints and Avengers*, p. 52.
36 See Buxton, *From The Avengers to Miami Vice*, p. 96; Chapman, *Saints and Avengers*, pp. 13, 21–22, 79, 86, 92.
37 Melly, *Revolt into Style*, p. 193.
38 See John Hill, *Sex, Class and Realism: British Cinema 1956–1963* (London, 1986), pp. 35ff.
39 Laing, 'The Production of Literature', p. 154; Hill, *Sex, Class and Realism*, pp. 35ff.
40 See *Daily Telegraph*, 1 March 1965; Chapman, *Licence to Thrill*, pp. 112–113; Cork and Scivally, *James Bond: The Legacy*, p. 79.
41 Tony Bennett and Janet Woollacott, *Bond and Beyond: The Political Career of a Popular Hero* (London, 1987), pp. 238–239; Chapman, *Licence to Thrill*, pp. 115–116.
42 On *Tom Jones*, see Jeffrey Richards, 'New Waves and Old Myths: British Cinema in the 1960s', in Bart Moore-Gilbert and John Seed, eds, *Cultural Revolution? The Challenge of the Arts in the 1960s* (London, 1992), p. 227; Walker, *Hollywood, England*,

p. 144; Anthony Aldgate and Jeffrey Richards, *Best of British: Cinema and Society from 1930 to the Present* (London, 1999), pp. 216–217. On *A Hard Day's Night*, see Rowena Agajanian, '"Nothing Like Any Previous Musical, British or American": The Beatles' Film *A Hard Day's Night*', in Aldgate, Chapman and Marwick, eds, *Windows on the Sixties*, pp. 103–104; Walker, *Hollywood, England*, p. 225; Ali Catterall and Simon Wells, *Your Face Here: British Cult Movies since the Sixties* (London, 2001), p. 4.

43 Chapman, *Licence to Thrill*, p. 97.
44 Walker, *Hollywood, England*, pp. 287, 339–341; Murphy, *Sixties British Cinema*, p. 258; Fiegel, *John Barry: A Sixties Theme*, p, 147.
45 Richards, 'New Waves and Old Myths', p. 232.
46 See the list of common devices in Murphy, *Sixties British Cinema*, p. 3.
47 See Marwick, *The Sixties*, p. 475; Roger Lewis, *The Life and Death of Peter Sellers* (London, 1994), pp. 400–401, 622; Ed Sikov, *Mr Strangelove: A Biography of Peter Sellers* (London, 2002), pp. 229–232,
48 Alexander Walker, *Peter Sellers: The Authorized Biography* (London, 1982), p. 173; Christopher Tookey, *The Critics' Film Guide* (London, 1994), p. 919; Marwick, *The Sixties*, pp. 474–475.
49 *Sight and Sound*, Summer 1966; Murphy, *Sixties British Cinema*, p. 277.
50 *Monthly Film Bulletin*, June 1966; Walker, *Hollywood, England*, pp. 298–299.
51 *The Times*, 13 August 1966; Walker, *Hollywood, England*, p. 302; Levy, *Ready, Steady, Go!*, pp. 170–171.
52 Marwick, *The Sixties*, p. 473.
53 Reviews quoted in Wells and Catterall, *Your Face Here*, pp. 40–41.
54 Walker, *Hollywood, England*, p. 331.
55 Walker, *Hollywood, England*, p. 361; Murphy, *Sixties British Cinema*, pp. 146, 264; Levy, *Ready, Steady, Go!*, pp. 337–338.
56 George Ornstein quoted in Walker, *Hollywood, England*, p. 395; see also Murphy, *Sixties British Cinema*, pp. 247, 260.
57 Film production statistics at <http://www.terramedia.co.uk/statistics/uk_film_productions.htm>.
58 *Sight and Sound*, Winter 1970; and see Murphy, *Sixties British Cinema*, pp. 2–3.
59 The exception being Arthur Marwick, as ever the rather indiscriminate champion of all things connected with the sixties: see Marwick, *The Sixties*, p. 470.
60 Aldgate and Richards, *Best of British*, pp. 216–217.
61 See Walker, *Hollywood, England*, p. 462.
62 See Dave Pirie, *A Heritage of Horror* (London, 1973); Alan Barnes and Marcus Hearn, *The Hammer Story* (London, 1998); Wayne Kinsey, *Hammer Films: The Bray Studio Years* (Richmond, 2002); Hill, *Sex, Class and Realism*, p. 48; Marcia Landy, *British Genres: Cinema and Society, 1930–1960* (Princeton, 1991), p. 403.
63 Ian Conrich, 'Traditions of the British Horror Film', in Robert Murphy, ed., *The British Cinema Book* (second edition; London 2001), p. 228; Durgnat, *A Mirror for England*, pp. 223–224; Murphy, *Sixties British Cinema*, pp. 162–163.
64 *The Times*, 6 May 1957.
65 *The Times*, 16 January 1964.

66 See Lez Cooke, 'British Cinema: A Struggle for Identity' in Bloom and Day, eds, *Literature and Culture in Modern Britain*, pp. 152–153.
67 Cooke, 'British Cinema: A Struggle for Identity', p. 153; Peter Hutchings, *Hammer and Beyond: The British Horror Film* (London, 1993), pp. 21, 65–70; Landy, *British Genres*, pp. 395, 425.
68 On the importance of colour, see Durgnat, *A Mirror for England*, p. 225.
69 Conrich, 'Traditions of the British Horror Film', p. 228.
70 See Hill, *Sex, Class and Realism*, p. 142; Landy, *British Genres*, pp. 362–364; Murphy, *Sixties British Cinema*, pp. 247–249; Sandbrook, *Never Had It So Good*, pp. 325–332.
71 Jeffrey Richards, *Films and British National Identity* (Manchester, 1997), p. 165; Landy, *British Genres*, pp. 368–369; Murphy, *Sixties British Cinema*, pp. 251–252.
72 Marion Jordan, 'Carry On . . . Follow that Stereotype', in James Curran and Vincent Porter, eds, *British Cinema History* (London, 1983), p. 327.
73 *The Times*, 16 March 1968.
74 Laing, 'The Production of Literature' p. 123.
75 Peter Mann, *Books, Buyers and Borrowers* (London, 1971), *passim*; Laing, 'The Production of Literature', pp. 128–129.
76 Laing, 'The Production of Literature', p. 139.
77 Michael Hayes, 'Popular Fiction 1930–55', in Day, ed., *Literature and Culture in Modern Britain: Volume Two*, p. 73.
78 John Sutherland, *Reading the Decades: Fifty Years of the Nation's Bestselling Books* (London, 2002), pp. 56–57.
79 Laing, 'The Production of Literature', pp. 125, 128.
80 Laing, 'The Production of Literature', pp. 125–127; Michael Denning, *Cover Stories: Narrative and Ideology in the British Spy Thriller* (London, 1987), p. 21.
81 John Sutherland, *Bestsellers: Popular Fiction of the 1970s* (London, 1981), pp. 96–98, 104.
82 Laing, 'The Production of Literature', p. 129; Sutherland, *Reading the Decades*, pp. 16–17.
83 Laing, 'The Production of Literature', p. 126.
84 Sutherland, *Reading the Decades*, p. 74.
85 Dave Harker, 'Still Crazy After All These Years: What *Was* Popular Music in the 1960s?', in Moore-Gilbert and Seed, eds, *Cultural Revolution?*, pp. 238–241. This brilliantly iconoclastic essay is essential reading for anyone interested in the music of the sixties.
86 *Daily Mirror*, *Daily Express*, *Daily Mail* and *Daily Sketch*, 27 December 1967.
87 *Evening News*, 27 December 1967.
88 Miles, *Paul McCartney*, p. 369.
89 Reprinted in *NME Originals: The Beatles*, 3 April 2002.
90 See McKibbin, *Classes and Cultures*, p. 389.
91 Harker, 'Still Crazy After All These Years', pp. 241–242.
92 Wybrow, *Britain Speaks Out*, pp. 77, 80, 85, 89, 93.
93 Harker, 'Still Crazy After All These Years', pp. 242–243.

20 THE POUND IN YOUR POCKET

1 Pimlott, *Harold Wilson*, p. 443.
2 Castle diary, 11 May 1967.

3   Castle diary, 25 June 1968.
4   Pimlott, *Harold Wilson*, p. 446; and see Ponting, *Breach of Promise*, pp. 179–182.
5   Castle diary, 20 June 1967.
6   King diary, 25 June 1967.
7   Quoted in Ponting, *Breach of Promise*, p. 287.
8   Susan Strange, *Sterling and British Policy* (London, 1971), p. 258.
9   Sked and Cook, *Post-War Britain*, p. 223; Ponting, *Breach of Promise*, pp. 286–287; Tomlinson, *Economic Policy*, p. 139.
10 Morgan, *Callaghan*, pp. 255, 261.
11 Castle diary, 22 July 1967.
12 Morgan, *Callaghan*, pp. 260, 280.
13 Quotation from *Let's Go With Labour for the New Britain*; and for Wilson's strategy in 1967, see Ponting, *Breach of Promise*, pp. 288–289.
14 *The Times*, 9 September 1967; Foot, *The Politics of Harold Wilson*, p. 188.
15 Crossman diary, 21 November 1967, 20 June and, 19 March 1968.
16 Crossman diary, 5 September 1967.
17 Ponting, *Breach of Promise*, p. 289; Morgan, *Callaghan*, p. 266.
18 Morgan, *Callaghan*, pp. 266–268.
19 Pimlott, *Harold Wilson*, p. 470.
20 Paterson, *Tired and Emotional*, pp. 193–194.
21 Crossman diary, 3 October 1967; Castle diary, 2 October 1967.
22 Wilson diary note, 2 November 1967, quoted in Pimlott, *Harold Wilson*, p. 471.
23 Wilson diary note, 2 November 1967, quoted in Pimlott, *Harold Wilson*, pp. 471–472.
24 Paterson, *Tired and Emotional*, pp. 198–199.
25 *Daily Express*, 1 November 1967; Paterson, *Tired and Emotional*, pp. 198–202.
26 *The Times*, 3 November 1967.
27 Crossman diary, 1 November 1967.
28 Crossman diary, 3 November 1967; on Wilson's reluctance to sack Brown, see Pimlott, *Harold Wilson*, pp. 472–473.
29 Paterson, *Tired and Emotional*, p. 192.
30 Paterson, *Tired and Emotional*, p. 195.
31 Paterson, *Tired and Emotional*, pp. 195–196.
32 Callaghan, *Time and Chance*, p. 218.
33 Cairncross diary, 4 November 1967, quoted in Morgan, *Callaghan*, p. 269.
34 Callaghan, *Time and Chance*, p. 219.
35 Crossman diary, 8 November 1967.
36 See Ponting, *Breach of Promise*, p. 290; Pimlott, *Harold Wilson*, pp. 475–478; Morgan, *Callaghan*, pp. 270–271.
37 From the accounts in Pimlott, *Harold Wilson*, pp. 479–481; Ziegler, *Wilson*, pp. 273–274.
38 Crossman diary, 13 November 1967.
39 Callaghan, *Time and Chance*, pp. 220–221; Morgan, *Callaghan*, p. 272.
40 Castle diary, 16 November 1967.
41 Castle and Crossman diaries, 16 November 1967.
42 Jenkins, *A Life at the Centre*, p. 213.

43 Crossman diary, 17 November 1967.
44 On the Sheldon question, see Crossman diary, 16 and 17 November 1967; Jenkins, *A Life at the Centre*, p. 213; Dell, *The Chancellors*, pp. 344–345; Morgan, *Callaghan*, pp. 272–273.
45 Pimlott, *Harold Wilson*, p. 482.
46 Ponting, *Breach of Promise*, p. 295; Dell, *The Chancellors*, p. 345; Morgan, *Callaghan*, p. 273.
47 Dell, *The Chancellors*, p. 321.
48 Holt, *Second Amongst Equals*, p. 236.
49 On the press and Callaghan's own verdict, see Morgan, *Callaghan*, pp. 280–281. For a more generous verdict, see Morgan, *Callaghan*, pp. 283–285.
50 Morgan, *Callaghan*, p. 276.
51 Crossman diary, 20 November 1967.
52 Crossman diary, 22 November 1967.
53 *The Times*, 22 November 1967; Morgan, *Callaghan*, p. 274.
54 Castle diary, 22 November 1967. Casca was one of Julius Caesar's assassins, immortalised by Shakespeare as 'envious Casca'.
55 See King and Wybrow, eds, *British Political Opinion*, pp. 233, 246–251.
56 Crossman diary, 19 November 1967.
57 Crossman diary, 17 November 1967.
58 Pimlott, *Harold Wilson*, p. 483.
59 Crossman diary, 19 November 1967.
60 Pimlott, *Harold Wilson*, pp. 482–483.
61 Transcribed by the author from a BBC recording. There are different versions, for example in Wilson, *The Labour Government*, pp. 587–589, but these are the words he used on the night.
62 Crossman diary, 19 November 1967.
63 Castle diary, 21 September 1967.
64 Castle diary, 20 November 1967; Crossman diary, 24 November 1967.
65 Pimlott, *Harold Wilson*, pp. 483–484.
66 King and Wybrow, eds, *British Political Opinion*, p. 330.
67 King and Wybrow, eds, *British Political Opinion*, pp. 168, 10.
68 Margach, *The Anatomy of Power*, pp. 178–179.
69 Marcia Williams to Herbert Wilson, 23 November 1967, quoted in Ziegler, *Wilson*, p. 286.

21 I WAS LORD KITCHENER'S VALET

1 *Daily Mirror*, 11 November 1966.
2 MacDonald, *Revolution in the Head*, p. 189.
3 *New Musical Express*, 31 December 1966.
4 Badman, *The Beatles off the Record*, p. 258.
5 Miles, *Paul McCartney*, pp. 303–304.
6 MacDonald, *Revolution in the Head*, p. 206.
7 Norman, *Shout!*, p. 286.
8 MacDonald, *Revolution in the Head*, pp. 193–194.

9 Badman, *The Beatles off the Record*, p. 263.
10 Badman, *The Beatles off the Record*, p. 268–269.
11 Quoted in MacDonald, *Revolution in the Head*, p. 220; Norman, *Shout!*, p. 287.
12 Allan F. Moore, 'The Brilliant Career of *Sgt. Pepper*', in Aldgate, Chapman and Marwick, eds, *Windows on the Sixties*, p. 139.
13 *New Musical Express*, 11 February 1967.
14 *New Musical Express*, 20 May 1967.
15 Quoted in Badman, *The Beatles off the Record*, p. 289.
16 Miles, *Paul McCartney*, pp. 383–384.
17 See MacDonald, *Revolution in the Head*, p. 212; Miles, *Paul McCartney*, pp. 311–312.
18 On George Martin, see Norman, *Shout!*, pp. 282–283; Miles, *Paul McCartney*, pp. 319, 330–331.
19 Miles, *Paul McCartney*, p. 346.
20 See Moore, 'The Brilliant Career of *Sgt. Pepper*', pp. 140–144; MacDonald, *Revolution in the Head*, pp. 188–220.
21 See MacDonald, *Revolution in the Head*, pp. 210–211.
22 On the cover, see Miles, *Paul McCartney*, pp. 304–306, 333–342; Vyner, *Groovy Bob*, pp. 173–175.
23 MacDonald, *Revolution in the Head*, p. 220.
24 MacDonald, *Revolution in the Head*, p. 217.
25 Green, *All Dressed Up*, pp. 212–215.
26 *Time*, 7 July 1967; Green, *All Dressed Up*, pp. 212–213. Barry Miles, *Hippie* (London, 2004) is the best overview of the movement.
27 See Pressley, *Changing Times*, pp. 30–31.
28 See Marwick, *The Sixties*, pp. 480–483.
29 Norman, *Shout!*, p. 290; Benson, *The Rise of Consumer Society*, p. 166; Fielding, *Labour and Cultural Change*, p. 16.
30 Quoted in Marwick, *The Sixties*, p. 488.
31 Jackson, *The Sixties*, pp. 52–53.
32 *International Times*, 17 May 1967.
33 Clayson, *Beat Merchants*, pp. 240, 244.
34 Bacon, *London Live*, p. 92.
35 Green, *All Dressed Up*, pp. 217–219; Bacon, *London Live*, pp. 99–101.
36 See Gillett, *The Sound of the City*, p. 394;. 'Procul Harum', in Larkin, ed., *The Virgin Encyclopedia of Sixties Music*, pp. 360–361.
37 *Melody Maker*, 22 October 1966. On their early performances at UFO, see Tim Willis, *Madcap: The Half-Life of Syd Barrett, Pink Floyd's Lost Genius* (London, 2002), p. 70.
38 *Melody Maker*, 7 January 1967.
39 On the middle-class background of Pink Floyd, see Willis, *Madcap*, pp. 28–32.
40 See Frith and Horne, *Art into Pop*, p. 96.
41 See Green, *All Dressed up*, pp. 212–223.
42 Willis, *Madcap*, p. 71.
43 The most cogent analysis of Barrett's plight is in Willis, *Madcap*, esp. pp. 140–143, which suggests that he may have suffered from Asperger's syndrome.
44 *Daily Mirror*, 6 November and 6 September 1963.

45 Badman, *The Beatles off the Record*, pp. 290–291, 289; Norman, *Shout!*, p. 289.
46 *New Musical Express*, 27 May 1967.
47 Quoted in MacDonald, *Revolution in the Head*, p. xvii.
48 MacDonald, *The People's Music*, pp. 87–89.
49 Melly, *Revolt into Style*, p. 128.
50 Taylor, *After the War*, pp. 5–6.
51 L. P. Hartley, *The Go-Between* (London, 1953), p. 7.
52 Wilson, *Late Call*, pp. 7–32.
53 Bergonzi, *The Situation of the Novel*, pp. 150–151.
54 *The Times*, 7 January 1967.
55 *The Times*, 12 January 1968.
56 *The Times*, 12 and 17 September 1968.
57 *The Times*, 10 August 1967, 19 February 1969.
58 *The Times*, 1 March 1969.
59 *The Times*, 7 March 1969.
60 Briggs, *Competition*, pp. 587–588.
61 *The Times*, 6 March 1969.
62 See Harrison, *Young Meteors*, p. 148, although he dates the transition to 1965 and the launch of the magazine *Nova*.
63 Jackson, *The Sixties*, p. 55.
64 See Simon Sadler, 'British Architecture in the Sixties', in Stephens and Stout, eds, *Art and the 60s*, p. 132.
65 *The Ambassador*, May 1966, quoted in Jackson, *The Sixties*, p. 207.
66 On the influence of Mucha and Beardsley, see Mellor, 'Tomorrow Starts Now', in Mellor and Gervereau, eds, *The Sixties*, pp. 21–23; Garner, *Sixties Design*, p. 60.
67 Jackson, *The Sixties*, pp. 207–208.
68 Jackson, *The Sixties*, p. 209.
69 John Fowles, *The French Lieutenant's Woman* (London, 1969); and see Gilbert Phelps, 'The Post-War English Novel', in Boris Ford, ed., *The New Pelican Guide to English Literature, Volume 8: From Orwell to Naipaul* (revised edition: London, 1998), pp. 439–440; Bradbury, *The Modern British Novel*, pp. 358–359.
70 Booker, *The Neophiliacs*, pp. 23–24.
71 Quoted in Bernard, *Fashion in the 60s*, p. 69.
72 Wilson, *Adorned in Dreams*, p. 192.
73 On Clark in this context, see Levy, *Ready, Steady, Go!*, pp. 218–219; Fogg, *Boutique*, pp. 160–164. The definitive work on his career in the sixties is Judith Watt, *Ossie Clark: 1965–74* (London, 2003).
74 *Daily Sketch*, 22 July 1967.
75 See Wilson, *Adorned in Dreams*, p. 162.
76 Unknown interviewee quoted in Pressley, *Changing Times*, p. 29.
77 See Fogg, *Boutique*, pp. 160, 172.
78 *New Musical Express*, 1 July 1967.
79 Fogg, *Boutique*, p. 172.
80 John Peacock, *Fashion Sourcebooks: The 1960s* (London, 1998), p. 8.
81 Advertisement reprinted in *NME Originals: The Beatles*, 3 April 2002.

82 Aitken, *The Young Meteors*, p. 21.
83 Quoted in Fogg, *Boutique*, p. 159.
84 Fogg, *Boutique*, p. 175.
85 Aitken, *The Young Meteors*, pp. 23–25. On the exterior, see Levy, *Ready, Steady, Go!*, pp. 214–216.
86 *Daily Mirror*, 4 May 1964; see also the interview with Hulanicki in Pressley, *Changing Times*, p. 26.
87 Jackson, *The Sixties*, p. 43; Fogg, *Boutique*, p. 81; Levy, *Ready, Steady, Go!*, p. 220. The definitive work on Biba is Alywn W. Turner, *Biba: The Biba Experience* (London, 2004), and see also Barbara Hulanicki, *From A to Biba* (London, 1983), as well as the store history page at <http://www.bibacollection.co.uk/history.htm>.
88 Lawson, *Twiggy in Black and White*, p. 43.
89 *Daily Telegraph*, 27 October 1965.
90 Wilson, *Adorned in Dreams*, p. 193; Jackson, *The Sixties*, pp. 43–44; Fogg, *Boutique*, p. 81.
91 Wilson, *Adorned in Dreams*, pp. 177, 193.
92 Alexandra Pringle, 'Chelsea Girl', in Sara Maitland, ed., *Very Heaven: Looking Back at the 1960s* (London, 1998) p. 39.
93 Lawson, *Twiggy in Black and White*, p. 42.
94 Aitken, *The Young Meteors*, p. 18; Levy, *Ready, Steady, Go!*, p. 221.
95 Quoted in Levy, *Ready, Steady, Go!*, p. 220.
96 Aitken, *The Young Meteors*, pp. 18–9.
97 Rosie Young quoted in Akhtar and Humphries, *The Fifties and Sixties*, p. 49.
98 Aitken, *The Young Meteors*, p. 20.
99 See Jackson, *The Sixties*, p. 44; Fogg, *Boutique*, p. 86; <http://www.bibacollection.co.uk/history.htm>.
100 Aitken, *The Young Meteors*, pp. 19–20.
101 Quoted in Harris, Hyde and Smith, *1966 and All That*, p. 112.
102 Jackson, *The Sixties*, p. 44; Fogg, *Boutique*, p. 86.
103 See Fogg, *Boutique*, pp. 178–179.
104 Jackson, *The Sixties*, p. 209.

22 HEAVENS ABOVE!

1 On the financial acquisitiveness and right-wing political links of the Maharishi, see Green, *All Dressed Up*, pp. 230–231; Miles, *Paul McCartney*, pp. 400–403.
2 Badman, *The Beatles off the Record*, pp. 300–301; Miles, *Paul McCartney*, pp. 401–402.
3 Norman, *Shout!*, p. 297.
4 Norman, *Shout!*, p. 297.
5 Marianne Faithfull with David Dalton, *Faithfull* (London, 1994), p. 188.
6 Lewis, *The Life and Death of Peter Sellers*, pp. 40–41.
7 Raymond Durgnat, 'St Smallwood: Or, Left of *Heaven's Above!*' in Alan Burton, Tim O'Sullivan and Paul Wells, eds, *The Family Way: The Boulting Brothers and Postwar British Film Culture* (Trowbridge, 2000), p. 219.
8 *Observer*, 14 November 1965.
9 Lawton, *1963*, p. 176.
10 Booker, *The Neophiliacs*, pp. 165, 179.

11 Alan Sinfield, 'Varieties of Religion', in Sinfield, ed., *Society and Literature 1945–1970*, p. 105.
12 See Eric James, *A Life of John Robinson: Scholar, Pastor, Prophet* (London, 1987); Lawton, *1963*, pp. 176–177.
13 C. H. Rolph, ed., *The Trial of Lady Chatterley* (Harmondsworth, 1961), pp. 70–71.
14 *Guardian*, 7 November 1960.
15 *Observer*, 6 November 1960.
16 *Observer*, 17 March 1963.
17 John Robinson, *Honest to God* (London, 1963), pp. 57, 7–8.
18 Robinson, *Honest to God*, pp. 52, 87.
19 Robinson, *Honest to God*, ch. 6; P. A. Welsby, *A History of the Church of England 1945–80* (Oxford, 1984), p. 113.
20 Levin, *The Pendulum Years*, p. 104; Lawton, *1963*, p. 177; David L. Edwards, ed., *The Honest to God Debate* (London, 1963).
21 Quoted in Sinfield, 'Varieties of Religion', p. 106.
22 Levin, *The Pendulum Years*, pp. 108–109.
23 *Sunday Telegraph*, 24 March 1963.
24 Levin, *The Pendulum Years*, p. 107.
25 Sinfield, 'Varieties of Religion', p. 107; Waugh, *Harvest of the Sixties*, p. 65.
26 Robinson, *Honest to God*, p. 43.
27 *Guardian*, 11 January 1963.
28 See Durgnat, *A Mirror for England*, pp. 99–100.
29 'Church-Going', in Philip Larkin, *Collected Poems* (London, 1990), pp. 97–98.
30 For example, 'Verses turned in aid of A Public Subscription (1952) towards the restoration of the Church of St Katherine, Chiselhampton, Oxon', or 'Church of England thoughts occasioned by hearing the bells of Magdalen Tower from the Botanic Gardens, Oxford, on St Mary Magdalen's Day', in John Betjeman, *Collected Poems* (London, 2001), pp. 149–151, 156–157.
31 See the discussion in C. B. Cox, 'Welsh Bards in Hard Times: Dylan Thomas and R. S. Thomas', in Ford, ed., *From Orwell to Naipaul*, pp. 208–213.
32 Sinfield, 'Varieties of Religion', p. 87; Grace Davie, *Religion in Britain since 1945: Believing Without Belonging* (Oxford, 1994), p. 31.
33 Sinfield, 'Varieties of Religion', p. 92; Adrian Hastings, *A History of English Christianity 1920–1985* (London, 1986), p. 454.
34 See Humphrey Carpenter, *The Inklings* (London, 1978), pp. 39–45, 226–228; Weight, *Patriots*, p. 224.
35 Peter Willmott and Michael Young, *Family and Class in a London Suburb* (London, 1960), pp. 82–83.
36 Willmott and Young, *Family and Class in a London Suburb*, p. 83.
37 Hastings, *A History of English Christianity*, p. 551; Davie, *Religion in Britain since 1945*, p. 53.
38 Marwick, *British Society since 1945*, pp. 101, 110; McKibbin, *Classes and Cultures*, p. 275.
39 Sinfield, 'Varieties of Religion', p. 109; Davie, *Religion in Britain since 1945*, p. 52.
40 See Peter Jupp, *From Dust to Ashes: The Replacement of Burial by Cremation in England 1840–1967* (London, 1990); Davie, *Religion in Britain since 1945*, pp. 81–82.

41 Sampson, *Anatomy of Britain*, pp. 169–170.
42 Davie, *Religion in Britain since 1945*, p. 61.
43 Sampson, *Anatomy of Britain*, pp. 170–171.
44 Davie, *Religion in Britain since 1945*, p. 58; Weight, *Patriots*, p. 443.
45 Weight, *Patriots*, p. 443.
46 Davie, *Religion in Britain since 1945*, p. 122.
47 Hastings, *A History of English Christianity*, p. 421. See also Davie, *Religion in Britain since 1945*, p. 33; Weight, *Patriots*, pp. 440–441.
48 Davie, *Religion in Britain since 1945*, p. 34.
49 Weight, *Patriots*, p. 447.
50 See Owen Chadwick, *Michael Ramsey: A Life* (London, 1990), p. 114.
51 Bryan R. Wilson, *Religion in Secular Society* (Harmondsworth, 1969), pp. 10–11.
52 Callum Brown, *The Death of Christian Britain: Understanding Secularisation 1800–2000* (London, 2001), p. 188.
53 Sinfield, 'Varieties of Religion', pp. 90–91.
54 Very oddly, one in six of those who did *not* believe in God, and one in five of those who did not believe that Jesus was divine, still *did* believe in the Virgin Birth, suggesting immense confusion in many minds: Mass Observation, *Puzzled People: A Study of Popular Attitudes to Religion, Ethics, Progress and Politics in a London Borough* (London, 1948), pp. 156ff.
55 Davie, *Religion in Britain since 1945*, pp. 78–79.
56 Davie, *Religion in Britain since 1945*, pp. 4, 12–13, 18–19.
57 Norman Davies, *The Isles: A History* (London, 1999), pp. 819–820.
58 Sutherland, *Reading the Decades*, p. 55.
59 Weight, *Patriots*, p. 445.
60 Quoted in Davie, *Religion in Britain since 1945*, p. 79.
61 See Edward Said, *Orientalism: Western Conceptions of the Orient* (London, 1995).
62 Landy, *British Genres*, pp. 417–418.
63 Agatha Christie, *Endless Night* (London, 1967), quoted in Robert Barnard, *A Talent to Deceive: An Appreciation of Agatha Christie* (London, 1990), p. 56.
64 Green, *All Dressed Up*, pp. 224–229; Akhtar and Humphries, *Some Liked It Hot*, pp. 130–149.
65 George Orwell, *The Road to Wigan Pier* (Harmondsworth, 1962), p. 152.
66 Levin, *The Pendulum Years*, p. 9.
67 See Green, *All Dressed Up*, pp. 227–228.
68 See Jonathan Bellman, 'Indian Resonances in the British Invasion', *Journal of Musicology* 15:1, Winter 1997, pp. 116–136. I am indebted to Dr Joe Street for bringing this invaluable article to my attention. For Harrison and the sitar, see Norman, *Shout!*, pp. 267–268; MacDonald, *Revolution in the Head*, pp. 144–147; Badman, *The Beatles off the Record*, pp. 190–191; Miles, *Paul McCartney*, p. 397.
69 Norman, *Shout!*, p. 269.
70 *New Musical Express*, 2 September 1966.
71 On the visit to Rishikesh, see Norman, *Shout!*, pp. 318–321; Miles, *Paul McCartney*, pp. 408–430.
72 Miles, *Paul McCartney*, p. 412.

73 McCartney interviewed in Miles, *Paul McCartney*, pp. 424–425.
74 Norman, *Shout!*, p. 320.
75 MacDonald, *Revolution in the Head*, pp. 262–263.
76 *New Musical Express*, 1 June 1968.
77 Anthony Powell, *Hearing Secret Harmonies*, in *A Dance to the Music of Time: IV, Winter* (London, 1997), p. 534.
78 Humphrey Carpenter, *J. R. R. Tolkien: A Biography* (London, 1977), pp. 77–78, 132; Humphrey Carpenter, *The Inklings* (London, 1978), pp. 156–159. See also Tom Shippey, *J. R. R. Tolkien: Author of the Century* (London, 2000), pp. 312–318, which argues that Tolkien's antipathy to modernism largely explains why professional literary critics sneer at his work.
79 Carpenter, *J. R. R. Tolkien: A Biography*, pp. 232–233.
80 Meredith Veldman, *Fantasy, the Bomb and the Greening of Britain: Romantic Protest 1945–1980* (Cambridge, 1994), pp. 107–108, 98.
81 See Shippey, *J. R. R. Tolkien: Author of the Century*, pp. vii–xxxv, 305–328.
82 Veldman, *Fantasy, the Bomb and the Greening of Britain*, pp. 45–49; Stevenson, *The British Novel since the Thirties*, p. 122; Taylor, *After the War*, p. 177.
83 Shippey, *J. R. R. Tolkien: Author of the Century*, p. 121. See also Patrick Curry, *Defending Middle-Earth: Tolkien: Myth and Modernity* (London, 1997), pp. 100–103.
84 Stevenson, *The British Novel since the Thirties*, p. 107.
85 See Bergonzi, *The Situation of the Novel*, p. 75; S. W. Dawson, 'Iris Murdoch: The Limits of Contrivance', in Ford, ed., *From Orwell to Naipaul*, pp. 214–216.
86 Steven Earnshaw, 'Novel Voices' in Bloom and Day, eds, *Literature and Culture in Modern Britain*, pp. 58–59.
87 Blake Morrison, *The Movement: English Poetry and Fiction of the 1950s* (Oxford, 1980), p. 244.
88 On the links between Pinter and Murdoch, see Waugh, *Harvest of the Sixties*, p. 65.
89 Bergonzi, *Wartime and Aftermath*, p. 205; Lacey, *British Realist Theatre*, p. 144.
90 Shellard, *British Theatre since the War*, pp. 92–93.
91 Taylor, *The Second Wave*, p. 206.
92 Peter Hall, *Making an Exhibition of Myself* (London, 1993), pp. 174–178; Waugh, *Harvest of the Sixties*, pp. 119–120; Shellard, *British Theatre since the War*, pp. 114–115.
93 See Bergonzi, *The Situation of the Novel*, p. 23; Bergonzi, *Wartime and Aftermath*, p. 190; Alan Sinfield, *Literature, Politics and Culture in Post-War Britain* (London, 1989), p. 142; Stevenson, *The British Novel since the Thirties*, p. 169.
94 See Bergonzi, *Wartime and Aftermath*, p. 191.
95 Harold Pinter, *The Caretaker* (London, 1960); see also John Russell Taylor, *Anger and After: A Guide to the New British Drama* (Harmondsworth, 1963), p. 299; Shellard, *British Theatre since the War*, p. 93.
96 See Konrad Lorenz, *On Aggression* (London, 1966); for the influence of Lorenz's ideas on contemporary English literature, see Waugh, *Harvest of the Sixties*, p. 58.
97 See Levin, *The Pendulum Years*, p. 409.
98 Sutherland, *Reading the Decades*, pp. 79–80.
99 Desmond Morris, *The Naked Ape* (London, 1967), p. 9.
100 Morris, *The Naked Ape*, p. 74.

101 Morris, *The Naked Ape*, p. 21.
102 Morris, *The Naked Ape*, p. 157.
103 Morris, *The Naked Ape*, pp. 158–159.
104 Morris, *The Naked Ape*, p. 56.
105 Morris, *The Naked Ape*, pp. 77–80.
106 Morris, *The Naked Ape*, p. 82.
107 Morris, *The Naked Ape*, 87.
108 Morris, *The Naked Ape*, p. 156.
109 *The Times*, 6 January 1968.

23 LOVE WITHOUT FEAR

1 Quoted in Jonathan Dollimore, 'The Challenge of Sexuality', in Sinfield, ed., *Society and Literature 1945–1970*, p. 51.
2 *The Times*, 10 August and 5 September 1967.
3 Weeks, *Sex, Politics and Society*, p. 11.
4 Akhtar and Humphries, *The Fifties and Sixties*, p. 11.
5 John Hopkins interviewed in Green, *Days in the Life*, p. 419.
6 Marwick, *The Sixties*, p. 95.
7 Green, *All Dressed Up*, p. 311.
8 Mary Whitehouse, *Whatever Happened to Sex?* (Hove, 1977), pp. 8–9.
9 Hera Cook, *The Long Sexual Revolution: English Women, Sex and Contraception 1800–1975* (Oxford, 2004), pp. 156, 178.
10 Tony Bennett in *Marxism Today*, June 1983, quoted in Hill, *Sex, Class and Realism*, p. 16.
11 Nina Fishman interviewed in Green, *Days in the Life*, p. 427.
12 Annan, *Our Age*, p. 184.
13 McKibbin, *Classes and Cultures*, p. 314.
14 Richard Hoggart, *The Uses of Literacy* (Harmondsworth, 1958), p. 98.
15 Michael Schofield, *The Sexual Behaviour of Young People* (London, 1965), pp. 84–85.
16 A friend of Amis junior, meanwhile, claimed to have been taken with his class of pubescent boys 'on a little tour of the supposed masturbation ward of the local hospital'. See Kingsley Amis, *Memoirs* (London, 1991), p. 11.
17 Amis, *Memoirs*, pp. 10–12; see also Jackson, *The Middle Classes*, pp. 222–223.
18 Jo Roffey interviewed in Akhtar and Humphries, *The Fifties and Sixties*, pp. 170–171. Her husband himself admitted that he was overexcited and slightly drunk, and that his behaviour had been 'right out of order': see the Victor Roffey interview on the same page.
19 There was a nurse present, so 'it was all above board'. Indeed, the woman reported that she was slightly disappointed when the specialist stopped arousing her. Anne Grundy interviewed in Akhtar and Humphries, *The Fifties and Sixties*, pp. 171–172.
20 Eve Moffat interviewed in Akhtar and Humphries, *The Fifties and Sixties*, p. 172.
21 George Mikes, *How to Be a Brit: A George Mikes Omnibus* (London, 1984), p. 35. According to Richard Weight, Mikes remarked that he received more letters agreeing with this observation than about any other: see Weight, *Patriots*, p. 769.
22 Paul Ferris, *Sex and the British: A Twentieth-Century History* (London, 1993), p. 14.

23 Eustace Chesser, *The Sexual, Marital and Family Relationships of the English Woman* (London, 1956), esp. pp. 311–313.
24 McKibbin, *Classes and Cultures*, p. 298.
25 Ferris, *Sex and the British*, p. 86.
26 Cate Haste, *Rules of Desire: Sex in Britain: World War I to the Present* (London, 1992), p. 69; Stevenson, *British Society 1914–45*, pp. 153–155; Cook, *The Long Sexual Revolution*, pp. 122–142.
27 Ferris, *Sex and the British*, p. 91.
28 Ferris, *Sex and the British*, p. 121.
29 Weeks, *Sex, Politics and Society*, pp. 205–206; Haste, *Rules of Desire*, p. 91.
30 Janet Chance, *The Cost of English Morals* (London, 1931), p. 35.
31 Lewis, *The Fifties*, p. 63; Ferris, *Sex and the British*, p. 129; Sutherland, *Reading the Decades*, pp. 10–11.
32 Weeks, *Sex, Politics and Society*, pp. 201, 257; McKibbin, *Classes and Cultures*, p. 299.
33 Eustace Chesser, *Love Without Fear: A Plain Guide to Sex Technique for Every Married Adult* (London, 1941); Sutherland, *Reading the Decades*, pp. 10–12; Cook, *The Long Sexual Revolution*, p. 226.
34 See Haste, *Rules of Desire*, p. 186.
35 McKibbin, *Classes and Cultures*, p. 299.
36 Haste, *Rules of Desire*, p. 109.
37 Renee Lester interviewed in Akhtar and Humphries, *The Fifties and Sixties*, pp. 175–176.
38 Ray Rochford interviewed in Akhtar and Humphries, *The Fifties and Sixties*, p. 176.
39 Haste, *Rules of Desire*, pp. 108–110; Ferris, *Sex and the British*, pp. 142–148.
40 Weeks, *Sex, Politics and Society*, p. 237.
41 David R. Mace, *Marriage Counselling* (London, 1948), p. 123; Weeks, *Sex, Politics and Society*, p. 237; Haste, *Rules of Desire*, pp. 144–145.
42 Maxine Davis, *The Sexual Responsibility of Women* (London, 1957), pp. 118–119.
43 Marie Robinson, *The Power of Surrender* (London, 1959), quoted in Haste, *Rules of Desire*, p. 156.
44 See Geoffrey Gorer, *Exploring English Character* (London, 1955), ch. 8.
45 Chesser, *The Sexual, Marital and Family Relationships of the English Woman*, pp. 312, 348.
46 Haste, *Rules of Desire*, pp. 72–73; McKibbin, *Classes and Cultures*, p. 297.
47 Jo Roffey interviewed in Akhtar and Humphries, *The Fifties and Sixties*, p. 169.
48 Hoggart, *The Uses of Literacy*, p. 99.
49 Gary Cross, ed., *Worktowners at Blackpool: Mass-Observation and Popular Leisure in the 1930s* (London, 1991), quoted in Ferris, *Sex and the British*, p. 136.
50 B. S. Rowntree and G. R. Lavers, *English Life and Leisure* (London, 1951), quoted in Marwick, *British Society since 1945*, pp. 70–71.
51 Weeks, *Sex, Politics and Society*, p. 240; Ferris, *Sex and the British*, pp. 27, 160–161.
52 Tim Newburn, *Permission and Regulation: Law and Morals in Post-War Britain* (London, 1992), p. 51.
53 John Wolfenden, *Turning Points: Memoirs* (London, 1976), p. 130.
54 Newburn, *Permission and Regulation*, pp. 53–54.
55 Haste, *Rules of Desire*, p. 172.

56 See Weeks, *Sex, Politics and Society*, p. 240; Dan Rebellato, *1956 and All That: The Making of Modern British Drama* (London, 1999), p. 158.
57 Weight, *Patriots*, p. 374.
58 Quoted in Weight, *Patriots*, p. 375.
59 *Report of the Committee on Homosexual Offences and Prostitution*, pp. 20, 22.
60 Wolfenden, *Turning Points*, pp. 141–142.
61 For two useful discussions of the legacy of the Wolfenden Report, see Weeks, *Sex, Politics and Society*, pp. 239–244; Newburn, *Permission and Regulation*, pp. 49–70.
62 Patrick Devlin, *The Enforcement of Morals* (Oxford, 1959), pp. 13–14.
63 Hopkins, *The New Look*, p. 205; Weight, *Patriots*, p. 375.
64 Annan, *Our Age*, pp. 186–187; Ferris, *Sex and the British*, pp. 162–163; White, *London in the Twentieth Century*, pp. 322–323, 344.
65 Quoted in Newburn, *Permission and Regulation*, p. 57.
66 See Max Caulfield, *Mary Whitehouse* (Oxford, 1975), p. 78.
67 Schofield, *The Sexual Behaviour of Young People*, p. 27.
68 Mary Ingham, *Now We Are Thirty: Women of the Breakthrough Generation* (London, 1981), p. 62.
69 *Daily Mirror*, 15 September 1958.
70 Masters, *The Swinging Sixties*, pp. 34–35.
71 Steve Abrams interviewed in Green, *Days in the Life*, p. 418.
72 Akhtar and Humphries, *The Fifties and Sixties*, p. 180.
73 Ferris, *Sex and the British*, pp. 200–201; Cook, *The Long Sexual Revolution*, p. 139.
74 Weeks, *Sex, Politics and Society*, p. 259.
75 *Daily Mirror*, 15 November 1963.
76 Ferris, *Sex and the British*, pp. 188, 200.
77 Cook, *The Long Sexual Revolution*, pp. 278–279, 268.
78 Geoffrey Gorer, *Sex and Marriage in England Today* (London, 1971), pp. 132–133, 216.
79 Margaret Bone, *Family Planning Services in England and Wales* (London, 1973), p. 58.
80 Ferris, *Sex and the British*, pp. 204–206.
81 See Cook, *The Long Sexual Revolution*, pp. 288–289.
82 Haste, *Rules of Desire*, pp. 216–217; Ferris, *Sex and the British*, p. 207; Cook, *The Long Sexual Revolution*, pp. 302–303, 268–269.
83 Masters, *The Swinging Sixties*, p. 35.
84 Quoted in Davies, *Permissive Britain*, p. 69. This preposterous claim was made, apparently, at the International Congress of Psychosomatic Medicine, but Davies does not give the date.
85 Haste, *Rules of Desire*, p. 151.
86 Jane Lewis, 'Marriage', in Zweiniger-Bargielowska, ed., *Women in Twentieth-Century Britain*, pp. 71–75; Weeks, *Sex, Politics and Society*, p. 252.
87 Ferris, *Sex and the British*, p. 185.
88 Aitken, *The Young Meteors*, p. 106.
89 Drusilla Beyfus, *The English Marriage: What It Is Like to Be Married Today* (London, 1968), pp. 73–101.
90 Schofield, *The Sexual Behaviour of Young People*, pp. 45–47.
91 Schofield, *The Sexual Behaviour of Young People*, p. 64.
92 Schofield, *The Sexual Behaviour of Young People*, pp. 78, 231.

93　Gorer, *Sex and Marriage in England Today*, p. 30.
94　Gorer, *Sex and Marriage in England Today*, pp. 39, 44–45.
95　Gorer, *Sex and Marriage in England Today*, pp. 51–54.
96　Gorer, *Sex and Marriage in England Today*, pp. 114–115, 217.
97　Gorer, *Sex and Marriage in England Today*, p. 116.
98　Schofield, *The Sexual Behaviour of Young People*, p. 242.
99　Schofield, *The Sexual Behaviour of Young People*, pp. 240, 253–254.
100　See, for example, T. R. Fyvel, *The Insecure Offenders* (Harmondsworth, 1964).
101　Schofield, *The Sexual Behaviour of Young People*, pp. 99–102.
102　Davies, *Permissive Britain*, p. 65; Schofield, *The Sexual Behaviour of Young People*, p. 108.
103　Gorer, *Sex and Marriage in England Today*, p. 214.
104　Gorer, *Sex and Marriage in England Today*, p. 206.
105　Gorer, *Sex and Marriage in England Today*, p. 30.
106　Clifford Allen, *Homosexuality: Its Nature, Causation and Treatment* (London, 1958), p. 34; Eustace Chesser, *Odd Man Out: Homosexuality in Men and Women* (London, 1959), p. 48.
107　Noel Currer-Briggs interviewed in Akhtar and Humphries, *The Fifties and Sixties*, p. 173.
108　Gorer, *Sex and Marriage in England Today*, pp. 190–191.
109　Gorer, *Sex and Marriage in England Today*, pp. 192–195.
110　Gorer, *Sex and Marriage in England Today*, p. 204.
111　Unknown interviewee quoted in Pressley, *Changing Times*, p. 82.
112　*The Times*, 7 March 1958.
113　Masters, *The Swinging Sixties*, pp. 120–127; Ferris, *Sex and the British*, p. 159; Newburn, *Permission and Regulation*, p. 56.
114　Quoted in Newburn, *Permission and Regulation*, p. 176.
115　Dollimore, 'The Challenge of Sexuality', p. 62.
116　Abse was also the author of the intriguing *Fellatio, Masochism, Politics and Love* (London, 2000).
117　See Masters, *The Swinging Sixties*, pp. 126–127.
118　Castle diary, 11 February 1966.
119　Quoted in Masters, *The Swinging Sixties*, pp. 127–128.
120　Stephen Jeffrey-Poulter, *Peers, Queers and Commons: The Struggle for Gay Law Reform from 1950 to the Present* (London, 1991), pp. 48–49; Weight, *Patriots*, p. 376.
121　Masters, *The Swinging Sixties*, p. 128.
122　Green, *All Dressed Up*, p. 389.
123　Lewis, 'Marriage', p. 74.
124　*Guardian*, 11 October 1967.
125　*The Times*, 16 June 1971.
126　Baston, *Reggie*, pp. 348–349.
127　*Evening News*, 24 September 1969.
128　Weeks, *Sex, Politics and Society*, p. 238.
129　Weeks, *Sex, Politics and Society*, p. 253.

24 THE ARCTIC WINTER OF THE TREASURY

1　Wilson to Johnson, 17 November 1967, quoted in Ziegler, *Wilson*, p. 284.
2　Crossman diary, 26 November 1967.

3. Quoted in Pearce, *Denis Healey*, p. 366.
4. Wybrow, *Britain Speaks Out*, p. 84.
5. Benn diary, 11 February 1968.
6. Crossman diary, 31 December 1967.
7. Callaghan, *Time and Chance*, p. 222.
8. Pimlott, *Harold Wilson*, p. 484.
9. Crossman diary, 5 January 1968; and see also Morgan, *Callaghan*, pp. 15–16, 290–294, 319–321.
10. Crossman diary, 6 February 1968.
11. Owen, *Time to Declare*, p. 156.
12. Pimlott, *Harold Wilson*, p. 488.
13. Callaghan, *Time and Chance*, p. 221.
14. S. Crosland, *Tony Crosland*, pp. 187–189.
15. Jenkins, *A Life at the Centre*, p. 218.
16. Jenkins, *A Life at the Centre*, p. 217; Radice, *Friends and Rivals*, p. 152. On Wilson's skill at playing off the two contenders against each other, see Pimlott, *Harold Wilson*, p. 403.
17. Paterson, *Tired and Emotional*, pp. 227–228; Healey, *The Time of My Life*, p. 335.
18. See Crossman diary, 14 September 1967; Paterson, *Tired and Emotional*, p. 228.
19. Ponting, *Breach of Promise*, p. 298.
20. Healey, *The Time of My Life*, pp. 335–336; and see Ponting, *Breach of Promise*, p. 299.
21. Wilson, *The Labour Government 1964–1970*, p. 470.
22. Castle diary, 13 December 1967.
23. Crossman diary, 13 December 1967.
24. Castle diary, 15 December 1967.
25. Castle and Crossman diaries, 15 December 1967; Healey, *The Time of My Life*, p. 335.
26. Crossman diary, 16 December 1967.
27. Castle diary, 16 December 1967.
28. Crossman diary, 16 December 1967.
29. Castle diary, 16 December 1967.
30. Crossman diary, 17 December 1967.
31. Castle diary, 18 December 1967.
32. Crossman diary, 18 December 1967.
33. Castle diary, 18 December 1967.
34. Crossman diary, 18 December 1967.
35. Brown, *In My Way*, p. 167; and see also Paterson, *Tired and Emotional*, pp. 231–232.
36. Healey, *The Time of My Life*, pp. 335–336.
37. Wright, *Britain in the Age of Economic Management*, pp. 161–162; Dell, *The Chancellors*, p. 345.
38. Jenkins, *A Life at the Centre*, p. 222.
39. Jenkins, *A Life at the Centre*, p. 230.
40. Jenkins, *A Life at the Centre*, p. 220.
41. Jenkins, *A Life at the Centre*, pp. 222–224.
42. Crossman diary, 20 December 1967; Ponting, *Breach of Promise*, p. 304.
43. Jenkins, *A Life at the Centre*, p. 227.

44 Jenkins, *A Life at the Centre*, pp. 224–225.
45 Benn diary, 3 January 1968.
46 S. Crosland, *Tony Crosland*, p. 194; Benn diary, 5 January 1968.
47 Benn and Crossman diaries, 5 January 1968.
48 Castle and Benn diaries, 12 January 1968.
49 Castle diary, 12 January 1968.
50 Crossman diary, 12 January 1968.
51 Benn diary, 12 January 1968.
52 Crossman diary, 12 January 1968.
53 Ponting, *Breach of Promise*, p. 308.
54 Benn diary, 12 January 1968.
55 Benn diary, 12 January 1968.
56 Pearce, *Denis Healey*, p. 351.
57 Hansard, 20 March 1968.
58 John le Carré, *A Small Town in Germany* (London, 1999), p. 73.
59 'Homage to a Government', in Larkin, *Collected Poems*, p. 171.
60 Bartlett, *The Special Relationship*, pp. 109–118; Alan Dobson, *Anglo-American Relations in the Twentieth Century* (London, 1995), p. 138; Young, *International Policy*, p. 20.
61 Quoted in Ponting, *Breach of Promise*, p. 59.
62 Quoted in Richard Aldrich, *The Hidden Hand: Britain, America and Cold War Secret Intelligence* (London, 2001), p. 644.
63 Morgan, *Callaghan*, p. 253.
64 Jenkins, *A Life at the Centre*, p. 220.
65 See Jenkins, *A Life at the Centre*, pp. 233–237; Ponting, *Breach of Promise*, pp. 372–373.
66 King diary, 13 March 1968.
67 Tomlinson, *Economic Policy*, p. 60.
68 Cairncross, *Managing the British Economy in the 1960s*, p. 209.
69 Crossman diary, 4 March 1968.
70 Jenkins, *A Life at the Centre*, pp. 234–236.
71 Jenkins, *A Life at the Centre*, p. 236; Pimlott, *Harold Wilson*, p. 494.
72 Castle diary, 14 March 1968.
73 Jenkins, *A Life at the Centre*, p. 237.
74 Pimlott, *Harold Wilson*, p. 495. The phrase 'office boy' comes from Jenkins, *A Life at the Centre*, p. 236.
75 Benn diary, 14 March 1968.
76 Pimlott, *Harold Wilson*, p. 497.
77 Jenkins, *A Life at the Centre*, p. 238.
78 Benn diary, 14 March 1968.
79 Jenkins, *A Life at the Centre*, p. 238; Pimlott, *Harold Wilson*, p. 499.
80 Marsh, *Off the Rails*, pp. 120–121.
81 Benn diary, 14 March 1968.
82 Benn diary, 14 March 1968.
83 Castle diary, 14 March 1968.
84 Castle diary, 14 March 1968.
85 Benn diary, 14 March 1968.

86 Castle diary, 14 March 1968.
87 Jim Prior, *A Balance of Power* (London, 1986), p. 46.
88 Benn diary, 14 March 1968.
89 Castle diary, 15 March 1968.
90 Pimlott, *Harold Wilson*, pp. 501–502.
91 Pimlott, *Harold Wilson*, p. 502.
92 Brown to Wilson, 15 March 1968, reprinted in Paterson, *Tired and Emotional*, pp. 251–252.
93 Paterson, *Tired and Emotional*, p. 253; and see Pimlott, *Harold Wilson*, pp. 501–503.
94 See *Daily Mirror* and *The Times*, 16 March 1968.
95 *The Times*, 14 January 1967.
96 Crossman diary, 17 March 1968.
97 Benn diary, 15 March 1968.
98 See Paterson, *Tired and Emotional*, pp. 256–287.
99 Patrick Marnham, *The Private Eye Story* (London, 1982), p. 117.
100 Crossman diary, 18 March 1968.
101 Castle diary, 13 June 1968; Ponting, *Breach of Promise*, pp. 373–374; Hennessy, *The Prime Minister*, p. 318.
102 Ponting, *Breach of Promise*, p. 374.
103 See Jenkins, *A Life at the Centre*, pp. 241–243.
104 Jenkins, *A Life at the Centre*, pp. 244–245.
105 See Jenkins, *A Life at the Centre*, p. 233; Ponting, *Breach of Promise*, p. 309; Dell, *The Chancellors*, p. 357; Tomlinson, *Economic Policy*, p. 208.
106 Crossman and Castle diaries, 19 March 1968.
107 *Spectator*, 5 April 1968; Jenkins, *A Life at the Centre*, p. 246.

25 PLAY POWER

1 Catterall and Wells, *Your Face Here*, pp. 50–51, 56.
2 Catterall and Wells, *Your Face Here*, pp. 45–46.
3 Aldgate and Richards, *Best of British*, p. 205.
4 See Aldgate and Richards, *Best of British*, pp. 207, 215.
5 *Daily Telegraph*, 19 December 1968; the other quotations are from Catterall and Wells, *Your Face Here*, pp. 60–61.
6 *The Times*, 19 December 1968.
7 See Green, *Days in the Life*, pp. 2–5.
8 Rowbotham, *Promise of a Dream*, pp. 6–8.
9 See Green, *Days in the Life*, x.
10 See Andrew Wilson, 'A Poetics of Dissent: Notes on a Developing Counterculture in London in the Early Sixties', in Stephens and Stout, eds, *Art and the 60s*, pp. 92–95; Hewison, *Too Much*, pp. 113–114; Green, *Days in the Life*, pp. 66–74.
11 Quoted in Green, *Days in the Life*, p. 70.
12 Hewison, *Too Much*, p. 114.
13 Sue Miles and Barry Miles quoted in Green, *Days in the Life*, pp. 70–71.
14 Green, *All Dressed Up*, pp. 132–133.
15 Michael White, *Empty Seats* (London, 1984), pp. 77–78.

16 Masters, *The Swinging Sixties*, pp. 153–154.

17 *New Society*, 27 July 1967; Wilson, 'A Poetics of Dissent', pp. 100–102; Hewison, *Too Much*, pp. 118–119.

18 *Exquisite Corpse* 11, Spring/Summer 2002, online at <http://www.corpse.org/issue_11/manifestos/levy.html>.

19 See Green, *Days in the Life*, pp. 76–77; Green, *All Dressed Up*, pp. 144–145; Miles, *Paul McCartney*, pp. 223–229.

20 Green, *All Dressed Up*, p. 146.

21 Craig Sams quoted in Green, *Days in the Life*, pp. 141–142.

22 Hewison, *Too Much*, pp. 94–95, 119; Green, *Days in the Life*, pp. 113–127; Green, *All Dressed Up*, pp. 148–152.

23 Hewison, *Too Much*, p. 121; Green, *Days in the Life*, pp. 119–121; Green, *All Dressed Up*, pp. 153–155.

24 Chris Rowley quoted in Green, *Days in the Life*, p. 114.

25 Green, *Days in the Life*, pp. 124–125; Green, *All Dressed Up*, pp. 156–159.

26 See Hewison, *Too Much*, p. 173; Green, *Days in the Life*, pp. 228–236.

27 Mark Williams quoted in Green, *Days in the Life*, p. 231.

28 See Hewison, *Too Much*, pp. 172–174.

29 Jerome Burne quoted in Green, *Days in the Life*, p. 400.

30 Quoted in Green, *Days in the Life*, p. 187.

31 Mark Williams quoted in Green, *Days in the Life*, p. 231.

32 Peter Roberts quoted in Green, *Days in the Life*, p. 49.

33 Quoted in Green, *Days in the Life*, p. 46.

34 Rowbotham, *Promise of a Dream*, p. 210.

35 Jenny Diski, 'A Long Forgotten War', *London Review of Books*, 6 July 2000, online at <http://www.lrb.co.uk/v22/n13/disk01.html>.

36 Nicola Lane quoted in Green, *Days in the Life*, p. 401.

37 Quoted in Green, *Days in the Life*, p. 187.

38 Rowbotham, *Promise of a Dream*, p. 134.

39 Quoted in Green, *Days in the Life*, p. 187.

40 Hewison, *In Anger*, p. 163; Rebellato, *1956 and All That*, p. 19; Veldman, *Fantasy, the Bomb, and the Greening of Britain*, pp. 180–186.

41 See Laing, *Representations of Working-Class Life*, pp. 197–202; Maurice Cowling, 'Raymond Williams in Retrospect', *New Criterion*, February 1990; Colls, *Identity of England*, pp. 362–364.

42 Eric Hobsbawm, *Interesting Times: A Twentieth-Century Life* (London, 2002), p. 211.

43 Krishan Kumar, 'The Social and Cultural Setting', in Ford, ed., *From Orwell to Naipaul*, pp. 44–45.

44 John Seed, 'Hegemony Postponed: The Unravelling of the Culture of Consensus in Britain in the 1960s', in Moore-Gilbert and Seed, eds, *Cultural Revolution?*, p. 37.

45 Quoted in Diski, 'A Long Forgotten War'.

46 *Guardian*, 24 June 1967.

47 Hobsbawm, *Interesting Times*, p. 254.

48 Pimlott, *Harold Wilson*, pp. 391–392.

49 Pimlott, *Harold Wilson*, p. 459.

50. *Spectator*, 21 October 1966; and see Hewison, *Too Much*, pp. 92–94; David Caute, *The Year of the Barricades: A Journey through 1968* (New York, 1988), pp. 274–275.
51. Michael Frayn, 'Festival', in Sissons and French, eds, *The Age of Austerity*, pp. 307–308.
52. See Rowbotham, *Promise of a Dream*, p. 172.
53. Quoted in Green, *Days in the Life*, p. 61.
54. Quoted in Green, *Days in the Life*, pp. 61–62.
55. Green, *All Dressed Up*, p. 260; Young, *International Policy*, p. 78.
56. See Cole, *As It Seemed to Me*, p. 48.
57. Rowbotham, *Promise of a Dream*, p. 179.
58. Adrian Henri, 'It Seemed Right, and Still Does', in John Minnion and Philip Bolsover, eds, *The CND Story* (London, 1983), p. 113.
59. *New Musical Express*, 12 April 1969.
60. Badman, *The Beatles off the Record*, pp. 435–436.
61. Nick Thomas, 'Challenging Myths of the 1960s: The Case of Student Protest in Britain', *Twentieth Century British History* 13: 3, 2002, pp. 287–278; Caute, *The Year of the Barricades*, p. 90; Green, *All Dressed Up*, pp. 260–263; Morgan, *Callaghan*, p. 315.
62. *The Times*, 18 and 19 March 1968; *Guardian*, 18 March 1968; and see also the various accounts in Green, *Days in the Life*, pp. 240–246; Green, *All Dressed Up*, pp. 263–265; Rowbotham, *Promise of a Dream*, p. 170.
63. Horace Ové quoted in Green, *Days in the Life*, pp. 244–245.
64. Caute, *The Year of the Barricades*, p. 89.
65. *Daily Mail*, *Sun* and *Daily Telegraph*, 19 March 1968.
66. Caute, *The Year of the Barricades*, p. 91; *Observer*, 21 April 1968.
67. *The Times*, 5 September 1968.
68. Callaghan, *Time and Chance*, p. 258.
69. *Daily Telegraph*, 24 October 1968.
70. Caute, *The Year of the Barricades*, p. 356.
71. *People*, 27 October 1968.
72. *The Times* and *Guardian*, 28 October 1968; and see Caute, *The Year of the Barricades*, p. 356; Green, *All Dressed Up*, p. 270.
73. *The Times* and *Daily Mirror*, 28 October 1968.
74. Morgan, *Callaghan*, pp. 315–316.
75. Crossman diary, 29 October 1968.
76. Davis, *Youth and the Condition of Britain*, pp. 107–108; Timmins, *The Five Giants*, pp. 200–202.
77. Harry Kidd, *The Trouble at LSE, 1966–1967* (London, 1969), pp. 51–119; Colin Crouch, *The Student Revolt* (London, 1970), pp. 36–49; Caute, *The Year of the Barricades*, pp. 357–360.
78. *Observer*, 19 May 1968; *Guardian*, 24 May 1968; Caute, *The Year of the Barricades*, pp. 345–347.
79. Crouch, *The Student Revolt*, p. 159.
80. Rowbotham, *Promise of a Dream*, p. 184.
81. See Caute, *The Year of the Barricades*, pp. 348–349.
82. See Students and Staff of Hornsey College of Art, *The Hornsey Affair* (Harmondsworth, 1969), *passim*; Hewison, *Too Much*, pp. 161–162; Caute, *The Year of the Barricades*, pp. 351–352.

83 Quoted in Hornsey College of Art, *The Hornsey Affair*, p. 207.
84 Quoted in Caute, *The Year of the Barricades*, p. 345.
85 Wybrow, *Britain Speaks Out*, p. 88.
86 *Sunday Telegraph*, 10 March 1968.
87 See Crouch, *The Student Revolt*, pp. 87–96.
88 Thomas, 'Challenging Myths of the 1960s', pp. 285–286.
89 *New Society*, 20 February 1969; Tiratsoo, 'Labour and Its Critics', pp. 176–177.
90 *Black Dwarf*, 23 March 1970.
91 Gallup survey cited in Thomas, 'Challenging Myths of the 1960s', pp. 282–283.
92 Marwick, *The Sixties*, p. 560.
93 Thomas, 'Challenging Myths of the 1960s', pp. 286–287.
94 See Tessa Blackstone, Kathleen Gales, Roger Hadley and Wyn Lewis, *Students in Conflict: LSE in 1967* (London, 1970); Thomas, 'Challenging Myths of the 1960s', pp. 295–296; Caute, *The Year of the Barricades*, pp. 360–361.
95 *Guardian*, 25 May 1968.
96 *Encounter*, May 1969.
97 Marwick, *The Sixties*, pp. 286–287.
98 Hewison, *Too Much*, pp. 174–175; Green, *Days in the Life*, pp. 382–398; Green, *All Dressed Up*, pp. 353, 363–364, 367–372.
99 Diski, 'A Long Forgotten War'; and see also Thomas, 'Challenging Myths of the 1960s', pp. 292–293.
100 Albert Hirschmann, 'Politics', in David Marquand and Anthony Seldon, eds, *The Ideas that Shaped Post-War Britain* (London, 1996), pp. 30–31; and see Sylvia Ellis, 'A Demonstration of British Good Sense? British Students during the Vietnam War', in Gerard J. DeGroot, ed., *Student Protest: The Sixties and After* (London 1998), pp. 54–69.
101 See Hirschmann, 'Politics', pp. 30–31, which touches on this argument.
102 Jeff Nuttall, *Bomb Culture* (London, 1968), p. 7.
103 Benson, *The Rise of Consumer Society*, p. 166; Fielding, *Labour and Cultural Change*, p. 16.
104 Mark Abrams and Alan Little, 'The Young Voter in British Politics', *British Journal of Sociology* 16, 1965, pp. 95–110; James Jupp, 'The Discontents of Youth', *Political Quarterly* 40, 1969; Davis, *Youth and the Condition of Britain*, p. 182; Fielding, *Labour and Cultural Change*, p. 17.
105 Quoted in Caute, *The Year of the Barricades*, p. 62.
106 Richard Neville, *Play Power* (London, 1970), quoted in Green, *All Dressed Up*, pp. 360–361.
107 *Daily Telegraph*, 7 August 1971.
108 *Observer*, 7 July 1968.
109 Marwick, *The Sixties*, p. 13.
110 Quoted in Green, *Days in the Life*, p. 432.
111 See Tiratsoo, 'Labour and Its Critics', p. 175.
112 Quoted in Green, *Days in the Life*, p. 439.

26 SYMPATHY FOR THE DEVIL

1 On the Redlands party, see Norman, *The Stones*, pp. 175–179; Wyman, *Stone Alone*, pp. 483–487.
2 Vyner, *Groovy Bob*, pp. 164–165.

3 Wyman, *Stone Alone*, p. 487.
4 Norman, *The Stones*, pp. 178–179; Vyner, *Groovy Bob*, pp. 164–165.
5 *News of the World*, 19 February 1967.
6 MacDonald, *The People's Music*, p. 59.
7 Wyman, *Stone Alone*, p. 262.
8 Quoted in Wyman, *Stone Alone*, p. 421.
9 Norman, *The Stones*, p. 187.
10 Norman, *The Stones*, p. 223.
11 Wyman, *Stone Alone*, pp. 13–14, 459.
12 Vyner, *Groovy Bob*, pp. 166–167.
13 Norman, *The Stones*, pp. 145–148.
14 Davies, *Permissive Britain*, pp. 140–141.
15 Green, *All Dressed Up*, p. 175.
16 Hewison, *Too Much*, p. 127.
17 Green, *All Dressed Up*, pp. 174–175.
18 HO 300/8, 'West End Jazz and Dance Clubs', 15 September 1964.
19 Aitken, *The Young Meteors*, p. 135; Davies, *Permissive Britain*, p. 151.
20 See Marwick, *British Society since 1945*, p. 147.
21 Aitken, *The Young Meteors*, p. 138.
22 Green, *All Dressed Up*, p. 97.
23 Green, *All Dressed Up*, pp. 97, 175.
24 Aitken, *The Young Meteors*, pp. 143–144.
25 Quoted in Green, *Days in the Life*, p. 180.
26 MacDonald, *Revolution in the Head*, pp. 253–254.
27 See Willis, *Madcap*, *passim*.
28 Morgan, *Callaghan*, pp. 319–320.
29 For the trial, see the detailed narratives in Norman, *The Stones*, pp. 194–205; Wyman, *Stone Alone*, pp. 514–528, as well as newspaper reports for 27–30 June 1967.
30 *Daily Telegraph*, 30 June 1967; Norman, *The Stones*, p. 197.
31 Norman, *The Stones*, pp. 204–206; Wyman, *Stone Alone*, pp. 530–531.
32 *Daily Mirror*, 30 June 1967.
33 *Evening Standard*, 29 June 1967.
34 Quoted in Vyner, *Groovy Bob*, p. 181.
35 Faithfull, *Faithfull*, p. 130.
36 *The Times*, 1 July 1967.
37 *Sunday Times*, 2 July 1967.
38 Paytress, *The Rolling Stones off the Record*, p. 143.
39 Norman, *The Stones*, p. 227.
40 Wyman, *Stone Alone*, p. 532.
41 On the polls, see Thompson, 'Labour's "Gannex Conscience"?', p. 143; Paytress, *The Rolling Stones off the Record*, p. 139.
42 Quoted in Wyman, *Stone Alone*, p. 532.
43 The letters are reprinted in Vyner, *Groovy Bob*, pp. 196–197.
44 Norman, *The Stones*, p. 224.
45 *New Musical Express*, 2 December 1967.

46 *New Musical Express*, 2 December 1967.
47 Jon Landau quoted in Wyman, *Stone Alone*, pp. 566–567; for other reviews, see Norman, *The Stones*, p. 228.
48 *International Times*, 17 May 1968.
49 See *New Musical Express*, 23 November 1968; Norman, *The Stones*, pp. 230, 244; Wyman, *Stone Alone*, pp. 606–607.
50 Quoted in Wyman, *Stone Alone*, p. 607.
51 See MacDonald, *Revolution in the Head*, pp. 249–250.
52 Chambers, *Urban Rhythms*, pp. 100, 107; Gillett, *The Sound of the City*, p. 386.
53 See Gillett, *The Sound of the City*, pp. 296, 402–403; Chambers, *Urban Rhythms*, pp. 110–111.
54 MacDonald, *Revolution in the Head*, p. 337.
55 Wyman, *Stone Alone*, pp. 594–595; Motion, *The Lamberts*, p. 335.
56 Norman, *The Stones*, p. 284; and see Gillett, *The Sound of the City*, pp. 375–7; Chambers, *Urban Rhythms*, pp. 84–85, 111–115.
57 Gillett, *The Sound of the City*, p. 375.
58 MacDonald, *Revolution in the Head*, pp. 175, 239.
59 Palmer, *All You Need Is Love*, p. 275.
60 On Led Zeppelin, see Palmer, *All You Need Is Love*, pp. 275–278; Gillett, *The Sound of the City*, pp. 386–387; Clayson, *Beat Merchants*, pp. 255–256. The standard work is Stephen Davis, *Hammer of the Gods: Led Zeppelin Unauthorized* (London, 2005): this is very sensationalist, but worth reading for the 'red snapper' story alone.
61 Wyman, *Stone Alone*, pp. 313–314.
62 Wyman, *Stone Alone*, p. 366.
63 See, for example, Wyman, *Stone Alone*, pp. 377, 423.
64 Oldham, *2Stoned*, p. 89.
65 On Pallenberg, see Norman, *The Stones*, pp. 146–147.
66 Norman, *The Stones*, pp. 151–152; Wyman, *Stone Alone*, p. 461.
67 Norman, *The Stones*, pp. 183–185; Wyman, *Stone Alone*, pp. 490–492.
68 Wyman, *Stone Alone*, pp. 492–493.
69 *Q*, October 1988.
70 Norman, *The Stones*, pp. 190–191; Wyman, *Stone Alone*, pp. 508–509.
71 Norman, *The Stones*, p. 193.
72 Norman, *The Stones*, pp. 193–194.
73 Paytress, *The Rolling Stones off the Record*, pp. 142–143; Wyman, *Stone Alone*, p. 559.
74 Wyman, *Stone Alone*, pp. 559–561.
75 Paytress, *The Rolling Stones off the Record*, pp. 145–146.
76 Paytress, *The Rolling Stones off the Record*, pp. 155–156; Wyman, *Stone Alone*, pp. 599–600.
77 See Norman, *The Stones*, pp. 238–240.
78 On Klein and the Stones, see Norman, *The Stones*, pp. 136–144.
79 See Catterall and Wells, *Your Face Here*, pp. 68–91; Colin McCabe, *Performance* (London, 1998); Mick Brown, *Performance* (London, 2000).
80 Vyner, *Groovy Bob*, p. 219.
81 Norman, *The Stones*, pp. 254–257.

82 Norman, *The Stones*, p. 273. The most reliable account of Jones's death is Norman, *The Stones*, pp. 258–275.
83 For a sample of the murder theories, see Anna Wohlin, *The Murder of Brian Jones* (London, 2000); Terry Rawlings, *Who Killed Christopher Robin: The Truth Behind the Murder of a Rolling Stone* (London, 2005).
84 Paytress, *The Rolling Stones off the Record*, p. 424.
85 Wyman, *Stone Alone*, p. 635.
86 Paytress, *The Rolling Stones off the Record*, p. 165.
87 Norman, *The Stones*, p. 267.
88 On the Hyde Park scene, see Norman, *The Stones*, pp. 268–70; Wyman, *Stone Alone*, pp. 636–639.
89 Norman, *The Stones*, p. 270.
90 *The Times*, 11 July 1969; Norman, *The Stones*, pp. 270–271.
91 Even Wyman (*Stone Alone*, p. 641) admits that they were 'dragging' and 'off-form'. See Norman, *The Stones*, p. 272.
92 On Altamont, see Stanley Booth, *The True Adventures of the Rolling Stones* (Chicago, 2000), *passim*; Greil Marcus, *The Dustbin of History* (Cambridge, MA, 1995), pp. 36–46; Norman, *The Stones*, pp. 290–308.
93 Wyman, *Stone Alone*, p. 7.

27 WHY LUCKY JIM TURNED RIGHT

1 *The Times*, 8 and 10 December 1965, 22 April 1966.
2 *The Times*, 27 April 1966.
3 Pamela Hansford Johnson, *On Iniquity* (London, 1967), p. 18.
4 Masters, *The Swinging Sixties*, p. 51.
5 See the letters page of the *New Statesman*, 6 May 1966.
6 *Spectator*, 13 May 1966.
7 *The Times*, 26 April 1971.
8 Marwick, *British Society since 1945*, p. 148.
9 See Diana Gittens, *The Family in Question* (London, 1985).
10 Landy, *British Genres*, p. 322.
11 Murphy, *Sixties British Cinema*, pp. 116–118.
12 See Hill, *Sex, Class and Realism*, pp. 106–108.
13 Hill, *Sex, Class and Realism*, pp. 106–107.
14 Murphy, *Sixties British Cinema*, p. 118.
15 See Jenkins, *A Life at the Centre*, pp. 120–124; Davies, *Permissive Britain*, p. 47; Newburn, *Permission and Regulation*, p. 83.
16 *The Times*, 16 November 1965; Briggs, *Competition*, pp. 531–532; Kathleen Tynan, *The Life of Kenneth Tynan* (second edition: London, 1988), ch. 24.
17 Levin, *The Pendulum Years*, p. 69.
18 By the end of the century Raymond owned the freeholds on almost two-thirds of all the property in Soho and was considered to be one of the richest men in Britain: see *Guardian*, 25 August 2001; Ferris, *Sex and the British*, p. 183.
19 Ferris, *Sex and the British*, pp. 5–7, 138–139; Weeks, *Sex, Politics and Society*, pp. 19–22.

20 See Ferris, *Sex and the British*, pp. 165–168; Newburn, *Permission and Regulation*, pp. 71–102.
21 John Sutherland, *Offensive Literature: Decensorship in Britain, 1959–82* (London, 1982), p. 4.
22 Sutherland, *Offensive Literature*, p. 165.
23 Sutherland, *Offensive Literature*, p. 6; Barry Cox, John Shirley and Martin Short, *The Fall of Scotland Yard* (Harmondsworth, 1977), pp. 140–211.
24 Quoted in Masters, *The Swinging Sixties*, p. 58.
25 Hansford Johnson, *On Iniquity*, p. 17.
26 Mary Whitehouse, *Who Does She Think She Is?* (London, 1972), ch. 5; Caulfield, *Mary Whitehouse*, pp. 19–23.
27 *Daily Telegraph*, 24 November 2001.
28 Michael Tracey and David Morrison, *Whitehouse* (London, 1979), p. 59.
29 On the early life of Mary Whitehouse, see Caulfield, *Mary Whitehouse*, pp. 28–36; Tracey and Morrison, *Whitehouse*, pp. 48–57; on Moral Rearmament, see Tracey and Morrison, *Whitehouse*, pp. 57–69.
30 Caulfield, *Mary Whitehouse*, p. 36.
31 Caulfield, *Mary Whitehouse*, pp. 40–41.
32 Caulfield, *Mary Whitehouse*, pp. 4–5.
33 Caulfield, *Mary Whitehouse*, p. 40; Tracey and Morrison, *Whitehouse*, pp. 198, 55.
34 Tracey and Morrison, *Whitehouse*, p. 40.
35 For the manifesto, see Tracey and Morrison, *Whitehouse*, pp. 42–43; Newburn, *Permission and Regulation*, pp. 17–18; Briggs, *Competition*, p. 333. On Norah Buckland, see Caulfield, *Mary Whitehouse*, pp. 59, 62.
36 *The Times*, 6 May 1964; Caulfield, *Mary Whitehouse*, pp. 68–70; Tracey and Morrison, *Whitehouse*, pp. 43–44.
37 Anthony Smith, *British Broadcasting* (Newton Abbott, 1974), p. 62.
38 A. W. Gordon, *Peter Howard: Life and Letters* (London, 1969), p. 302; Tracey and Morrison, *Whitehouse*, pp. 68–69.
39 Tracey and Morrison, *Whitehouse*, p. 44.
40 Tracey and Morrison, *Whitehouse*, p. 46.
41 Caulfield, *Mary Whitehouse*, p. 85.
42 John Tulloch and Manuel Alvarado, *Doctor Who: The Unfolding Text* (London, 1983), p. 158; Tracey and Morrison, *Whitehouse*, pp. 71, 85.
43 Briggs, *Competition*, p. 334.
44 Quoted in Tracey and Morrison, *Whitehouse*, p. 45.
45 *Daily Telegraph*, 24 November 2001; Caulfield, *Mary Whitehouse*, p. 46.
46 Caulfield, *Mary Whitehouse*, p. 45.
47 Caulfield, *Mary Whitehouse*, p. 110.
48 Caulfield, *Mary Whitehouse*, pp. 1, 4.
49 Whitehouse, *Whatever Happened to Sex?*, p. 72.
50 Tracey and Morrison, *Whitehouse*, p. 64.
51 See Tom Driberg, *The Mystery of Moral Rearmament* (London, 1964); Tracey and Morrison, *Whitehouse*, pp. 59–62.
52 *Daily Telegraph*, 24 November 2001.
53 Caulfield, *Mary Whitehouse*, p. 140.

54 Caulfield, *Mary Whitehouse*, p. 56.
55 Whitehouse, *Who Does She Think She Is?*, p. 11.
56 Tracey and Morrison, *Whitehouse*, pp. 188–189.
57 On the NVALA as a religious movement, see Dallas Cliff, 'Religion, Morality and the Middle Class', in Roger King and Neill Nugent, eds, *Respectable Rebels: Middle-Class Campaigns in Britain in the 1970s* (London, 1979), pp. 129–130; Tracey and Morrison, *Whitehouse*, pp. 22–38, 186–199; Newburn, *Permission and Regulation*, pp. 17–48.
58 Hugo Young, *One of Us: A Biography of Margaret Thatcher* (revised edition: London, 1990), p. 352. See also Campbell, *The Grocer's Daughter*, pp. 17–18, 378–379.
59 Tracey and Morrison, *Whitehouse*, p. 171.
60 *The Times*, 22 May 1967.
61 Weeks, *Sex, Politics and Society*, pp. 277–279.
62 Caulfield, *Mary Whitehouse*, p. 99.
63 *The Times*, 22 May 1967.
64 Amis, *Memoirs*, pp. 231–233. On Muggeridge, see Richard Ingrams, *Muggeridge: The Biography* (London, 1995); Gregory Wolfe, *Malcolm Muggeridge* (London, 1995).
65 Wolfe, *Malcolm Muggeridge*, p. 289.
66 Wolfe, *Malcolm Muggeridge*, pp. 326, 312.
67 Wolfe, *Malcolm Muggeridge*, pp. 330–332.
68 Malcolm Muggeridge, *Tread Softly for You Tread on My Jokes* (London, 1966), p. 57.
69 *The Times*, 11 November 1966.
70 *The Times*, 17 February 1967.
71 Wolfe, *Malcolm Muggeridge*, p. 352.
72 *The Times*, 15 January 1968. There is a slightly different version of this speech in Malcolm Muggeridge, *Jesus Rediscovered* (New York, 1968), pp. 54–55.
73 *The Times*, 16 January 1968.
74 See Wolfe, *Malcolm Muggeridge*, p. 353.
75 *The Times*, 12 July 1971.
76 *The Times*, 10 September 1971.
77 *The Times*, 27 September 1971; and see Cliff, 'Religion, Morality and the Middle Class', pp. 128–130; Newburn, *Permission and Regulation*, pp. 41–43; Wolfe, *Malcolm Muggeridge*, pp. 366–367; Green, *All Dressed Up*, pp. 348–349.
78 *The Times*, 11 October 1969.
79 *The Times*, 16 June 1971.
80 *The Times*, 14 June 1971. See also Newburn, *Permission and Regulation*, p. 42.
81 *The Times*, 20 and 21 April 1971.
82 *The Times*, 21 May 1971.
83 *The Times*, 25, 26 and 27 April 1971.
84 Newburn, *Permission and Regulation*, pp. 104–107; Wolfe, *Malcolm Muggeridge*, pp. 368–369.
85 Eric Jacobs, *Kingsley Amis: A Biography* (London, 1995), p. 12.
86 See Amis, *Lucky Jim*, p. 51.
87 Kingsley Amis, 'Socialism and the Intellectuals' (Fabian Society pamphlet: London, 1957), reprinted in Gene Feldman and Max Gartenberg, eds, *Protest: The Beat Generation and the Angry Young Men* (London, 1959), pp. 267–268.
88 Morrison, *The Movement*, p. 252.

89 Kingsley Amis, 'Why Lucky Jim Turned Right', reprinted in Kingsley Amis, *What Became of Jane Austen?* (London, 1970), p. 217.
90 Andrew Motion, *Philip Larkin: A Writer's Life* (London, 1993), p. 388.
91 Motion, *Philip Larkin*, pp. 409–410.
92 Quoted in Morrison, *The Movement*, p. 259.
93 Amis, *Memoirs*, p. 147.
94 Motion, *Philip Larkin*, p. 410.
95 See Zachary Leader, ed., *The Letters of Kingsley Amis* (London, 2000), especially the letters in 1967 and 1968; Jacobs, *Kingsley Amis*, pp. 182–183. The Soviet invasions of Hungary (1956) and Czechoslovakia (1968) were also instrumental in destroying the socialist sympathies of many party members and fellow-travellers.
96 Morrison, *The Movement*, p. 251.
97 Jacobs, *Kingsley Amis*, pp. 187–188.
98 Amis, *Lucky Jim*, pp. 169–170.
99 Morrison, *The Movement*, p. 261.
100 Amis to the Editor, *Observer*, 18 April 1965, in Leader, ed., *The Letters of Kingsley Amis*, p. 660.
101 Timmins, *The Five Giants*, pp. 269–271.
102 See C. B. Cox and A. E. Dyson, *The Black Papers on Education* (London, 1971).
103 *The Times*, 9 April 1969.
104 See Timmins, *The Five Giants*, pp. 270–274; Hewison, *Too Much*, pp. 295–296. For Kingsley Amis's contributions to the *Black Papers*, see Kingsley Amis, *The Amis Collection* (London, 1990), pp. 263–286.
105 Marwick, *The Sixties*, p. 501; Timmins, *The Five Giants*, p. 270.
106 Timmins, *The Five Giants*, p. 272.
107 See Timmins, *The Five Giants*, pp. 242–247, 272–274.
108 Taylor, *After the War*, p. 198.
109 Kingsley Amis, *I Want It Now* (London, 1968), p. 218.
110 Amis, *I Want It Now*, p. 248.
111 Amis, *Girl, 20*, pp. 126–127.
112 Amis, *Girl, 20*, p. 201.
113 See Taylor, *After the War*, pp. 201–205.
114 Powell, *Hearing Secret Harmonies*, p. 641.
115 See the discussion at the Anthony Powell Society's website, <http://www.anthonypowell.org.uk/dance/dancewho.htm>.
116 Levin, *The Pendulum Years*, pp. 9–10.
117 *Private Eye*, 25 June 1965; Booker, *The Neophiliacs*, pp. 318–319.
118 Booker, *The Seventies*, pp. 31–32.
119 Green, *All Dressed up*, pp. ix, 62, 397.

Part 4

28 THE OTHER ENGLAND

1 *Daily Express*, 5 January 1963.
2 George Brandt, *British Television Drama* (Cambridge, 1981), p. 16.

3 Briggs, *Competition*, p. 520.
4 Lacey, *British Realist Theatre*, p. 116.
5 See John Corner, 'Cathy Come Home', online at <http://www.museum.tv/archives/etv/index.html>.
6 *Guardian*, 13 January 1967.
7 *The Times*, 3 December 1966.
8 *The Times*, 17 November 1966.
9 Tony Pearson, 'Ken Loach', online at <http://www.museum.tv/archives/etv/index.html>.
10 Corner, 'Cathy Come Home'; and see also Lacey, *British Realist Theatre*, p. 122; Shellard, *British Theatre since the War*, p. 135.
11 Quoted in Ros Cranston, 'Up the Junction', online at <http://www.screenonline.org.uk/tv/id/440997/index.html>.
12 Walker, *Hollywood, England*, p. 376.
13 *The Times*, 2 December 1966; Timmins, *The Five Giants*, pp. 257–258.
14 Timmins, *The Five Giants*, p. 258.
15 *Guardian*, 13 January 1966; *The Times*, 3 December 1966.
16 Shelter full-page advertisement, *The Times*, 2 December 1966.
17 Shelter full-page advertisement, *The Times*, 2 December 1966.
18 Moorhouse, *The Other England*, pp. 11–28.
19 Moorhouse, *The Other England*, p. 107.
20 Moorhouse, *The Other England*, pp. 141–142.
21 Moorhouse, *The Other England*, pp. 155–156.
22 See Timmins, *The Five Giants*, p. 255; Fielding, *Labour and Cultural Change*, p. 7.
23 Brian Abel-Smith and Peter Townsend, *The Poor and the Poorest* (London, 1965); Coates and Silburn, *Poverty: The Forgotten Englishmen*, pp. 13–20; Clarke, *Hope and Glory*, p. 306.
24 Timmins, *The Five Giants*, pp. 255–256.
25 Calvocoressi, *The British Experience*, p. 124; Wright, *Britain in the Age of Economic Management*, p. 126.
26 Cassie McConachy quoted in Akhtar and Humphries, *The Fifties and Sixties*, p. 70.
27 Lawton, *1963*, p. 19.
28 Moorhouse, *The Other England*, pp. 99–100.
29 Coates and Silburn, *Poverty: The Forgotten Englishmen*, pp. 38, 66–67.
30 Coates and Silburn, *Poverty: The Forgotten Englishmen*, p. 66.
31 Coates and Silburn, *Poverty: The Forgotten Englishmen*, pp. 68–69.
32 Coates and Silburn, *Poverty: The Forgotten Englishmen*, pp. 70–71.
33 Coates and Silburn, *Poverty: The Forgotten Englishmen*, pp. 50, 54–55.
34 Coates and Silburn, *Poverty: The Forgotten Englishmen*, pp. 80–81.
35 Coates and Silburn, *Poverty: The Forgotten Englishmen*, pp. 47–48.
36 Jack Shaw, *On Our Conscience: The Plight of the Elderly* (Harmondsworth, 1971), p. 11–12.
37 Shaw, *On Our Conscience*, p. 11.
38 Shaw, *On Our Conscience*, pp. 27–29.
39 Shaw, *On Our Conscience*, p. 14.

40 Shaw, *On Our Conscience*, pp. 153–154.

41 Shaw, *On Our Conscience*, pp. 112–113.

42 Shaw, *On Our Conscience*, p. 55.

43 *Express and Star*, 13 June 1964; on consumerism for the elderly, see Benson, *The Rise of Consumer Society*, pp. 45–46.

44 See Mary Abbott, *Family Affairs: A History of the Family in 20th Century England* (London, 2003), p. 142.

45 Willmott and Young, *Family and Class in a London Suburb*, p. 58.

46 Willmott and Young, *Family and Class in a London Suburb*, p. 58.

47 Shaw, *On Our Conscience*, pp. 182–185.

48 Shaw, *On Our Conscience*, pp. 186–187.

49 Booker, *The Neophiliacs*, p. 304.

50 Booker, *The Neophiliacs*, pp. 305–306.

51 *New York Times*, 8 June 1966.

52 Frost and Jay, *To England with Love*, pp. 9–10.

53 Quoted in Young, *This Blessed Plot*, p. 200.

54 *The Times*, 1 and 3 January 1968.

55 *The Times*, 1 January 1968.

56 *The Times*, 3 January 1968.

57 *The Times*, 1 January 1968.

58 *The Times*, 8 January 1968.

59 *Guardian*, 4 January 1968.

60 See reports in *The Times*: 3, 5, 6 and 11 January 1968.

61 *The Times*, 4 January 1968.

62 *Guardian*, 9 January 1968.

63 *Daily Telegraph*, 11 January 1968.

64 Paul Foot, *The Rise of Enoch Powell* (Harmondsworth, 1969), p. 109.

65 Heffer, *Like the Roman*, p. 442.

66 See Paul Einzig, *Decline and Fall: Britain's Crisis in the Sixties* (London, 1969), p. 138.

67 *The Times*, 5 January 1968.

68 *The Times*, 8 January 1968.

69 *The Times*, 4 January 1968.

70 *The Times*, 7 and 12 February 1968.

71 Bergonzi, *The Situation of the Novel*, p. 57; Taylor, *After the War*, xii.

72 See Taylor, *After the War*, p. 171; Waugh, *Harvest of the Sixties*, p. 7; Sandbrook, *Never Had It So Good*, pp. 236–240.

73 Anthony Burgess, *The Right to an Answer* (London, 1960), quoted in Bergonzi, *The Situation of the Novel*, p. 181.

74 Laing, 'The Production of Literature', p. 154; Chambers, *Popular Culture*, pp. 110–111; Murphy, *Sixties British Cinema*, p. 275.

75 Steve Chibnall, *Get Carter* (London, 2003), pp. 18–19.

76 See Chibnall, *Get Carter*, pp. 17–25.

77 Quoted in Chibnall, *Get Carter*, pp. 11, 24–25.

78 See Chibnall, *Get Carter*, pp. 10, 50–51.

79 Moorhouse, *The Other England*, pp. 164–166.

80 Calvocoressi, *The British Experience*, p. 140.
81 Moorhouse, *The Other England*, pp. 168, 172.
82 Cockerell, *Live from Number 10*, pp. 148–149.
83 Caine, *What's It All About?*, p. 323.
84 Quoted in Chibnall, *Get Carter*, p. 36.
85 Chibnall, *Get Carter*, p. 10.
86 Chibnall, *Get Carter*, pp. 39–40.
87 See Weight, *Patriots*, p. 384.
88 See Chibnall, *Get Carter*, pp. 40–41; Ray Fitzwalter and David Taylor, *Web of Corruption: The Story of J. G. L. Poulson and T. Dan Smith* (London, 1981).
89 Chibnall, *Get Carter*, p. 47.
90 Quoted in Chibnall, *Get Carter*, p. 86.
91 Catterall and Wells, *Your Face Here*, pp. 116–117; and see Anthony Burgess, *Little Wilson and Big God* (London, 1987); Anthony Burgess, *You've Had Your Time* (London, 1990).
92 Anthony Burgess, *A Clockwork Orange* (Harmondsworth, 1972), p. 5.
93 Amis, *Memoirs*, pp. 277–278.
94 See the discussion of the novel in Waugh, *Harvest of the Sixties*, pp. 145–147.
95 Burgess, *A Clockwork Orange*, pp. 34–35.
96 See the commentaries in Stevenson, *The British Novel since the Thirties*, p. 180; Waugh, *Harvest of the Sixties*, pp. 146–147.
97 On the history of Thamesmead, see the University of Greenwich's online feature at <http://www.ideal-homes.org.uk/bexley/thamesmead.html>.
98 *Guardian*, 13 March 2000.
99 Quoted in Catterall and Wells, *Your Face Here*, pp. 129–130.
100 Catterall and Wells, *Your Face Here*, pp. 114–115, 127–134.

29 STREETS IN THE SKY

1 *The Times*, 17 May 1968.
2 *The Times*, 17 May 1968. For more on the explosion, see Patrick Dunleavy, *The Politics of Mass Housing in Britain, 1945–1975: A Study of Corporate Power and Professional Influence in the Welfare State* (Oxford, 1981), p. 242; White, *London in the Twentieth Century*, p. 56.
3 *The Times*, 17 May 1968; Dunleavy, *The Politics of Mass Housing*, p. 242.
4 See 'From Here to Modernity', online at <http://www.open2.net/modernity/3_13_frame.htm>.
5 White, *London in the Twentieth Century*, p. 56.
6 *The Times*, 20 May 1968.
7 Dunleavy, *The Politics of Mass Housing*, p. 245.
8 Peter Hall, *Cities of Tomorrow: An Intellectual History of Urban Planning and Design in the Twentieth Century* (Oxford, 1996), pp. 207–209.
9 See Hall, *Cities of Tomorrow*, pp. 220–221.
10 See Reyner Banham, *The New Brutalism* (London, 1966); Sutherland Lyall, *The State of British Architecture* (London, 1980), pp. 30ff.
11 See Nigel Warburton, *Ernö Goldfinger: The Life of an Architect* (London, 2002).

12 *Independent*, 23 January 2004.
13 Weight, *Patriots*, pp. 330–331.
14 Levin, *The Pendulum Years*, p. 95.
15 See Jackson, *The Sixties*, pp. 68–69, 78–80, 130.
16 See Simon Sadler, 'British Architecture in the Sixties', in Stephens and Stout, eds, *Art and the 60s*, pp. 127–129; Jackson, *The Sixties*, pp. 132–133.
17 Peter Mandler, 'New Towns for Old: The Fate of the Town Centre', in Conekin, Mort and Waters, eds, *Moments of Modernity*, p. 215.
18 Gordon E. Cherry, *Town Planning in Britain since 1900: The Rise and Fall of the Planning Ideal* (Oxford, 1990), p. 163.
19 Quoted in Sadler, 'British Architecture in the Sixties', p. 125.
20 Mandler, 'New Towns for Old', p. 219.
21 *The Times*, 14 June 1960.
22 Mandler, 'New Towns for Old, p. 221.
23 Moorhouse, *The Other England*, pp. 57–58.
24 See White, *London in the Twentieth Century*, pp. 51–52; Lyall, *The State of British Architecture*, pp. 27–28.
25 Dunleavy, *The Politics of Mass Housing*, pp. 108–110.
26 Lyall, *The State of British Architecture*, pp. 35–38.
27 *Independent*, 11 March 2004.
28 Moorhouse, *The Other England*, p. 94.
29 Stuart Jeffries, *Guardian*, 15 March 2004.
30 Moorhouse, *The Other England*, pp. 95, 97.
31 Moorhouse, *The Other England*, p. 157–158.
32 Hattersley, *Who Goes Home?*, p. 30.
33 *The Times*, 10 November 1969.
34 Sadler, 'British Architecture in the Sixties', p. 122; Hall, *Cities of Tomorrow*, p. 225; Moorhouse, *The Other England*, p. 158.
35 Hall, *Cities of Tomorrow*, p. 225.
36 Colls, *Identity of England*, pp. 344–346.
37 Cherry, *Town Planning in Britain*, p. 151.
38 Dunleavy, *The Politics of Mass Housing*, p. 36.
39 Ponting, *Breach of Promise*, pp. 121–122.
40 Timmins, *The Five Giants*, p. 185.
41 See Sadler, 'British Architecture in the Sixties', p. 132; Hall, *Cities of Tomorrow*, pp. 220–221.
42 Dunleavy, *The Politics of Mass Housing*, p. 103; Timmins, *The Five Giants*, p. 186.
43 Hall, *Cities of Tomorrow*, p. 233; Dunleavy, *The Politics of Mass Housing*, pp. 136–137.
44 Dunleavy, *The Politics of Mass Housing*, pp. 73, 101.
45 *Birmingham Evening Dispatch*, 6 April 1960; *Birmingham Gazette*, 10 February 1955; both quoted in Dunleavy, *The Politics of Mass Housing*, p. 268.
46 Dunleavy, *The Politics of Mass Housing*, p. 120.
47 Quoted in Mandler, 'New Towns for Old', p. 218.
48 See Dunleavy, *The Politics of Mass Housing*, pp. 66–67, 293–294.
49 Quoted in Timmins, *The Five Giants*, p. 185.

50 *The Times*, 20 and 22 June 1974; Dunleavy, *The Politics of Mass Housing*, pp. 293–294.
51 Dunleavy, *The Politics of Mass Housing*, p. 1.
52 Dunleavy, *The Politics of Mass Housing*, pp. 46–48, 259.
53 Sadler, 'British Architecture in the Sixties', p. 118.
54 *The Times*, 26 October 1966; Sadler, 'British Architecture in the Sixties', p. 118; Dunleavy, *The Politics of Mass Housing*, p. 126.
55 Nicholas Taylor, *The Village in the City* (London, 1973), p. 79.
56 See Dunleavy, *The Politics of Mass Housing*, pp. 95ff.
57 Hall, *Cities of Tomorrow*, p. 226.
58 *Newham Recorder*, 1 October 1966, quoted in Dunleavy, *The Politics of Mass Housing*, pp. 219–221.
59 *Newham Recorder*, 1 February 1968, quoted in Dunleavy, *The Politics of Mass Housing*, p. 221.
60 Dunleavy, *The Politics of Mass Housing*, pp. 222–223.
61 Barbara Adams and Jean Conway, *The Social Effects of Living off the Ground* (London, 1973), pp. 8ff; Dunleavy, *The Politics of Mass Housing*, p. 96.
62 Shaw, *On Our Conscience*, p. 92.
63 Dunleavy, *The Politics of Mass Housing*, pp. 94–95.
64 See Joan Maizels, *Two to Five in High Flats* (London, 1971); Elizabeth Gittus, *Flats, Families and the Under Fives* (London, 1976); Lyall, *The State of British Architecture*, pp. 42–43; Dunleavy, *The Politics of Mass Housing*, p. 149.
65 Lyall, *The State of British Architecture*, p. 43; Dunleavy, *The Politics of Mass Housing*, p. 97.
66 See Lyall, *The State of British Architecture*, p. 33.
67 Lyall, *The State of British Architecture*, pp. 42–43.
68 Ponting, *Breach of Promise*, p. 123; Dunleavy, *The Politics of Mass Housing*, p. 70.
69 *Building Design*, 5 January 1979; Lyall, *The State of British Architecture*, pp. 45, 50.
70 Crossman diary, 2 October 1965.
71 John le Carré, *The Looking-Glass War* (London, 1965), pp. 38–40.
72 See Whiteley, 'Shaping the Sixties', p. 32; Cherry, *Town Planning in Britain*, p. 159; Dunleavy, *The Politics of Mass Housing*, p. 58.
73 Norman Wilson, 'High Rise Is Inevitable', *Architect and Building News* 1, 1968, p. 37.
74 *The Times*, 8 August 1968.
75 Dunleavy, *The Politics of Mass Housing*, pp. 39–41, 122–123.
76 Geoffrey Strickland, 'F. R. Leavis and "English"', in Ford, ed., *From Orwell to Naipaul*, p. 176.
77 See *Daily Telegraph*, 10 July 2004; *Independent*, 13 July 2004.
78 Ian Nairn, *Your England Revisited* (London, 1964), p. 9.
79 *Observer*, 13 February 1966.
80 'The Town Clerk's Views', in Betjeman, *Collected Poems*, pp. 144–147.
81 'The Dear Old Village', in Betjeman, *Collected Poems*, pp. 187–188.
82 'Inexpensive Progress', in Betjeman, *Collected Poems*, pp. 286–287.
83 See *The Times*, 12 and 14 September 1966; Bevis Hillier, *John Betjeman: New Fame, New Love* (London, 2002); Bevis Hillier, *John Betjeman: The Bonus of Laughter* (London, 2004).
84 On thalidomide, see Newburn, *Permission and Regulation*, p. 140.
85 Jenkins, *A Life at the Centre*, pp. 207–208.

86 Benn diary, 21 March 1967.
87 Rowbotham, *Promise of a Dream*, p. 168.
88 See 'Doomwatch', in Evans, *The Penguin TV Companion*, pp. 212–213.
89 See Sandbrook, *Never Had It So Good*, pp. 236–240.
90 L. P. Hartley, *Facial Justice* (London, 1960); and see Bergonzi, *The Situation of the Novel*, p. 177.
91 Anthony Burgess, *The Wanting Seed* (London, 1983), pp. 8–9.
92 Burgess, *The Wanting Seed*, p. 6.
93 Burgess, *The Wanting Seed*, p. 2; and see the discussion of the novel in Bergonzi, *The Situation of the Novel*, pp. 185–186.
94 See Taylor, *After the War*, p. 171; Waugh, *Harvest of the Sixties*, p. 10.
95 See Waugh, *Harvest of the Sixties*, pp. 140–141.
96 J.G. Ballard, *High Rise* (London, 1975).
97 Quoted in Veldman, *Fantasy, the Bomb and the Greening of Britain*, p. 83.
98 Veldman, *Fantasy, the Bomb and the Greening of Britain*, p. 71, and see also pp. 79–83, 93.
99 Veldman, *Fantasy, the Bomb and the Greening of Britain*, pp. 107–108.
100 Barbara Ward, *Spaceship Earth* (New York, 1966), pp. 1, 15.
101 *The Times*, 14 February 1963.
102 Veldman, *Fantasy, the Bomb and the Greening of Britain*, pp. 217–220.
103 *Observer*, 17 March 1966.
104 Veldman, *Fantasy, the Bomb and the Greening of Britain*, p. 209.
105 Jackson, *The Sixties*, pp. 14, 55, 213.

30 WILSON MUST GO

1 Jenkins, *A Life at the Centre*, p. 243.
2 Ponting, *Breach of Promise*, pp. 316–317.
3 King and Wybrow, eds, *British Political Opinion*, pp. 168–169.
4 King and Wybrow, eds, *British Political Opinion*, p. 188.
5 See Alexander and Watkins, *The Making of the Prime Minister 1970*, p. 49.
6 Ponting, *Breach of Promise*, p. 263.
7 See Pimlott, *Harold Wilson*, p. 401.
8 Foot, *The Politics of Harold Wilson*, pp. 326–327, 333–334.
9 Tiratsoo, 'Labour and Its Critics', pp. 163–183; Rowbotham, *Promise of a Dream*, pp. 174–175.
10 'Wilsundra Trial Opens', reprinted in Ingrams, ed., *The Life and Times of Private Eye*, pp. 166–167.
11 Pimlott, *Harold Wilson*, pp. 447–448.
12 Pimlott, *Harold Wilson*, p. 448.
13 Castle diary, 11 May 1967.
14 Haines, *Glimmers of Twilight*, pp. 175, 179.
15 Cockerell, *Live from Number 10*, pp. 124–125.
16 See Cockerell, *Live from Number 10*, pp. 129–130.
17 Quoted in Cockerell, *Live from Number 10*, p. 132.
18 Cockerell, *Live from Number 10*, p. 141.
19 Cockerell, *Live from Number 10*, pp. 134–136.

20 Cockerell, *Live from Number 10*, pp. 151–152.
21 Benn diary, 11 February 1970.
22 Benn diary, 30 April 1968.
23 Jenkins, *A Life at the Centre*, pp. 258–259
24 Jenkins, *A Life at the Centre*, p. 259.
25 Crossman diary, 11 May 1968; Jenkins, *A Life at the Centre*, p. 257.
26 Crossman diary, 2 April 1968; see also Castle diary, 29 March, 2 and 3 April 1968; Jenkins, *A Life at the Centre*, p. 249.
27 Pimlott, *Harold Wilson*, p. 504.
28 Jenkins, *A Life at the Centre*, p. 257.
29 Dorril and Ramsay, *Smear!*, pp. 188–189; Pimlott, *Harold Wilson*, p. 505; Radice, *Friends and Rivals*, p. 167.
30 Owen, *Time to Declare*, p. 127.
31 Pimlott, *Harold Wilson*, pp. 507–508.
32 Quotations from Patrick Gordon Walker's diary; see Pimlott, *Harold Wilson*, pp. 507–508; Ziegler, *Wilson*, p. 295; Radice, *Friends and Rivals*, pp. 167–168.
33 Pimlott, *Harold Wilson*, p. 490.
34 Jenkins, *A Life at the Centre*, pp. 621–622.
35 Healey, *The Time of My Life*, p. 329.
36 Pimlott, *Harold Wilson*, pp. 490–491.
37 Healey, *The Time of My Life*, p. 329.
38 Desmond Donnelly, *Gadarene '68: The Crimes, Follies and Misdemeanours of the Wilson Government* (London, 1968), p. 140.
39 Donnelly, *Gadarene '68*, pp. 159, 12.
40 Pimlott, *Harold Wilson*, pp. 508–509.
41 See Pimlott, Harold Wilson, pp. 697–723. The most comprehensive, if sensational, discussion of the various Wilson plots is Dorril and Ramsay, *Smear!*, especially pp. 204–304.
42 See, for example, *The Times*, 3 November 1967, 20 January, 9 and 14 December 1968.
43 Healey, *The Time of My Life*, p. 340.
44 Benn diary, 8 February 1968.
45 Benn diary, 6 February 1968.
46 Dudley Edwards, *Newspapermen*, pp. 272–273; Greenslade, *Press Gang*, p. 158.
47 Quoted in Dudley Edwards, *Newspapermen*, p. 1.
48 See S. J. Taylor, *The Great Outsiders: Northcliffe, Rothermere and the* Daily Mail (London, 1996).
49 Dudley Edwards, *Newspapermen*, pp. 142–143.
50 See Dudley Edwards, *Newspapermen*, p. 38.
51 Dudley Edwards, *Newspapermen*, p. 119; Greenslade, *Press Gang*, p. 159.
52 Jenkins, *A Life at the Centre*, pp. 252–253.
53 Introduction to King diary, p. 11.
54 See Ziegler, *Wilson*, p. 212; Dudley Edwards, *Newspapermen*, pp. 340–347.
55 Dudley Edwards, *Newspapermen*, pp. 321, 286.
56 Dudley Edwards, *Newspapermen*, p. 324.
57 Quoted in Dudley Edwards, *Newspapermen*, p. 341.

58 Dudley Edwards, *Newspapermen*, p. 348; Hugh Cudlipp, *Walking on the Water* (London, 1976), p. 293.
59 Cudlipp, *Walking on the Water*, p. 294.
60 King diary, 22 August 1967.
61 Dudley Edwards, *Newspapermen*, pp. 357–359.
62 Cudlipp, *Walking on the Water*, pp. 304–305.
63 King diary, 22 February 1967.
64 King diary, 5 May 1967.
65 Benn diary, 11 February 1968.
66 Dudley Edwards, *Newspapermen*, p. 360.
67 Benn diary, 6 February 1968.
68 King diary, 12 August 1967.
69 Cudlipp to King, 29 and 30 April 1968, quoted in Dudley Edwards, *Newspapermen*, pp. 367–369.
70 The best summary is in Dudley Edwards, *Newspapermen*, pp. 369–372.
71 Cudlipp, *Walking on the Water*, p. 326.
72 King diary, unpublished entry, quoted in *Encounter*, September 1981.
73 Cudlipp, *Walking on the Water*, p. 326.
74 See Dudley Edwards, *Newspapermen*, p. 372.
75 *Daily Mirror*, 10 May 1968.
76 Dudley Edwards, *Newspapermen*, p. 374.
77 Pimlott, *Harold Wilson*, p. 507.
78 King diary, 11 May 1968.
79 *The Times*, 11 May 1968; *Observer* and *Sunday Express*, 12 May 1968.
80 *Private Eye*, 24 May 1968.
81 Crossman diary, 13 May 1968.
82 Dudley Edwards, *Newspapermen*, pp. 353–354, 380–385.
83 Cudlipp to King, 29 May 1968, reprinted in Cudlipp, *Walking on the Water*, p. 351; and see King diary, 8 June 1968.
84 Dudley Edwards, *Newspapermen*, pp. 385–389.
85 *Sunday Express*, 2 June 1968.
86 Castle diary, 11 July 1968.
87 See Jenkins, *A Life at the Centre*, pp. 261–270; Ponting, *Breach of Promise*, pp. 378–380; Dell, *The Chancellors*, pp. 358–359.
88 Jenkins, *A Life at the Centre*, pp. 270–271.
89 Dell, *The Chancellors*, p. 358.
90 King and Wybrow, eds, *British Political Opinion*, pp. 9–10.
91 Wybrow, *Britain Speaks Out*, p. 89.
92 *Daily Telegraph*, 13 December 1968.
93 See Pimlott, *Harold Wilson*, p. 527.
94 Crossman diary, 22 March 1967.
95 Anne Perkins, *Red Queen: The Authorized Biography of Barbara Castle* (London, 2003), p. 263.
96 Crossman diary, 29 March 1968. As we have seen, his original plan was to appoint her to the DEA, but this was vetoed by Jenkins. Employment was therefore a second choice.

97 Castle diary, 29 March 1968.
98 Quoted in Perkins, *Red Queen*, p. 262.
99 Castle diary, 5 April 1968.

31 BACK BRITAIN, NOT BLACK BRITAIN

1 Briggs, *Competition*, pp. 527–528. See also the BBC's website on the programme, at <http://www.bbc.co.uk/comedy/guide/articles/t/tilldeathusdopar_7776335.shtml>; Taylor, *Anger and After*, p. 272; Tracey and Morrison, *Whitehouse*, p. 106.
2 Briggs, *Competition*, p. 529.
3 Tracey and Morrison, *Whitehouse*, p. 115.
4 Johnny Speight, *The Thoughts of Chairman Alf: Alf Garnett's Little Blue Book, or Where Britain Went Wrong* (London, 1971), pp. 72–73.
5 Newburn, *Permission and Regulation*, p. 23.
6 *Daily Mirror*, 8 August 1968; *The Times*, 17 February 1968.
7 Quoted in Tracey and Morrison, *Whitehouse*, p. 109.
8 *Evening Standard*, 21 February 1968.
9 See Colin Holmes, *John Bull's Island: Immigration and British Society, 1871–1971* (London, 1988), pp. 262, 296.
10 Holmes, *John Bull's Island*, pp. 270, 295.
11 Quoted in Holmes, *John Bull's Island*, p. 314.
12 See Clifford S. Hill, *How Colour Prejudiced Is Britain?* (London, 1965).
13 Holmes, *John Bull's Island*, pp. 299–300; Colls, *Identity of England*, pp. 138, 143.
14 Robert Winder, *Bloody Foreigners: The Story of Immigration to Britain* (London, 2004), pp. 284–292.
15 Quoted in Dilwyn Porter, '"Never-Never Land": Britain under the Conservatives', in Nick Tiratsoo, ed., *From Blitz to Blair: A New History of Britain since 1939* (London, 1997), p. 118.
16 Fielding, *Labour and Cultural Change*, p. 14.
17 Holmes, *John Bull's Island*, pp. 261, 255.
18 W. W. Daniel, *Racial Discrimination in England* (Harmondsworth, 1968), p. 209.
19 Daniel Lawrence, *Black Migrants, White Natives: A Study of Race Relations in Nottingham* (Cambridge, 1974), pp. 39–40.
20 Shamit Saggar, *Race and Politics in Britain* (London, 1992), pp. 69–70.
21 *Daily Telegraph*, 11 October 1961.
22 *The Times*, 9 April 1963.
23 Saggar, *Race and Politics in Britain*, pp. 71; Fielding, *Labour and Cultural Change*, p. 144.
24 *The Times*, 9 November 1963.
25 Quoted in Paul Foot, *Immigration and Race in British Politics* (London, 1965), p. 212.
26 Paul Foot, *The Rise of Enoch Powell* (Harmondsworth, 1969), p. 46.
27 See Sandbrook, *Never Had It So Good*, pp. 298–299.
28 *Express and Star*, 19 January 1956.
29 Marwick, *The Sixties*, p. 231.
30 Childs, *Britain since 1945*, p. 200; Sandbrook, *Never Had It So Good*, pp. 299–301.
31 Heffer, *Like the Roman*, p. 359.
32 *Express and Star*, 9 April 1956.

33 Foot, *The Rise of Enoch Powell*, pp. 45–46.
34 *Express and Star*, 28 February 1957.
35 Foot, *The Rise of Enoch Powell*, pp. 51, 32–35.
36 Holmes, *John Bull's Island*, p. 261; Saggar, *Race and Politics in Britain*, p. 72.
37 Mike Phillips and Trevor Phillips, *Windrush: The Irresistible Rise of Multi-Racial Britain* (London, 1999), pp. 118, 248.
38 George Thomas quoted in Foot, *The Rise of Enoch Powell*, p. 56.
39 See Moorhouse, *The Other England*, pp. 102–104.
40 *The Times*, 9 March 1964; Moorhouse, *The Other England*, pp. 103–104.
41 *The Times*, 9 March 1964.
42 *The Times*, 17 September 1964.
43 Foot, *The Rise of Enoch Powell*, p. 68.
44 *The Times*, 13 October 1964.
45 *Express and Star*, 9 October 1964.
46 *Daily Mail*, 16 October 1964; Pimlott, *Harold Wilson*, p. 355.
47 Crossman diary, 5 February 1965.
48 On Powell's life and career to the end of 1963, see Heffer, *Like the Roman*, pp. 1–341.
49 *Sunday Express*, 4 April 1965.
50 Heffer, *Like the Roman*, p. 380.
51 Heffer, *Like the Roman*, p. 346.
52 Cockett, *Thinking the Unthinkable*, pp. 122–199; Heffer, *Like the Roman*, pp. 250–251, 367–368.
53 Quoted in Heffer, *Like the Roman*, pp. 389–390.
54 Campbell, *Edward Heath*, p. 239; Heffer, *Like the Roman*, pp. 390–397.
55 Campbell, *Edward Heath*, pp. 103, 249.
56 Campbell, *Edward Heath*, pp. 258–259.
57 Heath, *The Course of My Life*, pp. 272–274.
58 Campbell, *Edward Heath*, pp. 250–252.
59 See the chart in Butler and Pinto-Duschinsky, *The British General Election of 1970*, p. 64; Gilmour and Garnett, *Whatever Happened to the Tories*, p. 226.
60 Cockerell, *Live from Number 10*, pp. 137–138.
61 *The Times*, 7 April 1966.
62 Patrick Cosgrave, *The Lives of Enoch Powell* (London, 1989), p. 228.
63 *Express and Star*, 10 October 1964; Foot, *The Rise of Enoch Powell*, pp. 39, 70–71; Heffer, *Like the Roman*, pp. 360–361.
64 *Sunday Telegraph*, 18 October 1964.
65 Heffer, *Like the Roman*, p. 379.
66 Foot, *The Rise of Enoch Powell*, pp. 78–79, 85.
67 Heffer, *Like the Roman*, pp. 359, 445.
68 *Daily Telegraph*, 19 April 1965; Foot, *The Rise of Enoch Powell*, pp. 77–78.
69 Heffer, *Like the Roman*, pp. 378–379.
70 Foot, The Rise of Enoch Powell, pp. 61–62.
71 *Guardian*, 24 May 1966.
72 Foot, *The Rise of Enoch Powell*, p. 64.
73 Address to the Royal Society of St George, 1961, reprinted in John Wood, ed., *A*

Nation Not Afraid: The Thinking of Enoch Powell (London, 1965), p. 144; and see the discussion of this speech in Heffer, *Like the Roman*, pp. 334–340.
74. Heffer, *Like the Roman*, p. 504.
75. Heffer, *Like the Roman*, p. 434.
76. Winder, *Bloody Foreigners*, pp. 289–291.
77. *Daily Telegraph*, 25 July 1967; Foot, *The Rise of Enoch Powell*, pp. 102–107.
78. Foot, *The Rise of Enoch Powell*, pp. 103–104.
79. *Daily Telegraph*, 8 December 1967.
80. Foot, *The Rise of Enoch Powell*, pp. 113–114.
81. *International Times*, 17 May 1968.
82. Holmes, *John Bull's Island*, pp. 264–266.
83. Holmes, *John Bull's Island*, p. 265; Saggar, *Race and Politics in Britain*, p. 180.
84. Ponting, *Breach of Promise*, pp. 332–333.
85. Fielding, *Labour and Cultural Change*, pp. 155–156.
86. Morgan, *Callaghan*, pp. 308–311.
87. Quoted in Winder, *Bloody Foreigners*, p. 290.
88. Crossman diary, 13 February 1968.
89. See, for example, Morgan, *Callaghan*, p. 311.
90. Crossman diary, 16 January 1969.
91. Heffer, *Like the Roman*, pp. 447–448.
92. Heffer, *Like the Roman*, p. 449.
93. The best analysis of the speech is in Heffer, *Like the Roman*, pp. 450–455.
94. Foot, *The Rise of Enoch Powell*, p. 112; Heffer, *Like the Roman*, p. 450.
95. In 1998 a Wolverhampton solicitor came forward to say that he had acted for the woman in question. He refused to give names or details, however, and it is hard to see how so many reporters scouring such a relatively small area could have failed to find her. See Heffer, *Like the Roman*, p. 460.
96. Foot, *The Rise of Enoch Powell*, pp. 113–116.
97. Heffer, *Like the Roman*, pp. 445, 455.
98. Shepherd, *Iain Macleod*, p. 501.
99. Campbell, *Edward Heath*, pp. 243–244; Heffer, *Like the Roman*, pp. 457–458.
100. *The Times*, 22 April 1968.
101. *Daily Mirror*, 22 April 1968.
102. Castle diary, 21 April 1968.
103. *News of the World*, 21 April 1968.
104. Clem Jones interviewed in Phillips and Phillips, *Windrush*, pp. 250–251.
105. Greenslade, *Press Gang*, p. 234.
106. *The Times*, 23 April 1968.
107. Heffer, *Like the Roman*, pp. 467–468.
108. *Guardian*, 13 June 1969.
109. Crossman diary, 27 April 1968.
110. *The Times*, 24 April 1968.
111. Heffer, *Like the Roman*, pp. 462–464.
112. Heffer, *Like the Roman*, pp. 467, 474.
113. *The Times*, 1 May 1968.

114 See White, *London in the Twentieth Century*, pp. 151–152, 296–297.

115 Heffer, *Like the Roman*, pp. 503–504.

116 Heffer, *Like the Roman*, p. 465.

117 Wybrow, *Britain Speaks Out*, p. 86; King and Wybrow, eds, *British Political Opinion*, pp. 206–207.

118 Campbell, *Edward Heath*, pp. 244–245.

119 Heffer, *Like the Roman*, p. 493.

120 *The Times*, 18 and 22 November 1968.

121 Mervyn Jones, *Michael Foot* (London, 1994), pp. 308–309.

122 Shepherd, *Iain Macleod*, p. 501; Heffer, *Like the Roman*, pp. 544–545.

123 Heffer, *Like the Roman*, p. 506.

124 Heffer, *Like the Roman*, pp. 476–477, 484–486.

125 See Timmins, *The Five Giants*, pp. 252–255; Cockett, *Thinking the Unthinkable*, pp. 122–199.

126 Shepherd, *Iain Macleod*, pp. 440, 463, and see ch. 18 in general.

127 Cohen, *Folk Devils and Moral Panics*, p. 201.

128 White, *London in the Twentieth Century*, pp. 151–152; Winder, *Bloody Foreigners*, p. 300.

129 Heffer, *Like the Roman*, p. 960.

130 *Guardian*, 9 February 1998.

131 The other was Sir Keith Joseph; see Heffer, *Like the Roman*, p. 958.

132 Michael Foot, *Loyalists and Loners* (London, 1986), p. 192.

133 Heffer, *Like the Roman*, p. 514.

32 DESPERATE HOUSEWIVES

1 *The Times*, 16 September 1965.

2 Geraghty, 'Women and 60s British Cinema', p. 104.

3 Geraghty, 'Women and 60s British Cinema', p. 107.

4 See Geraghty, 'Women and 60s British Cinema', pp. 103–104; Walker, *Hollywood, England*, p. 282.

5 See Hill, *Sex, Class and Realism*, pp. 157–158; Murphy, *Sixties British Cinema*, pp. 124–125.

6 *Daily Mail*, 14 September 1965.

7 Julie Christie, 'Everybody's Darling', in Maitland, ed., *Very Heaven*, p. 171.

8 McKibbin, *Classes and Cultures*, p. 204.

9 Marwick, *British Society since 1945*, p. 68.

10 Hoggart, *The Uses of Literacy*, p. 35.

11 Willmott and Young, *Family and Class in a London Suburb*, p. 77.

12 John Newsom, *The Education of Girls* (London, 1948), p. 109.

13 John Newsom, *Half Our Future: A Report of the Central Advisory Council for Education (England)* (London, 1963), pp. 135–137.

14 *Observer*, 11 October 1964.

15 Newsom, *The Education of Girls*, pp. 116, 146.

16 *Woman's Own*, 21 January 1961, quoted in Haste, *Rules of Desire*, p. 152.

17 Pressley, *The Best of Times*, p. 8; Akhtar and Humphries, *The Fifties and Sixties*, p. 91.

18 Hoggart, *The Uses of Literacy*, pp. 42, 55.

19 Weeks, *Sex, Politics and Society*, p. 205; Jackson, *The Middle Classes*, p. 117; Gunn and Bell, *Middle Classes*, pp. 69–71.
20 Newsom, *The Education of Girls*, pp. 102–103.
21 Harris, Hyde and Smith, eds, *1966 and All That*, p. 149.
22 See the examples quoted in Akhtar and Humphries, *The Fifties and Sixties*, p. 108.
23 Christine Fagg interviewed in Akhtar and Humphries, *The Fifties and Sixties*, p. 93.
24 Hopkins, *The New Look*, pp. 325–326.
25 Norman Macrae, *Sunshades in October* (London, 1963), pp. 92–93.
26 Macrae, *Sunshades in October*, p. 98.
27 Ina Zweiniger-Bargielowska, 'Housewifery', in Zweiniger-Bargielowska, ed., *Women in Twentieth-Century Britain*, p. 153.
28 Elizabeth Wilson, *Only Halfway to Paradise: Women in Postwar Britain: 1945–1968* (London, 1980), p. 29.
29 Ingham, *Now We Are Thirty*, pp. 41–42.
30 Pat Mancini interviewed in Akhtar and Humphries, *The Fifties and Sixties*, p. 91.
31 Pamela Woodland interviewed in Akhtar and Humphries, *The Fifties and Sixties*, p. 91.
32 Beyfus, *The English Marriage*, pp. 73–101.
33 Vivien Allen interviewed in Akhtar and Humphries, *The Fifties and Sixties*, p. 93.
34 Wilson, *Only Halfway to Paradise*, p. 183.
35 Quoted in Ingham, *Now We Are Thirty*, p. 59.
36 Richard Titmuss, *Essays on 'The Welfare State'* (London, 1958), p. 91
37 Colls, *Identity of England*, p. 184; Weight, *Patriots*, p. 76.
38 See Hill, *Sex, Class and Realism*, p. 16.
39 Alan Sinfield, *Literature, Politics and Culture in Post-war Britain* (London, 1989), p. 206.
40 Marwick, *The Sixties*, p. 259; Weight, *Patriots*, p. 78.
41 Hill, *Sex, Class and Realism*, p. 17.
42 See Wilson, *Only Halfway to Paradise*, pp. 172–174.
43 *Observer*, 31 March 1968.
44 See Ingham, *Now We Are Thirty*, pp. 79–80.
45 *Picture Post*, 5 July 1947, quoted in Ingham, *Now We Are Thirty*, p. 35.
46 John Bowlby, *Child Care and the Growth of Love* (Harmondsworth, 1953), p. 105.
47 Wilson, *Only Halfway to Paradise*, p. 189.
48 Pearl Jephcott, Nancy Sear and J. H. Smith, *Married Women Working* (London, 1962), pp. 165–171.
49 D. E. Cooper, 'Looking Back on Anger', in Bogdanor and Skidelsky, eds, *The Age of Affluence*, pp. 257–258.
50 Walker, *Peter Sellers*, pp. 116–117; Lewis, *The Life and Death of Peter Sellers*, pp. 463–471; Hill, *Sex, Class and Realism*, p. 147.
51 Haste, *Rules of Desire*, p. 154.
52 *Woman's Own*, 28 January 1961, quoted in Haste, *Rules of Desire*, p. 154.
53 Unknown interviewee quoted in Pressley, *Best of Times*, p. 26.
54 Chapman, *Licence to Thrill*, pp. 117–118.
55 Haste, *Rules of Desire*, pp. 91, 109, 144–145; Weeks, *Sex, Politics and Society*, p. 237.
56 Mace, *Marriage Counselling*, p. 123.

57 Weeks, *Sex, Politics and Society*, p. 260.
58 Ronald Fletcher, *The Family and Marriage in Britain* (Harmondsworth, 1966), p. 139.
59 Ferdynand Zweig, *The Worker in an Affluent Society: Family Life and Industry* (London, 1961), pp. 23–31.
60 Willmott and Young, *Family and Class in a London Suburb*, pp. 24, 29.
61 Gorer, *Sex and Marriage in England Today*, pp. 62–65.
62 Gorer, *Sex and Marriage in England Today*, pp. 66–67.
63 Wendy Mitchell interviewed in Akhtar and Humphries, *The Fifties and Sixties*, pp. 29–30.
64 Ferris, *Sex and the British*, pp. 214–215.
65 Marwick, *British Society since 1945*, pp. 152–153; Ferris, *Sex and the British*, p. 215.
66 Lewis, 'Marriage', p. 73; Clarke, *Hope and Glory*, p. 366.
67 Diana Gittens, *Fair Sex: Family Size and Structure, 1900–1939* (London, 1983), pp. 171–172; Ferris, *Sex and the British*, p. 189; McKibbin, *Classes and Cultures*, p. 307.
68 Phyllis Willmott, *Growing up in a London Village* (London, 1979), p. 60.
69 Cook, *The Long Sexual Revolution*, p. 288.
70 Ingham, *Now We Are Thirty*, pp. 112–113.
71 Paul Ferris, *The Nameless: Abortion in Britain Today* (London, 1966); Ferris, *Sex and the British*, pp. 196–197.
72 Ingham, *Now We Are Thirty*, p. 113.
73 Akhtar and Humphries, *The Fifties and Sixties*, p. 170.
74 Newburn, *Permission and Regulation*, p. 154; Ferris, *Sex and the British*, p. 190.
75 Barbara Brookes, *Abortion in England, 1900–67* (Kent, 1988), p. 152.
76 Newburn, *Permission and Regulation*, p. 141.
77 Marwick, *British Society since 1945*, pp. 151–152; Newburn, *Permission and Regulation*, pp. 136–157.
78 Davies, *Permissive Britain*, p. 73.
79 Quoted in Wilson, *Only Halfway to Paradise*, pp. 184–185.
80 Sheila Rowbotham, *Women, Resistance and Revolution* (Harmondsworth, 1973), p. 12.
81 Quoted in Fielding, *Labour and Cultural Change*, p. 127.
82 Castle diary, 14 February 1968.
83 Barbara Castle, 'No Kitchen Cabinet', in Maitland, ed., *Very Heaven*, pp. 50–51.
84 Quoted in Marwick, *The Sixties*, p. 79.
85 Kingsley Amis, *Take a Girl Like You* (London, 1960), p. 185.
86 See Bergonzi, *The Situation of the Novel*, p. 167; Bradbury, *The Modern British Novel*, p. 323; Richard Bradford, *Lucky Him: The Life of Kingsley Amis* (London, 1991), pp. 169–190.
87 For a feminist critique of sexual mores in the late sixties, see Sheila Jeffreys, *Anticlimax: A Feminist Perspective on the Sexual Revolution* (London, 1990).
88 Unknown interviewee quoted in Pressley, *Changing Times*, p. 82.
89 Quoted in Haste, *Rules of Desire*, p. 207.
90 Nicola Lane interviewed in Green, *Days in the Life*, pp. 418–419.
91 See Green, *All Dressed Up*, pp. 398–417.
92 Alfred Roper interviewed in Akhtar and Humphries, *The Fifties and Sixties*, p. 184.
93 Linda Shanovitch interviewed in Akhtar and Humphries, *The Fifties and Sixties*, p. 181. One can only hope that she never encountered the predatory Mr Roper.

94 See Mark Donnelly, *Sixties Britain* (Harlow, 2005), pp. 158–159.
95 Rosie Boycott interviewed in Green, *Days in the Life*, pp. 407–408.
96 Marwick, *The Sixties*, p. 689.
97 Rowbotham, *A Century of Women*, pp. 347–349; Fielding, *Labour and Cultural Change*, pp. 129–130.
98 See Fielding, *Labour and Cultural Change*, pp. 131–132.
99 *The Times*, 2 March 1970.
100 Michelene Wandor interviewed in Green, *Days in the Life*, pp. 405–406; see also Green, *All Dressed Up*, pp. 403–406.
101 Greer, *The Female Eunuch*; on *The Female Eunuch* as a bestseller, see Sutherland, *Reading the Decades*, pp. 109–110.
102 *The Times*, 21 November and 23 December 1970.
103 Green, *All Dressed Up*, pp. 407–408.
104 Ferris, *Sex and the British*, p. 219.
105 Ingham, *Now We Are Thirty*, p. 132.

33 IN PLACE OF STRIFE

1 Castle diary, 9 April 1968; Pimlott, *Harold Wilson*, p. 527.
2 Perkins, *Red Queen*, pp. 11–13.
3 See Perkins, *Red Queen*, pp. 86–88.
4 Perkins, *Red Queen*, p. 231.
5 Hattersley, *Who Goes Home?*, p. 66.
6 See Perkins, *Red Queen*, pp. 261, 275–276.
7 Childs, *Britain since 1945*, p. 103; Sandbrook, *Never Had It So Good*, pp. 334–335.
8 *The Times*, 4 November 1959; and see Sandbrook, *Never Had It So Good*, pp. 327–337.
9 See Peter Jenkins, *The Battle of Downing Street* (London, 1970), xiv; Ponting, *Breach of Promise*, pp. 350–351.
10 See Stephen Milligan, *The New Barons: Union Power in the 1970s* (London, 1976), pp. 48–9; Ponting, *Breach of Promise*, pp. 73–74, 185–187; Tomlinson, *Economic Policy*, pp. 134–137.
11 *Sunday Telegraph*, 31 July 1966.
12 Castle diary, 22 February 1967.
13 Perkins, *Red Queen*, pp. 250, 269.
14 Glyn Jones and Michael Barnes, *Britain on Borrowed Time* (Harmondsworth, 1967), p. 133; Milligan, *The New Barons*, p. 19; Childs, *Britain since 1945*, p. 207.
15 Castle diary, 9 September 1968.
16 Clutterbuck, *Britain in Agony*, p. 293.
17 *The Times*, 10 October 1968.
18 Milligan, *The New Barons*, pp. 20, 25–27.
19 Milligan, *The New Barons*, pp. 21–23.
20 Milligan, *The New Barons*, pp. 22–23, 32–34.
21 Jenkins, *The Battle of Downing Street*, xii.
22 PREM 13/2724, Andrew Graham, 'The White Paper on Industrial Relations', 14 January 1969; Tomlinson, *Economic Policy*, p. 145.
23 See Geoffrey Owen, *From Empire to Europe: The Decline and Revival of British Industry Since the Second World War* (London, 1999), pp. 439–40.

24 Jenkins, *The Battle of Downing Street*, pp. 11–25; Gerald A. Dorfman, *Government versus Trade Unionism in British Politics since 1968* (London, 1979), pp. 10–15; Campbell, *Edward Heath*, p. 220.
25 *Sunday Telegraph*, 5 January 1969; Perkins, *Red Queen*, p. 277.
26 Castle diary, 13 June 1968.
27 Perkins, *Red Queen*, p. 268.
28 Jenkins, *The Battle of Downing Street*, pp. 31–32.
29 See Perkins, *Red Queen*, pp. 277–283.
30 Castle diary, 16 November 1968.
31 See *The Castle Diaries 1964–70*, pp. 549–50.
32 Department of Employment and Productivity, *In Place of Strife: A Policy for Industrial Relations* (London, 1969), pp. 1–40. See also the discussions in *The Castle Diaries 1964–70*, pp. 560–562; Jenkins, *The Battle of Downing Street*, pp. 26–43; Dorfman, *Government versus Trade Unionism*, pp. 15–23; Ponting, *Breach of Promise*, pp. 353–354.
33 Castle diary, 4 December 1968.
34 Perkins, *Red Queen*, pp. 285–286.
35 Crossman diary, 1 January 1969.
36 Crossman and Castle diaries, 3 January 1969.
37 See Castle diary, 14 January 1969; Pimlott, *Harold Wilson*, pp. 529–532.
38 Castle diary, 15 January 1969.
39 Dorfman, *Government versus Trade Unionism*, p. 27; Perkins, *Red Queen*, p. 291.
40 *Daily Telegraph*, 16 January 1968.
41 See Tiratsoo, 'Labour and Its Critics', p. 172; Jenkins, *The Battle of Downing Street*, p. 46; Milligan, *The New Barons*, p. 219.
42 Milligan, *The New Barons*, pp. 96–98; Perkins, *Red Queen*, p. 305.
43 Milligan, *The New Barons*, pp. 130–131.
44 Jenkins, *The Battle of Downing Street*, pp. 124–125; Milligan, *The New Barons*, pp. 196–197; Perkins, *Red Queen*, pp. 26, 290.
45 Perkins, *Red Queen*, pp. 304–305.
46 See Dorfman, *Government versus Trade Unionism*, pp. 28–29.
47 Jenkins, *The Battle of Downing Street*, p. 135; Perkins, *Red Queen*, p. 306.
48 Castle diary, 4 December 1968.
49 Castle diary, 28 September 1968.
50 Morgan, *Callaghan*, pp. 333–334.
51 Crossman diary, 11 November 1969; and see Morgan, *Callaghan*, pp. 319–321.
52 Pimlott, *Harold Wilson*, pp. 530–531; Morgan, *Callaghan*, pp. 333–334.
53 Morgan, *Callaghan*, p. 130.
54 Jenkins, *The Battle of Downing Street*, p. 82.
55 Castle diary, 5 February 1969.
56 See *The Times*, 19 and 27 February, 14 and 19 March 1969; Dorfman, *Government versus Trade Unionism*, pp. 30–31; Perkins, *Red Queen*, pp. 292–293.
57 *The Times*, 28 February 1969.
58 Pimlott, *Harold Wilson*, p. 532.
59 Ziegler, *Wilson*, p. 302.
60 Crossman diary, 27 April 1969.

61 Crossman diary, 6 and 9 March 1969. On the fate of the Parliament Bill, see Ponting, *Breach of Promise*, pp. 342–349.
62 Castle diary, 26 March 1969; Morgan, *Callaghan*, p. 334.
63 Quoted in Perkins, *Red Queen*, p. 294.
64 Castle diary, 2 April 1969; Jenkins, *A Life at the Centre*, p. 288.
65 Castle diary, 3 and 4 April 1969; Benn diary, 3 April 1969.
66 Perkins, *Red Queen*, p. 294.
67 Castle diary, 11 April 1969; Dorfman, *Government versus Trade Unionism*, pp. 33–34; Perkins, *Red Queen*, p. 295.
68 Jenkins, *The Battle of Downing Street*, pp. 90–91.
69 Ponting, *Breach of Promise*, p. 359.
70 *Tribune*, 18 April 1969.
71 Crossman diary, 27 April 1969.
72 Crossman diary, 29 April 1969.
73 Castle diary, 29 April 1969.
74 Castle to Wilson, 29 April 1969, reprinted in Perkins, *Red Queen*, p. 299.
75 Castle diary, 29 April 1969.
76 Crossman diary, 29 April 1969
77 Castle diary, 30 April 1969.
78 Crossman diary, 1 May 1969.
79 Crossman diary, 4 May 1969.
80 Pimlott, *Harold Wilson*, pp. 534–535.
81 S. Crosland, *Tony Crosland*, p. 204.
82 *The Times*, 2 May 1969.
83 On the Callaghan camp, see Jenkins, *The Battle of Downing Street*, pp. 111–112; Morgan, *Callaghan*, p. 340.
84 Jenkins, *The Battle of Downing Street*, pp. 109–112.
85 Pimlott, *Harold Wilson*, pp. 537–538.
86 *The Times*, 5 May 1969.
87 See *The Times*, 8 May 1969; Pimlott, *Harold Wilson*, pp. 538–539.
88 Jenkins, *The Battle of Downing Street*, pp. 116–117; Pimlott, *Harold Wilson*, pp. 535–539.
89 Crossman and Castle diaries, 8 May 1969.
90 Crossman diary, and 13 May 1969; Morgan, *Callaghan*, p. 336.
91 See Jenkins, *The Battle of Downing Street*, pp. 124–138; Dorfman, *Government versus Trade Unionism*, pp. 37–39; Ponting, *Breach of Promise*, pp. 360–361; Perkins, *Red Queen*, pp. 302, 308.
92 Jenkins, *A Life at the Centre*, p. 289.
93 Castle and Crossman diaries, 20 May 1969; Ponting, *Breach of Promise*, pp. 361–362.
94 Crossman diary, 20 May 1969.
95 Castle diary, 21 May 1969.
96 Castle diary, 23, 25 and 29 May 1969; Perkins, *Red Queen*, pp. 309–311.
97 Castle diary, 1 June 1969; Jenkins, *The Battle of Downing Street*, p. 140; Perkins, *Red Queen*, pp. 312–313.
98 Castle diary, 2 June 1969.
99 Castle diary, 8 June 1969.

100 Jenkins, *The Battle of Downing Street*, p. 147.
101 Castle diary, 9 and 10 June 1969.
102 Castle diary, 17 June 1969; Jenkins, *The Battle of Downing Street*, pp. 153–154; Pimlott, *Harold Wilson*, pp. 541–542.
103 Castle and Crossman diaries, 17 June 1969.
104 Pimlott, *Harold Wilson*, p. 541.
105 Jenkins, *A Life at the Centre*, p. 290.
106 Crossman diary, 17 June 1969.
107 Benn diary, 17 June 1969.
108 Benn diary, 18 June 1969.
109 Crossman and Castle diaries, 19 June 1969.
110 Castle diary, 19 June 1969; Dorfman, *Government versus Trade Unionism*, pp. 47–48; Perkins, *Red Queen*, pp. 321–322.
111 Quoted in Hennessy, *Muddling Through*, p. 257.
112 *The Times*, 19 June 1969.
113 *Sunday Times* and *Observer*, 22 June 1969.
114 See Morgan, *Labour People*, p. 255.
115 Castle diary, 18 June 1969.
116 S. Crosland, *Tony Crosland*, p. 204.
117 Jenkins, *A Life at the Centre*, p. 290.
118 See Campbell, *Edward Heath*, pp. 228–229; Gilmour and Garnett, *Whatever Happened to the Tories?* pp. 239–240.
119 Crossman diary, 2 July 1969.
120 Clutterbuck, *Britain in Agony*, p. 27.
121 Callaghan, *Time and Chance*, p. 277; and see Morgan, *Callaghan*, pp. 342–344.
122 See Ponting, *Breach of Promise*, pp. 368–369.
123 Crossman diary, 20 April 1969.
124 Benn diary, 24 July 1969.
125 Crossman diary, 18 June 1969.
126 Quoted in Cockerell, *Live from Number 10*, p. 146.
127 Crossman diary, 18 June 1969.
128 See Morgan, *Callaghan*, pp. 290–324.
129 Crossman diary, 5 September 1969.
130 See Crossman diary, 14 October 1969; Pimlott, *Harold Wilson*, pp. 549–550; Morgan, *Callaghan*, pp. 345, 356.
131 Benn diary, 15 December 1968.
132 See Jenkins, *A Life at the Centre*, pp. 273–274, 277–279; Ponting, *Breach of Promise*, pp. 380–381.
133 Crossman diary, 23 October 1969.
134 Ponting, *Breach of Promise*, pp. 378, 393; Tomlinson, *Economic Policy*, p. 220.
135 Woodward, 'Labour's Economic Performance, 1964–1970', pp. 96–97; Clutterbuck, *Britain in Agony*, pp. 39–40.
136 Castle diary, 5 November 1969.
137 Butler and Pinto-Duschinsky, *The British General Election of 1970*, pp. 128–129; Ponting, *Breach of Promise*, p. 378.

138 Hansard, 14 April 1970.
139 *The Times*, 15 April 1970.
140 *The Times*, 21 April 1970.
141 *The Times*, 30 April 1970.

34 CHILDREN OF WRATH

1 See Coogan, *The Troubles*, pp. 49–51; McKittrick and McVea, *Making Sense of the Troubles*, p. 39.
2 *The Times*, 12 April 1965.
3 McKittrick and McVea, *Making Sense of the Troubles*, pp. 36–7.
4 See Niall Ó Dochartaigh, *From Civil Rights to Armalites: Derry and the Birth of the Irish Troubles* (Cork, 1997), pp. 25–26; English, *Armed Struggle*, p. 91. On NICRA's origins and agenda, see Northern Ireland Civil Rights Association, *We Shall Overcome: The History of the Struggle for Civil Rights in Northern Ireland 1968–78* (Belfast, 1978).
5 Taylor, *Loyalists*, pp. 51–53.
6 English, *Armed Struggle*, p. 82.
7 English, *Armed Struggle*, p. 85.
8 Bob Purdie, *Politics in the Streets: The Origins of the Civil Rights Movement in Northern Ireland* (Belfast, 1990), pp. 130–132; English, *Armed Struggle*, pp. 85–90.
9 Coogan, *The Troubles*, p. 66; English, *Armed Struggle*, p. 91.
10 English, *Armed Struggle*, pp. 90–91; and see Bob Purdie, 'Was the Civil Rights Movement a Republican/Communist Conspiracy?', *Irish Political Studies* 3, 1988, pp. 33–36.
11 Coogan, *The Troubles*, p. 74; English, *Armed Struggle*, pp. 94–98.
12 See Taylor, *Loyalists*, pp. 48–50.
13 Bobby Norris quoted in Taylor, *Loyalists*, p. 49.
14 McKittrick and McVea, *Making Sense of the Troubles*, p. 34.
15 Bobby Norris quoted in Taylor, *Loyalists*, pp. 49–50.
16 These incidents are related in McKittrick and McVea, *Making Sense of the Troubles*, p. 36.
17 Taylor, *Loyalists*, pp. 13, 26–27.
18 Rose, *How the Troubles Came*, pp. 45–47; Greenslade, *Press Gang*, pp. 236–237.
19 Coogan, *The Troubles*, pp. 39, 61–63.
20 Quoted in Coogan, *The Troubles*, p. 61.
21 See Rose, *How the Troubles Came*, pp. 59–60.
22 Rose, *How the Troubles Came*, pp. 64–65.
23 Rose, *How the Troubles Came*, pp. 77–78, 175, 178.
24 Callaghan, *A House Divided*, pp. 1–4; Rose, *How the Troubles Came*, pp. 92–93.
25 Rose, *How the Troubles Came*, p. 107.
26 Quoted in Coogan, *The Troubles*, p. 39.
27 Coogan, *The Troubles*, p. 70.
28 Coogan, *The Troubles*, p. 71; Ó Dochartaigh, *From Civil Rights to Armalites*, p. 20.
29 On the march, see Coogan, *The Troubles*, pp. 70–72; Ó Dochartaigh, *From Civil Rights to Armalites*, pp. 20–21; McKittrick and McVea, *Making Sense of the Troubles*, pp. 41–42.
30 Quoted in McKittrick and McVea, *Making Sense of the Troubles*, p. 42.

31 See Ó Dochartaigh, *From Civil Rights to Armalites*, p. 26.
32 McKittrick and McVea, *Making Sense of the Troubles*, p. 42.
33 Ó Dochartaigh, *From Civil Rights to Armalites*, p. 21.
34 Publicly, though, he defended the police and described the march as 'a provocation': see *The Times*, 8 October 1968.
35 Stormont Cabinet minutes for 14 October 1968, quoted in McKittrick and McVea, *Making Sense of the Troubles*, pp. 42–43.
36 Minutes quoted in McKittrick and McVea, *Making Sense of the Troubles*, pp. 45–6; and see Rose, *How the Troubles Came*, pp. 121–123.
37 McKittrick and McVea, *Making Sense of the Troubles*, pp. 46–47; Rose, *How the Troubles Came*, p. 126.
38 See Coogan, *The Troubles*, p. 76.
39 McKittrick and McVea, *Making Sense of the Troubles*, p. 47.
40 Terence O'Neill, 'Ulster Stands at the Crossroads', in Terence O'Neill, *Ulster at the Crossroads* (London, 1969), pp. 140–146.
41 Coogan, *The Troubles*, p. 78; Ó Dochartaigh, *From Civil Rights to Armalites*, p. 32.
42 On the distrust of O'Neill in the Catholic community, see Ó Dochartaigh, *From Civil Rights to Armalites*, pp. 30–31.
43 On the culpability of the Wilson government, see Rose, *How the Troubles Came*, esp. pp. 169–179.
44 English, *Armed Struggle*, p. 99.
45 Kenneth Bloomfield, *Stormont in Crisis* (Belfast, 1994), p. 108.
46 Bernadette Devlin, *The Price of My Soul* (London, 1969), p. 120; on PD, see English, *Armed Struggle*, pp. 94–96.
47 Taylor, *Provos*, pp. 41–42.
48 Devlin, *The Price of My Soul*, p. 120.
49 Devlin, *The Price of My Soul*, pp. 139–141.
50 Michael Farrell quoted in Coogan, *The Troubles*, p. 81. On the Burntollet Bridge incident, see Bowes Egan and Vincent McCormack, *Burntollet* (London, 1969), esp. chs 6–9; Coogan, *The Troubles*, pp. 79–81; Taylor, *Loyalists*, pp. 56–57, as well as the official Cameron Commission report, *Disturbances in Northern Ireland: Report of the Commission Appointed by the Governor of Northern Ireland* (Belfast, 1969).
51 Coogan, *The Troubles*, pp. 81–82; Ó Dochartaigh, *From Civil Rights to Armalites*, pp. 39–41.
52 See Coogan, *The Troubles*, p. 79.
53 Quoted in English, *Armed Struggle*, p. 97.
54 Sean MacStiofain, *Memoirs of a Revolutionary* (Edinburgh, 1975), p. 116.
55 *New Statesman*, 10 January 1969.
56 *Belfast Telegraph*, 6 January 1969.
57 Rose, *How the Troubles Came*, pp. 134–136.
58 *Spectator*, 7 February 1969.
59 This is from the 9 February 1969 entry in Crossman's unedited, unpublished diary, held at the University of Warwick and quoted in Rose, *How the Troubles Came*, p. 136.
60 See the excellent section in Rose, *How the Troubles Came*, pp. 151–154.

61 Molony and Pollak, *Paisley*, pp. 170–171; Taylor, *Loyalists*, pp. 58–59.
62 Ó Dochartaigh, *From Civil Rights to Armalites*, pp. 33, 73–79.
63 The results are listed online at < http://cain.ulst.ac.uk/issues/politics/election/rs1969.htm >.
64 See Ó Dochartaigh, *From Civil Rights to Armalites*, pp. 86–87.
65 *The Times*, 25 February 1969; Rose, *How the Troubles Came*, pp. 137–138.
66 See Taylor, *Loyalists*, p. 60.
67 Quoted in Taylor, *Loyalists*, p. 61.
68 McKittrick and McVea, *Making Sense of the Troubles*, p. 50.
69 Coogan, *The Troubles*, p. 85; McKittrick and McVea, *Making Sense of the Troubles*, p. 53.
70 Ó Dochartaigh, *From Civil Rights to Armalites*, pp. 36–37.
71 Taylor, *Provos*, p. 44.
72 Hansard, 22 April 1969; on the events surrounding her election and maiden speech, see Coogan, *The Troubles*, pp. 85–86.
73 Taylor, *Provos*, p. 47; Ó Dochartaigh, *From Civil Rights to Armalites*, pp. 52–53, 111.
74 Wilson, *The Labour Government*, p. 692; Rose, *How the Troubles Came*, pp. 161–163.
75 See Rose, *How the Troubles Came*, pp. 161–163.
76 *Derry Journal*, 1 August 1969.
77 Taylor, *Provos*, p. 48.
78 *The Times*, 12 August 1969; Ó Dochartaigh, *From Civil Rights to Armalites*, pp. 112–119.
79 *The Times*, 13 August 1969; Coogan, *The Troubles*, pp. 87–88; Ó Dochartaigh, *From Civil Rights to Armalites*, pp. 119–122; Taylor, *Provos*, pp. 48–49.
80 Ó Dochartaigh, *From Civil Rights to Armalites*, p. 122.
81 Quoted in Taylor, *Provos*, p. 49.
82 Clive Limpkin, *The Battle of Bogside* (Harmondsworth, 1972), p. 19.
83 Taylor, *Loyalists*, pp. 64–65.
84 'Barricade Bulletin', quoted in Ó Dochartaigh, *From Civil Rights to Armalites*, p. 123.
85 See Ó Dochartaigh, *From Civil Rights to Armalites*, p. 123 and *passim*.
86 See Coogan, *The Troubles*, pp. 89–90, 116–117; Ó Dochartaigh, *From Civil Rights to Armalites*, pp. 123, 187.
87 *The Times*, 14 August 1969.
88 McKittrick and McVea, *Making Sense of the Troubles*, pp. 58–59; Ó Dochartaigh, *From Civil Rights to Armalites*, pp. 122–123.
89 Ó Dochartaigh, *From Civil Rights to Armalites*, pp. 124–125.
90 Taylor, *Loyalists*, pp. 66–67, and see *The Times*, 14 August 1969.
91 Limpkin, *The Battle of Bogside*, pp. 26–29.
92 *The Times*, 15 and 16 August 1969; Coogan, *The Troubles*, pp. 96–106; Taylor, *Provos*, pp. 52–53; Taylor, *Loyalists*, pp. 68–69.
93 Coogan, *The Troubles*, pp. 91–92, 106; Ó Dochartaigh, *From Civil Rights to Armalites*, p. 161.
94 *The Economist*, 16 August 1969.
95 Wilson, *The Labour Government*, p. 693.
96 *Irish News*, 13 August 1969.
97 Quoted in 'The Sparks That Lit the Bonfire', *Timewatch*, BBC2, 27 January 1992.
98 Hattersley, *Who Goes Home?*, p. 77.

99 Taylor, *Loyalists*, pp. 69–70; Peter Taylor, *Brits: The War against the IRA* (London, 2002), p. 29.
100 Crossman diary, 14 and 17 August 1969.
101 Quoted in 'The Sparks That Lit the Bonfire'.
102 Taylor, *Provos*, pp. 56–57.
103 Taylor, *Brits*, p. 25.
104 Taylor, *Provos*, pp. 57–59. See also Coogan, *The Troubles*, pp. 111–112, as well as almost any contemporary newspaper report.
105 Taylor, *Loyalists*, p. 70.
106 *The Times*, 30 August 1969.
107 There are different accounts of Paisley's precise words: see Callaghan, *A House Divided*, p. 82.
108 *The Times*, 22 September 1969; and see Coogan, *The Troubles*, pp. 108, 110; Ó Dochartaigh, *From Civil Rights to Armalites*, pp. 130–137.
109 See English, *Armed Struggle*, pp. 103–104.
110 See *Report of the Advisory Committee on Police in Northern Ireland* (Belfast, 1969), esp. ch. 10.
111 *The Times*, 13 October 1969. For other accounts of the Shankill riots, see Taylor, *Loyalists*, pp. 71–72; Taylor, *Brits*, pp. 35–36.
112 See Coogan, *The Troubles*, pp. 123–127; Ó Dochartaigh, *From Civil Rights to Armalites*, pp. 154–160, 176.
113 Ó Dochartaigh, *From Civil Rights to Armalites*, pp. 165–166.

35 THE CARNIVAL IS OVER

1 Edward Heath, *Sailing: A Course of My Life* (London, 1975), p. 54.
2 Heath, *Sailing*, p. 69.
3 Crossman diary, 25 January 1970.
4 *The Times*, 2 February 1970.
5 *The Economist*, 7 February 1970.
6 *The Times*, 7 February 1970; and see Wilson's version in Wilson, *The Labour Government*, pp. 952–956.
7 See Campbell, *Edward Heath*, p. 264.
8 Cockett, *Thinking the Unthinkable*, p. 203. For other analyses of the Selsdon myth, see Campbell, *Edward Heath*, pp. 264–267; Timmins, *The Five Giants*, pp. 275–276; E. H. H. Green, *Ideologies of Conservatism: Conservative Political Ideas in the Twentieth Century* (Oxford, 2004), pp. 231–232.
9 See Crossman diary, 8 February 1970.
10 Campbell, *Edward Heath*, pp. 266–267.
11 *The Times*, 9 September 1969.
12 Ponting, *Breach of Promise*, p. 324.
13 Reprinted in Butler and Pinto-Duschinsky, *The British General Election of 1970*, pp. 123–124.
14 *Daily Telegraph* and *Guardian*, 1 October 1969.
15 *The Times*, 1 October 1969.
16 Pimlott, *Harold Wilson*, p. 547; King and Wybrow, eds, *British Political Opinion*, pp. 9–10.
17 Castle diary, 30 June 1969.

18. Castle diary, 5 September 1969; see also Crossman diary, 2 July 1969.
19. Benn diary, 8 March 1970.
20. Jenkins, *A Life at the Centre*, p. 291.
21. Castle diary, 12 February 1970.
22. *The Times*, 15 April 1970.
23. Pimlott, *Harold Wilson*, p. 553.
24. Castle diary, 14 April 1970.
25. See Jenkins, *A Life at the Centre*, pp. 294–295.
26. Butler and Pinto-Duschinsky, *The British General Election of 1970*, pp. 133–134; *The Times*, 23 April 1970.
27. Jenkins, *A Life at the Centre*, pp. 295–296.
28. *The Times*, 23 April 1970.
29. Castle and Crossman diaries, 8 March 1970.
30. Crossman diary, 29 April 1970.
31. Pimlott, *Harold Wilson*, p. 553.
32. Castle diary, 14 May 1969.
33. Crossman diary, 1 January 1970.
34. *New Musical Express*, 15 March 1969.
35. Clayson, *Beat Merchants*, pp. 259–263.
36. MacDonald, *Revolution in the Head*, pp. 222–223, 229.
37. Norman, *Shout!*, p. 349.
38. Badman, *The Beatles off the Record*, pp. 412–413.
39. On Klein and the Beatles, see Norman, *Shout!*, pp. 351–374.
40. Badman, *The Beatles off the Record*, pp. 443–444.
41. Norman, *Shout!*, p. 265; MacDonald, *Revolution in the Head*, p. 170.
42. Norman, *Shout!*, pp. 337–338.
43. See MacDonald, *Revolution in the Head*, pp. 245–287.
44. MacDonald, *Revolution in the Head*, p. 295.
45. See Badman, *The Beatles off the Record*, pp. 379–380; MacDonald, *Revolution in the Head*, pp. 308–309.
46. Norman, *Shout!*, pp. 356–358.
47. Quoted in Miles, *Paul McCartney*, p. 491.
48. Norman, *Shout!*, p. 330; MacDonald, *Revolution in the Head*, pp. 303–304.
49. MacDonald, *Revolution in the Head*, p. 321.
50. Miles, *Paul McCartney*, pp. 562–566.
51. *Daily Mirror*, 10 April 1970; Miles, *Paul McCartney*, pp. 572–573.
52. Badman, *The Beatles off the Record*, pp. 493–495.
53. Miles, *Paul McCartney*, pp. 575–578; see also MacDonald, *Revolution in the Head*, p. 298.
54. *The Times*, 11 April 1970.
55. MacDonald, *The People's Music*, pp. 48–50; see also MacDonald, *Revolution in the Head*, pp. 9–10, 328.
56. Hattersley, *Who Goes Home?*, p. 89.
57. *The Economist*, 16 May 1970.
58. *Sunday Times*, 17 May 1970.
59. Benn diary, 8 May 1970.

60 Jenkins, *A Life at the Centre*, pp. 297–298; Pearce, *Denis Healey*, p. 387.
61 *Private Eye*, 22 May 1970.
62 Butler and Pinto-Duschinsky, *The British General Election of 1970*, pp. 143, 153–154.
63 Hopcraft, *The Football Man*, pp. 153–157; Holt, *Sport and the British*, p. 335; Benson, *The Rise of Consumer Society*, pp. 173–174.
64 See Hopcraft, *The Football Man*, pp. 17ff.; Jeff Dawson, *Back Home: England and the 1970 World Cup* (London, 2001), p. 23.
65 *The Times*, 28 May 1970.
66 Dawson, *Back Home*, p. 52.
67 Dawson, *Back Home*, pp. 107, 112–113.
68 Dawson, *Back Home*, pp. 68, 127, 71.
69 See Dawson, *Back Home*, pp. 91–106.
70 Dawson, *Back Home*, p. 105.
71 Pimlott, *Harold Wilson*, p. 555.
72 *Daily Express*, 1 June 1970.
73 *Sunday Times*, 14 June 1970.
74 Castle diary, 15 May 1970.
75 Crossman diary, 7 June 1970.
76 See Cockerell, *Live from Number Ten*, p. 161; Ziegler, *Wilson*, p. 349.
77 Paterson, *Tired and Emotional*, pp. 258–259.
78 *The Times*, 3 June 1970; Brown, *In My Way*, p. 267.
79 Butler and Pinto-Duschinsky, *The British General Election of 1970*, p. 231.
80 Cockerell, *Live from Number Ten*, p. 162.
81 Hattersley, *Who Goes Home?*, p. 90.
82 *The Times*, 20 June 1970.
83 Castle diary, 28 May 1970.
84 Mark Garnett and Ian Aitken, *Splendid! Splendid! The Authorized Biography of Willie Whitelaw* (London, 2003), pp. 83–84.
85 *The Times*, 4 June 1970.
86 Crossman diary, 7 June 1970.
87 *Daily Sketch*, 15 June 1970; *News of the World*, 14 June 1970.
88 See Butler and Pinto-Duschinsky, *The British General Election of 1970*, pp. 327–329.
89 See, for example, the table on the papers' lead stories during the campaign in Butler and Pinto-Duschinsky, *The British General Election of 1970*, pp. 238–239.
90 See *The Times*, 5 June 1970.
91 Heath, *The Course of My Life*, p. 305.
92 Dawson, *Back Home*, pp. 202–203.
93 Benn diary, 11 June 1970.
94 *The Times*, 20 June 1970.
95 *Spectator*, 13 June 1970.
96 Crossman diary, 14 June 1970.
97 Dawson, *Back Home*, p. 254.
98 On the coverage of the match, see Dawson, *Back Home*, pp. 260–268, from which the quotations are drawn.
99 Dawson, *Back Home*, p. 268.

100 Dawson, *Back Home*, pp. 269–270.
101 Dawson, *Back Home*, p. 279.
102 See, for example, *The Times* and *Daily Mail*, 15 June 1970.
103 Dawson, *Back Home*, p. 272.
104 Jenkins, *A Life at the Centre*, p. 301.
105 *The Times*, 16 June 1970; Jenkins, *A Life at the Centre*, pp. 299–300.
106 Alexander and Watkins, *The Making of the Prime Minister 1970*, p. 162.
107 *The Times*, 16 June 1970.
108 Benn diary, 15 June 1970.
109 *Observer*, 7 June 1970; *Sunday Times*, 14 June 1970; *Financial Times*, 15 June 1970; *Evening Standard*, 18 June 1970.
110 Butler and Pinto-Duschinsky, *The British General Election of 1970*, p. 165.
111 *The Times*, 17 June 1970.
112 Butler and Pinto-Duschinsky, *The British General Election of 1970*, p. 168; Cockerell, *Live from Number Ten*, pp. 165–166.
113 Butler and Pinto-Duschinsky, *The British General Election of 1970*, pp. 168–169, 194, 224; Cockerell, *Live from Number Ten*, pp. 166–168.
114 *Spectator*, 20 June 1970.
115 *The Times*, 17 June 1970.
116 *The Economist*, 20 June 1970.
117 Thorpe, *Alec Douglas-Home*, pp. 402–403; Garnett and Aitken, *Splendid! Splendid!*, p. 85.
118 Jenkins, *A Life at the Centre*, p. 301.
119 *The Times*, 19 June 1970.
120 Heath, *The Course of My Life*, p. 307.
121 Jenkins, *A Life at the Centre*, p. 301.
122 Williams, *Inside Number 10*, pp. 9–10, 272.
123 Crossman diary, 18 June 1970.
124 Williams, *Inside Number 10*, p. 10.
125 Benn diary, 18 June 1970.
126 Butler and Pinto-Duschinsky, *The British General Election of 1970*, pp. 172, 185.
127 Jenkins, *A Life at the Centre*, p. 297.
128 Crossman diary, 19 June 1970.
129 Butler and Pinto-Duschinsky, *The British General Election of 1970*, p. 339; Fielding, *Labour and Cultural Change*, pp. 221–225.
130 As argued in Ponting, *Breach of Promise*, p. 389; Campbell, *Edward Heath*, p. 281.
131 Kenneth O. Morgan, 'Symposium: The Labour Party's Record in Office', *Contemporary Record* 3:4, April 1990, p. 22.
132 Marquand, *The Progressive Dilemma*, p. 158.
133 Tomlinson, *Economic Policy*, p. 220.
134 Tomlinson, *Economic Policy*, pp. 201–202.
135 Timmins, *The Five Giants*, pp. 216, 247.
136 See, for example, David Coates, *The Labour Party and the Struggle for Socialism* (Cambridge, 1975), pp. 97–129; James Hinton, *Labour and Socialism: A History of the British Labour Movement* (Brighton, 1983), pp. 189–192; Ralph Miliband, *Parliamentary Socialism: A Study in the Politics of Labour* (London, 1972), pp. 350–359.

137 Ponting, *Breach of Promise*, pp. 399–400.
138 Butler and Pinto-Duschinsky, *The British General Election of 1970*, p. 351.
139 Dell, *A Strange Eventful History*, p. 318.
140 Williams, *Inside Number 10*, p. 12.
141 Pimlott, *Harold Wilson*, p. 558.
142 Jenkins, *A Life at the Centre*, p. 303.
143 Benn diary, 19 June 1970; Jenkins, *A Life at the Centre*, p. 304.
144 *The Times*, 20 June 1970.
145 Pimlott, *Harold Wilson*, p. 559.
146 Williams, *Inside Number 10*, p. 17.
147 *The Times*, 19 June 1970.
148 *Sun*, 19 June 1970.
149 *Daily Express*, 19 June 1970.
150 *The Economist*, 27 June 1970.
151 Campbell, *Edward Heath*, p. 284.
152 *The Times*, 20 June 1970; Heath, *The Course of My Life*, pp. 307–309.
153 *Finchley Press*, 26 June 1970, quoted in Campbell, *The Grocer's Daughter*, p. 210.

EPILOGUE

1 See Graham McCann, *Dad's Army: The Story of a Classic Television Show* (London, 2002), pp. 83–86.
2 McCann, *Dad's Army*, p. 77.
3 *Sunday Telegraph* and *Observer*, 4 August 1968.
4 *Daily Express*, 1 August 1968. For more on the reception of the pilot episode, see McCann, *Dad's Army*, pp. 87–88.
5 McCann, *Dad's Army*, pp. 100–101, 178–185.
6 *Guardian*, 14 November 1977.
7 On the lasting success of the series, see McCann, *Dad's Army*, pp. 3–9, 222–223.
8 See <www.bfi.org.uk/features/tv/100/>. The quotation is from the BFI's online encyclopedia of television at <www.screenonline.org.uk/tv/id/449057/index.html>.
9 On *Dad's Army* and the Ealing tradition, see Richards, *Films and British National Identity*, pp. 360ff.
10 Richards, *Films and British National Identity*, p. 360.
11 See McCann, *Dad's Army*, pp. 137–138.
12 *New Society*, 27 November 1969.
13 George Orwell, 'The Lion and the Unicorn: Socialism and the English Genius', online at <http://www.k–1.com/Orwell/lion.htm>.

SELECT BIBLIOGRAPHY

What follows is a list of the books cited in the Notes. The full details of academic articles, newspapers, government reports and other materials can be found in the notes themselves.

Mary Abbott, *Family Affairs: A History of the Family in Twentieth Century England* (London, 2003)
Brian Abel-Smith and Peter Townsend, *The Poor and the Poorest* (London, 1965)
Mark Abrams, *The Teenage Consumer* (London, 1959)
Mark Abrams, *Teenage Consumer Spending in 1959* (London, 1961)
Mark Abrams and Richard Rose, *Must Labour Lose?* (Harmondsworth, 1960)
Barbara Adams and Jean Conway, *The Social Effects of Living Off the Ground* (London, 1973)
Gerry Adams, *Before the Dawn: An Autobiography* (London, 1996)
Paul Addison, *Now the War is Over: A Social History of Britain 1945–51* (London, 1985)
Jonathan Aitken, *The Young Meteors* (London, 1967)
Miriam Akhtar and Steve Humphries, *Some Liked It Hot: The British on Holiday at Home and Abroad* (London, 2000)
Miriam Akhtar and Steve Humphries, *The Fifties and Sixties: A Lifestyle Revolution* (London, 2001)
Anthony Aldgate and Jeffrey Richards, *Best of British: Cinema and Society from 1930 to the Present* (London, 1999)
Anthony Aldgate, James Chapman and Arthur Marwick, eds, *Windows on the Sixties: Exploring Key Texts of Media and Culture* (London, 2000)
Richard J. Aldrich, *The Hidden Hand: Britain, America and Cold War Secret Intelligence* (London, 2001)
Peter Alex, *Who's Who in Pop Radio* (London, 1966)
Andrew Alexander and Alan Watkins, *The Making of the Prime Minister 1970* (London, 1970)
Clifford Allen, *Homosexuality: Its Nature, Causation and Treatment* (London, 1958)
Kingsley Amis, *Lucky Jim* (London, 1954)
Kingsley Amis, *I Like It Here* (London, 1958)
Kingsley Amis, *Take a Girl Like You* (London, 1960)
Kingsley Amis, *I Want It Now* (London, 1968)
Kingsley Amis, *Girl, 20* (London, 1971)
Kingsley Amis, *What Became of Jane Austen?* (London, 1970)
Kingsley Amis, *The Amis Collection* (London, 1990)
Kingsley Amis, *Memoirs* (London, 1991)

Kingsley Amis, *The King's English* (London, 1997)

Noël Annan, *Our Age: The Generation That Made Post-War Britain* (London, 1990)

Tony Bacon, *London Live: From the Yardbirds to Pink Floyd to the Sex Pistols* (London, 1999)

Keith Badman, *The Beatles off the Record: Outrageous Opinions and Unrehearsed Interviews* (London, 2001)

David Bailey, *David Bailey's Box of Pin-ups* (London, 1965)

J. G. Ballard, *High Rise* (London, 1975)

Reyner Banham, *The New Brutalism* (London, 1966)

Keith Banting, *Poverty, Politics and Policy: Britain in the 1960s* (London, 1979)

Robert Barnard, *A Talent to Deceive: An Appreciation of Agatha Christie* (London, 1990)

Alan Barnes and Marcus Hearn, *The Hammer Story* (London, 1998)

Richard Barnes, *Mods!* (London, 1989)

Correlli Barnett, *The Audit of War: The Illusion and Reality of Britain as a Great Power* (London, 1986)

Correlli Barnett, *The Lost Victory: British Dreams, British Realities, 1945–1950* (London, 1995)

Correlli Barnett, *The Verdict of Peace: Britain Between her Yesterday and the Future* (London, 2001)

C. J. Bartlett, *The Special Relationship: A Political History of Anglo-American Relations since 1945* (London, 1992)

Lewis Baston, *Reggie: The Life of Reginald Maudling* (London, 2004)

The Beatles, *The Beatles Anthology* (New York, 2000)

Tony Benn, *Out of the Wilderness: Diaries, 1963–67* (London, 1987)

Tony Benn, *Office Without Power: Diaries 1968–72* (London, 1988)

Alan Bennett, *Forty Years On* (London, 1969)

Tony Bennett and Janet Woollacott, *Bond and Beyond: The Political Career of a Popular Hero* (London, 1987)

John Benson, *The Rise of Consumer Society in Britain 1880–1980* (London, 1994)

Bernard Bergonzi, *The Situation of the Novel* (London, 1970)

Bernard Bergonzi, *Wartime and Aftermath: English Literature and its Background, 1939–1960* (Oxford, 1993)

Barbara Bernard, *Fashion in the 60s* (London, 1978)

John Betjeman, *Collected Poems* (London, 2001)

Reginald Bevins, *The Greasy Pole* (London, 1965)

Drusilla Beyfus, *The English Marriage: What It Is Like to Be Married Today* (London, 1968)

Michael Billington, *The Life and Work of Harold Pinter* (London, 1998)

Tessa Blackstone, Kathleen Gales, Roger Hadley and Wyn Lewis, *Students in Conflict: LSE in 1967* (London, 1970)

David Bleakley, *Faulkner: Conflict and Consensus in Irish Politics* (London, 1974)

Clive Bloom and Gary Day, eds, *Literature and Culture in Modern Britain: Volume Three: 1956–1999* (London, 2000)

Kenneth Bloomfield, *Stormont in Crisis* (Belfast, 1994)

Vernon Bogdanor and Robert Skidelsky, eds, *The Age of Affluence* (London, 1970)

Alan Bold, *MacDiarmid: Christopher Murray Grieve, A Critical Biography* (Boston, 1990)

Margaret Bone, *Family Planning Services in England and Wales* (London, 1973)

Christopher Booker, *The Seventies: Portrait of a Decade* (Harmondsworth, 1980)
Christopher Booker, *The Neophiliacs: The Revolution in English Life in the Fifties and Sixties* (Revised edition: London, 1992)
Stanley Booth, *The True Adventures of the Rolling Stones* (Chicago, 2000)
David Boulton, *The UVF 1966–73* (Dublin, 1973)
John Bowlby, *Child Care and the Growth of Love* (Harmondsworth, 1953)
Andrew Boyd, *Holy War in Belfast* (Tralee, 1969)
Duncan Brack and Iain Dale, eds, *Prime Minister Portillo, and Other Things that Never Happened* (London, 2003)
Malcolm Bradbury, *Possibilities: Essays on the State of the Novel* (London, 1972)
Malcolm Bradbury, *The Modern British Novel* (London, 1993)
Richard Bradford, *Lucky Him: The Life of Kingsley Amis* (London, 1991)
George Brandt, *British Television Drama* (Cambridge, 1981)
Roger Bray and Vladimir Raitz, *Flight to the Sun: The Story of the Holiday Revolution* (London, 2000)
Piers Brendon, *The Dark Valley: A Panorama of the 1930s* (London, 2000)
Piers Brendon and Phillip Whitehead, *The Windsors: A Dynasty Revealed 1917–2000* (London, 2000)
Lionel Brett, *Landscape in Distress* (London, 1965)
Asa Briggs, *The History of Broadcasting in the United Kingdom: Volume V: Competition* (Oxford, 1995)
Jacob Bronowski, *Exhibition of Science, South Kensington: A Guide to the Story It Tells* (London, 1951)
Barbara Brookes, *Abortion in England, 1900–67* (Kent, 1988)
Callum Brown, *The Death of Christian Britain: Understanding Secularisation 1800–2000* (London, 2001)
George Brown, *In My Way: The Political Memoirs of Lord George-Brown* (Harmondsworth, 1972)
Mick Brown, *Performance* (London, 2000)
Kevin Brownlow, *David Lean* (New York, 1996)
Arthur Bryant, *The National Character* (London, 1934)
Anthony Burgess, *The Right to an Answer* (London, 1960)
Anthony Burgess, *A Clockwork Orange* (Harmondsworth, 1972)
Anthony Burgess, *The Wanting Seed* (London, 1983)
Anthony Burgess, *Little Wilson and Big God* (London, 1987)
Anthony Burgess, *You've Had Your Time* (London, 1990)
Alan Burton, Tim O'Sullivan and Paul Wells, eds, *The Family Way: The Boulting Brothers and Postwar British Film Culture* (Trowbridge, 2000)
David Butler and Anthony King, *The British General Election of 1964* (London, 1965)
David Butler and Anthony King, *The British General Election of 1966* (London, 1966)
David Butler and Michael Pinto-Duschinsky, *The British General Election of 1970* (London, 1971)
R. A. Butler, *The Art of the Possible: The Memoirs of Lord Butler* (Harmondsworth, 1973)
David Buxton, *From The Avengers to Miami Vice: Form and Ideology in Television Series* (Manchester, 1990)

Michael Caine, *What's It All About? The Autobiography* (London, 1992)
Alec Cairncross, *The British Economy since 1945* (Oxford, 1992)
Alec Cairncross, *Managing the British Economy in the 1960s: A Treasury Perspective* (Basingstoke, 1996)
James Callaghan, *A House Divided* (London, 1973)
James Callaghan, *Time and Chance* (London, 1987)
Peter Calvocoressi, *The British Experience 1945–75* (Harmondsworth, 1978)
John Campbell, *Edward Heath: A Biography* (London, 1993)
John Campbell, *Margaret Thatcher: Volume One: The Grocer's Daughter* (London, 2000)
David Cannadine, *In Churchill's Shadow: Confronting the Past in Modern Britain* (London, 2002)
Humphrey Carpenter, *J.R.R. Tolkien: A Biography* (London, 1977)
Humphrey Carpenter, *The Inklings* (London, 1978)
Humphrey Carpenter, *Dennis Potter: A Biography* (London, 1999)
Humphrey Carpenter, *That Was Satire That Was: The Satire Boom of the 1960s* (London, 2000)
Humphrey Carpenter, *The Angry Young Men: A Literary Comedy of the 1950s* (London, 2002)
John le Carré, *A Small Town in Germany* (London, 1999)
Ernestine Carter, *Mary Quant's London* (London, 1973)
Barbara Castle, *The Castle Diaries, 1964–70* (London, 1984)
Barbara Castle, *Fighting All the Way* (London, 1993)
Ali Catterall and Simon Wells, *Your Face Here: British Cult Movies Since the Sixties* (London, 2001)
Max Caulfield, *Mary Whitehouse* (Oxford, 1975)
David Caute, *The Year of the Barricades: A Journey Through 1968* (New York, 1988)
Nigel Cawthorne, *Sixties Source Book: A Visual Guide to the Style of a Decade* (London, 1998)
Central Council of Physical Recreation, *Sport and the Community* (London, 1960)
Owen Chadwick, *Michael Ramsey: A Life* (London, 1990)
Iain Chambers, *Urban Rhythms: Pop Music and Popular Culture* (Basingstoke, 1985)
Iain Chambers, *Popular Culture: The Metropolitan Experience* (London, 1986)
Janet Chance, *The Cost of English Morals* (London, 1931)
James Chapman, *Licence to Thrill: A Cultural History of the James Bond Films* (London, 1999)
James Chapman, *Saints and Avengers: British Adventure Series of the 1960s* (London, 2002)
Gordon E. Cherry, *Town Planning in Britain since 1900: The Rise and Fall of the Planning Ideal* (Oxford, 1996)
Eustace Chesser, *Love Without Fear: A Plain Guide to Sex Technique for Every Married Adult* (London, 1947)
Eustace Chesser, *The Sexual, Marital and Family Relationships of the English Woman* (London, 1956)
Eustace Chesser, *Odd Man Out: Homosexuality in Men and Women* (London, 1959)
Steve Chibnall, *Get Carter* (London, 2003)
David Childs, *Britain since 1945: A Political History* (London, 1979)
Agatha Christie, *Endless Night* (London, 1967)
Mark Clapson, *Invincible Green Suburbs, Brave New Towns* (Manchester, 1998)
Mark Clapson, *A Social History of Milton Keynes: Middle England/Edge City* (London, 2004)
Peter Clarke, *Hope and Glory: Britain 1900–1990* (London, 1996)

Adam Clayson, *Beat Merchants: The Origins. History, Impact and Rock Legacy of the 1960s British Pop Groups* (London, 1995)

Richard Clutterbuck, *Britain in Agony: The Growth of Political Violence* (London, 1978)

David Coates, *The Labour Party and the Struggle for Socialism* (Cambridge, 1975)

Ken Coates and Richard Silburn, *Poverty: The Forgotten Englishmen* (Harmondsworth, 1970)

Richard Cockett, *Thinking the Unthinkable: Think-Tanks and the Economic Counter-Revolution, 1931–1983* (London, 1995)

Michael Cockerell, *Live From Number 10: The Inside Story of Prime Ministers and Television* (London, 1988)

Stanley Cohen, *Folk Devils and Moral Panics: The Creation of the Mods and Rockers* (London, 1972)

John Cole, *As It Seemed To Me: Political Memoirs* (London, 1995)

Nicholas Coleridge and Stephen Quinn, eds, *The Sixties in* Queen (London, 1997)

Jane Colin, *Jane Colin's Pocket Calorie Guide to Safe Slimming* (London, 1960)

Linda Colley, *Britons: Forging the Nation, 1707–1837* (New Haven, 1992)

Bruce Collins and Keith Robbins, eds. *British Culture and Economic Decline* (New York, 1990)

Michael Collins, *The Path to Freedom* (Cork, 1968)

Robert Colls, *Identity of England* (London, 2002)

Becky E. Conekin, *The Autobiography of a Nation: The 1951 Festival of Britain* (Manchester, 2003)

Becky E. Conekin, Frank Mort and Chris Waters, eds, *Moments of Modernity: Reconstructing Britain 1945–1964* (London, 1999)

Tim Pat Coogan, *Ireland Since the Rising* (London, 1966)

Tim Pat Coogan, *The IRA* (London, 1995)

Tim Pat Coogan, *The Troubles: Ireland's Ordeal 1966–1996 and the Search for Peace* (London, 1996)

Hera Cook, *The Long Sexual Revolution: English Women, Sex and Contraception, 1800–1975* (Oxford, 2004)

Chester L. Cooper, *The Lost Crusade: The Full Story of US Involvement in Vietnam from Roosevelt to Nixon* (London, 1980)

Richard Coopey, Steven Fielding and Nick Tiratsoo, eds, *The Wilson Governments 1964–1970* (London, 1993)

John Cork and Bruce Scivally, *James Bond: The Legacy* (London, 2002)

John Corner, ed., *Popular Television in Britain* (London, 1991)

Patrick Cosgrave, *The Lives of Enoch Powell* (London, 1989)

Patrick Cosgrave, *The Strange Death of Socialist Britain* (London, 1993)

Noël Coward, *The Noël Coward Diaries* (ed. Graham Payne and Sheridan Morley: London, 1982)

Barry Cox, John Shirley and Martin Short, *The Fall of Scotland Yard* (Harmondsworth, 1977)

C. B. Cox and A. E. Dyson, *The Black Papers on Education* (London, 1971)

Anthony Crosland, *The Future of Socialism* (London, 1956)

Anthony Crosland, *Socialism Now* (London, 1975)
Susan Crosland, *Tony Crosland* (London, 1983)
Richard Crossman, *The Diaries of a Cabinet Minister: Volume 1: Minister of Housing, 1964–66* (London, 1975)
Richard Crossman, *The Diaries of a Cabinet Minister: Volume 2: Lord President of the Council and Leader of the House of Commons, 1966–68* (London, 1976)
Richard Crossman, *The Diaries of a Cabinet Minister: Volume 3: Secretary of State for Social Services, 1968–70* (London, 1977)
Colin Crouch, *The Student Revolt* (London, 1970)
Thomas Crow, *The Rise of the Sixties: American and European Art in the Era of Dissent 1955–1969* (London, 1996)
Hugh Cudlipp, *Walking on the Water* (London, 1976)
James Curran and Vincent Porter, eds, *British Cinema History* (London, 1983)
Patrick Curry, *Defending Middle-Earth: Tolkien, Myth and Modernity* (London, 1997)
Karl F. Dallas, *Swinging London: A Guide to Where the Action Is* (London, 1967)
W. W. Daniel, *Racial Discrimination in England* (Harmondsworth, 1968)
John Darwin, *Britain and Decolonisation: The Retreat from Empire in the Post-War World* (London, 1988)
Martin Daunton, ed., *The Cambridge Urban History of Britain: Volume III, 1840–1950* (Cambridge, 2001)
Nicholas Davenport, *The Split Society* (London, 1964)
Grace Davie, *Religion in Britain since 1945* (Oxford, 1994)
Christie Davies, *Permissive Britain: Social Change in the Sixties and Seventies* (London, 1975)
Hunter Davies, ed., *The New London Spy: A Discreet Guide to the City's Pleasures* (London, 1967)
Norman Davies, *The Isles: A History* (London, 1999)
Ray Davies, *X-Ray: The Unauthorized Autobiography* (London, 1996)
John Davis, *Youth and the Condition of Britain: Images of Adolescent Conflict* (London, 1990)
Maxine Davis, *The Sexual Responsibility of Women* (London, 1957)
Stephen Davis, *Hammer of the Gods: Led Zeppelin Unauthorized* (London, 2005)
Jeff Dawson, *Back Home: England and the 1970 World Cup* (London, 2001)
Gary Day, ed., *Literature and Culture in Modern Britain: Volume Two: 1930–1955* (London, 1997)
Sir Robin Day, *Grand Inquisitor: Memoirs* (London, 1989)
Max Décharné, *King's Road: The Rise and Fall of the Hippest Street in the World* (London, 2005)
Gerard J. DeGroot, ed., *Student Protest: The Sixties and After* (London, 1998)
Len Deighton, ed., *Len Deighton's London Dossier* (London, 1967)
Edmund Dell, *The Chancellors: A History of the Chancellors of the Exchequer, 1945–90* (London, 1996)
Edmund Dell, *A Strange Eventful History: Democratic Socialism in Britain* (London, 2000)
Michael Denning, *Cover Stories: Narrative and Ideology in the British Spy Thriller* (London, 1987)
Paul Denver, *Black Stockings for Chelsea* (London, 1963)
Bernadette Devlin, *The Price of My Soul* (London, 1969)

Patrick Devlin, *The Enforcement of Morals* (Oxford, 1959)

Jonathan Dimbleby, *Richard Dimbleby: A Biography* (London, 1975)

Jonathan Dimbleby, *The Prince of Wales* (London, 1996)

Alan Dobson, *Anglo-American Relations in the Twentieth Century* (London, 1995)

Saki Dockrill, *Britain's Retreat from East of Suez: The Choice Between Europe and the World?* (London, 2002)

Desmond Donnelly, *Gadarene '68: The Crimes, Follies and Misdemeanours of the Wilson Government* (London, 1968)

Mark Donnelly, *Sixties Britain* (Harlow, 2005)

Gerald A. Dorfman, *Government versus Trade Unionism in British Politics since 1968* (London, 1979)

Stephen Dorril and Robin Ramsay, *Smear! Wilson and the Secret State* (London, 1992)

Stephen Dorril, *MI6: Fifty Years of Special Operations* (London, 2000)

Sir Alec Douglas-Home, *Peaceful Change* (London, 1964)

David Downing, *The Best of Enemies: England v. Germany, A Century of Football Rivalry* (London, 2000)

Margaret Drabble, *Angus Wilson: A Biography* (London, 1996)

Tom Driberg, *The Mystery of Moral Rearmament* (London, 1964)

Ruth Dudley Edwards, *The Faithful Tribe: An Intimate Portrait of the Loyal Institutions* (London, 2000)

Ruth Dudley Edwards, *Newspapermen: Hugh Cudlipp, Cecil Harmsworth King and the Glory Days of Fleet Street* (London, 2003)

Patrick Dunleavy, *The Politics of Mass Housing in Britain, 1945–1975: A Study of Corporate Power and Professional Influence in the Welfare State* (Oxford, 1981)

Raymond Durgnat, *A Mirror for England: British Movies from Austerity to Affluence* (London, 1970)

David L. Edwards, ed., *The Honest to God Debate* (London, 1963)

Bowes Egan and Vincent McCormack, *Burntollet* (London, 1969)

Paul Einzig, *Decline and Fall: Britain's Crisis in the Sixties* (London, 1969)

Richard English, *Armed Struggle: The History of the IRA* (London, 2004)

Martin Esslin, *Pinter the Playwright* (London, 2000)

Jeff Evans, *The Penguin TV Companion* (Second edition: London, 2003)

Roma Fairley, *A Bomb in the Collection: Fashion with the Lid Off* (Brighton, 1969)

Marianne Faithfull with David Dalton, *Faithfull* (London, 1994)

Marcia Falkender, *Downing Street in Perspective* (London, 1983)

Gene Feldman and Max Gartenberg, eds, *Protest: The Beat Generation and the Angry Young Men* (London, 1959)

Paul Ferris, *The Nameless: Abortion in Britain Today* (London, 1966)

Paul Ferris, *Sex and the British: A Twentieth-Century History* (London, 1993)

Georgina Ferry, *A Computer Called LEO: Lyons Teashops and the World's First Office Computer* (London, 2003)

Steven Fielding, *The Labour Governments 1964–1970: Volume 1: Labour and Cultural Change* (Manchester, 2003)

Eddi Fiegel, *John Barry: A Sixties Theme: From James Bond to Midnight Cowboy* (London, 2001)

David Fitzpatrick, *The Two Irelands 1912–1939* (Oxford, 1998)
Ray Fitzwalter and David Taylor, *Web of Corruption: The Story of J.G.L. Poulson and T. Dan Smith* (London, 1981)
Ronald Fletcher, *The Family and Marriage in Britain* (Harmondsworth, 1966)
Ken Flower, *Serving Secretly: An Intelligence Chief on Record: Rhodesia to Zimbabwe, 1964–1981* (London, 1987)
Marnie Fogg, *Boutique: A '60s Cultural Phenomenon* (London, 2003)
Michael Foot, *Loyalists and Loners* (London, 1986)
Paul Foot, *Immigration and Race in British Politics* (London, 1965)
Paul Foot, *The Politics of Harold Wilson* (Harmondsworth, 1968)
Paul Foot, *The Rise of Enoch Powell* (Harmondsworth, 1969)
Boris Ford, ed., *The Cambridge Cultural History of Britain, Volume 9: Modern Britain* (London, 1992)
Boris Ford, ed., *The New Pelican Guide to English Literature, Volume 8: From Orwell to Naipaul* (Revised edition: London, 1998)
Roy Foster, *Modern Ireland 1600–1972* (London, 1989)
John Fowles, *The French Lieutenant's Woman* (London, 1969)
Willi Frischauer, *David Frost: A Biography* (London, 1971)
Simon Frith and Howard Horne, *Art into Pop* (London, 1987)
David Frost and Antony Jay, *To England with Love* (London, 1967)
T.R. Fyvel, *The Insecure Offenders* (Harmondsworth, 1964)
Andrew Gamble, *Britain in Decline: Economic Policy, Political Strategy and the British State* (Fourth edition: Basingstoke, 1994)
Juliet Gardiner, *From the Bomb to the Beatles* (London, 1999)
Phillipe Garner, *Sixties Design* (Cologne, 1996)
Mark Garnett and Ian Aitken, *Splendid! Splendid! The Authorized Biography of Willie Whitelaw* (London, 2003)
Gary Gillatt, *Doctor Who from A to Z* (London, 1998)
Charlie Gillett, *The Sound of the City: The Rise of Rock and Roll* (Revised edition: London, 1983)
Ian Gilmour and Mark Garnett, *Whatever Happened to the Tories: The Conservatives since 1945* (London, 1997)
Diana Gittens, *Fair Sex: Family Size and Structure, 1900–1939* (London, 1983)
Diana Gittens, *The Family in Question* (London, 1985)
Elizabeth Gittus, *Flats, Families and the Under Fives* (London, 1976)
Brian Glanville, *The Story of the World Cup* (London, 1993)
Jim Goldbolt, *A History of Jazz in Britain, 1919–50* (London, 1984)
Tim Goodwin, *Britain's Royal National Theatre* (London, 1988)
A. W. Gordon, *Peter Howard: Life and Letters* (London, 1969)
Patrick Gordon Walker, *The Cabinet* (London, 1970)
Patrick Gordon Walker, *Political Diaries 1932–71* (ed. Robert Pearce: London, 1991)
Geoffrey Gorer, *Exploring English Character* (London, 1955)
Geoffrey Gorer, *Sex and Marriage in England Today* (London, 1971)
Jimmy Greaves and Norman Giller, *Don't Shoot The Manager: The Revealing Story of England's Soccer Bosses* (London, 1994)

E. H. H. Green, *Ideologies of Conservatism: Conservative Political Ideas in the Twentieth Century* (Oxford, 2004)

Jonathon Green, *Them: Voices from the Immigrant Community in Contemporary Britain* (London, 1990)

Jonathon Green, *Days in the Life: Voices From the English Underground, 1961–1971* (London, 1998)

Jonathon Green, *All Dressed Up: The Sixties and the Counter-Culture* (London, 1998)

Roy Greenslade, *Press Gang: How Newspapers Make Profits from Propaganda* (London, 2004)

Germaine Greer, *The Female Eunuch* (London, 1993)

John Selwyn Gummer, *The Permissive Society* (London, 1971)

Simon Gunn and Rachel Bell, *Middle Classes: Their Rise and Sprawl* (London, 2003)

Lord Hailsham, *A Sparrow's Flight: Memoirs* (London, 1990)

Joe Haines, *The Politics of Power: The Inside Story of Life at No. 10* (London, 1977)

Joe Haines, *Glimmers of Twilight: Harold Wilson in Decline* (London, 2003)

Piri Halasz, *A Swinger's Guide to London* (New York, 1967)

Peter Hall, *Making an Exhibition of Myself* (London, 1993)

Peter Hall, *Cities of Tomorrow: An Intellectual History of Urban Planning and Design in the Twentieth Century* (Oxford, 1996)

Richard Hamilton, *Collected Words: 1953–1982* (London, 1982)

Pamela Hansford Johnson, *On Iniquity* (London, 1967)

Jennifer Harris, Sarah Hyde and Greg Smith, eds, *1966 And All That* (London, 1986)

Nigel Harris, *Competition and the Corporate State: British Conservatives, the State and Industry, 1945–1964* (London, 1972)

Martin Harrison, *Young Meteors: British Photojournalism, 1957–1965* (London, 1998)

Cate Haste, *Rules of Desire: Sex in Britain: World War I to the Present* (London, 1994)

Anthony Hartley, *A State of England* (London, 1963)

L. P. Hartley, *The Go-Between* (London, 1953)

Adrian Hastings, *A History of English Christianity 1920–1985* (London, 1986)

Roy Hattersley, *Who Goes Home? Scenes From A Political Life* (London, 1995)

Denis Healey, *The Time of My Life* (London, 1989)

Edward Heath, *Sailing: A Course of My Life* (London, 1975)

Edward Heath, *The Course of My Life: My Autobiography* (London, 1998)

Simon Heffer, *Like the Roman: The Life of Enoch Powell* (London, 1998)

Thomas Hennessey, *A History of Northern Ireland 1920–1996* (Dublin, 1997)

Thomas Hennessey, *Dividing Ireland: World War One and Partition* (London, 1998)

Peter Hennessy, *Never Again: Britain 1945–1951* (London, 1992)

Peter Hennessy, *Muddling Through: Power, Politics and the Quality of Government in Postwar Britain* (London, 1996)

Peter Hennessy, *The Prime Minister: The Office and its Holders Since 1945* (London, 2000)

Peter Hennessy and Anthony Seldon, eds, *Ruling Performance: British Governments from Attlee to Thatcher* (Oxford, 1987)

Paolo Hewitt, ed., *The Sharper Word: A Mod Anthology* (Second edition: London, 2002)

Robert Hewison, *In Anger: Culture in the Cold War, 1945–60* (London, 1981)

Robert Hewison, *Too Much: Art and Society in the Sixties 1960–75* (London, 1986)

Clifford S. Hill, *How Colour Prejudiced Is Britain?* (London, 1965)
Jeffrey Hill, *Sport, Leisure and Culture in Twentieth-Century Britain* (London, 2002)
John Hill, *Sex, Class and Realism: British Cinema 1956–1963* (London, 1986)
Bevis Hillier, *John Betjeman: New Fame, New Love* (London, 2002)
Bevis Hillier, *John Betjeman: The Bonus of Laughter* (London, 2004)
James Hinton, *Labour and Socialism: A History of the British Labour Movement* (Brighton, 1983)
Peter Hitchens, *The Abolition of Britain* (Revised edition: London, 2000)
Eric Hobsbawm, *Industry and Empire* (Harmondsworth, 1969)
Eric Hobsbawm, *Age of Extremes: The Short Twentieth Century 1914–1991* (London, 1994)
Eric Hobsbawm, *Interesting Times: A Twentieth-Century Life* (London, 2002)
David Hockney, *That's the Way I See It* (London, 1999)
Stanley Hoffman and Patrick Kitromilides, eds, *Culture and Society in Contemporary Europe* (London, 1981)
Godfrey Hodgson, *In Our Time: America from World War II to Nixon* (New York, 1976)
Richard Hoggart, *The Uses of Literacy* (Harmondsworth, 1958)
Jonathan Hollowell, ed., *Twentieth-Century Anglo-American Relations* (Basingstoke, 2001)
Colin Holmes, *John Bull's Island: Immigration and British Society, 1871–1971* (London, 1988)
Richard Holt, *Sport and the British: A Modern History* (Oxford, 1990)
Richard Holt, *Second Amongst Equals: Chancellors of the Exchequer since the Second World War* (London, 2001)
Lord Home, *The Way The Wind Blows: An Autobiography* (London, 1976)
Arthur Hopcraft, *The Football Man: People and Passions in Soccer* (Harmondsworth, 1971)
Harry Hopkins, *The New Look: A Social History of the Forties and Fifties in Britain* (London, 1964)
Alistair Horne, *Macmillan 1957–1986: Volume II of the Official Biography* (London, 1989)
Students and Staff of Hornsey College of Art, *The Hornsey Affair* (Harmondsworth, 1969)
Anthony Howard, *RAB: The Life of R. A. Butler* (London, 1987)
Anthony Howard, *Crossman: The Pursuit of Power* (London, 1990)
Anthony Howard and Richard West, *The Making of the Prime Minister* (London, 1965)
David J. Howe and Stephen James Walker, *Doctor Who: The Television Companion* (London, 1998)
Georgina Howell, *In Vogue* (London, 1975)
Robert Hughes, *The Shock of the New: Art and the Century of Change* (Revised edition: London, 1991)
Barbara Hulanicki, *From A to Biba* (London, 1983)
Steve Humphries and John Taylor, *The Making of Modern London, 1945–1985* (London, 1986)
Peter Hutchings, *Hammer and Beyond: The British Horror Film* (London, 1993)
Roger Hutchinson, *It Is Now! The Real Story of England's 1966 World Cup Triumph* (Edinburgh, 1995)
Stuart Hylton, *Magical History Tour: The 1960s Revisited* (Stroud, 2000)
Mary Ingham, *Now We Are Thirty: Women of the Breakthrough Generation* (London, 1981)
Richard Ingrams, ed., *The Life and Times of Private Eye* (London, 1971)

Richard Ingrams, *Muggeridge: The Biography* (London, 1995)
Richard Ingrams and John Wells, *Mrs Wilson's Diaries* (London, 1966)
Richard Ingrams and John Wells, *Mrs Wilson's Second Diary* (London, 1966)
Alan A. Jackson, *The Middle Classes 1900–1950* (Nairn, 1991)
Brian Jackson, *Working-Class Community* (Harmondsworth, 1972)
Lesley Jackson, *The New Look: Design in the Fifties* (London, 1991)
Lesley Jackson, *Contemporary: Architecture and Interiors of the 1950s* (London, 1998)
Lesley Jackson, *The Sixties: Decade of Design Revolution* (London, 1998)
Eric Jacobs, *Kingsley Amis: A Biography* (London, 1995)
Eric James, *A Life of John Robinson: Scholar, Pastor, Prophet* (London, 1987)
Lawrence James, *The Rise and Fall of the British Empire* (London, 1994)
Douglas Jay, *Change and Fortune: A Political Record* (London, 1980)
Kevin Jefferys, *Retreat from New Jerusalem: British Politics, 1951–64* (London, 1997)
Kevin Jefferys, *Anthony Crosland* (London, 1999)
Sheila Jeffreys, *Anticlimax: A Feminist Perspective on the Sexual Revolution* (London, 1990)
Stephen Jeffrey-Poulter, *Peers, Queers and Commons: The Struggle for Gay Law Reform from 1950 to the Present* (London, 1991)
Peter Jenkins, *The Battle of Downing Street* (London, 1970)
Roy Jenkins, *The Labour Case* (Harmondsworth, 1959)
Roy Jenkins, *A Life at the Centre* (London, 1992)
Roy Jenkins, *Portraits and Miniatures: Selected Writings* (London, 1993)
Pearl Jephcott, Nancy Sear and J. H. Smith, *Married Women Working* (London, 1962)
Paul Johnson, ed., *The Oxford Book of Political Anecdotes* (Oxford, 1989)
Glyn Jones and Michael Barnes, *Britain on Borrowed Time* (Harmondsworth, 1967)
Matthew Jones, *Conflict and Confrontation in South East Asia, 1961–1965: Britain, the United States, Indonesia and the Creation of Malaysia* (Cambridge, 2001)
Mervyn Jones, *Michael Foot* (London, 1994)
Peter Jones, *America and the Labour Party: The Special Relationship at Work* (London, 1997)
Denis Judd, *Empire: The British Imperial Experience from 1765 to the Present* (London, 1996)
Peter Jupp, *From Dust to Ashes: The Replacement of Burial by Cremation in England 1840–1967* (London, 1990)
Ernest Kay, *Pragmatic Premier* (London, 1967)
Harry Kidd, *The Trouble at LSE, 1966–1967* (London, 1969)
Anthony King and Robert J. Wybrow, eds, *British Political Opinion 1937–2000: The Gallup Polls* (London, 2001)
Cecil King, *The Cecil King Diary, 1965–1970* (London, 1972)
Roger King and Neill Nugent, eds, *Respectable Rebels: Middle-Class Campaigns in Britain in the 1970s* (London, 1979)
Brian Y. Kingsworth, *Sensible Slimming* (London, 1964)
Wayne Kinsey, *Hammer Films: The Bray Studio Years* (Richmond, 2002)
Henry Kissinger, *The White House Years* (London, 1979)
U. W. Kitzinger, *The Second Try: Labour and the EEC* (London, 1968)
Arthur Koestler, ed., *Suicide of a Nation? An Enquiry Into the State of Britain Today* (London, 1963)

Maurice Kogan, *The Politics of Education* (Harmondsworth, 1971)
J. S. Kotschack, *The Radio Nord Story* (London, 1963)
Allan Kozinn, *The Beatles* (London, 1995)
Stephen Lacey, *British Realist Theatre: The New Wave in Context, 1956–1965* (London, 1995)
John Lahr, *Prick Up Your Ears: The Biography of Joe Orton* (Revised edition: London, 2002)
Margaret Laing, *Edward Heath, Prime Minister* (London, 1972)
Stuart Laing, *Representations of Working-Class Life 1957–1964* (Basingstoke, 1986)
Richard Lamb, *The Macmillan Years 1957–1963: The Unfolding Truth* (London, 1995)
Cecile Landau, ed., *Growing Up in the Sixties* (London, 1991)
Marcia Landy, *British Genres: Cinema and Society, 1930–1960* (Princeton, 1991)
Colin Larkin, ed., *The Virgin Encyclopedia of Sixties Music* (London, 1997)
Philip Larkin, *Collected Poems* (London, 1990)
Peter Laurie, *The Teenage Revolution* (London, 1965)
Daniel Lawrence, *Black Migrants, White Natives: A Study of Race Relations in Nottingham* (Cambridge, 1974)
Twiggy Lawson with Penelope Dening, *Twiggy in Black and White: An Autobiography* (London, 1997)
John Lawton, *1963: Five Hundred Days* (London, 1992)
Zachary Leader, ed., *The Letters of Kingsley Amis* (London, 2000)
F. R. Leavis, *Nor Shall My Sword: Discourses on Pluralism, Compassion, and Social Hope* (New York, 1972)
Peter Leslie, *Fab: The Anatomy of a Phenomenon* (London, 1965)
Bernard Levin, *The Pendulum Years: Britain and the Sixties* (Revised edition: London, 1977)
Shawn Levy, *Ready, Steady, Go! Swinging London and the Invention of Cool* (London, 2002)
Peter Lewis, *The Fifties* (London, 1978)
Peter Lewis, *The National: A Dream Made Concrete* (London, 1990)
Roger Lewis, *The Life and Death of Peter Sellers* (London, 1994)
Clive Limpkin, *The Battle of Bogside* (Harmondsworth, 1972)
Konrad Lorenz, *On Aggression* (London, 1966)
Jerry Lucky, *The Progressive Rock Files* (London, 2003)
Sutherland Lyall, *The State of British Architecture* (London, 1980)
John Lynch, *A Tale of Three Cities: Comparative Studies in Working-Class Life* (Basingstoke, 1998)
Humphrey Lyttleton, *I Play As I Please* (London, 1954)
Edward L. Macan, *Rocking the Classics; English Progressive Rock and the Counterculture* (Oxford, 1997)
Ian MacDonald, *Revolution in the Head* (Revised edition: London, 1997)
Ian MacDonald, *The People's Music* (London, 2003)
David R. Mace, *Marriage Counselling* (London, 1948)
Colin MacInnes, *Absolute Beginners* (London, 1980)
Harold Macmillan, *Riding the Storm, 1956–59* (London, 1971)
Harold Macmillan, *At the End of the Day, 1959–1961* (London, 1973)
Norman Macrae, *Sunshades in October* (London, 1963)
Sean MacStiofain, *Memoirs of a Revolutionary* (Edinburgh, 1975)

SELECT BIBLIOGRAPHY

Sara Maitland, ed., *Very Heaven: Looking Back at the 1960s* (London, 1988)
Joan Maizels, *Two to Five in High Flats* (London, 1971)
Jamie Mandelkau, *Buttons: The Making of a President* (London, 1971)
Peter Mann, *Books, Buyers and Borrowers* (London, 1971)
Greil Marcus, *The Dustbin of History* (Cambridge, Massachusetts, 1995)
James Margach, *The Anatomy of Power* (London, 1979)
Patrick Marnham, *The Private Eye Story* (London, 1982)
David Marquand, *The Progressive Dilemma: From Lloyd George to Blair* (Second edition: London, 1999)
David Marquand and Anthony Seldon, eds, *The Ideas that Shaped Post-War Britain* (London, 1996)
Andrew Marr, *The Battle for Scotland* (London, 1992)
Patrick Marrinan, *Paisley: Man of Wrath* (Tralee, 1973)
Dave Marsh, *Before I Get Old: The Story of the Who* (New York, 1983)
Richard Marsh, *Off the Rails: An Autobiography* (London, 1978)
Arthur Marwick, *Class: Image and Reality in Britain, France and the USA since 1930* (London, 1980)
Arthur Marwick, *British Society since 1945* (Harmondsworth, 1982)
Arthur Marwick, *The Sixties: Cultural Revolution in Britain, France, Italy, and the United States, c.1958–c.1974* (Oxford, 1998)
Mass-Observation, *Puzzled People: A Study of Popular Attitudes to Religion, Ethics, Progress and Politics in a London Borough* (London, 1948)
Brian Masters, *The Swinging Sixties* (London, 1985)
Reginald Maudling, *Memoirs* (London, 1978)
Colin McCabe, *Performance* (London, 1998)
Hugh McIlvanney, *McIlvanney on Football* (Edinburgh, 1994)
Ross McKibbin, *Classes and Cultures: England, 1918–1951* (Oxford, 1998)
David McKittrick and David McVea, *Making Sense of the Troubles* (London, 2001)
David Alan Mellor and Laurent Gervereau, eds, *The Sixties: Britain and France, 1962–1973: The Utopian Years* (London, 1997)
George Melly, *Revolt Into Style* (Oxford, 1989)
George Mikes, *How To Be A Brit: A George Mikes Omnibus* (London, 1984)
Barry Miles, *Paul McCartney: Many Years From Now* (London, 1997)
Barry Miles, *The Beatles Diary: Volume 1: The Beatles Years* (London, 2001)
Barry Miles, *Hippie* (London, 2004)
Ralph Miliband, *Parliamentary Socialism: A Study in the Politics of Labour* (London, 1972)
James Miller, *Flowers in the Dustbin: The Rise of Rock and Roll, 1947–1977* (New York, 1999)
Stephen Milligan, *The New Barons: Union Power in the 1970s* (London, 1976)
Tom Milne, *No Shining Armour* (London, 1977)
John Minnion and Philip Bolsover, eds, *The CND Story* (London, 1983)
Austin Mitchell and David Wienir, eds, *Last Time: Labour's Lessons from the Sixties* (London, 1997)
John Mitchinson, ed., *British Greats* (London, 2000)
Ed Molony and Andy Pollak, *Paisley* (Dublin, 1986)

Bart Moore-Gilbert and John Seed, eds, *Cultural Revolution? The Challenge of the Arts in the 1960s* (London, 1992)
Geoffrey Moorhouse, *Britain in the Sixties: The Other England* (Harmondsworth, 1964)
Paul Moorhouse, ed., *Bridget Riley* (London, 2003)
Kenneth O. Morgan, *Labour People: Leaders and Lieutenants, Hardie to Kinnock* (Revised edition: London, 1992)
Kenneth O. Morgan, *Callaghan: A Life* (Oxford, 1997)
Kenneth O. Morgan, *Rebirth of a Nation: Wales, 1880–1980* (Oxford, 1997)
Kenneth O. Morgan, *The People's Peace: British History since 1945* (Second edition: Oxford, 1999)
Desmond Morris, *The Naked Ape* (London, 1967)
Blake Morrison, *The Movement: English Poetry and Fiction of the 1950s* (Oxford, 1980)
Andrew Motion, *The Lamberts: George, Constant and Kit* (London, 1986)
Andrew Motion, *Philip Larkin: A Writer's Life* (London, 1993)
Malcolm Muggeridge, *Tread Softly for You Tread on My Jokes* (London, 1966)
Malcolm Muggeridge, *Jesus Rediscovered* (New York, 1968)
Robert Murphy, *Sixties British Cinema* (London, 1992)
Robert Murphy, ed., *The British Cinema Book* (Second edition: London, 2001)
Robin Neillands, *A Fighting Retreat: The British Empire 1947–97* (London, 1996)
Richard Neville, *Play Power* (London, 1970)
Tim Newburn, *Permission and Regulation: Law and Morals in Post-War Britain* (London, 1992)
John Newsom, *The Education of Girls* (London, 1948)
John Newsom, *Half Our Future: A Report of the Central Advisory Council for Education (England)* (London, 1963)
Philip Norman, *Shout! The True Story of the Beatles* (London, 1981)
Philip Norman, *The Stones* (London, 1993)
Philip Norman, *Everyone's Gone to the Moon* (London, 1995)
Northern Ireland Civil Rights Association, *We Shall Overcome: The History of the Struggle for Civil Rights in Northern Ireland 1968–78* (Belfast, 1978)
Jeff Nuttall, *Bomb Culture* (London, 1968)
Patrick Nuttgens, *The Home Front: Housing the People 1840–1990* (London, 1989)
Niall Ó Dochartaigh, *From Civil Rights to Armalites: Derry and the Birth of the Irish Troubles* (Cork, 1997)
Andrew Loog Oldham, *Stoned* (London, 2001)
Andrew Loog Oldham, *2Stoned* (London, 2003)
Paul Oliver, Ian Davis and Ian Bentley, eds, *Dunroamin: The Suburban Semi and its Enemies* (London, 1981)
Terence O'Neill, *Ulster at the Crossroads* (London, 1969)
George Orwell, *The Road to Wigan Pier* (Harmondsworth, 1962)
John Osborne, *The Entertainer* (London, 1957)
David Owen, *Time to Declare* (London, 1992)
Geoffrey Owen, *From Empire to Europe: The Decline and Revival of British Industry Since the Second World War* (London, 1999)
Tony Palmer, *All You Need Is Love: The Story of Popular Music* (London, 1977)

Peter Paterson, *Tired and Emotional: The Life of Lord George-Brown* (London, 1993)
Mark Paytress, *The Rolling Stones Off The Record* (London, 2003)
John Peacock, *Fashion Sourcebooks: The 1960s* (London, 1998)
Edward Pearce, *Denis Healey: A Life In Our Times* (London, 2002)
Geoffrey Pearson, *Hooligan: A History of Respectable Fears* (London, 1983)
Anne Perkins, *Red Queen: The Authorized Biography of Barbara Castle* (London, 2003)
Alan Butt Philip, *The Welsh Question: Nationalism in Welsh Politics, 1945–1970* (Cardiff, 1975)
Mike Phillips and Trevor Phillips, *Windrush: The Irresistible Rise of Multi-Racial Britain* (London, 1999)
John Pidgeon, *Eric Clapton* (London, 1976)
Ben Pimlott, ed., *The Political Diary of Hugh Dalton 1918–40, 1945–60* (London, 1986)
Ben Pimlott, *Harold Wilson* (London, 1992)
Ben Pimlott, *The Queen: A Biography of Elizabeth II* (London, 1997)
Harold Pinter, *The Caretaker* (London, 1960)
Dave Pirie, *A Heritage of Horror* (London, 1973)
Martin Polley, *Moving the Goalposts: A History of Sport and Society since 1945* (London, 1998)
Clive Ponting, *Breach of Promise: Labour in Power 1964–1970* (London, 1990)
Anthony Powell, *A Dance to the Music of Time: IV, Winter* (London, 1997)
Alison Pressley, *The Best of Times: Growing Up in Britain in the 1950s* (London, 1999)
Alison Pressley, *Changing Times: Being Young in Britain in the '60s* (London, 2000)
Jim Prior, *A Balance of Power* (London, 1986)
Bob Purdie, *Politics in the Streets: The Origins of the Civil Rights Movement in Northern Ireland* (Belfast, 1990)
Mary Quant, *Quant by Quant* (London, 1967)
Peter Raby, ed., *The Cambridge Companion to Harold Pinter* (Cambridge, 2001)
Giles Radice, *Friends and Rivals: Crosland, Jenkins and Healey* (London, 2002)
Michael Ramsey, *Image Old and New* (London, 1963)
Terry Rawlings, *Mod: A Very British Phenomenon* (London, 2000)
Terry Rawlings, *Who Killed Christopher Robin: The Truth Behind the Murder of a Rolling Stone* (London, 2005)
Dan Rebellato, *1956 And All That: The Making of Modern British Drama* (London, 1999)
Robin Renwick, *Fighting with Allies* (London, 1996)
R. A. W. Rhodes, ed., *Transforming British Government, Volume 1: Changing Institutions* (London, 2000)
Huw Richards, Peter Stead and Gareth Williams, eds, *Heart and Soul: The Character of Welsh Rugby* (Cardiff, 1998)
Jeffrey Richards, *Films and British National Identity* (Manchester, 1997)
Harry Ritchie, *Success Stories: Literature and the Media in England, 1950–1959* (London, 1988)
John Robinson, *Honest to God* (London, 1963)
Marie Robinson, *The Power of Surrender* (London, 1959)
The Rolling Stones, *The Rolling Stones: Our Own Story* (London, 1964)
C. H. Rolph, ed., *The Trial of Lady Chatterley* (Harmondsworth, 1961)
E. J. B. Rose, *Colour and Citizenship* (Oxford, 1969))
Peter Rose, *How the Troubles Came to Northern Ireland* (London, 2001)

Andrew Roth, *Heath and the Heathmen* (London, 1972)
Andrew Roth, *Sir Harold Wilson: The Yorkshire Walter Mitty* (London, 1977)
Sheila Rowbotham, *Women, Resistance and Revolution* (Harmondsworth, 1973)
Sheila Rowbotham, *A Century of Women: The History of Women in Britain and the United States* (London, 1999)
Sheila Rowbotham, *Promise of a Dream: Remembering the Sixties* (London, 2000)
Seebohm Rowntree and G. R. Lavers, *English Life and Leisure* (London, 1951)
W. D. Rubinstein, *Capitalism, Culture and Decline in Britain, 1750–1990* (London, 1993)
Deborah S. Ryan, *The Ideal Home Through the Twentieth Century* (London, 1997)
Roger Sabin, *Adult Comics: An Introduction* (London, 1993)
Shamit Saggar, *Race and Politics in Britain* (London, 1992)
Edward Said, *Orientalism: Western Conceptions of the Orient* (London, 1995)
Anthony Sampson, *Anatomy of Britain* (London, 1962)
Anthony Sampson, *Anatomy of Britain Today* (London, 1965)
Anthony Sampson, *The New Anatomy of Britain* (London, 1971)
Raphael Samuel, *Island Stories: Unravelling Britain* (London, 1998)
Dominic Sandbrook, *Never Had It So Good: A History of Britain from Suez to the Beatles* (London, 2005)
Vidal Sassoon, *I'm Sorry I Kept You Waiting, Madam* (London, 1967)
Jon Savage, *The Kinks: The Official Biography* (London, 1984)
Michael Schofield, *The Sexual Behaviour of Young People* (London, 1965)
P. H. Scott and A. C. David, eds, *The Age of MacDiarmid: Hugh MacDiarmid and His Influence on Contemporary Scotland* (Edinburgh, 1980)
Rosemary Scott, *The Female Consumer* (London, 1976)
Alex Seago, *Burning the Box of Beautiful Things: The Development of a Postmodern Sensibility* (Oxford, 1995)
G. R. Searle, *A New England? Peace and War 1886–1918* (Oxford, 2004)
Ronald Segal, *The Race War* (Harmondsworth, 1967)
Michael Shanks, *The Stagnant Society* (Harmondsworth, 1961)
Jack Shaw, *On Our Conscience: The Plight of the Elderly* (Harmondsworth, 1971)
Dominic Shellard, *British Theatre Since the War* (London, 1999)
Robert Shepherd, *Iain Macleod: A Biography* (London, 1994)
Tom Shippey, *J.R.R. Tolkien: Author of the Century* (London, 2000)
Anthony Short, *The Communist Insurrection in Malaya, 1948–1960* (London, 1975)
Jean Shrimpton, *The Truth About Modelling* (London, 1965)
Jean Shrimpton with Unity Hall, *An Autobiography* (London, 1990)
Ed Sikov, *Mr Strangelove: A Biography of Peter Sellers* (London, 2002)
Alan Sinfield, ed., *Society and Literature 1945–1970* (London, 1983)
Alan Sinfield, *Literature, Politics and Culture in Post-war Britain* (London, 1989)
Michael Sissons and Philip French, eds, *Age of Austerity* (Oxford, 1986)
Alan Sked and Chris Cook, *Post-War Britain: A Political History* (Second edition: London, 1984)
Anthony Smith, *British Broadcasting* (Newton Abbott, 1974)
David Smith, *From Boom to Bust: Trial and Error in British Economic Policy* (London, 1993)

David Smith and Gerald Chambers, *Inequality in Northern Ireland* (Oxford, 1991)
David Smith and Gareth Williams, *Fields of Praise: The Official History of the Welsh Rugby Union, 1881–1981* (Cardiff, 1980)
C. P. Snow, *The Two Cultures* (Cambridge, 1993)
Johnny Speight, *The Thoughts of Chairman Alf: Alf Garnett's Little Blue Book, or Where Britain Went Wrong* (London, 1971)
Johnny Speight, *Till Death Us Do Part: Scripts* (London, 1973)
Chris Stephens and Katharine Stout, eds, *Art and the 60s: This Was Tomorrow* (London, 2004)
Jane Stern and Michael Stern, *Sixties People* (New York, 1990)
John Stevenson, *British Society 1914–45* (Harmondsworth, 1984)
Randall Stevenson, *The British Novel Since the Thirties* (London, 1986)
Susan Strange, *Sterling and British Policy* (London, 1971)
John Subritzky, *Confronting Sukarno: British, American, Australian and New Zealand Diplomacy in the Malaysian-Indonesian Confrontation, 1961–5* (London, 2000)
John Sutherland, *Bestsellers: Popular Fiction of the 1970s* (London, 1981)
John Sutherland, *Offensive Literature: Decensorship in Britain, 1959–82* (London, 1982)
John Sutherland, *Reading the Decades: Fifty Years of the Nation's Bestselling Books* (London, 2002)
A. J. P. Taylor, *The Origins of the Second World War* (Harmondsworth, 1964)
D. J. Taylor, *After the War: The Novel and England since 1945* (London, 1993)
John Russell Taylor, *Anger and After: A Guide to the New British Drama* (Harmondsworth, 1963)
John Russell Taylor, *The Second Wave: British Drama of the Sixties* (London, 1978)
Peter Taylor, *Provos: The IRA and Sinn Fein* (Revised edition: London, 1998)
Peter Taylor, *Loyalists* (London, 2000)
Peter Taylor, *Brits: The War Against the IRA* (London, 2002)
S. J. Taylor, *The Great Outsiders: Northcliffe, Rothermere and the Daily Mail* (London, 1996)
Norman Tebbit, *Britain's Future: A Conservative Vision* (London, 1985)
Dave Thompson, *Cream: The World's First Supergroup* (London, 2005)
D. R. Thorpe, *Alec Douglas-Home* (London, 1996)
Nicholas Timmins, *The Five Giants: A Biography of the Welfare State* (London, 1995)
Nick Tiratsoo, ed., *From Blitz to Blair: A New History of Britain since 1939* (London, 1997)
Richard Titmuss, *Essays on 'The Welfare State'* (London, 1958)
John H. Tobe, *Garden Glimpses: Random Thoughts of an Enthusiastic Gardener* (London, 1957)
Jim Tomlinson, *The Politics of Decline: Understanding Post-war Britain* (Harlow, 2000)
Jim Tomlinson, *The Labour Governments 1964–70: Volume 3: Economic Policy* (Manchester, 2004)
Christopher Tookey, *The Critics' Film Guide* (London, 1994)
Sean Topham, *Where's My Space Age? The Rise and Fall of Futuristic Design* (Munich, 2003)
Michael Tracey and David Morrison, *Whitehouse* (London, 1979)
John Tulloch and Manuel Alvarado, *Doctor Who: The Unfolding Text* (London, 1983)
Alywn W. Turner, *Biba: The Biba Experience* (London, 2004)
Twiggy, *Twiggy on Twiggy* (London, 1976)

Kathleen Tynan, *The Life of Kenneth Tynan* (Second edition: London, 1988)
Meredith Veldman, *Fantasy, the Bomb and the Greening of Britain: Romantic Protest 1945–1980* (Cambridge, 1994)
Harriet Vyner, *Groovy Bob: The Life and Times of Robert Fraser* (London, 2001)
Hilary Wainwright, *Labour: A Tale of Two Parties* (London, 1987)
Alexander Walker, *Hollywood, England: The British Film Industry in the Sixties* (London, 1974)
Alexander Walker, *Peter Sellers: The Authorized Biography* (London, 1982)
Alexander Walker, *National Heroes: British Cinema in the Seventies and Eighties* (London, 1985)
Gerald Walters and Stephen Cotgrove, eds, *Scientists in British Industry* (Bath, 1967)
Nigel Warburton, *Ernö Goldfinger: The Life of an Architect* (London, 2002)
Barbara Ward, *Spaceship Earth* (New York, 1966)
Colin Ward, *Housing: An Anarchist Approach* (London, 1976)
Stuart Ward, ed., *British Culture and the End of Empire* (Manchester, 2001)
Alan Watkins, *A Short Walk Down Fleet Street* (London, 2001)
Colin Watson, *Snobbery with Violence: English Crime Stories and their Audience* (London, 1987)
Judith Watt, *Ossie Clark: 1965–74* (London, 2003)
Patricia Waugh, *Harvest of the Sixties: English Literature and its Background, 1960–1990* (Oxford, 1995)
Peter Webb, *Portrait of David Hockney* (London, 1990)
Jeffrey Weeks, *Sex, Politics and Society: The Regulation of Sexuality since 1800* (Second edition: London, 1989)
Richard Weight, *Patriots: National Identity in Britain 1940–2000* (London, 2002)
P. A. Welsby, *A History of the Church of England 1945–80* (Oxford, 1984)
Jerry White, *London in the Twentieth Century* (London, 2002)
Michael White, *Empty Seats* (London, 1984)
Phillip Whitehead, *The Writing on the Wall: Britain in the Seventies* (London, 1985)
Mary Whitehouse, *Who Does She Think She Is?* (London, 1972)
Mary Whitehouse, *Whatever Happened to Sex?* (Hove, 1977)
John Whyte, *Interpreting Northern Ireland* (Oxford, 1991)
David Widgery, *The Left in Britain 1956–68* (Harmondsworth, 1976)
Martin J. Wiener, *English Culture and the Decline of the Industrial Spirit 1850–1980* (Cambridge, 1981)
Lord Wigg, *George Wigg* (London, 1972)
Marcia Williams, *Inside Number 10* (London, 1975)
Philip M. Williams, *Hugh Gaitskell* (Oxford, 1982)
T. I. Williams, *A Short History of Twentieth Century Technology* (Oxford, 1982)
Tim Willis, *Madcap: The Half-Life of Syd Barrett, Pink Floyd's Lost Genius* (London, 2002)
Peter Willmott and Michael Young, *Family and Class in a London Suburb* (London, 1960)
Phyllis Willmott, *Growing up in a London Village* (London, 1979)
Angus Wilson, *Anglo-Saxon Attitudes* (Harmondsworth, 1958)
Angus Wilson, *A Bit off the Map* (Harmondsworth, 1968)
Angus Wilson, *The Middle Age of Mrs Eliot* (Harmondsworth, 1961)
Angus Wilson, *The Old Men at the Zoo* (London, 1979)
Angus Wilson, *Late Call* (London, 1982)

Bryan R. Wilson, *Religion in Secular Society* (Harmondsworth, 1969)
Elizabeth Wilson, *Only Halfway to Paradise: Women in Postwar Britain: 1945–1968* (London, 1980)
Elizabeth Wilson, *Adorned in Dreams: Fashion and Modernity* (London, 1995)
Harold Wilson, *The New Britain: Labour's Plan* (Harmondsworth, 1964)
Harold Wilson, *The Labour Government 1964–1970: A Personal Record* (London, 1971)
Robert Winder, *Bloody Foreigners: The Story of Immigration to Britain* (London, 2004)
Anna Wohlin, *The Murder of Brian Jones* (London, 2000)
Gregory Wolfe, *Malcolm Muggeridge* (London, 1995)
John Wolfenden, *Turning Points: Memoirs* (London, 1976)
John Wood, ed., *A Nation Not Afraid: The Thinking of Enoch Powell* (London, 1965)
J. F. Wright, *Britain in the Age of Economic Management: An Economic History since 1939* (Oxford, 1979)
Robert J. Wybrow, *Britain Speaks Out, 1937–87: A Social History As Seen Through the Gallup Data* (London, 1989)
Bill Wyman, with Ray Coleman, *Stone Alone: The Story of a Rock 'n' Roll Band* (London, 1991)
Dennis Young and Barbara Young, *Furniture in Britain Today* (London, 1964)
Hugo Young, *One of Us: A Biography of Margaret Thatcher* (Revised edition: London, 1990)
Hugo Young, *This Blessed Plot: Britain and Europe from Churchill to Blair* (London, 1998)
John W. Young, *The Labour Governments 1964–70: Volume 2: International Policy* (Manchester, 2003)
Michael Young and Peter Willmott, *Family and Kinship in East London* (London, 1957)
Michael Young and Peter Willmott, *The Symmetrical Family: Study of Work and Leisure in the London Region* (London, 1973)
John Yudkin, *This Slimming Business* (Harmondsworth, 1958)
Philip Ziegler, *Wilson: The Authorised Life* (London, 1993)
Ferdynand Zweig, *The Worker in an Affluent Society: Family Life and Industry* (London, 1961)
Ferdynand Zweig, *The Student in an Age of Anxiety: A Survey of Oxford and Manchester Students* (London, 1963)
Ina Zweiniger-Bargielowska, ed., *Women in Twentieth-Century Britain* (Harlow, 2001)

INDEX

Abel-Smith, Brian, 601
The Abominable Snowman, 467
abortion, 337, 338, 341, 698–700
Abortion Act (1967), 699, 700
About, 256
Abrams, Mark, 6, 54, 61, 62, 308
Abse, Leo, 341, 496, 497, 697
Abstract Expressionism, 70, 524
Academy Awards, 304
Ad Lib Club, 262–4, 275
Adam Adamant Lives!, 228, 274, 434
Adams, Gerry, 734
Adams, Ken, 79–80
Adams, Walter, 537, 539
Adamson, Jimmy, 309
Adeane, Sir Michael, 17
Aden, 372, 373, 374–7
AEU (Amalgamated Engineering Union), 708, 712, 713
affluence, xvi, xvii, 18, 54, 60, 82, 88, 191, 270; and dolly birds, 235; and fashion, 248; and New Towns, 191; and Pop Art, 71, 72; and the secret agent, 399; and spread of obscenity, 574; and success of contemporary design, 67, 68; and Swinging London, 255; and tastes and habits, 196–7; and technology, 48; teenage, 102
Aitken, Jonathan, 84, 228–9, 232, 239, 261, 271, 451–2, 477; LSD experiment, 551
Albu, Austen, 647
Aldiss, Brian, 611, 637
Alfie, 265, 403
Ali, Tariq, 528, 534–5, 536
Allen, Clifford, 494
Allen, Woody, 403

Alloway, Lawrence, 72, 73, 74
Altamont Raceway concert, 568
alternative society, 522–30, 543–5; elitism and sexism of, 530; establishment of, 526; 'happenings', 524–5, 526; and *IT*, 527–9; and New Left, 530–1; newspapers, 527–8; and *Oz*, 542, 544; and women, 702–3
Alvarez, A., 472
Alvaro's (restaurant), 261
Amalgamated Engineering Union (AEU), 708, 712, 713
Amaya, Mario, 72
American Federal Reserve, 94
Amis, Kingsley, 396, 434, 445, 450, 471, 472, 480, 570, 592, 611; contempt for Tony Benn, 588; *Girl, 20*, 245–6, 590–1; *I Want It Now*, 590, 661; *Lucky Jim*, 588; moves to the right, 585–6, 587; and pornography, 586, 588; *Take a Girl Like You*, 701–2; writes anti-permissive novels, 590–1
amphetamines, 550
Anderson, Lindsay, 520–1; *If . . .*, 520–2
Andress, Ursula, 403
Andrews, Julie, 304
Andrews, Pat, 141
Anglo-Irish Treaty, 344
the Animals, 118, 137, 138, 139, 154, 216; 'The House of the Rising Sun', 138
Annan, Noël, 8, 479
anti-permissive campaigns, 576–80; and Festival of Light (1971), 583–4; Longford's Commission on Pornography, 584–5; and Malcolm Muggeridge, 581–2
anti-permissive novels, 590–1

Antonioni, Michelangelo, 404–5, 527
Apple (boutique), 766
Apple Corps, 766
the Applejacks, 114
Architectural Review, 185, 628, 630
architecture: Brutalist movement, 67, 622–3, 625–6, 634; modernism and challenging of, 622–4; *see also* high-rise tower blocks
Arden, John, 219
Argentinean football team, 313–15
Argyll and Sutherland Highlanders, 376
Armstrong, Sir William, 86, 90, 285, 416
Arnold, Matthew, 53
Arran, Lord, 496, 498
Arsenal FC, 306
art, 70–8; booming of, 75; and commercialism, 77–8; Op Art, 77–8, 101, 404; Pop Art, 71–5, 101, 222, 401, 404; *see also individual artists*
Art and Artists, 72
art galleries, 75–6
Art Nouveau, 447
art schools, 70, 137–8, 222–3
Artaud, Antonin, 524
Arts Council, 75, 254, 306, 395
Arts Lab (Covent Garden), 526
Ash, John Beresford, 736
Ashcroft, David, 520
Asher, Jane, 215, 268–9
Ashley, Laura, 455–6
Aspinall, Neil, 435
Associated Newspapers, 650
Associated Rediffusion, 101
athletes, 306
Attlee, Clement, 161, 496
Auger, Claudine, 695–6
Austin Reed, 247
The Avengers, 44, 49, 78, 80, 219, 234–5, 274, 399, 400–2, 450; *see also* Blackman, Honor; Rigg, Diana
Avory, Mick, 117, 142, 143
Ayckbourn, Alan, 396
Ayer, A. J., 496

B Specials, 345, 346, 753, 757
the Bachelors, 114
Bacon, Francis, 70

Baden-Powell, Robert, 22
Bader, Douglas, 58
Bag o'Nails (Soho), 262
Bailey, David, 78, 149, 240, 241–2, 243, 251, 255, 263, 267, 275, 304; *Box of Pin-ups*, 269–70
Bakelite company, 68
Baker, Ginger, 136
Bakhramov, Tofik, 320
balance of payments, 86–8, 91–2, 280, 370–1, 416, 761, 779–80
Baldwin, Stanley, 772
Ball, Alan, 312, 313, 318, 320, 770
Ball, George, 124
Ballard, J. G., 396, 638; *High Rise*, 638
Balogh, Thomas, 18, 37, 90, 100, 416, 426, 429
Banham, Reyner, 72
Bank of England, 93, 94, 168, 282–3, 418, 423, 512
Banks, Gordon, 312, 318, 319, 770, 775, 777
Barber, Chris, 135
Barclay, Sir Roderick, 386
Barclaycard, 191
Bardot, Brigitte, 453
Barlow Committee (1946), 50
Barnett, Correlli, 53
Barnwood Court (West Ham), 631
Barrett, Syd, 137, 443, 444, 552
Barry, John, 262
Barstow, Stan: *A Kind of Loving*, 484
Bates. Alan, 270
Bates, John, 234, 245
Bath, 624
bathrooms, 83
Battle of the Sexes, 694–5
Bayley, Stephen, 85
Bazaar (boutique), 229–30, 231, 245, 453
BBC, xvi, 309, 398–9, 791; and Harold Wilson, 644–6; and Mary Whitehouse, 576–8
BBC Radio One, 104
the Beach Boys, 216, 223, 435
Beardsley, Aubrey, 447
beat music, 114, 116, 118
Beatle Buddies, 113
the Beatles, xvi, 119, 103, 105–15, 118, 145, 146, 148, 150, 154–5, 210–20, 223–6, 251,

257, 272, 273, 411, 765–9; *Abbey Road*, 413; American tour (1964), 108–10, 113; American tour (1966), 226; appearance on *The Ed Sullivan Show*, 111–12; awarded MBEs, 210–11, 304, 765; Beatlemania, 112; break-up of, 766–9; and death of Brian Epstein, 458; dissatisfaction amongst, 434–5; drawbacks of being famous, 211–13; drug experimentation, 216–17, 224, 438, 444; failure of non-musical ventures, 766; furore over Lennon's remarks about Christianity, 225–6; and George Martin, 217, 438; *A Hard Day's Night*, 403, 449–50; 'I Want to Hold Your Hand', 103, 108; imitating American models, 218; imitators, 113; Lennon-McCartney partnership, 108, 213–14, 219, 769; *Let It Be*, 768; limits to popular appeal, 411–12; 'Lucy in the Sky with Diamonds', 437, 438; lyrics, 219; *Magical Mystery Tour*, 411, 765; and Maharishi Mahesh Yogi, 457–8, 469; musical and studio experimentation, 214–16, 217, 436; 'Norwegian Wood', 469; in the Philippines, 225; *Please Please Me*, 412; and the press, 105, 107, 112, 145, 213, 224; retreat into the studio, 213, 218; *Revolver*, 224, 225, 434, 435, 436, 438, 439; and the Rolling Stones, 145, 549; *Rubber Soul*, 154–5, 217–18, 223, 439; *Sgt. Pepper's Lonely Hearts Club Band*, 74, 220, 436–40, 445, 450, 557; 'She Loves You', 103; 'Strawberry Fields Forever', 436, 437, 438; success and adulation of, 103, 108, 110–13, 114–15, 154, 210, 212–13, 223, 765, 768; success in the United States, 110–13, 114; theatricality and music-hall tradition, 219–20, 438–9; 'Tomorrow Never Knows', 224; transformation into hippies, 444; *The White Album*, 766; *With the Beatles*, 103; 'Yellow Submarine/Eleanor Rigby', 434; 'Yesterday', 218, 219
'beatnik' appearance, 232
Beck, Jeff, 137, 558
Beckenbauer, Franz, 777, 778
Bedford, Eric, 44
Belfast Telegraph, 366
Bell, Colin, 777, 778

Beloff, Nora, 415, 783
Benidorm, 193–4
Benn, Anthony 'Tony' Wedgwood, 6, 24, 36, 37, 96, 121, 290, 334, 457, 509, 510, 636, 649, 652, 684, 722, 776; addiction to gadgets and innovations, 169–70; on Alec Douglas-Home, 14; attack on Enoch Powell, 775; background, 169; and the Beatles, 210–11; called a cunt by Kingsley Amis, 588; character, 169; diary, 732; and election campaign (1963), 6–7, 8, 11, 12; and election campaign (1970), 783–4; on George Brown, 34, 35, 367, 518; on Harold Wilson, 26, 28, 179, 282, 299, 645, 715, 727, 728; on Edward Heath, 166; on Marcia Williams, 38; at Ministry of Technology, 326, 327, 328; as Postmaster General, 35, 45, 169; and Rhodesia, 129; and stamp redesign, 170; on the *Sun*, 62; and technology, 326–7; worships a rubber hovercraft, 326
Benn, Caroline, 7
Benson, John, 200
Bergman, Ingmar, 405
Bergonzi, Bernard, 184
Berlin, Isaiah, 496
Berry, Chuck, 136, 139, 147, 218
Best, George, 770
Best, Pete, 146
Betjeman, John, 396, 463, 523, 635–6; 'Inexpensive Progress', 635–6; 'The Town Clerk's Vision', 635
Bevan, Aneurin, 25–6, 336
Beveridge, Sir William, 24
Bhagwan Shree Rajneesh, 469
Biba, 236, 452–5
Biffen, John, 157
Bilk, Acker, 108, 154
Billy Budd, 265
Billy Liar!, 254
Birmingham, 627, 628–9, 630; immigrant population, 666; redevelopment of city centre, 626
Birmingham Immigration Control Association, 667, 675
birth rate, 491, 693
Birtwell, Celia, 449

Black Dwarf, 528, 529, 538, 540, 703
Black Papers, 589
The Black and White Minstrel Show, 399
Blackburn, Robin, 533
Blackett, Patrick, 56
Blackman, Honor, 17, 234, 401
Blackpool, 193
Blair, Lionel, 219
Blake, Peter, 73, 74, 255, 439; *Sgt. Pepper* cover, 74; *Toy Shop*, 74
Blakenham, Lord, 15
Blaney, Neil, 751
Block, Leslie, 552–3, 555
Bloomfield, Kenneth, 355, 700
Blow-Up, 404–5
Blues Incorporated, 135–6, 142
blues music/clubs, 135–7
the Bluesbreakers, 137, 262
Bogdanor, Vernon, 64
Bogside, Battle of, 748–54, 755
Bond, James, xvi, 59, 60, 78, 255, 399, 400, 402, 404, 410, 622–3, 695; *Casino Royale*, 395; *Goldfinger*, 402; *Thunderball*, 303–4, 402, 695
Bonetti, Peter, 777, 778
Bonham Carter, Mark, 336
Booker, Christopher, 59, 234, 592, 606; *The Neophiliacs*, 592
Booth, Pat, 260
Boothby, Lord, 53
Borneo, 372
Boshier, Derek, 74
boutiques, 232, 245–6; Bazaar, 229–30, 231, 245, 453; Biba, 236, 452–5; decline of, 455; hippy, 450; men's, 246–7; *see also individual shops*
Bowlby, John, 694
bowls, 198
Boxer, Mark, 239, 269
Boycott, Rosie, 702, 703
Boyd-Carpenter, John, 610
Boyle, Sir Edward, 333, 680
Boyle, Mark, 532
Boyle, Ron, 790
Bradbury, Malcolm, 183, 591
Brady, Ian, 570–1
Braine, John, 471, 587
Brandreth, Gyles, 585

brass bands, 198
Bratby, John, 70
Bristol, 624
British Association for the Advancement of Science, 50
British Council for Peace in Vietnam, 533
British Film Institute, 531
British Invasion, 302–3
British Leyland, 328
British National Party (BNP), 680
British Standard Time, 167–8
Britten, Benjamin, 396
Bronowski, Jacob, 56
Brook clinics, 490
Brook, Peter, 473
Brooke, Sir Basil, 351
Brooke, Henry, 339
Brown, Callum, 466
Brown, George, 27–30, 31, 32, 89, 92, 93–4, 97, 98, 124, 125, 194, 281; and arms sales to South Africa issue, 503–5; background, 27; character and qualities, 27–8, 33, 517–18; confesses marital woes to Harold Wilson, 419–20; dances the 'frug', 418; and the DEA, 35, 172, 283, 367; defeat by Harold Wilson in party leadership (1963), 29, 174; and devaluation, 90, 91, 283, 285, 287–9; and election campaign (1970), 773–4; and European integration, 387; fights Eli Wallach, 33; fights Richard Crossman, 28; as Foreign Secretary, 367, 383, 385–7; and Harold Wilson, 28, 174, 175, 287–8, 293–4, 383, 419, 422, 504, 506, 514–15; insults Belgian Army, 385–6; insults Lord Thomson, 420–1; insults President Sunay, 423; and James Callaghan, 283–5, 286, 292; and July crisis (1966), 283–5, 296; Kennedy incident, 33–4; leaves National Plan on back seat of Mini, 175–6; misbehaviour and drinking, 28, 33–5, 173–5, 385–7, 389, 418–19, 420–1, 425–6, 432, 513, 515, 518; and National Plan, 126, 175, 176–7, 288, 296; opposition to homosexual legislation reform, 497, 498; and the press, 418–19, 421–2; relations with officials, 173; resignation, 516–18; and school-leaving

age, 509; scuffles during 1970 campaign, 773; threatens to hit Harold Wilson, 515; threatens to resign, 175, 288, 289–90, 292–4, 419, 420; and trade unions, 707; tries to dance with Cardinal Archbishop of Lima, 387; and the World Cup (1966), 323

Brown, Sophie, 28, 419
Browne, Tara, 271, 275
Bruce, Jack, 136, 137
Brunswick Centre, 633
Brutalist movement, 67, 622–3, 625–6, 634
Bryant, Sir Arthur, 201
Buchanan, Colin: *Traffic in Towns*, 624
Buckland, Norah, 577, 578
Bucknell, Barry, 200
Buckton, Ray, 708
Budgets: (1964), 92–3; (1965), 97; (1968), 519, 641; (1969), 729, 730–1; (1970), 763
Bundy, McGeorge, 123–4
Burdon, Eric, 138, 139
Burgess, Anthony, 396, 472, 637; *A Clockwork Orange*, 597, 616–17; *The Right to an Answer*, 611; *The Wanting Seed*, 637–8, 639
Burnet, Alastair, 656
Burns, Wilfred, 614–15
Burton, Richard, 304
Butler, Rab, 10, 15–16, 18, 156–7, 331, 332, 339
Butlin, Sir Billy, 45
Butlin's, 193
Butskellism, 684
Butterflies, 189
by-elections, 96–7, 370
Byatt, A. S., 396, 591
the Byrds, 439, 440

Cage, John, 215
Cahill, Joe, 349–50
Caine, Michael, 251, 260, 262, 264–5, 269, 270, 272, 274; ejects Stamp and Shrimpton, 265; in *Get Carter*, 613, 614
Caine, Sir Sydney, 537
Cairncross, Sir Alec, 86, 88, 93, 423–4, 512
Callaghan, James, 31–3, 96, 172, 280, 426, 430; and Anglo-American relations, 121; and Anthony Crosland, 368; background and early political career,
29, 31–2; and Barbara Castle, 429, 712; Budget (1965), 97–8; as Chancellor, 32, 86, 88–9, 93–4, 370, 371, 416, 417, 418; character and abilities, 32–3; and the DEA, 173; and 'deal' with Washington (1965), 124–5; and decimalisation, 168; and devaluation, 284, 286, 423–4, 426–8; and emergency Budget (1964), 92–3; and George Brown, 284–5, 286, 292; and Harold Wilson, 26, 40, 284, 287, 367–8, 502, 714–15; as Home Secretary, 502, 552, 676, 729; and immigration, 676; and the July crisis (1966), 283, 284–8, 292; and the National Plan, 176, 177; and Northern Ireland, 348, 729, 737, 739, 745, 747–8, 752, 754–5, 756; and the polls, 295; resignation from Treasury, 429; and Rhodesia, 131; and Richard Crossman, 721–2; and Roy Jenkins, 425, 502–3, 721; and the trade unions, 712–13, 714–15, 728; and Vietnam War demonstrations, 536; and the World Cup (1966), 323

Cameron, James, 4
Cammell, Donald, 563
Campbell, Gregory, 750–1
Campbell, John, 160
cannabis, 550–1, 552
capital punishment *see* death penalty
Capitol, 108, 109
Caravan Club, 192
caravanning, 192–3
cardboard chairs, 81
Carnaby Street, 246, 248–50, 274–5, 303
Caro, Anthony, 75
Carr, Robert, 159, 670, 680
Carrington, Peter, 783
Carry On films, 194, 219, 407–9, 612
cars, 83, 192
Carson, Sir Edward, 344
Carson, Rachel: *Silent Spring*, 639
Carter, Angela, 472, 638
Carter, Ernestine, 245
Cartland, Barbara, 14, 410
Casino Royale, 395
Castle, Barbara, 35, 91, 97, 99, 100, 125, 287, 289, 343, 368, 501, 653, 681, 703; appointed Secretary of State for Employment and Productivity, 659–60;

Castle, Barbara — *continued*
  background and political career, 705–6;
  and the Beatles, 210; and devaluation,
  291–2; and the election (1966), 278; on
  feminism, 701; and George Brown,
  289–90; and Harold Wilson, 40, 42,
  414–15, 432, 643, 705–6, 714–15, 717, 718,
  722, 723–5; *In Place of Strife*, 710–16; and
  James Callaghan, 429, 712;
  Mediterranean cruise, 723; opposition
  to Common Market entry, 388;
  personality, 705, 706; and Rhodesia, 129,
  132; and South Africa, 504, 506; and
  trade unions, 659, 706, 709–16, 722–8
Catholic church, 464
Cathy Come Home, 598–9
Caulcott, Tom, 173–4
Cavern Club (Liverpool), 275, 533
censorship, 396
Centre Point building (London), 624
Chain, Ernst, 46
chairs, 80–1
Chalfont, Lord, 389
The Champions, 399
Chapman, Herbert, 306
Charles, Prince, 704
Charlie Girl, 397
Charlton, Bobby, 312, 313, 315, 317, 318,
  319, 322, 770, 777
Charlton, Jack, 312, 315–16, 318
Charteris, Sir Martin, 20
Chelsea, 274–5
Chelsea Set, 229
Chesser, Eustace, 481, 482, 484, 494
Chibnall, Steve, 614
Chichester-Clarke, James, 747, 748, 755
China, 372
Christie, Agatha, 410, 467; *Endless Night*, 468
Christie, Julie, 251, 272, 304, 453, 687, 688
Christopher, John, 611, 637
Churchill, Sir Winston, 95; death of, xiii–xv
cigarette lighter (Kenneth Grange), 79
cinema, 402–9; American investment in,
  403; and British Invasion, 303–4; and
  Carry On films, 194, 219, 407–9, 612; and
  Hammer studio, 406–7, 467, 612; sex in
  films, 407, 408; withdrawal of American
  investment, 405, 612; *see also individual films*

Civilisation, 398
Clacton (Essex), 203–4, 208
Clapton, Eric, 137, 558
Clark, Ossie, 246, 260, 449
Clark, Petula, 114, 119
Clarke, Allan, 310
Clayson, Alan, 114, 115
Clean Air Act (1956), 253
Clean-Up TV campaign, 577–8
Cleave, Maureen, 107, 150–1
Clemens, Brian, 401
Clermont Club, 259
A Clockwork Orange: book, 597, 616–17; film,
  616, 617–19
Coates, Ken, 602
cocaine, 550
coffee, 195
Cogan, Alma, 219
Coggan, Donald (Archbishop of York), 459
Cohen, George, 312, 314, 318, 322
Cold War, 121, 122, 371–2
Cole, John, 4, 25, 35
Coleman, David, 112
Colonial Office, 371
colour supplements, 255–6; *see also individual
  newspapers*
Colt Ventilation and Heating Ltd, 608,
  610–11
Comedy Playhouse, 661
commercialism: and art, 78; and design, 84;
  and youth culture, 102
Commission on Pornography (Lord
  Longford), 584–5
Common Market, 162, 167, 196, 283,
  387–91, 432
Commonwealth Immigrants Act (1962),
  664
Commonwealth Immigrants Bill (1968),
  676
Communist Party, 281–2, 708
comprehensive schools, 332–4, 335, 588
computers, 48, 49
Conan Doyle, Arthur, 467
condoms, 489
Connery, Sean, 257, 304, 400, 402
Connolly, Cyril, 253
Conquest, Robert, 587
Conran, Terence, 65–6, 78, 82, 84–5, 230, 239

conservation, 447
Conservation Society, 639–40
Conservative Party, 4; and election (1964), 10–11, 12–13, 14–15, 18; and election (1966), 278; leadership contest (1965), 157–9; and polls, 156, 166, 370, 432–3, 502, 658; and *Private Eye*, 297; wins 1970 election, 784; *see also* Heath, Edward
consumerism, 61, 66, 191–2, 690; link with technology, 48
Consumers' Association, 192, 489
Contemporary design, 68–9
contraception, 481, 489–90, 693, 698; the Pill, xvii, 478, 489–91
Coogan, Tim Pat, 356, 738
Cook, Hera, 479
Cooper, Chester, 383–4
Cooper, D. E., 694
Cooper, Terry, 770
Corbett, David, 311
Corbett, Harry, 12
Cornwall, 193
Coronation Street, xvi, 5, 790
council houses, 628
Council of Industrial Design, 69, 78
counter-culture *see* alternative society
Courrèges, André, 234, 244–5
Courtenay, Tom, 273
Cousins, Frank, 171, 282, 283, 328, 711
Coventry, Bishop of, 459
Coventry Cathedral, 623
Cowan, John, 241, 242
Cox, C. B., 588, 589
Cox, Harvey, 466
Craig, James, 346
Craig, William, 733, 738, 739, 740, 742, 746
Craigie, Jill, 700
Crawdaddy club (Richmond), 144, 146
Craxton, John, 70
Cream, 558, 559
credit cards, 191
Crick, Francis, 46–7
cricket, 307
crime: link with permissiveness, 571–2
Critical Quarterly, 588
Croft, David, 790
Cromer, Lord, 88, 90, 94, 95
Cromwellian (nightclub), 262

Crooks, Wade, 683
Crosby, John, 249, 250, 257–8, 304
Crosland, Anthony 'Tony', 22, 24, 29, 55, 59, 89, 91, 289, 326, 329–33, 502–3, 714; and abolition of grammar schools, 334, 335; background and character, 329–30, 334; and comprehensive system, 333; and economic policy, 99, 100; as Education Secretary, 331, 332, 333; *The Future of Socialism*, 55, 329, 333, 337; and George Brown, 173; on Harold Wilson, 30, 179, 369, 719; and James Callaghan, 368; love of *Match of the Day*, 330; and the National Plan, 176; rivalry with Roy Jenkins, 335, 342, 503; rudeness to women, 330; on Tony Benn, 169
Crosland, Susan, 173
Crossman, Richard, xiii, xv, 30, 37, 86, 92, 93, 94, 97, 99, 100, 120, 125, 177, 289, 501, 502, 628, 711; character, 35–6; and Common Market entry, 388; and devaluation, 291, 292, 427, 428; and economic policy, 284; on Edward Heath, 165, 759–60; and election (1966), 277–8; and election (1970), 776–7, 783, 784; on Enoch Powell, 682; on George Brown, 27–8, 34, 172, 296, 517–18; and Harold Wilson, 14, 23, 35, 26, 27, 39, 40, 41, 95, 96, 131, 179, 180, 297, 299, 368–9, 370, 432, 646, 659, 716, 718–19; in Harold Wilson's cabinet, 35; on high-rise blocks in Wigan, 633; on homosexuality, 338; and James Callaghan, 429, 430, 721–2; and Northern Ireland, 745; and Rhodesia, 129, 130; on Tony Benn, 169, 327–8; and Vietnam War, 383; and the World Cup (1966), 324–5
Cudlipp, Hugh, 61, 62, 650, 651, 653–4, 655, 657
Cumbernauld, 186, 187, 190
Curran, Charles, 555
Currie, Austin, 733, 738
The Curse of Frankenstein, 406
Cushing, Peter, 406, 407
Cusick, Ray, 80

D-Notice affair, 415
Dad's Army, 789–93, 794

Daily Express, xv, 5, 16, 58, 150, 208, 209, 241, 271, 296, 301, 415
Daily Herald, 4, 61, 62
Daily Mail, 105, 115, 158, 234, 316, 437, 522
Daily Mail Ideal Home Exhibition, 79; (1959), 66; (1962), 79; (1966), 81; House of the Future (1956), 67, 79
Daily Mirror, 48–9, 104, 105–6, 115, 164, 203, 204, 316, 434, 444, 649, 650–1, 662, 681; and the Beatles, 112
Daily Sketch, 148, 158, 164
Daily Telegraph, 5, 81, 104, 208, 324, 522, 539, 544
the Dakotas, 114
the Dales, 188
Dalton, Hugh, 27
Daltrey, Roger, 222
Dance, James, 488
Danger Man, 399
Darling, 687–8
'Dash for Growth', 87
the Dave Clark Five, 113, 115–16
Dave Dee, Dozy, Beaky, Mick and Tich, 220
Davie, Donald, 587, 588
Davie, Grace, 465, 466, 467
Davies, Christie, 340
Davies, Cyril, 135
Davies, Dave, 116, 117, 220
Davies, Maxine: *The Sexual Responsibility of Women*, 484
Davies, Ray, 116, 117, 137, 203, 220–1, 222
Davis, Gerry, 637
Davis, Miles, 206
Day, Robin (designer), 69, 80–1, 84
Day, Robin (interviewer), 13, 671
Day-Lewis, Cecil, 496
de Gaulle, President Charles, 388, 389, 370–1, 432, 522
DEA (Department of Economic Affairs), 171–3, 177–8, 283, 328, 329, 417–18
death penalty: abolition of, 337, 339–40, 342
Decca, 146, 209
decimalisation, 168–9, 191
decline: popular sense of, 607, 611
Dee, Simon, 104
Deedes, William, 112, 581
Deep Purple, 559

deflation, 98, 99, 283, 293, 294–5
Dell, Edmund, 32, 63, 89, 93, 99, 384, 428, 785–6
Department of Economic Affairs (DEA), 171–3, 177–8, 283, 328, 329, 417–18
Department S, 399
department stores: decline, 232
design: and Art Nouveau, 447; close links with science and technology, 78–9; Contemporary, 68–9; evolution of and consumer economy, 84; and historical revivalism, 447; influence of television and cinema, 79–80; and Victorianism, 447–8
Design, 69, 249, 634
Design Centre (London), 69
devaluation, (1967), 416–17, 423–5, 427–32, 501–2, 507–8, 512–13, 607, 634; debate on (1966), 284–92, 295; Wilson's initial opposition to, 89–91, 100
Devlin, Bernadette, 743, 744, 747, 755
Devlin, Patrick, 487
Devon, 193
Diamond, Jack, 86–7, 647
Dickens, Monica, 689, 695
Dienst, Gottfried, 319, 320, 321, 322
Dimbleby, Richard, xiii, xv
Dineley, Chief Inspector Gordon, 546
Diski, Jenny, 542
divorce and divorce laws, 337, 341, 697
Divorce Reform Act (1969), 697
Dixon, Willie, 148
DIY, 200
DNA, 46–7
Docherty, Noel, 360, 361–2
dockers' strike (1967), 418
Doctor Who, xvi, 45–6, 48, 50, 80, 274, 398, 578, 620, 790
dolly birds, 232, 235, 236, 239
domestic appliances, 48, 82, 83, 690
domesticity, 66, 192, 201
Donegan, Lonnie, 108
Donnelly, Desmond, 98, 648
Donovan, 470
Donovan, Terence, 240–1, 242, 251
Donovan Report, 709, 710
Doomwatch, 637
the Doors, 440

Douglas, Craig, 147
Douglas-Home, Alec *see* Home, Lord
Drabble, Margaret, 396, 445, 499
the Dreamers, 114
drinking habits, 195–6
drugs, 206, 216–17, 440, 549–50; cannabis, 550–1, 552; and legislation, 552; LSD, 216, 442–3, 444, 550, 551–2; rise in use of and addiction, 442, 550
Drugs (Prevention of Misuse) Act (1964), 550
du Cann, Edward, 164
Duffy, Brian, 240, 241, 242
Dunbar, John, 526, 529
Dunn, Nell, 597
Durgnat, Raymond, 459
Dylan, Bob, 216, 435
Dyson, A. E., 588, 589

Eagle, 58
earnings *see* wages
East of Suez *see* Aden; Far East
Eastern culture: fascination with, 467–8
Easton, Eric, 146, 147
The Economist, 53, 56, 60, 294, 331, 711, 760
economy, 86–100, 370–1, 416–18, 657–8, 784; austerity package and wage freeze (1966), 293, 294, 324, 325, 416; austerity package (1968), 508–9, 510, 657–8; balance of payments, 86–8, 91–2, 280, 370–1, 416, 761, 779–80; boom in, xvi, 11, 18, 60, 82; devaluation debate (1966), 283–92, 295; devaluation of 1967 and aftermath, 416–17, 423–5, 427–32, 501–2, 507–8, 512, 607, 634; effect of austerity programmes, 370–1; inflation, 730–1, 785; July crisis (1966), 282–99; and National Plan, 175–7, 296, 329; opposition to devaluation (1964), 89–91; sterling crises, 93–4, 121, 123–4, 418, 512–14, 516, 518–19, 729; *see also* budgets; DEA
The Ed Sullivan Show, 111–12
Eden, Sir Anthony, 162
Edinburgh, Duke of, 50
Edinburgh University, 582
education, 331–3, 588–90; abolition of eleven-plus and grammar schools, 331–5, 589–90; Black Papers on, 589; and Christianity, 465; and comprehensive schools, 331–4, 335, 588; and Open University, 331; politicisation of, 589; and women, 689
elderly, 603–6
Election Forum, 13
elections: (1964), 10–18; (1966), 277–8, 644; (1970), 772, 769, 776–7, 780–4
eleven-plus, 332, 334, 335
Elizabeth II, Queen, 20–1, 170
Elle, 243
Ellison, Dr S.E., 584
Encounter, 51, 53
English, Richard, 734
English National Opera, 396
English Rights Association, 675
Englishness, 201
Entwhistle, John, 222
environment, 639–40
Epstein, Brian, 108, 109, 212, 269, 457, 458
Epstein, Jacob, 623
Equal Pay Act (1970), 703
Esher, Viscount, 634–5
Europe, 387
European Economic Community (EEC) *see* Common Market
Eusebio, 315
Evans, Allen, 224, 437
Evans, Edward, 570–1
Evening Standard, 13, 105, 107, 150–1, 208, 246–7, 554, 566, 663
Everton, 309
expendability: fascination with, 81–2

F-111 aircraft, 508, 509, 510, 511
Fabulous, 104
facial hair, 450
Faith, Adam, 103, 459
Faithfull, Marianne, 268, 271, 272, 453, 458, 547, 549, 553, 554, 568
The Fall and Rise of Reginald Perrin, 189
family, institution of, 572
Family Planning Act (1967), 490
Family Planning Association (FPA), 490
Far East: Britain's military presence in, 372–3; withdrawal of troops from, 373, 387, 509, 510–11, 785

Far from the Madding Crowd, 405
fashion, 228–50; Courrèges' Clothes of the Future, 234, 244–5; hippy look, 232, 441–2, 448–53, 455; and the Look, 236–7; magazines, 238–40; men's, 246–7; the mini-skirt, xvii, 244; Op look, 234; prominence of in sixties, 248; and PVC, 233, 234; rise of the independent boutique, 232, 245–6; second wave of designers, 246; Space Age, 233–4; success of British fashion in the United States, 302–3; transformation of the industry, 230–1; *see also* Quant, Mary
Faulkner, Brian, 354–5, 739, 745, 746
Feather, Victor, 712, 715, 723
Fellini, Federico, 405
feminism, 700–1, 702–4
Ferris, Paul, 481, 698–9
Festival of Britain, 65
Festival of Light (1971), 583–4
Fielding, Steven, 197
films *see* cinema *and individual films*
Financial Times, 30, 51, 662–3, 692, 711
Finlay, Frank, 396
Finney, Albert, 396
Fisher, Alan, 708
Fisher, Roy: *City*, 638
fishing, 307
Fitt, Gerry, 732, 738, 754
Fleetwood, Mick, 137
Fleming, Anne, 288
Fleming, Ian, 60, 255, 304, 410, 622–3
Florey, Howard, 46, 56
'flower power', 440–2
Flymo, 201
Foale, Marion, 246, 260
food, 196
Foot, Michael, 282, 684, 685, 705, 716
Foot, Paul, 673, 680; *The Politics of Harold Wilson*, 642
football, 307–25, 769–72; *see also* World Cup *and individual players*
Ford Motor Company, 713
Formica, 80
Forster, Margaret: *Georgy Girl*, 270
The Forsyte Saga, 445–6
Forsyth, Bruce, 609
Forte, Sir Charles, 723

the Fortunes, 114
Foster, Roy, 355
Fowles, John, 396; *The French Lieutenant's Woman*, 448
France: and British Invasion, 303; Paris riots (1968), 522
Franco, Francisco, 193
Fraser, Robert, 271, 272; art dealer and gallery, 73, 76; Redlands drugs trial (1967), 547–8, 549, 552, 553–4, 556
Frayn, Michael, 459, 532
Free School (Notting Hill), 526
Freeland, General Sir Ian, 756
Freeman, Alan, 252
French, Christine, 608
French, Philip, 404
Frendz, 528
Friedman, Milton, 684
Friends, 528
Front for the Liberation of South Yemen, 375
Frost, David, 8, 198, 272, 477, 607, 683, 728
Fry, Carol, 608
Fuller, Roy, 446
Furlong, Monica, 462
furniture, 78; and Contemporary design, 68; G-Plan range, 69; and modernity, 82; paper, 81; Robin Day's chairs, 80–1; Summa range, 66
Fury, Billy, 103, 113

G-Plan range, 69
Gaitskell, Hugh, 24–5, 26, 28–9, 32, 54, 169, 288; death, 27, 29, 335
Galbraith, John Kenneth, 55
Gale, George, 15–16, 776, 782
Gallagher, Danny, 606
Gallery One, 77
Galsworthy, John: *The Forsyte Saga*, 445–6
Gambon, Michael, 396
Gardener's World, 201
gardening, 192, 200–2
Gardening Club, 201
Garner, Philippe, 72
Garnett, Tony, 598, 599
GEC, 328
Gee, Cecil, 247
genetic engineering, 47

Georgy Girl, 270
Germans: popular attitudes towards, 316; *see also* West Germany (football team)
Get Carter, 612–13, 614, 615–16
Getty, Paul, 420
Gibbs, Christopher, 271
Giles, Billy, 360
Gillett, Charlie, 221, 559
Gilmour, Sir Ian, 336
Ginsberg, Allen, 440, 523
Girling brake factory, 710
Gittens, Diana, 698
Glamour, 243
Glasgow, 627; high-rise flats in, 630; Mods in, 207
Gloucester, 625
Glynn, Prudence, 248
Goldfinger, 402
Goldfinger, Ernö, 622–3, 634
Golding, William, 396, 472, 473, 611; *Lord of the Flies*, 473, 474
Gomelsky, Giorgio, 144
Gomme and Sons, E. H., 69
The Good Life, 189
Goodman, Arnold, 395
Gordon Walker, Patrick, 121, 371, 509, 647, 720; Leyton defeat, 96–7; Smethwick defeat, 668–9
Gorer, Geoffrey, 484, 490, 696–7; *Sex and Marriage in England Today*, 491–4, 495
Gott, Richard, 533
Goulding, Cathal, 349, 733, 734
Grabowski Gallery, 76
Graham, Andrew, 709
Graham, Billy, 111
grammar schools, 331–2, 333, 334, 589
Grandstand, 112
Grange, Kenneth, 79, 83–4
Granny Takes a Trip (boutique), 451–2, 529
the Grateful Dead, 440
Great Train Robbery (1963), 572
The Great War, 398
Greaves, Desmond, 734
Greaves, Jimmy, 310, 312–13, 317, 323
Green, Jonathon, 237, 397, 478, 550, 592
Greene, Graham, 396, 411
Greene, Hugh Carleton, 16, 578–9, 580, 644

Greenwood, Arthur, 292
Greer, Germaine, 238, 702; *The Female Eunuch*, 704
Gres, Marie-Lise, 252
Griffiths, Peter, 96, 668–9, 673
Grimond, Jo, 17
Guardian, 4, 87, 158, 235–6, 541, 598, 599, 692, 790

Habitat, 65, 66, 84, 85, 452
Haden-Guest, Anthony, 263
Hailsham, Lord, 30, 50
Hain, Peter, 704
Haines, Joe, 37–8, 643–4
hairstyles, 233
Halasz, Piri, 258, 260, 275
Haley, Bill, 103
Hall, Peter, 473, 630–1
Hall, Stuart, 531
Halliwell, Kenneth, 477
Halsbury Committee (1961), 168
Hamilton, Richard, 70–2, 73
Hammer horror films, 406–7, 467, 612
Hammond, Celia, 242, 251, 269, 274
Hampshire, Susan, 445
happenings, 524–5, 526
A Hard Day's Night, 403, 449–50
Harker, Dave, 413
Harlow, 253
Harris, Kenneth, 34
Harrison, George, 111, 146, 210, 213, 216, 263, 272, 273, 434–5, 439, 444–5, 450, 469, 766–7; and Maharishi Mahesh Yogi, 469, 470; *see also* Beatles
Harrison, James, 666
Harrison, Rex, 304
Harrod, Rod, 264
Harrods, 245
Hartley, Anthony, 51
Hartley, L. P.: *Facial Justice*, 637; *The Go-Between*, 445
Hartwell, Lord, 255
Hastings, Adrian, 465
Hastings, Hubert de Cronin, 630
Hastings, Michael, 597
Hatch, Tony, 609
Hattersley, Roy, 289, 627, 706, 710, 723, 769
Haughey, Charles, 751

Haworth, Jann, 439
Hay, John, 196
Hayek, Friedrich, 684
Haynes, Jim, 523–4, 527
Hayward Art Gallery (London), 395
Healey, Denis, 97, 161, 166, 292, 372, 373, 427, 507, 649, 651; as Defence Secretary, 129–30, 508, 510; on Edward Heath, 163; on George Brown, 174–5; on Harold Wilson, 179, 369, 510–11; in Harold Wilson's first cabinet, 36–7, 42; opposition to Common Market entry, 388; on Roy Jenkins, 648
Heal's, 78–9
hearing aids, 47
Heath, Edward, 107, 159–67, 192, 296, 614, 642, 670–1; and Arsenal FC, 306; bachelorhood, 162–3; background and early life, 159–61; character and attributes, 158, 162–3, 165–6, 670–1; as a communicator, 166; disappointing Commons performances, 165; early political career, 161–2; election campaign (1966), 278; election campaign (1970), 774, 776, 780–3, 787; and Enoch Powell, 670, 672, 680–1, 683, 684; and Europe, 387, 389; and Harold Wilson, 164–5, 166; and 'I'm Backing Britain' campaign, 610; image and style, 158; and music, 160–1, 166; names dog after himself, 160; party leadership contest and election as leader (1965), 157–9, 164; and polls, 166; and the press, 164; and RPM, 10; and sailing, 166, 671, 759–60; and Second World War, 161; and Selsdon affair, 760–1; unpopularity of, 671, 683, 684; wins Sydney-Hobart race, 759–60
Heath, Ted (musician), 135
Heavens Above!, 459
Heffer, Simon, 680
Hell's Angels, 207
Hendrix, Jimi, 558
Henri, Adrian, 533–4
Herman's Hermits, 114, 115
heroin, 550
Heseltine, Michael, 256
Heyer, Georgette, 410

Hicks, David, 448
Higgins, Terence, 164
high-rise tower blocks, 190, 620–2, 627, 628, 629–30; Barnwood Court (West Ham), 631; problems associated with, 631–3; Ronan Point, 620–2, 634
Higham, Bruce, 251–2
higher education, 588
Hill, Charles, 644–5
Hill, Peter, 583
Hindley, Myra, 570–1
hippy culture 441–5; *see also* alternative society
hippy look, 232, 441–2, 448–53, 455
His Clothes (boutique), 247
historical revivalism, 447
Hitchcock, Alfred, 405
Hitchens, Peter, 338, 340
Hobsbawm, Eric, 531
Hobson's Choice, 572
Hockney, David, 73, 74–5, 269, 304; *Mr and Mrs Clark and Percy*, 75
Hodge, Ivy, 620
Hodges, Mike, 612, 615
Hodgkin, Dorothy, 46
Hodgkinson, Patrick, 625
Hodgson, Simon, 229
Hoffman, Dezo, 109
Hogg, Quentin, 14, 536, 608, 676, 680
Hoggart, Richard, 196, 201, 479–80, 485, 690; *The Uses of Literacy*, 689
holiday camps, 193
holidays, 192–5
the Hollies, 114, 220
Holly, Buddy, 113
The Holly and the Ivy, 572
Holt, Richard, 428
Home, Lord (Alec Douglas-Home), xvi, 5, 41, 107, 782; on the Beatles, 112; comeback in Edward Heath's government, 787; comparisons with Harold Wilson, 8–9, 13; election campaign (1964) and defeat, 9, 13, 14–15, 16–18; as Prime Minister, 10–11; resignation, 157; style and persona, 8, 13–14, 156; as successor to Macmillan, 8
home ownership, 66, 83, 192
'Home-Centred Society', 308

homeless, 63, 600; and Shelter, 599–600
homes: and bathrooms, 83; and Contemporary design, 67–9; and kitchens, 83, 691; renovations of, 82–3; *see also Daily Mail* Ideal Home Exhibition
Homosexual Law Reform Society, 496
homosexuality, 337, 338, 341, 486, 494–9, 784; attempt at reform, 496–7; attitudes towards, 494–5, 496; defending of, 495–6; legislation on, 497–8; and Wolfenden Report, 486–7
Honest to God (Robinson), 460–2, 474
Honey, 238–9
hooliganism, 204–5
Hopcraft, Arthur, 309, 310
Hope, Bob, 704
Hopkins, Harry, 691
Hopkins, John, 478
Hornby, Lesley *see* Twiggy
Hornsey College of Art, 538–9
Houghton, Douglas, 292, 647, 712, 720
House of the Future, 67, 79
House of Lords, 714
housewives, 689–92
housing: housing estates, 201; and Northern Ireland, 347; public, 627–8; *see also* high-rise tower blocks
Houston, Penelope, 405
Howard, Anthony, 14, 380
Howard, Terence, 251
Howe, Geoffrey, 164
Howell, David, 164
Howell, Denis, 300, 309
Howell, Georgina, 453
Huddersfield, 198–9
Huddersfield Town FC, 305–6
Hughes, Brendan, 756
Hughes, Robert, 73
Hughes, Ted, 396, 472, 638
Hulanicki, Barbara, 236, 452–3, 454–5
Hume, John, 733, 754
Humperdinck, Engelbert, 412, 436
Hung on You (boutique), 450
Hunt, Roger, 312, 318, 319, 320
Hunter, Meredith, 568
Hurd, Douglas, 787
Hurst, Geoff, 313, 314, 317, 318, 320, 321, 323, 325, 770

Hutchins, Chris, 213
Huxley, T. H., 53

I Was Lord Kitchener's Valet (boutique), 450
Ideal Home Exhibition *see Daily Mail* Ideal Home Exhibition
Idiot International, 528
If..., 520–2
Ifield, Frank, 154
I'm All Right Jack, 408
'I'm Backing Britain' campaign, 608–10, 792
immigrants/immigration, 661–86, 775; calls for greater control, 666; fears over, 674–5; and Kenyan Asians issue, 674–6; and the National Front, 675; and Enoch Powell, 667, 668, 672–86; and Enoch Powell's 'rivers of blood' speech (1968), 677–84, 685; racial prejudice and campaigns against, 664–7, 668
In Place of Strife, 710–29, 730
Independent Group, 72, 73
India, 468
Indica Gallery, 76, 526–7
Indonesia, 373
industrial relations, 706–31; *see also* trade unions
Industrial Relations Bill (1969), 721, 722, 723–6
Industrial Reorganisation Corporation, 328
inequality, 601–2
inflatable chairs, 81
inflation, 730–1, 785
Ingham, Mary, 699
Ingrams, Richard, 36, 297
Inklings, 471
Institute of Contemporary Arts (ICA), 72, 531
Institute of Economic Affairs (IEA), 670, 684
Institute for Race Relations, 663
Institute of Workers' Control, 531
International Marxist Group, 531
International Monetary Fund (IMF), 88, 418
International Poetry Festival (1965), 523–4

International Publishing Company *see* IPC Group
International Socialist Group, 531, 538
International Times (IT), 527–9
internationalism, 532
IPC Group, 62, 178, 649–50, 655
The Ipcress File, 265
IRA, 348–50, 363, 733–4, 753, 754
Iremonger, Tom, 536
Ironside, Virginia, 400
Issigonis, Sir Alec, 192
Italy: and British Invasion, 303
ITV, xvi, 255, 309, 398–9
the Ivy League, 114

Jackson, Brian, 198–9
Jackson, Glenda, 532
Jacobi, Derek, 396
Jaeger, 247
Jagger, Eva, 546
Jagger, Mick, 76, 133, 136, 138, 142, 143, 145, 147, 149, 151–2, 153, 218, 251, 260, 273, 411, 458, 520, 546, 548; and Altamont Raceway concert, 568; and aristocracy, 271; background, 139–40; and Chrissie Shrimpton, 267–8; and death of Brian Jones, 566–7; and drugs, 549; on immigration, 675; joins Rolling Stones, 142; and Mary Whitehouse, 579; and Paul McCartney, 268; in *Performance*, 563; and Redlands drugs raid and trial, 552–6; *see also* Rolling Stones
James Bond films *see* Bond, James *and individual films*
Jay, Antony, 198, 477, 607
Jay, Douglas, 124, 291
Jay, Peter, 416
jazz, 135, 137, 205
Jeff Beck Group, 220
Jefferson Airplane, 439, 440
Jenkins, Arthur, 161
Jenkins, Clive, 610
Jenkins, Peter, 681, 710, 712
Jenkins, Roy, 22, 91, 161, 166, 173, 285, 288, 289, 329, 335–41; and abolition of death penalty, 339; background, 335–6; Budget (1968), 519, 641; Budget (1969), 729, 730–1; Budget (1970), 763; as Chancellor, 503, 507–9, 512–13, 516, 518, 519, 657–8, 729, 779–80; and Common Market entry, 388; and devaluation, 427; and election campaign (1970), 782–3, 786; failure to commit to planned plot against Harold Wilson (1968), 647–8, 720–1; and Harold Wilson, 24, 30, 503, 516, 645–6; as Home Secretary, 336, 369; and homosexual legislation reform, 498; and immigration issue, 676; and James Callaghan, 425, 502–3, 721; *The Labour Case*, 326, 336–7; and Northern Ireland, 736–7; and plot to oust Harold Wilson (1969), 719–21; and rivalry with Anthony Crosland, 335, 342, 503; supporters of, 646–7; and trade unions, 715–16, 727–8
Johnson, President Lyndon, 120, 122, 123–4, 125, 379–80, 384, 425, 510
Johnson, Pamela Hansford, 571, 575, 584; *On Iniquity*, 571
Johnson, Paul, 101, 106
Johnston, Roy, 734
Jones, Brian, 135, 136, 140–2, 143, 144, 145, 146, 149, 151, 152, 153, 251, 548, 560–2, 723, 726; and Anita Pallenberg, 560–1; death, 564–5, 567–8; decline in mental state, 149–50, 560–2; drinking and drugs, 549, 560–2; sacked from Rolling Stones, 563–4; *see also* Rolling Stones
Jones, Clem, 667–8, 681
Jones, Jack, 708, 711, 712
Jones, Paul, 136
Jones, Peter, 133
Jordan, Colin, 97
Joseph, Sir Keith, 579
Journal of the Society of Industrial Arts, 79–80
Juke Box Jury, 106
July crisis (1966), 282–99, 367, 370, 373, 388, 415
The Jungle Book, 522
Just Looking (boutique), 245

Kaldor, Nicholas, 37, 100, 285, 416
Kasmin, John, 85
Kasmin Art Gallery, 76, 85
Kaufman, Gerald, 37
Kay, Ernest, 279
Keeley, Charles, 152

Keenan, Brigid, 232
Keenan, Sean, 748, 752
Kelly, Andrew, 364, 365
Kendall, Bill, 708
Kennedy, Jacqueline, 336
Kennedy, President John F., 6, 7, 14; assassination of, 33
Kennington, Jill, 242
Kenrick, Reverend Bruce, 600
Kenwood Chef food mixer, 84
Kenyan Asians, 674–6
Khrushchev, Nikita, 17
Kilfedder, Jim, 359–60
King, Cecil, 61, 62, 124, 130, 131–2, 158, 178–9, 378, 388, 415, 418, 512, 649–51, 705; background and character, 649–50; dismissal as chairman of IPC, 657; plan to topple Harold Wilson, 651–7
King, Michael, 419
King's Road, 229, 245
the Kinks, 115, 116–18, 119, 137, 154, 216, 220–2, 223, 304, 439, 445, 447; 'Autumn Almanac', 221–2; blacklisted by American unions, 117, 220; 'Dedicated Follower of Fashion', 228; and Englishness, 221, 304; experimentation with new techniques, 220; *The Kinks Are the Village Green Preservation Society*, 222; 'See My Friends', 220–1; 'Sunny Afternoon', 221, 305; theatricality of, 221; 'You Really Got Me', 116, 138
Kissinger, Henry, 26
kitchens, 83, 691
Klee, Paul, 68
Klein, Allen, 563, 766
The Knack, 403
Korner, Alexis, 135, 136, 141, 142
Kosygin, Alexei, 383
Kray brothers, 269–70, 572
Kreitlein, Rudolf, 313
Ku Klux Klan, 675
Kubrick, Stanley, 616, 617, 619
Kurosawa, Akira, 405

Labour Party, 3–4, 54; conference (1969), 761–2; and election (1964), 5–6, 11–12, 16–17; and election (1966), 278–9; leadership contest (1963), 29; liberal progressivism of, 56; losing of by-elections, 370; and modernisation project, 54, 56, 329; and polls, 295, 432; and trade unions, 706–8; and United States, 381
Labour Party (Northern Ireland), 352, 353
Lady Chatterley's Lover trial (1960), 460, 462, 573
lager, 195
Landy, Marcia, 407
Lane, Jackie, 609
Larkin, Philip, 396, 472, 586, 587; 'Church-Going', 463; 'Homage to a Government', 511
Lasdun, Denys, 623
Late Call (Wilson), 183–5, 188, 189, 191, 196, 397, 597
Laurie, Peter, 153, 235, 332
Law, Denis, 322
Lawrence, D. H.: *Lady Chatterley's Lover* trial, 460, 462
Le Carré, John: *The Looking-Glass War*, 633–4; *A Small Town in Germany*, 511
Le Corbusier, 622, 627, 628, 633, 639
Le Mesurier, John, 790
Lean, David, 405
Leavis, F. R., 52–3, 634
Lebel, Jean-Jacques, 525
Led Zeppelin, 559–60
Lee, Christopher, 407
Lee, Francis, 771
Leeds, 630
leisure, 192–5, 306; *see also* holidays
Lemass, Seán, 350, 356
Lennon, John, 109, 141, 213, 214, 215, 224, 269, 272, 304, 411, 414, 439, 450, 641, 766–7; and anti-war movement, 534; assassination of, 214; and break-up of the Beatles, 767–9; furore over remarks about Christianity, 225–6; and LSD, 216, 224, 438; and Maharishi Mahesh Yogi, 469–70; songwriting partnership with Paul McCartney, 108, 213–15, 219, 769; and Yoko Ono, 766, 767; *see also* Beatles
LEO (Lyons Electronic Office), 47, 48
Lessing, Doris, 396, 472, 703
Levin, Bernard, xiv–xv, 188, 256, 274, 325, 327, 397, 461–2, 468, 623–4; *The Pendulum Years*, 592

Lewis, Anthony, 607
Lewis, C. S., 463, 471; *The Last Battle*, 638–9
Lewis, Jerry Lee, 112
Lewis, Ted: *Jack's Return Home*, 612
Leyton by-election (1965), 96–7
Liaison Committee for the Defence of Trade Unions, 708
Liberal Party: and election (1964), 17
libraries, public, 409
Life magazine, 302, 396
literature, 396, 409–11; anti-permissive novels, 590–1; fables and religious imagery, 472; and nostalgia, 445; and religion, 463; rise of paperbacks, 409–10; vogue for popular anthropology, 474–8
Little Richard, 218
Liverpool, 627, 630
the Liverpool Kids, 113
the Liverpools, 113
Loach, Ken, 598, 599
local elections (1967), 370–1; (1968), 641; (1970), 764–5
Logue, Christopher, 545
London, 253–4; bias towards, 254; character of population, 253; depiction of in novels and plays, 254; and prostitution, 486; reinvigoration of, 253–4; *see also* Swinging London
London Fashion House Group, 78, 230
London Fashion Weeks, 230
London School of Economics (LSE), 537–8, 539–40
London Tourist Board, 260
Longford, Lord, 27, 583, 585, 591
the Look, 232, 233, 236–7, 239, 302
Look Back in Anger, 397
Lord of the Flies (Golding), 474
The Lord of the Rings (Tolkien), 471–2, 474, 638
Lorenz, Konrad: *On Aggression*, 474
Lorenzo, Peter, 316
Love Without Fear, 482
Lovell, Sir Bernard, 46
LSD, 216, 442–3, 444, 550, 551–2
Lucky Jim, 254
Luder, Owen, 625
Lynch, Jack, 751–2, 754
Lynn, Jack, 627

Lyons, Maura, 358
Lyttleton, Humphrey, 137

McCann, Gerald, 246
McCartney, Jim, 202, 220
McCartney, Linda, 262
McCartney, Paul, 76, 108, 110, 155, 202, 211, 214–15, 216–17, 223–5, 226–7, 268–9, 272, 273, 304, 435–6, 438, 439, 450, 766, 767; and break-up of the Beatles, 767–9; and counter-culture, 526, 527; enthusiasm for avant-garde, 214–16; and Indica, 526–7; and LSD, 444; and *Magical Mystery Tour*, 411; and Maharishi Mahesh Yogi, 469–70; and Mick Jagger, 268; and nightclubs, 262; songwriting partnership with John Lennon, 108, 213–15, 219, 769; *see also* Beatles
Maccioni, Alvaro, 261
McClean, Hugh, 364, 365
McConachy, Cassie, 601
MacDonald, Ian, 105, 119, 213–14, 224, 436, 551–2, 769
MacDonald, Kevin, 251, 252–3, 275
McDougall, Sir Donald, 175
McGoohan, Patrick, 189
McGowan, Cathy, 101–2, 251, 453
McHale, John, 70
McIlvanney, Hugh, 317, 322, 324
MacInnes, Colin: *Absolute Beginners*, 205
McKee, Billy, 350
McKibbin, Ross, 481
Mackintosh, John, 720
MacLean, Alistair, 410
Macleod, Iain, 299, 519, 676, 680, 684, 787
Macmillan, Harold, xvi, 5, 8, 18, 26, 30, 50, 51, 60, 54, 105, 121, 162, 168, 387, 776
McMillen, Liam, 358, 734
Macnee, Patrick, 400
Macrae, Norman, 691
Macrobiotic Restaurant, 527
McSharry, Deirdre, 301
MacStiofain, Sean, 744
magazines: teenage, 238; women's, 82, 238–40, 482, 690, 695
Maharishi Mahesh Yogi, 457–8, 468
Mailer, Norman, 441
make-up, 232

Malaysia, 122, 372–3
Man Alive, 631
Manchester Guardian, 691–2
Manchester United, 308
Manfred Mann, 304
Mankowitz, Gered, 241
Mann, Manfred, 101
Mann, William, 769
Marcos, Imelda, 225
Margach, James, 43, 769
Margaret, Princess, 239
Margate (Kent), 204
Marine Broadcasting (Offences) Act (1967), 104
Marowitz, Charles, 531
Marquand, David, 35, 295, 369, 648, 784
marriage, 482, 491, 695, 697–8
Marriage Guidance Council, 483, 696
Marsh, Richard, 171, 179, 368
Martin, David, 466
Martin, George, 108, 146, 155, 213, 217–18, 436, 438, 766
Martin, Leo, 364
Marwick, Arthur, 340, 341, 478, 540–1, 545, 520, 693
Mary Quant Ginger Group, 231
Mason, James, 304
Mason, Nick, 443
Masters, Brian, 489, 490, 498
Match of the Day, 330
Matrimonial Property Act (1970), 697
Maude, Angus, 167, 589
Maudling, Caroline, 499
Maudling, Reginald, 8, 18, 60, 87–8, 91, 649, 762, 787; and dash for growth, 11; and daughter's affair, 499; defeat in Conservative leadership election, 157–9
Maudsley, Alan, 629
Maxwell Davies, Peter, 396
May, Phil, 137
May Day Manifesto, 642
Mayall, John, 137
Mayhew, Christopher, 647
medical science, 46–7
Meher Baba (the 'Awakener'), 468–9
Mellish, Bob, 38, 423, 717, 725
Melly, George, 70, 102, 225, 241, 242, 249, 262–4, 272, 305, 402, 445

Melody Maker, 105, 151, 210, 443, 548–9
men: and fashion, 246–7
Menswear Association, 247
Menzies, Sir Robert, 286
Mercer, David, 396
Mercury, Freddie, 137
Michael, John, 247
Micklewhite, Maurice *see* Caine, Michael
Mikardo, Ian, 682
Mikes, George: *How to Be an Alien*, 480
Miles, Barry, 263, 524, 526, 527
Miles, Sarah, 572
Miles, Sue, 533
Miliband, Ralph, 531
Miller, Roger, 258
Milligan, Stephen, 708
Mills and Boon, 409, 410
Milton Keynes, 187–8, 190–1, 197, 201, 331
Mini, 192
mini-skirt, xvii, 244
Ministry of Housing, 634
Ministry of Technology (MinTech), 78, 171, 326, 327–9
Mirabelle, 239
Miró, Joan, 68
Miss World contest (1970), 704
Mitchell, Juliet, 703
Mitchell, Lieutenant-Colonel Colin, 376–7
Mitchell, Warren, 661, 662
The Mod, 207
modernity/modernisation, 167, 171, 178; and architecture, 622, 624; challenging of and reaction against, 447, 634; and furniture, 82; limits of, 169; public enthusiasm for, 59
Modesty Blaise, 403, 404
Mods, 204, 205–9, 246, 550
the Mojos, 114
the Monkees, 113
Monty Python, 398
Moon, Keith, 222
Moore, Bobby, 312, 318, 319, 321, 322, 770, 771–2, 775
Moore, Henry, 75
Moore, Roger, 399, 400
Moorhouse, Geoffrey, 197, 602, 613, 614, 625–7; *The Other England*, 254, 600
Moors murders, 538–9

Moral Rearmament, 576, 577, 579
More, Kenneth, 445
The Morecambe and Wise Show, 219
Morgan, Kenneth, 23, 784
Morley, Lewis, 241
Morris, Brian, 269
Morris, Desmond: *The Naked Ape*, 474–6
Mountbatten, Earl, 653–4, 655
the Move, 137
Mozambique, 132
Mrs Dale's Diary, 188
Mucha, Alphons, 447
Muggeridge, Malcolm, 269, 342, 581–4, 585, 592
Muir, Jean, 246
Mullery, Alan, 771, 777, 779
Mumford, Brenda, 608
Murder on the Orient Express, 397
Murdoch, Iris, 396, 411, 472, 638, 703
Murdoch, Peter, 81
Murdoch, Rupert, 62
Murphy, Robert, 275
Murray, Sue, 243, 251, 269
music, 70; *see also individual names/groups*; popular music
music hall, 219–20, 304
musical soundtracks, 412–13

Nabarro, Sir Gerald, 27, 579, 665–6
Nairn, Ian, 635
National Council for Civil Liberties, 663
National Economic Development Council, 171
National Front, 675, 680, 775
National Health Service (NHS), 25
National Housewives' Register, 692
National Jazz and Blues Festival, 137
National Liberation Front (NLF), 375, 377
National Parks Commission, 306
National Plan, 175–7, 296, 329
National Service, 209
National Theatre, 397
National Union of Seamen (NUS), 280, 281–2
National Viewers' and Listeners' Association (NVALA), 578–81, 584
National Women's Conference (1970), 703–4

nationalisation, 98
Neild, Robert, 100, 285, 289, 416
Neo-Romanticism, 70
Nescafé, 195
Neville, Richard, 542, 702; *Play Power*, 544
New Left, 530–3, 545, 642
New Left Review, 530, 702–3
New Musical Express (*NME*), 118, 147–8, 154, 210, 211, 220–1, 224–5, 304, 412, 435, 437, 557, 641, 765
New Right, 685
New Society, 51, 191, 199, 341, 540, 793
New Statesman, 53, 77, 183, 208, 522; and the Beatles, 106
New Towns, 185–91, 201, 253, 331, 628; and affluence, 191; criticism of, 185–6; Cumbernauld, 186, 187, 190; depiction of in *Late Call*, 184–5, 188, 189; depiction of in the media, 188–9, 190; Milton Keynes, 187–8, 190–1, 197, 201, 331; popularity of, 190–1; roots of, 185; Stevenage, 186, 253
New Towns Act (1946), 185
New Wave films, 599
New York Times, 607
Newcastle, 579–80, 613, 616
The Newcomers, 189
Newman, Sydney, 274, 597, 598
News of the World, 152, 158, 681; Redlands drugs raid, 546, 548
Newsom, John, 689, 690
newspapers: alternative, 527–8; impact of commercial television on, 255; and Sunday colour supplements, 255–6; *see also individual newspapers*
Newsweek, 437
Newton, Keith, 771, 777
NHS (National Health Service), 25, 47
Nichols, Dandy, 662
NICRA (Northern Ireland Civil Rights Association), 733–4, 738–9
nightclubs, 261–4; *see also individual clubs*
Nitsch, Hermann, 525
NME (*New Musical Express*), 118, 147–8, 154, 210, 211, 220–1, 224–5, 304, 412, 435, 437, 557, 641, 765
No Trees in the Street, 572
Nonconformists, 464

Norman, Philip, 210, 218, 441, 566, 559
Northcliffe, Viscount (Alfred Harmsworth), 650, 656
Northern England, 197–8, 613–14
Northern Ireland, 343–66, 732–58; attempt to appease civil rights movement and reforms by Terence O'Neill, 739–43; Battle of the Bogside, 748–54, 755; Battle of the Shankill, 757; bridge-building with Catholic community, 355–6; Catholic civil rights movement, 700, 733–5; complacency of Wilson government, 736–7, 742, 746, 747–8; demonstrations by civil rights movement and violence, 737–9, 743–5; deployment of British troops in, 754–6, 757; economy, 352; elections (1969), 745; 'hearts and minds' campaign, 757–8; and housing, 347; and Ian Paisley, 356–61, 735, 744, 745, 757; and IRA, 348–50, 363, 733–4, 753, 754; modernisation under Terence O'Neill, 353, 732; rioting over Irish tricolour (1964), 358–9; roots and beginning of Troubles, 343–8, 363–4; sectarian attacks and violence, 747–58; sectarianism, 344–8, 350, 732; and Ulster Volunteer Force (UVF), 344, 362–6, 735, 746; violence at Burntollet Bridge, 743–4
Northern Ireland Civil Rights Association *see* NICRA
nostalgia, 445–7
Nottingham: riots (1958), 664; survey on poverty, 602–3; West Indian community, 665
Nova, 81
nuclear technology/weapons, 121, 372
Nuttall, Jeff, 543–4

Ó Dochartaigh, Niall, 739
O'Brien, Sir Leslie, 283, 287
Obscene Publications Act (1959), 573, 574
obscenity: spread of, 574–5
Observer, xv, 5, 8, 59, 164, 234, 256, 295, 324, 325, 656
O'Donovan, Patrick, xv
office blocks, 624
O'Hea, Alan, 608

Oldham, Andrew Loog, 133–4, 139, 146, 149, 152–3, 251, 267, 269, 272, 560, 563
Oliver!, 397, 522
Olivier, Laurence, 396, 572, 592
Olympic Games, 306
O'Neill, Captain Terence, 361, 736–7, 739–43, 744–6; attitude towards Catholics, 355–6; background, 351–2; banning of UVF, 366; criticism of, 735–6; modernisation efforts, 352–4, 732, 739–42; resignation, 746
Ono, Yoko, 534, 766, 767
Op Art, 77–8, 101, 404
Op Art Look, 234
Open University, 331
open-plan housing, 82
Orange Order, 345–6, 736
Orient: vogue for, 467–8
Orton, Joe, 396, 477, 478; *Loot*, 478
Orwell, George, xvi, 468, 793, 794
Osborne, Cyril, 665, 667
Osborne, John, 396, 397, 545, 615; *The Entertainer*, 219
Othello, 396
O'Toole, Peter, 304, 403, 404
Owen, David, 339, 497, 502, 647
Oz, 542, 544

the Pacemakers, 114
package holidays, 194
Page, Jimmy, 137
Paisley, Ian, 356–61, 735, 736–7, 744, 745, 746, 757
'Paki-bashing', 683, 685
Pallenberg, Anita, 560–1, 563
Pan, 410
Panorama, 671
Paolozzi, Eduardo, 65, 71–2, 73
paper furniture, 81
Paris riots (1968), 543
Park, Cheryl, 530
Park, Jonathan, 530
Park Hill (Sheffield), 627
Parker, Charlie, 206
patriotism, 304–5
Patterson, Henry, 355
Pauling, Linus, 46
Paynter, Will, 610

peace movement, 532–9, 545
Peake, Mervyn, 472; *Gormenghast* trilogy, 472
Pearson, Geoffrey, 205
Pedler, Dr Kit, 50, 637
Peel, John, 442, 528, 551
Penguin Books, 410–11; *Lady Chatterley's Lover* trial, 460, 462, 573
penicillin, 46
Penney, J. C., 231
pensions, 179, 605
People, 34, 429, 536
People's Democracy (PD), 743–4
Percy Report (1945), 50
Performance, 563
permissive society, 571; concept of, 338–42; link with crime, 571–2; Mary Whitehouse's battle against, 576–80; *see also* anti-permissive campaigns; sex
Perry, Jimmy, 790
Peter and Gordon, 113
Peters, Martin, 312, 313, 314, 318, 319, 770, 777
Philip, Prince, 608
Phillips, Mike, 685
Phillips, Morgan, 56
photographers, 239–42
Pickwick (Great Newport Street), 262
Pill, 478, 489–91
Pimlott, Ben, 23, 41, 129, 384
Pink Floyd, 137, 443–4, 558, 559
Pinter, Harold, 219, 268, 397, 472–3, 638; *The Birthday Party*, 472; *The Caretaker*, 472, 473; *The Room*, 264, 472
pirate radio stations, 104
Pitney, Gene, 118
planning, 171, 177
plastic, 80, 637
Plath, Sylvia, 472
Play Power, 702
Plowright, Joan, 396
Plunket Greene, Alexander, 229, 251, 255
poetry, 523–4
Polaris, 121, 372
polypropylene, 80
polythene, 46
Pompidou, Georges, 283
Pontin, Fred, 193
Ponting, Clive, 785

Poole, Edward, 537
Poole, Lord, 13
Pop Art, 71–5, 101, 222, 401, 404
Pop Goes the Easel, 73
popular music, 102–19, 154, 411; accessibility of, 103–4; amateurishness of, 105; and art schools, 137–8, 222–3; establishment of pirate radio stations, 104; growth of, 102–4, 210; ideas of formal aesthetic merit, 558; influence of rhythm and blues, 134–7; pop-rock dichotomy, 558–9; and the press, 105, 112, 115, 119, 145, 150–1; reasons underlying devotion to, 104–5; record sales, 118, 411; singles and albums market, 558–9; success of British groups in America, 113–15; swing of pendulum away from Britain, 440–1; as symbol of style, 210; teenage affluence and development of, 102–3; *see also* individual names/groups
pornography, 574; Longford's Commission on, 584–5
Porter, Eric, 445
Porter, Nyree Dawn, 445
Portsmouth shopping centre (Tricorn), 625
Portugal (football team), 315
Post Office Tower, 44–6, 79
postcodes, 167
Potter, Dennis, 20, 120, 597; *Stand Up, Nigel Barton*, 20, 196; *Vote, Vote, Vote for Nigel Barton*, 120, 183, 661
Poulson, John, 615, 629
poverty, 63, 600–2; and the elderly, 604–5; North-east England, 614; survey of in Nottingham, 602–3
Powell, Anthony, 396, 445, 587; *Hearing Secret Harmonies*, 470–1, 591
Powell, Enoch, 123, 157, 159, 610, 669–75, 683–4; background and political career, 669–70; and Edward Heath, 670, 672, 680–1; and election campaign (1970), 774–5; and IEA, 670; and immigration, 667, 668, 672–86; and New Right, 685; patriotism of, 674; 'rivers of blood' speech (1968), 677–84, 685; sacking of, 680–1, 683; support for, 681–2, 685–6
prescription charges, 179

Presley, Elvis, 103, 113, 135, 148
the Pretty Things, 137
Price, Frederick, 608
Priestley, J.B., 496
The Prisoner, 189, 398
Private Eye, 20, 38, 59, 169, 251, 275–6, 327, 657; and *About*, 256–7; attacks on Harold Wilson, 297–8, 643; and the Beatles, 107; cartoon of Harold Wilson, 26, 126; and Common Market issue, 390; 'Mrs Wilson's Diary', 39, 120, 130–1, 156, 163, 277, 300, 641, 705; and Tony Benn, 45
Private's Progress, 408
Proby, P. J., 118
Procul Harum: 'A Whiter Shade of Pale', 442–3
Profumo sex scandal, xvi, 5, 14
Proops, Marjorie, 271
prostitution, 486; and Wolfenden Committee/Report, 486, 488, 574
Protestant Telegraph, 357, 360, 746
psychedelic vogue, 442–3
Public Libraries Act (1964), 409
'purple hearts', 206, 216, 550
Purser, Philip, 790
PVC: and fashion, 233, 234
Pye Records, 228

Quant, Mary, 60, 66, 78, 84, 133, 229–33, 236–7, 239, 245, 248, 251, 255, 267, 302, 303, 449; background, 229; haircut, 233; and the Look, 232, 233, 236–7; and make-up, 232–3; and the mini-skirt, 245; opening of Bazaar, 229–30, 231; success of, 230–1, 304; tastes and style of clothes, 230, 231–2
The Quatermass Xperiment, 406
Queen, 60, 234, 239, 256, 274

Race Relations Act (1968), 676–7, 678, 682
Racial Preservation Society, 675
racism: against immigrants, 664–7
radio: establishment of pirate stations, 104
Radio Caroline, 104
Radio City, 104
Radio Invicta, 104
Radio London, 104
Radio Scotland, 104

radio telescope, 46
Radio Times, 50
Railton, Ruth, 651
Ramblers' Association, 640
Ramsey, Alf, 309–10, 770; appointed England manager, 310; background, 309; during 1966 World Cup, 312, 313, 314, 317, 318, 319–20, 322, 323; during 1970 World Cup, 777, 779
Ramsey, Michael (Archbishop of Canterbury), 466
Rattin, Antonio, 313
Rave, 104
Raven, Kay, 163
Raven, Simon, 591
Raymond, Paul, 574
Raynor, Henry, 446
Read, Piers Paul, 591
Ready, Steady, Go!, 101–2, 210
Record Mirror, 147
Red Mole, 528
Redditch, 187
redevelopment schemes, 624–6
Redgrave, Lynn, 270
Redgrave, Vanessa, 12, 304, 703
Redlands drugs raid and trial (1967), 546–8, 552–6
Rees, Goronwy, 64
Rees-Mogg, William, 554–5
Reith, Lord, 420
Relf, Keith, 137
religion, 458–71; appeal of Oriental, 467–8; decline of Christianity and churchgoing, 463–6; and homosexuality, 496; and literature, 463; modernity and Christianity, 462; progressive churchmen, 459–60; rise of Indian gurus, 468–9; and Robinson's *Honest to God*, 460–2, 474
Resale Price Maintenance (RPM), 10
Responsible Society, 584
restaurants, 260–1
revolutions (1968), 543
Rhodes, Zandra, 246
Rhodesia, 122, 126–32, 378–9; background, 126–32; declaration of UDI, 128–9; peace negotiations, 378–9; sanctions against, 131–2, 166, 378; *see also* Smith, Ian

rhythm and blues, 134–7
Richard, Cliff, xvi, 103, 108, 113, 154, 147, 412, 583, 585
Richards, Jeffrey, 405
Richards, Keith, 136, 137, 142, 143, 145, 146–7, 149, 153–4, 212, 251, 273, 457, 546; and Anita Pallenberg, 561, 563; background, 139–40, 41; and drugs, 549; Redlands drugs raid and trial, 546–8, 552–6; *see also* Rolling Stones
Ridley, Nicholas, 157
Rigg, Diana, 234–5, 401
Riley, Bridget, 76–8; *Fall*, 77
Robert Fraser Gallery, 76
Robertson, Bryan, 70, 76
Robinson, Dr John, 460, 465; *Honest to God*, 460–2, 474
Robinson, Dr Marie: *The Power of Surrender*, 484
robots, 48–9
rock music, 559
rock and roll, 103, 105, 135, 219
Rockers, 207–9, 246
Rocket, 58
Rodgers, Bill, 30, 172, 173, 293, 517, 647, 720
Rogers, George, 666
Rogers, Peter, 407
Rolling Stone, 557, 559
Rolling Stones, 78, 113, 115, 117, 118, 119, 134, 137, 138–55, 212, 216, 218, 223, 263, 269, 273, 435, 546–58, 560–3; *Aftermath*, 548; Altamont Raceway concert, 568; and the Beatles, 145, 549; *Beggars' Banquet*, 557, 558; *Between the Buttons*, 549; and decline/death of Brian Jones, 149–50, 560–2, 565–8; discovery of by Andrew Loog Oldham, 134, 139, 146; and drugs, 549; early lack of success, 142–3; growth in popularity and success, 144–5, 147–8, 148–9; Hyde Park concert, 566–7; image, 152–3, 548; 'Jumping Jack Flash', 557; 'Little Red Rooster', 148; origins, 136, 139, 141–3; in the press, 145, 150–1; Redlands drugs raid and trial, 546–8, 552–6; sacking of Jones, 563–4; service station incident, 152; singles and albums, 148–9; 'Stupid Girl', 268; *Their Satanic Majesties Request*, 557; 'Under My Thumb', 267–8
Roman Catholicism, 464
Ronan Point block explosion (1968), 620–2, 634
Room at the Top, 406
Rooney, Patrick, 753
Rose, Paul, 343
Ross, Willie, 292, 498
Rostow, Walt, 384
Rothermere, Viscount, 650, 656
Rothwell, Talbot, 408
Rotunda (Birmingham), 79, 623–4, 626
Rowan, Sir Leslie, xiv
Rowbotham, Sheila, 523, 529, 530, 533, 538, 687, 700, 702, 703
Rowe, Dick, 146
Royal Academy, 74; Bonnard exhibition (1956), 75
Royal Ballet, 396
Royal College of Art (RCA), 73, 74, 75
The Royal Hunt of the Sun, 396
Royal Opera, 396
Royal Shakespeare Company, 397, 532
Royal Ulster Constabulary (RUC), 345, 346, 358–9, 361, 738–9, 749, 750–1, 752–3, 757
Runcorn, 187
Rusk, Dean, 122, 509, 511
Russell, Bertrand, 496
Russell, George, 69
Russell, John, 72–3
Russell, Ken, *Pop Goes the Easel*, 73

Saddle Room (Mayfair), 262, 271
Saga, 605
the Saint, 228, 399, 400
St John Stevas, Norman, 164, 341
St Pancras Station, 636
St Trinian's films, 408
Sampson, Anthony, 47, 49, 51, 57; *New Anatomy of Britain*, 202
Sandford, Jeremy, 598
Sandys, Duncan, 674
Sassoon, Vidal, 233, 269
Saturday Night and Sunday Morning, 406
Savile, Jimmy, 585
Savundra, Dr Emil, 297, 643
Sayers, Dorothy L., 463

INDEX

Scanlon, Hugh, 708, 711, 712, 723, 726, 727
Scarfe, Gerald, 126
Schlesinger, John, 687
Schneider, Werner, 316
Schofield, Michael, 480, 492–4; *The Sexual Behaviour of Young People*, 491–4
Schofield, Paul, 304
school-leaving age, 508–9
science, 61; and change in suburban home, 66; and design, 78–9; enthusiasm for, 57; golden age of, 46–50; government spending on research, 50; Harold Wilson's commitment to, xvii, 3–4, 54, 56–7; Snow-Leavis feud, 52–4, 57
science fiction, 611, 637
Scotch of St James's, 263–4
Scott, Paul, 446
scouting, 22–3
Scruton, Roger, 623
Scullion, John Patrick, 364
seamen's strike (1966), 280–2
the Searchers, 113, 114
Seaton, Reginald, 563
Second World War, 58, 316, 455
secondary-modern schools, 331–2
Sellers, Peter, 403, 404, 459
sex, 478–85, 498–500, 702; attitudes towards before 1960s, 479–80; and founding of Responsible Society, 584; outside marriage, 484–5, 494; and teenagers, 488–9; within marriage, 482–3; and women's magazines, 482; *see also* contraception; homosexuality
sex manuals, 482, 483–4
sex surveys, 491–4
Sexual Offences Act (1967), 498
the Shadows, xvi, 108
Shanks, Michael, 51, 731
Shaw, Jack, 604–5, 606
Shawcross, Lord, 731
Sheffield: Park Hill, 627
Sheffield Star, 208, 604–5, 606
Sheldon, Robert, 428
Shelter, 599–600
Shepherd's Bush police murders (1966), 572
Shergold, Reverend William, 459
shopping, 82, 191–2, 239

Shore, Peter, 37, 295, 327, 382, 417–18, 514, 682, 722, 725
Short, Edward, 501–2
Short, Ted, 589
Shrimpton, Chrissie, 267–8, 269
Shrimpton, Jean, 242–5, 255, 257, 263, 269, 300, 302, 304; relationship with Terence Stamp, 265–7
Shulman, Milton, 663
Sibylla's (nightclub), 251–2, 272
Silburn, Richard, 602
Silkin, John, 716–17
Sillitoe, Alan, 445
Silverman, Sidney, 340
Simpson, Dr George, 208–9
Simpson's of Piccadilly, 248
Singapore, 373
Sinn Fein, 358, 359
Six-Day War, 416, 417
Six-Five Special, 101
Skelmersdale, 187
Sketch, 208
'skinhead' phenomenon, 685
Skol, 195
slang, 441
slums, 602, 614; clearance of, 621, 627
Smashing Time, 405
Smethwick, 668–9
Smith, David, 570
Smith, Ian, 127–9, 131, 132, 378–9
Smith, Ivor, 627
Smith, Maggie, 396
Smith, Richard, 74
Smith, T. Dan, 614, 615, 629
Smithson, Alison, 67, 72, 622
Smithson, Peter, 67, 72, 622
Snow, C. P., 52–4, 57, 171, 334
Snowden, Philip, 22
Snowdon, Lord, 239, 257, 269–70
social problem films, 572–3
Soft Machine, 532
Soho, 574; London, 257
Solidarity Group, 531
Soper, Donald, 358
Soskice, Sir Frank, 336
The Sound of Music, 412–13, 434, 437
South Africa, 132, 378; arms sales issue, 503–7

South Pacific, 412
Southall Residents' Association, 666, 675
Southwell, Joan, 608
Space Age, 58–9, 62–4, 79, 83, 84, 233–4
Spain: taking holidays in, 193–4
Spectator, 53, 63, 167, 571, 676
Spector, Phil, 768
Speight, Johnny, 661, 662
Spence, Basil, 623, 624
Spence, Gusty, 363, 364, 365, 746
sport, 59, 305–25; see also football
Sports Council, 306
Springfield, Dusty, 118
Spurling, Hilary, 532
Sputnik, 58
The Spy with a Cold Nose, 311
Stamp, Terence, 242, 243, 260, 262, 269, 271, 272, 273, 404; relationship with Jean Shrimpton, 265–7
stamps, 170
Starke, Frederick, 80
Starr, Ringo, 111, 144, 212, 214, 263, 272, 434, 439, 450, 469, 766, 767; see also Beatles
steel: nationalisation issue, 98
Steel, David, 699–700
Steele, Tommy, 103, 219
Stephen, John, 247, 248, 249
Stephens, Robert, 396
Stepney, Alex, 777
Steptoe and Son, 16, 399, 661
sterling crises: (1964), 93–4, 121; (1965), 123–4; (1967), 418; (1968), 512–14, 516, 518–19; (1969), 729
Stevenage, 186, 253
Stevens, Jocelyn, 239
Stewart, Ian, 142, 146
Stewart, Michael, 121–2, 292, 367, 371, 514, 725; as Foreign Secretary, 517
Stiles, Nobby, 312, 313, 315, 317, 318, 319, 322
Stockhausen, Karlheinz, 215
Stokes, Sir Donald, 420
Stone, Pauline, 241
Stopes, Marie, 481
Stoppard, Tom, 396, 790
Street Offences Act (1959), 488
'streets in the sky', 627
strikes, 706, 707–8, 709–10, 728, 730; dockers' strikes (1967), 418; economic impact and number of days lost to, 707–8, 709–10, 728; seamen's strikes (1966), 280–2; wildcat, 706, 708
student unrest, 537–41
Suez Crisis, xv
suicide, 337
Summa furniture range, 66
Sun, 3, 61–2, 132, 316
Sunay, President, 422–3
Sunday Express, 157, 324, 656, 657
Sunday Night at the London Palladium, 6, 213, 219
Sunday Pictorial, 162
Sunday Telegraph, 60, 158, 255, 256, 296, 323, 790
Sunday Times, 59, 60, 157, 275, 555, 769
Sunday Times Colour Section, 73, 75, 82, 240, 255–6
Sunderland, 614
supermarkets, 191
the Supremes, 119
Sutherland, Graham, 70, 75, 623
Sutherland, John, 411, 574
Swinging London, 254–5, 257–74, 403; and *Adam Adamant Lives!*, 274; and affluence, 255; American enthusiasm for, 257–8; backlash against, 274; and *Blow Up*, 404–5; forging of 'new class', 271; guidebooks on, 260; nightclubs and restaurants, 261–4; *Time* article on, 258–60; and upper classes, 271, 273; and working classes, 270

Tate Gallery, 75
Taverne, Dick, 13–14, 647
Taylor, A. J. P., 496
Taylor, D. J., 445
Taylor, Dick, 137, 139, 140, 142, 143
Taylor, John Russell, 397, 405, 408–9, 473
Taylor, Mick, 137, 566
Tebbit, Norman, 342
technology, 57; and affluence, 48; changing of people's daily lives, 62–3; and consumerism, 48; see also Ministry of Technology
Teddy Boys, 205, 207, 246
teenagers see young people
telephones, 167

television, 398–402, 791; book adaptations, 445–6; and football, 308, 309; growth of, xvi, xvii; introduction of colour (1967), 398; semi-fantastic adventure series genre, 399; viewing figures, 398; *see also* individual programmes

Term of Trial, 572–3, 592

Terry, Walter, 26

TGWU (Transport and General Workers Union), 708, 712, 713

thalidomide scandal (1961–2), 636, 699

Thamesmead, 618, 619

Thank Your Lucky Stars, 150

That Was The Week That Was, 8, 687

Thatcher, Margaret, 41, 580, 592, 685, 787

Thatcherism, 684

theatre, 396–7, 473

Thomas, Gerald, 407

Thomas, Peter, 571–2

Thomas, R. S., 'In Church', 463

Thompson, E. P., 531, 642; *The Making of the English Working Class*, 530–1

Thomson, Roy, 255, 420–1

Thorogood, Frank, 564, 565

Thrower, Percy, 200–1

Thunderball, 304, 402, 695

Till Death Us Do Part, 661–3

Time, 57, 258–60, 440

Time Out, 528

The Times, 158, 186, 193, 195, 209, 291–2, 343, 348, 395, 398, 404, 406, 429, 501, 535–6, 598, 599–600, 627, 649, 656, 681, 706, 719, 731, 760; on Alec Douglas-Home, 11; and the Beatles, 107, 437; and Edward Heath, 782; and election campaign (1964), 14; on Enoch Powell, 684; film reviews, 522; and Harold Wilson, 4, 63, 415; and 'I'm Backing Britain' campaign, 609; and immigration issue, 668–9, 676; and Northern Ireland, 356, 359, 366, 732, 746; and the Rolling Stones, 554; on unions, 713; on Winston Churchill's funeral, xiv; women's page, 238

Times Education Supplement, 331

Times Literary Supplement, 437

Tinling, Teddy, 67

Tippett, Michael, 396

Titmuss, Richard, 601

Tizard, Henry, 50

To England with Love, 607

Tolkien, J. R. R., 411, 471–2; *The Hobbit*, 638; *The Lord of the Rings*, 471–2, 474, 638

Tom Jones, 403

Tomlinson, Jim, 52

Ton-up boys, 207

Top Gear (shop), 260

the Tornados, 58

Torrey Canyon disaster (1967), 636

Tottenham Hotspur, 59, 308

Town, 240, 256

town planning, 624

Townsend, Peter, 601

Townshend, Pete, 137, 209, 220, 222, 304, 469

trade, 87, 418

trade unions, 706–31; and Communist participation, 708; and Harold Wilson 282, 659, 705, 714, 715–16, 722, 724, 725–6; and *In Place of Strife*, 710–29, 730; and James Callaghan, 712–13, 714–15, 728; and Labour Party, 706–7; negotiations with government over Industrial Relations bill and settlement, 722, 723–9; opposition to 'I'm Backing Britain' campaign, 610–11; rise in public disaffection with, 706; *see also* strikes

transcendental meditation, 470

Transport and General Workers Union (TGWU), 708, 712, 713

Trattoria Terrazza, 260–1

Traverse Theatre (Edinburgh), 523, 526

Trellick Tower, 633

Trench, Richard, 545

Trevelyan, John, 406

Tribune, 4, 178, 282, 716

Trimble, David, 354

TUC, 715, 716, 722

Tuffin, Sally, 246, 260

Twiggy, 59, 231, 243, 300–2, 303, 304, 325, 453

Tynan, Kenneth, 268, 396, 437, 573

UFO (nightclub), 442

Ulster Constitution Defence Committee, 361–2

Ulster Protestant Volunteers (UPV), 362, 746
Ulster Unionist Party, 343, 345, 346, 350–1, 353–4
Ulster Volunteer Force see UVF
the Undertakers, 114
unemployment, 11, 18, 82, 88, 179, 191, 305, 416, 785
uniforms, 450–1
Union Jack, 304–5
unions see trade unions
United States: British invasion of, 302–3; enthusiasm for Swinging London, 257–8; and the Labour Party, 381; racial codes, 138; relations with Britain, 120–6, 509, 511–12; success of Beatles in, 109–12; success of other British groups in, 113–15; see also Vietnam War
urban development, 624–6
Utley, T. E., 461
UVF (Ulster Volunteer Force), 344, 362–6, 735, 746

Valentine, 239
Venice Biennale, 77
vernacular tradition, 634
Victorianism, 447–8, 449
Vidal Sassoon, 78
Vietnam Solidarity Campaign, 533, 534–5
Vietnam War, 122–3, 126, 130, 178, 372, 379, 440, 587; and Harold Wilson, 122–3, 126, 381–5; non-commitment of British troops to, 382; peace proposals, 382–3, 384; protests against, 381–2, 522, 532–7
Viewers' and Listeners' Council, 570
Villeneuve, Justin de, 301
Violent Playground, 572
Vitti, Monica, 404, 527
Voelcker, John, 70
Vogue, 231, 233, 238, 240, 241, 242, 243, 245, 451

Waddington Galleries, 76
wages, 191, 707, 708, 730,
Walden, Brian, 289
Walker, Alexander, 405
Walker, Peter, 164
Wallach, Eli, 33
Warbey, William, 123
Ward, Barbara: *Spaceship Earth*, 639
Ward, Peter, 365, 366
Warner, Sir Pelham, 307
The Wars of the Roses, 473
Washington, 187
Waters, Roger, 443
Watkins, Alan, 159, 166, 330
Watson, James, 46–7
Watton, Harry, 629
Watts, Charlie, 137, 144, 147, 153, 154, 565; and drugs, 549; see also Rolling Stones
Waymouth, Nigel, 451–2, 529
Wedge, James, 260
The Wednesday Play, 597–8
Weekend Telegraph, 257, 258, 249
Weeks, Jeffrey, 477, 580–1
Weight, Richard, 305
Welch, Robert, 69
Wenner, Jann, 557
Wesker, Arnold, 396
West Germany (football team), 317–22
What's New, Pussycat?, 403–4
Which?, 192
Whistle Down the Wind, 462–3
Whitcombe, Noel, 271
White, Jerry, 257
White, Michael, 524–5
White, Valerie, 608
Whitechapel Art Gallery, 70; 'This is Tomorrow' exhibition (1956), 70, 72
Whitechapel New Generation programme, 77
Whitehouse, Ernest, 576, 579
Whitehouse, Mary, 342, 478–9, 488, 575–80, 583, 592, 598; background, 575–6; criticises *Doctor Who*, 578; founds Clean-Up TV, 577–8; and NVLA, 578; and religion, 576–7
Whitelaw, Willie, 782, 787
The Who, 115, 118, 154, 209–10, 216, 220, 222–3, 304, 305, 469
Wiener, Martin, 53
Wigg, George, 37, 291, 293
Wilcox, Desmond, 644
The Wild One, 207
Williams, Marcia, 14, 16, 25, 40–1, 131, 169, 278, 279–80, 289, 433, 783, 786–7;

background, 37; and George Brown, 174, 175; relationship with Harold Wilson, 3, 14, 37–8; rumours of scandal, 38

Williams, Raymond, 196, 530–1, 642; *Culture and Society*, 530–1

Williams, Shirley, 341, 700

Williamson, Robert, 365

Willis, Ted, 33

Willmott, Peter, 463–4, 689, 696

Wilson, Angus, 183–5, 188, 445, 496; *Late Call*, 183–5, 188, 189, 191, 196, 397, 597

Wilson, Bryan, 466

Wilson, Des, 599

Wilson, Elizabeth, 423–4

Wilson, Harold, xiii, xvi, xvii, 3–19, 35, 157, 192; and Alec Douglas-Home, 10–11; allegations of being a Soviet agent, 649; and Anglo-American relations, 120–6; and Anthony Crosland, 330; and arms sales to South Africa issue, 503–7; assessment of government record of, 784–5; attributes, 26–7, 179–80; background and early political career, 4–5, 21–5, 41; and the BBC, 644–6; cabinets, 31, 36, 86, 92; Cecil King's plan to topple, 651–7; character and image, 21–4, 25–7, 40–1, 786; collapse of reputation after July crisis (1966), 297–9, 415; commitment to science and modernisation, xvii, 3–4, 54, 56–7; and Common Market entry, 387–9, 390–1; comparison with Alec Douglas-Home, 8–9, 13; comparison with Edward Heath, 160–1; criticism of and dissatisfaction with, 25–6, 28, 63, 90, 178–9, 288, 368–9, 380–1, 642, 648–9, 728; and D-Notice Affair, 415; and 'deal' with US arising from pressure on sterling (1965), 123–5; and decimalisation, 168; and devaluation, 89–91, 284–6, 291–2, 295, 424–5, 427, 430–2, 501; early popularity and persona, 5–6, 8–9; economic policy, 89–96, 98–9, 171–2, 176, 177, 284–7, 292–3, 294–5, 324–5, 370, 417; and Edward Heath, 164–5; and election campaign (1964), 6–8, 12, 14, 16–17; and election campaign (1966), 278–9; and election campaign (1970), 772, 776, 781, 782; ending of honeymoon period and decline in polls, 97–9; foreign policy, 371–2, 373, 385; and George Brown, 29, 174, 175, 287–8, 293–4, 383, 419, 422, 504, 506, 514–15; home life and interests, 23–5, 39–40; and Hugh Gaitskell, 24; and *In Place of Strife*, 711; infatuation with Kennedy, 6; interest in football, 305–6; and James Callaghan, 26, 40, 284, 287, 367–8, 502, 714–15; and July crisis (1966), 282–99, 296–7; 'Kitchen Cabinet', 37; leadership speculation over (1969), 719–21; loses election and leaves Downing Street (1970), 783–6; losing interest in modernisation project, 178; nearing collapse, 717–18; Northern Ireland, 348, 365, 739–40; and Open University, 331; and opening of the Post Office Tower, 44–5; at Oxford University, 21–3; paranoia and belief in plot against, 369–70, 504, 645–6, 647–8; and party conference address (1969), 761–2; party leadership contest (1963), 29; planned plots to oust, 647, 719–21; playing off colleagues against each other, 335, 646; political philosophy, 25; and the polls, 131, 179, 295, 367, 762; praise for 'I'm Backing Britain' campaign, 609–10; and relations with America, 379–80; relationship with Marcia Williams, 3, 14, 37–8; relationship with Queen, 20–1; and Rhodesia, 126–32, 378–9; rise in popularity of government (1970), 763–4, 769; rise in public disaffection with, 706–7; and Roy Jenkins, 24, 30, 503, 645–6; and seamen's strike, 280–2; style of leadership, 40–1; successor issue, 647; tastes, 23; 'ten faces' of, 26; tensions and distrust within government of, 368, 369, 507; and trade unions, 282, 659, 706–8, 714–15, 722, 723–4, 725–6; treatment of by press, 414–15, 643–4; trip to Moscow, 289; unpopularity of government, 641, 658; unpopularity of, 100, 641–2, 648–9, 719, 762, 785–6;

Wilson, Harold – *continued*
  and Vietnam War, 122–3, 381–5, 532; 'White Heat' speech (1963), 3–4, 63; wins 1964 election and becomes Prime Minister, 16–19, 20–1; and World Cup (1966), 323
Wilson, Hugh, 186, 187
Wilson, Mary, 20, 23–4, 37, 39–40
Wilson, Ray, 312, 314, 318, 319, 320
Wilson, Robin, 20
wine drinking, 195
Wings, 262
winter (1962-3), 143
Winters, Frank and Bernie, 219
Wisdom, Norman, 408
Wohlin, Anna, 564, 565
Wolfe Tone societies, 734
Wolfenden, Jeremy, 486–7
Wolfenden, Sir John, 486–7
Wolfenden Committee/Report (1957), 328, 486–7, 574
Wolff, Michael, 79–80
Wolstenholme, Kenneth, 320, 321, 322
Wolverhampton, 630; immigrant population, 666–7, 673
Wolverhampton Wanderers, 308
Woman, 238
Woman's Own, 690, 695
women, 688–704; and advertising, 690; and alternative scene, 702–3; distrust of modern, 694; and education, 689; and employment, 692–5; fashion, 449; and feminism, 700–1, 702–4; as housewives, 689–92; as mothers and homemakers in 1950s, 688–9; and National Women's Conference (1970), 703–4; and sexual politics of counter-culture, 702–3; working mothers, 209
Women's Illustrated, 690
women's liberation movement, 703
women's magazines, 82, 238–40, 482, 690, 695
Women's Mirror, 301
Wood, Ronnie, 137
Woodward, Nicholas, 730
Wootton, Baroness, 497–8
Wootton Committee (1968), 551, 552
Worboys Committee (1963), 167

working classes, 197–8, 270
working men's clubs, 198–9
World Cup (1966), 305, 309, 310–22; early matches, 311–12; final against West Germany, 316–22; players, 312–13; quarter-final against Argentina, 313–15; semi-final against Portugal, 315; theft of Cup, 311
World Cup (1970), 769–72, 775–6; quarter-final against West Germany, 777–8
Worsley, Peter, 662–3
Worsthorne, Peregrine, 380–1
Wright, Peter, 649
Wright, Rick, 443
Wyatt, Woodrow, 98
Wyman, Bill, 141, 143–4, 145, 146, 147, 149, 152, 153, 273, 555, 558, 568; and drugs, 549; *see also* Rolling Stones
Wyndham, Francis, 240, 263, 269, 270
Wyndham, John, 611, 637

X-ray equipment, 47

the Yardbirds, 118, 137, 154
Yardley, 302, 303
Yemen, 377
Yorkshire, 198
Young, Hugh, 388, 555
Young, Michael, 463–4, 689, 696
Young, Terence, 695
Young Contemporaries Exhibition (1961), 73
young people, 101–2, 198–9, 200, 440–2, 537–43; attitude towards homosexuality, 495; and drugs, 550; fears over adolescent misbehaviour, 203–5, 208–10; importance of shopping to teenagers, 239; magazines for, 238; Mods and Rockers, 204, 205–9, 246, 550; sexual behaviour of, 488–9, 492–4

Z Cars, 188, 189
Zeffirelli, Franco, 396
Ziegler, Philip, 25, 38
Zuckerman, Sir Solly, 50, 420, 654, 655
Zulu, 265
Zweig, Ferdynand, 696